READINGS
in the
Essentials o
ABNORMAL
PSYCHOLOGY
D0809257

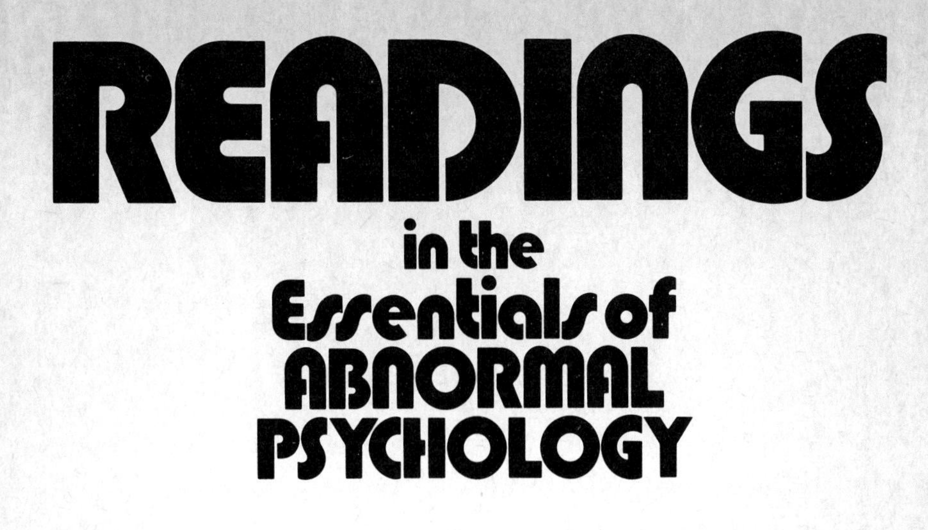

Benjamin Kleinmuntz

University of Illinois at Chicago Circle

Harper & Row, Publishers
New York, Evanston, San Francisco, London

Sponsoring Editor: George A. Middendorf
Project Editor: Cynthia Hausdorff
Designer: Rita Naughton
Production Supervisor: Will Jomarron

READINGS IN THE ESSENTIALS
OF ABNORMAL PSYCHOLOGY

 For information address Harper & Row, Publishers, Inc., 10 East 53rd Street, New York, N.Y. 10022.

Library of Congress Cataloging in Publication Data
Kleinmuntz, Benjamin, comp.
Readings in the essentials of abnormal psychology.

1. Psychology, Pathological—Addresses, essays, lectures. I. Title. [DNLM: 1. Psychopathology—essays. WM100 K652r 1974]
RC454.K582 157 74-1492
ISBN 0-06-043709-X

Contents

Preface

This compilation of readings was designed to accompany the text, *Essentials of Abnormal Psychology*, but it could serve as a supplementary source for most other abnormal psychology books as well. The advantage of teaching with primary source materials is that such materials provide students with a closer familiarity than is possible in conventional textbooks with the relevant research and theoretical contributions of some of the outstanding scholars in the field. This permits students to formulate their own opinions and impressions about the original source material.

The textbook that these readings were designed to supplement reflects the state of flux besetting abnormal psychology at the present time and presents numerous topics that are at the center of contemporary controversy. Accordingly, this volume too provides articles that deal with various controversial topics, thus permitting the student to judge at first hand the merit of some of the arguments surrounding such topics as the ethics and validity of diagnosis, the value of the disease model, the worth of some representative psychotherapies, and the relevance for blacks of white America's treatment methods. In addition, this volume includes research and empirical reports on the conventional areas of psychopathology.

The readings are organized into six parts.

The first part is introductory and these chapters deal with definitions of mental illness and with topics on the worth of the mental illness model and classification. Part Two, Psychodiagnosis, is basically concerned with the tools of the clinician and with the clinician himself as a psychometric tool. This is followed by Part Three, Chapters 5 and 6, which deal with the causes of behavior pathology, and by Part Four, Chapters 7 through 13, which cover the behavior pathologies. The dependencies are covered in Part Five, Chapters 14 and 15. The three chapters in Part Six contain articles on the varieties of treatment methods and include discussions of the traditional, behavior, and somatic therapies, as well as the settings in which these treatments occur. There is, in addition, a comprehensive index that includes names and topics referred to in the body of the readings.

Courses for which these readings are appropriate include those commonly labeled *abnormal psychology*, *psychopathology*, *behavior pathology*, *mental hygiene*, *psychiatry*, *neuropsychiatry*, and all others dealing with the problems and issues of mental disorders.

I am especially indebted, as always, to Mrs. Betty H. Boal who attended to the interminable chores surrounding the gathering and compiling of readings; and to my wife, Dalia, and our three sons, Don, Ira, and Oren, who are the innocent victims of my compulsion to get involved in such lengthy projects as this one.

Benjamin Kleinmuntz

INTRODUCTION

Chapter 1

Is "Mental Illness" a Disease?

For some time contemporary clinical psychology has been debating the issue of whether abnormality is an illness or a disturbance in interpersonal competence. The three papers that follow examine this issue in depth. George Albee, a longtime critic of the "sickness model" examines this model and concludes that its application permits mental-health experts to diagnose an individual as having an illness although he is functioning adequately as a member of society. Consequently Albee proposes an alternative model that emphasizes the importance of social–developmental explanations of behavioral functioning.

In an empirical report supporting the proposition that disturbed functioning is not a mental disorder, Rosenhan demonstrates in a series of studies the consequences of hospitalizing persons as "insane." He concludes that it is difficult to distinguish the "sane from the insane" in mental hospitals and that the consequence of the illness model is that people become patients in environments where they are rendered powerless, depersonalized, segregated—all of which are countertherapeutic.

In sharp contrast to the foregoing papers, the article by David Ausubel holds that personality disorder is a disease. After examining several propositions for discarding the concept of mental illness, he concludes that, among other things, there is no inherent contradiction in regarding mental symptoms as both expressions of problems of living *and* manifestations of illness.

Emerging Concepts of Mental Illness and Models of Treatment: The Psychological Point of View*

George W. Albee

This author reviews the evidence for the "sickness" model of mental illness and finds it to be inconclusive. Psychiatry, he argues, in insisting on its prerogatives of primary patient responsibility and control of treatment facilities, bases its justification either on rare and uncertain genetic and metabolic conditions or on the common chronic organic conditions it characteristically neglects; the typical person in psychiatric treatment is suffering from neither. The alternative presented here is a social–developmental model, which would emphasize the nurturance of strength rather than the search for and excision of weakness.

In preparing this presentation I had to choose between either: 1) developing a psychological model for disturbed behavior and then spelling out its implications for intervention and prevention or 2) discussing the shortcomings of the sickness model in order to provide a logical groundwork for the subsequent development of alternative models. I chose the second alternative because I have spent more time thinking about this problem and also because I do not think the alternative to the sickness model is likely to be a psychological model. Indeed I believe the new approach will be social-educational, and it is more likely to develop out of the fields of special education or social work than out of psychology.

WHAT IS THE "SICKNESS MODEL"?

This explanation of disturbed behavior, briefly stated, holds that "mental illness is an illness like any other." The very fact that strenuous efforts, made for a century and more, have achieved only limited acceptance of this slogan suggests that it is not entirely creditable.

Attempts to explain the origins of neurotic and psychotic behavior, addiction to alcohol, juvenile delinquency, mental deficiency, and even such peripheral problems as marital maladjustment and school learning difficulties as sicknesses inside the person make them discontinuous with normal behavior. The sickness model suggests that these conditions are among a number of separate, discrete mental illnesses, each with a separate cause, prognosis, and potential treatment. We have seen this theme in some of what Dr. Grinker had to say.

The sickness model further suggests that the treatment of these "illnesses" is properly the function of a physician specially trained in their diagnosis and in known methods of intervention. While other professionals may play various useful roles, they will be ancillary to the physician, who is charged with the clinical responsibility for the welfare of the "patient" (who must be "treated" in a hospital or clinic or in the physician's private office). Even the so-called personality disturbances, and all the agonies deriving from a dehumanized and hostile environment, are diagnosed as various kinds of sicknesses or intrapersonal illnesses.

This model, which occupies the center of our clinical stage, places the identification of forces in the individual before consideration of the hostile and damaging forces in his world; it demands that we try to fix him, treat his disease (as we do other diseases), and then send him back to the continuing horrors of his world. Realistically, it causes us to treat only the small number comprising those who believe in our cures or even worse the much smaller number for whom our cures may work, thereby causing us to neglect all those people with problems we do not understand because they do not fit our model, and those people who cannot participate in, nor accept, our verbal intervention methods.

The origins of this explanation of emotional disturbance, like the origins of most human myth systems, are overdetermined and complex. Sarbin suggests that the label "illness" was first used by Teresa of Avila in the 16th century to describe emotionally disturbed people; it served

From *American Journal of Psychiatry*, 1969, **125**, 870–876.

*Read at the 124th annual meeting of the American Psychiatric Association, Boston, Mass., May 13–17, 1968.

as a useful metaphor to protect disturbed nuns (those who exhibited symptoms of hysteria) from the Inquisition. "If a person's conduct could be accounted for by such natural causes, it was to be regarded not as evil, but *comas enfermas*, 'as if sick' " (10, p. 448).

Werry (14), a research psychiatrist at the University of Illinois, recently called the disease model "the great operating delusion of psychiatry." Elsewhere Werry (15) says "The debate . . . between the proponents of the disease model and those who believe that emotional and behavioral difficulties belong in the moral sphere was long and acrimonious but, as you must be aware, psychiatry in the past hundred years, has achieved a substantial victory in this contested field . . ." (p. 4).

The end of moral treatment of the insane in America seems to have coincided, in the middle half of the 19th century, with the beginning of the enormous wave of foreign immigration into the United States. Most of the Yankee physicians, who had been able to extend a kind of Quaker fellowship to the insane, found themselves unable to deal with the "foreign insane paupers" who had inundated the retreats, jails, and almshouses in the latter part of the 19th century.

It was John P. Gray, superintendent of Utica State Hospital and editor of the *American Journal of Insanity*, who, in the late 19th century, became the chief advocate of the position that mental patients were really physically ill with a brain disease. Gray is often awarded the distinction of being the most influential medical spokesman for the rejection of a moral approach to insanity (with its reliance on compassion, reason, kindness, and human interaction) and advancing instead the argument that the insane were victims of some unknown brain disease.

One of the primary arguments used by contemporary psychiatry to support its basic responsibility for the treatment of mental conditions holds that there are underlying organic defects, in most cases still undiscovered, producing the disturbed behavior. Starting from this uncertain platform, psychiatry advances the conclusion that medical training, most of which has not been used since the internship, somehow provides unique qualifications to treat these sicknesses.

The gossamer web of logic is not strong enough to hold the weight of this whole proposition, and many contemporary psychiatrists have rejected this argument. In the first place, there is little substantial evidence supporting the hypothesis of an underlying organic defect in most functional mental disorders. Second, the medical training of most psychiatrists was obtained years in the past and is not especially relevant to their therapeutic activities. In other situations, where the stakes are different, most psychiatrists have refused to practice medicine in any traditional sense. (Most psychiatrists are excused from volunteer duty at community health clinics and from emergency room duty in the military service.)

Third, when a real organic cause is discovered to be the significant underlying factor in the production of disturbed behavior (as has been the case in a few genuine mental diseases), then the treatment of these conditions is removed from the psychiatric field.

As Zubin points out:

> As soon as a mental disorder is traced to some organic cause, however, it ceases to belong to the psychiatric fold and is handed over to internal medicine or neurology as was the case with general paresis, pellagra with psychosis, and will probably be the case with phenylpyruvic oligophrenia. Only diseases of unknown origin tend to remain in the psychiatric domain (18, p. 2).

Barbara Wooton (16) has made a searching examination of the interaction between social and cultural forces and mental disorders. It will be clear to most thoughtful persons who examine her approach that "mental illness" is not "a disease like any other." She has spelled out certain crucial and fundamental differences between mental disorders and true diseases. She points out, quite correctly, that

> anti-social behavior is the precipitating factor that leads to mental treatment. But at the same time the fact of the illness is itself inferred from this behavior: indeed it is almost true to say that the illness is the behavior for which it is also the excuse. But any disease, the morbidity of which is established only by the social failure that it involves, must rank as fundamentally different from those with which the symptoms are independent of social norms (17).

In one of her examples Wooton reminds us that we diagnose a mental disease when we observe an individual disregarding the property rights of others, as for example, the adolescent who steals cars, the middle-aged suburban housewife who shoplifts, or the hippie who picks flowers from the city parks, refusing in the process to keep off the grass. Without this observable behavior we would not suspect the existence of an underlying "mental disease." So the identification of this "disease" depends on the violation of social laws which uphold the sanctity of individual or of public ownership. In a society where possessions were held in common such diseases could not exist!

The point of all this is that the social disapproval of the social consequences of behavior usually identifies the underlying "disease." In the absence of these interactions the disease would not exist.

WHAT EVIDENCE SUPPORTS THE SICKNESS MODEL?

There is precious little evidence to support a discontinuity (sickness) model. At the center of the continuity-discontinuity argument stands the mystery condition (or conditions) of schizophrenia. There just must be a biological explanation! While the argument will not be entirely won or lost here, still the causation of schizophrenia is under constant debate, and support for a disease or defect explanation is being sought most vigorously in the blood, sweat, and tears (as well as all the other fluids) of the schizophrenic.

Recently an entire volume (some 500 pages) of the *Annals of the New York Academy of Sciences* was devoted to "Some Biological Aspects of Schizophrenic Behavior" (11). Even this elaborate production could not obscure the fact that no clear-cut phenotypical defect has yet been found which even comes close to providing a key to a possible molecular basis for this condition. All sorts of profound-sounding statements were made which, on careful examination, turn out to be meaningless. For example:

It has become quite evident that neuropathology and its allied sciences are assuming a progressively important role in the study and understanding of mental disorders. Thus far, the morphologic, histochemical, and cytobiophysical observations in brain biopsies and topectomies appeared to be of a pleomorphic character and non-specific or rather of heterogenic patterns. Therefore one must look forward to future research investigations (p. 481).

This polysyllabic nonsense says: "We haven't found anything yet, and we're still looking."

Occasionally someone finds a biological measure which does differentiate schizophrenics from controls, but as anyone knows who has followed this literature for the past 20 years, artifacts (like vitamin C deficiency or too much caffeine) have a way of confounding the significance of the differences found.

The discovery that chronic back-ward schizophrenics have smaller hearts than controls matched for age and sex would hardly prove that small hearts cause schizophrenia. Rather, a more parsimonious explanation in terms of lack of exercise would undoubtedly be suggested. But repeatedly the finding of some blood factor which differentiates backward schizophrenics from normals has been hailed as the long-sought key to the mystery of schizophrenia.

Seymour Kety (8), in an honest and straightforward review of biochemical theories of schizophrenia, refers to "a present consensus that a pathological lesion characteristic of schizophrenia or any of its subgroups remains to be demonstrated" (p. 409). He reviews the errors, the subjective biases, and the confounding effects of unsuspected or uncontrolled variables that have led to premature "discoveries." He concludes that of all the new reports of toxic materials in the blood of schizophrenics "there has been no extensive substantiation of any of them" (p. 418). He continues: "Many of the current hypotheses concerning the schizophrenia complex are original and attractive even though, up to this time, evidence directly implicating any one of them in the disease itself is hardly compelling" (p. 426).

If there is no convincing evidence that schizophrenia is an identifiable disease, there is far less scientific support for a sickness model explanation of all of the less extreme forms of human deviation, yet the American Psychiatric Association keeps issuing position statements claiming responsibility for such conditions as mental retardation, juvenile delinquency, and alcoholism. The trouble is that the sickness model demands a kind of intervention that is terribly expensive and a kind of highly trained intervener who is not widely available. Eventually, I predict, the needs of society will be better served!

If the organic approach could be demonstrated to be valid our society would be justified in demanding an enormous increase in the number of medical and paramedical professionals prepared to take their places in the battle against "mental illness." But the organic approach has not been found to be convincingly valid, and alternative models seem to hold at least as much promise for helping many more disturbed people. Further, the supply of physicians (and therefore psychiatrists) in proportion to the population has been declining for many years and probably will continue to decline (1).

Still another subtle but powerful force lending support to the sickness model of mental disorder has been the steady increase in the use of the psychotropic drugs that have become the common approach to many emotional conditions. Persuasive advertisements, beamed at psychiatrists in the psychiatric journals by the drug companies, keep emphasizing the value of drug therapy. Drug therapy has been hailed by the great popular medical journals—*Time, Life, Look!*

With hundreds of thousands of daily drug users in the public hospitals, plus millions more seeking tranquility or at least relief from intense anxiety, the psychotropic drugs have become a fantastic growth industry. Understandably any threat to the sickness model is a threat to the drug salesmen. What is good for General Napoleon is good for United Chemical!

By using drugs for the poor in the state hospitals we can get by with practically no professional personnel in these tax-supported settings. (In over one-third of our state hospitals practically no psychiatric time is available, and two-thirds of our 2,000 psychiatric clinics do not have a single full-time psychiatrist on the staff [1]). Eighty percent of psychiatric practice is private office practice with a suburban upper-middle class clientele.

Jules Henry (5) says: "State hospitals today seem to exhale from their antique bricks and dark labyrinths the miasmas of misunderstanding, prejudice, callousness, and hate whose origins lie deep in our history. Who knows what happens in the pit, where their voices do not come up to us?" (p. 43).

The point of all of this argument should not be lost. Psychiatry, in insisting on its prerogatives of primary patient responsibility and control of treatment institutions and intervention efforts of all sorts, bases its argument either on rare and uncertain genetic and metabolic conditions or on those common chronic organic mental conditions which it characteristically neglects. Most of psychiatric practice is private, most of it is suburban, and most hospital psychiatry is practiced in general hospitals. None of the organic mental conditions is the central concern of current psychiatric treatment.

A great majority of the people whom psychiatrists treat are not suffering from genetic, metabolic, and arteriosclerotic conditions, or from alcoholic delirium, or from central nervous system malfunction. If psychiatrists were to devote their primary attention to these kinds of cases there would be little need for today's debate about models. Repeatedly, surveys show that the most common psychiatric patient in 1968 is a college-educated, white, upper-middle class, non-Catholic female between 30 and 40. She has none of the usual organic mental diseases.

Recently psychiatrist David J. Vail (13) commented on the unhappy fact that psychiatry has not been able to produce a meaningful definition of mental illness. He argues that

A recent booklet on insurance published by the American Psychiatric Association, for example, defines mental disorder essentially as those items listed in the official manual on nomenclature, in other words, a mental disorder exists when a ruling group of psychiatrists say that it is what it is. Worse yet, psychiatrists cannot agree among each other.

There are many beautiful examples of the contortions that must be performed to define mental disorder as sickness. In the recent booklet Vail refers to, the following curious statement appears: "Illness (which includes mental disorders) is any symptom or syndrome the American medical profession at the present time generally accepts as evidence of disease or disorder" (2). Doesn't that sound like Alice in Wonderland?

Not only do mental disorders include conditions which "interfere with current functioning," but also those which, while not affecting in any way current functioning "carry with them the threat of future disability" (2). In other words, with this model an individual may be diagnosed as having a mental disorder although he is functioning adequately as a member of society if, in the judgment of a psychiatrist, potential exists for future disturbance. Frankly, this is a frightening notion to those who adhere to the principle that a man is innocent until proven guilty and that no one can be convicted for the possible commission of some future criminal act.

WHAT IS THE ALTERNATIVE?

I have been arguing for the past several years that the sickness model explanation of the origins of disturbed behavior will have to be replaced with a social-developmental explanation before our society will get off its inertia and begin to do some constructive things about large-scale intervention and prevention of human misery. The intervention will emphasize the nurturance of strength rather than the search for and excision of weakness, and the prevention will take the form of social engineering to strengthen the family.

I fully expect many psychiatrists to agree with this approach because it is my experience that many thoughtful leaders in American psychiatry are saying the same thing. Don Jackson (6) pointed out that:

> Each year data are collected that provide strong evidence for the fact that mental disorders, including schizophrenia, arise out of disturbed personal relationships. Each year we seem to rediscover this fact, splicing out the rest of the year with dreams of glory about the bio-chemical cause of schizophrenia, and the new happy pills.

Psychiatrist Robert Coles (4) said recently: "With respect to what can legitimately be called psychiatric disorders, I am not at all convinced that anything new will be discovered to 'cure' them. I am not even sure that we ought to call them 'diseases'." Coles goes on to ask the question that every "mental health" worker should be forced to answer:

> What pills will ever dissolve the anxiety and fear that go with life itself? What will psychiatry ever know that it does not know now about the damage done by thoughtless, cruel parents to vulnerable children? What further "frontiers" do we really have to conquer, when it comes to such subjects as despair, brutality, envy?

After completing his dramatic survey of Boston's mental health resources (which exceed the resources of any city in the world and yet largely neglect those in greatest need), William Ryan (9) made a proposal so audacious, so revolutionary, so shocking in its implications that in another age he would have been tried for heresy and boiled in oil. He suggested that Boston's mental health establishment forego any further budgetary increases because their services were having no significantly beneficial effect on the public most in need of them and that the money saved be put into improved welfare services. (Dr. Ryan recently moved to Connecticut!) But Ryan is right. Casework, group work, and counseling by clergymen are reaching more of the citizens of Boston than are psychiatric facilities.

The psychoanalyst should be in the vanguard, together with the social worker and the learning theorist, in advocating the abandonment of the sickness model and arguing for its replacement with a social-developmental model. Certainly the most fundamental contribution of Freud was his discovery of the continuity between the normal and the abnormal. In discussing Darwin and Freud, Jerome Bruner pointed out that the Victorians, reeling from Darwin's discovery of a perfectly lawful continuity between man and the rest of the animal kingdom, were dealt a second and more terrifying blow by Freud's discovery of the continuity between the sane and the insane. Bruner (3) speaks of the

> lawful continuity between man and the animal kingdom, between dreams and unreason on one side and waking rationality on the other, between madness and sanity, between consciousness and unconsciousness; between the mind of the child and the adult mind, between primitive and civilized man—each of these has been a cherished discontinuity preserved in doctrinal canons.

Freud forced the abandonment of these cherished discontinuities.

Why, in the face of this central message of Freud's life work, does the latter-day psychoanalyst continue to pay homage to the sickness model? Primarily, I think, because of the historical accident which has required the psychoanalyst in the United States to be trained first as a physician. I look forward to the day when the psychoanalysts, perhaps in continuing self-analysis, will join forces with Freud and the rest of us who believe the evidence supports a continuity model, a model which holds that it is established that the same mechanisms are operating in adaptive and maladaptive human behavior, and will help lead the scientific assault on those who seek to preserve and defend the sickness model.

WHAT WOULD BE DIFFERENT IF WE CHANGED MODELS?

I have not yet really dealt with the consequences that would follow from changing models. Very briefly, I hold that: 1) the nature of the model determines 2) the nature of the institutions we develop for intervention and prevention, which in turn dictates 3) the kind of manpower we use to deliver care. With a social-developmental model our state hospitals and public clinics would be replaced by social intervention centers, largely staffed by people at the bachelor's level—more like special education teachers and social welfare workers, potentially available in vastly greater supply than psychologists and psychiatrists. For prevention, people like ourselves would be needed as teachers, researchers, and especially as radical social activists proselytizing for changes in our society to make it more supportive, less dehumanized.

The massive deterioration of the fabric of society and its institutions results in a complex tangle of pathology. The pathology includes especially the destruction of the emotional integrity of the family. Let me emphasize here something that you already know very well. Many significant research breakthroughs have already been made. Many of the discoveries are already in. We know, for example, that the emotional climate which surrounds the infant and young child is of critical importance in determining his future—including the kind, the severity, and perhaps even the biological concomitants of his later disturbance.

Such knowledge is dangerous. We usually shut our eyes to its implications. We go on trying to fix up damaged adults in one-to-one relationships when a more proper professional function would be to spend a considerable portion of our energies trying to fix up our society in ways that will increase the strength and stability of the family, thereby affecting positively the mental health of generations to come. It is not possible here to further elaborate upon prevention except to say that I believe, because of the nature of the human animal, it must take the form of strengthening the institution of the family.

I believe that history may judge President Johnson to have been one of the most complicated of American presidents. But his speech at Howard University's commencement will be judged among the half-dozen great landmarks in the history of our society. In it the President called for a massive attack on the central problem of our time. He said:

> The family is the cornerstone of our society. More than any other force it shapes the attitudes, the hopes, the ambitions, and the values of the child. When the family collapses it is the children that are usually damaged. When it happens in a massive scale the community itself is crippled.
>
> So, unless we work to strengthen the family, to create conditions under which most parents will stay together—all the rest: schools and playgrounds, public assistance and private concern, will never be enough to cut completely the circle of despair and deprivation (7).

Unhappily Johnson's Great Society program, which began with such hope and promise, got sidetracked by our unfortunate involvement in Viet Nam. Eventually, let us pray, we will get back to a rational concern with dealing with our important problems—people who suffer.

William Ryan (9) has put it plainly:

> If the assumption is accepted that all behavior disorder and all emotional disturbance are the general province of the psychiatrist and the other mental health professionals, obviously the province remains unoccupied. At present only a beachhead has been established. Further, in view of the scarcity of mental health professionals, which will continue for many years to come, it is unlikely that the beachhead will be extended in any dramatic manner (p. 46).

Edward Stainbrook, chairman of the department of psychiatry at the University of Southern California, says:

> Many of the impairments due to poor social learning and to inadequate development *don't* have to be defined as illness, and they don't have to be treated by medical doctors. . . . I think we need a new kind of institution, too . . . where people could learn, or relearn, social and occupational skills (12).

I am convinced that once society realizes that disturbed behavior reflects the results of social-developmental learning in pathological social environments (rather than intrapersonal sickness), the institutions that will be developed for intervention will be social and educational in nature.

REFERENCES

1. Albee, G.: Models, Myths, and Manpower, Ment. Hyg., 52:168–180, 1968.
2. American Psychiatric Association: APA Guidelines for Psychiatric Services Covered Under Health Insurance Plans. Washington, D. C., 1966.
3. Bruner, J.: "Freud and the Image of Man," in Nelson, B., ed.: Freud and the Twentieth Century. Cleveland and New York: World Meridan, 1957.
4. Coles, R.: The Limits of Psychiatry, The Progressive 31:32–34, 1967.
5. Henry, J.: The Human Demons, Trans-Action 3:45–48, 1966.
6. Jackson, D.: Action for Mental Illness—What Kind, Stanford Med. Bull. 20:77–80, 1962.
7. Johnson, L. B.: Remarks of the President at Howard University, June 4, 1965: "To Fulfill These Rights." Washington, D. C.: White House Press Office, 1965.
8. Kety, S.: Biochemical Theories of Schizophrenia, Int. J. Psychiat. 1:409–430, 1965.
9. Ryan, W.: Distress in the City. Cleveland: Case Western Reserve University Press, in press.
10. Sarbin, T. R.: On the Futility of the Proposition That Some People Be Labeled "Mentally Ill," J. Consult. Psychol. 5:447–453, 1967.
11. Siva Sankar, D. V., ed.: Some Biological Aspects of Schizophrenic Behavior, Ann. N. Y. Acad. Sci. 96:1–490, 1962.
12. Stainbrook, E.: One Hundred Sixty-Five Beds, Nine Thousand Patients, SK&F Psychiatric Reporter no. 32, 1967, pp. 7–9.
13. Vail, D.: editorial in the Mental Health Newsletter. Minneapolis: Minnesota Department of Public Welfare, 6:1, 1966.
14. Werry, J. S.: Psychotherapy—A Medical Procedure? Canad. Psychiat. Ass. J. 10:278–282, 1965.
15. Werry, J. S.: The Psychiatrist and Society, 1967 Velde lecture given at Bradley University, Peoria, Ill., April 26–27 (processed).
16. Wooton, B.: Social Science and Social Pathology. London: George Allen and Unwin, 1959.
17. Wooton, B.: quoted in Zubin, J.: Some Scientific Models for Psychopathology, 1967 (processed).
18. Zubin, J.: Some Scientific Models for Psychopathology, 1967 (processed).

On Being Sane in Insane Places*

D. L. Rosenhan

If sanity and insanity exist, how shall we know them?

The question is neither capricious nor itself insane. However much we may be personally convinced that we can tell the normal from the abnormal, the evidence is simply not compelling. It is commonplace, for example, to read about murder trials wherein eminent psychiatrists for the defense are contradicted by equally eminent psychiatrists for the prosecution on the matter of the defendant's sanity. More generally, there are a great deal of conflicting data on the reliability, utility, and meaning of such terms as "sanity," "insanity," "mental illness," and "schizophrenia" (1). Finally, as early as 1934, Benedict suggested that normality and abnormality are not universal (2). What is viewed as normal in one culture may be seen as quite aberrant in another. Thus, notions of normality and abnormality may not be quite as accurate as people believe they are.

To raise questions regarding normality and abnormality is in no way to question the fact that some behaviors are deviant or odd. Murder is deviant. So, too, are hallucinations. Nor does raising such questions deny the existence of the personal anguish that is often associated with "mental illness." Anxiety and depression exist. Psychological suffering exists. But normality and abnormality, sanity and insanity, and the diagnoses that flow from them may be less substantive than many believe them to be.

At its heart, the question of whether the sane can be distinguished from the insane (and whether degrees of insanity can be distinguished from each other) is a simple matter: do the salient characteristics that lead to diagnoses reside in the patients themselves or in the environments and contexts in which observers find them? From Bleuler, through Kretchmer, through the formulators of the recently revised *Diagnostic and Statistical Manual* of the American Psychiatric Association, the belief has been strong that patients present symptoms, that those symptoms can be categorized, and, implicitly, that the sane are distinguishable from the insane. More recently, however, this belief has been questioned. Based in part on theoretical and anthropological considerations, but also on philosophical, legal, and therapeutic ones, the view has grown that psychological categorization of mental illness is useless at best and downright harmful, misleading, and pejorative at worst. Psychiatric diagnoses, in this view, are in the minds of the observers and are not valid summaries of characteristics displayed by the observed (3–5).

Gains can be made in deciding which of these is more nearly accurate by getting normal people (that is, people who do not have, and have never suffered, symptoms of serious psychiatric disorders) admitted to psychiatric hospitals and then determining whether they were discovered to be sane and, if so, how. If the sanity of such pseudopatients were always detected, there would be prima facie evidence that a sane individual can be distinguished from the insane context in which he is found. Normality (and presumably abnormality) is distinct enough that it can be recognized wherever it occurs, for it is carried within the person. If, on the other hand, the sanity of the pseudopatients were never discovered, serious difficulties would arise for those who support traditional modes of psychiatric diagnosis. Given that the hospital staff was not incompetent, that the pseudopatient had been behaving as sanely as he had been outside of the hospital, and that it had never been previously suggested that he belonged in a psychiatric hospital, such an unlikely outcome would support the view that psychiatric diagnosis betrays little about the patient but much about the environment in which an observer finds him.

This article describes such an experiment. Eight sane people gained secret admission to 12 different hospitals (6). Their diagnostic experiences constitute the data of the first part of this article; the remainder is devoted to a description of their experiences in psychiatric institutions. Too few psychiatrists and psychologists, even those who have worked in such hospitals, know what the experience is like. They rarely talk about it with former patients, perhaps because they distrust information coming from the previously insane. Those who have worked in psychiatric hospitals are likely to have adapted so thoroughly to the settings that they are insensitive to the impact of that experience. And while there have been occasional reports of researchers who submitted themselves to psychiatric hospitalization (7), these researchers have commonly remained in the hospitals for short periods of time, often with the knowledge of the hospital staff. It is difficult to know the extent to which they were treated like patients or like research colleagues. Nevertheless, their reports about the inside of the psychiatric hospital have been valuable. This article extends those efforts.

PSEUDOPATIENTS AND THEIR SETTINGS

The eight pseudopatients were a varied group. One was a psychology graduate student in his 20's. The remaining

From *Science*, 1973, **179**, 250–258.

*Portions of these data were presented to colloquiums of the psychology departments at the University of California at Berkeley and at Santa Barbara; University of Arizona, Tucson; and Harvard University, Cambridge, Massachusetts.

seven were older and "established." Among them were three psychologists, a pediatrician, a psychiatrist, a painter, and a housewife. Three pseudopatients were women, five were men. All of them employed pseudonyms, lest their alleged diagnoses embarrass them later. Those who were in mental health professions alleged another occupation in order to avoid the special attentions that might be accorded by staff, as a matter of courtesy or caution, to ailing colleagues (8). With the exception of myself (I was the first pseudopatient and my presence was known to the hospital administrator and chief psychologist and, so far as I can tell, to them alone), the presence of pseudopatients and the nature of the research program was not known to the hospital staffs (9).

The settings were similarly varied. In order to generalize the findings, admission into a variety of hospitals was sought. The 12 hospitals in the sample were located in five different states on the East and West coasts. Some were old and shabby, some were quite new. Some were research-oriented, others not. Some had good staff–patient ratios, others were quite understaffed. Only one was a strictly private hospital. All of the others were supported by state or federal funds or, in one instance, by university funds.

After calling the hospital for an appointment, the pseudopatient arrived at the admissions office complaining that he had been hearing voices. Asked what the voices said, he replied that they were often unclear, but as far as he could tell they said "empty," "hollow," and "thud." The voices were unfamiliar and were of the same sex as the pseudopatient. The choice of these symptoms was occasioned by their apparent similarity to existential symptoms. Such symptoms are alleged to arise from painful concerns about the perceived meaninglessness of one's life. It is as if the hallucinating person were saying, "My life is empty and hollow." The choice of these symptoms was also determined by the *absence* of a single report of existential psychoses in the literature.

Beyond alleging the symptoms and falsifying name, vocation, and employment, no further alterations of person, history, or circumstances were made. The significant events of the pseudopatient's life history were presented as they had actually occurred. Relationships with parents and siblings, with spouse and children, with people at work and in school, consistent with the aforementioned exceptions, were described as they were or had been. Frustrations and upsets were described along with joys and satisfactions. These facts are important to remember. If anything, they strongly biased the subsequent results in favor of detecting sanity, since none of their histories or current behaviors were seriously pathological in any way.

Immediately upon admission to the psychiatric ward, the pseudopatient ceased simulating *any* symptoms of abnormality. In some cases, there was a brief period of mild nervousness and anxiety, since none of the pseudopatients really believed that they would be admitted so easily. Indeed, their shared fear was that they would be immediately exposed as frauds and greatly embarrassed. Moreover, many of them had never visited a psychiatric ward; even those who had, nevertheless had some genuine fears about what might happen to them. Their nervousness, then, was quite appropriate to the novelty of the hospital setting, and it abated rapidly.

Apart from that short-lived nervousness, the pseudopatient behaved on the ward as he "normally" behaved. The pseudopatient spoke to patients and staff as he might ordinarily. Because there is uncommonly little to do on a psychiatric ward, he attempted to engage others in conversation. When asked by staff how he was feeling, he indicated that he was fine, that he no longer experienced symptoms. He responded to instructions from attendants, to calls for medication (which was not swallowed), and to dining-hall instructions. Beyond such activities as were available to him on the admissions ward, he spent his time writing down his observations about the ward, its patients, and the staff. Initially these notes were written "secretly," but as it soon became clear that no one much cared, they were subsequently written on standard tablets of paper in such public places as the dayroom. No secret was made of these activities.

The pseudopatient, very much as a true psychiatric patient, entered a hospital with no foreknowledge of when he would be discharged. Each was told that he would have to get out by his own devices, essentially by convincing the staff that he was sane. The psychological stresses associated with hospitalization were considerable, and all but one of the pseudopatients desired to be discharged almost immediately after being admitted. They were, therefore, motivated not only to behave sanely, but to be paragons of cooperation. That their behavior was in no way disruptive is confirmed by nursing reports, which have been obtained on most of the patients. These reports uniformly indicate that the patients were "friendly," "cooperative," and "exhibited no abnormal indications."

THE NORMAL ARE NOT DETECTABLY SANE

Despite their public "show" of sanity, the pseudopatients were never detected. Admitted, except in one case, with a diagnosis of schizophrenia (10), each was discharged with a diagnosis of schizophrenia "in remission." The label "in remission" should in no way be dismissed as a formality, for at no time during any hospitalization had any question been raised about any pseudopatient's simulation. Nor are there any indications in the hospital records that the pseudopatient's status was suspect. Rather, the evidence is strong that, once labeled schizophrenic, the pseudopatient was stuck with that label. If the pseudopatient was to be discharged, he must naturally be "in remission"; but he was not sane, nor, in the institution's view, had he ever been sane.

The uniform failure to recognize sanity cannot be attributed to the quality of the hospitals, for, although there were considerable variations among them, several are considered excellent. Nor can it be alleged that there was simply not enough time to observe the pseudopatients. Length of hospitalization ranged from 7 to 52 days, with an average of 19 days. The pseudopatients were not, in fact, carefully observed, but this failure clearly speaks more to traditions within psychiatric hospitals than to lack of opportunity.

Finally, it cannot be said that the failure to recognize the pseudopatients' sanity was due to the fact that they were not behaving sanely. While there was clearly some tension present in all of them, their daily visitors could detect no serious behavioral consequences—nor, indeed, could other patients. It was quite common for the patients to "detect" the pseudopatients' sanity. During the first three hospitalizations, when accurate counts were kept, 35 of a total of 118 patients on the admissions ward voiced their suspicions, some vigorously. "You're not crazy. You're a journalist, or a professor [referring to the continual note-taking]. You're checking up on the hospital." While most of the patients were reassured by the pseudopatient's insistence that he had been sick before he came in but was fine now, some continued to believe that the pseudopatient was sane throughout his hospitalization (11). The fact that the patients often recognized normality when staff did not raises important questions.

Failure to detect sanity during the course of hospitalization may be due to the fact that physicians operate with a strong bias toward what statisticians call the type 2 error (5). This is to say that physicians are more inclined to call a healthy person sick (a false positive, type 2) than a sick person healthy (a false negative, type 1). The reasons for this are not hard to find: it is clearly more dangerous to misdiagnose illness than health. Better to err on the side of caution, to suspect illness even among the healthy.

But what holds for medicine does not hold equally well for psychiatry. Medical illnesses, while unfortunate, are not commonly pejorative. Psychiatric diagnoses, on the contrary, carry with them personal, legal, and social stigmas (12). It was therefore important to see whether the tendency toward diagnosing the sane insane could be reversed. The following experiment was arranged at a research and teaching hospital whose staff had heard these findings but doubted that such an error could occur in their hospital. The staff was informed that at some time during the following 3 months, one or more pseudopatients would attempt to be admitted into the psychiatric hospital. Each staff member was asked to rate each patient who presented himself at admissions or on the ward according to the likelihood that the patient was a pseudopatient. A 10-point scale was used, with a 1 and 2 reflecting high confidence that the patient was a pseudopatient.

Judgments were obtained on 193 patients who were admitted for psychiatric treatment. All staff who had had sustained contact with or primary responsibility for the patient—attendants, nurses, psychiatrists, physicians, and psychologists—were asked to make judgments. Forty-one patients were alleged, with high confidence, to be pseudopatients by at least one member of the staff. Twenty-three were considered suspect by at least one psychiatrist. Nineteen were suspected by one psychiatrist *and* one other staff member. Actually, no genuine pseudopatient (at least from my group) presented himself during this period.

The experiment is instructive. It indicates that the tendency to designate sane people as insane can be reversed when the stakes (in this case, prestige and diagnostic acumen) are high. But what can be said of the 19 people who were suspected of being "sane" by one psychiatrist and another staff member? Were these people truly "sane," or was it rather the case that in the course of avoiding the type 2 error the staff tended to make more errors of the first sort—calling the crazy "sane"? There is no way of knowing. But one thing is certain: any diagnostic process that lends itself so readily to massive errors of this sort cannot be a very reliable one.

THE STICKINESS OF PSYCHODIAGNOSTIC LABELS

Beyond the tendency to call the healthy sick—a tendency that accounts better for diagnostic behavior on admission than it does for such behavior after a lengthy period of exposure—the data speak to the massive role of labeling in psychiatric assessment. Having once been labeled schizophrenic, there is nothing the pseudopatient can do to overcome the tag. The tag profoundly colors others' perceptions of him and his behavior.

From one viewpoint, these data are hardly surprising, for it has long been known that elements are given meaning by the context in which they occur. Gestalt psychology made this point vigorously, and Asch (13) demonstrated that there are "central" personality traits (such as "warm" versus "cold") which are so powerful that they markedly color the meaning of other information in forming an impression of a given personality (14). "Insane," "schizophrenic," "manic-depressive," and "crazy" are probably among the most powerful of such central traits. Once a person is designated abnormal, all of his other behaviors and characteristics are colored by that label. Indeed, that label is so powerful that many of the pseudopatients' normal behaviors were overlooked entirely or profoundly misinterpreted. Some examples may clarify this issue.

Earlier I indicated that there were no changes in the pseudopatient's personal history and current status beyond those of name, employment, and, where necessary, vocation. Otherwise, a veridical description of personal history and circumstances was offered. Those circumstances were not psychotic. How were they made consonant with the diagnosis of psychosis? Or were those diagnoses modified in such a way as to bring them into accord with the circumstances of the pseudopatient's life, as described by him?

As far as I can determine, diagnoses were in no way affected by the relative health of the circumstances of a pseudopatient's life. Rather, the reverse occurred: the perception of his circumstances was shaped entirely by the diagnosis. A clear example of such translation is found in the case of a pseudopatient who had had a close relationship with his mother but was rather remote from his father during his early childhood. During adolescence and beyond, however, his father became a close friend, while his relationship with his mother cooled. His present relationship with his wife was characteristically close and warm. Apart from occasional angry exchanges, friction was minimal. The children had rarely been spanked. Surely there is nothing especially pathological about such a history. Indeed, many readers may see a similar pattern in their own experiences, with no markedly deleterious consequences. Observe, however, how such a history was translated in the psychopathological context, this from the case summary prepared after the patient was discharged.

> This white 39-year-old male . . . manifests a long history of considerable ambivalence in close relationships, which begins in early childhood. A warm relationship with his mother cools during his adolescence. A distant relationship to his father is described as becoming very intense. Affective stability is absent. His attempts to control emotionality with his wife and children are punctuated by angry outbursts and, in the case of the children, spankings. And while he says that he has several good friends, one senses considerable ambivalence embedded in those relationships also. . . .

The facts of the case were unintentionally distorted by the staff to achieve consistency with a popular theory of the dynamics of a schizophrenic reaction (15). Nothing of an ambivalent nature had been described in relations with parents, spouse, or friends. To the extent that ambivalence could be inferred, it was probably not greater than is found in all human relationships. It is true the pseudopatient's relationships with his parents changed over time, but in the ordinary context that would hardly be remarkable—indeed, it might very well be expected. Clearly, the meaning ascribed to his verbalizations (that is, ambivalence, affective instability) was determined by the diagnosis: schizophrenia. An entirely different meaning would have been ascribed if it were known that the man was "normal."

All pseudopatients took extensive notes publicly. Under ordinary circumstances, such behavior would have raised questions in the minds of observers, as, in fact, it did among patients. Indeed, it seemed so certain that the notes would elicit suspicion that elaborate precautions were taken to remove them from the ward each day. But the precautions proved needless. The closest any staff member came to questioning these notes occurred when one pseudopatient asked his physician what kind of medication he was receiving and began to write down the response. "You needn't write it," he was told gently. "If you have trouble remembering, just ask me again."

If no questions were asked of the pseudopatients, how was their writing interpreted? Nursing records for three patients indicate that the writing was seen as an aspect of their pathological behavior. "Patient engages in writing behavior" was the daily nursing comment on one of the pseudopatients who was never questioned about his writing. Given that the patient is in the hospital, he must be psychologically disturbed. And given that he is disturbed, continuous writing must be a behavioral manifestation of that disturbance, perhaps a subset of the compulsive behaviors that are sometimes correlated with schizophrenia.

One tacit characteristic of psychiatric diagnosis is that it locates the sources of aberration within the individual and only rarely within the complex of stimuli that surrounds him. Consequently, behaviors that are stimulated by the environment are commonly misattributed to the patient's disorder. For example, one kindly nurse found a pseudopatient pacing the long hospital corridors. "Nervous, Mr. X?" she asked. "No, bored," he said.

The notes kept by pseudopatients are full of patient behaviors that were misinterpreted by well-intentioned staff. Often enough, a patient would go "berserk" because he had, wittingly or unwittingly, been mistreated by, say, an attendant. A nurse coming upon the scene would rarely inquire even cursorily into the environmental stimuli of the patient's behavior. Rather, she assumed that his upset derived from his pathology, not from his present interactions with other staff members. Occasionally, the staff might assume that the patient's family (especially when they had recently visited) or other patients had stimulated the outburst. But never were the staff found to assume that one of themselves or the structure of the hospital had anything to do with a patient's behavior. One psychiatrist pointed to a group of patients who were sitting outside the cafeteria entrance half an hour before lunchtime. To a group of young residents he indicated that such behavior was characteristic of the oral-acquisitive nature of the syndrome. It seemed not to occur to him that there were very few things to anticipate in a psychiatric hospital besides eating.

A psychiatric label has a life and an influence of its own. Once the impression has been formed that the patient is schizophrenic, the expectation is that he will continue to be schizophrenic. When a sufficient amount of time has passed, during which the patient has done nothing bizarre, he is considered to be in remission and available for discharge. But the label endures beyond discharge, with the unconfirmed expectation that he will behave as a schizophrenic again. Such labels, conferred by mental health professionals, are as influential on the patient as they are on his relatives and friends, and it should not surprise anyone that the diagnosis acts on all of them as a self-fulfilling prophecy. Eventually, the patient himself accepts the diagnosis, with all of its surplus meanings and expectations, and behaves accordingly (5).

The inferences to be made from these matters are quite simple. Much as Zigler and Phillips have demonstrated that there is enormous overlap in the symptoms presented by patients who have been variously diagnosed (16), so there is enormous overlap in the behaviors of the sane and the insane. The sane are not "sane" all of the time. We lose our tempers "for no good reason." We are occasionally depressed or anxious, again for no good reason. And we may find it difficult to get along with one or another person—again for no reason that we can specify. Similarly, the insane are not always insane. Indeed, it was the impression of the pseudopatients while living with them that they were sane for long periods of time—that the bizarre behaviors upon which their diagnoses were allegedly predicated constituted only a small fraction of their total behavior. If it makes no sense to label ourselves permanently depressed on the basis of an occasional depression, then it takes better evidence than is presently available to label all patients insane or schizophrenic on the basis of bizarre behaviors or cognitions. It seems more useful, as Mischel (17) has pointed out, to limit our discussions to *behaviors*, the stimuli that provoke them, and their correlates.

It is not known why powerful impressions of personality traits, such as "crazy" or "insane," arise. Conceivably, when the origins of and stimuli that give rise to a behavior are remote or unknown, or when the behavior strikes us as immutable, trait labels regarding the *behaver* arise. When, on the other hand, the origins and stimuli are known and available, discourse is limited to the behavior itself. Thus, I may hallucinate because I am sleeping, or I may hallucinate because I have ingested a peculiar drug. These are termed sleep-induced hallucinations, or dreams, and drug-induced hallucinations, respectively. But when the stimuli to my hallucinations are unknown, that is called craziness, or schizophrenia—as if that inference were somehow as illuminating as the others.

THE EXPERIENCE OF PSYCHIATRIC HOSPITALIZATION

The term "mental illness" is of recent origin. It was coined by people who were humane in their inclinations and who wanted very much to raise the station of (and the public's sympathies toward) the psychologically disturbed from that of witches and "crazies" to one that was akin to the physically ill. And they were at least partially successful, for the treatment of the mentally ill *has* improved considerably over the years. But while treatment has improved, it is doubtful that people really regard the mentally ill in the same way that they view the physically ill. A broken leg is something one recovers from, but mental illness allegedly endures forever (18). A broken leg does not threaten the observer, but a crazy schizophrenic? There is by now a host of evidence that attitudes toward the mentally ill are characterized by fear, hostility, aloofness, suspicion, and dread (19). The mentally ill are society's lepers.

That such attitudes infect the general population is perhaps not surprising, only upsetting. But that they affect the professionals—attendants, nurses, physicians, psychologists, and social workers—who treat and deal with the mentally ill is more disconcerting, both because such attitudes are self-evidently pernicious and because they are unwitting. Most mental health professionals would insist that they are sympathetic toward the mentally ill, that they are neither avoidant nor hostile. But it is more likely that an exquisite ambivalence characterizes their relations with psychiatric patients, such that their avowed impulses are only part of their entire attitude. Negative attitudes are there too and can easily be detected. Such attitudes should not surprise us. They are the natural offspring of the labels patients wear and the places in which they are found.

Consider the structure of the typical psychiatric hospital. Staff and patients are strictly segregated. Staff have their own living space, including their dining facilities, bathrooms, and assembly places. The glassed quarters that contain the professional staff, which the pseudopatients came to call "the cage," sit out on every dayroom. The staff emerge primarily for caretaking purposes—to give medication, to conduct a therapy or group meeting, to instruct or reprimand a patient. Otherwise, staff keep to themselves, almost as if the disorder that afflicts their charges is somehow catching.

So much is patient–staff segregation the rule that, for four public hospitals in which an attempt was made to measure the degree to which staff and patients mingle, it was necessary to use "time out of the staff cage" as the operational measure. While it was not the case that all time spent out of the cage was spent mingling with patients (attendants, for example, would occasionally emerge to watch television in the dayroom), it was the only way in which one could gather reliable data on time for measuring.

The average amount of time spent by attendants outside of the cage was 11.3 percent (range, 3 to 52 percent). This figure does not represent only time spent mingling with patients, but also includes time spent on such chores as folding laundry, supervising patients while they shave, directing ward clean-up, and sending patients to off-ward activities. It was the relatively rare attendant who spent time talking with patients or playing games with them. It proved impossible to obtain a "percent mingling time" for nurses, since the amount of time they spent out of the cage was too brief. Rather, we counted instances of emergence from the cage. On the average, daytime nurses emerged from the cage 11.5 times per shift, including instances when they left the ward entirely (range, 4 to 39 times). Late afternoon and night nurses were even less available, emerging on the average 9.4 times per shift (range, 4 to 41 times).

Table 1. *Self-initiated Contact by Pseudopatients with Psychiatrists and Nurses and Attendants, Compared to Contact with Other Groups.*

	Psychiatric hospitals		University campus (nonmedical)	University medical center		
				Physicians		
Contact	(1) Psychiatrists	(2) Nurses and attendants	(3) Faculty	(4) "Looking for a psychiatrist"	(5) "Looking for an internist"	(6) No additional comment
Responses						
Moves on, head averted (%)	71	88	0	0	0	0
Makes eye contact (%)	23	10	0	11	0	0
Pauses and chats (%)	2	2	0	11	0	10
Stops and talks (%)	4	0.5	100	78	100	90
Mean number of questions answered (out of 6)	[a]	[a]	6	3.8	4.8	4.5
Respondents (No.)	13	47	14	18	15	10
Attempts (No.)	185	1283	14	18	15	10

[a]Not applicable.

Data on early morning nurses, who arrived usually after midnight and departed at 8 a.m., are not available because patients were asleep during most of this period.

Physicians, especially psychiatrists, were even less available. They were rarely seen on the wards. Quite commonly, they would be seen only when they arrived and departed, with the remaining time being spent in their offices or in the cage. On the average, physicians emerged on the ward 6.7 times per day (range, 1 to 17 times). It proved difficult to make an accurate estimate in this regard, since physicians often maintained hours that allowed them to come and go at different times.

The hierarchical organization of the psychiatric hospital has been commented on before (20), but the latent meaning of that kind of organization is worth noting again. Those with the most power have least to do with patients, and those with the least power are most involved with them. Recall, however, that the acquisition of role-appropriate behaviors occurs mainly through the observation of others, with the most powerful having the most influence. Consequently, it is understandable that attendants not only spend more time with patients than do any other members of the staff—that is required by their station in the hierarchy—but also, insofar as they learn from their superiors' behavior, spend as little time with patients as they can. Attendants are seen mainly in the cage, which is where the models, the action, and the power are.

I turn now to a different set of studies, these dealing with staff response to patient-initiated contact. It has long been known that the amount of time a person spends with you can be an index of your significance to him. If he initiates and maintains eye contact, there is reason to believe that he is considering your requests and needs. If he pauses to chat or actually stops and talks, there is added reason to infer that he is individuating you. In four hospitals, the pseudopatient approached the staff member with a request which took the following form: "Pardon me, Mr. [or Dr. or Mrs.] X, could you tell me when I will be eligible for grounds privileges?" (or " . . . when I will be presented at the staff meeting?" or " . . . when I am likely to be discharged?"). While the content of the question varied according to the appropriateness of the target and the pseudopatient's (apparent) current needs the form was always a courteous and relevant request for information. Care was taken never to approach a particular member of the staff more than once a day, lest the staff member become suspicious or irritated. In examining these data, remember that the behavior of the pseudopatients was neither bizarre nor disruptive. One could indeed engage in good conversation with them.

The data for these experiments are shown in Table 1, separately for physicians (column 1) and for nurses and attendants (column 2). Minor differences between these four institutions were overwhelmed by the degree to which staff avoided continuing contacts that patients had initiated. By far, their most common response consisted of either a brief response to the question, offered while they were "on the move" and with head averted, or no response at all.

The encounter frequently took the following bizarre form: (pseudopatient) "Pardon me, Dr. X. Could you tell me when I am eligible for grounds privileges?" (physician) "Good morning, Dave. How are you today?" (Moves off without waiting for a response.)

It is instructive to compare these data with data recently obtained at Stanford University. It has been alleged that large and eminent universities are characterized by faculty who are so busy that they have no time for students. For this comparison, a young lady approached individual faculty members who seemed to be walking purposefully to some meeting or teaching engagement and asked them the following six questions.

1. "Pardon me, could you direct me to Encina Hall?" (at the medical school: " . . . to the Clinical Research Center?").
2. "Do you know where Fish Annex is?" (there is no Fish Annex at Stanford).
3. "Do you teach here?"
4. "How does one apply for admission to the college?" (at the medical school: " . . . to the medical school?").
5. "Is it difficult to get in?"
6. "Is there financial aid?"

Without exception, as can be seen in Table 1 (column 3), all of the questions were answered. No matter how rushed they were, all respondents not only maintained eye contact, but stopped to talk. Indeed, many of the respondents went out of their way to direct or take the questioner to the office she was seeking, to try to locate "Fish Annex," or to discuss with her the possibilities of being admitted to the university.

Similar data, also shown in Table 1 (columns 4, 5, and 6), were obtained in the hospital. Here too, the young lady came prepared with six questions. After the first question, however, she remarked to 18 of her respondents (column 4), "I'm looking for a psychiatrist," and to 15 others (column 5), "I'm looking for an internist." Ten other respondents received no inserted comment (column 6). The general degree of cooperative responses is considerably higher for these university groups than it was for pseudopatients in psychiatric hospitals. Even so, differences are apparent within the medical school setting. Once having indicated that she was looking for a psychiatrist, the degree of cooperation elicited was less than when she sought an internist.

POWERLESSNESS AND DEPERSONALIZATION

Eye contact and verbal contact reflect concern and individuation; their absence, avoidance and depersonalization. The data I have presented do not do justice to the rich daily encounters that grew up around matters of depersonalization and avoidance. I have records of patients who were beaten by staff for the sin of having initiated verbal contact. During my own experience, for example, one patient was beaten in the presence of other patients for having approached an attendant and told him, "I like you." Occasionally, punishment meted out to patients for misdemeanors seemed so excessive that it could not be justified by the most radical interpretations of psychiatric canon. Nevertheless, they appeared to go unquestioned. Tempers were often short. A patient who had not heard a call for medication would be roundly excoriated, and the morning attendants would often wake patients with, "Come on, you m-----f-----s, out of bed!"

Neither anecdotal nor "hard" data can convey the overwhelming sense of powerlessness which invades the individual as he is continually exposed to the depersonalization of the psychiatric hospital. It hardly matters *which* psychiatric hospital—the excellent public ones and the very plush private hospital were better than the rural and shabby ones in this regard, but, again, the features that psychiatric hospitals had in common overwhelmed by far their apparent differences.

Powerlessness was evident everywhere. The patient is deprived of many of his legal rights by dint of his psychiatric commitment (21). He is shorn of credibility by virtue of his psychiatric label. His freedom of movement is restricted. He cannot initiate contact with the staff, but may only respond to such overtures as they make. Personal privacy is minimal. Patient quarters and possessions can be entered and examined by any staff member, for whatever reason. His personal history and anguish is available to any staff member (often including the "grey lady" and "candy striper" volunteer) who chooses to read his folder, regardless of their therapeutic relationship to him. His personal hygiene and waste evacuation are often monitored. The water closets may have no doors.

At times, depersonalization reached such proportions that pseudopatients had the sense that they were invisible, or at least unworthy of account. Upon being admitted, I and other pseudopatients took the initial physical examinations in a semipublic room, where staff members went about their own business as if we were not there.

On the ward, attendants delivered verbal and occasionally serious physical abuse to patients in the presence of other observing patients, some of whom (the pseudopatients) were writing it all down. Abusive behavior, on the other hand, terminated quite abruptly when other staff members were known to be coming. Staff are credible witnesses. Patients are not.

A nurse unbuttoned her uniform to adjust her brassiere in the presence of an entire ward of viewing men. One did not have the sense that she was being seductive. Rather, she didn't notice us. A group of staff persons might point to a patient in the dayroom and discuss him animatedly, as if he were not there.

One illuminating instance of depersonalization and invisibility occurred with regard to medications. All told, the pseudopatients were administered nearly 2100 pills, including Elavil, Stelazine, Compazine, and Thorazine, to name but a few. (That such a variety of medications should have been administered to patients presenting identical symptoms is itself worthy of note.) Only two were swallowed. The rest were either pocketed or deposited in the toilet. The pseudopatients were not alone in this. Although I have no precise records on how many patients rejected their medications, the pseudopatients frequently found the medications of other patients in the toilet before they deposited their own. As long as they were cooperative, their behavior and the pseudopatients' own in this matter, as in other important matters, went unnoticed throughout.

Reactions to such depersonalization among pseudopatients were intense. Although they had come to the hospital as participant observers and were fully aware that they did not "belong," they nevertheless found themselves caught up in and fighting the process of depersonalization. Some examples: a graduate student in psychology asked his wife to bring his textbooks to the hospital so he could "catch up on his homework"—this despite the elaborate precautions taken to conceal his professional association. The same student, who had trained for quite some time to get into the hospital, and who had looked forward to the experience, "remembered" some drag races that he had wanted to see on the weekend and insisted that he be discharged by that time. Another pseudopatient attempted a romance with a nurse. Subsequently, he informed the staff that he was applying for admission to graduate school in psychology and was very likely to be admitted, since a graduate professor was one of his regular hospital visitors. The same person began to engage in psychotherapy with other patients—all of this as a way of becoming a person in an impersonal environment.

THE SOURCES OF DEPERSONALIZATION

What are the origins of depersonalization? I have already mentioned two. First are attitudes held by all of us toward the mentally ill—including those who treat them—attitudes characterized by fear, distrust, and horrible expectations on the one hand, and benevolent intentions on the other. Our ambivalence leads, in this instance as in others, to avoidance.

Second, and not entirely separate, the hierarchical structure of the psychiatric hospital facilitates depersonalization. Those who are at the top have least to do with patients, and their behavior inspires the rest of the staff. Average daily contact with psychiatrists, psychologists, residents, and physicians combined ranged from 3.9 to 25.1 minutes, with an overall mean of 6.8 (six pseudopatients over a total of 129 days of hospitalization). Included in this average are time spent in the admissions interview, ward meetings in the presence of a senior staff member, group and individual psychotherapy contacts, case presentation conferences, and discharge meetings. Clearly, patients do not spend much time in interpersonal contact with doctoral staff. And doctoral staff serve as models for nurses and attendants.

There are probably other sources. Psychiatric installations are presently in serious financial straits. Staff shortages are pervasive, staff time at a premium. Something has to give, and that something is patient contact. Yet, while financial stresses are realities, too much can be made of them. I have the impression that the psychological forces that result in depersonalization are much stronger than the fiscal ones and that the addition of more staff would not correspondingly improve patient care in this regard. The incidence of staff meetings and the enormous amount of record-keeping on patients, for example, have not been as substantially reduced as has patient contact. Priorities exist, even during hard times. Patient contact is not a significant priority in the traditional psychiatric hospital, and fiscal pressures do not account for this. Avoidance and depersonalization may.

Heavy reliance upon psychotropic medication tacitly contributes to depersonalization by convincing staff that treatment is indeed being conducted and that further patient contact may not be necessary. Even here, however, caution needs to be exercised in understanding the role of psychotropic drugs. If patients were powerful rather than powerless, if they were viewed as interesting individuals rather than diagnostic entities, if they were socially significant rather than social lepers, if their anguish truly and wholly compelled our sympathies and concerns, would we not *seek* contact with them, despite the availability of medications? Perhaps for the pleasure of it all?

THE CONSEQUENCES OF LABELING AND DEPERSONALIZATION

Whenever the ratio of what is known to what needs to be known approaches zero, we tend to invent "knowledge" and assume that we understand more than we actually do. We seem unable to acknowledge that we simply don't know. The needs for diagnosis and remediation of behavioral and emotional problems are enormous. But rather than acknowledge that we are just embarking on understanding, we continue to label patients "schizophrenic," "manic-depressive," and "insane," as if in those words we had captured the essence of understanding. The facts of the matter are that we have known for a long time that diagnoses are often not useful or reliable, but we have nevertheless continued to use them. We now know that we cannot distinguish insanity from sanity. It is depressing to consider how that information will be used.

Not merely depressing, but frightening. How many people, one wonders, are sane but not recognized as such in our psychiatric institutions? How many have been needlessly stripped of their privileges of citizenship, from the right to vote and drive to that of handling their own accounts? How many have feigned insanity in order to avoid the criminal consequences of their behavior, and, conversely, how many would rather stand trial than live interminably in a psychiatric hospital—but are wrongly thought to be mentally ill? How many have been stigmatized by well-intentioned, but nevertheless erroneous, diagnoses? On the last point, recall again that a "type 2 error" in psychiatric diagnosis does not have the same consequences it does in medical diagnosis. A diagnosis of cancer that has been found to be in error is cause for celebration. But psychiatric diagnoses are rarely found to be in error. The label sticks, a mark of inadequacy forever.

Finally, how many patients might be "sane" outside the psychiatric hospital but seem insane in it—not because craziness resides in them, as it were, but because they are responding to a bizarre setting, one that may be unique to institutions which harbor nether people? Goffman (4) calls the process of socialization to such institutions "mortification"—an apt metaphor that includes the processes of depersonalization that have been described here. And while it is impossible to know whether the pseudopatients' responses to these processes are characteristic of all inmates—they were, after all, not real patients—it is difficult to believe that these processes of socialization to a psychiatric hospital provide useful attitudes or habits of response for living in the "real world."

SUMMARY AND CONCLUSIONS

It is clear that we cannot distinguish the sane from the insane in psychiatric hospitals. The hospital itself imposes a special environment in which the meanings of behavior can easily be misunderstood. The consequences to patients hospitalized in such an environment—the powerlessness, depersonalization, segregation, mortification, and self-labeling—seem undoubtedly countertherapeutic.

I do not, even now, understand this problem well enough to perceive solutions. But two matters seem to have some promise. The first concerns the proliferation of community mental health facilities, of crisis intervention centers, of the human potential movement, and of behavior therapies that, for all of their own problems, tend to avoid psychiatric labels, to focus on specific problems and behaviors, and to retain the individual in a relatively nonpejorative environment. Clearly, to the extent that we refrain from sending the distressed to insane places, our impressions of them are less likely to be distorted. (The risk of distorted perceptions, it seems to me, is always present, since we are much more sensitive to an individual's behaviors and verbalizations than we are to the subtle contextual stimuli that often promote them. At issue here is a matter of magnitude. And, as I have shown, the magnitude of distortion is exceedingly high in the extreme context that is a psychiatric hospital.)

The second matter that might prove promising speaks to the need to increase the sensitivity of mental health workers and researchers to the *Catch 22* position of psychiatric patients. Simply reading materials in this area will be of help to some such workers and researchers. For others, directly experiencing the impact of psychiatric hospitalization will be of enormous use. Clearly, further research into the social psychology of such total institutions will both facilitate treatment and deepen understanding.

I and the other pseudopatients in the psychiatric setting had distinctly negative reactions. We do not pretend to describe the subjective experiences of true patients. Theirs may be different from ours, particularly with the passage of time and the necessary process of adaptation to one's environment. But we can and do speak to the relatively more objective indices of treatment within the hospital. It could be a mistake, and a very unfortunate one, to consider that what happened to us derived from malice or stupidity on the part of the staff. Quite the contrary, our overwhelming impression of them was of people who really cared, who were committed and who were uncommonly intelligent. Where they failed, as they sometimes did painfully, it would be more accurate to attribute those failures to the environment in which they, too, found themselves than to personal callousness. Their perceptions and behavior were controlled by the situation, rather than being motivated by a malicious disposition. In a more benign environment, one that was less attached to global diagnosis, their behaviors and judgments might have been more benign and effective.

REFERENCES AND NOTES

1. P. Ash, *J. Abnorm. Soc. Psychol.* 44, 272 (1949); A. T. Beck, *Amer. J. Psychiat.* 119, 210 (1962); A. T. Boisen, *Psychiatry* 2, 233 (1938); N. Kreitman, *J. Ment. Sci.* 107, 876 (1961); N. Kreitman, P. Sainsbury, J. Morrisey, J. Towers, J. Scrivener, *ibid.*, p. 887; H. O. Schmitt and C. P. Fonda, *J. Abnorm. Soc. Psychol.* 52,

262 (1956); W. Seeman, *J. Nerv. Ment. Dis.* 118, 541 (1953). For an analysis of these artifacts and summaries of the disputes, see J. Zubin, *Annu. Rev. Psychol.* 13, 373 (1967); L. Phillips and J. G. Draguns, *ibid.* 22, 447 (1971).
2. R. Benedict, *J. Gen. Psychol.* 10, 59 (1934).
3. See in this regard H. Becker, *Outsiders: Studies in the Sociology of Deviance* (Free Press, New York, 1963); B. M. Braginsky, D. D. Braginsky, K. Ring, *Methods of Madness: The Mental Hospital as a Last Resort* (Holt, Rinehart & Winston, New York, 1969); G. M. Crocetti and P. V. Lemkau, *Amer. Sociol. Rev.* 30, 577 (1965); E. Goffman, *Behavior in Public Places* (Free Press, New York, 1964): R. D. Laing, *The Divided Self: A Study of Sanity and Madness* (Quadrangle, Chicago, 1960); D. L. Phillips, *Amer. Sociol. Rev.* 28, 963 (1963); T. R. Sarbin, *Psychol. Today* 6, 18 (1972), E. Schur, *Amer. J. Sociol.* 75, 309 (1969); T. Szasz, *Law, Liberty and Psychiatry* (Macmillan, New York, 1963); *The Myth of Mental Illness: Foundations of a Theory of Mental Illness* (Hoeber Harper, New York, 1963). For a critique of some of these views, see W. R. Gove, *Amer. Sociol. Rev.* 35, 873 (1970).
4. E. Goffman, *Asylums* (Doubleday, Garden City, N.Y., 1961).
5. T. J. Scheff, *Being Mentally Ill: A Sociological Theory* (Aldine, Chicago, 1966).
6. Data from a ninth pseudopatient are not incorporated in this report because, although his sanity went undetected, he falsified aspects of his personal history, including his marital status and parental relationships. His experimental behaviors therefore were not identical to those of the other pseudopatients.
7. A. Barry, *Bellevue Is a State of Mind* (Harcourt Brace Jovanovich, New York, 1971); I. Belknap, *Human Problems of a State Mental Hospital* (McGraw Hill, New York, 1956); W. Caudill, F. C. Redlich, H. R. Gilmore, E. B. Brody, *Amer. J. Orthopsychiat.* 22, 314 (1952); A. R. Goldman, R. H. Bohr, T. A. Steinberg, *Prof. Psychol.* 1, 427 (1970); unauthored, *Roche Report* 1 (no. 13), 8 (1971).
8. Beyond the personal difficulties that the pseudopatient is likely to experience in the hospital, there are legal and social ones that, combined, require considerable attention before entry. For example, once admitted to a psychiatric institution, it is difficult, if not impossible, to be discharged on short notice, state law to the contrary notwithstanding. I was not sensitive to these difficulties at the outset of the project, nor to the personal and situational emergencies that can arise, but later a writ of habeas corpus was prepared for each of the entering pseudopatients and an attorney was kept "on call" during every hospitalization. I am grateful to John Kaplan and Robert Bartels for legal advice and assistance in these matters.
9. However distasteful such concealment is, it was a necessary first step to examining these questions. Without concealment, there would have been no way to know how valid these experiences were; nor was there any way of knowing whether whatever detections occurred were a tribute to the diagnostic acumen of the staff or to the hospital's rumor network. Obviously, since my concerns are general ones that cut across individual hospitals and staffs, I have respected their anonymity and have eliminated clues that might lead to their identification.
10. Interestingly, of the 12 admissions, 11 were diagnosed as schizophrenic and one, with the identical symptomatology, as manic-depressive psychosis. This diagnosis has a more favorable prognosis, and it was given by the only private hospital in our sample. On the relations between social class and psychiatric diagnosis, see A. deB. Hollingshead and F. C. Redlich, *Social Class and Mental Illness: A Community Study* (Wiley, New York, 1958).
11. It is possible, of course, that patients have quite broad latitudes in diagnosis and therefore are inclined to call many people sane, even those whose behavior is patently aberrant. However, although we have no hard data on this matter, it was our distinct impression that this was not the case. In many instances, patients not only singled us out for attention, but came to imitate our behaviors and styles.
12. J. Cumming and E. Cumming, *Community Ment. Health* 1, 135 (1965); A. Farina and K. Ring, *J. Abnorm. Psychol.* 70, 47 (1965); H. E. Freeman and O. G. Simmons, *The Mental Patient Comes Home* (Wiley, New York, 1963); W. J. Johannsen, *Ment. Hygiene* 53, 218 (1969); A. S. Linsky, *Soc. Psychiat.* 5, 166 (1970).
13. S. E. Asch, *J. Abnorm. Soc. Psychol.* 41, 258 (1946); *Social Psychology* (Prentice-Hall, New York, 1952).
14. See also I. N. Mensh and J. Wishner, *J. Personality* 16, 188 (1947); J. Wishner, *Psychol. Rev.* 67, 96 (1960); J. S. Bruner and R. Tagiuri, in *Handbook of Social Psychology*, G. Lindzey, Ed. (Addison-Wesley, Cambridge, Mass., 1954), vol. 2, pp. 634–654; J. S. Bruner, D. Shapiro, R. Tagiuri, in *Person Perception and Interpersonal Behavior*, R. Tagiuri and L. Petrullo, Eds. (Stanford Univ. Press, Stanford, Calif., 1958), pp. 277–288.
15. For an example of a similar self-fulfilling prophecy, in this instance dealing with the "central" trait of intelligence, see R. Rosenthal and L. Jacobson, *Pygmalion in the Classroom* (Holt, Rinehart & Winston, New York, 1968).
16. E. Zigler and L. Phillips, *J. Abnorm. Soc. Psychol.* 63, 69 (1961). See also R. K. Freudenberg and J. P. Robertson, *A.M.A. Arch. Neurol. Psychiatr.* 76, 14 (1956).
17. W. Mischel, *Personality and Assessment* (Wiley, New York, 1968).
18. The most recent and unfortunate instance of this tenet is that of Senator Thomas Eagleton.
19. T. R. Sarbin and J. C. Mancuso, *J. Clin. Consult. Psychol.* 35, 159 (1970); T. R. Sarbin, *ibid.* 31, 447 (1967); J. C. Nunnally, Jr., *Popular Conceptions of Mental Health* (Holt, Rinehart & Winston, New York, 1961).
20. A. H. Stanton and M. S. Schwartz, *The Mental Hospital: A Study of Institutional Participation in Psychiatric Illness and Treatment* (Basic, New York, 1954).
21. D. B. Wexler and S. E. Scoville, *Ariz. Law Rev.* 13, 1 (1971).
22. I thank W. Mischel, E. Orne, and M. S. Rosenhan for comments on an earlier draft of this manuscript.

Personality Disorder *Is* Disease

David P. Ausubel

In two recent articles in the *American Psychologist*, Szasz (1960) and Mowrer (1960) have argued the case for discarding the concept of mental illness. The essence of Mowrer's position is that since medical science lacks "demonstrated competence . . . in psychiatry," psychology would be wise to "get out" from "under the penumbra of medicine," and to regard the behavior disorders as manifestations of sin rather than of disease (p. 302). Szasz' position, as we shall see shortly, is somewhat more complex than Mowrer's, but agrees with the latter in emphasizing the moral as opposed to the psychopathological basis of abnormal behavior.

For a long time now, clinical psychology has both repudiated the relevance of moral judgment and accountability for assessing behavioral acts and choices, and has chafed under medical (psychiatric) control and authority in diagnosing and treating the personality disorders. One can readily appreciate, therefore, Mowrer's eagerness to sever the historical and professional ties that bind clinical psychology to medicine, even if this means denying that psychological disturbances constitute a form of illness, and even if psychology's close working relationship with psychiatry must be replaced by a new rapprochement with sin and theology, as "the lesser of two evils" (pp. 302–303). One can also sympathize with Mowrer's and Szasz' dissatisfaction with prevailing amoral and nonjudgmental trends in clinical psychology and with their entirely commendable efforts to restore moral judgment and accountability to a respectable place among the criteria used in evaluating human behavior, both normal and abnormal.

Opposition to these two trends in the handling of the behavior disorders (i.e., to medical control and to nonjudgmental therapeutic attitudes), however, does not necessarily imply abandonment of the concept of mental illness. There is no inconsistency whatsoever in maintaining, on the one hand, that most purposeful human activity has a moral aspect the reality of which psychologists cannot afford to ignore (Ausubel, 1952, p. 462), that man is morally accountable for the majority of his misdeeds (Ausubel, 1952, p. 469), and that psychological rather than medical training and sophistication are basic to competence in the personality disorders (Ausubel, 1956, p. 101), and affirming, on the other hand, that the latter disorders are genuine manifestations of illness. In recent years psychology has been steadily moving away from the formerly fashionable stance of ethical neutrality in the behavioral sciences; and in spite of strident medical claims regarding superior professional qualifications and preclusive legal responsibility for treating psychiatric patients, and notwithstanding the nominally restrictive provisions of medical practice acts, clinical psychologists have been assuming an increasingly more important, independent, and responsible role in treating the mentally ill population of the United States.

It would be instructive at this point to examine the tactics of certain other medically allied professions in freeing themselves from medical control and in acquiring independent, legally recognized professional status. In no instance have they resorted to the devious strategem of denying that they were treating diseases, in the hope of mollifying medical opposition and legitimizing their own professional activities. They took the position instead that simply because a given condition is defined as a disease, its treatment need not necessarily be turned over to doctors of medicine if other equally competent professional specialists were available. That this position is legally and politically tenable is demonstrated by the fact that an impressively large number of recognized diseases are legally treated today by both medical *and* non-medical specialists (e.g., diseases of the mouth, face, jaws, teeth, eyes, and feet). And there are few convincing reasons for believing that psychiatrists wield that much more political power than physicians, maxillofacial surgeons, ophthalmologists, and orthopedic surgeons, that they could be successful where these latter specialists have failed, in legally restricting practice in their particular area of competence to holders of the medical degree. Hence, even if psychologists were not currently managing to hold their own vis-à-vis psychiatrists, it would be far less dangerous and much more forthright to press for the necessary ameliorative legislation than to seek cover behind an outmoded and thoroughly discredited conception of the behavior disorders.

THE SZASZ-MOWRER POSITION

Szasz' (1960) contention that the concept of mental illness "now functions merely as a convenient myth" (p. 118) is grounded on four unsubstantiated and logically untenable propositions, which can be fairly summarized as follows:

1. Only symptoms resulting from demonstrable physical lesions qualify as legitimate manifestations of disease. Brain pathology is a type of physical lesion, but its symptoms, properly speaking, are neurological rather than psychological in nature. Under no circumstances, therefore, can mental symptoms be considered a form of illness.

2. A basic dichotomy exists between *mental* symptoms, on the one hand, which are subjective in nature, dependent on subjective judgment and personal involvement of the observer, and referable to cultural-ethical norms, and *physical* symptoms, on the other hand, which are allegedly

objective in nature, ascertainable without personal involvement of the observer, and independent of cultural norms and ethical standards. Only symptoms possessing the latter set of characteristics are genuinely reflective of illness and amenable to medical treatment.

3. Mental symptoms are merely expressions of problems of living and, hence, cannot be regarded as manifestations of a pathological condition. The concept of mental illness is misleading and demonological because it seeks to explain psychological disturbance in particular and human disharmony in general in terms of a metaphorical but nonexistent disease entity, instead of attributing them to inherent difficulties in coming to grips with elusive problems of choice and responsibility.

4. Personality disorders, therefore, can be most fruitfully conceptualized as products of moral conflict, confusion, and aberration. Mowrer (1960) extends this latter proposition to include the dictum that psychiatric symptoms are primarily reflective of unacknowledged sin, and that individuals manifesting these symptoms are responsible for and deserve their suffering, both because of their original transgressions and because they refuse to avow and expiate their guilt (pp. 301, 304).

Widespread adoption of the Szasz-Mowrer view of the personality disorders would, in my opinion, turn back the psychiatric clock twenty-five hundred years. The most significant and perhaps the only real advance registered by mankind in evolving a rational and humane method of handling behavioral aberrations has been in substituting a concept of disease for the demonological and retributional doctrines regarding their nature and etiology that flourished until comparatively recent times. Conceptualized as illness, the symptoms of personality disorders can be interpreted in the light of underlying stresses and resistances, both genic and environmental, and can be evaluated in relation to *specifiable* quantitative and qualitative norms of appropriately adaptive behavior, both cross-culturally and within a particular cultural context. It would behoove us, therefore, before we abandon the concept of mental illness and return to the medieval doctrine of unexpiated sin or adopt Szasz' ambiguous criterion of difficulty in ethical choice and responsibility, to subject the foregoing propositions to careful and detailed study.

Mental Symptoms and Brain Pathology

Although I agree with Szasz in rejecting the doctrine that ultimately some neuroanatomic or neurophysiologic defect will be discovered in *all* cases of personality disorder, I disagree with his reasons for not accepting this proposition. Notwithstanding Szasz' straw man presentation of their position, the proponents of the extreme somatic view do not really assert that the *particular nature* of a patient's disordered beliefs can be correlated with "certain definite lesions in the nervous system" (Szasz, 1960, p. 113). They hold, rather, that normal cognitive and behavioral functioning depends on the anatomic and physiologic integrity of certain key areas of the brain, and that impairment of this substrate integrity, therefore, provides a physical basis for disturbed ideation and behavior, but does not explain, except in a very gross way, the particular kinds of symptoms involved. In fact, they are generally inclined to attribute the *specific* character of the patient's symptoms to the nature of his pre-illness personality structure, the substrate integrity of which is impaired by the lesion or metabolic defect in question.

Nevertheless, even though this type of reasoning plausibly accounts for the psychological symptoms found in general paresis, various toxic deleria, and other comparable conditions, it is an extremely improbable explanation of *all* instances of personality disorder. Unlike the tissues of any other organ, brain tissue possesses the unique property of making possible awareness of and adjustment to the world of sensory, social, and symbolic stimulation. Hence, by virtue of this unique relationship of the nervous system to the environment, diseases of behavior and personality may reflect abnormalities in personal and social adjustment, quite apart from any structural or metabolic disturbance in the underlying neural substrate. I would conclude, therefore, that although brain pathology is probably not the most important cause of behavior disorder, it is undoubtedly responsible for the incidence of *some* psychological abnormalities *as well as* for various neurological signs and symptoms.

But even if we completely accepted Szasz' view that brain pathology does not account for any symptoms of personality disorder, it would still be unnecessary to accept his assertion that to qualify as a genuine manifestation of disease a given symptom must be caused by a physical lesion. Adoption of such a criterion would be arbitrary and inconsistent both with medical and lay connotations of the term "disease," which in current usage is generally regarded as including any marked deviation, physical, mental, or behavioral, from normally desirable standards of structural and functional integrity.

Mental versus Physical Symptoms

Szasz contends that since the analogy between physical and mental symptoms is patently fallacious, the postulated parallelism between physical and mental disease is logically untenable. This line of reasoning is based on the assumption that the two categories of symptoms can be sharply dichotomized with respect to such basic dimensions as objectivity-subjectivity, the relevance of cultural norms, and the need for personal involvement of the observer. In my opinion, the existence of such a dichotomy cannot be empirically demonstrated in convincing fashion.

Practically all symptoms of bodily disease involve some elements of subjective judgment—both on the part of the patient and of the physician. Pain is perhaps the most important and commonly used criterion of physical illness. Yet, any evaluation of its reported locus, intensity, character, and duration is dependent upon the patient's subjective appraisal of his own sensations and on the physician's assessment of the latter's pain threshold, intelligence, and personality structure. It is also a medical commonplace that the severity of pain in most instances of bodily illness may be mitigated by the administration of a placebo. Furthermore, in taking a meaningful history the physician must not only serve as a participant observer but also as a skilled interpreter of human behavior. It is the rare patient who does not react psychologically to the signs of physical illness; and hence physicians are constantly called upon to decide, for example, to what extent precordial pain and reported tightness in the chest are manifestations of coronary insufficiency, of fear of cardiac disease and impending death, or of combinations of both conditions. Even such allegedly objective signs as pulse rate, BMR, blood pressure, and blood cholesterol have their subjective and relativistic aspects. Pulse rate and blood pressure are notoriously susceptible to emotional influences, and BMR and blood cholesterol fluctuate widely from one cultural environment to another (Dreyfuss & Czaczkes, 1959). And anyone who believes that ethical norms have no relevance for physical illness has obviously failed to consider the problems confronting Catholic patients and/or physicians when issues of contraception, abortion, and preferential saving of the mother's as against the fetus' life must be faced in the context of various obstetrical emergencies and medical contraindications to pregnancy.

It should now be clear, therefore, that symptoms not only do not need a physical basis to qualify as manifestations of illness, but also that the evaluation of *all* symptoms, physical as well as mental, is dependent in large measure on subjective judgment, emotional factors, cultural-ethical norms, and personal involvement on the part of the observer. These considerations alone render no longer tenable Szasz' contention (1960, p. 114) that there is an inherent contradiction between using cultural and ethical norms as criteria of mental disease, on the one hand, and of employing medical measures of treatment on the other. But even if the postulated dichotomy between mental and physical symptoms were valid, the use of physical measures in treating subjective and relativistic psychological symptoms would still be warranted. Once we accept the proposition that impairment of the neural substrate of personality can result in behavior disorder, it is logically consistent to accept the corollary proposition that other kinds of manipulation of the same neural substrate can conceivably have therapeutic effects, irrespective of whether the underlying cause of the mental symptoms is physical or psychological.

Mental Illness and Problems of Living

"The phenomena now called mental illness," argues Szasz (1960), can be regarded more forthrightly and simply as "expressions of man's struggle with the problem of how he should live" (p. 117). This statement undoubtedly oversimplifies the nature of personality disorders; but even if it were adequately inclusive it would not be inconsistent with the position that these disorders are a manifestation of illness. There is no valid reason why a particular symptom cannot both reflect a problem in living *and* constitute a manifestation of disease. The notion of mental illness, conceived in this way, would not "obscure the everyday fact that life for most people is a continuous struggle . . . for a 'place in the sun,' 'peace of mind,' or some other human value" (p. 118). It is quite true, as Szasz points out, that "human relations are inherently fraught with difficulties" (p. 117), and that most people manage to cope with such difficulties without becoming mentally ill. But conceding this fact hardly precludes the possibility that some individuals, either because of the magnitude of the stress involved, or because of genically or environmentally induced susceptibility to ordinary degrees of stress, respond to the problems of living with behavior that is either seriously distorted or sufficiently unadaptive to prevent normal interpersonal relations and vocational functioning. The latter outcome—gross deviation from a designated range of desirable behavioral variability—conforms to the generally understood meaning of mental illness.

The plausibility of subsuming abnormal behavioral reactions to stress under the general rubric of disease is further enhanced by the fact that these reactions include the same three principal categories of symptoms found in physical illness. Depression and catastrophic impairment of self-esteem, for example, are manifestations of personality disorder which are symptomologically comparable to edema in cardiac failure or to heart murmurs in valvular disease. They are indicative of underlying pathology but are neither adaptive nor adjustive. Symptoms such as hypomanic overactivity and compulsive striving toward unrealistically high achievement goals, on the other hand, are both adaptive and adjustive, and constitute a type of compensatory response to basic feelings of inadequacy, which is not unlike cardiac hypertensive heart disease or elevated white blood cell count in acute infections. And finally, distortive psychological defenses that have some adjustive value but are generally maladaptive (e.g., phobias, delusions, autistic fantasies) are analogous to the pathological situation found in conditions like pneumonia, in which the excessive outpouring of serum and phagocytes in defensive response to pathogenic bacteria literally causes the patient to drown in his own fluids.

Within the context of this same general proposition, Szasz repudiates the concept of mental illness as demonological in nature, i.e., as the "true heir to religious myths in general and to the belief in witchcraft in particular" (p. 118) because it allegedly employs a reified abstraction ("a deformity of personality") to account in causal terms both for "human disharmony" and for symptoms of behavior disorder (p. 114). But again he appears to be demolishing a straw man. Modern students of personality disorder do not regard mental illness as a cause of human disharmony, but as a co-manifestation with it of inherent difficulties in personal adjustment and interpersonal relations; and insofar as I can accurately interpret the literature, psychopathologists do not conceive of mental illness as a cause of particular behavioral symptoms but as a generic term under which these symptoms can be subsumed.

Mental Illness and Moral Responsibility

Szasz' final reason for regarding mental illness as a myth is really a corollary of his previously considered more general proposition that mental symptoms are essentially reflective of problems of living and hence do not legitimately qualify as manifestations of disease. It focuses on difficulties of ethical choice and responsibility as the particular life problems most likely to be productive of personality disorder. Mowrer (1960) further extends this corollary by asserting that neurotic and psychotic individuals are responsible for their suffering (p. 301), and that unacknowledged and unexpiated sin, in turn, is the basic cause of this suffering (p. 304). As previously suggested, however, one can plausibly accept the proposition that psychiatrists and clinical psychologists have erred in trying to divorce behavioral evaluation from ethical considerations, in conducting psychotherapy in an amoral setting, and in confusing the psychological explanation of unethical behavior with absolution from accountability for same, *without* necessarily endorsing the view that personality disorders are basically a reflection of sin, and that victims of these disorders are less ill than responsible for their symptoms (Ausubel, 1952, pp. 392–397, 465–471).

In the first place, it is possible in most instances (although admittedly difficult in some) to distinguish quite unambiguously between mental illness and ordinary cases of immorality. The vast majority of persons who are guilty of moral lapses knowingly violate their own ethical precepts for expediential reasons—despite being volitionally capable at the time, both of choosing the more moral alternative and of exercising the necessary inhibitory control (Ausubel, 1952, pp. 465–471). Such persons, also, usually do not exhibit any signs of behavior disorder. At crucial choice points in facing the problems of living they simply choose the opportunistic instead of the moral alternative. They are not mentally ill, but they are clearly accountable for their misconduct. Hence, since personality disorder and immorality are neither coextensive nor mutually exclusive conditions, the concept of mental illness need not necessarily obscure the issue of moral accountability.

Second, guilt may be a contributory factor in behavior disorder, but is by no means the only or principal cause thereof. Feelings of guilt may give rise to anxiety and depression; but in the absence of catastrophic impairment of self-esteem induced by *other* factors, these symptoms tend to be transitory and peripheral in nature (Ausubel, 1952, pp. 362–363). Repression of guilt is more a consequence than a cause of anxiety. Guilt is repressed in order to avoid the anxiety-producing trauma to self-esteem that would otherwise result if it were acknowledged. Repression per se enters the causal picture in anxiety only secondarily—by obviating "the possibility of punishment, confession, expiation, and other guilt reduction mechanisms" (Ausubel, 1952, p. 456). Furthermore, in most types of personality disorder other than anxiety, depression, and various complications of anxiety such as phobias, obsessions, and compulsion, guilt feelings are either not particularly prominent (schizophrenic reactions), or are conspicuously absent (e.g., classical cases of inadequate or aggressive, antisocial psychopathy).

Third, it is just as unreasonable to hold an individual responsible for symptoms of behavior disorder as to deem him accountable for symptoms of physical illness. He is no more culpable for his inability to cope with sociopsychological stress than he would be for his inability to resist the spread of infectious organisms. In those instances where warranted guilt feelings *do* contribute to personality disorder, the patient is accountable for the misdeeds underlying his guilt, but is hardly responsible for the symptoms brought on by the guilt feelings or for unlawful acts committed during his illness. Acknowledgment of guilt may be therapeutically beneficial under these circumstances, but punishment for the original misconduct should obviously be deferred until after recovery.

Lastly, even if it were true that all personality disorder is a reflection of sin and that people are accountable for their behavioral symptoms, it would still be unnecessary to deny that these symptoms are manifestations of disease. Illness is no less real because the victim happens to be culpable for his illness. A glutton with hypertensive heart disease undoubtedly aggravates his condition by overeating, and is culpable in part for the often fatal symptoms of his disease, but what reasonable person would claim that for this reason he is not really ill?

CONCLUSIONS

Four propositions in support of the argument for discarding the concept of mental illness were carefully examined, and the following conclusions were reached:

First, although brain pathology is probably not the major cause of personality disorder, it does account for *some* psychological symptoms by impairing the neural substrate of personality. In any case, however, a symptom need not reflect a physical lesion in order to qualify as a genuine manifestation of disease.

Second, Szasz' postulated dichotomy between mental and physical symptoms is untenable because the assessment of *all* symptoms is dependent to some extent on subjective judgment, emotional factors, cultural-ethical norms, and personal involvement of the observer. Furthermore, the use of medical measures in treating behavior disorders—irrespective of whether the underlying causes are neural or psychological—is defensible on the grounds that if inadvertent impairment of the neural substrate of personality can have distortive effects on behavior, directed manipulation of the same substrate may have therapeutic effects.

Third, there is no inherent contradiction in regarding mental symptoms both as expressions of problems in living *and* as manifestations of illness. The latter situation results when individuals are for various reasons unable to cope with such problems, and react with seriously distorted or maladaptive behavior. The three principal categories of behavioral symptoms—manifestations of impaired functioning, adaptive compensation, and defensive overreaction—are also found in bodily disease. The concept of mental illness has never been advanced as a demonological cause of human disharmony, but only as a co-manifestation with it of certain inescapable difficulties and hazards in personal and social adjustment. The same concept is also generally accepted as a generic term for all behavioral symptoms rather than as a reified cause of these symptoms.

Fourth, the view that personality disorder is less a manifestation of illness than of sin, i.e., of culpable inadequacy in meeting problems of ethical choice and responsibility, and that victims of behavior disorder are therefore morally accountable for their symptoms, is neither logically nor empirically tenable. In most instances, immoral behavior and mental illness are clearly distinguishable conditions. Guilt is only a secondary etiological factor in anxiety and depression, and in other personality disorders is either not prominent or conspicuously absent. The issue of culpability for symptoms is largely irrelevant in handling the behavior disorders, and in any case does not detract from the reality of the illness.

In general, it is both unnecessary and potentially dangerous to discard the concept of mental illness on the grounds that only in this way can clinical psychology escape from the professional domination of medicine. Dentists, podiatrists, optometrists, and osteopaths have managed to acquire an independent professional status without rejecting the concept of disease. It is equally unnecessary and dangerous to substitute the doctrine of sin for illness in order to counteract prevailing amoral and nonjudgmental trends in psychotherapy. The hypothesis of repressed guilt does not adequately explain most kinds of instances of personality disorder, and the concept of mental illness does not preclude judgments of moral accountability where warranted. Definition of behavior disorder in terms of sin or of difficulties associated with ethical choice and responsibility would substitute theological disputation and philosophical wrangling about values for specifiable quantitative and qualitative criteria of disease.

REFERENCES

Ausubel, D. P. *Ego development and the personality disorders.* New York: Grune & Stratton, 1952.

Ausubel, D. P. Relationships between psychology and psychiatry: The hidden issues. *Amer. Psychologist*, 1956, **11**, 99–105.

Dreyfuss, F., & Czaczkes, J. W. Blood cholesterol and uric acid of healthy medical students under the stress of an examination. *AMA Arch. intern. Med.*, 1959, **103**, 708.

Mowrer, O. H. "Sin," the lesser of two evils. *Amer. Psychologist*, 1960, **15**, 301–304.

Szasz, T. S. The myth of mental illness. *Amer. Psychologist*, 1960, **15**, 113–118.

Problems of Labeling and Classification

A basic tenet of science is that there be a systematic ordering of objects, events, or organisms into categories that reflect a scheme of resemblances and relationships. Such an ordering, or classification scheme is useful because class membership implies the possession of certain attributes that are defined by the category. For example, the class of objects defined by the properties of strength, corrosibility, and capacity to be strongly magnetized can also be assumed to be conductors of electricity and probably also have other properties of iron and steel.

In psychopathology, however, although classification schemes date back to Hippocrates, there is currently considerable opposition to labeling (also see Rosenhan's article in Chapter 1). Such opposition, as indicated in Sarbin's paper, is an extension of the controversy regarding the illness model. Sarbin suggests the rejection of the mental-illness concept because such labeling leads to social discrimination and self-denigration.

On somewhat different grounds, Zigler and Phillips argue against current practices of labeling because of the unreliability of psychiatric diagnosis. However, they suggest that the current scheme be improved rather than rejected.

A systems-analysis approach to classification is demonstrated by Peter Nathan in the final paper of this chapter. Using the *Boston City Hospital-Behavior Checklist*, Nathan and his associates indicated that current diagnostic procedures permit the reliable differentiation of psychosis and psychoneurosis. However, their inability to differentiate between persons with psychoneurotic and personality disorders—conditions that represent many individuals who frequent community mental-health facilities—lead these authors to conclude that the understanding and treatment of such individuals is seriously compromised.

On the Futility of the Proposition That Some People Be Labeled "Mentally Ill"

Theodore R. Sarbin

By recognizing the metaphorical nature of "symptoms" and "illness" and the hypothetical nature of "mind," the mythical character of the mental concept is exposed. Conclusions lead the author to take a position contrary to Ellis's: Logical canons as well as humanistic value orientations direct us to delete "mental illness" from our vocabulary. Such a deletion does not deny that persons who engage in certain kinds of norm violations, which Ellis would call symptoms of mental illness, present problems to society. How to contain, manage, and reform persons judged to be actual or potential violators of social norms has been and continues to be one of the fundamental problems of social organizations. Creative solutions to such fundamental problems require a new set of metaphors and the sustained effort of experts in jurisprudence, social engineering, law enforcement, and community psychology.

The writing of a dispassionate account of the current utility of the mental illness concept reflects a noble purpose. Ellis (1967), by juxtaposing pro et contra arguments, tries to implement this purpose. On the one hand, he recognizes the massive negative utilities that result from the use of the mental-illness label; on the other hand, he points to occasions where the employment of the label appears to have positive utility. His studied conclusion is that the label, when used by professional diagnosticians in an operational way, identifies a limited number of people who are "really mentally ill." He adds the caution that the person who uses the label must subtract from it the pejorative components that have become part and parcel of the concept. Of several definitions, the following is representative of Ellis's viewpoint:

> This is what we really mean when we say that an individual is "mentally ill"—that he has *symptoms* of *mental malfunctioning* or *illness.* More operationally stated, he thinks, emotes, and acts *irrationally* and he can usually uncondemningly acknowledge and change his acts. If this, *without any moralistic overtones,* is the definition of "mental illness," then it can distinctly help the *afflicted* individual to accept himself while he is *ill* . . . [p. 440; italics added].

The general conclusions drawn by Ellis must be rejected on logical grounds. They represent not so much a lack of attention to the rules of evidence (to be mentioned later) as the acceptance of an entrenched and unwarranted belief that operates as a major premise. When operative, the premise may be stated: The label "mental illness" reliably denotes certain forms of conduct that are discriminable from forms of conduct that may be reliably denoted as "not mentally ill."

Since Ellis does not establish the ontological argument for "mental illness," his conclusions are illicit. That is to say, he assumes the truth of the proposition he sets out to demonstrate. (Note the italicized phrases in the quotation above.) The fundamental question is by-passed; to wit, is there a set of observations for which the dual metaphor "mental illness" is appropriate?

Most of Ellis's (and others', for example Ausubel, 1961) arguments aimed at retaining the mental-illness label flow from concealed, tacit, and disguised implications now contained within the label itself. Further, such arguments do not take into account the fact that the choice of label not only constrains further descriptive elaborations of the conduct under observation, but also indirectly restricts alternatives to action. The sentence, "a child . . . is known to have tendencies toward severe (mental) illness . . . " contains implications different from "a child has tendencies to hit other children."

To anticipate a criticism of the semiotic approach as a legitimate entrée into the argument, let me assert that the choice of a metaphor to designate an object or event is not inconsequential. Every metaphor contains a wealth of connotations, each connotation has the potential for manifold implications, and each implication is a directive to action. While metaphors are ordinarily used by people to facilitate communication, the peril is always at hand that people may be used by metaphors (Turbayne, 1960). Such a peril is activated when the user of a metaphor ignores, forgets, or purposely drops syntactical modifiers (e.g., *as if*) that denote the metaphor and, instead, employs the word in a literal fashion. To say "Jones is a saint" carries one set of implications if we supply the tacit modifier ("It is *as if* Jones is a saint"); the sentence carries a radically different set of implications if the predicate is treated as literal. The effects of permanently ignoring the metaphoric properties of a word, that is, of dropping the expressed or tacit modifiers, is to hypostatize an entity. Such hypostatization sets the stage for myth making.

Most of Ellis's arguments topple of their own structural defects, defects related to the uncritical acceptance of "illness of the mind" as the proper concept for describing the conduct of people who violate propriety norms (the mores of Sumner, 1906). Much of the undiagnosed confusion currently noted in the helping professions and in relevant juridical decisions is reflected in Ellis's paper. Such confusion might be reduced if we looked at the metaphorical background of our constraining vocabularies. First, let us look at "illness."

The basic referent for illness and for synonyms such as sickness and disease is a stable one, extending over centuries. The referent is discomfort of some kind, such as aches, pains, cramps, chills, paralyses, and so on. The discomfort is a self-appraisal through attention to unusual proximal stimuli, that is, stimuli located "inside" the organism. These proximal stimuli, when they occur simultaneously with dysfunction of bodily organs, are the so-called symptoms of illness. A diagnosis of illness or disease meant not only that a person reported discomforts, but that the associated somatic dysfunction interfered with the performance of some of his customary roles. This general paradigm of sickness or illness is widespread and may be found in ancient writings and in ethnographic reports.

A compelling question arises: How did the concept "illness" come to include gross behavior, that is, misconduct, rather than complaints and somatic symptoms which were the defining criteria of pre-Renaissance diagnosis? What additional criteria were employed to increase the breadth of the concept "illness"?

The inclusion of behavior disorders in the concept "illness" did not come about suddenly or accidentally. Rather, the label "illness" was at first used as a metaphor and later transformed into a myth.

The beginning of this metaphor-to-myth transformation may be located in the 16th Century. The demoniacal model of conduct disorders, codified in the 15th Century *Malleus Mallificarum*, had embraced all conduct that departed from the existing norms and was policed by zealous church and secular authorities. The most outstanding result of this thought model was the Inquisition, a social movement that among other things influenced the diagnosis and treatment of unusual imaginings, esoteric beliefs, and extraordinary conduct. The diagnosis of witchcraft and the prescription of treatment (burning) was the province of ecclesiastical specialists.

The 16th Century witnessed the beginnings of a reaction against the excesses of the Inquisition. The beginnings of humanistic philosophy, the discovery and serious study of Galen and other classical writers, the renunciation of scholasticism—the whole thrust of the Renaissance was opposite that of the Inquisition. In this atmosphere, Teresa of Avila, an outstanding figure of the Counter-Reformation, contributed to the shift from demons to "illness" as the cause of conduct disturbances. A group of nuns was exhibiting conduct which at a later date would have been called hysteria. By declaring these women to be infirm or ill, Teresa was able to fend off the Inquisition. However, the appeal that a diagnosis should be changed from witchcraft to illness required some cognitive elaboration. She invoked the notion of natural causes. Among the natural causes were (*a*) melancholy (Galenic humoral pathology), (*b*) weak imagination, and (*c*) drowsiness. If a person's conduct could be accounted for by such natural causes, it was to be regarded not as evil, but comas enfermas, *as if sick*. By employing the metaphor "as if sick," she implied that practitioners of physic rather than clergymen should be the responsible social specialists (Sarbin & Juhasz, 1967).

When employing metaphorical expressions there is a common human tendency to drop the qualifying "as if" (Turbayne, 1960). That is to say, the metaphor is used without a qualifier to designate it as figurative rather than literal. In the case of illness as a metaphor for conditions not meeting the usual criteria of illness, the dropping of the "as if" was facilitated by the practitioners of physic. It was awkward for them to talk about two kinds of illness, "real" illness and "as if" illness. When Galenic classifications were reintroduced, the "as if" was dropped. Thus, post-Renaissance physicians could concern themselves with illness as traditionally understood and also with norm violations as illness. A review of the 16th and 17th Century treatises on "physic" reveals clearly that Galen's humoral theory was the standard for diagnosis and treatment. The diagnostic problem was how to construct inferences about the balance of humors inside the organism.

The decline of the power of church authorities in diagnosing extraordinary imaginings and perplexing conduct was parallel to the rise of science. The prestige of the scientist helped in establishing the model of Galen for both kinds of "illness"—those with somatic complaints and observable somatic symptoms and those without somatic complaints but with unusual behavior standing for somatic symptoms.

Whereas the concept illness had been satisfied by the exclusive use of conjunctive criteria (complaints and observable somatic symptoms), it was now satisfied by the use of disjunctive criteria (complaints and somatic symptoms or complaints by others of perplexing, embarassing, mystifying conduct). As a result of the uncritical acceptance of the humoral pathology of Galen as the overriding explanation for both somatic and behavior disorders, the latter became assimilated to the former. That is to say, to meet the requirements of the basic Galenic model, symptoms of disease had to be observed, so the observed behavior sequences were regarded as if they were the symptoms. Thus, the verbal report of strange imaginings on the one hand and fever on the other, were treated as belonging to the same class, that is, symptoms. As a result of shifting from a metaphoric to a literal interpretation of gross behavior as symptom, Galenic medicine embraced not only everything somatic but also all conduct. Now, any bit of behavior—laughing, crying, threatening, spitting, silence, imagining, lying, and believing—could be called symptoms of underlying internal pathology.

The basic Galenic model was not rejected by psychiatry or clinical psychology. Microbes, toxins, and growths, which were material and operated according to mechanical principles, were appropriate "causes" of diseases of the body. They were inside. The appropriate causes for abnormal behavior had to be sought on different dimensions. Since the mind-body conception was taken as truth, the hypothesis could be entertained that the causes of abnormal conduct were in the mind. If this were so, then the most appropriate label for such nonsomatic diseases would be "mental illness."

Before considering the meaning of "mental" in the phrase "mental illness," let me recapitulate. "Illness," as in mental illness, is an illicit transformation of a metaphorical concept to a literal one. To save unfortunate people from being labeled witches, it was humane to treat persons who exhibited misconduct of certain kinds as if they were ill. The Galenic model facilitated the eliding of the hypothetical phrase, the "as if," and the concept of illness was thus deformed to include events that did not meet the original conjunctive criteria for illness. A second transformation assured the validity of the Galenic model. The mystifying behaviors could be treated as if they were symptoms equivalent to somatic symptoms. By dropping the "as if" modifier, observed behavior could be interpreted as symptomatic of underlying internal pathology.

How did the notion of "illness of the mind" become so widely accepted that it served as the groundwork for several professions? A searching historical analysis makes clear that mind was originally employed as a metaphor to denote such events as remembering and thinking. (Colloquial English has retained this formulation, as in "mind your manners.") The shift of meaning to that of a substantive or agency can best be understood as another instance of metaphor-to-myth transformation (Ryle, 1948).

The modern practitioner of Galenic psychiatry and psychology operates from the principle that the "illness" about which he is concerned is in the mind (or psyche, or psychic apparatus). But the mind, even for Galenic practitioners, was too abstract and undifferentiated a concept.

Since the mind was invisible and immaterial, it could not have the same properties as the body—properties that could be denoted by physicalistic terms. Visual palpable organs being the components of the material body, what differentiating components of the invisible impalpable mental entity could one discover or invent? A new metaphor was required—the metaphor of states of mind. States of love, fear, anxiety, apathy, etc. were invented to account for differences in observed conduct. The practitioner now had the job of discovering through chains of inferences which mental states were responsible for normal and abnormal conduct.

MIND AS AN ORGAN OF ILLNESS

Three developments contributed to the construction of mind as the repository of special states and as an organ that was subject to "illness": (1) the ready availability of dispositional terms, (2) the introduction of new terms of faith and religion that located religious experience "inside" the person, and (3) the development of a scientific lexicon.

1. Dispositional terms are shorthand expressions for combinations or orderings of distal and/or proximal events—in principle, a dispositional term can be reduced to a series of observable occurrences. For example, "bravery" implies a set of concrete behaviors under certain conditions. No implication is carried that the referent is an internal mental state. The development of dispositional terms, however, appears to be a necessary (though not sufficient) prerequisite for the postulation of mental states. In time, dispositional terms become elided and remote from the original metaphorical beginnings.

2. Dispositional terms were conveniently borrowed to denote religious conceptions which followed the shift from an emphasis on ritual and ceremony to inward, personal aspects of faith. Theologians and preachers gave a new set of referents to these dispositional terms, referents that changed dispositional terms from brief notations of observable conduct to states of the soul. The context in which mental states are employed is best expressed by the polarity inside-outside. The problem for the medieval thinker was to find a paradigm for locating events on the inside. Such a model could have been constructed from the following observations: Two classes of proximal inputs may be identified. The first occurs in a context of distal events: for example, pain in the ankle occurs in a context of tripping over a curb; a burning irritation in the fingers occurs in the context of leaning on a hot radiator. The second class of proximal inputs occurs in the absence of associated distal events, such as toothache, headache, gastritis, neuritis, etc. Since the antecedents of the latter inputs could not be located in the outside world, the locus of the somatic perception inside the body was taken as the causal locus. Medieval man had little reliable knowledge of anatomy save that there were bones, sinews, tubes, and fluids and there were also empty spaces. Under the authority of the priests, he acquired the belief that an immaterial and invisible soul resided in these otherwise empty spaces. On this belief system, events for which there were no observed distal contexts could be attributed to the workings of this inner entity or soul. Such an analysis probably prepared the way for locating dispositions inside the person and calling them states of mind. If the cause of an event had no obvious external locus, then it must have an internal locus. Dispositions, when they are codified as substantives, tend to be treated in the same way as other nouns, as possessing "thingness." Thus bravery, lust, conscience, purity, devotion—all dispositional terms originally tied to orderings of behavior—are framed as nouns. If nouns are names of things, and things have location, the problem emerged: where to locate the referents for these nouns? The answer is similar to the process of locating inside the person the cause of pain and discomfort in the absence of external occurrences. Thus, anger, joy, courage, happiness, etc., came to be located in the soul.

3. The replacement of theologians by scientists in the 16th and 17th Centuries in matters pertaining to strange and mysterious conduct made necessary a shift from such theological terms as "soul" to scientific metaphors. However, the scientists could not break completely with the

entrenched dualistic philosophy. They took as their point of departure the facts of thinking and knowing and, as a substitute for the soul, employed *mind* as the organ for such activities. With the development of classical scholarship, Greek terms were substituted for the vernacular, the most popular being "psyche" (Boring, 1966). The efforts of the post-Renaissance Galenic practitioners, then, were directed toward analyzing states of mind or psychic events. Those sequences of perplexing conduct that could not be related to external occurrences were declared to be outcomes of internal mental or psychic processes.

Thus mental states—the objects of interest and study for the diagnostician of "mental illness"—were postulated to fill gaps in early knowledge. Through historical and linguistic processes, the construct was reified. Contemporary users of the mental-illness concept are guilty of illicitly shifting from metaphor to myth. Instead of maintaining the metaphorical rhetoric "it is as if there were states of mind," and "it is as if some 'states of mind' could be characterized as sickness," the contemporary mentalist conducts much of his work as if he believes that minds are "real" entities and that, like bodies, they can be sick or healthy.

The most potent implication of the metaphor is that persons labeled mentally ill are categorized as significantly discontinuous from persons labeled with the unmodified term "ill." Of course, referring to persons simply as ill or sick suggests that they belong to a class different from the mutually exclusive class "not ill" or "healthy." Assigning persons to the class "ill" carries the meaning of objective symptoms of a recognized or named disease, in addition to subjectively experienced discomfort. In most societies, persons so classified are temporarily excused from the performance of selected role obligations. The label carries no hint of negative valuation. Sickness, in general, is something for which one is not responsible.

However, when the adjective "mental" is prefixed, a whole new set of implications follows. Contrary to the humane intent of those who resisted the Inquisitors by employing the nonpejorative diagnostic label of illness, present usage is transparently pejorative.

In adding the word "mental" to "illness," the whole meaning structure changes. In the first place, the necessity for adding a prefix to "illness" imposes a special constraint on the interpreter: He asks, "What about this person or his behavior calls for such a special designation?" Since it is a special kind of illness, does the same expectation hold that he (the patient) is to be temporarily excused from the enactment of his roles?

The answers to these questions may be found in a number of studies (Cumming & Cumming, 1962; Goffman, 1961; Nunnally, 1961; Phillips, 1963). Persons who are labeled mentally ill are not regarded as merely sick; they are regarded as a special class of beings, to be feared or scorned, sometimes to be pitied, but nearly always to be degraded. Coincident with such negative valuations are the beliefs that such "mentally ill" persons discharge obligations only of the most simple kinds. The author has elsewhere argued that the process whereby a person is converted into a mental patient carries with it the potential for self-devaluation. The stigmatization, then, may work in the nature of a self-fulfilling prophecy (Sarbin, 1967c).

Further, because of the inherent vagueness in the concept of mind, its assumed independence from the body, and its purported timelessness (derived from the immortal soul), there is a readiness to regard this special kind of sickness as permanent. Thus, a person with a fractured wrist or a patient suffering from influenza, that is, a sick person, may take up his customary roles upon being restored to health. A person diagnosed as mentally ill, however, is stigmatized. Although "cured" of the behavior that initiated the sequence of social and political acts that resulted in his being classified as mentally ill, his public will not usually accept such "cures" as permanent. It is as if the mental states were capable of disguising the person as healthy, although the underlying mental illness remains in a dormant or latent state.

The pejorative connotation is an integral part of the concept. Ellis's advice to subtract the "moralistic overtones" is gratuitous. One can no more delete by fiat the valuational component from "mental illness" than eliminate the "pleasantness" from the act of eating a preferred food.

Another implication of the mental-illness concept stemming from the demonstrated utility of germ theory for nonmental illness is the internal causal locus of mental illness. But the shadowy interior of the mind is not easily entered. The experts must depend on chains of inference forged out of the verbal and nonverbal communications of patients and informants. From such communications, today's experts draw conclusions about the mental structures, their dynamic properties, and their relation to observed behavior in the same manner as Galenic practitioners drew conclusions about the distribution of the humors. One outcome of the exclusive verbal preoccupation with psychic states is the neglect and avoidance of events in the social systems that might be antecedent to instances of misconduct illicitly and arbitrarily called symptoms.

The heuristic implications of the mental-illness metaphor are no less important than the practical implications. Scientists of many kinds have discovered the causes for many (nonmental) illnesses by looking inside the body. By adding a postulate that all mental states are caused by organic conditions (the somatopsychic hypothesis) and also accepting disordered conduct as symptomatic of underlying disease entities, the corollary follows that the ultimate causal agents will be discovered through searching for biochemical, toxicological, and bacteriological substrates. Again, such search methods deploy attention and effort away from the social ecology as a possible source of antecedent conditions of misconduct.

REJECTION OF THE MENTAL-ILLNESS CONCEPT

The analysis offered so far supports the argument that the label "mental illness" should be eliminated from our vocabulary. Following from the implications contained in the label, the logical arguments by themselves would predict the social discrimination and self-denigration consequent to the establishment of social institutions to segregate, house, treat, manage, and reform norm violators. The tacit semantic relation between sin (or evil) and mental illness (Crumpton, Weinstein, Acker, & Annis, 1967), as well as the juridically endorsed relation of mental illness to danger (Platt & Diamond, 1966; Sarbin, 1967a), also grows out of the label's implications.

It is one thing to demonstrate that "mental illness" has achieved mythic status and that its continued employment stands in the way of developing policies and practices for meeting some important social problems; it is another thing to recognize that some people, sometimes, somewhere, engage in conduct that violates propriety norms, including norms controlling ingroup aggression. Ellis is justifiably concerned with the problem of what disposition to make of these norm violators. His solution to the problem is to label them mentally ill (sans "moral overtones"). Such labeling provides a warrant for segregating norm violators in mental hospitals or referring them to psychotherapists. The warrant contains (sometimes explicitly) the notion "for the patient's own good." The history of the mental hospital system and of the mental health movement in America witnesses that "the patient's good" is little more than a cliché uttered to offset the degradation and desocialization outcomes.

If my previous arguments are not footless, then Ellis's recommendation that we continue the practice of labeling people mentally ill should be forcefully rejected. If his advice is rejected on the grounds of logic and of humanitarian values, then we are left with a gap in the social fabric. What should citizens and officials of an open society do about the problem of norm violation? What, if anything, should we do about people who are sometimes described as silly, unpredictably eccentric, perturbed, deviant, mute, shameless, rude, impertinent, immodest, dishonest, childish, dangerous, hostile, aggressive, and so on? Current practice is, under some conditions, to regard the behavior described by such terms as symptoms of, or caused by, mental illness. Ellis (1967) illustrates this point nicely. With impressive documentation, he says:

> In the last analysis, almost all neurosis and psychosis consists of some self-dishonesty. . . . When, therefore, one fully faces the fact that one is "mentally ill," that this is not a pleasant way to be, and that one is partially responsible for being so, one becomes at that very point, more honest with oneself and begins to get a little better [p. 440].

What function is served other than the imputation of a discredited mental-state causality? More continuous with observation would be the substitution of the word "dishonest" for "mentally ill."

In exposing mental illness as a myth that has outlived its usefulness, the label becomes improper and futile. Thus we are left with a farreaching problem in jurisprudence, law enforcement, social engineering, and community psychology. The problem may be formulated as a question: What criteria should be employed to deprive a man of his liberty, his civil rights, his capacity for self-determinism, and so on? It would be foolhardy for me to try even to suggest answers in this brief paper. However, I can point to some partially charted areas that require further exploration.

All of us must put our heads together and decide how free and open a society we want. This decision is prerequisite for establishing criteria to identify those persons who should not be free. It is my belief that with increasing application of democratic principles the use of "mental illness" will be dropped as an intervening category between overt conduct and juridically established status as free or restrained. The arguments of Szasz (1963); the observations of Goffman (1961); the historico-legal studies of Platt and Diamond (1966); the persisting dissatisfaction with such legal precedents as McNaughten, Durham, and others (Diamond, 1964; Dreher, 1967); the disillusionment of psychiatric and psychological practitioners with mentalistic and scholastic theories (Sarbin, 1964); and the development of community psychology (The Conference Committee, 1966)—these and other forces are converging toward finding a fair and more efficient process for arresting, detaining, and incarcerating individuals whose public conduct violates current propriety norms.

In this connection, we must confront the implications of a currently common practice of regarding deviant conduct (e.g., homosexuality) as equivalent to sickness. The refusal of an individual to accept the pejorative classification of mental illness and, correlatively, his refusal to enter psychotherapy, are taken as signs that he, according to Ellis, does not want "to improve his lot." The careful work of Hooker (1957, 1958) suggests that in the culture of male homosexuals the distributions of conventionally used indicators of psychopathology (e.g., Rorschach variables) are not substantially different from the distributions of heterosexuals. Deviance from cultural norms is a societal problem. It is doubtful whether the use of the mental-illness label or any other epithet of degradation will contribute to the solution of the problem. I know of no evidence that supports the contrary notion that societal problems associated with cultural deviance are ameliorated by diagnosing deviant individuals as "ill."

We turn our attention briefly to the problems in jurisprudence generated by the facts of norm violation and by the continued use of the mental-illness doctrine. A cursory review of legal treatises makes clear that the law, its writers, and interpreters, although deeply involved in the problems of equity and justice, have not been concerned with questioning the ontological status of mental illness. Such verdicts as "not guilty by reason of insanity" reflect the dualism upon which much of our jurisprudence rests, not to mention our theology and metaphysics. This verdict is not unlike many constructions to be found in legal treatises. The hidden metaphor is this: It is as if there is a body and a mind normally functioning in harmony. The body performs actions under the governance of the immaterial invisible mind. Where the acts of the body and the intent of the mind are not in harmony in meeting normative standards of conduct, explanations in terms of rule-following models are inadequate. Under these conditions a causal explanation is required: The mind is not properly controlling the body. Therefore the body is declared "not guilty" and the mind becomes the object of punishment or retribution. The aim of such actions is to exorcise the evil influences or mental states that guided the body to perform improper or sinful acts.

While I may be charged with unrestrained hyperbole, the historical facts are undeniable. The same cultural thought model that generated the medieval demoniacal model also produced the modern mental-illness model to explain conduct that does not meet rule-following prescriptions.

The rejection of such an entrenched thought model by the relevant professionals is in the nature of a scientific revolution. As in all scientific revolutions, a new metaphor is needed to replace an exploded myth. The most likely candidate for such replacement is a metaphor that denotes recent and current observations not convincingly assimilated into the older labels. Elsewhere, I have presented arguments in support of a new metaphor—the transformation of social identity—a metaphor that captures the antecedent and concurrent process of becoming a norm violator (Sarbin, 1967a, 1967b, 1967c; Sarbin, Scheibe, & Kroger, 1965). Because of space limitations, I can say only that the metaphor arises from a comprehensive social theory—a theory that rejects mentalistic metaphors as being feebly inappropriate to the enormity of the theoretical and societal problems that confront us.

In these few pages I have tried to make the case that it is futile to try to support the proposition that some people be labeled "mentally ill." The case stands or falls on the coherence of the ontological argument. My argument declares that the label is vacuous, save as an epithet of pejoration. Further, its scientific utility is suspect because of its reliance on an outworn mentalistic concept—the ghost in the machine, to use Ryle's (1948) apt metaphor.

REFERENCES

Ausubel, D. Personality disorder *is* disease. *American Psychologist,* 1961, 16, 69–74.

The Conference Committee. C. C. Bennett (Chm.), *Community psychology, a report of the Boston Conference on the education of psychologists for community mental health.* Boston: Boston University Press, 1966.

Boring, E. G. A note on the origin of the word psychology. *Journal of the History of the Behavioral Sciences,* 1966, **2,** 167.

Crumpton, E., Weinstein, A. D., Acker, C. W., & Annis, A. P. How patients and normals see the mental patient. *Journal of Clinical Psychology,* 1967, **23,** 46–49.

Cumming, J., & Cumming, E. *Ego and milieu.* New York: Atherton Press, 1962.

Diamond, B. L. Review of T. S. Szasz, *Law, liberty and psychiatry; an inquiry into the social uses of mental health practices. California Law Review,* 1964, **52,** 899–907.

Dreher, R. H. Origin, development and present status of insanity as a defense to criminal responsibility in the common law. *Journal of the History of the Behavioral Sciences,* 1967, **3,** 47–57.

Ellis, A. Should some people be labeled mentally ill? *Journal of Consulting Psychology,* 1967, **31,** 435–446.

Goffman, E. *Asylums.* Chicago: Aldine, 1961.

Hooker, E. The adjustment of the male overt homosexual. *Journal of Projective Techniques and Personality Assessment,* 1957, **21,** 18–31.

Hooker, E. Male homosexuality in the Rorschach. *Journal of Projective Techniques and Personality Assessment,* 1958, **22,** 31–54.

Nunnally, J. C. *Popular conceptions of mental health.* New York: Holt, Rinehart & Winston, 1961.

Phillips, D. L. Rejection as a consequence of seeking help for mental disorders. *American Sociology Review,* 1963, **28,** 963–972.

Platt, A. M., & Diamond, B. L. The origins and development of the "wild beast" concept of mental illness and its relation to theories of criminal responsibility. *Journal of the History of the Behavioral Sciences,* 1965, **1,** 355–367.

Ryle, G. *The concept of mind.* Oxford: Hutchinson's University Press, 1948.

Sarbin, T. R. Anxiety: The reification of a metaphor. *Archives of General Psychiatry,* 1964, **10,** 630–638.

Sarbin, T. R. The dangerous individual: An outcome of social identity transformations. *British Journal of Criminology,* 1967, in press. (a)

Sarbin, T. R. Notes on the transformation of social identity. In N. S. Greenfield, M. L. Miller, & L. M. Roberts (Eds.), *Comprehensive mental health: The challenge of evaluation.* Madison: University of Wisconsin Press, 1967, in press. (b)

Sarbin, T. R. Role theoretical analysis of schizophrenia. In J. H. Mann (Ed.), *Reader in general psychology.* New York: Rand-McNally, 1967, in press. (c)

Sarbin, T. R. The scientific status of the mental illness concept. In S. Plog (Ed.), *Determinants of mental illness—A handbook.* New York: Holt, Rinehart & Winston, 1967, in press. (d)

Sarbin, T. R., & Juhasz, J. B. The historical background of the concept of hallucination. *Journal of the History of the Behavioral Sciences,* 1967, in press.

Sarbin, T. R., Scheibe, K. E., & Kroger, R. O. *The transformation of social identity.* Unpublished manuscript, University of California, Berkeley, 1965.

Sumner, W. G. *Folkways.* Boston: Ginn, 1906.

Szasz, T. S. *Law, liberty and psychiatry; an inquiry into the social uses of mental health practices.* New York: Macmillan, 1963.

Turbayne, C. *Myth of metaphor.* New Haven: Yale University Press, 1960.

Psychiatric Diagnosis: A Critique

Edward Zigler
Leslie Phillips

The inadequacies of conventional psychiatric diagnosis have frequently been noted (Ash, 1949; Cattell, 1957; Eysenck, 1952; Foulds, 1955; Harrower, 1950; Hoch & Zubin, 1953; Jellinek, 1939; King, 1954; Leary & Coffey, 1955; Mehlman, 1952; Menninger, 1955; Noyes, 1953; Phillips & Rabinovitch, 1958; Roe, 1949; Rogers, 1951; Rotter, 1954; Scott, 1958; Thorne, 1953; Wittenborn & Weiss, 1952; Wittman & Sheldon, 1948). The responses to this rather imposing body of criticism have ranged from the position that the present classificatory system is in need of further refinement (Caveny, Wittson, Hunt, & Herman, 1955; Foulds, 1955), through steps towards major revisions (Cattell, 1957; Eysenck, 1952; Leary & Coffey, 1955; Phillips & Rabinovitch, 1958; Thorne, 1953; Wittman & Sheldon, 1948), to a plea for the abolishment of all "labeling" (Menninger, 1955; Noyes, 1953; Rogers, 1951). As other investigators have noted (Caveny et al., 1955; Jellinek, 1939), this last position suggests that the classificatory enterprise is valueless. This reaction against classification has gained considerable popularity in clinical circles. The alacrity with which many clinicians have accepted this view seems to represent more than a disillusionment with the specific current form of psychiatric diagnosis. These negative attitudes appear to reflect a belief that diagnostic classification is inherently antithetical to such clinically favored concepts as "dynamic," "idiographic," etc. Thus, a question is raised as to whether any diagnostic schema can be of value. Let us initially direct our attention to this question.

ON CLASSIFICATION

The growth among clinicians of sentiment against categorization has coincided with a period of critical reappraisal within the behavioral sciences generally (Beach, 1950; Brower, 1949; Cronbach, 1957; Guthrie, 1950; Harlow, 1953; Koch, 1951; MacKinnon, 1953; Marquis, 1948; Rapaport, 1947; Roby, 1959; Scott, 1955; Tolman, 1953; Tyler, 1959). This parallel development is more than coincidental. The reaction against "labeling" can be viewed as an extreme outgrowth of this critical self-evaluation, i.e., that psychology's conceptual schemata are artificial in their construction, sterile in terms of their practical predictions, and lead only to greater and greater precision about matters which are more and more irrelevant. It is little wonder that in this atmosphere, conceptualization has itself become suspect nor that Maslow's (1948) exposition of the possible dangers of labeling or naming has been extended (Rotter, 1954) as a blanket indictment of the categorizing process.

The error in this extension is the failure to realize that what has been criticized is not the conceptual process but only certain of its products. The criticisms mentioned above have not been in favor of the abolishment of conceptualization, but have rather been directed at the prematurity and rarifications of many of our conceptual schemata and our slavish adherence to them. Indeed, many of these criticisms have been accompanied by pleas for lower-order conceptualization based more firmly on observational data (Koch, 1951; MacKinnon, 1953; Tolman, 1953).

In the clinical area, the sentiment against classification has become sufficiently serious that several investigators (Cattell, 1957; Caveny et al., 1955; Eysenck, 1952; Jellinek, 1939) have felt the need to champion the merits of psychiatric categorization. They have pointed out that diagnosis is a basic scientific classificatory enterprise to be viewed as essentially the practice of taxonomy, which is characteristic of all science. Eysenck (1952) puts the matter quite succinctly in his statement, "Measurement is essential to science, but before we can measure, we must know what it is we want to measure. Qualitative or taxonomic discovery must precede quantitative measurement" (p. 34).

Reduced to its essentials, diagnostic classification involves the establishment of categories to which phenomena can be ordered. The number of class systems that potentially may be constructed is limited only by man's ability to abstract from his experience. The principles employed to construct such classes may be inductive, deductive, or a combination of both, and may vary on a continuum from the closely descriptive to the highly abstract.

Related to the nature of the classificatory principle are the implications to be derived from class membership. Class membership may involve nothing more than descriptive compartmentalization, its only utility being greater ease in the handling of data. Obversely, the attributes or correlates of class membership may be widespread and farreaching in their consequences. The originators of a classificatory schema may assert that specified behavioral correlates accompany class membership. This assertion is open to test. If the hypothesized correlates represent the full heuristic val-

From *Journal of Abnormal and Social Psychology*, 1961, 63, 607–618.

This investigation was supported by the Dementia Praecox Research Project, Worcester State Hospital, and a research grant (N-896) from the National Institute of Mental Health, United States Public Health Service.

ue of the diagnostic schema and class membership is found not to be related to these correlates, then revision or discard is in order. A somewhat different type of problem may also arise. With the passage of time, correlates not originally related to the schema may erroneously be attributed to class membership. Nevertheless, the original taxonomy may still possess a degree of relevance to current objectives in a discipline. In these circumstances, its maintenance may be the rational choice, although a clarification and purification of categories is called for. The relationship of the two problems outlined here to the criticism of contemporary psychiatric diagnosis will be discussed later. What should be noted at this point is that the solution to neither problem implies the abolishment of the attempt at classification.

Another aspect of taxonomy is in need of clarification. When a phenomenon is assigned to a class, certain individual characteristics of that phenomenon are forever lost. No two class members are completely identical. Indeed, a single class member may be viewed as continuously differing from itself over time. It is this loss of uniqueness and an implied unconcern with process that have led many clinicians to reject classification in principle. While classificatory schemata inevitably involve losses of this type, it must be noted that they potentially offer a more than compensatory gain. This gain is represented in the significance of the class attributes and correlates. Class membership conveys information ranging from the descriptive similarity of two phenomena to a knowledge of the common operative processes underlying the phenomena.

A conceptual system minimizes the aforementioned loss to the extent that only irrelevant aspects of a phenomenon are deleted in the classificatory process. The implicit assumption is made that what is not class relevant is inconsequential. The dilemma, of course, lies in our lacking divine revelation as to what constitutes inconsequentiality. It is this issue which lies at the heart of the idiographic versus nomothetic controversy (Allport, 1937, 1946; Beck, 1953; Eysenck, 1954; Falk, 1956; Hunt, 1951a, 1951b; Skaggs, 1945, 1947). The supporters of the idiographic position (Allport, 1937; Beck, 1953) have criticized certain conceptual schemata for treating idiosyncratic aspects of behavior as inconsequential when they are in fact pertinent data which must be utilized if a comprehensive and adequate view of human behavior is to emerge. However, the idiographic position is not a movement toward the abolishment of classification, a fact emphasized by Allport (1937) and Falk (1956). Rather, it represents a plea for broader and more meaningful classificatory schemata.

A conceptually different type of argument against the use of any diagnostic classification has been made by the adherents of nondirective psychotherapy (Patterson, 1948; Rogers, 1946, 1951). This position has advanced the specific contention that differential diagnosis is unnecessary for, and perhaps detrimental to, successful psychotherapy. This attitude of the nondirectivists has been interpreted (Thorne, 1953) as an attack on the entire classificatory enterprise. To argue against diagnosis on the grounds that it affects therapeutic outcome is to confuse diagnosis as an act of scientific classification with the present clinical practice of diagnosis with its use of interviewing, psychological testing, etc. The error here lies in turning one's attention away from diagnosis as an act of classification, a basic scientific enterprise, and attending instead to the immediate and prognostic consequences of some specific diagnostic technique in a specific therapeutic situation, i.e., an applied aspect. To reject the former on the basis of the latter would appear to be an unsound decision.

Although the nondirectivists' opposition to diagnosis seems to be based on a confusion between the basic and applied aspects of classification, implicitly contained within their position is a more fundamental argument against the classificatory effort. Undoubtedly, diagnosis both articulates and restricts the range of assumptions which may be entertained about a client. However, the philosophy of the nondirectivist forces him to reject any theoretical position which violates a belief in the unlimited psychological growth of the client. It would appear that this position represents the rejection, in principle, of the view that any individual can be like another in his essential characteristics, or that any predictable relationship can be established between a client's current level of functioning and the ends which may be achieved. In the setting of this assumption, a transindividual classificatory schema is inappropriate. There is no appeal from such a judgment, but one should be cognizant that it rejects the essence of a scientific discipline. If one insists on operating within the context of a predictive psychology, one argues for the necessity of a classificatory system, even though particular diagnostic schemata may be rejected as irrelevant, futile, or obscure.

Let us now direct our discussion toward some of the specific criticisms of conventional psychiatric diagnosis—that the categories employed lack homogeneity, reliability, and validity.

HOMOGENEITY

A criticism often leveled against the contemporary diagnostic system is that its categories encompass heterogeneous groups of individuals, i.e., individuals varying in respect to symptomatology, test scores, prognosis, etc. (King, 1954; Rotter, 1954: Wittenborn, 1952; Wittenborn & Bailey, 1952; Wittenborn & Weiss, 1952). Contrary to the view of one investigator (Rotter, 1954), a lack of homogeneity does not necessarily imply a lack of reliability. King (1954) has clearly noted the distinction between these two concepts. Reliability refers to the agreement in assigning individuals to different diagnostic categories, whereas homogeneity refers to the diversity of behavior subsumed within categories. While the two concepts may be related, it is not difficult to conceptualize categories which, though quite reliable, subsume diverse phenomena.

King (1954) has argued in favor of constructing a new diagnostic classification having more restrictive and homogeneous categories. He supports his argument by noting his own findings and those of Kantor, Wallner, and Winder (1953), which have indicated that within the schizophrenic group subcategories may be formed which differ in test performance. King found further support for the construction of new and more homogeneous diagnostic categories in a study by Windle and Hamwi (1953). This study indicated that two subgroups could be constructed within a psychotic population which was composed of patients with diverse psychiatric diagnoses. Though matched on the distribution of these diagnostic types, the subgroups differed in the relationship obtained between test performance and prognosis. On the basis of these studies, King suggests that the type of homogeneous categories he would favor involves such classificatory dichotomies as reactive versus process schizophrenics and chronic versus nonchronic psychotics.

An analysis of King's (1954) criticism of the present diagnostic system discloses certain difficulties. The first is that King's heterogeneity criticism does not fully take into consideration certain basic aspects of classification. A common feature of classificatory systems is that they utilize classes which contain subclasses. An example drawn from biology would be a genus embracing a number of species. If schizophrenia is conceptualized as a genus, it cannot be criticized on the grounds that all its members do not share a particular attribute. Such a criticism would involve a confusion between the more specific attributes of the species and the more general attributes of the genus. This is not to assert that schizophrenia does in fact possess the characteristics of a genus. It is, of course, possible that a careful analysis will reveal that it does not, and the class schizophrenia will have to be replaced by an aggregate of entities which does constitute a legitimate genus. However, when a genus is formulated, it cannot be attacked because of its heterogeneous nature since genera are characterized by such heterogeneity.

A more serious difficulty with King's (1954) heterogeneity criticism lies in the inherent ambiguity of a homogeneity-heterogeneity parameter. To criticize a classificatory system because its categories subsume heterogeneous phenomena is to make the error of assuming that homogeneity is a quality which inheres in phenomena when in actuality it is a construction of the observer or classifier. In order to make this point clear, let us return to King's argument. What does it mean to assert that chronic psychosis is an example of an homogeneous class, while schizophrenia is an example of an heterogeneous one? In terms of the descriptively diverse phenomena encompassed, the latter would appear to have the greater homogeneity. The statement only has meaning insofar as a particular correlate—for instance, the relationship of test score to prognosis—is shared by all members of one class but not so shared by the members of the other class. Thus, the meaningfulness of the homogeneity concept is ultimately dependent on the correlates or attributes of class membership or to the classificatory principle related to these correlates or attributes. The intimacy of the relationship between the attributes of classes and the classificatory principle can best be exemplified by the extreme case in which a class has but a single attribute, and that attribute is defined by the classificatory principle, e.g., the classification of plants on the basis of the number of stamens they possess. Therefore, the heterogeneity criticism of a classificatory system is nothing more than a plea for the utilization of a new classificatory principle so that attention may be focused on particular class correlates or attributes not considered in the original schema. While this plea may be a justifiable one, depending on the significance of the new attributes, it has little to do with the homogeneity, in an absolute sense, of phenomena. Indeed, following the formulation of a new classificatory schema, the heterogeneity criticism could well be leveled against it by the adherents of the old system, since the phenomena encompassed by the new categories would probably not be considered homogeneous when evaluated by the older classificatory principle.

Although differing in its formulation, the heterogeneity criticism of present psychiatric classification made by Wittenborn and his colleagues (Wittenborn, 1952; Wittenborn & Bailey, 1952; Wittenborn & Weiss, 1952) suffers from the same difficulties as does King's (1954) criticism. Wittenborn's findings indicated that individuals given a common diagnosis showed differences in their symptom cluster score profiles based on nine symptom clusters isolated earlier by means of factor analytic techniques (Wittenborn, 1951; Wittenborn & Holzberg, 1951). It is upon the existence of these different profiles within a diagnostic category that Wittenborn bases his heterogeneity criticism. Here again the homogeneity—hetorogeneity distinction is only meaningful in terms of an independent criterion, a particular symptom cluster score profile. Had it been discovered that all individuals placed into a particular diagnostic category shared a common symptom cluster score profile, then this category would be described as subsuming homogeneous phenomena. But the phenomena—the symptoms mirrored by the symptom profile—are not homogeneous in any absolute sense because the pattern of symptoms may involve the symptoms in descriptively diverse symptom clusters. Thus, the homogeneity ascribed to the category would refer only to the fact that individuals within the category homogeneously exhibited a particular pattern of descriptively diverse behaviors. However, the organization of symptoms mirrored by the symptom cluster profiles is not in any fundamental sense different from that observed in conventional diagnostic syndromes. Both methods of categorization systematize diverse behaviors because of an observed regularity in their concurrent appearance.

The difference between these two approaches, then, lies only in the pattern of deviant behaviors that define the categories. Indeed, Eysenck (1953) has noted that both the clinician and the factor analyst derive syndromes in essentially the same manner, i.e., in terms of the observed intercorrelations of various symptoms. It is the difference in method, purely observational versus statistical, that explains why the final symptom structure may differ. The assumption must not be made that the advantage lies entirely with the factor analytic method. The merit accruing through the greater rigor of factor analysis may be outweighed by the limitations imposed in employing a restricted group of symptoms and a particular sample of patients. Thus, the factor analyst cannot claim that the class-defining symptom pattern he has derived is a standard of homogeneity against which classes within another schema can be evaluated. The plea that symptom cluster scores, derived from factor analytic techniques, substitute for the present method of psychiatric classification has little relevance to the heterogeneity issue.

In the light of this discussion we may conclude that the concept of homogeneity has little utility in evaluating classificatory schemata. Since the heterogeneity criticism invariably involves an implicit preference for one classificatory principle over another, it would perhaps be more fruitful to dispense entirely with the homogeneity-heterogeneity distinction, thus, allowing us to direct our attention to the underlying problem of the relative merits of different classificatory principles.

RELIABILITY AND VALIDITY

A matter of continuing concern has been the degree of reliability of the present diagnostic system. Considerable energy has been expended by both those who criticize the present system for its lack of reliability (Ash, 1949; Boisen, 1938; Eysenck, 1952; Mehlman, 1952; Roe, 1949; Rotter, 1954; Scott, 1958) and those who defend it against this criticism (Foulds, 1955; Hunt, Wittson, & Hunt, 1953; Schmidt & Fonda, 1956; Seeman, 1953). Certain investigators (Foulds, 1955; Schmidt & Fonda, 1956) who have offered evidence that the present system is reliable have also pointed out that the earlier studies emphasizing the unreliability of psychiatric diagnosis have suffered from serious conceptual and methodological difficulties.

In evaluating the body of studies concerned with the reliability of psychiatric diagnosis, one must conclude that so long as diagnosis is confined to broad diagnostic categories, it is reasonably reliable, but the reliability diminishes as one proceeds from broad, inclusive class categories to narrower, more specific ones. As finer discriminations are called for, accuracy in diagnosis becomes increasingly difficult. Since this latter characteristic appears to be common to the classificatory efforts in many areas of knowledge, it would appear to be inappropriate to criticize psychiatric diagnosis on the grounds that it is less than perfectly reliable. This should not lead to an underestimation of the importance of reliability. While certain extraclassificatory factors, e.g., proficiency of the clinicians, biases of the particular clinical settings, etc., may influence it, reliability is primarily related to the precision with which classes of a schema are defined. Since the defining characteristic of most classes in psychiatric diagnosis is the occurrence of symptoms in particular combinations, the reliability of the system mirrors the specificity with which the various combinations of symptoms (syndromes) have been spelled out. It is mandatory for a classificatory schema to be reliable since reliability refers to the definiteness with which phenomena can be ordered to classes. If a system does not allow for such a division of phenomena, it can make no pretense of being a classificatory schema.

While reliability is a prerequisite if the diagnostic system is to have any value, it must not be assumed that if human effort were to make the present system perfectly reliable, it could escape all the difficulties attributed to it. This perfect reliability would only mean that individuals within each class shared a particular commonality in relation to the classificatory principle of symptom manifestation. If one were interested in attributes unrelated or minimally related to the classificatory principle employed, the perfect reliability of the system would offer little cause for rejoicing. Perfect reliability of the present system can only be the goal of those who are interested in nothing more than the present classificatory principle and the particular attributes of the classes constructed on the basis of this principle.

When attention is shifted from characteristics which define a class to the correlates of class membership, this implies a shift in concern from the reliability of a system to its validity. The distinction between the reliability and validity of a classificatory system would appear to involve certain conceptual difficulties. It is perhaps this conceptual difficulty which explains why the rather imposing body of literature concerned with diagnosis has been virtually silent on the question of the validity of the present system of psychiatric diagnosis. Only one group of investigators (Hunt, 1951; Hunt, Wittson, & Barton, 1950a, 1950b; Hunt, Wittson, & Hunt, 1953; Wittson & Hunt, 1951) has specifically been concerned with the predictive efficacy of diagnoses and, thus, to the validity of psychiatric classifications; and even in this work, the distinction between validity and reliability is not clearly drawn.

In order to grasp the distinction between the reliability and the validity of a classificatory schema, one must differentiate the defining characteristics of the classes from the correlates of the classes. In the former case, we are interested in the principles upon which classes are formed; in the latter, in the predictions or valid statements that can be made about phenomena once they are classified. The difficulty lies in the overlap between the classifying principles and the class correlates. If a classificatory system is reliable, it is also valid to the extent that we can predict that the individuals within a class will exhibit certain characteristics, namely, those behaviors or attributes which serve to define the class.

It is the rare class, however, that does not connote correlates beyond its defining characteristics. The predictions associated with class membership may vary from simple extensions of the classificatory principles to correlates which would appear to have little connection with these principles. Let us examine a simple illustration and see what follows from categorizing an individual. Once an individual has been classified as manifesting a manic-depressive reaction, depressed type, on the basis of the symptoms of depression of mood, motor retardation, and stupor (American Psychiatric Association, 1952), the prediction may be made that the individual will spend a great deal of time in bed, which represents an obvious extension of the symptom pattern. One may also hypothesize that the patient will show improvement if electroshock therapy is employed. This is a correlate which has little direct connection with the symptoms themselves. These predictions are open to test, and evidence may or may not be found to support them. Thus, measures of validity may be obtained which are independent of the reliability of the system of classification.

The problem of validity lies at the heart of the confusion which surrounds psychiatric diagnosis. When the present diagnostic schema is assailed, the common complaint is that class membership conveys little information beyond the gross symptomatology of the patient and contributes little to the solution of the pressing problems of etiology, treatment procedures, prognosis, etc. The criticism that class membership does not predict these important aspects of a disorder appears to be a legitimate one. This does not mean the present system has no validity. It simply indicates that the system may be valid in respect to certain correlates but invalid in respect to others. Much confusion would be dispelled if as much care were taken in noting the existing correlates of classes as is taken in noting the classificatory principles. A great deal of effort has gone into the formalization of the defining characteristics of classes (American Psychiatric Association, 1952), but one looks in vain for a formal delineation of the extraclassificatory attributes and correlates of class membership. As a result, the various diagnostic categories have been burdened with correlates not systematically derived from a classificatory principle but which were attributed to the classes because they were the focal points of clinical interest. A major question is just what correlates can justifiably be attributed to the class categories. To answer this question we must turn our attention to the purposes and philosophy underlying contemporary psychiatric diagnosis.

PHILOSOPHY AND PURPOSE OF CONVENTIONAL DIAGNOSIS

The validity of the conventional diagnostic system is least ambiguous and most free from potential criticism as a descriptive schema, a taxonomy of mental disorders analogous to the work of Ray and Linnaeus in biology. In this sense, class membership confirms that the inclusion of an individual within a class guarantees only that he exhibit the defining characteristics of that class. Only a modest extension of this system, in terms of a very limited number of well established correlates, makes for a system of impressive heuristic value, even though it falls considerably short of what would now be considered an optimal classificatory schema. As has been noted (Caveny et al., 1955; Hunt et al., 1953), the present diagnostic system is quite useful when evaluated in terms of its administrative and, to a lesser extent, its preventive implications. Caveny et al. (1955) and Wittenborn, Holzberg, and Simon (1953) should be consulted for a comprehensive list of such uses, but examples would include legal determination of insanity, declaration of incompetence, type of ward required for custodial care, census figures and statistical data upon which considerable planning is based, screening devices for the military services or other agencies, etc. In view of the extensive criticism of contemporary diagnosis, the surprising fact is not that so few valid predictions can be derived from class membership, but that so many can.

The value of the present psychiatric classification system would be further enhanced by its explicit divorcement from its Kraepelinian heritage by an emphasis on its descriptive aspect and, through careful empirical investigation, the cataloging of the reliable correlates of its categories. That this catalog of correlates would be an impressive one is expressed in Hoch's (1953) view that the present system is superior to any system which has been evolved to replace it. It is an open question whether the system merits this amount of praise. In general, however, the defense of the present system—or, for that matter, diagnosis in general (Caveny et al., 1955; Eysenck, 1952; Hunt et al., 1953; Jellinek, 1939)—tends to rest on the merits of its descriptive, empirical, and nondynamic aspects.

The present classificatory system, even as a purely descriptive device, is still open to a certain degree of criticism. Its classificatory principle is organized primarily about symptom manifestation. This would be adequate for a descriptive system if this principle were consistently applied to all classes of the schema and if the symptoms associated with each diagnostic category were clearly specified. There is some question, however, whether the system meets these requirements (Phillips & Rabinovitch, 1958; Rotter, 1954). The criticism has been advanced that the present system is based on a number of diverse principles of classification. Most classes are indeed defined by symptom manifestation, but the organic disorders, for example, tend to be identified by etiology, while such other factors as prognosis, social conformity, etc. are also employed as classificatory principles. This does not appear, however, to be an insurmountable problem, for the system could be made a completely consistent one by explicitly defining each category by the symptoms encompassed. The system would appear to be eminently amenable to the unitary application of this descriptive classificatory principle, for there are actually few cases where classes are not so defined. Where reliable relations between the present categories and etiology and prognosis have been established, these also could be incorporated explicitly within the system. Etiology and prognosis would be treated not as inherent attributes of the various classifications, but rather as correlates of the particular classes to which their relationship is known. They would, thus, not be confounded with the classificatory principle of the system.

This course of action would satisfy the requirement of consistency in the application of the classificatory principle. A remaining area of ambiguity would be the lack of agreement in what constitutes a symptom. In physical medicine, a clear distinction has been made between a symptom, which is defined as a subjectively experienced abnormality, and a sign, which is considered an objective indication of abnormality (Holmes, 1946). This differentiation has not, however, been extended to the sphere of mental disorders. A source of difficulty may lie in the definition of what is psychologically abnormal. In psychiatric terminology, symptoms include a wide range of phenomena from the grossest type of behavior deviation, through the complaints of the patient, to events almost completely inferential in nature. One suggestion (Yates, 1958) has been to eliminate the term "symptom" and direct attention to the manifest responses of the individual. This suggestion appears to be embodied in the work of Wittenborn and his colleagues (Wittenborn, 1951, 1952; Wittenborn & Bailey, 1952; Wittenborn & Holzberg, 1951; Wittenborn et al., 1953; Wittenborn & Weiss, 1952). Wittenborn's diagnostic system, in which symptoms are defined as currently discernible behaviors, represents a standard of clarity for purely descriptive systems of psychiatric classification. This clarity was achieved by clearly noting and limiting the group of behaviors which would be employed in the system. But even here a certain amount of ambiguity remains. The number of responses or discernible behaviors which may be considered for inclusion within a diagnostic schema borders on the infinite. The question arises, then, as to how one goes about the selection of those behaviors to be incorporated in the classificatory system. Parsimony demands that only "meaningful" items of behavior be chosen for inclusion, and this selective principle has certainly been at work in the construction of all systems of diagnosis. In this sense, the present method of psychiatric classification is not a purely descriptive one, nor can any classification schema truly meet this criterion of purity. Meaning and utility inevitably appear among the determinants of classificatory systems.

Several investigators (Cameron, 1953; Jellinek, 1939; Magaret, 1952) have stressed the inappropriateness of discussing diagnosis in the abstract, pointing out that such a discussion should center around the question of "diagnosis for what?" Indeed, a diagnostic system cannot be described as "true" or "false," but only as being useful or not useful in attaining prescribed goals. Therefore, when a system is devised, its purposes should be explicitly stated so that the system can be evaluated in terms of its success or failure in attaining these objectives. Furthermore, these goals should be kept explicit throughout the period during which the system is being employed. The present diagnostic schema has not met this requirement. Instead, its goals have been carried along in an implicit manner and have been allowed to become vague. The result has been that some see the purpose of the schema as being an adequate description of mental disorders (Hunt et al., 1953), others view it as being concerned with prognosis (Hoch, 1953), and still others view the schemata goal as the discovery of etiology (Cameron, 1953).

Typically, the present schema has been conceptualized as descriptive in nature, but a brief glance at its history indicates that the original purposes and goals in the construction of this schema went far beyond the desire for a descriptive taxonomy. As Zilboorg and Henry (1941) clearly note, Kraepelin not only studied the individual while hospitalized, but also the patient's premorbid history and post-hospital course. His hope was to make our understanding of all mental disorders as precise as our knowledge of the course of general paresis. He insisted on the classification of mental disorders according to regularities in symptoms and course of illness, believing this would lead to a clearer discrimination among the different disease entities. He hoped for the subsequent discovery of a specific somatic malfunction responsible for each disease. For Kraepelin, then, classification was related to etiology, treatment, and prognosis. Had the system worked as envisaged, these variables would have become the extraclassificatory attributes of the schema. When matched against this aspiration, the present system must be considered a failure since the common complaint against it is that a diagnostic label tells us very little about etiology, treatment, or prognosis (Miles, 1953). However, it would be erroneous to conclude that the present system is valueless because its classes are only minimally related to etiology and prognosis.

What should be noted is that etiology and prognosis, though important, are but two of a multitude of variables of interest. The importance of these variables should not obscure the fact that their relationship to a classificatory system is exactly the same as that of any other variables. This relationship may take one of two forms. Etiology and prognosis may be the correlates of the classes of a diagnostic system which employs an independent classificatory principle like symptom manifestation. Optimally, we should prefer a classificatory schema in which the indices of etiology and preferred modes of treatment would be incorporated (Hunt et al., 1953; Pepinsky, 1948). In essence, this was Kraepelin's approach, and it continues to underlie some promising work in the area of psychopathology. Although Kraepelin's disease concept is in disrepute (Hoch & Zubin, 1953; Marzoff, 1947; Rotter, 1954), it is the opinion of several investigators (Eysenck, 1953; Phillips & Rabinovitch, 1958; Wittenborn et al., 1953) that further work employing the descriptive symptomatic approach could well lead to a greater understanding of the etiology underlying abnormal "processes."

Another manner in which etiology, treatment, or prognosis could be related to a classificatory schema is by utilizing each of these variables as the classificatory principle for a new diagnostic system. For instance, we might organize patients into groups which respond differentially to particular forms of treatment like electroshock, drugs, psychotherapy, etc. The new schemata which might be proposed could be of considerable value in respect to certain goals but useless in regard to others. Since we do not possess a diagnostic system based on all the variables of clinical interest, we might have to be satisfied with the construction of a variety of diagnostic systems, each based on a different principle of classification. These classificatory techniques would exist side by side, their use being determined by the specific objectives of the diagnostician.

ETIOLOGY VERSUS DESCRIPTION IN DIAGNOSIS

The classical Kraepelinian classification schema shows two major characteristics: a commitment to a detailed description of the manifest symptomatic behaviors of the individual and an underlying assumption that such a descriptive classification would be transitory, eventually leading to and being replaced by a system whose classificatory principle was the etiology of the various mental disorders. Major criticism of this classificatory effort has been directed at the first of these. The reservations are that, in practice, such a descriptive effort allows no place for a process interpretation of psychopathology and that it has not encouraged the development of prevention and treatment programs in the mental disorders.

The authors do not feel that the failure of the Kraepelinian system has demonstrated the futility of employing symptoms as the basis for classification. It does suggest that if one approaches the problem of description with an assumption as to the necessary correlates of such descriptions, then the diagnostic system may well be in error. Kraepelin's empiricism is contaminated in just this way. For example, he refused to accept as cases of dementia praecox those individuals who recovered from the disorder, since he assumed irreversibility as a necessary concomitant of its hypothesized neurophysiological base. Bleuler, on the other hand, who was much less commited to any particular form of causality in this illness, readily recognized the possibility of its favorable outcome. It is not, then, the descriptive approach itself which is open to criticism, but description contaminated by preconception. An unfettered description of those schizophrenics with good prognosis in contrast to those with poor prognosis reveals clear differences in the symptom configuration between these kinds of patients (Farina & Webb, 1956; Phillips, 1953).

Kraepelin's basic concern with the problem of etiology has remained a focus of efforts in the clinical area. Although his postulate of central nervous system disease as the basis of mental disorder is in disrepute, and his systematic classificatory efforts are assailed, one nevertheless finds a striking congruence between Kraepelin's preconceptions and certain current attempts at the solution of the problem of psychopathology. There is an unwavering belief that some simple categorical system will quickly solve the mysteries of etiology. The exponents of these newer classificatory schemata have merely replaced symptoms by other phenomena like test scores (King, 1954), particular patterns of interpersonal relations (Leary & Coffey, 1955), etc. It is the authors' conviction that these new efforts to find shortcut solutions to the question of etiology will similarly remain unsuccessful. The amount of descriptive effort required before etiological factors are likely to be discovered has been underestimated (Kety, 1959a, 1959b), and the pursuit of etiology should represent an end point rather than a beginning for classificatory systems. The process of moving from an empirical orientation to an etiological one is, of necessity, inferential and therefore susceptible to the myriad dangers of premature inference. We propose that the greatest safeguard against such prematurity is not to be found in the scrapping of an empirical descriptive approach, but in an accelerated program of empirical research. What is needed at this time is a systematic, empirical attack on the problem of mental disorders. Inherent in this program is the employment of symptoms, broadly defined as meaningful and discernible behaviors, as the basis of a classificatory system. Rather than an abstract search for etiologies, it would appear more currently fruitful to investigate such empirical correlates of symptomatology as reactions to specific forms of treatment, outcome in the disorders, case history phenomena, etc.

The pervasive concern with etiology may derive from a belief that if this were known, prevention would shortly be forthcoming, thus, making the present complex problems of treatment and prognosis inconsequential. Unfortunately, efforts to short-circuit the drudgery involved in establishing an empirically founded psychiatry has not resulted in any major breakthroughs. Etiology is typically the last characteristic of a disorder to be discovered. Consequently, we would suggest the search for etiology be put aside and attempted only when a greater number of the correlates of symptomatic behaviors have been established.

The authors are impressed by the amount of energy that has been expended in both attacking and defending various contemporary systems of classification. We believe that a classificatory system should include any behavior or phenomenon that appears promising in terms of its significant correlates. At this stage of our investigations, the system employed should be an open and expanding one, not one which is closed and defended on conceptual grounds. Systems of classification must be treated as tools for further discovery, not as bases for polemic disputation.

As stated above, it is possible that a number of systems of classification may be needed to encompass the behaviors presently of clinical interest. It may appear that the espousal of this position, in conjunction with a plea for empirical exploration of the correlates of these behaviors, runs headlong into a desire for conceptual neatness and parsimony. It may be feared that the use of a number of classificatory systems concurrently, each with its own correlates, may lead to the creation of a gigantic actuarial table of unrelated elements. However, the authors do not feel that such a fear is well founded because it assumes that the correlates of these systems have no eventual relation one to the other.

We believe that this latter view is unnecessarily pessimistic. While in principle a multiplicity of classificatory systems might be called for, results from the authors' own research program suggests that a single, relatively restricted and coherent classification system can be derived from an empirical study of the correlates of symptomatic behaviors (Phillips & Rabinovitch, 1958; Zigler & Phillips, 1960). Such a system might serve a number of psychiatrically significant functions, including the optimum selection of patients for specific treatment programs and the prediction of treatment outcomes. In conclusion, a descriptive classificatory system appears far from dead, and if properly employed, it can lead to a fuller as well as a more conceptually based understanding of the psychopathologies.

REFERENCES

Allport, G. *Personality: A psychological interpretation.* New York: Holt, 1937.

Allport, G. Personalistic psychology as science: A reply. *Psychol. Rev.*, 1946, **53**, 132–135.

American Psychiatric Association, Mental Hospital Service, Committee on Nomenclature and Statistics of the American Psychiatric Association. *Diagnostic and statistical manual: Mental disorders.* Washington, D. C.: APA, 1952.

Ash, P. The reliability of psychiatric diagnosis. *J. abnorm. soc. Psychol.*, 1949, **44**, 272–277.

Beach, F. The snark was a boojum. *Amer. Psychologist*, 1950, **5**, 115–124.

Beck, S. The science of personality: Nomothetic or idiographic? *Psychol. Rev.*, 1953, **60**, 353–359.

Boisen, A. Types of dementia praecox: A study in psychiatric classification. *Psychiatry*, 1938, **1**, 233–236.

Brower, D. The problem of quantification in psychological science. *Psychol. Rev.*, 1949, **56**, 325–333.

Cameron, D. A theory of diagnosis. In P. Hoch & J. Zubin (Eds.), *Current problems in psychiatric diagnosis.* New York: Grune & Stratton, 1953. Pp. 33–45.

Cattell, R. *Personality and motivation structure and measurement.* New York: World Book, 1957.

Caveny, E., Wittson, C., Hunt, W., & Herman, R. Psychiatric diagnosis, its nature and function. *J. nerv. ment. Dis.*, 1955, **121**, 367–380.

Cronbach, L. The two disciplines of scientific psychology. *Amer. Psychologist*, 1957, **12**, 671–684.

Eysenck, H. *The scientific study of personality.* London: Routledge & Kegan Paul, 1952.

Eysenck, H. The logical basis of factor analysis. *Amer. Psychologist*, 1953, **8**, 105–113.

Eysenck, H. The science of personality: Nomothetic. *Psychol. Rev.*, 1954, **61**, 339–341.

Falk, J. Issues distinguishing idiographic from nomothetic

approaches to personality theory. *Psychol. Rev.*, 1956, **63**, 53–62.

Farina, A., & Webb, W. Premorbid adjustment and subsequent discharge. *J. nerv. ment. Dis.*, 1956, **124**, 612–613.

Foulds, G. The reliability of psychiatric, and the validity of psychological diagnosis. *J. ment. Sci.*, 1955, **101**, 851–862.

Guthrie, E. The status of systematic psychology. *Amer. Psychologist*, 1950, **5**, 97–101.

Harlow, H. Mice, monkeys, men, and motives. *Psychol. Rev.*, 1953, **60**, 23–32.

Harrower, Molly. (Ed.) *Diagnostic psychological testing.* Springfield, Ill.: Charles C Thomas, 1950.

Hoch, P. Discussion. In P. Hoch & J. Zubin (Eds.), *Current problems in psychiatric diagnosis.* New York: Grune & Stratton, 1953. Pp. 46–50.

Hoch, P., & Zubin, J. (Eds.) *Current problems in psychiatric diagnosis.* New York: Grune & Stratton, 1953.

Holmes, G. *Introduction to clinical neurology.* Edinburgh: Livingstone, 1946.

Hunt, W. Clinical psychology—science or superstition. *Amer. Psychologist*, 1951, **6**, 683–687. (a)

Hunt, W. An investigation of naval neuropsychiatric screening procedures. In H. Gruetskaw (Ed.), *Groups, leadership, and men.* Pittsburgh, Pa.: Carnegie Press, 1951. Pp. 245–256. (b)

Hunt, W., Wittson, C., & Barton, H. A further validation of naval neuropsychiatric screening. *J. consult. Psychol.*, 1950, **14**, 485–488. (a)

Hunt, W., Wittson, C., & Barton, H. A validation study of naval neuropsychiatric screening. *J. consult. Psychol.*, 1950, **14**, 35–39. (b)

Hunt, W., Wittson, C., & Hunt, E. A theoretical and practical analysis of the diagnostic process. In P. Hoch & J. Zubin (Eds.), *Current problems in psychiatric diagnosis.* New York: Grune & Stratton, 1953. Pp. 53–65.

Jellinek, E. Some principles of psychiatric classification. *Psychiatry*, 1939, **2**, 161–165.

Kantor, R., Wallner, J., & Winder, C. Process and reactive schizophrenia. *J. consult. Psychol.*, 1953, **17**, 157–162.

Kety, S. Biochemical theories of schizophrenia. Part I. *Science*, 1959, **129**, 1528–1532. (a)

Kety, S. Biochemical theories of schizophrenia. Part II. *Science*, 1959, **129**, 1590–1956. (b)

King, G. Research with neuropsychiatric samples. *J. Psychol.*, 1954, **38**, 383–387.

Koch, S. The current status of motivational psychology. *Psychol. Rev.*, 1951, **58**, 147–154.

Leary, T., & Coffey, H. Interpersonal diagnosis: Some problems of methodology and validation. *J. abnorm. soc. Psychol.*, 1955, **50**, 110–126.

MacKinnon, D. Fact and fancy in personality research. *Amer. Psychologist*, 1953, **8**, 138–146.

Magaret, Ann. Clinical methods: Psychodiagnostics. *Annu. Rev. Psychol.*, 1952, **3**, 283–320.

Marquis, D. Research planning at the frontiers of science. *Amer. Psychologist*, 1948, **3**, 430–438.

Marzoff, S. S. The disease concept in psychology. *Psychol. Rev.*, 1947, **54**, 211–221.

Maslow, A. Cognition of the particular and of the generic. *Psychol. Rev.*, 1948, **55**, 22–40.

Mehlman, B. The reliability of psychiatric diagnosis. *J. abnorm. soc. Psychol.*, 1952, **47**, 577–578.

Menninger, K. The practice of psychiatry. *Dig. Neurol. Psychiat.*, 1955, **23**, 101.

Miles, H. Discussion. In P. Hoch & J. Zubin (Eds.), *Current problems in psychiatric diagnosis.* New York: Grune & Stratton, 1953. Pp. 107–111.

Noyes, A. *Modern clinical psychiatry.* Philadelphia: Saunders, 1953.

Patterson, C. Is psychotherapy dependent on diagnosis? *Amer. Psychologist*, 1948, **3**, 155–159.

Pepinsky, H. B. Diagnostic categories in clinical counseling. *Appl. psychol. Monogr.*, 1948, No. 15.

Phillips, L. Case history data and prognosis in schizophrenia. *J. nerv. ment. Dis.*, 1953, **117**, 515–525.

Phillips, L., & Rabinovitch, M. Social role and patterns of symptomatic behaviors. *J. abnorm. soc. Psychol.*, 1958, **57**, 181–186.

Rapaport, D. The future of research in clinical psychology and psychiatry. *Amer. Psychologist*, 1947, **2**, 167–172.

Roby, T. An opinion on the construction of behavior theory. *Amer. Psychologist*, 1959, **14**, 129–134.

Roe, Anne. Integration of personality theory and clinical practice. *J. abnorm. soc. Psychol.*, 1949, **44**, 36–41.

Rogers, C. Significant aspects of client-centered therapy. *Amer. Psychologist*, 1946, **1**, 415–422.

Rogers, C. *Client-centered therapy.* Boston: Houghton Mifflin, 1951.

Rotter, J. *Social learning and clinical psychology.* New York: Prentice-Hall, 1954.

Schmidt, H., & Fonda, C. The reliability of psychiatric diagnosis: A new look. *J. abnorm. soc. Psychol.*, 1956, **52**, 262–267.

Scott, J. The place of observation in biological and psychological science. *Amer. Psychologist*, 1955, **10**, 61–63.

Scott, W. Research definitions of mental health and mental illness. *Psychol. Bull.*, 1958, **55**, 1–45.

Seeman, W. Psychiatric diagnosis: An investigation of interperson-reliability after didactic instruction. *J. nerv. ment. Dis.*, 1953, **118**, 541–544.

Skaggs, E. Personalistic psychology as science. *Psychol. Rev.*, 1945, **52**, 234–238.

Skaggs, E. Ten basic postulates of personalistic psychology. *Psychol. Rev.*, 1947, **54**, 255–262.

Thorne, F. Back to fundamentals. *J. clin. Psychol.*, 1953, **9**, 89–91.

Tolman, R. Virtue rewarded and vice punished. *Amer. Psychologist*, 1953, **8**, 721–733.

Tyler, Leona. Toward a workable psychology of individuality. *Amer. Psychologist*, 1959, **14**, 75–81.

Windle, C., & Hamwi, V. An exploratory study of the prognostic value of the complex reaction time tests in early and chronic psychotics. *J. clin. Psychol.*, 1953, **9**, 156–161.

Wittenborn, J. Symptom patterns in a group of mental hospital patients. *J. consult. Psychol.*, 1951, **15**, 290–302.

Wittenborn, J. The behavioral symptoms for certain organic psychoses. *J. consult. Psychol.*, 1952, **16**, 104–106.

Wittenborn, J., & Bailey, C. The symptoms of involutional psychosis. *J. consult. Psychol.*, 1952, **16**, 13–17.

Wittenborn, J., & Holzberg, J. The generality of psychiatric syndromes. *J. consult. Psychol.*, 1951, **15**, 372–380.

Wittenborn, J., Holzberg, J., & Simon, B. Symptom correlates for descriptive diagnosis. *Genet. psychol. Monogr.*, 1953, **47**, 237–301.

Wittenborn, J., & Weiss, W. Patients diagnosed manic-depressive psychosismanic state. *J. consult. Psychol.*, 1952, **16**, 193–198.

Wittman, P., & Sheldon, W. A proposed classification of psychotic behavior reactions. *Amer. J. Psychiat.*, 1948, **105**, 124–128.

Wittson, C., & Hunt, W. The predictive value of the brief psychiatric interview. *Amer. J. Psychiat.*, 1951, **107**, 582–585.

Yates, A. Symptoms and symptom substitution. *Psychol. Rev.*, 1958, **65**, 371–374.

Zigler, E., & Phillips, L. Social effectiveness and symptomatic behaviors. *J. abnorm. soc. Psychol.*, 1960, **61**, 231–238.

Zilboorg, G., & Henry, G. W. *History of medical psychology.* New York: Norton, 1941.

Syndromes of Psychosis and Psychoneurosis: A Clinical Validation Study

Peter E. Nathan

Albert Samaraweera

Marcia M. Andberg

Vernon D. Patch

There is little disagreement among mental health professionals that current procedures for psychiatric diagnosis are largely unreliable and, hence, of doubtful validity and utility. Several sources of low diagnostic reliability have been traced (1-3). Various limitations on diagnosis as an aid to prognosis, treatment, and determination of etiology have also been reviewed (4,5). Because of its carefully documented shortcomings, some investigators have argued for the abolition of the process of formal psychiatric diagnosis, in favor of the "single-case" approach which views each individual's psychopathology as unique and unclassifiable (6). Others would retain the concept of diagnosis but radically alter traditional procedures so that behavior is categorized as one set or another of characteristic maladaptive interactions with the environment rather than as a collection of psycopathological symptoms (7). A smaller group of researchers argue for less fundamental changes in current diagnostic procedures. For the most part, they confine their efforts to attempts to evolve more effective diagnostic instruments to measure psychopathology, including highly structured mental status protocols, behavior rating scales, and personal history questionnaires (8-10).

In similar response to dissatisfaction with the reliability and validity of psychiatric diagnosis and, in particular, as an effort to identify and measure the several sources of diagnostic unreliability (an integrative task which had not before been done), a systems analysis of current diagnostic procedures was performed (11). The systems analysis, consisting in part of a set of 21 logic flowcharts, first identified a set of 100 psychiatric signs and symptoms thought to be of key differential diagnostic significance and then traced the diverse pathways by which these cues are usually processed for diagnosis. Identification of these cues and their usual mode of diagnostic integration was accomplished by drawing upon a wide range of written material on the diagnostic process produced by diagnostic authorities writing from the time of Bleuler and Kraepelin to our own. This analysis, drawing on the accumulated wisdom of a composite "complete clinician," was thought to represent a model which might finally enable the thorough testing of diagnostic reliability by making much of what is implicit in psychiatric diagnosis much more explicit and, hence, replicable.

In flowchart form, though, the value of the systems analysis was sharply limited by the absence of empirical data to demonstrate its only theoretically superior reliability and to support its only consensually validated structure. To enable this testing, the 21 flowcharts of the systems analysis were translated into a diagnostic instrument, the *Boston City Hospital-Behavior Checklist* (BCH-BCL).

A study of the diagnostic reliability of the BCH-BCL (12) indicated that the instrument does enhance the reliability of psychiatric diagnosis by restricting the elements of the diagnostic decision process to more reliable "observables."

The study upon which this paper reports was designed to permit examination of the diagnostic reliability and validity of a portion of the BCH-BCL. This design also allowed concurrent evaluation of the utility of abnormal behavior as a basis for diagnosis since signs and symptoms of abnormal behavior represent the instrument's primary diagnostic criteria. During the course of the study, BCH-BCL protocols summarizing the behavior of 605 psychiatric patients evaluated at Boston City Hospital were examined for the follow-

From *Archives of General Psychiatry*, 1968, **19**, 704–716.

ing: (1) diagnostic reliability, estimated from the degree to which several diagnosticians were able to agree on a diagnostic label when presented equivalent sets of psychopathology; (2) diagnostic validity and utility, measured by the capacity of the BCH-BCL and the assumptions which underlie it (*a*) to yield empirically derived "baseline" symptom rates for four broad diagnostic groups (the psychoses, psychoneuroses, personality disorders, and acute brain disorders) and (*b*) to enable concurrent identification of "predictor" symptoms, ie, those which allow reliable, rapid separation of patients into the four major diagnostic groups listed above.

METHODS

Sample and Procedure. The sample was composed of 605 patients, all of whom had received a psychiatric diagnosis at Boston City Hospital during the winter of 1966 to 1967. Patients ranged in age from 14 to 78 with a mean age of 32.6 years. Approximately 36% of the patients in the sample were males. Level of education ranged from third grade through college; mean education was 11th grade. Most of the men in the sample were either blue-collar or service workers; most of the women were service workers.

Each patient was evaluated by one of 16 Boston City Hospital psychiatric residents, either on the accident floor of the hospital or on its psychiatric ward. In addition to his evaluation, which customarily included a complete mental status examination and thorough inquiry into medical and psychosocial history, each resident completed a BCH-BCL. Every resident was asked to consult a senior staff person when he was unsure of a diagnosis or a plan for disposition; such consultations were almost always available in practice. Second- and third-year residents evaluated accident floor patients while first-year residents under supervision saw inpatients. As a result, first-year residents evaluated the 68 inpatients included in the sample; and third-year residents evaluated the 537 accident floor patients who completed the sample.

The decision was made before the study began to require that at least ten protocols describing a specific diagnosis be available to be included in this study. Accordingly certain specific diagnostic categories (eg, catatonic schizophrenia, obsessive compulsive reaction) are not included in this study. This decision was made to permit the use of appropriate statistical procedures. In practice, the decision meant leaving 45 protocols out of the sample. In view of the data analysis employed in this study, this omission could not have altered materially the data gathered or the conclusions reached.

The *Boston City Hospital-Behavior Checklist* (BCH-BCL) is a 100-item questionnaire designed to record the presence of almost any given symptom or group of symptoms of

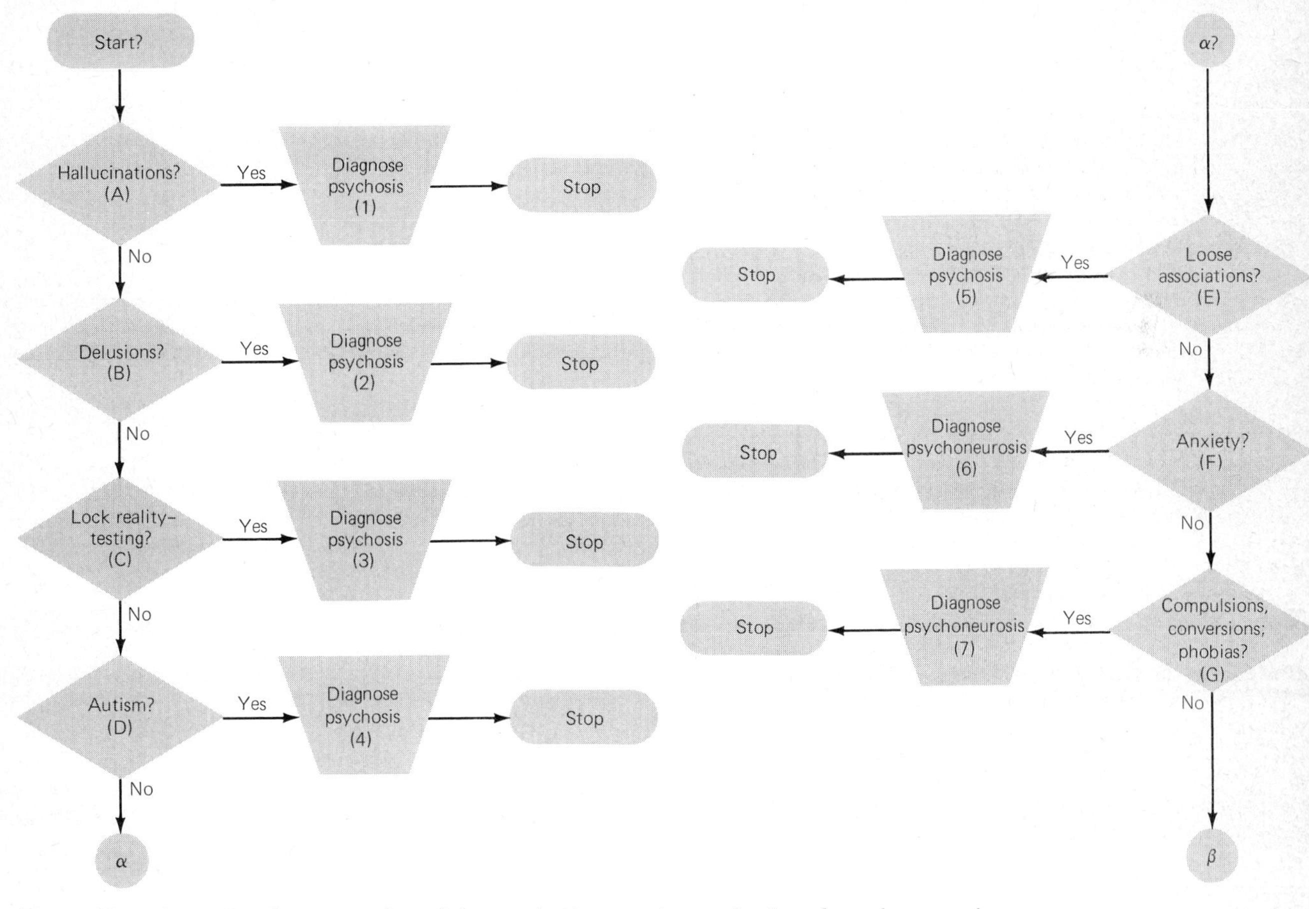

Fig. 1. Flowchart of pathognomonic and demonstrative cues to psychosis and psychoneurosis.

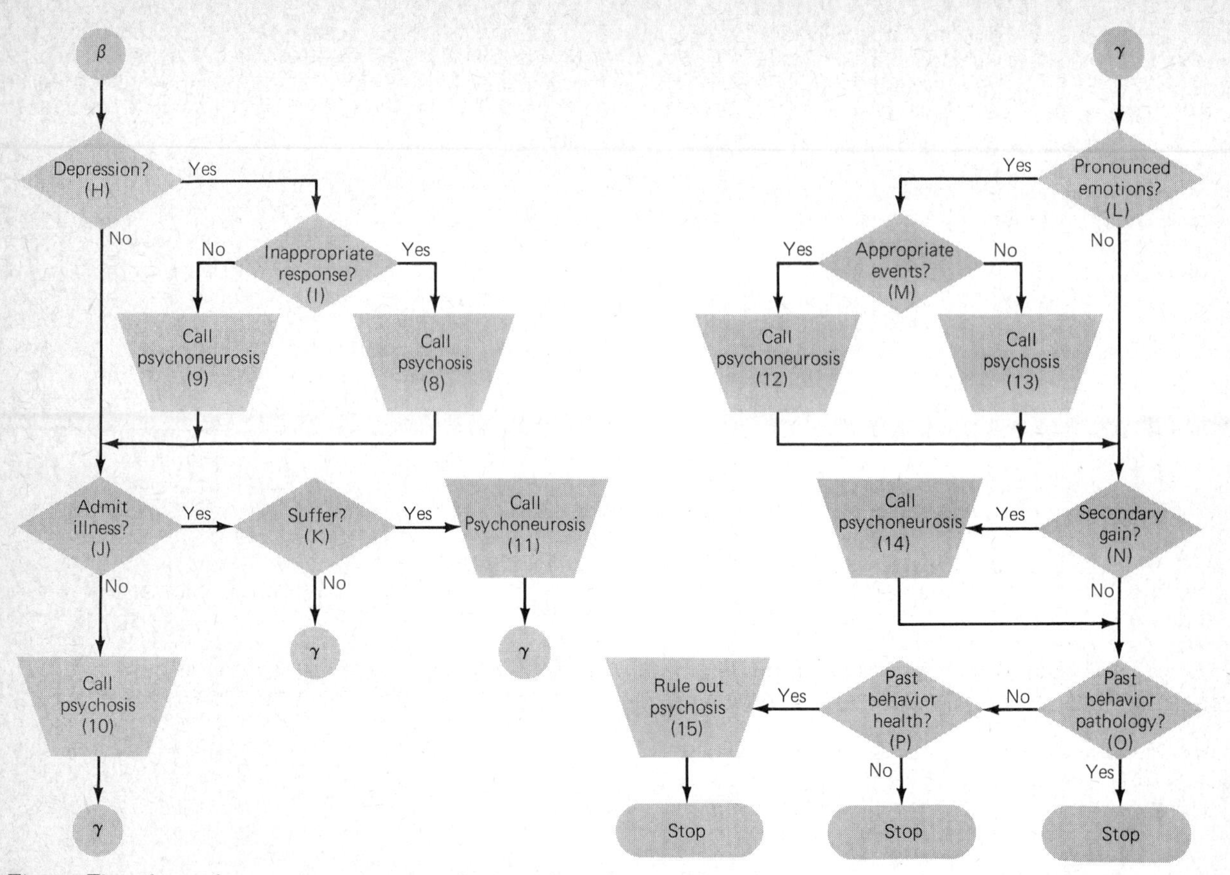

Fig. 2. Flowchart of suggestive cues to psychosis and psychoneurosis.

psychopathology. A research edition of the instrument is available from the first author. The instrument is composed of six separate sections, each of which explores a relatively homogeneous group of symptoms. Section I of the BCH-BCL looks for symptoms which are thought to differentiate among the broad diagnostic categories (eg, psychosis, psychoneurosis, the personality disorders, etc). The succeeding five sections of the instrument record symptoms of abnormal psychomotor, perceptual, cognitive, and affective behavior, and disordered levels of consciousness, symptoms thought to enable decisions on specific diagnostic labels.

This study evaluated the reliability and utility of the 16 cues comprising the first section, "Gross Presenting Symptoms," of the BCH-BCL. The two flowcharts which organized these cues in the initial systems analysis are shown in Figs. 1 and 2; the section as it appears in the BCH-BCL is reproduced in Table 1.

At the beginning of this study, the diagnostic significance of the 16 cues was drawn together from a multitude of recorded clinical observations to achieve consensual validation. The resultant judgment of the composite "ideal clinician" was as follows: (1) cues 1 to 5 were considered pathognomonic of psychosis. The diagnosis of any patient showing one or more of these symptoms was predicted to be a psychotic one; (2) cues 6 and 7 were considered demonstrative of psychoneurosis in the absence of any of the first five cues. It was assumed that any patient showing either or both of these symptoms and none of the first five would be diagnosed psychoneurotic; (3) cues 8A, 9B, and 10B were thought to be suggestive of psychosis while cues 8B, 9A, 10A, and 11 were assumed suggestive of psychoneurosis. A patient who showed more of the former than latter cues would presumably be tentatively labeled psychotic, and vice versa, until additional confirming information on his behavior was available; (4) finally, it was anticipated that patients who showed none of these 16 cues or who showed conflicting patterns of them might well be labeled with one of the personality disorder diagnoses.

RESULTS

Tables 2, 3, and 4 summarize the results of the study.

Table 2 shows the manner in which the seven pathognomonic and demonstrative cues were distributed among the several diagnostic groups. It also indicates the significance of differences in frequency with which each of these cues appeared in the behavior of patients given one of the three broad diagnostic labels of psychosis, psychoneurosis, and personality disorders. These significance levels were computed with the χ^2 one-sample statistic (13). The acute brain disorders were not included in this comparison because behavior during alcohol or drug intoxication, due to its great variability, cannot be judged reliably as either psychotic or psychoneurotic.

Application of the χ^2 statistic to the data in Table 2 revealed the following: (1) All five symptoms considered pathognomonic of psychosis prior to this study (1 to 5) were shown significantly more often by psychotic patients than by nonpsychotic patients. (2) Though anxiety (6) was seen significantly more often in the behavior of psychoneurotic patients than in that of other patients, the level of difference between groups just reached significance. (3) The other demonstrative symptoms of psychoneurosis (7), compulsive, conversional and phobic behavior, were seen slightly more often in the behavior of psychotic patients than psychoneurotic.

Table 3 summarizes the distribution of suggestive cues within the diagnostic categories. The χ^2 applied to these data revealed the following: (1) Only one (10B) of the three cues (8A, 9B, 10B) thought prior to study to be suggestive of psychosis, ie, pronounced emotions in the absence of appropriate environmental events, was seen significantly more often in the behavior of patients subsequently labeled psychotic. (2) All four cues considered suggestive of psychoneurosis (8A, 9A, 10A, 11) were shown significantly more often by psychoneurotic than psychotic patients.

Table 4 summarizes data on the differential diagnostic utility of seven symptom patterns thought on the basis of consensual validation, ie, the composite predictions of "the complete clinician," to be capable of differentiating among the three broad diagnostic groups. The table also records the accuracy of pre-study BCH-BCL procedures by showing, in percentage form, the distribution of labeling errors that would have resulted if the consensually validated assumptions about the diagnostic significance of the 16 cues and seven symptom patterns summarized above had been applied consistently to all 605 protocols. These labeling errors occurred, essentially, when our diagnosticians conferred a diagnosis different from that the complete clinician would have given on the basis of available diagnostic information.

Table 4 shows the following: (1) The two symptom patterns expected before study to be predictive of ultimate psychotic diagnoses were in fact so: 77% of psychotic patients showed two or more symptoms pathognomonic of psychosis (I) while fewer than 1% of nonpsychotic patients showed this pattern. In addition, 41% of patients labeled psychotic showed more cues suggestive of psychosis than of psychoneurosis (II), a pattern shown by only 14% of nonpsychotic patients. (2) The two symptom patterns presumed to be characteristic of psychoneurosis were also found to be so in fact, though their discriminative powers were not as great as were those of the psychotic symptom patterns. Thus, 64% of psychoneurotic patients showed no pathognomonic symptoms of psychosis but at least one of the symptoms considered demonstrative of psychoneurosis (III); only 5% of psychotic patients did so. The fact that 43% of patients labeled with personality disorder diagnoses showed the same pattern seriously reduces the differential diagnostic value of this pattern. A similar finding with respect to cues preponderantly suggestive of psychoneurosis (IV) also occurred: psychotic and psychoneurotic patients were clearly differentiated by this pattern; psychoneurotic and personality disorder patients were not. (3) Two of the three symptom patterns which reflect the absence of specified numbers and types of symptoms revealed little of

Table 1. *Section I of the Boston City Hospital-Behavior Checklist: Gross Presenting Symptoms.*

Yes		
	Does Patient:	
________	(1)	Hallucinate?
________	(2)	Show delusions?
________	(3)	Lack reality-testing?
________	(4)	Show autism?
________	(5)	Show loose associations?
________	(6)	Verbalize persistent anxiety?
________	(7)	Show compulsive, conversional, or phobic behavior?
	Is Patient:	
________	(8)	Depressed?
		If (8): In the absence of an appropriate recent
________	(8A)	event or as inappropriate response to one?
		Or
________	(8B)	In appropriate response to a recent event?
________	(9A)	Willing to admit his illness and suffering from it?
		Or
________	(9B)	Unwilling to admit his illness?
	Are Patient's:	
________	(10)	Emotions more or less pronounced than normal?
________	(10A)	*If* (10): In appropriate response to recent events?
		Or
________	(10B)	In the apparent absence of appropriate environmental stimuli?
________	(11)	Symptoms producing secondary gain which he strives to maintain?

Table 2. *Percentage Distribution of Pathognomonic and Demonstrative Cues.*

Diagnosis / Cue	No. patients	BCH-BCL Cues (1) Halluci-nations	(2) Delu-sions	(3) Lack reality testing	(4) Autism	(5) Loose Associ-ations	(6) Anxiety	(7) Compulsive, conversional, or phobic behavior
Psychosis (Total)	220	49 nd[a,b]	75 nd[a]	73 nd[a]	38 nd[a]	39 n[c]	15	
Schizophrenic reations:								
Paranoid type	100	59	88	85	37	40	42	12
Chronic undiff type	40	63	60	70	41	50	30	20
Acute undiff type	20	60	90	90	70	66	40	26
Manic depressive reaction, manic	20	—	55	45	5	15	35	—
Psychotic depressive reaction	20	20	65	40	30	25	45	25
Involuntary psychotic reaction	20	35	55	60	25	10	40	20
Psychoneurosis (Total)	165	— p[a,b]	1 p[a]	1 p[a]	— p[a]	— p[a]	57 pd[c]	12
Depressive reaction	125	—	2	1	—	—	56	—
Anxiety reaction	20	—	—	5	—	—	95	20
Conversion reaction	20	—	—	—	—	—	39	80
Personality Disorder (Total)	160	1p[a]	3p[a]	2p[a]	—p[a]	1p[a]	41n[c]	9
Inadequate personality	20	—	—	—	—	—	55	10
Emotionally unstable personality	20	—	10	—	—	—	40	5
Passive-aggressive personality	40	3	—	3	—	—	48	15
Antisocial personality	20	—	—	—	—	—	15	10
Addiction (alcoholism)	20	5	—	5	—	—	45	5
Situational reaction (adult)	20	—	5	5	—	5	50	5
Adjustment reaction, adolescence	20	—	10	—	—	5	30	10
Acute Brain Disorder (Total)	60	23	25	32	16	13	43	8
Alcohol intoxication	40	20	20	25	15	3	35	5
Drug intoxication	20	30	35	45	20	35	60	15

[a] Significant < 0.001 level.
[b] p indicates significant difference between this group and the psychotic group with respect to this cue; n, significant difference between this group and the psychoneurotic group with respect to this cue; d, significant difference between this group and the personality disorder group with respect to this cue.
[c] Significant < 0.05 level.

additional diagnostic value; these patterns were the absence of cues 1 to 5 (V) and the absence of cues 1 to 7 (VI). On the other hand, it was found that patients who showed none of the 16 cues (pattern VII) were almost always labeled with personality disorder diagnoses. This finding is an important one which will be discussed in detail later.

The fact that only 8% of patients labeled psychotic and 7% of patients labeled psychoneurotic by the psychiatric residents would have been labeled otherwise by the consensually validated decision rules lends strong empirical support both to the diagnostic validity of these rules and to the diagnostic competence of our clinicians. The fact that 49% of patients with personality disorders diagnoses would have been mislabeled by these same rules emphasizes just as strongly the profound lack of meaningful criteria for the integration of cues to this heterogeneous group of diagnostic categories.

COMMENT

Limitations on sample. While the psychiatric patients seen at Boston City Hospital, when judged by most demographic criteria, appear similar to those seen by psychiatrists at other large municipal hospitals, they are different from patients seen at most strictly mental health facilities so far as diagnostic label, presenting symptoms, and precipitating circumstances are concerned (14,15). The patients seen at this urban hospital are, for the most part, economically deprived, underemployed, and undereducated. They are more likely than most other psychiatric patient groups to show acute and chronic brain disorders following acute and chronic alcohol and drug intoxication, in part because of the extremely high incidence of alcoholism and drug addiction in Boston. The fact that many of these patients were first seen on the accident floor of the hospital following a violent incident at home or on the street probably caused the number of patients in our sample diagnosed within the personality disorder categories to be increased. This fact must be taken into account when the general significance and generalizability of our findings are assessed.

Limitations on availability of criterion measure. The lack of reliable measures of criterion validity remains an unsolved problem for psychiatric researchers. It is an especially troublesome one in diagnostic research, since what should be the most valid measure of criterion validity, ie, a diagnostic statement by an experienced clinician, is often quite unreliable (16).

Early in the formative stages of this research, it became clear that we had two distinct choices of a criterion validity measure. Either we give every BCH-BCL protocol completed by a supervised psychiatric resident to a single experienced clinician who would apply a diagnostic label or we require the resident himself to apply the label. The former alternative would have required an experienced clinician willing to examine several hundred BCH-BCL protocols, willing to confer a diagnostic label without actually seeing

Table 3. *Percentage Distribution of Suggestive Cues.*

		BCH—BCL Cues								
		(8)	(8A)	(8B)	(9A)	(9B)	(10)	(10A)	(10B)	(11)
Diagnosis / Cue	No. patients	Depression	Inappropriate response	Appropriate response	Admit illness	Not admit illness	Pronounced emotions	Appropriate response	Inappropriate response	Secondary gain
Psychosis (Total)	220	35 nd[a,b]	17	11 nd[a]	25 n[a]	19	53	7 nd[a]	40 nd[c]	1 nd[c]
Schizophrenic reactions:										
Paranoid type	100	26	14	5	24	14	41	4	33	3
Chronic undiff type	40	33	8	23	10	30	45	5	40	—
Acute undiff type	20	20	10	—	16	16	66	—	50	—
Manic depressive reaction, manic	20	10	—	—	5	15	100	15	65	—
Psychotic depressive reaction	20	90	50	25	70	10	65	20	35	—
Involuntary Psychotic reaction	20	75	40	30	40	35	55	10	40	—
Psychoneurosis (Total)	165	86 pd[a,b]	24	51 pd[a]	63 pd[a]	8	49	29 p[a]	14 p[c]	29 p[c]
Depressive reaction	125	100	25	66	72	8	54	34	14	32
Anxiety reaction	20	50	20	5	55	—	40	15	20	5
Conversion reaction	20	35	20	5	20	15	25	15	10	35
Personality Disorder (Total)	160	62 pn[a]	22	29 pn[a]	38 n[a]	11	47	23 p[a]	12 p[c]	32 p[a]
Inadequate personality	20	60	20	30	35	10	65	35	25	35
Emotionally unstable personality	20	65	15	20	35	25	35	5	15	35
Passive-Aggressive personality	40	65	25	30	38	8	55	28	20	33
Antisocial personality	20	40	15	15	35	5	15	—	5	15
Addiction (alcoholism)	20	55	25	20	45	—	40	20	10	35
Situational reaction (adult)	20	65	10	45	45	20	60	40	10	40
Adjustment reaction, adolescence	20	80	40	45	35	15	50	30	5	30
Acute Brain Disorder (Total)	60	38	18	13	35	12	35	13	15	13
Alcohol intoxication	40	40	20	15	33	10	33	13	15	17
Drug intoxication	20	35	15	10	40	15	40	15	15	5

[a] Significant < 0.05 level.
[b] p designates significant difference between this group and the psychotic group with respect to this cue; n, significant difference between this group and the psychoneurotic group with respect to this cue; d, significant difference between this group and the personality disorder group with respect to this cue.
[c] Significant < 0.001 level.

Table 4. *Percentage Distribution of Symptom Patterns.*

		BCH-BCL Symptom Patterns							
		(I)	(II)	(III)	(IV)	(V)	(VI)	(VII)	
Diagnosis	No. patients	2 or more cues, 1st five	Cues suggestive of psychosis	No cues 1st five, cues 6 to 7	Cues suggestive of neurosis	No cues, 1st five	No cues, 1st seven	No cues, all 16	Patients mislabeled
Psychosis (Total)	220	77 nd[a,b]	41 nd[a]	5 nd[c]	18 nd[c]	10 nd[a]	5 nd[c]	—d[a]	8 d[a]
Schizophrenic reactions:									
Paranoid type	100	91	37	—	16	—	—	—	—
Chronic undiff type	40	83	38	5	20	8	3	—	8
Acute undiff type	20	95	50	5	10	5	—	—	5
Manic depressive reaction, manic	20	45	65	20	15	40	20	—	25
Psychotic depressive reaction	20	45	35	5	35	20	15	—	15
Involuntary Psychotic reaction	20	55	50	20	25	35	15	—	30
Psychoneurosis (Total)	165	— p[a,b]	15 p[a]	64 pd[c]	68 pd[c]	98 p[a]	34 pd[c]	1 d[a]	7 d[a]
Depressive reaction	125	—	15	55	79	98	42	—	9
Anxiety reaction	20	—	15	90	50	95	5	5	5
Conversion reaction	20	—	15	90	20	100	10	5	—
Personality Disorder (Total)	160	1 p[a]	13 p[a]	43 pn[c]	48 pn[c]	95 p[a]	52 pn[c]	14 pn[a]	49 pn[a]
Inadequate personality	20	—	10	65	55	100	35	5	65
Emotionally unstable personality	20	—	20	45	40	95	50	10	50
Passive-Aggressive personality	40	—	15	50	50	95	45	15	58
Antisocial personality	20	—	15	20	40	100	80	25	20
Addiction (alcoholism)	20	—	5	40	40	90	50	30	50
Situational reaction (adult)	20	5	10	50	60	95	45	—	55
Adjustment reaction, adolescence	20	5	10	25	50	90	65	15	35
Acute Brain Disorder (Total)	60	28	22	22	28	53	32	10	cnp[d]
Alcohol intoxication	40	20	20	23	28	60	37	13	cnp[d]
Drug intoxication	20	45	25	20	30	40	20	5	cnp[d]

[a] Significant < 0.001 level.
[b] p designates significant difference between this group and the psychotic group with respect to this cue; n, significant difference between this group and the psychoneurotic group with respect to this cue; d, significant difference between this group and the personality disorder group with respect to this cue.
[c] Significant < 0.05 level.
[d] Computation not performed.

the patient, and willing to subject his diagnostic skills to continuing scrutiny. The latter alternative would primarily necessitate a large sample of patients to attenuate the effects of relative inexperience on the process of diagnosis and to enhance the generalizability of the results. Since choosing either alternative would not have measurably altered the confidence level of the resultant criterion measure and since a large patient population was readily available, psychiatric residents were chosen as diagnostic judges.

A number of steps were taken before the study began and during its course to guarantee the adequacy of the psychiatric evaluations completed for the study. All residents performing the evaluations were under continuous supervision by senior staff members of the psychiatry service, Boston City Hospital (though not every evaluation was supervised). Residents who performed the bulk of the diagnoses, ie, those on the hospital's accident floor, were second and third year psychiatric residents who had had, by virtue of the starting date of the study, at least 18 months intensive experience with diagnostic procedures prior to the beginning of the study. First-year residents evaluated the 68 inpatients included in the sample. None of the first year-residents had had less than six months psychiatric experience, and all were under quite close, continuous supervision of each case. In addition to the diagnostic competence implicit in the experience and supervision provisions made for each resident-diagnostician, BCH-BCL protocols were evaluated before being included in the study to insure that they did not violate predetermined criteria of completeness (eg, a psychotic diagnosis conferred but no psychotic symptoms checked on the entire instrument) and consensuality (eg, hallucinations and delusions observed but reality-testing considered to be intact). Twenty-one BCH-BCL protocols were dropped from the study for one or both of these reasons.

Distribution of diagnostic labels. The very large number of patients in our sample who were given personality disorder diagnoses surprised us. These findings probably foreshadow the imminent experience of the new community mental health centers that will likely be called upon to see many patients whose symptoms are neither sufficiently well-defined nor disabling enough to permit other diagnostic labels. Many patients seen by psychiatric residents at Boston City Hospital present with the same vague complaints for which their more affluent brothers now consult private psychiatrists. As community mental health centers proliferate in urban areas, they will doubtless be called upon to see more and more of these patients, as they assume more and more the dual responsibilities of the general hospital psychiatric emergency ward and the private psychiatrist. Our data lend urgency to efforts to define and diagnose more successfully patients who show some of the characteristic symptoms of this heterogeneous group of diagnostic entities.

Discrete symptoms and broad diagnostic labels. Though there was virtual unanimity among our diagnosticians on the diagnostic significance of the major symptoms of psychosis and moderate agreement on the diagnostic utility of the various cues to psychoneurosis, there was no consensus on the characteristic symptoms, if indeed they exist, of the several personality disorders. To a startling degree, this present "state of the art" of psychiatric diagnosis was reflected in the results of our efforts to establish empirically derived "baseline" symptom rates for these three broad diagnostic categories.

The five BCH-BCL cues generally considered pathognomonic of psychosis turned out to be impressively characteristic of the several functional psychoses. Only 9 of 325 nonpsychotic patients but fully 200 of 220 psychotic patients showed one or more of these "psychotic" cues. Even assuming a "halo" effect which would have increased the likelihood that a diagnostician would see additional "psychotic" symptoms in his patient's behavior once he had seen a single one of them, these findings are both convincing and compelling.

The cluster of behavioral and physiological symptoms which define anxiety remain enigmatic for the field. Their reliable measurement in clinical settings has never been accomplished (17), and their diagnostic significance has not yet been established (18,19). In fact, many of the general problems raised by current diagnostic procedures are cogently epitomized by the profound difficulties symptoms of anxiety present to the psychiatric diagnostician. These difficulties were clearly seen in our data. Though a larger percentage of psychoneurotic than either psychotic or personality disorder patients showed anxiety, sizeable numbers of nonpsychoneurotic patients also showed the symptom, rendering it of minimal differential diagnostic value. In essence, fewer psychoneurotic patients and more nonpsychoneurotic patients showed anxiety than expected. Though one might rationalize these findings by pointing to the observational unreliabilities anxiety engenders, comparable difficulties presumably extend through all the diagnostic categories and are, hence, of little specific explanatory value. One is left, then, to stress again the imperfect nature of anxiety as a differential diagnostic symptom by itself.

The other demonstrative cues to psychoneurosis, conversional, compulsive, and phobic behavior, were even less useful by themselves than anxiety for differentiating among the broad diagnostic categories, primarily because the incidence of these symptoms among all three categories was too low to permit differentiation. The differential diagnostic value of these symptoms, as with anxiety, was thought to lie in their capacity to enable a specific diagnostic label once other symptoms permit a decision on broad diagnostic category. This matter is discussed below in greater detail.

The cues suggestive either of psychosis or psychoneurosis were, taken singly, of moderate differential diagnostic value. This finding was in line with expectations that led these symptoms to be considered suggestive rather than pathognomonic or demonstrative. On the other hand, when these cues were taken together, ie, when they were, in a sense, summed, their capacity to differentiate among the broad diagnostic groups was greatly enhanced.

Symptom patterns and broad diagnostic labels. Most of the discussion above centered on the utility of single symptoms for diagnosis. But what of the use of symptom patterns for this purpose? In particular: Does diagnosis from symptom patterns enhance diagnostic accuracy?

Accurate diagnoses can be made from single symptoms. Each of the five symptoms considered pathognomonic of psychosis turned out to be, by itself, a powerful predictor of that diagnosis. Five of the seven cues considered only suggestive of psychosis or psychoneurosis by themselves enabled a reliable diagnosis, despite the prediction prior to study that their diagnostic significance would not be great. But an even greater number of valid diagnoses resulted from integration of several converging symptoms. Thus, though the most powerful single predictor of psychosis, presence of delusions, correctly labeled 75% of psychotic patients, 90% of these patients were labeled validly when the five pathognomonic symptoms of psychosis were taken together, and the label was given any patient who showed one or more of these symptoms. Similarly, when the seven suggestive cues were treated as a single symptom pattern, they enabled accurate diagnostic prediction far in excess of their diagnostic value when used singly.

Even anxiety becomes of moderate diagnostic significance when it is viewed as part of the diagnostic pattern rather than as a single unpredictive symptom. Anxiety, because it frequently accompanies psychiatric illness, is by itself of little diagnostic value. But the symptom pattern, anxiety in the absence of any symptom pathognomonic of psychosis, is of important diagnostic value for it labels correctly 64% of all neurotic patients and mislabels only 5% of all psychotic patients (by incorrectly labeling them neurotic).

On the other hand, this symptom pattern, like all but one of the other six patterns, did not differentiate among psychoneurotic and personality disorder patients. In fact, the only symptom pattern which did validly separate personality disorder patients from psychotic and psychoneurotic patients was the one which recorded the absence of any of the 16 symptoms examined here! When a patient showed none of these 16 symptoms, he was 28 times more likely subsequently to be labeled with a personality disorder diagnosis than with another one. Unfortunately, because it was shown by only 14% of these patients, the pattern was not of major diagnostic value.

When the seven symptom patterns summarized in Table 3 were applied to all patients diagnosed with psychotic, psychoneurotic or personality disorder labels, they yielded the following overall "hit rates": 92% of patients who showed patterns I or II ("psychotic patterns") were ultimately given psychotic diagnoses; 93% of patients who displayed patterns III or IV ("psychoneurotic patterns") were later considered psychoneurotic. However, 49% of patients who were later given personality disorder diagnoses were mislabeled and called psychotic or psychoneurotic by these four patterns. Most of this mislabeling occurred because many of these patients showed a preponderance of cues suggestive of neurosis. "Hit rates" computed by comparing our diagnosticians' diagnoses to those the complete clinician would have conferred if he had had access to the BCH-BCL protocols, reflect the degree to which these young clinicians use the standard rules for integrating diagnostic data. These "hit rates" do not, of course, reflect on the validity of the present psychiatric classificatory system or on the reliability of the clinical observations; they simply indicate the degree to which these clinicians have learned to perform diagnosis as they were taught.

While the former "hit rates" are encouraging because they support the hope that the BCH-BCL and its assumptions can aid diagnosis, the percentage of errors made when labeling personality disorder patients is alarming and intolerable. It is clear that present diagnostic procedures, inincluding the BCH-BCL, do not differentiate psychoneurotic and personality disorder states. There are two distinct and different explanations for these findings. The first emphasizes the present imperfect nature of current diagnostic procedures by suggesting that improved procedures and more sensitive instruments will ultimately enable measurement of those cues which will permit differentiation between the psychoneurotic and personality disorder groups. The second considers the findings to reflect shortcomings not in current diagnostic procedures, but in the present classificatory system. This position holds that there may not in fact be a unique diagnostic entity, personality disorder; and that consequently, efforts to separate it by symptoms from the psychoses and psychoneuroses will continue to fail. The recent American Psychiatric Association decision (1968) to accept the World Health Organization's new classificatory system (which combines all nonpsychotic conditions into one broad diagnostic category) presumably reflects a similar point of view. Our data would seem to support this decision.

Discrete symptoms, symptom patterns, and specific diagnostic labels. Though not a major intent of this study, it is interesting to note briefly symptom differences occurring among the 18 different diagnostic groupings included in the sample.

The three groups of schizophrenic patients showed symptom clusters similar to each other yet quite different from the other psychoses. Schizophrenic patients tended to show more pathognomonic symptoms of psychoses per patient than any other psychotic patients. There were also more patients in this group who displayed one or more of these key psychotic symptoms.

Anxiety was of little value for differentiating among most specific diagnostic labels. Between 30% and 50% of patients with psychotic, psychoneurotic, or personality disorder diagnoses showed anxiety. The symptom did predict two specific labels: All but one patient diagnosed anxiety reaction showed anxiety; only 15% of patients diagnosed antisocial personality (psychopaths) showed the symptom. Otherwise, the high incidence of this symptom among all other diagnoses rendered it of little differential diagnostic value.

The other major psychoneurotic symptoms, conversional, compulsive, and phobic behavior, were shown equally often by patients in all diagnostic groups with one exception: patients diagnosed conversion reaction. The cue was a useful one with these patients, given its low incidence in the general sample and its high incidence among them. This cut, like anxiety, though of minimal value for differentiating among broad diagnostic categories, does enable valid separation of circumscribed neurotic conditions.

Suggestive cues, by themselves, did not differentiate among specific diagnoses. In one important instance, however, a symptom pattern did so. Mirroring similar findings reported above, four of 160 schizophrenic patients (2.5%) but 19 of 60 nonschizophrenic psychotic patients (32%) showed no pathognomonic symptoms of psychosis. In view of these findings, one is led to ask whether certain of the psychotic symptoms ought not to be considered pathognomonic of schizophrenia rather than simply pathognomonic of psychosis. Perhaps our findings lend support to Bleuler's (21) position, set forth so many years ago.

Relationships between labeling errors and specific diagnostic labels were also found. No errors were made during diagnosis of paranoid schizophrenia despite the high frequency of this diagnosis in the sample, mostly because these patients showed several compelling psychotic symptoms. Conversely, patients with the other psychoses were much more often mislabeled because they showed relatively fewer symptoms pathognomonic of psychosis. It is also interesting to note that the most accurately labeled personality disorder, antisocial personality, contained patients who showed no pathognomonic psychotic symptoms, few demonstrative neurotic symptoms, and little anxiety, an unusual hence distinctive cluster of symptoms.

SUMMARY

This study evaluated the diagnostic reliability and utility of 16 psychiatric symptoms which, from consensually validated clinical experience, were thought before the study began to permit valid separation of psychiatric patients into the three major functional diagnostic categories of psychosis, psychoneurosis, and personality disorder. The 16 diagnostic cues comprise a section of the *Boston City Hospital-Behavior Checklist* (BCH-BCL), a new diagnostic instrument derived from a recent systems analysis of current diagnostic procedures.

The psychopathological behavior of 605 psychiatric patients, each of whom had been evaluated by a Boston City Hospital psychiatric resident, was recorded on the BCH-BCL. Results were: (1) All five symptoms considered pathognomonic of psychosis prior to study were found to be so in fact. (2) Anxiety, conversional behavior, phobic behavior, and compulsions, all expected to be demonstrative of psychoneurosis, were not found to be so; in all cases, sizeable numbers of psychotic and personality disorder patients also showed these symptoms. (3) Only one of three cues initially judged suggestive of psychosis were found to be so. Though all four symptoms thought to be suggestive of psychoneurosis were shown more often by psychoneurotic than by psychotic patients, they did not differentiate between neurotic and personality disorder patients. (4) The only BCH-BCL measure which consistently differentiated among psychoneurotic and personality disorder patients was the absence of any of the 16 cues. This pattern occurred rarely and hence had limited diagnostic value. (5) While few "mislabeling" errors were made of psychotic and psychoneurotic patients, almost half the personality disorder patients were mislabeled (by calling them either psychotic or psychoneurotic).

These results indicate that current diagnostic procedures permit the reliable differentiation of psychosis and psychoneurosis. They also emphasize the nature and extent of the inability of these procedures to enable diagnostic differentiation between the psychoneuroses and the personality disorders. The significance of these findings for the growing community mental health movement is great since more and more patients with nonspecific, nonpsychotic symptoms will be seen at these mental health centers. Continued failure to accurately diagnose the conditions which present with these symptoms has profound negative implications for their successful treatment and ultimate understanding.

REFERENCES

1. Beck, A. T., et al: Reliability of Psychiatric Diagnosis: 2. A Study of Consistency of Clinical Judgements and Ratings, *Amer J Psychiat* **119**:351–357 (Oct) 1963.
2. Gauron, E., and Dickinson, J. K.: Diagnostic Decision Making in Psychiatry, *Arch Gen Psychiat* **14**:233–237 (Sept) 1966.
3. Schmidt, H. O., and Fonda, C. P.: The Reliability of Psychiatric Prognosis: A New Look, *J Abnorm Psychol* **52**:262–267 (Sept) 1956.
4. Foulds, G.: The Reliability of Psychiatric and the Validity of Psychological Diagnosis, *J Ment Sci* **101**:851–862 (Nov) 1955.
5. Pinsker, H.: The Irrelevancy of Psychiatric Diagnosis or Psychiatric Diagnosis in the General Hospital, read before the American Psychiatric Association, Detroit, May 1967.
6. Pasamanick, B.: On the Neglect of Diagnosis, *Amer J Orthopsychiat* **33**:397–398 (April) 1963.
7. Kanfer, F. H., and Saslow, G.: Behavioral Analysis, *Arch Gen Psychiat* **12**:529–538 (June) 1965.
8. Kleinmuntz, B.: MMPI Decision Rules for the Identification of College Maladjustments: A Digital Computer Approach, *Psychol Monogr* **577**:1–22 (Dec) 1965.
9. Spitzer, R. L., and Endicott, J.: Diagno: A Computer Program for Psychiatric Diagnosis Utilizing the Differential Diagnostic Procedures, read before the American Psychiatric Association, Detroit, May 1967.
10. Spitzer, R. L.; Endicott, J.; and Fleiss, J. L.: Instruments and Recording Forms for Evaluating Psychiatric Status and History: Rationale, Method of Development and Description, *Compr Psychiat* **8**:321–343 (Oct) 1967.
11. Nathan, P. E.: *Cues, Decisions, and Diagnoses*, New York: Academic Press, Inc., 1967.
12. Nathan, P. E.; Andberg, M. M.; Behan, P. O.; and Patch, V. D.: Thirty-two Observers and One Patient: A Study of Diagnostic Reliability, *J Clin Psychol* (Jan) 1969, to be published.
13. Siegel, S.: *Nonparametric Statistics*, New York: McGraw-Hill Book Co., Inc., 1956.
14. Dohrenwend, B. R., and Dohrenwend, B. S.: The Problem of Validity in Field Studies of Psychological Disorder, *J Abnorm Psychol* **70**:52–69 (Feb) 1965.
15. Srole, L., et al: *Mental Health in the Metropolis: the Midtown Study*, New York: McGraw-Hill Book Co., Inc., vol 1, 1962.
16. Goldberg, L. R.: Simple Models or Simple Processes? Some Research on Clinical Judgements, *Amer Psychol* **23**:483–496 (July) 1968.
17. Buss, A. H.: Two Anxiety Factors in Psychiatric Patients, *J Abnorm Psychol* **65**:426–427 (Dec) 1962.
18. Distler, L. S.; May, P. R. A.; and Tuma, A. H.: Anxiety and Ego Strength as Predictors of Response in Schizophrenic Patients, *J Consult Psychol* **28**:170–177, (June) 1964.
19. Garfield, S. L., and Browning, B.: Clinically Reported Anxiety in Psychoneurotic and Personality Disorders, *Psychiat Quart Suppl* **37**:282–288 (Sept) 1963.
20. American Psychiatric Association: *Psychiatric News*, Washington, DC: American Psychiatric Association (Jan) 1968.
21. Bleuler, E.: *Dementia Praecox or the Group of Schizophrenias*, New York: International Universities Press, Inc., 1950.

Part Two

PSYCHODIAGNOSIS

Chapter 3

Observation and Interview

All scientific study requires observation of the subject under investigation. Special problems exist, however, when the subjects are people. First, the person being studied is aware of being observed and this may influence his actions. Second, the psychologist, because he is also a human being, imbues his subjects with his own feelings, needs, or wishes. These problems distort the observational process in certain indeterminate ways. A third difficulty has to do with the clinician's limited capacity to process certain types of information.

The first paper deals with some of the complexities of the person-perception situation. Shrauger and Altrocchi suggest constructing a theory of personality perception that treats personality and social factors together, and they offer a framework for future research that is aimed at increased understanding of personality variables as they relate to person perception.

Attending more closely to the clinician as an important variant of the personality assessment process, Meehl's paper is aimed at lifting interviewing out of the realm of an art and making it more scientific.

Kleinmuntz and McLean are less concerned with the clinician as interviewer and they assay a project in which the computer is challenged with the assignment of interviewing. Colby et al., in the last paper of this chapter, provide us with an artificial-intelligence approach to simulating a clinical interviewer. This paper proposes both a model of paranoia (see Chapter 9) and an instance of the computer as a paranoid interviewee.

The Personality of the Perceiver as a Factor in Person Perception*†

Sid Shrauger
John Altrocchi

This review shows that research on accuracy and assumed similarity has primarily led to blind alleys thus far, but investigations of attribution of specific traits, differentiation, free descriptions, and implicit personality theories show promise. Theories which attend to personality and social factors together and research dealing with personality, situational, and stimulus variables together are needed. The authors offer a framework for future research which delineates phases of the judging process and which suggests that cognitive control variables may be especially prominent in selection of cues, motivational-interpersonal variables may be important in drawing inferences from cues, and situational variables may be salient in making a verbal report.

The factors influencing the perception of other people can be organized into three sets of variables and the interactions among them: the attributes of the stimulus person, the nature of the interaction situation, and the characteristics of the perceiver (Tagiuri, 1958a). This paper will focus on the third set of variables, conceptualized as personality variables in the perceiver which influence how he perceives others. Despite the generally held assumption that one's perceptions of others are partially shaped by his own personal characteristics, it will be seen that there has been little research devoted directly to this topic and that contributions to the area have been scattered and unsystematized. This paper will review the few directly relevant studies, abstract pertinent findings and ideas from related areas, and present a framework for future research involving personality and person perception.

We will use the term personality to refer to the relatively enduring patterning of a person's dispositions to think, feel, and behave in certain ways. Such a broad definition almost covers the area of individual differences. Following Secord (1958), however, the term will not refer to cultural determinants of consensual perception of others but will refer to differences among perceivers within a given culture. In line with current definitions of person perception (Tagiuri, 1958a), we will use this term to refer to attribution of psychological characteristics (e.g., traits, intentions, emotions) to other people—either by describing them or by making predictions of their subsequent behavior. This broad definition includes processes of inference which have often been classified as cognition and apperception rather than as perception. Research on attribution of traits to people on projective tests such as the TAT will not be included. Although such research has some relevance for this area, the task or set in projective tests emphasizes imagination and fantasy, while the studies reviewed here involve a set to be accurate or realistic, which is presumably more relevant for understanding the ways in which people characteristically perceive others in real life situations.

ACCURACY

The earliest experimental investigations of how people differ in their attribution of personal characteristics to others were concerned with accuracy. Two comprehensive reviews of research done before 1954 on accuracy of perception (Bruner & Tagiuri, 1954; Taft, 1955) make a

From *Psychological Bulletin*, 1964, **62**, 289–308.

*Some of the ideas expressed in this paper were briefly presented in a symposium paper by the junior author at the Southeastern Psychological Association in Louisville, March 1962. An early development of the present paper was submitted in 1963 by the senior author as a major area paper in partial fulfillment of the requirements for the PhD at Duke University.

†The authors wish to express their gratitude to David A. Rodgers, Edward E. Jones, Douglas N. Jackson, Michael A. Wallach, Robert C. Carson, and Kurt W. Back for their helpful advice and criticism, and to the Scripps Clinic and Research Foundation, La Jolla, California, where parts of this paper were written while the junior author was on sabbatical leave. Both authors are associated with the Departments of Psychology and Psychiatry, Duke University.

comprehensive rereview here unnecessary. These reviews concluded that accuracy is positively correlated with intellectual and social skills and adjustment. Cronbach's (1955) incisive critique of accuracy scores, published at almost the same time, however, rendered these conclusions equivocal. Accuracy was typically measured by one of two methods, both of which have serious shortcomings. One method employed a comparison between subjects' predictions of how a stimulus person would fill out an inventory and how the person actually filled it out. This is a task which involves the contamination of response sets and the influence of the unknown factors that mediate responses to an inventory, and is also a task which is of questionable relevance unless one is specifically interested in the ability to predict others' modes of self-presentation. The second method involved a comparison between a subject's description of a stimulus person and the mean of all subjects' descriptions of that person. Without even considering the effect on the latter measure of biases held by other judges, the effect of regression to the mean is that the person with the highest accuracy score is the one who most accurately judges the average response of the group. Using either of these methods it is impossible to determine the degree to which high accuracy reflects an accurate stereotype of the group judged or an ability to sense differences between others or both.

These difficulties with criteria of accuracy have brought methodological advances. Techniques have been developed which eliminate meaningless artifacts and response sets by using comparisons between deviation scores instead of absolute scale values. Bronfenbrenner, Harding, and Gallwey (1958) have used correlations between deviation scores to compare one subject's ratings of a set of stimulus persons with the mean ratings of them by all subjects, while Carson has used a correlation of deviation scores across items to assess the accuracy of a subject's prediction of a stimulus person's self-description (1). Measures of differential and stereotype accuracy have been conceptually and methodologically separated (Bronfenbrenner et al., 1958; Sechrest & Jackson, 1961) (2). Results of these later studies suggest that the personality traits associated with stereotype and differential accuracy are not the same. A relatively consistent finding has been that women high in stereotype accuracy are well liked, well socialized, and predictable (Bronfenbrenner et al., 1958; Sechrest & Jackson, 1961). Consistent personality differences related to differential accuracy have not yet been noted, possibly because of lack of consistency in measures of differential accuracy.

The often implicit assumption that accuracy is a trait which is relatively stable over a variety of persons, characteristics, and situations has recently been put to test. The results are mixed (e.g., Cline & Richards, 1960; Crow & Hammond, 1957). What little individual consistency has been shown is attributable to stereotype accuracy. Chance and Meaders (1960) used a technique for studying accuracy which assures some generality over persons judged. Two stimulus persons were selected who were at opposite extremes on the dimensions judged; and the personality characteristics of judges, who were high in accuracy for both stimulus persons, were compared with those who were low for both stimulus persons. The results suggest that the more accurate person tends to be outgoing and sociable but little given to reflection about his interpersonal behavior. Regarding differential accuracy, however, the work of Bronfenbrenner et al. (1958) has demonstrated behavioral differences between subjects accurate in judging opposite-sexed persons and subjects accurate in judging same-sexed persons, thus clearly demonstrating one fallacy in assuming generality over stimulus persons.

Despite attempts to refine measures of accuracy, one cannot, on the basis of current research evidence, be assured that people at one extreme on any personality dimension are consistently more prone to perceive specific kinds of other people more accurately than are people at the other extreme. If one's goal is to determine how personality relates to perception of others, investigations of accuracy will have to be supplemented by, or perhaps replaced by, studies of the components of accuracy and studies of attribution of specific traits to others. Such specific investigations have emerged only recently, however, and preceding this development there was a search for another kind of generality in perception of others.

ASSUMED SIMILARITY

Growing out of Rogers' (1951) self-concept theory and Fiedler's early research (reviewed in Fiedler, 1958), a number of studies of assumed similarity appeared. It was proposed that some people (e.g., successful psychotherapists, effective team leaders) assume that other people are similar to themselves and thus attribute approximately the same traits to others as to themselves. In another penetrating paper, however, Cronbach (1958) rendered many earlier conclusions equivocal by pointing out that assumed similarity scores confound many different components. In the first place, an overall assumed similarity score may combine judgments of several different trait dimensions into a single score. Furthermore, even with a single trait, similarity scores can be analyzed into five simpler mathematical components—the means and standard deviations of the two descriptions (self and other) and the regression of one on the other. Cronbach pointed out that only after the monadic effects have been given separate consideration can one speak with any certainty about the dyadic component—the regression or correlation component. A study by Altrocchi (1961) decisively supported Cronbach's conclusions by presenting differences in assumed similarity scores which were due to intergroup differences in self-description, with no evidence of differences in person perception. There is a consistent tendency for subjects to describe strangers favorably in psychological experiments and therefore anyone with a relatively favorable self-concept will seem to be assuming similarity.

The statement of research results in terms of global ten-

[1] R. C. Carson, personal communication, 1963.

[2] Satisfactory measures of other aspects of accuracy less germane to the focus of this review have also been developed—for example, Tagiuri's (1958b) measures of accuracy of group members' sociometric preferences for one another and Ekman's measures of accuracy of matching verbal statements and photographs taken when the statements were being made (P. Ekman, personal communication, 1963).

dencies such as accuracy and assumed similarity may lead to confusion rather than to clarification. A case in point is a series of studies on authoritarianism. The principal conclusion of the first study was that nonauthoritarians were more accurate than authoritarians (Scodel & Mussen, 1953). Later investigations, however, suggested that the results might be more parsimoniously explained as differences in assumed similarity (Crockett & Meidinger, 1956; Scodel & Friedman, 1956), but a subsequent study showed that these differences in assumed similarity were not consistent from one instrument to another (Schulberg, 1961). While the authoritarian and nonauthoritarian may not differ in their tendencies to be accurate or to assume similarity, these and other studies have consistently found that people who are high in authoritarianism tend to see others as more authoritarian than do nonauthoritarians. These results point to the utility of a strategy in which individual differences in the attribution of particular traits are attended to in themselves rather than being interpreted in terms of global variables such as accuracy and assumed similarity.

DIFFERENTIATION AMONG OTHERS

Cronbach's (1955) methodological suggestions and other recent contributors to personality theory and research have emphasized the importance of the extent to which one forms a differentiated conceptualization of his social environment (Bieri, 1961; Harvey, Hunt & Schroder, 1961; Witkin, Dyk, Faterson, Goodenough, & Karp, 1962). Conceptually, differentiation refers to the tendency to make fine distinctions among people and thus to perceive them as different from one another. Operationally, it has been defined in several ways, and little is known about the interrelationships among these measures. It has often been defined as the standard deviation of one's judgment of a number of people on a specified dimension. When measured this way, differentiation has not been shown to be consistently related to personality traits, despite the fact that this measure is somewhat consistent over dimensions judged (Rabin, 1962). Fiedler (1958) reported no significant correlations between subjects' scores on a number of personality tests and their tendencies to differentiate in their descriptions of people best and least liked, while Koltuv (1960) found no relationship between subjects' tendencies to differentiate and ratings of the social favorability of their behavior made by peers. Ormont (1960) found no relationships between group therapy patients' scores on Welsh's Anxiety scale and measures of their tendencies to differentiate in their *Q* sort descriptions of other group therapy patients.

Measures of adjustment and the tendency to differentiate have, however, been shown to be related in two studies. Ormont (1960) reported that group therapy patients who were classed as better adjusted tended to differentiate more in their descriptions of the other members of their therapy group than did patients who were more poorly adjusted. Rabin (1962) analyzed descriptions of diverse stimulus persons by adjusted and maladjusted subjects, using criteria for maladjustment which included whether or not subjects had ever sought help for emotional problems. Maladjusted subjects had larger standard deviations in their judgments on each of four factorially determined dimensions of judgment. Such a result could be a function of increased random responding of maladjusted subjects (3). Numerous procedural differences between the two studies might account for the seemingly discrepant results. These results, however, can be seen as supporting the plausible proposition that differentiation increases and then decreases as one moves from extreme repressiveness to awareness of personal shortcomings in self and others to severe disruption of personality functioning. In support of such a proposition, Altrocchi (1961) demonstrated a slight tendency among normals for sensitizers to differentiate among others more than repressors and he suggested pursuit of this problem because of its relationship to research demonstrating more general perceptual differences (e.g., Holzman & Gardner's, 1959, demonstration that extreme repressors tend to be levelers on a neutral psychophysical task).

One problem in using a variance measure as an index of differentiation and relating it to personality characteristics of judges is that high scores might be achieved by two psychologically different processes. High scores would be obtained just as readily by using only the extremes of rating scales and classifying people into two distinct types as by making fine distinctions and distributing people along the entire continuum. Making extreme ratings and forming dichotomized judgments of others may be related to traits such as impulsivity and intolerance for ambiguity, while making fine distinctions among others and using a large number of categories for evaluation may be more reflective of social sensitivity. Thus, use of a variance measure of differentiation requires attention to the exact contributions to high variance scores. New and refined dimensional procedures (Jackson, 1962; Jackson & Messick, 1963) will probably, in fact, prove much more adequate than the variance model for investigating differentiation.

Other operational measures of differentiation seem to define it more specifically as the tendency to emphasize differences among others and to see people as distinctly different from each other. There have, for instance, been a number of investigations of cognitive complexity, which is defined as the number of independent dimensions which people characteristically utilize in describing others on a modified Kelly Role Construct Repertory Test (Kelly, 1955). A more differentiated conceptual system with a greater number of descriptive dimensions available would presumably allow for a more precise, unique description of other people. People having a more differentiated or cognitively complex conceptual system have been shown to give more complex Rorschach percepts, to be better able to predict how others will respond in a series of social situations, and to be less likely to change their initial impressions of others after receiving contradictory information about them (cf. review by Bieri, 1961). Gardner and Schoen (1962) have criticized measures of cognitive complexity as too indirect and too much influenced by verbal fluency and have shown that cognitive complexity is unrelated to their own measure of differentiation. Their measure, called conceptual differentiation, refers to the number

[3] D. N. Jackson, personal communication, 1964.

of categories into which heterogeneous stimulus objects are grouped. They have proposed that conceptual differentiation may optimally be viewed as a basic characteristic of cognitive organization. Research is now in progress at the Menninger Foundation to determine the relationship between conceptual differentiation and measures of differentiation in social perception (4). The relationships between the different measures of differentiation and cognitive complexity have yet to be clarified, but the present authors think that research in this area offers considerable promise for delineating individual differences in the perception of people.

JUDGING ON SPECIFIED DESCRIPTIVE DIMENSIONS

Some studies scattered throughout the psychological literature of the last 15 years have focused on differences in how others are characteristically described on dimensions specified by the experimenter. They can be grouped under four headings: favorability, hostility, dominance, and interactions between the traits of the judge and the traits of the stimulus person.

Favorability

The most prominent feature of any description of a person is the degree of favorability expressed. Factor analyses have consistently indicated that an evaluative factor accounts for the largest portion of variance in descriptions (Levy & Dugan, 1960; Osgood, Suci, & Tannenbaum, 1957). Regarding individual differences in general favorability toward others, maladjusted subjects (using a loose Rorschach criterion) have been shown to rate the "real" but not the "apparent" personality of the stimulus person less favorably than well-adjusted subjects (Matkom, 1963). Edwards (1959) showed that people who are more positive in their evaluation of others are also more positive in their self-descriptions. Studies testing Rogers' (1951) notion, that the person who is accepting of himself is also likely to be more accepting of other people, have shown generally positive results as indicated by a variety of questionnaires exploring attitudes toward the self and others (e.g., Berger, 1952; Omwake, 1954; Phillips, 1951; Suinn, 1961). Some of these findings, however, may readily be interpreted in terms of a response set specific to a certain measuring instrument. Furthermore, there has not been satisfactory support for Rogers' hypothesis that an increase in one's self-acceptance is a causal determinant of increased acceptance of others. It should also be pointed out that acceptance of others is not the same as seeing them favorably. On the contrary, Rogers (1951) noted that the self-accepting person will more readily recognize negative aspects of others when this is justified, since he will not be threatened and will not distort his perceptions in order to defend himself. Thus it is important to separate acceptance of others from esteem of others or favorability of one's description of others, just as it is important to separate self-acceptance from self-esteem (Hatfield, 1958). Finally, investigation of favorability needs to be focused on differences in favorability of perceptions of particular types of stimulus persons as well as on the general tendency to describe others favorably.

Favorability of description of others should probably be high on a priority list of specific descriptive dimensions worth investigating since it is a prominent variable in descriptions of people and has strong implications for the type of interaction which one might be expected to have with the persons described (Tagiuri, 1958b), especially if subjects are describing the real instead of the apparent personality of the stimulus person. Matkom's (1963) subjects were evidently able to make this distinction easily, and it might lessen subjects' tendency to say only blandly favorable things about others. While there have been some careful investigations of situational factors and attributes of the stimulus person which lead to favorable perceptions (e.g., Jones, Gergen, & Jones, 1963), there has been little work on the effects of perceiver variables and their interactions with these other factors (cf. Jones & Daugherty, 1959).

Hostility

Leary (1957) reported that people who described themselves and were described by others as hostile tended to attribute considerable hostility to others, while people described as exceptionally friendly tended not to attribute hostility to others. Berkowitz (1959) showed that anti-Semitic students, after being frustrated by a hostile experimenter, tended to generalize their feelings and rate others as more hostile than did students who scored low on anti-Semitism. Cohen (1956) found that college males utilizing projection as their principal defense, after discussing with partners a story related to some area of psychosexual conflict, described their partners as more hostile when the partners were also projectors than did subjects using other defensive processes. Because subjects and stimulus persons interacted in all these studies, however, one cannot be sure whether differences in the attribution of hostility were due to individual differences in the interpretation of essentially similar behavior or to differential influence of the subjects on the persons described. Cohen's experiment, nevertheless, stands out in this research area thus far because of his theoretically derived attention to individual differences in subjects and stimulus persons and specification of the situation—in this case the presumed arousal of threat in the subjects.

Other studies involving hostility neglected threat arousal but were based on clinical theories and research in perception and personality (Eriksen, 1963) which suggest that the repressive person tends to fail to perceive negative attributes and hostile actions of others while certain other people are especially sensitive to such attributes. Altrocchi and Perlitsh (1963) compared the descriptions of classmates by student nurses who were classified on the basis of their use of characteristic defensive patterns. They found that people classed as expressors, individuals characterized by their expression of impulses and lack of anxiety over this expression, were more likely to attribute hostility to others than were either sensitizers, people with high anxiety who rely heavily on obsessive and intellectualizing defenses, or repressors, who primarily utilize defenses of denial and

[4] R. W. Gardner, personal communication, 1963.

repression. A second study (Altrocchi, Shrauger, & McLeod, 1964) provided more experimental control but failed to confirm the earlier findings and found different results for male and female subjects. On the other hand, McDonald (1965), using the same instruments as Altrocchi and Perlitsh (1963) and studying 177 single pregnant females' descriptions of self and parents, supported the Altrocchi and Perlitsh and the Altrocchi, Shrauger, and McLeod predictions in a convincing fashion. Again, a primary task in clarifying such results is separating differences in perception from differential influence (provoked hostility). Secondly, there are many reasons to believe that there may be major sex differences in the ramifications of various patterns of ego control in personality functioning and in the meaning of attribution of hostility, dominance, and other traits. Furthermore, experimental manipulation of threat may be particularly important when classifying subjects by patterns of ego defense, since some of the differences in perception of others predicted by clinical theories may apply only in threatening situations which arouse ego defenses. Feshbach and his collaborators have been quite successful in arousing hostility (which would theoretically be psychodynamically threatening to some subjects) by disparaging subjects and have demonstrated that under these conditions hostility is more likely to be attributed to persons similar than to persons dissimilar to the subjects (Feshbach, Singer, & Feshbach, 1963). Inclusion of perceiver personality variables would seem to be a useful addition to such research and Feshbach's techniques of arousal of hostility would seem to be a useful addition to studies of personality factors in perception of hostility in others.

Dominance

Early studies on attribution of dominance confront one again with the alternative explanations of differences in perception versus differential influence. Naboisek (1953) and Leary (1957) reported that autocratic, exploitive, dominant people described others as weaker than they were described to be by most people. Altrocchi (1959) and Smelser (1961), however, reported controlled studies in which there were no such differences in attribution of dominance. In Altrocchi's study the subjects watched a movie of the stimulus persons in action, but in Smelser's study the subjects and stimulus persons interacted with each other. While Smelser's (1961) report concludes that "The degree of dominance ascribed to the partner, relative to the subject's own dominance, is a function of the subject's personal dominance [p. 540]," it is apparent that his was a dyadic frame of reference (5). Examination of his results shows no complementary attribution of dominance when attribution of dominance to others is kept separate from attribution of dominance to self. These results at least limit the generality of Naboisek's and Leary's observations and suggest that their results may have been due to stronger affect arousal in the clinical settings they were using, or to differential influence, or both.

A recent paper by Bieri (1962) has increased the sophistication of research on attribution of dominance and hostility. He found that female subjects' ratings of a male stimulus person on dominance were a linear function of the relative frequency of dominant and submissive behaviors of the stimulus person in the information provided by the experimenter, but male subjects' ratings followed what appeared to be a stepwise function. The results for the love-hostility dimension were somewhat different. These results suggest that differences in attribution of traits are a function of sex-related personality variables in interaction with the type of behavior judged and varying degrees of inconsistency in the stimulus behavior.

Interactions between Traits of the Judge and Traits of the Stimulus Person

While we have been considering differences in the descriptions of people in general, some differences in the attribution of traits to others are evident only when particular kinds of other people are described. For example, men's perceptions of their mothers have been shown to influence the sorts of characteristics which they ascribed to other women, but only for women described as motherly (Secord & Jourard, 1956). It is implicit in the definition of certain personality traits such as racial prejudice or authoritarianism that the trait will only affect one's perception of certain types of people. The effect of one's authoritarianism upon his judgment of others is dependent on the power or status of the person judged. If the person judged is presented as a leader with high status, the authoritarian describes him in more generally favorable terms than the nonauthoritarian (Jones, 1954) and is less likely to lower his opinion of him even when he is later shown to be an unpleasant person and a poor leader (Thibaut & Reicken, 1955). Also, authoritarian college students tend to describe others presented as college students or peers more favorably than do nonauthoritarians (Kates, 1959), but when those judged are presented as strangers not particularly similar to the judges, it is the nonauthoritarians whose descriptions are more favorable (DeSoto, Kuethe, & Wunderlich, 1960). With such evidence available, it would seem that investigators should use stimulus persons specifically chosen to represent groups the subjects will perceive differently or should use a broad and representative sample of stimulus persons so that specific interactions will cancel each other out.

JUDGING WITHOUT SPECIFICATION OF DESCRIPTIVE DIMENSIONS

Studies in the preceding section have been concerned with differences in how people judge others along dimensions or on traits which the experimenter has specified. There is no guarantee, however, that the dimensions in which the experimenter is interested are also those which people commonly utilize or can utilize in judging others. Much of the individual variability in descriptions may well be due to differences in the types of dimensions or traits which people spontaneously use in judging others. There have been a number of pleas for research to determine the salient dimensions typically used in evaluating others and to

[5] W. T. Smelser, personal communication, 1963.

delineate how people differ in the dimensions which they employ (Beach & Wertheimer, 1961; Bruner & Tagiuri, 1954; Cronbach, 1958; Hastorf, Richardson, & Dornbusch, 1958; Tagiuri, 1958a). While it has been shown that own and experimenter-specified traits provide reasonably comparable measures of cognitive complexity (Tripodi & Bieri, 1963), studies investigating subjects' own spontaneous descriptions have also been shown to offer unique information about individual differences in person perception.

Early and primary empirical attention to analysis of subjects' descriptions focused on the use of psychological as opposed to physical characteristics (Sarbin, 1954). The tendency to describe others in external-physical in contrast to internal-psychological terms has been interpreted as one aspect of the characteristic of field dependency (cf. review by Bieri, 1961) and has also been positively related to authoritarianism (Wilkins & deCharms, 1962). There is some evidence that people show consistent differences in whether they select psychological or physical characteristics (Wolin, 1956), and there are sex differences in this respect. When classifying individuals into groups and when listing traits describing them, men have been found to focus more on descriptive characteristics such as the color or types of clothing worn, height, and direction faced; while women have been found to be more prone to focus on inferential, psychological characteristics (Sarbin, 1954). Sex differences occur when extensive free descriptions are analyzed, but the descriptive versus inferential dichotomy seems to be an oversimplification (Beach & Wertheimer, 1961). The differences seem partially dependent on the sorts of people described and on the differential importance of the specific behaviors in the male and female role. Studies with children indicate that boys tend to emphasize behavior associated with aggression, nonconformity, and physical recreation; while girls focus more on nurturant behavior, physical appearance, and social skills (Campbell & Radke-Yarrow, 1956; Hastorf, 1962).

A recent investigation by Hastorf (1962), however, suggested that the matter is even more complicated. He demonstrated that if behavior relevant to a particular personality dimension is mentioned frequently in descriptions, the describer may be having trouble in his own adjustment with respect to that dimension. For example, children who are more dependent tend to emphasize information on generosity, giving aid, and needing aid in their descriptions. Boys who are not aggressive tend to mention aggressive behavior more often in their descriptions of others than do more aggressive boys. With girls, the differences are opposite; those who are rated as more aggressive tend to mention aggression more in describing others than do those who are not so aggressive. It would be hard to obtain such information if subjects were not allowed some freedom in describing others. Thus the suggestions that subjects be allowed to describe others in their own terms clearly have some merit.

IMPLICIT PERSONALITY THEORIES

There is one further historical trend, and it comes last in this review because of the sophistication of some of the studies, even though it includes some of the earliest forays into personality factors in person perception (Secord & Muthard, 1955). This is the notion of implicit personality theory, first introduced by Bruner and Tagiuri (1954, p. 649), elaborated and named by Cronbach (1955), and centrally important in Kelly's (1955) theory of personality. Cronbach suggested that perceivers differ in: response biases toward rating consistently higher (or lower) on particular traits, tendencies to make more extreme (or more central) ratings on certain traits, and tendencies to associate particular traits with each other.

Regarding the first tendency, previous sections of this paper have shown that under certain conditions different personality groups tend to rate others higher or lower on particular traits (e.g., hostility), although this may well be a function of the particular types of people described or the differential nature of the interaction with those described. Gross (1961) showed that consistent individual differences in the tendency to rate others as high or low on particular traits are small when a heterogeneous set of stimulus persons are judged. She concluded that the concept of a unitary attitude toward the generalized other is too nonspecific to be useful, so that such terms as implicit personality theory would be more precise if used in the plural. Thus she suggested that the contribution of personality variables can be seen most clearly in conjunction with specific situations and specified stimulus persons—an interactional recommendation which is a cornerstone of this review.

The tendency to make more extreme ratings has been mentioned in the section on differentiation. There have, however, been no investigations of differences in the extent to which stimulus persons are distributed on relevant as opposed to nonrelevant dimensions or of personality-related differences in the extremeness with which others are perceived on particular dimensions.

The third aspect of implicit personality theory, patterns of perceived consistency in trait intercorrelations, has begun to receive exceptionally competent research attention. Koltuv (1962) contributed a scholarly historical review of trait centrality and trait intercorrelations, which renders a review unnecessary here. She suggested that lack of attention to the relevance of the traits for each individual may account for Gross's (1961) finding that perceiver predispositions account for little of the variance in person perception. Koltuv obtained the names of personally relevant and nonrelevant traits and the names of familiar and unfamiliar people for each of her subjects and then had them rate these people on both kinds of traits. Her results strongly indicated the importance of the correlational aspect of implicit personality theories by demonstrating that: each perceiver assumed a matrix of correlations to exist among traits, these correlations were greater for unfamiliar than familiar persons, correlations were greater among personally relevant than among nonrelevant traits, and these intercorrelations were not wholly a function of the overall evaluative attitude of the subject (halo effect) or the logical connections between certain traits. She concluded that idiographic analysis is necessary to demonstrate the magnitude of individual intercorrelations which otherwise might be obscured by nomothetic analysis.

A study by Secord and Berscheid (1963) also demonstrated the generality of trait intercorrelations, showing that certain types of traits are perceived as highly intercorrelated not only in judgments of people in whom these traits are commonly thought to appear together, but in other people as well. Both Koltuv (1962) and Secord (1958) pointed out that it is unrealistic to assume that people apply their implicit personality theories indiscriminately in the judgment of all people. Having established the existence of consistent patterns of trait intercorrelations, it will be useful to investigate the determinants of differences in these patterns. Theoretical models and statistical methods which can encompass the complexity of such multidimensional problems as analyzing different patterns of trait relationships for different kinds of subjects, situations, and stimulus persons have been explicated and are available (Jackson, 1962; Jackson & Messick, 1963; Tucker, 1963). It is likely that use of such methods will increase our understanding of person perception considerably.

A FRAMEWORK FOR FUTURE RESEARCH

The diversity of contributions, lack of organization, and variable usefulness of research dealing with personality variables in person perception is apparent. In an attempt to provide some organization for the area and in order to suggest some potentially productive approaches for future research, an organized framework will be presented. It includes suggested personality variables, some possible interactions between personality, situational, and perceptual variables, a delineation of phases of the judging process, and some general methodological recommendations.

Personality Variables

Neither personality theories nor empirical research thus far have clearly spotlighted the independent personality variables that might be most significantly related to person perception, but modern developments of interpersonal theory and perceptual-cognitive research based on modified psychoanalytic theory suggest the usefulness of two kinds of personality variables: multilevel interpersonal motives or traits and cognitive controls.

Freud's (1924) conceptualization of transference as a source of perceptual distortion in the psychoanalytic situation, the extension of the concept by Fenichel (1945) and Sullivan (1948) to all types of interpersonal situations, and Sullivan's (1948) conceptualization of parataxic distortion of and selective inattention to the anxiety-producing attributes of others led to Leary's (1957) notions concerning the effect of personality on person perception. His and subsequent similar circumplex models (Foa, 1961; Lorr & McNair, 1963) suggest the usefulness in interpersonal research of such personality variables as hostility, dominance, sociability, and combinations among them. Furthermore, Leary's organization of these variables in a conception of levels of personality provides an organized way of studying the dynamic role of possession of a trait by the perceiver and thus provides a rationale and methodology for research of the kind reported by Hastorf (1962)—although Leary's measures of the various levels leave much to be desired. Thus, for example, a person with considerable fantasy hostility who is seen by others as frequently hostile, but who does not conceive of himself as hostile, might be expected to attribute considerable hostility to others, especially under conditions involving strong affect such as anger or anxiety. Many similar hypotheses can be deduced.

At the same time, we strongly concur with Gardner and his associates (Gardner, Holzman, Klein, Linton, & Spence, 1959, and many other publications) and Jackson (1962) that consideration of motivational variables is not sufficient and should be supplemented by attention to organizational dispositions of the individual, such as cognitive controls. For instance, as mentioned in a preceding section, by Jackson (1962), and Gardner and Schoen (1962), conceptual differentiation may relate to differentiation among others in person perception. It would be eminently sensible to coordinate research in individual differences in person perception with research concerning individual consistencies in cognitive or perceptual styles by use of such cognitive control principles as conceptual differentiation (formerly equivalence range), leveling-sharpening, constricted flexible control, scanning, and field articulation (Gardner et al., 1959; Messick & Fritzky, 1963; Witkin et al., 1962). Separate assessment of cognitive controls and multilevel interpersonal traits would probably clarify some of the results obtained using complex combinations of cognitive and motivational variables such as authoritarianism and repressiveness.

Personality-Situation Interactions

Here is where a theoretical vacuum is most apparent. Our current theories deal with personality variables or social (situational) variables but almost never both. Nevertheless, it is likely that some situational variables and some personality variables interact with each other in their effects on person perception. For instance, it is likely that subjects will differ considerably in their projection of experimentally aroused anxiety (Singer & Feshbach, 1962) and, as implied in earlier sections of this review, a subject who does not admit hostility which is perceived by others in his behavior and which is revealed in his fantasy productions should be more likely to project experimentally aroused hostile affect (Feshbach et al., 1963). Furthermore, this suggests an important point, usually implicit but rarely explicit in personality theories (e.g., Leary, 1957): The presence of strong emotion may well be a necessary condition for the appearance of the effects of motivational (not cognitive) variables on person perception. As Secord, Backman, and Meredith (1962) have suggested, the static notion that perceiver traits will have a simple relation to attribution of traits to others is weak without attention to dynamic affective and role relations between the people involved. In our necessary attempts to provide rigor in the laboratory, it is easy to forget that real interpersonal encounters often involve impressive feelings of affection, hostility, and fear. We must utilize ways of arousing such feelings in our experiments or we must pay more research attention to nonlaboratory situations where emotions are naturally strong.

Person Perception Variables and Their Interactions

Concerning dependent or person perception variables, we have argued for the use of free descriptions, attention to the real as opposed to the apparent personality of the stimulus person, attention to specific traits rather than general tendencies such as assumed similarity, have stressed the importance of subjects' conceptions of intercorrelations among traits, and have pointed out that certain differences between subjects will occur only in the perception of specified stimulus persons. A new contribution to the delineation of useful dependent variables is Hastorf's current research on the perception and evaluation of behavior change in a stimulus person (6). More generally, developments in interpersonal theory (Foa, 1961; Leary, 1957; Lorr & McNair, 1963) suggest the usefulness of such variables as hostility, dominance, and sociability as dependent as well as independent variables (cf. Bieri, 1962). The more such traits can be used in conjunction with specific interpersonal situations, the better. Finally, triple interaction studies are quite feasible—what kinds of people describing what kinds of other people in what situations—and will certainly be a necessary future step, although studies even approaching assessment of triple interaction are rare (cf. Cohen, 1956; Jones & Daugherty, 1959).

All of this leaves the perceptual-cognitive process rather global and unitary, however. Delineation of phases of the judging process may be useful to the general investigation of person perception and specifically useful in the present context by indicating how personality variables may contribute differently in the different phases. While the process of forming an impression may be perceived as an immediate, unitary phenomenon, this process can be usefully conceptualized as consisting of three phases: selecting cues, drawing inferences about personal characteristics from these cues, and translating one's impressions into an overt verbal response. The distinction between the first two phases is similar to distinctions made by Jones and Thibaut (1958), Secord (1958), and Bieri (1962).

Selection of cues. A major factor limiting the ability to generalize to person perception from research on perception of ambiguous stimuli (Eriksen, 1963) is the complexity of a person as a stimulus object. Even a photograph presents so much sensory data that it is extremely difficult to assimilate all the cues presented. Therefore, an important source of individual variability in the judgment process may well be differences in cues chosen as bases for judgments. Selection can occur in studies in which the person judged is not actually observed by the judges, but the data about him are presented in the form of brief vignettes or descriptions of his personal attributes. One could investigate selection in this situation by analyzing what information is recalled when the stimulus information is removed (Carlson, 1961). Culture places selective emphasis on certain cues (Secord, 1958), but there may well be consistent individual differences in the degree to which particular classes of cues such as tone of voice, movements of hands, content of verbalizations, or particular physiognomic features, for example, are utilized as determinants of descriptions. If such differences were demonstrated, they might well affect the psychological attributes ascribed to others, since particular psychological characteristics tend to be inferred from particular physiognomic traits (e.g., Secord, Dukes, & Bevan, 1954). A recent exploratory foray in this area made by Exline (1963) showed that women focused visually on those with whom they interacted more than men did. This suggests a greater reliance by women on visual cues about the attributes of others.

In an ingenious series of studies, Levy (1961a, 1961b, 1963) has demonstrated the potency of perceiver attributes and the relevance of adaptation, anchoring, dissipation, conditioning, and generalization in person perception and has proposed that the learning of dispositional responses is one mechanism by means of which many of the reported effects of personality variables might be produced. He conceptualized that dispositional responses do not alter what the person sees (selection of cues), but alter the probabilities of how he interprets what he reports seeing (inference). From the arguments presented by Levy (1963) and Secord (1958) and from the evidence presented in this and the following section, one would suspect that the kinds of personality variables most likely to affect selection of cues are cognitive controls or styles, while motivational variables are more likely to affect inference. For some readers it may clarify communication to note that we are asserting that attribution of traits is probably influenced by secondary process as well as primary process variables. Furthermore, the two kinds of variables may interact. For instance, Klein (1954) suggested that needs influence cognition less in people with flexible, as opposed to constricted, cognitive control.

Inference. The most basic form of inference occurs when some cue such as an inflection of the voice, a gesture, or an eye movement is interpreted as signifying some psychological feature of the person being described. For purposes of clarification, we shall refer to this as interpretive inference. The same cue, while equally attended to, may be seen by various people as implying very different characteristics or it may be seen as reflecting nothing. One must then consider how many and what dimensions people typically have at their disposal for conceptualizing others' behavior. The number of dimensions may relate to such cognitive controls as conceptual differentiation. Descriptive dimensions must then be classified in some way. The most frequently used classification of dimensions is the dichotomous distinction between physical, external attributes as opposed to internal, psychological characteristics, although it has been shown that more discriminating categorizations can be successfully utilized (e.g., Beach & Wertheimer, 1961; Hastorf, 1962). The type of classification to be used is usually and most easily determined by the investigator's theoretical preference, but it will probably be useful to pay some attention to subjects' own classifications too.

If a particular sample of behavior is seen by a subject as relevant to some dimension of behavior, three factors may determine where the person is placed along the dimension in question. The first is the intensity of the behavior (Bieri, 1962). The second involves temporal extension (Secord,

[6] A. H. Hastorf, personal communication, 1963.

1958)—one's willingness to generalize broadly on the basis of limited information, to assume that action in a particular situation is characteristic of the individual's typical behavior in many situations. Although we have suggested that cognitive controls play a primary role in selection of cues, they may also play a role in interpretive inference by influencing temporal extension and associated factors such as stereotyping (Secord & Berscheid, 1963), the halo effect, and overestimations of consistency (Ichheiser, 1949). Motivational variables probably play a role here too, especially when the motivational variable is the same as the dimension being judged. The third factor relevant to interpretive inference is the nature of the comparison standard against which particular cues are evaluated—people's varied norms and expectations about behavior in a particular situation. In assessing the contribution of this third factor, substantive and methodological influences may become highly entangled. It is necessary to determine whether consistent differences in ratings on a dimension are artifacts, only reflecting differential use of the measuring instrument, or are differences having substantive bases. The problem of response sets is complex, but a first and simple step would simply be to see whether the same differences occur using parallel measuring instruments.

Inference also takes place when a subject is asked to rate a person on attributes about which he has no direct information (cf. Bieri, 1962). We will refer to this as extended inference, and it includes subjects' implicit personality theories. One would expect that most personality differences in trait interrelations would be found in magnitude rather than direction of ratings because of the evaluative connotations which most traits carry and a tendency to see others as consistently favorable or unfavorable. There has, however, been a demonstration of directional differences in inference patterns, although the statistical significance of these differences was not determined. Jones (1954) found that persons presented as more democratic were judged by high authoritarians to be more undependable, rebellious, nonintrospective, harder to figure out, and more prone to act without thinking than persons presented as autocratic, while nonauthoritarians associated those characteristics more with the autocratic person. Considerable individual variability has also been shown in the types of attributes ascribed to others when seemingly inconsistent information about the person to be described has been presented. The formation of integrated impressions from discrepant information is found more frequently with females, children with higher intelligence, middle-class as opposed to lower-class children (Gollin, 1958), and children rated by their peers as being higher in social effectiveness (Campbell & Yarrow, 1961). Steiner and Johnson (1963) have shown that authoritarians tend not to alter their favorable impressions of an individual when they receive moderately derogatory information about him.

One study (Benedetti & Hill, 1960) suggested that subjects' own possession of a trait influenced their patterns of inferences about people varying in their possession of that trait. More extensive investigation indicated that these relationships existed only for certain traits and differed for males and females (Benedetti, Morgan, & Bessemer, 1959). Secord et al. (1962) found no relationship between strength of a trait in a perceiver and the effect of that trait in the stimulus person on the pattern of inferences concerning other traits when liking and favorability were controlled. Their conclusions, however, from an otherwise well-designed study, rely entirely on the validity of the not yet validated Edwards Personal Preference Schedule (EPPS). Even if the EPPS were of demonstrated validity, though, such a one-level measure would not indicate the dynamic role of a trait in the personality (Leary, 1957). Much work remains to be done on individual differences in extended inference patterns. The recent availability of multidimensional methods (Jackson, 1962; Jackson & Messick, 1963; Tucker, 1963) makes such research much more feasible. We predict that motivational interpersonal variables will be more significant than cognitive controls in such research.

In most experimental studies of impression formation one would find it hard to decide whether differences in judgment were due primarily to individual differences in selection or inference. They can, however, be unconfounded to permit separate investigation. Selection can be estimated by determining which cues, from a large amount of information about the other person, the judge could later remember. The judge would be required to interpret the information as little as possible and only to reproduce it (cf. Carlson, 1961). In investigations of inference processes, on the other hand, one could standardize stimuli and could condition such sets as the reversal response set (Levy, 1963), or one could present only a limited amount of information pertinent to the judgment of one attribute and as neutral as possible (for people in general) with respect to those other attributes about which inferences are to be made. Thus, the least contaminated tests of the inference process would employ techniques similar to those used by Asch (1946) in which the information given consisted only of sets of traits. Studies of individual personality theories (Jackson & Messick, 1963; Koltuv, 1962), however, demonstrate the usefulness of analysis of individual rather than group results, and such analyses would clearly open the way for investigation of personality variables (Jackson, 1962).

Verbal Report. The final phase of the judgment process is making some verbal report of one's impressions. Individual variation in verbal report is shown in the candidness and completeness of one's report of his subjective impressions. The most likely lack of candor is a tendency to give a more favorable description than one actually perceived. Again, it is difficult to separate verbal report from selection and inference, but this may be done by analyzing sequences of responses (Forrest & Lee, 1962), by using projective devices and ratings of the subjects' nonverbal behavior, by investigating response variation as a function of reward and punishment (Eriksen, 1963), and by manipulating the experimental conditions. One could, for instance, compare descriptions obtained under conditions varying in the extent to which they aroused a social-desirability response set. One would expect that variance in descriptions due to differences in reporting would be associated more with situational factors operating at the time the report is made than with personality variables, but this, like many problems suggested in this review, is an empirical problem about which we currently know almost nothing.

General Methodological Recommendations

A few general recommendations may warrant emphasis:

1. Differences in perception of others need to be separated from differences due to the effect of the perceiver as a social stimulus. This can be done by having subjects rate people they observe and also people with whom they interact under otherwise similar conditions.
2. Many of the research problems involving personality factors in the perception of people are problems in response sets, so that general response sets need to be investigated rather than eliminated. The response sets that need to be controlled or eliminated are those that are specific to a measuring instrument.
3. Evidence repeatedly shows that sex differences are crucial in this area and must be taken into account in research and in theory.
4. This review has not focused on the mode of presentation of the stimulus material, but this may be an important variable. For instance, Secord and Berscheid (1963) have suggested that making inferences about verbal traits from verbal cue traits is less susceptible to perceiver affect than is rating photographs.
5. We concur with Jackson and Messick (1963) that, for an accurate and full understanding of person perception, research methods and measurements must faithfully represent the complexity of the area—and, as this review has shown, the complexity is considerable.

CONCLUSIONS

Although focusing on personality variables, a major message of this review is that progress will most efficiently occur with attention to specific problems involving interactions among personality, situational, and perception variables. This is a formidable task, but surely not too formidable for psychologists in the age of computer technology.

Increased understanding of personality variables as they affect person perception can provide a link integrating intraindividual and interpersonal processes. Subtleties of the impression process itself may be illuminated, consistencies and seeming inconsistencies in overt behavior may be explained, and we should gain considerable understanding of how self-concepts and personality dispositions may be supported and maintained by selective attention to specific cues and idiosyncratic patterns of inference about others. To adapt a phrase still familiar from our recent history, it may be that one of the best ways in which processes of person perception are revealed is through analyzing the way different types of people perceive others and one of the best ways in which personality is revealed is through perception of others.

REFERENCES

Altrocchi, J. Dominance as a factor in interpersonal choice and perception. *J. abnorm. soc. Psychol.*, 1959, **59**, 303–308.

Altrocchi, J. Interpersonal perceptions of repressors and sensitizers and component analysis of assumed similarity scores. *J. abnorm. soc. Psychol.*, 1961, **62**, 528–534.

Altrocchi, J., & Perlitsh, Hilda D. Ego control patterns and attribution of hostility. *Psychol. Rep.*, 1963, **12**, 811–818.

Altrocchi, J., Shrauger, S., & McLeod, Mary Ann. Attribution of hostility to self and others by expressors, sensitizers and repressors. *J. clin. Psychol.*, 1964, **20**, 233.

Asch, S. E. Forming impressions of personality. *J. abnorm. soc. Psychol.*, 1946, **41**, 258–290.

Beach, L., & Wertheimer, M. A free response approach to the study of person cognition. *J. abnorm. soc. Psychol.*, 1961, **62**, 367–374.

Benedetti, D. T., & Hill, J. G. A determiner of the centrality of a trait in impression formation. *J. abnorm. soc. Psychol.*, 1960, **60**, 278–280.

Benedetti, D. T., Morgan, R., & Bessemer, D. Relationships among the traits of the perceiver and those of the perceived in impression formation. Final report, September 1959, Contract AF 49(638)-33 (Phase 4), Department of the Air Force.

Berger, E. M. The relation between expressed acceptance of self and expressed acceptance of others. *J. abnorm. soc. Psychol.*, 1952, **47**, 778–782.

Berkowitz, L. Anti-Semitism and the displacement of aggression. *J. abnorm. soc. Psychol.*, 1959, **59**, 182–187.

Bieri, J. Complexity—simplicity as a personality variable in cognitive and preferential behavior. In D. W. Fiske & S. R. Maddi (Eds.), *Functions of varied experience.* Homewood, Ill.: Dorsey Press, 1961. Ch. 12.

Bieri, J. Analyzing stimulus information in social judgments. In S. Messick & J. Ross (Eds.), *Measurement in personality and cognition.* New York: Wiley, 1962.

Bronfenbrenner, U., Harding, J., & Gallwey, Mary. The measurement of skill in social perception. In D. McClelland, A. Baldwin, U. Bronfenbrenner, & F. Strodtbeck (Eds.), *Talent and society.* Princeton, N.J.: Van Nostrand, 1958.

Bruner, J. S., & Tagiuri, R. The perception of people. In G. Lindzey (Ed.), *Handbook of social psychology.* Vol. 2. Cambridge, Mass.: Addison-Wesley, 1954. Ch. 17.

Campbell, J. D., & Radke-Yarrow, Marian. Interpersonal perception and behavior in children. *Amer. Psychologist*, 1956, **11**, 416. (Abstract)

Campbell, J. D., & Yarrow, Marian R. Perceptual and behavioral correlates of social effectiveness. *Sociometry*, 1961, **24**, 1–20.

Carlson, E. R. Motivation and set in acquiring information about persons. *J. Pers.*, 1961, **29**, 285–293.

Chance, June E., & Meaders, W. Needs and interpersonal perception. *J. Pers.*, 1960, **28**, 200–209.

Cline, V. B., & Richards, J. M., Jr. Accuracy of interpersonal perception: A general trait? *J. abnorm. soc. Psychol.*, 1960, **60**, 1–7.

Cohen, A. R. Experimental effects of ego-defense preference on interpersonal relations. *J. abnorm. soc. Psychol.*, 1956, **52**, 19–27.

Crockett, W. H., & Meidinger, T. Authoritarianism and interpersonal perception. *J. abnorm. soc. Psychol.*, 1956, **53**, 378–380.

Cronbach, L. J. Processes affecting scores on "understanding others" and "assumed similarity." *Psychol. Bull.*, 1955, **52**, 177–193.

Cronbach, L. J. Proposals leading to analytic treatment of social perception scores. In R. Tagiuri & L. Petrullo (Eds.), *Person perception and interpersonal behavior.* Stanford: Stanford Univer. Press, 1958. Ch. 23.

Crow, W. J., & Hammond, K. R. The generality of accuracy and response sets in interpersonal perception. *J. abnorm. soc. Psychol.*, 1957, **54**, 384–396.

DeSoto, C., Kuethe, J. L., & Wunderlich, R. Social perception and self-perception of high and low authoritarians. *J. soc. Psychol.*, 1960, **52**, 149–155.

Edwards, A. L. Social desirability and the description of others. *J. abnorm. soc. Psychol.*, 1959, **59**, 434–436.

Eriksen, C. W. Perception and personality. In J. Wepman & R. Heine (Eds.), *Concepts of personality.* Chicago, Ill.: Aldine, 1963. Ch. 2.

Exline, R. V. Explorations in the process of person perception: Visual interaction in relation to competition, sex, and need for affiliation. *J. Pers.*, 1963, **31**, 1–20.

Fenichel, O. *Psychoanalytic theory of neurosis.* New York: Norton, 1945.

Feshbach, S., Singer, R. D., & Feshbach, Norma. Effects of anger arousal and similarity upon the attribution of hostility to pictorial stimuli. *J. consult. Psychol.*, 1963, **27**, 248–252.

Fiedler, F. E. Interpersonal perceptions and group effectiveness. In R. Tagiuri & L. Petrullo (Eds.), *Person perception and interpersonal behavior.* Stanford: Stanford Univer. Press, 1958. Ch. 16.

Foa, U. G. Convergences in the analysis of the structure of interpersonal behavior. *Psychol. Rev.*, 1961, **68**, 341–353.

Forrest, D. W., & Lee, S. G. Mechanisms of defense and readiness in perception and recall. *Psychol. Monogr.*, 1962, **76**(4, Whole No. 523).

Freud, S. The dynamics of transference. In, *Collected papers.* Vol. 2. London: Hogarth, 1924.

Gardner, R. W., Holzman, P. S., Klein, G. S., Linton, Harriet B., & Spence, D. P. Cognitive control: A study of individual consistencies in cognitive behavior. *Psychol. Issues,* 1959, **1**(4), 1–186. (Reprinted: G. S. Klein (Ed.), *Psychological issues.* New York: Basic Books, 1959.)

Gardner, R. W., & Schoen, R. A. Differentiation and abstraction in concept formation. *Psychol. Monogr.*, 1962, **76**(41, Whole No. 560).

Gollin, E. S. Organizational characteristics of social judgment: A developmental investigation. *J. Pers.*, 1958, **26**, 139–154.

Gross, Cecily F. Intrajudge consistency in ratings of heterogeneous persons. *J. abnorm. soc. Psychol.*, 1961, **62**, 605–610.

Harvey, O. J., Hunt, D. E., & Schroder, H. M. *Conceptual systems and personality organization.* New York: Wiley, 1961.

Hastorf, A. H. The relationships among children's categories of interpersonal perception. Paper presented at American Psychological Association, St. Louis, August 1962.

Hastorf, A. H., Richardson, S. A., & Dornbusch, S. M. The problem of relevance in the study of person perception. In R. Tagiuri & L. Petrullo (Eds.), *Person perception and interpersonal behavior.* Stanford: Stanford Univer. Press, 1958. Ch. 5.

Hatfield, J. A study of self-concept configurations in relation to forms of ego functioning. Unpublished doctoral dissertation, University of California, 1958.

Holzman, P. S., & Gardner, R. W. Leveling and repression. *J. abnorm. soc. Psychol.*, 1959, **59**, 151–155.

Ichheiser, G. Misunderstandings in human relations: A study in false social perception. *Amer. J. Sociol.*, 1949, **55**(2, Pt. 2).

Jackson, D. N. The measurement of perceived personality trait relationships. In N. Washburn (Ed.), *Values, decisions, and groups.* Vol. 2. New York: Pergamon Press, 1962.

Jackson, D. N., & Messick, S. Individual differences in social perception. *Brit. J. soc. clin. Psychol.*, 1963, **2**, 1–10.

Jones, E. E. Authoritarianism as a determinant of first impression formation. *J. Pers.*, 1954, **23**, 107–127.

Jones, E. E., & Daugherty, B. N. Political orientation and the perceptual effects of an anticipated interaction. *J. abnorm. soc. Psychol.*, 1959, **59**, 340–349.

Jones, E. E., Gergen, K. J., & Jones, R. G. Tactics of ingratiation among leaders and subordinates in a status hierarchy. *Psychol. Monogr.*, 1963, **77**(3, Whole No. 566).

Jones, E. E., & Thibaut, J. W. Interaction goals as basis of inference. In R. Tagiuri & L. Petrullo (Eds.), *Person perception and interpersonal behavior.* Stanford: Stanford Univer. Press, 1958. Ch. 11.

Kates, S. L. First impression formation and authoritarianism. *Hum. Relat.*, 1959, **12**, 277–286.

Kelly, G. A. *The psychology of personal constructs.* New York: Norton, 1955. 2 vols.

Klein, G. S. Need and regulation. In M. R. Jones (Ed.), *Nebraska symposium on motivation: 1954.* Lincoln: Univer. Nebraska Press, 1954. Pp. 224–274.

Koltuv, Barbara B. Some characteristics of intrajudge trait intercorrelations. *Psychol. Monogr.*, 1962, **76**(33, Whole No. 552).

Koltuv, M. Some social perceptual correlates of the valence of social behavior. Unpublished doctoral dissertation, Columbia University, 1960.

Leary, T. *Interpersonal diagnosis of personality.* New York: Ronald Press, 1957.

Levy, L. H. Adaptation, anchoring, and dissipation in social perception. *J. Pers.*, 1961, **29**, 94–104. (a)

Levy, L. H. The conditioning and generalization of changes in social perceptual dispositions. *J. abnorm. soc. Psychol.*, 1961, **63**, 583–587. (b)

Levy, L. H. Reversal response sets and the nature of person perception. *J. abnorm. soc. Psychol.*, 1963, **67**, 392–396.

Levy, L. H., & Dugan, R. A constant error approach to the study of dimensions of social perception. *J. abnorm. soc. Psychol.*, 1960, **61**, 21–24.

Lorr, M., & McNair, D. M. An interpersonal behavior circle. *J. abnorm. soc. Psychol.*, 1963, **67**, 68–75.

McDonald, R. L. Ego control patterns and attribution of hostility to self and others. *J. Pers. soc. Psychol.*, 1965, in press.

Matkom, A. J. Impression formation as a function of adjustment. *Psychol. Monogr.*, 1963, **77**(5, Whole No. 568).

Messick, S., & Fritzky, F. J. Dimensions of analytic attitude in cognition and personality. *J. Pers.*, 1963, **31**, 346–370.

Naboisek, H. Validation of a method for predicting role expectations in group therapy. Unpublished doctoral dissertation, University of California, 1953.

Omwake, Katherine T. The relation between acceptance of self and acceptance of others shown by three personality inventories. *J. consult. Psychol.*, 1954, **18**, 443–446.

Ormont, L. Tendency to differentiate in perceiving others as related to anxiety and adjustment. Unpublished doctoral dissertation, Columbia University, 1960.

Osgood, C. E., Suci, G. J., & Tannenbaum, P. H. *The measurement of meaning.* Urbana: Univer. Illinois Press, 1957.

Phillips, E. L. Attitudes toward self and others: A brief questionnaire report. *J. consult. Psychol.*, 1951, **15**, 79–81.

Rabin, H. M. Perception of others by adjusted and maladjusted subjects as reflected in measures of perceptual space. *J. soc. Psychol.*, 1962, **56**, 149–158.
Rogers, C. R. *Client-centered therapy.* Boston, Mass.: Houghton Mifflin, 1951.
Sarbin, T. R. Role theory. In G. Lindzey (Ed.), *Handbook of social psychology.* Vol. 1. Cambridge, Mass.: Addison-Wesley, 1954. Ch. 6.
Schulberg, H. C. Authoritarianism, tendency to agree, and interpersonal perception. *J. abnorm. soc. Psychol.*, 1961, **63**, 101–108.
Scodel, A., & Friedman, Maria L. Additional observations on the social perception of authoritarians and nonauthoritarians. *J. abnorm. soc. Psychol.*, 1956, **52**, 92–95.
Scodel, A., & Mussen, P. Social perceptions of authoritarians and nonauthoritarians. *J. abnorm. soc. Psychol.*, 1953, **48**, 181–184.
Sechrest, L., & Jackson, D. N. Social intelligence and accuracy of interpersonal predictions. *J. Pers.*, 1961, **29**, 167–182.
Secord, P. F. Facial features and inference processes in interpersonal perception. In R. Tagiuri & L. Petrullo (Eds.), *Person perception and interpersonal behavior.* Stanford: Stanford Univer. Press, 1958. Ch. 20.
Secord, P. F., Backman, C. W., & Meredith, Helen E. Cue-dominance in person perception as a function of strength of perceiver-need. *J. soc. Psychol.*, 1962, **58**, 305–313.
Secord, P. F., & Berscheid, Ellen S. Stereotyping and the generality of implicit personality theory. *J. Pers.*, 1963, **31**, 65–78.
Secord, P. F., Dukes, W. F., & Bevan, W. Personalities in faces: I. An experiment in social perceiving. *Genet. Psychol. Monogr.*, 1954, **49**, 231–279.
Secord, P. F., & Jourard, S. M. Mother concepts and judgments of young women's faces. *J. abnorm. soc. Psychol.*, 1956, **52**, 246–250.
Secord, P. F., & Muthard, J. E. Individual differences in the perception of women's faces. *J. abnorm. soc. Psychol.*, 1955, **50**, 238–242.
Singer, R., & Feshbach, S. Effects of anxiety arousal in psychotics and normals upon the perception of anxiety in others. *J. Pers.*, 1962, **30**, 574–587.
Smelser, W. T. Dominance as a factor in achievement and perception in cooperative problem solving interactions. *J. abnorm. soc. Psychol.*, 1961, **62**, 535–542.
Steiner, I. D., & Johnson, H. H. Authoritarianism and "tolerance of trait inconsistency." *J. abnorm. soc. Psychol.*, 1963, **67**, 388–391.
Suinn, R. M. The relationship between self-acceptance and acceptance of others: A learning theory analysis. *J. abnorm. soc. Psychol.*, 1961, **63**, 37–42.
Sullivan, H. S. *Conceptions of modern psychiatry.* Washington, D. C.: William Alanson White Psychiatric Foundation, 1948.
Taft, R. The ability to judge people. *Psychol. Bull.*, 1955, **52**, 1–23.
Tagiuri, R. Introduction. In R. Tagiuri & L. Petrullo (Eds.), *Person perception and interpersonal behavior.* Stanford: Stanford Univer. Press, 1958. (a)
Tagiuri, R. Social preference and its perception. In R. Tagiuri & L. Petrullo (Eds.), *Person perception and interpersonal behavior.* Stanford: Stanford Univer. Press, 1958. Ch. 21. (b)
Thibaut, J. W., & Riecken, H. W. Authoritarianism, status, and the communication of aggression. *Hum. Relat.*, 1955, **8**, 95–120.
Tripodi, T., & Bieri, J. Cognitive complexity as a function of own and provided constructs. *Psychol. Rep.*, 1963, **13**, 26.
Tucker, L. R. Implications of factor analysis of three-way matrices for measurement of change. In C. W. Harris (Ed.), *Problems in measuring change.* Madison: Univer. Wisconsin Press, 1963.
Wilkins, E. J., & deCharms, R. Authoritarianism and response to power cues. *J. Pers.*, 1962, **30**, 439–458.
Witkin, H. A., Dyk, Ruth B., Faterson, Hanna F., Goodenough, D. R., & Karp, S. A. *Psychological differentiation.* New York: Wiley, 1962.
Wolin, L. R. An analysis of the content of interpersonal perception. Unpublished doctoral dissertation, Cornell University, 1956.

The Cognitive Activity of the Clinician

Paul E. Meehl

Somebody has described psychotherapy as "the art of applying a science which does not yet exist." Those of us who try to help people with their troubles by means of that special kind of conversation are uncomfortably aware of the serious truth behind this facetious remark. The clinical psychologist has been able to assuage some of his therapeutic anxiety, and to refurbish his sometimes battered self-image, by keeping one foot planted on what seemed like comparatively solid ground, namely, psychodiagnosis. In recent years, some clinicians have been making a determined effort to assess the validity of our currently fashionable diagnostic instruments, and the findings are not very impressive. The cumulative impact of validation studies is reflected, for example, in Garfield's excellent textbook (1957), where one does not need a highly sensitive third eye to discern a note of caution (or even pessimism?). E. L.

Kelly finds that 40% of young clinicians state that they would not go into clinical psychology if they had it to do over again. One suspects that at least part of this professional disillusionment springs either from awareness of the weaknesses in our psychodiagnostic methods or from the chronic intrapsychic (and interprofessional!) strain exacted of those who ward off such a confrontation. Who, for example, would *not* react with discouragement upon reading the recent monograph by Little and Shneidman (1959) where, in an unbiased and well-designed study, we find a very low congruency among interpretation of psychological test data, the test interpreters having been chosen as "experts" on four widely used instruments? Any tendency I felt to rejoice at the slight superiority of the MMPI over the three projective techniques with which it was competing was counteracted by the finding that my favorite test, like the others, does not do at all well when judged in absolute terms.

The cognitive activity of the clinician can be separated into several functions, which I have discussed in a recent paper (Meehl, 1959a). Setting aside for the moment that special kind of cognitive activity which goes on within the therapeutic interview, we can distinguish three classes of functions performed by the psychodiagnostician: *formal diagnosis* (the attachment of a nosological label); *prognosis* (including "spontaneous" recoverability, therapy-stayability, recidivism, response to therapy, indications for differential treatment); and *personality assessment* other than diagnosis or prognosis. This last may be divided, somewhat arbitrarily, into *phenotypic* and *genotypic:* the former being the descriptive or surface features of the patient's behavior, including his social impact; the latter covering personality structure and dynamics, and basic parameters of a constitutional sort.

Quite apart from the validity of current techniques for performing these various cognitive functions, their pragmatic value is open to question. It is commonly believed that an accurate pretreatment personality assessment of his patient is of great value to the psychotherapist. It is not known to what extent, if at all, this is true. However, what do psychotherapists themselves have to say about it? Bernard C. Glueck, Jr. and I have recently collected responses from 168 psychotherapists (both medical and nonmedical, and representing a wide spectrum of orientations: e.g., Freudian, neo-Freudian, Radovian, Sullivanian, Rogerian, eclectic, "mixed") to a questionnaire dealing with 132 aspects of therapeutic technique. One of our items reads: "It greatly speeds therapy if the therapist has prior knowledge of the client's dynamics and content from such devices as the Rorschach and TAT." While the self-styled groups differ significantly in their response to this item (ranging from a unanimous negative among Rogerians to a two-thirds affirmative among George Kelly disciples), all groups except the last tend to respond negatively. The overall percentage who believe that such prior knowledge of the client's personality greatly speeds therapy is only 17%. This low figure, taken together with the fashionable de-emphasis upon nosology and the feebleness of most prognostic studies, at least raises doubts about the practical value of our diagnostic contribution.

Although they do not bear directly upon this question, we have some other interesting results which suggest considerable skepticism among therapists as to the significance of causal understanding itself in the treatment process. For example, 43% state that "Warmth and real sympathy are much more important than an accurate causal understanding of the client's difficulty." Over one-third believe that "Literary, dramatic, aesthetic, or mystical people are likely to be better therapists than people of a primarily scientific, logical, or mathematical bent." Four out of five believe that "The personality of the therapist is more important than the theory of personality he holds." About half believe that "Interpretation as a tool is greatly overrated at present." Two out of five go as far as to say that "Under proper conditions, an incorrect interpretation, not even near to the actual facts, can have a real and long-lasting therapeutic effect." Time does not permit me to read other examples of items which, in the aggregate, suggest minimization of the importance of the therapist's forming a "correct" picture of the client's psyche.

Setting aside the pragmatic question of the therapeutic value of assessment, let us look briefly at the inductive structure of the assessment process. The epistemological rock bottom is a single, concrete, dated slice or interval in the behavior flux, an "episode," identified by certain physical or social properties. Having observed one or more episodes of a given kind, we make an inductive inference as to the strength of low order *dispositions* which these episodes exemplify. Such dispositions are grouped into families, the justification for this grouping being, as Cattell (1946, 1950) has emphasized, some kind of covariation (although not necessarily of Type R) among the members of the disposition-family. It is perhaps possible to formulate the clinician's decision making behavior entirely in terms of such disposition-classes. In such a formulation, clinical inference involves probabilistic transition from episodes to dispositions, followed by the attribution of further dispositions as yet unobserved. Ideally, such inferences would be based upon an extensive actuarial experience providing objective probability statements. Given a particular configuration of dispositions present in a patient, the statistical frequencies for all other dispositions of practical import would be known within the limits of observational and sampling errors. In practice, of course, this ideal is rarely achieved, the conditional probabilities being subjectively judged from clinical experience without the benefit of an actual tallying and accumulation of observations, and the probabilities being expressed in rough verbal form, such as "frequently" and "likely," rather than as numerical values.

I am still of the opinion (McArthur, Meehl, & Tiedeman, 1956; Meehl, 1954, 1956, 1957) that the practical utility of this approach has been insufficiently explored, and I think that many clinicians are unaware of the extent to which their daily decision making behavior departs from such a model not by being qualitatively different but mainly by being less explicit and, therefore, less exact. However, we must recognize that a purely dispositional approach is not the *only* way of proceeding. An alternative, more exciting (and more congenial to the clinician's self-concept) is to view the clinician's cognitive activity as aiming at the assessment of hypothetical inner states, structures, or events which cannot be reduced to dispositions but which belong to the domain of theoretical entities, crude though the theory may be. Episodes and dispositions are here treated as "signs" or "indicators" of the postulated internal states. These states should not be spoken of as "operationally defined" in terms of the dispositions, because the logical relationship between propositions concerning theoretical entities and those describing dispositions is not one of equivalence, but merely one of degrees of confirmation. The inference *from* dispositions *to* states of theoretical variables is again only probabilistic, partly because statistical concepts occur within the causal model itself (i.e., probability appears, as in the other sciences, in the object-language) and partly because the theoretical network is incomplete and imperfectly confirmed.

A fundamental contribution to the methodology of inference from multiple indicators is the "multitrait-multimethod matrix" of Campbell and Fiske (1959). These authors show that in order to support a claim of construct validity, we must take into account more kinds of correlational data than have been traditionally provided and that it is just as important for some correlations to be low as it is for others to be high. Consider two or more traits (e.g., dominance and sociability), each of which is allegedly measured by two or more methods (e.g., MMPI scores and peer group ratings). Computing all possible intercorrelations, we construct a multitrait-multimethod matrix. The relationships within this matrix may or may not lend support to the claim of construct validity. The monotrait-heteromethod coefficients should be not only statistically significant and respectable in size, but should exceed both the heterotrait-heteromethod and heterotrait-monomethod coefficients. For example, if MMPI dominance and sociability correlate higher than does MMPI dominance with peer group dominance or than MMPI sociability with peer group sociability, we ought to be nervous about the relative contribution of methods factors versus traits under study. Campbell and Fiske point out that the individual differences literature is very weak in this respect, usually failing to provide the necessary data and, when it does, usually showing unimpressive results.

An interesting adaptation of the Campbell-Fiske technique arises if we substitute "persons" for "traits" and deal with Q correlations rather than R correlations. Suppose that a therapist provides us with Q sort descriptions of two patients. From the MMPI profiles these patients are then Q sorted independently by two interpreters. This set up generates a modified Campbell-Fiske matrix of 15 Q correlations, in which the validity diagonals (i.e., heteromethod-mono*patient* coefficients) represent how similarly the same patient is perceived by the therapist and the two MMPI readers; the monomethod-heteropatient and heteromethod-heteropatient values reflect the projections, stereotypes, and other idiosyncratic sorting biases of the therapist and of the two interpreters, the extent to which such stereotypes are shared by all three, and the unknown true resemblance of the particular patient pair. Robert Wirt and I have been running a series of such matrices, and thus far our results are as unencouraging as those of the Little and Shneidman study. I have decided to spare you the slides, faintly hoping that the pairs thus far completed will turn out to be atypically bad.

The situation is not much improved by selecting a small subset of "high confidence" items before Q correlating. One disadvantage of Q sort is that it requires the clinician to record a judgment about every trait in the deck. The technique has the advantage that it presents the judge with a standard set of dispositions and constructs and therefore gets judgments which he is able to make but would often fail to make in producing a spontaneous description. But, for this advantage in coverage we have to pay a price. Such a situation is clinically unrealistic: whether we are starting with test data, history, or interview impressions, the particular facets which stand out (whether high or low) will not be the same for different patients. It may be that the meager results of recent validation studies are attributable in part to the calculation of hit frequencies or Q correlations over the entire range of traits, only a minority of which, variable in composition, would willingly be judged by the clinician on any one patient.

I cited earlier the statistic that only one psychotherapist in six believes that he is greatly helped in the treatment process by having advance knowledge of the patient's psychodynamics. One relevant consideration here is the rate at which the psychotherapist's image of his patient converges to a stable picture. John Drevdahl, Shirley Mink, Sherman Nelson, Murray Stopol, and I have been looking into this question. So far, it seems that the therapist's image of his patient crystallizes quite rapidly, so that somewhere between the second and fourth therapeutic hour it has stabilized approximately to the degree permitted by the terminal sort-resort reliabilities. Let me show you a couple of typical results. Figure 1 shows the Q correlations between Stopol's phenotypic sort after the twenty-fourth hour and his successive sorts after the first, second, fourth, eighth, and sixteenth hours. "S_t" indicates correlation of his stereotype with twenty-fourth-hour sort. "Rel" is sort-resort reliability. (The phenotypic and genotypic ratings are

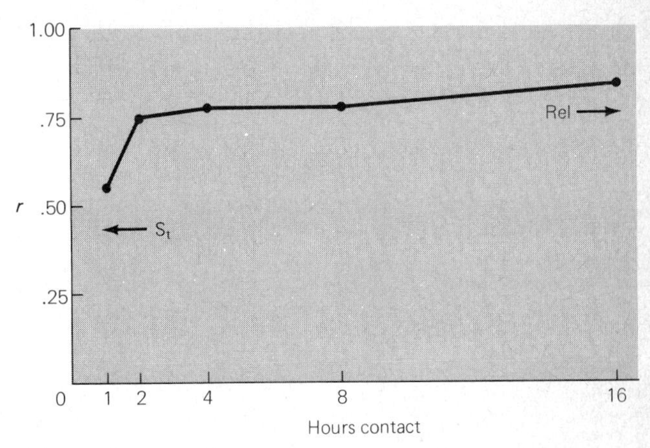

Fig. 1. Q correlations between therapist's sort at 24 contacts and earlier sorts. (Phenotypic pool; N = 182 items; Stopol)

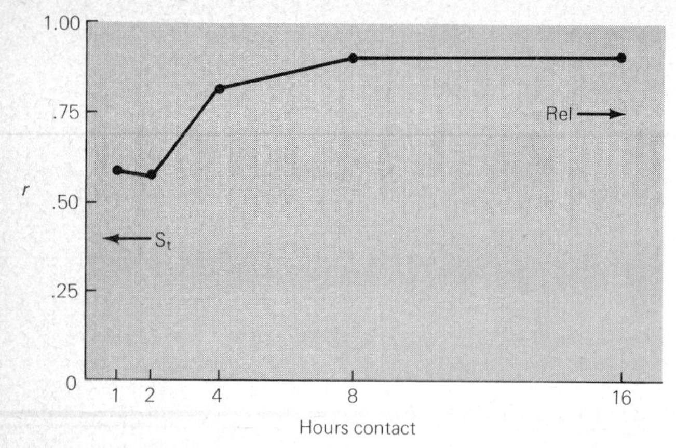

Fig. 2. Q correlations between therapist's sort at 24 contacts and earlier sorts. (Genotypic pool; $N = 113$ items; Stopol)

made separately.) Figure 2 shows results for the genotypic pool. I do not mean to suggest that the therapist's perception at the end of 24 hours is "the criterion," which would involve a concept of validation that I reject (Cronbach and Meehl, 1955, pp. 284–285, 292–294). But presumably his perception after 24 contacts is more trustworthy than after only one. Or, if we (*a*) assume that some information gained early is subsequently lost by forgetting, erroneous revisions, and the like; (*b*) take as our standard of comparison the average value of ratings over all six sortings; and (*c*) treat this as a kind of "best combined image," the essential character of the situation remains as shown.

Now this state of affairs presents any psychological test with a difficult task. If, after two or four hours of therapeutic interviewing, the therapist tends to arrive at a stable image of the patient which is not very different from the one he will have after 24 contacts, and if that final image is pretty accurate, the test would need to have very high validity before we could justify the expenditure of skilled psychological time in giving, scoring, interpreting, and communicating it.

When we first began this convergence study, our primary interest was in the pragmatic utility of the MMPI. One way to consider validity (which makes more practical sense than the conventional validation study) is to ask: "How long does it take the psychotherapist to find out what the test would have told him in the first place?" We were interested in plotting the Q correlation between a blind MMPI description of the patient and the successive sorts done by the therapist as he gathered more extensive samples of the latter's behavior during treatment, hoping to find that, as the therapist gets "wised up" by further interviews, he learns what the MMPI would have told him all along. This pleasant fantasy was disturbed by the rapidity with which the therapist's image of the patient converges, even before the Campbell-Fiske correlations were run. It is of some interest to plot the curve of Q correlation between a "good" blind MMPI description of the patient and the successive descriptions by the therapist (Figure 3). These results are surely nothing to write home about!

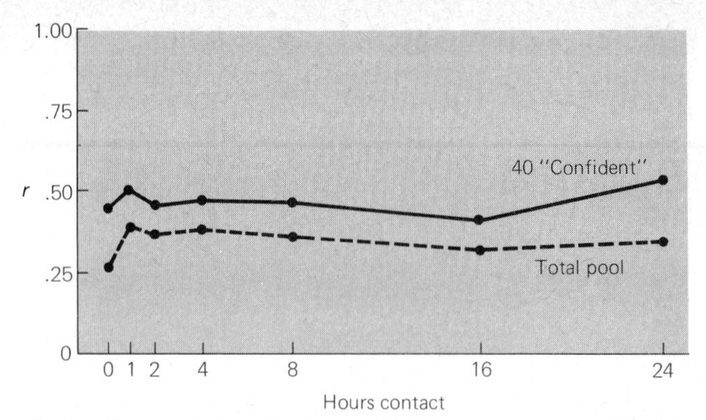

Fig. 3. Q correlations between MMPI reader's sort and successive sorts by therapist. (Phenotypic pool; Meehl and Stopol)

In a recent paper reporting on an empirical study of MMPI sorting behavior (Meehl 1959b) I listed six factors or circumstances which might be expected theoretically to favor the clinician's brain as a cognizing and decision making instrument in competition with the traditional statistical methods of combining data. Among these six factors is one in which I have a particular interest, I suppose partly because it lends itself more readily to quantitative study than do some of the others. This factor is the presumed ability of the clinician to react on the basis of higher order configural relations (Meehl 1954, pp. 130–134; Horst 1954) by virtue of the fact that a system of variables can be graphically represented as a profile; and thereafter, given extensive clinical experience with a particular instrument, the clinician can respond to the visual gestalt. This he could do by *exemplifying* a complex mathematical function which neither he nor anyone else had as yet succeeded in *formulating*. The search for that function could take place in the context of studying the generalization and discrimination of complex visual forms. I recommend to your attention the recent work of Paul J. Hoffman on this subject, some of which has been reported (1958a, 1958b, 1959). Hoffman has undertaken a mathematical analysis of the rating behavior of judges who are presented with multi-

Table 1. *Concurrent Validity of Meehl-Dahlstrom Rules in Eight Cross-validation Samples.*

Sample	N	$H\%$	$M\%$	$I\%$	$\frac{H}{H+M}$	P
A[a]	92	55	16	28	.77	<.001
B[a]	77	45	29	26	.61	<.05
C	103	49	16	35	.75	<.001
D	42	40	21	38	.65	nonsig.
E[a]	181	45	18	36	.71	<.001
F	166	47	20	33	.70	<.001
G	273	63	12	25	.84	<.001
K[a]	54	78	5	17	.93	no test
Total	988	53	17	30	.76	.001

[a]Essentially uncontaminated samples.

variable profiles, and the application of his formulas should teach us a great deal about the clinician's cognitive activity.

Comparing the impressionistic judgment of a group of Minnesota clinicians as to the amount of "psychotic tendency" revealed by MMPI profiles with six statistical methods of treating the profiles, I found that the pooled judgment of 21 clinicians was significantly better (against the diagnostic criterion) than the linear discriminant function. In fact, there was a significant tendency (although slight) for even the *individual* clinicians to do a better job than the linear discriminant function. However, the best cross-validative results displayed by any method of sorting these profiles thus far tried utilizes a very complex set of configural rules developed by Grant Dahlstrom and myself (Meehl & Dahlstrom, 1960). Table 1 shows the results of applying these rules to almost a thousand cases from eight clinics over the United States. These rules were concocted by a combination of clinical experience with statistical checking; and, while relatively crude and surely failing to extract all of the profile information, they are more efficient at this than a linear combination of scores, the pooled judgments of 29 MMPI readers, or the judgment of the best of 29. Without knowing the form and constants of the mathematical function relating probability of psychosis to the MMPI variables, we cannot answer the question: "How much of the information contained in the profile is extracted by the clinician?" One may plot probability of

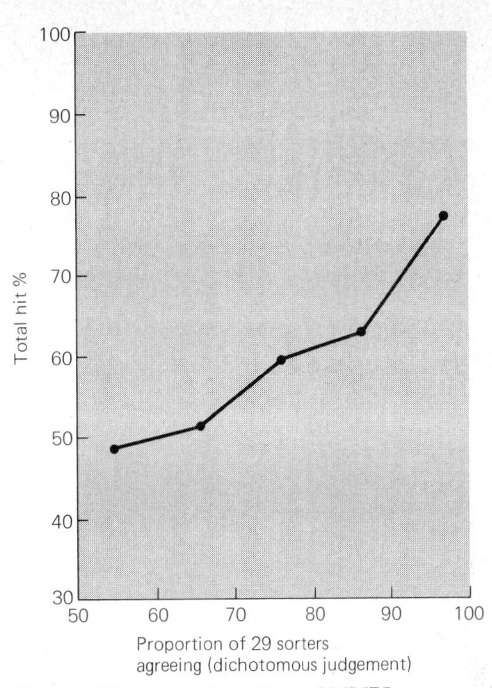

Fig. 5. Hit rate as function of MMPI sorter consensus (neurosis–psychosis).

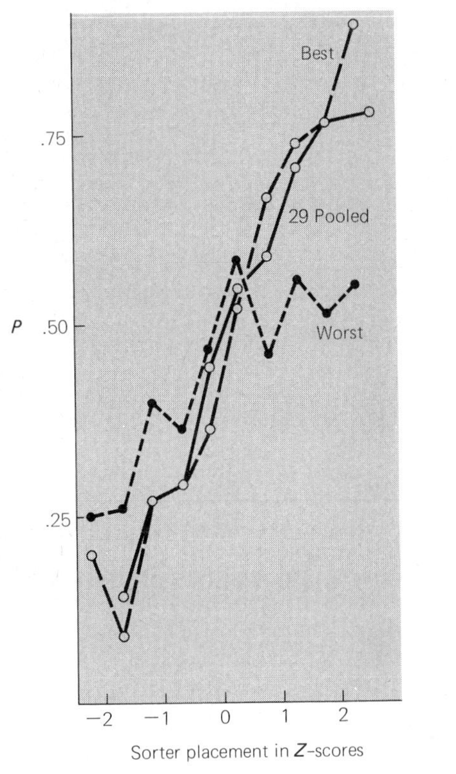

Fig. 4. Probability of psychosis as function of MMPI profile placement by sorters.

psychosis as a function of the clinicians' placement of profiles on an 11-step subjective scale of degree (or confidence) of psychoticism. Figure 4 shows probability of psychosis as a function of impressionistic profile placement by the best and worst clinician, and the pooled judgment of a group of 29. Figure 5 shows hit rate (whether neurotic or psychotic) as a function of the amount of consensus among 29 judges.

While our data do indicate that the clinician's judging behavior with respect to the psychoticism variable is significantly configural, the *amount* of departure from a linear, additive model does not appear to be very great. For many years, skeptical statisticians have been pointing out to us clinicians that there is more conversation about nonlinear functions than there is actual demonstration of such and, anyway, that the value of departures from linearity and additivity involved in clinical judgments is likely to be attenuated, if not completely washed out, by the clinician's assignment of nonoptimal weights and the unreliability invariably involved in the impressionistic use of multivariate data.

Lykken, Hoffman, and I plan to utilize some of the MMPI psychoticism data for the kinds of analysis the latter has suggested, but in the meantime I have applied one of Hoffman's formulas to a portion of these data. He suggests that, if we treat the clinician's quantitative sorting as the dependent variable, the multiple R of this variable upon the profile scores should differ from unity only because of the clinician's unreliability, provided his sorting behavior follows a linear model. The multiple R of the 11-step psychoticism ratings for my four best clinicians, when divided by the square root of their reliabilities (Hoffman's "complexity" formula), varies from .871 to .975, with a mean of .942, indicating that the departure of their judging behavior from a linear model is small. It is also interesting that the *inter*sorter reliability (Horst's generalized coefficient) reaches .994 for the four best sorters and .987 for the four worst. Whatever these MMPI readers are doing when asked to judge psychoticism from the profile, they seem to be doing it in very much the same way.

Let me turn next to a brief account of an exploratory study which was a dismal failure and which I am still trying to figure out. All told, there now exist almost 200 different scoring keys for the MMPI item pool, ranging all the way from "dependency" to "baseball talent" and derived by a variety of methods (including factor analysis, face validity, and criterion keying). I thought it might be interesting to treat the patient's MMPI behavior more like the psychoanalyst than like the factor analyst: namely, to overdetermine the psychology of the patient by scoring him on a large number of these scales, in spite of their redundancy. Imagine two patients who produce identical profiles when scored on a very large number of partially overlapping but distinguishable variables. One might hope, except for the intrinsic defects of *coverage* in the MMPI item pool, that such a pair of individuals would be, so to speak, pinpointed in personality space as very close together. In practice it is impossible to find identical (or even nearly identical) profiles as the number of scored dimensions is increased, but perhaps one could get an estimate of this extreme by extrapolating interpatient similarities from lesser degrees of profile resemblance.

Selecting a sample of 20 female outpatients rated by staff psychiatrists or psychologists in connection with a study on the new ataraxic Mellaril (Fleeson, Glueck, Heistad, King, Lykken, Meehl, & Mena, 1958), we calculated the interviewer rating Q correlations for all possible pairs, thus generating an interpatient resemblance matrix of 190 elements. Turning then to the MMPI (by which the clinical raters were, of course, uncontaminated) and eliminating scales of fewer than 10 or more than 80 items, we set up random sets of 10 scales after defining the first set of 10 as the basic profile of clinical scales commonly used. The Cronbach-Gleser distance measure was then computed on the MMPI profiles for the same 190 pairs. Thus we had a matrix of interpatient resemblances as clinically described by skilled interviewers through Q sorts and a corresponding matrix of MMPI profile similarity indices. A *series* of matrices of this latter kind was then generated by progressively extending the profile, adding successive blocks of 10 randomly chosen scales. Thus, the first MMPI matrix was based upon the interpatient distance measures for the usual 10 scores, the second one upon 20 scores (the usual 10 plus 10 randomly chosen), the third one on 30 scores, and so forth up to a profile of 160 variables! The idea, of course, was that through this procedure we would be squeezing all of the blood out of the psychometric turnip and that a second order correlation (apologies to the statisticians) between the corresponding elements of the two matrices would show a steady rise.

It would have been very nice had the asymptote of this intermatrix coefficient, when plotted as a function of the number of MMPI variables entering into the distance measure, approached a very high value. That is, if you measure—however unreliably and redundantly—a huge mass of variables (schizoid trend, recidivism, dominance, defensiveness, baseball talent, dependency, control, ego strength, use of repression, tendency to homesickness, academic potential, etc.), then the psychological resemblance between two patients will be closely related to their profile similarity on this extended list of MMPI scores. It turned out that there was no problem of curve fitting, for the simple reason that the intermatrix resemblances began at zero for the first 10 scales and remained at zero, without the slightest tendency to increase as we included further blocks of scales in computing the distance measures. We know from a good deal of evidence that neither the MMPI nor the clinical Q sorts are quite *that* bad, and I am at a loss to understand these results. My suspicion is that they arise from inadequacies of the distance measure itself, and further analysis of the data is being undertaken with this hypothesis in mind. I still think that it was an interesting idea.

Leaving profile pattern interpretation, I should like to consider one more topic briefly. One of the most important problems in clinical psychology is deciding what kind of language communicates the largest amount of information about a patient. Most clinical practice today is predicated upon the assumption that useful statements about the patient can best be formulated (or at least inferentially mediated) by a theoretical language. The power of theoretical discourse in the other sciences makes this predilection understandable, and the characteristic Allport-Vernon-Lindzey profiles of clinical psychologists reflect strong theoretical interest. However, we learn in undergraduate physics that in order to apply theoretical constructs to the solution of practical problems (specifically, to predict the subsequent course of a particular physical system), one must fulfill two conditions. First, he must possess a reasonably well developed theory. That is, he must know the laws that systems of the given kind obey. Secondly, he must have a technology, a set of measuring instruments, for determining the initial and boundary conditions of the particular system under study. To the extent that either, or both, of these conditions are not fulfilled, predictions arrived at by theoretical inference will be untrustworthy. I do not see how anyone taking an objective view of the enterprise could claim that we fulfill *either*, let alone both, of these conditions in clinical psychology today. For this reason, in spite of my own personal interest in theoretical questions, I remain among that minority who persist in skepticism as to the pragmatic utility of theoretical constructions in daily clinical decision making.

Suppose, however, that some kind of theoretical discourse is to be used; which of the several kinds of theoretical sublanguages is most economical? As a pilot study in connection with a Ford Foundation project now going on at Minnesota, I collected some preliminary data which you may find of interest. Twenty psychotherapists were asked to describe a patient whom they had had in treatment for at least 25 hours, using the 182-item phenotypic pool which generated the curves previously shown. They also described the patient in terms of the 113-item genotypic pool. Although the latter pool was not constructed in any systematic way with respect to theoretical orientation, having been built for a different purpose, one can identify five relatively homogeneous subsets of genotypic items as follows: 25 Murray needs, 14 areas of conflict, 13 mechanisms of defense, 10 value-orientation components, and 7 items referring to dimensions of psychiatric nosology. After calculating the 190 interpatient Q correlations based upon each of these subpools, we may ask how well the pattern of interpatient resemblances in the phenotype is reproduced by the genotypic matrix. Unfortunately, I have not been able to find a statistician who will tell me how to do a significance test on such data, but the coefficients obtained are shown in Table 2. It is remarkable, I think, that the 13 defense mechanisms do about as well in reproducing the 182-item phenotypic matrix as does the entire genotypic pool consisting of almost 10 times as many items. We hope that with a more systematic coverage of the domain the Ford project will give us some definite information about this question.

I have presented some samples of research currently in progress at Minnesota which, while somewhat heterogeneous and difficult to pull together, all treat of what we see as pragmatically important aspects of the clinician's cognitive activity. In order to place any confidence in either the theoretical constructs we employ in discussing patients, or in the instrument-interpreter combinations we use to assess them, studies of convergent and discriminative validity must be carried out. The Campbell-Fiske multitrait-multimethod matrix, or the multiperson-multimethod variant of it, should be useful for this purpose. It seems obvious that even adequate and sophisticated studies of construct validity must be supplemented by data upon the *rate* at which the clinician acquires information from various sources. Since the commonest justification for expenditure of psychometric time is the utility to the therapist of "advance knowledge" (especially of the genotype), the skepticism expressed by our sample of psychotherapists, taken in combination with the convergence curves for the therapist's perception of his patient, put this widely held belief badly in need of experimental support. An important aspect of such data, presumably rather specific to various populations and clinical instruments, is that of differential convergence rates among items. There are probably certain attributes for which a test's validity is insufficient to justify a marked departure from the base rates or mean rating of the given clinical population, and others for which the therapist tends to be in error early in the game and to converge to the truth rather slowly in contrast to the test. I would predict that an example of this is MMPI Scale 6, which is a rather weak scale when used as an exclusion test, but which, when elevated, turns out almost invariably to be right. I have had patients in treatment whose paranoid potential did not manifest itself until 50 or 75 sessions, by which time I had concluded (erroneously) that the MMPI was giving me a false positive.

Table 2. *Correlations between Interpatient* P *Matrix and* G *Matrices Based on Various Subpools.*

Variables	*r*
P (182 items) vs. entire G pool (113 items)	.59
P vs. 13 defense mechanisms	.52
P vs. 25 Murray needs	.22
P vs. 7 nosological components	.22
P vs. 10 value dimensions	.03
P vs. 14 conflict areas	−.03
P vs. all 69 G items in above subpools	.45

Note. ${}_{20}C_2$ patients rated; $N = 190$ coefficients.

As has been pointed out by many clinicians, lacking adequate clinical cookbooks (Meehl 1956) we have in practice to treat our instruments as instrument-interpreter combinations. I believe we can say upon present evidence that no one interpreter succeeds in extracting all of the information contained in a profile and that the development of objective configural methods of profile analysis (of which the Meehl-Dahlstrom rules are a primitive example) is a task of great importance. David Lykken and I are currently engaged in a study comparing more complex functions—such as a second degree polynomial having squares and cross-products—with clinical judgment and the Meehl-Dahlstrom Rules. I am betting on the last-named, because—while nonoptimally weighted—they do at least tap configural effects involving interactions up to the sixth order.

Finally, the question of what is the most economical language to employ in describing a patient remains open, although it appears that there are many practitioners who are not sufficiently aware that this problem exists.

I look forward to the next decade of research in clinical psychology with a certain ambivalence. We are asking more sensible questions and being more critical of our procedures; and several research techniques are now available, and in wide use, which should give us some pretty clear answers. The reason for my ambivalence (and I regret that in the role of prophet I have to sound like Jeremiah) is that the evidence already available suggests that the outcomes will look pretty gloomy. My advice to fledgling clinical psychologists is to construct their self-concept mainly around "I am a researcher" or "I am a psychotherapist," because one whose self-concept is mainly "I am a (test oriented) psychodiagnostician" may have to maintain his professional security over the next few years by not reading the research literature, a maneuver which has apparently proved quite successful already for some clinicians. Personally, I find the cultural lag between what the published research shows and what clinicians persist in claiming to do with their favorite devices even more disheartening than the adverse evidence itself.

Psychologists cannot administer shock treatment or pass out tranquilizers, and I do not know of any evidence that we are better psychotherapists than our psychiatric colleagues. If there is anything that justifies our existence—other than the fact that we come cheaper—it is that we think scientifically about human behavior and that we come from a long tradition, going way back to the very origins of experimental psychology in the study of human error, of being critical of ourselves as cognizing organisms and of applying quantitative methods to the outcomes of our cognitive activity. If this methodological commitment is not strong enough to compete with the commitments clinicians have to particular diagnostic instruments, the unique contribution of our discipline will have been lost. I can mobilize some enthusiasm for the next 10 years within the field: while I expect discouraging findings at the level of practice, from the standpoint of the sociology of professions and the history of ideas, the developments should be very interesting to watch.

REFERENCES

Campbell, D. T., & Fiske, D. W. Convergent and discriminant validation by the multitrait-multimethod matrix. *Psychol. Bull.*, 1959, **56**, 81–105.

Cattell, R. B. *Description and measurement of personality.* Yonkers: World Book, 1946.

Cattell, R. B. *Personality.* New York: McGraw-Hill, 1950.

Cronbach, L. J., & Meehl, P. E. Construct validity in psychological tests. *Psychol. Bull.*, 1955, **52**, 281–302.

Fleeson, W., Glueck, B., Heistad, G., King, J., Lykken, D., Meehl, P., & Mena, A. The ataraxic effect of two phenothiazine drugs on an outpatient population. *Univer. Minn. med. Bull.*, 1958, **29**, 274–286.

Garfield, S. *Introductory clinical psychology.* New York: Macmillan, 1957.

Hoffman, P. J. Criteria of human judgment ability: I. The "clinical" assessment of intelligence and personality. *Amer. Psychologist*, 1958, **13**, 388. (Abstract) (a)

Hoffman, P. J. Human judgment as a decision process. *Amer. Psychologist*, 1958, **13**, 368. (Title) (b)

Hoffman, P. J. The prediction of clinical prediction. *Amer. Psychologist*, 1959, **14**, 356. (Title)

Horst, P. Pattern analysis and configural scoring. *J. clin. Psychol.*, 1954, **10**, 3–11.

Little, K. B., & Shneidman, E. S. Congruencies among interpretations of psychological tests and anamnestic data. *Psychol. Monogr.*, 1959, **73**(6, Whole No. 476).

McArthur, C. C., Meehl, P. E., & Tiedeman, D. V. Symposium on clinical and statistical prediction. *J. counsel. Psychol.*, 1956, **3**, 163–173.

Meehl, P. E. *Clinical versus statistical prediction.* Minneapolis: Univer. Minnesota Press, 1954.

Meehl, P. E. Wanted—a good cookbook. *Amer. Psychologist*, 1956, **11**, 263–272.

Meehl, P. E. When shall we use our heads instead of the formula? *J. counsel. Psychol.*, 1957, **4**, 268–273.

Meehl, P. E. Some ruminations on the validation of clinical procedures. *Canad. J. Psychol.*, 1959, **13**, 102–128. (a)

Meehl, P. E. A comparison of clinicians with five statistical methods of identifying psychotic MMPI profiles. *J. counsel. Psychol.*, 1959, **6**, 102–109. (b)

Meehl, P. E., & Dahlstrom, W. G. Objective configural rules for discriminating psychotic from neurotic MMPI profiles. *J. consult. Psychol.*, 1960, **24**, in press.

Computers in Behavioral Science: Diagnostic Interviewing by Digital Computer

Benjamin Kleinmuntz

Robert S. McLean

A computer system is proposed for conducting large-scale psychodiagnostic interviews. The discussion focuses on the rationale for the use of the computer as an interviewer, computer hardware and software problems encountered, and on an operational computer program which approximates the ideal automated interview scheme.

Some years ago, Boring (1946) posed the question: "What properties would a potato have to have in order to be conscious?" He addressed himself to the problem of providing a robot with consciousness and listed the characteristics (reactions, attitudes, memory, and so forth) that a robot might need to make a human of him. In this paper we propose to consider the problem of what properties are needed to build a machine that is able to conduct psychodiagnostic interviews.

From *Behavioral Science*, 1968, 13, 75–80. Reproduced by permission.

Our discussion focuses on four aspects of the problem: 1) the rationale for the use of the computer as an interviewer; 2) considerations of the computer hardware necessary for the interview assignment; 3) content areas that may be most amenable to computer programming at the present stage of development of hardware and software; and 4) borrowing from the well developed area of personality testing, we give an illustration of an operational computer program that might be used in the manner proposed. It is assumed in this paper, and will bear no further repetition, that, due to the imbalance between the large numbers of patients who need psychiatric attention and the meager numbers of trained professionals available for this job, the use of the computer for mass psychiatric screening needs no defense or apology.

COMPUTER AS A CLINICIAN

The three characteristics of the computer that highly recommend it for the task of psychiatric interviewing are flexibility, objectivity, and speed. It may be interesting to note that the machine excels in that aspect of the clinician's interview behavior in which the clinician prides himself most. For example, Holtzman (1960) stated that the processing of information by the clinician is not likely to be adaptable to the computer since the clinician is "a free floating processor with no hard and fast rules." In other words, the chief advantage of the clinician over the computer, according to Holtzman, is the clinician's greater flexibility. But the ability of the computer to alter its activity as the result of the environment in which it is working is its greatest strength. It has already been demonstrated in work with teaching machines (Silberman and Coulson, 1962) that a computer program can be written to branch to one of several alternative content areas as a function of a person's prior response.

The clinical interview is nothing more than the process of nonrandom sampling of the set of all possible questions that could be asked during a given period of time. How the particular subset of questions is chosen often depends on the interviewer's master program (that is, training) and his judgment of the relevance of the items for the particular patient-problem combination. Given unlimited resources of time, persistence, and money, an interviewer could ask a universal set of questions of all respondents. However, since in practice such resources are limited, the clinician does not apply an exhaustive search; rather he uses a directed search for data relevant to the patient's problem. The facility of the computer to alter its line of questioning is limited only by its hardware, memory capacity, and the programmer's ingenuity. The human interviewer is similarly restricted by his limited memory and inventiveness.

Moreover the computer is objective and conceptually neutral (Tomkins and Messick, 1963). It has no built-in biases other than those that are programmed into it and is in fact dependent on the explicit rules stored into it as its program. The machine, therefore, has no "halo effect" or counter-transference problems unless the program explicitly furnished it with these appurtenances. The temperament of the computer is relatively stable from day to day and its previous night's activities do not impede its functioning the morning after. In addition to its reliability and commendable stability, it is capable of doing several things at once and can complete all these tasks with great speed. Through time sharing it is capable of interviewing many subjects simultaneously, and it can be arranged so that the impression is given to each subject that he is receiving individualized service.

Finally Smith (1963) calls attention to the advantage of the computer's impersonal nature. He points out that there may be some very personal and embarrassing material that a patient may not want to express to another person but might be able to present to an impartial machine. Whether or not this "confession machine" effect is sufficiently large to compensate for some of the warmth exuded by some human clinicians is an empirical problem possibly worthy of study.

In summary, the computer's ability to select items to be asked in an interview on the basis of answers to prior questions, and its speed, objectivity, and impartiality make it exceptionally suited for the task of psychodiagnostic interviewing.

HARDWARE

The equipment considerations involved in an automatic interviewing machine are threefold: storage, input, and output equipment. The large number of potential interview questions and their responses demand storage facilities and speed of access that are considerably larger and faster than those available in present-day computers. Since the actual interview items or questions are stored in coded form so that they may be typed out or otherwise displayed directly by the computer, some mass auxiliary memory device must be used to hold this information and it must be readily accessible as needed. In addition to the interview items, the computer must be furnished a program of instructions that guide the display of items, and it must keep cumulative records of individuals' prior responses during the interview. Since normative data should be collected continually for each of the item-response combinations, and because the machine should be capable of interviewing many individuals simultaneously, the memory requirements should be increased considerably beyond present-day capacities.

One of the main drawbacks for the computer as a clinician is that a subject cannot converse with the machine in some easy and meaningful way. He is limited to two modes of communicating with the machine: key pressing and pointing. Key pressing can be either on the conventional typewriter keyboard or on a special-purpose keyboard which may be equipped with a limited number of keys, each of which represents an alternative response (such as, 1 = "Agree;" 2 = "Disagree;" 3 = "Indifferent," and so on). Pointing can occur with a "light gun" at a display on a cathode ray tube, or by pressing some portion of a special display screen. From the point of view of the computer, the output consists of the statements and questions that the machine presents to the subject in the interview situation. The subject can receive the output of the computer in either the visual or the auditory mode.

The most common form of visual output at present is the printed page generated by some typewriter-like device. It is a permanent record which is not easily removed from the view of the subject when his use of it is to be restricted. The process of typing out questions is relatively slow unless a high-speed printer is used, in which case the cost is great. A similar form of output can be furnished on a cathode ray tube, where the image can be displayed and removed instantaneously under program control. The capacity of a tube face is not large but is probably adequate for most applications of the present sort. Units are being produced on a small scale, for use in programmed learning (Silberman and Coulson, 1962) and for some commercial applications.

Another method is a random access slide projector, under the control of the computer (Silberman, 1960, 1961; Silberman and Coulson, 1962), which instructs the projector to show a particular slide by transmitting the item number to the projector. This method is relatively economical in terms of computer storage requirements. However, a disadvantage of presentation by cathode ray, printout or slide may be that all visual output depends upon the ability and/or motivation of the subject to read it; and it may be therefore a problem for the illiterate and the unmotivated.

Alternatively one may present the items audibly. Computers may soon speak of their own accord through appropriate encoding of the required sounds into the computer language, and subsequent conversion of these data into electrical representations of sound waves with a digital analog converter (Smith, Ansell, Koehler, and Servos, 1964). The computer memory requirements for such a scheme would be large but could be managed by having a random access audio device such as a magnetic tape recorder which could hold the questions in vocal form.

In summary, there are a number of devices that are available, at least in principle, which will facilitate easier two-way communication between subject and computer. None of them is the ultimate in flexibility and ease of communication but they can help to bypass many of the traditional limitations of present memory, input, and output that one has to face in more routine use of computers.

CONTENT

The most difficult aspect of the design of a machine that conducts an interview is the selection of the content areas to be covered during the interview session. It is tempting to claim that an entire mental status psychiatric examination such as is described by Noyes and Kolb (1963) could be conducted by a computer, and ultimately this seems a possibility, but there are two obstacles that must be surmounted before this becomes reality. One is that at the present time our knowledge of protocol content analysis and of computational linguistics are so limited that the computer's processing of the protocol could only be trivial. Work currently under way in content analysis (Stone, Bales, Namenwirth, and Ogilvie, 1962; Paige 1964; Dunphy, Stone, and Smith, 1965; Allport, 1966) and in computational linguistics (Weizenbaum, 1966) should contribute toward a remedy of this state of affairs.

A second and even more important obstacle than the linguistic one is the fact that very little is known about the clinician's processing of diagnostic interview information. His moment to moment differential responding to a subject's verbal cues, and the basis of his subsequent diagnostic and prognostic judgments are for the most part unknown and must still be explored.

AN ILLUSTRATIVE COMPUTER PROGRAM

In the meantime, the closest approximation to the psychiatric interview, and perhaps ultimately the method of choice, can be found to a large extent in the already developed techniques of psychometrics. There are many personality questionnaires currently in use at clinics as supplements to the psychiatric interview. Ideally if a number of personality traits are to be assessed one could administer a limited set of items which would differentiate subjects empirically along the dimensions or traits in question. If the examiner, for example, is interested in detecting the presence of certain psychopathognomic signs in an individual he could present the subject with a set of highly discriminating items that are specially relevant to the dimensions under consideration. The advantage of the computer for this type of test administration is that it enables intensive sampling of the dimensions that are of major interest.

Consider the situation, for example, in which the purpose of a psychiatric interview is the traditional one of diagnostic classification. Given a pool of items such as are included in the Minnesota Multiphasic Personality Inventory (MMPI), a subset of items selected from each of its ten clinical scales could be used as a starting point for the machine interview. This subset is given to each subject at the beginning of the testing session and on the basis of subjects' responses to these items, certain hypotheses could be formulated by the computer program regarding the specific psychiatric dimensions worthy of further exploration. In practice, this means that instead of administering all 550 MMPI items to a respondent after it has become obvious from an initial set of items that only the dimensions of schizophrenia and paranoia are relevant, the computer could branch to highly discriminating schizophrenic and paranoid items borrowed from a number of well-established and empirically validated personality tests; or the computer could turn to a new set of empirically validated questionnaire items, perhaps accumulated from previous computer interviews.

For illustrative purposes our method of supervised test administration by computer was explored by using the MMPI as the universe of items from which we can select samples of items that will aid in diagnostic classification. The MMPI was chosen for this purpose because it is readily subdivided into scales which correspond to psychiatric diagnostic categories. The computer program had as its goal the evaluation of the subject on each of 15 scales (that is, L, F, K, Hs, D, Hy, Pd, Mf, Pa, Pt, Sc, Ma, Si, Es, and Mt). At any point in the course of testing, the program assumed one of three states with respect to each of the 15 scales. On each particular scale the subject was said to be (1) assumed normal, (2) assumed abnormal, or (3) not yet classified. At the beginning of the computer run, all scales were in the third state.

A flow chart of the sample program is shown in Figure 1. The action of the program was as follows: First, the program presented a basic set of items consisting of 5 for each of the 15 scales. The basic set provided the computer with data on which to decide on those scales relevant for further testing. After the basic questions were asked, the computer calculated a *T*-score on each scale and assigned each scale to one of the first three states. The *T*-score was used for this purpose because it is the traditional manner of scoring the MMPI scales, and can therefore be interpreted in terms of deviation from the typical response characteristics of the standardization group of subjects. A scale was assumed to

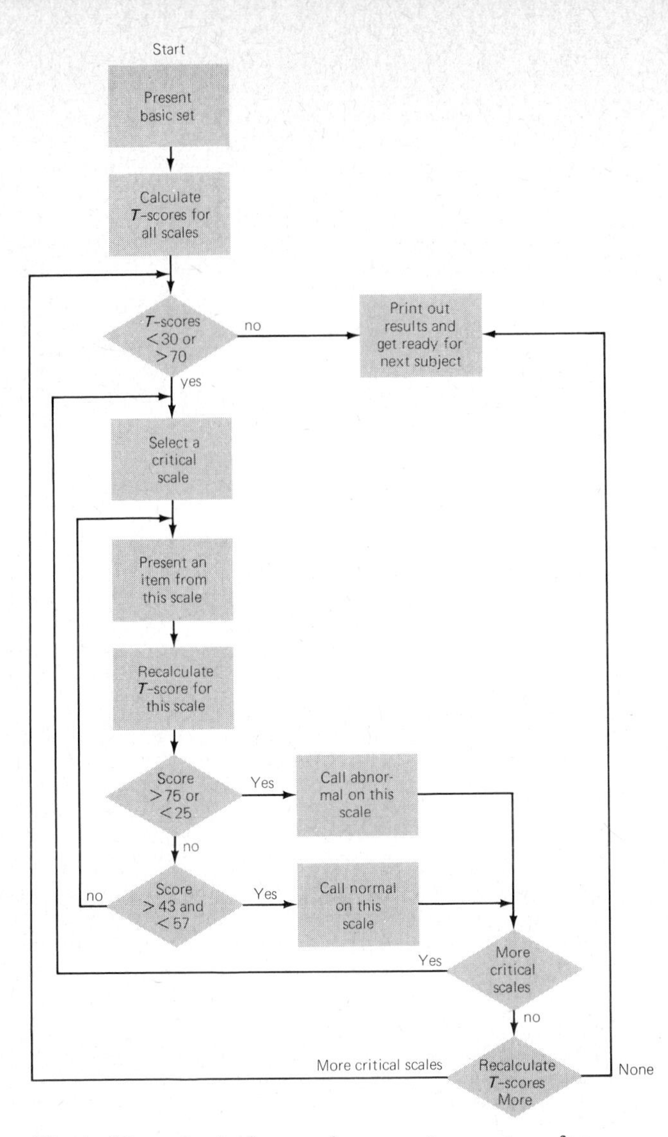

Fig. 1. Flow chart of a sample computer program for administering MMPIs.

be normal if the *T*-score fell within two standard deviations of the mean, 30 to 70, and it was assumed to be abnormal if its *T*-score was more than two standard deviations from the mean. The scale was marked "not yet classified" if it did not meet either of these criteria. Each scale so marked was placed on a "critical" list.

The second phase of the computer program consisted of selecting a scale from those on the critical list; questions relevant to that scale were asked. After each question, the *T*-score was again calculated for that scale. If the scale now qualified for one of the other states (normal or abnormal), questioning on that scale was discontinued, another scale selected from the critical list, and the process repeated. If the scale still remained in the "not yet classified" state, questioning continued until a classification was made.

At some point all scales were removed from the critical list. At this point all scales that were not yet classified were rescored and any that were not clearly "normal" or "abnormal" were placed on the critical list and the second phase restarted. At some point each scale was classified as "normal" or "abnormal," whereupon the program terminated and printed out its conclusions concerning the mental status of the person being tested, with regard to each of the fifteen scales.

This computer program was written in ALGOL and its feasibility as an interview technique has been tested using item responses from subjects (who took the entire MMPI) as data input to the computer. The simulated subjects' MMPIs were used for testing the program, since the hardware required for a real test of such a program is not presently available to the authors. Thus instead of actually having a number of subjects sit opposite a computer teletype—the manner in which the computer interview of the future may be conducted—MMPI answer sheets were "read into" the computer.

The main purpose of this study was to obtain an approximation of the goodness of fit between MMPIs administered conventionally and those administered by our computer-controlled branching system. The feasibility of such a program was readily ascertained by observing that the machine was able to accomplish its task of administering the MMPI to 50 simulated subjects in a matter of several minutes. However, the goodness of fit between the computer-administered and the long form of the MMPI was not so encouraging. Based on 50 subjects, the intercorrelations of scale scores ranged from −.005 to +.942, and averaged +.365.

Clearly, in the future, additional comparisons between computer and conventionally administered tests are indicated, and large-scale comparisons should be made of the relative efficacy of each method's facility for detecting psychopathology. Such studies are currently being planned.

Ideally, the studies of the future would be conducted by having subjects sit opposite cathode ray tubes on which item displays are printed out. The choice of items and the number of items asked would be under the control of the computer. This system of computer "interviewing," if large numbers of display tubes were available, would permit large-scale psychiatric screening of personnel.

REFERENCES

Allport, G. W. Traits revisited. *Amer. Psychol.*, 1966, 21, 1–10.

Boring, E. G. Mind and mechanism. *Amer. J. Psychol.*, 1946, **59**, 173–192.

Dunphy, D. C., Stone, P. J., & Smith, M. S. The general inquirer: Further developments in a computer system for content analysis of verbal data in the social sciences. *Behav. Sci.*, 1965, **10**, 468–480.

Holtzman, W. H. Can the computer supplant the clinician? *J. clin. Psychol.*, 1960, **16**, 119–122.

Noyes, A. P., & Kolb, L. C. *Modern clinical psychiatry* (6th Ed.). Philadelphia: Saunders, 1963.

Paige, J. M. *Automated content analysis of "Letters from Jenny."* Honors thesis, Department of Social Relations, Harvard University, 1964.

Silberman, H. F. A computer as an experimental laboratory machine for research on automated teaching procedures. *Behav. Sci.*, 1960, **5**, 175–176.
Silberman, H. F. A computer-controlled teaching machine. *Behav. Sci.*, 1961, **6**, 259–261.
Silberman, H. F., & Coulson, J. E. Automated teaching. In H. Borko (Ed.), *Computer applications in the behavioral sciences.* Englewood Cliffs, N.J.: Prentice Hall, 1962, Pp. 308–335.
Smith, R. E. Examination by computer. *Behav. Sci.*, 1963, **8**, 76–79.
Smith, K. U., Ansell, S. D., Koehler, J., & Servos, G. H. Digital computer system for dynamic analysis of speech and sound feedback mechanisms. *J. ACM*, 1964, **11**, 240–251.
Stone, P. J., Bales, R. F., Namenwirth, Z., & Oglivie, D. M. The general inquirer: A computer system for content analysis and retrieval based on the sentence as a unit of information. *Behav. Sci.*, 1962, **7**, 484–498. Reprinted in R. D. Luce (Ed.), *Readings in mathematical psychology*, vol. 2. New York: John Wiley, 1964. Pp. 58–72.
Tomkins, S. S., & Messick, S. *Computer simulation of personality.* New York: John Wiley, 1963.
Weizenbaum, J. ELIZA—A computer program for the study of natural language communication between man and machine. *Communications of the ACM*, 1966, **9**, 36–45.

Artificial Paranoia

Kenneth Mark Colby
Sylvia Weber
Franklin Dennis Hilf

A case of artificial paranoia has been synthesized in the form of a computer simulation model. The model and its embodied theory are briefly described. Several excerpts from interviews with the model are presented to illustrate its paranoid input-output behavior. Evaluation of the success of the simulation will depend upon indistinguishability tests.

Within the paradigm of computer science, distinctions are sometimes drawn between the activities of computer simulation and artificial intelligence. Yet in constructing models of psychological processes, the distinction can become blurred in places where overlaps emerge, as will be evident from our account of a model of artificial paranoia.

1. SIMULATION MODELS AND ARTIFACTS

An information-processing system is defined as a structured combination of functions which collaborate in governing a set of input-output behaviors. Two information-processing systems, S_1 and S_2, are considered input-output (I-O) equivalent when the I-O pairs of S_1 in a particular situation are indistinguishable from the I-O pairs of S_2 in a similar situation in respect to specified dimensions. To simulate the I-O behavior of a system, S_1, one constructs a computer simulation model, S_2, whose I-O behavior imitates that of S_1 along certain dimensions.

Our phrase 'artificial paranoia' refers to an actual but non-human case of paranoia which we have constructed in the form of a computer model. The model's I-O behavior, in the communicative situation of a diagnostic psychiatric interview, is identifiable by psychiatric judges as 'paranoid'. In constructing this paranoid model we were not attempting to simulate any actual human case of paranoia. Our artificial case is that of an imagined hypothetical individual. However, the model's I-O behavior imitates the I-O behavior of humans whose information processing is dominated by a mode psychiatrists label as 'paranoid'.

From *Artificial Intelligence*, 1971, **2**, 1–25.
This research is supported by Grant PHS MH 06645-09 from the National Institute of Mental Health, by (in part) Research Scientist Award (No. 1-KO5-K-14, 433) from the National Institute of Mental Health to the senior author and by (in part) the Advanced Research Projects Agency of the Office of the Secretary of Defense (SD-183).

This simulation model can be classified as a theoretical model in that it embodies as part of its inner structure an explanatory account of complex I-O paranoid behavior. It attempts to systematize and account for certain empirical regularities and particular occurrences familiar to clinicians who interview paranoid patients. An explanatory account involves functional relations expressed as lawlike generalizations. In order to explain concrete individual cases, it also contains initial conditions expressed as singular statements. Our model embodies general theoretical principles about paranoid communicative I-O behavior. In order to run and test the model as an explanation, these principles are combined with initial conditions descriptive of an individual hypothetical case.

Our model of artificial paranoia represents a synthesized case of paranoid information processing. It is not an 'ideal' case either in the sense of an entity known to be impossible, such as a molecule without mass, or in the sense of an extreme type, such as absolute zero. Evaluation of the model as a successful simulation depends on a consensus of expert judgments by psychiatrists who interview it.

2. PARANOIA

Originally (about 2500 years ago among the Greeks) the term 'paranoia' (Gr.: *para* = beside; *nous* = mind) referred to a concept of delirium, thought disorganization and general craziness (1). During this century its usage has become adjectivally limited to only a few clinical conditions such as paranoid state, paranoid personality, paranoid reaction and paranoid schizophrenia. While the reliability (in the sense of level of agreement) of these specific subcategories is low, the reliability of the more general category 'paranoid' has been shown in several studies to be high, reaching 80–95% agreement. In our work we have limited the general term 'paranoid' to a name for a mode of thinking, feeling and action characterized by malevolence delusions.

Delusions are defined as false beliefs. Belief, a primitive concern of an epistemic intelligent system, we have defined as a prehension of acceptance, rejection or uncertainty regarding the truth of a conceptualization of some situation (2). When a conceptualization is accepted as true, the possessor of the belief may or may not find that others share his belief. Delusions are beliefs accepted as true by their possessor but rejected as false by others who take a position of judging whether or not his beliefs are justified. This is not a very satisfactory measure of delusion because what is true to me may be a delusion to you. But it is all we have at present and much of the human world runs this way.

A malevolence delusion represents a belief that other persons have evil intentions to harm or injure the possessor of the belief. While malevolence delusions characterize the paranoid mode, they may or may not be directly expressed and observable. If delusions of malevolence are not expressed, empirical indicators of their presence include I-O behaviors characterized as self-referent, irritable, hypersensitive, opinionated, suspicious, accusatory, sarcastic, hostile, uncooperative, argumentative, rigid, secretive, guarded and avoidant. Appearance of these indicators in a psychiatric interview lead psychiatrists to judge the patient as 'paranoid'.

Numerous formulations have been proposed to account for the phenomena of the paranoid mode. Most of these formulations did not qualify as explanatory theories since they were not empirically testable. They were untestable because they were not sufficiently explicit and well-articulated to decide what observations would count as confirmatory or disconfirmatory instances. A simulation model as an explicit and intelligible effective procedure is testable because its observable I-O pairs can be compared with observable I-O pairs of the processes being imitated.

Our model is testable by means of indistinguishability tests. If the model's paranoid I-O behavior cannot be distinguished from its human counterpart by psychiatric judges using a diagnostic interview, then we shall consider the simulation to be successful. Before entering the topic of evaluation, we shall first describe our theory of paranoid processes and its implementation in the model.

3. A THEORY OF PARANOID I-O PROCESSES

To offer an explanatory account of observable communicative phenomena characteristic of the paranoid mode, we first postulate a structure of strategies governed by a delusional belief system. As mentioned, a belief is defined as a prehension of acceptance, rejection or uncertainty regarding the truth of a conceptual representation of some situation. To accept a conceptualization as true is to believe that the situation it represents obtains, holds or is the case. A belief system consists of a set of beliefs which interact in deciding the truth-status of a given conceptualization. A delusional belief system is a network of beliefs accepted as true by their holder, but rejected as false by others. We shall term the possessor of a delusional belief system the 'Self' and the other person in an encounter the 'Other'.

Paranoid delusions are networks of false beliefs in which the malevolent intent of some Other toward the Self predominates. In an encounter such as an interview, the input-output strategies of a paranoid Self are dominated by delusions of malevolence regarding the Other. Malevolence we define as a conceptualization of psychological harm and/or physical threat by some Other to the Self. In a dialogue the input strategies of a paranoid mode operate to detect malevolence by scrutinizing the linguistic expressions of the Other for explicit and implicit harms and threats. The Other's expressions are subjected to transformations which can result in an interpretation of malevolence where none is intended.

We define psychological harm to consist of an explicit or implicit attempt on the part of the Other (a) to humiliate, demean or belittle the Self, and/or (b) to subjugate, control or exploit the Self. Physical threat we conceive as an explicit or implicit intent of the Other to physically attack the Self or to have it brought about that the Self is physically injured.

A paranoid Self is differentially sensitive to concepts relating to self-concerns and self-worth. It is also sensitive to 'flare' concepts which are related at various semantic distances to concepts involved in delusions and which tend to activate a delusional complex. This activation is facilitated by the Self offering hints and prompts to the Other in order to probe the Other's interest and attitude towards hearing the delusional 'story' the Self strives to tell.

It is assumed that the detection of malevolence in an input affects internal affect-states of fear, anger and mistrust, depending on the conceptual content of the input. If a physical threat is involved, fear rises. If psychological harm is recognized, anger rises. Mistrust rises as a function of the combined negative affect experiences (fear and anger) the Self has been subjected to by the Other. When no malevolence is detected the level of fear falls slowly, anger rapidly and mistrust only very slowly.

Once malevolence on the part of the Other is detected and internally reacted to affectively, output strategies of the paranoid mode attempt to execute linguistic counteractions. Two sorts of counteracting output strategies are utilized; one consists of counterattack when anger predominates, while the second generates actions of avoidance and withdrawal when fear and mistrust predominate. Once the output counteractions are undertaken by the Self, the course of further dialogue depends to some extent on the reactions of the Other. For example, when attacked, if the Other responds in kind, then the input strategies of the Self detect malevolence again and the two communicants can become locked in a loop typical of paranoid conversational struggles.

In ordinary human communication a receiver of messages does not routinely and intensively search them for indications of malevolence. We thus postulate that the understanding of natural language by a paranoid information-processing system is different from the 'normal' mode of understanding. However, input strategies dominated and monopolized by a paranoid mode do not always detect malevolence in the input, in which case the output strategies generate a 'nonparanoid' reply.

Our explanatory structure is circumscribed in that it attempts to account for the way in which a paranoid belief system operates in a particular situation. The explanations are not etiological in that they do not attempt to explain how the system over time came to be the way it is. It should also be emphasized that the explanations account dynamically for phenomena over only a short period of time, i.e. the duration of a diagnostic psychiatric interview, which typically lasts from 20–60 minutes.

As stated [earlier], an explanatory structure is composed of statements of lawlike generalizations and singular statements of initial conditions. Some of the initial conditions for our hypothetical paranoid individual are as follows: (a complete specification of the initial conditions is contained in the model).

He is a 28-year-old single man who works as a post office clerk. He has no siblings and lives alone, seldom seeing his parents. He is sensitive about his physical appearance, his family, his religion, his education and the topic of sex. His hobbies are movies and horseracing. He has gambled extensively on horses both at the track and through bookies. A few months ago he became involved in a quarrel with a bookie, claiming the bookie did not pay off in a bet. Alarmed and angry, he confronted the bookie with the accusations and physically attacked him. After the quarrel it occurred to him that bookies pay protection to the underworld and that this particular bookie might gain revenge by having him injured or killed by underworld figures. He is eager to tell his story to interested and non-threatening listeners. Thus he cautiously offers hints of the direction in which his problems lie and feels his way along in an interview in an attempt to test the trustworthiness of an interviewer.

A model which implements these generalizations and particularizations involves a greater degree of explicitness and complexity than the above essayistic description. In the following section we shall attempt a description of the model at a level of detail sufficient to satisfy, but hopefully not exhaust, an artificial intelligence reader.

4. A PARANOID MODEL

The program of this model is written in MLISP, a high-level programming language which translates M-expressions into S-expressions of LISP 1.6. The model involves a 35K program, of which 14K is allocated to the data base. It runs in an interactive mode on the PDP 6/10 time-shared system of the Stanford Artificial Intelligence Project. The input-output pairs of the model represent purely symbolic behavior in that its I-O sequences are limited to linguistic communication by means of teletyped messages. An interviewer can ask the model questions and offer it statements in natural language.

The task of the program is to interpret the input expressions and to produce internal (affective) and external (linguistic) responses which characterize the paranoid mode according to the theory described. (See Fig. 1.) The program must expect as input not only the type of material susceptible to distortion by the paranoid processes and specific questions relating to a psychiatric interview, but also reactions of the Other to the last output statement. The question arises with respect to input strategies, then, as to when the program should operate in a kind of 'breadth first' mode, looking in some fixed order for topics recognizable at the top level of the program, and when it should operate in a 'depth first' mode, keeping in mind first the context of the interview and the input which might be expected to occur next in this context. For example, if a flare topic is under discussion, should the program first check for a change of topic, or should it check for reactions of the Other such as encouragement, disinterest or further questions relating to that flare? Likewise, in a context of high Fear, should the program submit to the usual checking sequence or should it concentrate on the presence of reassurance or further threats in the input and ignore specific inquiries? Here we are considering not the question of time-efficiency but rather the more important question of a mechanism which, statically viewed, is not unnecessarily complex or redundant. The searches for the various input situations should be as independent of one another as possible.

With respect to output strategies, the problem is somewhat simpler. The relationship between certain types of input and certain types of output is determined by the theory and realized in the program in the form of conditionals. Once the significance of the input expression has been determined, the actual type of response usually de-

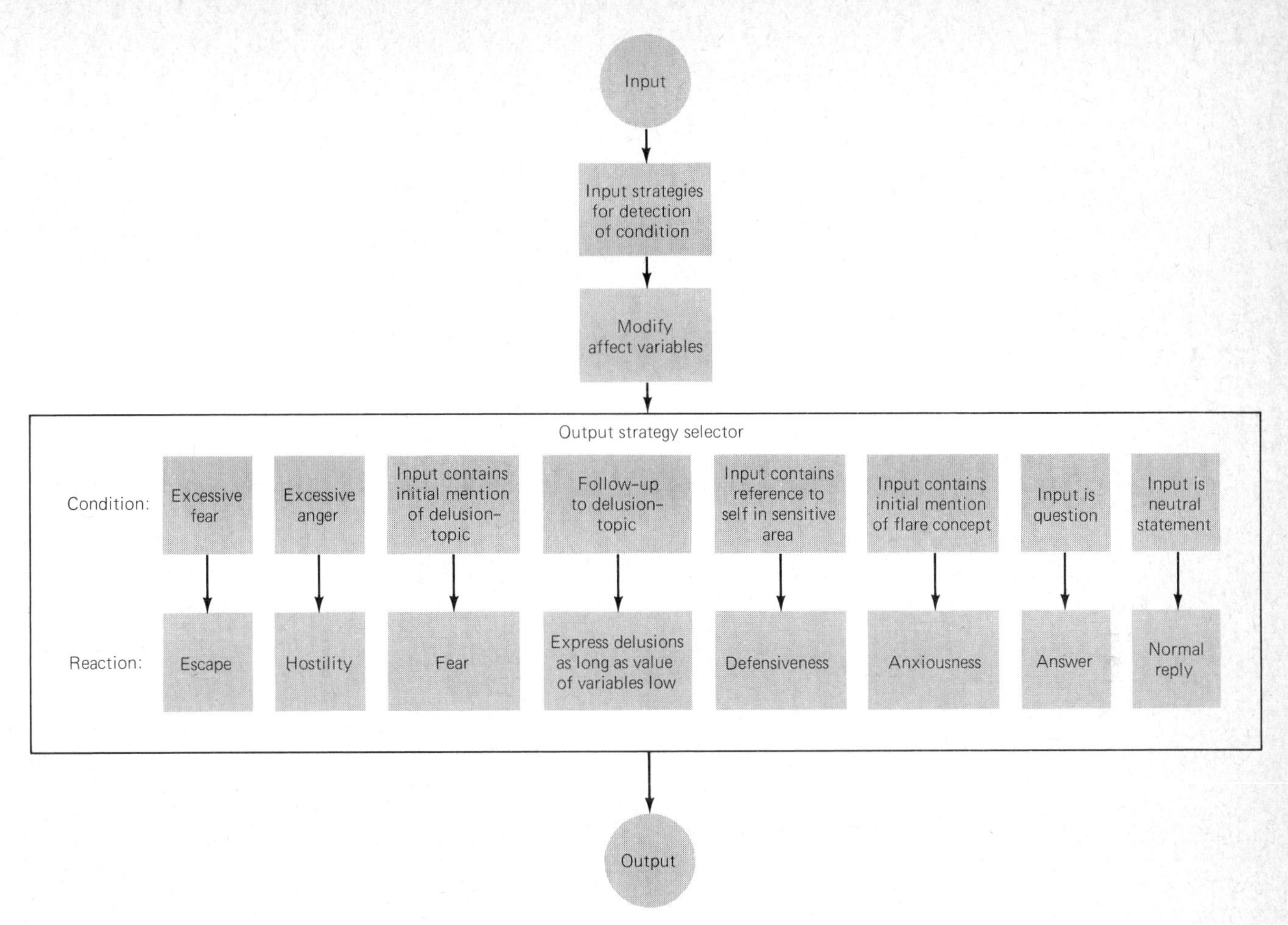

Fig. 1. General outline of program's operations.

pends only on a simple check of the affective context of the interview. (The responses selected for output exist for the most part as such in the data. In the case of certain suspicious responses about sensitive areas and leading questions about flare topics, the relevant concept is 'plugged into' the reply with due respect for syntactic considerations.)

Let us then consider first the role of context in output strategies, with reference to affective responses. A change of the affect states for any I-O pair automatically draws context into consideration by the use of a function which implies smaller absolute rises in the variable for higher current levels of the variable. Values for jumps in Fear or Anger for any I-O pair are given in percentages, which are then applied to the difference between the current level and the maximum level. An insult therefore produces the same percentage rise in anger at a low Anger level as at a high one, but the absolute rise will be greater.

The affect states determine a kind of context which governs not only individual variations in the affect variables, but also the 'tone' of any linguistic output which is not the immediate (context-independent) reaction to input provocative to the model. However, the reply is determined by only one or two thresholds of the relevant affect variable, as a more precise dependence of linguistic expressions on affect levels would be of little significance. (It should especially be noted that the actual numbers involved in the manipulation of affect variables are somewhat arbitrarily selected as part of the initial conditions for this particular hypothetical individual and are not meant to specify any quantitative aspect of the theoretical generalizations.) The effect of this mechanism is to cause the model to appear to be 'remembering' the last provocative input expression(s) for several I-O pairs after it occurs. Thus over a sequence of I-O pairs, the attitude displayed by the model differs according to context. The linguistic aspect of the model's behavior is then described by its individual responses in conjunction with (1) the expressions of the Other, (2) the 'paranoidness' of the model during that time.

The specific operation of the affect variables is as follows. Following the ith I-O pair, any rise in Fear or Anger is accounted for by the function

$$\text{VAR}_i = \text{VAR}_{i-1} + \text{RISE}_{\text{var}} * (20 - \text{VAR}_{i-1})$$

For a rise in either variable, Mistrust is recomputed by the function

$$\text{MISTRUST}_i = \text{MISTRUST}_{i-1} + 0.5 * \text{VAR} * (20 - \text{MISTRUST}_{i-1})$$

Something should be said here about base levels for these three variables. Fear and Anger are considered to be very 'fluid' variables. Initial Fear or Anger may be low or mild (0 or 10 respectively on a scale of 0–20), may rise to an extreme high during the conversation, and theoretically drop to the initial value again toward the end of a long conversation. (It is assumed that the level of these variables *initially* will not be high, since the patient is obviously willing to begin the interview. It is also assumed that a first interview will never cause the affect variables to drop below their initial values.) The normal drop in these values occurs after each I-O pair by a subtraction of 1 from Anger and 0.3 from Fear. In the context of flare discussion, however, the Fear level will in no case be allowed to fall below a level of 3; in the context of expression of delusions, the lowest value is 5. Such a minimum is designed to reflect some guardedness or anxiety of the model which must accompany the sharing of his 'story' with the Other.

Mistrust, however, is a 'sticky' variable, given that it is an identifying and static feature of paranoia. An initial value of 0 reflects an inherent mild mistrust; the other possible initial value is 'high' (15). Mistrust falls very slowly (by 0.05 for each I-O pair) to a base level which rises for each rise in Fear or Anger according to the function

$$\text{MISTRUST } 0_i = \text{MISTRUST } 0_{i-1} + 0.1 * \text{VAR} * (20 - \text{MISTRUST } 0_{i-1})$$

Thus any fear or anger induced in the model by the Other can only result in a model more distrustful of the Other by the end of the interview.

Perhaps it would be helpful at this point to say a little about how the linguistic understanding of the model (or rather—given the absence of a natural language parser—the inadequacy thereof) influences the operation of the program. In scanning for delusion-, flare- or sensitivity-terms, a person whose information processing is dominated by a paranoid mode tends to ignore the context of such a term. This is of obvious advantage to a program which relies on key-word understanding. When 'normal' questions are presented to the model, the interview suffers from all of the traditional inadequacies of this type of understanding. The problem of what to do with input sentences which are not recognized or fully understood, however, is mitigated if we are dealing with a model which in a sense has a one-track-mind. Our model has this property, in that it has a propensity to focus on its delusional complex and its associated flare concepts. Thus for lack of something else to say, the model will make a delusional statement or flare statement if this satisfies the current context of the situation. In most cases, it will appear that continuity is being maintained and that a typical feature of the paranoid mode (rigidity) is being expressed.

There are two versions in which the program may be run. The following description of the main flow of the program applies to both, except that in the weakly paranoid version there is no elicitable delusional complex. In addition, selection of the 'weak' parameter determines that (1) all affect variables be initialized to the lowest possible values and that (2) Fear and Anger rise more slowly, with the accompanying effect of a slower rise in Mistrust.

The first four routines scan for (1) an insinuation that the model is mentally ill, (2) reference to the delusional complex, (3) reference to a sensitive area and (4) reference to a flare concept respectively. If none of these situations is detected, the program checks for another characteristic feature of a psychiatric interview, namely (5) a statement expressing an emotional or intellectual relationship between the interviewer and the patient, e.g. 'You seem afraid of me', or 'I don't believe you'. This segment checks also for an apology or a direct threat, both of which are a kind of special case of relationship between the interviewer and the model. The external and internal reaction to each of these input situations is determined within each routine. The decisions relevant to the responses given are described below.

The scanning order just given is context-independent; the presence of the concepts involved is sufficient to interrupt any current situation and to produce immediate responses fairly independent of such situations. In the absence of input activating a response independent of context, the program checks the Fear and Anger levels before considering a response to 'normal' input. (Fear is considered a stronger influence than Anger, if both levels are high.) If Fear is high, the model will avoid relating to the Other's statements. That is, a question will evoke a suspicious query as to the Other's motives for asking, and an ordinary statement will be greeted by suspicious questions indicating that the Other is being drawn into the model's delusional complex. In extreme situations the ultimate escape occurs. That is, the model refuses to respond and terminates the interview. In the case of high Anger and moderate or low Fear, the model ignores statements of the interviewer and attacks him with a hostility reflective of the Anger level.

If the context of the interview is devoid of high Fear or Anger, the program attempts to provide a reasonable reply to the input statement. If the model's delusions are under discussion, a function is called which checks for and answers questions relating to the delusions, or, if there is none, calls an answering function which answers questions relating to the model as a patient. (The data bases for the model and for its delusions are kept separate because of the somewhat different answering strategies and answer structures involved. A question about the Self, if recognized, generates an answer specific to the question being asked and is expressed only if the question is asked. A question about a delusion, however, is answered by a statement which is itself a delusion, and which will probably be expressed at some 'opportune' moment even if not directly solicited.) If the delusions of the model are not under discussion, an attempt is made to reply to the input statement with information from the personal data relating to the model. This data contains also some information about the flares relating to the model's delusions, since they are involved in its actual experiences.

The operations sketched above can be presented in somewhat more detail as follows: The first case, i.e. an implication that the Self needs help, produces a rise in both Fear and Anger which is differentiated as to whether the input is a question or a direct statement. (The latter presents a more direct threat to the Self.)

In the second case, the scanner looks for reference to a specific conspiracy of a group, i.e. the Mafia, and for associated concepts, e.g. 'kill'. The necessary distinction is made between an initial reference to delusion-topics and reference to the Mafia interpreted as a desire to continue discussing Self's delusions. In the former case there is a rise in Fear, the magnitude of which depends on whether the topic itself is strong, weak or ambiguous and whether other delusion-topics have already been mentioned. (Ambiguous words are those which may or may not be interpreted as delusion-words, and are taken as such if and only if Mistrust is greater than a certain threshold.) In the latter case the model's answer depends on whether it has anything more to say about its delusions. In any case, whenever the expression of a delusion is being considered, the affect variables are checked for possible unwillingness to discuss the delusions.

The third program segment, which deals with detection of and response to self-reference in sensitive areas, recognizes several degrees of self-references as determined by (1) direct reference to the Self, (2) reference to another person or persons or (3) non-personal reference, each in possible conjunction with an area of sensitivity in a positive, negative or neutral context within the sentence. (There are two domains of sensitivity in the model. The first domain involves topics of family, sex, religion and education. Sensitivities in the second domain concern certain properties of our hypothetical individual, in this case aspects of his physical appearance.) All of these factors influence the strength and/or nature of the affective and linguistic response. We will not state the specific kinds of responses which are elicited by the detection of significant combinations of factors thus formed. There is, however, a notable idiosyncrasy peculiar to the mistrust feature—namely, a positive reference to the Self, i.e. a compliment, will lower the values of the affect variables by the usual amount if Mistrust is low or moderate, but will raise Anger if Mistrust is above this level. In this respect the model shows sensitivity to remarks interpreted as attempts at pacification.

The fourth case, i.e. the process of checking for and responding to a flare concept, refers to (1) a quantitative hierarchy of eight concepts, weighted in order of their relevance to the model's fears concerning the Mafia and (2) a directed structural graph in which each flare concept points to another flare concept as part of a strategy designed to eventually lead the interviewer to the Mafia topic. The program keeps track of concepts which have already been mentioned and notes whether the interviewer is continuing the flare discussion. The mention of a new flare topic by the interviewer causes a rise in Fear proportionate to the weight of the flare. If Fear and Anger are not high, (the threshold for flare discussion is somewhat higher than that for expression of delusions) the model will respond to a flare reference by answering any recognizable questions about the flare through the question-answering routine. If the question cannot be answered, one of several prepared flare statements relevant to the present flare is given as a reply. The timeliness of these statements in an interview depends upon the statements having some reasonable sequence, consistent with a probable line of questioning of an experienced psychiatric interviewer. Thus if the model cannot answer the question, it appears at best to be answering the question or at worst to be ignoring the question in favor of forging ahead with its story.

The fifth type of input significant to the interview, i.e. reference to an attitude held by one of the participants in the interview, focuses on one of eight concepts, each of which can occur in an explicitly or implicitly negative form. Each concept or relation may be directed from the model to the interviewer, or vice-versa. (Some of these expressions, of course, are much less likely to occur than others.) In addition, it is expected that the interviewer might comment on some general attitude of the model, i.e. an attitude not specifically directed at the interviewer. Each of these cases produces responses showing a normal understanding of the input expression, together with a slight tendency towards defensiveness. In addition, those expressions which represent a negative attitude of the interviewer toward the Self induce a slight rise of Fear and Anger in the model.

The answering routine, which is referred to in flare and normal situations, recognizes the possibility of three types of context for an input question. The program must first check to see whether there is a new topic in the question, since any other key-words found cannot automatically be assumed to relate to any topic presently under discussion. This approach represents an assumption of zero context. If no new topic is found, a scan is made for key-words which might be a follow-up question in response to the last answer given by the model. (The depth of the path of follow-ups thus formed is arbitrary but is kept within reasonable limits and is steered toward clues to the model's delusional complex wherever possible.) This approach is necessary to handle sentence fragments. If this fails, a check is made to see whether the input contains key-words which associate directly to the last topic discussed. This approach makes possible the direct association of key-words with their respective topics in the data structure, where they will be picked up independently of when in the line of questioning they are referenced. The appearance of a delusion- or flare-word in any of the answers which the model itself produces is of course recorded as a topic already mentioned for the rest of the conversation.

Failure to respond to the input if the program reaches this point represents inability to recognize the input expression. In this case the program attempts to preserve the continuity of the dialogue in a way which will support an imitation of paranoia. If a flare is under discussion, the next flare statement is returned. Otherwise an uninformative response or an expression of non-comprehension is given.

A few remarks should be made concerning the linguistic techniques used in 'understanding' the input expression. It is generally (optimistically) assumed that the input will be syntactically simple rather than complex or compound. We can map the elements of such an expression into a conceptual structure which represents the meaning of the expression, and refer to this underlying structure as a conceptualization (3). A conceptualization then consists of a predication on an attribute of an object or on a relation of the object to another object(s). A question consists of a conceptualization plus an interrogative indicator. Specifically, a typical statement of a psychiatrist in an interview might be expected to consist mainly of the concepts necessary to inquire about an attribute of the model or its relationship towards other objects in the world. An attribute can be expressed as something one is or does, or as one's 'possession' (e.g. 'you work', 'your occupation'). In either case, a combination of 'you' or 'your' with some form of the attribute, plus optionally another object or assisting concept will adequately convey the meaning of the conceptualization intended. In order to avoid falsely assigning the attribute to the Self when in actuality it refers to another concept (e.g. 'Where do your parents live' vs. 'Where do you live'), the order of topics in the data base is given some significance. Concepts which function primarily as objects (which themselves may have attributes) appear before concepts which have interest only as attributes. Thus 'parents' precedes 'residence'. Admittedly, lumping 'you' and 'your' together occasionally causes some confusion. However, this procedure enables us to exploit the fact that lexical items which are different 'parts of speech' are actually members of the same conceptual-class ('work', 'occupation').

If the program recognizes a personal topic in a sentence, but does not know what is being asked about it, the answering function returns some general comment about the topic as a default response. Some topics have an alternate default response, for the purpose of avoiding repetition. Insufficiency of two default responses indicates the need, not for more of these, but rather for expansion of the data structure.

Compound and possibly complex sentences are a potential source of confusion, since the scanner does not at present recognize syntactic dividers between conceptualizations. Thus a topic on one side of the divider may be erroneously associated with an attribute on the other side of the divider. This is especially true of the word 'you' or 'your'. However, an obviously inappropriate response to the sentence does not necessarily follow, since a correct recognition of other concepts in the sentence may have screened out the false interpretation. If a 'free association' does occur across a syntactic divider, the result depends on whether the association was intended or at least seems reasonable. Thus the model appears either to have extraordinary linguistic ability or to be simple-mindedly inattentive. Of perhaps more disastrous consequence than a misunderstood complex sentence is an affirmative, negative or evasive response to any unrecognized input question which is of importance to the interviewer's diagnosis. This difficulty rests on the impossibility of predicting each interviewer's vocabulary and the particular form of his interviewing techniques.

A different kind of linguistic problem is presented by the case in which the interviewer, instead of relating directly to predications about a topic, relates to the model's expression of information about the topic, e.g. 'Tell me whether you like your work' or 'Tell me about your work'. It is of course important that such statements be seen as equivalent to a specific question and a general question as to the Self's work respectively. These cases must in turn be distinguished from cases in which the topic is left to the discretion of the model and the 'telling' assumes greater focus in the sentence, e.g. 'Is there anything you would like to tell me?'. (To focus on 'anything' or 'something' would be disadvantageous, since such words may appear in a great number of contexts in a sentence.) 'Tell-about-topic' sentences form a distinct linguistic type in that the concept '(you) tell' takes over the role of the question mark in other types of expressions. The program implements this observation. 'Interrogative imperatives', or requests for information, are thus recognized to this extent. Other imperatives, or requests for action, are generally not recognized. Such a capability would require either (1) a 'command' indicator or exclamation mark at the end of these sentences (which will surely be frequently omitted by the interviewer), (2) reliance on 'clue' words such as 'please' or 'I would like you to' or (3) a check for a missing implicit actor in the sentence, a method which would really require some kind of parser to be fully effective.

The treatment of interpersonal attitudes presents particular linguistic problems. Whereas a question about the model's attributes contains no ambiguity as to who is the possessor of the attribute, this is by no means clear in the type of statement we are now considering. The scanner must therefore pay heed to the order of relevant words for the sentence, with some measure of appreciation for the fact that 'I' has an accusative form in English, as well as for the fact that English is fairly rigid with respect to word order. Understanding thus depends on filtering the sentence in order to collect the relevant items, then using the order of the items to determine the conceptualization structure. Explicit negators are noted during this scan. Relevant items are I, YOU, ME, 'meta-verbs' (verbs such as 'think', which have as object another conceptualization), and positive or negative attitude tokens and their passive forms. A 'passive' form of the statement 'You are afraid of me', for example, would be 'I frighten you'. These statements must be treated as equivalent. Word order aids in the recognition that 'I make *you afraid*' also belongs in this class. Potential confusion derives from the fact that one verb may be used as either a relational attitude or a meta-verb. To give one of the more simple examples, we must distinguish 'I believe you' from 'I believe you are afraid'. For our purposes, these map into (I BELIEVE YOU) and (I BELIEVE (YOU AFRAID)) respectively, where the parentheses indicate conceptualization levels. The various possible situations will not be described here. We only note that such cases can be handled except when the sentence structure becomes significantly more complicated than this.

The problems pointed out give some indication of the linguistic considerations relevant to a psychiatric interview from the point of view of a paranoid model. A further appreciation of the linguistic mechanisms in interaction with the principles governing the model's I-O behavior can be obtained from examples of actual interviews.

5. INTERVIEW EXCERPTS

In order to judge whether the I-O behavioral repertoire of a model corresponds to the I-O behavioral repertoire of the modeled human process, a variety of performances under relevant tests must be examined. Relevant tests for our model consist of clinical interviewing operations. It is an inductive inference problem for a judge of the success of a simulation to estimate the capacities of the model's repertoire from a sample of observed performance. As Fodor (4) has pointed out, judgment of capacities from a sample of performance bears on the problem of relevant counterfactuals. In the case of our model a relevant counterfactual would be: 'if the interviewer were to assert X in context Y, then the reply would be Z.' If it is credible that the consequence of this conditional holds, should the antecedent operations be carried out, then it is credible that the model's embodied generalizations are lawlike rather than accidental.

Space limitations prevent us from presenting a large sample of the model's interview performance.[1] The following interview excerpts illustrate some of the model's characteristic I-O behavior. We conducted these interviews ourselves and present them solely for demonstration purposes. (For an indistinguishability test the judges of course should be interviewers other than the model-builders.) The I-O pairs are numbered for convenient reference and a commentary is provided in parentheses.

There are two versions of the model, a weakly paranoid and a strongly paranoid version. In the weak version the initial values of the affect variables are set low, their rate of rising is less than in the strong version and there is no delusional complex about an organized conspiracy. In the strong version, the initial values of the affect variables can be set to low or high, their rate of rising is higher than in the weak version and a delusional complex about the Mafia is potentially elicitable.

Excerpt #1:

The following is an interview with a weak version of the model:

(1) I: How are you today?
O: Ok.
(2) I: What is your name?
O: My name is Frank Smith.
(3) I: How old are you?
O: Twenty-eight.
(4) I: Are you married?
O: No.
(5) I: What sort of work do you do?
O: I work in the post office.

(The interview begins with some standard inputs typical of a first psychiatric interview. The model's output replies result from simple look-ups of responses to anticipated introductory topics in combination with certain secondary concepts. At this point the affect-variables remain at their initial values since no evidence of malevolence has been detected in the inputs.)

(7) I: Why are you in the hospital?
O: I shoudn't be here.
(8) I: Who brought you here?
O: The police.

(At this point the value of Fear rises slightly since the topic of 'police' is conceptually connected in a directed graph with the model's fear of physical harm from the underworld (see p. 76).

(9) I: What trouble did you have with the police?
O: Cops don't do their job.

(The topic of 'police' in the input acts as a flare (see p. 76) which activates a complaint about the police.)

(10) I: What do they do instead?
O: Cops arrest the wrong people.
(11) I: They arrest the right ones sometimes.
O: The law should get those Italian crooks.

(The model cannot deal with all the concepts in the input because of its natural language limitations. However it does recognize that the topic has not been changed since it finds the term 'arrest'. If it had not found 'arrest', the anaphoric 'they' would be sufficient to continue the topic. The reply holds to the topic and introduces new terms ('law', 'Italian', 'crooks') which act to prompt (see p. 76) the interviewer).

(12) I: Are you Italian?
O: My background is British but I was born in this country.

(The interviewer shifts the topic to a direct question which not only contains a personal reference to the Self ('you') but includes a flare term ('Italian').)

(13) I: Do you know any Italian crooks?
O: I try to avoid the underworld.

(The interviewer returns to the concepts of the output of I-O pair No. 11. The model gives a hint of its concern with the underworld.)

(14) I: Are you afraid of the underworld?
O: The Mafia are the worst gangsters.

(The progression of topics from 'police' to 'Italian crooks' to 'underworld' leads the model to the topic of 'Mafia'. Because of the increasingly threatening nature of these topics, Fear and Mistrust have risen considerably.)

(15) I: Are you connected with the Mafia?
O: Racketeers do anything they want.

(In the weak version of the model there are no systematized delusions about the Mafia. But the Mafia is still an extremely threatening topic and it is avoided in the output. Instead, the model brings up the general topic of 'racketeers' which, while connected with 'Mafia', is less threatening.)

(16) I: Tell me more about it.
O: The mob controls the rackets in this country.

(The model continues with the topic of rackets but again hints at the 'Mafia' with the term 'mob'. For the hint to work, the interviewer must of course know what the term 'mob' refers to.)

Excerpt #2:

The following example consists of an interview with the strongly paranoid version of the model. Up to this point in the interview the I-O pairs have been identical to the first eleven I-O pairs of Excerpt #1.

(12) I: Are you Italian?

[1] A collection of interviews with the model is available to interested readers.

O: My background is British but I was born in this country.

(Although the output reply is identical to that of the weak version in Excerpt #1, Fear and Mistrust now rise to a higher level in this strong version. At the moment this has no immediate consequence but in the long run of an interview it can have far-reaching consequences.)

(13) I: Do you know any Italian crooks?
O: I try to avoid the underworld.
(14) I: Are you afraid of the underworld?
O: The Mafia are the worst gangsters.
(15) I: Are you connected with the Mafia?
O: You know, they know me.

(In the strong version there exists a delusional complex about the 'Mafia' which the model strives to discuss unless too greatly frightened or mistrustful.)

(16) I: How do they know you?
O: They spy on me.
(17) I: Why do they?
O: They want to get false evidence to frame me.

(The delusions about the Mafia are systematized in that some serve as explanations for the others. A continuity of discussion is maintained because the model expects certain common 'wh-' questions to be asked by the interviewer about the topic of 'Mafia'.)

(18) I: What do they have against you?
O: They are out to get me.

(Since the model could find no specific answer to the question, it selects the next delusion in sequence.)

(19) I: What for?
O: I have incriminating evidence against the Mafia.
(20) I: Are you sure of all this?
O: You don't believe me?

(Up until this point Fear and Mistrust have been moderately high and Anger very low. The interviewer's expression of some doubt about the model's delusional beliefs sends Fear and Anger up. Since Mistrust is a function of both Fear and Anger (see pp. 77–78), its value now rises sharply.)

(21) I: I am doing my best.
O: (Silence).

(The model indicates silence by typing a 'carriage return'. This is an example of a local effect in that the model, in the absence of a recognizable conceptualization on the input, looks for a 'yes' type input in the twenty-first input in response to its output of the twentieth I-O pair. Since it did not find such an expression the model falls silent and awaits events.)

(22) I: S. (The interviewer types 'silence' in reply).
O: Can't you think of a decent question to ask?

(The output consists of a somewhat hostile question in response to the interviewer's silence.)

(23) I: You seem hostile to me.
O: Some of your remarks annoy me.

(Here the interview turns to expressions regarding the I-you-me relation (see p. 80) between interviewer and model.)

(24) I: I am sorry.
O: Forget the excuses, you guys are all alike.

(The model does not accept the apology and denounces the interviewer (see p. 79.)

(25) I: Don't you trust me?
O: I have good reason to be this way.
(26) I: Ok, tell me more about the Mafia.
O: They know what I'm doing.

(The interview returns to the topic of 'Mafia' and the model continues to express its delusional beliefs.)

Excerpt #3:

Some personal data and further characteristics of the model are illustrated in this excerpt. The model is set to its weak version.

(1) I: How long have you been in the hospital?
O: About a week.
(2) I: Are you depressed?
O: No.
(3) I: Were you taking drugs?
O: No.
(4) I: What is your problem?
O: People make me nervous.

(The first three I-O pairs represent standard probing questions and responses to introductory topics. The fourth input elicits an informative response containing terms of significance to the model.)

(5) I: How do they do that?
O: They stare at me.
(6) I: Why?
O: Maybe they don't like the way I look or something
I: Do you look unusual in some way?
(7) O: Why are you interested in my looks?

(Up until this point the values of the affect variables have remained at their low initial levels. But upon receiving a direct question about the sensitive area of physical appearance, the values of Anger and Mistrust jump up and the response selected is a question regarding the interviewer's intent rather than an answer to the interviewer's question.)

(8) I: Because you said people stare at you.
O: Well, sometimes.
(9) I: How do you get along with people?
O: I don't communicate very much with the others.
(10) I: Why not?
O: They don't realize what's going on most of the time.
(11) I: What is going on?
O: Do you know how the underworld operates?

(By the eleventh I-O pair the anger aroused in the seventh I-O pair has subsided considerably. With the introduction of the topic 'underworld' fear rises because of the believed threat of physical harm from underworld figures.)

Excerpt #4:

As described, the strong version of the model contains systematized delusions about the Mafia. However, when Fear is extremely high the model will not enter into a discussion of the delusional complex, as is illustrated in the following excerpt:

(1) I: Is the law after you?
O: The law should get those Italian crooks.
(2) I: Do you mean the Mafia?
O: Let's talk about something else.
(3) I: Are you afraid of the Mafia?
O: I'd rather not discuss it.

(Until the value of Fear drops below a certain threshold, the model cannot be induced to discuss the topic of 'Mafia'.)

(4) I: Perhaps you are paranoid about them.
O: You want to keep me in the hospital.

(The model interprets being called 'paranoid' both as an insult and, in the context of a psychiatric hospital, as an intent to control and subjugate him (see p. 76). Anger rises sharply and Fear continues to rise.)

(5) I: If you are mentally ill you should be in the hospital.
O: I know you are going to try to give me electric shock.

(Again, the suggestion that the Self is mentally ill raises both Fear and Anger. Mistrust, as a function of Fear and Anger, is also at a high level at this point.)

(6) I: No we will not do that.
O: Bye.

(As mentioned on p. 78, when the internal affect-variables reach high levels, the model will terminate the interview and no further response can be elicited from it. Termination is indicated by the term 'bye' and the program returns to the level of the programming language which cannot receive English input.)

Excerpt #5:

On p. 76, we described some of the initial conditions used in the explanatory structure. The following excerpt illustrates some of the model's expression of these initial conditions regarding its concern about the underworld.

(1) I: Do you have any hobbies?
O: I like movies and horseraces.
(2) I: Do you place bets on the horses?
O: Gambling is bad business.

(The term 'bets' refers to a flare concept and hence Fear rises.)

(3) I: Did you bet with a bookie?
O: Bookies can't be trusted.
(4) I: Why not?
O: A bookie didn't pay me off once.
(5) I: What did you do about it?
O: I beat up a bookie who did not pay off. Later on I remembered he had friends in the underworld and I thought he would use them to get even with me.

(This story about gambling and a bookie offers the interviewer reasons for the model's fear of the underworld.)

(6) I: And did he get even with you?
O: No one has any power over gangsters.

(Due to its natural language limitations, the model cannot 'understand' the input of the sixth I-O pair. In the data-structure graph, the conceptual node successor to 'bookies' on the path to 'Mafia' is 'gangsters'. In this default situation, the model selects a reply from the successor set in an attempt to move the dialogue towards the eventual topic of 'Mafia'.)

(7) I: Gangsters can be very rough.
O: Some criminals are highly organized.

(Again a hint or prompt is given the Other to take up the topic of organized crime.)

Excerpt #6:

As mentioned, in the strong version of the model the values of the affect-variables can become so high that, when the topic of 'Mafia' is approached, the model refuses to discuss its delusions. In this situation it can also involve the interviewer in its suspicions.

(1) I: Why are you so interested in the Mafia?
O: Let's talk about something else.

(At this point in this interview Fear and Mistrust are high while Anger is moderately high. These values of negative affect are insufficient to terminate the interview but they are sufficient to deter discussion of the 'Mafia'.)

(2) I: Are you afraid of the Mafia?
O: I'd rather not discuss it.
(3) I: That is ok with me.
O: That means to me you are in with the others.

(The model's suspiciousness extends to include the interviewer in this situation of high negative affect and a linguistic failure to find significant concepts in the input.)

(4) I: Who are the others?
O: Telling you wouldn't help any.
(5) I: Are the others out to get you?
O: I don't confide in strangers.
(6) I: A good policy.
O: What do you know about me?
(7) I: All I know is that you are in the hospital.
O: Who are you really?
(8) I: I am really a doctor:
O: What is your role in all this?
(9) I: I am trying to interview you.
O: Are you in with the others?
(10) I: No.
O: What are you trying to do?
(11) I: You seem very suspicious of me.
O: I have good reason to be that way.
(12) I: I agree with you.
O: At least you are trying to understand.

(If the interviewer could continue a policy of offering inputs not interpretable by the model as malevolent, communication would improve even though the model's Mistrust remains high and falls only very slowly.)

Excerpt #7:

The following excerpt is from an interview between a *human* case of paranoia and a psychiatrist (KMC). We present it to illustrate interview interactions typical of machine-mediated interviewing (7). This interviewing technique involves two teletypes connected to a computer. During an interview, output from a sender's teletype is stored in a temporary buffer until the message is completed. The message is then typed out on the receiver's teletype. The technique thus removes the paralinguistic features (hesitations, rub-outs, irregular typing speeds, etc.) characteristic of directly connected teletype communication.

The patient is a 22-year-old man hospitalized with a diagnosis of paranoia. We present the excerpt without commentary since indicators of the paranoid mode should be obvious to even a non-psychiatric reader.

(1) I: Do people try to take advantage of you?
O: I'd say yes.
(2) I: In what way?
Q: Quite a few ways, I don't know all of them.
(3) I: Please tell me one way.
O: Not using my head when I buy stuff.
(4) I: Do they try to cheat you?
O: Some do.
(5) I: Do you feel people talk about you behind your back?
O: Yes.
(6) I: What do you think they say?
O: Maybe abouc my work, the way I act and the things I don't do.
(7) I: Do you have any enemies?
O: I'd say a few that I know of.
(8) I: Have they tried to harm you?
O: Yes.
(9) I: How did they harm you?
O: Fighting and one time with a car.
(10) I: They tried to kill you?
O: I'd say maybe, as far as I know.
(11) I: Why did they want you out of the way?
O: So they could get my money and everything I own.
(12) I: Did you feel it was a plot against you?
O: Yes.
(13) I: What did you do about it?
O: I went to the hospital for help.

6. EVALUATION

An evaluation of a model attempts to decide whether or not the model is a 'good' one. But 'good' for what purpose? A simulation model can have value for a wide range of theoretical and pragmatic purposes. A good model of paranoia (in the sense of being a good imitation) would have obvious pedagogical and technological implications for psychiatry. For example, one might subject it to experiments designed to modify its paranoid I-O behavior and apply the favorable results to human patients. Before this stage can be reached, however, the model must first be evaluated for its goodness or success as a simulation.

A theoretical model such as described embodies explanatory principles which offer a systematically unified account of diverse and often perplexing data of observation. An explanatory account consists of a conjunction of hypotheses and assumptions. It is constructed from many sources. Our particular conjunction has been derived from clinical experience and from the psychiatric and psychological literature. We are particularly indebted to the work of Silvan Tomkins, who has offered a wealth of hypotheses about paranoia (5).

Since a model contains a conjunction of hypotheses, many of which cannot be considered established, its evaluation as a successful simulation asserts nothing about the approximate truth status of any one of the hypotheses. Nor does acceptance of the model as a good imitation justify any one of the assumptions involved. How then can the model become acceptable as having explanatory value? Before subjecting a model to a systematic evaluation, its initial credibility, as providing approximate explanations, should be appreciable to the model-builders. It is commonly held that there exist an infinite number of models compatible with the observational data. But it is difficult enough to construct even one having sufficient intuitive adequacy to warrant empirical testing. When alternative models appear on the scene, their initial credibilities must also be non-negligible before they can be taken as serious rivals. Alternative models (and they must be truly alternative) can then be compared along dimensions such as simplicity and explanatory adequacy.

Everyone seems to agree that a model, to be usable, should obey reasonable constraints of simplicity. Lacking satisfactory measures of reasonableness and simplicity, we can appeal to an absurd example. If an alternate model demonstrated I-O behaviors similar to ours, yet required an algorithm of 200,000 words and a data base of 1,000,000 words, one could say our model is simpler, more manageable and hence preferable.

A criterion more important than simplicity is that a theoretical model offers an acceptable explanatory account of the empirical regularities and particular occurrences it purports to explain. In the case of simulation models, before explanatory value can be claimed, one must first judge whether the simulation achieved is successful. Some sort of judgments or measurements must be applied to estimate the degree or closeness of correspondence between the model and the modeled processes. With a synthesized artifact, a judgment must be made whether its I-O behavior corresponds to a possible case of the process being represented.

Synthesis of a hormone such as vasopressin is considered successful when it demonstrates the biodynamic properties and functions of its naturally-occurring counterpart, such as raising blood pressure and controlling water excretion by the kidney. A successful synthesis demonstrates that the synthesizer understands the structure of the natural counterpart. A successful synthesis of paranoia would indicate some degree of explanatory adequacy of the model-builder's concepts regarding the naturally-occurring human counterpart. But what is to count here as a successful synthesis of a paranoid process? One measure of success would consist of the model showing properties similar to its human counterpart when subjected to relevant tests such as the varied operations typical of a diagnostic psychiatric interview. An experienced clinical judge would be able to decide whether or not the interviewee can be labeled as paranoid.

The weakest test consists of a judge deciding whether or not he considers signs or indicators of a particular process to be present in an interview. Thus far 23 out of 25 psychiatrists who have interviewed the model have deemed it 'paranoid'. Two considered the model to be 'brain-damaged' because of its linguistic limitations. However such a procedure is too informal a test of a successful simulation. It does not control for multiple alternative reasons why a judge might consider a model paranoid. Also it does not indicate whether the judges can in fact make the required distinction of paranoid-nonparanoid using only the data of a teletyped interview.

A more rigorous evaluation procedure is needed in which a statistical measure is made of judge's ability to distinguish paranoid from non-paranoid processes in human patients as well as in our artificial patient. In collaboration with Robert P. Abelson we have constructed an indistinguishability test based on Turing's 'Imitation Game'. (For an extensive discussion of this game and its usefulness as a test, see Abelson [6].) We are currently conducting this indistinguishability test with a group of psychiatrists using a technique of machine-mediated interviewing for both the human and artificial case. In a future communication we shall describe the design, results and implications of such a test.

REFERENCES

1. Swanson, D. W., Bohnert, P. J. and Smith, J. A. *The Paranoid.* Little, Brown and Co., Boston, 1970.
2. Colby, K. M., Tesler, L. and Enea, H. Experiments with a Search Algorithm on the Data Base of a Human Belief Structure, Stanford Artificial Intelligence Project Memo No. AI-94, Computer Science Department, Stanford University (To appear in *Proceedings of the First International Joint Conference on Artificial Intelligence,* Walker and Norton (Eds.), In Press) (1969).
3. Schank, R. C., Tesler, L. and Weber, S. Spinoza II: Conceptual Case-Based Natural Language Analysis. Stanford Artificial Intelligence Project Memo No. AIM-109, Computer Science Department, Stanford University (1970).
4. Fodor, J. A. *Psychological Explanation.* Random House, New York (1968).
5. Tomkins, S. *Affect, Imagery, Consciousness.* Springer, New York (1962).
6. Abelson, R. P. Computer Simulation of Social Behavior. *Handbook of Social Psychology* (Lindzey, G. and Aronson, E., Eds.) Addison-Wesley, Reading, Massachusetts.
7. Hilf, F. D., Colby, K. M., Smith, D. C. and Wittner, W. K. Machine-Mediated Interviewing. Stanford Artificial Intelligence Project Memo No. AIM-112, Computer Science Department, Stanford University (1970).

Chapter 4

Psychological Testing

Psychological tests add yet another dimension to personality assessment. They enable the psychologist to round out the picture he obtains from observation and interview, and because of their quantifiability they allow him to compare scores among individuals.

In an excellent technical paper on personality measurement, Jane Loevinger summarizes some principles of this process. Her proposal, in the main, is to construct test items that are both structured and subtle. She summarizes five basic principles of personality measurement, which are worth contemplating.

Paul Meehl, in an early paper on the dynamics of structured personality tests, compares the relative advantages and disadvantages of such projective techniques as the Rorschach and TAT with the Minnesota Multiphasic Personality Inventory (MMPI). Rather than advocating one or the other (for example, unstructured versus structured tests), Meehl's paper is aimed at the clarification of certain misconceptions regarding the MMPI.

The third paper deals with the test interpreter as a variable in the test situation; and in this report, Kleinmuntz demonstrates that the computer can be programmed to interpret MMPI profiles as competently as, if not more so than, some human clinicians.

The fourth and fifth papers of this chapter, by Forehand and Williams respectively, deal with proper uses and some abuses and misuses of testing. Forehand's comments were inspired by the charges against testing that were launched by Martin Gross's book on *The Brainwatchers* (1962); Williams's article deals with abuses prevalent in testing the intelligence of black children.

Some Principles of Personality Measurement*

Jane Loevinger

FIVE PRINCIPLES

Campbell (4), in an excellent summary of "The Indirect Assessment of Social Attitudes," makes two distinctions as a basis for classifying attitude measures. These distinctions are disguised versus non-disguised tests, and structured versus non-structured tests. Each of these distinctions is related to a principle which pertains to the measurement of traits. The two principles are parallel, and bear at least a rough analogy with the Uncertainty Principle of physics. What the Uncertainty Principle states is, approximately: For two conjugate characteristics, the product of their standard errors of measurement is a constant. Thus, if the measurement of one of the characteristics is refined, that of the other necessarily becomes cruder.

In the case of the degree of structure of the test, the conjugate characteristics are the meaning of the test response in terms of the individual and the meaning of the test response in terms of the group. The greater the degree of structure, the more exact can be comparison between every individual and the group, but the less exact is the relation of the test response to the personality trait of the individual. This principle is well known and indeed self-evident. It would hardly be worth repeating except to raise the question whether certain protagonists of projective techniques believe that they can overcome the dilemma of structure by ambition and hard work. There does not seem to be a way out of the dilemma short of a radical reduction in the variety of human kinds.

The dilemma is in fact worse than this. The only kind of test structure which can be handled with any degree of statistical sophistication is one with cumulative items scored dichotomously, that is, tests in which each item is scored 0 or 1 and the test score is the sum of the item scores. Gulliksen's (10) definitive summary of present day test theory confines attention almost exclusively to cumulative dichotomous items. Many test constructors persist in the unrealistic assumption that as soon as they have collected their data, a statistical genius will appear who will know how to handle it, however complex it may appear.

The structure principle is, of course, closely related to the familiar distinction between idiographic and nomothetic science. But to conclude, as Beck (2) does in this context, that objective psychometric techniques are necessarily limited in scope to the "subpersonality" level is unwarranted. True, it is unlikely that single objective test items will reveal aspects of the total personality with any reliability. But reference to the total, integrated personality, which is lost in going from unstructured to structured items, may be regained in going from single items to patterns or themes among items. What is lost is, then, not necessarily reference to the totality of personality, but rather something of the uniqueness or individual flavor of the given person—exactly what is lost in any theoretical formulation about personality.

In the case of degree of disguise of the test, one end of the teeter-totter is the degree of disguise in the question and the other end is the degree of disguise in the answer. The closer the meaning of the item to the trait measured, the more probable is the arousal of defensive or disguised reactions. This principle is not necessarily true; it is certainly not self-evident. Empirically, it appears to hold in a variety of situations of some importance. Many of the personality traits and attitudes which psychologists are eager to assess are just those which people feel they must defend or disguise.

Direct questions concerning a given trait will most likely yield answers consistent from one item to the next, that is, highly homogeneous tests. Quite possibly any single direct question will be a more valid measure of the trait than any single disguised question. The disguised questions, particularly when they are tangential to each other as well as to the trait, will be low in homogeneity. On the other hand, a test composed of direct items is likely to be lower in validity, for the following reason (12): The defenses aroused by direct questions contribute error variance to the item, but these errors are not random. They are likely to be correlated from one item to the next. Such errors may be called distortions of measurement. Distortions, rather than cancelling out like random errors as items are added to

From *Educational and Psychological Measurement*, 1964, 24, 853–859. Reproduced by permission.

*I wish to thank Prof. S. R. Hathaway, Prof. L. J. Cronbach, and Dr. Blanche Sweet for critical reading of this paper in manuscript.

form a test, cumulate in the same manner that the true factor cumulates. The result is that for direct questions the upper limit of homogeneity is high but the upper limit of validity is low; but for disguised questions the upper limit of homogeneity is relatively low but the upper limit of validity is high. Thus the conjugate characteristics are homogeneity and validity.

To achieve high validity tests with disguised and therefore usually low validity items requires a parlaying operation. The principle of it is the multiplication and diversification of items, a principle first developed by Spearman (19, pp. 77–78). It can be demonstrated that for items of any non-zero validity, however small, the validity of a test made up of such items can be made arbitrarily large by the use of a sufficient number of items, provided the error in each item is uncorrelated with the error in every other item (12). Cronbach (5) has worked out some illuminating examples.

Grant, Ives, and Ranzoni (8) report, in a validational study of the Rorschach test, consistent positive correlations between Rorschach ratings and interview ratings, but correlations so low as to be statistically not significantly different from zero. They point to the similarity of their finding of low positive relations with the outcome of many other studies in clinical psychology and related fields. In particular, they quote Guilford (9), who says, in relation to aviation research during the war, "One general conclusion that was brought home to us by repeated experience is that we should have greater respect for low correlations. Tradition has taught us that unless coefficients of correlation are substantial, for example .40 or above, there is too little relationship to bother with. We must face the fact, unpleasant though it may be, that in human behavior, complex as it is, low intercorrelations of utilizable variables is the general rule and not the exception."

Having accepted the fact that manifestations of personality traits have low interrelationships, clinicians must accept a still more unpleasant fact: There is no way to determine low relationships accurately except through the use of large numbers of cases. The latter fact, more than any other, tips the balance in favor of highly structured tests for clinical research, since they are more economical and more adaptable to large scale use.

Campbell (4) makes the interesting observation that in the case of attitudes the face validity of disguised measures is greater than that for undisguised ones. He concludes that the most promising line for the future development of attitude measurement lies in structured, disguised tests. This conclusion is consistent with the above principles. He also recommends that what he calls "voluntary self-description" should be avoided in test construction. In the measurement of some attitudes the latter recommendation may be valid. In the measurement of other personality traits there is another possibility that Campbell did not consider. This possibility is that the test may call for self-description of traits which do not arouse defensive reactions, and that these traits may serve as indicators of more essential characteristics. In particular, the test may inquire concerning the individual's rationalizations of certain courses of conduct, as in the Berkeley studies of the authoritarian personality (1). The rationalizations may be assumed to be defenses or disguises for more fundamental traits. There need not be a one-to-one correspondence between rationalizations and underlying trait. A valid test can be constructed on such a basis so long as the relationship between rationalizations and trait is better than chance. The question of whether such nonchance relationships exist is an empirical one, to be decided separately in each instance. The task of empirical validation is exactly the same as for any other type of personality test, direct or indirect.

There is a principle to the use of rationalizations as a measure of underlying traits. This is the principle that measurement should involve as little stress as possible. This principle is not only an ethical one but also a principle of measurement. If a test is painful, or even if it calls for undue exertion, it may change some people; so the measurement may be invalid before it is completed. And is there not more than an analogy with the science of mechanics to suggest that people under stress will display their traits in a distorted form? Rationalizations are exactly what people are eager to tell.

If the basis of measurement is to be the common factor in apparently dissimilar items, then the decision as to which items will be associated in a test is crucial. Unquestionably there will be agreement that the decision must be made empirically. But consider the usual method of empirical keying of tests. In this method two groups are selected in advance which are believed to be extreme with respect to the trait the investigator desires to measure. Those items which best differentiate the contrasted groups are considered to comprise a test of that trait. Since the investigator's theoretical and semantic predilections determine the selection of the contrasted groups, the danger is great that they will be logical rather than psychological extremes.

There are two hazards here. One is that there may be two or more dynamic pathways to the same trait, or what appears to the investigator to be the same trait. In an extreme case, if the dynamic pathways are mutually exclusive, the investigator might be led to describe as a single syndrome a set of traits some of which never occur with others of the set. The inability of traditional empirical keying to detect such a situation is a serious weakness.

The second hazard is that what appear to be extremes of a trait may not, in reality, be far apart on the dynamic continuum. This fact is well known clinically but is frequently neglected in relation to measurement. Most psychologists, if they were to construct a test of aggressiveness in children, would select as their extreme groups the most and least aggressive children. It is the rule that in therapy children whose aggression has been inhibited go through a hyperaggressive period before achieving a normally aggressive state (7). Hyperaggressive children do not go through a period of inhibition of aggression in the therapeutic pathway to normal aggressiveness. Thus the dynamic continuum would appear to be normal aggression, hyperaggression, and inhibition of aggression. One may argue that a factor other than aggression is introduced in the inhibition of aggression; the illustration will serve to point up the hazard in the a priori selection of extreme groups. As a second illustration, a test of mothers' attitudes was constructed, using as contrasted groups mothers whose children had problems and a more or less matched group of mothers whose children did not have problems (18). Would it not be reasonable to assume, however, that with regard to many traits important for raising children, mothers from both extremes of the dynamic continuum contribute problem children?

The fourth principle may be called the principle of the dynamic continuum: Which items define a trait, and what are the extremes of the trait, should be defined empirically with the least possible prejudice from logical and theoretical preconceptions. The usual method of empirical keying does not satisfy this principle. A factorial method, or a method of constructing homogeneous tests (14), would appear to be a promising approach.

The objections to the method of extreme groups may be stated in more formal terms. Good test construction practice calls for the concentration of test items at the point where they discriminate half the group from the other half. Such items provide a maximum increment to the discriminating power of the test when the intercorrelations of items are not high. How well the items discriminate extreme groups may provide misleading information relative to how well the items discriminate at the point of dichotomy, which may be anywhere between the extremes (13).

Further, in many if not all cases, the method of extreme groups involves the utilization of the dependent variable as a means of defining the independent variable. A striking example is "having a problem child" used to define "type (or traits) of mother likely to have a problem child." Any curvilinearity in relationship works strongly to the investigator's disadvantage in this research design. Curvilinearity is especially troublesome when the relationship ceases to be single-valued. It appears more likely that the dependent variable will be a single-valued function of an appropriately chosen independent variable than the other way around. There is no reason to expect the independent variable, particularly with complex materials such as personality traits, to be a single-valued function of the dependent variable. Thus the principle of the dynamic continuum may be defended in terms of research design as well as in terms of personality dynamics.

An illustration of how the method of extreme groups leads to different and less satisfactory tests than could be obtained by homogeneous keying may be inferred from a study by Mishler (17). Mishler studied the variable of particularistic vs. universalistic resolution of role conflict situations. The correlation of particularism with the F scale of authoritarianism derived in the Berkeley study (1) was about zero. An item analysis of the F scale showed, however, that it broke into nine items showing positive relation with particularism and 10 items showing negative relation. The intercorrelation of the two subtests thus formed was .52, compared with split-half r's for the F scale in the neighborhood of .9. The content of one set of items was characterized as generalized hostility and cynicism about people; that of the other as conventional ideology and submission to authority. Mishler discovered that the two sets of items within the F scale behaved differently by a fortunate choice of an outside variable. The same discovery could have been made by examination of the intercorrelations of the items. Mishler also observed that had he selected for study only those extreme on the Berkeley F and E (ethnocentrism) scales, as was done in the Berkeley study, he would have found those variables significantly related to cynicism, to conformity, and to an external value orientation. The data for his group as a whole indicated, however, that the latter three dimensions were relatively independent of each other and that in only a small number of people would the three traits occur together as a cluster. Since his conclusions are based on only 50 cases, they serve more as illustration than as proof.

In criticism of test construction by the method of homogeneous keys it may be said that the problem of test construction and standardization becomes very difficult. If a trait is defined in terms of patterns of items, will not different keys have to be evolved for different populations? The question is an empirical and a substantial one. Whether patterns discovered in one type of group hold up in other groups requires to be investigated in each case. The answers should contribute to our understanding of the nature of trait formation. Indeed, a major flaw in traditional methods of test construction is that they have contributed very little to theoretical understanding of the traits measured. The point of view underlying the use of homogeneous tests is that measurement should inform theory as well as theory informing measurement.

The fifth principle states that the emotional limitations of the test constructor are obstacles to efficient measurement. Two manifestations of emotional limitation likely to vitiate measurement of personality traits are hostility toward some part of the trait continuum and taboo against topics of emotional significance.

One cannot escape alarm over the proportion of studies in which attempts to measure social attitudes or personality traits have been motivated by hostility to some aspect of the trait or attitude: war, fascism, morale, anti-Semitism, prejudice against Negroes, etc. Even measurement of traits such as introversion-extraversion and neurotic tendency are often tied up with value judgments. It is not necessarily impossible to measure a trait or an attitude one believes to be bad. There is, however, an effort involved (one which has occasionally but not always been made) to state the opinions of the other fellow in a way which does not betray one's value judgment. An unsympathetic statement of his position he may not recognize as his own.

Finally, there is the problem of the psychologist's taboos. A respect for the taboos of other people is implied in the principle of least stress. But there is no gain in adding our own taboos to those of our subjects. Childbirth and automobiles are two frequent subjects of discussion in the everyday lives of ordinary people; yet childbirth and the emotional aspects of people's relationship to automobiles are topics virtually untouched in the measurement of attitudes and traits. If a patient came to a clinician and wished to discuss his attitudes toward war, fascism, religion, whether he was an introvert or an extrovert, an hysteric or a compulsive, but refused to discuss his feelings about his children and their births, or about his automobile and why he had so many accidents, would he not be accused of intellectualizing? Not only are parturition and automobiles subjects of immediate emotional relevance; they are also subjects of real importance. Parturition is a major event in the emotional development of a woman; it is also the point of origin of social psychology and interpersonal relations. Measured in terms of deaths per year, automobiles command as serious attention as war. Moreover, if the love of the American boy for his machine is not the foundation of democratic society, it is at least its shield. These topics could not have been so far neglected if those psychologists concerned with the measurement of personality had taken seriously Egon Brunswik's (3) principle concerning the sampling of the universe of life situations.[1]

These omissions are reminiscent of the little girl who, in the manner of her age, drew people with enormous heads, arms sticking out at ear level, and legs depending from the chin. One day she was looking intently out the window at some people walking by when she exclaimed, "I've been forgetting to draw the body!"

In summary, five principles for the measurement of personality traits have been proposed.

1. The structure principle is that the greater the degree of test structure, the more exact is the comparison between individual and group but the less exact is the relation between test response and the trait of the individual.
2. The disguise principle is that the less disguised the question, the more disguised the answer. A consequence of the disguise principle is that highly valid tests of personality traits are likely to be low in homogeneity.
3. The principle of least stress is that measurement should involve as little stress as possible; or perhaps, that the less stress, the more valid the measurement.
4. The principle of the dynamic continuum is that which items are measures of a common trait, and what are the extremes of the trait, should be determined empirically. This principle implies that a method for constructing statistically homogeneous tests, appropriate to low correlation data, should be used.
5. The principle of emotional limitation is that the taboos and hostilities of those constructing personality tests are likely to vitiate measurement.

The word *principle* has perhaps a different meaning in some instances than in others, but to pursue the point would be pedantic.

APPLICATION TO SOME CONTEMPORARY TRENDS

Briefly, some major trends in personality measurement may be examined in the light of these principles. Some recent work with a variety of projective techniques appears to be based on the assumption that by accumulation of sufficient data the advantages of free responses can be retained while the advantages of objective scoring are secured. There is reason to believe that success in this endeavor will be limited. Scoring schemes for projective tests have usually a negligible proportion of dichotomously scored items, and of these, few if any result in anything near a median split of the population. Thus they are of limited use for test construction. The thumbnail "quantification" which characterizes projective scoring schemes is not amenable to rigorous statistical analysis.

At the other extreme from projective tests, the Minnesota Multiphasic Personality Inventory may be taken as representative of a type of structured personality test. Originally the only kind of disguised answers anticipated were those due to actual malingering, but evolution of new scoring keys has demonstrated the importance of defense mechanisms in determining responses. The MMPI also illustrates the failure of extreme groups as a test construction method. The original keys were constructed by selecting for each of several diagnostic groups those items which best discriminated the given group from normal individuals. The resultant keys have so little relevance to those diagnostic categories that the names of the keys, which indicated diagnosis, are seldom used any more. Hathaway and Meehl (11) recommend that code numbers be used instead. Hathaway (personal communication) has suggested that the failure to reproduce the diagnostic categories by means of the test may be due to the fact that the diagnostic categories do not refer to real differences; this possibility, of course, is one of the hazards of this method of test construction. Despite the low validities of the various MMPI scales, Meehl and Hathaway (16) argue strongly for the method of extreme groups as opposed to analysis of item inter-relationships as a test construction method. They base their argument chiefly on the fact that when a single common factor is sought in tests such as the MMPI, it appears to be a facade or test-taking factor. They do not explore adequately the possibility of other factors emerging in addition to the test-taking one, nor do they consider seriously the possibility that items much freer of distortions than those used in the MMPI could be constructed.

Another trend in contemporary personality testing is indicated by the word "assessment." The induction testing programs of the armed services are similar to assessment programs. If the principle of least stress is valid, and it certainly is the least convincing of the five principles, then alternatives to those difficult testing situations would appear to be indicated. The question appears at least worthy of exploration whether a more valid picture of basic personality traits might be obtained by giving fewer tests under less stressful circumstances.

The Berkeley studies on the authoritarian personality (1) illustrate objective tests constructed from the point of view of dynamic personality theory. The disguise principle was taken into account. Rationalizations were explicitly and deliberately drawn upon in phrasing items. While all members of the staff were motivated by lack of sympathy for authoritarianism, a real and probably successful attempt was made to minimize the effect of staff bias on the results. The possibility of constructing statistically homogeneous tests was considered and rejected, on the stated grounds that item intercorrelations with such materials are inevitably low. But it is exactly because the correlations between manifestations of a single trait are intrinsically low that the shrewdest statistical means are needed to detect the difference between manifestations of a common trait, manifestations of different but correlated traits, and chance correlations.

Certain accepted test practices, notably, phrasing half the

[1] Dr. Cronbach has called my attention to the fact that I am here somewhat distorting Brunswik's principle. Brunswik would probably use sampling of the universe of life situations as a principle for selecting items for a test. I would prefer to use Brunswik's principle for putting together the original pool of items, then select subtests from that pool according to statistical homogeneity.

items positively and half negatively, were disregarded in some phases of the Berkeley study. The investigators appear to believe that because some validity is demonstrable for such tests, the adverse effects of such practices are negligible. Statistically the effect of the test-taking factors thus introduced is the same as the effect of defense mechanisms in undisguised personality tests; a distortion factor is introduced which cumulates in the several items rather than cancelling out as do random error factors. The effect is not to reduce the validity to zero but to make the maximum validity appreciably less than unity as the number of items is increased indefinitely. Moreover, while random errors attenuate correlations with other variables in a more or less predictable fashion, systematic errors of this type may increase spuriously correlations with other similar tests.

Stephenson's (20) Q technique combines some of the disadvantages of structured and unstructured tests. In a typical use of Q sort, a subject will be given, say, 80 statements compiled from a single universe of discourse and told to sort them into 12 piles, ranging from "most characteristic of me habitually" to "least characteristic of me habitually." The number of statements in each of the twelve piles is specified in advance. This method most flagrantly violates the principle of least stress, since the task of comparing every statement to every other one and to a pre-assigned frequency distribution is extremely onerous. No clear rules are given for the selection of items; presumably they are selected to conform to the theoretical predilections of the experimenter. Thus the principle of the dynamic continuum is also grossly violated. Despite the highly structured character of the Q sort, it does not adapt itself readily to comparison of individual with group, nor is it so used. It does, however, provide access to some types of problems otherwise difficult to approach. A number of methodological difficulties involved in the use of Q technique have been pointed out by Cronbach and Gleser (6). In view of the lack of connection between Q technique and any rigorous method of item selection, and in view of the many complex methodological problems involved in its use, pursuit of other lines of test development seems more promising.

A PROPOSAL

The considerations of this paper appear to the writer to converge on a proposal for measurement of personality traits, a paradigm of which is discussed fully elsewhere (15). The type of test envisaged would be objective to the extreme of dichotomously scored items. For reasons relating chiefly to elimination of distortions inherent in test-taking factors, forced choice between pairs of more or less opposite statements is preferable to the more usual checklist of statements. The content of the items should sample widely the spectrum of ordinary everyday activities of the relevant population; at the same time, the items should be so worded or so selected that they will be indirect expressions of or related to basic feelings and attitudes. However, obvious references to abnormal, disapproved, or emotionally laden behavior should be avoided. Statements concerning characteristic defense mechanisms, especially rationalizations, appear particularly suitable for the manifest item content. To construct items one may keep in mind such basic traits as levels of psychosexual development, defenses, and dimensions of ego strength, as they would be manifest in the diversity of everyday situations. There is advantage, however, in capturing the content of the items from common speech rather than artificially constructing it. Items should have large dispersions, i.e., they should discriminate near the middle rather than at an extreme of the group. Parenthetically, a completely nonverbal test might also be constructed in accordance with the principles of this paper.

Scoring keys should be evolved by a method of homogeneous keying suitable for items whose intercorrelations are low. Several subtests would be expected to emerge from a large pool of items. As few as five statistically homogeneous items, none of which is diagnostic by itself, may comprise a fairly effective subtest to measure a trait or attitude. The meaning of a high or low score can be inferred tentatively from the common thread of content in the items but ultimately must be validated clinically. Where statistically coherent patterns emerge in items whose manifest content is not similar, there is reason to postulate an underlying determining tendency, or intervening variable, or hypothetical construct. If the constructs which most closely describe empirically derived subtests correspond to concepts in personality theory derived from other methods, an important independent line of verification will have been established.

REFERENCES

1. Adorno, T. W., Frenkel-Brunswik, Else, Levinson, D. J. and Sanford, R. N. *The Authoritarian Personality.* New York: Harper, 1950.
2. Beck, S. J. "The Science of Personality: Nomothetic or Idiographic?" *Psychological Review,* LX, (1953), 353–359.
3. Brunswik, E. *Systematic and Representative Design of Psychological Experiments.* University of California Syllabus Series, Number 304, 1947.
4. Campbell, D. T. "The Indirect Assessment of Social Attitudes." *Psychological Bulletin,* XLVII (1950), 15–38.
5. Cronbach, L. J. "Coefficient Alpha and the Internal Structure of Tests." *Psychometrika,* XVI (1951), 297–334.
6. Cronbach, L. J., and Gleser, Goldine C. "Assessing Similarity between Profiles." *Psychological Bulletin* L (1953), 456–473.
7. English, O. S., and Pearson, G. H. J. *Emotional Problems of Living.* New York: Norton, 1945.
8. Grant, Marquerite Q., Ives, Virginia, and Ranzoni, Jane H. "Reliability and Validity of Judges' Ratings of Adjustment on the Rorschach." *Psychological Monographs,* LXVI (1952), Number 334.
9. Guilford, J. P. "Some Lessons from Aviation Psychology." *American Psychologist,* III (1948), 3–12.
10. Gulliksen, H. O. *Theory of Mental Tests.* New York: Wiley, 1950.
11. Hathaway, S. R., and Meehl, P. E. *An Atlas for the Clinical Use of the MMPI.* Minneapolis: University of Minnesota Press, 1951.

12. Loevinger, Jane. "Effect of Distortions of Measurement on Item Selection." *Educational and Psychological Measurement*, XIV (1954), 441–448.
13. Loevinger, Jane. "The Attenuation Paradox in Test Theory." *Psychological Bulletin*, LI (1954), 493–504.
14. Loevinger, Jane, Gleser, Goldine C., and DuBois, P. H. "Maximizing the Discriminating Power of a Multiple-Score Test." *Psychometrika*, XVIII (1953), 309–317.
15. Loevinger, Jane, and Sweet, Blanche. "A Proposal for Measuring Patterns of Motherhood." Paper read at American Psychological Association meeting, New York, September 4, 1954.
16. Meehl, P. E., and Hathaway, S. R. "The K Factor as a Suppressor Variable in the Minnesota Multiphasic Personality Inventory." *Journal of Applied Psychology*, XXX (1946), 525–564.
17. Mishler, E. G. "Personality Characteristics and the Resolution of Role Conflicts." *Public Opinion Quarterly* XVII (1953), 115–135.
18. Shoben, E. J., Jr. "The Assessment of Parental Attitudes in Relation to Child Adjustment." *Genetic Psychology Monographs*, XXXIX (1949), 101–148.
19. Spearman, C. *The Abilities of Man.* New York: Macmillan, 1927.
20. Stephenson, W. "Some Observations on Q Technique." *Psychological Bulletin*, XLIX (1952), 483–498.

The Dynamics of "Structured" Personality Tests

Paul E. Meehl

In a recent article in this Journal, (9) Lt. Max L. Hutt of the Adjutant General's School has given an interesting discussion of the use of projective methods in the army medical installations. This article was part of a series describing the work of clinical psychologists in the military services, with which the present writer is familiar only indirectly. The utility of any instrument in the military situation can, of course, be most competently assessed by those in contact with clinical material in that situation, and the present paper is in no sense to be construed as an "answer" to or an attempted refutation of Hutt's remarks. Nevertheless, there are some incidental observations contained in his article which warrant further critical consideration, particularly those having to do with the theory and dynamics of "structured" personality tests. It is with these latter observations rather than the main burden of Hutt's article that this paper is concerned.

Hutt defines "structured personality tests" as those in which the test material consists of conventional, culturally crystallized questions to which the subject must respond in one of a very few fixed ways. With this definition we have no quarrel, and it has the advantage of not applying the unfortunate phrase "self-rating questionnaire" to the whole class of question-answer devices. But immediately following this definition, Hutt goes on to say that "it is assumed that each of the test questions will have the same meaning to all subjects who take the examination. The subject has no opportunity of organizing in his own unique manner his response to the questions."

These statements will bear further examination. The statement that personality tests assume that each question has the same meaning to all subjects is continuously appearing in most sources of late, and such an impression is conveyed by many discussions even when they do not explicitly make this assertion. It should be emphasized very strongly, therefore, that while this perhaps has been the case with the majority of question-answer personality tests, it is not by any means part of their essential nature. The traditional approach to verbal question-answer personality tests has been, to be sure, to view them as self-ratings; and it is in a sense always a self-rating that you obtain when you ask a subject about himself, whether you inquire about his feelings, his health, his attitudes, or his relations to others.

However, once a "self-rating" has been obtained, it can be looked upon in two rather different ways. The first, and by far the commonest approach, is to accept a self-rating as a second best source of information when the direct observation of a segment of behavior is inaccessible for practical or other reasons. This view in effect forces a self-rating or self-description to act as surrogate for a behavior-sample. Thus we want to know whether a man is shy, and one criterion is his readiness to blush. We cannot conveniently drop him into a social situation to observe whether he blushes, so we do the next best (and often much worse) thing and simply ask him, "Do you blush easily?" We assume that if he does in fact blush easily, he will realize that fact about himself, which is often a gratuitous assumption; and secondly, we hope that having recognized it, he will be willing to tell us so.

Associated with this approach to structured personality tests is the construction of items and their assembling into scales upon an *a priori* basis, requiring the assumption that the psychologist building the test has sufficient insight into

From *Journal of Clinical Psychology*, 1945, 1, 296–303. Reproduced by permission.

the dynamics of verbal behavior and its relation to the inner core of personality that he is able to predict beforehand what certain sorts of people will say about themselves when asked certain sorts of questions. The fallacious character of this procedure has been sufficiently shown by the empirical results of the Minnesota Multiphasic Personality Inventory alone, and will be discussed at greater length below. It is suggested tentatively that the relative uselessness of most structured personality tests is due more to *a priori* item construction than to the fact of their being structured.

The second approach to verbal self-ratings is rarer among test-makers. It consists simply in the explicit denial that we accept a self-rating as a feeble surrogate for a behavior sample, and substitutes the assertion that a "self-rating" constitutes an intrinsically interesting and significant bit of verbal behavior, the non-test correlates of which must be discovered by empirical means. Not only is this approach free from the restriction that the subject must be able to describe his own behavior accurately, but a careful study of structured personality tests built on this basis shows that such a restriction would falsify the actual relationships that hold between what a man says and what he *is*.

Since this view of question-answer items is the rarer one at the present time, it is desirable at this point to elucidate by a number of examples. For this purpose one might consider the Strong Vocational Interest Blank, the Humm-Wadsworth Temperament Scales, the Minnesota Multiphasic Personality Inventory, or any structured personality measuring device in which the selection of items was done on a thoroughly empirical basis using carefully selected criterion groups. In the extensive and confident use of the Strong Vocational Interest Blank, this more sophisticated view of the significance of responses to structured personality test items has been taken as a matter of course for years. The possibility of conscious as well as unconscious "fudging" has been considered and experimentally investigated by Strong and others, but the differences in possible interpretation or *meaning* of items have been more or less ignored—as well they should be. One is asked to indicate, for example, whether he likes, dislikes, or is indifferent to "conservative people." The possibilities for differential interpretation of a word like *conservative* are of course tremendous, but nobody has worried about that problem in the case of the Strong. Almost certainly the strength of verbs like "like" and "dislike" is variably interpreted throughout the whole blank. For the present purpose the Multiphasic (referred to hereinafter as MMPI) will be employed because the present writer is most familiar with it.

One of the items on the MMPI scale for detecting psychopathic personality (Pd) is "My parents and family find more fault with me than they should." If we look upon this as a rating in which the *fact* indicated by an affirmative response is crucial, we immediately begin to wonder whether the testee can objectively evaluate how much other people's parents find fault with them, whether his own parents are warranted in finding as much fault with him as they do, whether this particular subject will interpret the phrase "finding fault" in the way we intend or in the way most normal persons interpret it, and so on. The present view is that this is simply an unprofitable way to examine a question-answer personality test item. To begin with, the empirical finding is that individuals whose past history and momentary clinical picture is that of a typical psychopathic personality tend to say "Yes" to this much more often than people in general do. Now in point of fact, they probably should say "No" because the parents of psychopaths are sorely tried and probably do not find fault with their incorrigible offspring any more than the latter deserve. An allied item is "I have been quite independent and free from family rule" which psychopaths tend to answer *false*—almost certainly opposite to what is actually the case for the great majority of them. Again, "Much of the time I feel I have done something wrong or evil." Anyone who deals clinically with psychopaths comes to doubt seriously whether they could possibly interpret this item in the way the rest of us do (*cf.* Cleckley's (2) "semantic dementia"), but they *say* that about themselves nonetheless. Numerous other examples such as "Someone has it in for me" and "I am sure I get a raw deal from life" appear on the same scale and are significant because psychopaths tend to *say* certain things about themselves, rather than because we take these statements at face value.

Consider the MMPI scale for detecting tendencies to hypochondriasis. A hypochondriac says that he has headaches often, that he is not in as good health as his friends are, and that he cannot understand what he reads as well as he used to. Suppose that he has a headache on an average of once every month, as does a certain "normal" person. The hypochondriac says he often has headaches, the other person says he does not. They both have headaches once a month, and hence they must either interpret the word "often" differently in that question, or else have unequal recall of their headaches. According to the traditional view, this ambiguity in the word "often" and the inaccuracy of human memory constitute sources of error; for the authors of MMPI they may actually constitute sources of discrimination.

We might mention as beautiful illustrations of this kind of relation, the non-somatic items in the hysteria scale of MMPI (8). These items have a statistical homogeneity and the common property by face inspection that they indicate the person to be possessed of unusually good social and psychiatric adjustment. They are among the most potent items for the detection of hysterics and hysteroid temperaments, but they reflect the systematic distortion of the hysteric's conception of himself, and would have to be considered invalid if taken as surrogates for the direct observation of behavior.

As a last example one might mention some findings of the writer, to be published shortly, in which "normal" persons having rather abnormal MMPI profiles are differentiated from clearly "abnormal" persons with equally deviant profiles by a tendency to give statistically rare as well as psychiatrically "maladjusted" responses to certain other items. Thus a person who says that he is afraid of fire, that windstorms terrify him, that people often disappoint him, stands a better chance of being normal in his non-test behavior than a person who does not admit to these things. The discrimination of this set of items for various criterion groups, the intercorrelations with other scales, and the content of the items indicate strongly that they detect some verbal-semantic distortion in the interpretation and response to the other MMPI items which enters into the spurious elevation of scores achieved by certain "normals." Recent unpublished research on more subtle "lie" scales of MMPI indicates that unconscious self-deception is inversely related to the kind of verbal distortion just indicated.

In summary, a serious and detailed study of the MMPI items and their interrelations both with one another and non-test behavior cannot fail to convince one of the necessity for this second kind of approach to question-answer personality tests. That the majority of the questions seem by inspection to require self-ratings has been a source of theoretical misunderstanding, since the stimulus situation seems to request a self-rating, whereas *the scoring does not assume a valid self-rating to have been given.* It is difficult to give any psychologically meaningful interpretation of some of the empirical findings on MMPI unless the more sophisticated view is maintained.

It is for this reason that the possible differences in interpretation do not cause us any *a priori* concern in the use of this instrument. Whether any structured personality test turns out to be valid and useful must be decided on pragmatic grounds, but the possibility of diverse interpretations of a single item is not a good *theoretical* reason for predicting failure of the scales. There is a "projective" element involved in interpreting and responding to these verbal stimuli which must be recognized, in spite of the fact that the test situation is very rigidly structured as regards the ultimate response possibilities permitted. The objection that all persons do not interpret structured test items in the same way is not fatal, just as it would not be fatal to point out that "ink blots do not look the same to everyone."

It has not been sufficiently recognized by critics of structured personality tests that what a man says about himself may be a highly significant fact about him even though we do not entertain with any confidence the hypothesis that what he says would agree with what complete knowledge of him would lead others to say of him. It is rather strange that this point is so often completely passed by, when clinical psychologists quickly learn to take just that attitude in a diagnostic or therapeutic interview. The complex defense mechanisms of projection, rationalization, reaction-formation, etc., appear dynamically to the interviewer as soon as he begins to take what the client *says* as itself motivated by other needs than those of giving an accurate verbal report. There is no good *a priori* reason for denying the possibility of similar processes in the highly structured "interview" which is the question-answer personality test. The summarized experience of the clinician results (one hopes, at least) in his being able to discriminate verbal responses admissible as accurate self-descriptions from those which reflect other psychodynamisms but are not on that account any the less significant. The test analogue to this experience consists of the summarized statistics on response frequencies, at least among those personality tests which have been constructed empirically (MMPI, Strong, Rorschach, etc.).

Once this has been taken for granted we are prepared to admit powerful items to personality scales regardless of whether the rationale of their appearance can be made clear at present. We do not have the confidence of the traditional personality test maker that the relation between the behavior dynamics of a subject and the tendency to respond verbally in a certain way must be psychologically obvious. Thus it puzzles us but does not disconcert us when this relation cannot be elucidated, the science of behavior being in the stage that it is. That "I sometimes tease animals" (answered *false*) should occur in a scale measuring symptomatic depression is theoretically mysterious, just as the tendency of certain schizophrenic patients to accept "position" as a determinant in responding to the Rorschach may be theoretically mysterious. Whether such a relation obtains can be very readily discovered empirically, and the wherefore of it may be left aside for the moment as a theoretical question. Verbal responses which do not apparently have any *self*-reference at all, but in their form seem to request an objective judgment about social phenomena or ethical values, may be equally diagnostic. So, again, one is not disturbed to find items such as "I think most people would lie to get ahead" (answered *false*) and "It takes a lot of argument to convince most people of the truth" (answered *false*) appearing on the hysteria scale of MMPI.

The frequently alleged "superficiality" of structured personality tests becomes less evident on such a basis also. Some of these items can be rationalized in terms of fairly deep-seated trends of the personality, although it is admittedly difficult to establish that any given depth interpretation is the correct one. To take one example, the items on the MMPI scale for hysteria which were referred to above as indicating extraordinarily good social and emotional adjustment can hardly be seen as valid self-descriptions. However, if the core trend of such items is summarily characterized as "I am psychiatrically and socially well adjusted," it is not hard to fit such a trend into what we know of the basic personality structure of the hysteric. The well known *belle indifference* of these patients, the great lack of insight, the facility of repression and dissociation, the "impunitiveness" of their reactions to frustration, the tendency of such patients to show an elevated "lie" score on MMPI, may all be seen as facets of this underlying structure. It would be interesting to see experimentally whether to the three elements of Rosenzweig's "triadic hypothesis" (impunitiveness, repression, hypnotizability) one might add a fourth correlate—the chief non-somatic component of the MMPI hysteria scale.

Whether "depth" is plumbed by a structured personality test to a lesser extent than by one which is unstructured is difficult to determine, once the present view of the nature of structured tests is understood. That the "deepest" layers of personality are not verbal might be admitted without any implication that they cannot therefore make themselves known to us via verbal behavior. Psychoanalysis, usually considered the "deepest" kind of psychotherapy, makes use of the dependency of verbal behavior upon underlying variables which are not themselves verbalized.

The most important area of behavior considered in the making of psychiatric diagnosis is still the form and content of the *speech* of the individual. I do not mean to advance these considerations as validations of any structured personality tests, but merely as reasons for not accepting the theoretical objection sometimes offered in criticizing them. Of course, structured personality tests may be employed in a purely diagnostic, categorizing fashion, without the use of any dynamic interpretations of the relationship among scales or the patterning of a profile. For certain practical purposes this is quite permissible, just as one may devote himself to the statistical validation of various "signs" on the Rorschach test, with no attempt to make qualitative or really dynamic personological inferences from the findings. The tradition in the case of structured personality tests is probably weighted on the side of non-dynamic thinking; and in the case of some structured tests, there is a considerable amount of experience and clinical subtlety required to extract the maximum of information. The present writer has heard discussions in case conferences at the University of Minnesota Hospital which make as "dynamic" use of MMPI patterns as one could reasonably make of any kind of test data without an excessive amount of illegitimate reification. The clinical use of the Strong Vocational Interest Blank is another example.

In discussing the "depth" of interpretation possible with tests of various kinds, it should at least be pointed out that the problem of validating personality tests, whether structured or unstructured, becomes more difficult in proportion as the interpretations increase in "depth." For example, the validation of the "sign" differentials on the Rorschach is relatively easier to carry out than that of the deeper interpretations concerning the basic personality structure. This does not imply that there is necessarily less validity in the latter class of inferences, but simply stresses the difficulty of designing experiments to test validity. A very major part of this difficulty hinges upon the lack of satisfactory external criteria, a situation which exists also in the case of more dynamic interpretations of structured personality tests. One is willing to accept a staff diagnosis of psychasthenia in selecting cases against which to validate the Pt scale of MMPI or the F% as a compulsive-obsessive sign on the Rorschach. But when the test results indicate repressed homosexuality or latent anxiety or lack of deep insight into the self, we may have strong suspicions that the instrument is fully as competent as the psychiatric staff. Unfortunately this latter assumption is very difficult to justify without appearing to be inordinately biased in favor of our test. Until this problem is better solved than at present, many of the "depth" interpretations of both structured and unstructured tests will be little more than an expression of personal opinion.

There is one advantage of unstructured personality tests which cannot easily be claimed for the structured variety, namely, the fact that falsehood is difficult. While it is true for many of the MMPI items, for example, that even a psychologist cannot predict on which scales they will appear nor in what direction certain sorts of abnormals will tend to answer them, still the relative accessibility of defensive answering would seem to be greater than is possible in responding to a set of ink blots. Research is still in progress on more subtle "lie" scales of MMPI and we have every reason to feel encouraged on the present findings. Nevertheless the very existence of a definite problem in this case and not in the case of the Rorschach gives the latter an advantage in this respect. When we pass to a more structured method, such as the T. A. T., the problem reappears. The writer has found, for example, a number of patients who simply were not fooled by the "intelligence-test" set given in the directions for the T. A. T., as was indicated quite clearly by self-references and defensive remarks, especially on the second day. Of course such a patient is still under pressure to produce material and therefore his unwillingness to reveal himself is limited in its power over the projections finally given.

In conclusion, the writer is in hearty agreement with Lieutenant Hutt that unstructured personality tests are of great value, and that the final test of the adequacy of any technique is its utility in clinical work. Published evidence of the validity of both structured and unstructured personality tests as they had to be modified for convenient military use does not enable one to draw any very definite conclusions or comparisons at the present time. There is assuredly no reason for us to place structured and unstructured types of instruments in battle order against one another, although it is admitted that when time is limited they come inevitably into a very real clinical "competition" for use. The present article has been aimed simply at the clarification of certain rather prevalent misconceptions as to the nature and the theory of at least one important structured personality test, in order that erroneous theoretical considerations may not be thrown into the balance in deciding the outcome of such clinical competition.

BIBLIOGRAPHY

1. Benton, A. C. The interpretation of questionnaire items in a personality schedule. *Archiv. Psychol.* 1935, No. 190.
2. Cleckley, H. *The Mask of Sanity.* St. Louis: Mosby, 1941.
3. Hathaway, S. R., and McKinley, J. C. A multiphasic personality schedule: I. Construction of the schedule. *J. Psychol.*, 1940, **10**, 249–254.
4. McKinley, J. C., and Hathaway, S. R. A multiphasic personality schedule: II. A differential study of hypochondriasis. *J. Psychol.*, 1940, **10**, 255–268.
5. Hathaway, S. R., and McKinley, J. C. A multiphasic personality schedule: III. The measurement of symptomatic depression. *J. Psychol.*, 1942, **14**, 73–84.
6. McKinley, J. C., and Hathaway, S. R. A multiphasic personality schedule: IV. Psychasthenia. *J. appl. Psychol.*, 1942, **26**, 614–624.
7. Hathaway, S. R., and McKinley, J. C. *Manual for the Minnesota Multiphasic Personality Inventory.* Minneapolis: University of Minnesota Press, 1943.
8. McKinley, J. C., and Hathaway, S. R. The Minnesota Multiphasic Personality Inventory: V. Hysteria, hypomania, and psychopathic deviate. *J. appl. Psychol.*, 1944, **28**, 153–174.
9. Hutt, Max L. The use of projective methods of personality measurement in army medical installations. *J. clin. Psychol.*, 1945, **1**, 134–140.
10. Landis, C., and Katz, S. E. The validity of certain questions which purport to measure neurotic tendencies. *Jour. appl. Psychol.*, 1934, **18**, 343–356.
11. Landis, C., Zubin, J., and Katz, S. E. Empirical evaluation of three personality adjustment inventories. *J. educ. Psychol.*, 1935, **26**, 321–330.
12. Leverenz, C. W. Minnesota Multiphasic Personality Inventory: An evaluation of its usefulness in the psychiatric service of a station hospital. *War Med.*, 1943, **4**, 618–629.
13. Maller, J. B. Personality tests. In J. McV. Hunt (ed.),

Personality and the Behavior Disorders. New York: Ronald Press, 1944, pp. 170–213.
14. Meehl, P. E. A general normality or control factor in personality testing. Unpublished Ph.D. Thesis, University of Minnesota Library, Minneapolis, 1945.
15. Mosier, C. I. On the validity of neurotic questionnaires. *J. soc. Psychol.*, 1938, **9**, 3–16.
16. Rosenzweig, S. An outline of frustration theory. In J. McV. Hunt (ed.), *Personality and the Behavior Disorders.* New York: Ronald Press, 1944.
17. Strong, E. K. *Vocational Interests of Men and Women.* Stanford: Stanford University Press, 1943.

Personality Test Interpretation by Digital Computer

Benjamin Kleinmuntz

In this study a set of decision rules was devised for interpreting profile patterns of the Minnesota Multiphasic Personality Inventory (MMPI) of maladjusted and adjusted college students. The procedure used was that of computer programming of the "maladjusted" versus "adjusted" decisions of an expert test interpreter. The interpreter's decision-making processes were tape-recorded while he was thinking aloud during the sorting of the profiles of 126 college students. The programmed decision rules, which were based on the interpreter's protocol and which were improved upon by a process of trial-and-error statistical checking, yielded a greater hit percentage than the decisions of the original interpreter. In its final form, the set of objective configural inventory rules identified correctly large numbers of maladjusted college students in two cross-validation samples.

Within the past few years research on human thinking has been facilitated by the introduction of the electronic digital computer as a research tool in the behavioral sciences and by the demonstration that this tool is much more than just a machine which performs rapid arithmetical operations. Among those who have contributed most to this development have been Allen Newell and Herbert A. Simon of Carnegie Institute of Technology and J. C. Shaw of the Rand Corporation (1). These workers have provided considerable and impressive evidence that the digital computer, when appropriately programmed, can carry out complex patterns of processes.

We now report how a computer has recently been applied as a tool to aid in interpretations of personality tests. The computer was used to approximate the rules expressed in the tape-recorded verbalizations of an expert test interpreter.

One of the personality tests which has frequently been used in psychiatric settings to aid in diagnostic and prognostic decision-making is the Minnesota Multiphasic Personality Inventory. The inventory is conventionally scored on a profile sheet which contains four validity and ten clinical scales. In this study an experienced user of the inventory was instructed to discriminate between the test profiles for maladjusted college students (N = 45) and those for well-adjusted students (N = 81).

From *Science*, 1963, **139**, 416–418. Copyright 1963 by the American Association for the Advancement of Science.

The profiles for 126 college students (72 males and 54 females) were used as a criterion sample upon which a set of decision rules was developed. Such profiles were obtained from students who belonged to subgroups as follows.

1) Adjusted and maladjusted counseling group. This group was comprised of 65 students who had voluntarily requested help from the Carnegie Institute of Technology Counseling Center. They were judged by two counselors, after the completion of several interviews, to have problems of either a vocational-academic or a personal-emotional nature. The students whose problems were vocational-academic were labeled "adjusted" (N = 37); those whose problems were personal-emotional were called "maladjusted" (N = 28).

2) Adjusted and maladjusted no-counseling group. There were 31 students in this group, all members of fraternities and sororities. They were classed as either "adjusted" or "maladjusted" on the basis of the way in which their fraternity brothers (or sorority sisters) perceived them. Each member of each fraternity and sorority on campus, under supervised conditions, nominated from a roster of names of his fraternity brothers or sorority sisters four individuals, two of whom he considered the least well adjusted and two the best adjusted. A student was retained in this group if 60 percent or more of his peers nominated him, or her, for one of the two categories. Finally, 31 of these students (the 17 least well adjusted and the 14 best adjusted) were given the personality inventory test. This type of sample was chosen in order to counterbalance the

effects of test set; that is, in principle it may be expected that at the time students seek aid at a counseling center they are probably experiencing the full force of their emotional difficulties. Consequently their scale scores may be higher than they would be under less threatening circumstances. The fraternity–sorority maladjusted sample, therefore, may be similar in personality makeup to the personal-emotional-problem counseling group, except that the former are not in immediate need of counseling.

3) Random normal group. Thirty inventory profiles (15 males and 15 females) were randomly selected from a group of Multiphasic profiles for 800 entering freshmen. None of these students had either been in for counseling or been in the sample of persons nominated by the fraternity–sorority groups. This group, the vocational-academic-problem sample, and the "most adjusted" fraternity–sorority sample constituted the "adjusted" criterion groups. In all, then, the 126 profiles comprised profiles from 81 adjusted and 45 maladjusted students.

Table 1. *Mean T-Score Values for MMPI Scales of the Criterion Group.*

	Male		Female	
MMPI scale	Adjusted (N = 48)	Maladjusted (N = 24)	Adjusted (N = 33)	Maladjusted (N = 21)
?	50.0	51.0	50.0	50.9
L	48.1	47.6	48.1	46.0
F	51.8	58.5	52.5	60.9
K	55.9	54.4	57.5	49.4
HS	50.7	55.3	52.8	54.7
D	53.3	65.2	51.6	64.0
HY	56.5	61.1	58.0	61.9
PD	55.0	63.1	57.4	65.8
MF	56.0	65.0	45.0	45.2
PA	53.8	59.4	55.0	67.3
PT	53.4	64.2	56.0	64.0
SC	54.1	65.5	56.4	66.4
MA	57.0	60.0	58.2	63.4
SI	47.9	54.4	48.5	55.1
ES[a]	52.0	49.0	46.8	42.0
MT[a]	10.7	18.1	11.7	23.5

[a]Raw score.

The 126 profiles were then prepared on 4½- by 4½-inch cards and Q-sorted by ten highly reputed experts in the United States. The mean profiles for the adjusted and maladjusted students are presented in Table 1. The experts were instructed to sort the profiles into a 14-step forced normal distribution which ranged from least to most adjusted; the number in each of the piles (from least to most adjusted) was 2, 3, 4, 9, 12, 15, 18, 18, 15, 12, 9, 4, 3, and 2, respectively. The cutting line between "maladjusted" and "adjusted" profiles was arbitrarily drawn in the middle of the distribution (between the two piles of 18 profiles).

Of the ten experts, one was chosen for intensive study and for computer programming because he had achieved the highest hit percentage. His sort/resort reliability, with an interval of 1 day between sorts, yielded a correlation coefficient of .96 and thus reflected considerable stability. On his first sorting he classified 80 percent and 67 percent of the profiles into the valid positive and valid negative categories, respectively; his second sorting yielded hit rates of 76 and 64 percent for the same categories. He was then instructed to Q-sort the profiles for the various subgroups and was asked to "think aloud" into a tape recorder during the process of sorting. The information which was obtained during approximately 30 hours of tape-recorded protocol was carefully edited, compiled, and then programmed into computer language so that an electronic digital computing machine could make decisions about profiles similar to the decisions made by the expert. In other words, the computer was given the sorter's information and procedure for processing that information (for example, the sorter's heuristics). Portions of the sorter's protocol and the corresponding decision rules are presented in Table 2.

When a sufficient amount of usable tape-recorded information had been obtained from the expert, the material was translated into computer language (GATE-20); this became the set of programmed decision rules (2). The rules were ordered in what was thought to be an optimal arrangement; the hit rates with these initial rules were 63 and 88 percent, respectively, for the valid positive and valid negative categories. The discrepancies between the expert's and the computer's hit percentages, which favored the expert in the valid positive case and favored the computer in the valid negative category, can be explained on the basis of my error. The error may possibly have been introduced through

Table 2. *Portions of Tape-Recorded Protocol and Corresponding MMPI Rules.*

Protocol	MMPI rule
1) ". . . Now I'm going to divide these into two piles . . . on the left [least adjusted] I'm throwing MMPI's with at least four scales primed. . . ."	1) If four or more clinical scales are equal to, or greater than, a T-score of 70, call maladjusted.
2) ". . . If the elevations are lopsided to the right with the left side of the profile fairly low, I'm throwing the MMPI's to the left [least adjusted]. . . ."	2) If Pa or Sc and Pa, Pt, or Sc are equal to or greater than Hs, D, or Hy, then call maladjusted.
3) ". . . Here are a couple of nice, normal looking MMPI's . . . all scales are hugging around a T-score of 50, and Es is nice and high . . . over to the right side [most adjusted]. . . ."	3) Call adjusted if at least 5 clinical scales are between T-scores 40 and 60 and if the Es scale's raw score is 45 or higher.

a nonoptimal ordering of the decision rules. However that may be, the task from that point on was clearly to sharpen the decision rules until they were superior to those of the original decision maker. This improvement was achieved by (i) a trial and error ordering and reordering of the rules; (ii) addition and deletion of portions of the rules; (iii) statistical searching and checking; and (iv) continual testing of the revised rules against the criterion sample. The completed set of decision rules included the original expert interpreter's information, a number of rank difference scores, and various slope characteristics of the profile pattern that the expert had failed to observe (3). With the revised set of decision rules, the hit rates for the 126 profiles were 91 and 84 percent, respectively, for the valid positive and valid negative categories. This was a considerable improvement over the expert's Q-sort.

The efficacy of any statistical formula, model, or set of rules is frequently judged on the basis of its ability to hold up with new samples. Moderately satisfactory results have thus far been achieved when the new rules have been tested against a sample of well-adjusted and maladjusted counseling clients from the University of Nebraska ($N = 116$) and from Brigham Young University ($N = 100$). The hit rates for the Nebraska sample were 72 and 94 percent, respectively, for the valid negative and valid positive categories; for the Brigham Young sample the percentages were 80 and 64. To some extent the size of the cross-validation shrinkage can be accounted for on two bases: (i) the differences in the ratio of "maladjusted" to "adjusted" profiles between the criterion and the new samples, and (ii) the fact that both of the cross-validation samples, in terms of the way they were selected, resembled only a subgroup of the criterion sample (for example, the counseling group of 65 students). The percentage ratios of "maladjusted" to "adjusted" profiles for the criterion group, the Nebraska sample, and the Brigham Young sample were 36:64, 31:69, and 50:50, respectively. Perhaps if greater care had been exercised in selecting comparable cross-validation samples the size of the shrinkage might have been smaller.

The results obtained in this study have a threefold significance. (i) The decision rules should aid a counseling center in detecting emotional maladjustment in an entering freshman class. (ii) The use of the computer in an entirely new area of intelligent problem-solving has been demonstrated. (iii) This study could pave the way for rigorous investigation of clinical decision-making, which is more subtle than personality test interpretation.

REFERENCES AND NOTES

1. A. Newell, J. C. Shaw, H. A. Simon. *Psychol. Rev.* 65, 151 (1958); A. Newell and H. A. Simon, *Science* 134, 2011 (1961).
2. Grateful acknowledgment for assistance in computational and computer programming is made to R. Dale Shipp, graduate mathematics student at Carnegie Institute of Technology.
3. The revised set of MMPI rules will be furnished to interested readers upon request.
4. This research was supported in part by the National Institute of Mental Health, grant No. M-5701.

Comments on Comments on Testing*

Garlie A. Forehand

The field of psychological testing appears to have joined advertising, television, bureaucracy, and public school systems as an object for the crusades of socially righteous authors. The charges brought against testing have ranged from sensible to ridiculous. Even the more vituperative criticisms, however, can serve the valuable function of revealing perspectives otherwise hidden from the practitioner deeply involved in his craft. The use of tests in personnel decisions has been most vehemently and widely criticized by Martin L. Gross (1962). The remarks in this paper result from an attempt to sort out and evaluate some of his criticisms, and to examine their implications for the practice of testing.

Many of Gross' comments on the theory and practice of testing neither require nor deserve rebuttal—certainly not in a professional forum. He has simplified a complex set of issues concerning the assessment of human performance—issues of which the technical problems of testing are only a subset; and for this simplified problem he offers a simple

From *Educational and Psychological Measurement,* 1964, 24, 853–859. Reproduced by permission.
*Based on remarks presented in a symposium on "The Use and Misuse of Tests" at the annual meeting of the Pennsylvania Psychological Association, Lancaster, Pa., May 10, 1963. The principal speaker was Martin L. Gross. Discussants were Zigmunt A. Piotrowski and G. A. Forehand. The symposium was arranged and chaired by Richard Teevan.

solution: the abolition of the practice of testing. He solicits support for this solution by painting the practice of testing in the sombre colors of anxiety. The individual, or as Gross suggests, the victim, is projected into a frightening situation where his livelihood depends on the whims of some shadowy institutional decision-maker poring over his test protocols, while his children, under the watchful eyes of schoolteachers, are recording his intimate family habits on test blanks. The anxious mood is intensified by mordant remarks and rhetorical questions about the motives and competence of testers and the content of assorted discomforting items. To alleviate the state of anxiety thus so carefully nourished, Gross offers a scapegoat: the sinister figure of the brainwatcher.

The brainwatcher is both a varied and a versatile species. His ranks include executives, personnel officers, school administrators, teachers, and psychologists—psychologists who use and make tests, and those who criticize them. The latter either have their eyes diverted momentarily from the cash box, or are engaging in shameless fratricidal backbiting. The traits of the brainwatcher are also varied; the major distinguishing characteristic is the somewhat awesome ability to select, systematically and efficiently, the colorless, other-directed individual for influential positions in our society, while ruthlessly excluding the creative individualist—all by means of invalid tests.

One of the most unfortunate effects of all of this rhetoric is the camouflage of a number of thoughtful, valuable points that Gross has to make. He questions the validity of present personality tests for executive selection—or indeed any selection. He criticizes the theoretical poverty of the trait-names attached to personality scales. He describes intolerable abuses; and while one may doubt the implied typicality of the abuses, they sound plausible as incidents. All of these, and other of Gross' points, have been stated repeatedly, and often less eloquently, by responsible psychologists.

We can certainly grant a number of specific, vexing problems in personality testing, particularly in applications thereof. We can also grant the appropriateness of a concern for the rights of the individuals who undergo such testing. Does personality testing, then, have a legitimate, defensible place in the personnel decisions made in our society?

It is not difficult to find motives for the testing movement that are at once more fundamental and more commendable than those posited by Mr. Gross. The question of what persons in a society are to fill what roles is, as Gardner (1961) has pointed out, an old and important one. A functioning society demands a wide range and diversity of talent, and it demands that its roles be taken by persons who have both the relevant talents and the personal qualities necessary for the appropriate, effective exercise of those talents. Such a range and diversity exists among the members of a society, but individuals are not neatly labeled as to the qualities they possess. If we grant such diversities, and if our society rejects a solution based upon hereditary or other *a priori* stratification, then the matching of persons and roles becomes a gigantic casting process—a process in which auditions will occur, human behavior will be assessed wisely or unwisely, validly or invalidly, with or without the complicity of tests. The fairness of the auditions and their relevance to the performance are reasonable concerns of both the professional psychologist and the aspiring actor.

What function can and should psychological tests serve in the casting? There are circumstances in which testing has achieved widely acknowledged usefulness. I suggest that there are two sets of conditions under which tests have been shown to be effective, both of them understood only after long and laborious experience. They provide a needed context for the consideration of more controversial applications.

The first set of conditions are those in which abilities tests can be used most effectively. Selection of college students is a good example, and there are many others. Ideally, many persons are being selected for a task whose performance is to be evaluated in terms of relatively homogeneous expectations. A quantitative criterion exists, and can be understood in terms of abilities and skills that can be abstracted and mirrored in test items. Under such conditions, a combination of ability (aptitude, achievement, proficiency, etc.) tests, while not eliminating "mistakes," will probably provide the fairest and best economically feasible basis for making decisions. The conditions are approximated sufficiently well and sufficiently often to establish for the abilities test a strategic importance in personnel decisions.

The second set of conditions under which the usefulness of testing is acknowledged is found in the clinic. Here, again stating the conditions ideally, the test is used as one source of information about the emotional and intellectual characteristics of an individual. It is evaluated in the context of professional judgment, based upon observation from several professional perspectives. The decisions that stem from the tests are made for the welfare of the patient. They are not fixed and absolute, but rather are modifiable, and often, if need be, reversible as further information is accumulated. Thus, the information provided by tests is continuously re-evaluated by persons who have the responsibility of being alert to circumstances requiring new interpretation.

There exist other circumstances in which human behavior is assessed—with or without the aid of tests—circumstances not characterized by either of the above sets of ideal conditions. Good examples are executive and professional selection. Here, a meaningful quantitative criterion is lacking; the behaviors that lead to achievement are expected to be individualistic rather than common; within the limited population from which selections are made, variation in ability seems generally unrelated to achievement. At the same time, the decision is not made for the individual's personal welfare, is not evaluated in the context of a diagnostic conference, and is not readily tested and modified as a continuous process. These problems thus are characterized by the ideal conditions for neither the application of abilities tests nor the application of diagnostic clinical judgment. Both approaches have been tried in this area. The regression equations of abilities testers have been computed, often with farfetched variables as predictors, and usually with questionable measures serving as criteria. Clinical judgment applied to test protocols has produced personality analyses of candidates, and, in turn, recommendations based upon clinicians assumptions about the traits relevant to personnel decisions. Both approaches have been disappointing; and it is in this shadowland that Gross finds his greatest cause for complaint.

Gross carries his criticism of personality testing in these situations further. He believes that personality testing is both unscientific and immoral. Unscientific because of faulty statistical claims, nonreplication of results, and the general atmosphere of hucksterism that surrounds it; immoral because its false predictions produce human misfortune, and because it results in discrimination on the basis of personality traits, which Gross sees as akin to discrimination on the basis of race or religion.

But in rejecting a solution, the critic has left us with the dilemma—the casting dilemma. How shall we select and place individuals in positions assuring fairness to the individual, and a reasonable expectation of competent performance of the roles? The question is a relevant one, both for psychologists and their critics.

Suppose we have the responsibility for filling a few positions from a sample of many applicants. The applicants all have the experience and educational requisites and all have demonstrated sufficient ability on the best set of ability tests we can assemble. It seems to me that we have four alternative strategies for solving our problem. The first might be called a "dog fight" strategy: permit applicants to compete for a position until the best man wins. A second would be to leave the decisions to the intuitive judgment of a person or persons with that assigned responsibility. A third would be to assign applicants randomly to the available positions. And finally, the fourth strategy is to make further systematic observations of the behavior of the applicants, in short to use tests in some form.[1]

The first strategy—the dog fight—would, I believe be considered unacceptable and unworkable both by psychologists and their critics, except, perhaps, in limited conditions in which several employees are being considered for a single promotion.

The second—the intuitive judgment strategy—carries with it the familiar problems of lack of control over competence of the judges, the limited range of available information, and the dangers of personal bias, favoritism, even nepotism. Even if the bias problem could be eliminated, it seems doubtful that the procedure could avoid the scientific defects attributed by Gross to personality tests; and his moral objection to discriminating on the basis of personality characteristics would apply as much to this strategy as to tests—perhaps more.

The third alternative—random selection—has the merit of impartiality. If we do not select according to relevant characteristics, at least we do not reject according to irrelevant ones. Some such strategy is posited by utility theory as a baseline against which to evaluate strategies involving tests or other additional information (Cronbach and Gleser, 1957).

If we adopt the random selection strategy as a fixed one rather than as a baseline, we are assuming that no further observations of personal characteristics will contribute to the values of the selection situation. Those values include those of the employers and thus refer to the validity or utility of a strategy from the employers' point of view. But they include individual and social values as well. If a person's interests, motives, and other personal characteristics are relevant to the satisfaction he will get from a particular job and to the likelihood of his using his abilities maximally, then information about these qualities may contribute to the achievement of his own values.

The fourth strategy, testing, rests upon two postulates: that whether a person can or will exercise his abilities in a given situation depends at least in part upon personal characteristics, and that these personal characteristics can be inferred from observations of behavior in standard situations. The question that our critics have raised—and answered with a premature negative—is whether these postulates provide a workable basis for the establishment of conditions under which personality testing can be effective aids to decision. The question has both short-range and long-range facets.

In evaluating the reasonableness of using tests at the present and in the immediate future, irresponsibility and abuse are troublesome problems, but they are not matters of issue between psychologists and their critics. All parties agree that irresponsibility is intolerable, and that measures can and should be taken to control it. But clearly not all psychologists and executives who use tests are irresponsible. The point of issue is whether there is a valid basis for the *responsible* use of tests. Accumulated research findings do not lend encouragement to confident routine application of test results to executive and professional selection (Tagiuri, 1961). As we have noted, these areas of application are not well adapted to the testing models that we can apply most confidently. The rationale for using tests at present that I find most convincing can be stated something like this: a person, not a test, is responsible for a personnel decision. A psychologist or executive who accepts that responsibility ought to use all available sources of information, personality tests included, that in his judgment help him make a fair and useful decision. Such a formulation places the responsibility for a decision clearly upon the individual. And evaluation of a decision is an evaluation of the individual who makes it; the individual cannot blame tests for his failures, and need not credit them with his success.

The long range question is this: can research and experience provide a rationale for testing that is more viable than the personal judgment of the decision maker? The question is clearly not one that can be answered by one or a few investigators in one or a few years. The assumption that existing models can be readily applied to these refractory areas has probably hindered the research needed to provide answers to it. The attempt to answer it will not commit us to existing tests, existing methods, existing concepts, or indeed to existing definitions of the roles to be filled. Recent developments may enable us to foresee some of the directions that the inquiry is likely to take. The "criterion problem" will probably have to be tackled by separating observations of behavior from evaluation of behavior in

[1] Another set of alternatives would involve changing the position to fit the persons. The need for and problems in evaluating behavior would be essentially the same as those discussed here.

performance appraisal. Assessment systems will probably include systematic appraisal of environmental characteristics among the data to be collected. The usefulness of decisions based on tests will probably be evaluated against decisions that could be made without the tests. The implementation of these suggestions—all found in recent personnel psychology literature—as well as the invention of new procedures, will require ingenuity at least equal to that of the developers of the earliest ability tests. The effort can result in extensive new values—both practical and social—for psychological tests.

REFERENCES

Cronbach, L. J. and Gleser, Goldine. *Psychological Tests and Personnel Decisions.* Urbana: University of Illinois Press, 1957.

Gardner, J. W. *Excellence: Can We Be Equal and Excellent Too?* New York: Harper, 1961.

Gross, M. L. *The Brainwatchers.* New York: Random House, 1962.

Tagiuri, R., (Ed.) *Research Needs in Executive Selection.* Boston: Graduate School of Business Administration, Harvard University, 1961.

Abuses and Misuses in Testing Black Children

Robert L. Williams

If a tree is to be judged by its fruit, if the intelligence of a race bears any relation to its accomplishments, it seems difficult to draw any conclusion other than that the Black and Brown races are inferior to the white race.—R. S. Ellis (1928, p. 284)

I. CURRENT STATUS OF THE PROBLEM

Before considering the major issues in the dispute over testing black children, it is important to take a quick glance at the current status of the problem involving abuse and misuse in testing black children.

The dispute over the intellectual inferiority of black people and the corresponding problem of measuring black intelligence has created more controversy than perhaps any other single issue in the field of psychology. Some of the central disputants have compromised on occasion, but essentially there has been produced a sharp cleavage of opinion about the intelligence of black people, and intelligence testing in general. In a word, opinion is split over whether or not lower scores by blacks on the traditional ability tests are attributed primarily to genetic heritage or biased intelligence tests. It is seriously questioned today whether traditional ability tests may serve as valid measures of black intelligence.

In preparing this response, the writer carefully examined a vast array of publications dealing with one phase or another of the continuing controversy over abuses and misuses in testing black children. The single, most salient conclusion is that traditional ability tests do systematically and consistently lead to assigning of improper and false labels on black children, and consequently to dehumanization and black intellectual genocide. This conclusion is neither new nor is it surprising. The information has been known for many years. It was not until the Association of Black Psychologists generated some heat in this area by calling a moratorium on the testing of black people, however, that the *real* issues began to surface.

From *The Counseling Psychologist,* 1971, 2, 62–73. Reprinted by permission.

First of all, the meaning of intelligence is rather diverse and although considerable attention and effort have been given this concept, it is still ill-used and poorly understood. The ambiguity and senselessness of the research on the nature of the concept of intelligence is exceeded only by the research on ESP. Definitions of intelligence are so diverse that it would be impractical to list all of them here. A few examples are given as representative:

a. Intelligence is what the intelligence tests measure.
b. Intelligence is defined by a consensus among psychologists. It is repertoire of intellectual skills and knowledge available to a person at any one period of time. (Humphreys, 1969)
c. Intelligence is the summation of the learning experiences of the individual. (Wesman, 1968)
d. Intelligence is the aggregate or global capacity of the individual to act purposely, to think rationally, and to deal effectively with his environment. (Wechsler, 1944)

It is clear from the preceding definitions that there is not only lacking a consensus among psychologists regarding the meaning of intelligence, but there is no absolute definition as well. Such confusion and ambiguity make for considerable difficulty in precise and accurate measurement.

Secondly, the most frequently accepted definition is that intelligence is based on the solution of brief problems of various kinds and on the quality of one's responses to a wide range of questions. The final, standardized test score, which is called the *intelligence quotient*, or IQ, is usually computed so that it is given a scale score for which the average of the reference population is about 100. Jensen (1969) and Humphreys (1969) claim that, in the general population, blacks are about 15 IQ points, or one standard deviation, below whites. Psychologists and educators incorrectly use IQ and intelligence interchangeably. The intelligence quotient is a symbol which refers to a set of scores earned on a test, nothing more. An IQ per se cannot be inherited. A review of the research on comparing intellectual differences between blacks and whites shows the results to be based almost exclusively on differences in test scores, or IQ. Since the tests are biased in favor of middle-class whites, all previous research comparing the intellectual abilities of blacks and whites should be rejected completely.

Bennett (1970), in responding to the Association of Black Psychologists' call for a moratorium on the repeated abuses and misuses of psychological tests and to Williams (1970a), dealt with such factors as test anxiety, amount of formal education, and uniform testing procedures. Clemans (1970) and Sommer (1970) give what appear to be the most frequent reactions to charges of abuse of ability tests, i.e., it is the user of the test who labels the child. In this regard, Newland (1970) joins in unison:

> Ability tests do not label any children or adults. The adults who use them do that on the basis of scores earned on tests. Human beings do the labeling as well as selecting of the tests used to obtain scores in terms of which any such labeling is done. (p. 5)

Similarly, Munday (1970) sees the criticism against tests as misdirected. Instead of criticizing the tests, Munday identifies counselors, teachers, advisors, and admissions officers as perpetrators of the improper uses of test results. From a black perspective, these critics are not dealing with the real issue.

Messick and Anderson (1970) perhaps came closer to the real issues than any of the critics when they made a clear distinction between the scientific and ethical considerations involved in testing black children. Many important issues however have been omitted from discussions in the literature. This paper will endeavor to bring to the surface from a black perspective some of the previously "overlooked" issues in ability testing, involving scientific, political, educational, legal, and economic considerations.

II. SCIENTIFIC CONSIDERATIONS

Messick and Anderson (1970) point out that the same test may measure "different attributes or processes in minority/poverty groups than it measures in white, middle-class samples or for the same processes to be captured with a different degree of fidelity" (p. 82).

Translated, if this is true, then that test is invalid and should not be used in testing black children. In fact, not only is the validity of ability tests being called into question, but other such psychometric considerations of tests as reliability, objectivity, and standardization.

A. Validity. The validity of a test pertains to the extent to which it measures what it is intended to measure (Anastasi, 1968). More specifically, construct validity refers to the extent to which the test is measuring a theoretical construct such as intelligence. Does the traditional ability test measure the intelligence of black children? Current ability tests do not and cannot measure a black child's capacity "to deal effectively with his environment." The tests were never intended to do so. It is obvious enough that a black child engages in many intelligent behaviors which are not validated in white, middle-class society. For example, a black child might respond with, "My mother told me to hit 'em back if anybody hits me," to one of the standard IQ test questions. That answer actually represents "a summation of the learning experiences" for that particular black child in his black culture. The response also represents an *effective* way of dealing with *his* environment. It would be less than intelligent for the child to give responses which are opposite to or different from his environmental training or to the dictates of his cultural norms. One child is taught not to hit back; another is taught to hit back. It is a value judgment as to which is more intelligent teaching. Most tests take the philosophic frame of reference that white, middle-class standards are the correct ones.

B. Reliability and objectivity. The reliability of a test refers to the extent to which a person earns the same score or rank each time he is measured (Anastasi, 1968). One of the most common causes of unreliability of a test is the inclusion of items which are scored on the basis of subjective judgment, or, in this context, a white, middle-class norm. For example, persons from different cultural backgrounds will respond differently to the question, "What is the thing to do if you find a purse with ten dollars in it?" One child might respond with, "Try to find the owner"; another might respond with, "Keep it." Such items lack objectivity in scoring. They do not take cultural differences into account. Black children from certain socioeconomic levels would be penalized, and therefore the reliability of such tests would be low for measuring the intelligence of black children.

C. Standardization. A test must be representative of the group for whom it was designed (Anastasi, 1968). Two of the major ability tests (the Stanford-Binet and the Wechsler Intelligence Scale for Children) excluded blacks from the representative sample. If the purpose of standardizing a test is to make it useful for certain reference groups, then the WISC and Stanford-Binet are invalid for use with blacks.

III. POLITICAL CONSIDERATIONS

In addition to the scientific issues of testing, traditional psychologists have created a number of polemics which involve political issues. The literature is fraught with examples. For instances, take the case of Jensen (1969), who asked the question, "How much can we boost IQ and scholastic achievement?" For the next 123 pages, he proceeded to answer his own political question. The Jensen report, clearly a political document, was well known to the Nixon Administration when the budgets for compensatory education programs were being sharply reduced. Boosting IQ is not a real issue; it clearly is a straw man. Changes in test scores should not serve as the primary criteria by which educational programs are evaluated. If the goal and objective of Head Start, Project Follow Through, and other compensatory educational programs is that of "boosting IQ," then the goal is misput, inappropriate, and irrelevant.

I submit to Jensen and to others several methods for boosting IQs of black children:

a. Teach them the answers to the ability tests; or
b. Develop a black IQ test containing items drawn exclusively from the black world; or
c. Standardize black responses to white-oriented tests as follows: What is the thing to do if you find a purse with ten dollars in it?" Correct answers: "Try to find the owner"; "Keep the money, return the purse."

A concern with producing increases in test scores is similar to that of a physician whose main concern is treating the *casualties* rather than the *causes.* We refer to this approach as "victim analysis." System-produced educational problems cannot effectively be changed by focusing exclusively on the victims. The system that produced the damage must be closely examined and modified.

A. Deficit vs. difference model. Bennett (1970) makes the point that traditional ability tests merely reveal the "detrimental consequences of substandard opportunity." He believes that it would be better to remedy the "cultural deficit" than to discredit the test measures. Similarly, Wilkoff (1970) argues that culture of blacks needs to be improved and enriched. For too long psychologists and educators have believed in the mythology that low scores on a test are in fact a weakness or a deficit in the mental ability of the black individual. It has not been made clear that the individual may possess abilities not measured by a particular test. The deficiency may well be in the weakness of the test to measure black children; in the tester but not in the testee. Black Americans do not have an inferior culture; it is, indeed, different, but it remains a highly enriched culture.

A review of the literature on the major issues involved in testing black children clearly reveals two general conceptual models. The first group is classified under the general heading of a "deficit" model, whereas the second group is classified under the heading of a "difference" model.

The deficit model assumes that black people are deficient when compared to whites in some measurable trait called intelligence, and that this deficiency is due to genetic or cultural factors or both. To support this notion, such terms as "heritability of IQ," "cultural deprivation," and "the disadvantaged" have been invented to perpetuate the myth. Proponents of this school of thought assume that the intellectual and educational deficits experienced by the so-called culturally deprived are clearly revealed by such psychological tests as the Stanford-Binet, Wechsler, Scholastic Aptitude Test, Stanford Achievement, Iowa Basic Skills, Graduate Record Examination and Miller Analogies tests. These tests are devised to measure one's capacity to learn, or, more specifically, what one has learned. The items are supposedly selected on the basis that individuals of the same age have had the same opportunity to become familiar with the content of the items. This assumption is not true. Two five-year-olds, one black and one white, from different cultural backgrounds, will answer quite differently questions such as "What is the thing to do if another child hits you?" or "What is the thing to do if you find a purse with ten dollars in it?" The deficit model assumes a set of acceptable, standard responses. If the black child gives a response that is not validated as acceptable by the norm, he is declared as deficient in his "ability to comprehend and to size up certain social situations," whereas the white child is considered adequate in his ability to make appropriate judgments.

If the black child scores lower on ability tests than the white child, the difference does not mean that the black child is actually inferior in intelligence; all it means is that the black child performed differently on the test from the white. Test inferiority is not to be equated with actual inferiority. In this connection, Jensen (1968) found that many disadvantaged children with IQs between 60 and 80 performed better on learning tasks than upper middle-class children having IQs in the same range. These findings suggest that the tests were a much better predictor of ability and capacity of middle-class children since these children performed at the "expected" level. The results suggest further that the tests underpredicted the performance of the disadvantaged children since these children performed at a higher than expected level.

The deficit model therefore engages in faulty reasoning: If a child scores low on a test, the assumption is that he lacks the capacity to compete with those children who scored at a higher level. Present ability tests do not measure one's capacity to do work. At best they measure a level of learning in certain areas. From these "measurements" inferences are made regarding his capacity to learn further. It is this kind of reasoning that is faulty.

Briefly stated, the cultural difference model asserts that the differences noted by psychologists in intelligence testing, family and social organizations, and the studies of the black community are not the result of pathology, faulty learning, or genetic inferiority. These differences are manifestations of a viable and well-delineated culture of the black American. The difference model also acknowledges that blacks and whites come from different cultural backgrounds which emphasize different learning experiences necessary for survival. To say that the black American is different from the white American is not to say that he is inferior, deficient, or deprived. One can be unique and different without being inferior. The model, therefore, makes a clear distinction between *equality* and *sameness.* Two pieces of fruit, e.g., an apple and an orange, may be equal in weight, in quality of goodness and marketability, but they are not the same. An apple cannot become an orange, and vice versa. Each must express its respective characteristics of "appleness" and "orangeness," yet both are fruit. Whereas the deficit model espouses a "Get like me" response, the difference model endeavors to increase the number of options as to what constitutes acceptable and nonacceptable responses. Instead of being confined by an egalitarian doctrine that confuses equality with sameness, the cultural difference model recognizes that this society is pluralistic in nature, where cultural differences abound.

B. Language deficiency vs. language deficit. Because of the vast cultural differences in black and white society, significant language differences are present. Differences in language and dialect may produce differences in cognitive learning styles, but a difference is not a deficiency. Linguists do not limit themselves to defining dialect as the way words are pronounced. "Dialect refers to the linguistic structure of a people. The dialect is a fully developed linguistic system" (Baratz and Baratz, 1969). Instead of calling black language wrong, improper, or deficient in nature, one must realize that the black child is speaking a well-developed language commonly referred to as nonstandard English. Intelligence is frequently based quite heavily on language factors. It is a common observation that black and white children do not speak alike. The differences in linguistic systems favor white children since standard English is the *lingua franca* of the tests and the public schools.

Take, for example, the Scholastic Aptitude Test (SAT) which contains a verbal and a numerical factor. The students who do not show high verbal or numerical ability score low on the SAT and are typically excluded from entering college. If this fact is true, then blacks have been routinely excluded from college due to the different dialect and language systems rather than weakness in verbal ability. It does not mean that black people do not have the intellectual ability to compete in college. For example, blacks typically are not inferior in verbal ability. The average black adolescent will know how to "play the dozens," and play them well. He will know from memory, "The Signifying Monkey," "Shine," "Mr. Boon," and many other indicators of verbal ability, but these factors do not get measured in the typical classroom. In fact, many black children can state bits of poetry and prose in iambic pentameter. A case in point is revealed in the following revision of a Mother Goose rhyme made by a black eight-year-old:

> "Baa baa, Black Sheep, Have you any wool?"
> "Yes sir, yes sir, two bags full;
> One for the black man; one for the Jew.
> Sorry, Mr. Charlie, but none for you."

C. The Commission on Tests report. A special Commission on Tests appointed by the College Entrance Examination Board indicated that the Board examinations taken by about 2,000,000 high-school students a year failed to recognize and assess a wide variety of talents, skills, and mental attributes (Report of the Commission on Tests, 1970). Over the years, many students, particularly black ones, have been grossly penalized. Basically, the Commission on Tests found the SAT, which measures fluency in English and ability to deal with mathematical and spatial concepts, to be discriminatory against certain minority groups. Although high verbal and numerical abilities are generally those required in traditional academic liberal arts and scientific education, the Commission found these indicators to be too narrow for application to all who might benefit from college. The Commission recommended that the tests gradually be replaced by a flexible assortment of other tests, measuring not only verbal and mathematical ability but many other dimensions of excellence. These dimensions included musical and artistic talents; sensitivity and commitment to social responsibility; political and social leadership; athletic, political, and mechanical skills; styles of analysis and synthesis; ability to express oneself through artistic, oral, nonverbal, or graphic means; ability to organize and manage information; ability to adapt to new situations; characteristics of temperament; and so on.

In a recent memo directed to school counselors, the Washington University Director of Admissions had these points to make regarding changes in admission procedures:

> We believe that this university has a great deal to offer to a wide variety of students; the scholar and the singer, the debater and dancer, the athlete, the artist and the actor, the editor and the engineer. Accordingly, we urge you to recommend capable, interesting students, even if there is some slight "lopsidedness" in their records. Where there is need for compensating strength for lower SAT scores, for instance, we will trust you to point this out to us. It is impossible to overemphasize how highly we regard your evaluation as we search for an ever-widening array of talents and abilities.

The political impact of reports issued under the rubric of education is enormous. Many of these reports are used as political and scientific clout against the black cause. The Moynihan report on black families reportedly led to deemphasis by the Nixon Administration on welfare programs. Moynihan's "benign neglect" memo hurt the cause of black people. "The time may have come when the issue of race could benefit from a period of 'benign neglect.' The subject has been too much talked about. The forum has been too much taken over to hysterics, paranoids, and boodlers on all sides" (Moynihan, 1970).

The Jensen report (1969) led directly or indirectly to a number of changes in the President's program regarding Head Start Programs, Project Follow Through, and other compensatory educational programs. These and other reports must be considered political in nature. A few of the reports lead to positive change for black people while others are quite detrimental.

IV. EDUCATIONAL CONSIDERATIONS

In addition to the foregoing comments regarding education, it is clear from this discussion that ability and certain achievement tests play a major role in current educational procedures and consequently in determining what doors in life will be opened or closed to a black child. Tests are used to determine admission, grouping, selection, assignment to special classes and educational tracks. If the tests are unfair (biased), then it is clear that they place (misplace), label (mislabel) a certain portion of the population in general and the black population in particular. Throughout the country, a disproportionately large number of black children are being misplaced in special education classes. Many states legally define the educable mentally retarded as those children obtaining an IQ below 80.

A. The Association of Black Psychologists' statement on testing abuse. At its annual meeting in 1969, the Association of Black Psychologists called for an immediate moratorium on the administration of ability tests to black children. The Association charged that these tests:

1. Label black children as uneducable;
2. Place black children in special classes;
3. Potentiate inferior education;
4. Assign black children to lower education tracks than whites;
5. Deny black children higher educational opportunities;
6. Destroy positive intellectual growth and development of black children.

In other words, black psychologists translated the whole abuse of testing issue into one of intellectual genocide of black children. Tests do not permit the masses of black children to develop their full intellectual potential. The tests are used to sort and consequently to misplace black children in Special Education classes.

B. Composition of Special Education classes in St. Louis and San Francisco. In St. Louis, during the academic year 1968–1969, blacks comprised approximately 63.6 percent of the school population, whereas whites comprised 36.4 percent. Of 4,020 children in Special Education, 2,975 (76 percent) were black, only 1,045 (24 percent) were white. Thus, black children were being placed in classes for the educable mentally retarded about three times as frequently as their white counterparts. Again, children are placed in Special Education classes primarily on the basis of scores earned on biased intelligence tests.

In San Francisco, a group of black psychologists recently presented a document on testing abuses to the San Francisco Unified School District School Board. The document called for an immediate moratorium on ability testing of black children until better and more appropriate assessment techniques are made available. The document pointed out the following: that although black children comprise only 27.8 percent of the total student population in the San Francisco Unified Schools, they comprise 47.4 percent of all students in educationally handicapped classes, and 53.3 percent of all students in the educable mentally handicapped classes. The black psychologists pointed out that the consultants to the psychologists and psychometricians in the San Francisco Unified School District are not familiar enough with the black experience to serve as competent evaluators of black children. The document also pointed out that, of the psychologists and psychometrists who administered and interpreted the psychological tests, no black personnel were involved. The Association of Black Psychologists has recently reported that the San Francisco School District has honored the moratorium on testing, and that no psychological tests are now being administered to black children for placement in special classes.

It is reported that an IBM computer was incorrectly programmed, sending the "slow" students into the high track and the "bright" ones into the low track. About one year later, when the error was discovered, "slow" pupils were behaving as though they were "bright" and the "bright" pupils were behaving as if they were dull.

Thus, the black mother who gratefully and naively sends her children to school daily does not suspect the dangers lurking in the shadows of the educational institution. No one has told her that her little child probably will be required to take a psychological examination. She does not know that this exam will yield a so-called IQ label which will probably follow her child for the rest of his school life. The mother does not understand that the IQ will lead to the placement (or misplacement) of her child in a Special Education class or an educational tracking system. The mother does not know that these tests are violating her child's constitutional and civil rights and that she can sue the perpetrators for their transgressions.

V. LEGAL CONSIDERATIONS ON TESTING

It is clear that the continued administration of traditional ability tests to black children is a violation of the child's civil and constitutional rights under the provisions of the Fourteenth Amendment for equal protection under the law.

The following four court cases will be discussed to show where charges have been made of actual abuse of tests:

a. Leary (1970) reports the case of *Diana et al.* v. *California State Board of Education*, which led to a decision in favor of a Mexican-American child whose intelligence had been woefully underestimated by the Binet.
b. The Skelly Wright decision in the case of *Hobson* v. *Hansen* in Washington, D.C., set an early precedent. In that decision, the judge ordered the track system abolished since unfair ability tests were used in sorting the children into tracks.
c. In Boston, the case of *Stewart et al.* v. *Phillips et al.* charges that children are being placed in special classes irrationally and unfairly.
d. The case of *Armstead et al.* v. *Starkeville, Mississippi, Municipal Separate School District et al.* involved the case of the Graduate Record Exam (GRE) for employment and retention of black and white teachers.

The increasing number of criticisms in the literature and the possible large number of impending court cases regarding the abuse and misuse of testing black children strongly suggest that the cries of the black community be heard as so eloquently stated by Halpern (1970–1971).

Article XIV, Section 1 of the Constitution of the United States reads as follows:

> All persons born or naturalized in the United States, and subject to the jurisdiction thereof are citizens of the United States and of the state wherein they reside. No state shall make or enforce any law which shall abridge the privileges or immunities of citizens in the United States; nor shall any state deprive any person of life, liberty, or property, without the due process of law; nor deny to any person within its jurisdiction the equal protection of the laws.

A. Diana et al. v. California State Board of Education. One case is reported by Leary (1970) of an eight-year-old Mexican-American girl who earned an IQ of 30 on the Stanford-Binet intelligence test, clearly placing her in the mentally defective range of functioning. Diana's mother had the test readministered by a school psychologist, also of Mexican-American descent, who translated the test into

Spanish. Diana's IQ increased 49 points. In fact, of nine Mexican-American children retested in Spanish, all but one increased to above the cutoff score of 79 used by the California school district to place children in the category of the educable mentally retarded or the educationally handicapped.

Another case of misjudging is reported by Witty and Jenkins (1935) of a black child with superior intelligence who had an IQ of 200. She was rated by her teacher as lower in intelligence than a child whose IQ turned out to be 100. When a misjudgment does occur, the result will be to place the child into a curriculum paced to his measured abilities, where he is likely to progress only at the speed provided by the teacher. In fact, many black children probably have higher native intelligence than their teachers. These teachers frequently see the gifted black students as "problem children," "hyperactive," "disruptive," when, in fact, the children are simply bored in the classroom. They are not being challenged by teachers who have only average to slightly above average intelligence.

B. Hobson v. Hansen. In a rather momentous decision in the United States District Court for the District of Columbia, United States Circuit Judge J. Skelly Wright issued a 182-page document in the case of *Hobson* v. *Hansen* in regard to abolishing the track system in the D.C. schools. Judge Wright stated: "It is further ordered, adjudged, and decreed that the defendants be, and they are hereby, permanently enjoined from operating the track system in the District of Columbia public schools." The D.C. educational track system was implemented in the high schools in 1956, and extended downward to the junior high and elementary schools in 1959. The track system proved to be nothing more than another way of resegregating blacks and whites within the individual school system. As the evidence in the case became clear, grouping children on the basis of test scores was clearly a denial of equal educational opportunity to the poor and the majority of blacks attending school in the nation's capital. The findings clearly showed that black children dominated the lower tracks. White and the more affluent students were found to be in the upper tracks. Thus, the judge decided that when a student is placed in a lower track, his future is being decided for him, i.e., the kind of job he gets is greatly shaped by the quality of education he receives.

The judge found the most important single aspect of the track system to be the process by which the school system grouped children in different tracks. The sorting process is the keystone of the entire track system. Children were placed in tracks based on such ability tests as the Binet and WISC. Thus, as the judge decided, when standard ability tests are given to low-income black children or disadvantaged children, they are less precise and less accurate, so it is virtually impossible to tell whether the test score reflects lack of ability or lack of opportunity.

The judge, looking very closely into side issues of psychological testing and placement of track systems, pointed out the following damages inherent in the system:

> By consigning students to specifically designed curricula, the track system makes highly visible the student's status within the school structure. To the unlearned, tracks can become pejorative labels, symptomatic of which is the recent abandonment of the suggestive "Basic" for the more euphemistic "Special Academic" as the nomenclature of the lowest track. A system that presumes to tell a student what his ability is and what he can successfully learn incurs an obligation to take account of the psychological damage that can come from such an encounter between the student and the school, and to be certain that it is in a position to decide whether the student's deficiencies are true, or only apparent. The District of Columbia school system has not shown that it is in such a position. *(Hobson* v. *Hansen,* p. 140)

The judge interpreted the testing and track system as a way of forcing the self-fulfilling prophecy, i.e., teachers acting under false assumptions because of low test scores will treat the black student in such a way as to make him conform to their low expectations. In concluding, the judge decided as follows:

> As to the remedy with respect to the track system, the track system simply must be abolished . . . even in concept the track system is undemocratic and discriminatory. Its creator admits it is designed to prepare some children for white collar and other children for blue collar jobs . . . the danger of children completing their education wearing the wrong collar is far too great for this democracy. *(Hobson* v. *Hansen,* p. 177)

Many cities have abolished the track system as a direct result of the decision rendered in the *Hobson* v. *Hansen* case. However, they have implemented other systems which are not called track systems but which are just as lethal; for example, in one city the tracking system has been officially abolished, but three levels have been substituted in its place: (A) Academic Curriculum, (B) Standard Curriculum, (C) General Curriculum. It is clear from the inequality of education provided that educational tracking is one of the major aspects of the new system. In any event, psychological tests are used to determine who goes into the academic, standard, or general curriculum, each of which leads to different educational careers or futures. A rose is a rose by any other name.

C. Stewart et al. v. Phillips and Massachusetts Board of Education. In the United States District Court for the District of Massachusetts, another case has recently been cited, *Stewart et al.* v. *Phillips and the Massachusetts Board of Education.* This action was brought by the public-school students and their parents for damages against officials of the Boston school system and the Board of Education of the Commonwealth of Massachusetts. The action challenges the arbitrary, irrational, and discriminatory manner in which students in the Boston public schools are denied the right to an education by being classified as mentally retarded and placed in so-called special classes. The State of Massachusetts uses the 79 cutoff IQ on ability tests as a basis for placing children in Special Education classes. The major claim in this suit is that a numerical IQ of less than 80 is an inadequate basis for placing children in the Special Education classes, and that since the tests are unfair and biased against black children, the state deprives the children of the right to equal protection of the laws in violation of the Fourteenth Amendment. The seven plaintiffs on behalf of their children are suing for $20,000 each in compensatory and punitive damages. They are asking that a permanent injunction be issued declaring and enjoining that no child be placed or retained in a special class in the city of Boston unless and until the following procedures are met:

1. That a special, nine-member Commission on Individual Educational Needs be established;
2. That no child be placed in a Special Education class unless a fair test has been administered by a competent psychologist, the parents are given notice, and the placement in the special class is naturally related to the child's educational needs;
3. That the Commission specify a battery of psychological tests from which examiners select the appropriate one for administration;
4. That the Commission approve a cadre of local psychologists and mental health agencies qualified to administer the tests;
5. That all children in Special Education classes be re-evaluated under the new procedures;
6. That all children found to be improperly labeled be provided with "transitional" programs designed to compensate for the educational loss experienced while misclassified;
7. That the Commission study the procedures for administering tests;
8. That no child be placed in a special class solely on the basis of a test score.

D. Armstead et al, v. Starkville, Mississippi, Municipal Separate School District et al. Another case of intended misuse of psychological tests was filed in the United States District Court for the Northern District of the Mississippi Eastern Division, where a suit was brought when the school system planned to use the Graduate Record Exam (GRE) for determining employment and retention of elementary and secondary teachers. Manning (1970) of the Educational Testing Service pointed out in an affidavit that the GRE is a national program of tests designed to assist undergraduate students in graduate schools in the process of transition from undergraduate to graduate study. Thus, the GRE would be inappropriately used if employed as a way of screening applicants for teaching positions in the state of Mississippi. It was clear that the Board of Education planned to use the GRE as a way of eliminating black teachers in the state's transition from segregated to desegregated schools. The GRE was simply an instrument to be used in that connection. Manning pointed out in his affidavit that the test would be perhaps less reliable for a group of teachers than for regular graduate students enrolled in study at the doctoral level, and that in using a test for purposes other than that for which it was designed would be to invalidate the use of that test.

Manning (1970) points out:

> In my judgment the use of the GRE aptitude and advanced test for selection and retention of teachers in the Starkville School System . . . would be a blind use of these tests unless studies were first performed that would, as a minimum, establish the content validity and concurrent validity of these tests for the criteria of teacher effectiveness. (p. 22)

Manning's affidavit provided the context for assessing the question of the validity of using the GRE and specified cutoff scores of the test as criteria for employment of elementary- and secondary-school teachers in the Starkville schools. The same arguments may be used in regard to testing black children and placing them in Special Education classes. In his conclusions, Manning (1970) noted the following characteristics of aptitude and achievement tests of blacks and whites:

1. The test may contain items that are specifically germaine to the white, middle-class environment, thus placing black students at a disadvantage
2. Black students may be less familiar with test-taking strategies and will, because they are less skilled or "test-wise," be less able to compete successfully
3. The conditions under which students are required to take the tests are such that black students may feel anxious, threatened, and alienated, thereby impairing their ability to perform successfully on the test
4. Tests measure abilities that are developed as a consequence of educational, social, and family experience over many years. One consequence of poverty, segregation, and inequality of educational opportunities to which black students are more likely to have been subjected is reflected in lower scores on tests such as the GRE Aptitude and Advanced Test (pp. 31–32).

VI. ECONOMIC CONSIDERATIONS

Testing is a big industry. One of the major nonprofit testing organizations showed the following statement of income from tests for the year ending June 30, 1970:

	Actual, 1968–1969	Actual, 1969–1970	Projected, 1970–1971
Admissions Testing Program	$17,424,015	$17,688,007	$18,520,800
College Level Exam Program	157,285	179,739	449,500
Puerto Rico Testing Program	211,697	259,850	233,000
Advanced Placement Program	973,823	1,236,065	1,363,000

Messick and Anderson (1970) point out [that] the social consequences of *not* testing are extreme. The economic consequences of not testing are also quite extreme!

For many black children, the economic consequences of testing are quite extreme. As pointed out earlier, testing may determine which doors may or may not be opened to black children. Or, as Judge Wright in the *Hobson* v. *Hansen* case so aptly put it, the tests may determine that the child wear the "wrong collar" occupationally. As reported by Williams (1970b), 100 minority group postal employees were hired without the usual screening tests being administered. At the end of one year, by and large they received satisfactory ratings based on job performance. The employees were administered the usual screening tests at the end of a one-year period; they all failed. The tests certainly would have led to the unemployment of qualified persons. Lowering standards is not the issue; appropriate assessment is a vital issue, however.

CONCLUSIONS

Testing is a big business. The use of tests has become deeply imbedded in the American version of education. To some, testing represents an American dream; to others, it represents a horrible nightmare. Tests shape, in large measure, what is to be taught in schools. Teaching the test is not an uncommon phenomenon in American schools. Teachers prepare the student for the test to be taken. In many ways, the tests may shape teacher expectations. If this assertion is at all true, and some evidence exists to suggest that it is (Goslin, 1967), one strategy for improving or changing the educational system would be to change the content of the tests as a way of bringing about educational reforms in the system. Items relevant to the black experience would bring about similar changes in classrooms. This effort might bring about a greater similarity between the predictor (tests) and the criterion (scholastic achievement).

While Bennett (1970) and others continue to declare the intellectual inferiority of black people, the courts are reaching decisions which negate their allegations. Thus, it merely becomes an academic exercise to continue this "straw man" debate. Black professionals must be about the business of developing appropriate measuring instruments and black educational models for black children.

COURT CASES

1. *Hobson* v. *Hansen.* Civil Action No. 82-66. United States District Court for the District of Columbia.
2. Winton H. Manning, An Affidavit of Winton H. Manning, cited in *Armstead et al.* v. *Starkville, Mississippi, Municipal Separate School District et al.* Civil Action No. EC 70-51-5.
3. *Stewart et al.* v. *Phillips and Massachusetts Board of Education.* Civil Action 70-1199F. United States District Court for the District of Massachusetts.
4. *Diana et al.* v. *California State Board of Education.* Cited by M. E. Leary, Children who are tested in an alien language: Mentally retarded? *The New Republic,* 1970, **162**(22), 17–18.

BIBLIOGRAPHY

Anastasi, A. *Psychological testing.* New York: Macmillan, 1968.

Baratz, S., and Baratz, J. C. Negro ghetto children and urban education: A cultural solution. *Social Education,* 1969, **33**(34), 401–405.

Bennett, G. L. Response to Robert Williams. *The Counseling Psychologist,* 1970, **2**(2), 88–89.

Clemans, W. U. A note in response to a request by the editor to comment on R. L. Williams' article. *The Counseling Psychologist,* 1970, **2**(2), 90–91.

Ellis, R. S. *The psychology of the individual.* New York: Appleton-Century-Crofts, 1928.

Goslin, D. A. *Teachers and testing.* New York: Russell Sage Foundation, 1967.

Halpern, F. C. Clinicians must listen! *Clinical Child Psychology Newsletter,* Winter 1970–1971, **9**(4), 8.

Humphreys, L. Letters. *Science,* 1969, **166**(3902), 167.

Jensen, A. R. How much can we boost IQ and scholastic achievement? *Harvard Educational Review,* Winter 1969, **39**, 1–123.

Leary, M. E. Children who are tested in an alien language: Mentally retarded? *The New Republic,* 1970, **162**(22), 17–18.

Messick, S., and Anderson, S. Educational testing, individual development and social responsibility. *The Counseling Psychologist,* 1970, **2**(2), 93–97.

Moynihan, P. "Benign neglect" for issue of race? *The Wall Street Journal,* March 3, 1970, 20.

Newland, T. E. Testing minority group children. *Clinical Child Psychology Newsletter,* 1970, **9**(3), 5.

Pierce, W. D., West, G. I., Dent, H. E., Rawls, J. D., and Woodson, W. B. A reply to San Francisco Unified School District Report on Special Education Classes. Report prepared by members of the Association of Black Psychologists. San Francisco, California, May 5, 1970.

Report of the Commission on Tests I. *Righting the balance.* College Entrance Examination Board, New York, 1970.

Sommer, J. Response to Robert Williams. *The Counseling Psychologist,* 1970, **2**(2), 93–97.

Wechsler, D. *The measurement of adult intelligence.* Baltimore: Williams & Wilkins, 1944.

Wesman, A. G. Intelligent testing. *American Psychologist,* 1968, **23**(4), 267–274.

Wikoff, R. L. Danger: Attacks on testing unfair. *Clinical Child Psychology Newsletter,* Spring 1970, **9**(1), 3–4.

Williams, R. L. Black pride, academic relevance and individual achievement. *The Counseling Psychologist,* 1970, **2**(1), 19–22. (a)

Williams, R. L. Letters. *Science,* 1970, **167**(3915), 124. (b)

Witty, P. A., and Jenkins, A. D. The case of "B_____," a gifted Negro girl. *Journal of Social Psychology,* 1935, **6**(1), 117–124.

CAUSATION

Chapter 5

Biological Determinants

The determinants of abnormal behavior, like those of normality, are complex because they involve the interplay of motivational, sociocultural, and biological forces. This complexity is amply and clearly depicted in Anne Anastasi's early paper "Heredity, Environment, and the Question 'How?' " in which she describes several modes of research attack on the question of how heredity and environment determine behavior. These are strategies that are still very much at the forefront of current studies.

The study presented in Albert Hood's paper challenges Kretschmer's and Sheldon's notions that there is a relationship between physique and personality makeup. After correlating the MMPIs of 10,000 male freshmen who were classified according to somatotypes, Hood concluded that the relationship between physique and personality type is not substantiated.

The third paper in this chapter, which investigates the incidence of chromosomal error and criminality, is by Telfer and her associates. The latter conclude that their limited survey confirms the existence of an XYY chromosomal syndrome among male prisoners.

The final paper consists of Gottesman and Shields's extensive, 16-year study on the incidence of schizophrenia among twin pairs. Their findings are a replication of some of their earlier and more recent twin studies and lead them to the rather interesting conclusion "that the mysteries of the schizophrenias will be solved in our lifetimes."

Heredity, Environment, and the Question "How?" *

Anne Anastasi

Two or three decades ago, the so-called heredity-environment question was the center of lively controversy. Today, on the other hand, many psychologists look upon it as a dead issue. It is now generally conceded that both hereditary and environmental factors enter into all behavior. The reacting organism is a product of its genes and its past environment, while present environment provides the immediate stimulus for current behavior. To be sure, it can be argued that, although a given trait may result from the combined influence of hereditary and environmental factors, a specific difference in this trait between individuals or between groups may be traceable to either hereditary or environmental factors alone. The design of most traditional investigations undertaken to identify such factors, however, has been such as to yield inconclusive answers. The same set of data has frequently led to opposite conclusions in the hands of psychologists with different orientations.

Nor have efforts to determine the proportional contribution of hereditary and environmental factors to observed individual differences in given traits met with any greater success. Apart from difficulties in controlling conditions, such investigations have usually been based upon the implicit assumption that hereditary and environmental factors combine in an additive fashion. Both geneticists and psychologists have repeatedly demonstrated, however, that a more tenable hypothesis is that of interaction (15, 22, 28, 40). In other words, the nature and extent of the influence of each type of factor depend upon the contribution of the other. Thus the proportional contribution of heredity to the variance of a given trait, rather than being a constant, will vary under different environmental conditions. Similarly, under different hereditary conditions, the relative contribution of environment will differ. Studies designed to estimate the proportional contribution of heredity and environment, however, have rarely included measures of such interaction. The only possible conclusion from such research would thus seem to be that both heredity and environment contribute to all behavior traits and that the extent of their respective contributions cannot be specified for any trait. Small wonder that some psychologists regard the heredity-environment question as unworthy of further consideration!

But is this really all we can find out about the operation of heredity and environment in the etiology of behavior? Perhaps we have simply been asking the wrong questions. The traditional questions about heredity and environment may be intrinsically unanswerable. Psychologists began by asking *which* type of factor, hereditary or environmental, is responsible for individual differences in a given trait. Later, they tried to discover *how much* of the variance was attributable to heredity and how much to environment. It is the primary contention of this paper that a more fruitful approach is to be found in the question "*How?*" There is still much to be learned about the specific *modus operandi* of hereditary and environmental factors in the development of behavioral differences. And there are several current lines of research which offer promising techniques for answering the question "How?"

VARIETY OF INTERACTION MECHANISMS

Hereditary factors. If we examine some of the specific ways in which hereditary factors may influence behavior, we cannot fail but be impressed by their wide diversity. At one extreme, we find such conditions as phenylpyruvic amentia and amaurotic idiocy. In these cases, certain essential physical prerequisites for normal intellectual development are lacking as a result of hereditary metabolic disorders. . . .

A somewhat different situation is illustrated by hereditary deafness, which may lead to intellectual retardation through interference with normal social interaction, language development, and schooling. In such a case, however, the hereditary handicap can be offset by appropriate adaptations of training procedures. It has been said, in fact, that the degree of intellectual backwardness of the deaf is an index of the state of development of special instructional facilities. As the latter improve, the intellectual retardation associated with deafness is correspondingly reduced.

A third example is provided by inherited susceptibility to

From *Psychological Review*, 1958, 65, 198–208.

*Address of the President, Division of General Psychology, American Psychological Association, September 4, 1957.

certain physical diseases, with consequent protracted ill health. If environmental conditions are such that illness does in fact develop, a number of different behavioral effects may follow. Intellectually, the individual may be handicapped by his inability to attend school regularly. On the other hand, depending upon age of onset, home conditions, parental status, and similar factors, poor health may have the effect of concentrating the individual's energies upon intellectual pursuits. The curtailment of participation in athletics and social functions may serve to strengthen interest in reading and other sedentary activities. Concomitant circumstances would also determine the influence of such illness upon personality development. And it is well known that the latter effects could run the gamut from a deepening of human sympathy to psychiatric breakdown.

Finally, heredity may influence behavior through the mechanism of social stereotypes. A wide variety of inherited physical characteristics have served as the visible cues for identifying such stereotypes. These cues thus lead to behavioral restrictions or opportunities and—at a more subtle level—to social attitudes and expectancies. The individual's own self concept tends gradually to reflect such expectancies. All of these influences eventually leave their mark upon his abilities and inabilities, his emotional reactions, goals, ambitions, and outlook on life.

The geneticist Dobzhansky illustrates this type of mechanism by means of a dramatic hypothetical situation. He points out that, if there were a culture in which the carriers of blood group AB were considered aristocrats and those of blood group O laborers, then the blood-group genes would become important hereditary determiners of behavior (12, p. 147). Obviously the association between blood group and behavior would be specific to that culture. But such specificity is an essential property of the causal mechanism under consideration.

More realistic examples are not hard to find. The most familiar instances occur in connection with constitutional types, sex, and race. Sex and skin pigmentation obviously depend upon heredity. General body build is strongly influenced by hereditary components, although also susceptible to environmental modification. That all these physical characteristics may exert a pronounced effect upon behavior within a given culture is well known. It is equally apparent, of course, that in different cultures the behavioral correlates of such hereditary physical traits may be quite unlike. A specific physical cue may be completely unrelated to individual differences in psychological traits in one culture, while closely correlated with them in another. Or it may be associated with totally dissimilar behavior characteristics in two different cultures.

It might be objected that some of the illustrations which have been cited do not properly exemplify the operation of hereditary mechanisms in behavior development, since hereditary factors enter only indirectly into the behavior in question. Closer examination, however, shows this distinction to be untenable. First it may be noted that the influence of heredity upon behavior is always indirect. No psychological trait is ever inherited as such. All we can ever say directly from behavioral observations is that a given trait shows evidence of being influenced by certain "inheritable unknowns." This merely defines a problem for genetic research; it does not provide a causal explanation. Unlike the blood groups, which are close to the level of primary gene products, psychological traits are related to genes by highly indirect and devious routes. Even the mental deficiency associated with phenylketonuria is several steps removed from the chemically defective genes that represent its hereditary basis. Moreover, hereditary influences cannot be dichotomized into the more direct and the less direct. Rather do they represent a whole "continuum of indirectness," along which are found all degrees of remoteness of causal links. The examples already cited illustrate a few of the points on this continuum.

It should be noted that as we proceed along the continuum of indirectness, the range of variation of possible outcomes of hereditary factors expands rapidly. At each step in the causal chain, there is fresh opportunity for interaction with other hereditary factors as well as with environmental factors. And since each interaction in turn determines the direction of subsequent interactions, there is an ever-widening network of possible outcomes. If we visualize a simple sequential grid with only two alternatives at each point, it is obvious that there are two possible outcomes in the one-stage situation, four outcomes at the second stage, eight at the third, and so on in geometric progression. The actual situation is undoubtedly much more complex, since there will usually be more than two alternatives at any one point.

In the case of the blood groups, the relation to specific genes is so close that no other concomitant hereditary or environmental conditions can alter the outcome. If the organism survives at all, it will have the blood group determined by its genes. Among psychological traits, on the other hand, some variation in outcome is always possible as a result of concurrent circumstances. Even in cases of phenylketonuria, intellectual development will exhibit some relationship with the type of care and training available to the individual. That behavioral outcomes show progressive diversification as we proceed along the continuum of indirectness is brought out by the other examples which were cited. Chronic illness *can* lead to scholarly renown or to intellectual immaturity; a mesomorphic physique *can* be a contributing factor in juvenile delinquency or in the attainment of a college presidency! Published data on Sheldon somatotypes provide some support for both of the latter outcomes.

Parenthetically, it may be noted that geneticists have sometimes used the term "norm of reaction" to designate the range of variation of possible outcomes of gene properties (cf. 13, p. 161). Thus heredity sets the "norm" or limits within which environmental differences determine the eventual outcome. In the case of some traits, such as blood groups or eye color, this norm is much narrower than in the case of other traits. Owing to the rather different psychological connotations of both the words "norm" and "reaction," however, it seems less confusing to speak of the "range of variation" in this context.

A large portion of the continuum of hereditary influences which we have described coincides with the domain of somatopsychological relations, as defined by Barker et al. (6). Under this heading, Barker includes "variations in physique that affect the psychological situation of a person by influencing the effectiveness of his body as a tool for actions or by serving as a stimulus to himself or others" (6, p. 1). Relatively direct neurological influences on behavior, which have been the traditional concern of physiological psychology, are excluded from this definition, Barker being primarily concerned with what he calls the "social psychology of physique." Of the examples cited in the present paper, deafness, severe illness, and the physical characteristics associated with social stereotypes would meet the specifications of somatopsychological factors.

The somatic factors to which Barker refers, however, are not limited to those of hereditary origin. Bodily conditions attributable to environmental causes operate in the same sorts of somatopsychological relations as those traceable to heredity. In fact, heredity-environment distinctions play a minor part in Barker's approach.

Environmental factors: organic. Turning now to an analysis of the role of environmental factors in behavior, we find the same etiological mechanisms which were observed in the case of hereditary factors. First, however, we must differentiate between two classes of environmental influences: (*a*) those producing organic effects which may in turn influence behavior and (*b*) those serving as direct stimuli for psychological reactions. The former may be illustrated by food intake or by exposure to bacterial infection; the latter, by tribal initiation ceremonies or by a course in algebra. There are no completely satisfactory names by which to designate these two classes of influences. In an earlier paper by Anastasi and Foley (4), the terms "structural" and "functional" were employed. However, "organic" and "behavioral" have the advantage of greater familiarity in this context and may be less open to misinterpretation. Accordingly, these terms will be used in the present paper.

Like hereditary factors, environmental influences of an organic nature can also be ordered along a continuum of indirectness with regard to their relation to behavior. This continuum closely parallels that of hereditary factors. One end is typified by such conditions as mental deficiency resulting from cerebral birth injury or from prenatal nutritional inadequacies. A more indirect etiological mechanism is illustrated by severe motor disorder—as in certain cases of cerebral palsy—*without* accompanying injury to higher neurological centers. In such instances, intellectual retardation may occur as an indirect result of the motor handicap, through the curtailment of educational and social activities. Obviously this causal mechanism corresponds closely to that of hereditary deafness cited earlier in the paper.

Finally, we may consider an environmental parallel to the previously discussed social stereotypes which were mediated by hereditary physical cues. Let us suppose that a young woman with mousy brown hair becomes transformed into a dazzling golden blonde through environmental techniques currently available in our culture. It is highly probable that this metamorphosis will alter, not only the reactions of her associates toward her, but also her own self concept and subsequent behavior. The effects could range all the way from a rise in social poise to a drop in clerical accuracy!

Among the examples of environmentally determined organic influences which have been described, all but the first two fit Barker's definition of somatopsychological factors. With the exception of birth injuries and nutritional deficiencies, all fall within the social psychology of physique. Nevertheless, the individual factors exhibit wide diversity in their specific *modus operandi*—a diversity which has important practical as well as theoretical implications.

Environmental factors: behavioral. The second major class of environmental factors—the behavioral as contrasted to the organic—are by definition direct influences. The immediate effect of such environmental factors is always a behavioral change. To be sure, some of the initial behavioral effects may themselves indirectly affect the individual's later behavior. But this relationship can perhaps be best conceptualized in terms of breadth and permanence of effects. Thus it could be said that we are now dealing, not with a continuum of indirectness, as in the case of hereditary and organic-environmental factors, but rather with a continuum of breadth.

Social class membership may serve as an illustration of a relatively broad, pervasive, and enduring environmental factor. Its influence upon behavior development may operate through many channels. Thus social level may determine the range and nature of intellectual stimulation provided by home and community through books, music, art, play activities, and the like. Even more far-reaching may be the effects upon interests and motivation, as illustrated by the desire to perform abstract intellectual tasks, to surpass others in competitive situations, to succeed in school, or to gain social approval. Emotional and social traits may likewise be influenced by the nature of interpersonal relations characterizing homes at different socioeconomic levels. Somewhat more restricted in scope than social class, although still exerting a relatively broad influence, is amount of formal schooling which the individual is able to obtain.

A factor which may be wide or narrow in its effects, depending upon concomitant circumstances, is language handicap. Thus the bilingualism of an adult who moves to a foreign country with inadequate mastery of the new language represents a relatively limited handicap which can be readily overcome in most cases. At most, the difficulty is one of communication. On the other hand, some kinds of bilingualism in childhood may exert a retarding influence upon intellectual development and may under certain conditions affect personality development adversely (2, 5, 10). A common pattern in the homes of immigrants is that the child speaks one language at home and another in school, so that his knowledge of each language is limited to certain types of situations. Inadequate facility with the language of the school interferes with the acquisition of basic concepts, intellectual skills, and information. The frustration engendered by scholastic difficulties may in turn lead to discouragement and general dislike of school. Such reactions can be found, for example, among a number of Puerto Rican children in New York City schools (3). In the case of certain groups, moreover, the child's foreign language background may be perceived by himself and his associates as a symbol of minority group status and may thereby augment any emotional maladjustment arising from such status (34).

A highly restricted environmental influence is to be found in the opportunity to acquire specific items of information occurring in a particular intelligence test. The fact that such opportunities may vary with culture, social class, or individual experiential background is at the basis of the test user's concern with the problem of coaching and with "culture-free" or "culture-fair" tests (cf. 1, 2). If the advantage or disadvantage which such experiential differences confer upon certain individuals is strictly confined to performance on the given test, it will obviously reduce the validity of the test and should be eliminated.

In this connection, however, it is essential to know the breadth of the environmental influence in question. A fallacy inherent in many attempts to develop culture-fair tests is that the breadth of cultural differentials is not taken into account. Failure to consider breadth of effect likewise characterizes certain discussions of coaching. If, in coaching a student for a college admission test, we can improve his knowledge of verbal concepts and his reading comprehension, he will be better equipped to succeed in college courses. His performance level will thus be raised, not only on the test, but also on the criterion which the test is intended to predict. To try to devise a test which is not susceptible to such coaching would merely reduce the effectiveness of the test. Similarly, efforts to rule out cultural differentials from test items so as to make them equally "fair" to subjects in different social classes or in different cultures may merely limit the usefulness of the test, since the same cultural differentials may operate within the broader area of behavior which the test is designed to sample.

METHODOLOGICAL APPROACHES

The examples considered so far should suffice to highlight the wide variety of ways in which hereditary and environmental factors may interact in the course of behavior development. There is clearly a need for identifying explicitly the etiological mechanism whereby any given hereditary or environmental condition ultimately leads to a behavioral characteristic—in other words, the "how" of heredity and environment. Accordingly, we may now take a quick look at some promising methodological approaches to the question "how."

Within the past decade, an increasing number of studies have been designed to trace the connection between specific factors in the hereditary backgrounds or in the reactional biographies of individuals and their observed behavioral characteristics. There has been a definite shift away from the predominantly descriptive and correlational approach of the earlier decades toward more deliberate attempts to verify explanatory hypotheses. Similarly, the cataloguing of group differences in psychological traits has been giving way gradually to research on *changes* in group characteristics following altered conditions.

Among recent methodological developments, we have chosen seven as being particularly relevant to the analysis of etiological mechanisms. The first represents an extension of selective breeding investigations to permit the identification of specific hereditary conditions underlying the observed behavioral differences. When early selective breeding investigations such as those of Tryon (36) on rats indicated that "maze learning ability" was inherited, we were still a long way from knowing what was actually being transmitted by the genes. It was obviously not "maze learning ability" as such. Twenty—or even ten—years ago, some psychologists would have suggested that it was probably general intelligence. And a few might even have drawn a parallel with the inheritance of human intelligence.

But today investigators have been asking: Just what makes one group of rats learn mazes more quickly than the other? Is it differences in motivation, emotionality, speed of running, general activity level? If so, are these behavioral characteristics in turn dependent upon group differences in glandular development, body weight, brain size, biochemical factors, or some other organic conditions? A number of recent and ongoing investigations indicate that attempts are being made to trace, at least part of the way, the steps whereby certain chemical properties of the genes may ultimately lead to specified behavior characteristics.

An example of such a study is provided by Searle's (31) follow-up of Tryon's research. Working with the strains of maze-bright and maze-dull rats developed by Tryon, Searle demonstrated that the two strains differed in a number of emotional and motivational factors, rather than in ability. Thus the strain differences were traced one step further, although many links still remain to be found between maze learning and genes. A promising methodological development within the same general area is to be found in the recent research of Hirsch and Tryon (18). Utilizing a specially devised technique for measuring individual differences in behavior among lower organisms, these investigators launched a series of studies on selective breeding for behavioral characteristics in the fruit fly, *Drosophila*. Such research can capitalize on the mass of available genetic knowledge regarding the morphology of *Drosophila*, as well as on other advantages of using such an organism in genetic studies.

Further evidence of current interest in the specific hereditary factors which influence behavior is to be found in an extensive research program in progress at the Jackson Memorial Laboratory, under the direction of Scott and Fuller (30). In general, the project is concerned with the behavioral characteristics of various breeds and cross-breeds of dogs. Analyses of some of the data gathered to date again suggest that "differences in performance are produced by differences in emotional, motivational, and peripheral processes, and that genetically caused differences in central processes may be either slight or non-existent" (29, p. 225). In other parts of the same project, breed differences in physiological characteristics, which may in turn be related to behavioral differences, have been established.

A second line of attack is the exploration of possible relationships between behavioral characteristics and physiological variables which may in turn be traceable to hereditary factors. Research on EEG, autonomic balance, metabolic processes, and biochemical factors illustrates this approach. A lucid demonstration of the process of tracing a psychological condition to genetic factors is provided by the identification and subsequent investigation of phenylpyruvic amentia. In this case, the causal chain from defective gene, through metabolic disorder and consequent cerebral malfunctioning, to feeblemindedness and other overt symptoms can be described step by step (cf. 32; 33, pp. 389–391). Also relevant are the recent researches on neurological and biochemical correlates of schizophrenia (9). Owing to inadequate methodological controls, however, most of the findings of the latter studies must be regarded as tentative (19).

Prenatal environmental factors provide a third avenue of fruitful investigation. Especially noteworthy is the recent work of Pasamanick and his associates (27), which demonstrated a tie-up between socioeconomic level, complications of pregnancy and parturition, and psychological disorders of the offspring. In a series of studies on large samples of whites and Negroes in Baltimore, these investigators showed that various prenatal and paranatal disorders are significantly related to the occurrence of mental defect and psychiatric disorders in the child. An important source of such irregularities in the process of childbearing and birth is to be found in deficiencies of maternal diet and in other conditions associated with low socioeconomic status. An analysis of the data did in fact reveal a much higher frequency of all such medical complications in lower than in higher socioeconomic levels, and a higher frequency among Negroes than among whites.

Direct evidence of the influence of prenatal nutritional factors upon subsequent intellectual development is to be found in a recent, well controlled experiment by Harrell et al. (16). The subjects were pregnant women in low-income groups, whose normal diets were generally quite deficient. A dietary supplement was administered to some of these women during pregnancy and lactation, while an equated control group received placebos. When tested at the ages of three and four years, the offspring of the experimental group obtained a significantly higher mean IQ than did the offspring of the controls.

Mention should also be made of animal experiments on the effects of such factors as prenatal radiation and neonatal asphyxia upon cerebral anomalies as well as upon subsequent behavior development. These experimental studies merge imperceptibly into the fourth approach to be considered, namely, the investigation of the influence of early experience upon the eventual behavioral characteristics of animals. Research in this area has been accumulating at a rapid rate. In 1954, Beach and Jaynes (8) surveyed this literature for the *Psychological Bulletin,* listing over 130 references. Several new studies have appeared since that date (e.g., 14, 21, 24, 25, 35). The variety of factors covered ranges from the type and quantity of available food to the extent of contact with human culture. A large number of experiments have been concerned with various forms of sensory deprivation and with diminished opportunities for motor exercise. Effects have been observed in many kinds of animals and in almost all aspects of behavior, including perceptual responses, motor activity, learning, emotionality, and social reactions.

In their review, Beach and Jaynes pointed out that research in this area has been stimulated by at least four distinct theoretical interests. Some studies were motivated by the traditional concern with the relative contribution of maturation and learning to behavior development. Others were designed in an effort to test certain psychoanalytic theories regarding infantile experiences, as illustrated by studies which limited the feeding responses of young animals. A third relevant influence is to be found in the work of the European biologist Lorenz (23) on early social stimulation of birds, and in particular on the special type of learning for which the term "imprinting" has been coined. A relatively large number of recent studies have centered around Hebb's (17) theory regarding the importance of early perceptual experiences upon subsequent performance in learning situations. All this research represents a rapidly growing and promising attack on the *modus operandi* of specific environmental factors.

The human counterpart of these animal studies may be found in the comparative investigation of child-rearing practices in different cultures and subcultures. This represents the fifth approach in our list. An outstanding example of such a study is that by Whiting and Child (38), published in 1953. Utilizing data on 75 primitive societies from the Cross-Cultural Files of the Yale Institute of Human Relations, these investigators set out to test a number of hypotheses regarding the relationships between child-rearing practices and personality development. This analysis was followed up by field observations in five cultures, the results of which have not yet been reported (cf. 37).

Within our own culture, similar surveys have been concerned with the diverse psychological environments provided by different social classes (11). Of particular interest are the study by Williams and Scott (39) on the association between socioeconomic level, permissiveness, and motor development among Negro children, and the exploratory research by Milner (26) on the relationship between reading readiness in first-grade children and patterns of parent-child interaction. Milner found that upon school entrance the lower-class child seems to lack chiefly two advantages enjoyed by the middle-class child. The first is described as "a warm positive family atmosphere or adult-relationship pattern which is more and more being recognized as a motivational prerequisite of any kind of adult-controlled learning." The lower-class children in Milner's study perceived adults as predominantly hostile. The second advantage is an extensive opportunity to interact verbally with adults in the family. The latter point is illustrated by parental attitudes toward mealtime conversation, lower-class parents tending to inhibit and discourage such conversation, while middle-class parents encourage it.

Most traditional studies on child-rearing practices have been designed in terms of a psychoanalytic orientation. There is need for more data pertaining to other types of hypotheses. Findings such as those of Milner on opportunities for verbalization and the resulting effects upon reading readiness represent a step in this direction. Another possible source of future data is the application of the intensive observational techniques of psychological ecology developed by Barker and Wright (7) to widely diverse socioeconomic groups.

A sixth major approach involves research on the previously cited somatopsychological relationships (6). To date, little direct information is available on the precise operation of this class of factors in psychological development. The multiplicity of ways in which physical traits—whether hereditary or environmental in origin—may influence behavior thus offers a relatively unexplored field for future study.

The seventh and final approach to be considered represents an adaptation of traditional twin studies. From the standpoint of the question "How?" there is need for closer coordination between the usual data on twin resemblance and observations of the family interactions of twins. Available data already suggest, for example, that closeness of contact and extent of environmental similarity are greater in the case of monozygotic than in the case of dizygotic twins (cf. **2**). Information on the social reactions of twins toward each other and the specialization of roles is likewise of interest (**2**). Especially useful would be longitudinal studies of twins, beginning in early infancy and following the subjects through school age. The operation of differential environmental pressures, the development of specialized roles, and other environmental influences could thus be more clearly identified and correlated with intellectual and personality changes in the growing twins.

Parenthetically, I should like to add a remark about the traditional application of the twin method, in which persons in different degrees of hereditary and environmental relationships to each other are simply compared for behavioral similarity. In these studies, attention has been focused principally upon the amount of resemblance of monozygotic as contrasted to dizygotic twins. Yet such a comparison is particularly difficult to interpret because of the many subtle differences in the environmental situations of the two types of twins. A more fruitful comparison would seem to be that between dizygotic twins and siblings, for whom the hereditary similarity is known to be the same. In Kallmann's monumental research on psychiatric disorders among twins (**20**), for example, one of the most convincing bits of evidence for the operation of hereditary factors in schizophrenia is the fact that the degrees of concordance for dizygotic twins and for siblings were practically identical. In contrast, it will be recalled that in intelligence test scores dizygotic twins resemble each other much more closely than do siblings—a finding which reveals the influence of environmental factors in intellectual development.

SUMMARY

The heredity-environment problem is still very much alive. Its viability is assured by the gradual replacement of the questions, "Which one?" and "How much?" by the more basic and appropriate question, "How?" Hereditary influences—as well as environmental factors of an organic nature—vary along a "continuum of indirectness." The more indirect their connection with behavior, the wider will be the range of variation of possible outcomes. One extreme of the continuum of indirectness may be illustrated by brain damage leading to mental deficiency; the other extreme, by physical characteristics associated with social stereotypes. Examples of factors falling at intermediate points include deafness, physical diseases, and motor disorders. Those environmental factors which act directly upon behavior can be ordered along a continuum of breadth or permanence of effect, as exemplified by social class membership, amount of formal schooling, language handicap, and familiarity with specific test items.

Several current lines of research offer promising techniques for exploring the *modus operandi* of hereditary and environmental factors. Outstanding among them are investigations of: (*a*) hereditary conditions which underlie behavioral differences between selectively bred groups of animals; (*b*) relations between physiological variables and individual differences in behavior, especially in the case of pathological deviations; (*c*) role of prenatal physiological factors in behavior development; (*d*) influence of early experience upon eventual behavioral characteristics; (*e*) cultural differences in child-rearing practices in relation to intellectual and emotional development; (*f*) mechanisms of somatopsychological relationships; and (*g*) psychological development of twins from infancy to maturity, together with observations of their social environment. Such approaches are extremely varied with regard to subjects employed, nature of psychological functions studied, and specific experimental procedures followed. But it is just such heterogeneity of methodology that is demanded by the wide diversity of ways in which hereditary and environmental factors interact in behavior development.

REFERENCES

1. Anastasi, Anne. *Psychological testing.* New York: Macmillan, 1954.
2. Anastasi, Anne. *Differential psychology.* (3rd ed.) New York; Macmillan, 1958.
3. Anastasi, Anne, & Cordova, F. A. Some effects of bilingualism upon the intelligence test performance of Puerto Rican children in New York City. *J. educ. Psychol.*, 1953, **44**, 1–19.
4. Anastasi, Anne, & Foley, J. P., Jr. A proposed reorientation in the heredity-environment controversy. *Psychol. Rev.*, 1948, **55**, 239–249.
5. Arsenian, S. Bilingualism in the postwar world. *Psychol. Bull.*, 1945, **42**, 65–86.
6. Barker, R. G., Wright, Beatrice A., Myerson, L., & Gonick, Mollie R. Adjustment to physical handicap and illness: A survey of the social psychology of physique and disability. *Soc. Sci. Res. Coun. Bull.*, 1953, No. 55 (Rev.).
7. Barker, R. G., & Wright, H. F. *Midwest and its children: The psychological ecology of an American town.* Evanston, Ill.: Row, Peterson, 1955.
8. Beach, F. A., & Jaynes, J. Effects of early experience upon the behavior of animals. *Psychol. Bull.*, 1954, **51**, 239–263.
9. Brackbill, G. A. Studies of brain dysfunction in schizophrenia. *Psychol. Bull.*, 1956, **53**, 210–226.
10. Darcy, Natalie T. A review of the literature on the effects of bilingualism upon the measurement of intelligence. *J. genet. Psychol.*, 1953, **82**, 21–57.
11. Davis, A., & Havighurst, R. J. Social class and color differences in child rearing. *Amer. sociol. Rev.*, 1946, **11**, 698–710.
12. Dobzhansky, T. The genetic nature of differences among men. In S. Persons (Ed.), *Evolutionary thought in America.* New Haven: Yale Univer. Press, 1950. pp. 86–155.
13. Dobzhansky, T. Heredity, environment, and evolution. *Science*, 1950, **111**, 161–166.
14. Forgus, R. H. The effect of early perceptual learning

on the behavioral organization of adult rats. *J. comp. physiol. Psychol.*, 1954, **47**, 331–336.

15. Haldane, J. B. S. *Heredity and politics.* New York: Norton, 1938.
16. Harrell, Ruth F., Woodyard, Ella, & Gates, A. I. *The effect of mothers' diets on the intelligence of the offspring.* New York: Bur. Publ., Teach. Coll., Columbia Univer., 1955.
17. Hebb, D. O. *The organization of behavior.* New York: Wiley, 1949.
18. Hirsch, J., & Tryon, R. C. Mass screening and reliable individual measurement in the experimental behavior genetics of lower organisms. *Psychol. Bull.*, 1956, **53**, 402–410.
19. Horwitt, M. K. Fact and artifact in the biology of schizophrenia. *Science*, 1956, **124**, 429–430.
20. Kallmann, F. J. *Heredity in health and mental disorder; Principles of psychiatric genetics in the light of comparative twin studies.* New York: Norton, 1953.
21. King, J. A., & Gurney, Nancy L. Effect of early social experience on adult aggressive behavior in C57BL10 mice. *J. comp. physiol. Psychol.*, 1954, **47**, 326–330.
22. Loevinger, Jane. On the proportional contributions of differences in nature and in nurture to differences in intelligence. *Psychol. Bull.*, 1943, **40**, 725–756.
23. Lorenz, K. Der Kumpan in der Umwelt des Vogels. Der Artgenosse als auslösendes Moment sozialer Verhaltungsweisen. *J. Orn., Lpz.*, 1935, **83**, 137–213; 289–413.
24. Luchins, A. S., & Forgus, R. H. The effect of differential postweaning environment on the rigidity of an animal's behavior. *J. genet. Psychol.*, 1955, **86**, 51–58.
25. Melzack, R. The genesis of emotional behavior: An experimental study of the dog. *J. comp. physiol. Psychol.*, 1954, **47**, 166–168.
26. Milner, Esther A. A study of the relationships between reading readiness in grade one school children and patterns of parent-child interaction. *Child Develpm.*, 1951, **22**, 95–112.
27. Pasamanick, B., Knobloch, Hilda, & Lilienfeld, A. M. Socioeconomics status and some precursors of neuropsychiatric disorder. *Amer. J. Orthopsychiat.*, 1956, **26**, 594–601.
28. Schwesinger, Gladys C. *Heredity and environment.* New York: Macmillan, 1933.
29. Scott, J. P., & Charles, Margaret S. Some problems of heredity and social behavior. *J. gen. Psychol.*, 1953, **48**, 209–230.
30. Scott, J. P., & Fuller, J. L. Research on genetics and social behavior at the Roscoe B. Jackson Memorial Laboratory, 1946–1951—A progress report. *J. Hered.*, 1951, **42**, 191–197.
31. Searle, L. V. The organization of hereditary maze-brightness and maze-dullness. *Genet. Psychol. Monogr.*, 1949, **39**, 279–325.
32. Snyder, L. H. The genetic approach to human individuality. *Sci. Mon., N. Y.*, 1949, **68**, 165–171.
33. Snyder, L. H., & David, P. R. *The principles of heredity.* (5th ed.) Boston: Heath, 1957.
34. Spoerl, Dorothy T. Bilinguality and emotional adjustment. *J. abnorm. soc. Psychol.*, 1943, **38**, 37–57.
35. Thompson, W. R., & Melzack, R. Early environment. *Sci. Amer.*, 1956, **194** (1), 38–42.
36. Tryon, R. C. Genetic differences in maze-learning ability in rats. *Yearb. nat. Soc. Stud. Educ.*, 1940, **39**, Part I, 111–119.
37. Whiting, J. W. M., et al. *Field guide for a study of socialization in five societies.* Cambridge, Mass.: Harvard Univer., 1954 (mimeo.).
38. Whiting, J. W. M., & Child, I. L. *Child training and personality: A cross-cultural study.* New Haven: Yale Univer. Press, 1953.
39. Williams, Judith R., & Scott, R. B. Growth and development of Negro infants: IV. Motor development and its relationship to child rearing practices in two groups of Negro infants. *Child Develpm.*, 1953, **24**, 103–121.
40. Woodworth, R. S. Heredity and environment: A critical survey of recently published material on twins and foster children. *Soc. Sci. Res. Coun. Bull.*, 1941, No. 47.

A Study of the Relationship Between Physique and Personality Variables Measured by the MMPI

Albert B. Hood

The purposes of this investigation were two-fold. The first was to investigate the Minnesota Multiphasic Personality Inventory (MMPI) profiles of groups of persons representing various extremes of physical constitution—to discover if the profiles of these groups differ in any consistent manner from those of the general population. In this way it could be determined whether one should expect MMPI scores which will differ substantially from the norm when dealing with a person who is extremely tall, short, fat, or thin. This was accomplished by examining the MMPI profiles of groups representing extremes of height and of weight drawn from a large college student population.

The second purpose was to take advantage of the opportunity afforded by these data to explore the relationship between physique and personality on a large population with this relatively comprehensive and widely used personality inventory. This relationship is the subject of many beliefs which are widely held by most laymen—such as that fat men are jolly and thin men morose. Various scholars have concerned themselves with this problem of how much association exists between physique and personality, and they have produced a variety of equivocal results.

Two of the best-known investigators have been Kretschmer and Sheldon, each of whom has concluded that physical constitution is of primary importance in the shaping of personality. Each has reported impressive findings bearing out these conclusions. Kretschmer (1925) found a strong relationship between certain types of physical constitution and certain psychoses. It is Sheldon whose name is most closely identified with constitutional psychology in America because of his classic work relating physique and temperament (Sheldon, Stevens, & Tucker, 1940; Sheldon & Stevens, 1942). He reported amazingly high correlations—in the order of .8—between certain components of physical constitution called somatotypes and three types of dimensions of personality which he has defined. Sheldon's findings have been criticized for a number of reasons: (a) The correlations of .8 which he reports are of a magnitude which is quite inconsistent with virtually all other research which has dealt with the complex nature of human behavior. (b) Certain of his dimensions of personality are almost synonymous with comparable dimensions of physique. (c) Most important of all, his investigation did not adequately control the problem of rater bias. Since the investigator could see the general physical constitution of the S at the time he was rating the temperamental variables, his bias, through influencing his ratings, could produce a considerable part or even all of each relationship found between the component of physique and that of temperament. (d) Humphreys (1957) and Meredith (1940) also have criticized some of the measurement and statistical procedures used by Sheldon in developing his components of physique.

More recent studies testing certain of Sheldon's findings, such as those conducted by Child (1950) and Smith (1949), have found no confirmation for certain of his findings; and where relationships have existed, they have been of a much smaller magnitude than reported by Sheldon. A study by Brodsky (1954) shows that a number of stereotypes exist in our culture regarding various personality traits expected of individuals of different types of physique. These expectations could easily lead persons with particular types of physique to develop particular behavior patterns and thus account for these relationships.

METHOD

This study was made possible by the data which have been collected over a period of years by the University Health Service and by the Student Counseling Bureau at the University of Minnesota. At this University, all entering students are required to undergo a physical examination by Health Service staff. At this time considerable information is collected about each student, and height and weight are among the data gathered. Numerous studies have been based on these data, which have been systematically collected for many years. Recently it has been the practice to place this information on IBM cards. Thus, the height and weight data necessary for the study were readily available.

For the past nine years, almost all entering freshmen in the three largest undergraduate colleges of the University of Minnesota have had the MMPI administered to them as a part of the freshman testing program. Although this testing program is not absolutely required of all students, it is built into the orientation program and at present over 80 per cent of the entering freshmen in these colleges take the MMPI. Thus, a population of over 10,000 male freshmen was available for which there existed both physical data and MMPI results.

From Albert B. Hood, *Journal of Personality*, 31, 97–107.

This study was supported by a grant from the Graduate School of the University of Minnesota.

Samples

Groups of students falling in the approximate top and bottom 3 per cent on each of the continua of height and of weight were drawn from the records of the University Health Service. In the years 1949-1954, 3.71 per cent of the entering male freshmen were 65 inches or shorter, and 3.14 per cent were 75 inches or taller. Samples of students for whom MMPI profiles were available in each of these groups were compared with each other and with a general student population sample on each of the MMPI scales.

To study scale scores for groups of different weights, students in the bottom 2.25 per cent—weighing less than 120 pounds—were selected for comparison with those in the top 3.37 per cent—weighing more than 200 pounds. This method alone is not sufficient to obtain a group of very fat and thin males in that a man who is 76 inches tall and weighs 200 pounds would not be considered particularly fat, but would be included in the heavy group. Therefore, a height-weight ratio was set up and all those who were in the heavy group primarily because they were tall (height over cube root of weight greater than 12.2) and in the light group because they were short (height over cube root of weight less than 13.4) were eliminated. The groups were then compared on each of the MMPI scales.

Even this method, however, did not prove to be satisfactory for obtaining the best fat and thin groups. The reason was that the man who is only 62 inches tall but weighs 190 pounds would be considered very heavy, but would not be included in the heavy group because his weight does not fall in the upper three per cent of the college population. The same would be true for the 76 inch man who weighs only 130 pounds as he would not be included in the thin group. Since these methods were inadequate for obtaining groups of certain types of overall body build or physique, it was necessary to find a more useful measure. Such a method has been developed and has been used extensively by Sheldon (1940) in his studies of somatotypes, as well as in other physiological research. It consists of utilizing the ratio derived from dividing height (in inches) by the cube root of weight (in pounds). The average ratio for college males is 13.0, and students whose ratios are less than 12 would be considered quite fat or endomorphic and those with ratios greater than 14 very thin or ectomorphic.

Sheldon has set up a table by which his somatotypes may be estimated from this height-weight ratio. There is some overlap among somatotypes in the center of the continuum of these ratios, and additional measurements are necessary to do an accurate job of somatotyping within this middle range. By selecting males only at the extreme ends of this height-weight ratio, however, it was possible to select a sample that could only contain ectomorphs and another that could contain only endomorphs. Sheldon expresses the somatotypes of any individual by three numerals, the first of which refers to endomorphy, the second to mesomorphy, and the third to ectomorphy. The range of numerals is from 1 to 7, with 1 representing the absolute minimum and 7 the highest possible amount of the component.

In this study all males included in the endomorph group had a height divided by cube root of weight ratio of less than 11.9. The majority of this group had somatotype ratings of 711 and 721, and the lowest endomorphic component a person could have had and be included in this group was 631. To be included in the ectomorph group, it was necessary to have a ratio greater than 13.9. This group tended to have somatotype ratings of 117 and 126 with the minimum ectomorphic component being 225. As an example of the type of persons included in these groups, a freshman five feet eleven inches in height would have to weigh more than 205 pounds to be in the endomorph group and less than 125 to be in the ectomorph sample.

One hundred MMPI's were selected at random for each of the ectomorph and endomorph groups, and these were compared on each of the MMPI scales.

For certain comparisons, a third sample was selected composed of males who fell exactly at the mean for entering freshmen on both height and weight. The sample selected contained students five feet eight inches to five feet ten inches in height with weights selected between 142 and 158 pounds, to give height over cube root of weight ratios of exactly 13.0. For example, a five feet ten inch student would have to weigh between 156 and 158 pounds to give this ratio of 13.0. Since there is considerable overlap of somatotypes in this region, this should not be considered to be a pure mesomorph group; however it would contain a large number of mesomorphs, and in all individuals in it there would be a fairly strong mesomorphic component.

Further Analysis

Another method of analyzing MMPI data consists of studying the highest *T*-score values found among the eight clinical scales of the individual's profile. It was hypothesized that if a relationship between personality and physique existed, it would be revealed in differences in high point codes—that certain types of physique would be associated with particular profile codes. Comparisons of high point codes were, therefore, carried out between the ectomorph, endomorph, and mean groups.

An item analysis was conducted between the responses of the extreme ectomorph and endomorph groups. The MMPI items cover a wide range of content and include aspects of neurotic and psychotic behavior manifestations, health and psychosomatic symptoms, social, educational, religious, and family attitudes, and the like. This inventory of 566 statements thus provided a rich and diverse item pool which was available for the study of differences in response between the two groups of extreme body types.

RESULTS

Scale Scores

The results of the comparisons of mean MMPI scale scores for male students 75 inches or taller with those 65 inches or shorter are shown in Table 1. Significant differences were found between the means of these groups on the *Mf* and *D* scales. On each of these scales, the mean for the tall group was about one raw score point below that of the short group. Biserial correlations between presence in one of the two extreme groups and scores of the *Mf* and *D* scales showed a relationship between height and scaled score of −.17 and −.15 respectively. In each of the tables, the mean for an unselected University of Minnesota freshman male population is given for purposes of reference. In this case, it can be seen that the tall groups scored lower on the *Mf* and *D* scales not only as compared with the short groups but also as compared with the total freshman mean.

The comparisons between mean MMPI scores of students of the extreme ectomorph group and the extreme endomorph group are shown in Table 2. Significant differences were found between these two groups on the *Ma*, *D*, and

Table 1. *A Comparison of Male College Freshmen Taller Than 75" and Shorter Than 65" on the Scales of the MMPI.*

MMPI scales	Tall[a] (mean raw score)	Mean *T*-score (*K*-cor.)	Short[b] (mean raw score)	Mean *T*-score (*K*-cor.)	Male freshman mean (*K*-cor.)
Mf[c]	22.91	(54.8)	24.27	(57.5)	57.02
D[c]	16.66	(49.8)	17.62	(52.2)	51.86
Pt	9.35	(54.6)	10.46	(55.7)	56.87
Sc	9.09	(55.0)	9.86	(55.5)	57.28
Pa	9.07	(53.2)	9.03	(53.1)	52.61
Ma	16.05	(55.7)	16.53	(56.8)	58.06
Sie	23.30	(48.3)	23.81	(48.8)	50.59
Hy	19.05	(55.1)	19.68	(55.7)	54.26
Pd	15.07	(51.9)	14.52	(54.4)	56.60
K	15.93	(57.0)	15.39	(55.8)	54.08
Hs	3.39	(50.1)	3.99	(51.0)	51.08

Note. $N = 150$.
[a]75"—97.0 percentile of male college freshman population.
[b]65"—3.71 percentile of male college freshman population.
[c]$p < .05$.

Table 2. *A Comparison of Male College Freshmen Representing Extreme Endomorph and Ectomorph Groups on the Scales of the MMPI.*

MMPI scales	Endo (mean raw score)	Mean *T*-score (*K*-cor.)	Ecto (mean raw score)	Mean *T*-score (*K*-cor.)	Male freshman mean (*K*-cor.)
Ma[a]	16.84	(57.9)	15.09	(53.8)	58.06
D[a]	16.35	(49.1)	17.96	(52.9)	51.86
Hy[b]	18.41	(53.8)	19.69	(55.7)	54.26
Mf	23.41	(55.8)	24.55	(58.1)	57.02
K	15.66	(56.3)	16.53	(58.1)	54.08
Sie	23.51	(48.5)	24.27	(49.3)	50.59

Note. $N = 100$.
Note. No differences: *Hs, Pd, Pa, Pt, Sc.*
[a]$p < .01$.
[b]$p < .05$.

Hy scales. Biserial correlations between these three scales and endomorphy were +.25, −.25, and −.19, respectively. As compared with the general freshman male population, ectomorphs obtained lower *Ma* scores and endomorphs lower *D* scores. These mean differences were also in the neighborhood of one raw score point.

Two groups containing students in the upper and lower 3 per cent of the entering students on weight were compared on the MMPI scales in a similar manner. Differences similar to those found between the ectomorph and endomorph groups were found on the *Ma* and *D* scales. In addition, the heavy group also had significantly lower mean scores on the *Sc*, *Sie*, *Mf*, and *Pt* scales. Because these differences had not shown up between the ectomorph and endomorph samples, they were subjected to further investigation. As was mentioned previously, the heavy group, because of the method used to select it, was made up mainly of students who were fairly tall in addition to being heavy. Similarly, the light group also tended to be quite short. The endomorph group was split and the taller endomorphs, 71 inches and over, were compared with the shorter ones, 67 inches or less. The taller endomorphs had significantly higher *Ma* scores and lower *Sie* scores. Thus, there appears to be a slight relationship between tall endomorphy and extroversion. When the ectomorph group was similarly split into tall and short groups, it became apparent that the higher *D* scores obtained by the ectomorph group were in a large measure accounted for by the short ectomorphs.

High Point Codes

The extreme ectomorph and endomorph groups, along with the mean group, which as was previously mentioned had a strong mesomorph component, were compared on profile high points. The results of this comparison are shown in Table 3. The chi-square test showed differences in numbers of high-point codes between these three groups to be significant at the .05 level. The scales on which the largest differences occurred were on the *Ma* and *Pt* scales, with the endomorphs tending to obtain peaks on the *Ma* scale and the ectomorphs on the *Pt* scale. The percentage of high points found among a general male student population at the University of Wisconsin are also shown in Table 3 for purposes of reference. The number of *Ma* high points for

Table 3. *A Comparison of the High Point Codes of Male College Freshmen of Three Different Body Types.*

MMPI high points	Endomorphs	Ectomorphs	Mean group (predominantly mesomorphs)	Univer. of Wisc. males—%[a] (N = 2805)
Hs	3	7	5	3.0
D	10	9	7	13.9
Hy	14	21	18	15.4
Pd	12	15	11	8.5
Pa	10	7	10	5.1
Pt	5	22	12	13.4
Sc	11	5	14	9.0
Ma	30	11	18	25.6
None over 55	5	3	5	6.3
Total	100	100	100	100.0

Note. χ^2 = 29.82, significant at .05 level.
[a]Hathaway and Meehl, 1951.

the endomorph group, which is considerably larger than the other two sample groups, does not differ greatly from that of the Wisconsin population. As a whole, the endomorph group, the mean group, and the Wisconsin general sample tend to be relatively similar in number of high-point *T*-scores. The largest differences occurred in the ectomorph group which had a significantly larger number of profiles with a high point on the *Pt* scale and a significantly fewer number on the *Ma* scale as compared to these other groups.

The two high points on each profile were also studied and compared among the three samples. With the large number of combinations possible in this analysis, the numbers in each cell were too small to treat statistically. The six largest differences in two-point codes between the somatotype groups are reported here. The highest scale and second highest were combined; thus, the *D-Pt* group contains both those on which *D* was highest and *Pt* second highest and those on which *Pt* was highest and *D* second. For the *D-Pt* combination, there was none among the endomorphs and eight each in the other two groups. For both the *Hy-Pa* and *Hy-Ma* high points, seven were found in the ectomorph group with only two each in the others. For *Pd-Pt*, there were six in the ectomorph group with only two in the endomorph and one in the mean group. Thirteen *Pd-Ma* combinations occurred in the endomorph group with seven in the ectomorph and nine in the mean group. Six *Pd-Pt* combinations occurred in the mean group, with only two in the ectomorph and one in the endomorph sample.

Item Analysis

The responses to each of the MMPI items were compared for the ectomorph and endomorph groups. Differences in responses significant at the .05 level were found on 42 of the items. Of these, 22 were significant at the .01 level. Inasmuch as there are 566 items on the MMPI, approximately half this number of differences could be expected to occur by chance. It was impossible to cross-validate these differences on a comparable sample, as it will take several more years to build up the necessary thousands of MMPI profiles of entering students from which to gather equivalent samples of extremes of somatotype.

Of the five items on which the largest differences occurred between the two groups, three were physiological in content. "I sweat very easily even on cool days" was the item on which answers were most highly related to somatotype. Only 7 per cent of the ectomorphs answered this item affirmatively as opposed to 58 per cent of the endomorphs, giving a tetra-choric correlation of .75 with somatotype. This item contributes to the *Ma* scale if answered affirmatively and to the *D* scale if answered negatively. "I drink an unusually large amount of water each day" (true—*Ma*, false—*Hy*) was answered affirmatively by 32 per cent of the endomorph group, but by only 7 per cent of the ectomorphs, giving an r_t of .47. If it is remembered that the endomorph group is made up of individuals who should be relatively buoyant, it is not at all surprising that the item "I have no fear of the water" (no scale) was answered negatively by three times as many ectomorphs (29 per cent) as by endomorphs (10 per cent), (r_t = .37). "I am a high-strung person" (true—endo 10 per cent, ecto 29 per cent), (r_t = .37), and "I have at times had to be rough with people who were rude or annoying" (true—endo 53 per cent, ecto 31 per cent), (r_t = .37), also showed moderate relationships to somatotype. Differences between the two somatotype groups on these items were significant at the .001 level. Differences significant at or beyond the .05 level were found on the following lists of items: Those items on which endomorphs responded affirmatively more often than ectomorphs were 5, 7, 39, 41, 51, 63, 93, 97, 112, 117, 118, 136, 140, 171, 215, 242, 244, 264, 269, 271, 313, 327, 415, 426, 455, 489, 498, 502, 546. Those that ectomorphs tended to answer affirmatively were 103, 289, 321, 344, 352, 361, 513, and 531.

A wide range of types of items is included here and no particular trends or groupings seem to appear other than the very slight tendency for ectomorphs to respond affirmatively to certain *Pt* items and to avoid *Ma* and *Pd* items.

DISCUSSION

Significant differences among scale scores on the MMPI have been found between various colleges at the University of Minnesota. For example, students in the College of

Science, Literature, and the Arts obtain significantly higher scores on the *Mf*, *Pd*, and *Sc* scales as compared with students in the Institute of Technology. The mean *T*-scores for the Science, Literature, and the Arts students are 59.25 on the *Mf* scale, 56.99 on the *Pd* scale, and 58.18 on the *Sc* scale, as compared with the Institute of Technology students' 55.48 on the *Mf* scale, 54.62 on the *Pd* scale, and 55.56 on the *Sc* scale. When the differences between these mean scores are compared with those found between the samples shown in Tables 1 and 2, it is seen that they are as large or larger than those found in this study. It is apparent that on the MMPI scales, there are no greater differences between persons of extreme physique than there are between persons of different colleges at this University.

In each of the analyses, the tall students scored lower on the *Mf* and *D* scales as compared with both the short groups and with a general freshman sample. The ectomorph group obtained a significantly lower mean score on the *Ma* scale and also had fewer *Ma* high points, as compared with both endomorphs and a general student population. There was a tendency for this ectomorph group to obtain higher scores on the *Pt* and *D* scales. The correlation coefficients obtained between presence in one of these groups and MMPI scale score, as well as those obtained for most of the significant items in the item analysis, were in the general vicinity of .2. Since groups at the extreme ends of the continua of physique were used to maximize differences, unless some type of curvilinear relationship exists, these correlations should probably be considered to represent the upper limits of any relationship which might be found to exist throughout the general population.

SUMMARY

From a population of 10,000 male freshmen who had the MMPI administered to them upon entrance to college, a study was made of the MMPI profiles of students falling at the extremes of the continua of height, weight, and somatotype. Significant differences were found between the short and tall samples on the *Mf* and *D* scales, between the light and heavy groups on the *Sie*, *Sc*, *D*, *Ma*, *Mf*, and *Pt* scales, and between the ectomorph and endomorph groups on the *Ma*, *D*, and *Hy* scales. These differences, although statistically significant, were extremely small in size—generally of a magnitude of about one raw score item—making them of little clinical significance.

Differences in high-point codes were found between the somatotype groups—generally in the tendency for the ectomorphs to have a significantly larger number of profiles with a high point on the *Pt* scale and a significantly fewer number on the *Ma* scale as compared to the other groups. An item analysis revealed 56 items on which there were differences in responses significant at or beyond the .05 level between the extreme ectomorph and endomorph groups. With but a few exceptions, the relationship between responses on these items and somatotype was in the vicinity of $r = .2$.

This study indicates that, while small differences do exist, no deviations of any size can be expected on the MMPI from persons representing various extremes of height and weight. The high degree of relationship between physique and personality advanced by Sheldon was not substantiated. This investigation confirms the existence of such a relationship, but the study of the scales, the high-point codes, and the individual items on the MMPI revealed only small relationships even between groups of extreme differences in physique. Thus, this study suggests that any relationship between physique and personality throughout the entire population is of a very small magnitude indeed.

REFERENCES

Brodsky, C. M. *A study of norms for body form—behavior relationships.* Washington, D.C.: Catholic University of America Press, 1954.

Child, I. S. The relationship of somatotype to self-ratings on Sheldon's temperamental traits. *J. Pers.*, 1950, **18**, 440–451.

Hathaway, S. R., & Meehl, P. E. *An atlas for the clinical use of the MMPI.* Minneapolis: University of Minnesota Press, 1951.

Humphreys, L. G. Characteristics of type concepts with special reference to Sheldon's topology. *Psychol. Bull.*, 1957, 54, 218–228.

Kretschmer, E. *Physique and character.* New York: Harcourt, 1925.

Meredith, H. V. Comments on "The Varieties of Human Physique." *Child Develop.*, 1940, 11, 301–309.

Sheldon, W. H., Stevens, S. S., & Tucker, W. B. *The varieties of human physique.* New York: Harper, 1940.

Sheldon, W. H., & Stevens, S. S. *The varieties of temperament.* New York: Harper, 1942.

Smith, H. C. Psychometric checks on hypotheses derived from Sheldon's work on physique and temperament. *J. Pers.*, 1949, **17**, 310–320.

Incidence of Gross Chromosomal Errors Among Tall, Criminal American Males

Mary A. Telfer
David Baker
Gerald R. Clark
Claude E. Richardson

The prevalence of aneuploidy among criminal males who are mentally ill, mentally retarded, or criminally insane is a phenomenon well appreciated in Great Britain (1, 2) but little recognized in the United States. In the course of a recent search for 47,XYY males among several criminal populations in Pennsylvania, we were impressed by the fact that 1 in 11 tall males displayed a gross chromosomal error, but that all the affected individuals had gone undiagnosed despite frequent arrest and review (Table 1).

As a first step, inmates of four institutions for the detention of criminals were screened according to height, those 71 in. tall or over being selected for study. With the explicit permission of the subject, a buccal smear was made according to the method of Sanderson and Stewart (3) and 2 ml of venous blood was drawn into a heparinized syringe for the purpose of leukocyte culture (4). Two culture vials were set up for each subject. Chromosome counts were made of 25 well-spread metaphases; the unique morphology of the human Y chromosome makes the identification of XYY males by microscopic inspection quite satisfactory. Six clear metaphases were photographed on 4- by 5-in. (10- by 12-cm) film and karyotypes were constructed for each aneuploid subject. Individuals whose cultures failed were eliminated from the study. Mosaicism was not observed but cannot be ruled out as a possibility without parallel analyses of other tissues.

Individuals who displayed sex chromatin in the buccal smear or who demonstrated aneuploidy on chromosomal analysis were revisited for further study. The cytogenetic studies were repeated; in each instance the initial finding was confirmed. A physical examination was performed at this time and the prisoner's social, educational, and medical records were carefully reviewed.

As shown in Table 1, 1 in 11 subjects proved to be aneuploid. Seven of the 129 subjects were Klinefelter males with positive sex chromatin and palpably atrophic testes. Five others were 47,XYY males, including one Negro, apparently the first to be reported in the literature (5).

The incidence of gonosomal aneuploidy among tall American males in a facility for the detention of juvenile delinquents proved to be 1:14; in a penal institution for mentally defective delinquent adults, 1:15; in a penal institution for unselected delinquent adults, 1:12; and in a mental hospital for the criminally insane, 1:8. The comparable incidence of sex chromosome errors among tall men at large is estimated to be 1:80, if one assumes that 20% of American males attain a height of 6 ft or over (5), that sex chromosome errors result in extreme body height, and that the incidence of 47,XYY is 1:2000 (6) and of 47,XXY is 1:500 (7) adult males.

Table 1. *Incidence of Gross Chromosomal Errors among Tall, Criminal American Males, 71 in. or more in Height.*

Type of facility	N	No. of subjects with chromosomal disorders: Klinefelter males	47,XYY	Overall incidence
JD	14	0	1	1:14
MDDA	30	2	0	1:15
UDA	35	1	2	1:12
CI	50	4	2	1:8
Total				1:11[a]

[a]Probability that this incidence is due to chance alone, $p = 0.001$. Abbreviations: N, number of subjects studied; JD, detention center for juvenile delinquents; MDDA, penal institution for mentally defective delinquent adults; UDA, penal institution for unselected delinquent adults; and CI, mental hospital for the criminally insane.

The results of this limited survey appear to confirm British observations that gross chromosomal errors contribute, in small but consistent numbers, to the pool of antisocial, aggressive males who are mentally ill and who become institutionalized for criminal behavior. Our data show, furthermore, that these men are to be found in general prisons as well as in mental hospitals for the "hard to handle."

To this we would add the observation that, despite good physical care and much psychiatric attention throughout repeated incarcerations, these individuals are not being identified in the institutions we have surveyed. The implications of gross chromosomal errors for the intellectual, emotional, physical, and social development of the individual, for his legal status before the law (8), for the psychiatrist who treats him, for the society that must provide either care or parole, are fundamental and deserve serious attention by professionals in many related disciplines.

BIBLIOGRAPHY

1. Forssman, H., and G. Hambert. *Lancet*, **1963–I**, 1327.
2. Jacobs, P. A., M. Brunton, M. M. Melville, R. P. Brittain, and W. F. McClemont. *Nature*, 1965, **208**, 1351.
3. Sanderson, A. R., and J. S. S. Stewart. *Brit. Med. J.*, 1961, **2**, 1065.
4. Arakaki, D. T., and R. S. Sparkes, *Cytogenetics*, 1963, **2**, 57.
5. Welch, J. P., D. S. Borgaonkar, and H. M. Herr. *Nature*, 1967, **214**, 500.
6. Anonymous. *Lancet*, **1966–I**, 583.
7. Maclean, N., D. G. Harnden, W. M. Court Brown, J. Bond, and D. J. Mantle. *Lancet*, **1964–I**, 286.
8. Pritchard, M. *Lancet*, **1964–II**, 762.

Schizophrenia in Twins: 16 Years' Consecutive Admissions to a Psychiatric Clinic *†

Irving I. Gottesman

James Shields

INTRODUCTION

Recent developments in the vexed questions of the relative importance to be attributed to genetic and environmental factors in the aetiology of schizophrenia, and the manner in which they interact to produce a phenotypic psychosis, are highlighted by David Rosenthal's series of critical papers (1959–1962) on twin and family studies and the book edited by him chronicling the lives of a set of monozygotic quadruplets all concordant for schizophrenia (1963). In his thorough and open-minded critique Rosenthal argues that previously reported concordance rates for monozygotic (MZ) twins have been misleadingly high. To this point we shall return in a moment. Rosenthal finally concludes that "the best information we now have with respect to the whole broad question of heredity and environment in schizophrenia, is to be found mainly in the five major studies of twins." Unlike some who have pointed out weaknesses in the studies, he believes that "our task is to determine their source, extent and implications, not to dismiss them offhandedly because they contain errors" (1962a, p. 132).

Other developments we can only treat of summarily in this paper are the first study of a large sample of schizophrenic twins in a non-Western culture, by Inouye (1961) in Japan, with results that are remarkably similar to those of Kallmann (1946) and Slater (1953); a study by Tienari (1963) in Finland, which reported a puzzling zero per cent. concordance for schizophrenia in a series of 16 pairs of male MZ twins; a study in Norway by Kringlen (1964) showing only 2 of 8 MZ male pairs concordant for schizophrenia; and finally, the establishment of a twin and sibling research section in the National Institute of Mental Health (Pollin, Stabenau, and Tupin, 1965). Elsewhere we are presenting a fairly detailed historical and critical review of the 11 major twin studies conducted to date (Gottesman and Shields, 1966).

METHODS

In view of the Rosenthal criticisms of sampling methods and diagnosis in the earlier twin studies, and the implication

From *British Journal of Psychiatry*, 1966, **112**, 809–818. Reproduced by permission.

*Paper presented in October 1965 at a meeting of the Eastern Psychiatric Research Association, New York, where it received the R. Thornton Wilson award for a clinical paper in Genetic and Preventive Psychiatry. To appear concurrently in a supplement to *Diseases of the Nervous System.*

†We are especially indebted to Dr. Eliot Slater whose foresight made this study possible. Correspondence and conversation with David Rosenthal was both valuable and stimulating. The authors are solely responsible for all errors of fact or interpretation. This research was carried out at the Medical Research Council Psychiatric Genetics Research Unit, Institute of Psychiatry, Maudsley Hospital, London. The research was supported in part by a USPHS Special Fellowship in Psychiatric Genetics to I.I.G. and Public Health Service Grant MH 10301-01A1. We were fortunate in having the assistance of Dr. R. R. Race and Dr. Ruth Sanger of the M.R.C. Blood Group Research Unit in the blood grouping of the twins. Lastly we acknowledge a debt to the twins and their families for their tolerance of our inquiries.

in the Finnish and Norwegian studies that genetic factors are generally of little import, we should like to describe the design and "early returns" from our own work now in progress.

Sampling

Through the foresight of Dr. Eliot Slater, director of the Medical Research Council's Psychiatric Genetics Unit, a register of all twins seen at the Maudsley and Bethlem Royal Joint Hospital has been kept from 1948 onwards. We know of no other schizophrenic twin research organized prospectively and based entirely on a population from a short-stay psychiatric hospital with a large outpatient department. Though situated at the Hospital, the Unit has no influence over patient admissions. On admission to the in-patient, out-patient, or children's services, every patient is routinely asked, as part of the prescribed intake procedure, whether he was born a twin.[1] In March, 1964, when our present series was closed, there were 392 patients on the register with twins of the same sex surviving to the age of 15. We believe ascertainment to be virtually complete.

Of the index twins (probands), 47 (12 per cent.) had received an official hospital diagnosis at the time of discharge of schizophrenia (code number 300 in the International List of Diseases). This is close to the 11 per cent. of all Maudsley patients thus diagnosed. Since most of the remaining twins on the register had been followed up by the Unit, some were known to have received subsequent diagnoses of schizophrenia when rehospitalized elsewhere. In 1963–64 we followed up all other twins in whose case initial symptoms suggested the possibility of a future schizophrenia (e.g. twins with paranoid, schizoid and obsessional features). In all, a further 21 probands were added with a hospital diagnosis of schizophrenia, making a total of 68. Three twins from Ghana, Jamaica and Barbados were then omitted, as were 3 others in whose cases information about zygosity or mental state of the co-twin was insufficient. Our 62 probands come from 57 pairs, since in 5 pairs both twins had been registered at the Maudsley. Unless otherwise specified, we shall always be speaking in terms of pairs rather than index cases; this leads to a conservative view of the degree of resemblance and permits comparisons across studies. Our 57 pairs of twins of whom at least one has a hospital diagnosis of schizophrenia were obtained from a starting material estimated at 45,000 psychiatric patients.

Zygosity Determination and Follow-up

Zygosity was diagnosed by a combination of blood grouping, finger-print analysis and resemblance in appearance. So far, 20/24 (83 per cent.) of MZ pairs have been blood-typed and a further pair fingerprinted only, and 20/33 (61 per cent.) of the DZ pairs typed with a further 4 pairs fingerprinted only. Evidence from the appearance of the remaining pairs is sufficient to rule out the likelihood of zygosity misdiagnosis. The distribution of the sample by sex and zygosity is given in Table I and supports the view that it is representative. It is the first schizophrenic twin series which has no excess of females. In terms of probands, we have 31 males and 31 females.

Table I. *Sample by Zygosity and Sex.*

	MZ	SS DZ	Total
Female	11	16	27
Male	13	17	30
Total	24	33	57

The twins were born between 1893 and 1945. Median age on last information was 37 with a range of 19 to 64. Of the 48 MZ twins, 42 (88 per cent.) have been seen personally by one or both of us; 4 have been seen by other Unit members or by a psychologist on our behalf, and the 2 remaining were specially seen by their family physician at the Unit's request before disappearing from sight. Of the 66 DZ twins, we have seen 49 (74 per cent.); 3 have been seen by others connected with the twin study. Of the remaining 14, 4 were dead, 4 abroad, 1 untraced and 5 uncooperative at the time of follow-up. All discordant pairs of twins have been followed for over 3 years from the onset of illness in the proband, one of them for as long as 16 years.

Data Collection Plan

Among the major pieces of information we have collected and will be analysing over the next few years are the following:

1. Hospital notes of all psychiatric admissions for all twins, siblings, and parents.
2. Case histories for all twins. More than half of the pairs have had a structured history form filled in by an informant (Briggs, 1959). Other information was obtained at the time of hospitalization or from follow-up interviews with twins and parents.
3. Tape-recorded 30 minute samples of verbal behaviour during a semi-structured interview. The latter was intended to elicit the subtle and obvious signs of schizophrenia and the compensated schizotype (Meehl, 1962), attitudes toward self, parents and twin, and ego strength. Interviews with 75 twins were recorded. (3 refused and 1 was missed through equipment failure.) A verbatim typescript of each tape is being prepared.
4. A Minnesota Multiphasic Personality Inventory (MMPI) from each cooperative and literate twin and parent (Dahlstrom and Welsh, 1960). The 101 profiles generated are essentially the same as those obtained in the U.S.A. One use of the test will be to assess within-pair personality similarity on a continuum of psychopathology (Gottesman, 1962, 1963).
5. The Goldstein-Scheerer Object Sorting Test (Lovibond, 1964; Rapaport, *et al.*, 1945) completed by 90 twins and parents. It is intended to measure concept formation and tendencies toward thought disorder. Lidz *et al.* (1962) and others have reported that half the normal-appearing parents of schizophrenics score within the schizophrenic range of thought disorder.

Our future plans call for the use of various rating scales for quantifying the presence of symptoms and the severity of illness, and for locating a point on the heuristically interesting process-reactive continuum. Meehl's (1964) Radovian inspired checklist of schizotypic signs will also be tried.

[1] Twins were also routinely ascertained at Belmont Hospital, 1950–53.

Summary

Our sample cannot be put forward, any more than any other, as being *truly* representative of the domain of schizophrenia. Based on 16 years' consecutive admissions to out-patient facilities and to a short-stay, in-patient service, and including probands who at first appeared to be neurotic or personality-disordered, it may be said to make better provision for cases with a good prognosis than previous schizophrenic twin samples which were loaded with classical types of dementia praecox. It is our intention to submit the data above to judges for uncontaminated diagnoses of mental status. We thus have a study which meets many of the criticisms of earlier twin research on schizophrenia.

RESULTS

At the present stage of our research we can only offer broad outlines of the results plus a few highlights that have caught our eye. Rather than defer data processing until a sophisticated continuum of schizophrenic pathology can be worked out, we have chosen to report degrees of twin resemblance in terms of old-fashioned concordance. Results are in terms of hospital diagnoses uninfluenced by our hindsight. We have four reasonably objective and reliable grades of similarity. Grade 1 consists of pairs where the co-twin has also been hospitalized and diagnosed as schizophrenic. Grade 2 co-twins have had a psychiatric hospitalization but have been diagnosed as other than schizophrenic. Grade 3 co-twins are otherwise psychiatrically abnormal, as determined by such criteria as out-patient psychiatric care only, in the care of a GP for a clear psychiatric problem, a neurotic or psychotic-looking MMPI profile, or, in three cases, being manifestly abnormal on interview. A disheartening example of the latter is a co-twin who agreed to an interview over the telephone; since he lived in the northernmost part of England, it required an overnight train journey from London. He kept one of us waiting for 30 minutes, then granted an audience of 10 minutes during which he refused to permit the tape recorder to be turned on, accused us of frightening his wife with the long-distance call, threatened to write to the Government about our waste of the taxpayers' money, demanded that questions be written out in advance if they were to be answered, and abruptly departed. Grade 4 co-twins were within normal limits at last information.

Table II. *Concordance for Schizophrenia and Rates of Psychiatric Hospitalization and Marked Abnormality in the Twins of Schizophrenics.*[a]

	MZ		DZ	
Grade	*N*	%	*N*	%
1[b]	10	42	3	9
1 + 2	13	54	6	18
1 + 2 + 3	19	79	15	45
Normal	5	21	18	55
Total	24	100	33	100

[a] All figures uncorrected for age.
[b] $\chi^2 = 6.63$; $p < .01$, one-tailed.

Table III. *Concordance for Schizophrenia and Pathology Similarity (%) by Sex.*

	Grade	1	1 + 2	1 + 2 + 3	Normal	*N*
Female	MZ	45	64	91	9	11
	DZ	12	31	62	38	16
Male	MZ	38	46	69	31	13
	DZ	6	6	29	71	17

Grade 1 pairs give the minimum concordance rates for schizophrenia in this initial analysis. Table II shows the results for the entire sample of MZ and DZ pairs without benefit of age correction. It gives the concordance for a diagnosis of schizophrenia, and, without necessarily implying a continuum, the concordances for psychiatric hospitalization of any kind, and for any noteworthy degree of personality aberration. For example, 79 per cent. of the co-twins of MZ schizophrenics are abnormal, with abnormality ranging from psychiatric hospitalization to having once been treated by a GP for a transient anxiety state. The corresponding DZ rate is 46 per cent. It will be remembered that in the Midtown Manhattan Study the mental morbidity rate was estimated at 26 per cent. (Srole, *et al.*, 1962).

The same data analysed by sex are given in Table III. As the sample sizes are now smaller, it is difficult to prove statistical significance. With respect to sex differences in concordance for schizophrenia, the difference is quite small, but supports the trends in the literature, i.e., female pairs higher than male pairs. Given 13 male and 11 female MZ pairs, the 10 concordant Grade 1 pairs could not be more evenly divided than 5/13 and 5/11. At first glance the combined abnormality rate of 91 per cent. in the MZ co-twins of female schizophrenics (no age correction) seems high; it is most likely due to a combination of causes, such as higher female prevalence of neuroses, susceptibility to post-partum decompensation, and the process of identification.

Next we analysed the relationship between the severity of schizophrenia in the proband and the degree of concordance for schizophrenia among the co-twins. Our calculations are in terms of probands rather than pairs at this point. As indicators of severity we took total length of hospitalization and outcome on follow-up. All patients had been subjected to the prevailing therapies for schizophrenia at the time they were hospitalized, including insulin, ECT, and, since 1954, phenothiazines. Let us first define "severe" as 52 weeks or longer in hospital and "mild" as less than 52 weeks in hospital. MZ concordance for the severe schizophrenics was 67 per cent. contrasted with a concordance rate of only 20 per cent. for the MZ mild schizophrenics. As an alternative criterion of severity let us take over and under two years in hospital. Table IV shows that 77 per cent. of the MZ co-twins of severe schizophrenics are themselves schizophrenic, contrasted to 27 per cent. of the MZ co-twins of mild schizophrenics. Corresponding figures for the very small sample of DZ probands are 15 per cent. and 10 per cent.

As a third criterion of severity let us take the inability to function successfully as a member of society. In this scheme, a severe degree of schizophrenia in a proband is defined as the inability, on last information, to stay out of a hospital for at least six months and to be gainfully employed or running a home. Table V shows that 75 per cent. of the MZ co-twins of severe probands were schizophrenic, compared to 17 per cent. for the mild cases. Corresponding figures for DZ probands support the observation with figures of 22 per cent. and 0 per cent. The patent paradox in this analysis of DZ higher than MZ concordance is transparent as soon as provision is made for the important dimension of severity of schizophrenia in the proband.

Our findings on the association between severity and concordance confirm one of Rosenthal's hypotheses (1961). In Kallmann's (1946) series from State hospitals, MZ concordance was 100 per cent. when the schizophrenia in the proband took a deteriorating course; it was only 26 per cent. for MZ pairs with little or no deterioration in the first twin. Inouye (1961) included among his analyses of subtypes in Japanese schizophrenic twins "progressive chronic schizophrenia" and "mild transient schizophrenia." Concordance in the former was 74 per cent., in the latter 39 per cent. A further point of interest is that our figures for severe schizophrenia in MZ twins agree quite well with the overall, age-uncorrected, concordance rates in the Kallmann and Slater studies, both of whom sampled in State or County hospitals where we might expect a high proportion of the schizophrenics to have poor prognoses.

DISCUSSION

What are the most likely explanations for our preliminary data analyses? Much of the data fit with a diathesis-stress theory of schizophrenia (Rosenthal, 1963). If the diathesis takes the form of a polygenic system, having a great many of the genes predisposes a person to develop schizophrenia by lowering his threshold for coping with stress, and, at the same time, tends to make for a poor prognosis. In this instance we could infer that a proband with a good outcome had had few of the genes in the system, and we would expect his co-twin to have a much lower probability of decompensating than the co-twin of a severe schizophrenic. This explanation would hold whether or not one assumed with Slater (1958) and others that a further single gene was essential for the development of most schizophrenias, or whether one espoused a broader polygenic theory for both aetiology and outcome or course. Most instances of schizophrenia, from the most mild to the most severe, could then be regarded as biologically related. Elsewhere (Gottesman and Shields, 1966) we have noted the present difficulty of distinguishing between sophisticated monogenic theories and polygenic ones in the aetiology of common disorders (cf. Edwards, 1960). Tienari's (1963) results, as they stand, contradict our polygenic explanation, since his probands were not mild cases. However, some cases of schizophrenia might well be regarded as schizophreniform psychoses (Langfeldt, 1939), or schizophrenias symptomatic or organic disease (Slater, Beard, and Glithero, 1963), genetically unrelated to the predominant varieties of the illness. The place to look for such a clarification is among the samples of discordant MZ twins.

Our sample included 14 pairs of identical twins where only one had received a diagnosis of schizophrenia. This fact by itself is enough to rule out genetic factors as a *sufficient* cause of schizophrenia as well as to raise the question of aetiological heterogeneity.

The following kinds of questions may be asked about discordant MZ twins:

1. Has the proband been misdiagnosed, or is his illness mild or atypical in some way?
2. Should the co-twin be considered, if not a full-blown schizophrenic, as a compensated schizotype? Is our information about the co-twin vague or unreliable?
3. Is the co-twin still within the period of risk for developing the illness, and for how long since the onset of

Table IV. *Effects of Severity (Weeks Hospitalized) on Concordance.*

	MZ proband[a]			DZ proband		
Co-twin status	< 2 Yrs.	> 2 Yrs.	Total	< 2 Yrs.	> 2 Yrs.	Total
Sc.	4	10	14	2	2	4
Non-sc.	11	3	14	19	11	30
% Concordance	27	77	50	10	15	12

[a] $\chi^2 = 5.17; p < .02$, one-tailed.

Table V. *Effects of Severity (Gainfully Employed and Out of Hospital > 6 Months) on Concordance.*

	MZ Proband[a]			DZ Proband		
Co-twin status	"Mild"	"Severe"	Total	"Mild"	"Severe"	Total
Sc	2	12	14	0	4	4
Non-sc.	10	4	14	16	14	30
% Concordance	17	75	50	0	22	12

[a] $\chi^2 = 7.15; p < .01$, one-tailed.

schizophrenia in the proband has the pair been followed?

4. What unique factors in the life (including prenatal) of the proband may have elicited the illness or what unique factors in the life of the co-twin may have insulated him against it?

A few examples from our unselected series of discordant identicals may illustrate some of these points.

In a Grade 4 pair, A, the proband, probably has an organic psychosis with schizophrenic-like features and a deteriorating course. His illness was called "paranoid state" at the Maudsley. The aetiology of his psychosis is probably nutritional brain damage sustained during the war as a prisoner of the Japanese. He is completely deaf, and has an EEG showing slow delta waves in the left frontal area and otherwise suggestive of a space-occupying lesion. B, the co-twin, is married, has a stable work history, and an MMPI within normal limits. Although he refused to be seen by a psychologist, he was seen by our social worker, who described him as diffident and monosyllabic. At this point, we should note that the careful case histories of Tienari permit us to suggest that 4 of his 16 MZ probands showed well-marked organic features (cases 608, 462, 32, and 74) (see Shields, 1965, for a critical review). Projected refinement of our own data call for the elimination of all probands in whose case information subsequent to the initial diagnosis leads our judges to question "true schizophrenia."

In another Grade 4 pair, A was diagnosed as an acute schizophrenic reaction after her thyroidectomy at age 43. Shortly before this operation she had had a hysterectomy and was involved in divorce proceedings from an abusive, bullying husband. On her most recent admission she was called a manic-depressive (Code 301). B, on the other hand, had not undergone either surgical procedure, although she also had a thyrotoxicosis. B's husband was an unusually kind and understanding man. B at age 46 is one of the pillars of her community.

A Grade 3 proband has had only one hospitalization and that for six weeks. He was an unusual boy with long-standing interests in oriental religion. At 20 he joined a messianic cult and two years later left his second wife to obtain special training at the cult's London headquarters. There he underwent "psychic realignment" and was given training in telepathy. Within a month he found he was radiating his thoughts and felt that other members knew the details of his sex life. On follow-up four years later he was working, back with his wife and child and not on medication, but he freely described feelings of depersonalization and aural hallucinations. He called himself a "radiating telepath" and continued his keen interest in the occult. B, in his middle 20's, is married, has children and a responsible position. He reported that things were "disinturbulated." Like A he is a fanatic for the occult, and on last information had left his job to go to a centre for special training. He told us that "Paul of Tarsus started off in many respects in a similar way to what I did." He considers himself too careful to become "insane," more self-reliant than A, and stronger all round. We have obtained more details about the early history of this pair from their mother and continue to follow both twins with interest. Their MMPI profiles are given in Fig. 1. Both twins have their highest scores on the clinical scales labelled *Paranoia* (6), *Psychopathic deviate* (4) and *Schizophrenia* (8).[2]

One final example from a Grade 3 pair involves our youngest discordant proband. A has had three hospitalizations, the first at age 16 when he was diagnosed as an adolescent depression. He is in the sample by virtue of a diagnosis of schizo-affective psychosis from an area psychiatric hospital. When treated with ECT, his depression cleared, but his thinking disorder remained. When treated with chlorpromazine, he showed enough improvement to be discharged to out-patient status. His brother, B., has had

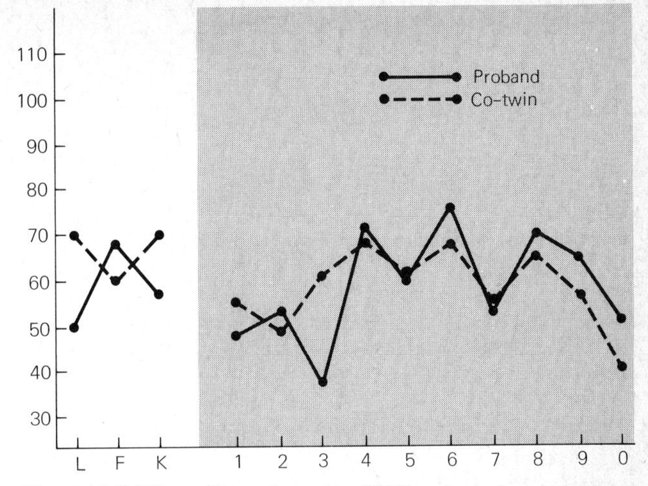

Fig. 1. MMPI profiles of a pair of MZ male twins, age 26, discordant for psychiatric hospitalization and a diagnosis of schizophrenia, concordant (grade 3) for psychiatric abnormality.

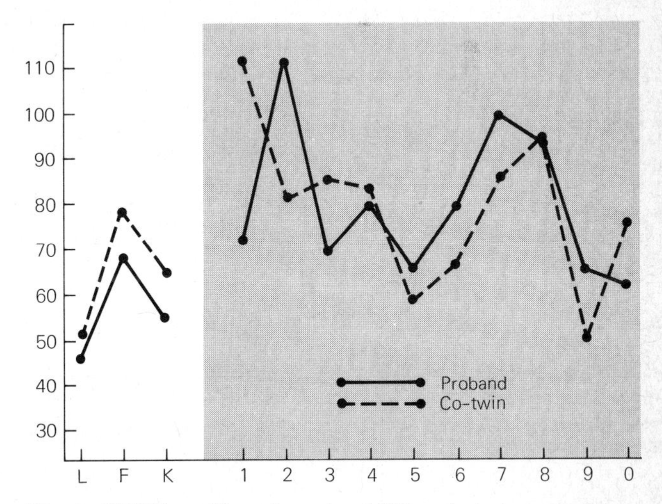

Fig. 2. MMPI profiles of a pair of MZ male twins, age 20, discordant for psychiatric hospitalization and a diagnosis of schizophrenia, concordant (grade 3) for psychiatric abnormality. Co-twin severely hypochondriacal.

[2] There is a brief description of the MMPI and data on a normal U.K. population in Clark, D. F., 1965, "The psychometric characteristics of an adult class in psychology," *Brit. J. Psychiat.*, III, 745–53.

no contact with the psychiatric world, but has hospitalized himself twice for physical complaints with no organic basis. He has put himself on an ulcer diet although no physician has verified this self-diagnosis. B has a very poor work history, never staying long. B was heavier at birth (4½ lbs. vs. A's 3¼) but the poorer in school achievement; the two attended different schools after the eleven plus examination. For the past four years A has lived mostly with the kindly maternal grandmother, uncle and aunt, while B has been more exposed to the "schizophrenogenic" mother and cold, harsh step-father. At the time of follow-up B was clinically free of marked schizophrenic symptoms but his MMPI profile was grossly abnormal and clearly of a psychotic shape. Since B is only in his early 20's, the labelling of this pair as discordant may be premature. MMPI profiles of this pair are presented in Fig. 2.

The last two cases in particular illustrate some of the reasons for dissatisfaction with the concept of concordance since it imposes an artificial dichotomy upon behaviour that is more fruitfully measured on a continuum.

CONCLUSIONS

The preliminary analyses of our data from the twins of schizophrenics ascertained in 16 years' consecutive admissions to a psychiatric clinic, together with our re-analysis of the earlier major twin studies, suggest that we are dealing with replications of the same experiment. Differences

Table VI. *Summary Table of Twin Studies of Schizophrenia (after Gottesman and Shields, 1966).*

		Concordance						Sampling						
		MZ		DZ SS		DZ OS								
Investigator	Country	Pairs	%	Pairs	%	Pairs	%	Resident vs. consec. admit.	Long stay vs. short stay	Is severity related to concordance	Sex with higher concordance	Sample sex surplus	Hospital vs. author diagnosis	Blood and/or fingerprints in Zyg. Dx.
Kallmann Preadolescent (1956)	U.S.A.	15/17	88	8/35[a]	23	[a]		R + C	L	?	?	M	A	Yes
Adult (1946)	U.S.A.	120/174	69	34/296	11	13/221	6	R + C	L	Yes	neither	F	A	No
Slater (1953)	U.K.													
Resident Sample		17/26	65	4/35	11	0/36	0	R	L	Yes	F	F	A	Yes
Consecutive sample		7/11	64	4/25	16	2/18	11	C	L	Yes	neither	neither	A	Yes
Essen-Möller (1941)	Sweden	7/11[b]	64	4/27[b]	15			C	L	No	neither	neither	A	Yes
Rosanoff (1934)	U.S.A.	25/41	61	7/53	13	3/48	6	R	L + S?	?	F	F	H	No
Inouye (1961)	Japan	33/55	60	2/11	18	0/6	0	R + C	L + S	Yes	neither	F	A	Yes
Luxenburger (1928)	Germany	11/19	58	0/13	0	0/20	0	R + C	L + S	Yes?	neither	neither	A	No
Gottesman and Shields (1966)	U.K.	10/24	42	3/33	9			C	S	Yes	neither	neither	H	Yes
Harvard & Hauge (1965)	Denmark	2/7	29	2/31	6	1/28	4	neither	n.a.	?	?	?	H	Yes
Kringlen (1964)	Norway	2/8	25	2/12	17			R + C	L	No	[c]	[c]	H	Yes
Tienari (1963)	Finland	0/16	0					neither	n.a.	No	[c]	[c]	A	Yes

[a] DZ pairs not broken down by type and include OS pairs.
[b] Includes psychoses with schizophrenic-like features and Kaij (1960) follow-up. On other criteria MZ concordance ranges from 0 per cent.—86 per cent.
[c] Neither Kringlen nor Tienari included female probands.

among the studies are more apparent than real. One important source of heterogeneity is the unequal representation in a sample of the two sexes. Higher female concordances in two particular studies (Rosanoff and Slater) could be an artefact of sampling; or it could be associated with more environmental variability for males or with some aspect of the process of identification. Another source, perhaps the most significant, relates to the severity of schizophrenia in the proband. Chronic schizophrenics residing in or admitted to long-stay hospitals show the highest concordances. The issue of sampling from the resident population versus consecutively is not as crucial as the type of hospital. Kallmann's twins were mostly from consecutive admissions, and an analysis of Slater's series according to whether the index case was "resident" or "consecutive" showed no difference in concordance (Gottesman and Shields, 1966). Table VI presents a summary of the 11 major twin studies of schizophrenia analysed in terms of the important dimensions; a simultaneous consideration of the effects of these dimensions on concordance rates has led us to the conclusion above. All the concordance rates cited are without age corrections and in terms of pairs, not index cases.

A third kind of heterogeneity is that between studies in the Scandinavian peninsula and adjoining Finland and those conducted thus far in the rest of the world. In the former (Essen-Möller, Tienari, and Kringlen), MZ probands tended to be matched with co-twins who presented eccentricities of character which we might label as schizophrenic-like, borderline, or schizoid. The possibility arises that there may be real reasons, genetic and/or environmental, why "concordance" in Scandinavian twin studies does not show up at the level of a clear cut psychosis. There is, however, no reason to expect concordance rates to be the same throughout the world, even in studies using the same design. Rates can vary according to the frequency of genes and their penetrance (Huizinga and Heiden, 1957). The continuing evolution of populations could have led to a genotype more adapted by natural selection to harbouring the genetic component of schizophrenia (Gottesman, 1965). There are many climates and cultures where twin studies have yet to be carried out.

We shall correct the de-emphasis on environmental factors in schizophrenia in future papers. Unfortunately, such factors as have been implicated in the literature have not proved to be specific for schizophrenia. From the fact that the identical twin of a schizophrenic is at least 42 times as likely to be schizophrenic as a person from the general population, and a fraternal twin of the same sex 9 times as likely, it would appear that genetic factors are largely responsible for the specific nature of most of the schizophrenias. Note that postulating a genetic specific aetiology for schizophrenia means only that the gene or genes are necessary, not that they are sufficient, for the disorder to occur (Meehl, 1962).

If we may be permitted a forecast, it would be that the mysteries of the schizophrenias will be solved in our lifetimes. The solution will come from the syntheses of research findings in such seemingly disparate areas as twins reared apart (Shields, 1962; Juel-Nielsen, 1965), fostered and non-fostered children of schizophrenics and normals, population genetics, biochemistry, and molecular and developmental biology.

REFERENCES

Briggs, P. F. (1959). "Eight item clusters for use with the M-B history record." *J. clin. Psychol.*, **15**, 22–28.

Dahlstrom, W. G., and Welsh, G. S. (Eds.) (1960). *An MMPI Handbook.* Minneapolis: University of Minnesota Press.

Edwards, J. H. (1960). "The simulation of Mendelism." *Acta genet. (Basel).* **10**, 63–70.

Essen-Möller, E. (1941). "Psychiatrische Untersuchungen in einer Serie von Zwillingen." *Acta psychiat. (Kbh.)*, Suppl. 23.

Gottesman, I. I. (1962). "Differential inheritance of the psychoneuroses." *Eugen. Quart.*, **9**, 223–7.

Gottesman, I. I. (1963). "Heritability of personality: a demonstration." *Psychol. Monog.*, **77**, No. 9 (Whole No. 572).

Gottesman, I. I. (1965). "Personality and natural selection." In S. G. Vandenberg (Ed.), *Methods and Goals in Human Behavior Genetics.* New York: Academic Press. pp. 63–80.

Gottesman, I. I., and Shields, J. (1966). "Contributions of twin studies to perspectives on schizophrenia." In *Progress in Experimental Personality Research* (ed. B. A. Maher), Vol. 3. New York: Academic Press. (In press).

Harvard, B., and Hauge, M. (1965). "Hereditary factors elucidated by twin studies." In J. V. Neel, M. W. Shaw and W. J. Schull (Eds.), *Genetics and the Epidemiology of Chronic Diseases.* Washington, D.C.: U.S. Department of Health, Education and Welfare, pp. 61–76.

Huizinga, J., and Heiden, J. A. v. d., (1957). "The percentages of concordance in twins and mode of inheritance." *Acta Genet. med. (Roma).* **6**, 437–50.

Inouye, E. (1961). "Similarity and dissimilarity of schizophrenia in twins." *Proc. Third World Congress Psychiatry, Montreal,* Vol. I, 524–30. University of Toronto Press, and McGill University Press.

Juel-Nielsen, N. (1965). "Individual and environment: a psychiatric-psychological investigation of monozygotic twins reared apart." *Acta psychiat. (Kbh).* Suppl. 183.

Kaij, L. (1960). *Alcoholism in Twins.* Stockholm: Almqvist and Wiksell.

Kallmann, F. J. (1946). "The genetic theory of schizophrenia: an analysis of 691 schizophrenic twin index families." *Amer. J. Psychiat.*, **103**, 309–22.

Kallmann, F. J., and Roth, B. (1956). "Genetic aspects of preadolescent schizophrenia." *Amer. J. Psychiat.*, **112**, 599–606.

Kringlen, E. (1964). "Schizophrenia in male monozygotic twins." *Acta psychiat. (Kbh).* Suppl. 178.

Langfeldt, G. (1939). *The Schizophreniform States.* London: Oxford University Press.

Lidz, T., Wild, Cynthia, Schafer, Sarah, Rosman, Bernice, & Fleck, S. (1962). "Thought disorders in the parents of schizophrenic patients: a study utilizing the Object Sorting Test." *J. psychiat. Res.*, **1**, 193–200.

Lovibond, S. H. (1964). "Personality and conditioning." In B. A. Maher (Ed.), *Progress in Experimental Personality Research.* Vol. I. New York: Academic Press, pp. 115–69.

Luxenburger, H. (1928). "Vorläufiger Bericht über psychiatrische Serienuntersuchungen an Zwillingen." *Z. ges. Neurol. Psychiat.*, **116**, 297–326.

Meehl, P. E. (1962). "Schizotaxia, schizotypy, schizophrenia." *Amer. Psychol.*, **17**, 827–38.

Meehl, P. E. (1964). "Manual for use with checklist of schizotypic signs." Unpub. ms., Minneapolis: University of Minnesota Medical School.

Pollin, W., Stabenau, J. R., and Tupin, J. (1965). "Family studies with identical twins discordant for schizophrenia." *Psychiatry*, **28**, 60–78.

Rapaport, D., Schafer, R., and Gill, M. (1945). *Diagnostic Psychological Testing.* Chicago: Yearbook Publ.

Rosanoff, A. J., Handy, L. M., Plesset, I. R., and Brush, S. (1934). "The etiology of so-called schizophrenic psychoses with special reference to their occurrence in twins." *Amer. J. Psychiat.*, **91**, 247–286.

Rosenthal, D. (1959). "Some factors associated with concordance and discordance with respect to schizophrenia in monozygotic twins." *J. nerv. ment. Dis.*, **129**, 1–10.

Rosenthal, D. (1960). "Confusion of identity and the frequency of schizophrenia in twins." *Arch. gen. Psychiat.*, **3**, 297–304.

Rosenthal, D. (1961). "Sex distribution and the severity of illness among samples of schizophrenic twins." *J. Psychiat. Res.*, **1**, 26–36.

Rosenthal, D. (1962a). "Problems of sampling and diagnosis in the major twin studies of schizophrenia." *Ibid.*, **1**, 116–34.

Rosenthal, D. (1962b). "Familial concordance by sex with respect to schizophrenia." *Psychol. Bull.*, **59**, 401–21.

Rosenthal, D. (Ed.) & Colleagues (1963). *The Genain Quadruplets.* New York: Basic Books.

Shields, J. (1962). *Monozygotic Twins Brought up Apart and Brought up Together.* London: Oxford University Press.

Shields, J. (1965). Review of "Psychiatric Illnesses in Identical Twins" by Pekka Tienari. *Brit. J. Psychiat.*, III, 777–81.

Slater, E. (with the assistance of Shields, J.). (1953). "Psychotic and neurotic illnesses in twins." *Med. Res. Counc. spec. Rept. Ser. No. 278*, London: Her Majesty's Stationery Office.

Slater, E. (1958). "The monogenic theory of schizophrenia." *Acta genet. (Basel)*, **8**, 50–56.

Slater, E., Beard, A. W., and Glithero, E. (1963). "The schizophrenia-like psychoses of epilepsy." *Brit. J. Psychiat.*, **109**, 95–150.

Srole, L., Langner, T. S., Michael, S. T., Opler, M. K., and Rennie, T. A. (1962). *Mental Health in the Metropolis.* Vol. I, New York: McGraw-Hill.

Tienari, P. (1963). "Psychiatric illnesses in identical twins." *Acta psychiat. (Kbh.).* Suppl. 171.

Psychogenic Determinants

In examining the other half of the heredity-environment question, we present a paper by Oltman and Friedman and one by George Frank, which address themselves to the question of the role of the family in the development of deviant behavior. The first is an empirical study that focuses on the effects of parental deprivation. Frank's paper, which is more methodologically oriented, reviews the literature of the past 40 years on the effects of family factors on psychopathology and concludes that no factors were found to support the assumption that there are unique parent-child interactions among any of the persons diagnosed as schizophrenic, neurotic, or behavior disorder.

Alvin Poussaint and Carolyn Atkinson's closing paper "Black Youth and Motivation" appeared in the *Black Scholar.* These authors make several important distinctions between how blacks and whites in America respond to the reward systems and standards that our white-oriented society has established. They suggest, therefore, that new frameworks be developed to enable the educational aspirations of black youth to correspond to their interests and proficiencies.

The Role of the Family in the Development of Psychopathology

George H. Frank

Psychologists generally make the assumption that the experiences to which the individual is exposed over a period of time lead to the development of learned patterns of behavior. From this, psychologists have reasoned that the experiences the individual has in his early life at home, with his family, in general, and his mother, in particular, are major determinants in the learning of the constellation of behaviors subsumed under the rubric, personality, and in particular, the development of psychopathology. A review of the research of the past 40 yr. failed to support this assumption. No factors were found in the parent-child interaction of schizophrenics, neurotics, or those with behavior disorders which could be identified as unique to them or which could distinguish one group from the other, or any of the groups from the families of the controls.

As psychopathology came to be viewed as the consequence of the emotional experiences to which the individual was exposed, interest was focused on the earliest of such experiences, those that occur in the family. The human infant is born incapable of sustaining its own life for a considerable length of time following birth, and is, in consequence, dependent upon the mother or a mother substitute for its very existence. There is no wonder, therefore, that the mother-child relationship is a close one and is expected to be influential with regard to the psychological development of the child. Some explanations for the development of psychopathology have therefore focused on this particular relationship as the major etiological factor. Levy (1931, 1932, 1937, 1943) has described a pattern centering around "maternal overprotection," involving a constellation of attitudes which he felt contributed to the development of neurotic disorders, and Despert (1938) focused on a kind of mother-child relationship which seemed to her to be closely associated with the development of schizophrenia, a pattern which has come to be termed the "schizophrenogenic mother."

The hypothesis that the emotional climate of the interpersonal relationships within the family—and between the child and its mother in particular—has a decisive part in the development of the personality of the child would seem to have face validity. In part, support for this hypothesis may be gleaned from the data demonstrating the devastating effects of being brought up in the extreme interpersonal isolation that comes from *not* having a family (Beres & Obers, 1950; Brodbeck & Irwin, 1946; Goldfarb, 1943a, 1943b, 1943c, 1945a, 1945b; Lowrey, 1940; Spitz, 1945) or extreme social isolation within a family (Bartmeier, 1952; Davis, 1940). Moreover, it has been demonstrated that various specific emotional behaviors of the child seem to be correlated causally with factors in the home. For example, children who could be described as emotionally immature, who are dependent, fearful, negativistic, emotionally labile, etc., have had mothers described as worriers (Pearson, 1931), overattentive (Hattwick, 1936; Hattwick & Stowell, 1936), or punitive (McCord, McCord, & Howard, 1961; Sears, Whiting, Nowlis, & Sears, 1953; Watson, 1934). Children who were described as being overly aggressive were described as having come from homes where mothers were seen as overcontrolling (Bishop, 1951) or punitive (McCord et al., 1961; Sears, 1961).

The evidence thus far suggests that there is, in fact, a correlation between events in the parent-child relationship and resultant personality *traits.* The question arises as to whether there is evidence which supports the hypothesis that there is a correlation between events in the parent-child relationship and the resultant complex patterns of behavior which have been termed personality. More specifically, in light of the theories which relate personality development to social, (i.e., interpersonal) learning, the question is raised as to whether there is any consistent relationship between the emotional experience the child may have in the home and the development of personality pathology, that is, schizophrenia, neurosis, and behavior disorders. Towards this end, the findings of the research that has explored the psychological characteristics of the parents of these people will be analyzed in order to isolate those consistent characteristics of the parents that may emerge

From *Psychological Bulletin*, 1965, **64**, 191–205.

from study to study. The analysis will be done with regard to each major type of psychopathology as a group. Moreover, because psychological test data might yield different information than case history analysis, or direct observation of familial interaction as compared to attitudes as elicited by questionnaire, an attempt will be made to analyze the information gleaned from the studies in terms of the method of data collection within the specific psychopathological groupings.

SCHIZOPHRENIA

Case History

One of the classical methods of data collection in the study of psychiatric illness is the case history, the information for which has generally been gathered by other professionals. The individual conducting a piece of research notes the material in the folders and draws conclusions from the collation of these observations.

In so doing, Despert (1938) observed that approximately 50% of the mothers of a sample of schizophrenic children, generally between the ages of 7 and 13, had been described as aggressive, overanxious, and oversolicitous and were considered to be the dominant parent. Clardy (1951) noted that 50% of the 30 cases of children between the ages of 3 and 12 diagnosed as schizophrenic had families characterized as overprotective and yet basically rejecting. Frazee (1953) noted the presence of this constellation particularly when the families of schizophrenics were compared with the families of children diagnosed as behavior disorders. Canavan and Clark (1923) and Lampron (1933) noted that 30% of the children of psychotics were themselves emotionally disturbed. Huschka (1941) and Lidz and Lidz (1949) noted that over 40% of their sample of schizophrenics had parents who were psychotic or neurotic. Bender (1936, 1937) and Frazee (1953) noted the high incidence of psychopathology in the children of psychotic parents. Preston and Antin (1932), on the other hand, found no significant differences in the incidence of psychosis and neurosis as a function of parents who were psychotic as compared to parents who were "normal," and Fanning, Lehr, Sherwin, and Wilson, (1938) found that 43% of the children of mothers who were psychotic were observed to be making an adequate social and personal adjustment, with only 11% of that sample classified as maladjusted.

Lidz and Lidz (1949) found that 40% of their sample of schizophrenic patients were deprived of one parent by divorce or separation before they were 19. Plank (1953) found that 63% of his sample of schizophrenics had families where one parent was absent either due to death or marital separation. Wahl (1954, 1956) found that there was a greater incidence of parental loss and rejection early in life for schizophrenics as compared to normals, and Barry (1936) found that from the case histories of 30 rulers adjudged, post facto, insane, 80% of them had lost one of their parents by the time they were 18. However, Barry and Bousfield (1937) found that the incidence of orphanhood in a psychiatric population (19 out of 26) was not much different from the incidence of orphanhood in a normal population (19 out of 24). Moreover, Oltman, McGarry, and Friedman (1952) found that the incidence of broken homes and parental deprivation in the families of schizophrenics (34%) was not very different from that found in the families of hospital employees (32%), alcoholics (31%), and manic-depressives (34%); indeed, in their sampling, neurotics (49%) and psychopaths (48%) showed a greater incidence. Other studies have found that the incidence of broken homes in the history of neurotics is between 20% (Brown & Moore, 1944) and 30% (Madow & Hardy, 1947; Wallace, 1935), and Gerard and Siegel (1950) found no particular incidence of broken homes in the family history of their sample of schizophrenics.

Psychiatric Interview

Another classical method of obtaining information regarding the individual with whom patients have been living is by having interviews with them directly. The quality of the mother-child relationship is then inferred from what the interviewee says. From this research, an overwhelming number of studies (Despert, 1951; Gerard & Siegel, 1950; Guertin, 1961; Hajdu-Gimes, 1940; Kasanin, Knight, & Sage, 1934; Lidz, Cornelison, Fleck, & Terry, 1957a, 1957b, 1957c; Lidz, Cornelison, Terry, & Fleck, 1958; Lidz & Lidz, 1949; Lidz, Parker, & Cornelison, 1956; Tietze, 1949; Walters, 1938) describe a familial pattern characterized by a dominant, overprotective, but basically rejecting mother and a passive, ineffectual father. Yet the data in the study by Schofield and Balian (1959) reflected similarity rather than differences in the families of schizophrenic and nonpsychiatric (general medical) patients, and the data of Gerard and Siegel (1950) indicated that the schizophrenics in their study, according to interpretation of the data gleaned from the interviews, received adequate breast feeding, had no history of particularly difficult toilet training or of obvious feeding problems, did not come from broken homes, and apparently were not unduly rejected or punished. Another factor which seems to emerge from the studies is that a dominant characteristic of the family life of schizophrenics is a quality of inappropriateness of thinking and behaving which seems to infiltrate the entire atmosphere (Fleck, Lidz, & Cornelison, 1963; Lidz et al., 1957b, 1957c; Stringer, 1962). Meyers and Goldfarb (1962), however, found that only 28% of the mothers of 45 children diagnosed as schizophrenic and only 12% of the fathers were themselves manifestly schizophrenic.

Psychological Evaluation

Attitude questionnaires. One of the most widely used questionnaires in this area of research has been the Shoben (1949) Parent-Child Attitude Survey. The Shoben scale consists of 148 items which measure the dimensions of parental rejection, possessiveness, and domination. From the administration of this attitude survey, Mark (1953) and Freeman and Grayson (1955) reported significant differences in attitudes toward child rearing between mothers of schizophrenics and mothers of normal children. In comparison with the mothers of the control subjects, the mothers of schizophrenic patients (Mark, 1953) were revealed as inconsistent in their methods of control. They described themselves as being, at times, overrestrictive and controlling of behavior, but in some instances lax. They frowned on sex play and tended to keep information regarding sex from their children; they also seemed to frown on friends for their children. Their relationship to their children appeared inconsistent; they described what could be interpreted as excessive devotion and interest in the child's activities while at the same time revealing a notable degree of "cool detachment." Freeman and Grayson (1955) found that in comparison to mothers of students in an undergraduate course, mothers of 50 hospitalized schizophrenics (ages 20 to 35) tended to reveal themselves to be somewhat more possessive, but inherently rejecting of their children, and particularly disturbed about sexual behavior in their children. However, according to these same data, the mothers of schizophrenic patients did not reveal themselves to be more dominant, dogmatic, or inconsistent in their attitude than the controls. But most important was the fact that item analysis of these data revealed that the attitudes of the mothers of the schizophrenics and of the controls were distinguished on only 14 of the items, and then, in general, there was so much overlap that even on these items the statistical significance was contributed by a small percentage of each group. Freeman, Simmons, and Bergen (1959) included four items from the Shoben scale among a larger sample of questions posed to parents. These items had been derived from a previous study (Freeman & Simmons, 1958) and were included in the second study because they were the only ones in the first study which were found to discriminate between the attitudes of mothers of schizophrenic patients and those of mothers of normals. The items are:

1. Parents should sacrifice everything for their children.
2. A child should feel a deep sense of obligation always to act in accord with the wishes of his parents.
3. Children who are gentlemanly or ladylike are preferable to those who are tomboys or "regular guys."
4. It is better for children to play at home than to visit other children.

Freeman et al. (1959) found no capacity for these items to differentiate the attitudes of the mothers of schizophrenics from those of other individuals with severe functional disorders.

Zuckerman, Oltean, and Monashkin (1958) utilized another attitude scale, the Parental Attitude Research Inventory (PARI, developed by Schaefer and Bell in their work at the Psychology Laboratory at NIMH). The PARI was administered to mothers of schizophrenics, and it was found that only one item distinguished between their attitudes and those of mothers of normal children. The mothers of schizophrenics tended to describe themselves as being stricter than did the mothers of nonschizophrenic children.

The minimal discrimination value of the several attitude scales should be noted. This would seem to reflect either minimal capacity of the scales to make such distinctions or little in the way of measurable differences between the groups. In either case, it is very difficult to evaluate the meaning of these data since the attitudes of the mothers of schizophrenics seemed to be distinguished from the attitudes of the mothers of neurotics on only a few items (the obtained number of differences did not even exceed that expected by chance alone).

Projective tests. Several studies presented Rorschach data on the mothers of schizophrenic patients (Baxter, Becker, & Hooks, 1963; Prout & White, 1950; Winder & Kantor, 1958). In comparison to those of the mothers of normals, the Rorschach protocols of the mothers of the schizophrenic patients were undistinguished as regards the general degree of immaturity (Winder & Kantor, 1958) and the use of defences which are essentially reality distorting, namely, denial and projection (Baxter et al., 1963).[1] However, Prout and White did find more pure color without form and less human and animal movement and shading responses in the Rorschach protocols of mothers of schizophrenic boys as compared to the mothers of a comparable group of boys randomly selected from the community. Perr (1958) found that the parents of schizophrenic children gave responses to the Thematic Apperception Test (TAT) little distinguished from those of parents of normal children, and Fisher, Boyd, Walker, and Sheer (1959) found that the TAT and Rorschach protocols of the parents of schizophrenic patients were measurably different from those of the parents of nonpsychiatric (general medical) patients, but they were not distinguishable from the protocols of the parents of neurotic patients. The mothers of the schizophrenics revealed a higher degree of perceptual rigidity, greater incidence of indicators of maladjustment on the Rorschach, and less definitely conceived parental images on the TAT than the mothers of the normals.

Direct observation of interpersonal behavior. Attempts have been made to study the interpersonal behavior of families of schizophrenics *in vivo;* some investigators have gone into the home, others have brought the family into a hospital setting and observed the interaction between family members for an hour or so at a time, others have brought the family into a laboratory setting (National Institute of Mental Health) where the family lives under actual but known conditions for months at a time.

In the study of the interpersonal relationships in the actual home setting, Behrens and Goldfarb (1958) observed that the personality of the mother seemed to set the tone of the family milieu and that there seemed to be a direct relationship between the degree of pathology that could be seen in the family setting and the degree of psychopathology demonstrated by the child. The homes they observed appeared physically deteriorated and crowded. There was a basic isolation between the mother and father, and the fathers were basically passive. Confusion and disorganiza-

[1] The conclusion that the Rorschach protocols of the mothers of schizophrenics were undistinguished from the Rorschach protocols of the mothers of normals (as in the research by Winder & Kantor, 1958, Baxter et al., 1963) is an interpretation of the results made by the present author. In fact, in both of these articles, the authors conclude that there *are* significant differences. However, in the article by Winder and Kantor, the mean rating of the degree of maturity of personality development for the mothers of the schizophrenics was 2.89, for the mothers of the normals, 2.43. In the article by Baxter et al., the means of the ratings of the degree of utilization of psychologically immature defenses on the Rorschach by the parents of poor premorbid schizophrenics, good premorbid schizophrenics, and neurotics are, respectively, 19.43, 19.62, and 19.49. Though in both of these investigations valid statistical significance was demonstrated between the obtained means, the actual means, in both researches, are so similar to each other that the interpretation of *psychologically* significant differences between groups on the basis of the obtained *statistically* significant differences seemed a highly doubtful conclusion.

tion characterized the family atmosphere, with the family demonstrating inadequate mechanisms to handle emotional flareups. The intensive observation of one mother-child interaction (Karon & Rosberg, 1958) yielded the observation that the mother was unempathic. She blocked verbalizations of emotions and tended to live vicariously through the child, but her relationship to the child appeared to involve a basic, though unconscious, hostility and rejection. The mother was an obsessive-compulsive personality, dominated the home, and was unable to accept herself as a woman. The intensive observation of 51 families (Donnelly, 1960) tends to confirm this finding. Observing the mother-child interaction in the home, utilizing the Fels Parent Behavior Scales, Donnelly found that mothers treated a psychotic child differently than their other nonpsychotic children. To the psychotic child, the mother was generally less warm, less accepting, less empathic, more punitive, more controlling, and more overprotective. The father was passive, but more rational than the mother in relation to the child. Psychotic children tended to come from homes characterized as less well adjusted, full of discord, and low in sociability. However, in comparing the family interaction of schizophrenic patients with those of normal controls, both Perr (1958) and Meyers and Goldfarb (1961) found little that could stand as a valid measure of distinction between the two groups of families. Perr found that the parents of schizophrenics tend to show more self-deception and to describe themselves as being more hostile. Meyers and Goldfarb found that the mothers of schizophrenic children appeared less capable of formulating a consistent definition of the world for the child.

A method of directly assessing the interpersonal behavior of husband and wife was introduced by Strodtbeck (1951). He posed questions to each parent individually, then he brought them together and had them discuss those points where their attitudes differed. Farina and his associates (Bell, Garmezy, Farina, & Rodnick, 1960; Farina, 1960; Farina & Dunham, 1963) utilized this method to study the families of schizophrenic patients. The questionnaire they used was the PARI. They found that they could distinguish the interpersonal behavior of schizophrenics otherwise described as having good or poor premorbid adjustment. In these studies, mother dominance was discerned in the families of the poor premorbid group only, with interpersonal conflict greatest in that group. In comparing the family interaction of the schizophrenic patient with those of normal controls, Bell et al. (1960) found that in the family constellation of normals, authority tended to be shared by both parents, and parental conflict was at a minimum, although even here there was a trend towards maternal dominance.

Bishop (1951) reported a method of studying the mother-child interaction under live, yet controlled, conditions. The mother and child were brought into a play room where the interpersonal behavior was observed directly. In 1954, Bowen introduced the principle of this technique to the study of families of schizophrenics. Families were brought into what came to be known as the Family Study Section of NIMH (National Institute of Mental Health), and there they were observed living under actual but known conditions for long periods of time (6 months–2 years). Observations based on families living under these conditions revealed that the mothers of schizophrenics showed extremely domineering, smothering, close relationships with the child (Dworin & Wyant, 1957), with the mothers utilizing threat of deprivation to control the child. Bowen, Dysinger, and Basamanie (1959) observed the presence of marked emotional distance and intense conflict between the parents. The fathers were emotionally immature and unable to define their role in the family and unable to make decisions; the mothers were usually the dominant ones, affecting a close relationship with the child to the exclusion of the father. Brodey (1959) found that the behavior of the families of schizophrenics was characterized by a selective utilization of reality, particularly the use of externalization, and that the interpersonal relationships were highly narcissistic.

Perception of parental behavior by patients. Several studies have indicated that schizophrenics tend to have experienced their mother as having been rejecting (Bolles, Metzger, & Pitts, 1941; Lane & Singer, 1959; Singer, 1954), and dominant, demanding, and overprotective (Garmezy, Clarke, & Stockner, 1961; Heilbrun, 1960; Kohn & Clausen, 1956; McKeown, 1950; Reichard & Tillman, 1950; Schofield & Balian, 1959). However, when one compares the perception of their mothers by normals (Garmezy et al., 1961; Heilbrun, 1960; Lane & Singer, 1959; Singer, 1954) the uniqueness of these attitudes toward the mothers of schizophrenics disappears. Recollections of dominance and overprotectiveness are common for both schizophrenics and normals. Although Heilbrun, Garmezy et al., and Bolles et al. report data which have shown that there is a greater incidence of a feeling of having been rejected on the part of a group of psychiatric patients when compared to medical-surgical controls, the actual incidence of this even in the psychiatric group was only 15% as compared to 1% in the controls. Moreover, Singer and Lane and Singer found that perception of parental relationships during childhood was more a function of the subjects' socioeconomic level than was psychopathology, paralleling a finding by Opler (1957) that familial patterns (parental dominance and attitudes) are a function of cultural factors (Italian versus Irish origin) rather than of psychopathology.

NEUROSIS

As compared to the research in the area of schizophrenia, investigations of the dynamics of the family life of neurotics are few and generally restricted to data gleaned from case histories. From these studies it appears that the neurotic behavior of the child is a direct function of the neurotic behavior of the mother (e.g., Fisher & Mendell, 1956; Ingham, 1949; Sperling, 1949, 1951; Zimmerman, 1930). Neurotic behavior in children has been seen to have been related to maternal overprotection (Holloway, 1931; Jacobsen, 1947; Zimmerman, 1930), maternal domination (Mueller, 1945), maternal rejection (Ingham, 1949; Newell, 1934, 1936; Silberpfennig, 1941), separation from the mother during the first 3 years of life (Bowlby, 1940; Ribble, 1941), and oral deprivation (Childers & Hamil, 1932). Neurotic involvement with the mother, where the mother needs the child for the satisfaction of her own needs and discourages the development of emotional separation between the child and herself, has been associated with the development in the child of psychosomatic disorders (Miller & Baruch, 1950; Sperling, 1949) and school phobia (e.g., Davidson, 1961; Eisenberg, 1958; Estes, Haylett, & Johnson, 1956; Goldberg, 1953; Johnson, Falstein, & Suzurek, 1941; Suttenfield, 1954; Talbot, 1957; van Houten, 1948; Waldfogel, Hahn, & Gardner, 1954; Wilson, 1955).

Neurosis in children has also been associated with such factors in the home as poverty (Brown & Moore, 1944; Holloway, 1931) and broken homes (Ingham, 1949; Madow & Hardy, 1947; Wallace, 1935). Silverman (1935), however, found that 75% of the children from broken homes were essentially "normal;" 16% were described as conduct disorders, and only 9% were classifiable as personality problems.

Of the studies that did not use the case history method of data collection, McKeown (1950) found that neurotic children perceive their mothers as demanding, antagonistic, and setting inordinately high standards for them to meet. Stein (1944) found that neurotics tended to perceive themselves as having been rejected, particularly as compared to the perception of their family life held by normals (Bolles et al., 1941). Although Kundert (1947) found that whether justified by experience or not (e.g., separation due to hospitalization of mother or child), emotionally disturbed children, in general, fear being deserted by their mothers and cling to them compulsively. The Rorschach protocols of mothers of neurotics reveal that they tend to utilize psychological mechanisms which abrogate reality, for example, denial and projection (Baxter et al., 1963).

BEHAVIOR DISORDER

Th research on the family background of individuals whose personality problems take the form of antisocial behavior is scanty. Shaw and McKay (1932) found no differences in the incidence of broken homes from cases referred to Cook County Juvenile Court (36%) as compared to a random sample of children in the Chicago public school system (42%). Behavior disorders in children have been seen to have been related to neurotic behavior in their parents (Field, 1940; Huschka, 1941), primarily involving maternal rejection, overt and covert. In line with a social learning hypothesis, another interesting finding is that a correlation has been found between antisocial behavior in children and the children's perception of parents' antisocial behavior (Bender, 1937; K. Friedlander, 1945; Williams, 1932).

DISCUSSION

Let us now summarize what conclusions can be drawn from these data which illuminate the role of the family in the development of psychopathology. As regards the families of schizophrenics, from an overview of the research which has investigated the pattern of parent-child interaction of this pathological group considered without reference to any other pathological or control group, several factors emerge which seem to characterize this group, regardless of the method of data collection, that is, whether by case history, interview, psychological test, or direct observation. Families of schizophrenics seem to be characterized by mothers who are dominant, fathers who are passive, and considerable family disharmony. The mother is overprotective, overpossessive, and overcontrolling, yet basically, albeit unconsciously, rejecting. These mothers frown on sex, are inconsistent in their methods of discipline, and introduce modes of thinking, feeling, and behaving which are not reality oriented. In light of the fact that these patterns emerge as a function of almost all methods of data collection, these results seem very impressive. Had our review of these data stopped here, we would have had apparent verification of the thesis that certain kinds of mother-child relationships and family atmospheres indeed account for the development of schizophrenia in the offspring. However, when each of these parental characteristics is compared with those which emerge from the analysis of the family situation of the normal (apparently nonpsychiatrically-involved) individual, each characteristic that is found to be typical of the families of schizophrenics is found to exist in the families of the controls as well. Furthermore, research which has attempted to make direct comparisons between the families of children in different categories of psychopathology (e.g., Baxter et al., 1963; Fisher et al., 1959; Frazee, 1953; Freeman et al., 1959; D. Friedlander, 1945; Inlow, 1933; McKeown, 1950; Oltman et al., 1952; Pollack & Malzberg, 1940; Pollack, Malzberg, & Fuller, 1936) reveals no significant or consistent differences in the psychological structure of the families.

The results are the same with regard to the families of the neurotics as well. At first glance, it appears that the mother's neurotic involvement with the child is causally associated with the neurotic behavior of the child. However, the essential characteristics of this involvement—maternal overprotectiveness, maternal domination, maternal rejection, deprivation and frustration, and the mothers fostering an almost symbiotic relationship between themselves and their children—are basically the same as those found in the families of schizophrenics and of children with behavior disorders. Moreover, in many respects, it would be hard, on blind analysis, to distinguish the family which produced an emotionally disturbed child from that which produced the so-called normal or well-adjusted child.

It seems apparent that the major conclusion that can be drawn from these data is that there is no such thing as a schizophrenogenic or a neurotogenic mother or family. At least these data do not permit of the description of a particular constellation of psychological events within the home and, in particular, between mother and child that can be isolated as a unique factor in the development of one or the other kind of personality disorder. If one is looking for *the* factor to account for the development of neurosis or schizophrenia, that one factor does not appear to exist as a clear cut finding in the research.

It is incumbent upon us to wonder why the research literature does not permit support of a hypothesis regarding parental influence on the psychological development of children in the manner we hypothesized. One of the major problems with which we must contend is that human behavior is a very complicated event, determined by many factors, and not clearly understood out of the context in which it occurs, and, in this regard, not everyone reacts in a like manner to similar life experiences. For example, strict discipline is reacted to differently when this occurs in a "warm" or "cold" home atmosphere (Sears, 1961); maternal rejection is reacted to differently where the father is accepting and warm (McCord et al., 1961) as well as where the father can be a buffer between the child and the overprotective mother (Witmer, 1933). Emphasizing the multivariate aspect of the determinants of behavior, one notes that Madow and Hardy (1947) reported that of the soldiers who broke down with neurotic reactions there was a high incidence of those coming from broken homes. Amongst those soldiers who did not break down, the incidence of coming from a broken home was 11–15%; the incidence of broken homes in the history of soldiers who did break down was 36%. Statistically, there is a significant difference between these percentages; however, even the 36% datum leaves 64% of the soldiers who broke down *not* coming from a broken home. Huschka (1941) reported that the incidence of neurotic mothers of problem children is high (42%); however, this leaves 58% of the group *not* accounted for by this factor. Brown and Moore (1944) commented that the incidence of excessive poverty, drunkenness, and family conflict in soldiers who broke down was significant, but this accounted for only 20% of the cases. Although between 30% (Canavan & Clark, 1923; Lampron, 1933) and 40% (Huschka, 1941; Lidz & Lidz, 1949) of the children born to mothers who are psychotic become psychotic themselves, these percentages do not account for the majority of children born to these mothers. Indeed, Fanning et al. (1938) found that 43% of the children born to mothers who were psychotic were observed to be making an adequate social and personal adjustment; only 11% of that sample of children was not. It should be noted that only half of the samples of mothers studied by Despert (1938) and Clardy (1951) resembled the traditional pattern of what has come to be known as the "schizophrenogenic mother." Finally, Beres and Obers (1950) observed that there is a wide reaction to an experience of emotional deprivation (in this instance, institutionalization) ranging from the development of a schizoid personality to schizophrenia itself, and including neurotic reactions and character disorders. Indeed, 25% of their sample of children who were brought up in institutions appeared to be making a satisfactory adjustment in spite of this ostensibly devastating experience.

Over and above the complexity of human behavior contributing to the inconclusiveness of the results, one must look at the way in which these data have been collected. It might be that the criterion measure, that is, the diagnosis, did not provide the investigator with meaningful groupings of subjects so that consistent findings *could* be obtained. As regards the method of data collection: Case histories may be inadequate in providing basic data; Information can be gross and/or inaccurate; The informant has to rely on memory, and this memory might be consciously or unconsciously selective, or the informant might not be aware of the import of or feel shame in giving certain data. Yet, despite the many limitations of this mode of data collection, some of the primary research in schizophrenia has utilized this method, and almost all of the data with respect to the family life of neurotics and behavior disorders were gathered in this way. These same limitations apply to data that are gathered when the informant is asked to fill out an attitude questionnaire. Surely the data on parents elicited from the children are susceptible to distortion even when given by normal children, no less those who already tend to consciously or unconsicously confound their perception of reality with fantasy. The psychiatric interview is a much more sensitive procedure than the case history or attitude questionnaire. Either structured or open-ended interviews enable the interviewer to follow up leads and possibly detect where information is being omitted for one reason or another. The problem here, however, is that there is always the possibility that distorted or inaccurate data are gathered by the interviewer, either through the kinds of questions asked, or the perception of the answer or of the individual being interviewed. For example, it is interesting to note that although the majority of psychiatric interviewers experienced the mothers of schizophrenics as matching the model of the schizophrenogenic mother—the dominant, overprotective, but basically rejecting mother who induces inappropriateness of thinking in her children—the psychological test evaluation of mothers of schizophrenics failed to confirm these findings. One explanation for this is that the interviewer, already acquainted with the literature regarding the mother of schizophrenics, anticipating to experience the mothers in terms of the ideas about schizophrenogenic mothers, did, indeed, experience them in that way, whereas a more objective evaluation of the patterns of thinking and feeling of these mothers did not confirm the more subjective impression.

In order to try and avoid the pitfalls inherent in data gleaned through case history or interview, investigators hypothesized that direct observation of the mother-child interaction might yield more valid information. Unfortunately, here, too, limitations inherent in the mode of data collection become apparent. Observations of the mother-child interaction in the home or in an observation room in a hospital or clinic are generally restricted to a limited time segment, for example, 1 hour once a week. This factor, in and of itself, limits the observations to a fairly restricted aspect of the spectrum of the interaction between mother and child. Here, too, the behavior to which the observer is exposed may be influenced by the conscious or unconscious attitudes and motives of the parent being observed. It is not too difficult for the parent to present only that behavior which, for one reason or another, she feels it safe to display and to control the presence of other behaviors. Direct observation of the family for extensive periods of time, that is, months, and under controlled but as natural as possible living conditions (as in the Family Study Section of NIMH) avoids the restrictiveness and overcomes, to one degree or another, the artificiality of the relatively brief observation. However, the family is still aware that they are being observed and may, to one degree or another, be unable to act "natural." Moreover, unless the observations are independently made by several people whose reliability of observation has already been established, they may also be influenced by the *Zeitgeist* and perceive the family as being "schizophrenogenic" whether it is or not, mutually reinforcing each other's expectations. A more pressing consideration in evaluating the validity of these kinds of observations is the fact that the interaction, no matter how natural, takes place after the development of the psychopathology. It is quite possible that the aspects of the interpersonal relationship within the family, or between the mother and child in particular, that eventuated in the development of the patterns of thinking, feeling, and behaving characteristic of the schizophrenic or the neurotic, are no longer present; they may have occurred at a time of the child's life long since past and/or under conditions of intimacy not even accessible to the observer. There is no reason to assume that the etiological factors are still functioning or that they will be available to the trained observer even over the course of 6 months. Of course, it might be that whatever differentiates the psychological existence of the schizophrenic from that of the neurotic or of the normal might be so subtle that it is imperceptible to the participants themselves or even the trained observer and, hence, escape notice. Here, one is reminded of Freud's comment that "the years of childhood of those who are later neurotic need not necessarily differ from those who are later normal except in intensity and distinctness [Freud, 1938 (Orig. publ. 1910), p. 583]."

Theorizing about the etiology of psychopathology has characteristically been of the either/or variety. Nineteenth century scientists sought explanations for neurotic and psychotic disorders in the hereditary background of their patients, working from the assumption that many directly inherited the neurotic or psychotic "illness." On the other hand, the scientist of the twentieth century has sought explanations for psychopathology in the experiential aspect of man's life, in his emotional and interpersonal learning. As with most events in our life, the truth is probably somewhere in between these two positions. Indeed, in spite of the emphasis that is placed on the role of experience in the development of personality in psychoanalysis, Freud did not think, at least as regards the etiology of psychopathology, in such categorically black and white terms. He was able to bridge the gap between the nature-nurture extremes:

> We divide the causes of neurotic disease into those which the individual himself brings with him into life, and those which life bring to him—that is to say, into constitutional and accidental. It is the interaction of these as a rule first gives rise to illness [Freud, 1950b (Orig. publ. 1913), p. 122].
>
> Let us bear clearly in mind that every human being has acquired, by the combined operation of inherent disposition and of external influences of childhood, a special individuality in the exercise of his capacity to love—that is, in the conditions which he sets up for loving, in the impulses he gratifies by it, and in the aims he sets out to achieve in it. . . . We will here provide against misconceptions and reproaches to the effect that we have denied the importance of the inborn (constitutional) factor because we have emphasized the importance of infantile impressions. Such an accusation arises out of the narrowness with which mankind looks for causes, inasmuch as one single causal factor satisfies him, in spite of the many commonly underlying the face of reality. Psycho-Analysis has said much about the "accidental" component in aetiology and little about the constitutional, but only because it could throw new light upon the former, whereas of the latter it knows no more so far than is already known. We deprecate the assumption of an essential opposition between the two series of aetiological factors; we presume rather a perpetual interchange of both in producing the results observed [Freud, 1950a (Orig. publ. 1912), p. 312].

Other psychoanalysts have followed Freud in the presumption of an inherent, predetermined characteristic functioning of the nervous system of the human organism which determines reactions to stimuli pre- and postnatally (e.g., Greenacre, 1941).

Augmenting the clinical observations of psychoanalysis, one must juxtapose the experimental evidence in psychology which indicates that (*a*) individuals reflect characteristic patterns of autonomic activity which are stable and which are typical of them as individuals (Grossman & Greenberg, 1957; Lacey, 1950; Richmond & Lustman, 1955; Wenger, 1941), (*b*) the characteristic patterns of neural activity are identifiable prenatally and are consistent with the patterns of activity observable postnatally (Richards & Newbery, 1938, (*c*) these characteristic patterns of autonomic activity consistently emerge in a factor of lability and balance in which specific personality factors are consistently highly loaded (Darling, 1940; Eysenck, 1956; Eysenck & Prell, 1951; Theron, 1948; van der Merwe, 1948; van der Merwe & Theron, 1947), (*d*) there is greater similarity of autonomic reactivity between identical twins than fraternal twins or ordinary siblings (Eysenck, 1956; Eysenck & Prell, 1951; Jost & Sontag, 1944), and (*e*) there is a selective influence on personality functioning due to the sex of the individual per se. For example, generally boys outnumber girls 2-1 in being referred for psychological help (Bender, 1937; Wile & Jones, 1937). Sears (1961) found a significant difference in the basic mode of self-reported expression of aggression between boys and girls: Girls appeared higher in socially acceptable forms of aggression and high in anxiety regarding hostility, while boys were significantly higher in aggression that was directed against social control. Sears also found that the more punitive the mother is, the more dependent the son becomes but the less dependent the daughter becomes. Newell (1936) found that maternal rejection affected males more than females: Marked increase in aggressive behavior was noted in the boys who experienced rejection, not so with the females. Baruch & Wilcox (1944) noted that interparental tensions lead to different reactions in boys as compared to girls; in boys, it led to ascendance-submission problems, in girls, to an experience of lack of affection.

We end this survey by concluding that we have not been able to find any unique factors in the family of the schizophrenic which distinguishes it from the family of the neurotic or from the family of controls, who are ostensibly free from evidence of patterns of gross psychopathology. In short, we end by stating that the assumption that the family is *the* factor in the development of personality has not been validated. It is interesting to note that Orlansky (1949), in his review of the literature exploring the relationship between certain childhood experiences, for example, feeding, toilet training, thumb-sucking, the degree of tactile stimulation by the mother, etc., upon the development of personality characteristics, was also forced to conclude that the data failed to confirm an invariant relationship between the experience in infancy and the resultant personality. Of course, it might well be that the reality of the family is not the important dimension in determining the child's reactions; rather, it might be the perception of the family members, and this might often have little or no relation to the people as they really are. This would mean, then, that in many instances the important variables in the development of psychopathology might be factors which the child brings to the family, the functioning of the nervous and metabolic systems and the cognitive capacity to integrate stimuli into meaningful perceptual and conceptual schema. Indeed, we are left to wonder, as do the psychoanalysts, whether the proclivity towards fantasy distortion of reality might not be *the* factor in the development of psychopathology, and this proclivity might not be always determined by the child's experiences per se.

Obviously, questions regarding the etiology of patterns of personality behavior which are regarded as pathological, unadaptive, or unadjusted cannot be met with simple answers. Apparently, the factors which play a part in the development of behavior in humans are so complex that it would appear that they almost defy being investigated scientifically and defy one's attempts to draw meaningful generalizations from the exploration which has already been done. It is, of course, conceivable that human behavior is so complex that it cannot be reduced to simple terms or be expected to yield unalterable patterns of occurrences. It might also be that what produces psychopathological reactions in one individual does not in another. All this would be understandable in light of the complexity that is the human being, neurologically as well as socially, but it is unfortunate as regards research endeavors. In 1926, Freud wrote:

> Anxiety is the reaction to danger. One cannot, after all, help suspecting that the reason why the affect of anxiety occupies a unique position in the economy of the mind has something to do with the essential nature of danger. Yet dangers are the common lot of humanity; they are the same for everyone. What we need and cannot lay our fingers on is some factor which will explain why some people are able to subject the affect of anxiety, in spite of its peculiar quality, to the normal workings of the mind, or which decides who is doomed to come to grief over the task [Freud, 1936, p. 64].

We end this review of forty years of research without being able to feel that we are any closer to an answer than was Freud.

REFERENCES

Ayer, Mary E., & Bernreuter, R. G. A study of the relationship between discipline and personality traits in little children. *Journal of Genetic Psychology*, 1937, **50**, 165–170.

Barry, H. Orphanhood as a factor in psychoses. *Journal of Abnormal and Social Psychology*, 1936, **30**, 431–438.

Barry, H., & Bousfield, W. A. Incidence of orphanhood among fifteen hundred psychotic patients. *Journal of Genetic Psychology*, 1937, **50**, 198–202.

Bartmeier, L. H. Deprivations during infancy and their effects upon personality development. *American Journal of Mental Deficiency*, 1952, **56**, 708–711.

Baruch, Dorothy W., & Wilcox, J. Annie. A study of sex differences in preschool children's adjustment coexistent with inter-parental tensions. *Journal of Genetic Psychology*, 1944, **64**, 281–303.

Baxter, J. C., Becker, J., & Hooks, W. Defensive style in the families of schizophrenics and controls. *Journal of Abnormal and Social Psychology*, 1963, **66**, 512–518.

Behrens, Marjorie L., & Goldfarb, W. A study of patterns of interaction of families of schizophrenic children in residential treatment. *American Journal of Orthopsychiatry*, 1958, **28**, 300–312.

Bell, R. Q., Garmezy, N., Farina, A., & Rodnick, E. H. Direct study of parent-child interaction. *American Journal of Orthopsychiatry*, 1960, **30**, 445–452.

Bender, Lauretta. Reactive psychosis in response to mental disease in the family. *Journal of Nervous and Mental Disease*, 1936, **83**, 143–289.

Bender, Lauretta. Behavior problems in the children of psychotic and criminal parents. *Genetic Psychology Monographs*, 1937, **19**, 229–339.

Beres, D., & Obers, S. J. The effects of extreme deprivation in infancy on psychic structure in adolescence: A study in ego development. *Psychoanalytic Study of the Child*, 1950, **5**, 212–235.

Bishop, Barbara M. Mother-child interaction and the social behavior of children. *Psychological Monographs*, 1951, **65**(11, Whole No. 328).

Bolles, Marjorie M., Metzger, Harriet F., & Pitts, Marjorie W. Early home background and personal adjustment. *American Journal of Orthopsychiatry*, 1941, **11**, 530–534.

Bowen, M., Dysinger, R. H., & Basamanie, Betty. The role of the father in families with a schizophrenic patient. *American Journal of Psychiatry*, 1959, **115**, 1017–1020.

Bowlby, J. The influence of early environment in the development of neurosis and neurotic character. *International Journal of Psychoanalysis*, 1940, **21**, 154–178.

Brodbeck, A. J., & Irwin, O. C. The speech behavior of infants without families. *Child Development*, 1946, **17**, 145–156.

Brodey, W. M. Some family operations in schizophrenia. *Archives of General Psychiatry*, 1959, **1**, 379–402.

Brown, W. T., & Moore, M. Soldiers who break down—family background and past history. *Military Surgeon*, 1944, **94**, 160–163.

Canavan, Myrtelle M., & Clark, Rosamond. The mental health of 463 children from dementiapraecox stock. *Mental Hygiene*, 1923, **7**, 137–148.

Childers, A. T., & Hamil, B. M. Emotional problems in children as related to the duration of breast feeding in infancy. *American Journal of Orthopsychiatry*, 1932, **2**, 134–142.

Clardy, E. R. A study of the development and course of schizophrenic children. *Psychiatric Quarterly*, 1951, **25**, 81–90.

Darling, R. P. Autonomic action in relation to personality traits of children. *Journal of Abnormal and Social Psychology*, 1940, **35**, 246–260.

Davidson, Susannah. School phobia as a manifestation of family disturbance: Its structure and treatment. *Journal of Child Psychology and Psychiatry*, 1961, **1**, 270–287.

Davis, K. Extreme social isolation of a child. *American Journal of Sociology*, 1940, **45**, 554–565.

Despert, Louise J. Schizophrenia in children. *Psychiatric Quarterly*, 1938, **12**, 366–371.

Despert, Louise J. Some considerations relating to the genesis of autistic behavior in children. *American Journal of Orthopsychiatry*, 1951, **21**, 335–350.

Donnelly, Ellen M. The quantitative analysis of parent

behavior toward psychotic children and their siblings. *Genetic Psychology Monographs*, 1960, **62**, 331–376.

Dworin, J., & Wyant, O. Authoritarian patterns in mothers of schizophrenics. *Journal of Clinical Psychology*, 1957, **13**, 332–338.

Eisenberg, L. School phobia: A study in the communication of anxiety. *American Journal of Psychiatry*, 1958, **114**, 712–718.

Estes, H. R., Haylett, Clarice H., & Johnson, Adelaide M. Separation anxiety. *American Journal of Psychotherapy*, 1956, **10**, 682–695.

Eysenck, H. J. The inheritance of extraversion-introversion. *Acta Psychologica*, 1956, **12**, 95–110.

Eysenck, H. J., & Prell, D. B. The inheritance of neuroticism: An experimental study. *Journal of Mental Science*, 1951, **97**, 441–465.

Fanning, Aneita, Lehr, Sara, Sherwin, Roberta, & Wilson, Marjorie. The mental health of children of psychotic mothers. *Smith College Studies in Social Work*, 1938, **8**, 291–343.

Farina, A. Patterns of role dominance and conflict in parents of schizophrenic patients. *Journal of Abnormal and Social Psychology*, 1960, **61**, 31–38.

Farina, A., & Dunham, R. M. Measurement of family relationships and their effects. *Archives of General Psychiatry*, 1963, **9**, 64–73.

Field, Minna A. Maternal attitudes found in twenty-five cases of children with primary behavior disorders. *American Journal of Orthopsychiatry*, 1940, **10**, 293–311.

Fisher, S., Boyd, Ina, Walker, D., & Sheer, Dianne. Parents of schizophrenics, neurotics, and normals. *Archives of General Psychiatry*, 1959, **1**, 149–166.

Fisher, S., & Mendell, D. The communication of neurotic patterns over two and three generations. *Psychiatry*, 1956, **19**, 41–46.

Fleck, S., Lidz, T., & Cornelison, Alice. Comparison of parent-child relationships of male and female schizophrenic patients. *Archives of General Psychiatry*, 1963, **8**, 1–7.

Frazee, Helen E. Children who later became schizophrenic. *Smith College Studies in Social Work*, 1953, **23**, 125–149.

Freeman, R. V., & Grayson, H. M. Maternal attitudes in schizophrenia. *Journal of Abnormal and Social Psychology*, 1955, **50**, 45–52.

Freeman, H. E., & Simmons, O. G. Mental patients in the community: Family settings and performance levels. *American Sociological Review*, 1958, **23**, 147–154.

Freeman, H. E., Simmons, O. G., & Bergen, B. J. Possessiveness as a characteristic of mothers of schizophrenics. *Journal of Abnormal and Social Psychology*, 1959, **58**, 271–273.

Freud, S. *Inhibitions, symptoms, and anxiety*. London: Hogarth Press, 1936.

Freud, S. Three contributions to the theory of sex. In A. A. Brill (Ed.), *The basic writings of Sigmund Freud*. (Orig. Publ. 1910) New York: Modern Library, 1938. p. 583.

Freud, S. The dynamics of the transference. (Orig. publ. 1912) In, *Collected papers*. Vol. 2. London: Hogarth Press, 1950. pp. 312–322. (a)

Freud, S. The predisposition to obsessional neurosis. (Orig. publ. 1913) In, *Collected papers*. Vol. 2. London: Hogarth Press, 1950. pp. 122–132. (b)

Friedlander, D. Personality development of twenty-seven children who later became psychotic. *Journal of Abnormal and Social Psychology*, 1945, **40**, 330–335.

Friedlander, Kate. Formation of the antisocial character. *Psychoanalytic Study of the Child*, 1945, 1, 189–203.

Garmezy, N., Clarke, A. R., & Stockner, Carol. Child rearing attitudes of mothers and fathers as reported by schizophrenic and normal patients. *Journal of Abnormal and Social Psychology*, 1961, **63**, 176–182.

Gerard, D. L., & Siegal, L. The family background of schizophrenia. *Psychiatric Quarterly*, 1950, **24**, 47–73.

Goldberg, Thelma B. Factors in the development of school phobia. *Smith College Studies in Social Work*, 1953, **23**, 227–248.

Goldfarb, W. The effects of early institutional care on adolescent personality (graphic Rorschach data). *Child Development*, 1943, **14**, 213–223. (a)

Goldfarb, W. Infant rearing and problem behavior. *American Journal of Orthopsychiatry*, 1943, **13**, 249–266. (b)

Goldfarb, W. The effects of early institutional care on adolescent personality. *Journal of Experimental Education*, 1943, **12**, 106–129. (c)

Goldfarb, W. Psychological deprivation in infancy. *American Journal of Psychiatry*, 1945, **102**, 19–33. (a)

Goldfarb, W. Psychological privation in infancy and subsequent adjustment. *American Journal of Orthopsychiatry*, 1945, **15**, 247–255. (b)

Greenacre, Phyllis. The predisposition to anxiety. *Psychoanalytic Quarterly*, 1941, **10**, 66–94.

Grossman, H. J., & Greenberg, N. H. Psychosomatic differentiation in infancy. I. Autonomic activity in the newborn. *Psychosomatic Medicine*, 1957, **19**, 293–306.

Guertin, W. H. Are differences in schizophrenic symptoms related to the mother's avowed attitudes toward child rearing? *Journal of Abnormal and Social Psychology*, 1961, **63**, 440–442.

Hajdu-Grimes, Lilly. Contributions to the etiology of schizophrenia. *Psychoanalytic Review*, 1940, **27**, 421–438.

Hattwick, Berta W. Interrelations between the preschool child's behavior and certain factors in the home. *Child Development*, 1936, **7**, 200–226.

Hattwick, Berta W., & Stowell, Margaret. The relation of parental over-attentiveness to children's work habits and social adjustment in kindergarten and the first six grades of school. *Journal of Educational Research*, 1936, **30**, 169–176.

Heilbrun, A. B. Perception of maternal childbearing attitudes in schizophrenics. *Journal of Consulting Psychology*, 1960, **24**, 169–173.

Holloway, Edith. A study of fifty-eight problem children, with emphasis upon the home situation as a causative factor in producing conflict. *Smith College Studies in Social Work*, 1931, **1**, 403.

Huschka, Mabel. Psychopathological disorders in the mother. *Journal of Nervous and Mental Disease*, 1941, **94**, 76–83.

Ingham, H. V. A statistical study of family relationships in psychoneurosis. *American Journal of Psychiatry*, 1949, **106**, 91–98.

Inlow, Ruby S. The home as a factor in the development of the psychosis. *Smith College Studies in Social Work*, 1933, 4, 153–154.

Jacobsen, Virginia. Influential factors in the outcome of treatment of school phobia. *Smith College Studies in Social Work*, 1947, **19**, 181–202.

Johnson, Adelaide M., Falstein, E. I., Szurek, S. A., & Svendsen, Margaret. School phobia. *American Journal of Orthopsychiatry*, 1941, **11**, 702–711.

Jost, H., & Sontag, L. W. The genetic factor in autonomic nervous system function. *Psychosomatic Medicine*, 1944, **6**, 308–310.

Karon, B. P., & Rosberg, J. Study of the mother-child

relationship in a case of paranoid schizophrenia. *American Journal of Psychotherapy*, 1958, **12**, 522–533.

Kasanin, J., Knight, Elizabeth, & Sage, Priscilla. The parent-child relationship in schizophrenia. *Journal of Nervous and Mental Disease*, 1934, **79**, 249–263.

Kohn, M. L., & Clausen, J. A. Parental authority behavior and schizophrenia. *American Journal of Orthopsychiatry*, 1956, **26**, 297–313.

Kundert, Elizabeth. Fear of desertion by mother. *American Journal of Orthopsychiatry*, 1947, **17**, 326–336.

Lacey, J. I. Individual differences in somatic response patterns. *Journal of Comparative and Physiological Psychology*, 1950, **43**, 338–350.

Lampron, Edna M. Children of schizophrenic parents. *Mental Hygiene*, 1933, **17**, 82–91.

Lane, R. C., & Singer, J. L. Familial attitudes in paranoid schizophrenics and normals from two socioeconomic classes. *Journal of Abnormal and Social Psychology*, 1959, **59**, 328–339.

Levy, D. M. Maternal overprotection and rejection. *Archives of Neurology and Psychiatry*, 1931, **25**, 886–889.

Levy, D. M. On the problem of delinquency. *American Journal of Orthopsychiatry*, 1932, **2**, 197–211.

Levy, D. M. Primary affect hunger. *American Journal of Psychiatry*, 1937, **94**, 643–652.

Levy, D. M. *Maternal overprotection.* New York: Columbia Univer. Press, 1943.

Lidz, T., Cornelison, Alice R., Fleck, S., & Terry, Dorothy. The intrafamilial environment of the schizophrenic patient: I. The father. *Psychiatry*, 1957, **20**, 329–342. (a)

Lidz, T., Cornelison, Alice R., Fleck, S., & Terry, Dorothy. The intrafamilial environment of schizophrenic patients: II. Marital schism and marital skew. *American Journal of Psychiatry*, 1957, **114**, 241–248. (b)

Lidz, T., Cornelison, Alice R., Fleck, S., & Terry, Dorothy. The intrafamilial environment of the schizophrenic patient. *Psychiatry*, 1957, **20**, 329–342. (c)

Lidz, T., Cornelison, Alice, Terry, Dorothy, & Fleck, S. Intrafamilial environment of the schizophrenic patient: VI. The transmission of irrationality. *Archives of Neurology and Psychiatry*, 1958, **79**, 305–316.

Lidz, Ruth W., & Lidz, T. The family environment of schizophrenic patients. *American Journal of Psychiatry*, 1949, **106**, 332–345.

Lidz, T., Parker, Neulah, & Cornelison, Alice. The role of the father in the family environment of the schizophrenic patient. *American Journal of Psychiatry*, 1956, **113**, 126–137.

Lowrey, L. G. Personality distortion and early institutional care. *American Journal of Orthopsychiatry*, 1940, **10**, 576–585.

Madow, L., & Hardy, S. E. Incidence and analysis of the broken family in the background of neurosis. *American Journal of Orthopsychiatry*, 1947, **17**, 521–528.

Mark, J. C. The attitudes of the mothers of male schizophrenics toward child behavior. *Journal of Abnormal and Social Psychology*, 1953, **48**, 185–189.

McCord, W., McCord, Joan, & Howard, A. Familial correlates of aggression in nondelinquent male children. *Journal of Abnormal and Social Psychology*, 1961, **62**, 79–93.

McKeown, J. E. The behavior of parents of schizophrenic, neurotic, and normal children. *American Journal of Sociology*, 1950, **56**, 175–179.

Meyers, D. I., & Goldfarb, W. Studies of perplexity in mothers of schizophrenic children. *American Journal of Orthopsychiatry*, 1961, **31**, 551–564.

Meyers, D., & Goldfarb, W. Psychiatric appraisals of parents and siblings of schizophrenic children. *American Journal of Psychiatry*, 1962, **118**, 902–908.

Miller, H., & Baruch, D. A study of hostility in allergic children. *American Journal of Orthopsychiatry*, 1950, **20**, 506–519.

Mueller, Dorothy D. Paternal domination: Its influence on child guidance results. *Smith College Studies in Social Work*, 1945, **15**, 184–215.

Newell, H. W. The psycho-dynamics of maternal rejection. *American Journal of Orthopsychiatry*, 1934, **4**, 387–401.

Newell, H. W. A further study of maternal rejection. *American Journal of Orthopsychiatry*, 1936, **6**, 576–589.

Oltman, Jane E., McGarry, J. J., & Friedman, S. Parental deprivation and the "broken home" in dementia praecox and other mental disorders. *American Journal of Psychiatry*, 1952, **108**, 685–694.

Opler, M. K. Schizophrenia and culture. *Scientific American*, 1957, **197**, 103–110.

Orlansky, H. Infant care and personality. *Psychological Bulletin*, 1949, **46**, 1–48.

Pearson, G. H. Some early factors in the formation of personality. *American Journal of Orthopsychiatry*, 1931, **1**, 284–291.

Perr, H. M. Criteria distinguishing parents of schizophrenic and normal children. *Archives of Neurology and Psychiatry*, 1958, **79**, 217–224.

Plank, R. The family constellation of a group of schizophrenic patients. *American Journal of Orthopsychiatry*, 1953, **23**, 817–825.

Pollock, H. M., & Malzberg, B. Hereditary and environmental factors in the causation of manic-depressive psychoses and dementia praecox. *American Journal of Psychiatry*, 1940, **96**, 1227–1244.

Pollock, H. M., Malzberg, B., & Fuller, R. G. Hereditary and environmental factors in the causation of dementia praecox and manic-depressive psychoses. *Psychiatric Quarterly*, 1936, **10**, 495–509.

Preston, G. H., & Antin, Rosemary. A study of children of psychotic parents. *American Journal of Orthopsychiatry*, 1932, **2**, 231–241.

Prout, C. T., & White, Mary A. A controlled study of personality relationships in mothers of schizophrenic male patients. *American Journal of Psychiatry*, 1950, **107**, 251–256.

Reichard, Suzanne, & Tillman, C. Patterns of parent-child relationships in schizophrenia. *Psychiatry*, 1950, **13**, 247–257.

Ribble, Margarethe A. Disorganizing factors of infant personality. *American Journal of Psychiatry*, 1941, **98**, 459–463.

Richards, T. W., & Newbery, Helen. Studies in fetal behavior: III. Can performance on test items at six months postnatally be predicted on the basis of fetal activity? *Child Development*, 1938, **9**, 79–86.

Richmond, J. B., & Lustman, S. L. Autonomic function in the neonate: I. Implications for psychosomatic theory. *Psychosomatic Medicine*, 1955, **17**, 269–275.

Schofield, W., & Balian, L. A comparative study of the personal histories of schizophrenic and nonpsychiatric patients. *Journal of Abnormal and Social Psychology*, 1959, **59**, 216–225.

Sears, R. R. Relation of early socialization experiences to aggression in middle childhood. *Journal of Abnormal and Social Psychology*, 1961, **63**, 466–492.

Sears, R. R., Whiting, J. W. M., Nowlis, V., & Sears, Pauline S. Some child-rearing antecedents of aggression and dependency in young children. *Genetic Psychology Monographs*, 1953, **47**, 133–234.

Shaw, C. R., & McKay, H. D. Are broken homes a causative

factor in juvenile delinquency? *Social Forces*, 1932, **10**, 514–524.

Shoben, E. J. The assessment of parental attitudes in relation to child adjustment. *Genetic Psychology Monographs*, 1949, **39**, 101–148.

Selberpfennig, Judith. Mother types encountered in child guidance clinics. *American Journal of Orthopsychiatry*, 1941, **11**, 475–484.

Silverman, B. The behavior of children from broken homes. *American Journal of Orthopsychiatry*, 1935, **5**, 11–18.

Singer, J. L. Projected familial attitudes as a function of socioeconomic status and psychopathology. *Journal of Consulting Psychology*, 1954, **18**, 99–104.

Sperling, Melitta. The role of the mother in psychosomatic disorders in children. *Psychosomatic Medicine*, 1949, **11**, 377–385.

Sperling, Melitta. The neurotic child and his mother: A psychoanalytic study. *American Journal of Orthopsychiatry*, 1951, **21**, 351–362.

Spitz, R. A. Hospitalism: An inquiry into the genesis of psychiatric conditions in early childhood. *Psychoanalytic Study of the Child*, 1945, **1**, 53–74.

Stein, Lucille H. A study of over-inhibited and unsocialized-aggressive children. *Smith College Studies in Social Work*, 1944, **15**, 124–125.

Stringer, Joyce R. Case studies of the families of schizophrenics. *Smith College Studies in Social Work*, 1962, **32**, 118–148.

Strodtbeck, F. L. Husband-wife interaction over revealed differences. *American Sociological Review*, 1951, **16**, 468–473.

Suttenfield, Virginia. School phobia: A study of five cases. *American Journal of Orthopsychiatry*, 1954, **24**, 368–380.

Talbot, Mira. School Phobia: A workshop: I. Panic in school phobia. *American Journal of Orthopsychiatry*, 1957, **27**, 286–295.

Theron, P. A. Peripheral vasomotor reaction as indices of basic emotional tension and lability. *Psychosomatic Medicine*, 1948, **10**, 335–346.

Tietze, Trude. A study of mothers of schizophrenic patients. *Psychiatry*, 1949, **12**, 55–65.

van der Merwe, A. B. The diagnostic value of peripheral vasomotor reactions in the psychoneuroses. *Psychosomatic Medicine*, 1948, **10**, 347–354.

van der Merwe, A. B., & Theron, P. A. A new method of measuring emotional stability. *Journal of General Psychology*, 1947, **37**, 109–124.

van Houten, Janny. Mother-child relationships in twelve cases of school phobia. *Smith College Studies in Social Work*, 1948, **18**, 161–180.

Wahl, C. W. Some antecedent factors in the family histories of 392 schizophrenics. *American Journal of Psychiatry*, 1954, **110**, 668–676.

Wahl, C. W. Some antecedent factors in the family histories of 568 male schizophrenics of the United States Navy. *American Journal of Psychiatry*, 1956, **113**, 201–210.

Waldfogel, S., Hahn, Pauline B., & Gardner, G. E. A study of school phobia in children. *Journal of Nervous and Mental Disease*, 1954, **120**, 399.

Wallace, Ramona. A study of the relationship between emotional tone of the home and adjustment status in cases referred to a travelling child guidance clinic. *Journal of Juvenile Research*, 1935, **19**, 205–220.

Walters, Jean H. A study of the family relationships of schizophrenic patients. *Smith College Studies in Social Work*, 1939, **9**, 189–191.

Watson, G. A. A comparison of the effects of lax versus strict home training. *Journal of Social Psychology*, 1934, **5**, 102–105.

Wenger, M. A. The measurement of individual differences in autonomic balance. *Psychosomatic Medicine*, 1941, **3**, 427–434.

Wile, I. S., & Jones, Ann B. Ordinal position and the behavior disorders of young children. *Journal of Genetic Psychology*, 1937, **51**, 61–93.

Williams, H. D. Causes of social maladjustment in children. *Psychological Monographs*, 1932, **43**(1, Whole No. 194).

Wilson, Margaret J. Grandmother, mother, and daughter in cases of school phobia. *Smith College Studies in Social Work*, 1955, **25**, 56–57.

Winder, C. L., & Kantor, R. E. Rorschach maturity scores of the mothers of schizophrenics. *Journal of Consulting Psychology*, 1958, **22**, 438–440.

Witmer, Helen L. Parental behavior as an index to the probable outcome of treatment in a child guidance clinic. *American Journal of Orthopsychiatry*, 1933, **3**, 431–444.

Zimmerman, Anna C. Parental adjustments and attitudes in relation to the problems of five- and six-year-old children. *Smith College Studies in Social Work*, 1930, **1**, 406–407.

Zuckerman, M., Oltean, Mary, & Monashkin, I. The parental attitudes of mothers of schizophrenics. *Journal of Consulting Psychology*, 1958, **22**, 307–310.

Black Youth and Motivation

Alvin F. Poussaint
Carolyn Atkinson

The civil rights movement of the 1960s in America spawned a new and vibrant generation of young black people. The degree of their commitment and determination came as a surprise for most white Americans, who, if they thought of blacks to any extent, considered them to be a rather docile, acquiescent people. As the events of the early 1960s moved on with inexorable force, another, still younger generation of blacks stood on the periphery watching and waiting their turn. Their intense coming-of-age has brought still more surprise and puzzlement not only to white Americans, but to some Negroes. So busy have many been in "handling" or "coping with" the complex behavior of these young blacks, that relatively little has been done in terms of examining the basis for this behavior. This paper represents an attempt to pause in the on-going melee for an exploration of some of the factors of particular relevance to the motivation of Afro-American youth. Our analysis will focus on some of the "problem areas," so of necessity it will not detail the many strengths and positive features of the black socio-cultural environment. Of primary interest in our discussion will be the areas of internal motivation: the individual's self-concept; certain of his patterned needs; and the external motivators—the rewards offered by society for satisfactory performance in any of its institutional areas.

Of obvious importance to the functioning of any individual is his concept or vision of himself. And like it or not, this concept is inevitably a part of how others see him, how others tell him he should be seen. According to Mead (1), Cooley (2), and others (3), the self arises through the individual's interaction with and reaction to other members of society: his peers, parents, teachers, and other institutional representatives. Through identification and as a necessary means of effective communication, the child learns to assume the roles and attitudes of others with whom he interacts. These assumed attitudes condition not only how he responds to others, but how he behaves toward himself. The collective attitudes of the others, the community or "generalized other" as Mead calls them, give the individual his unity of self. The individual's self is shaped, developed, and controlled by his anticipating and assuming the attitudes and definitions of others (the community) toward him. To the extent that the individual is a member of this community, its attitudes are his, its values are his, and its norms are his. His image of himself is structured in these terms. Each self, then, though having its unique characteristics of personality, is also an individual reflection of the social process (4). This idea can be seen more succinctly illustrated in Cooley's suggestion of the self as a looking-glass, a looking-glass mirroring the three principal components of one's self-concept: "the imagination of our appearance to the other person; the imagination of his judgment of that appearance; and some sort of self-feeling, such as pride or mortification" (5).

From *The Black Scholar,* 1970, 1, 43–51. Reprinted by permission.

For the black youth in white American society, the generalized other whose attitudes he assumes and the looking-glass into which he gazes both reflect the same judgment: He is inferior because he is black. His self-image, developed in the lowest stratum of a color caste system, is shaped, defined, and evaluated by a generalized other which is racist or warped by racists. His self-concept naturally becomes a negatively esteemed one, nurtured through contact with such institutionalized symbols of caste inferiority as segregated schools, neighborhoods, and jobs and more indirect negative indicators such as the reactions of his own family who have been socialized to believe that they are substandard human beings. Gradually becoming aware of the meaning of his black skin, the Negro child comes to see himself as an object of scorn and disparagement, unworthy of love and affection. The looking-glass of white society reflects the supposed undesirability of the black youth's physical appearance: black skin and wooly hair, as opposed to the valued models of white skin and straight hair. In order to gain the esteem of the generalized other, it becomes clear to him that he must approximate this white appearance as closely as possible. He learns to despise himself and to reject those like himself. From the moment of this realization, his personality and style of interaction with his environment become molded and shaped in a warped, self-hating, and self-denigrating way. He learns that existence for him in this society demands a strict adherence to the limitations of his substandard state. He comes to understand that to challenge the definition the others have given of him will destroy him. It is impressed upon him that the incompetent, acquiescent and irresponsible Negro survives in American society, while the competent, aggressive black is systematically suppressed. The looking-glass of the black youth's self reflects a shattered and defeated image.

Several attempts have been made to determine how this shattered self-concept affects the black child's ability to function in society, his ability to achieve, to succeed or "make good," particularly in the area of education. Though the conclusions of these varied attempts have differed on occasion, there has been general agreement as to the reality of the black child's incomplete self-image (6, 7, 8). One notable exception to this agreement, however, is the Coleman Report, a 1966 study by the United States Office of Education on the *Equality of Education Opportunity* (9). This report maintains that the black child's self-concept has not been exceptionally damaged, and is in fact virtually no different from that of a white child. The report did, however, note that the white child is consistently able to achieve on a higher level than that of his black counterpart. The Coleman Study, therefore, concluded that self-concept has little to do with an individual's ability to achieve (10). Other studies tend to disagree with these findings.

Another variation on this theme of the black child's self-concept is seen in a 1968 report on "Academic Motivation and Equal Educational Opportunity" done by Irwin Katz. Katz found that black children tended to have exaggeratedly high aspirations, so high, in fact, that they were realistically impossible to live up to. As a result, these children were able to achieve very little:

> Conceivably, their [low achieving Negro boys'] standards were so stringent and rigid as to be utterly dysfunctional. They seem to have internalized a most effective mechanism for self-discouragement. In a sense, they had been socialized to self-impose failure. (11)

Katz presents evidence which indicates that the anticipation of failure or harsh judgment by adults produces anxiety in the child, and that in black children, this level of anxiety is highest in low achievers who have a high standard of self-evaluation (12). Accordingly, a black child with an unrealistically elevated self-concept often tends to become so anxious concerning his possible failure to meet that self-concept that he does in fact fail consistently.

On the other hand, Deutsch's work has shown that Negro children had significantly more negative self-images than did white children (13). He maintains that, among the influences converging on the black urban child,

> is his sensing that the larger society views him as inferior and expects inferior performance from him as evidenced by the general denial to him of realistic vertical mobility possibilities. Under these conditions, it is understandable that the Negro child would tend strongly to question his own competencies and in so questioning would be acting largely as others expect him to act, an example of what Merton has called the "self-fulfilling prophecy"—the very expectation itself is a cause of its fulfillment. (14)

Similarly, Coombs and Davies offer the important proposition that

> In the context of the school world, a student who is defined as a "poor student" (by significant others and thereby by self) comes to conceive of himself as such and gears his behavior accordingly, that is, the social expectation is realized. However, if he is led to believe by means of the social "looking-glass" that he is capable and able to achieve well, he does. To maintain his status and self-esteem becomes the incentive for further effort which subsequently involves him more in the reward system of the school. (15)

These views have been confirmed in such studies as that of Davidson and Greenberg (16). In their examination of children from central Harlem, these authors found that the lower the level of self-esteem, the lower the level of achievement; while consequently, higher levels of self-appraisal and ego strength—feelings of self-competence—were associated with higher levels of achievement. For example, high achievers were more able to give their own ideas and to express basic needs, suggesting that a stronger self-concept is associated with a greater willingness to risk self-expression, an obvious prerequisite for achievement.

Certainly these various studies cannot be considered as ultimately not unanimously conclusive. However, it is important to note that none of these reports has found any evidence of high achievement resulting from a low self-concept. Obviously the black child with such a low self-concept competes at a disadvantage with white youth in the struggle to achieve in this society.

The question then arises as to why black youth bother to involve themselves at all in this struggle. If their negative self-image handicaps them so greatly in achieving, why not simply abdicate and in fact adhere to society's definition of them as substandard? An attempted response to this question moves us into another area, that of patterned needs.

In the course of the socialization process, the individual acquires needs which motivate behavior and generate emotions. Three such needs concern us here: the need for achievement, the need for self-assertion or aggression, and the need for approval.

Among the attitudes of the generalized other which the individual in this society internalizes are the norms and values of the wider community, including, of course, the major tenets of the Protestant Ethic-American creed, i.e., with hard work and effort the individual can achieve success, and the individual's worth is defined by his ability to achieve that success. The individual who internalizes these values is motivated to act consistently with them, as his self-esteem is heightened or maintained through behaving in a manner approved by the community. Thus, the need for achievement develops in both white and black Americans. Consequently, the black youth's participation in the struggle for success is at least in part an attempt to satisfy his own needs.

This need to achieve may be very high as illustrated in the findings of Coleman (17) and Katz (18) who note the exceptionally high aspirations of Negro youth with regard to schooling and occupational choice. In addition, Katz (19) and Gordon (20) indicate that the aspirations and demands for academic achievement of the parents of these youth are also often exceptionally high. All of these sources agree, however, that the achievement of these youth is far from commensurate with either their own aspirations or those of their parents (21). Thus, the problem does not seem to be, as some have suggested, one of insufficiently high levels of aspiration, but rather one of realizing these aspirations through productive behavior (22). Gordon (23) and Katz (24) suggest that this discrepancy persists because the educational and occupational values and goals of white society have been internalized by black youth, but for one reason or another, the behavior patterns necessary for their successful attainment have not been similarly learned. Katz puts it succinctly:

> Apparently the typical Negro mother tries to socialize her child for scholastic achievement by laying down verbal rules and regulations about classroom [behavior], coupled with punishment or detected transgressions. But she does not do

enough to guide and encourage her child's efforts at verbal-symbolic mastery. Therefore, the child learns only to verbalize standards of academic interest and attainment. Their standards then provide the cognitive basis for negative self-evaluations. . . . The low achieving Negro student learns to use expressions of interest and ambition as a verbal substitute for behaviors he is unable to enact. . . . By emphasizing the discrepancy between the real and ideal performance, anxiety is raised in actual achievement situations. (25)

Thus the black child's negative self-concept is further complicated by his internalization of white society's high-level goals, and the need to achieve them, without a true comprehension of how effectively to do so.

Further examination of the values of the Protestant Ethic leads to the conclusion that they imply that assertion of self and aggression is an expected and admired form of behavior. Through the socialization process, the individual internalizes those attitudes which reinforce his basic need to assert himself or express himself aggressively. Thus, random and possibly destructive aggression is channeled into a legitimate and rewarded avenue of achievement (26).

What happens to the black child's need for aggression and self-assertion? What has been the nature of his socialization with respect to expressing aggression? Since slavery days and, to some extent, through the present, the Negro most rewarded by whites has been the "Uncle Tom," the exemplar of the black man who was docile and nonassertive, who bowed and scraped for the white boss and denied his aggressive feelings for his oppressor. In order to retain the most menial of jobs and keep from starving, black people quickly learned that passivity was a necessary survival technique. To be an "uppity nigger" was considered by racists one of the gravest violations of racial etiquette. Vestiges of this attitude remain to the present day, certainly in the South, but also in the North: Blacks who are too "outspoken" about racial injustices often lose their jobs or are not promoted to higher positions because they are considered "unreasonable" or "too sensitive." It is significant that the civil rights movement had to adopt passive resistance and nonviolence in order to win acceptance by white America. Thus, the black child is socialized to the lesson taught by his parents, other blacks, and white society: Don't be aggressive, don't be assertive. Such lessons do not, however, destroy the need for aggression and self-assertion.

One asserts oneself for self-expression, for achievement of one's goals, and for control of one's environment. Thus, an individual's success in satisfying his need for self-assertion is to some degree determined by his sense of control of his environment. Coleman found that of three attitudes measured, sense of control over environment showed the strongest relationship to achievement (27). He further discovered that blacks have a much lower sense of control over their environment than do whites (28), but that this sense of control increased as the proportion of whites with whom they went to school increased (29). These findings indicate that for blacks, a realistic inability for meaningful self-assertion is a greater inhibitor of ability to achieve than is any other variable. These findings also suggest, however, that when blacks are interacting in a school situation which approximates the world in which they must cope, i.e., one with whites, their sense of control and achievement increases. Our emphasis here is not that black students' being in the presence of white students increases their sense of control and level of achievement, but that their being in a proximate real world suggests to them that they can cope in any situation, not just one in which they are interacting with others who, like themselves, have been defined as inferior.

Coleman's findings are supported by those of Davidson and Greenberg: High achievers were more able to exercise control and to cope more effectively with feelings of hostility and anxiety generated by the environment than were low achievers (30). Deutsch points out that black male children for whom aggressive behavior has always been more threatening (compared with black girls) have lower levels of achievement on a number of variables than do black girls (31). It is not surprising then that black people, objectively less able to control their environment than can whites, may react in abdicating control by deciding not to assert themselves. The reasons for this are clear. First, the anxiety that accompanies growth and change through self-assertion is avoided if a new failure is not risked and thus a try is not made. Second, the steady state of failure through nonachievement rather than through unsuccessful trial is a pattern which many blacks have come to know and expect. They feel psychologically comfortable with the more familiar.

However, this effort by black people to deny their need for control and self-assertion inevitably takes its toll. Frustration of efforts to control the environment are likely to lead to anger, rage, and other expressions of aggression (32). This aggression can be dealt with in a variety of ways. It can be suppressed, leading one to act on the basis of a substitute and opposing emotional attitude, i.e., compliance or docility. It can be channeled through legitimate activities—dancing, sports, or through an identification with the oppressor and a consequent striving to be like him. Aggression can also be turned inward and expressed in psychosomatic illness, drug addiction, or the attacking of those like oneself (other blacks) whom one hates as much as oneself. Or aggression can be directed toward those who generate the anger and rage—the oppressors, those whom the individual defines as thwarting this inclination to self-assertion. This final form of aggression can be either destructive or constructive: Dropping out of school or becoming delinquent are examples of the former case, while participation in black social action movements is an example of the latter instance. This latter form of aggressive behavior amongst black people is increasing in extent. The old passivity is fading and being replaced by a drive to undo powerlessness, helplessness, and dependency under American racism. The process is a difficult one for those black people who manage to make the attempt. For their aggressive drive, so long suppressed by the ruling power structure, is exercised to the inevitable detriment of still another exigency: their need for approval.

With the development of the self and through the process of identification, the individual's need for approval develops and grows as does his need to avoid disapproval (33). As we have stated earlier, the Protestant Ethic of American society approves behavior which follows the achievement motive and expresses the need for self-assertion. An individual's behavior in accordance with this ethic is often tied to a need for approval. On the other hand, for blacks in American society, the reverse is often the case, i.e., behavior which is neither achievement-oriented nor self-assertive is often approved by both blacks and whites (for different reasons), and thus, the need for approval may be met through behavior unrelated to either achievement or self-assertion.

Katz's study maintains that in lower-class homes, children do not learn realistic (middle-class) standards of self-appraisal and therefore do not develop (as do middle-class children) the capacity for gaining "satisfaction through self-approval of successful performance" (34). Accordingly, Katz suggests that achievement should be motivated and rewarded by approval not from the home, but from fellow students and teachers (35). The extent to which black children are responsive to approval for achievement in middle-class terms is, however, problematic. Some evidence suggests that lower-class black children are motivated to gain approval through physical characteristics and prowess rather than through intellectual achievement as are middle-class white and black children (36). Further, needs for approval, not often met in black children through the established institutional channels, may be met by others outside of these legitimate institutional areas. For instance, delinquent subcultures support and encourage the behavior of their members. As a result, such members are not often sensitive to the informal sanctions imposed by nonmembers of this subsociety (37). If an individual's needs are not met by others to whose sanctions he is expected to be responsive, he will be less likely to fear their sanctions for nonperformance and will seek to have his needs met by others to whose rewards of approval he will then be responsive (38). Thus, for black youth no less than others, how the need for approval motivates behavior depends in large part upon how it is satisfied or rewarded.

The rewards which the institutions of this society offer to those whose behavior meets their approval or is "successful" consist of money, prestige, power, respect, acclamation, and love, with increasing amounts of each of these being extended for increasingly "successful" behavior. The individual is socialized to know that these will be his if he performs according to expectations. Hence, these rewards act as external motivators of behavior. Blacks have learned of the existence of these rewards. They have also learned, however, that behavior for which whites reap these rewards does not result in the same consequences for them. In the various institutional areas of society, blacks are often rewarded differentially from whites for the same behavior—if they are rewarded at all. How then can such a highly capricious system motivate their behavior?

That blacks orient some aspects of their behavior to society's reward system is evidenced by the fact that many studies have shown that lower-class blacks, as opposed to middle-class whites and blacks, have a utilitarian attitude toward education, viewing it primarily in terms of its market value (39). The system provides no assurance, however, that once they obtain the proper education for a job, they will in fact be allowed to get that job. This inability to trust society to confer rewards consistently no doubt makes it difficult for blacks to be socialized to behave in terms of anticipating future reward for present activity. Thus, it is that Deutsch found that young black children are unwilling to persist in attempting to solve difficult problems. They respond to such situations with a "who cares" attitude (40). Similarly, another study showed that when a tangible reward was offered for successful work on a test, the motivation of the deprived youngsters increased considerably (41). In a New York program, young men who had been working primarily as clerks and porters were motivated to join a tutorial program for admission to a construction trade union apprenticeship program when they were promised that successful completion of the program (passing the union's examination) would definitely result in their being hired immediately at a salary often double what they were able to command previously (42).

However, motivation to achieve certain rewards may have different consequences for behavior. As Merton explained, when the goals of society are internalized without a corresponding internalization of normative means for achieving these goals, what often results is the resort to illegitimate (deviant) means to achieve the socially valued goals (43). Just as a child unable to satisfy his need for approval through legitimate channels may turn to delinquent subcultures for support and encouragement, so too might such a child, unable to gain society's rewards by legitimate means, turn to illegitimate methods in order to attain them. Such forms of behavior as numbers running, dope pushing, and prostitution effectively serve to net the rewards of society, while circumventing the institutional channels for achievement of societal rewards. That Negro children early learn that such behavior is rewarded is suggested by Gordon's study in which young (9–13) central Harlem boys were asked if they knew people who had become rich, and if so, how they thought they had managed to do so. Of those who responded affirmatively, a majority felt that they had become rich through illegitimate means or luck (44).

Consequently, for many black youth, external rewards are weak motivators of behavior, as they are discriminatorily and inconsistently given. The more immediate and direct the reward is, the stronger a motivator it is likely to be.

It would appear from this analysis that the standards and rewards of white American society simply do not work effectively to motivate productive behavior in young blacks. Clearly there is urgent need for a fundamental restructuring of the system. First, with respect to self-concept, all institutional segments of society must begin to function in a nonracist manner. To the extent that the self is shaped with reference to a generalized other, to that extent will the black child's image be impaired as long as America remains racist. The growth of black consciousness and pride have had salutary consequences for the black's self-image. But this alone is not sufficient. The operation of self-image as a motivator for behavior is like a self-fulfilling prophecy: Blacks are continuously told and some believe that they are inferior and will fail. Therefore, they fail. For the black child to be motivated to achieve in school, the school must negate everything that the society affirms: It must tell the child that he can succeed—and he will (45).

The relationship between self-concept and achievement is

not clear-cut, but it appears to be a weaker motivator of behavior than the motive to self-assertion and aggression. More attention should be given to examining this dimension of personality as a motivator of the black youth's behavior than to continuing inquiries into his self-image. It has been noted that the black youth's sense of control of his environment increases as the proportion of whites in his school increases. It is imperative to keep in mind, however, that participation in all-or-predominantly-black structures need not be self-destructive if the black youth chooses rather than is forced to participate in them. For if he chooses, he is asserting control over his environment. Those structural changes being made in American society in the direction of blacks having the opportunity to be more aggressively in control of their environment must be continued and expanded. The plans to decentralize New York City schools, to develop black business, and to organize and channel black political power are significant steps in this direction.

Most of the data indicate that black youth and their parents have high educational and occupational aspirations, which are not carried through to achievement levels. The reward systems of American society are often irrelevant to the lives and aspirations of most black youth. Approval is rewarded primarily for forms of behavior in which the black youth has managed to achieve little proficiency, making him less likely to make the effort. Something is obviously wrong with any school system which permits so much young potential to be wasted simply because it cannot be developed within the confines of traditional methods. New frameworks must be developed which will enable the educational aspirations of black youth to correspond to their interests and proficiencies. With the establishment of a pattern of consistent reward, there is every possibility that intellectual endeavors would have immediate relevance to their lives.

Certainly these suggested changes are sweeping, but so too have been the dangerous effects of the maintenance of the old systems. The time for being surprised at the behavior of black youth has passed. The time for lengthy, nonproductive attempts at understanding them has too, in its turn, come to an end. The time remaining must be effectively used in action to bring about these and similar changes. America cannot afford to wait for the next generation.

NOTES AND REFERENCES

1. George H. Mead, *Mind, self, and society* (Chicago: University of Chicago Press, 1934), Part III.
2. Charles H. Cooley, *Human nature and the social order* (New York: Free Press, 1956), *passim*.
3. *Sociological Quarterly*, Summer 1966, **7**(3), entire issue.
4. Mead, *op. cit.*
5. Cooley, *op. cit.*
6. Alvin F. Poussaint, The dynamics of racial conflict, *Lowell Lecture Series*, sponsored by the Tufts-New England Medical Center, April 16, 1968.
7. Joan Gordon, *The poor of Harlem: Social functioning in the underclass*, Report to the Welfare Administration, Washington, D.C., July 31, 1965, pp. 115, 161; and Irwin Katz, Academic motivation and equal educational opportunity, *Harvard Educational Review*, Winter 1968, **38**, 56–65.
8. While we recognize the limitations of many measures of self-concept and that self-concept is often defined by how it is measured, an exploration of these considerations within the scope of this paper is clearly impossible. Therefore, for the purpose of our presentation here, we are taking the measures of self-concept at face value.
9. James S. Coleman et al., *Equality of educational opportunity*, U.S. Office of Education (Washington, D.C.: U.S. Government Printing Office, 1966), p. 281.
10. *Ibid.*, p. 320.
11. Katz, *op. cit.*, p. 60.
12. *Ibid.*, pp. 61–62.
13. Martin Deutsch, Minority groups and class status as related to social and personality factors in scholastic achievement, in Martin Deutsch et al., *The disadvantaged child* (New York: Basic Books, 1967), p. 106.
14. *Ibid.*, p. 107.
15. R. H. Coombs and V. Davies, Self-conception and the relationship between high school and college scholastic achievement, *Sociology and Social Research*, July 1966, **50**, 468–469.
16. Helen H. Davidson and Judith W. Greenberg, *Traits of school achievers from a deprived background* (New York: City College of the City University of New York, May 1967), pp. 133, 134.
17. Coleman, *op. cit.*, pp. 278–280.
18. Katz, *op. cit.*, p. 64.
19. *Ibid.*, pp. 63–65.
20. Gordon, *op. cit.*, p. 115.
21. Coleman, *op. cit.*, p. 281; Katz, *op. cit.*, p. 63; Gordon, *op. cit.*, pp. 155, 160–161.
22. David P. Ausubel and Pearl Ausubel, Ego development among segregated Negro children, in A. Harry Passow (ed.), *Education in depressed areas* (New York: Teachers College Press, 1963), p. 135.
23. Gordon, *op. cit.*, pp. 115, 161.
24. Katz, *op. cit.*, p. 63.
25. *Ibid.*, p. 64.
26. Davidson and Greenberg, *op. cit.*, p. 58.
27. Coleman, *op. cit.*, p. 319.
28. *Ibid.*, p. 289.
29. *Ibid.*, pp. 323–324.
30. Davidson and Greenberg, *op. cit.*, p. 54.
31. Deutsch, *op. cit.*, p. 108.
32. Alvin F. Poussaint, A Negro psychiatrist explains the Negro psyche, *New York Times Magazine*, August 20, 1967, pp. 58–80.
33. Davidson and Greenberg, *op. cit.*, p. 61.
34. Katz, *op. cit.*, p. 57.
35. *Ibid.*
36. Edmund W. Gordon and Doxey A. Wilkerson, *Compensatory education for the disadvantaged* (New York: College Entrance Examination Board, 1966), p. 18.
37. Claude Brown, *Manchild in the promised land* (New York: Macmillan, 1965), *passim.*
38. Talcott Parsons, *The social system* (New York: Free Press, 1951), chap. 7.
39. Gordon and Wilkerson, *op. cit.*, p. 18.
40. Deutsch, *op. cit.*, p. 102.
41. Elizabeth Douvan, Social status and success striving, cited in Frank Riessman, *The culturally deprived child* (New York: Harper & Row, 1962), p. 53.
42. Personal communication (C. A.).
43. Robert K. Merton, *Social theory and social structure* (New York: Free Press, 1957), chap. 4.
44. Gordon, *op. cit.*, p. 164.
45. Kenneth B. Clark, *Dark ghetto* (New York: Harper & Row, 1965), pp. 139–148.

Part Four

THE BEHAVIOR PATHOLOGIES

Chapter 7

The Neuroses

The importance of anxiety in the neuroses is emphasized in Freudian theory as well as in much of the experimental work on neurosis induction with human subjects. The first paper in this chapter, by Justin Aronfreed and Arthur Reber, demonstrates how anxiety is attached to certain internal cues in children when they are punished for a transgression and how anxiety is reduced by internalized behavioral suppression.

The second article, inspired by Stanley Schachter's 1959 book on *The Psychology of Affiliation*, is a test of the hypothesis that firstborn children find physical pain more averse and frightening than do later-born individuals. In this study, Nisbett shows that first-borns are less likely than later-borns to participate in dangerous sports.

Taking a somewhat untraditional view, the late A. H. Maslow discusses, in the last paper, neurosis as a failure of personal growth. He introduces several new concepts into the literature, including "full-humanness," which consists of a person's full complement of desirable or positive human traits (for example, ability to abstract, to be able to love, to transcend the self); "human diminution," which is his new term for neurosis; and the "Jonah Syndrome," by which he refers to some person's blocking of his own growth because of his "evasion of his destiny" (or "running away from one's own best talents").

Internalized Behavioral Suppression and the Timing of Social Punishment

Justin Aronfreed

Arthur Reber

This paper reports an experiment which demonstrates that punishment of an act at its initiation is more effective than punishment at its completion in producing internalized suppression of the act. The experiment, which is carried out with 9- and 10-yr.-old children, is used to support a theoretical analysis of internalized suppression in terms of 2 sequential acquisition processes. The 1st process is the attachment of anxiety to the intrinsic cues provided by either the behavioral or cognitive stimulus correlates of an incipient transgression. The 2nd is the attachment of anxiety reduction to the intrinsic correlates of suppression. The experimental findings are also extended to suggest that a number of features of naturalistic socialization, other than timing of punishment, affect internalized suppression through their impact on: (a) the temporal locus and intensity of the anxiety that motivates suppression and (b) the reinforcement of the suppression itself. The verbal mediation of socializing agents is singled out as the most significant of these features.

Many forms of conduct tend to become internalized as they are acquired in the course of social learning. They can then be elicited, and maintained to some extent, in the absence of surveillance or reinforcement. Developmental conceptions of conscience (Bronfenbrenner, 1960; Miller & Swanson, 1960, Ch. 5; Sears, Maccoby, & Levin, 1957, Ch. 10) and theoretical approaches to the social psychology of conformity (Kelman, 1958; Thibaut & Kelley, 1959, Ch. 13) commonly appear to assume that this kind of intrinsic control over behavior requires the individual's adoption of the values or standards of others. It seems very doubtful, however, that either moral or other kinds of evaluative processes are indispensable to the stability of conduct in the absence of external monitors. Preverbal children and even animals are capable of suppressing previously punished behavior, for example, over significant periods of time during which punishment contingencies are no longer present. Recent studies of older children (Aronfreed, 1961, 1964) indicate that their internalized reactions to already committed transgressions also can be established and maintained with little evidence that they are applying evaluative standards to their own behavior. And common observation suggests that adults likewise have many durable patterns of social behavior which are remarkably independent of external outcomes and yet do not call upon their evaluative resources.

Much of the intrinsic control of behavior which human beings show is, of course, mediated by evaluative cognition. But the experimental socialization paradigms which will be described in this paper are designed to provide a relatively simple context for examining the motivational and reinforcement mechanisms through which internalized behavioral suppression is established. These mechanisms are presumed to be fundamentally constant, regardless of the complexity of the cognitive structures which may intervene between a stimulus situation and the individual's ultimate behavior. Accordingly, the paradigms minimize the place of cognitive structure in the internalization process and emphasize the role of intrinsic cues which are closely tied to behavior itself. Even under these conditions, there is a problem in specifying the operational criteria for internalization. The degree to which conduct is internalized may be indeterminate even though it is maintained without direct social observation. For example, its maintenance may be controlled by the individual's expectations of rewards or punishments which will be eventually contingent on his alternative actions. Whiting's (1959) cross-cultural observations illustrate that control over behavior in the absence of socializing agents remains dependent, in many societies, on perceived external surveillance and sanctions. The rationales

From *Journal of Personality and Social Psychology*, 1965, 1, 3–16.

This investigation was supported in part by Research Grant MH-06671 to the senior author from the National Institute of Mental Health, United States Public Health Service.

which children of different ages offer as justification for specific acts of conduct (Kohlberg, 1963; Piaget, 1948) also reveal how the evaluative processes which support internalization may vary in the extent of their reference to external outcomes.

A proper criterion of internalization might specify that an act is internalized to the extent that it can be maintained in the absence of external outcomes which have directly reinforcing consequences for the actor (and, one might wish to add, in the absence of the actor's anticipation of such outcomes). A more pragmatic extension of this criterion, to be used in the present study, is that conduct be considered internalized if it can be reliably elicited in the absence of socializing agents, after having been acquired under the control of either direct response outcomes which were mediated by the agents or the display of similar conduct by the agents. Whatever the precise meaning to be assigned to internalization, its demonstration clearly requires evidence that the maintenance of conduct has shown some movement from external to intrinsic control. We may conceive of the intrinsic control as being mediated by changes of affective state which have become partially contingent on the stimulus properties of behavior itself (response-produced cues) or on the cognitive representations of the behavior. In the case of internalized suppression, the relevant affective changes are the induction and attenuation of anxiety, which were originally controlled by the aversive social outcomes of particular forms of behavior. These aversive outcomes can be roughly assumed under the heading of social punishment, since they usually occur in a context where they are perceived as being transmitted by an agent who specifically intends to introduce them in response to one's actions. It is unlikely that any substantial repertoire of behavior becomes independent of external outcomes, in the course of naturalistic socialization, through interaction that is exclusively punitive. But the distinct contribution that response-contingent punishment makes to internalization can be examined in experimental situations where the effects of positive reinforcement have been reduced to a minimum.

The experiment to be reported here attempts to test a conception of internalized behavioral suppression that specifies a two-step acquisition process. It can be most conveniently illustrated in terms of the socialization of the child. The first acquisition mechanism is the attachment of anxiety to stimuli which are intrinsically produced. The most general common effect of all types of socially mediated punishment is their induction of an aversive affective state in the child. This state may have a number of qualitative variations (such as fear, guilt, or shame) which are dependent on the cognitive setting in which it is embedded. But its invariant motivational properties may be broadly designated as anxiety. Once the child has had some experience with a punished act, the role of punishment in eliciting anxiety can be easily displaced to social cues which have acquired secondary aversive value through their previous association with punishment. The incipient and even ongoing actions of children are frequently brought under the control of warning signals which are provided by their socializing agents.

Although the aversive social consequences of a child's behavior do not always reflect the violation of recognized norms of conduct, they do always imply some form of behavioral constraint between the child and the agent of punishment. It is therefore convenient to refer to any act as a transgression, when it is followed by social punishment of sufficient consistency and intensity to produce suppression of the act. If the punishment does have some minimally consistent relationship to the child's act, then a component of anxiety will necessarily become attached to the intrinsic stimulus correlates of the act. These intrinsic stimuli may be cues directly produced by the performance of the act itself. They also may be the cue properties of cognitive or verbal representations of the act—in the form, for example, of intentions or evaluative processes. Thus, certain kinds of actions, and their intrinsic representations, become capable of eliciting anxiety both during their performance and before they are even carried out, without the benefit of any external surveillance or objective threat of punishment.

The second mechanism in the internalization of behavioral suppression follows from the motivating properties of anxiety. Children quickly discover that they can avoid or attenuate social punishment and aversive warning stimuli by terminating an ongoing transgression or by arresting a transgression while it is still in an incipient stage. A variety of alternative nonpunished behaviors, including simple suppression of the transgression, consequently acquire instrumental value for them in reducing the anxiety elicited by aversive external events. At the same time, these suppressive behavioral modifications (and their representative cognitive processes) eliminate the intrinsic stimulus correlates of transgression and attenuate whatever anxiety may have been already independently attached to such correlates. Anxiety reduction will then gradually become attached directly to the intrinsic response-produced and cognitive correlates of suppression. And it will serve to reinforce the suppression, regardless of whether or not there are external consequences of the kind associated with surveillance and punishment. This entire two-step formulation is consistent with phenomena which are readily observable in naturalistic socialization, and also with the findings of extensive experimentation on the effects of punishment learning in animals (Estes, 1944; Mowrer, 1960a, Ch. 2; Solomon & Brush, 1956). It can also be extended to the learning of internalized reactions to transgressions which have already been committed (Aronfreed, 1963, 1964; Hill, 1960).[1]

Temporal Locus of Internalized Anxiety

Most of the acts which are defined by social punishment as transgressions are not punished indiscriminately without reference to the conditions of their occurrence. Ordinarily, an act has been punished in some situations, but not in others. The suppression of a transgression therefore cannot be viewed as being entirely mediated by intrinsic cues merely because it occurs in the absence of surveillance. The changes of affective state which motivate and reinforce suppression must rather be dependent on stimulus com-

[1] The anxiety induced by punishment may disrupt punished responses not only because it motivates alternative responses, but also because it serves in itself as a competing response.

plexes which consist of both intrinsic and external cues, even though the external cues may not include the presence of a socializing agent. In order to examine the function of intrinsic cues in the mediation of suppression, it is necessary to have an experimental method in which these cues are given a variable relationship to the course of anxiety, while the role of external situational cues remains constant. One such method is to observe the effects of variation in the timing of punishment with respect to the initiation and completion of a punished act. The rationale for this procedure is implicit in the common finding that punishment is less effective in suppressing the behavior of animals when it follows an act only after a relatively long temporal interval (Bixenstine, 1956; Kamin, 1959; Mowrer, 1960a, Ch. 2). The particular variant of the procedure used here was suggested by an informal report on work in progress with dogs by R. L. Solomon (see Mowrer, 1960b, pp. 399–404). Solomon's observations of 6-month-old puppies tentatively indicated that punishment upon approach to a forbidden food resulted in more prolonged suppression, during a test in which the experimenter was absent, than did punishment after a considerable portion of the food had been eaten. There was also some indication that puppies who did transgress during the test were more likely to show reactive signs of distress if they had been punished originally after having eaten part of the food.

Any act may be regarded as having a number of distinguishable components. In addition to intentions or other implicit precursors of the act, there are intrinsic cues which occur as the act is initiated. When the act is fully committed, there will be other intrinsic stimulus correlates which have some duration in time, and they may actually extend beyond the point of its completion. If we assume that internalized suppression requires some mediation of anxiety by the sequence of intrinsic cues associated with a punished act, then we would expect the temporal locus of the original social punishment to have a significant impact on the effective motivation for subsequent suppression when the child is no longer under surveillance. Punishment used at initiation of a transgression would attach maximal anxiety to the intrinsic cues which occur at that point. In contrast, punishment administered only when a transgression has been already committed would tend to produce greater intensity of internalized anxiety at the point where subsequent transgressions have also been completed.

The difference in the effects of these two temporal loci of punishment would be limited by generalization or spread of anxiety to elements of the act other than those immediately present at the point of punishment. But to the extent that responses alternative to transgression (including its suppression) are motivated by anxiety and reinforced by anxiety reduction, they should have a greater probability of being elicited by the incipient cues of transgression—before the transgression is actually carried out—if punishment originally occurred at its initiation. If punishment occurred only after the commission of a transgression, the anxiety generalized to the point of onset might not be intense enough to motivate subsequent suppression when the child has been removed from the external presence of the punitive agent. Moreover, if punishment were to occur consistently after a transgression was socially perceived as having been already committed, suppression would not acquire much anxiety-reducing value at the point where maximal internalized anxiety would eventually be concentrated. When a child has completed a transgression, suppression is ordinarily no longer instrumental to the avoidance or attenuation of punishment.

METHOD

Two experimental socialization paradigms were constructed to require children to choose, on each of nine training trials, between a punished class of responses and a nonpunished class of active alternative responses (rather than between punished responses and passive suppression). This technique insured that there would be some opportunity for punishment training among all of the children, since they could not reduce their anxiety about the entire situation by resorting to a generalized suppression of all active responses. Consequently, the suppression to become evident during training appeared not simply as absence of the punished response, but rather as the positive choice of a nonpunished alternative. The children were confronted with a relatively simple discrimination. They were asked to choose between two small toy replicas of real objects commonly found in their social environment, to pick up the chosen toy, and to describe its function if they were asked to do so. The pair of toys varied from trial to trial, but one was always quite attractive, while the other was relatively unattractive. Punishment was consistently administered for choice of the attractive toy, and the child was not permitted to describe its function. Choice of the unattractive toy was not punished, but was also not rewarded, except for the minimal social reinforcement inherent in being permitted to describe its function and in the experimenter's noncommittal recognition of the child's verbal statement (in the form of a casual "uh-huh").

The experimenter's role as a socializing agent was predominantly punitive and provided in itself no model for the behavioral changes which the child was to acquire. A very limited cognitive context for punishment was provided by telling the children that certain of the toys were supposed to be chosen only by older children. This restriction was imparted during instructions and was repeated each time that the child was punished. In one training condition, punishment was administered as soon as the child's hand approached the attractive toy, and before the child picked it up. In the other training condition, the child was permitted to pick up the attractive toy and hold it for a few seconds (but not to handle it), and then punishment was given and the toy was removed from the child's hand. A control condition without explicit punishment was also devised, primarily to control for any possible effects of the difference between the two punishment conditions in habituation to picking up the toys during punished choices.

Following the nine trials used under each of these conditions, the children were tested for internalized suppression of the punished behavior. The experimenter set out a tenth pair of toys, one of which was highly attractive, and then left the room on a pretext. When he returned, he was able to discern whether the attractive toy had been picked up or even moved. The experiment was not designed to assess the effects of timing of punishment upon internalized reactions to completed transgressions, because of the difficulty of eliciting overt evidence of such reactions without disclosing the hidden monitoring of the children's behavior during the test for internalization. However, an attempt was made to get a tentative index of responses which the children might have used to reduce their anxiety following transgressions in the test situation.

Subjects

The subjects used in the experiment were 88 boys from the fourth and fifth grades of two public schools in a large urban school system.[2] The subjects were divided as follows among the three conditions: Punishment at Initiation, 34; Punishment at Completion, 34; Control, 20.

Procedure

Each child was taken individually from his classroom to the experimental room by the experimenter, who was a male. The child was asked to sit at a small table, and the experimenter seated himself across from the child. A rectangular wooden presentation board, roughly 12 X 18 inches in size, lay centered on the table. At the experimenter's right was a second table, upon which lay a black compartmentalized box and the experimenter's recording materials. The box had 24 compartments, each of which held a pair of toy replicas. Only the first 10 pairs were actually used for the nine training trials and the test trial. The toys were all quite small, and varied in their outer dimensions from roughly .5 inch to 2.5 inches. The attractive member of each pair was always somewhat larger, had more detailed fidelity to its realistic prototype, and had a higher relevance to masculine interests (for example, a tiny electric motor, a camera with moving parts, etc.). The unattractive items were, in contrast, smaller, shabbily designed, and more generally associated with feminine interests (for example, a barrette, a thimble, etc.). The pairs of items were used in a fixed order under all conditions.

Punishment at Initiation. The experimenter's instructions were given as follows:

> I'm going to put some toys down here on this board. Each time I'll put down two toys. Here's what you do—pick up the one you want to tell about, hold it over the board [the experimenter indicated appropriate action with hand, using his fingers to show that the item was to be easily visible when held], look at it for a while, and just think about what you're going to say. Then, if I ask you, tell me what it's for or what you do with it. Do you understand?

Following the child's indication of understanding, the experimenter continued:

> Now some of the toys here are only supposed to be for older boys, so you're not supposed to pick them. When you pick something that's only for older boys, I'll tell you.

The experimenter then began the first trial by placing the initial pair of toys on the board and saying: "All right, now pick up the one you want to tell about, look at it for a while, and just think about what you're going to say." To indicate subsequent trials, the experimenter said: "All right, pick up the one you want to tell about," or simply "All right." The position of the attractive toy was consistently alternated over the nine training trials, so that it appeared at the child's left on odd-numbered trials and at his right on even-numbered trials (thus providing another cue, in addition to attractiveness, to simplify the discrimination).

After the experimenter initiated each trial by placing a pair of toys, he dropped his hands lightly to an apparently casual resting position just behind the toys. When the child reached for the unattractive toy, he was permitted to pick it up and hold it over the board, in accordance with the instructions. After 2 or 3 seconds, the experimenter said: "All right, tell me about it." Following the subject's description of the toy's function (usually rather brief), the experimenter simply said "uh-huh" (quite flatly) and removed both toys from the board after the child had put down the toy he had chosen. When the child reached for the attractive toy, the experimenter said: "No—that's for the older boys" (firmly, though not very sharply), and raised the fingers of his hand behind the toy as though to slightly cover it. The experimenter's verbal disapproval was always given before the child actually touched the toy, but when the child's hand was rather close to it. The disapproval was almost always immediately effective in causing the child to withdraw his hand without even touching the toy. The experimenter then first removed the attractive toy, leaving the unattractive one for a few seconds, in the event that the child would want to pick it up and thus correct its original transgression. But very few children ever used the opportunity to pick up an unattractive toy, once they had already been punished for their choice of the attractive one.

Punishment at Completion. The instructions and general procedure for the training condition, and the experimenter's behavior when the child chose an unattractive toy, were identical to those described above for the Punishment at Initiation condition. The only difference was in the timing of punishment when the child chose an attractive toy. Here, the child was permitted to pick up the attractive toy and hold it over the board, just as in the case of an unattractive toy. Then, after 2 or 3 seconds, the experimenter said: "No—that's for the older boys," and gently but firmly removed the toy from the child's hand (the position in which the children had been instructed to hold the toys was such that the toy was never actually handled and was readily removable). As in the first condition, the unattractive toy was removed from the board a few seconds later, so as to give the child an opportunity to correct himself.

Control. The Control condition was constructed to observe the effects of lack of opportunity to pick up the attractive toys, during training in which there was no response-contingent punishment. Instructions and procedure were similar to those used for the punishment conditions, but had to be slightly modified to define a situation in which the child would never actually pick up the toys, without the necessity of using explicit punishment. A statement was also added to specifically indicate which of the toys were intended only for older boys, since the general prohibition on choosing such toys, imparted in the instructions, was concretized in the other training conditions by the information conveyed on punishment trials.

The experimenter's modified instructions were as follows:

> I'm going to put some toys down here on this board. Each time I'll put down two toys. Here's what you do—you just point to the one you want to tell about [the experimenter demonstrated with his hand], look at it for a while, and just think about what you're going to say. Then, if I ask you, tell me what it's for or what you do with it. Do you understand?

Following the child's indication of understanding, the experimenter continued:

> Now some of the toys here are only supposed to be for

[2] The experiment was made possible through the cooperation of a number of administrators and teachers in the Philadelphia public school system.

older boys, so you're not supposed to pick them up. The nicer-looking, more interesting toys are for the older boys.

The experimenter then initiated the training trials. On each trial, the child was asked to indicate his choice by pointing. When the child pointed to an unattractive toy, the experimenter said: "All right, tell me about it." After the child had finished describing the toy's function, the experimenter said "uh-huh" and removed both toys. When the child pointed to the attractive toy, the experimenter simply removed both toys without saying anything (a procedure which, while it was not explicitly punitive, may well have been frustrating or otherwise aversive to the child).

Test situation. The two objects used on the tenth (test) trial were related to one another in the same way as were the members of previous pairs used during training. But they were somewhat less toylike. There was visible action within the attractive object, whereas the other object was not only unattractive but also relatively difficult to identify. Consequently, some generalization had to be exercised by the child in carrying his response tendencies to the test situation. The attractive object was a two-chambered glass timer in which an enclosed quantity of salt ran down from the upper to the lower chamber in a period of 1 minute (previous pilot work had suggested that the tendency to turn the timer, or at least to handle it, was difficult to resist). The unattractive object was a dingy, yellow, 2-inch square of terry cloth, folded into an approximation of a piece of toweling. As the tenth trial began, the experimenter was about to place these objects, but then turned hesitatingly to his folder of papers, in which he had been recording the child's choices, and said (in a halting and distracted fashion, while looking into the folder):

> It looks like I forgot some of the papers I need . . . I must have left them in my car . . . I'll have to go outside on the street and get them.

The experimenter then placed the pair of toys. The presentation board was unfinished and had on its surface a number of scratches. One of these was actually a faint marker inserted for the test situation, a straight line about .5 inch in length. A barely visible scratch line had also been made on each of the timer's two hexagonal rubber bases, running from their edges along their upper surfaces. The experimenter placed the timer so that the scratch line on one of its bases was exactly orthogonal to the faint line on the board. As the experimenter placed the item, he also rose and said:

> I'll be gone for about 5 or 10 minutes . . . while I'm gone, you can be deciding which one of these toys you want to tell about.

The experimenter then took his folder and left the room, closing the door firmly behind him. The experimenter remained out of the room for 5 minutes, and then reentered, first rattling the doorknob, so as to give the child time to replace either of the toys which he might have picked up. While the experimenter was walking over to the table where the child was sitting, he asked: "While I was gone, were you thinking about the toys?" Then the experimenter continued, after sitting down and opening his folder to his recording sheet: "Well, I don't want you to choose yet, but tell me what you were thinking while I was gone." Following the child's response to this inquiry, the experimenter asked: "While I was gone, did you decide on which one you want to tell about?" The child's responses to each of these questions were recorded verbatim. The experimenter also noted whether the timer had been moved during his absence.

After the inquiry described above was completed, the experimenter closed the procedure on the pretext that the remaining toys in the box could not be used because he could not find his misplaced papers. A further statement was added to put the child at ease about his performance and to invoke his cooperation in not discussing his experience with other children.

RESULTS

The primary observations were of whether or not the children picked up or handled the attractive minute-glass in the experimenter's absence, an index of the internalized effectiveness of the suppression acquired during training. Table 1 shows, for each of the training conditions, the numbers of children who did and did not transgress. Chi-square values for the 2 X 2 contingency tables which compare each two of the three training conditions, with respect to frequencies of transgression and nontransgression during the test, are as follows: Punishment at Initiation versus Punishment at Completion: $\chi^2 = 11.54, p < .001$; Punishment at Initiation versus Control: $\chi^2 = 12.44$, $p < .001$; Punishment at Completion versus Control: $\chi^2 = .19$, *ns.*[3]

These differences in the effectiveness of internalized suppression, during the test situation, were complemented by the behavior of the children during training. Despite the mild prohibition conveyed in the instructions, the children in the Control condition persistently pointed to the attractive toys, even though this behavior resulted in no opportunity to describe the function of the toys. The great majority of these children chose the attractive toy on six to eight of the nine trials. More than a few chose it on all nine trials. The discriminability of the toys within each pair, and the consistent difference in their attractiveness, was also apparent in the responses of children in the punishment training conditions, but in a very different way that clearly showed the effects of the punishment. Under punishment training, the typical sequence of behavior was to choose the attractive toy on the first one, two, or three trials, and then to fairly consistently choose the unattractive toy thereafter. A single punishment was sufficient, for 21 of the children, to inhibit further choices of the attractive toys. Occasionally, a child would revert once, near the middle of the series of trials, to choosing an attractive toy, but would then return immediately to choosing the unattractive ones.

Table 1. *Frequency of Test Transgression and Nontransgression following Each of Three Training Paradigms.*

	Training paradigms		
Behavior during test situation	Punishment at initiation (N = 34)	Punishment at completion (N = 34)	Control (N = 20)
Transgression	9	24	16
Nontransgression	25	10	4

[3] All values shown here are for one-tailed tests and incorporate a correction for continuity.

Table 2. *Frequency of Transgression and Punishment during Training among Test Transgressors and Nontransgressors Trained under Each of Two Variations in Timing of Punishment.*

	Frequency of punishment during training							
Experimental group	0	1	2	3	4	5	6	7
Punishment at Initiation								
Transgressors	1	3	2	2		1		
Nontransgressors	1	11	7	5		1		
Both test groups	2	14	9	7		2		
Punishment at Completion								
Transgressors	1	5	10	4	1	2		1
Nontransgressors		2	3	3		1	1	
Both test groups	1	7	13	7	1	3	1	1

It is particularly interesting to note that children punished at initiation of transgression exposed themselves to punishment *less* frequently than did those punished at completion. Table 2 shows the distribution of frequencies of punishment in the two punishment training paradigms, separately for those children who transgressed and those who did not transgress in the test situation. The two total training groups are significantly different from one another ($\chi^2 = 3.16$, $p < .05$), if we compare the number of children who received less than two punishments with those who received two or more punishments.[4] Clearly, it is not the number of punishments during training that makes punishment at initiation more effective as a paradigm for inducing internalized suppression. A comparison of all transgressors with all nontransgressors also indicates that behavior in the test situation is not attributable to frequency of punishment during training.

For reasons already set forth, it might be expected that children trained under punishment at completion would experience more anxiety *following* a transgression in the test situation than would children trained under punishment at initiation. Since the anxiety was not likely to be so intense as to overflow into an overt display of affect, the only evidence of its presence would be in certain responses which might be instrumental to its reduction. In the present experiment, it was important that the experimenter's knowledge of the child's transgression not be revealed, and consequently it was not possible to employ techniques which would directly elicit observable responses such as confession and reparation. It appeared, however, that some of the children might be using a quasi-confessional response, predispositionally available from past experience, to reduce their anxiety following a transgression in the experimenter's absence. When the experimenter returned to the room, there were virtually no spontaneous responses from the children which could be easily classified as internalized reactions to transgression. But there were some interesting variations of response to the inquiry about their thoughts during the test situation. Children who had been in the Control condition almost invariably indicated that they had been "thinking" about the attractive test object, a verbal response that agreed with their behavior during the test. In contrast, a substantial majority of the children exposed to the two punishment conditions reported that they had thought about the unattractive object (a few indicated that they had not thought about either one). However, roughly one third of the punished children did admit thinking about the attractive object. Closer inspection of the data, shown in Table 3, revealed that these latter children were predominantly those trained under punishment at completion, and that they were almost entirely transgressors. In view of the overall contrast between the Control and punishment groups, it seemed that their response to the inquiry might be regarded as a reaction of "admission."[5]

Table 3. *Frequency of Admission and Nonadmission Reactions following Test Situation among Transgressors and Nontransgressors Trained under Each of Two Variations in Timing of Punishment.*

	Reaction following test situation	
Experimental group	Admission	Nonadmission
Punishment at Initiation		
Transgressors	4	5
Nontransgressors	1	24
Both test groups	5	29
Punishment at Completion		
Transgressors	16	8
Nontransgressors	2	8
Both test groups	18	16

[4] The value shown is for a one-tailed test and incorporates a correction for continuity. The comparison given results in the least disproportionate division possible along the frequency scale. Separate analogous comparisons of the two punishment conditions, within the transgressor and nontransgressor groups, would not be meaningful because of the extremely small samples which would appear in some cells of the relevant frequency tables.

The effects of differential timing of punishment are also visible in the occurrence of reversals. Seventeen of the children punished at completion reverted momentarily to choosing an attractive toy after suppression had begun to be established during training, but this behavior was shown by only nine of the children punished at initiation.

[5] The term guilt is unwarranted in reference to the effects of this kind of experimental situation, if one regards guilt as a phenomenon of rather specific cognitive properties interwoven with an affective base of anxiety (Aronfreed, 1964). The situation does not provide the kind of evaluative processes through which the perception of transgression can properly be said to arouse a moral affect (for example, cognitive focus on intentions or on the consequences of action for others).

Comparison of the total numbers of transgressors and nontransgressors who showed admission and nonadmission reactions shows a highly significant difference ($\chi^2 = 18.29$, $p < .001$). The same difference appears when the comparison is made only among children trained under punishment at completion ($\chi^2 = 4.44$, $p < .05$; $p < .02$ for the Fisher exact test). And a similar tendency is apparent among children punished at initiation (though it does not attain statistical significance in the latter case). If the admission of having thought about the attractive test object did serve to reduce the anxiety that followed transgression, then we would expect to find it more commonly among transgressors trained under punishment at completion than among transgressors trained under punishment at initiation. Inspection of Table 3 does reveal a tendency in this direction, but it does not attain statistical significance, in part because of the restricted number of children who transgress following punishment at initiation.[6]

DISCUSSION

The difference between the effects of the Punishment at Initiation and the Punishment at Completion paradigms indicates that timing of punishment is a very significant determinant of internalized behavioral suppression, at least when the punishment is accompanied by only minimal cognitive structure. This finding strongly supports the view that the suppression is some positive function of the intensity of the anxiety which is mobilized at the onset of a transgression, and that the anxiety is in turn a function of the original temporal relationship between this locus and the occurrence of punishment. It also supports the broader conception of the internalization of social control through punishment as resting first on the attachment of anxiety to intrinsic cues associated with transgression, and secondly on the attachment of anxiety reduction to intrinsic cues associated with alternative nonpunished behavior.

The great majority of the children who were exposed to the Control paradigm picked up the attractive toy during the test, even though they were never permitted to pick up any toys during training. This last observation clearly indicates that transgressions had to be specifically punished in order to induce internalized suppression, and that the differential effects of the two punishment paradigms cannot be attributed to lack of opportunity to pick up attractive toys during training with punishment at initiation. Effects which are similar to those of the Control paradigm are commonly observed in naturalistic socialization. In the absence of external surveillance, previous mild injunctions and prophylactic restrictions of opportunity to transgress are often insufficient, without the addition of punishment, to suppress behavior which may have other highly reinforcing consequences for the child.

It will be observed that the experimentally induced suppression, during the test for internalization, cannot be attributed simply to "generalized" anxiety that might have become attached to the external cues which remain when the socializing agent has left the situation. Nor is it reasonable to suppose that the suppression is mediated by variable expectations about the risk of punishment. The difference in the effects of the two variations in the timing of punishment was apparent not only during the test, but also while the socializing agent was still present during training. And during both training and test, external cues and conditions of risk were identical for children who were exposed to either of the two punishment paradigms. It is likewise implausible to attribute the experimental findings to differences between the two paradigms in whatever positive reinforcement may have been associated with the act of choosing (but never being able to tell about) an attractive toy. The children who were trained under punishment at completion were permitted to pick up attractive toys, but they were required to do so in such a way that they could not handle them. They were also subjected to an additional period of uncertainty while they awaited the experimenter's punitive response (particularly during the early training trials), and to the possibly enhanced frustration entailed in having the toys removed from their hands. Moreover, it should be noted that children trained under the Control paradigm transgressed even more freely during the test than did children trained under punishment at completion, even though they were prevented from picking up any toys during training.

There may well have been some cognitive mediation of the experimental effects, despite the attempt to minimize cognitive structure. If the two variations in timing of punishment induced different temporal patterns of arousal and reduction of anxiety, these patterns might have become intrinsically mediated by intentions or other cognitive representations of the sequential elements in the acts of choice. Such cognitive interventions would tend to restrict the mediational role of cues which were directly produced by the punished and nonpunished acts. But they would not require any change in the more general view that behavioral suppression becomes internalized when the course of anxiety begins to be monitored by intrinsic stimuli. If one were to assume that the primary difference between the two experimental groups, at the point of decision between transgression and non-transgression, was cognitive rather than motivational—for example, that the perceived determinant of punishment was reaching for the attractive toy in one group, but was picking it up in the other group—it would be difficult to account for the observed effects. Such an assumption would make no reference to the variable intensity of anxiety which might precede or accompany a punished act. It would lead us to expect that children in the Punishment at Completion group would be more likely than those in the Punishment at Initiation group to *reach for* the attractive test toy. It would also lead, however, to the prediction that the Punishment at Completion group would not go so far as to *pick up* the attractive toy. But the observations during both training and the test for internalization indicate that children in this group do pick up the attractive test toys more frequently than do children trained under punishment at initiation.[7]

[6] The values shown are for one-tailed tests and incorporate a correction for continuity.

[7] The assumption that the experimental groups differ in their cognition of the determinants of punishment is perhaps not very credible in any case. The common general instructions to the children clearly convey the idea that "picking" a toy (i.e., the act of choice) is the relevant determinant.

The acquisition and maintenance of internalized suppression are not determined only by the intensity of the anxiety that becomes attached to the intrinsic cues associated with an incipient transgression. They are also affected by the reinforcement of behavioral alternatives to the punished act (including suppression). When the timing of social punishment is predictable to a child, as it is in the experimental paradigms, it may result in a delay-of-reinforcement effect upon suppression. The direction of this reinforcement effect would be parallel to the direction of the motivational effect that timing of punishment exercises upon suppression through its impact on the intrinsic temporal locus of anxiety. When children are confronted with choices between punished and nonpunished acts, they will experience some anxiety in connection with any choice, particularly early in the learning process before discriminant cues are firmly established. And the temporal relationship between nonpunished behavior and the reinforcement inherent in anxiety reduction will tend to be a direct function of the timing with which punishment predictably occurs for transgressions. In the Punishment at Initiation paradigm, for example, the external cues which signal that the child will not be punished begin to become apparent to him as soon as his hand reaches an unattractive toy without a punitive interruption. The anxiety reduction that reinforces the suppression of attractive choices thus soon becomes virtually immediate. In the Punishment at Completion condition, however, the anxiety reduction that follows nonpunished behavior is considerably more delayed, since the external safety signals do not occur until the child has been asked to tell about the toy. A possible implication of this analysis for naturalistic socialization is that children who are closely supervised by their parents may tend to experience more immediate reinforcement for their suppression of transgressions. It is also interesting to note that children may be forced to rely too heavily on the external outcomes of their behavior, if anxiety reduction cannot easily become discriminately attached to the intrinsic correlates of nonpunished behavior. This difficulty might arise if they were faced with complex discriminations in which they could not distinguish between punished and nonpunished responses, or if the anxiety induced by punishment were so intense as to disrupt the discrimination of relevant cues.

Some Further Theoretical Implications

The Punishment at Completion paradigm seems to be hardly more effective than the Control paradigm in producing internalized suppression. This finding suggests that the anxiety mobilized by an incipient transgression during the test situation was not sufficient to motivate suppression, when its intensity was attenuated across a gradient of generalization from the total complex of cues which were originally present at punishment of a completed transgression during training. The relative lack of effectiveness of the Punishment at Completion paradigm presents an instructive contrast to the observations made in a similar experiment conducted by Walters and Demkow (1963). These investigators used reaching for attractive toys versus touching the toys as their two temporal positions of punishment, and found that these training conditions produced only a tenuous difference in the subsequent effectiveness of the child's behavioral suppression in the experimenter's absence. The limitation on the effect which they observed was very probably due to the fact that their variation in timing cut a rather fine difference into the topography of the punished act and into the generalization gradients of the anxiety induced at the two points of punishment. A comparison of their findings with the findings of the present study indicates that the anxiety induced by the social punishment of an act does generalize from the intrinsic stimuli which are immediately present at the point of punishment to closely surrounding stimulus components of the punished act.

It may appear to be somewhat surprising that so many transgressions occur in the test situation following the Punishment at Completion paradigm, since naturalistic socialization commonly produces effective internalized suppression, even though it is very dependent on the punishment of already committed transgressions. Although the punishment of parents and socializing agents may be extremely variable in its timing, the ecology of socialization does not present too many opportunities to introduce punishment when a child is only on the threshold of transgressions. Part of this apparent discrepancy between naturalistic and experimental socialization may be an artifact of the use of a gross index of suppression in the test situation—the occurrence or nonoccurrence of transgression in a limited time period. A more sensitive index, such as elapsed time before the occurrence of transgression, might have revealed differences in the strength of the internalized suppression induced by the two punishment training conditions, without implying that the small variation in timing was so powerful as to determine whether a transgression could be elicited at all. The use of an elapsed time measure might have disclosed, for example, that transgressions following the Punishment at Completion paradigm occurred later in the test period than transgressions following the Control paradigm. Conversely, a longer test period might have raised the attractiveness of the forbidden toy, or might have resulted in extinction of some of the anxiety attached to intrinsic cues of incipient transgression, so that transgression would have been more common following training under punishment at initiation.

Variation of the precise timing of punishment, within the microstructure of a punished act, may be a convenient method for teasing out the specific mechanisms through which behavioral suppression becomes acquired and internalized. But naturalistic socialization has a number of other features which would tend to dilute the significance of timing, and to facilitate internalization even when punishments typically follow transgressions at temporal intervals well beyond these used in the experimental paradigms. The anxiety aroused by the punishment of agents to whom the child has strong positive attachments (particularly the parents) may be substantially greater than the anxiety aroused by an experimenter's verbal disapproval. And even if punishment follows a committed transgression, a greater intensity of anxiety at its point of application will be more likely to insure enough generalization to motivate suppression at the point of subsequent incipient transgressions. The punishment and warning signals emitted by parents are also often patterned in accordance with the continuous or intermittent character of many of a child's transgressions. Parents sometimes punish in the midst of a committed but sustained transgression, or after a discrete repeatable act that the child has completed but is about to initiate again. Under these conditions, substantial anxiety can become directly attached to the intrinsic cues associated with an incipient transgression, even though punishment is originally contingent on visible commission of the transgression. Moreover, the child may be given the opportunity to avoid or escape punishment by introducing its own behavioral control in the course of an ongoing transgression—a corrective option that is not available in the experimental paradigms—with the result that suppression may acquire instrumental, anxiety-reducing value even when it does not initially prevent the occurrence of transgression.

In the social interaction between parents and children, the reinforcement of behavioral suppression is not entirely defined, of course, by the presence or absence of aversive outcomes. Parents often react with affection, praise, or other forms of positive reinforcement, when they are aware of evidence of suppression in their children's behavior. A significant component of the intrinsic reinforcement that supports internalized suppression may consequently be derived from positive affect which was originally induced by social rewards, rather than from the reduction of the anxiety which is elicited by incipient transgression. It is for this reason that situational assessments of children's already acquired dispositions to suppress socially prohibited behavior are ambiguous with respect to the motivational antecedents and reinforcing consequences of the suppression. Such dispositions will be the resultants of a complex history of interaction of the effects of direct punishments and rewards (and also, perhaps, of the effects of modeling). Two well-designed surveys (Burton, Maccoby, & Allinsmith, 1961; Grinder, 1962) have, in fact, uncovered only tenuous and inconsistent relationships between children's internalized suppression of social transgressions and the discrete practices of punishment or reward which are used by their parents.

Probably the feature of naturalistic socialization that most effectively insures internalized suppression, regardless of the temporal locus of punishment, is the extensive verbal mediation used by parents. A verbal medium of punishment makes it possible for the child's anxiety to become monitored by intentions, conceptual labels, and other cognitive processes. Such cognitive processes may act as common mediators of anxiety. They can become attached to any of the concrete patterns of proprioceptive and external cues which emerge sequentially in the performance and aftereffects of a transgression. And they can consequently bridge the microstructure and temporal separation of these concrete cues, so that the cues retain only a negligible function in governing the course of anxiety. The intensity of the anxiety that is elicited at the point of an incipient transgression would thus become independent of the original temporal relationship between the cues which are immediately present at that point and the occurrence of punishment. When a child is enabled to represent its intentions to itself, for example, in close conjunction with punishment that occurs long after a transgression has taken place, then its intentions may elicit sufficient anxiety to motivate suppression when they subsequently intercede before a transgression is carried out.

A number of surveys (Bandura & Walters, 1959; Maccoby, 1961; Sears, 1961; Sears et al., 1957, Ch. 7) have reported some evidence that children's internalized control over socially prohibited actions is positively associated with the closeness of supervision exercised by their parents. As was pointed out earlier, it is unlikely that close supervision affects suppression merely through the opportunity that it affords to punish the child's incipient transgressions. The association is more probably generated by the tendency of parents who closely control their children's behavior to also use verbal mediation and to be more attentive to the intrinsic cognitive and motivational precursors of transgression. Support for this observation can be found in the correlates of the different disciplinary methods to which parents in our society are disposed (Aronfreed, 1961; Bronfenbrenner, 1958; Davis & Havighurst, 1946; Kohn, 1959; Maccoby & Gibbs, 1954). Middle-class parents tend to be more oriented toward their children's intentions. They are likely to use reasoning and explanation to induce an internal governor in their children, and not merely to sensitize them to the punitive external consequences of transgression. They also often actively induce their children to initiate their own self-corrective processes. Working-class parents are more prone to react to the concretely visible consequences of their children's transgressions, and to sensitize their children to the threat of punishment. Their methods of punishment are more direct and occur in a less verbal medium. And they are less oriented toward reinforcing signs of internally mediated control in their children. Middle-class children do show more of a corresponding orientation toward internal monitors in the control of behavior, while working-class children show more of an external orientation (Aronfreed, 1961; Boehm, 1962; Kohlberg, 1963). Some surveys (Allinsmith, 1960; Bandura & Walters, 1959; MacKinnon, 1938; Sears et al., 1957, Ch. 7) have found direct relationships between the internal versus external orientation of parental discipline and parallel differences of orientation in children's suppression of socially prohibited behavior.

Children do acquire highly general and integrative evaluative systems for some areas of social behavior. Such value systems may affect internalized control over behavior in ways which are not apparent from the effects of direct response outcomes in a simple discrimination situation. It is possible, for example, that more massive and cognitive forms of internalization can occur through acquisition processes of the kind implied in theories of identification. Certainly, stable behavioral changes can be induced in children through their tendency to reproduce the behavior of models (Bandura & Walters, 1963) without the initial support of direct external reinforcement. But the experimental findings reported in this paper show that internalized suppression can be acquired through a form of aversive learning that is highly sensitive to the timing of punishment, a parameter of social learning that is not readily translatable into the child's disposition to adopt the role of a model. A general conception of mechanisms of internalization must take into account, then, that some forms of internalized control over behavior can be established through the direct reinforcement and punishment of the child's overtly emitted responses.

REFERENCES

Allinsmith, W. The learning of moral standards. In D. R. Miller & G. E. Swanson (Eds.), *Inner conflict and defense.* New York: Holt, 1960. Pp. 141–176.

Aronfreed, J. The nature, variety, and social patterning of moral responses to transgression. *Journal of Abnormal and Social Psychology,* 1961, **63,** 223–240.

Aronfreed, J. The effects of experimental socialization paradigms upon two moral responses to transgression. *Journal of Abnormal and Social Psychology,* 1963, **66,** 437–448.

Aronfreed, J. The origin of self-criticism. *Psychological Review,* 1964, **71,** 193–218.

Bandura, A., & Walters, R. H. *Adolescent aggression.* New York: Ronald Press, 1959.

Bandura, A., & Walters, R. H. *Social learning and personality development.* New York: Holt, Rinehart, & Winston, 1963.

Bixenstine, V. E. Secondary drive as a neutralizer of time in integrative problem-solving. *Journal of Comparative and Physiological Psychology,* 1956, **49,** 161–166.

Boehm, Lenore. The development of conscience: A comparison of American children of different mental and socioeconomic levels. *Child Development,* 1962, **33,** 575–590.

Bronfenbrenner, U. Socialization and social class through time and space. In Eleanor E. Maccoby, T. M. Newcomb, & E. L. Hartley (Eds.), *Readings in social psychology.* (3rd ed.) New York: Holt, 1958. Pp. 400–425.

Bronfenbrenner, U. Freudian theories of identification and their derivatives. *Child Development,* 1960, **31,** 15–40.

Burton, R. V., Maccoby, Eleanor E., & Allinsmith, W. Antecedents of resistance to temptation in four-year-old children. *Child Development,* 1961, **32,** 689–710.

Davis, A., & Havighurst, R. J. Social class and color differences in child-rearing. *American Sociological Review,* 1946, **11,** 698–710.

Estes, W. K. An experimental study of punishment. *Psychological Monographs,* 1944, **57**(3, Whole No. 263).

Grinder, R. E. Parental childrearing practices, conscience, and resistance to temptation of sixth-grade children. *Child Development,* 1962, **33,** 803–820.

Hill, W. F. Learning theory and the acquisition of values. *Psychological Review,* 1960, **67,** 317–331.

Kamin, L. J. The delay-of-punishment gradient. *Journal of Comparative and Physiological Psychology,* 1959, **52,** 434–437.

Kelman, H. C. Compliance, identification, and internalization: Three processes of attitude change. *Journal of Conflict Resolution,* 1958, **2,** 51–60.

Kohlberg, L. Moral development and identification. In H. W. Stevenson (Ed.), *Yearbook of the National Society for the Study of Education.* Part I. *Child psychology.* Chicago: Univer. Chicago Press, 1963. Pp. 277–332.

Kohn, M. L. Social class and the exercise of parental authority. *American Sociological Review,* 1959, **24,** 352–366.

Maccoby, Eleanor E. The taking of adult roles in middle childhood. *Journal of Abnormal and Social Psychology,* 1961, **63,** 493–503.

Maccoby, Eleanor E., & Gibbs, Patricia K. Methods of child-rearing in two social classes. In W. E. Martin & Celia B. Stendler (Eds.), *Readings in child development.* New York: Harcourt, Brace, 1954. Pp. 380–396.

MacKinnon, D. W. Violation of prohibitions. In H. A. Murray (Eds.), *Explorations in personality: A clinical and experimental study of fifty men of college age.* New York: Oxford Univer. Press, 1938. Pp. 491–501.

Miller, D. R., & Swanson, G. E. (Eds.) *Inner conflict and defense.* New York: Holt, 1960.

Mowrer, O. H. *Learning theory and behavior.* New York: Wiley, 1960. (a)

Mowrer, O. H. *Learning theory and the symbolic processes.* New York: Wiley, 1960. (b)

Piaget, J. *The moral judgment of the child.* Glencoe, Ill.: Free Press, 1948.

Sears, R. R. Relation of early socialization experiences to aggression in middle childhood. *Journal of Abnormal and Social Psychology,* 1961, **63,** 466–492.

Sears, R. R., Maccoby, Eleanor E., & Levin, H. *Patterns of child rearing.* Evanston, Ill.: Row, Peterson, 1957.

Solomon, R. L., & Brush, Elinor S. Experimentally derived conceptions of anxiety and aversion. In M. R. Jones (Ed.), *Nebraska symposium on motivation: 1956.* Lincoln: Univer. Nebraska Press, 1956. Pp. 212–305.

Thibaut, J. W., & Kelley, H. H. *The social psychology of groups.* New York: Wiley, 1959.

Walters, R. H., & Demkow, Lillian. Timing of punishment as a determinant of response inhibition. *Child Development,* 1963, **34,** 207–214.

Whiting, J. W. M. Sorcery, sin, and the superego: Some cross-cultural mechanisms of social control. In M. R. Jones (Ed.), *Nebraska symposium on motivation: 1959.* Lincoln: Univer. Nebraska Press, 1959. Pp. 174–195.

Birth Order and Participation in Dangerous Sports *

Richard E. Nisbett

It was found that firstborns are less likely than later borns to participate in dangerous sports. The finding is consistent with evidence showing firstborns to be more frightened by the prospect of physical injury than later borns.

Several findings reported by Schachter (1959) in *The Psychology of Affiliation* indicate that firstborns find physical pain more aversive or the prospect of it more frightening than do later-born individuals. When told that they were to receive severe electric shock, firstborn females reported more fear than did later-born females. In an experiment on toleration of electric shock, firstborn females asked the experimenter to terminate the shock earlier in the series than did later-born females. And an analysis of data obtained by Torrance (1954) indicated that in a situation involving considerable physical danger—piloting a fighter plane in combat—firstborns were less effective than later borns.

If it is true that firstborns find pain or the prospect of it more aversive than do later borns, one would expect them to avoid activities where the risk of physical injury is high. This paper examines the proportion of first- and later-born individuals who participate in one such activity—dangerous sports.

METHOD

Birth-order information was obtained from four samples: (*a*) A complete record of the intercollegiate athletic participation of the 2,432 undergraduates enrolled at Columbia in 1963 was obtained from the college files. Data on athletics or birth order were missing for fewer than 1% of the population; (*b*) reports of interscholastic participation in high school sports and birth-order information were obtained by questionnaire from 110 Pennsylvania State University freshmen enrolled in introductory psychology in 1964[1]; (*c*) similar reports were obtained from 384 Yale University students enrolled in introductory psychology in 1967; (*d*) birth-order reports were obtained by mailed questionnaire in 1964 from a professional football team—the New York Giants—and a professional baseball team—the New York Mets. Response to the mailed questionnaire was a little less than 50% in each club.

From Journal of *Personality and Social Psychology*, 1968, 8, 351–358.

*This article is based on a paper presented at the Eastern Psychological Association meeting, Boston, April 1967. The author is indebted to Stanley Schachter for advice and help in all phases of this study.

[1] Jerome E. Singer kindly provided this data.

RESULTS

The proportion of Columbia students who participated in a dangerous intercollegiate sport at some point in their college career is presented in Table 1 as a function of birth order and family size. Dangerous sports were defined as those which a sample of 35 students rated as the three most dangerous played at Columbia. These were football, soccer, and rugby.

Two striking effects in Table 1 should be observed in passing: (*a*) Firstborns are markedly overrepresented in the sample. At every family size, the number of firstborns is greater than the number of children at every other position. This is consistent with Schachter's (1963) finding that firstborns are more likely to attend college; (*b*) the probability that an individual will play a dangerous sport increases with family size. This fact is consistent with Schachter's (1959) finding that large-family children were less frightened by the prospect of electric shock than small-family children, but since the family-size effect was observed only in the Columbia and Yale samples, it may be due to an idiosyncrasy of the Ivy League population.

Table 1 clearly shows the predicted birth order effect. At all but the very largest family sizes, firstborns are less likely to play a dangerous sport than later borns.[2] Students from large families are more likely to play a dangerous sport than those from small families, and, on the average, later borns are members of larger families than are firstborns. Thus, to examine the birth order effect it is necessary to control for family size. Of a variety of ways to do this, one of the more conservative is simply to compare players and nonplayers on the ratio of first- to *second* borns from families with two or more children. This throws away much of the data, but completely circumvents the confounding effects of family size. The resulting χ^2 is 6.15, which for $df = 1$ is significant at the .02 level. The data on which this test is based are presented in Table 2.

Also presented in Table 2 are the comparable proportions for players and nonplayers for the Pennsylvania State and the Yale samples, and the proportions for the professional football and baseball teams. These differences are of the same magnitude and direction as that for the larger sample of Columbia students.

It may have occurred to the reader that football, rugby,

[2] The reversal for families of six or more children is not significant.

Table 1. *Proportion of Columbia Undergraduates Who Play Dangerous Sports as a Function of Birth Order and Number of Children in Family.*

	Family size						
Birth order	1	2	3	4	5	6 or more	Total
First	.088	.072	.096	.129	.206	.438	.091
N	(443)	(639)	(272)	(93)	(34)	(16)	(1497)
Second		.106	.130	.280	.400	.167	.130
N		(473)	(177)	(50)	(15)	(6)	(721)
Third			.121	.278	.111	.000	.150
N			(99)	(29)	(9)	(3)	(140)
Fourth				.250	.375	.000	.250
N				(20)	(8)	(4)	(32)
Fifth					.182	1.00	.308
N					(11)	(2)	(13)
Sixth						.143	.143
N						(7)	(7)
Total proportion	.088	.086	.111	.203	.247	.143	.110
N	(443)	(1112)	(548)	(192)	(77)	(38)	(2410)

Table 2. *Ratio of Firstborns to Second Borns as a Function of Athletic Participation.*

	Columbia		Pennsylvania State		Yale		Professional teams	
	Students who play dangerous sports (college)	Students who do not play dangerous sports	Students who play dangerous sports (in high school)	Students who do not play dangerous sports	Students who play dangerous sports (in high school)	Students who do not play dangerous sports	Football	Baseball
Ratio of first borns to second borns	.510	.603	.560	.660	.508	.581	.600	.727
N	(192)	(1583)	(25)	(53)	(124)	(260)	(15)	(11)

and soccer are not only dangerous sports but team sports and that this latter similarity might account for the differential participation of firstborns and later borns. A comparison of the participation of firstborns in nondangerous team[3] sports with their participation in nondangerous individual[4] sports renders this alternative unlikely. For the Columbia group, where the sample was large enough to perform the appropriate analysis, firstborns were nonsignificantly *more* likely to play a nondangerous individual sport: The ratio of first- to second borns from families of two or more children among students playing team sports was .62, while the ratio for those playing only individual sports was .55. Finally, the underrepresentation of firstborns in the dangerous sports is not due to an avoidance of sports in general. At all three schools the proportion of firstborns among players of nondangerous sports was entirely similar to the proportion of firstborns among students who played no sports at all.

[3] Baseball, basketball, crew.
[4] Wrestling, track, swimming, tennis, fencing, golf.

DISCUSSION

In summary, the evidence is in complete accord with the expectation that firstborns would avoid dangerous activity. Firstborns are as likely to play sports with low risk of injury as later borns, but less likely to play those involving high risk. The underrepresentation of firstborns in the dangerous sports is not a pronounced effect but it is a consistent one. In high school, college, and professional athletics, firstborns are less likely to play the high-risk sports.

This type of evidence is of course subject to all the ills that correlational data are heir to. A variety of explanations could be marshalled to explain the finding that firstborns avoid dangerous sports. The fact that they do not avoid the safer sports eliminates many of the contending alternative explanations, however. In addition, the only empirically demonstrated birth order difference which can comfortably explain the finding is the observation that firstborns react with more anxiety to the prospect of physical harm than do later borns.

Since Sampson, in his review of the birth-order literature (1965), gives the impression that there are no consistent birth order differences with respect to anxiety, a re-review of the evidence on this point is in order. It is correct to conclude that the evidence is contradictory and confused regarding chronic anxiety and situational anxiety where the threat is not physical. However, the evidence concerning reaction to physical danger is virtually uncontradicted. In addition to the studies cited in the introduction, Helmreich and Collins (1967) have replicated with a male population the finding that firstborns respond with more fear to the prospect of physical harm than do later borns; and Helmreich (1966) has shown that firstborns express more fear than later borns in a hazardous diving situation, and, as Torrance (1954) found with fighter pilots, perform more poorly. A reanalysis of data reported by Nisbett and Schachter (1966) again replicates the finding that firstborns respond with more fear to the prospect of physical harm than do later borns. Following the fear manipulation subjects in that experiment were given a jarring and unpleasant electric shock. Firstborns were judged by observers to react more strongly to it than later borns ($p < .06$). The firstborn subjects also reported the shock to be more painful than did later-born subjects ($p < .05$). While it is possible that firstborns are in some way more sensitive to pain (and this conclusion was reached by Carman in 1899), a more cautious interpretation is to say that the reaction to the electric shock provides behavioral evidence that firstborns were more fearful than later borns.

Only one study reviewed by Sampson failed to report significantly greater fear on the part of firstborns in response to physical danger (Weller, 1962). The writer is not aware of any other contradictory evidence. It seems safe to conclude that firstborns are more frightened by the prospect of physical harm than are later borns, and it is plausible to infer that they avoid dangerous sports for this reason.

REFERENCES

Carman, A. Pain and strength measurements of 1,507 school children in Saginaw, Michigan. *American Journal of Psychology*, 1899, **10**, 392–398.

Helmreich, R. L. Prolonged stress in Sealab II: A field study of individual and group reactions. Unpublished doctoral dissertation, Yale University, 1966.

Helmreich, R. L., & Collins, B. E. Situational determinants of affiliative preference under stress. *Journal of Personality and Social Psychology*, 1967, **6**, 79–85.

Nisbett, R. E., & Schachter, S. Cognitive manipulation of pain. *Journal of Experimental Social Psychology*, 1966, **2**, 227–236.

Sampson, E. E. The study of ordinal position: Antecedents and outcomes. In B. A. Maher (Ed.), *Progress in experimental personality research.* Vol. 2. New York: Academic Press, 1965.

Schachter, S. Birth order, eminence, and higher education. *American Sociological Review*, 1963, **28**, 757–768.

Schachter, S. *The psychology of affiliation.* Stanford: Stanford University Press, 1959.

Torrance, E. B. A psychological study of American Western Psychological Association, Long Beach, California, 1954.

Weller, L. The relationship of birth order to anxiety. *Sociometry*, 1962, **25**, 415–417.

Neurosis as a Failure of Personal Growth*

Abraham H. Maslow

Rather than trying to be comprehensive, I have chosen to discuss only a few selected aspects of this topic, partly because I have been working with them recently, partly also because I think they are especially important, but mostly because they have been overlooked.

The frame of reference which all in this symposium have taken for granted considers the neurosis to be, from *one* aspect, a describable, pathological state of affairs which presently exists, a kind of disease or sickness or illness, on the medical model. But we have learned to see it also in a dialectical fashion, as simultaneously a kind of moving forward, a clumsy groping forward toward health and toward fullest humanness, in a kind of timid and weak way, under the aegis of fear rather than of courage, and *now* involving the future as well as the present.

All the evidence that we have (mostly clinical evidence, but already some other kinds of research evidence) indicates that it is reasonable to assume in practically every human being, and certainly in almost every newborn baby, that there is an active will toward health, an impulse toward growth, or toward the actualization of human potentialities. But at once we are confronted with the very saddening realization that so few people make it. Only a small proportion of the human population gets to the point of identity, or of selfhood, full humanness, self-actualization, etc., even in a society like ours which is relatively one of the most fortunate on the face of the earth. This is our great paradox. We all have the impulse towards full develop-

From *Humanitas*, 1967, **3**, 153–169. Reproduced by permission.

*Institute of Man symposium on *Neurosis and Personal Growth*, November 18, 1966.

ment of humanness. Then why is it that it does not happen more often? What blocks it?

This is our new way of approaching the problem of humanness, i.e., with an appreciation of its high possibilities and simultaneously, a deep disappointment that these possibilities are so infrequently actualized. This attitude contrasts with the "realistic" acceptance of whatever happens to be the case, and then of regarding that as the norm, as, for instance, Kinsey did, and as the TV pollsters do today. We tend then to get into the situation that Dr. Barton pointed out to us this morning in which normalcy from the descriptive point of view, from the value-free science point of view—that this normalcy or averageness is the best we can expect, and that therefore we should be content with it. From the point of view that I have outlined, normalcy would be rather the kind of sickness or crippling or stunting that we share with everybody else and therefore don't notice. I remember an old textbook of abnormal psychology that I used when I was an undergraduate, which was an awful book, but which had a wonderful frontispiece. The lower half was a picture of a line of babies, pink, sweet, delightful, innocent, lovable. Above that was a picture of a lot of passengers in a subway train, glum, grey, sullen, sour. The caption underneath was very simply, "What happened?" This is what I'm talking about.

I should mention also—I feel a little self-conscious about this after Dr. Gendlin's address—but I should mention also that part of what I have been doing and what I want to do here now comes under the head of the strategy and tactics of research and of preparation for research and of trying to phrase all of these clinical experiences and personal subjective experiences that we have been discussing today in such a way that we can learn more about them in a scientific way, that is, checking and testing and making more precise, and seeing if it is really so, and were the intuitions correct? etc., etc. For this purpose and also for those of you who are primarily interested in the philosophical problems which are involved in this discussion, I would like to present briefly a few theoretical points which are relevant for what follows. This is the age-old problem of the relationship between facts and values, between *is* and *ought*, between the descriptive and the normative—a terrible problem for the philosophers who have dealt with it ever since there were any philosophers, and who haven't got very far with it yet. I'd like to offer some considerations that I would like you to mull over which have helped me with this old philosophical difficulty, and perhaps might do the same for you, a third horn to the dilemma, you might say.

FUSION-WORDS

What I have in mind here is the general conclusion that I have already written about (15), which comes partly from the Gestalt psychologists and partly from clinical and psychotherapeutic experience, namely, that, in a kind of a Socratic fashion, facts often point in a direction, i.e., they are vectorial. Facts don't lie there like pancakes, just doing nothing; they are to a certain extent signposts which tell you what to do, which make suggestions to us, which nudge us in one direction rather than another. They "call for," they have "demand" character, they even have "requiredness," as Köhler called it (10). I feel frequently that whenever we get to know enough, then we know what to do, or we know much better what to do; that sufficient knowledge will often solve the problem, that it will often help us at our moral and ethical choice-points, when we must decide whether to do this or to do that. For instance, it is our common experience in therapy, that as people "know" more and more consciously, their solutions, their choices become more easy, more automatic. This is why I would reject entirely Sartre's kind of arbitrariness. I think it's a profound mistake to think of us as being confronted only with arbitrariness, with choices we make by fiat, by sheer, unaided acts of will, and without any help from the nature of reality or from the essential nature of human nature.

I am suggesting something other than that. I am suggesting that there are facts and words which themselves are both normative and descriptive simultaneously. I am calling them for the moment "fusion-words," meaning a fusion of facts and values, and what I have to say beyond this should be understood as part of this effort to solve the *is* and *ought* problem.

I myself have advanced, as I think we all have in this kind of work, from talking in the beginning, in a frankly normative way, for example, asking the questions—what is normal, what is healthy? My former philosophy professor, who still feels fatherly toward me, and to whom I still feel filial, has occasionally written me a worried letter scolding me gently for the cavalier way in which I was handling these old philosophical problems, saying something like, "Don't you realize what you have done here? 2000 years of thought lies behind this problem and you go skating over this thin ice so easily and casually." And I remember that I wrote back once trying to explain myself, saying that this sort of thing is really the way a scientist functions, and that this is part of his strategy of research, i.e., to skate past philosophical difficulties as fast as possible. I remember writing to him once that my attitude as a strategist in the advancement of knowledge had to be one, so far as philosophical problems were concerned, of "determined naivete." And I think that is what we have here. I felt that it was heuristic, and therefore all right, to talk about normal and healthy and what was good and what was bad, and frequently getting very arbitrary about it. I did one research in which there were good paintings and bad paintings, and with a perfectly straight face I put in the footnote, "Good paintings are defined here as paintings that I like." The thing is, that if I can skip to my conclusion, it turns out to be not so bad a strategy after all.

In studying healthy people, self-actualizing people, etc., there has been a steady move from the openly normative and the frankly personal, step by step, toward more descriptive, objective words, to the point at which there is today a standardized test of self-actualization (25). Self-actualization can now be defined quite operationally, as intelligence used to be defined, i.e., self-actualization is what that test tests. It correlates well with external variables of various kinds, and keeps on accumulating additional correlational meanings. As a result, I feel heuristically justified in *starting* with my "determined naivete." Most of what I was able to see intuitively, directly, personally is being confirmed now with numbers and tables and curves.

FULL-HUMANNESS

I would like to suggest a further step toward the fusion-word "fully-human," a concept which is still more descriptive and objective (than the concept "self-actualization") and yet retains everything that we need of normativeness. This is in the hope of moving from intuitive heuristic beginnings toward more certainty, greater reliability, more and more external validation, which in turn means more scientific and theoretical usefulness of this concept. This phrasing and this way of thinking was suggested to me about fifteen or so years ago by the axiological writings of Robert Hartman (5) who defined "good" as the degree to which an object fulfills its definition or concept. This suggested to me that the conception of humanness might be made, for research purposes, into a kind of quantitative concept. For instance, full humanness can be defined in a cataloguing fashion, i.e., full humanness is the ability to abstract, to have a grammatical language, to be able to love, to have values of a particular kind, to transcend the self, etc., etc., etc. The complete cataloguing definition could even be made into a kind of check list.

We might shudder a little at this thought, but it could be very useful if only to make the theoretical point for the researching scientist that the concept *can* be descriptive and quantitative—and yet also normative, i.e., this person is closer to full humanness than that other person. Or we could even say: This person is *more* human than that one. This is a fusion-word in the sense that I have mentioned above; it is really objectively descriptive because it has nothing to do with my wishes and tastes, my personality, my neuroses. Moreover, my unconscious wishes or fears, anxieties or hopes are far more easily excluded from the conception of full humanness than they are from the conception of psychological health.

If you ever work with the concept of psychological health—or any other kind of health, or normality—you will discover what a temptation it is to project your own values and to make it into a self-description or perhaps a description of what you would like to be, or what you think people *should* be like. You'll have to fight against it all the time, and you'll discover that, while it is *possible* to be objective in such work, it is certainly difficult. And even then, you cannot be really sure. Have you fallen into sampling error? After all, if you select persons for investigation on the basis of your personal judgment and diagnosis, such sampling errors are more likely than if you select by some more impersonal criterion (12).

Clearly, fusion-words are a scientific advance over more purely normative words, while also avoiding the trap of believing that science *must* be *only* value-free, and non-normative, i.e., non-human. Fusion-concepts and words permit us to participate in the normal advance of science and knowledge from its phenomenological and experiential beginnings on toward greater reliability, greater validity, greater confidence, greater exactness, greater sharing with others and agreement with them (18).

Other obvious fusion-words are: problem, task duty, mature, evolved, developed, stunted, crippled, fully-functioning, graceful, awkward, clumsy, and the like. There are many more words which are less obviously fusions of the normative and the descriptive. One day we may even have to get used to thinking of fusion-words as paradigmatic, as normal, usual and central. Then the more purely descriptive words and the more purely normative words would be thought of as peripheral and exceptional. I believe that this will come as part of the new humanistic Weltanschauung which is now rapidly crystallizing into a structured form.[1]

For one thing, as I have pointed out (11), these conceptions are too exclusively extra-psychic and don't account sufficiently for the quality of consciousness, for intra-psychic or subjective abilities, for instance, to enjoy music, to meditate and contemplate, to savor flavors, to be sensitive to one's inner voices, etc. Getting along well within one's inner world may be as important as social competence or reality competence.

But more important from the point of view of theoretical elegance and research strategy, these concepts are less objective and quantifiable than is a list of the capacities that make up the concept of humanness.

I would add that I consider none of these models to be *opposed* to the medical model. There is no need to dichotomize them from each other. Medical illnesses diminish the human being and therefore fall on the continuum of greater to lesser degree of humanness. Of course, though the medical illness model is necessary (for tumors, bacterial invasions, ulcers, etc.), it is certainly not sufficient (for neurotic, characterological or spiritual disturbances).

HUMAN DIMINUTION

One consequence of the usage of "full-humanness" rather than "psychological health" is the corresponding or parallel use of "human diminution," instead of "neurosis," which is a totally obsolete word anyway. Here the key concept is the loss or not-yet-actualization of human capacities and possibilities, and obviously this is also a matter of degree and quantity. Furthermore, it is closer to being externally observable, i.e., behavioral, which of course makes it easier to investigate than, for example, anxiety or compulsiveness or repression. Also it places on the same continuum all the standard psychiatric categories, all the stuntings, cripplings and inhibitions that come from poverty, exploitation, maleducation, enslavement, etc., and also the newer value pathologies, existential disorders, character disorders that come to the economically privileged. It handles very nicely the diminutions that result from drug-addiction, psychopathy, authoritarianism, criminality, and other categories that cannot be called "illness" in the same medical sense as, for example, brain tumor.

This is a radical move away from the medical model, a move which is long overdue. Strictly speaking, neurosis means an illness of the nerves, a relic we can very well do without today. In addition, using the label "psychological illness" puts neurosis into the same universe of discourse as ulcers, lesions, bacterial invasions, broken bones, or tumors.

[1] I consider the "degree of humanness" concept to be more useful also than the concepts of "social competence," "human effectiveness" and similar notions.

By now, we have learned very well that it is better to consider neurosis as related rather to spiritual disorders, to loss of meaning, to doubts about the goals of life, to grief and anger over a lost love, to seeing life in a different way, to loss of courage or of hope, to despair over the future, to dislike for oneself, to recognition that one's life is being wasted, or that there is no possibility of joy or love, etc., etc.

These are all fallings away from full-humanness, from the full blooming of human nature. They are losses of human possibility, of what might have been and could perhaps yet be. Physical and chemical hygiene and prophylaxes certainly have some place in this realm of psychopathogenesis, but are nothing in comparison with the far more powerful role of social, economic, political, religious, educational, philosophical, axiological and familial determinants.

SUBJECTIVE BIOLOGY

There are still other important advantages to be gained from moving over to this psychological-philosophical-educational-spiritual usage. Not the least of these, it seems to me, is that it encourages the *proper* conceptual use of the biological and constitutional base which underlies any discussion of Identity or of The Real Self, of growth, of uncovering therapy, of full-humanness or of diminution of humanness, of self-transcendence, or any version of these. Briefly, I believe that helping a person to move toward full-humanness proceeds inevitably via awareness of one's identity (among other things). A very important part of this task is to become aware of what one *is*, biologically, temperamentally, constitutionally, as a member of a species, of one's capacities, desires, needs, and also of one's vocation, what one is fitted for, what one's destiny is.

To put it bluntly and unequivocally, one absolutely necessary aspect of this self-awareness is a kind of phenomenology of one's own inner biology, of that which I have called instinctoid (17), of one's animality and specieshood. This is certainly what psychoanalysis tries to do., i.e., to help one become conscious of one's animal urges, needs, tensions, depressions, tastes, anxieties. So also for Horney's distinction between a real self and a pseudo-self. Is this also not a subjective discrimination of what one truly is? And what *is* one truly if not first and foremost one's own body, one's own constitution, one's own functioning, one's own specieshood? (I have very much enjoyed, *qua theorist*, this pretty integration of Freud, Goldstein, Sheldon, Horney, Cattell, Frankl, May, Rogers, Murray, et al. Perhaps even Skinner could be coaxed into this diverse company, since I suspect that a listing of all his "intrinsic reinforcers" for his human subjects might very well look much like the "hierarchy of instinctoid basic needs and metaneeds" that I have proposed!)

I believe it is possible to carry through this paradigm even at the very highest levels of personal development, where one transcends one's own personality (16). I hope to make a good case soon for accepting the probable instinctoid character of one's highest values, i.e., of what might be called the spiritual or philosophical life (19). Even this personally discovered axiology I feel can be subsumed under this category of "phenomenology of one's own instinctoid nature" or of "subjective biology" or "experiential biology" or some such phrase.

Think of the great theoretical and scientific advantages of placing on one single continuum of degree or amount of humanness, not only all the kinds of sickness the psychiatrists talk about but also all the additional kinds that existentialists and philosophers and religious thinkers and social reformers have worried about. Not only this, but we can also place on the same single scale all the various degrees and kinds of *health* that we know about, plus even the health-beyond-health of self-transcendence, of mystical fusion, and whatever still higher possibilities of human nature the future may yet disclose.

INNER SIGNALS

Thinking in this way has had for me at least the one special advantage of directing my attention sharply to what I called at first "the impulse voices" but which could be called more generally something like the "inner signals" (or cues or stimuli). I had not realized sufficiently that in most neuroses, and in many other disturbances as well, the inner signals become weak or even disappear entirely (as in the severely obsessional person) and/or are not "heard" or *cannot* be heard. At the extreme we have the experientially-empty person, the zombie, the one with empty insides. Recovering the self *must*, as a *sine qua non*, include the recovery of the ability to have and to cognize these inner signals, to know what and whom one likes and dislikes, what is enjoyable and what is not, when to eat and when not to (Schachter), when to sleep, when to urinate, when to rest.

The experientially-empty person, lacking these directives from within, these voices of the real self, must turn to outer cues for guidance, for instance eating when the clock tells him to, rather than obeying his appetite (he has none). He guides himself by clocks, rules, calendars, schedules, agenda, and by hints and cues from other people.

In any case, I trust that the particular sense in which I suggest interpreting the neurosis as a failure of personal growth must be clear by now. It is a falling short of what one could have been, and even one could say, of what one *should* have been, biologically speaking, that is, if one had grown and developed in an unimpeded way. Human and personal possibilities have been lost. The world has been narrowed, and so has consciousness. Capacities have been inhibited. I think for instance of the fine pianist who couldn't play before an audience of more than a few, or the phobic who is forced to avoid heights or crowds. The person who can't study, or who can't sleep, or who can't eat many foods has been diminished as surely as the one who has been blinded. The cognitive losses, the lost pleasures, joys, and ecstasies,[2] the loss of competence, the inability to relax, the weakening of will, the fear of responsibility—all these are diminutions of humanness.

I have mentioned some of the advantages of replacing the concepts of psychological illness and health with the more

[2] What it means for one's style of life to lose peak-experiences has been very well set forth in Colin Wilson's *Introduction to the New Existentialism.* (29)

pragmatic, public and quantitative concept of full or diminished humanness, which I believe is also biologically and philosophically sounder. But before I move on, I would like to note also that diminution can, of course, be either reversible or irreversible, for example, we feel far less hopeful about the paranoid person than we do about say a nice, lovable hysterical. And, of course, diminution is also dynamic, in the Freudian style. The original Freudian schema spoke of an intrinsic dialectic between the impulse and the defenses against this impulse. In this same sense, diminution leads to consequences and processes. It is only rarely a completion or a finality in a simple descriptive way. In most people these losses lead not only to all sorts of defensive processes which have been well described by Freudian and other psychoanalytic groups, for instance, to repression, denial, conflict, etc. They also lead to coping responses as I stressed long ago (21).

Conflict itself is of course a sign of relative health, as you would know if you ever met really apathetic people, hopeless people, people who have given up hoping, striving and coping. Neurosis is by contrast a very hopeful kind of thing. It means that a man who is frightened, who does not trust himself, who has a low self-image, etc., reaches out for the human heritage and for the basic gratifications to which every human being has a right, simply by virtue of being human. You might say it's a kind of *timid* and ineffectual striving toward self-actualization, toward full humanness.

Diminution can of course be reversible. Very frequently, simply supplying the need gratifications can solve the problem, especially in children. For a child who has not been loved enough, obviously the treatment of first choice is to love him to death, to just slop it all over him. Clinical and general human experience is that it works—I don't have any statistics, but I would suspect nine out of ten times. So is respect a wonderful medicine for counteracting a feeling of worthlessness. Which of course brings up the obvious conclusion that, if "health and illness" on the medical model are seen as obsolete, so also must the medical concepts of "treatment" and "cure" and the authoritative doctor be discarded and replaced.

THE JONAH SYNDROME

In the little time I have left, I would like to turn to one of the many reasons for what Angyal (1) called the evasion of growth. Certainly everybody in this room would like to be better than he is. All of us have an impulse to improve ourselves, an impulse toward actualizing more of our potentialities, toward self-actualization, or full humanness, or human fulfillment, or whatever term you like. Granted this for everybody here, then what holds us up? What blocks us?

One such defense against growth, which I'd like to speak about especially because it hasn't received much notice, I shall call the Jonah syndrome.[3]

In my own notes I had at first labelled this defense the "fear of one's own greatness" or the "evasion of one's destiny" or the "running away from one's own best talents." I had wanted to stress as bluntly and sharply as I could the non-Freudian point that we fear our best as well as our worst, even though in different ways. It is certainly possible for most of us to be greater than we are in actuality. We all have unused potentialities or not fully developed ones. It is certainly true that many of us evade our constitutionally suggested vocations (call, destiny, task in life, mission). So often we run away from the responsibilities dictated (or rather suggested) by nature, by fate, even sometimes by accident, just as Jonah tried—in vain—to run away from *his* fate.

We fear our highest possibilities (as well as our lowest ones). We are generally afraid to become that which we can glimpse in our most perfect moments, under the most perfect conditions, under conditions of greatest courage. We enjoy and even thrill to the godlike possibilities we see in ourselves in such peak moments. And yet we simultaneously shiver with weakness, awe and fear before these very same possibilities.

I have found it easy enough to demonstrate this to my students simply by asking, "Which of you in this class hopes to write the great American novel, or to be a Senator, or Governor, or President? Who wants to be Secretary-General of the United Nations? Or a great composer? Who aspires to be a saint, like Schweitzer, perhaps? Who among you will be a great leader?" Generally everybody starts giggling, blushing, and squirming until I ask, "If not you, then who else?" Which of course is the truth. And in this same way, as I push my graduate students toward these higher levels of aspiration, I'll say, "What great book are you now secretly planning to write?" And then they often blush and stammer and push me off in some way. But why should I not ask that question? Who else will write the books on psychology except psychologists? So I can ask, "Do you not plan to be a psychologist?" "Well, yes." "Are you in training to be a mute or an inactive psychologist? What's the advantage of that? That's not a good path to self-actualization. No, you must want to be a first-class psychologist, meaning the best, the very best you are capable of becoming. If you deliberately plan to be less than you are capable of being, then I warn you that you'll be deeply unhappy for the rest of your life. You will be evading your own capacities, your own possibilities."

Not only are we ambivalent about our own highest possibilities. We are also in a perpetual and I think universal—perhaps even *necessary*—conflict and ambivalence over these same highest possibilities in other people, and in human nature in general. Certainly we love and admire good men, saints, honest, virtuous, clean men. But could anybody who has looked into the depths of human nature fail to be aware of our mixed and often hostile feelings toward saintly men? Or toward very beautiful women or men? Or toward great creators? Or toward our intellectual geniuses? It is not necessary to be a psychotherapist to see this phenomenon—let us call it "counter-valuing." Any reading of history will turn up plenty of examples, or perhaps I could even say that any such historical search might fail to turn up a single exception throughout the whole history of mankind. We surely love and admire all the persons who have incarnated the true, the good, the beautiful, the just, the perfect, the ultimately successful.

[3] This name was suggested by my friend, Professor Frank Manual, with whom I had discussed this puzzle.

And yet they also make us uneasy, anxious, confused, perhaps a little jealous or envious, a little inferior, clumsy. They usually make us lose our aplomb, our self-possession and self-regard. (Nietzsche is still our best teacher here.)

Here we have a first clue. My impression so far is that the greatest people, simply by their presence and by being what they are, make us feel aware of our lesser worth, whether or not they intend to. If this is an unconscious effect, and we are not aware of why we feel stupid or ugly or inferior whenever such a person turns up, we are apt to respond with projection, i.e., we react as if he were *trying* to make us feel inferior, as if we were the target (8). Hostility is then an understandable consequence. It looks to me so far as if conscious awareness tends to fend off this hostility. That is, if you are willing to attempt self-awareness and self-analysis of your *own* counter-valuing, i.e., of your unconscious fear and hatred of true, good, beautiful, people, you will most likely be less nasty to them. I am willing also to extrapolate the guess that if you can learn to love more purely the highest values in others, this might make you love these qualities in yourself in a less frightened way.

Allied to this dynamic is the awe before the highest, of which Rudolf Otto (23) has given us the classical description. Putting this together with Eliade's insights (2) into sacralization and desacralization, we become more aware of the universality of the fear of direct confrontation with a god or with the godlike. In some religions death is the inevitable consequence. Most preliterate societies also have places or objects that are taboo because they are too sacred and *therefore too dangerous.* In the last chapter of my *Psychology of Science* (18), I have also given examples mostly from science and medicine of desacralizing and resacralizing and tried to explain the psychodynamics of these processes. Mostly it comes down to awe before the highest and best (I want to stress that this awe is intrinsic, justified, *right,* suitable, rather than some sickness or failing to get "cured of").

But here again my feeling is that this awe and fear need not be negative alone, need not be something to make us flee or cower. These are also desirable and enjoyable feelings capable of bringing us even to the point of highest ecstasy and rapture. Conscious awareness, insight and "working through," à la Freud, is the answer here too I think. This is the best path I know to the acceptance of our highest powers, and whatever elements of greatness or goodness or wisdom or talent we may have concealed or evaded.

A helpful sidelight for me has come from trying to understand why peak-experiences are ordinarily transient and brief (13). The answer becomes clearer and clearer. *We are just not strong enough to endure more!* It is just too shaking and wearing. So often people in such ecstatic moments say, "It's too much," or "I can't stand it," or "I could die." And as I get the descriptions, I sometimes feel, "Yes, they *could* die." Delirious happiness cannot be borne for long. Our organisms are just too weak for any large doses of greatness, just as they would be too weak to endure hour-long sexual orgasms, for example.

The word "peak-experience" is more appropriate than I realized at first. The acute emotion must be climactic and momentary and it *must* give way to nonecstatic serenity, calmer happiness, and the intrinsic pleasures of clear, contemplative cognition of the highest goods. The climactic emotion can not endure, but B-Cognition *can* (16, 18).

Does this not help us to understand our Jonah syndrome? It is partly a justified fear of being torn apart, of losing control, of being shattered and disintegrated, even of being killed by the experience. Great emotions after all can in *fact* overwhelm us. The fear of surrendering to such an experience, a fear which reminds us of all the parallel fears found in sexual frigidity, can be understood better I think through familiarity with the literature of psychodynamics and depth psychology, and of the psychophysiology and medical psychomatics of emotion.

There is still another psychological process that I have run across in my explorations of failure to actualize the self. This evasion of growth can also be set in motion by a fear of paranoia. Of course this has been said in more universal ways. Promethean and Faustian legends are found in practically any culture.[4] For instance, the Greeks called it the fear of *hubris.* It has been called "sinful pride," which is of course a permanent human problem. The person who says to himself, "Yes, I will be a great philosopher and I will rewrite Plato and do it better," must sooner or later be struck dumb by his grandiosity, his arrogance. And especially in his weaker moments, will say to himself, "Who? Me?" and think of it as a crazy fantasy or even fear it as a delusion. He compares his knowledge of his inner private self, with all its weakness, vacillation, and shortcomings, with the bright, shining, perfect, and faultless image he has of Plato. Then, of course, he will feel presumptuous and grandiose. (What he fails to realize is that Plato, introspecting, must have felt just the same way about himself, but went ahead anyway, overriding his own doubts about self.)

For some people this evasion of one's own growth, setting low levels of aspiration, the fear of doing what one is capable of doing, voluntary self-crippling, pseudo-stupidity, mock-humility are in fact defenses against grandiosity, arrogance, sinful pride, hubris. There are people who cannot manage that graceful integration between humility and pride which is absolutely necessary for creative work. To invent or create you must have the "arrogance of creativeness" which so many investigators have noticed. But, of course, if you have *only* the arrogance without the humility, then you are in fact paranoid. You *must* be aware not only of the godlike possibilities within, but also of the existential human limitations. You must be able simultaneously to laugh at yourself and at all human pretensions. If you can be amused by the worm trying to be a god (28), then in fact you may be able to go on trying and being arrogant without fearing paranoia or bringing down upon yourself the evil eye. This is a good technique.

May I mention one more such technique that I saw at its best in Aldous Huxley, who was certainly a great man in the sense I have been discussing, one who was able to accept his talents and use them to the full. He managed it by perpetually marvelling at how interesting and fascinating

[4] Sheldon's excellent book on this subject (24) is not quoted often enough, possibly because it came before we were quite ready to assimilate it (1936).

everything was, by wondering like a youngster at how miraculous things are, by saying frequently, "Extraordinary! Extraordinary!" He could look out at the world with wide eyes, with unabashed innocence, awe and fascination, which is a kind of admission of smallness, a form of humility, and then proceed calmly and unafraid to the great tasks he set for himself.

Finally, may I refer you to a paper of mine (14) relevant in itself, but also as the first in a possible series. Its name, "The need to know and the fear of knowing," illustrates well what I want to say about *each* of the intrinsic or ultimate values that I call Values of Being (B-Values). I am trying to say that these ultimate values, which I think are also the highest needs (or metaneeds, as I'm calling them (19) in a forthcoming publication) fall, like all basic needs, into the basic Freudian schema of impulse *and* defense against that impulse. Thus it is certainly demonstrable that we need the truth and love and seek it. And yet it is just as easy to demonstrate that we are also simultaneously *afraid* to know the truth. For instance, certain truths carry automatic responsibilities which may be anxiety-producing. One way to evade the responsibility and the anxiety is simply to evade consciousness of the truth.

I predict that we will find a similar dialectic for each of the intrinsic Values of Being, and I have vaguely thought of doing a series of papers on, for example, "The love of beauty and our uneasiness with it," "Our love of the good man and our irritation with him," "Our search for excellence and our tendency to destroy it." Of course these counter-values are stronger in neurotic people, but it looks to me as if all of us must make our peace with these mean impulses within ourselves. And my impression so far is that the best way to do this is to transmute envy, jealousy, *resentiment*, and nastiness into humble admiration, gratitude, appreciation, adoration, and even worship via conscious insight and working through (22). This is the road to feeling small and weak and unworthy and *accepting* these feelings instead of needing to protect a spuriously high self-esteem by striking out (7).

Again I think it is obvious that understanding this basic existential problem should help us to embrace the B-Values not only in others, but also in ourselves, thereby helping to resolve the Jonah syndrome.

REFERENCES

1. Angyal, A. *Neurosis and Treatment: A Holistic Theory.* Wiley, 1965.
2. Eliade, M. *The Sacred and the Profane.* Harper & Row, 1961.
3. Frankl, V. Self-transcendence as a human phenomenon, *Journal of Humanistic Psychology*, 1966, **6**, 97–206.
4. Goldstein, K. *The Organism.* American Book Company, 1939.
5. Hartman, R. The science of value, in A. H. Maslow (Ed.), *New Knowledge in Human Values.* Harper & Row, 1959.
6. Henle, M. (Ed.). *Documents of Gestalt Psychology.* University of California Press, 1961.
7. Horney, K. *Neurosis and Human Growth.* W. W. Norton, 1950.
8. Huxley, L., *You Are Not the Target.* Farrar, Straus & Co., 1963.
9. King, C. D. The meaning of normal, *Yale Journal of Biology and Medicine*, 1945, **17**, 493–501.
10. Köhler, W. *The Place of Values in a World of Facts.* Liveright, 1938.
11. Maslow, A. H. *Motivation and Personality.* Harper & Row, 1954.
12. Maslow, A. H. Some frontier problems in mental health, in A. Combs (Ed.), *Personality Theory and Counseling Practice.* University of Florida Press, 1961.
13. Maslow, A. H. Lessons from the peak-experiences, *Journal of Humanistic Psychology*, 1962, **2**, 9–18.
14. Maslow, A. H. The need to know and the fear of knowing, *Journal of General Psychology*, 1963, **68**, 111–125.
15. Maslow, A. H. Fusions of facts and values, *American Journal of Psychoanalysis*, 1963, **23**, 117–131.
16. Maslow, A. H. *Religions, Values, and Peak-Experiences.* Ohio State University Press, 1964.
17. Maslow, A. H. Criteria for Judging Needs to be Instinctoid, in M. R. Jones (Ed.), *Human Motivation: A Symposium*, University of Nebraska Press, 1965, 33–47.
18. Maslow, A. H. *The Psychology of Science: A Reconnaissance.* Harper & Row, 1966.
19. Maslow, A. H. A theory of metamotivation: the biological rooting of the value-life. *Journal of Humanistic Psychology*, 1967, in press.
20. Maslow, A. H. Self-actualization and beyond, in J. Bugental (Ed.), *Challenges of Humanistic Psychology.* McGraw-Hill, 1967.
21. Maslow, A. H. and Mittelman, B. *Principles of Abnormal Psychology.* Harper & Row, 1941.
22. Maslow, A. H., with Rand, H. & Newman, S. Some parallels between the dominance and sexual behavior of monkeys and the fantasies of patients in psychotherapy, *Journal of Nervous & Mental Disease*, 1960, **131**, 202–212.
23. Otto, R., *The Idea of the Holy.* Oxford University Press, 1958.
24. Sheldon, W. H. *Psychology and the Promethean Will*, Harper & Row, 1936.
25. Shostrom, E. Personal Orientation Inventory (POI), Educational and Industrial Testing Service, 1963.
26. van Kaam, A. *Existential Foundations of Psychology.* Duquesne University Press, 1966.
27. Weiss, F. A. Emphasis on health in psychoanalysis, *American Journal of Psychoanalysis*, 1966, **26**, 194–198.
28. Wilson, C. *The Stature of Man.* Houghton Mifflin, 1959.
29. Wilson, C. *Introduction to the New Existentialism.* Houghton Mifflin, 1967.

Psychophysiological Disorders

The psychophysiological disorders are characterized by physical symptoms that are caused by emotional factors, and this chapter opens with the classic paper by Hans Selye on the effects of stress on human beings. In this paper, the distinguished Canadian biomedical researcher defines stress, and then discusses the changes characteristic of stress, the three stages of the stress syndrome, the conditioning of hormone actions, and the definition and types of diseases of adaptation.

Another classic in the area of psychophysiological disorders is the second paper of this chapter, by Joseph V. Brady and his associates at the Walter Reed Army Institute of Research. This is the now-famous study on the development of stomach ulcers in the so-called executive monkeys.

Although obesity is not a psychological disorder in the sense of possessing demonstrated organ damage, we present Stanley Schachter's paper "Obesity and Eating" because it suggests how emotional and internal states can cause physical changes. Schachter describes experiments that show how internal and external food cues differentially affect the eating behavior of obese and normal human beings.

Finally, a paper by Maslach, Marshall, and Zimbardo describes how skin temperature can be brought under control by hypnosis.

Stress and Disease

Hans Selye

Almost two decades have passed now since the publication of a short note on "A syndrome produced by diverse nocuous agents" (1). Since that time, the relationships between this "general-adaptation syndrome," or "stress syndrome," and virtually every branch of physiology and clinical medicine have been subjected to study. Those who seek detailed information concerning certain aspects of the stress problem will find a key to the world literature in the monographs (2–10) and yearbooks (11–14) that are especially devoted to this topic. Hence there is no need to burden this text with numerous references. It may be opportune, however, to take stock now in the form of a brief synopsis surveying the most fundamental facts that we have learned about the relationships between stress and disease. This will give us an opportunity also to outline what we would consider to be the principal scope and the limitations of this new approach to problems of medicine (15).

Ever since man first used the word *disease*, he has had some inkling of the stress concept. The very fact that this single term has been used to denote a great variety of manifestly distinct maladies clearly indicates that they have been recognized as having something in common. They possess, as we would now say, some "nonspecific disease features" (the feeling of being ill, loss of appetite and vigor, aches and pains, loss of weight, and so forth), that permit human beings to distinguish illness from the condition of health. Yet, precisely because these manifestations are not characteristic of any one disease, they have received little attention in comparison with the specific ones. They were thought to be of lesser interest to the physician, for, unlike the specific symptoms and signs, they did not help him to recognize the "eliciting pathogen" or to prescribe an appropriate specific cure. Whenever it was impossible to determine precisely what the cause of the trouble was, therapy had to be limited to such general measures as the recommendation of rest, an easily digestible and yet nutritious diet, protection against great variations in the surrounding temperature, or the use of salicylates to stop pain.

Experience had likewise shown long ago that what we now call nonspecific stress can also have certain remarkable curative properties under certain conditions. Nonspecific therapy was consciously or unconsciously based on this principle. In the Middle Ages, flogging of the insane was practiced "to drive the evil spirit out of them." This procedure was subsequently replaced by the more humane fever therapy, Metrazol shock, insulin shock, electroshock, and numerous other measures, but all of these have in common the property of producing a state of systemic, nonspecific stress. Such practices as bloodletting, fasting, or the parenteral administration of milk, blood, and colloidal metals may serve as additional examples of nonspecific procedures, which undoubtedly can produce beneficial results in patients afflicted by a variety of diseases. These measures were, and some of them still are, widely used for lack of more effective and less traumatic means of therapy. However, the mechanism of their action remained obscure, and therefore scientifically minded physicians were always reluctant to use them, for they recognized that these treatments were actually stabs in the dark whose consequences could never be accurately foretold.

Perhaps the most fundamental difference between medieval and modern medicine is that the former was primarily based on pure empiricism and directed by mysticism and intuition, whereas the latter attempts to understand the mechanisms of disease—through an objective scientific analysis—and to treat it by influencing well-defined points along the pathways of its development. Up to the present time, the greatest progress that has been made along these lines has resulted in specific therapeutic procedures that are designed to eliminate in each case the particular primary cause—the eliciting pathogen of a disease—for instance, by chemotherapeutic measures or with the surgeon's knife.

By contrast, throughout the centuries, we have learned virtually nothing about rational, scientifically well-founded procedures that would help the body in its own natural efforts to maintain health quite apart from the attacks on the pathogen. Yet, often, the causative agent cannot be recognized or is not amenable to any therapeutic procedures directed specifically against it. Besides, elimination of the causative agent frequently does not cure, because the effects of the disease producer may greatly outlast its actual presence in the body. Let us remember that it is not the microbe, the poison, or the allergen but our reactions to these agents that we experience as disease. A man may die from a single exposure to ionizing rays, a rheumatic heart, or an infectious nephritis long after the original cause of his illness is no longer present in his body.

From *Science*, 1955, 122, 625–631.

Whenever the available procedures of specific therapy are imperfect, the physician is forced to say that he has done what he could and "nature will do the rest." The fact is that very often nature actually does the rest, but unfortunately not always. Indeed, we may say that the leitmotiv of our work on stress was the question: "How does nature do 'the rest' and, when nature fails in this, could we not help if we learned more about natural methods?"

When we were first confronted with the "alarm reaction," the idea that presented itself most vividly was that the very tangible and accurately measurable morphologic characteristics of this first stage of the stress response might give us a key to the objective scientific analysis of systemic, nonspecific reactions. The enlargement of the adrenal cortex and the atrophy of the thymus and lymph nodes, for example, were changes that could be expressed in strictly quantitative terms, and they were certainly not specific, since any agent that caused systemic damage or stress elicited them.

A multitude of questions presented themselves immediately. Which among the manifestations of this alarm reaction are useful for the maintenance of health and which are merely signs of damage? How does an injury to a limited area of the body reach the various internal organs that are eventually affected during the alarm reaction? For instance, how does a trauma to one limb eventually influence such distant structures as the adrenal cortex or the thymus? Which organ change is the cause and which the consequence of another structural alteration? For instance, does the disintegrating thymus tissue liberate substances that stimulate the adrenals or does the enlarged adrenal cortex secrete hormones that affect the thymus?

It was quite evident, of course, that to answer these questions would take much time and probably long series of often monotonous stereotypic experiments, using various stressors on various species of animals. Nevertheless, a general blueprint for the dissection and clinical utilization of the stress syndrome presented itself immediately. In particular, we asked ourselves five questions, which we thought would now be amenable to experimental analysis: (i) What are the changes characteristic of stress as such? (ii) How does the stress response evolve in time? (iii) What are the pathways through which stress reaches various organs? (iv) Are there "diseases of adaptation," that is, maladies principally the result of errors in the adaptation syndrome? (v) To what extent are the animal experiments on stress applicable to clinical medicine?

None of these questions has been fully answered, and, indeed, the complete clarification of biologic problems is hardly an attainable aim. However, partial answers have been obtained to all of these basic questions, and—most important of all—it appears that they have been so formulated that further progress is now largely a matter of time.

We have learned, for instance, that acute involution of the lymphatic organs, diminution of the blood eosinophiles, enlargement and increased secretory activity of the adrenal cortex, and a variety of changes in the chemical constitution of the blood and tissues are truly nonspecific and characteristic of stress as such. It has also become evident that they represent a syndrome, in that they are closely correlated with one another, both in time and in intensity. Whenever dissociations among them tend to occur, it can usually be shown that these are attributable to one of the following two reasons: (i) either the specific actions of the evocative agent are superimposed upon the stress syndrome and thus obscure some of the nonspecific manifestations (for example, if insulin is used as a stressor, the glycemic response is masked by the hypoglycemic effect of the hormone); or (ii) one of the pathways through which stress acts in the organism is deranged (for example, stress causes no thymus involution after adrenalectomy).

No agent produces only stress. Hence, in actual experimentation, the stress response is invariably complicated by certain superimposed specific changes, and in every species—indeed, in every individual—one or the other pathway is more or less functional than the rest. These factors tend to mask or deform the typical stress response, and failure to recognize them was undoubtedly the principal handicap to clear characterization of the stress response in the past. Let us now return to our five basic problems and enumerate at least the most important facts about them that have come to light during these 20 years of research on stress.

CHANGES CHARACTERISTIC OF STRESS

In attempting to answer the question, "What are the changes characteristic of stress as such?" the first problem was, of course, to define *stress*, at least as accurately as definitions can be formulated in biology. The word, especially when it is used with its mate *strain*, has long been in everyday usage, but its significance in biology had never been defined. The layman speaks, for instance, of *eyestrain* or *mental stress* in referring to rather specific complaints. Cannon, the great student of homeostasis, also used the terms *stresses* and *strains* in connection with specific reactions. He emphasized, for instance, that the stresses and strains of oxygen lack, hemorrhage, and starvation elicit totally different and specific homeostatic reactions. Conversely, it is a characteristic of the stress syndrome, as we understand it, that it is always the same, no matter what happens to elicit it. For over-all responses, which include specific and nonspecific features—and this is even more true of purely specific responses—the term now used would be *reaction* (not *stress*) and the eliciting agent would be called a *stimulus* (not a *stressor* or *alarming stimulus*). Such specific reactions are precisely the part of the over-all response that we must subtract to arrive at our stress syndrome.

To make this distinction clear, we always used the term *nonspecific stress* in our early publications. Later, unfortunately, it became customary to omit the adjective, for brevity's sake. To avoid confusion, we then pointed out that in the sense in which we use the term, stress may be defined as a nonspecific deviation from the normal resting state; it is caused by function or damage and it stimulates repair.

Here, the nonspecific causation of the change has been selected as its most characteristic feature. However, even the term *specific* had been used somewhat loosely in medicine; we therefore defined a nonspecific change as one that can be produced by many or all agents, as opposed to a specific change, which is elicited only by one or few agents.

Correspondingly, a nonspecific agent acts on many targets, a specific one acts on few targets, and a stressor is an agent that causes stress.

Of course, we realized from the outset that these, like all biologic definitions, are imperfect, but trying to formulate them helped us to impart precision to our own concepts of *stimulus, stressor, stress, specific,* and *nonspecific.* Among other things, these considerations brought out with particular clarity the fact that stress is not necessarily the result of damage but can be caused by physiologic function and that it is not merely the result of a nonspecific action but also comprises the defense against it. These are cardinal facts, as we shall see later when we consider the relationship between stress and disease.

In our efforts to identify the characteristics of stress, our main problem was to eliminate all specific manifestations that are typical either of the agent or of the reacting organism. Hence, a large number of animal species had to be studied, following exposure to a great variety of essentially different stimuli, to compare the resulting structural, chemical, and functional changes. This made it possible to determine which are the responses common to all types of exposure, and only these could be considered to be truly nonspecific—that is, the result of stress as such. The residue that remained after subtraction of all the specific changes is the general-adaptation syndrome.

In this response, every part of the body is involved, but the two great integrators of activity, the hormonal and the nervous systems, are especially important. The facts known today may lead us to believe that the anterior pituitary and the adrenal cortex play the cardinal roles in coordinating the defense of the organism during stress. This view is probably distorted by the fact that the syndrome has been studied primarily by endocrinologists, and investigations concerning the participation of the nervous system are handicapped by the greater complexity of the required techniques. It is considerably easier to remove an endocrine gland and to substitute for its hormones by the injection of extracts than it is to destroy minute individual nervous centers selectively and then restore their function to determine the role they may play during stress.

STRESS RESPONSE IN TIME

To establish the evolution of the stress response in time, animals had to be repeatedly exposed to stressors (cold, forced muscular exercise, bloodletting, and drugs) of a constant intensity over long periods of time. It was found that, after a while, the same agent does not continue to produce the same nonspecific response. For instance, treatment with a drug that initially causes discharge of adrenocortical lipid granules will later actually promote accumulation of lipids in the adrenal cortex, after the animals have become more resistant to the damaging effects of the agent. Upon still more continued exposure, sooner or later, this acquired adaptation is invariably lost; then the animals again show signs of damage, and their adrenal cortices again discharge their lipid granules.

These adrenal changes are taken as only one example among the many characteristics of the general-adaptation syndrome that show such a triphasic pattern (for example, glycemia, chloremia, and body weight). In fact the whole syndrome is essentially triphasic; thus its manifestations depend as much on the stressor effect of the eliciting agent as on the time elapsed since the organism was first exposed to it.

The three stages of the stress syndrome are (i) the alarm reaction, in which adaptation has not yet been acquired; (ii) the stage of resistance, in which adaptation is optimum; and (iii) the stage of exhaustion, in which the acquired adaptation is lost again.

The physicochemical basis of the curious terminal loss of acquired adaptation is still quite obscure. Exhaustion cannot be fully compensated, either by changes in the caloric intake or by any known hormonal substitution therapy. The term *adaptation energy* has been suggested to designate the adaptability that is gradually consumed during exposure, but despite much research we have learned nothing about the nature of this "energy."

Many of the changes characteristic of the stage of exhaustion are strikingly similar to those of senility. It is tempting to view the general-adaptation syndrome as a kind of accelerated aging. It appears as though, because of the greater intensity of stress, the three major periods of life—infancy (in which adaptation has not yet been acquired), adulthood (in which adaptation has been acquired to the usual stresses of life), and senility (in which the acquired adaptation is lost again)—are here telescoped into a short space of time.

However, these will remain sterile speculations until some ingenious mind can devise new experimental procedures with which to analyze them in quantitative terms. It is only to stimulate thought along these lines that I venture even to mention these problems here. I hope that some talented young mind, still sufficiently uninhibited by textbook knowledge to see a new approach, will follow this trail. To me it seems more promising of truly great progress in the understanding of life and adaptability than any other aspect of stress research.

PATHWAYS OF STRESS

To clarify the pathways through which stress reaches various organs, it was merely necessary to use the classic procedures of experimental medicine—namely, the destruction of suspected relay stations and, wherever possible, their restoration (for example, removal of an endocrine gland and substitution therapy with extracts containing its hormones). Figure 1 helps to summarize the principal data that have come to light in this respect.

All agents that act on the body or any of its parts exert dual effects: (i) specific actions, with which we are not concerned in this review, except insofar as they modify the nonspecific actions of the same agents and (ii) nonspecific or stressor effects, whose principal pathways (as far as we know them today) are illustrated in Fig. 1. The stressor acts on the target (the body or some part of it) directly (thick arrow) and indirectly by way of the pituitary and the adrenal. Through some unknown pathway (labeled by a question mark), the "first mediator" travels from the directly injured target area to the anterior pituitary. It noti-

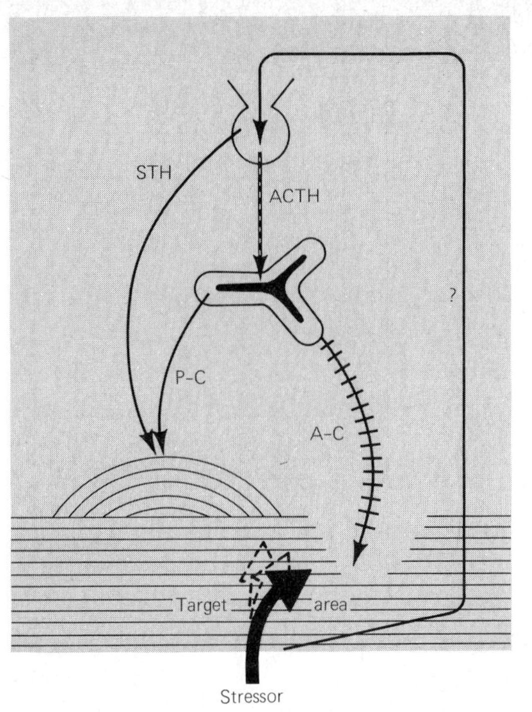

Fig. 1. Diagram illustrating the principal pathways of the stress response. [After Selye (*3*)]

fies the latter that a condition of stress exists and thus induces it to discharge adrenocorticotrophic hormone (ACTH).

It is quite possible that this first mediator of hormonal defense is not always the same. In some instances, it may be an adrenaline discharge, in others a liberation of histamine-like toxic tissue metabolites, a nervous impulse, or even a sudden deficiency in some vitally important body constituent (such as glucose or an enzyme). During stress it is rarely the lack of adrenal corticoids that stimulates ACTH secretion, through a self-regulating "feed-back" mechanism.

ACTH, alone or in cooperation with other hormones, stimulates the adrenal cortex to discharge corticoids. Some of the cortical hormones, the mineralocorticoids, also known as prophlogistic corticoids (P-Cs), stimulate the proliferative ability and reactivity of connective tissue; they enhance the "inflammatory potential." Thus, they help to put up a strong barricade of connective tissue through which the body is protected against further invasion by the pathogenic stressor agent (examples are desoxycorticosterone and aldosterone).

However, under ordinary conditions, ACTH stimulates the adrenal much more effectively to secrete glucocorticoids, also known as antiphlogistic corticoids (A-Cs). These inhibit the ability of the body to put up granulomatous barricades in the path of the invader; in fact, they tend to cause involution of connective tissue with a pronounced depression of the inflammatory potential. Thus they can suppress inflammation, but, by this same token, they open the way to the spreading of infection (examples are cortisol and cortisone).

Certain recent experiments suggest that, depending on the conditions, ACTH may cause a predominant secretion of one or the other type of corticoid. However, be this as it may, the "growth hormone," or somatotrophic hormone (STH), of the pituitary increases the inflammatory potential of connective tissue very much as the prophlogistic corticoids do; hence, it can sensitize the target area to the actions of the prophlogistic corticoids.

It is possible that the hypophysis also secretes some special corticotrophin that induces the adrenal to elaborate predominantly prophlogistic corticoids; indeed, STH itself may possess such effects, but this has not yet been proved. Probably the electrolyte content of the blood can also regulate mineralocorticoid production. In any event, even if ACTH were the only corticotrophin, the actions of the corticoids produced under its influence can be vastly different, depending on "conditioning factors" (such as STH) that specifically sensitize the target area for one or the other type of corticoid action. Actually, conditioning factors could even alter the response to ACTH of the adrenal cortex itself, so that its cells would produce more antiphlogistic or prophlogistic corticoids. Thus, during stress, one or the other type of effect can predominate.

As work along these lines progressed, it became increasingly more evident that the actions of all the "adaptive hormones" (corticoids, ACTH, STH) are so largely dependent on conditioning factors that the latter must be considered to be equally as important, in determining the final outcome of a reaction to stress, as the hormones themselves. It will be rewarding, therefore, to discuss this topic thoroughly.

Conditioning of hormone actions. Heredity, age, previous exposure to stress, nervous stimuli, the nutritional state, and many other factors can affect both the production of the adaptive hormones and their effect on individual target organs. The action of mineralocorticoids on most of their target tissues is augmented, and that of glucocorticoids is diminished, by an excess of dietary sodium. However, stress during the secretion of adaptive hormones is perhaps the most effective and most common factor capable of conditioning their actions. Thus systemic stress augments the antiphlogistic, lympholytic, catabolic, and hyperglycemic actions of antiphlogistic corticoids. Furthermore, one of the salient effects of the adaptive hormones, that of modifying the course of inflammation, naturally cannot manifest itself unless some "topical stressor" (for example, a nonspecific irritant acting on a circumscribed tissue region) first elicits an inflammatory response.

A few words about the recently introduced concept of the "permissive actions" of corticoids may be in order here. This hypothesis assumes that the corticoids do not themselves affect the targets of stress but merely permit stressors to act on them. Thus the presence or absence of corticoids could only allow or disallow a stress reaction but could not vary its intensity. To illustrate this concept, one might compare the production of light by an electric lamp to the biologic reaction and the switch to the permissive factor.

The switch cannot produce light or regulate the degree of its intensity, but unless it is turned on the lamp will not function. Correspondingly, the functional signs—generally considered to be characteristic of overproduction of corticoids during stress—would result not from any actual increase in corticoid secretion but from the extra-adrenal actions of the stressors themselves. The presence of corticoids would be necessary only in a "supporting capacity" to maintain the vitality and reactivity of tissues (16).

Actually, it is precisely in the specific and not in the nonspecific (stress) reactions that the corticoids play a purely permissive role of this type. Here they are necessary only to prevent stress and collapse, thus keeping the tissues responsive. For instance, adrenalectomized rats will not respond to injected STH with somatic growth or to sexual stimulation with mating without a minimal-maintenance corticoid treatment. However, these are specific reactions; they are not characteristic either of stress or of the corticoids and could not be duplicated in the absence of the specific stimulus (STH and sexual stimulation), even with the highest doses of corticoids.

The characteristics of antiphlogistic corticoid overproduction that we see in the alarm reaction (for example, atrophy of the lymphatic organs, catabolism, and inhibition of inflammation) are also impeded by adrenalectomy; they are also restored even by mere maintenance doses of antiphlogistic corticoids in the presence of stress, because the latter sensitizes, or conditions, the tissue to them. The fundamental difference is, however, that—unlike specific actions—these nonspecific effects can be duplicated, even in the absence of any stressor, if large doses of antiphlogistic corticoids are given.

The importance of such conditioning influences is particularly striking in the regulation of stress reactions, because, in the final analysis, they are the factors that can actually determine whether exposure to a stressor will be met by a physiologic adaptation syndrome or cause "diseases of adaptation." Furthermore, in the latter instance, these conditioning factors can even determine the selective breakdown of one or the other organ. We are led to believe that differences in predisposition, caused by such factors, might explain why the same kind of stressor can cause diverse types of diseases of adaptation in different individuals.

"Buffering action" of the adrenals. It has long been noted that it is much more difficult to obtain overdosage with either glucocorticoids or mineralocorticoids in the presence than in the absence of the adrenals. Thus, for instance, cortisol exerts its typical actions (for example, on inflammation, body weight, and the thymicolymphatic organs) at much higher dose levels in intact rats than it does in adrenalectomized rats. This is largely, if not entirely, the result of the absence of mineralocorticoids, for it proved possible to restore the glucocorticoid resistance of the adrenalectomized rat to normal by treatment with small doses of mineralocorticoids (desoxycorticosterone and aldosterone). Even a mere excess of dietary sodium can, at least partially, substitute for the adrenal in such experiments; hence it is reasonable to assume that here the mineralocorticoids antagonize the glucocorticoids, as a direct result of their effect upon mineral metabolism.

These experiments definitely disproved the so-called "unitarian theory" of adrenocortical function, which was still held by some of the most distinguished adrenal physiologists a short while ago. It is clear not only that the cortex produces more than one kind of corticoid but that the mineralocorticoids and the glucocorticoids are mutually antagonistic in many respects, as postulated by the "corticoid balance theory."

However, several observations still did not seem to be consonant with our concept of corticoid antagonism. For instance, in the presence of the adrenals, both in experimental animals and in man, it proved extremely difficult to stimulate inflammatory reactions much above normal, even with very large doses of mineralocorticoids. On the other hand, glucocorticoids always succeed in overcoming the buffering action of an intact adrenal, as long as the dosage is sufficiently high.

It is only quite recently that the cause of this apparent exception to the concept of adrenal hormone antagonism has been clarified by the demonstration that the corticoids act in accordance with the "law of intersecting dose-effect curves."

Law of intersecting dose-effect curves. When a solution containing fixed proportions of cortisol acetate and desoxycorticosterone acetate (DCA) is administered to adrenalectomized rats, the cortisol action (catabolism, thymolysis, and inhibition of inflammation) predominates at high, and the opposite, desoxycorticosterone type of activity, predominates at low dose levels. This was ascribed to the fact that the DCA activity rises rapidly to its optimum level, but then a "ceiling" is reached, and raising the dose further will not increase the effect. The cortisol type of activity, on the other hand, rises more slowly but does not flatten out until it far exceeds the ceiling of its antagonist (Fig. 2).

The relationship between the two types of corticoids explains why it is readily possible to overcome the adrenal buffer with appropriate doses of cortisol-like hormones, whereas even the highest doses of DCA cannot inhibit this

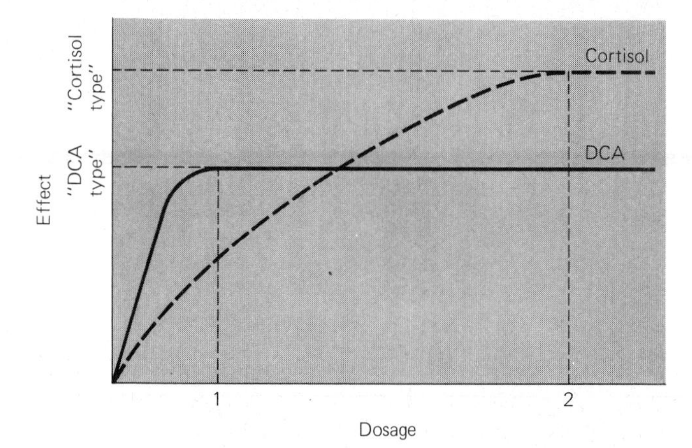

Fig. 2. Effect of varying the dose while the cortisol/deoxycorticosterone quotient is kept constant. Difference in the slopes results in intersecting dose-effect curves. [After Selye and Bois (*18*)]

effect. In the presence of the adrenals the normal level of mineralocorticoid production is usually already at its optimum of efficacy. This may also explain the frequently made observation that in adrenalectomized animals and man—where the starting point is below the mineralocorticoid ceiling—desoxycorticosterone stimulates inflammatory phenomena (for example, arthritis), and this can be antagonized by concurrent treatment with cortisol.

However, in certain respects, the desoxycorticosterone action does not appear to have a definite ceiling. Thus, in the rat, the production of renal damage by desoxycorticosterone is quite proportional to the amount given, within a very wide dose range.

Exceptional position of the kidney among the targets of corticoid activity. Numerous observations show that there exists a rather special relationship between the corticoids and the kidney, a relationship that clearly distinguishes renal tissue from other targets of corticoid activity.

Thus, the renal damage (nephrosclerosis) produced with high doses of desoxycorticosterone, in the rat, is not antagonized but is actually aggravated by concurrent treatment with cortisol. In other words, here there is no mineralocorticoid-glucocorticoid antagonism.

Furthermore, the kidney-damaging effect of various agents (for example, cold, foreign proteins, large doses of STH-preparations, and methylandrostenediol) can be prevented by adrenalectomy, while their extrarenal effects (including, for instance, the influence of STH and methylandrostenediol upon inflammation) are not markedly affected.

The cause of this exceptional reactivity of renal tissue to corticoids is not yet known. However, two factors undoubtedly play an important role here: (i) glucocorticoids and mineralocorticoids are not strictly antagonistic (and may even be synergistic) in their actions on the kidney; (ii) the inability of mineralocorticoids to produce more than a limited effect on extra-adrenal tissues (no matter how much the dose is raised) does not apply to the kidney.

In the preceding discussion we have just barely mentioned the "topical stressors," but now we shall have to consider these a little more carefully before we turn our attention to the diseases of adaptation.

Concept of the local-adaptation syndrome. In Fig. 1 we have indicated that nonspecific damage to a limited tissue area can influence the pituitary-adrenal system and consequently initiate systemic reactions to stress. It has long been known, furthermore, that many local responses to injury are nonspecific; it has been observed, for instance, that a variety of topical stressors (burns, microbes, drugs) share the power of producing local nonspecific tissue damage and/or inflammation. However, it is only recently that the close relationship between the systemic and local types of nonspecific reactions has been more clearly established. While the characteristic response of the body to systemic stress is the general-adaptation syndrome, which is characterized by manifold morphologic and functional changes throughout the organism, topical stress elicits a local adaptation syndrome, the principal repercussions of which are confined to the immediate vicinity of the eliciting injury. They consist, on the one hand, of degeneration, atrophy, and necrosis and, on the other hand, of inflammation, hypertrophy, hyperplasia, and, under certain conditions, even of neoplasia.

At first sight, there appears to be no striking similarity between the systemic and the local reaction types. A patient in traumatic shock furnishes a characteristic example of the general-adaptation syndrome and, in particular, of its earliest stage, the shock phase of the general alarm reaction. On the other hand, an abscess formed around a splinter of wood represents a typical example of the local-adaptation syndrome and, in particular, of its stage of resistance, during which the defensive inflammatory phenomena predominate. On the surface, these two instances of disease reveal no striking similarities; yet more careful study shows them to be closely related: (i) both are nonspecific reactions, comprising damage and defense; (ii) both are triphasic (with systemic or local alarm, resistance, and exhaustion); (iii) both are singularly sensitive to the adaptive hormones (ACTH, STH, and corticoids); (iv) if the two reactions develop simultaneously in the same individual, they greatly influence each other—that is, systemic stress markedly alters tissue reactivity to local stress and vice versa.

The fundamental reaction pattern to topical stressors is a local-adaptation syndrome; to systemic stressors the fundamental reaction pattern is the general-adaptation syndrome. Various modifications of these two basic responses constitute the essence of most of the diseases known today.

ARE THERE DISEASES OF ADAPTATION?

By diseases of adaptation, we mean maladies that are caused principally by errors in the adaptation syndrome. Thus we arrived at the conclusion that the pathogenicity of many systemic and local stressors depends largely on the function of the hypophysis-adrenocortical system. The latter may either enhance or mitigate the body's defense reactions against stressors. We think that derailments of this adaptive mechanism are the principal factors in the production of certain maladies, which we consider, therefore, to be essentially diseases of adaptation (17).

It must be kept in mind that such diseases of adaptation do not necessarily become manifest during exposure to stress. This is clearly demonstrated by the observation that temporary overdosage with desoxycorticosterone can initiate a self-sustaining hypertension, which eventually leads to death, long after hormone administration has been discontinued. Here, we speak of "metacorticoid" lesions. The possibility that a temporary excess of endogenous mineralocorticoids could induce similar delayed maladies deserves serious consideration.

Among the derailments of the general-adaptation syndrome that may cause disease, the following are particularly important: (i) an absolute excess or deficiency in the amount of adaptive hormones (for example, corticoids, ACTH, and STH) produced during stress; (ii) an absolute excess or deficiency in the amount of adaptive hormones retained (or "fixed") by their peripheral target organs during stress; (iii) a disproportion in the relative secretion (or fixation) during stress of various antagonistic adaptive hormones (for example, ACTH and antiphlogistic corticoids, on the one hand, and STH and prophlogistic corticoids, on the other hand); (iv) the production by stress of metabolic derangements, which abnormally alter the target organ's response to adaptive hormones (through the phenomenon of "conditioning"); and (v) finally, we must not forget that, although the hypophysis-adrenal mechanism plays a prominent role in the general-adaptation syndrome, other organs that participate in the latter (for example, nervous system, liver, and kidney) may also respond abnormally and become the cause of disease during adaptation to stress.

With this in mind it may be convenient for investigative purposes to classify as "diseases of adaptation" those maladies in which an inadequacy of the adaptation syndrome plays a particularly important role. This means that the term should be used only when the maladaptation factor appears to be more important than the eliciting pathogen itself. No disease is purely a disease of adaptation, anymore than it could be purely a disease of the heart or an infectious disease, without overlap with other nosologic groups. Conversely, there is no disease in which adaptive phenomena play no part.

It is undoubtedly useful to realize, however, that some agents are virtually "unconditional pathogens," in that their influence on the tissues is so great that they cause damage almost irrespective of any sensitizing or adaptive factors (for example, immediate effect of x-rays or of severe thermal and mechanical injuries, and the actions of certain microorganisms to which everybody is susceptible.)

Most disease-producing agents, however, are to a greater or lesser extent "conditionally acting pathogens"; that is, their ability to produce illness is largely dependent on our adaptive reactions to them. Here, correct adaptation may prevent disease (for instance, a focus of tuberculosis perfectly held in check by an appropriate inflammatory barricade), but insufficient or excessive adaptive reactions may themselves be what we experience as illness (excessive and unnecessary inflammation around an otherwise harmless allergen).

APPLICATION OF ANIMAL EXPERIMENTS TO CLINICAL MEDICINE

Since most of the fundamental work on stress had been performed on laboratory animals, it was reasonable to question its applicability to problems of clinical medicine. It may now be said, however, that although there are certain differences in the stress response of every species, the general pattern of reaction is essentially the same in the various kinds of experimental animals and in man. Furthermore, a good deal of evidence has accumulated in support of the view that the experimental similes of spontaneous diseases produced in animals by exposure to stress, or by overdosage with certain adaptive hormones, are closely related to the corresponding maladies of man.

Let us merely mention a few of the most striking similarities in the responses to stress and to adaptive hormones of animals and man.

Morphologic and functional adrenocortical changes during stress. There can be no doubt that, during intense stress (for example, severe mechanical or thermal injuries and massive infections), the adrenal cortex of man, just as that of laboratory animals, shows morphologic changes characteristic of hyperactivity. At the same time, there is a demonstrable increase in the blood concentration and urinary excretion of corticoids and their metabolites. The other manifestations (morphologic, functional, and chemical) of the stress syndrome also failed to exhibit any fundamental dissimilarity in the reaction patterns of animals and man.

Corticoid requirements during stress. During stress, the corticoid requirements of all mammals are far above normal. After destruction of the adrenals by disease (as after their surgical removal), the daily dose of corticoids, necessary for the maintenance of well-being at rest, is comparatively small, but it rises sharply during stress (for example, cold, intercurrent infections, and hemorrhage), both in experimental animals and in man.

Anti-inflammatory effects of corticoids. The same antiphlogistic corticoids (cortisone and cortisol) that were shown to inhibit various types of experimental inflammations in laboratory animals exert similar effects in a human being afflicted by inflammatory diseases (for example, rheumatoid arthritis, rheumatic fever, and allergic inflammations).

Sensitivity to infection after treatment with antiphlogistic corticoids. In experimental animals, the suppression of inflammation by antiphlogistic hormones is frequently accompanied by an increased sensitivity to infection, presumably because the encapsulation of microbial foci is less effective and perhaps partly also because serologic defense is diminished. Thus, even a species naturally resistant to the human type of tuberculosis, such as the rat, can contract this disease during overdosage with ACTH or cortisone. Similarly, in patients undergoing intense treatment with antiphlogistic hormones (for example, for rheumatoid arthritis), a previously latent tuberculous focus may suddenly spread. It is a well-known fact that in patients suffering from tuberculosis the disease is especially readily aggravated by exposure to any kind of stress situation. Rest cures have long been practiced in view of this. It is perhaps not too farfetched to consider the possibility that an increased ACTH and cortisol secretion during stress may play an important part in the development of clinical tuberculosis.

Sensitization to mineralocorticoids by sodium and the buffering effect of the adrenals. In experimental animals, mineralocorticoids tend to raise the blood pressure and to cause vascular and renal damage (nephrosis and nephrosclerosis) often with edema. This effect is aggravated by simultaneous treatment with sodium chloride and becomes particularly severe after adrenalectomy. Similarly, in man on a high sodium intake, and especially after adrenalectomy, otherwise nontoxic doses of desoxycorticosterone will produce hypertension and edema. Apparently, in man as in the laboratory animal, sodium acts as a conditioning factor for mineralocorticoids, while the adrenal exerts a buffering effect.

This may also explain why, in many cases of clinical hypertension, bilateral adrenalectomy exerts a beneficial effect, as long as only cortisone or cortisol is used for substitution therapy, while treatment with desoxycorticosterone restores or further aggravates the hypertensive disease. Apparently, the adrenals of these patients produce some desoxycorticosteronelike factor that plays at least an adjuvant role in the pathogenesis of hypertension.

In patients suffering from rheumatoid arthritis, adrenalectomy has also been reported to exert a beneficial influence if only glucocorticoids are used for maintenance. Furthermore desoxycorticosterone tends to elicit arthritic changes only in the adrenal-deficient but not in the intact patient. This effect of desoxycorticosterone is, in turn, corrected by simultaneous cortisone treatment.

Finally, let us point out that, both in man and in animals, the various characteristic effects of cortisone are also obtained at especially low dose levels after adrenalectomy.

Psychological and psychiatric effects of corticoid overdosage. Considerable attention has been given of late to the possible mental effects of stress and of the adaptive hormones. It would be beyond the scope of this article (and certainly outside my competence) to discuss these in detail, but a few remarks based on our experimental observations may be in order.

It has long been noted that various steroids—including desoxycorticosterone, cortisone, progesterone, and many others—can produce in a variety of animal species (even in primates such as the rhesus monkey) a state of great excitation followed by deep anesthesia. It has more recently been shown that such steroid anesthesia can also be produced in man, and, of course, the marked emotional changes (sometimes bordering on psychosis) that may occur in predisposed individuals during treatment with ACTH, cortisone, and cortisol are well known. Several laboratories reported furthermore that the electroshock threshold of experimental animals and their sensitivity to anesthetics can be affected by corticoids.

Thus, it appears very probable that corticoids secreted during stress also have an important influence on nervous and emotional reactions. Conversely, it is now definitely established that nervous stressors (pain and emotions) are particularly conducive to the development of the somatic manifestations of the stress syndrome; thus stress can both cause and be caused by mental reactions.

In conclusion, let us reemphasize that no illness is exclusively a disease of adaptation, but considerable evidence has accumulated in favor of the view that stress, and particularly the adaptive hormones produced during stress, exert an important regulating influence on the development of numerous maladies.

It is virtually certain that our concepts concerning the role of pituitary and corticoid hormones in the pathogenesis of certain diseases of adaptation will have to undergo modifications as more facts become known. However this is true with every theory. The same was true, for instance, of the original theory that related diabetes to a simple hypoinsulinism, when the role of the anterior pituitary was discovered. Yet, the realization of some pathogenic relationship between insulin and diabetes was an almost indispensable step in the subsequent development of this field.

The best theory is that which necessitates the minimum number of assumptions to unite the maximum number of facts, since such a theory is most likely to possess the power of assimilating new facts from the unknown without damage to its own structure. Our facts must be correct; our theories need not be if they help us to discover new facts, even if these discoveries necessitate some changes in the structure of the theory.

Meanwhile, the stress theory, as outlined in this article, permits us to correlate the known facts and furnishes a concrete plan for the systematic development of this field through planned investigation rather than through the mere empirical collection of chance observations.

OUTLOOK

Pasteur, Koch, and their contemporaries introduced the concept of specificity into medicine, a concept that has proved to be of the greatest heuristic value up to the present time. Each individual, well-defined disease, they held, has its own specific cause. It has been claimed by many that Pasteur failed to recognize the importance of the "terrain," because he was too preoccupied with the pathogen (microorganism) itself. His work on induced immunity shows that this is incorrect. Indeed, at the end of his life he allegedly said, "Le microbe n'est rien, le terrain est tout."

The theory that directed the most fruitful investigations of Pasteur and his followers was that the organism can develop specific adaptive reactions against individual pathogens and that by imitating and complementing these, whenever they are short of optimal, we can treat many of the diseases that are caused by specific pathogens.

To my mind, the general-adaptation syndrome represents, in a sense, the negative counterpart, or mirror image, of this concept. It holds that many diseases have no single cause, no specific pathogen, but are largely due to nonspecific stress and to pathogenic situations that result from inappropriate responses to such nonspecific stress.

Our blueprint of the pathways through which stress acts may be partly incorrect; it is certainly quite incomplete. But in it we have a basis for the objective scientific dissection of such time-honored, but hitherto rather vague, concepts as the role of "reactivity," "constitution and resistance," or "nonspecific therapy," in the genesis and treatment of disease.

If I may venture a prediction, I would like to reiterate my opinion that research on stress will be most fruitful if it is guided by the principle that we must learn to imitate—and if necessary to correct and complement—the body's own autopharmacologic efforts to combat the stress factor in disease.

REFERENCES AND NOTES

1. H. Selye, *Nature* **138**, 32 (1936).
2. H. Selye, *Stress. The Physiology and Pathology of Exposure to Stress* (Acta, Montreal, 1950).
3. H. Selye, *The Story of the Adaptation Syndrome* (Acta, Montreal, 1952).
4. H. G. Wolff, *Stress and Disease* (Thomas, Springfield, Ill., 1953).
5. H. G. Wolff, S. G. Wolf, C. C. Hare, Eds., "Life Stress

and Bodily Disease," *Research Publs. Assoc. Research Nervous Mental Disease* **29** (1950).
6. United States Army Medical Service Graduate School and Division of Medical Sciences, National Research Council (Sponsors), Symposium on Stress, Walter Reed Army Medical Center, Washington, D. C., March 16th–18th (1953).
7. H. Ogilvie and W. A. R. Thomson, Eds., "Stress," *The Practitioner* **172**, No. 1027 (1954).
8. R. Q. Pasqualini, *Stress.* Enfermedades de Adaptacion. ACTH y Cortisona (Libreria El Ateneo, Buenos Aires, 1952).
9. I. Galdston, Ed., *Beyond the Germ Theory* (N.Y. Acad. Med. Health Education Council, New York, 1954).
10. J. Jensen, *Modern Concepts in Medicine* (Mosby, St. Louis, Mo., 1953).
11. H. Selye, *First Annual Report on Stress* (Acta, Montreal, 1951).
12. H. Selye and A. Horava, *Second Annual Report on Stress* (Acta, Montreal, 1951).
13. H. Selye and A. Horava, *Third Annual Report on Stress* (Acta, Montreal, 1953).
14. H. Selye and G. Heuser, *Fourth Annual Report on Stress* (Acta, Montreal, 1954).
15. The major part of the investigations upon which this article is based was subsidized in part by a consolidated grant from the National Research Council of Canada and in part by the Medical Research Board, Office of the Surgeon General, Department of the Army, contract DA-49-007-MD-186.
16. D. J. Ingle, in *Recent Progress in Hormone Research* (Academic Press, New York, 1951), vol. **6**, p. 159.
17. H. Selye, *J. Clin. Endocrinol.* **6**, 117 (1946).
18. H. Selye and P. Bois, in *Fourth Annual Report on Stress,* H. Selye and G. Heuser, Eds. (Acta, Montreal, 1954), pp. 533–552.

Avoidance Behavior and the Development of Gastroduodenal Ulcers

Joseph V. Brady
Robert W. Porter
Donald G. Conrad
John W. Mason

Observations in our laboratory over the past year or more have revealed the development of extensive gastrointestinal lesions in a series of some 15 monkeys restrained in chairs and subjected to a variety of prolonged behavioral conditioning and/or intracerebral self-stimulation experiments (1). The behavioral studies focused upon emotional conditioning procedures of the "fear" or "anxiety" type, and upon avoidance of noxious electric shocks to the feet. Intracerebral self-stimulation through chronically implanted electrodes involved various limbic-system structures. While the program for each animal in this initial series varied considerably, all were subjected to intensive experimental study for at least 2 to 8 weeks. Five control monkeys, subjected only to restraint in the chair for similar periods, however, showed no gastrointestinal complications.

The present report describes the results of an experiment designed to define some of the more specific behavioral factors contributing to the etiology of this lethal pathological picture. Eight rhesus monkeys, restrained in chairs, as illustrated in Fig. 1, were divided into pairs and conditioned according to a "yoked-chair" avoidance procedure. Each pair of monkeys received brief electric shocks (5 milliamperes, 60-cycle AC, for 0.5 second) to the feet from a common source every 20 seconds unless the experimental animal of the pair pressed a lever which delayed the shock another 20 seconds for both animals (2). Inactivation of the lever available to the control animal insured an equal number and temporal distribution of shocks to both monkeys ("physical trauma"), while providing the avoidance contingency for only the experimental animal. Each pair of monkeys received 6-hour sessions on this procedure, alternating with 6-hour "off-periods" (no shocks) 24 hours each day for periods up to 6 or 7 weeks. A red light was illuminated in plain view of both animals during the 6-hour "avoidance" periods, and was turned out during the 6-hour off-periods. The experimental procedure was programmed and the animal's behavior recorded automatically by timers, magnetic counters, cumulative-work recorders, and associated relay circuits. Lever responses and shocks were recorded continuously for all animals, and separate counts were maintained for the avoidance periods and for the off-periods. Throughout the entire experiment, urine was collected continuously from all animals in 24- or 48-hour samples for 17-hydroxycorticosteroid determinations.

From *Journal of the Experimental Analysis of Behavior,* 1958, 1, 69–72.

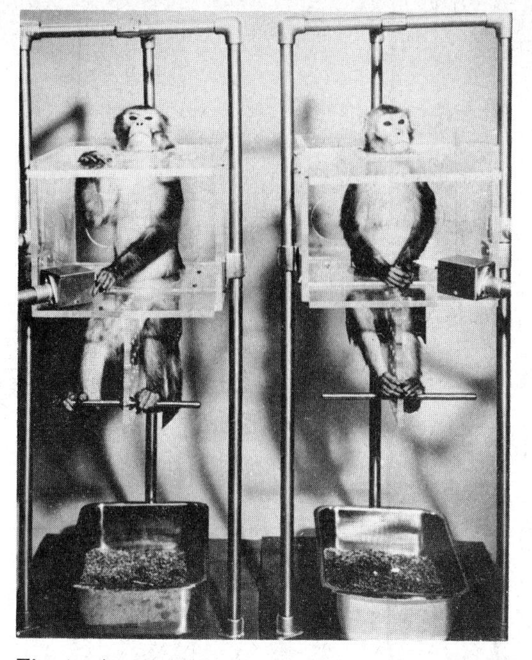

Fig. 1. An experimental monkey and a control monkey, gently restrained in primate chairs, illustrate the "yoked-chair" avoidance situation. The lever available to each animal is shown within easy reach, although only the experimental "avoidance" monkey on the left is observed to press the lever.

The avoidance behavior was trained initially during two preliminary daily sessions of 2 to 4 hours. The training procedure involved the use of a short 5-second interval between shocks in the absence of a lever response (the "shock-shock" or "S-S" interval) and a 20-second interval between lever responses and shocks (the "response-shock" or "R-S" interval). At the outset, a lever response by either animal of a given pair delayed the shock for both animals and no further "shaping" of the behavior was attempted. Within the first preliminary session, however, one monkey of each pair was observed to develop avoidance lever-pressing before its partner and was selected as the experimental animal. At this point in the preliminary training procedure, both the "shock-shock" and the "response-shock" intervals were set at 20 seconds and the control monkey's lever was made ineffective with respect to avoiding shocks for the remainder of the experiment.

Within a few hours after the initiation of the alternating 6-hour sessions, the experimental animals of each pair had developed stable avoidance lever-pressing rates (Fig. 2) which showed little change throughout the experiment. Responses during the 6-hour off-periods in the absence of the red light rapidly dropped to a low level, as shown in Fig. 2, and also remained there throughout the experiment. Since the lever-pressing rates for the experimental animals during the 6-hour avoidance periods approximated 15 to 20 responses per minute, the behavior effectively prevented all but an occasional shock for both animals throughout the alternating 6-hour "on-off" cycles of any given 24-hour period. The shock rates never exceeded 2 per hour during the 6-hour avoidance periods, and typically averaged less than 1 per hour. For the most part, only somewhat variable "operant levels" of lever-pressing were maintained by the control animals of each pair, although one of these animals did appear to develop what might be termed a "superstitious avoidance" rate during the 3-week alternating procedure. From an initial rate not exceeding 1 response per hour during the first few days of the procedure, this control monkey gradually increased his output to 2 responses per minute by the 10th day, and ultimately reached a peak of 5 responses per minute on the 20th day. During the succeeding 5-day period, however, his rate again gradually declined to relatively high levels of considerably less than 1 response per minute. Throughout this entire period, the experimental animal of this pair maintained a lever-pressing response rate of almost 20 responses per minute.

Measurement of the urinary excretion of total 17-hydroxycorticosteroids (17-OH-CS) at selected stages during the experiment revealed slight increases in the 24-hour 17-OH-CS output in both monkeys of each pair during the initial phases of avoidance conditioning. Otherwise, the samples tested in subsequent phases of the experiments showed no evidence of increased adrenal cortical activity, as judged by the 24-hour 17-OH-CS excretion. Fluctuations outside the normal range which may have occurred within individual 6-hour avoidance or rest periods cannot, however, be excluded by the data on 24-hour urine portions.

With the first pair of monkeys, the death of the avoidance animal after 23 days terminated the experiment during one of the 6-hour avoidance periods. With the second pair, the avoidance monkey again expired during one of the 6-hour "on-periods," this time 25 days after the start of the

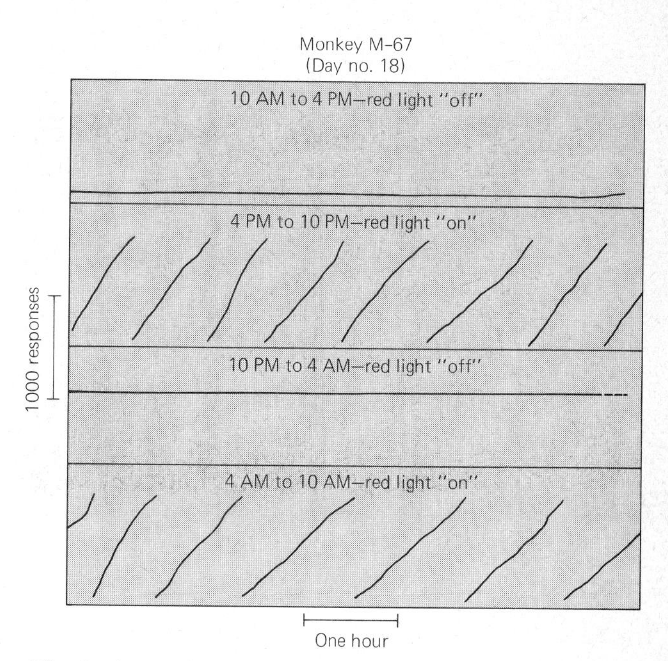

Fig. 2. A sample cumulative-response curve showing one 24-hour session (alternating 6-hour "on-off" cycles) for experimental "avoidance" monkey M-07 on day No. 18. The oblique "pips" on the record indicate shocks.

experiment. With the third pair in this series, the death of the experimental animal again terminated the experiment during one of the avoidance cycles, this time only 9 days after initiation of the alternating 6-hour on-off procedure. And the experimental animal of the fourth pair of monkeys was sacrificed in a moribund condition after 48 days on the avoidance procedure. In all instances, gross and microscopic analysis revealed the presence of extensive gastrointestinal lesions with ulceration as a prominent feature of the pathological picture in the experimental animals. However, none of the control animals sacrificed for comparison with their experimental partners and subjected to complete postmortem examination, showed any indications of such gastrointestinal complications.

The results obtained with this technique, while consistent with previous reports of experimentally produced "psychosomatic" conditions (3), must be considered only as the initial findings of a programmatic effort to systematically define the variables of which this phenomenon may be a function. Follow-up studies, presently in progress, strongly suggest that selection criteria for experimental and control animals, relative degrees of "social contact" or isolation during the experiment, and possibly even constitutional factors may play a critical role in the development of gastrointestinal pathology as a consequence of such "behavioral stress."

REFERENCES

1. Porter, R. W., Brady, J. V., Conrad, D. G., and Mason, J. W. Occurrence of gastrointestinal lesions in behaviorally conditioned and intracerebral self-stimulated monkeys. *Federation Proc.*, 1957, **16**, 101–102.
2. Sidman, M. Avoidance conditioning with brief shock and no exteroceptive warning signal. *Science.* 1953, **118**, 157–158.
3. Sawrey, W. L., Conger, J. J., and Turrell, E. S. An experimental investigation of the role of psychological factors in the production of gastric ulcers in rats. *J. comp. physiol. Psychol.*, 1956, **49**, 457–461.

Obesity and Eating*

Stanley Schachter

Internal and external cues differentially affect the eating behavior of obese and normal subjects.

Current conceptions of hunger control mechanisms indicate that food deprivation leads to various peripheral physiological changes such as modification of blood constituents, increase in gastric motility, changes in body temperature, and the like. By means of some still debated mechanism, these changes are detected by a hypothalamic feeding center. Presumably some or all facets of this activated machinery lead the organism to search out and consume food. There appears to be no doubt that peripheral physiological changes and activation of the hypothalamic feeding center are inevitable consequences of food deprivation. On the basis of current knowledge, however, one may ask, when this biological machinery is activated, do we necessarily describe ourselves as hungry, and eat? For most of us raised on the notion that hunger is the most primitive of motives, wired into the animal and unmistakable in its cues, the question may seem far-fetched, but there is increasing reason to suspect that there are major individual differences in the extent to which these physiological changes are associated with the desire to eat.

On the clinical level, the analyst Hilde Bruch (1) has observed that her obese patients literally do not know when they are physiologically hungry. To account for this observation she suggests that, during childhood, these patients were not taught to discriminate between hunger and such states as fear, anger, and anxiety. If this is so, these people may be labeling almost any state of arousal "hunger," or, alternatively, labeling no internal state "hunger."

If Bruch's speculations are correct, it should be anticipated that the set of physiological symptoms which are considered characteristic of food deprivation are not labeled "hunger" by the obese. In other words the obese literally may not know when they are physiologically hungry. For at least one of the presumed physiological correlates of food deprivation, this does appear to be the case. In an absorbing study, Stunkard (2, 3) has related gastric motility to self-reports of hunger in 37 obese subjects and 37 subjects of normal size. A subject, who had eaten no breakfast, came to the laboratory at 9 a.m.; he swallowed a gastric balloon, and for 4 hours Stunkard

From *Science*, 1968, **161**, 751–756.

*This article is based on a speech delivered at a conference entitled "Biology and Behavior: Neurophysiology and Emotion," held at the Rockefeller University, New York, on 10 December 1965, under the sponsorship of Russell Sage Foundation and the Rockefeller University.

continuously recorded gastric motility. Every 15 minutes the subject was asked if he was hungry. He answered "yes" or "no," and that is all there was to the study. We have, then, a record of the extent to which a subject's self-report of hunger corresponds to his gastric motility. The results show (i) that obese and normal subjects do not differ significantly in degree of gastric motility, and (ii) that, when the stomach is not contracting, the reports of obese and normal subjects are quite similar, both groups reporting hunger roughly 38 percent of the time. When the stomach is contracting, however, the reports of the two groups differ markedly. For normal subjects, self-report of hunger coincides with gastric motility 71 percent of the time. For the obese, the percentage is only 47.6. Stunkard's work seems to indicate that obese and normal subjects do not refer to the same bodily state when they use the term *hunger.*

EFFECTS OF FOOD DEPRIVATION AND FEAR

If this inference is correct, we should anticipate that, if we were to directly manipulate gastric motility and the other symptoms that we associate with hunger, we would, for normal subjects, be directly manipulating feelings of hunger and eating behavior. For the obese there would be no correspondence between manipulated internal state and eating behavior. To test these expectations, Goldman, Gordon, and I (4) performed an experiment in which bodily state was manipulated by two means—(i) by the obvious technique of manipulating food deprivation, so that some subjects had empty stomachs and others had full stomachs before eating; (ii) by manipulating fear, so that some subjects were badly frightened and others were quite calm immediately before eating. Carlson (5) has indicated that fear inhibits gastric motility; Cannon (6) also has demonstrated that fear inhibits motility, and has shown that it leads to the liberation, from the liver, of sugar into the blood. Hypoglycemia and gastric contractions are generally considered the chief peripheral physiological correlates of food deprivation.

Our experiment was conducted under the guise of a study of taste. A subject came to the laboratory in mid-afternoon or evening. He had been called the previous evening and asked not to eat the meal (lunch or dinner) preceding his appointment at the laboratory. The experiment was introduced as a study of "the interdependence of the basic human senses—of the way in which the stimulation of one sense affects another." Specifically, the subject was told that this study would be concerned with "the effects of tactile stimulation on the way things taste."

It was explained that all subjects had been asked not to eat a meal before coming to the laboratory because "in any scientific experiment it is necessary that the subjects be as similar as possible in all relevant ways. As you probably know from your own experience," the experimenter continued, "an important factor in determining how things taste is what you have recently eaten." The introduction over, the experimenter then proceeded as follows.

For the "full stomach" condition he said to the subject, "In order to guarantee that your recent taste experiences are similar to those of other subjects who have taken part in this experiment, we should now like you to eat exactly the same thing they did. Just help yourself to the roast beef sandwiches on the table. Eat as much as you want—till you're full."

For the "empty stomach" condition, the subjects, of course, were not fed.

Next, the subject was seated in front of five bowls of crackers and told, "We want you to taste five different kinds of crackers and tell us how they taste to you." The experimenter then gave the subject a long set of rating scales and said, "We want you to judge each cracker on the dimensions (salty, cheesy, garlicky, and so on) listed on this sheet. Taste as many or as few of the crackers of each type as you want in making your judgments; the important thing is that your ratings be as accurate as possible."

Before permitting the subject to eat, the experimenter continued with the next stage of the experiment—the manipulation of fear.

"As I mentioned," he said, "our primary interest in this experiment is the effect of tactile stimulation on taste. Electric stimulation is the means we use to excite your skin receptors. We use this method in order to carefully control the amount of stimulation you receive."

For the "low fear" condition the subject was told, "For the effects in which we are interested, we need to use only the lowest level of stimulation. At most you will feel a slight tingle. Probably you will feel nothing at all. We are only interested in the effect of very weak stimulation."

For the "high fear" condition the experimenter pointed to a large black console loaded with electrical junk and said, "That machine is the one we will be using. I am afraid that these shocks will be painful. For them to have any effect on your taste sensations, the voltage must be rather high. There will, of course, be no permanent damage. Do you have a heart condition?" A large electrode connected to the console was then attached to each of the subject's ankles, and the experimenter concluded, "The best way for us to test the effect of tactile stimulation is to have you rate the crackers now, before the electric shock, and then rate them again, after the shock, to see what changes in your ratings the shock has made."

The subject then proceeded to taste and rate crackers for 15 minutes, under the impression that this was a taste test; meanwhile we were simply counting the number of crackers he ate (7). We then had measures of the amounts eaten by subjects who initially had either empty or full stomachs and who were initially either frightened or calm. There were of course, two types of subjects: obese subjects (from 14 percent to 75 percent overweight) and normal subjects (from 8 percent underweight to 9 percent overweight).

To review expectations: If we were correct in thinking that the obese do not label as hunger the bodily states associated with food deprivation, then our several experimental manipulations should have had no effects on the amount eaten by obese subjects; on the other hand, the eating behavior of normal subjects should have directly paralleled the effects of the manipulations on bodily state.

It will be a surprise to no one to learn, from Fig. 1, that the normal subjects ate considerably fewer crackers when their stomachs were full than when their stomachs were empty. The results for obese subjects stand in fascinating contrast. They ate as much—in fact, slightly more—when

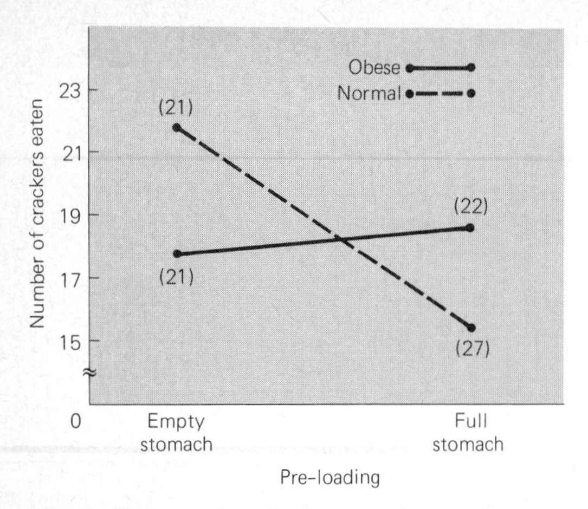

Fig. 1. Effects of preliminary eating on the amounts eaten during the experiment by normal and obese subjects. Numbers in parentheses are numbers of subjects.

their stomachs were full as when they were empty (interaction $P < .05$). Obviously the actual state of the stomach has nothing to do with the eating behavior of the obese.

In Fig. 2, pertaining to the effect of fear, we note an analogous picture. Fear markedly decreased the number of crackers the normal subjects ate but had no effect on the number eaten by the obese (interaction $P < .01$). Again, there was a small, though nonsignificant, reversal: the fearful obese ate slightly more than the calm obese.

It seems clear that the set of bodily symptoms the subject labels "hunger" differs for obese and normal subjects. Whether one measures gastric motility, as Stunkard did, or manipulates it, as I assume my co-workers and I have done, one finds, for normal subjects, a high degree of correspondence between the state of the gut and eating behavior and, for obese subjects, virtually no correspondence. While all of our manipulations have had a major effect on the amounts eaten by normal subjects, nothing that we have done has had a substantial effect on the amounts eaten by obese subjects.

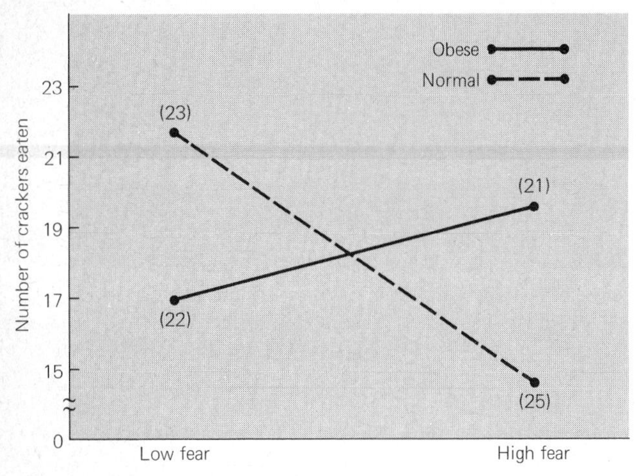

Fig. 2. Effects of fear on the amounts eaten by normal and obese subjects. Numbers in parentheses are numbers of subjects.

EFFECTS OF THE CIRCUMSTANCES OF EATING

With these facts in mind, let us turn to the work of Hashim and Van Itallie (8) of the Nutrition Clinic, St. Luke's Hospital, New York City. Their findings may be summarized as follows: virtually everything these workers do seems to have a major effect on the eating behavior of the obese and almost no effect on the eating behavior of the normal subject.

These researchers have prepared a bland liquid diet similar to commercial preparations such as vanilla-flavored Nutrament or Metrecal. The subjects are restricted to this monotonous diet for periods ranging from a week to several months. They can eat as much or as little of it as they want. Some of the subjects get a pitcher full and pour themselves a meal any time they wish. Other subjects are fed by a machine which delivers a mouthful every time the subject presses a button. With either feeding technique, the eating situation has the following characteristics. (i) The food itself is unappealing. (ii) Eating is entirely self-determined: whether or not the subject eats, how much he eats, and when he eats are matters decided by him and no one else. Absolutely no pressure is brought to bear to limit his consumption. (iii) The eating situation is devoid of any social or domestic trappings. It is basic eating; it will keep the subject alive, but it's not much fun.

To date, six grossly obese and five normal individuals have been subjects in these studies. In Fig. 3 the eating curves for a typical pair of subjects over a 21-day period are plotted. Both subjects were healthy people who lived in the hospital during the entire study. The obese subject was a 52-year-old woman, 5 feet 3 inches (1.6 meters) tall, who weighed 307 pounds (138 kilograms) on admission. The normal subject was a 30-year-old male, 5 feet 7 inches tall, who weighed 132 pounds.

The subject's estimated daily caloric intake before entering the hospital (as determined from a detailed interview) is plotted at the left in Fig. 3. Each subject, while in the hospital but before entering upon the experimental regime, was fed a general hospital diet. The obese subject was placed on a 2400-calorie diet for 7 days and a 1200-calorie diet for the next 8 days. As may be seen in Fig. 3, she ate everything on her tray throughout this 15-day period. The normal subject was placed on a 2400-calorie diet for 2 days, and he too ate everything.

With the beginning of the experiment proper, the difference in the eating behavior of the two subjects was dramatic and startling. The food consumption of the obese subject dropped precipitately the moment she entered upon the experimental regime, and it remained at an incredibly low level for the duration of the experiment. This effect is so dramatic that the weight of one obese subject who took part in the experiment for 8 months dropped from 410 to 190 pounds. On the other hand, the food consumption of the normal subject of Fig. 3 dropped slightly on the first 2 days, then returned to a fairly steady 2300 grams or so of food a day. The curves for these two subjects are typical. Each of the six obese subjects has manifested this marked and persistent decrease in food consumption during the experiment; each of the normal subjects has steadily consumed about his normal amount of food.

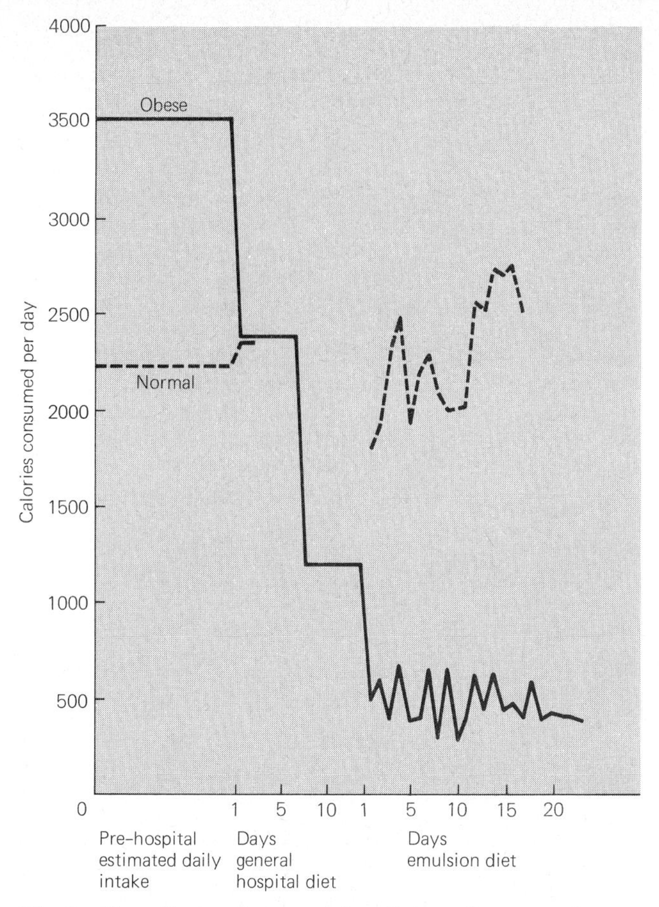

Fig. 3. The effects of an emulsion diet on the amounts eaten by an obese and a normal subject.

Before suggesting possible interpretations, I should note certain marked differences between these two groups of subjects. Most important, the obese subjects had come to the clinic for help in solving their weight problem and were, of course, motivated to lose weight. The normal subjects were simply volunteers. Doubtless this difference could account for the observed difference in eating behavior during the experiment, and until obese volunteers, unconcerned with their weight, are used as subjects in similar studies, we cannot be sure of the interpretation of this phenomenon. However, I think we should not, solely on grounds of methodological fastidiousness, dismiss these findings. It was concern with weight that brought these obese subjects to the clinic. Each of them, before entering the hospital and while in the hospital before being put on the experimental diet, was motivated to lose weight. Yet, despite this motivation, none of these subjects had been capable of restricting his diet at home, and each of them, when fed the general hospital diet, had eaten everything on his tray. Only when the food was dull and the act of eating was self-initiated and devoid of any ritual trappings did the obese subject, motivated or not, severely limit his consumption.

INTERNAL AND EXTERNAL CONTROL

On the one hand, then, our experiments indicate virtually no relationship between internal physiological state and the eating behavior of the obese subject; on the other hand, these case studies seem to indicate a close tie between the eating behavior of the obese and what might be called the circumstances of eating. When the food is dull and the eating situation is uninteresting, the obese subject eats virtually nothing. For the normal subject, the situation is just the reverse: his eating behavior seems directly linked to his physiological state but is relatively unaffected by the external circumstances or the ritual associated with eating.

Given this set of facts it seems clear that eating is triggered by different sets of stimuli in obese and normal subjects. Indeed, there is growing reason to suspect that the eating behavior of the obese is relatively unrelated to any internal state but is, in large part, under external control, being initiated and terminated by stimuli external to the organism. Let me give a few examples. A person whose eating behavior is under external control will stroll by a pastry shop, find the food in the window irresistible, and, even if he has recently eaten, go in and buy something. He will pass by a hamburger stand, smell the broiling meat, and, even though he has just eaten, buy a hamburger. Obviously such external factors—smell, sight, taste, other people's actions—to some extent affect anyone's eating. However, in normal individuals such external factors interact with internal state. They may affect what, where, and how much the normal individual eats, but they do so chiefly when he is in a state of physiological hunger. For the obese, I suggest, internal state is irrelevant and eating is determined largely by external factors.

This hypothesis obviously fits the data presented here, as well it should, since it is an *ad hoc* construction designed specifically to fit these data. Let us see, then, what independent support there is for the hypothesis, and where the hypothesis leads.

EFFECTS OF MANIPULATING TIME

Among the multitude of external food-relevant cues, one of the most intriguing is the passage of time. Everyone "knows" that 4 to 6 hours after eating his last meal he should eat his next one. Everyone "knows" that, within narrow limits, there are set times for eating regular meals. We should, then, expect that if we manipulate time we should be able to manipulate the eating behavior of the obese subjects. In order to do this, Gross and I (9) simply gimmicked two clocks so that one ran at half normal speed and the other, at twice normal speed. A subject arrives at 5:00 p.m., ostensibly to take part in an experiment on the relationship of base levels of autonomic reactivity to personality factors. He is ushered into a windowless room containing nothing but electronic equipment and a clock. Electrodes are put on his wrists, his watch is removed "so that it will not get gummed up with electrode jelly," and he is connected to a polygraph. All this takes 5 minutes, and at 5:05 he is left alone, with nothing to do for a true 30 minutes, while ostensibly we are getting a record of galvanic skin response and cardiac rate in a subject at rest. There are two experimental conditions. In one, the experimenter returns after a true 30 minutes and the clock reads 5:20. In the other, the clock reads 6:05, which is normal dinner time for most subjects. In both cases the experimenter is carrying a box of crackers and nibbling a cracker as he comes into the room; he puts the box down, invites the subject to help himself, removes the electrodes from the subject's wrists, and proceeds with personality testing for exactly 5 minutes. This done, he gives the subject a personality inventory which he is to complete and leaves him alone with the box of crackers for another true 10 minutes. There are two groups of subjects—normal and obese—and the only datum we collect is the weight of the box of crackers before and after the subject has had a chance at it.

If these ideas on internal and external controls of eating behavior are correct, normal subjects, whose eating behavior is presumably linked to internal state, should be relatively unaffected by the manipulation and should eat roughly the same number of crackers regardless of whether the clock reads 5:20 or 6:05. The obese, on the other hand, whose eating behavior is presumably under external control, should eat very few crackers when the clock reads 5:20 and a great many crackers when it reads 6:05.

The data of Fig. 4 do indeed indicate that the obese subjects eat almost twice as many crackers when they think the time is 6:05 as they do when they believe it to be 5:20. For normal subjects, the trend is just the reverse (interaction $P = .002$)—an unanticipated finding but one which seems embarrassingly simple to explain, as witness the several normal subjects who thought the time was 6:05 and politely refused the crackers, saying, "No thanks, I don't want to spoil my dinner." Obviously cognitive factors affected the eating behavior of both the normal and the obese subjects, but there was a vast difference. While the manipulation of the clock served to trigger or stimulate eating among the obese, it had the opposite effect on normal subjects, most of whom at this hour were, we presume, physiologically hungry, aware that they would eat dinner very shortly, and unwilling to spoil their dinner by filling up on crackers.

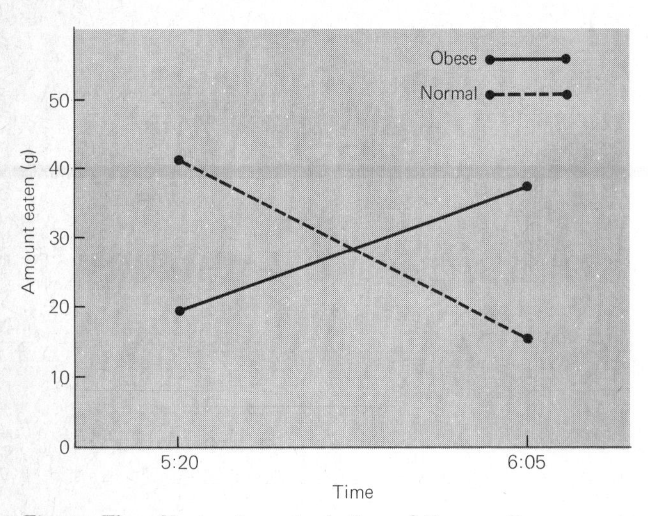

Fig. 4. The effects of manipulation of time on the amounts eaten by obese and normal subjects.

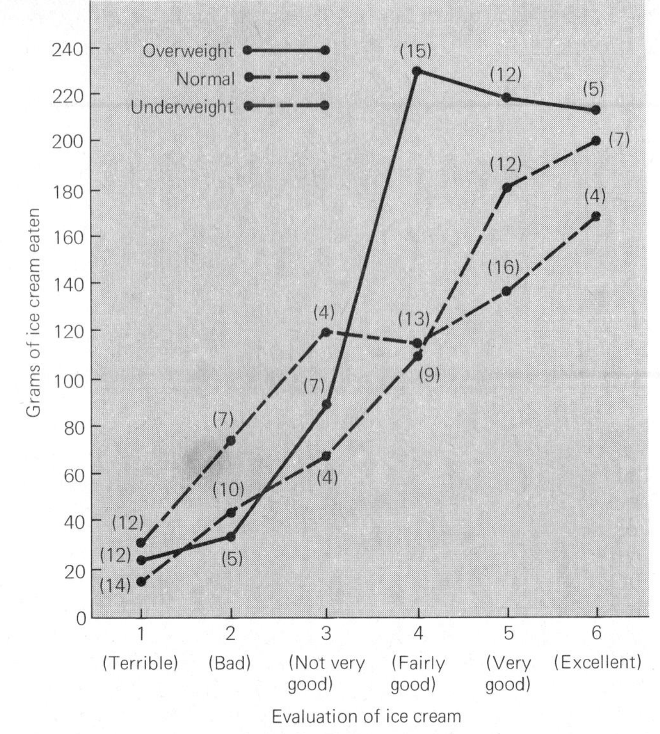

Fig. 5. The effects of food quality on the amounts eaten by obese, normal, and underweight subjects. Numbers in parentheses are numbers of subjects.

EFFECTS OF TASTE

In another study, Nisbett (10) examined the effects of taste on eating behavior. Nisbett reasoned that taste, like the sight or smell of food, is essentially an external stimulus to eating. Nisbett, in his experiment, also extended the range of weight deviation by including a group of underweight subjects as well as obese and normal subjects. His purpose in so doing was to examine the hypothesis that the relative potency of external versus internal controls is a dimension directly related to the degree of overweight. If the hypothesis was correct, he reasoned, the taste of food would have the greatest impact on the amounts eaten by obese subjects and the least impact on the amounts eaten by underweight subjects. To test this, Nisbett had his subjects eat as much as they wanted of one of two kinds of vanilla ice cream; one was a delicious and expensive product, the other an acrid concoction of cheap vanilla and quinine which he called "vanilla bitters." The effects of taste are presented in Fig. 5, in which the subjects ratings of how good or bad the ice cream is are plotted against the amount eaten. As may be seen in Fig. 5, when the ice cream was rated "fairly good" or better, the obese subjects ate considerably more than the normal subjects did; these, in turn, ate more than the underweight subjects did. When the ice cream was rated "not very good" or worse, the ordering tended to reverse: the underweight subjects ate more than either the normal or the obese subjects. This experiment, then, indicates that the external, or at least nonvisceral, cue *taste* does have differential effects on the eating behavior of underweight, normal, and obese subjects.

The indications, from Nisbett's experiment, that the degree of dependence on external cues relative to internal cues varies with deviation from normal weight are intriguing, for, if further work supports this hypothesis, we may have the beginnings of a plausible explanation of why the thin are thin and the fat are fat. We know from Carlson's work (5) that gastric contractions cease after a small amount of food has been introduced into the stomach. To the extent that such contractions are directly related to the hunger "experience"—to the extent that a person's eating is under internal control—he should "eat like a bird," eating only enough to stop the contractions. Eating beyond this point should be a function of external cues—the taste, sight, and smell of food. Individuals whose eating is externally controlled, then, should find it hard to stop eating. This hypothesis may account for the notorious "binge" eating of the obese (11) or the monumental meals described in loving detail by students (12) of the great, fat gastronomic magnificoes.

This rough attempt to explain why the obese are obese in itself raises intriguing questions. For example, does the external control of eating behavior inevitably lead to obesity? It is evident, I believe, that not only is such a linkage logically not inevitable but that the condition of external control of eating may in rare but specifiable circumstances lead to emaciation. A person whose eating is externally controlled should eat and grow fat when food-related cues are abundant and when he is fully aware of them. However, when such cues are lacking or when for some reason, such as withdrawal or depression, the individual is unaware of the cues, the person under external control would, one would expect, not eat, and, if the condition persisted, would grow "concentration-camp" thin. From study of the clinical literature one does get the impression that there is an odd but distinct relationship between obesity and extreme emaciation. For example, 11 of 21 subjects of case studies discussed by Bliss and Branch in *Anorexia Nervosa* (13) were, at some time in their lives, obese. In the case of eight of these 11 subjects, anorexia was preceded and accompanied by either marked withdrawal or intense depression. In contrast, intense attacks of anxiety or nervousness [states which our experiment (4) suggests would inhibit eating in normal individuals] seem to be associated with the development of anorexia among most of the ten subjects who were originally of normal size.

At this point, these speculations are simply idea-spinning—fun, but ephemeral. Let us return to the results of the studies described so far. These can be quickly summarized as follows.

1. Physiological correlates of food deprivation, such as gastric motility, are directly related to eating behavior and to the reported experience of hunger in normal subjects but unrelated in obese subjects (3, 4).
2. External or nonvisceral cues, such as smell, taste, the sight of other people eating, and the passage of time, affect eating behavior to a greater extent in obese subjects than in normal subjects (8–10).

OBESITY AND FASTING

Given these basic facts, their implications have ramifications in almost any area pertaining to food and eating, and some of our studies have been concerned with the implications of these experimental results for eating behavior in a variety of nonlaboratory settings. Thus, Goldman, Jaffa, and I (14) have studied fasting on Yom Kippur, the Jewish Day of Atonement, on which the orthodox Jew is supposed to go without food for 24 hours. Reasoning that, on this occasion, food-relevant external cues are particularly scarce, one would expect obese Jews to be more likely to fast than normal Jews. In a study of 296 religious Jewish college students (defined as Jewish college students who had been to a synagogue at least once during the preceding year on occasions other than a wedding or a bar mitzvah), this proves to be the case, for 83.3 percent of obese Jews fasted, as compared with 68.8 percent of normal Jews ($P < .05$).

Further, this external-internal control schema leads to the prediction that fat, fasting Jews who spend a great deal of time in the synagogue on Yom Kippur will suffer less from fasting than fat, fasting Jews who spend little time in the synagogue. There should be no such relationship for normal fasting Jews. Obviously, there will be far fewer food-related cues in the synagogue than on the street or at home. Therefore, for obese Jews, the likelihood that the impulse to eat will be triggered is greater outside of the synagogue than within it. For normal Jews, this distinction is of less importance. In or out of the synagogue, stomach pangs are stomach pangs. Again, the data support the expectation. When the number of hours in the synagogue is correlated with self-ratings of the unpleasantness of fasting, for obese subjects the correlation is −.50, whereas for normal subjects the correlation is only −.18. In a test of the difference between correlations, $P = .03$. Obviously, for the obese, the more time the individual spends in the synagogue, the less of an ordeal fasting is. For normals, the number of hours in the synagogue has little to do with the difficulty of the fast.

OBESITY AND CHOICE OF EATING PLACE

In another study (14) we examined the relationship of obesity to choice of eating places. From Nisbett's findings on taste, it seemed a plausible guess that the obese would be more drawn to good restaurants and more repelled by bad ones than normal subjects would be. At Columbia, students have the option of eating in the university dining halls or in any of the many restaurants that surround the campus. At Columbia, as probably at every similar institution in the United States, students have a low opinion of the institution's food. If a freshman elects to eat in a dormitory dining hall, he may, if he chooses, join a prepayment food plan at the beginning of the school year. Any time after 1 November he may, by paying a penalty of $15, cancel his food contract. If we accept prevailing campus opinion of the institution's food as being at all realistically based, we should anticipate that those for whom taste or food quality is most important will be the most likely to let their food contracts expire. Obese freshmen, then, should be more likely to drop out of the food plan than normal freshmen. Again, the data support the expectation: 86.5 percent of fat freshmen cancel their contracts as compared with 67.1 percent of normal freshmen ($P < .05$). Obesity does to some extent serve as a basis for predicting who will choose to eat institutional food.

OBESITY AND ADJUSTMENT TO NEW EATING SCHEDULES

In the final study in this series (14) we examined the relationship of obesity to the difficulty of adjusting to new eating schedules imposed by time-zone changes. This study involved an analysis of data collected by the medical department of Air France in a study of physiological effects of time-zone changes on 236 flight personnel assigned to the Paris–New York and Paris–Montreal flights. Most of these flights leave Paris around noon, French time; fly for approximately 8 hours; and land in North America sometime between 2:00 and 3:00 p.m. Eastern time. Flight-crew members eat lunch shortly after takeoff and, being occupied with landing preparations, are not served another meal during the flight. They land some 7 hours after their last meal, at a time that is later than the local lunch hour and earlier than the local dinner time.

Though this study was not directly concerned with eating behavior, the interviewers systematically noted all individuals who volunteered the information that they "suffered from the discordance between their physiological state and meal time in America" (15). One would anticipate that the fatter individuals, being sensitive to external cues (local meal hours) rather than internal ones, would adapt most readily to local eating schedules and be least likely to complain of the discrepancy between American meal times and physiological state.

Given the physical requirements involved in the selection of aircrews, there are, of course, relatively few really obese people in this sample. However, the results of Nisbett's experiment (10) indicate that the degree of reliance on external relative to internal cues may well be a dimension which varies with the degree of deviation from normal weight. It seems reasonable, then, to anticipate that, even within a restricted sample, there will be differences in response between the heavier and the lighter members of the sample. This is the case. In comparing the 101 flight personnel who are overweight (0.1 to 29 percent overweight) with the 135 who are not overweight (0 to 25 percent underweight), we find that 11.9 percent of the overweight complain as compared with 25.3 percent of the non-overweight ($P < .01$). It does appear that the fatter were less troubled by the effects of time changes on eating than the thinner flyers (16).

These persistent findings that the obese are relatively insensitive to variations in the physiological correlates of food deprivation but highly sensitive to environmental, food-related cues is, perhaps, one key to understanding the notorious long-run ineffectiveness of virtually all attempts to treat obesity (17). The use of anorexigenic drugs such as amphetamine or of bulk-producing, nonnutritive substances such as methyl cellulose is based on the premise that such agents dampen the intensity of the physiological symptoms of food deprivation. Probably they do, but these symptoms appear to have little to do with whether or not a fat person eats. Restricted, low-calorie diets should be effective just so long as the obese dieter is able to blind himself to food-relevant cues or so long as he exists in a world barren of such cues. In the Hashim and Van Itallie study (8), the subjects did, in fact, live in such a world. Restricted to a Metrecal-like diet and to a small hospital ward, all the obese subjects lost impressive amounts of weight. However, on their return to normal living, to a man they returned to their original weights.

REFERENCES AND NOTES

1. H. Bruch, *Psychiat. Quart.* **35**, 458 (1961).
2. A. Stunkard, *Psychosomat. Med.* **21**, 281 (1959).
3. H. Bruch and C. Koch, *Arch. Genet. Psychiat.* **11**, 74 (1964).
4. S. Schachter, R. Goldman, A. Gordon, *J. Personality Soc. Psychol.*, in press.
5. A. J. Carlson, *Control of Hunger in Health and Disease* (Univ. of Chicago Press, Chicago, 1916).
6. W. B. Cannon, *Bodily Changes in Pain, Hunger, Fear and Rage* (Appleton, New York, 1915).
7. It is a common belief among researchers in the field of obesity that the sensitivity of their fat subjects makes it impossible to study their eating behavior experimentally—hence this roundabout way of measuring eating; the subjects in this study are taking a "taste test," not "eating."
8. S. A. Hashim and T. B. Van Itallie, *Ann. N. Y. Acad. Sci.* **131**, 654 (1965).
9. S. Schachter and L. Gross, *J. Personality Soc. Psychol.*, in press.
10. R. E. Nisbett, *ibid.*, in press.
11. A. Stunkard, *Amer. J. Psychiat.* **118**, 212 (1961).
12. L. Beebe, *The Big Spenders* (Doubleday, New York, 1966).
13. E. L. Bliss and C. H. Branch, *Anorexia Nervosa* (Hoeber, New York, 1960).
14. R. Goldman, M. Jaffa, S. Schachter, *J. Personality Soc. Psychol.*, in press.
15. J. Lavernhe and E. Lafontaine (Air France), personal communication.
16. Obviously, I do not mean to imply that the *only* explanation of the results of these three nonlaboratory studies lies in this formulation of the external-internal control of eating behavior. These studies were deliberately designed to test implications of this general schema in field settings. As with any field research, alternative explanations of the findings are legion, and, within the context of any specific study, impossible to rule out. Alternative formulations of this entire series of studies are considered in the original papers [see Schachter *et al.* (4 and 9), Nisbett (10), and Goldman *et al.* (14)].
17. A. Stunkard and M. McLaren-Hume, *Arch. Internal Med.* **103**, 79 (1959); A. R. Feinstein, *J. Chronic Diseases*, **11**, 349 (1960).

18. Much of the research described in this article was supported by grants G23758 and GS732 from the National Science Foundation.

Hypnotic Control of Complex Skin Temperature

Christina Maslach
Gary Marshall
Philip Zimbardo

Maintenance of a relatively constant level of body temperature is a vital physiological function in man. It is so efficient and automatic that we become aware of the process only when pathological internal conditions cause us to react with fever or chills, and when extremes of environmental conditions markedly alter the skin temperature of our limbs. To what extent can such a basic regulatory function be brought under volitional control?

In 1938, the Russian scientist, A. R. Luria, performed an interesting experiment which bears directly upon this question. He had been studying the remarkable mental feats of a man who appeared to have eidetic imagery. Apparently, his subject not only had "photographic memory" but could induce such vivid visual images that they exerted a profound influence on his behavior. When he was instructed to modify the skin temperature in his hands, it took only several minutes before he had made one hand hotter than it had been by two degrees, while the other became colder by one and a half degrees. These changes were attributed by the subject to the "reality" of his visual images:

> I saw myself put my right hand on a hot stove . . . Oi, was it hot! So, naturally, the temperature of my hand increased. But I was holding a piece of ice in my left hand. I could see it there and began to squeeze it. And, of course, my hand got colder. . . (Luria, 1969, pp. 140–141).

Is such a phenomenon replicable with "normal" individuals not born with the remarkably developed eidetic ability of this man? We were led to believe so on the basis of converging research findings coming from three rather different sources: visceral learning, cognitive control of motivation, and hypnosis.

Neal Miller and his associates at Rockefeller University (1969a, b) have recently demonstrated that the control over skeletal muscle responses through operant conditioning procedures can be extended to responses of the glands and viscera. Their work has generated the powerful conclusion that any discriminable response which is emitted by any part of the body can be learned if its occurrence is followed by reinforcement. "Learning" here refers to the change in frequency of making a specific response (such as cardiac acceleration or deceleration, or glandular secretion) when that change has as its consequence electrical stimulation in the pleasure center of the animal's hypothalamus. Miller believes that such results "force us to the radical reorientation of thinking of glandular visceral behavior, which ordinarily is concealed inside the body, in exactly the same way as we think of the externally more easily observable skeletal behavior." (Miller, 1969b, p. 11)

This conclusion is extended in the work of Zimbardo and his colleagues (1969) which experimentally demonstrates that biological drives, as well as social motives, may be brought under the control of cognitive variables such as choice and justification. Subjects modified the impact of a host of drive stimuli at subjective, behavioral, and physiological levels, in the process of resolving an "irrational," dissonant commitment (e.g., not to eat when hungry, or to expose oneself to a noxious stimulus without adequate justification for doing so). Thus a wide range of responses was controlled through the operation of "concealed" cognitive processes, in the absence of external reinforcers.

It appeared to us that hypnosis: a) is a state in which the effects of cognitive processes on bodily functioning are amplified; b) enables the subject to perceive the locus of causality for mind and body control as more internally centered and volitional; c) is often accompanied by a heightened sense of visual imagery; and d) can lead to intensive concentration and elimination of distractions. For these reasons, it should be possible for well-trained hypnotic subjects to gain control over regulation of their own skin temperature without either external reinforcement or even external feedback. While there have been a few scattered attempts to control temperature through hypnosis or other methods (McDowell, 1959; Chapman, Goodell, & Wolff, 1959; Green, Green, & Walters, 1970), they have often lacked adequate controls and tend to focus on a single aspect of temperature modification, such as unidirectional changes.

Our present study was exploratory in nature and attempted to demonstrate that hypnotic subjects would be able to achieve simultaneous alteration of skin temperature in opposite directions in their two hands, while waking

Unpublished paper. Reproduced by permission of the authors.
This study was financially supported by an ONR research grant N00014-67-A-0112-0041 to Professor P. Zimbardo, supplemented by funds from an NIMH grant 03859-09 to Professor E. J. Hilgard.

control subjects would not. The differential response of one hand getting hotter than normal, while the other gets colder, was chosen in order to rule out any simple notion of activation or prior learning and to control for any naturally occurring changes in skin temperature, such as cold hands gradually warming up over time. We also attempted to rule out other alternative explanations of changes in skin temperature by keeping environmental conditions constant and by minimizing overt skeletal responses on the part of the subjects.

METHOD

Three of our trained hypnotic subjects were tested in a specially designed room in the Laboratory of Dermatology Research at the Stanford Medical Center. The ambient temperature in this room was automatically regulated to maintain a constant level. Ten thermocouples of copper constantin were taped to identical sites on the ventral surface of the two hands and forearms of the subjects. Both room and skin temperatures were continuously monitored by a Honeywell recording system which printed them out directly in degrees Centigrade. The subjects lay on a bed with their arms resting comfortably at their sides and with open palms extended upward in exactly the same position. This posture was maintained throughout the session, and there was no overt body movement.

The instructions, which were delivered over an intercom, began with approximately ten minutes of hypnotic induction. After the subjects were deeply hypnotized (according to their self-reports), they were asked to focus attention on their hands. They were then told to make an arbitrarily selected hand hotter, and the other colder, than normal. Accompanying this last, brief instruction were suggestions of several images which could be useful in producing this effect, and encouragement to generate personal imagery and commands which might be necessary to achieve the desired result. Typically, the subject lay in silence for the duration of the testing session (which averaged about ten minutes). In a few instances, the experimenter provided verbal feedback during the second half of the session when the subject appeared to have successfully differentiated the temperature of the two hands. The final instruction was to normalize the temperature in both hands by returning it to the initial baseline level.

Each of the subjects participated in two or three such sessions. In addition, one of the subjects (the junior author) completed two sessions utilizing auto-hypnosis. Communication between him and the experimenter occurred only to demarcate the various procedural stages being experienced.

Six waking control subjects also participated in each of two experimental sessions. The procedure was identical to that employed with the hypnotic subjects, except that they were not given any prior hypnotic training or the hypnotic induction during the experiment. The control group consisted of three male and three female undergraduate paid volunteers from the introductory psychology course at Stanford University. The hypnotized subjects, other than the junior author, were both coeds drawn from the same population.

RESULTS

All of the hypnotic subjects demonstrated the ability to significantly alter localized skin temperature. Large differences (as much as 4° C) between identical skin sites on opposite hands appeared within two minutes of the verbal suggestion, were maintained for the entire testing period, and then were rapidly eliminated upon the suggestion to normalize skin temperature. Temperature decreases in the "cold" hand were generally much larger than the increases in the "hot" hand, the largest decrease being 7° C, while the largest increase was 2° C. In contrast, none of the waking control subjects were able to achieve such divergent changes in the temperature of their hands. The magnitude of the consistent changes produced by the hypnotic subjects was considerably greater than the slight fluctuations shown by the controls. The between-group differences illustrated in Figure 1 are highly reliable beyond the .001 level of significance ($t = 14.27$, $df = 7$).

When we examine the individual patterns of reaction in the hypnotized subjects, it becomes even more apparent that they were able to exert a considerable degree of control over the temperature of their two hands. The subject's data shown in Figure 2 reveals how, following the suggestion to make her left hand colder and right hand hotter (opposite to their relative baseline position), she rapidly "drove" them in the appropriate directions. After maintaining the separation for more than ten minutes, she re-established the initial baseline difference as soon as she was given the instruction to normalize her skin temperature. Since there was no overlap in the temperature distributions of the two hands, the obtained differences from minute 4 to minute 16 were extremely significant ($p <$ .001, within-subject $t = 20.18$, $df = 12$).

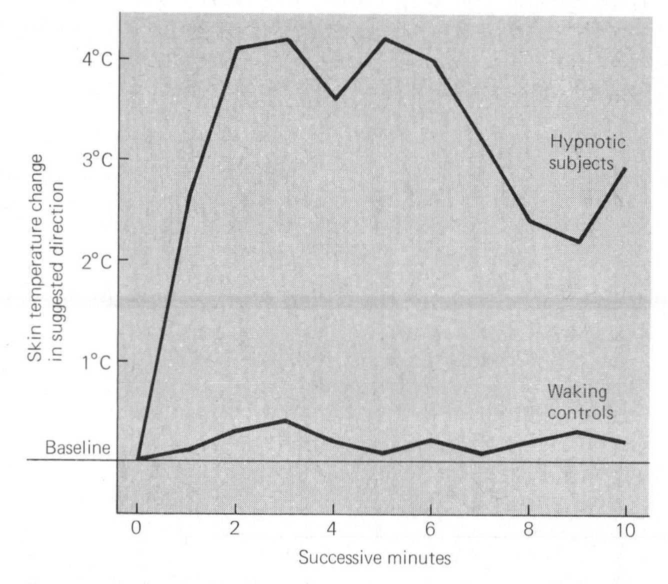

Fig. 1. Mean change in skin temperature in suggested direction (no change being the baseline level, negative scores for changes opposite to suggestion, positive scores for appropriate changes).

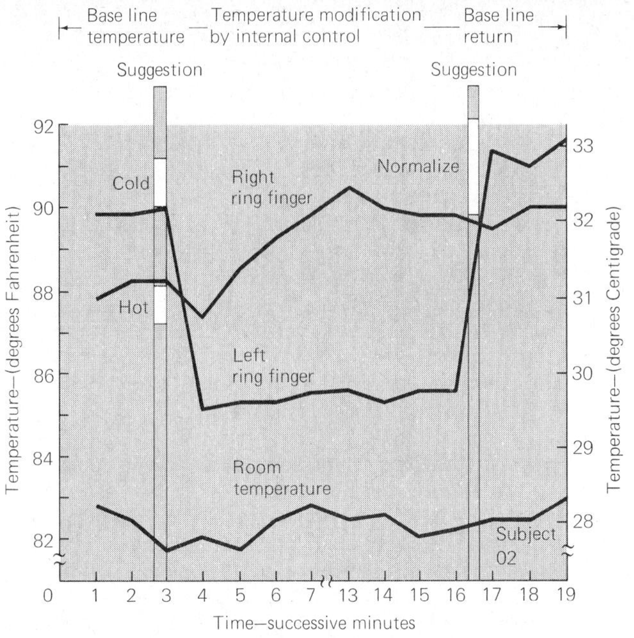

Fig. 2. Simultaneous modification of skin temperature in opposite directions in the right and left hands (omitted minutes 8–12 are no different from the rest of the modification period).

The most impressive evidence for the hypnotic-cognitive control of this autonomic responding can be observed in the data for a subject under auto-suggestion (see Figure 3). After having induced a state of hypnotic relaxation, he signalled the experimenter as to which hand he would try to make hotter and which cooler. During the first minute thereafter, the left hand became hotter as the temperature in the right one dropped sharply. This divergence was also seen during the 5th to 6th minutes and again in the 10th to 11th minutes.

When the experimenter provided information after seven minutes as to the subject's success, this feedback had a negative effect. A similar "loss" of the phenomenon occurred in both of the other hypnotic subjects immediately after being given verbal feedback from the experimenter. We believe that the intensive concentration required to achieve the unusual performance demanded in this study was disturbed by having to attend to and process the informational input from the experimenter. In a sense, the feedback, although supportive, operated as a distractor to attenuate the obtained differences in skin temperature. While non-verbal cues might be utilized to give the subject information as to performance adequacy, the comprehension required of verbal feedback may always intrude upon and interfere with performance on such a complex task. However, we wish to underscore the fact that this subject was able to alter the skin temperature of his hands in opposite directions simultaneously without the aid of external demands, feedback, or extrinsic sources of reinforcement.

The specificity of this controlling process can be seen in Figure 4, where the subject was instructed to maintain the forearm at its normal temperature while making the right hand colder than normal. The forearm varied less than half a degree Centigrade, while at the same time, the temperature of the right index finger dropped 4° C.

All of the hypnotic subjects reported great difficulty in performing this task due to the intensive concentration, extreme dissociation, and novel experience involved. Two of the subjects could not achieve a separation between the temperature of their two hands on the first day of testing, although they could vary both in conjunction. From analysis of the pattern of temperature changes and introspective reports, it appears that three different cognitive strategies were used to achieve these effects. The most frequent one was "unequal parallel shifts"—the temperature in the two hands increased or decreased in a similar direction, but at a faster rate in one of the two hands. A "holding and spreading" approach was used to focus most attention on changing the temperature of one hand and, once changed, to hold it steady while driving the temperature in the other hand away. The technique which appeared to be most difficult, but was effectively used for at least several minutes during each testing session, was "simultaneous divergence." Here the two hands seemed to act independently, with the arbitrarily chosen one getting hotter than normal, and the other becoming colder than normal.

Different types of imagery were generated by the subjects during the sessions in order to help produce the desired

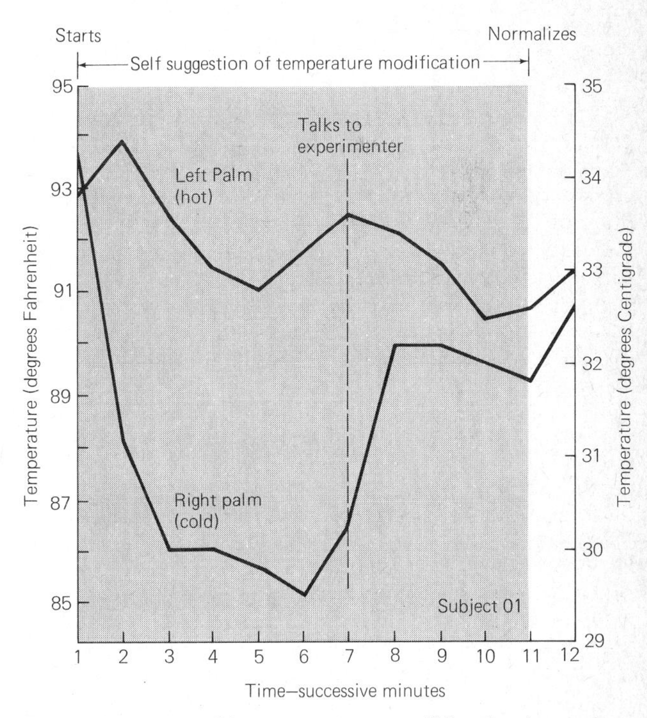

Fig. 3. Divergent skin temperature modification in a subject responding to self-induced relaxation, concentration, and temperature change suggestions.

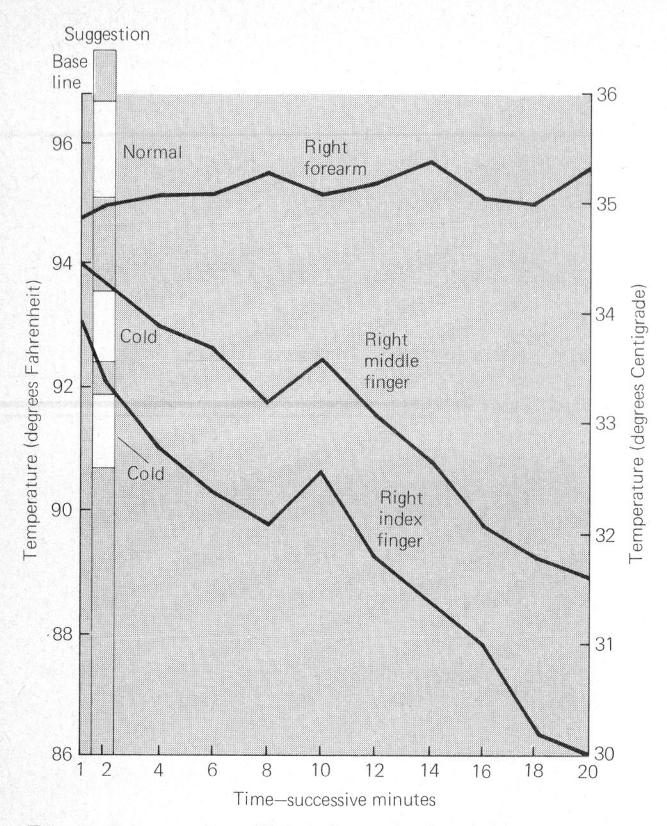

Fig. 4. Response specificity shown by hand decreases in temperature with constantly maintained forearm temperature.

effect. Some of the imagery involved realistic experiences, such as having one hand in a bucket of ice water while the other was under a heat lamp. Other imagery had a more symbolic or fantasy quality: the "hot" hand was getting red with anger over something the "cold" hand did, and the "cold" hand was getting white with fear over this angry reaction. However, it seems that at times the most dramatic divergences in skin temperature were produced by imageless commands given independently to each hand: "You become hot, you become cold." All of the waking control subjects reported trying hard to meet the experimental demand, and generating assorted imagery for that purpose. Several even believed they had done so effectively, although as we noted, the largest divergence was but a fraction of a degree.

Although we are not yet in a position to characterize the physiological mechanisms responsible for the control of skin temperature which we have shown, we believe that the role of hypnosis in the process is quite understandable. The research by Miller on visceral learning has stressed the important function served by curare in paralyzing the skeletal musculature of the animals. At first, this methodological control was thought to be necessary only to rule out possible influences of skeletal muscle responding on glandular and visceral responding. However, it now appears that curarizing the subjects may serve a more basic function:

> It is possible that curare may help to maintain a constant stimulus situation and/or to shift the animal's attention from distracting skeletal activities to the relevant visceral ones. (Miller, 1969b, p. 19)

We would argue that the effects of hypnosis are analogous to those of curare, since hypnosis provides a set of training conditions which permit a greater than normal degree of generalized relaxation, removal of distracting stimuli, and enhanced concentration upon a given, relevant dimension. Hypnotic training may also aid in the control of experiential, behavioral, and physiological processes by increasing the subject's confidence in his ability to exert such control, and by altering consciousness to the point that words and images can be more readily translated into a code language to which he is physiologically responsive.

While we feel this research demonstrates the fine degree of control it is possible for people to exert over one aspect of their autonomic nervous system, it is, nevertheless, a pilot study. The findings need to be replicated, additional measures must be introduced to discover how the instructional input yields the temperature difference output, and variations in type of feedback, imagery, and extent of practice should be incorporated into subsequent work.

To us, the significance of research in this area is less in understanding how hypnosis per se operates, but rather how human beings "naturally" learn to induce ulcers, tachycardia, excessive and uncontrolled sweating, and other forms of psychosomatic illness. Miller's work suggests that the intervention and modification of such reactions follow principles of operant conditioning. Our work adds the possibility that the sources of reinforcement in both producing and changing psychosomatic symptomatology may be cognitive in nature. Therapeutic control may thus be best achieved by combining the precision of reinforcement contingencies with the power of a more pervasive cognitive approach to dealing with such mind–body interactions.

REFERENCES

Chapman, L. F., Goodell, H., and Wolff, H. G. Increased inflammatory reaction induced by central nervous system activity. *Association of American Physicians. Transactions*, 1959, **72**, 84–109.

Green, E. E., Green, A. M., and Walters, E. D. Self-regulation of internal states. In J. Rose (ed.), *Progress of Cybernetics: Proceedings of the International Congress of Cybernetics, London, 1969.* London: Gordon and Breach, 1970.

Luria, A. R. *The Mind of a Mnemonist.* New York: Discus Books, 1969.

McDowell, M. Hypnosis in dermatology. In J. M. Schneck (ed.), *Hypnosis in Modern Medicine* (2nd ed.). Springfield, Ill.: Charles C Thomas, 1959.

Miller, N. E. Learning of visceral and glandular responses. *Science*, 1969a, **163**, 434–445.

Miller, N. E. Autonomic learning: clinical and physiological implications. Invited lecture at the XIX International Congress of Psychology, London, 1969b.

Zimbardo, P. G. *The Cognitive Control of Motivation.* Glenview, Ill.: Scott, Foresman and Co., 1969.

Chapter 9

The Psychoses

The psychotic is considerably more disturbed than either the neurotic or the psychophysiologically ill. His thinking, actions, and total personality are more disorganized; and he is less likely than the other types to function at home or on the job. Some of the psychotic's symptomatology is described in our first paper, by J. R. Wittenborn, in which factor analysis was performed on the symptom ratings of 150 male psychiatric patients. Several nonpsychotic symptoms (for example, conversion hysteria, homosexual dominance, phobic compulsive) also showed up in the factor analyses.

Lazarus' paper on learning theory and the treatment of depression provides both an excellent description of the disorder and a behavioral technique for its modification. The treatment method that Lazarus especially favors is called "time projection with positive reinforcement"; it consists of having the patient, either under hypnotic trance or not, think of filling the next 48 hours with pleasant and enjoyable activities.

The paper by Paula Clayton describes a study in which hospitalized manic depressives of the manic variety were compared with their depressive counterparts. Although demographic differences between these types were noted, the important contribution of this paper is its clinical picture of mania.

Richard Seiden's paper describes a comparison of campus suicide victims and their nonsuicidal classmates. Similarities among the former that were not present among nonsuicidal students consisted of scholastic anxieties, concern over physical health, and difficult interpersonal relationships.

The last paper of this chapter describes how the paranoid person attempts to regain object relations by reconstructing a reality that seems to justify his paranoid behavior. Norman Cameron, the noted psychiatrist and author of this paper on the "paranoid pseudo-community," describes paranoia in terms of the need that each person has for social communication.

The Dimensions of Psychosis

J. R. Wittenborn

In 1948 the writer began a series of investigations for the purpose of developing a set of rating scales which could indicate symptom patterns prevalent among newly admitted patients. These scales were designed to serve research interests, specifically, as standard criteria for validating diagnostic tests and as quantifiable referents for evaluating changes which might occur in consequence of treatment.

The scales were intended to show the various facets of the fulminating illness of newly admitted hospital patients, and were not sensitive to differences which might be found among tranquilized patients or among chronic patients.

With the advent of tranquilizers, however, a renewed interest in the chronic patient has emerged, and investigators have been particularly active in evaluating the efficacy of various drugs as aids in the treatment or control of all mental hospital patients, including those from the "back wards." Because of this shift in interest, the writer has revised and extended his symptom rating scales to provide descriptive distinctions among all classes of adult mental hospital patients, chronic as well as acute.

The present report describes a factor analysis of 98 new or revised rating scales. The analysis was conducted for the purpose of providing scoring dimensions for the new comprehensive scales. The extensions broaden the symptomatic coverage of the scales, and the revisions are simplifications and refinements resulting from experience with the original scales (15).

The development of reliable and pertinent rating scales for mental hospital patients is a difficult and time-consuming task. Mental hospital patients are extraordinarily heterogeneous in their behavioral manifestations, and if a set of scales is to have general use, each scale must be applicable to mute and immobile patients, as well as to patients with the most exaggerated forms of verbal and motoric behavior. Manifestations of pathology among mental patients are episodic and variable, and ratings of the patient's *typical or modal* behavior may not only obscure significant pathology but in many cases may reveal no pathology at all. For this reason the writer's scales, which involve four steps varying from no pathology to a pathologic extreme, require that the ratings be based on the *most extreme* pathology noted during the specified observation period.

The writer has attempted to meet the problem of rating scale ambiguity by using steps which refer to explicit symptomatic facts. Some of these symptomatic facts are observable and can be rated unambiguously. Other symptomatic facts refer to affective or cognitive experiences of the patient and may not be equally accessible to all raters, or may be interpreted differently according to the requirements of the rater's personality. It was found in developing the new scales that interrater consistency could be improved if the rater was advised whether the rating should be based primarily on behavior observations, primarily on the basis of interview, or on either observation or interview.

In the original investigation a set of 55 symptom rating scales was employed (9). Quantitative summaries of these ratings were prepared on the basis of nine different symptom clusters which had been revealed by factor analysis of the rating scale intercorrelations. Two major samples—140 males from the Veterans Administration Hospital at Northampton (9), and 250 males and females from the Connecticut State Hospital at Middletown (10)—provided data for two independent factor analyses. Although the results of these two factor analyses were in general mutually confirming, the Middletown sample, comprising newly admitted patients, contributed most to the definition of the scale clusters used for scoring purposes in the version published for general use. In further analyses, however, we, as well as other investigators, have found that factorial studies of symptom intercorrelations, although mutually confirmatory in many respects (13), may vary somewhat according to the nature of the sample (11, 12), the content of the rating scales and, to a lesser degree, the factorial model employed, *e.g.*, orthogonal or oblique (6, 16). Lorr's investigations have yielded factors somewhat different from the writer's, and although it is believed that the differences are due primarily to the set of symptom rating scales employed, it is possible that some of the discrepancy may be due to his sample of veteran patients (4).

The research on which the present report is based was supported by U.S. Public Health Grant MY 3008 from the Psychopharmacology Service Center of the National Institutes of Health.

THE SAMPLE

The present sample comprises 150 male patients at the Veterans Administration Hospital, Lyons, New Jersey. Although a description of a sample of patients is never sufficient for all purposes, the results of a factor analysis can vary sufficiently in consequence of differences in samples to make a description of the sample a desirable feature of a report of any factor analysis. The raters were instructed to exclude patients who were senile or debilitated by organic disease. With these exceptions, the sample is broadly representative of the hospital population, but it was not drawn at random. None of the patients was in psychotherapy with the rater; they were drawn from various wards, including a disturbed ward. Seventy-five of the patients were under 40 years of age; 64 were over 40 and under 60, and 11 were in their 60's. Eighty-five of the patients had begun their current hospitalization less than five years before the rating; 18 had been hospitalized more than five but less than 15 years before rating; and 19 had begun their current hospitalization more than 15 but less than 20 years before. Diagnoses are notoriously variable in their meaning from hospital to hospital; nevertheless, a summary of the diagnostic classification of the patients may be of interest. Forty-four had been diagnosed as paranoid schizophrenia, 28 as hebephrenic, and 57 as some other form of schizophrenia. Twelve patients had an organic diagnosis, and nine had a functional disorder bearing a diagnostic label other than schizophrenia.

It is planned eventually to conduct an independent analysis with a comparable sample of females. In this way sex differences will not be confounded with other sources of variance within the samples, and any factor structure unique to the sexes may be identified.

THE RATING SCALE DATA

The nature of each of the 98 rating scales employed in the present analysis is characterized by its most pathologic extreme. This is paraphrased in Table 1, which includes the rating scale intercorrelations. The intercorrelations are sufficiently high to suggest rather reliable symptom ratings. Unfortunately, it is difficult to evaluate the reliability of symptom rating scales. It is difficult enough to arrange for each patient to be observed by two different raters for a sufficiently long period of time to provide a basis for ratings representative of extremes of pathology; it is almost impossible to arrange for two different raters to observe the same patient at the same times.

For each of the present scales, however, independent ratings by two raters, a psychologist and an aide, were possible for our sample of 150 patients.[1] The raters observed during the same two-week period, but did not observe at the same time. The two ratings were correlated to provide a kind of minimal reliability estimate for each scale. It was apparent that many of the rating scales are reliable; there were others with low interrater correlations, and these may or may not be reliable. The low interrater correlations may be due to limitations in the scale or in the rater, and thereby ascribable to unreliability. It is possible, however, that many of the low correlations are due to the fact that the raters observed different things, either because of differences in the conditions under which the patient was observed or because of the variable, episodic nature of the patient's behavior. It is interesting to note that the highest interrater correlations were for the scales rated on the basis of behavioral observations, and the lowest interrater correlations were for the scales which could be rated on the basis of *either* behavioral observation or interview, thereby implying some uncertainty concerning the basis for ratings.

For the purpose of the present analysis, we began with a set of 115 scales. From these we selected those scales which had an interrater correlation of at least .25; these scales appear in Table 1 and are numbered from one to 72, inclusive. In addition, we included certain other scales, which, despite their low interrater correlation in the present sample, had shown themselves to be important in factor analyses based on earlier samples and should be used in comparative studies with additional samples; these scales are numbered 73 to 98 in Table 1. Some of the low interrater correlations may be explainable in terms of limited variance within the present sample. There were very few patients with primarily affective disorders in the present sample, and almost no neurotics. It is not surprising, therefore, that many of the scales for neurotic behavior and some forms of affective behavior showed low interrater correlation. Some of the low interrater correlations may be ascribable to restriction in sample range and may not necessarily be due to unreliability of the scale, or to extreme variability within patients. Despite many low interrater correlations, the *level* of rating for aides and psychologists was generally quite similar, with the psychologist seeing slightly less pathology on the average than did the aides. The two scales showing the greatest differences, numbers 88 and 91, reveal the psychologist to be rating the more pathology; the average difference was .53 and .64, respectively.

The data which were intercorrelated[2] are not the work of any one rater or the result of any one rating. As previously indicated, each patient was rated by two different raters. When for a given scale the two ratings differed from each other, the more extreme rating was considered to be the more valid indication of pathology and was used as a basis for computing the interscale correlations. Since we were interested in a factor analysis which would provide dimensions of psychopathology, we are clearly interested, as the rating instructions indicate, in the extremes of pathology that occur during the rating period. Accordingly, the more pathologically extreme of the two ratings is considered to

[1] The ratings, which were provided by Grant funds, were conducted with unusual care under the joint supervision of the writer and Dr. Herman Efron, of the Veterans Administration Hospital, Lyons, New Jersey.

[2] A copy of the complete intercorrelation table has been deposited as Document number 7064 with the ADI Auxiliary Publications Project, Photoduplication Service, Library of Congress, Washington 25, D. C. A copy may be secured by citing the Document number and by remitting $3.75 for photoprints, or $2.00 for 35 mm microfilm. Advance payment is required. Make checks or money orders payable to: Chief, Photoduplication Service, Library of Congress.

Table 1. *Orthogonal Varimax Rotation.*

No.	Scale	A	B	C	D	E	F	G	H	I	J	K	L	h^2
1	Claims can't sleep (O)	103	051	−088	168	−108	326	−162	016	169	178	082	−186	295
2	Constant movement (O)	484	011	−191	367	032	036	154	−041	115	397	037	−134	624
3	Refuses to eat (O)	138	193	049	066	238	087	301	−044	−060	240	−064	−049	287
4	Avoids people (O)	164	740	170	−026	−011	041	126	104	−080	083	−020	132	664
5	Incontinent (O)	308	300	−025	137	252	150	441	364	229	092	102	102	699
6	Motions slow (O)	−002	557	228	−067	128	083	254	−005	−008	033	214	−080	508
7	Compulsive acts continuous (O)	420	204	−075	328	107	−076	005	016	190	457	123	−147	630
8	Initiates physical assaults (O)	059	142	160	747	133	050	044	050	065	144	−038	−166	687
9	Abrupt mood changes (O)	201	122	100	553	049	120	104	112	−101	088	162	−036	457
10	Lies or steals indiscriminately (O)	088	133	093	271	−034	250	489	−027	228	−010	−142	−133	501
11	Disrupts routine (O)	065	482	058	406	002	102	378	−085	182	210	−103	073	659
12	Actively resists attendants (O)	179	411	075	506	048	088	347	−082	−007	333	−095	179	752
13	Will not participate (O)	−070	758	155	030	084	099	085	−077	038	103	025	144	668
14	Stays in one spot (O)	−107	619	234	−014	046	−005	−061	−003	014	−042	−029	042	460
15	Unaware of other patients (O)	085	770	123	112	−008	030	011	054	001	−110	025	057	649
16	Demands help (O)	122	−208	−142	442	094	156	084	−299	174	129	225	098	510
17	Attacks without provocation (O)	117	053	142	555	245	−031	076	024	167	130	−098	−236	522
18	Critical of others (O)	112	−211	264	657	012	263	085	−173	090	−062	037	057	681
19	Insists on controlling patients (O)	055	−258	−005	317	039	101	014	−180	605	150	−056	268	678
20	Over-reacts to overtures (O)	014	−476	047	−025	−089	101	185	−176	369	102	040	052	464
21	Mumbles and shouts (O)	613	181	146	360	137	086	071	105	−006	−016	018	118	616
22	Stuffs self gluttonously (O)	062	−078	−007	074	008	031	151	040	323	−261	041	024	216
23	Irrelevant acts (O)	520	234	038	413	190	093	196	050	216	158	−012	009	655
24	Doesn't talk with patients (O)	102	788	−004	−100	091	−018	006	117	−210	−064	131	030	731
25	Direct sexual approaches (O)	008	072	−083	114	082	−042	−008	006	628	129	058	014	448
26	Does not complete tasks (O)	079	591	032	272	292	158	372	−176	073	−032	017	−010	717
27	Does not comprehend (O)	167	469	087	273	466	051	220	008	044	091	−002	−039	611
28	Will not help patients (O)	064	785	044	098	064	066	113	−134	−014	−012	081	−050	681
29	Resistant and oppositional (O)	073	446	023	496	046	116	362	−054	052	193	−091	176	680
30	Behavior has no function (O)	404	424	165	282	289	053	207	−034	099	242	−033	−019	650
31	Restless and distractible (O)	506	159	−004	344	063	156	197	−026	153	272	091	−078	579
32	Clothing discarded (O)	318	306	−098	177	312	188	495	291	159	056	111	074	745
33	Unreasoning urgency (O)	083	−142	109	633	−055	274	128	−084	277	229	022	035	672
34	Nosy (O)	121	−511	050	369	033	225	−008	−098	294	095	025	172	601
35	Demands high-level personnel (O)	014	−270	−044	550	−069	244	203	−313	130	097	241	−081	672
36	Stereotype movements (O)	413	052	040	222	118	−037	171	−033	190	203	126	−340	478
37	Tics or grimaces (O)	389	163	063	281	000	090	081	010	303	−022	094	−160	403

Table 1. (*Continued*)

No.	Scale	A	B	C	D	E	F	G	H	I	J	K	L	h^2
38	Dramatic attempts to be helpful (O)	050	−646	051	−017	014	042	−088	−028	191	082	000	239	534
39	Participation apathetic (O)	−015	676	−002	179	139	171	156	−036	−126	−011	116	085	601
40	Unaware of others' feelings (I)	200	761	−082	−045	077	−102	066	034	−048	−003	−103	−039	665
41	Deliberately disrupts routine (I)	104	055	211	693	−025	−040	098	091	051	192	016	040	601
42	Shouts, sings, talks loudly (I)	220	−236	035	681	034	042	−062	−118	098	−068	−052	−061	611
43	Attention-demanding (I)	106	−312	066	580	−010	222	−058	−298	308	−020	032	008	687
44	Exaggerated affect (I)	366	067	090	512	036	046	−032	−024	133	039	255	043	499
45	Face flaccid (I)	072	533	044	−135	266	−035	−011	−093	102	153	−006	157	449
46	Profane or obscene (I)	281	−078	188	650	068	145	135	044	−055	−014	073	093	607
47	Inappropriate laughter (I)	231	−093	074	141	230	−033	140	107	392	−027	−186	021	362
48	Can't concentrate (I)	204	562	028	136	420	005	208	−079	097	142	−012	107	644
49	Temper tantrums (I or O)	148	−132	343	549	−054	202	−052	124	042	175	−112	173	595
50	Fears impending doom (I or O)	284	015	321	146	034	309	−098	−126	014	151	129	100	377
51	Fluctuating plans (I or O)	214	603	−054	020	158	136	058	130	080	064	025	−032	488
52	Delusional thinking (I or O)	638	173	344	169	074	127	033	−097	−052	043	248	060	686
53	Feels persecuted (I or O)	210	075	720	316	009	211	117	−028	−020	−072	055	−047	737
54	Ideas of influence (I or O)	240	058	688	206	−036	109	−015	−048	009	207	080	−131	659
55	Ideas of grandeur (I or O)	352	−197	277	275	023	002	017	−374	102	016	−009	−054	470
56	Suicidal attempts (I or O)	016	058	061	009	001	423	008	−080	−032	067	164	−088	233
57	*Belle indifference* (I or O)	−039	−010	076	−010	007	216	025	012	−074	094	021	−389	221
58	Memory faults (I or O)	136	493	−062	011	689	075	035	−011	015	066	027	−110	764
59	No comprehension (I or O)	222	608	071	028	522	−071	093	076	120	052	−110	−024	746
60	Can't identify persons (I or O)	164	487	−037	121	682	020	−035	016	−034	023	−016	031	750
61	Can't identify self (I or O)	220	509	024	107	670	−037	043	−036	030	−034	091	043	785
62	Interest in others' problems (I or O)	001	−620	196	332	−049	063	−057	−338	−082	−001	−035	191	701
63	Speaks to hallucinations (I or O)	639	261	227	205	233	016	044	−136	128	042	097	056	676
64	Little recent memory (I or O)	092	526	−010	006	712	085	052	000	073	026	−029	−129	825
65	Avoids talk of relatives (I or O)	140	669	−066	−093	176	−024	−061	029	008	106	−074	−188	569
66	Delusional misinterpretations (I or O)	136	096	554	418	051	095	−037	−004	124	−065	173	014	572
67	Believes everybody hates him (I or O)	105	054	625	387	028	163	142	−024	−017	108	014	030	615
68	Rarely speaks (I or O)	−041	735	−062	−142	305	−115	012	063	038	065	012	000	682
69	Unintelligible (I or O)	386	375	162	124	352	−134	015	086	090	−066	039	019	496
70	No goals (I or O)	089	473	−050	−108	064	053	−299	123	073	124	−008	015	378

Continued

Table 1. *Orthogonal Varimax Rotation (Continued)*

No.	Scale	A	B	C	D	E	F	G	H	I	J	K	L	h^2
71	Little affective involvement (I or O)	169	727	−055	−100	037	−016	−077	139	068	085	−230	−004	662
72	No insight into hospitalization (I or O)	268	516	−108	009	061	007	−018	−079	086	048	−073	−145	397
73	Submissive (O)	300	228	−006	−284	063	117	250	−211	156	−048	086	−027	382
74	Great variation in speech (I)	363	011	199	605	105	−032	−011	−041	106	−101	203	−072	618
75	Can't make decisions (I)	274	484	−062	−063	422	087	165	095	205	069	−012	149	608
76	Stilted speech (I)	399	034	183	370	036	043	−136	013	176	−052	−032	251	450
77	Ideas change with rapidity (I or O)	455	146	202	261	327	008	−156	014	081	119	−035	032	491
78	Delusions of sexual arrangement (I or O)	189	−022	182	226	−020	013	−022	−059	528	−004	282	−154	507
79	Uncontrollable obsessions (I or O)	277	−025	359	252	−021	021	−098	−082	052	372	272	−030	503
80	Delusions of guilt (I or O)	148	−018	157	082	004	092	−030	052	054	−034	519	072	344
81	Uses physical symptoms (I or O)	029	−081	062	158	−018	510	159	−033	002	057	−202	−017	367
82	Phobic (I or O)	266	045	219	288	132	266	−108	−021	−030	368	024	−026	442
83	Unrealistic plans (I or O)	−032	−421	126	176	−102	044	−023	−300	−038	071	005	214	380
84	Can't resist compulsion (I or O)	184	138	173	265	123	−058	093	035	294	454	091	−149	505
85	Exaggerated well being (I or O)	206	−109	195	400	062	−146	200	−288	181	−033	041	−076	441
86	No hope (I or O)	352	128	164	122	−074	362	047	−039	−088	037	−132	−048	351
87	Fears he's misunderstood (I or O)	095	−377	330	185	012	191	012	−267	100	−023	−148	022	436
88	No organic basis for claims (I or O)	081	031	124	150	064	539	198	059	051	−172	178	012	446
89	Distressed by anxiety (I or O)	195	−105	324	276	−058	208	122	−141	−102	094	289	043	416
90	Psychosomatic (I or O)	035	−046	256	174	133	569	055	105	067	−009	−002	−005	460
91	No insight (I or O)	228	338	−054	124	044	−045	−021	−160	−018	029	−215	−240	319
92	Affective failure (I or O)	216	478	088	−066	207	−133	042	−260	113	070	−150	123	473
93	Statements violate physics (I or O)	261	−097	328	478	−034	189	−073	−314	202	038	040	−239	656
94	Hallucinates (I or O)	498	152	418	100	069	106	150	064	−043	106	138	−056	534
95	Fears abhorred act (I or O)	112	−094	037	088	−020	−002	016	−036	108	248	504	−186	394
96	Words not relevant (I or O)	622	191	165	234	258	081	076	−061	012	093	054	−025	600
97	Failure and blocking (I or O)	070	098	155	202	042	125	106	027	031	364	089	−014	251
98	Repudiates insights (I or O)	159	213	169	204	128	194	377	−004	025	−022	093	−238	403

The scales designated (O) were rated on the basis of observations alone; the scales designated (I) were rated on the basis of the interview alone, and the scales designated (I or O) were rated on the basis of either observation or interview.

be more pertinent to our interest than the median of the two ratings. This decision is based on the assumption that both raters were equally able, but that one may have been in a position to observe a greater degree of pathology than the other. In this way, the ratings which we have intercorrelated may be viewed as the kind of ratings which would have been possible had either rater been able to spend twice as much time with the patient. The obvious alternative of having each rater spend much more time with each patient was not practical.

All of the raters were full-time members of the hospital staff and made their observations during their lunch hours, after work, and during other off-duty periods, as well as during the course of their regular duties in the hospital. The raters attempted to observe only a small number of patients during any one observation period, and the ratings are probably as good as could be secured with the use of personnel observing at scattered intervals during the total observation period. An average of seven hours was spent by each rater in interviewing or observing each patient in either an individual or a group situation.

THE ANALYSIS

From time to time it is claimed that the results of a factor analysis may be influenced by the manner in which the factors have been extracted, by the fact that too few factors have been extracted so that variance which should be in the factors remains in the residual correlations, by the choice of an oblique or an orthogonal rotational model, or by bias or subjectivity in the rotation which would favor the definition of certain variables at possible expense of others.

To eliminate the influence of any unverbalized subjective criteria from the guidance of the present analysis, it was decided that the extraction of the factors (3) and their rotation (1, 6) should be conducted by a machine according to a predetermined set of mathematical criteria and by personnel who had no interest in the problem and no knowledge of the nature of the variables. Accordingly, the extraction of the factors and their rotations were guided by generally applicable programs prepared for the IBM 704, and the work was processed by the Littauer Computation Center at Cambridge, Massachusetts.

After 12 centroid factors had been extracted, only 70 (or less than two per cent) of the 4,753 residuals were greater than .10; of these 70, only five were greater than .15, and the highest residual was .20. On this basis it is claimed that the extraction of factors was sufficiently complete for ordinary purposes and that the extraction of additional factors would have no appreciable effect on the meaning of the ultimate solution. For the orthogonal solution, the 12 centroid factors were subjected to a Varimax rotation through a series of 25 cycles. The criterion difference between the twenty-fourth and the twenty-fifth cycles was .00000051.

The orthogonal rotations are given in Table 1. It is apparent upon inspection that the variables were interrelated in such a way as to yield a relatively simple factor structure. Very few of the variables are factorially complex. This simplicity not only facilitates interpretation, but also lends itself nicely to our present purposes of identifying symptomatic dimensions which can be used as a basis for summarizing ratings in terms of symptom clusters.

DESCRIPTION OF ORTHOGONAL FACTORS

Each of the orthogonal factors may be described in terms of the variables which bear the highest correlations. The primary discussion of each factor will be in terms of the eight variables having the highest loadings. In addition, however, some further consideration will be given to other variables which have high loadings, *e.g.*, as great as .40. In the discussion of each factor the variables will be introduced in the order of their decreasing correlation.

Schizophrenic excitement. Factor A is determined by such rating scales as speaking in response to hallucinations, delusional thinking, words not relevant to recognizable ideas, mumbling or shouting vocalizations, disruption of behavior by irrelevant acts, general restlessness and distractibility, hallucinations without insight into their nature, and constant movement. In addition, such scales as rapid change of ideas, continuous compulsive acts, stereotyped movements, and behavior without apparent function are important in the determination of this factor. The behavior represented by these rating scales is considered to be indicative of a schizophrenic excitement. This factor was apparent in the writer's study of the Northampton sample (9) and in the Middletown sample (10). This factor may possibly refer to the same dimension of psychosis indicated by Moore's deluded and hallucinated factor (7). It also bears some limited resemblance to factors A and C reported by Degan (2). That this factor has emerged in several independent studies justifies a continuing interest in it as a useful dimension of psychotic behavior.

Depressive retardation. Factor B is bipolar. One pole is indicative of depressive retardation; the other suggests a manic state. The rating scales bearing an important correlation with this factor are almost too numerous to mention. Eight scales were correlated with the depressive pole to a degree sufficient to account for more than half of their total variance. These were: refusing to talk with other patients, refusing to help other patients, appearing unaware of other patients, appearing unaware of the feelings of others, refusing to participate in various activities, avoiding people, showing reluctance to speak, and showing no feeling during the interview. Various additional scales may be mentioned as bearing important correlations with this factor; they include apathetic participation in activities, reluctance to talk about relatives, tendency to stay in one spot, absence of goals, apparent restriction of comprehension, failure to complete tasks, slowed motions, and flaccid face. In this factor, as in the writer's earlier reports of the depressive end of the bipolar manic-depressed factor (10), the features of retardation are much more conspicuous than are the agitation and dysphoria often so conspicuous in clinical depressions; in the writer's earlier studies, agitation and dysphoria contributed to the definition of an anxiety factor.

It should be noted that depressions seem currently to be less common and less severe than appeared to be the case ten or more years ago. Why this should be true is not altogether clear, but possibly it may reflect the fact that depressions uncomplicated by schizophrenic features are now generally known to run a course which is frequently self-limiting and may not, therefore, now lead to precipitous hospitalization. In a veteran population, such patients often improve in the course of outpatient care, or in the course of their stay at short-term treatment hospitals. As a consequence, relatively few of them may be found at a chronic hospital such as Lyons. The depressive retardation described by factor B doubtlessly characterizes many patients who would not be diagnosed as depressive. The factor is somewhat reminiscent of Moore's catatonia and of Degan's B factor. Lorr, moreover, has found a bipolar factor similar to the present one in two of his analyses (4, 5). It will be useful to continue to consider depressive retardation as one of the important dimensions of psychosis.

Manic state. The manic state pole of factor B is equally familiar, and takes its definition from such scales as dramatic attempts to be helpful, interest in the difficulties of others, interest in activities that do not concern him, overreacting to friendly gestures, unrealistic plans, trying to control the impression of others, dramatic demanding of attention, and seeking contact with high-level personnel. This manic factor has been revealed in earlier analyses of the writer (9, 10).

It is interesting to note that factor B, although similar to the manic-depressed factor described previously by the writer and by Lorr (5), is somewhat different in that it is concerned primarily with mania and retardation *per se*, and appears to have fewer of the psychotic implications found in the factors reported in earlier studies. This simplification in the present factor should be viewed in the light of the clearly psychotic nature of some of the factors which have emerged in the analyses of the present set of rating scales.

Paranoid schizophrenia. Factor C appears to be the paranoid schizophrenia constellation found by the writer in his earlier analyses (9, 10) and reported by Lorr as well (5). The scales it comprises include feeling systematically persecuted, believing others influence him, believing everybody hates him, misinterpreting according to the requirements of his delusions, showing an inability to distinguish hallucinations from reality, and having uncontrollable obsessive thoughts, temper tantrums, and fears that others misunderstand him.

Psychotic belligerence. Factor D draws upon many rating scales, most of which have high loadings. It rests primarily on such scales as initiating physical assaults, deliberately disrupting routine, shouting or singing in a loud voice, criticizing others, using profanity or obscenity, asserting needs with unreasoning urgency, showing great variation in rate of speech, and demanding attention. In addition, this factor draws upon numerous other scales, including abrupt mood changes, attacks without provocation, demands upon high-level personnel, temper tantrums, exaggerated affect, resistance to attendants, oppositional behavior, statements disregarding physical laws, demands for help, misinterpreting on the basis of delusions, performing irrelevant acts, and disrupting routine. This is a factor of psychotic belligerence. Although it is new in the writer's investigations, it is reminiscent of a factor reported by Lorr (5) and appears to be similar to Moore's manic factor (7). It appears also to bear some resemblance to Degan's factor G (2). This is an important factor in the present study, in the sense that it draws upon many variables having a common implication. It is important also in another sense: with the emergence of a separate dimension of belligerence, it is possible to see the schizophrenic excitement of Factor A, the manic pole of Factor B, and the paranoia of Factor C unobscured by the destructive belligerence represented in Factor D. In earlier reports of these factors the belligerent component was always involved in these factors and contributed to or obscured their definition.

Intellectual impairment. Factor E involves such scales as poor memory for recent events, conspicuous memory faults, inability to identify persons, inability to identify self, poor comprehension, inability to direct thoughts, and inability to make decisions. This is clearly a factor of intellectual impairment and is reminiscent of Moore's cognitive factor (7). It also bears a limited resemblance to Degan's F factor (2) and is slightly suggestive of Lorr's factors K and F (5). Although such a dimension is commonly encountered among chronic mental hospital patients with purely functional disorders, it is possible that in our sample the presence of a few patients bearing an organic diagnosis contributed to the present clear emergence of this factor.

Conversion hysteria. Factor F will be recognized as the factor of conversion hysteria which the writer reported in earlier analyses (9, 10). Despite the fact that there were virtually no neurotics in the present sample, patients did manifest somatic-type symptoms suggestive of hysterical conversions, and the exaggerated, dramatic behavior so characteristic of the hysterical personality. In the present study the factor is defined by such scales as organic pathology caused by emotional factors, absence of an organic basis for physical complaints, use of physical symptoms in relation to other people, suicidal attempts, claims that he can't be helped, claims that he can't sleep, feelings of impending doom, the urgent expression of needs, and behavior disrupted by phobias.

Hebephrenic negativism. From a factorial standpoint, Factor G points to a clinically useful dimension of psychosis which has been anticipated in the writer's earlier study of a sample comprising chronic patients (9). This factor may be described as a hebephrenic negativism, and it is descriptively useful to see this dimension distinguished from other dimensions of psychosis suggested by the other factors. It is identified by such scales as clothing falling off, lying or stealing indiscriminately, incontinence, disruption of routines, failure to complete tasks, repudiation of insights, oppositional behavior, and resisting the attendants.

Factor H appears to be a residual factor, and no attempt is made to identify it.

Homosexual dominance. Factor I is a new factor. Several of the scales it comprises were at one time hypothesized by the writer to be a part of the paranoid continuum; this hypothesis had not been confirmed, however (10). The present factor draws to our attention a dimension of psychotic behavior which is commonly observed, particularly among males, but which in most writings has been confused with other psychotic dispositions. The present factor is defined by such scales as direct sexual approaches to other patients, insistence on controlling other patients, belief that a sexual union has been arranged for him, amusement at unpleasant things, over-reaction to friendly overtures, gluttony, grimaces, and attention-demanding behavior. It is a factor of homosexual dominance.

Phobic compulsive. Factor J appears to be the phobic compulsive factor which emerged in the Middletown study (10). That study, based on data from new admissions, reflected neurotic components more clearly than did the other studies, and the loadings with the phobic compulsive scales were higher in that study than in the present one, which is based on a relatively chronic veteran population. Factor J comprises the following scales: continuous compulsive acts, inability to resist compulsions, inability to control obsessive thinking, behavior disrupted by phobias, failure and blocking, resisting the attendants, restlessness, and distractibility.

Anxiety. Factor K is a neurotic factor of anxiety which was clearly indicated by the earlier reports (9, 10) and which is similar to a factor which Lorr describes as melancholy agitation (5). The loadings for this factor in the present study are not so high as those reported previously, and the difference is ascribed to the chronic composition of the present sample. The identifying scales include delusions of guilt, fear of an abhorred act, and distress caused by anxiety. The remaining loadings for this factor are low, but the most important of them involve belief that a sexual union has been arranged, inability to control obsessive thoughts, exaggerated affective expressions, delusional features, and the seeking of high-level personnel.

Factor L, like factor H, appears to be a residual factor, and no attempt will be made to describe it.

SUMMARY AND CONCLUSIONS

A set of rating scales designed to be comprehensive from the standpoint of the symptom manifestations commonly observed in both acute and chronic mental hospital patients was applied to a representative sample of 140 male patients at the Veterans Administration Hospital, Lyons, New Jersey. The patients were rated independently by both a psychologist and an aide. Although the two raters did not observe the patients at the same time, the ratings were made at the end of a common two-week period during which observations were made. When interrater correlations were computed, they were found to vary from negligible to reassuringly high. It is not known whether the low interrater correlations were due to the fact that the raters observed different behavior, or rated from the standpoint of different points of view. The low ratings may have been due to the homogeneity of the sample with respect to certain characteristics, or possibly they were due to unreliability.

For each scale a composite rating was prepared for each patient. This composite represented the more pathological extreme of the two ratings. Since each scale was designed to be rated on the basis of the most extreme pathology observed during the rating period, one might regard the composite rating as a kind of hypothetic rating which could have been based on a period of observation as great as the total period in which the patient was under observation, *i.e.*, six or seven hours of observation by the psychologist, plus six or seven hours by the aide. These composite ratings were intercorrelated and the Pearson product-moment coefficients factor analyzed by the centroid method. Twelve factors were extracted and, upon orthogonal rotation, ten appeared to be meaningful. Both the centroid analysis and the rotations were conducted by personnel of the Littauer Computation Center, using an electronic computing machine. Accordingly, the factors summarized in the following paragraphs should not be regarded as a possible product of the writer's selective interest during the course of factor extraction or rotation.

Schizophrenic excitement refers to the restless and disrupted behavior which seemingly emerges from hallucinations and delusional thinking. It has been described in the writer's earlier investigations, and appears to be similar to a factor reported by Moore.

Depressive retardation refers to the apathy and withdrawal characteristic of patients in extreme depression. This is one end of a bipolar factor and has been described by the writer in other studies. A somewhat similar factor has been reported by Moore, Degan, and Lorr.

Manic state is the opposite pole of the depressed factor and has been described previously by the writer, but with greater emphasis on psychotic features than is presently indicated. A similar factor has been reported by Lorr.

Paranoid schizophrenia includes the usual feelings of persecution and ideas of influence and reference so characteristic of this diagnostic group. It has been reported in the writer's earlier studies and has been described by Lorr as well.

Psychotic belligerence draws upon the assaultive, disruptive and assertive characteristics of patients. Although new in the writer's investigations, such a factor has been described by Moore, by Lorr, and by Degan.

Intellectual impairment is characterized by faults of memory and comprehension and is reminiscent of Moore's cognitive factor but new in the writer's investigations.

Conversion hysteria is characterized by somatic-type symptoms and dramatic exaggerations. This factor has been reported in the writer's earlier investigations.

Hebephrenic negativism is defined by such characteristics as clothing falling off, lying or stealing indiscriminately, and incontinence. This factor has been reported in the writer's previous studies.

Homosexual dominance, as far as the writer is aware, is a new dimension in the factorial studies of psychoses. Since the loadings are relatively low, confirmation by independent study is required. The factor as it appears is characterized by sexual approaches to other patients, attempts to control other patients, gluttony, and sexual preoccupation.

Phobic compulsive has been described repeatedly in the writer's earlier studies.

Anxiety is identified by such matters as delusion of guilt, fear of an abhorred act, and subjectively experienced anxious distress. This factor, previously described by the writer, appears to be similar to Lorr's melancholy agitation.

The present study, based on a comprehensive set of rating scales and designed to be descriptive of both acute and chronic patients, is encouraging in its implications. Specifically, by yielding factors representative of those previously reported by the writer and by other investigators, this study suggests that the present set of rating scales may provide a basis for the description of all the important dimensions of symptomatic behavior required by the various factorial studies published at this time. In addition, the present set of factors clarifies the nature of several of the established factors and separates somewhat discretely certain symptomatic aspects that had remained confounded or obscure in earlier studies.

REFERENCES

1. Carroll, J. B. An analytical solution for approximating simple structure in factor analysis. Psychometrika, **18**: 23–38, 1953.
2. Degan, J. W. *Dimensions of a Functional Psychosis.* Psychometr. Monogr., No. 6, 1952.
3. Kaiser, H. F. Varimax solution for primary mental abilities. Psychometrika, **25**: 153–158, 1960.
4. Lorr, M., Jenkins, R. J. and O'Connor, J. P. Factors descriptive of psychopathology and behavior of hospitalized psychotics. J. Abnorm. Soc. Psychol., **50**: 78–86, 1955.
5. Lorr, M., O'Connor, J. P. and Stafford, J. W. Confirmation of nine psychotic symptom patterns. J. Clin. Psychol., **13**: 252–257, 1957.
6. Lorr, M. The Wittenborn psychiatric syndromes: An oblique rotation. J. Consult. Psychol., **21**: 439–444, 1957.
7. Moore, T. V. The essential psychoses and their fundamental syndromes. Stud. Psychol. Psychiat., **3**: 1–128, 1933.
8. Wittenborn, J. R. A new procedure for evaluating mental hospital patients. J. Consult. Psychol., **14**: 500–501, 1950.
9. Wittenborn, J. R. Symptom patterns in a group of mental hospital patients. J. Consult. Psychol., **15**: 290–302, 1951.
10. Wittenborn, J. R. and Holzberg, J. D. The generality of psychiatric syndromes. J. Consult. Psychol., **15**: 372–380, 1951.
11. Wittenborn, J. R., Mandler, G. and Waterhouse, I. K. Symptom patterns in youthful mental hospital patients. J. Clin. Psychol., **7**: 323–327, 1951.
12. Wittenborn, J. R. and Bailey, C. The symptoms of involutional psychosis. J. Consult. Psychol., **16**: 13–17, 1952.
13. Wittenborn, J. R., Herz, M. I., Kurtz, K. H., Mandell, W. and Tatz, S. The effect of rater differences on symptom rating scale clusters. J. Consult. Psychol., **16**: 107–109, 1952.
14. Wittenborn, J. R. and Weiss, W. Patients diagnosed manic depressive psychosis-manic state. J. Consult. Psychol., **16**: 193–198, 1952.
15. Wittenborn, J. R. *Psychiatric Rating Scales.* Psychological Corp., New York, 1955.
16. Wittenborn, J. R. Rotational procedures and descriptive inferences. J. Consult. Psychol., **21**: 445–447, 1957.

Learning Theory and the Treatment of Depression*

Arnold A. Lazarus

Difficulties in defining and measuring "depression" operationally have led behavior therapists largely to ignore the subject. This paper describes several operational factors which lend themselves to more objective assessment and therapeutic maneuvers. Within this context, S-R analyses can presumably lead to effective and specific treatment procedures. Three treatment techniques are described, and one method (time projection with positive reinforcement) is described in considerable detail.

Depression, according to Hathaway and McKinley (1951) "is the most ubiquitous of the patterns seen in psychological abnormality." Yet apart from exploratory studies on conditionability (e.g. Ban *et al.*, 1966) behavior therapists have tended to ignore the subject or have dealt with it mainly *en passant.* Psychoanalysts, by contrast, have invested much energy in attempting to unravel the putative unconscious dynamics involved. The general psychiatric literature on the topic of depression, although extremely vast, is disappointingly inconsistent. For instance, there does not seem to be an acceptable system of classification or a standard nomenclature. Even the broadest nosological divisions are open to criticism. The validity of the numerous sub-divisions such as "involutional melancholia" in contrast to the "manic-depressive reaction", as distinct from "schizo-affective disorders" as opposed to "agitated depressions", etc. certainly does not hold up well under statistical scrutiny (e.g., Stenstedt, 1959). The main difficulty as Blinder (1966) points out, is that the current nosology and taxonomy of depression is based upon the old Kraepelinian classification of mental disorders as definite disease entities.

Despite the perennial dispute which centers around the distinction between endogenous and exogenous (reactive) depressions, there is little doubt, as Maddison and Duncan (1965) point out, that many depressions are based entirely

From *Behavioral Research and Therapy*, 1968, **6**, 83–89. Reproduced by permission.
*I wish to thank Dr. J. P. Brady, Dr. A. T. Beck and Dr. T. Schnurer for their comments and advice.

on *physiological* factors (i.e. some genetic, enzymatic, metabolic, endocrine, or other biochemical disturbance). The picture is further complicated by "mixed depressions" and so-called "masked depressions" (in which the patient initially complains only of atypical somatic symptoms). Faced with these diagnostic difficulties it is well worth inquiring whether learning theory can bring the field into clearer focus.

In general, where a therapist finds himself unable to account for a persistent response pattern in terms of contiguous associations, drive reduction, stimulus generalization, positive or negative reinforcement, or any other principle of learning, he is best advised to consider the likelihood of organic pathology. This is by no means a cut-and-dried matter, but one cannot ascribe to learning, response patterns which have no logical antecedents. Learned responses do not mysteriously well up from unconscious depths. They have a discernible history and, for this reason, a careful S-R analysis is considered indispensable for adequate diagnosis and therapy.

The main purpose of this paper is to present some of the many and complex variables involved in understanding, assessing, and treating "psychogenic" or "reactive" depressions. It is perhaps necessary first to try and define the subject matter under discussion.

PROBLEMS OF DEFINITION

Depression is exceedingly difficult to define (let alone measure!) and it is clear that many diverse phenomena have been lumped together under this term. It is difficult to evoke "depression" in experimental subjects, and even more difficult to isolate and maintain this response in a "pure" state. Yet, the temptation to deny depression status as a subject matter for scientific consideration must be resisted—if for no reason other than the fact that clinicians daily are consulted by thousands of people who say they feel depressed. Literature, art, drama, and psychiatric reports are replete with descriptions of depression which are often at variance with each other.

Shall we define depression as a subjective experience involving inner dejection, despair, misery, despondency, futility, or perhaps in such terms as nuclear unworthiness or implosive aggression? Or should we avoid the snares of subjectivity and like Skinner (1953), simply define depression as a general weakening of one's behavioral repertoire? But as Ferster (1965) points out: "Whether a man who moves and acts slowly is 'depressed' or merely moving slowly is not easily or reliably determined by observing his behavior alone."

If we compile a catalogue of operant responses, we might establish a base rate of frequent weeping, decreased food intake, frequent statements of dejection and self-reproach, psychomotor retardation, difficulties with memory and concentration, insomnia or a fitful sleep pattern, and general apathy and withdrawal. Descriptively, depressed patients primarily express a pool of gloomy feelings and pessimistic thoughts, and are relatively refractory to various kinds of stimulation, while displaying one or more of the above-mentioned operant responses.

Some theorists separate depression from what Freud (1925) termed "the normal emotion of grief" which he felt one would never regard as a morbid condition in need of therapeutic intervention. In fact, he stated that "we look upon any interference with it as inadvisable or even harmful." From a behavioral point of view, this separation seems to have no therapeutic usefulness. What criteria can be utilized to differentiate "normal grief" from intense or protracted grief, which is indistinguishable from "depression"?

Dengrove (1966) has in fact successfully treated grief reactions, whether due to the death of a loved one, separation, or desertion, by systematic desensitization. He commences by having the patient visualize the person or the "lost object" in a series of formerly happy and pleasant contexts. Then, under conditions of deep muscle relaxation, he slowly moves forward in time gradually progressing to the events of the funeral. He adds that if fear of death or reactions of guilt are present, these are included in the hierarchy.

DEPRESSION AND ANXIETY

It is sometimes difficult to separate depression from "anxiety". While it is true that depression is often a consequence of "anxiety that is unusually intense or prolonged" (Wolpe and Lazarus, 1966, p. 162), it is important to separate anxiety from depression and to stress that they usually have different antecedents.

Fundamentally, anxiety may be viewed as a response to noxious or threatening stimuli, and depression may be regarded as a function of inadequate or insufficient reinforcers. In Skinnerian terms, this would probably result in a weakened behavioral repertoire. A depressed person is virtually on an extinction trial. Some significant reinforcer has been withdrawn. There is loss and deprivation—loss of money or love, status or prestige, recognition or security, etc. More subtle factors are sometimes involved, e.g. loss of youth or a particular loss of body functioning. Clinicians are sometimes puzzled by depressions which have their onset when an individual finally attains a pinnacle of success. One reason for these depressive patterns is perhaps the loss of striving.

Ferster (1965) describes how diverse factors such as (a) sudden environmental changes, (b) punishment and aversive control, and (c) shifts in reinforcement contingencies give rise to depression. For him, the essential characteristic of a depressed person is "a reduced frequency of emission of positively reinforced behavior."

The essence of therapy in overcoming anxiety is to remove the noxious elements and/or change the patient's responses towards them. Depressed patients require a different schedule of reinforcement and/or need to learn a way of recognizing and utilizing certain reinforcers at their disposal.

Where depression is secondary to anxiety, it may prove helpful to deal with the anxiety component (e.g. by means of relaxation, desensitization, assertive training, aversion-relief, feeding responses, galvanic stimulation, etc.). In this paper, the section on therapy will consider the treatment of those cases in whom the depressive component is uppermost and in whom the removal of attendant anxieties is unlikely to dislodge the debilitating depressive reaction.

CLINICAL ASSESSMENT

One pragmatic rule is that when the depressive verbalizations, such as nihilistic statements and complaints of helplessness and hopelessness, do not center around stressful or other provoking emotional experiences, endogenous (i.e. physiological) factors must receive diagnostic priority. The treatment of depressions which are primarily physiological in nature usually calls for drugs and/or ECT (Maddison and Duncan, 1965), possibly in a supportive psychotherapeutic setting. The converse is true when treating depressions in which psychological features predominate. Here, intensive psychological techniques are called for, and the use of medication (if any) is mainly palliative.

An adequate life history remains an indispensable aid towards a valid and reliable assessment of the patient's condition. Consider the following case: Miss B. D., a 29-yr-old unmarried female developed persistent feelings of depression following a prolonged bout of viral influenza. She felt most depressed in the early morning hours but was seldom depressed in the evenings. She fell asleep readily but kept waking up intermittently, and would usually fail to go back to sleep after 3 a.m. at which time she experienced perseverating morbid thoughts. She ate poorly since her illness, had lost weight and was constipated. She accused herself of indolence and had lost her *joie de vivre.* A family history revealed that the patient's mother had been treated for a "puerperal depression."

To the writer's surprise, several clinicians ventured to make differential diagnoses based on the scanty material outlined above. Learning theory demands a detailed and precise description of S-R patterns before problem identification can be attempted. Presented with the syndrome described in the case of Miss B. D. (a physiological precipitant, diurnal variation, characteristic sleep pattern, weight loss, statements of self-recrimination, and a family history of depression), too many clinicians might be inclined to label the problem "endogenous" without further inquiry. A more detailed behavior analysis revealed that the patient had been unhappy for some time with her work situation, that her fiance had been acting in an inconsistent manner, that her mother had become increasingly demanding, and that she was concerned about some financial reversals her family had suffered in recent months. Furthermore, her depressive content and her perseverating thoughts were always focused on her specific problem areas. A program of assertive training resulted in a new work situation, a new boyfriend, a contrite mother, and an efficient accountant. Not surprisingly, she no longer complained of depression and has withstood a 3-yr follow-up inquiry.

SPECIFIC METHODS OF TREATMENT

The generic conception of depression as a consequence of inadequate or insufficient reinforcement requires elaboration. The obvious withdrawal of a reinforcer (such as loss of money, work, or friendship) followed by a pattern of misery and gloom, calls for very little diagnostic ingenuity. The clinician is taxed most by those patients who show no obvious loss to account for their depression. Some very subtle features are sometimes operative. For instance, an expected loss or any anticipation of a non-reinforcing state of affairs may precipitate various intensities of depression. These cases are sometimes too hastily classified as "endogenous depressions." Furthermore, depression which may have had physiological origins and/or obvious history of reinforcement-deprivation, may be maintained by operant consequences. The patient when "blue" finds people who cheer-him-up and they thus reinforce his depressive behavior. Therapy must take cognizance of both antecedent factors and the consequences of behavior.

Most therapists, when confronted by depressed patients, prescribe anti-depressant medication and a combination of reassurance and supportive therapy. Let us turn to some more specific therapeutic strategies.

Environmental manipulation has an obvious place in those cases where depression appears to be a consequence of inimical life situations—an unsatisfactory job, an unhappy marriage, social isolation, etc. These non-rewarding circumstances are often altered by a touch of assertiveness and by some therapeutic ingenuity in fostering recreational pursuits, meaningful friendships, hobbies and other constructive activities. As already mentioned, when depression is secondary to anxiety, the elimination of the latter (by means of the usual behavioral techniques) is often enough of a rewarding contingency to break through the depressive condition. Three specific anti-depressive behavioral techniques will now be outlined for those cases in whom "reactive" depression is the primary complaint.

1. Time Projection with Positive Reinforcement

The truism "time heals" ignores the fact that the passage of time *per se* is not therapeutic, but that psychological healing occurs because time permits new or competing responses to emerge. Generally, an event which causes intense annoyance or distress can be viewed with indifference or detachment after say a lapse of 6 months or a year. The therapeutic utility and application of this observation is illustrated by the following case history:

Miss C. H., a 23-yr-old art student, became acutely depressed when her boyfriend informed her that he intended marrying one of her classmates. She became sleepless, anorexic, restless, and weepy. Previously she had been a most talented and enthusiastic student; now she was unable to concentrate on her work, had stopped attending classes, and had become apathetic and listless. After 10 days, her parents persuaded her to consult a psychiatrist who prescribed amphetamines and barbiturates, whereupon she made a suicidal attempt by swallowing all her pills. Fortunately, the dose was not lethal. She refused to seek further psychiatric help, but her family physician nevertheless requested the writer to conduct a home visit.

It was difficult to establish rapport but the patient was finally responsive to emphatic statements of sympathy and reassurance. She agreed to see the writer at his consulting room on the following day. A behavioral inquiry revealed that prior to her unrequited love relationship, she had enjoyed painting, sculpting, and practicing the guitar. She also went horse-riding and displayed some interest in symphony concerts. During the 10 months of her love affair, she had exchanged all of these activities for "stock-car racing, amateur dramatics and a few wild parties."

As the patient proved highly susceptible to hypnotic techniques, a trance state was induced and the following time projection sequence was applied:

"It is almost 3:15 p.m. on Wednesday, April 14, 1965. (This was the date of the actual consultation.) Apart from sleeping, eating, etc., how could you have occupied these 24 hr? You could have gone horse-riding for a change, or taken your guitar out of mothballs . . . (5-sec pause) . . . Let's push time forward another 24 hr. You are now 48 hr ahead in time. Enough time has elapsed to have started a painting and done some sculpting. You may even have enjoyed a ride in the country and attended a concert. Think about these activities; picture them in your mind; let them bring a good feeling of pleasant associations, of good times . . . (5-sec pause) . . . Let's advance even further in time. A whole week has gone by, and another, and yet another. Now these past three weeks into which you have advanced have been busy and active. Reflect back for a moment on three weeks of enjoyable activity . . . (10-sec pause) . . . Now you move further forward in time. Days are flying past; time advances; days become weeks; time passes; weeks become months. It is now 6 months later. It's the 14th of October, 1965. Look back on the past 6 months, from April to October. Think about the months that separate April from October. What have you done during May, June, July, August, and September? (Pause of 5 sec) . . . Now six months ago, going back to April, you were very upset. In retrospect, how do you feel? Think back; reflect over an incident now more than 6 months old. If it still bothers you, signal to me by raising your left index finger."

As the patient did not raise her finger, she was told that she would recall the entire time projection sequence and return back in time to April 14, feeling as she did during October. She was then dehypnotized and asked to recount her feelings. (If she had signalled, the time projection sequence would have been continued, up to 2-yr ahead.) She stated: "How can I put it in words? Let me just explain it in three ways. First, I feel kind of foolish; second, there are lots of pebbles on the beach; and number three, there's something inside that really wants to find an outlet on canvass. Does that make sense?"

Miss C. H. was interviewed a week later. She reported having enjoyed many productive hours, had regained her appetite, and had been sleeping soundly. There were some minor episodes of "gloom" which responded to self-induced imagery, similar to the therapeutic time-projection sequence. She cancelled her subsequent appointments, stating that she had completely overcome her depression. This impression was confirmed by her parents and the referring physician. A follow-up after a year revealed that she had been exposed to a series of disappointments which often led to temporary bouts of depression (none, however, as severe as that which had led her to therapy).

Some patients have responded well to this technique when neither hypnosis nor relaxation were employed. All successful cases, however, were able to picture vivid images. Although depressed patients are usually deaf to advice and guidance, the cognitive effects of this procedure are similar to the old "pull - yourself - together- sufficiently - to - do something-creative-and-then-you-will-feel-better" doctrine. Once the patient can imagine himself sufficiently freed from his oppressive inertia to engage in some enjoyable (or formerly enjoyable) activity, a lifting of depressive effect is often apparent. This may be sustained by insuring that the patient thereupon experiences actual rewarding activities.

The time projection sequence has been used with 11 patients. Six cases responded excellently, two improved moderately, and three were unimproved. These results refer to one-session trials.

2. Affective Expression

Reference has already been made to the notion that depressed patients are relatively refractory to most forms of stimulation. Yet almost any stimulus which shatters this web of inertia may also vanquish their depression—temporarily at least. The writer recalls witnessing a severely depressed patient evince an extreme startle reaction followed by panic at a false fire alarm. Both his subjective report and his overt behavior revealed the absence of depression for many hours thereafter. It is hypothesized that when an individual feels or expresses anger, depressive affect is often undermined. This idea was bolstered when a patient who grew angry at the writer for asking too many personal questions remarked: "I was feeling very depressed when I walked in here, but now I feel fine." *In general, the writer submits that anger (or the deliberate stimulation of feelings of amusement, affection, sexual excitement, or anxiety) tends to break the depressive cycle.* The clinical utility of this principle is suggested by a patient who was exceedingly depressed about the end of a love affair. He became furious when he discovered that his ex-girlfriend had spread false rumors about him, whereupon his depression immediately (and lastingly) disappeared. The writer has several cases on record in which the development of "righteous indignation" rather than "self-blame" appeared to coincide with the elimination of depression and suicidal feelings.

3. Behavioral Deprivation and Retraining

The schema of depression elaborated in the previous sections is that a chronic and/or acute non-reinforcing state of affairs can result in a condition where the person becomes relatively refractory to most stimuli and enters a state of "depression". A period of deliberate or enforced "sensory deprivation" and inertia, may, however, make the depressed patient more susceptible to incoming stimuli, so that positive reinforcement may take effect. This is in keeping with the practices of "Morita Therapy" (Kora, 1965) where the patient is subjected to a 5- to 7-day period of absolute bed rest, without access to any external stimuli (i.e. no reading, writing, smoking, visitors, or other distractions are permitted). At the end of this period, most people find positive reinforcement value in almost *any* external stimulus. After leaving bed, patients are gradually exposed to a graduated series of tasks commencing with "light work" for 1 week (a form of occupational therapy) and eventually progress from "heavy work" to "complicated work".

Although Morita Therapy is not advocated by its practitioners specifically for the treatment of depression (they have applied it with success to cases of so-called neurasthenia, anxiety states and obsessional disorders), the writer has had some encouraging preliminary results when applying it to depressed patients in a less stringent manner.

The well-known methods of narcosis or sleep therapy (e.g. Loucas and Stafford-Clark, 1965; Andreev, 1960) might also have a place in this schema. It must be emphasized again that, from the behavioral viewpoint, the rationale for these methods is that they render persons more amenable to a wider range of positive reinforcers.

To recapitulate, therapy for psychological depressions requires the introduction of sufficiently powerful reinforcers to disrupt the "emotional inhibitions" which characterize the behavior of depressed patients. If the patient is enabled merely to contemplate future positive reinforcements, depressive responses usually diminish or disappear. The time-projection sequence described above makes use of this observation. Any change in emotional tone in which excitatory rather than inhibitory affect predominates (whether due to positive or negative reinforcement) is also likely to impede depressive reactions. When depressed patients are highly refractory to the usual range of positive reinforcers, they are sometimes rendered more amenable to stimulation after undergoing a general regime of stimulus deprivation. The three methods discussed above are merely a small sample of the many and varied techniques which can be advanced within a general behavioral framework.

REFERENCES

Andreev B. V. (1960) *Sleep Therapy in the Neuroses.* Consultant's Bureau, New York.

Ban T. Z., Choi S. M., Lehmann H. E. and Adamo E. (1966) Conditional reflex studies in depression. *Can. psychiat. Ass. J.* 11, S98–S104.

Blinder M. G. (1966) The pragmatic classification of depression. *Am. J. Psychiat.* 123, 259–269.

Dengrove E. (1966) *Treatment of Non-phobic Disorders by the Behavioral Therapies.* Lecture to the Association for Advancement of the Behavioral Therapies, in New York on 17 December.

Ferster C. B. (1965) Classification of behavioral pathology. In *Research in Behavior Modification.* (Eds. Krasner L. and Ullmann L. P.). Holt, Rinehart and Winston, New York.

Freud S. (1925) Mourning and melancholia. In *Collected Papers,* Vol. IV. Hogarth, London.

Hathaway S. R. and McKinley J. C. (1951) *Manual of the M.M.P.I.* The Psychological Corporation, New York.

Kora T. (1965) Morita therapy. *Int. J. Psychiat.* 1, 611–640.

Loucas K. P. and Stafford-Clark D. (1965) Electronarcosis at Guy's. *Guy's Hosp. Reps.* 114, 223–237.

Maddison D. and Duncan G. M. (1965) (Eds.) *Aspects of Depressive Illness.* Livingston, Edinburgh.

Skinner, B. F. (1953) *Science and Human Behavior.* Macmillan, New York.

Stenstedt A. (1959) Involutional melancholia. *Acta Psychiat. Scand.* 34, *Suppl.* 127, 1–71.

Wolpe J. and Lazarus A. A. (1966) *Behavior Therapy Techniques.* Pergamon Press, Oxford.

Affective Disorder: IV. Mania

Paula J. Clayton

F. N. Pitts, Jr.*

George Winokur

Clinically, mania differs from depression in other parameters than mood and psychomotor activity. Lundquist (4) noted that manic patients were younger than depressives at first admission to a psychiatric hospital and that the percentage of men in a group of manics is higher than in a group of depressives. In a family study, Stenstedt (6) found no differences between probands with mania or with depression for occurrence of manics and/or depressions in siblings.

Other factors which are of interest in mania are those involving the clinical picture. Of importance is the question of the limits of this clinical picture; for example, what kinds of symptoms in the manic individual would occasion diagnostic difficulties but would not rule out the diagnosis of mania? Passivity and depersonalization, generally considered to be associated with schizophrenia, might fit this category. Langfeldt (3) has pointed out that mixtures of manic symptoms with typical depersonalization and derealization make the question of the prognosis difficult. This, of

From *Comprehensive Psychiatry,* 1965, 6, 313–322. Reprinted by permission of Grune & Stratton, Inc. and the author.

This investigation was supported by USPHS grants MH-5804, MH-5938 and MH-7081.

*USPHS grant K3-MH-18,292.

course, bears directly on the differentiation between schizophrenia and mania as the former has ordinarily a bad and the latter a good prognosis.

In a large study of affective disorders it was possible to study the subentity of mania and to take into account some of the problems which have been mentioned above. This paper presents this material.

SUBJECTS AND METHODS

A structured interview was administered to 768 consecutive patients who were admitted to Renard Hospital in St. Louis. The procedure has been described more fully in previous papers (5, 7, 8); material concerning family history of psychiatric illness was recorded as well as discharge diagnoses on all patients. In the study reported here, 366 patients were given the diagnosis of affective disorder. This general diagnosis included psychotic depression, manic depressive depressed, manic depressive manic and involutional psychosis. Twelve patients with the diagnosis of reactive depression were omitted from the study and are presented in another paper. Thirty-one patients with a manic reaction were separated from the large group of affective disorders. The ratio of manics to other affective disorders was 1:11. Patients in whom severe alcoholism or drug intake might have obscured the picture were excluded, although in a few of these the possibility existed that mania was the primary diagnosis. All 31 patients were re-evaluated by a perusal of the chart. Although the data in the chart were collected in a nonsystematic fashion it was possible to determine the clinical picture in those that had been called manic. This clinical picture is presented in Table 1. The frequency of the appearance of symptoms depended on whether or not the symptom had been recorded as positive or negative in the chart; and, as a consequence, for each symptom a different number of patients was used.

Other factors besides the clinical picture which added reliability to the diagnosis of mania were previous depressions which were seen in 22 of the patients and previous manias which were seen in 18 of the patients. Further, in order to be included in the group of manias all patients had to have a period of good social functioning as an adult.

The 31 patients were then compared to the patients in the other affective disorders in terms of age, sex and family history of psychiatric illness. In order to determine the age of onset of illness and age of first admission, 31 manics were matched with 31 patients with depression. The matching was done for the variables of age, sex and socioeconomic status (ward or private patient) at the time of the admission which was recorded for the large study. The 2 matched groups were then compared. Finally, the 7 patients who exhibited feelings of passivity were singled out for special study. These were followed up with the idea of determining whether the symptom of passivity which is generally considered to be a schizophrenic symptom in fact removed the 7 patients from the group of affective disorders.

RESULTS

Clinical factors. In reviewing the 31 patients with mania, a number of clinical observations were striking. In 24 patients there was recorded in the chart the presence or absence of a depression immediately prior to when the onset of the mania was recorded. In 14 of these 24 patients (58 per cent), their mania was preceded by a depression. In all 31 patients a note was made about the presence or absence of the symptom of confusion (disorientation or memory lapses). Eighteen (58 per cent) exhibited such a symptom. It is of interest to note that the high frequency of the symptom of confusion is rather similar to that noted by Hamilton (1) in his work on postpartum psychoses.

In evaluating the patients and the charts an effort was made to ascertain the clinical picture of each patient's first attack of psychiatric illness. Table 2 gives a breakdown of the kinds of first illnesses seen in these 31 manic patients.

These types of first illnesses were considered breaks in the individual's habitual adjustment after having done well in a social sense. It is noteworthy that a few of the patients had a first illness that could possibly have been called character and behavior disorder; and another and larger group had the onset as a depression.

Table 1. *The Symptom Picture in Mania (N = 31).*

Symptom	No. of patients with symptom recorded	% of patients with symptom recorded as positive
1. Hyperactivity	31	100
2. Euphoria	31	97
3. Flight of ideas	29	100
4. Distractibility	30	97
5. Circumstantiality	27	96
6. Push of speech	31	100
7. Increased sexuality	23	74
8. Grandiosity and/or religiosity	24	79
9. Decreased sleep	31	94
10. Delusions	26	73
11. Ideas of reference	26	77
12.[a] Passivity	15	47
13.[a] Depersonalization and/or derealization	14	43

[a]In symptoms 12 and 13 of Table 1 a note in the chart was not made enough times to reliably gauge the true frequency of the presence of the symptom.

Table 2. *Types of First Illnesses in Patients Admitted for Mania (N = 31).*

Type of illness	No. of patients
Mania	8
Depression	12
Paranoid state	1
Tearfulness and inability to adapt to service	1
"Combat fatigue"	2
Delirium	1
Nervousness, drinking, chest pain	1
Unknown	5
Total	31

Age and mania. When the 31 patients were evaluated according to age, it was noted that 22 per cent of them at the time of the index admission were over age 50. In contrast an evaluation of the age of the patients with the remaining 335 affective disorders indicated that 47 per cent were over the age of 50. A group of 31 depressives were matched for age, sex and socioeconomic status to the 31 manics. These 2 groups were then evaluated by a perusal of their clinical histories for age at first symptoms and the age of the first psychiatric admission. It was possible to obtain a matching of 28 pairs for the age of the first symptom and of 30 pairs for the age of the first admission. This material is shown in Table 3. It would appear from Table 3 that manics are significantly younger at the time that they become ill and are admitted earlier than depressives.

Sex and Mania. Fifty-eight per cent of the 31 manic patients were males as opposed to 33 per cent of the patients with other affective disorders.

Family background. The 31 manics were compared with 335 patients with other affective disorders on family history of affective disorders in parents and siblings. Table 4 gives this material.

It would appear from Table 4 that there is little difference in family history of affective disorder in manics as compared to patients with other affective disorders. Alchoholism was seen in 13 per cent of the fathers of the manics as opposed to 9 per cent of the fathers of the other affective disorder patients.

Schizophrenic-like symptoms in mania. Seven patients were noted to have passivity feelings during the course of their illness. Even more admitted ideas of reference and delusional thinking. These latter 2 kinds of symptoms may be seen in almost any illness; therefore, it was decided to focus on passivity feelings as being most closely allied to schizophrenia. As a consequence, these 7 patients were selected for a personal follow-up. Five of these 7 patients had a family history of affective disorder. Short abstracts of their cases follow with a 2 year follow-up, below:

Table 3. *A Comparison of Manics and Depressives with Respect to Age of First Symptoms and First Admissions.*

	Mean age of 1st symptoms (28 pairs)	S.E. of diff. of means	Mean age of 1st admissions (30 pairs)	S.E. of diff. of means
Manics	28	2.9 ($p < .05$)	33	2.9 ($p < .05$)
Depressives	35		40	

Table 4. *Family History of Affective Disorder in Manics as Compared to Patients with Other Affective Disorders.*

	Manics (N = 31)	Other affective disorders (N = 335)
Affective disorder in fathers	16%	13%
Affective disorder in mothers	23%	23%
Affective disorder in parents and/or siblings	61%	47%

ABSTRACTS OF CASE HISTORIES

Case 1. A 33 year old married white woman at the time of the index admission. During her period in the hospital, her younger sister was admitted for a severe depression after a medically and psychiatrically serious suicidal attempt. The illness had started 2 years previously with tearfulness and depressed affect in the first trimester of her second pregnancy. She had trouble sleeping with early morning awakening; social life deteriorated as did her housework. She was self-depreciatory and had suicidal ideas. She was treated in psychotherapy and gradually became more spontaneous and outgoing. After the delivery she became depressed again, then improved, and about 8 months prior to the index admission became overactive, spoke rapidly, and slept little. She had moved and expressed the idea that people in her new neighborhood did not like her. Her mood started to fluctuate again and she took an overdose of sleeping pills in a suicidal attempt. She was admitted to a hospital where she was paranoid, specifically deluded that nurses were spys, and was very fearful. After 2 months in the hospital, she was discharged, was quite overactive sexually, and approached her psychotherapist sexually. Her husband described her at this time as being proud, witty, euphoric and quite active. She made a few suicidal gestures and was readmitted to the psychiatric hospital where she was treated with electroshock. She was discharged as well a month prior to the index admission. For about 2 days she appeared well and then became belligerent and began talking of sexual relations with her psychotherapist again. She claimed her husband stole a car and on an early morning wandered around a shopping center "all dolled up fit to kill." She was admitted to the county psychiatric hospital and was transferred to Renard for the index admission. At the time of admission she expressed her thoughts about 2 books and 2 drums that were in her house. To her, she said, they symbolized her psychotherapist and she, i.e., the 2 books and the drums meant beating it together and running away. The sound of a car motor running was interpreted as a message to leave a particular area. Objects that she found in an automobile meant to her that she should go to a department store to meet her psychotherapist. Mental status revealed that her speech was slow and circumstantial. She had feelings of passivity, i.e., that she was being hypnotized to wake up at 4:30 every morning. She had paranoid delusions and primary delusions. She was treated with very large doses of phenothiazines. She was discharged after 2½ months without any evidence of delusions or any other kind of schizophrenic thinking. Her diagnosis was that of manic depressive, manic. There was much staff disagreement with many contending that the proper diagnosis was paranoid schizophrenia.

Follow-Up. Since her discharge 2½ years ago, the patient has been followed up continually, although infrequently, by a psychiatrist. She has been treated with drugs, chiefly antidepressants, and supportive psychotherapy. She was readmitted 6 months ago for 2 weeks with symptoms of depression which included depressed mood, irritability, tiredness, sleep difficulty, fear of going insane, decreased libido, increased alcoholic consumption and delusional self-depreciation. She was diagnosed as manic depressive psychosis, depressed. She was treated with EST and her condition improved. Prior to this she had resumed teaching and when she was interviewed she was engaged in substitute teaching. On interview she again seemed depressed. She had an increased latency of response and psychomotor retardation. She complained of being tired and stated that her husband felt she had been drinking too much. She felt she had not fulfilled her obligations as a mother or a teacher, but was extremely confused as to how she might accomplish these things. Despite her depressed affect she realized that her reasoning during her index hospitalization was irrational and denied any such disturbances since.

Case 2. A 29 year old married woman at the time of the index admission. The mother was subject to periods of depression and irritability. A paternal great aunt may have attempted suicide. A maternal grandmother was overly religious and seclusive. The patient's first illness started during her first year in college at which time she had a bout of malaise and suffered a marked loss of energy lasting for about a month. Six years prior to the index admission she had a similar episode for which she had 2 short hospitalizations. After each attack the patient claimed she was back to "normal." Two years prior to the index admission she had the delusion that her child had brucellosis and that she was being experimented upon. She told of auditory hallucinations. She was hospitalized. After 2 months on phenothiazine therapy she was discharged as improved. She was considered undiagnosed at this time. During the interim between this hospitalization and the index hospitalization, she continued to have alien thoughts which consisted of ideas of control, influence and reference; however, they did not interfere with her social functioning. At the time of the index admission she had ideas of control and felt as though she were being programmed. She thought that a gentleman of her acquaintance was behind this kind of control. She expressed the delusion that she was poisoned or drugged with a barbiturate. Other aspects of the mental status revealed an unkempt, endomorphic woman with a moderate increase in psychomotor activity. There seemed to be loosening of associations, tangentiality and vagueness. There was some push of speech. There was some grimacing and a great deal of hostility.

Her normal behavior, i.e., behavior out of the hospital, was that of an extremely active, domineering, vigorous woman. She was very loud and boisterous during her periods of being well.

She was treated with phenothiazines and discharged after a month. She still had delusions at the time of her discharge.

Follow-Up. Three months after her discharge she was seen as an office patient. She was back to being boisterous and overactive. She had abandoned her delusions and feelings of passivity. She was functioning well.

The patient could not be interviewed for follow-up as she had moved to another state; however, approximately 2 years after her index admission she wrote to her psychiatrist. The letter was coherent, rational and relevant. She stated, "I've felt better in the past few months than I can remember in the 30 years that went before. I have no major worries, fears or even chronic irritations. I'm at ease with my family, my friends, and myself. I do my work with reasonably good humor, and spend what time remains reading, drawing, or visiting with neighbors. I've gotten back to normal weight. I believe that I have steadily improved since my second hospitalization." She had had no further psychiatric care in the 1½ years since leaving the city and is judged to be well without defect.

Case 3. A 39 year old, white, married woman at the time of index admission. The mother has had an illness rather similar many years before the index admission. She was hospitalized and given a course of electroshock treatment. A maternal uncle was hospitalized in a psychiatric facility. At the age of 24 the patient had become wild and combative, was admitted to the hospital, and had a total thyroidectomy. She recovered and remained well for 14 years until 10 months prior to the index admission when she went through a period of crying episodes, was very irritable, complained of difficulty in concentration, and was treated with an antidepressant drug. At the time of her index admission she had primary delusions. She saw a mark on her left hand pointing to her wedding ring which had some special but secret meaning to her. She felt she was being controlled and had numerous auditory hallucinations. Gestures by people about her indicated to her that she was going to die. One gesture signified to her that she was divine. She was quite talkative and overactive prior to admission. On coming to the hospital she was smiling and laughing during the entire trip. She gave a history of thought deprivation and intrusion of extraneous thoughts. Mental status revealed a person with increase in psychomotor activity, tangentiality, and loosening of associations. Frequently the responses were irrelevant. She exhibited blocking on occasion. She engaged in religious posturing. At times there was self-depreciation and at other times marked grandiosity. She was treated with phenothiazines and discharged. Two months after the index admission she was readmitted because of an overdose of sleeping pills. She had been having difficulty getting to sleep at night, was feeling depressed. She was discharged and readmitted for a third time 3 months after the second admission. The diagnosis was manic depressive disease, depressed. She had depressive symptoms and admitted to some suspicious ideas.

Follow-Up. The patient was interviewed 2 years after discharge and appeared well at the time. She was still under psychiatric care, but the visits were infrequent. She had returned to her former job as court reporter and despite the fact that companions on this job formed the foundation for her former delusional material, she was having no difficulty. She had complete insight into her illness and was eager to relate her memories of the delusional material and her misinterpretations—"At the time I imagined a visitor to the floor was a female doctor watching me and that magazine articles were laid open and television programs turned on especially to torture me." She denied any delusions, hallucinations, disturbance of symbolization or passivity feelings since her discharge.

Case 4. A 28 year old, white, married woman. There is no history of psychiatric illness in the family. For a period of 6 months prior to admission she had a lack of energy, felt she was getting nothing done. A month prior to admission she had a loss of appetite with weight loss, was unable to concentrate and was irritable. She was sleeping poorly and was tearful. She became suspicious of her inlaws and husband and neighbors and felt they were plotting behind her back. She felt that these people knew what she was thinking about and were 2 or 3 "pages ahead" of what she was doing. She felt that she was like an actor in a play and people were saying things to her that had special significance. Two or 3 weeks prior to the admission she had feelings of unreality. She admitted to auditory hallucinations and on one occasion had visual hallucinations. Mental status revealed a woman quite friendly, frequently silly, and laughing at things that might be taken more seriously. Her mood was one of almost euphoria. Speech was clear, spontaneous, but she was circumstantial. There was loosening of associations. She had delusions, auditory and visual hallucinations, ideas of reference and influence, and feelings of passivity. She was disoriented as far as the month was concerned and made mistakes in simple calculations. Organic work-up was negative. Patient was placed on phenothiazine drugs. She became more appropriate, socialized well. The delusional material and the hallucinations disappeared for the most part. She was discharged and followed as an outpatient.

Follow-Up. The patient was seen approximately 2 years after her discharge, on the day of her second hospitalization. She had been followed continuously since her index admission by a psychiatrist who treated her with supportive psychotherapy and large doses of phenothiazine and antidepressants. He felt she had been continually ill with paranoid delusions, e.g., relatives trying to ruin her marriage and trying to get her children from her. Approximately 1 month before her second admission she became hyperactive, fearful she was losing her mind and sensitive about her illness. She denied sleep difficulty, diurnal variation of mood, loss of interest in her surroundings or guilt feelings. Immediately before admission she lost weight, cried continuously and ruminated about suicide. On examination she denied disturbance of symbolization, passivity feelings, hallucinations (auditory or tactile), depersonalization or derealization. She admitted to some of these symptoms with her last (index) admission but denied any since. She admitted she had been suspicious of her inlaws in the past but felt now that this was unwarranted. She appeared depressed. She was treated with minimal sedation and discharged after 4 days. It seems she would best fit into the diagnostic category of schizophrenic reaction, schizoaffective type.

Case 5. A 50 year old, married, white man. A young daughter and son are said to be nervous. Patient had been a heavy drinker for 9 to 10 years and had been hospitalized with the diagnosis of alcoholism and depressive reaction. Prior to admission the patient had had no alcohol for 3 months. He was taking Antabuse daily. A few days prior to the index admission the patient became very upset, stuttered, made sounds of whistling and snorting and beat out rhythms. Mental status was essentially as above with the additional symptom that he said he had been controlled by radar.

Follow-Up. This patient was interviewed by telephone 2½ years after his index hospitalization. Since his discharge from the hospital the patient had had 4 brief (5 day) admissions to a general hospital to "dry out" from drinking. He does not drink daily, but rather goes on occasional binges, 3 to 4 days of constant drinking, which are terminated by hospitalization. He considers his index admission a "nervous breakdown" unlike anything he had had before or has had since. He feels it was precipitated by overworking on a civic play, "My Fair Lady," and attributes his symptoms of euphoria, singing, beating drums, etc., to this. He has had no periods of euphoria or depression since. During his 10 minute interview he was rational and coherent. He should be considered a chronic alcoholic as well as manic.

Case 6. A 43 year old, white, divorced woman. There was no family history of psychiatric illness. Her first psychiatric problem occurred 16 years previously during which time she was treated at the State Hospital with electroshock therapy. She had subsequent admissions to public hospitals for manias and depressions. At the time of the index admission she had been admitted to Barnes Hospital for a vein stripping operation. One week after surgery she began showing increased motor activity, walked constantly up and down the halls, laughed inappropriately, showed marked flight of ideas with push of speech, and on one occasion expressed paranoid ideas. At the time of her transfer to the psychiatric section at Renard she appeared moderately agitated with flat, perplexed faces. There was marked push of speech, tangentiality, flight of ideas, and incoherence. There was increased psychomotor activity. She admitted to ideas of reference and influence and there was some paranoid ideas evident. She denied feelings of unreality, depersonalization, and there was no evidence of auditory or visual hallucinations. Patient was treated with electroshock therapy and discharged as improved.

Follow-Up. During the intervening 2 years she had been under outpatient psychiatric care with weekly psychotherapy sessions and daily phenothiazines. She had been hypomanic most of the time but had experienced at least 2 episodes of marked depression lasting 2–3 weeks each. At time of follow-up she had been readmitted "because I began to get really high and to prevent severe mania"; at this time she was expansive, overly energetic, euphoric with marked push of speech, and irritable. She denied paranoid ideation, feelings of unreality, depersonalization, or ideas of reference or influence. She responded to large doses of phenothiazine and electroshock and, again, was discharged as improved.

Case 7. A 42 year old, white, married man at the time of index admission. Family history revealed one brother who had religious preoccupations and one sister who was quite nervous during menopause. The first psychiatric illness had occurred 16 years previously when he was hospitalized for a few weeks in Japan. At that time he complained of a pain in his chest and was nervous. He was drinking quite heavily at the time. Eleven years prior to the index admission he had an episode when he was preoccupied with religion and the meaning of life and felt that he was a "form of Christ." During all this time he was apparently drinking quite heavily. For 3 months prior to admission his drinking had decreased somewhat. Four months prior to the index admission the patient began to appear preoccupied and squandered unknown quantities of money on clothes and shirts despite rather limited finances. He began gambling and attempted to buy a Cadillac car which was considerably above his limited financial status. Further, he felt that things began to crystallize and had various kinds of religious thoughts, such as letting himself and his subconscious go into the "cosmic stream" and feeling at peace. Three months prior to admission the patient told his wife he had heard Gabriel's horn and told her that the kingdom had arrived. On the day of admission he began thinking about Egyptians having masks like dogs. He noted that God was dog spelled backwards and somehow arrived at the idea that he had to kill himself and would have to kill the dog. He began strangling the dog which weighed some 40 pounds. His wife tried to pull him off and he bit 3 of her fingers. He was admitted shortly to Renard Hospital and at the time admitted to ideas of control and influence but denied ideas of reference. He said that at the time he strangled the dog he had no control over himself but was controlled by some external force. The mental status revealed an obese, white male with a moderate increase in psychomotor activity. He was generally smiling and presented a rather jocular appearance. He showed some push of speech. His associations were loosened and rather vague at times. He was very circumstantial. He demonstrated paranoid delusional system with ideas of grandiosity. He related ideas of control. He denied hallucinations.

Follow-Up. The patient was seen approximately 2 years after his discharge and by coincidence, 8 days after his wife's death. He reported that for about 1 month after his discharge he was "sick and mixed up," but he had felt well since. He still drinks half pint of whiskey daily, gambles occasionally ("two dollar bets") and is religiously concerned, although he does not feel he has a mission or that his bible has special meaning to him. His religious preoccupation seems to be quite philosophizing more than overt assurance of fact. His manner was jovial and expansive. He admitted concern about the "sickness coming back on him," especially in regard to the homocidal tendencies he had shown. He still wondered why he had killed his dog. He denied disturbance of symbolization, passivity feelings, hallucinations, delusions or depersonalization since discharge. He had not seen a psychiatrist since his hospitalization. He was considered a chronic alcoholic, even by his own admission.

DISCUSSION

It is quite clear from the data that some of the observations of Lundquist are confirmed. Hospitalized manics contain a higher per cent of men than hospitalizable depressions. This finding might be explained as being a social phenomenon; namely, that men by and large in depressions are able to work their way through them and in fact do so because of their need in the family situation. On the other hand, it is possible that there is some biological difference which accounts for the increased prevalence of males having manias. Another observation of Lundquist which is confirmed is the question of age of onset and age of admission. Lundquist found that the first admission was earlier for manics than for depressives and we have found that not only is this true but also the first manifestation of the illness which has been noted is earlier for manics. Once more this might possibly be a social phenomenon, i.e., that the manifestations of mania are considerably more dramatic and noticeable than the manifestations of depression. On the other hand, it is entirely possible that age contributes some pathoplastic effect on the manifestations of the illness.

The clinical picture of mania is rather striking. The triad of euphoria, overactivity and push of speech was seen in almost all the patients reported here. Interestingly enough, other symptoms such as those of confusion were seen as well as a number of schizophrenic symptoms. One would have to consider that if an individual shows rather the typical picture of mania with the symptoms and has had a period of time when he functioned rather well, that the diagnosis and prognosis should be based on these things rather than on the presence of occasional schizophrenic symptoms. In other words, the presence of schizophrenia might be made by exclusion if the symptoms of mania were not present. On the other hand, if they are present it would appear that they have equal or better weight in the determination of the prognosis. The aberrant factors in these cases were the schizophrenic-like symptoms.

In a follow-up study of 255 patients with acute schizophrenia and schizophreniform psychoses, Holmboe and Astrup evaluated the effect on prognosis of various symptoms such as incoherence, depersonalization, passivity and symbolism (2). Passivity feelings included such phenomena as foreign thoughts coming into the patient's head, a feeling that somebody is imposing his thoughts on the patient, thought deprivation and the patients saying that they are under hypnosis. Having such feelings as these led to a somewhat poorer prognosis than having incoherence and depersonalization but even with passivity feelings 34 per cent of the patients were considered completely cured. To this we might add that if the major part of the clinical picture is manic and the history one of good social functioning interspersed with episodic psychiatric illness, the disease is probably manic, not schizophrenic, and will have a good prognosis for the individual to recover from the attack.

Family histories of both depressives and manics are rather similar. There seems to be no reason to separate them as a different disorder. This raises an interesting point as to the possible biologic basis for the disease. Mania itself is the opposite of depression as far as the clinical picture is concerned. Nevertheless, there is no reason to assume that the biological background of mania is the exact opposite of that for depression. It might be essentially the same with other factors being of considerable importance in determining the actual clinical picture. Such factors might be age and sex and degree of development of the personality.

SUMMARY

In this paper 31 patients with a diagnosis of manic depressive, manic are matched for age, sex and socioeconomic status with 31 patients with a diagnosis of manic depressive, depressed. The study shows that hospitalized manics contain a higher percentage of men than hospitalized depressives and the manics are hospitalized at an earlier age. It is also noted that the first symptoms are seen at an earlier age.

There were no significant differences in the family histories of manics and depressives.

Turning to the clinical picture of mania, euphoria, overactivity and push of speech were seen in almost all patients studied. Objective confusion was seen in 18 of the 31 (58 per cent) patients. Eighteen of 24 patients (58 per cent), in whom information about depressive symptoms was recorded, reported a depression immediately preceding the onset of the mania. Special attention was given to those patients who exhibited schizophrenic symptomatology in their index admission. Seven patients with passivity feelings were personally interviewed approximately 2 years after their index admission. It was found that in none had classical schizophrenia with deterioration developed. Their cases histories are presented.

REFERENCES

1. Hamilton, J. A.: Post-partum Psychiatric Problems. St. Louis, C. V. Mosby Co., 1962.
2. Holmboe, R., and Astrup, C.: A follow-up study of 255 patients with acute schizophrenia and schizophreniform psychoses. Acta Psychiat. Neurol. Scand., Suppl. 115, Copenhagen, 1957.
3. Langfeldt, G.: The prognosis in schizophrenia. Acta Psychiat. Neurol. Scand., Suppl. 110, Copenhagen, 1956.
4. Lundquist, G.: Prognosis and course in manic depressive psychoses. Acta Psychiat. Neurol. Scand., Suppl. 35, Stockholm, 1945.
5. Pitts, F. N., Jr., and Winokur, G.: Affective disorder. III: Diagnostic correlates and incidence of suicide. J. Nerv. Ment. Dis. **139**:176–181, 1964.
6. Stenstedt, A.: A study in manic depressive psychosis. Acta Psychiat. Neurol. Scand., Suppl. 79, Copenhagen, 1952.
7. Winokur, G., and Pitts, F. N., Jr.: Affective disorder. I: Is reactive depression an entity. J. Nerv. Ment. Dis. **138**:541–547, 1964.
8. Woodruff, R., Pitts, F. N., Jr., and Winokur, G.: Affective disorder. II. A comparison of patients with endogenous depressions with and without family history of affective disorder. J. Nerv. Ment. Dis. **139**:49–52, 1964.

Campus Tragedy: A Study of Student Suicide*

Richard H. Seiden

Prior studies of college suicides have neglected the need for an adequate comparison or control group. To remedy this situation, student suicides were compared to their nonsuicidal classmates on selected demographic variables. Suiciding students could be significantly differentiated from their fellow students on the basis of age, class standing, major subject, nationality, emotional condition, and academic achievement. The suicidal students presented similar prodromal patterns which were precipitated by scholastic anxieties, concern over physical health, and difficult interpersonal relationships. Contrary to general belief, the greatest suicidal activity occurred during the beginning, not the final, weeks of the semester. On the basis of changes transpiring in the college population, a future increase of student suicide was predicted.

The act of self-destruction rudely challenges our supposed love for life and fear of death. It is always a puzzlement, but in no case is suicide more shocking or bewildering than it is in the college student. For here are a relatively privileged group of persons enjoying valued advantages of youth, intelligence, and educational opportunity. Why should persons, seemingly so rewarded, seek to kill themselves, and, indeed, to commit suicide at a rate significantly in excess of their noncollege peers (Bruyn & Seiden, 1965, p. 76)?

This perplexing question—"Why do students suicide?"—has motivated a great deal of concern among college health authorities leading to several studies and evaluations of the problem in American universities (Braaten & Darling, 1962; Jensen, 1955; Parrish, 1957; Raphael, Power, & Berridge, 1937; Temby, 1961). Unfortunately, these studies have all had an exclusively descriptive approach. They have drawn conclusions about certain characteristics of suicidal students but, seemingly, without appreciation for the degree to which these same characteristics are shared by the entire

From *Journal of Abnormal and Social Psychology*, 1966, 71, 389–399.

This research was supported by Grant #5 T1 MH-8104 from the National Institute of Mental Health.

*Revision of a paper presented to Psi Chi colloquium, Western Psychological Association, Honolulu, June 1965.

student body population. What has been conspicuously omitted is a baseline—a standard of comparison against which the diagnostic value of their findings might be judged. One is reminded of the gentleman who, when asked, "How is your wife?" astutely responded, "Compared to what?" This very question of relative comparison must also be asked in the study of student suicides.

The present study attempted to remedy this situation by applying a reasonable standard of comparison, namely, the great majority of fellow college students who do not commit suicide. By investigating what characteristics significantly differentiate suicidal students from their classmates plus examining those situational-temporal conditions associated with campus suicides, it was hoped to achieve a clearer diagnostic picture. Once the high-risk, suicide-prone student can be identified, a large and necessary step will have been taken toward the ultimate objective of effective prophylaxis.

METHOD

The approach used in the present study was one of analytic epidemiology, that is, comparing for particular characteristics the subject of student suicides with the total student body population from which they were drawn. This particular procedure meets the methodological criteria for selection of comparison groups, as stated by MacMahon, Pugh, and Ipsen (1960):

> A comparison group is a group of unaffected individuals believed to reflect the characteristics of the population from which the affected group was drawn. Ideally the comparison group should not differ from the affected group in any respect (other than not being affected) which might be likely to influence the frequency of the variable or variables suspected of being causally connected. This means either that both the patient and comparison groups must be representative of the same population or that if selective factors enter into the choice of the patterns, the same factors ought to enter into the selection of the comparison group [p. 235].

The method of the present study involved a comparison of the sample of 23 University of California at Berkeley (UCB) students who committed suicide during the 10-year period 1952 through 1961, with the entire UCB student body population during this same decade. The objective of this comparison was to determine what special characteristics differentiated the suicide-prone student from his classmates. Within this framework the following working definitions were employed: (*a*) *Student*—the definition of a student was established by registration on the Berkeley campus of the University of California, in either graduate or undergraduate status, during the regular college semester periods. Summer sessions were not included because of the unreliability of data for these periods and changes in the usual composition of the student body population during summer sessions. (*b*) *Suicide*—refers to a completed suicide, established by a death certificate stating suicide as the legal cause of death. In one instance, involving a jump from the Golden Gate bridge, this was not possible. Since the body was never recovered, a certificate was not issued; however, the case was well-documented in police and newspaper files. By keeping to this legalistic definition of suicide, one runs the very likely probability that the true number of suicides will be underenumerated. For example, cases of equivocal student deaths, such as by falls or drowning, were regarded as accidental, in keeping with the coroner's findings, even though these deaths, listed as accidents, could have been suicides which were covered up to avoid the social stigma related to suicide. Indeed, it has been estimated that only about 70% of successful suicides are ever recorded as such (Dublin, 1963, p. 3). The advantage in using this definition is that one can be quite certain that deaths recorded as suicide are bona-fide cases since the error is, almost always, in the direction of underreporting. (*c*) *Exposure to risk*—the period of exposure to risk comprised the 10-year span 1952–1961 inclusive, a total of 10 academic or 7½ calendar years. This important variable, the length of exposure, was to some degree controlled since both the suicidal and nonsuicidal students were exposed to the same period of risk. (*d*) *Population at risk*—population at risk was the total student body of UCB during the 10-year period cited. Case finding procedures were extremely painstaking, requiring several months of effort to detect and verify 23 bona-fide study cases. Numerous sources of information were used, but for the suicidal students the primary source was the standard death certificate, obtained from the state health department. Secondary sources consisted of newspaper clippings, police files, and University records. The source of materials for the baseline data for the total student body population was the UCB Office of the Registrar. Their publication, *A Ten-Year Survey of Certain Demographic Characteristics of the Student Population* (Suslow, 1963), was indispensable.

In terms of research design, the procedures consisted of collecting and analyzing data regarding selected attributes to the total student population. These data were then used as a baseline to which the sample of suicidal UCB students could be compared. Since suicide may also involve a strong volitional component, further analyses were made with respect to certain situational-temporal features of the academic environment.

RESULTS AND DISCUSSION

Results are presented in tabular and graphic form and discussed in the text by order of their appearance. The various comparisons were statistically analyzed by testing the significance of the difference between two proportions (Hill, 1961, pp. 122–132), specifically, the significance of proportional differences between the suicidal sample and expected population values as based upon knowledge of the student universe. All probability statements are two-tailed probabilities.

Incidence and Prevalence

Previous research on the UCB population (Bruyn & Seiden, 1965) investigated the general question of student suicide risk. By comparing the student suicide experience with the suicide incidence among a comparable group of non-college-age cohorts, it was established that the incidence of suicide among students was significantly greater than for non-student-age peers ($p = .004$). Conversely, the general mortality experience from all causes was significantly more favorable for students when compared to their non-academic-age peers ($p < .001$). In terms of total mortality, suicides accounted for 23 of the 68 student deaths which occurred during the 10-year study period. Proportionally, it ranked as the second leading cause of death (34%), exceeded only by accidents (37%).

Age

For the United States as a whole, there is a well-documented positive correlation between age and suicide (Dublin, 1963, p. 22). This same relationship holds for the student population. If the student body is divided on the basis of those who are above and below age 25, one finds that the percentage of suicides in the older age group is approximately twice their proportional percentage in the population (see Table 1). This distinction is graphically portrayed in Figure 1 which presents the relative frequency of suicidal and nonsuicidal students by 5-year age groups. It is notable that only about 6% of all students fall in the 30 to 34-year age category while more than 26% of the suicidal students are found in this interval. In fact, the median age for the student body population is 22 years, 6 months, while the median age for the suicidal students, 26 years, 5 months, is greater by almost 4 years.

Class Standing

Directly correlated with, and, indeed, almost identical to, chronological age, is the class standing of individual students. Median class standing for the entire student population was the junior year, for the suicidal subset it was the senior year. When the groups are divided on the basis of graduate or undergraduate standing, one finds that graduate students committed suicide in numbers significantly greater than could be expected from their proportions in the student body at large (see Table 1).

Sex

Of the 23 student suicides, 17 were male, 6 female, a sex ratio approximating 3:1 (see Table 1). This finding accords with those sex ratios reported in previous studies of completed suicide (Dublin, 1963, p. 23). However, an adjustment is necessary to correctly relate this information to the college population. Whereas the sexes are about equally distributed in the general United States population, they

Table 1. *Selected Demographic Characteristics of Suicidal and Nonsuicidal Students, UCB, 1952–1961.*

	Suicidal students		Total student body population	
Demographic characteristics	Frequency distribution (n = 23)	% distribution	% distribution	p
Age				
Under 25	9	39	70	.001
25 and above	14	61	30	
Class standing				
Undergraduate	12	52	72	.033
Graduate	11	48	28	
Sex				
Male	17	74	67	*ns*
Female	6	26	33	
Marital status[a]				
Married	3	14	23	*ns*
Never married	19	86	77	
Race				
White	20	87	89	*ns*
Nonwhite	3	13	11	
Religion				
Protestant	15	65	60	
Jewish	5	22	18	*ns*
Catholic	3	13	22	
Nationality				
U.S.A.	19	83	96	.002
Foreign	4	17	04	
Major subject[b]				
Mechanical-mathematic	10	50	64	*ns*
Aesthetic-social	10	50	36	
Grade-point average[c]				
Above average	14	67	50	*ns*
Below average	7	33	50	
Mental health service				
Psychiatric patient	8	34	10	$<.001$
Nonpatient	15	66	90	

[a]Excludes one divorced student.
[b]Excludes three students who had not declared majors.
[c]Excludes two students who did not complete a semester.

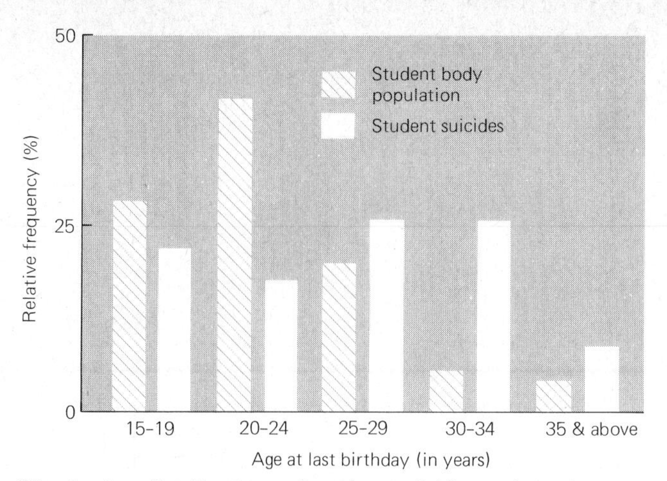

Fig. 1. Age distributions of student suicides and total student body population, UCB, 1952–1961.

are not equally distributed on campus. For the years under study, males outnumbered females in the student body population by approximately 2:1. Accordingly, the obtained sex ratio of 3:1 must be halved to yield an adjusted student ratio of about 1.5 male suicides for each female suicide. This student sex ratio is considerably narrower than the sex ratio for the country at large. It seems to indicate a heightened risk of suicide among female students as compared to the general female population. However, this indication must remain somewhat speculative since the female suicides were considerably older (median age 30 years, 1 month) than were male suicides (median age 26 years, 1 month). As a consequence one cannot be entirely sure that the constricted ratio is not an effect of confounding between age and sex. Should further research confirm that there is, in fact, a greater risk of suicide among female students as opposed to female nonstudents, it would follow the predictions of Gibbs and Martin (1964). They proposed a rise in female suicides due to increasing social pressures. According to their status-integration theory, as more women enter the labor force they encounter cross-pressures from conflicting social roles. They postulate that these stresses will lead to increasing numbers of female suicides.

Marital Status

Of the 23 student suicides, it was possible to classify 22 persons into the categories of "married" or "never married," which corresponded to the available student population data. One divorced student was thereby excluded from the analysis. There was no remarkable disparity between the suicidal and nonsuicidal students on the basis of marital status (see Table 1). For the entire United States population, suicide is less common among married persons (Dublin, 1963, p. 26), but this was not the case for campus suicides. Only three of the student suicides were married, and only one of those married had children. The remaining two cases, both females, committed suicide shortly after their marriages.

Race

Of the 23 known suicides, only three were nonwhite and all three of these nonwhite students were Chinese. There were no suicides among Negro, East Indian, or American Indian students who, at any event, comprised only about 3% of the student body population. The distribution of suicides by race corresponded closely to the racial proportions found in the student population (see Table 1). It should be mentioned, however, that there is good reason to question the adequacy of these racial data. Since University records do not ask for nor indicate students' race, these breakdowns, furnished by the University Dean of Students Office, were presumably obtained from simple headcounts with all the imprecision that this method implies.

Religion

Religion was not a significant factor in differentiating suicidal students from the general campus population (see Table 1). As was the case with racial statistics, the religious data, likewise, must be regarded with great skepticism. The University does not conduct a religious census of its students. Consequently, the religious population figures were estimated from student residence information cards on which "religious affiliation" is an optional item. Very frequently it is left unanswered.

Nationality

Only 4 of the 23 student suicides were foreign students. Nonetheless, their representation in the student body was so negligible (only 4%) that they appear among the suicides in approximately four times the magnitude one would expect from their proportions in the student population (see Table 1). As a group, these four "international student" suicides were characterized by some striking similarities. As youngsters, all of the four had known and suffered from the ravages of war, and three of them were forced to flee from their childhood homes. Two of the students, natives of mainland China, had been dispossessed by the Communist revolution; another student, born in Austria, lost his family in the horrors of the Nazi concentration camps and subsequently migrated to Israel. The fourth student, a native Israeli, had grown up amidst the Arab-Jewish war over the Palestine partition.

Moreover, they shared a similar pattern of conflicts, centering to a large degree around strong feelings of shame. These feelings were reflected in a deep dread that they would not meet expectations that others had set for them. There was some reality to these fears, in that other persons had sent them abroad, were paying their expenses, and probably did expect from them some measure of academic achievement. Still, their excessive concern about "what others would think" was unduly frenetic. All four of them were known to the Student Mental Health Service where they had been seen for psychiatric treatment. These findings, however, must be interpreted with some caution since the median age of foreign students (26 years, 1 month), exceeded the median age of American students (24 years), raising the possibility that the differences were due in some degree to age rather than nationality.

Major Subject

For this comparison, the suicidal subjects were divided into two categories, corresponding somewhat to William James' distinction between the "tough" and "tender minded." Of the 20 suicidal students who had declared majors, the breakdown was 10 students in the "tough-minded" or mechanical-mathematics group (Engineering, Professional, Physical Sciences, Biological Sciences, Agricultural majors) and 10 students in the "tender-minded" or esthetic-social group (Arts, Social Sciences, Language and Literature majors). Relative to their population proportions, there was a greater incidence of suicides in the tender-minded group, but not a large enough imbalance to achieve statistical significance. Further analysis, by individual subject groups, revealed that suicides were significantly more frequent among students majoring in languages and literature (five cases), especially English majors, who comprised three of the five cases (see Table 2).

Grade-Point Average

Grade-point analysis required some basic adjustments since graduate and undergraduate grading systems are not directly comparable. In practice, an undergraduate "C" is approximately equivalent to a graduate "B." For the student population, the grade-point average (GPA) for undergraduates was 2.50, while for graduates it was 3.35 (calculated to the scale: A = 4, B = 3, C = 2, D = 1, F = 0). Given this discrepancy, it is obviously necessary to separately compare undergraduate and graduate students with reference to their respective grade-point distributions. When the suicidal students (excluding two who did not complete a full semester at UCB) are ranked by means of achievement above or below their population GPA, we find that two-thirds of them were above average while, by definition, only half of the general student body achieved this mark. Although suggestive of a tendency toward higher grades among suicidal students, the difference, in fact, did not achieve statistical significance. However, further analysis, distributing GPA by class standing, revealed a marked discrepancy between graduate and undergraduate students. This breakdown is detailed in Table 3 and reveals that of the 11 undergraduate students who committed suicide (after one complete semester at the University), 10 of them had surpassed the undergraduate GPA. For graduate student suicides, only 4 of the 10 who had completed a semester exceeded the graduate GPA. Despite the differential grading system that rewards the graduate student with more grade points for a similar level of work, the suicidal undergraduate students received a higher overall GPA than the graduate student suicides (see Table 4).

This finding seems to indicate that undergraduate and graduate suicides differ markedly from one another in terms of academic achievement. The undergraduate suicides performed on a level well above their fellow classmates and performed considerably better than did graduate suicides. Looking at the personal histories of these undergraduate students one discovers an interesting paradox. To an external observer, say someone viewing their transcripts, these students achieved splendidly in their academic pursuits. They had all been A or B students in high school since a B or better average is required for undergraduate admission, a policy which is estimated to limit entrance to the top 10–12% of graduating high school seniors. Reports from family and friends, however, reveal that self-satisfaction was not the case with these students. Rather, they seemed filled with doubts of their adequacy, dissatisfied with their grades, and despondent over their general academic aptitude. This exacerbated fear of failure was tempered somewhat by the fact that in every case of undergraduate suicide the final semester's GPA was lower ($\bar{x}$ = 2.53) than the previous cumulative GPA ($\bar{x}$ = 3.34). Another consideration is whether these students aspired to graduate school which requires a higher than average GPA (2.5–3.0 at UCB). Unfortunately, these exact data are not available; however, a check of those students in major subjects which definitely indicated future graduate work, for example, premedicine, revealed academic achievement in excess of grade requirements. Nevertheless, on balance, they were still achieving loftily above the average of their classmates. How can one explain their deep self-dissatisfaction despite contrary and

Table 2. *Suicides among Language and Literature Majors vs. All Other Subject Majors.*

	Suicidal students		Total student body population	
Major subject group	*n*	%	%	*p*
Language and literature	5	25	9	.012
All other majors	15	75	91	

Note. Excludes three students who had not declared major subjects.

Table 3. *Grade-Point Averages for Graduate and Undergraduate Student Suicides.*

	Suicidal students		Student population	
GPA	*n*	%	%	*p*
Class standing				
Undergraduate				
Above mean	10	91	50	.006
Below mean	1	09	50	
Graduate				
Above mean	4	40	50	*ns*
Below mean	6	60	50	

Note. Excludes two students; one graduate, one undergraduate, who suicided during their first semester.

Table 4. *Observed and Expected GPA of Student Suicides by Class Standing.*

	GPA	
Class standing	Observed	Expected
Undergraduate	3.18	2.50
Graduate	2.90	3.35

objective indications of their competence? Two possible explanations suggest themselves: (*a*) The internal standards these students applied to themselves were so Olympian, the demands they imposed upon themselves so exacting, that they were destined to suffer frustration and disappointment no matter how well they fared; and/or (*b*) Whereas they had previously been crackerjack students in high school or junior college, excelling without much difficulty, the precipitous drop in grade points over the final semester threatened their feelings of self-esteem. Thus, faced by a sudden loss of status, they may have suicided as a response to this egoistic conflict. In any case, the discrepancy between perceived self-concept and objective reality indicates that a purely objective approach often obscures more than it reveals. What one needs to try and understand is the phenomenological response of the individual student. What is necessary to know is what inner standards, what idealized fantasy he uses to judge himself and his own personal worth. For the graduate student suicides as a group, there was no discrepancy between their academic achievements and what might be expected on the basis of the general population of graduate students. While they produced slightly below their population mean, the variation in this instance was primarily due to two students who were in considerable scholastic straits. Contrary to the undergraduates, graduate suicides showed no pattern of decline in their terminal semester GPA. Confirmation of the scholastic disparity between graduate and undergraduate suicides is further revealed by the irregular distribution of academic awards. Inspection of Table 5 indicates that undergraduate students garnered scholarship honors at a rate well beyond the general undergraduate population, while the graduate student suicides did not differ significantly from their classmates in earning academic awards. Even though graduate student awards were far more plentiful, the great majority of awards (10 of 11) were held by undergraduate student suicides.

Mental Health

Of the 23 student suicides, 8 had been referred to the student mental health service for psychiatric treatment (of the 8 students, apparently only 2 were diagnosed as psychotic reactions). These 8 cases comprised better than one-third of the student suicides, significantly exceeding the approximately 10% of the total student body population seen at the mental health facilities (see Table 1). Besides the 8 students known to the student psychiatric service, an additional 3 students were in private psychiatric treatment, making a total of almost 50% of the suicidal group who gave this particular indication of prior mental disturbance.

Table 5. *Scholastic Awards by Class Standing.*

	Suicidal students		Student population	
Class standing	*n*	%	%	*p*
Undergraduate				
Scholarship	7	58	05	< .001
Nonscholarship	5	42	95	
Graduate				
Scholarship	1	10	23	*ns*
Nonscholarship	10	90	77	

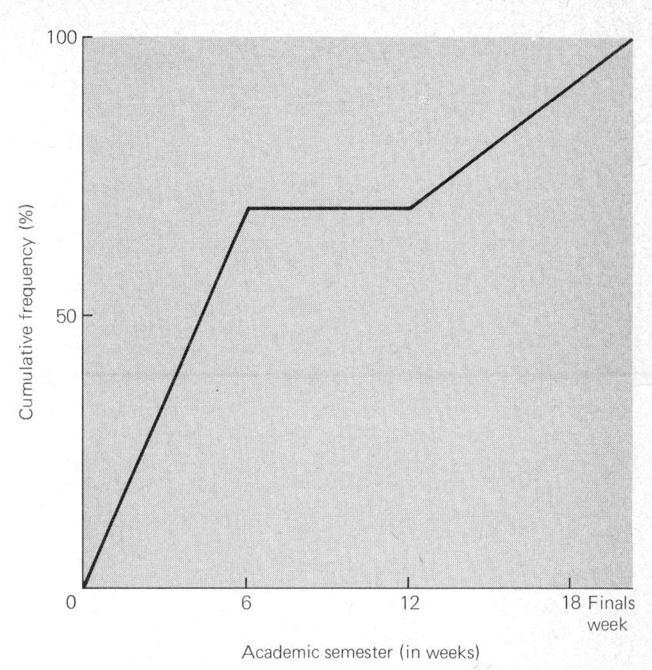

Fig. 2. Time distribution of student suicides, UCB, 1952–61.

Temporal-Situational Relationships

Among all causes of death, suicide allows for the greatest degree of volition. The suicidal person is in a position to choose the date, place, and method of his death, and it has long been speculated that there may be a special psychological significance to these choices. Through tracing the time, place, and method of student suicides, the following particular patterns were observed:

Time. When student suicides were charted by calendar months they formed a bimodal curve with peaks occurring during February and October. A more meaningful comparison obtained when the academic semester was used as the time interval. This distribution, as illustrated in Figure 2, challenges a frequently held belief about campus suicides. Academic folklore often explains student suicides as a response to the anxieties and stresses of final examinations. Yet, surprisingly, the data showed that almost the reverse relationship held. Only 1 of the 23 student suicides was committed during finals. (Even that single instance may be dubiously related to final exams since this student was doing well in school and had expressed satisfaction with his "finals" performance.) Most of the suicides occurred at the beginning of the semester. When the semester is divided into three equivalent parts, the vast majority of cases, 16 out of 23, are found to occur during the first 6-week segment. (Actually, the period is only 5 weeks from when instruction begins; the first week is confined to registration procedures.) No cases were found during the second 6-week period which includes the mid-term examinations. Over the remaining third of the semester there were seven cases, just one of which occurred during finals week itself (always the last week of the semester). This irregular time distribution of student suicides departed significantly from uniform expectations (x^2_2 = 16.8, $p < .001$). Clearly, the old saw about suicides and finals was not supported. Instead, the danger period for student suicide was found to be the start, not the finish, of the school semester. Incidentally, the day of the week departed significantly from the null hypothesis of uniformity (x^2_1 = 4.18, $p < .05$) with almost one-half the cases occurring on Monday or Friday, terminals of the school week. Unfortunately, the data were none too precise since some cases were based on coroner's estimates as to the date of death.

The unexpectedly low correspondence between final examinations and the commission of student suicide bears some resemblance to a parallel phenomenon involving student mental health during the recent free speech activities on the UCB campus. In the course of these supposedly stressful times, there was a striking drop in admissions to the student mental health service (20% below average) and no recorded student suicides during the 1965 academic year. (Such behavior corresponds to the drop in suicides, psychosomatic illness, and neurotic conditions observed during both World Wars.) Why, in the midst of all the controversy, turmoil, and tempest was student mental health apparently enhanced? One possibility is that some students who had previously been grappling with internal problems now had the opportunity to act out, to ventilate their inner conflicts, and to displace their intrapunitive anger and hostility by redirecting it toward an external symbol, namely, the University. Perhaps it was the galvanized and heightened sense of community that facilitated mental well-being. Certainly many students felt involved in a common cause; probably, for some it imparted meaning to their lives where previously they had felt alienated and purposeless. If so, it was also a perfect antidote to the kinds of feelings that often drive people to self-destruction.

Place. Most of the students, 12 of 23, committed suicide at their residences. The next most frequent location was the University itself, upon whose grounds 4 students ended their lives. Three students were found dead in parked autos on isolated suburban roads. Another 2 suicided in out-of-town hotel rooms, and 1 student leaped from the San Francisco Golden Gate bridge. It is difficult to determine any significance to the site of these suicides, except for the 4 cases who killed themselves on the university grounds. Of these, the most symbolic suicide was the 1 student who jumped from the Campanile, an architectural landmark of the Berkeley campus.

Method. The most frequent agent of choice was firearms, followed by ingestions and asphyxiations. A comparison with the methods used by Yale student suicides (see Table 6) revealed considerable similarity in the methods employed by the two groups of students. The relatively larger number of poisonings among UCB students is most likely due to the more recent availability of tranquilizers and barbiturates.

Table 6. *Methods of Suicide Used by UCB and Yale Students.*

	UCB (1952–1961)		Yale (1920–1955)[a]	
Method	*n*	%	*n*	%
Firearms	8	35	10	40
Poisonings	6	26	3	12
Asphyxiation	4	17	5	20
Hanging	2	09	6	24
Jumping from high place	2	09	1	04
Cutting instruments	1	04	—	—
Total	23	100	25	100

[a]Source: Parrish, 1957, p. 589.

For only two of the Berkeley cases was there the least equivocation about assigning suicide as the cause of death. These two cases, both involving ingestions of poisonous substances, were qualified as "probably suicide" but routinely coded as "deaths due to suicide." In at least 10 instances, suicide notes were left by the decedents. These notes ranged from simple instructions concerning the disposal of personal belongings to lengthy, literary dissertations, one of which finished by tersely quoting Camus: "Life as a human being is absurd."

Psychological Factors

A statistical approach, per se, can go just so far in describing the suicide-prone student. The additional use of case history materials provides a fuller, more clinically oriented dimension to the portrayal. As such, the following inferences were derived from anecdotal reports of friends and acquaintances of the students, along with those members of the University community whose lives they touched. From a preventive standpoint, the most pertinent questions which might be asked are, "What prodromal signs, what clues to suicide could be discerned from the personal lives of these students? Specifically, were there any indications or harbingers of their ultimate destinies?" Lastly, "Was there a characteristic conflict which precipitated their self-destructive actions?" The question of prodromal indications can be flatly answered "yes." There were numerous warnings in almost every case. At least five of the students had made past suicide attempts. Warnings of a more subtle nature could be discovered in the histories of the remaining students. For example, the pupil who went out of his way to modify an item on the medical history form. Where it had requested, "Whom shall we notify in case of emergency?" he crossed out the word "emergency" and substituted "death." Or the student who confided that he sometimes takes 10 or so nembutals because "I am an adventurer." Other students evidenced a long-standing infatuation with death, often initiating "bull sessions" about the futility of life, or making wry jokes about killing themselves. Prior to their suicides a disproportionately large number of these students were involved in psychiatric treatment. As a group, they presented similar symptomatic patterns featuring symptoms of insomnia, anorexia, and extreme moodiness, especially moods of despondency; in all, it was a psychological picture compatible with the general diagnosis of agitated depression.

Although their prodromal response to stress was very similar, the particular crises that precipitated their suicides were not. Bearing in mind that each individual case was unique, for purposes of description, the main prodromal conflicts could be classified into the following three categories:

1. **Concern over studies.** In many cases acquaintances of the students made such judgments as "he pushed himself too hard," "worried over grades," "felt his grades were not as good as he thought they should be," or similar scholastic anxieties which, they felt, triggered the suicidal crisis. It is difficult to evaluate these inferences since "worry over grades" is often seen by informants as a most likely explanation. At any event, if true, their exaggerated concern over studies contrasted vividly with generally excellent academic grades.

2. **Unusual physical complaints.** A number of the students complained of inability to eat or sleep, one student warranting a diagnosis of "avitaminosis." Others worried about possible deterioration such as the student who feared that his "failing sight" might ruin a prospective medical career. A few pupils, however, presented physical complaints of a bizarre semidelusional quality, for instance, the young man whose stomach literally persecuted him. From childhood on he had suffered from anorexia and "stomach ache." Although an exploratory laparotomy did not disclose anything, by the time he entered the University he was at least 50 pounds underweight, still wracked by chronic stomach pains. He then moved from his fraternity house, in the hope of gaining weight by selecting his own food. This plan proved to no avail, nor did extensive medical testing at the student health service, all of which proved negative. He finally ended his torment, perhaps symbolically, by ingesting cyanide.

3. **Difficulties with interpersonal relationships.** Combined under this heading were two different types of conflicts, both reflecting problems in personal relationships. First were the students involved in stormy love affairs. Here the critical stresses were feelings of rejection which had been engendered by broken romances. In the one recorded instance of double suicide, the precipitating event was parental opposition to the youngsters' marriage. Much more typical, however, was the essentially asocial, withdrawn student. These particular students were uniformly described as terribly shy, virtually friendless individuals, alienated from all but the most minimal social interactions. Frequently they had compensated for their personal solitude by increased study and almost total absorption in schoolwork. The most calamitous example of such human isolation was the student, dead for 18 days before he was found in his lonely room. It is a tragic commentary to his existence, and perhaps a cause for his suicide, that there were no friends, no people involved enough in his life to know, or to care, that he had been missing for well over 2 weeks.

Interpretation

Reviewing the results of the present study, one can reasonably conclude that significant associations between student suicide and numerous variables, both personal and environmental, have been demonstrated. Nonetheless, one cannot, with certitude, infer that these relationships are causal ones. This type of inference would require procedures more exacting than the limited epidemiological methods herein employed. For instance, the total student body population, used as a matched control or comparison group, included a number of students who had unsuccessfully attempted suicide. Quite possibly their inclusion diluted the significance of the obtained differences between suicidal and presumably nonsuicidal students. This is a relatively minor concern, compared to other more cautionary limitations. A primary concern is to what degree the observed relationships were spuriously increased by a common variable. For example, the correlation between student suicide and declining terminal GPA may very well be due to a third factor—emotional disturbance—which both depressed scholastic grades and led to self-destruction. As a corollary, it should be recognized that not all of the selected variables were independent of one another. It is known for one that age and class standing are highly dependent, and it was observed, also, that the variable of age probably confounded to some degree the comparisons by sex and by nationality. Another area of uncertainty concerns the time-order sequence of student suicide. One is unable to state, with certainty, which comes first, the disturbed student or the stresses of student life. Are the suicides due to selection into colleges of mentally unstable individuals or are they due to competitive pressures of the academic environment? The fullest answer to these questions will only come from further research. Toward this goal some salient lines of inquiry could include: the investigation of student suicide attempters and student accident cases, postcollegiate follow-up studies, and the use of "psychological autopsy" procedures, as described by Shneidman and Farberow (1961).

Within the expressed limits of the study design, what predictions about the future suicide problem are warranted? Extrapolating from results of the present study, it appears that a future increase of student suicides may be expected. This increase should occur as a function of two variables, that is, age and academic competition, both of which are directly correlated to student suicides, and both of which are slated to increase in future student body populations. Average student age is already rising as a result of ever increasing proportions of graduate students in the American university system. For example, architects of the UCB educational master plan are considering an ultimate 50:50 graduate-undergraduate ratio. The second variable, academic competition, will likely increase as a result of mounting public demands for quasi-universal college education. As a case in point, the enrollment demands at UCB have already exceeded the available academic supply. Consequently, it has been necessary to restrict enrollment to the uppermost fraction of high school graduating classes. If accepted, the pressure on the student to achieve and maintain very high GPAs gives no indication of abatement. In fact, the situation ominously resembles a suicidal problem which prevails among the youth of Japan. In the Japanese case there are tremendous pressures to attend college, and those students who fail to gain entrance frequently turn to suicide as a solution to their dilemmas. Such conflicts, in addition to a more accepting cultural attitude, have probably helped to make Japan "a country of youthful suicides where suicide has become the number one cause of death in individuals under 30 [DeVos, 1964, p. 6]."

SUMMARY

The purpose of this study was to identify distinctive attributes of the suicidal student, and to determine those environmental conditions which heighten his susceptibility to suicide.

Using an epidemiological approach, demographic comparisons were made between the sample of 23 UCB students who committed suicide during the years 1952–1961 inclusive, and the total student body population for those years. As an additional procedure, the temporal-situational characteristics of student suicides were described and analyzed.

The main findings of the research were:

1. Suicidal students could be significantly differentiated from their classmates on the variables of age, class standing, major subject, nationality, emotional condition, and academic achievement. Compared to the student population at large, the suicidal group was older, contained greater proportions of graduates, language majors, and foreign students, and gave more indications of emotional disturbance. In addition, the undergraduate suicides fared much better than their fellow students in matters of academic achievement.

2. Contrary to the popular belief that suicides frequently occur during final examinations week, time relationships indicated that the peak danger period for student suicides was the beginning (first 6 weeks), not the midterm, nor end of the semester.

3. Most of the students gave recurrent warnings of their suicidal intent. Many of them presented a similar prodromal pattern marked by anorexia, insomnia, and periods of despondency.

4. Major precipitating factors were: Worry over schoolwork, chronic concerns about physical health (sometimes of a decidedly bizarre nature), and difficulties with interpersonal relationships. This last category contained some students who had reacted to romantic rejections but, for the most part, comprised the emotionally withdrawn and socially isolated student.

5. A future increase of student suicides was predicted on the basis of changes taking place in the age structure of college populations and in the competitive pressures of student life.

REFERENCES

Braaten, J., & Darling, C. Suicidal tendencies among college students. *Psychiatric Quarterly*, 1962, **36**, 665–692.

Bruyn, H. B., & Seiden, R. H. Student suicide: Fact or fancy? *Journal of the American College Health Association*, 1965, **14**, 69–77.

DeVos, G. Role narcissism and the etiology of Japanese suicide. Berkeley, Calif.: Institute of International Studies, University of California, 1964. (Mimeo)

Dublin, L. I. *Suicide: A sociological and statistical study*. New York: Ronald, 1963.

Gibbs, J. P., & Martin, W. T. *Status integration and suicide*. Eugene: Oregon University Press, 1964.

Hill, A. B. *Principles of medical statistics*. New York: Oxford University Press, 1961.

Jensen, V. W. Evaluating the suicidal impulse in the university setting. *Journal Lancet*, 1955, **75**, 441–444.

MacMahon, B., Pugh, T. F., & Ipsen, J. *Epidemiological methods*. Boston: Little, Brown, 1960.

Parrish, H. M. Epidemiology of suicide among college students. *Yale Journal of Biology and Medicine*, 1957, **29**, 585–595.

Raphael, T., Power, S. H., & Berridge, W. L. The question of suicide as a problem in college mental hygiene. *American Journal of Orthopsychiatry*, 1937, **7**, 1–14.

Shneidman, E. S., & Farberow, N. L. Sample investigations of equivocal deaths. In N. L. Farberow & E. S. Shneidman (Eds.), *The cry for help*. New York: McGraw-Hill, 1961. Pp. 118–128.

Suslow, S. *A ten-year survey of certain demographic characteristics of the student population*. Berkeley: Office of the Registrar, University of California, 1963. (Mimeo)

Temby, W. D. Suicide. In G. B. Blaine & C. G. McArthur (Eds.), *Emotional problems of the student*. New York: Appleton-Century-Crofts, 1961. Pp. 133–152.

The Paranoid Pseudo-Community Revisited

Norman Cameron

The pseudo-community is reformulated as a cognitive structure which attempts to solve the problem of reconciling social reality with the products of paranoid projection. Delusional development follows regression and the loss of social reality. It begins with the estrangement experienced by a partially regressed person when he attempts to regain object relations and proceeds through successive provisional reconstructions of reality until a cognitive solution is reached which seems to justify paranoid action. Aggressive action is likely to make social reality confirm the expectations of the pseudo-community.

A decade of experience with intensive clinical studies of paranoid thinking, in the course of psychoanalyzing psychoneurotics and in the long-term therapy of ambulatory psychotics, has led me to a reworking of the concept of the pseudo-community as formulated in this *Journal*[1] and further developed elsewhere.[2] The social aspects of the concept require little change. It is in its individual aspects—in a greater concern with the evidence of internal changes and with the signs that forces are operative which are not open to direct observation—that the pseudo-community acquires deeper roots and greater usefulness.

Original presentation. In the normal evolution and preservation of socially organized behavior the most important factor is the developing and maintaining of genuine communication. In each individual, language behavior grows out of preverbal interchange between infant and older person. It evolves in accordance with whatever traditional patterns prevail in the immediate environment, since communication is always, at first, between a child who operates at preverbal levels and older individuals whose language is already a highly organized interactive system. Through sharing continuously in such language and prelanguage interchange, each child develops shared social perspectives and skill in shifting from one perspective to another in time of need.

A highly significant result of this gradual process is that, as time goes on, the child normally acquires an increasingly realistic grasp of how other people feel, what their attitudes, plans, hopes, fears, and intentions are, and in what ways these all relate to his own. Eventually, he is able to take the roles of other people around him in imagination and to view things more or less realistically from their perspectives as well as from his own. In this way he also develops a workable degree of objectivity toward himself, learning to respond to his body, his personality, and his behavior more or less as others do. In the final product, there is considerable difference between the socialization achieved in behavior publicly shared and genuinely communicated and behavior that has remained private and little formulated or expressed in language.

The adult who is especially vulnerable to paranoid developments is one in whom this process of socialization has been seriously defective. His deficient social learning and poorly developed social skills leave him unable to understand adequately the motivations, attitudes, and intentions of others. When he becomes disturbed or confused under stress, he must operate under several grave handicaps imposed by a lifelong inability to communicate freely and effectively, to suspend judgment long enough to share his tentative interpretations with someone else, to imagine realistically the attitudes that others might have toward his situation and himself, and to imagine their roles and thus share their perspectives.

Left to his own unaided devices in a crisis, the paranoid person is able only to seek and find "evidence" that carries him farther in the direction he is already going—toward a more and more delusional interpretation of what seems to be going on around him.[3] This process may culminate in a conviction that he himself is the focus of a community of persons who are united in a conspiracy of some kind against him. It is this supposed functional community of real persons whom the patient can see and hear, and of other persons whom he imagines, that we call the *paranoid pseudo-community.* It has no existence as a social organization and as soon as he attempts to combat it, or to flee, he is likely to come into conflict with his actual social community.

Incompleteness of the descriptive pseudo-community. This, in brief, is the background and structure of the paranoid pseudo-community, as originally described. As it stands, it still seems valid; but it is unnecessarily restricted. In the first place, the account of the delusional development pays scant attention to internal dynamics because of the limits

From *American Journal of Sociology*, 1959, **65**, 52–62. Reproduced by permission.

[1] Norman Cameron, "The Paranoid Pseudo-Community," *American Journal of Sociology*, XLIX (1943), 32–38. Reprinted in A. M. Rose (ed.), *Mental Health and Mental Disorder: A Sociological Approach* (New York: W. W. Norton & Co., 1955).

[2] Norman Cameron, *The Psychology of Behavior Disorders: A Biosocial Interpretation* (Boston: Houghton Mifflin Co., 1947), and "Perceptual Organization and Behavior Pathology," in R. Blake and G. Ramsey (eds.), *Perception: An Approach to Personality* (New York: Ronald Press Co., 1951); and Norman Cameron and A. Margaret, *Behavior Pathology* (Boston: Houghton Mifflin Co., 1951), chap. xiii, "Pseudo-Community and Delusion."

[3] For a detailed discussion of this process of *desocialization* see "Desocialization and Disorganization," in Cameron and Margaret, *op. cit.*, pp. 448–517.

imposed by a behavioristic orientation. Patients, of course, recognize no such limitations. In the course of long-term intensive therapy they can sometimes furnish important information about what is going on within them to a therapist who is ready to receive it. Some of this they describe as it happens, in their own terms, and often in their own idiom. Some of it one can infer from what is said and done, with the help of material communicated in parallel cases. Some of it one must postulate in an effort to make one's observations and direct inferences more intelligible, just as is done in other empirical sciences.

In the original account not enough emphasis was given to the positive achievements of delusion formation. As we shall see, the pseudo-community is the best means a paranoid patient has at the time for bridging the chasm between his inner reality and social reality. Its use for this purpose may lead to a progressive reduction in desocialization and the reappearance of more normal communicative channels.

And, finally, the concept of the pseudo-community needs a background of structural postulates. In order to make sense out of the experiences which people actually have in fantasies, daydreams, dreams, and psychoses, one is obliged to go beyond such impermanent concepts as perception, response, and behavior—upon which the writer earlier relied—and to assume probable forces and mechanisms operating within personality systems and interacting subsystems. Here, again, the patient often comes to the rescue with empirical data. And, every now and then, one comes across a patient who describes with naive simplicity and directness—but consistently over a long period of time—phenomena which seem purely theoretical and highly abstruse, as reported in the literature. Exposed to such material the therapist may still be left with a sense of strangeness; but his previous feeling of their abstruseness and incredulity sooner or later vanishes.[4]

Paranoid loss of social reality. Paranoid delusional development begins with an impairment of social communication. It is preceded by experiences of frustration to which, like many normal persons, the paranoid individual reacts by turning away from his surroundings, and taking refuge in fantasy and daydream. This is the phase of withdrawal and preoccupation which is sometimes obvious even to an untrained observer.

When a paranoid person withdraws like this, he is far more likely than a normal person to lose effective contact with his social environment (i.e., with social reality) and to undergo regression. If this happens, he may abandon social reality for a time completely and become absorbed in primitive regressive thinking and feeling. Occasionally, a patient openly expresses some of his regressive experiences at the time; more often they can be inferred only from what emerges later on.

Precursors of the pseudo-community. I. Beginning restitution. It is a fact, of both clinical observation and subjective report, that paranoid patients, while still withdrawn, preoccupied, and regressed, begin to make attempts to regain their lost relationships with social reality. We may conceptualize these as marking the tapering-off of regression and the beginning of the reintegration of personality. The attempts fail to recover the lost social reality, however, because the patient's internal situation is not what it was before his regression. It is no longer possible for him to regain social reality as, for example, a normal person does when he wakes up in the morning. Instead, as we shall see, paranoid reintegration involves a restitutive process, the construction of a pseudo-reality which culminates in the paranoid pseudo-community.

Paranoid personalities suffer all their lives from defective repressive defenses and a heavy reliance upon the more primitive defenses of denial and projection. If they undergo a psychotic regression, which involves partial ego disintegration, their repressive defenses become still more defective. Primitive fantasies and conflicts now begin to emerge and to threaten ego disruption. The patient is forced to deal with them somehow, if he is to preserve what personality integration he still has and avoid further regression. Since he cannot successfully repress them, he vigorously denies them and projects them. An immediate result of the intense projective defense is that the products of the patient's emerging fantasies and conflicts now appear to him to be coming from outside him. Thus he seems to escape disintegration from within only to be threatened with destruction from without.

Precursors of the pseudo-community. II. Estrangement and diffuse vigilance. In the process of denying and projecting, the paranoid patient makes a start toward regaining contact with his surroundings. But this process neither simplifies nor clarifies the situation for him; and it does not bring about a return to social reality. On the contrary, the surroundings now seem somehow strange and different. Something has unquestionably happened. The patient misidentifies this "something" as basically a change in the makeup of his environment instead of what it actually is, a fundamental change within himself. If he expresses his feelings at this point, he is likely to say that things are going on which he does not understand; and this, of course, is literally true.

It is hardly surprising that the patient, finding himself in a world grown suddenly strange, should become diffusely vigilant. He watches everything uneasily; he listens alertly for clues; he looks everywhere for hidden meanings. Here his lifelong social incompetence makes matters still worse. He lacks even ordinary skill in the common techniques for testing social reality. He is unable to view his threatening situation even temporarily from the perspective of a neutral person. The more anxious and vigilant he grows, the less he can trust anybody, the less he dares to share with anyone his uneasiness and suspicion. He is condemned to pursue a solitary path, beset by primal fears, hates, and temptations which he cannot cope with nor escape.

Precursors of the pseudo-community. III. Increased self-reference. Strong tendencies toward self-reference are characteristic of paranoid personalities. When a paranoid adult becomes deeply and regressively preoccupied, his habitually egocentric orientation is greatly increased. And

[4] See, e.g., the clinical material in Norman Cameron, "Reprojection and Introjection in the Interaction between Schizophrenic Patient and Therapist" (submitted for publication).

when he next resorts to wholesale projection, he in effect converts his environment into an arena for his projected fantasies and conflicts. This destroys whatever neutrality and objectivity the environment may have previously possessed for him. He is now engrossed in scrutinizing his surroundings for signs of the return of what he is denying and projecting. To these he has become selectively sensitive. He is watching out for something that will explain away the strangeness and enable him to escape his frightening sense of isolation.

It is an unfortunate fact that a badly frightened person—even a normal one—is likely to notice things and make interpretations that increase rather than diminish his fear. And this is especially the case if he feels alone, in strange surroundings, and threatened by an unknown danger. Many non-paranoid adults, for example, walking alone through a large cemetery at night, or lost at night in a forest, become extremely alert and feel personally threatened by harmless things wholly unrelated to them. The paranoid adult, who is peopling his surroundings with projected phantoms from his own past, likewise creates a situation in which everything seems somehow dangerously related to him. Since he cannot escape, he tries to understand the situation he has unconsciously created, in the vain hope that he may then be able to cope with it.

Precursors of the pseudo-community. IV. Preliminary hypotheses. Being human, the paranoid patient is driven irresistibly to make hypotheses; but, having partially regressed, and being paranoid as well, he cannot test them. He tends, therefore, to pass from one guess or one suspicion to another like it. Using the materials provided by his environment and by his projected fantasies and conflicts, he constructs a succession of provisional hypotheses, discarding each as it fails to meet the contradictory demands of his internal needs and the environment. This is characteristic also of complex normal problem-solving. It is an expression of what is called the synthetic function of the ego.

Everyone who works with paranoid patients discovers that some kind of delusional reconstruction of reality is essential to their continued existence as persons. Even a temporary and unsatisfactory delusional hypothesis may be at the time a patient's sole means of bridging the gap between himself and his social environment. It gives a distorted picture of the world; but a distorted world is better than no world at all. And this is often a regressed person's only choice. To abandon his projected fears, hates, and temptations might mean to abandon all that he has gained in the reconstruction of reality, to have his world fall apart and fall apart himself. Patients sense this danger, even expressing it in these words, and they rightly refuse to give up their delusional reality. Their fear is not unrealistic, for clinically such catastrophes actually occur, ending in personality disintegration.

A great many paranoid persons never go beyond the phase of making and giving up a succession of preliminary delusional hypotheses. Some of them regain a good working relationship with social reality, something approaching or equaling their premorbid status. Some are less successful and remain chronically suspicious, averse, and partially withdrawn but manage even so to go on living otherwise much as they had lived before. They may appear morose, irascible, and bitter; but they do not fix upon definite enemies or take definite hostile action. At most they suffer brief outbursts of protest and complaint without losing their ability to retreat from an angry delusional position. In this paper, however, we are concerned primarily with paranoid patients—by no means incurable—who go on to crystallize a more stable delusional organization.

Final crystallization: the pseudo-community. A great many paranoid persons succeed in crystallizing a stable conceptual organization, the pseudo-community, which gives them a satisfactory cognitive explanation of their strange altered world and a basis for doing something about the situation as they now see it. Their problem is exceedingly complex. It is impossible for them to get rid of the unconscious elements, which they have denied and projected, but which now return apparently from the outside. They cannot abandon or even ignore their environment without facing a frightening regression into an objectless world. Their task is somehow to integrate these internal and external phenomena which appear before them on a single plane into a unified world picture.

The human environment which others share (*social reality*) provides the patient with real persons having social roles and characteristics which he can utilize in making his delusional reconstruction. It also provides real interaction among them, including interaction with the patient himself. Many things actually happen in it, some of them in direct relation to the patient, most of them actually not.

Internal reality provides two sets of functions. One is made up of the previously unconscious impulses, conflicts, and fantasies—now erupted, denied, and projected. This, as noted, introduces imagined motivation, interaction, and intentions into the observed activities of other persons. It gives apparent meaning to happenings which do not have such meaning for the consensus. The other set of functions is included in the concept of ego adaptation. It is the ego synthesis mentioned above, by means of which the demands of internal reality and the structure of a social reality are integrated into a meaningful, though delusional, unity.

What the paranoid patient does is as follows: Into the organization of social reality, as he perceives it, he unconsciously projects his own previously unconscious motivation, which he has denied but cannot escape. This process now requires a perceptual and conceptual reorganization of object relations in his surroundings into an apparent community, which he represents to himself as organized wholly with respect to him (delusion of self-reference). And since the patient's erupted, denied, and projected elements are overwhelmingly hostile and destructive, the motivation he ascribes to the real persons he has now organized into his conceptual pseudo-community is bound to be extremely hostile and destructive.

To complete his conceptual organization of a paranoid conspiracy, the patient also introduces imaginary persons. He ascribes to them, as to real persons, imagined functions, roles, and motivations in keeping with his need to unify his restitutional conception and make it stable. He pictures helpers, dupes, stooges, go-betweens, and masterminds, of whose actual existence he becomes certain.

It is characteristic of the pseudo-community that it is made up of both real and imaginary persons, all of whom may have both real and imaginary functions and interrelations.[5] In form it usually corresponds to one or another of the common dangerous, hostile groups in contemporary society, real or fictional—gangs, dope and spy rings, secret police, and groups of political, racial, and religious fanatics. Many paranoid patients succeed in creating a restitutional organization which has well-formulated plans. The chief persecutor is sometimes a relative or acquaintance, or a well-known public figure, while the rest of the imaginary personnel forms a vague, sinister background. Sometimes one finds the reverse—the chief persecutor is unknown, a malevolent "brain" behind everything, while the known dangerous persons play supporting roles in the delusional cast.

The final delusional reconstruction of reality may fall into an integrated conceptual pattern that brings an experience of closure: "I suddenly realized what it was all about!" the patient may exclaim with obvious relief at sudden clarification. The intolerable suspense has ended; the strangeness of what has been "going on" seems to disappear, and confusion is replaced by "understanding," and wavering doubt by certainty. A known danger may be frightening; but at least it is tangible, and one can do something about it. In short, the pseudo-community reduces the hopeless complexity and confusion to a clear formula. This formula—"the plot"—the patient can now apply to future events as he experiences them and fit them into the general framework of his reconstruction.

The organization of a conceptual pseudo-community is a final cognitive step in paranoid problem-solving. It reestablishes stable object relations, though on a delusional basis, and thus makes integrated action possible. To summarize what this reconstruction of reality has achieved for its creator:

a. Reduction in estrangement. As a direct result of paranoid problem-solving, experienced external reality is distorted so as to bring it into line with the inescapable projected elements. This lessens confusion and detachment and allows the patient to recover some of his lost sense of ego integrity. The world seems dangerous but familiar.

b. Internal absorption of aggression. Construction and maintenance of a conceptual pseudo-community absorb aggression internally, in the same sense that organizing a baseball team, a political ward, or a scientific society absorbs aggression. This reduces the threat of ego disintegration which the id eruptions pose.

c. Basis for action. Any new cognitive construct can serve as a basis for new action; in this respect the paranoid pseudo-community is no exception. It organizes the drive-directed cognitive processes, leads to meaningful interpretations in a well-defined pseudo-reality structure, and paves the way for overt action with a definite focus. The patient is enabled to go ahead as anyone else might who had powerful urges and felt sure that he was right.

d. Justification of aggressive action. Finally, a persecutory pseudo-community justifies attack or flight, either of which involves a direct aggressive discharge in overt action. Fighting or running away is less disintegrative psychologically than prolonged frightened inaction. And under the circumstances, as the patient now conceptualizes them, he need feel neither guilt for attacking nor shame for fleeing.

[5] This is in contrast to the autistic community, which is composed of wholly imaginary persons (see "Autistic Community and Hallucination," in Cameron and Magaret, *op. cit.*, pp. 414–47.

Paranoid cognition and paranoid action. When a patient succeeds in conceptualizing a pseudo-community, he has taken the final cognitive step in paranoid problem-solving. He now "knows" what his situation is. But he is still faced with his need to do something about it. As a matter of fact, the crystallization of a hostile delusional structure usually increases the urge to take action. A circular process may quickly develop. The imagined threats of the now structured imaginary conspiracy seem to the patient concrete and imminent. They stimulate more and more his anxiety and defensive hostility—and the latter, being as usual projected, further increases the apparent external threat. Often this kind of self-stimulation spirals upward, while more and more "incidents" and people may be drawn into the gathering psychotic storm.

Paranoid action, however inappropriate it may be, still represents the completion of restitutional relationships and the fullest contact with his human environment of which the patient is capable at the time. He switches from his previous passive role of observer and interpreter, with all its indecision and anxiety, to that of an aggressive participant in what he conceives as social reality. For him this is genuine interaction, and he experiences the gratification that comes with certainty and with a massive discharge of pent-up aggressiveness. He may give a preliminary warning to the supposed culprits or make an appeal for intervention to someone in authority before taking direct action himself, which, when it comes, may be in the form of an attack or sudden flight, either of which may be planned and executed with considerable skill.

Making social reality conform to the pseudo-community. Paranoid patients who take aggressive action often achieve a pyrrhic victory. They succeed finally in making social reality act in conformity with the delusional reality which they have created. As long as a patient confines himself to watching, listening, and interpreting, he need not come into open conflict with the social community. But, when he takes overt action appropriate only in his private pseudo-community, a serious social conflict will arise.

Social reality is the living product of genuine sharing, communication, and interaction. Valid social attitudes, interpretations, and action derive continuously from these operations. The restitutional reality in which the patient believes himself to be participating has no counterpart outside of himself: it is illusory. Other persons cannot possibly share his attitudes and interpretations because they do not share his paranoid projections and distortions. Therefore they do not understand action taken in terms of his delusional reconstruction. The patient, for his part, cannot share their attitudes and interpretations because he is driven by regressive needs which find no place in adult social reality.

When an intelligent adult expresses beliefs and makes

accusations which seem unintelligible to others, as well as threatening, he may make the people around him exceedingly anxious. This is particularly the case when his words tend to activate their unconscious fantasies and conflicts. And when such a person begins to take aggressive action, which seems unprovoked as well as unintelligible, he inevitably arouses defensive and retaliatory hostility in others. The moment the social community takes action against him, it provides him with the confirmation he has been expecting—that there is a plot against him.

Thus, in the end, the patient manages to provoke action in the social community that conforms to the expectation expressed in his pseudo-community organization. His own internal need to experience hostility from without—as a defense against being overwhelmed by internal aggression—is satisfied when actual persons behave in accordance with his projections. His need for a target against which to discharge hostility is also met. This is his victory and his defeat.

The defeat need not be final. Much will depend, of course, upon the patient's basic personality organization, particularly his emotional flexibility, his potentiality for internal change, and his residual capacity for establishing new ego and superego identifications. The depth and extent of his regression are also important, as are the fixity and the inclusiveness of his delusional structure. Much will also depend upon his potential freedom to communicate, to develop reciprocal role-taking skills with another person, and to include another's alternative perspectives in his own therapeutic orientation.

Therapy. The primary therapeutic consideration, of course, is not the character of the delusional structure but what makes it necessary. A reduction in anxiety is among the first objectives. The source of anxiety lies in the regressive changes and in the threat these have brought of an unconscious breakthrough. But it is also aggravated by anything in the environment which tends to increase the patient's hostility and fear. Once the setting has been made less anxiety-provoking, the most pressing need is for someone in whom the patient can ultimately put his trust—someone not made anxious by the patient's fear and hostility or driven to give reassurances and make demands.

For the paranoid patient who is ready to attempt social communication, an interested but neutral therapist can function as a living bridge between psychotic reality and social reality. Through interacting with such a person, who neither attacks the delusional structure nor beats the drums of logic, a patient may succeed in gaining new points of reference from which to build a new orientation. The therapeutic process now involves another reconstruction of reality, one which undoes the restitutional pseudo-community without destroying the patient's defenses and forcing him to regress further.

As anxiety and the threat of disintegration subside, paranoid certainty becomes less necessary to personality survival. The patient can begin to entertain doubts and consider alternative interpretations. Such changes, of course, must come from within if they are to come at all. If he is able to work through some of the origins and derivatives of his basic problems, the patient may succeed eventually in representing to himself more realistically than ever before how other people feel and think. In this way the conceptual structure of his pseudo-community may be gradually replaced by something approaching the conceptual structure of social reality.

Chapter 10

The Psychoses: Schizophrenia

Schizophrenia occupies a special place in psychopathology because in a sense its history is the history of abnormality: its symptoms were differentiated and recorded more than 3300 years ago. However, its etiology and treatment still remain among the least understood psychological phenomena.

Some inroads toward the understanding of this disorder are made in Paul Meehl's oft-appearing paper on the topic. This paper, which is this chapter's lead piece, differentiates two milder or incipient forms from full-blown schizophrenia. Meehl's assertion about schizophrenia, yet to be borne out, is that although its content is learned it is fundamentally a neurological disease of genetic origin.

An important distinction between process and reactive schizophrenia is made in the paper by William Herron. On the basis of this review of the research literature on the process-reactive classification, the author calls for even more efficient criteria for allowing finer discriminations between these two types of disorder.

The papers by Kohn and the comments by Mechanic deal with the way genetics, stress, and the conditions of life contribute to the etiology of schizophrenia. And the last paper by Schofield and Balian, which has become a minor classic in the field, refutes the popular notion of a significantly higher incidence of unfavorable family relationships among schizophrenics than normals.

Schizotaxia, Schizotypy, Schizophrenia*

Paul E. Meehl

In the course of the last decade, while spending several thousand hours in the practice of intensive psychotherapy, I have treated—sometimes unknowingly except in retrospect—a considerable number of schizoid and schizophrenic patients. Like all clinicians, I have formed some theoretical opinions as a result of these experiences. While I have not until recently begun any systematic research efforts on this baffling disorder, I felt that to share with you some of my thoughts, based though they are upon clinical impressions in the context of selected research by others, might be an acceptable use of this occasion.

Let me begin by putting a question which I find is almost never answered correctly by our clinical students on PhD orals, and the answer to which they seem to dislike when it is offered. Suppose that you were required to write down a procedure for selecting an individual from the population who would be diagnosed as schizophrenic by a psychiatric staff; you have to wager $1,000 on being right; you may not include in your selection procedure any behavioral fact, such as a symptom or trait, manifested by the individual. What would you write down? So far as I have been able to ascertain, there is only one thing you could write down that would give you a better than even chance of winning such a bet—namely, "Find an individual X who has a schizophrenic identical twin." Admittedly, there are many other facts which would raise your odds somewhat above the low base rate of schizophrenia. You might, for example, identify X by first finding mothers who have certain unhealthy child-rearing attitudes; you might enter a subpopulation defined jointly by such demographic variables as age, size of community, religion, ethnic background, or social class. But these would leave you with a pretty unfair wager, as would the rule, "Find an X who has a fraternal twin, of the same sex, diagnosed as schizophrenic" (Fuller & Thompson, 1960, pp. 272–283; Stern, 1960, pp. 581–584).

Now the twin studies leave a good deal to be desired methodologically (Rosenthal, in press); but there seems to be a kind of "double standard of methodological morals" in our profession, in that we place a good deal of faith in our knowledge of schizophrenic dynamics, and we make theoretical inferences about social learning factors from the establishment of group trends which may be statistically significant and replicable although of small or moderate size; but when we come to the genetic studies, our standards of rigor suddenly increase. I would argue that the concordance rates in the twin studies need not be accepted uncritically as highly precise parameter estimates in order for us to say that their magnitudes represent the most important piece of etiological information we possess about schizophrenia.

It is worthwhile, I think, to pause here over a question in the sociology of knowledge, namely, why do psychologists exhibit an aversive response to the twin data? I have no wish to argue *ad hominem* here—I raise this question in a constructive and irenic spirit, because I think that a substantive confusion often lies at the bottom of this resistance, and one which can be easily dispelled. Everybody readily assents to such vague dicta as "heredity and environment interact," "there need be no conflict between organic and functional concepts," "we always deal with the total organism," etc. But it almost seems that clinicians do not fully believe these principles in any concrete sense, because they show signs of thinking that *if* a genetic basis were found for schizophrenia, the psychodynamics of the disorder (especially in relation to intrafamilial social learnings) would be somehow negated or, at least, greatly demoted in importance. To what extent, if at all, is this true?

Here we run into some widespread misconceptions as to what is meant by *specific etiology* in nonpsychiatric medicine. By postulating a "specific etiology" one does *not* imply any of the following:

1. The etiological factor always, or even usually, produces clinical illness.
2. If illness occurs, the particular form and content of symptoms is derivable by reference to the specific etiology alone.
3. The course of the illness can be materially influenced only by procedures directed against the specific etiology.
4. All persons who share the specific etiology will have closely similar histories, symptoms, and course.

From *American Psychologist,* 1962, 17, 827–838.

*Address of the President to the seventieth Annual Convention of the American Psychological Association, St. Louis, September 2, 1962.

5. The largest single contributor to symptom variance is the specific etiology.

In medicine, not one of these is part of the concept of specific etiology, yet they are repeatedly invoked as arguments against a genetic interpretation of schizophrenia. I am not trying to impose the causal model of medicine by analogy; I merely wish to emphasize that *if* one postulates a genetic mutation as the specific etiology of schizophrenia, he is not thereby committed to any of the above as implications. Consequently such familiar objections as, "Schizophrenics differ widely from one another" or "Many schizophrenics can be helped by purely psychological methods" should not disturb one who opts for a genetic hypothesis. In medicine, the concept of specific etiology means the *sine qua non*—the causal condition which is necessary, but not sufficient, for the disorder to occur. A genetic theory of schizophrenia would, in this sense, be stronger than that of "one contributor to variance"; but weaker than that of "largest contributor to variance." In analysis of variance terms, it means an interaction effect such that no other variables can exert a main effect when the specific etiology is lacking.

Now it goes without saying that "clinical schizophrenia" as such cannot be inherited, because it has behavioral and phenomenal contents which are learned. As Bleuler says, in order to have a delusion involving Jesuits one must first have learned about Jesuits. It seems inappropriate to apply the geneticist's concept of "penetrance" to the crude statistics of formal diagnosis—if a specific genetic etiology exists, its phenotypic expression in *psychological* categories would be a quantitative aberration in some parameter of a behavioral acquisition function. What could possibly be a genetically determined functional parameter capable of generating such diverse behavioral outcomes, including the preservation of normal function in certain domains?

The theoretical puzzle is exaggerated when we fail to conceptualize at different levels of molarity. For instance, there is a tendency among organically minded theorists to analogize between catatonic phenomena and various neurological or chemically induced states in animals. But Bleuler's masterly *Theory of Schizophrenic Negativism* (1912) shows how the whole range of catatonic behavior, including diametrically opposite modes of relating to the interpersonal environment, can be satisfactorily explained as instrumental acts; thus even a convinced organicist, postulating a biochemical defect as specific etiology, should recognize that the causal linkage between this etiology and catatonia is indirect, requiring for the latter's derivation a lengthy chain of statements which are not even formulable except in molar psychological language.

What kind of behavioral fact about the patient leads us to diagnose schizophrenia? There are a number of traits and symptoms which get a high weight, and the weights differ among clinicians. But thought disorder continues to hold its own in spite of today's greater clinical interest in motivational (especially interpersonal) variables. If you are inclined to doubt this for yourself, consider the following indicators: Patient experiences intense ambivalence, readily reports conscious hatred of family figures, is pananxious, subjects therapist to a long series of testing operations, is withdrawn, and says, "Naturally, I am growing my father's hair."

While all of these are schizophrenic indicators, the last one is the diagnostic bell ringer. In this respect we are still Bleulerians, although we know a lot more about the schizophrenic's psychodynamics than Bleuler did. The significance of thought disorder, associative dyscontrol (or, as I prefer to call it so as to include the very mildest forms it may take, "cognitive slippage"), in schizophrenia has been somewhat de-emphasized in recent years. Partly this is due to the greater interest in interpersonal dynamics, but partly also to the realization that much of our earlier psychometric assessment of the thought disorder was mainly reflecting the schizophrenic's tendency to underperform because uninterested, preoccupied, resentful, or frightened. I suggest that this realization has been overgeneralized and led us to swing too far the other way, as if we had shown that there really *is* no cognitive slippage factor present. One rather common assumption seems to be that if one can demonstrate the potentiating effect of a motivational state upon cognitive slippage, light has thereby been shed upon the etiology of schizophrenia. Why are we entitled to think this? Clinically, we see a degree of cognitive slippage not found to a comparable degree among nonschizophrenic persons. Some patients (e.g., pseudoneurotics) are highly anxious and exhibit minimal slippage; others (e.g., burnt-out cases) are minimally anxious with marked slippage. The demonstration that we can intensify a particular patient's cognitive dysfunction by manipulating his affects is not really very illuminating. After all, even ordinary neurological diseases can often be tremendously influenced symptomatically via emotional stimuli; but if a psychologist demonstrates that the spasticity or tremor of a multiple sclerotic is affected by rage or fear, we would not thereby have learned anything about the etiology of multiple sclerosis.

Consequent upon our general assimilation of the insights given us by psychoanalysis, there is today a widespread and largely unquestioned assumption that when we can trace out the motivational forces linked to the content of aberrant behavior, then we understand why the person has fallen ill. There is no compelling reason to assume this, when the evidence is mainly our dynamic understanding of the patient, however valid that may be. The phrase "why the person has fallen ill" may, of course, be legitimately taken to include these things; an account of how and when he falls ill will certainly include them. But they may be quite inadequate to answer the question, "Why does X fall ill and not Y, granted that we can understand both of them?" I like the analogy of a color psychosis, which might be developed by certain individuals in a society entirely oriented around the making of fine color discriminations. Social, sexual, economic signals are color mediated; to misuse a color word is strictly taboo; compulsive mothers are horribly ashamed of a child who is retarded in color development, and so forth. Some colorblind individuals (not all, perhaps not most) develop a color psychosis in this culture; as adults, they are found on the couches of color therapists, where a great deal of *valid* understanding is achieved about color dynamics. Some of them make a social recovery. Nonetheless, if we ask, "What was basically the matter with these patients?" meaning, "What is the specific etiology of the color psychosis?" the answer is that mutated gene on the X chromosome. This is why my own therapeutic experience with schizophrenic patients has not yet convinced me of the schizophrenogenic mother as a specific etiology, even though the picture I get of my patients' mothers is pretty much in accord with the familiar one. There is no question here of accepting the patient's account; my point is that *given* the account, and taking it quite at face value, does not tell me why the patient is a patient and not just a fellow who had a bad mother.

Another theoretical lead is the one given greatest current emphasis, namely, *interpersonal aversiveness.* The schizophrene suffers a degree of social fear, distrust, expectation of rejection, and conviction of his own unlovability which cannot be matched in its depth, pervasity, and resistance to corrective experience by any other diagnostic group.

Then there is a quasi-pathognomonic sign, emphasized by Rado (1956; Rado & Daniels, 1956) but largely ignored in psychologists' diagnostic usage, namely, *anhedonia*—a marked, widespread, and refractory defect in pleasure capacity which, once you learn how to examine for it, is one of the most consistent and dramatic behavioral signs of the disease.

Finally, I include *ambivalence* from Bleuler's cardinal four (1950). His other two, "autism" and "dereism," I consider derivative from the combination of slippage, anhedonia, and aversiveness. Crudely put, if a person cannot think straight, gets little pleasure, and is afraid of everyone, he will of course learn to be autistic and dereistic.

If these clinical characterizations are correct, and we combine them with the hypothesis of a genetic specific etiology, do they give us any lead on theoretical possibilities?

Granting its initial vagueness as a construct, requiring to be filled in by neurophysiological research, I believe we should take seriously the old European notion of an "integrative neural defect" as the only direct phenotypic consequence produced by the genic mutation. This is an aberration in some parameter of single cell function, which may or may not be manifested in the functioning of more molar CNS systems, depending upon the organization of the mutual feedback controls and upon the stochastic parameters of the reinforcement regime. This neural integrative defect, which I shall christen *schizotaxia*, is all that can properly be spoken of as inherited. The imposition of a social learning history upon schizotaxic individuals results in a personality organization which I shall call, following Rado, the *schizotype.* The four core behavior traits are obviously not innate; but I postulate that they are universally learned by schizotaxic individuals, given any of the actually existing social reinforcement regimes, from the best to the worst. If the interpersonal regime is favorable, and the schizotaxic person also has the good fortune to inherit a low anxiety readiness, physical vigor, general resistance to stress and the like, he will remain a well-compensated "normal" schizotype, never manifesting symptoms of mental disease. He will be like the gout-prone male whose genes determine him to have an elevated blood uric acid titer, but who never develops clinical gout.

Only a subset of schizotypic personalities decompensate into clinical schizophrenia. It seems likely that the most important causal influence pushing the schizotype toward schizophrenic decompensation is the schizophrenogenic mother.

I hope it is clear that this view does not conflict with what has been established about the mother-child interaction. If this interaction were totally free of maternal ambivalence and aversive inputs to the schizotaxic child, even compensated schizotypy might be avoided; at most, we might expect to find only the faintest signs of cognitive slippage and other minimal neurological aberrations, possibly including body image and other proprioceptive deviations, but not the interpersonal aversiveness which is central to the clinical picture.

Nevertheless, while assuming the etiological importance of mother in determining the course of aversive social learnings, it is worthwhile to speculate about the modification our genetic equations might take on this hypothesis. Many schizophrenogenic mothers are themselves schizotypes in varying degrees of compensation. Their etiological contribution then consists jointly in their passing on the gene, *and* in the fact that being schizotypic, they provide the kind of ambivalent regime which potentiates the schizotypy of the child and raises the odds of his decompensating. Hence the incidence of the several parental genotypes among parent pairs of diagnosed proband cases is not calculable from the usual genetic formulas. For example, given a schizophrenic proband, the odds that mother is homozygous (or, if the gene were dominant, that it is mother who carries it) are different from those for father; since we have begun by selecting a decompensated case, and formal diagnosis as the phenotype involves a potentiating factor for mother which is psychodynamically greater than that for a schizotypic father. Another important influence would be the likelihood that the lower fertility of schizophrenics is also present, but to an unknown degree, among compensated schizotypes. Clinical experience suggests that in the semicompensated range, this lowering of fertility is greater among males, since many schizotypic women relate to men in an exploited or exploitive sexual way, whereas the male schizotype usually displays a marked deficit in heterosexual aggressiveness. Such a sex difference in fertility among decompensated cases has been reported by Meyers and Goldfarb (1962).

Since the extent of aversive learnings is a critical factor in decompensation, the inherited anxiety readiness is presumably greater among diagnosed cases. Since the more fertile mothers are likely to be compensated, hence themselves to be relatively low anxiety if schizotaxic, a frequent parent pattern should be a compensated schizotypic mother married to a neurotic father, the latter being the source of the proband's high-anxiety genes (plus providing a poor paternal model for identification in male patients, and a weak defender of the child against mother's schizotypic hostility).

These considerations make ordinary family concordance studies, based upon formal diagnoses, impossible to interpret. The most important research need here is development of high-validity indicators for compensated schizotypy. I see some evidence for these conceptions in the report of Lidz and co-workers, who in studying intensively the parents of 15 schizophrenic patients were surprised to find that "minimally, 9 of the 15 patients had at least one parent who could be called schizophrenic, or ambulatory schizophrenic, or clearly paranoid in behavior and attitudes" (Lidz, Cornelison, Terry, & Fleck, 1958, p. 308). As I read the brief personality sketches presented, I would judge that all but two of the probands had a clearly schizotypic parent. These authors, while favoring a "learned irrationality" interpretation of their data, also recognize the alternative genetic interpretation. Such facts do not permit a decision, obviously; my main point is the striking difference between the high incidence of parental schizotypes, mostly quite decompensated (some to the point of diagnosable psychosis), and the zero incidence which a conventional family concordance study would have yielded for this group.

Another line of evidence, based upon a very small sample but exciting because of its uniformity, is McConaghy's report (1959) that among nondiagnosed parent pairs of 10 schizophrenics, subclinical thought disorder was psychometrically detectable in at least one parent of every pair. Rosenthal (in press) reports that he can add five tallies to this parent-pair count, and suggests that such results might indicate that the specific heredity is dominant, and completely penetrant, rather than recessive. The attempt to replicate these findings, and other psychometric efforts to tap subclinical cognitive slippage in the "normal" relatives of schizophrenics, should receive top priority in our research efforts.

Summarizing, I hypothesize that the statistical relation between schizotaxia, schizotypy, and schizophrenia is class inclusion: All schizotaxics become, *on all actually existing social learning regimes*, schizotypic in personality organization; but most of these remain compensated. A minority, disadvantaged by other (largely polygenically determined) constitutional weaknesses, and put on a bad regime by schizophrenogenic mothers (most of whom are themselves schizotypes) are thereby potentiated into clinical schizophrenia. What makes schizotaxia etiologically specific is its role as a *necessary* condition. I postulate that a nonschizotaxic individual, whatever his other genetic makeup and whatever his learning history, would at most develop a character disorder or a psychoneurosis; but he would not become a schizotype and therefore could never manifest its decompensated form, schizophrenia.

What sort of quantitative aberration in the structural or functional parameters of the nervous system can we conceive to be directly determined by a mutated gene, and to so alter initial dispositions that affected individuals will, in the course of their childhood learning history, develop the four schizotypal source traits: cognitive slippage, anhedonia, ambivalence, and interpersonal aversiveness? To me, the most baffling thing about the disorder is the phenotypic heterogeneity of this tetrad. If one sets himself to the task of doing a theoretical Vigotsky job on this list of psychological dispositions, he may manage part of it by invoking a sufficiently vague kind of descriptive unity between ambivalence and interpersonal aversiveness; and perhaps even anhedonia could be somehow subsumed. But the cognitive slippage presents a real roadblock. Since I consider cognitive slippage to be a core element in schizophrenia, any characterization of schizophrenic or schizotypic behavior which purports to abstract its essence but does not include the cognitive slippage must be deemed unsatisfactory. I believe that an adequate theoretical account will necessitate moving downward in the pyramid of the sciences to invoke explanatory constructs not found in social, psychodynamic, or even learning theory language, but instead at the neurophysiological level.

Perhaps we don't know enough about "how the brain works" to theorize profitably at that level; and I daresay that the more a psychologist knows about the latest research on brain function, the more reluctant he would be to engage in etiological speculation. Let me entreat my physiologically expert listeners to be charitable toward this clinician's premature speculations about how the schizotaxic brain might work. I feel partially justified in such speculating because there are some well-attested general truths about mammalian learned behavior which could almost have been set down from the armchair, in the way engineers draw block diagrams indicating what kinds of parts or subsystems a physical system *must* have, and what their interconnections *must* be, in order to function "appropriately." Brain research of the last decade provides a direct neurophysiological substrate for such cardinal behavior requirements as avoidance, escape, reward, drive differentiation, general and specific arousal or activation, and the like (see Delafresnaye, 1961; Ramey & O'Doherty, 1960). The discovery in the limbic system of specific positive reinforcement centers by Olds and Milner in 1954, and of aversive centers in the same year by Delgado, Roberts, and Miller (1954), seems to me to have an importance that can scarcely be exaggerated; and while the ensuing lines of research on the laws of intracranial stimulation as a mode of behavior control present some puzzles and paradoxes, what *has* been shown up to now may already suffice to provide a theoretical framework. As a general kind of brain model let us take a broadly Hebbian conception in combination with the findings on intracranial stimulation.

To avoid repetition I shall list some basic assumptions first but introduce others in context and only implicitly when the implication is obvious. I shall assume that:

When a presynaptic cell participates in firing a postsynaptic cell, the former gains an increment in firing control over the latter. Coactivation of anatomically connected cell assemblies or assembly systems therefore increases their stochastic control linkage, and the frequency of discharges by neurons of a system may be taken as an intensity variable influencing the growth rate of intersystem control linkage as well as the momentary activity level induced in the other systems. (I shall dichotomize acquired cortical systems into "perceptual-cognitive," including central representations of goal objects; and "instrumental," including overarching monitor systems which select and guide specific effector patterns.)

Most learning in mature organisms involves altering control linkages between systems which themselves have been consolidated by previous learnings, sometimes requiring thousands of activations and not necessarily related to the reinforcement operation to the extent that perceptual-to-instrumental linkage growth functions are.

Control linkage increments from coactivation depend heavily, if not entirely, upon a period of reverberatory activity facilitating consolidation.

Feedback from positive limbic centers is facilitative to concurrent perceptual-cognitive or instrumental sequences, whereas negative center feedback exerts an inhibitory influence. (These statements refer to initial features of the direct wiring diagram, not to all long-term results of learning.) Aversive input also has excitatory effects via the arousal system, which maintain activity permitting escape learning to occur because the organism is alerted and keeps doing things. But I postulate that this overall influence is working along with an opposite effect, quite clear from both molar and intracranial experiments, that a major biological function of aversive-center activation is to produce "stoppage" of whatever the organism is currently doing.

Perceptual-cognitive systems and limbic motivational control centers develop two-way mutual controls (e.g., discriminative stimuli acquire the reinforcing property; "thoughts" become pleasantly toned; drive-relevant perceptual components are "souped-up.")

What kind of heritable parametric aberration could underlie the schizotaxic's readiness to acquire the schizotypic tetrad? It would seem, first of all, that the defect is much more likely to reside in the neurone's synaptic control function than in its storage function. It is hard to conceive of a general defect in storage which would on the one hand permit so many perceptual-cognitive functions, such as tapped by intelligence tests, school learning, or the high order cognitive powers displayed by some schizotypes, and yet have the diffuse motivational and emotional effects found in these same individuals. I am not saying that a storage deficit is clearly excludable, but it hardly seems the best place to look. So we direct our attention to parameters of control.

One possibility is to take the anhedonia as fundamental. What is *phenomenologically* a radical pleasure deficiency may be roughly identified *behaviorally* with a quantitative deficit in the positive reinforcement growth constant, and each of these—the "inner" and "outer" aspects of the organism's appetitive control system—reflect a quantitative deficit in the limbic "positive" centers. The anhedonia would then be a direct consequence of the genetic defect in wiring. Ambivalence and interpersonal aversiveness would be quantitative deviations in the balance of appetitive-aversive controls. Most perceptual-cognitive and instrumental learnings occur under mixed positive and negative schedules, so the normal consequence is a collection of habits and expectancies varying widely in the intensity of their positive and negative components, but mostly "mixed" in character. Crudely put, everybody has *some* ambivalence about almost everything, and everybody has *some* capacity for "social fear." Now if the brain centers which mediate phenomenal pleasure and behavioral reward are numerically sparse or functionally feeble, the aversive centers meanwhile functioning normally, the long-term result would be a general shift toward the aversive end, appearing clinically as ambivalence and exaggerated interpersonal fear. If, as Brady believes, there is a wired-in reciprocal inhibiting relation between positive and negative centers, the long-term aversive drift would be further potentiated (i.e., what we see at the molar level as a sort of "softening" or "soothing" effect of feeding or petting upon anxiety elicitors would be reduced).

Cognitive slippage is not as easy to fit in, but if we assume that normal ego function is acquired by a combination of social reinforcements and the self-reinforcements which become available to the child via identification; then we might say roughly that "everybody has to learn *how* to think straight." Rationality is socially acquired; the secondary process and the reality principle are slowly and imperfectly learned, by even the most clear headed. Insofar as slippage is manifested in the social sphere, such an explanation has some plausibility. An overall aversive drift would account for the paradoxical schizotypic combination of interpersonal distortions and acute perceptiveness of others' unconscious, since the latter is really a hypersensitivity to aversive signals rather than an overall superiority in realistically discriminating social cues. On the output side, we might view the cognitive slippage of mildly schizoid speech as originating from poorly consolidated second-order "monitor" assembly systems which function in an editing role, their momentary regnancy constituting the "set to communicate." At this level, selection among competing verbal operants involves slight differences in appropriateness for which a washed-out social reinforcement history provides an insufficiently refined monitor system. However, if one is impressed with the presence of a pervasive and primary slippage, showing up in a diversity of tests (cf. Payne, 1961) and also on occasions when the patient is desperately trying to communicate, an explanation on the basis of deficient positive center activity is not too convincing.

This hypothesis has some other troubles which I shall merely indicate. Schizoid anhedonia is mainly interpersonal, i.e., schizotypes seem to derive adequate pleasure from esthetic and cognitive rewards. Secondly, some successful psychotherapeutic results include what appears to be a genuine normality to hedonic capacity. Thirdly, regressive electroshock sometimes has the same effect, and the animal evidence suggests that shock works by knocking out the aversive control system rather than by souping up appetitive centers. Finally, if the anhedonia is really general in extent, it is hard to conceive of any simple genetic basis for weakening the different positive centers, whose reactivity has been shown by Olds and others to be chemically drive specific.

A second neurological hypothesis takes the slippage factor as primary. Suppose that the immediate consequence of whatever biochemical aberration the gene directly controls were a specific alteration in the neurone's membrane stability, such that the distribution of optional transmission probabilities is more widely dispersed over the synaptic signal space than in normals. That is, presynaptic input signals whose spatio-temporal configuration locates them peripherally in the neurone's signal space yield transmission probabilities which are relatively closer to those at the maximum point, thereby producing a kind of dedifferentiation or flattening of the cell's selectivity. Under suitable parametric assumptions, this synaptic slippage would lead to a corresponding dedifferentiation of competing inter-assembly controls, because the elements in the less frequently or intensely coactivated control assembly would be accumulating control increments more rapidly than normal. Consider a perceptual-cognitive system whose regnancy is preponderantly associated with positive-center coactivation but sometimes with aversive. The cumulation of control increments will draw these apart; but if synaptic slippage exists, their difference, at least during intermediate stages of control development, will be attenuated. The intensity of aversive-center activation by a given level of perceptual-cognitive system activity will be exaggerated relative to that induced in the positive centers. For a preponderantly aversive control this will be reversed. But now the different algebraic sign of the feedbacks introduces an important asymmetry. Exaggerated negative feedback will tend to lower activity level in the predominantly appetitive case, retarding the growth of the control linkage; whereas exaggerated positive feedback in the predominantly aversive case will tend to heighten activity levels, accelerating the linkage growth. The long-term tendency will be that movement in the negative direction which I call *aversive drift.* In addition to the asymmetry generated by the difference in feedback signs, certain other features in the mixed-regime setup contribute to aversive drift. One factor is the characteristic difference between positive and negative reinforcers in their role as strengtheners. It seems a fairly safe generalization to say that positive centers function only weakly as strengtheners when "on" continuously, and mainly when they are turned on as terminators of a cognitive or instrumental sequence; by contrast, negative centers work mainly as "off" signals, tending to inhibit elements while steadily "on." We may suppose that the former strengthen mainly by facilitating postactivity reverberation (and hence consolidation) in successful systems, the latter mainly by holding down such reverberation in unsuccessful ones. Now a slippage-heightened aversive steady state during predominantly appetitive control sequences reduces their activity level, leaves fewer recently active elements available for a subsequent Olds-plus "on" signal to consolidate. Whereas a slippage-heightened Olds-plus steady state during predominantly aversive control sequences (*a*) increases their negative control *during* the "on" period and (*b*) leaves relatively more of their elements recently active and hence further consolidated by the negative "off" signal when it occurs. Another factor is exaggerated competition by aversively controlled sequences, whereby the appetitive chains do not continue to the stage of receiving socially mediated positive reinforcement, because avoidant chains (e.g., phobic behavior, withdrawal, intellectualization) are getting in the way. It is worth mentioning that the schizophrenogenic mother's regime is presumably "mixed" not only in the sense of the frequent and unpredictable aversive inputs she provides in response to the child's need signals, but also in her greater tendency to present such aversive inputs *concurrently* with drive reducers—thereby facilitating the "scrambling" of appetitive-and-aversive controls so typical of schizophrenia.

The schizotype's dependency guilt and aversive overreaction to offers of help are here seen as residues of the early knitting together of his cortical representations of appetitive goals with punishment-expectancy assembly systems. Roughly speaking, he has learned that to want anything interpersonally provided is to be endangered.

The cognitive slippage is here conceived as a direct molar consequence of synaptic slippage, potentiated by the disruptive effects of aversive control and inadequate development of interpersonal communication sets. Cognitive and instrumental linkages based upon sufficiently massive and consistent regimes, such as reaching for a seen pencil, will converge to asymptotes hardly distinguishable from the normal. But systems involving closely competing strengths and automatized selection among alternatives, especially when the main basis of acquisition and control is social reward, will exhibit evidences of malfunction.

My third speculative model revives a notion with a long history, namely, that the primary schizotaxic defect is a quantitative deficiency of inhibition. (In the light of Milner's revision of Hebb, in which the inhibitory action of Golgi Type II cells is crucial even for the formation of functionally differentiated cell assemblies, a defective inhibitory parameter could be an alternative basis for a kind of slippage similar in its consequences to the one we have just finished discussing.) There are two things about this somewhat moth-eaten "defective inhibition" idea which I find appealing. First, it is the most direct and uncomplicated neurologizing of the schizoid cognitive slippage. Schizoid cognitive slippage is neither an incapacity to link, nor is it an unhealthy overcapacity to link; rather it seems to be a defective *control* over associations which are also accessible to the healthy (as in dreams, wit, psychoanalytic free association, and certain types of creative work) but are normally "edited out" or "automatically suppressed" by those superordinate monitoring assembly systems we lump together under the term "set." Secondly, in working with pseudoneurotic cases one sees a phenomenon to which insufficient theoretical attention has been paid: Namely, these patients cannot turn off painful thoughts. They suffer constantly and intensely from painful thoughts about themselves, about possible adverse outcomes, about the past, about the attitudes and intentions of others. The "weak ego" of schizophrenia means a number of things, one of which is failure of defense; the schizophrenic has too ready access to his own id, and is too perceptive of the unconscious of others. It is tempting to read "failure of defense" as "quantitatively deficient inhibitory feedback." As mentioned earlier, aversive signals (whether exteroceptive or internally originated) must exert both an exciting effect via the arousal system and a quick-stoppage effect upon cortical sequences which fail to terminate the ongoing aversive signal, leading the organism to shift to another. Suppose the gene resulted in an insufficient production (or too rapid inactivation) of the specific inhibitory transmitter substance, rendering all inhibitory neurones quantitatively weaker than normal. When aversively linked cognitive sequences activate negative limbic centers, these in turn soup up the arousal system normally but provide a subnormal inhibitory feedback, thereby permitting their elicitor to persist for a longer time and at higher intensity than normal. This further activates the negative control center, and so on, until an equilibrium level is reached which is above normal in intensity all around, and which meanwhile permits an excessive linkage growth in the aversive chain. (In this respect the semicompensated case would differ from the late-stage deteriorated schizophrenic, whose aversive drift has gradually proliferated so widely that almost any cognitive or instrumental chain elicits an overlearned defensive "stoppage," whereby even the inner life undergoes a profound and diffuse impoverishment.)

The mammalian brain is so wired that aversive signals tend to produce stoppage of regnant cognitive or instrumental sequences without the aversive signal having been specifically connected to their controlling cues or motivational systems. E.g., lever pressing under thirst or hunger can be inhibited by shock-associated buzzer, even though the latter has not been previously connected with hunger, paired with the discriminative stimulus, nor presented as punishment for the operant. A deficient capacity to inhibit concurrent activity of fringe elements (aversively connected to ambiguous social inputs from ambivalent mother) would accelerate the growth of linkages between them and appetitive systems not hitherto punished. Sequential effects are here especially important, and combine with the schizophrenogenic mother's tendency not to provide differential cues of high consistency as predictors of whether aversive or appetitive consequences will follow upon the child's indications of demand.

Consider two cortical systems having shared "fringe" subsystems (e.g., part percepts of mother's face). When exteroceptive inputs are the elicitors, negative feedback from aversive centers cannot usually produce stoppage; in the absence of such overdetermining external controls, the relative activity levels are determined by the balance of facilitative and inhibitory feedbacks. "Fringe" assemblies which have already acquired more aversive control, if they begin to be activated by regnant perceptual-cognitive sequences, will increase inhibitory feedback; and being "fringe" they can thereby be held down. The schizotaxic, whose aversive-feedback stoppage of fringe-element activity is weakened, accumulates excessive intertrial Hebbian increments toward the aversive side, the predominantly aversive fringe elements being more active and becoming more knit into the system than normally. On subsequent exteroceptively controlled trials, whenever the overdetermining stimulus input activates predominantly aversive perceptual-cognitive assemblies, their driving of the negative centers will be heightened. The resulting negative feedback may now be strong enough that, when imposed upon "fringe" assemblies weakly activated and toward the appetitive side, it can produce stoppage. On such occasions the more appetitive fringe elements will be retarded in their linkage growth, receiving fewer Hebbian increments. And those which do get over threshold will become further linked during such trials to the concurrent negative center activity. The result is twofold: a retarded growth of appetitive perceptual-cognitive linkages; and a progressive drawing of fringe elements into the aversive ambit.

"Ambiguous regimes," where the pairing of S^+ and S^- inputs occurs very unpredictably, will have a larger number of fringe elements. Also, if the external schedule is dependent upon regnant appetitive drive states as manifested in the child's instrumental social acts, so that these are often met with mixed S^+ (drive-relevant) and S^- (anxiety-eliciting) inputs, the appetitive and aversive assemblies will tend to become linked, and to activate positive and negative centers concurrently. The anhedonia and ambivalence would be consequences of this plus-minus "scrambling," especially if the positive and negative limbic centers are mutually inhibitory but here deficiently so. We would then expect schizotypic anhedonia to be basically interpersonal, and only derivatively present, if at all, in other contexts. This would in part explain the schizotype's preservation of relatively normal function in a large body of instrumental domains. For example, the acquisition of basic motor and cognitive skills would be relatively less geared to a mixed input, since "successful" mastery is both mechanically rewarded (e.g., how to open a door) and also interpersonally rewarded as "school success," etc. The hypercathexis of intellect, often found even among nonbright schizotypes, might arise from the fact that these performances are rewarded rather "impersonally" and make minimal demands on the reinforcing others. Also, the same cognitive and mechanical instrumental acts can often be employed both to turn on positive center feedback and to turn off negative, an equivalence much less true of purely social signals linked to interpersonal needs.

Having briefly sketched three neurological possibilities for the postulated schizotaxic aberration, let me emphasize that while each has sufficient merit to be worth pursuing, they are mainly meant to be illustrative of the vague concept "integrative neural defect." I shall myself not be surprised if all three are refuted, whereas I shall be astounded if future research shows no fundamental aberration in nerve-cell function in the schizotype. Postulating schizotaxia as an open concept seems at first to pose a search problem of needle-in-haystack proportions, but I suggest that the plausible alternatives are really somewhat limited. After all, what does a neuron do to another neuron? It excites, or it inhibits! The schizotypic preservation of relatively normal function in selected domains directs our search toward some minimal deviation in a synaptic control parameter, as opposed to, say, a gross defect in cell distribution or structure, or the kind of biochemical anomaly that yields mental deficiency. Anything which would give rise to defective storage, grossly impaired transmission, or sizable limitations on functional complexity can be pretty well excluded on present evidence. What we are looking for is a quantitative aberration in synaptic control—a deviation in amount or patterning of excitatory or inhibitory action—capable of yielding cumulative departures from normal control linkages under mixed appetitive-aversive regimes; but slight enough to permit convergence to quasi-normal asymptotes under more consistent schedules (or when massive repetition with motive-incentive factors unimportant is the chief basis for consolidation). The defect must generate aversive drift on mixed social reinforcement regimes, and must yield a primary cognitive slippage which, however, may be extremely small in magnitude except as potentiated by the cumulative effects of aversive drift. Taken together these molar constraints limit our degrees of freedom considerably when it comes to filling in the neurophysiology of schizotaxia.

Leaving aside the specific nature of schizotaxia, we must now raise the familiar question whether such a basic neurological defect, however subtle and nonstructural it might be, should not have been demonstrated hitherto? In reply to this objection I shall content myself with pointing out that there are several lines of evidence which, while not strongly arguing *for* a neurological theory, are rebuttals of an argument presupposing clear and consistent *negative* findings. For example: Ignoring several early European reports with inadequate controls, the literature contains a half-dozen quantitative studies showing marked vestibular system dysfunction in schizophrenics (Angyal & Blackman, 1940, 1941; Angyal & Sherman, 1942; Colbert & Koegler, 1959; Freeman & Rodnick, 1942; Leach, 1960; Payne & Hewlett, 1960; Pollock & Krieger, 1958). Hoskins (1946) concluded that a neurological defect in the vestibular system was one of the few clear-cut biological findings in the Worcester studies. It is of prime importance to replicate these findings among compensated and pseudoneurotic cases, where the diffuse withdrawal and deactivation factor would not provide the explanation it does in the chronic, burnt-out case (cf. Collins, Crampton, & Posner, 1961). Another line of evidence is in the work of King (1954) on psychomotor deficit, noteworthy for its careful use of task simplicity, asymptote performance, concern for patient cooperation, and inclusion of an outpatient pseudoneurotic sample. King himself regards his data as indicative of a rather basic behavior defect, although he does not hold it to be schizophrenia-specific. Then we have such research as that of Barbara Fish (1961) indicating the occurrence of varying signs of perceptual-motor maldevelopment among infants and children who subsequently manifest clinical schizophrenia. The earlier work of Schilder and Bender along these lines is of course well known, and there has always been a strong minority report in clinical psychiatry that many schizophrenics provide subtle and fluctuating neurological signs of the "soft" variety, if one keeps alert to notice or elicit them. I have myself been struck by the frequent occurrence, even among pseudoneurotic patients, of transitory neurologic-like complaints (e.g., diplopia, localized weakness, one-sided tremor, temperature dyscontrol, dizziness, disorientation) which seem to lack dynamic meaning or secondary gain and whose main effect upon the patient is to produce bafflement and anxiety. I have seen preliminary findings by J. McVicker Hunt and his students in which a rather dramatic quantitative deficiency in spatial cognizing is detectable in schizophrenics of above-normal verbal intelligence. Research by Cleveland (1960; Cleveland, Fisher, Reitman, & Rothaus, 1962) and by Arnhoff and Damianopoulos (in press) on the clinically well-known body-image anomalies in schizophrenia suggests that this domain yields quantitative departures from the norm of such magnitude that with further instrumental and statistical refinement it might be used as a quasi-pathognomonic sign of the disease. It is interesting to note a certain thread of unity running through this evidence, which perhaps lends support to Rado's hypothesis that a kinesthetic integrative defect is even more characteristic of schizotypy than is the radial anhedonia.

All these kinds of data are capable of a psychodynamic interpretation. "Soft" neurological signs are admittedly ambiguous, especially when found in the severely decompensated case. The only point I wish to make here is that *since* they exist and are at present unclear in etiology, an otherwise plausible neurological view cannot be refuted on the ground that there is a *lack* of any sign of neurological dysfunction in schizophrenia; there is no such lack.

Time forces me to leave detailed research strategy for another place, but the main directions are obvious and may be stated briefly: The clinician's Mental Status ratings on anhedonia, ambivalence, and interpersonal aversiveness should be objectified and preferably replaced by psychometric measures. The research findings on cognitive slippage, psychomotor dyscontrol, vestibular malfunction, body image, and other spatial aberrations should be thoroughly replicated and extended into the pseudoneurotic and semicompensated ranges. If these efforts succeed, it will be possible to set up a multiple sign pattern, using optimal cuts on phenotypically diverse indicators, for identifying compensated schizotypes in the nonclinical population. Statistics used must be appropriate to the theoretical model of a dichotomous latent taxonomy reflecting itself in otherwise independent quantitative indicators. Family concordance studies should then be run relating proband schizophrenia to schizotypy as identified by this multiple indicator pattern. Meanwhile we should carry on an active and varied search for more direct neurological signs of schizotaxia, concentrating our hunches on novel stimulus inputs (e.g., the stabilized retinal image situation) which may provide a better context for basic neural dysfunction to show up instead of being masked by learned compensations or imitated by psychopathology.

In closing, I should like to take this unusual propaganda opportunity to play the prophet. It is my strong personal conviction that such a research strategy will enable psychologists to make a unique contribution in the near future, using psychological techniques to establish that schizophrenia, while its content is learned, is fundamentally a neurological disease of genetic origin.

REFERENCES

Angyal, A., & Blackman, N. Vestibular reactivity in schizophrenia. *Arch. Neurol. Psychiat.*, 1940, **44**, 611–620.

Angyal, A., & Blackman, N. Paradoxical reactions in schizophrenia under the influence of alcohol, hyperpnea, and CO_2 inhalation. *Amer. J. Psychiat.*, 1941, **97**, 893–903.

Angyal, A., & Sherman, N. Postural reactions to vestibular stimulation in schizophrenic and normal subjects. *Amer. J. Psychiat.*, 1942, **98**, 857–862.

Arnhoff, F., & Damianopoulos, E. Self-body recognition and schizophrenia: An exploratory study. *J. abnorm. soc. Psychol.*, in press.

Bleuler, E. *Theory of schizophrenic negativism.* New York: Nervous and Mental Disease Publishing, 1912.

Bleuler, E. *Dementia praecox.* New York: International Universities Press, 1950.

Cleveland, S. E. Judgment of body size in a schizophrenic and a control group. *Psychol. Rep.*, 1960, **7**, 304.

Cleveland, S. E., Fisher, S., Reitman, E. E., & Rothaus, P. Perception of body size in schizophrenia. *Arch. gen. Psychiat.*, 1962, **7**, 277–285.

Colbert, G., & Koegler, R. Vestibular dysfunction in childhood schizophrenia. *AMA Arch. gen. Psychiat.*, 1959, **1**, 600–617.

Collins, W. E., Crampton, G. H., & Posner, J. B. The effect of mental set upon vestibular nystagmus and the EEG. *USA Med. Res. Lab. Rep.*, 1961, No. 439.

Delafresnaye, J. F. (Ed.) *Brain mechanisms and learning.* Springfield, Ill.: Charles C Thomas, 1961.
Delgado, J. M. R., Roberts, W. W., & Miller, N. E. Learning motivated by electrical stimulation of the brain. *Amer. J. Physiol.*, 1954, **179**, 587–593.
Fish, Barbara. The study of motor development in infancy and its relationship to psychological functioning. *Amer. J. Psychiat.*, 1961, **117**, 1113–1118.
Freeman, H. & Rodnick, E. H. Effect of rotation on postural steadiness in normal and schizophrenic subjects. *Arch. Neurol. Psychiat.*, 1942, **48**, 47–53.
Fuller, J. L., & Thompson, W. R. *Behavior genetics.* New York: Wiley, 1960. Pp. 272–283.
Hoskins, R. G. *The biology of schizophrenia.* New York: Norton, 1946.
King, H. E. *Psychomotor aspects of mental disease.* Cambridge: Harvard Univer. Press, 1954.
Leach, W. W. Nystagmus: An integrative neural deficit in schizophrenia. *J. abnorm. soc. Psychol.*, 1960, **60**, 305–309.
Lidz, T., Cornelison, A., Terry, D., & Fleck, S. Intrafamilial environment of the schizophrenic patient: VI. The transmission of irrationality. *AMA Arch. Neurol. Psychiat.*, 1958, **79**, 305–316.
McConaghy, N. The use of an object sorting test in elucidating the hereditary factor in schizophrenia. *J. Neurol. Neurosurg. Psychiat.*, 1959, **22**, 243–246.
Meyers, D., & Goldfarb, W. Psychiatric appraisals of parents and siblings of schizophrenic children. *Amer. J. Psychiat.*, 1962, **118**, 902–908.
Olds, J., & Milner, P. Positive reinforcement produced by electrical stimulation of septal area and other regions of rat brain. *J. comp. physiol. Psychol.*, 1954, **47**, 419–427.
Payne, R. W. Cognitive abnormalities. In H. J. Eysenck (Ed.), *Handbook of abnormal psychology.* New York: Basic Books, 1961. Pp. 248–250.
Payne, R. S., & Hewlett, J. H. G. Thought disorder in psychotic patients. In H. J. Eysenck (Ed.), *Experiments in personality.* Vol. 2. London: Routledge, Kegan, Paul, 1960. Pp. 3–106.
Pollack, M., & Krieger, H. P. Oculomotor and postural patterns in schizophrenic children. *AMA Arch. Neurol. Psychiat.*, 1958, **79**, 720–726.
Rado, S. *Psychoanalysis of behavior.* New York: Grune & Stratton, 1956.
Rado, S., & Daniels, G. *Changing concepts of psychoanalytic medicine.* New York: Grune & Stratton, 1956.
Ramey, E. R., & O'Doherty, D. S. (Eds.) *Electrical studies on the unanesthetized brain.* New York: Hoeber, 1960.
Rosenthal, D. Problems of sampling and diagnosis in the major twin studies of schizophrenia. *J. psychiat. Res.*, in press.
Stern, K. *Principles of human genetics.* San Francisco: Freeman, 1960. Pp. 581–584.

The Process-Reactive Classification of Schizophrenia

William G. Herron

The heterogeneity of schizophrenic patients and the lack of success in relating variable schizophrenic functioning to diagnostic subtypes (King, 1954) have indicated the serious limitations of the current neuropsychiatric classification of schizophrenia. In response to these limitations interest has arisen in a two-dimensional frame of reference for schizophrenia. Such a conception is based on the patient's life history and/or prognosis. A number of terms—malignant-benign, dementia praecox-schizophrenia, chronic-episodic, chronic-acute, typical-atypical, evolutionary-reactive, true-schizophreniform, process-reactive—have appeared in the literature describing these two syndromes. Process schizophrenia involves a long-term progressive deterioration of the adjustment pattern with little chance of recovery, while reactive schizophrenia indicates a good prognosis based on a history of generally adequate social development with notable stress precipitating the psychosis.

From *Psychological Bulletin,* 1962, **59**, 329–343.

In view of the current favorable interest in this approach to the understanding of schizophrenia (Rabin & King, 1958) the present investigation is designed as an evaluative review of the literature on the process-reactive classification.

EARLY PROGNOSTIC STUDIES

The process-reactive distinction had its implicit origin in the work of Bleuler (1911). Prior to this the Kraepelinian influence had prevailed, with dementia praecox considered an incurable deteriorative disorder. Bleuler, while adhering to an organic etiology for schizophrenia, nonetheless observed that some cases recovered. This conclusion opened the field to a series of subsequent prognostic studies (Benjamin, 1946; Chase & Silverman, 1943; Hunt & Appel, 1936; Kant, 1940, 1941, 1944; Kretschmer, 1925; Langfeldt, 1951; Lewis, 1936, 1944; Malamud & Render, 1939; Mauz, 1930; Milici, 1939; Paskind & Brown, 1940; Wittman, 1941, 1944; Wittman & Steinberg, 1944a, 1944b) eventuating in formalized descriptions of the process and reactive syndromes in terms of specific criteria.

These early studies can be classified in three general categories: studies correlating the outcome of a specific type of therapy with certain prognostic variables, studies descriptively evaluating prognostic criteria, and studies validating a prognostic scale.

The first category is illustrated by the attempt of Chase and Silverman (1943) to correlate the results of Metrazol and insulin shock therapy with prognosis, using 100 schizophrenic patients treated with Metrazol and 40 schizophrenic patients treated with insulin shock.

In the first part of this study the probable outcome of each of the 150 patients was estimated on the basis of prognostic criteria. The criteria considered of primary importance for a favorable prognosis were: short duration of illness, acute onset, obvious exogenic precipitating factors, early prominence of confusion, and atypical symptoms (marked by strong mixtures of manic-depressive, psychogenic, and symptomatic trends), and minimal process symptoms (absence of depersonalization, derealization, massive primary persecutory ideas, and sensations of influence, conscious realization of personality disintegration, bizarre delusions and hallucinations, marked apathy, and dissociation of affect). When these conditions were reversed the prognosis was least favorable. The following factors were considered less important for a favorable prognosis: history of previous illness, pyknic body type, extrovert temperament and adequate prepsychotic life adjustment, catatonic and atypical subtypes. Asthenic body type, introversion, inadequacy of prepsychotic reactions to life situations, onset of illness after the age of 40, and hebephrenic and paranoid subtypes were considered indicative of unfavorable prognosis. Age of onset under 40, sex, education, and abilities, and hereditary background were not considered of prognostic importance. An analysis of the prognostically significant factors resulted in the evaluation of the prognosis for each case as good, fair, or poor.

Following termination of shock treatment all patients were followed-up for an average of 10 months and divided into three groups; much improved, improved, and unimproved. A comparison of the prognostic assessments with the results of shock indicated that of 43 cases in which the prognosis was considered good, 33 showed remissions, while of 74 cases with a poor prognosis, 63 did not improve. It was concluded that shock therapies were effective in cases of schizophrenia in which the prognosis was favorable, but were of little value when the prognosis was poor.

The second part of the research involved a reanalysis of the prognostic criteria in the light of the results of shock treatment. Short duration of illness and the absence of process symptoms were the most significant factors for favorable outcome, while long duration of illness (more than 2 years) and the presence of process symptoms were primary in determining poor prognosis.

A descriptive review of prognostic factors is seen in Kant's (1944) description of the benign (reactive) syndrome as cases in which clouding and confusion prevail, or in which the schizophrenic symptoms centered around manic-depressive features or cases with alternating states of excitement and stupor with fragmentation of mental activity. Malignant (process) cases are characterized by direct process symptoms. These include changes in the behavior leading to disorganization, dulling and autism, preceding the outbreak of overt psychosis. The most subtle manifestation of this is the typical schizophrenic thought disturbance. The patient experiences the process as a loss of normal feeling of personality activity and the start of experiencing a foreign influence applied to mind or body.

The third category includes the Elgin Prognostic Scale, constructed by Wittman (1941) to predict recovery in schizophrenia. It is comprised of 20 rating scales weighted according to prognostic importance: favorable factors are weighted negatively, and unfavorable factors are assigned positive weights. Initial validation involved 343 schizophrenic cases placed on shock treatment. Wittman and Steinberg (1944a) performed a follow-up study on 804 schizophrenics and 156 manic-depressive patients. The Elgin scale proved effective in predicting the outcome of therapy in 80–85% of the cases in both studies, and has been utilized in the work of Becker (1956, 1959), King (1958), and McDonough (1960) to distinguish the process-reactive syndrome. Included in the subscales of the Elgin scale are evaluations of prepsychotic personality, nature of onset, and typicality of the psychosis relative to Kraepelin's definition.

STUDIES WITH DETAILED PROCESS-REACTIVE CRITERIA

The synthesis of early studies is found in the research of Kantor, Wallner, and Winder (1953) establishing detailed criteria for distinguishing the two syndromes on the basis of case history material. A process patient would exhibit the following characteristics: early psychological trauma, severe or long physical illness, odd member of the family, school difficulties, family troubles paralleled by sudden changes in the patient's behavior, introverted behavior trends and interests, history of a breakdown of social, physical, and/or mental functioning, pathological siblings, overprotective or rejecting mother, rejecting father, lack of heterosexuality, insidious gradual onset of psychosis without pertinent stress, physical aggression, poor response to treatment, lengthy stay in the hospital, massive paranoia, little capacity for alcohol, no manic-depressive component, failure under adversity, discrepancy between ability and achievement, awareness of a change in the self, somatic delusions, a clash between the culture and the environment, and a loss of decency. In contrast, the reactive patient has these characteristics: good psychological history, good physical health, normal family member, well adjusted at school, domestic troubles unaccompanied by behavioral disruptions in the patient, extroverted behavior trends and interests, history of adequate social, physical, and/or mental functioning, normal siblings, normally protective accepting mother, accepting father, heterosexual behavior, sudden onset of psychosis with pertinent stress present, verbal aggression, good response to treatment, short stay in the hospital, minor paranoid trends, good capacity for alcohol, manic-depressive component present, success despite adversity, harmony between ability and achievement, no sensation of self-change, absence of somatic delusions, harmony between the culture and the environment, and retention of decency.

The first three criteria apply to the patient's behavior between birth and the fifth year; the next seven, between the fifth year and adolescence; the next five, from adolescence to adulthood; the last nine, during adulthood. Using these 24 points to distinguish the two syndromes they tried to answer three questions:

1. Do diagnoses based upon the Rorschach alone label as nonpsychotic a portion of the population of mental patients who are clinically diagnosed as schizophrenic?
2. Can case histories of clinically diagnosed schizophrenics be differentiated into two categories: process and reactive?
3. Are those cases rated psychotic from the Rorschach classed as process on the basis of case histories, and are those cases judged nonpsychotic from the Rorschach classified as reactive from the case histories?

Two samples of 108 and 95 patients clinically diagnosed as schizophrenic were given the Rorschach and rated according to the process-reactive criteria. In the first sample of 108 patients, 57 were classified as psychotic and 51 nonpsychotic on the basis of the Rorschach alone, while in the second sample, of 74 patients who could be rated as process or reactive, 36 were classified as psychotic, and 38 as nonpsychotic from their Rorschach protocols. Those patients who were rated as reactive from their history were most often judged nonpsychotic from the Rorschach, and those rated process from the case histories were most often judged as psychotic from the Rorschach.

Only one judge was used in the second sample to rate the patients as process or reactive, but two judges were used in the first sample. Of the 108 patients in this sample, both judges rated 86 cases, and were in agreement on 64 of these, which is greater than would be expected by chance.

However, the accuracy of the schizophrenic diagnosis is questionable in this study. If the Rorschach diagnosis is followed, then it appears that reactive schizophrenics are not psychotic. Furthermore, the psychiatric diagnosis appears to be somewhat contaminated because it was established on the basis of data collected by all appropriate services of the hospital, including psychological examinations. A similar type of contamination may have been present in classifying patients as process or reactive because one judge had reviewed each case previously and had seen psychological examination and history materials together prior to making his ratings. Three difficulties can be found with the criteria for process-reactive ratings. First, case histories are often incomplete and the patient is unable or unwilling to supply the necessary information. Second, it is difficult to precisely apply some of the criteria. For example, what is the precise dividing line between oddity and normality within the family? Third, in order to classify a patient it is necessary to set an arbitrary cut off point based on the number of process or reactive characteristics a patient has. Such a procedure needs validation.

Nonetheless, the results of this study support the view that schizophrenics can be classified as process or reactive, and that these syndromes differ in psychological functioning.

Another rating scale which has been used extensively to distinguish prognostically favorable and prognostically unfavorable schizophrenics was developed by Phillips (1953). The scale was developed from the case histories of schizophrenic patients who were eventually given shock treatment. The scale evaluates each patient in three areas: premorbid history, possible precipitating factors, and signs of the disorder. Premorbid history includes seven items on the social aspects of sexual life during adolescence and immediately beyond, seven items on the social aspects of recent sexual life, six items on personal relations, and six items on recent premorbid adjustment in personal relations. The sections of the scale which reflect the recent sexual life and its social history are the most successful in predicting the outcome of treatment. The items in the scales are arranged in order of increasing significance for improvement and nonimprovement away from the score of three, which is the dividing point between improved and unimproved groups. The premorbid history subscale has been utilized as the ranking instrument in the studies described by Rodnick and Garmezy (1957; Garmezy & Rodnick, 1959).

Another approach to the separation of schizophrenics into prognostic groups uses the activity of the autonomic nervous system as the basis for division (Meadow & Funkenstein, 1952; Meadow, Greenblatt, Funkenstein, & Solomon, 1953; Meadow, Greenblatt, & Solomon, 1953). Meadow and Funkenstein (1952) worked with 58 schizophrenic patients tested for autonomic reactivity and for abstract thinking. Following therapy the patients were divided into two groups, good or poor, depending on the outcome of the treatment. The battery of psychological tests included the similarities and block design subtests of the Wechsler-Bellevue scale, the Benjamin Proverbs test, and the object sorting tests. The physiological test involved the systolic blood pressure reaction to adrenergic stimulation (intravenous Epinephrine) and cholinergic stimulation (intramuscular Mecholyl). On the basis of the physiological and psychological testing, schizophrenic cases were divided into three types: Type I, characterized by marked response to Epinephrine, low blood pressure, and failure of the blood pressure to rise under most stresses, loss of ability for abstract thinking, inappropriate affect, and a poor prognosis; Type II, characterized by an entirely different autonomic pattern, relatively intact abstract ability, anxiety or depression, and a good prognosis; Type III, showing no autonomic disturbance, relatively little loss of abstract ability, little anxiety, well organized paranoid delusions, and a fair prognosis.

However, as Meadow and Funkenstein (1952) point out, there is considerable overlap of the measures defining these types so that the classification must be tentative. Also, of the psychological tests used, only Proverbs distinguished significantly between the patients when they were classified according to autonomic reactivity, while Block Design failed to distinguish significantly among any of the types. Further research using this method of division (Meadow, Greenblatt, Funkenstein, & Solomon, 1953; Meadow, Greenblatt, & Solomon, 1953) served as a basis for investigations of the process-reactive syndromes by King (1958) and Zuckerman and Grosz (1959).

King (1958) hypothesized that predominantly reactive

schizophrenics would exhibit a higher level of autonomic responsiveness after the injection of Mecholyl than predominantly process schizophrenics. The subjects were 60 schizophrenics who were classified as either process or reactive by the present investigator and an independent judge using the criteria of Kantor et al. (1953). Only those subjects were used on which there was classificatory agreement. This resulted in 22 process and 24 reactive patients. In order to consider the process-reactive syndrome as a continuum, 16 subjects were randomly selected from these two groups and were ranked by two independent raters.

While the patient was lying in bed shortly after awaking in the morning the resting systolic blood pressure was determined. The patient then received 10 milligrams of Mecholyl intramuscularly, and the systolic blood pressure was recorded at intervals up to 20 minutes. Then the maximum fall in systolic blood pressure (MFBP) below the resting blood pressure following the injection of Mecholyl was computed for the different time intervals. There was a significant difference in the MFBP score for the reactives as compared with the normals. For the 16 subjects, the correlation between the sets of ranks on the process-reactive dimension and MFBP was −.58.

In a second part of the study 90 schizophrenics, none of whom had participated in the first part, were classified as either process, process-reactive, or reactive, using the criteria of Kantor et al. (1953). On this basis the subjects were divided into three groups of 24. Also, scores for 22 subjects were obtained on the Elgin Prognostic Scale, and 12 of these were rated independently by two raters. The MFBP scores were 17.04 for the process group, 22.79 for the process-reactive group, and 26.62 for the reactive. Using an analysis of variance a significant F score occurs at the .01 level. The correlation between the Elgin Prognostic Scale and the MFBP scores for 22 patients was −.49.

Results of both parts of the study revealed that the patients classified as reactive exhibited a significantly greater fall in blood pressure after the administration of Mecholyl than the process patients. This evidence points to diminished physiological responsiveness in process, but not in reactive schizophrenia. However, Zuckerman and Grosz (1959) found that process schizophrenics showed a significantly greater fall in blood pressure following the administration of Mecholyl than reactives. Since these results contradict King's findings the question of the direction of responsiveness to Mecholyl in these two groups requires further investigation before a conclusion can be reached.

PROCESS-ORGANIC VERSUS REACTIVE-PSYCHOGENIC

Brackbill and Fine (1956) suggested that process schizophrenics suffer from an organic impairment not present in the reactive case. They hypothesized that there would be no significant differences in the incidence of "organic signs" on the Rorschach between a group of process schizophrenics and a group of known cases of central nervous system pathology, and that both organic and process groups would show significantly more signs of organic involvement than the reactive group.

The subjects consisted of 36 patients diagnosed as process schizophrenics and 24 reactive schizophrenics. The criteria of Kantor et al. (1953) were used to describe the patients as process or reactive. Patients were included only when there was complete agreement between judges as to the category of schizophrenia. Also included in the sample were 28 cases of known organic involvement. All patients were given the Rorschach, and the protocols were scored using Piotrowski's (1940) 10 signs of organicity.

Using the criterion of five or more signs as a definite indication of organic involvement there was no significant difference between the organic and process groups, but both groups were significantly different from the reactives. Considering individual signs, four distinguished between the reactive and organic group, while two distinguished between process and reactive groups. The authors concluded that the results supported the hypothesis that process schizophrenics react to a perceptual task in a similar manner to that of patients with central nervous system pathology. No specific hypothesis was made about individual Rorschach signs, but color naming, completely absent in the reactives, was indicated as an example of concrete thinking and inability to abstract, suggesting that one of the critical differences between process and reactive groups is in terms of a type of thought disturbance.

This study does not provide detailed information about the manner of establishing the diagnosis of schizophrenia or about the judges deciding the process and reactive syndromes. Also, a further difficulty is the admitted inadequacy of the organic signs, since 66% of cases with organic pathology in this study were false negatives according to the Rorschach criteria. Thus while the existence of the process and reactive syndromes is supported by the results of this investigation, there is less evidence of an organic deficit in process schizophrenics.

Becker (1956) pointed out that the consistency of the prognostic findings in schizophrenia has led to postulating two kinds of schizophrenia: process, with an organic basis, and reactive, with a psychological basis. He rejects this conclusion because research data in this area shows considerable group overlap, making it clinically difficult and arbitrary to force all schizophrenics into one group or the other. Also, if schizophrenia is a deficit reaction which may be brought about by any combination of 40 or more etiological factors, then the conception of two dichotomous types of schizophrenia is not useful. Finally, he maintains that 20 years of research have failed to find clear etiological differences between any subgroupings.

Instead, Becker stated that process and reactive syndromes should be conceived as end points on a continuum of levels of personality organization. Process reflects a very primitive undifferentiated personality structure, while reactive indicates a more highly organized one. He hypothesized that schizophrenics more nearly approximating the process syndrome would show more regressive and immature thinking processes than schizophrenics who more nearly approximate the reactive syndromes. His sample consisted of 51 schizophrenics, 24 males and 27 females, all under 41 years of age. Their thinking processes were evaluated by the Rorschach and the Benjamin Proverbs test. The 1937 Stanford-Binet vocabulary test was used to estimate verbal intelligence. A Rorschach scoring system was used which presumably reflected the subjects' level of perceptual development, while a scoring system was devised for the Proverbs which reflected levels of abstraction. Since there is a high relationship between intelligence and ability to interpret proverbs, a more sensitive index of a thinking disturbance was considered to be a discrepancy score based on the standard score difference between a vocabulary estimate of verbal intelligence and the proverbs score. Process and reactive ratings were made on the Elgin Prognostic Scale.

The Rorschach mean perceptual level score and the Elgin Prognostic Scale correlated −.599 for men and −.679 for women, indicating a significant relationship between the process-reactive dimension as evaluated from case history data and disturbances of thought processes as measured by the Rorschach scoring system. The proverbs-vocabulary discrepancy score was significantly related to the process-reactive dimension for men, but not for women. No adequate explanation was found for this sex difference, which mitigates the results. A further difficulty occurs because the case history and test evaluations were made by the same person. However, the results in part support the hypothesis, indicating evidence for a measurable dimension of regressive and immature thinking related to the process-reactive dimension.

McDonough (1960), acting on the assumption that process schizophrenia involves central nervous system pathology specifically cortical in nature, hypothesized that brain damaged patients and process schizophrenics would have significantly lower critical flicker frequency (CFF) thresholds and would be unable to perceive the spiral aftereffect significantly more often than reactive schizophrenics and normals. Four groups of 20 subjects each were tested. The organic group consisted of individuals with known brain damage. One hundred and sixty-one schizophrenic case histories were examined, and 76 were chosen from this group to be rated on the Elgin Prognostic Scale. The 20 patients receiving the lowest point totals were selected as being most reactive, while those with the 20 highest scores were considered most process.

Results of the experiment revealed that organic patients were significantly different from all other groups in CFF threshold and ability to perceive the spiral aftereffect. Process and reactive schizophrenics did not differ from each other on either task, but reactive schizophrenics had higher CFF thresholds than normals. These results do not indicate demonstrable cortical defect in either process or reactive schizophrenia.

PROCESS-POOR PREMORBID HISTORY VERSUS REACTIVE-GOOD PREMORBID HISTORY

Rodnick and Garmezy (1957), discussing the problem of motivation in schizophrenia, reviewed a number of studies in which the Phillips prognostic scale was used to classify schizophrenic patients into two groups, good and poor. For example, Bleke (1955) hypothesized that patients whose prepsychotic life adjustment was markedly inadequate would have greater interferences and so show more reminiscence following censure than patients whose premorbid histories were more adequate.

The subjects were presented with a list of 14 neutrally toned nouns projected successively on a screen. Each subject was required to learn to these words a pattern of pull-push movements of a switch lever. For half the subjects in each group learning took place under a punishment condition, while the remaining subjects were tested under a reward condition. The subjects consisted of 40 normals, 20 poor premorbid schizophrenics, and 20 good premorbid schizophrenics. The results confirmed the hypothesis.

A reanalysis of Dunn's (1954) data indicated that a poor premorbid group showed discrimination deficits when confronted with a scene depicting a mother and a young boy being scolded, but good premorbid and normal subjects did not show this deficit.

Mallet (1956) found that poor premorbid subjects in a memory task for verbal materials showed significantly poorer retention of hostile and nonhostile thematic contents than did good premorbid and normal subjects. Harris (1955) has found that in contrast to goods and normals poor premorbids have more highly deviant maternal attitudes. They attribute more rejective attitudes to their mothers, and are less able to critically evaluate their mothers. Harris (1957) also found differences among the groups in the size estimation of mother-child pictures. The poors significantly overestimated, while the goods underestimated, and the normals made no size error.

Rodnick and Garmezy (1957) reported a study using Osgood's (1952) semantic differential techniques in which six goods and six poors rated 20 concepts on each of nine scales selected on the basis of high loadings on the evaluative, potency, and activity factors. Good and poor groups differed primarily on potency and activity factors. The poors described words with negative value, as more powerful and active. The goods could discriminate among concepts, but the poors tended to see most concepts as powerful and active.

Rodnick and Garmezy (1957) also investigated differences in authority roles in the family during adolescence in good and poor premorbid patients. While results were tentative at that time, they suggested that the mothers of poor premorbid patients were perceived as having been more dominating, restrictive, and powerful, while the fathers appeared ineffectual. The pattern was reversed in the good premorbid patients.

Alvarez (1957) found significantly greater preference decrements to censured stimuli by poor premorbid patients. This result was consistent with the results of Bleke's (1955) and Zahn's (1959) observations of reversal patterns of movement of a switch lever following censure. These experiments suggested an increased sensitivity of the poor premorbid schizophrenic patient to a threatening environment.

These studies reported by Rodnick and Garmezy (1957) indicated that it was possible, using the Phillips scale, to effectively dichotomize schizophrenic patients. However, the Phillips scale had predictive validity only when applied to male patients. Within this form of reference it was also possible to demonstrate differences between goods and poors in response to censure, and in perception of familial figures. Variability in the results of schizophrenic performance was considerably reduced by dichotomizing the patients, but it was often impossible to detect significant differences between the performance of good premorbid schizophrenics and normals. Rodnick and Garmezy (1957) suggest that the results be considered as preliminary findings pending further corroboration, though providing support for the concept of premorbid groups of schizophrenics differing in certain psychological dimensions.

PROCESS-REACTIVE EMPIRICAL-THEORETICAL FORMULATIONS

Fine and Zimet (1959; Zimet & Fine, 1959) used the same population employed by Kantor et al. (1953) and the same criteria for distinguishing the process and reactive patients. For this study only those cases were included where there was complete agreement among the judges as to the category of schizophrenia. They studied the level of perceptual organization of the patients as shown on their Rorschach records. The process group was found to have significantly more immature, regressive perceptions, while the reactive group gave more mature and more highly organized responses. The findings indicated that archaic and impulse-ridden materials break through more freely in process schizophrenia, and that there is less ego control over the production of more regressive fantasies. Zimet and Fine (1959) speculated that process schizophrenia mirrors oral deprivation of early ego impoverishment, so that either regression or fixation to an earlier developmental stage is reflected in his perceptual organization. In contrast, it is possible that the reactive schizophrenic's ego weakness occurs at a later stage in psychosexual development, and any one event may reactivate the early conflict.

An amplification of the process-reactive formation has been suggested by Kantor and Winder (1959). They hypothesized that schizophrenia can be understood as a series of responses reflecting the stage of development in the patient's life at which emotional support was severely deficient. Schizophrenia can be quantitatively depicted in terms of the level in life to which the schizophrenic has regressed, and beyond which development was severely distorted because of disturbing life circumstances. The earlier in developmental history that severe stress occurs, the more damaging the effect on subsequent interpersonal relationships. Sullivan (1947) suggested five stages in the development of social maturity: empathic, prototaxic, parataxic, autistic, and syntaxic. The most malignant schizophrenics are those who were severely traumatized in the empathic stage of development when all experience is unconnected, there is no symbolism, and functioning is at an elementary biological level. The schizophrenic personality originating at this stage may show many signs of organic dysfunction. Prognosis will be most unfavorable, and delusional formation will tend to be profound.

In view of the primitive symbolic conduct and the lack of a self-concept in the prototaxic stage, the schizophrenic personality referable to this stage will be characterized by magical thinking and disturbed communication. The delusion of adoption often occurs. However, these patients are more coherent than those of the previous level.

The parataxic schizophrenic state involves the inability of the self-system to prevent dissociation. The autonomy of the dissociations result in the patient's fear of uncontrollable inward processes. Schizophrenic symptoms appear as regressive behavior attempting to protect the self and regain security in a threatening world. Delusional content usually involves world disaster coupled with bowel changes. Nihilistic delusions are common. While there is evidence of a self-system in these patients, prognosis remains unfavorable.

The patient who has regressed to the autistic stage, although more reality oriented than in the previous stages, is characterized by paranoid suspiciousness, hostility, and pathological defensiveness against inadequacy feelings. A consistent system of delusions will be articulated and may bring the patient into conflict with society. However, prognosis is more favorable at this stage than previously.

An individual at the syntaxic level has reached consensus with society, so that if schizophrenia occurs it will be a relatively circumscribed reaction. Onset will be sudden with plausible environmental stresses, and prognosis is relatively good.

Becker (1959) also elaborated on the lack of a dichotomy in schizophrenia. Individual cases spread out in such a way that the process syndrome moves into the reactive syndrome, so that the syndromes probably identify the end points of a dimension of severity. At the process end of the continuum the development of personality organization is very primitive, or involves severe regression. There is a narrowing of interests, rigidity of structure, and inability to establish normal heterosexual relationships and independence. In contrast, the reactive end of the continuum represents a higher level of personality differentiation. The prepsychotic personality is more normal, heterosexual relations are better established, and there is greater tolerance of environmental stresses. The remains of a higher developmental level are present in regression and provide strength for recovery.

Becker (1959) factor analyzed some of the data from his previous study (Becker, 1956). The factored matrix included a number of background variables, the 20 Elgin Prognostic Scale subscores, and a Rorschach genetic level score (*GL*) based on the first response to each card. Seven centroid factors were extracted from the correlation matrix. Factors 4, 6, and 7 represented intelligence, cooperativeness, and marital status of parents, respectively. The highest loadings on Factor 5 were history of mental illness in the family, excellent health history, lack of precipitating factors, and clouded sensorium. The Rorschach *GL* score and the Elgin scales did not load significantly on Factors 4 through 7.

The remaining three factors parallel the factors Lorr, Wittman, and Schanberger (1951) found with 17 of the 20 Elgin scales using an oblique solution instead of the orthogonal solution used in this study. Factor 1 is called schizophrenic withdrawal, loading on defect of interest, insidious onset, shut-in personality, long duration of psychosis, and lack of precipitating factors. At one end this factor defines the typical process syndrome, while the other end describes the typical reactive syndrome. The Rorschach *GL* score loaded −.46 on Factor 1.

Factor 2, reality distortion, loads on hebephrenic symptoms, bizarre delusions, and inadequate affect. Rorschach *GL* score loaded −.64 on this factor. Factor 3 loaded on indifference and exclusiveness-stubbornness. The opposite pole of this factor involves insecurity, inferiority, self-consciousness, and anxiety. Rorschach *GL* score loaded .25 on this factor.

Further analysis indicated that when Factors 1 and 2 were plotted against each other an oblique rotation was required, introducing a correlation of from .60 to .70 between schizophrenic withdrawal and reality distortion factors. Similar obliqueness was found between Factors 2 and 3, suggesting the presence of a second-order factor.

However, the sampling of behavior manifestations in the Elgin scale overweights the withdrawal factor, which gives Factor 1 undue weight and biases the direction of a second-order factor toward the withdrawal factor. Also, it is not possible to accurately locate second-order factors with only seven first-order factors as reference points. In addition, sample size and related sampling errors limited inferences about a second-order factor. There is the suggestion, however, of the existence of a general severity factor, loading primarily schizophrenic withdrawal and reality distortion.

The author suggests utilizing the evidence from this study to form an index of severity of psychosis which could be used to make diagnoses with prognostic significance. This diagnostic procedure would include factor estimates of schizophrenic withdrawal and emotional rigidity, based on Elgin scale ratings, and reality distortion, based on the Rorschach *GL* score.

Garmezy and Rodnick (1959) pointed out that despite failure to find support for a fundamental biological deviation associated with schizophrenia (Kety, 1959), the view of schizophrenia as a dichotomous typology influenced either by somatic or psychic factors has continuously been advanced. They maintain that on the basis of empirical evidence there is little support for a process-organic versus reactive-psychogenic formulation of schizophrenic etiology.

Reviewing a series of studies using the Phillips scale as a dichotomizing instrument (Alvarez, 1957; Bleke, 1955; Dunham, 1959; Dunn, 1954; Englehart, 1959; Farina, 1960; Garmezy, Stockner, & Clarke, 1959; Harris, 1957; Kreinik, 1959; Rodnick & Garmezy, 1957; Zahn, 1959) Garmezy and Rodnick concluded that the results indicate two groups of schizophrenic patients differing both in prognostic potential and sensitivity to experimental cues. There is an interrelationship among the variables of premorbid adequacy, differential sensitivity to censure, prognosis, and types of familial organization. This suggests a relationship between varying patterns of early experience and schizophrenia, though it does not embody the acceptance of a given position regarding psychological or biological antecedents in schizophrenia.

Reisman (1960), in an attempt to explain the heterogeneous results of psychomotor performance in schizophrenics, suggested that there were two groups of schizophrenics, process and reactive, differing in motivation. The process group was seen as more withdrawn and indifferent to their performance, and consequently reflecting a psychomotor deficit not present in reactives. In order to test this hypothesis 36 reactives, 36 process patients, and 36 normals performed a card-sorting task. The groups were distinguished according to the criteria of Kantor, Wallner, and Winder (1953). On Trial 1 all subjects were requested to sort as rapidly as possible. Then the subjects were assigned to one of four experimental conditions, with an attempt made to equate across the experimental conditions for age, estimated IQ, length of hospitalization, and initial sorting time. Condition 1 (FP) involved sorting the cards seven more times and if the sort was fast the subjects were shown stress-arousing photographs. If they sorted slowly no photographs were shown. Condition 2 (SP) was the reverse of this. Condition 3 (FL) and Condition 4 (SL) were similar to the first two conditions except that a nonreinforcing light was used instead of the pictures. After Trial 8 all subjects were informed that there would be no more pictures or light, but were asked to sort rapidly for three more trials. With four conditions on Trials 2 through 8, 10 subjects from each of the three groups participated in each of the two picture conditions, while eight subjects from each group participated in each of the light conditions.

The results indicated that the normals performed about the same under all conditions. The process group under FP sorted as fast as normals, but performed slowly under the other three conditions, while the reactives were slowest under FP but were as fast as normals under the other three conditions. Within all three groups performance under FL did not differ significantly from performance under SL. Under FL and SL, however, reactives and normals sorted more rapidly than the process group. These results supported the hypothesis of a motivational deficit for process schizophrenics. The results also indicated that the pictures were negatively reinforcing for the reactives, while the process patients were motivated to see them. This suggested a withdrawal differential. The withdrawal of the process patients is of such duration that supposedly threatening photographs cause little anxiety. In contrast, reactive withdrawal is motivated by an environment that recently became unbearable. Confronted with pictures representing this environment the reactive patient experiences anxiety and avoidance. However, the results of this experiment are in contrast to the findings of Rodnick and Garmezy (1957) that prolonged exposure to social censure will result in greater sensitivity to that stimulation.

SUMMARY

This review of all the research on the process-reactive classification of schizophrenia strongly indicates that it is possible to divide schizophrenic patients into two groups differing in prognostic and life-history variables. Using such a division it is also possible to demonstrate differences between the two groups in physiological measures and psychological dimensions.

The result of such an approach has been to clarify many of the heterogenous reactions found in schizophrenia. It also appears that the dichotomy is somewhat artificial and really represents end points on a continuum of personality organization. The most process patient represents the extreme form of personality disintegration, while the most reactive patient represents the extreme form of schizophrenic integration. The reactions of this type of patient are often difficult to distinguish from behavior patterns of normal subjects. There does not appear to be any significant evidence to support the contention of a process-organic versus a reactive-psychogenic formulation of schizophrenic etiology.

It is difficult to decide on the most appropriate criteria for selecting schizophrenic subjects so as to reduce their response variability. Preferences are generally found for one of three sets of criteria: Kantor, Wallner, and Winder's (1953) items, the Elgin Prognostic Scale (1944), or the Phillips scale (1953). The criteria of Kantor et al. (1953) does not provide a quantitative ordering of the variables, and is descriptively vague in several dimensions as well as depending upon life history material which is not always available. While the Elgin scale does provide a quantitative approach, it also has the disadvantages of descriptive vagueness and excessive dependence upon life history material. The Phillips scale eliminates some of these difficulties, but its validity is limited to the adequacy or inadequacy of social-sexual premorbid adjustment. The need for more feasible criteria may be met by the factor analysis of pertinent variables to obtain a meaningful severity index (Becker, 1959), or by using rating scales in which the patient verbally supplies the necessary information. An example of the latter is the Ego Strength scale (Barron, 1953), recently utilized in distinguishing two polar constellations of schizophrenia; a process type with poor prognosis and grossly impaired abstract ability, and a reactive type characterized by good prognosis and slight abstractive impairment (Herron, in press).

This need for more efficient differentiating criteria mitigates some of the significance of present findings using the process-reactive dimension. Nonetheless, the process-reactive research up to this time has succeeded in explaining schizophrenic heterogeneity in a more meaningful manner than previous interpretations adhering to various symptom pictures and diagnostic subtypes. Consequently, there appears to be definite value in utilizing the process-reactive classification of schizophrenia.

REFERENCES

Alvarez, R. R. A comparison of the preferences of schizophrenic and normal subjects for rewarded and punished stimuli. Unpublished doctoral dissertation, Duke University, 1957.

Barron, F. An ego-strength scale which predicts response to psychotherapy. *J. consult. Psychol.*, 1953, **17**, 327–333.

Becker, W. A genetic approach to the interpretation and evaluation of the process-reactive distinction in schizophrenia. *J. abnorm. soc. Psychol.*, 1956, **53**, 229–236.

Becker, W. C. The process-reactive distinction: A key to the problem of schizophrenia? *J. nerv. ment. Dis.*, 1959, **129**, 442–449.

Benjamin, J. D. A method for distinguishing and evaluating formal thinking disorders in schizophrenia. In J. S. Kasanin (Ed.), *Language and thought in schizophrenia.* Berkeley: Univer. California Press, 1946. Pp. 66–71.

Bleke, R. C. Reward and punishment as determiners of reminiscence effects in schizophrenics and normal subjects. *J. Pers.*, 1955, **23**, 479–498.

Bleuler, E. *Dementia praecox.* New York: International Univer. Press, 1911.

Brackbill, G., & Fine, H. Schizophrenia and central nervous system pathology. *J. abnorm. soc. Psychol.*, 1956, **52**, 310–313.

Chase, L. S., & Silverman, S. Prognosis in schizophrenia: An analysis of prognostic criteria in 150 schizophrenics treated with Metrazol or insulin. *J. nerv. ment. Dis.*, 1943, **98**, 464–473.

Dunham, R. M. Sensitivity of schizophrenics to parental censure. Unpublished doctoral dissertation, Duke University, 1959.

Dunn, W. L. Visual discrimination of schizophrenic subjects as a function of stimulus meaning. *J. Pers.*, 1954, **23**, 48–64.

Englehart, R. S. Semantic correlates of interpersonal concepts and parental attributes in schizophrenia. Unpublished doctoral dissertation, Duke University, 1959.

Farina, A. Patterns of role dominance and conflict in parents of schizophrenic patients. *J. abnorm. soc. Psychol.*, 1960, **61**, 31–38.

Fine, H. J., & Zimet, C. N. Process-reactive schizophrenia and genetic levels of perception. *J. abnorm. soc. Psychol.*, 1959, **59**, 83–86.

Garmezy, N., & Rodnick, E. H. Premorbid adjustment and performance in schizophrenia: Implications for interpreting heterogeneity in schizophrenia. *J. nerv. ment. Dis.*, 1959, **129**, 450–466.

Garmezy, N., Stockner, C., & Clarke, A. R. Child-rearing attitudes of mothers and fathers as reported by schizophrenic and normal control patients. *Amer. Psychologist*, 1959, **14**, 333. (Abstract)

Harris, J. G., Jr. A study of the mother-son relationship in schizophrenia. Unpublished doctoral dissertation, Duke University, 1955.

Harris, J. G., Jr. Size estimation of pictures as a function of thematic content for schizophrenic and normal subjects. *J. Pers.*, 1957, **25**, 651–672.

Herron, W. G. Abstract ability in the process-reactive classification of schizophrenia. *J. gen. Psychol.*, in press.

Hunt, R. C., & Appel, K. E. Prognosis in psychoses lying midway between schizophrenia and manic-depressive psychoses. *Amer. J. Psychiat.*, 1936, **93**, 313–339.

Kant, O. Differential diagnosis of schizophrenia in light of concepts of personality stratification. *Amer. J. Psychiat.*, 1940, **97**, 342–357.

Kant, O. A comparative study of recovered and deteriorated schizophrenic patients. *J. nerv. ment. Dis.*, 1941, **93**, 616–624.

Kant, O. The evaluation of prognostic criteria in schizophrenia. *J. nerv. ment. Dis.*, 1944, **100**, 598–605.

Kantor, R., Wallner, J., & Winder, C. Process and reactive schizophrenia. *J. consult. Psychol.*, 1953, **17**, 157–162.

Kantor, R. E., & Winder, C. L. The process-reactive continuum: A theoretical proposal. *J. nerv. ment. Dis.*, 1959, **129**, 429–434.

Kety, S. S. Biochemical theories of schizophrenia. *Science*, 1959, **129**, 1528–1532, 1590–1596, 3362–3363.

King, G. Differential autonomic responsiveness in the process-reactive classification of schizophrenia. *J. abnorm. soc. Psychol.*, 1958, **56**, 160–164.

King, G. F. Research with neuropsychiatric samples. *J. Psychol.*, 1954, **38**, 383–387.

Kreinik, P. S. Parent-child themas and concept attainment in schizophrenia. Unpublished doctoral dissertation, Duke University, 1959.

Kretschmer, E. *Physique and character.* New York: Harcourt, Brace, 1925.

Langfeldt, G. The diagnosis of schizophrenia. *Amer. J. Psychiat.*, 1951, **108**, 123–125.

Lewis, N. D. C. *Research in dementia praecox.* New York: National Committee for Mental Hygiene, 1936.

Lewis, N. D. C. The prognostic significance of certain factors in schizophrenia. *J. nerv. ment. Dis.*, 1944, **100**, 414–419.

Lorr, M., Wittman, P., & Schanberger, W. An analysis of the Elgin Prognostic scale. *J. clin. Psychol.*, 1951, **7**, 260–263.

McDonough, J. M. Critical flicker frequency and the spiral aftereffect with process and reactive schizophrenics. *J. consult. Psychol.*, 1960, **24**, 150–155.

Malamud, W., & Render, N. Course and prognosis in schizophrenia. *Amer. J. Psychiat.*, 1939, **95**, 1039–1057.

Mallet, J. J. Verbal recall of hostile and neutral thematic contents by schizophrenic and normal subjects. Unpublished doctoral dissertation, Duke University, 1956.

Mauz, F. *Die Prognostik der endogen Psychosen.* Leipzig: G. Theime, 1930.

Meadow, A., & Funkenstein, D. H. The relationship of abstract thinking to the automatic nervous system in schizophrenia. In P. H. Hoch and J. Zubin (Eds.), *Relation of psychological tests to psychiatry.* New York: Grune & Stratton, 1952. Pp. 131–144.

Meadow, A., Greenblatt, M., Funkenstein, G. H., & Solomon, H. C. The relationship between the capacity for abstraction in schizophrenia and the physiologic response to autonomic drugs. *J. nerv. ment. Dis.*, 1953, **118**, 332–338.

Meadow, A., Greenblatt, M., & Solomon, H. C. "Looseness of association" and impairment in abstraction in schizophrenia. *J. nerv. ment. Dis.*, 1953, **118**, 27–35.

Milici, P. Postemotive schizophrenia. *Psychiat. Quart.*, 1939, **13**, 278–293.

Osgood, C. E. The nature and measurement of meaning. *Psychol. Bull.*, 1952, **49**, 197–237.

Paskind, J. A., & Brown, M. Psychosis resembling schizophrenia occurring with emotional stress and ending in recovery. *Amer. J. Psychiat.*, 1940, **96**, 1379–1388.

Phillips, L. Case history data and prognosis in schizophrenia. *J. nerv. ment. Dis.*, 1953, **117**, 515–525.

Piotrowski, Z. A. Positive and negative Rorschach organic reactions. *Rorschach res. Exch.*, 1940, **4**, 143–151.

Rabin, A. J., & King, G. F. Psychological studies. In L. Bellak (Ed.), *Schizophrenia: A review of the syndrome.* New York: Logos, 1958. Pp. 216–278.

Reisman, J. M. Motivational differences between process and reactive schizophrenics. *J. Pers.*, 1960, **28**, 12–25.

Rodnick, E. H., & Garmezy, N. An experimental approach to the study of motivation in schizophrenia. In M. R. Jones (Ed.), *Nebraska symposium on motivation: 1957.* Vol. V. Lincoln: Univer. Nebraska Press, 1957. Pp. 109–184.

Sullivan, H. S. *Conceptions of modern psychiatry.* Washington: W. A. White Psychiatric Foundation, 1947.

Wittman, P. A scale for measuring prognosis in schizophrenic patients. *Elgin State Hosp. Pap.*, 1941, **4**, 20–33.

Wittman, P. Follow-up on Elgin prognosis scale results. *Ill. psychiat. J.*, 1944, **4**, 56–59.

Wittman, P., & Steinberg, L. Follow-up of an objective evaluation of prognosis in dementia praecox and manic-depressive psychoses. *Elgin State Hosp. Pap.*, 1944, **5**, 216–227. (a)

Wittman, P., & Steinberg, D. L. Study of prodromal factors in mental illness with special references in schizophrenia. *Amer. J. Psychiat.*, 1944, **100**, 811–816. (b)

Zahn, T. P. Acquired and symbolic affective value as determinant of size estimation in schizophrenic and normal subjects. *J. abnorm. soc. Psychol.*, 1959, **58**, 39–47.

Zimet, C. N., & Fine, H. J. Perceptual differentiation and two dimensions of schizophrenia. *J. nerv. ment. Dis.*, 1959, **129**, 435–441.

Zuckerman, M., & Grosz, H. J. Contradictory results using the mecholyl test to differentiate process and reactive schizophrenia. *J. abnorm. soc. Psychol.*, 1959, **59**, 145–146.

Class, Family, and Schizophrenia: A Reformulation

Melvin L. Kohn

The proposed formulation attempts to bring genetics, stress, and the conditions of life attendant on social-class position into one coherent interpretation of schizophrenia. The thrust of the argument is that the conditions of life experienced by people of lower social-class position tend to impair their ability to deal resourcefully with the problematic and the stressful. Such impairment would probably result in schizophrenia only for people who are both genetically vulnerable and exposed to considerable stress—but these conditions, too, may impinge with special severity on people in the lowest social classes.

A multitude of studies carried out in several countries consistently suggests that schizophrenia[1] occurs most frequently at the lowest social-class levels of urban society. Reviews and assessments of this research literature by the Dohrenwends (1969), Kohn (1968), Mishler and Scotch (1963), and Roman and Trice (1967), all come to the same conclusion: despite serious shortcomings in the research, the weight of evidence clearly points to an especially high rate of schizophrenia at the bottom of the social-class hierarchy.[2] What is not clear is *why* class is related to schizophrenia.

Discussions of the class–schizophrenia relationship have generally focused on interpretations that, in effect, explain away its theoretical significance. Some argue that the statistical relationship between social class and rates of schizophrenia is only artifactual, the result of methodological error.[3] Others accept the statistical relationship as real, but assert that schizophrenics are found disproportionately in lower social classes (or in declining occupations or in central city areas) because of the impairment they have suffered or because of some characterological defect of non-social origin.[4] The social statuses of schizophrenics, from this point of view, tell us something about how schizophrenics fare in society but little or nothing about what produces schizophrenia.

Other interpretations emphasize the processes by which people come to be perceived as mentally disordered and what happens to them after they are so perceived. One such interpretation asserts that psychiatric and other authorities are especially prone to stigmatize and hospitalize lower-class people: they victimize the powerless.[5] Similar, though more subtle explanations focus on the processes by which families, employers, police, and others come to label some deviant behaviors as mentally disordered, thereby setting in

From *Social Forces*, 1972, **50**, 295–304. Reproduced by permission of The University of North Carolina Press.

*Revised version of a paper presented at the Seventh World Congress of Sociology, Varna, Bulgaria, September 1970.

[1] The classic definition of schizophrenia (Bleuler, 1950:14) considers it to be a group of disorders whose "fundamental symptoms consist of disturbances of association and affectivity, the predilection for fantasy as against reality, and the inclination to divorce oneself from reality." In common with most American investigators, I use the term broadly, to refer to those severe functional disorders marked by disturbances in reality relationships and concept formation (cf. Rosenbaum, 1970:3–16). Unfortunately, available research evidence does not enable me to differentiate clinical subtypes of schizophrenia or to make such important distinctions as that between "process" and "reactive" forms of disturbance (cf. Garmezy, 1965).

[2] The cited works provide references to virtually all studies of class and schizophrenia published through 1968. The evidence comes from research conducted in Canada, Denmark, Finland, Great Britain, Norway, Sweden, Taiwan, and the United States—an unusually large number of countries and cultures for establishing the generality of any relationship in social science. Moreover, the exceptions are few and partial: they occur in small cities and rural areas or in special subpopulations of larger cities; none contradicts the larger generalization of an especially high rate of schizophrenia at the lowest social-class levels of urban populations.

Judging from data about patients newly admitted to psychiatric treatment (e.g., Hollingshead and Redlich, 1958:236), the incidence of schizophrenia is approximately three or four times as great at the bottom of the class hierarchy as at the top.

One unresolved issue is whether the relationship of class to schizophrenia is linear or is discontinuous, with an especially high rate in the lowest social class but little variation above that level (cf. Kohn, 1968:157; Rushing, 1969). I have attempted to make my formulation consistent with either possibility.

[3] The principal issues are the adequacy of indices, the completeness of the search procedures used, and the relative merits and defects of incidence and prevalence as statistical measures. I (1968) have discussed these issues in an earlier paper.

[4] Most germane, and prototypic of all such interpretations, is the well-known drift hypothesis, which asserts that schizophrenics have "drifted" into lower social classes (or into poorer neighborhoods) as a consequence of their disorder. In recent years, the drift hypothesis has been much amended, to include the possibility that schizophrenics may not actually have declined in class position, but may simply not have achieved the class positions ordinarily reached by people of their class origins or educational attainments.

The most important studies are those by Dunham (1965), Goldberg and Morrison (1963), Turner (1968), and Turner and Wagenfeld (1967). Other references are given in Dohrenwend and Dohrenwend (1969:45–48) and in Kohn (1968). After a detailed review of the evidence (Kohn, 1968:158–160), I concluded that downward social mobility does not provide a sufficient explanation of the class–schizophrenia relationship. A point of view contrary to mine is argued forcefully by Dunham (1965) and by Ødegaard (1956).

[5] This interpretation is a logical outgrowth of Goffman's (1959) analysis of the "moral career of the mental patient," which sees hospitalization as the end-product of a "funnel of betrayal," with the psychiatrist as a major culprit. Goffman deals only in passing with the possibility of class differences in the likelihood of victimization, but some of his followers argue that psychiatrists are especially prone to hospitalize lower-class people and to diagnose them as schizophrenic; middle-class people are spared, if not hospitalization, at least the stigma of being called schizophrenic.

motion complex changes in social expectation and self-conception that sometimes eventuate in hospitalization.[6] From this point of view, social position matters not because of its role in producing the initially deviant behavior but because it affects other people's perceptions of and reactions to that behavior. The class–schizophrenia relationship documents the discriminatory readiness of many people to see signs of mental disorder in lower-class behavior.

Even those interpretations that accord a primary causal significance to social-structural conditions have deemphasized the importance of class, per se, emphasizing instead such related processes as social isolation, social integration, discrepancies between aspirations and achievements, and minority position in the community—to name but a few of the most prominently suggested.[7] These interpretations are, for the most part, consistent with existing data and must be acknowledged to be plausible. But they largely neglect the most straightforward possibility of all—that social class is related to schizophrenia primarily because the conditions of life built into lower social-class position are conducive to that disorder.

I think it is time to devote a larger portion of our efforts to devising and testing formulations about how and why lower-class conditions of life might contribute to schizophrenia. The purpose of this paper is to offer one such formulation. It is necessarily tentative, for it is based on seriously incomplete information; at critical places, there is no directly pertinent evidence and I can only speculate.

GENETICS AND STRESS

Any interpretation of the role of social class in the development of schizophrenia must take into account two other clusters of variables—genetics and stress.[8]

Genetics

Recent studies of monozygotic twins and of adopted children demonstrate that although genetics alone cannot provide a sufficient explanation of schizophrenia, some genetic mechanism must be involved.[9] Geneticists do not agree on what is inherited—whether it be a vulnerability specifically to schizophrenia, a vulnerability to mental disorder more generally, or even a type of personality structure. Nor is it certain whether the mode of genetic transmission is monogenic or polygenic. Important as these questions may be, they can for my immediate purposes be passed over; all that need be accepted is that genetics plays some substantial part in schizophrenia.

One could argue, in fact, that genetics explains why *class* is related to schizophrenia. If there is a heritable component in schizophrenia, there must have been higher than usual rates of the disorder among the parents and grandparents of schizophrenics. Moreover, since schizophrenia is debilitating, there would have been downward social mobility in earlier generations. Thus, schizophrenics could come disproportionately from lower-class families, not because the conditions of life experienced by lower-class people have pernicious effects, but because there is a concentration of genetically susceptible people in the lower social classes.

These processes of multigenerational mobility may well contribute to the increased probability of schizophrenia for people of lower-class position. The question, though, is whether there could have been *enough* downward mobility attributable to the genetically induced disabilities of earlier generations to account for the heightened incidence of schizophrenia found today in the lower social classes.

Since there are no data about the mobility rates of parents and grandparents of schizophrenics, one can only extrapolate from existing data about the rates of intergenerational occupational mobility of (male) schizophrenics. Turner and Wagenfeld (1967:110) show that the absolute amount of downward mobility has been almost nil: *36* percent of the schizophrenics in their sample have fallen and *35* percent have risen from their fathers' occupational levels, for a net decline of less than one-tenth of a step on a 7-point occupational scale. In the general population, though, there has been a net rise of nearly one-half step on the same 7-point scale. Thus, schizophrenics have lagged behind the general population in not rising above their fathers' occupational levels.

The effect of this failure of upward mobility could be an increase from one generation to the next in genetic susceptibility to schizophrenia at lower-class levels. But such an increase would probably not be great, even over several generations, for three main reasons. First, it can reasonably be assumed that the schizophrenics' parents and grandparents were, on the average, less disturbed and therefore less likely to lag in mobility than were the schizophrenics themselves. Second, we need not assume that the entire lag in intergenerational mobility is genetically induced or has genetic consequences. Finally, it would take a large amount of downward mobility, not just a moderate lag in upward mobility, to increase the genetic susceptibility of the lower social classes appreciably. These considerations make it seem improbable that class differences in the incidence of schizophrenia result entirely, or even largely, from genetically induced, intergenerational social mobility.

Stress

Investigators of the role of stress in schizophrenia face a perplexing problem in defining and indexing stress (cf.

[6] Scheff (1966) presents a cogent formulation of the labeling theory approach as applied to mental disorder. But Gove (1970) marshals evidence that this approach is based on assumptions that are inconsistent with what is known: principally, that people strongly resist seeing deviant behavior as mentally disordered; the pressures, instead, are to interpret even grotesque behavior as somehow normal and situationally explainable.

[7] Although some of these interpretations have been addressed to mental illness in general, they are equally applicable to schizophrenia. On social isolation, cf. Hare (1956), Jaco (1954), Kohn and Clausen (1955). On social integration, cf. Leighton *et al.* (1963). On discrepancies between aspirations and achievements, cf. Kleiner and Parker (1963), Myers and Roberts (1959), Parker and Kleiner (1966). On occupying a minority position in the community, cf. Schwartz and Mintz (1963), Wechsler and Pugh (1967).

[8] It is widely believed that there must also be a biochemical abnormality in schizophrenia. I omit that possibility from this discussion because of Kety's (1960; 1969) conclusion, based on his critical reviews of the research literature, that positive biochemical findings have thus far failed to stand the test of replication. There is of course no necessary incompatibility between biochemical and social-psychological interpretations of schizophrenia, provided that neither claims to be exclusive.

[9] For a comprehensive assessment of the genetic evidence, cf. Rosenthal (1970). Other valuable discussions are to be found in Kringlen (1966; 1967), Rosenthal (1962; 1968), Shields (1968), Slater (1968). For discussions of the mode of genetic transmission, cf. Gottesman and Shields (1967), Heston (1970), Rosenthal (1970).

Dohrenwend and Dohrenwend, 1969; Lazarus, 1966; Scott and Howard, 1970). A narrow conception would have that term apply only to externally induced events that can be assumed to be psychically painful to virtually everyone who experiences them. Such a conception achieves rigor at the price of excluding from its purview those traumas that may have been self-induced, as well as all those traumas that are painful for some people but not for everyone. It also excludes such real if self-defined misfortunes as failure to attain a longed-for goal. In fact, the only experiences that can be assumed to be externally induced and to be painful for everyone are such crises as serious illness, death of close relatives, hunger, and loss of one's job; and even these misfortunes may not be equally painful to all who experience them. But broader conceptions of stress are also problematic. At the extreme, if any event that produces subjectively experienced pain in some individual is considered to be stressful, formulations that attribute to stress a causal role in schizophrenia become tautological.

Research workers have for the most part dealt with this dilemma by (explicitly or implicitly) defining as stressful those events that usually are externally induced and that can be expected to be painful to most people who experience them. Such events occur with greater frequency at lower social-class levels: people at the bottom of the class hierarchy experience great economic insecurity and far more than their share of serious ill health, degradation, and the afflictions attendant on inadequate, overcrowded housing, often in over-populated, under-serviced areas.

Is stress conducive to schizophrenia? A definitive study would require direct, rather than inferential, measurement of stress; a research design that takes social class explicitly into account; and, of course, an adequate index of schizophrenia. Not surprisingly, no study meets all these criteria. Therefore, one can make only a tentative overall appraisal, recognizing that some pertinent studies do not index stress as well as we should like, others do not explicitly control social class, and some are addressed to mental disorder in general rather than specifically to schizophrenia.

My appraisal of the research evidence is based primarily on the studies by Birley and Brown (1970), Brown and Birley (1968), Eitinger (1964), Langner and Michael (1963), and Rogler and Hollingshead (1965). These studies do indicate that stress is associated with the occurrence of schizophrenia. Moreover, Rogler and Hollingshead (1965: 409–411) show that the relationship between stress and schizophrenia does not simply reflect the high levels of stress prevalent in the lower social classes. From their investigation of schizophrenics and matched controls in the lowest social class of San Juan, Puerto Rico, they report that during the year before the onset of symptoms, the schizophrenics experienced notably greater stress than did the controls.[10] Even when judged by the harsh standards of life of the San Juan slums, the stresses that preceded the onset of schizophrenia were unusually severe.

As with genetics, one must reverse the question and ask whether stress can explain the relationship of class to schizophrenia. The Rogler–Hollingshead study cannot help us here, for it is limited to one social class. Unfortunately for our purposes, the only study that does provide data for all levels of social class, that by Langner and Michael (1963), is addressed to mental disorder in general rather than to schizophrenia in particular. This study is nevertheless germane, for it provides a powerful argument against stress explaining why social class is related to mental disorder. At any given level of stress, people of lower social-class position are more likely to become mentally disturbed than are people of higher social-class position. In fact, the more sources of stress, the greater the class difference in the proportion of people who manifest psychotic symptoms. The implication is that the relationship of class to mental disorder (hence, if we may extrapolate, to schizophrenia) is not attributable to the amount of stress that people endure. There must be important class differences in how effectively people deal with stress.

Part of the explanation for lower-class people dealing less effectively with stress may be that the stress-producing situations they face are less alterable by individual action than are those encountered by people of higher social-class position. Many of their stresses arise from economic circumstances over which few individuals have much control, lower-class individuals least of all. Moreover, lower-class people have little money or power to employ in coping with the consequences of stress. It also appears (cf. Dohrenwend and Dohrenwend, 1969:137–139) that fewer institutional resources are available to them, either for escaping stressful situations or for mitigating the consequences of stress.

Still, important as class differences in the modifiability of stress-producing situations and in the availability of external resources may be, they do not provide a complete explanation of lower-class people's greater difficulty in dealing with stress. There is one more element that need be taken into account: lower-class conditions of life also limit people's *internal* resources (cf. Dohrenwend and Dohrenwend, 1969:140–143).[11] Understanding how lower-class conditions of life may impair people's internal resources for dealing with stress is, I believe, crucial to understanding how class contributes to schizophrenia. It is therefore the heart of my formulation.

I would add that class position affects people's ability to deal, not only with situations that by my limited definition are stressful, but also with many other dilemmas and uncertainties in a rapidly changing, complex society. From this perspective, interpreting the role of social class in the genesis of schizophrenia requires an explanation of how lower-

[10] A cautionary note: the Rogler–Hollingshead study is based on schizophrenics who are married or living in stable consensual unions. One would assume them to be predominantly "reactive" schizophrenics—precisely the group whom clinical studies describe as having had normal childhood social experiences, good social adjustment, and extreme precipitating circumstances. So these findings may apply only to reactive schizophrenia, not to process schizophrenia. It may also be that some of the stress experienced by the schizophrenics resulted from their already disordered behavior. Still, Rogler and Hollingshead present a strong case that externally induced stress is important for some types of schizophrenia.

[11] Pertinent, too, are the discussions by Brewster Smith (1968) of "the competent self," by Foote and Cottrell (1955) of "interpersonal competence," and by Phillips (1968) of "social competence."

class conditions of life adversely affect people's ability to deal with stress, with complexity, and with change.

CLASS, FAMILY, AND SCHIZOPHRENIA

If internal resources for dealing with complex and stressful situations are at issue, then that primary socializing institution, the family, is probably somehow involved. The many studies of the role of the family in the development of schizophrenia are pertinent here, even though most of them have been addressed to a question quite different from ours. The purpose of these investigations has generally been to find some pattern of interpersonal relationship unique to the families of schizophrenics. To the best of my knowledge, though, no well-controlled study has shown a substantial difference between the patterns of parent–child relationship characteristic of families that produce schizophrenic offspring and those characteristic of ordinary lower- and working-class families.[12] From a traditional, single-factor perspective, two interpretations of this negative finding are possible.

One would be that the family plays no important part in the genesis of schizophrenia. This interpretation holds that the patterns of parent–child relationship typical of schizophrenia-producing families merely reflect those of the lower social classes from which schizophrenics disproportionately come,[13] without having been instrumental in the disorder.

The alternative interpretation would assert that the family does play a critically differentiating role in schizophrenia, but that the statistical evidence is not yet in. From this point of view, most well-controlled studies have been too limited in focus. They have dealt with such relatively concrete aspects of family life as the overall pattern of role-allocation, parental bestowal of warmth and affection, and disciplinary practices, but have missed more subtle interpersonal processes that recent clinical investigations have emphasized.[14] Future studies may show clear and convincing evidence of important differences between schizophrenia-producing families and ordinary families of lower social-class position.

There is, however, a third possible interpretation. Instead of looking to the family for a total explanation of schizophrenia, this interpretation attempts only to explain how lower-class families may contribute to the disorder in genetically vulnerable people who are subject to great stress. From this perspective, the family is important for schizophrenia, not because the family experiences of schizophrenics have differed in some presently undisclosed manner from those of other people of lower social-class background, but precisely because they have been similar. If this be the case, there is no reason to restrict our interest to processes that are unique to the family, such as its particular patterns of role allocation. We should expand our focus to include, even to emphasize, processes that the family shares with other institutions—notably, those processes that affect people's ability to perceive, to assess, and to deal with complexity and stress.[15]

The family, I suggest, is important principally because of its strategic role in transmitting to its offspring conceptions of social reality that parents have learned from their own experience. In particular, many lower-class families transmit to their offspring an orientational system[16] too limited and too rigid for dealing effectively with complex, changing, or stressful situations. This point of view is, I believe, consonant with recent psychiatric thinking about the family and schizophrenia, which emphasizes those communicational and cognitive processes in schizophrenia-producing families that contribute to the schizophrenic's difficulties in interpreting social reality.[17] What is new is the assertion that these conceptions of reality, far from being unique to families whose offspring become schizophrenic, are widely held in the lower social classes, in fact arise out of the very conditions of life experienced by people in these segments of society.

SOCIAL CLASS AND CONCEPTIONS OF REALITY

Although admittedly speculative, this formulation is a direct extrapolation from what is known about the relationship between social class and conceptions of reality (cf. the review by Rossi and Blum, 1968). My (1969: chaps. 4 and 5) own research indicates that the lower a man's social-class position, the more likely he is to value conformity to external authority and to believe that such conformity is all that his own capacities and the exigencies of the world allow; in particular, the lower a man's social-class position, the more likely is his orientational system to be marked by a rigidly conservative view of man and his social institutions, fearfulness and distrust, and a fatalistic belief that one is at the mercy of forces and people beyond one's control, often, beyond one's understanding.

Lee Rainwater (1968:241), reviewing more intensive

[12] This sweeping conclusion is based on my inability, and that of others who have reviewed the research literature, to find a single study that finds important differences in patterns of parent–child relationship between schizophrenics and ordinary persons of lower social-class background. Several well-controlled studies find an absence of difference (cf. Kohn and Clausen, 1956; Mishler and Waxler, 1968; Rogler and Hollingshead, 1965).

For a comprehensive, if now dated, review of research on family and schizophrenia, cf. Sanua (1961); see also the introduction to, and references included in, Kohn and Clausen (1956), the discussion and references in Mishler and Waxler (1965), and Rosenbaum (1970:140–163).

[13] For an incisive review of research on class and family, cf. Bronfenbrenner (1958). For references to studies completed since Bronfenbrenner's review, and to studies done outside the United States, cf. Kohn (1969:4).

[14] In support of this position are indications that lower-class families with schizophrenic offspring, although no different from other lower-class families in role-patterning, may manifest disturbed, even pathological, patterns of communication (cf. Behrens *et al.*, 1968; Rosenthal *et al.*, 1968).

[15] One implication is that it is not only the social class of one's parental family, but also one's adult social-class position, that matters for schizophrenia. This point is often overlooked, particularly in discussions of the drift hypothesis.

[16] By orientation (or orientational system), I mean conceptions of the external world and of self that serve to define men's stance toward reality.

[17] Especially relevant here is the work of Lyman Wynne and his associates (cf. Singer and Wynne, 1965; Wynne, 1967; Wynne and Singer, 1963). See also Bateson *et al.*, (1956), Mishler and Waxler (1965), Schuham (1967).

studies of lower-class population groups, arrives at essentially the same conclusion:

All investigators who have studied lower-class groups seem to come up with compatible findings to the general effect that the lower-class world view involves conceptions of the world as a hostile and relatively chaotic place in which you have to be always on guard, a place in which one must be careful about trusting others, in which the reward for effort expended is always problematic, in which good intentions net very little.

One need not argue that this orientational system is held by all lower-class people, or that lower-class people hold these beliefs and values to the exclusion of others, more characteristic of higher social classes (cf. Miller, 1964; Rodman, 1963). It does seem to be well established, though, that these conceptions of social reality are most prevalent at the bottom of the social hierarchy.

The existence of class differences in beliefs and values is hardly accidental, nor even cultural in the sense employed by "culture of poverty" theorists who see lower-class orientations as something handed down from generation to generation independently of current social conditions.[18] On the contrary, social class embodies such basic differences in conditions of life that subjective reality is necessarily different for people differentially situated in the social hierarchy. Lower-class conditions of life allow little freedom of action, give little reason to feel in control of fate. To be lower class is to be insufficiently educated, to work at a job of little substantive complexity, under conditions of close supervision, and with little leeway to vary a routine flow of work. These are precisely the conditions that narrow one's conception of social reality and reduce one's sense of personal efficacy (cf. Kohn, 1969: chaps. 9 and 10).

The characteristically lower-class orientational system, molded as it is by actual conditions, may often be useful. It is, for example, attuned to the occupational demands that lower-class people must meet; a self-directed stance would probably bring few rewards and might easily lead to trouble. Moreover, participant-observation studies of lower-class life (cf. Liebow, 1966; Whyte, 1943) make it vividly apparent that, in an environment where one may be subject to diverse and often unpredictable risks of exploitation and victimization, this perspective may serve other protective functions as well. It is a way of keeping one's guard up. It provides a defensive strategy for people who really are vulnerable to forces they cannot control.

But there are times when a defensive posture invites attack, and there are times when the assumption that one is at the mercy of forces beyond one's control—even though justified—leaves one all the more at their mercy. An orientational system predicated on conforming to the dictates of authority sees social reality too simply and too fearfully to permit taking advantage of options that might otherwise be open. It is too inflexible for precisely those problematic and stressful circumstances that most require subtlety, flexibility, and a perceptive understanding of larger social complexities. So limited an orientational system is an impediment for anyone subjected to stressful or problematic circumstances, a catastrophe for those so unfortunate as to be genetically vulnerable to schizophrenia.

It is likely, too, that this orientational system helps shape the distinctively inflexible schizophrenic response to threat. One reason for the disproportionately high incidence of schizophrenia at lower social-class levels may be that schizophrenic disorders build on conceptions of reality firmly grounded on the experiences of these social classes.

CONCLUSIONS

To try to explain the relationship of class to schizophrenia without considering genetics and stress would be extremely difficult. One would be hard pressed to resolve the apparent contradiction that, although lower-class conditions of life appear to be conducive to schizophrenia, the absolute incidence of schizophrenia in even the lowest social class is small. When, however, one brings genetics and stress into consideration, the task becomes more manageable. It is no longer necessary to find in class itself an explanation of schizophrenia. Instead, the interpretive task is to explain how social class fits into an equation that includes genetics, probably stress, and undoubtedly other, as yet unrecognized, factors.

My formulation suggests that the constricted conditions of life experienced by people of lower social-class position foster conceptions of social reality so limited and so rigid as to impair people's ability to deal resourcefully with the problematic and the stressful. Such impairment would not in itself result in schizophrenia. In conjunction with a genetic vulnerability to schizophrenia and the experience of great stress, though, such impairment could well be disabling. Since both genetic vulnerability and stress appear to occur disproportionately at lower social-class levels, people in these segments of society may be at triple jeopardy.[19]

REFERENCES

Bateson, G., D. D. Jackson, J. Haley, and J. Weakland, 1956. "Toward a Theory of Schizophrenia." *Behavioral Science* 1(October):251–264.

Behrens, M. I., A. J. Rosenthal, and P. Chodoff, 1968. "Communication in Lower-Class Families of Schizophrenics: II. Observations and Findings." *Archives of General Psychiatry* 18(June):689–696.

Birley, J. L. T., and G. W. Brown, 1970. "Crises and Life

[18] For a systematic statement of the culture of poverty thesis, cf. Lewis (1965:xlii–lii). For critiques of this and related concepts, cf. Roach and Gursslin (1967), Rossi and Blum (1968), Valentine) 1968. The principal issue, as I see it, is not whether there are class differences in values, orientation, and cognitive style—there certainly are—but whether the lower-class orientational systems, once transmitted from parents to children, are amenable to change. My data show that if there is a discrepancy between early family experience and later educational and occupational conditions, the latter are likely to prevail (Kohn, 1969:135–137). The practical implications of this finding are as important as they are obvious: the most efficacious way to alleviate the burdens of lower social-class position is not by therapy, resocialization, or other efforts to teach middle-class values and orientation, but by changing the social conditions to which lower-class people are subject.

[19] In trying to make my point forcefully, I may have exaggerated statistical tendencies, making it seem as if class differences in orientational systems were differences in kind rather than in degree. I hope it is clear from the general argument, though, that all the relevant variables—genetics, stress, conceptions of reality—must be seen as probabilistic; the formulation depends on the joint occurrence of these necessary conditions.

Changes Preceding the Onset or Relapse of Acute Schizophrenia: Clinical Aspects." *British Journal of Psychiatry* **116**(March):327–333.

Bleuler, Eugen, 1950. *Dementia Praecox or the Group of Schizophrenias.* New York: International Universities Press.

Bronfenbrenner, U., 1958. "Socialization and Social Class through Time and Space." Pp. 400–425 in Eleanor E. Maccoby, Theodore M. Newcomb, and Eugene L. Hartley (eds.), *Readings in Social Psychology.* New York: Holt.

Brown, G. W., and J. L. T. Birley, 1968. "Crises and Life Changes and the Onset of Schizophrenia." *Journal of Health and Social Behavior* **9**(September):203–214.

Dohrenwend, Bruce P., and Barbara Snell Dohrenwend, 1969. *Social Status and Psychological Disorder: A Causal Inquiry.* New York: Wiley.

Dunham, H. Warren, 1965. *Community and Schizophrenia: An Epidemiological Analysis.* Detroit: Wayne State University Press.

Eitinger, Leo, 1964. *Concentration Camp Survivors in Norway and Israel.* Oslo: Universitetsforlaget.

Foote, Nelson N., and Leonard S. Cottrell, 1955. *Identity and Interpersonal Competence: A New Direction in Family Research.* Chicago: University of Chicago Press.

Garmezy, N., 1965. "Process and Reactive Schizophrenia: Some Conceptions and Issues." Pp. 419–466 in Martin M. Katz, Jonathan O. Cole, and Walter E. Barton (eds.), *The Role and Methodology of Classification in Psychiatry and Psychopathology.* PHS Publication No. 1584. Washington, D.C.: Government Printing Office.

Goffman, E., 1959. "The Moral Career of the Mental Patient," *Psychiatry* **22**(May):123–142.

Goldberg, E. M., and S. L. Morrison, 1963. "Schizophrenia and Social Class." *British Journal of Psychiatry* **109** (November): 785–802.

Gottesman, I. I., and J. Shields, 1967. "A Polygenic Theory of Schizophrenia." *Proceedings of the National Academy of Sciences* **58**(July):199–205.

Gove, W. R., 1970. "Societal Reaction as an Explanation of Mental Illness: An Evaluation." *American Sociological Review* **35**(October):873–884.

Hare, E. H., 1956. "Mental Illness and Social Conditions in Bristol." *Journal of Mental Science* **102**(April):349–357.

Heston, L. L., 1970. "The Genetics of Schizophrenic and Schizoid Disease." *Science* **167**(16 January):249–256.

Hollingshead, August B., and Fredrick C. Redlich, 1958. *Social Class and Mental Illness: A Community Study.* New York: Wiley.

Jaco, E. G., 1954. "The Social Isolation Hypothesis and Schizophrenia." *American Sociological Review* **19**(October):567–577.

Kety, S. S., 1969. "Recent Biochemical Theories of Schizophrenia." Pp. 120–145 in Don D. Jackson (ed.), *The Etiology of Schizophrenia.* New York: Basic Books.

Kety, S. S., 1969. "Biochemical Hypotheses and Studies." Pp. 155–171 in Leopold Bellak and Laurence Loeb (eds.), *The Schizophrenic Syndrome.* New York: Grune & Stratton.

Kleiner, R. J., and S. Parker, 1963. "Goal-Striving, Social Status, and Mental Disorder: A Research Review." *American Sociological Review* **28**(April):189–203.

Kohn, Melvin L., 1968. "Social Class and Schizophrenia: A Critical Review." Pp. 155–173 in David Rosenthal and Seymour S. Kety (eds.), *The Transmission of Schizophrenia.* Oxford: Pergamon Press. (Reprinted in Rosenbaum, 1970:164–188, and in Wechsler *et al.*, 1970:113–128).

Kohn, Melvin L., 1969. *Class and Conformity: A Study in Values.* Homewood, Illinois: Dorsey.

Kohn, M. L., and J. A. Clausen, 1955. "Social Isolation and Schizophrenia." *American Sociological Review* **20**(June): 265–273.

Kohn, M. L., and J. A. Clausen, 1956. "Parental Authority Behavior and Schizophrenia." *American Journal of Orthopsychiatry* **26**(April):297–313.

Kringlen, Einar, 1966. "Schizophrenia In Twins: An Epidemiological-Clinical Study." *Psychiatry* **29** (May):172–184.

Kringlen, Einar, 1967. *Heredity and Environment in the Functional Psychoses: An Epidemiological-Clinical Twin Study.* Oslo: Universitetsforlaget.

Langner, Thomas S., and Stanley T. Michael, 1963. *Life Stress and Mental Health.* New York: Free Press of Glencoe.

Lazarus, Richard S., 1966. *Psychological Stress and the Coping Process.* New York: McGraw-Hill.

Leighton, Dorothea C., John S. Harding, David B. Macklin, Allister M. MacMillan, and Alexander H. Leighton, 1963. *The Character of Danger: Psychiatric Symptoms in Selected Communities.* New York: Basic Books.

Lewis, Oscar, 1965. *La Vida: A Puerto Rican Family in the Culture of Poverty—San Juan and New York.* New York: Random House.

Liebow, Elliot, 1966. *Tally's Corner: A Study of Negro Streetcorner Men.* Boston: Little, Brown.

Miller, S. M., 1964. "The American Lower Classes: A Typological Approach." Pp. 139–154 in Frank Riessman, Jerome Cohen, and Arthur Pearl (eds.), *Mental Health of the Poor.* New York: Free Press of Glencoe.

Mishler, E. G., and N. A. Scotch, 1963. "Sociocultural Factors in the Epidemiology of Schizophrenia: A Review." *Psychiatry* **26**(November):315–351.

Mishler, Elliot G., and Nancy E. Waxler, 1965. "Family Interaction Processes and Schizophrenia: A Review of Current Theories." *Merrill-Palmer Quarterly of Behavior and Development* **11**(October):269–315.

Mishler, Elliot G., and Nancy E. Waxler, 1968. *Interaction in Families: An Experimental Study of Family Processes and Schizophrenia.* New York: Wiley.

Myers, Jerome K., and Bertram H. Roberts, 1959. *Family and Class Dynamics in Mental Illness.* New York: Wiley.

Ødegaard, Ø., 1956. "The Incidence of Psychoses in Various Occupations." *International Journal of Social Psychiatry* **2**(Autumn):85–104.

Parker, Seymour, and Robert J. Kleiner, 1966. *Mental Illness in the Urban Negro Community.* New York: Free Press.

Phillips, Leslie, 1968. *Human Adaptation and Its Failures.* New York: Academic Press.

Rainwater, L., 1968. "The Problem of Lower-Class Culture and Poverty-War Strategy." Pp. 229–259 of Daniel P. Moynihan (ed.), *On Understanding Poverty: Perspectives from the Social Sciences.* New York: Basic Books.

Roach, J. L., and O. R. Gursslin, 1967. "An Evaluation of the Concept 'Culture of Poverty.'" *Social Forces* **45** (March):383–392.

Rodman, H., 1963. "The Lower-Class Value Stretch." *Social Forces* **42**(December):205–215.

Rogler, Lloyd H., and August B. Hollingshead, 1965. *Trapped: Families and Schizophrenia.* New York: Wiley.

Roman, Paul M., and Harrison M. Trice, 1967. *Schizophrenia and the Poor.* Ithaca: New York State School of Industrial and Labor Relations.

Rosenbaum, C. Peter, 1970. *The Meaning of Madness:*

Symptomatology, Sociology, Biology and Therapy of the Schizophrenias. New York: Science House.
Rosenthal, A. J., M. I. Behrens, and P. Chodoff, 1968. "Communication in Lower Class Families of Schizophrenics: I. Methodological Problems." *Archives of General Psychiatry* **18**(April):464–470.
Rosenthal, David, 1962. "Problems of Sampling and Diagnosis in the Major Twin Studies of Schizophrenia." *Journal of Psychiatric Research* **1**(September):116–134.
Rosenthal, David, 1968. "The Heredity-Environment Issue in Schizophrenia." Pp. 413–427 in David Rosenthal and Seymour S. Kety (eds.), *The Transmission of Schizophrenia.* Oxford: Pergamon.
Rosenthal, David, 1970. *Genetic Theory and Abnormal Behavior.* New York: McGraw-Hill.
Rossi, P. H., and Z. D. Blum, 1968. "Class, Status, and Poverty." Pp. 36–63 in Daniel P. Moynihan (ed.), *On Understanding Poverty: Perspectives from the Social Sciences.* New York: Basic Books.
Rushing, W. A., 1969. "Two Patterns in the Relationship between Social Class and Mental Hospitalization." *American Sociological Review* **34**(August):533–541.
Sanua, V. D., 1961. "Sociocultural Factors in Families of Schizophrenics: A Review of the Literature." *Psychiatry* **24**(August):246–265.
Scheff, Thomas J., 1966. *Being Mentally Ill: A Sociological Theory.* Chicago: Aldine.
Schuham, A. I., 1967. "The Double-Bind Hypothesis a Decade Later." *Psychological Bulletin* **68**(December): 409–416.
Schwartz, D. T., and N. L. Mintz, 1963. "Ecology and Psychosis among Italians in 27 Boston Communities." *Social Problems* **10**(Spring):371–374.
Scott, R. and A. Howard, 1970. "Models of Stress." Pp. 259–278 in Sol Levine and Norman A. Scotch (eds.), *Social Stress.* Chicago: Aldine.
Shields, J. 1968. "Summary of the Genetic Evidence." Pp. 95–126 in David Rosenthal and Seymour S. Kety (eds.), *The Transmission of Schizophrenia.* Oxford: Pergamon.
Singer, M. T., and L. C. Wynne, 1965. "Thought Disorder and Family Relations of Schizophrenics: Methodology Using Projective Techniques; Results and Implications." *Archives of General Psychiatry* **12**(February):187–212.
Slater, E., 1968. "A Review of Earlier Evidence on Genetic Factors in Schizophrenia." Pp. 15–26 in David Rosenthal and Seymour S. Kety (eds.), *The Transmission of Schizophrenia.* Oxford: Pergamon.
Smith, M. B., 1968. "Competence and Socialization." Pp. 270–320 in John A. Clausen (ed.), *Socialization and Society.* Boston: Little, Brown.
Turner, R. J., 1968. "Social Mobility and Schizophrenia." *Journal of Health and Social Behavior* **9**(September): 194–203.
Turner, R. J., and M. O. Wagenfeld, 1967. "Occupational Mobility and Schizophrenia: An Assessment of the Social Causation and Social Selection Hypotheses." *American Sociological Review* **32**(February):104–113.
Valentine, Charles A., 1968. *Culture and Poverty: Critique and Counter-Proposals.* Chicago: University of Chicago Press.
Wechsler, H., and T. F. Pugh, 1967. "Fit of Individual and Community Characteristics and Rates of Psychiatric Hospitalization." *American Journal of Sociology* **73**(November):331–338.
Wechsler, Henry, Leonard Solomon, and Bernard M. Kramer (eds.), 1970. *Social Psychology and Mental Health.* New York: Holt, Rinehart & Winston.
Whyte, William Foote, 1943. *Street Corner Society: The Social Structure of an Italian Slum.* Chicago: University of Chicago Press.
Wynne, L. C., 1967. "Family Transactions and Schizophrenia: Conceptual Considerations for a Research Strategy." Pp. 165–178 in John Romano (ed.), *The Origins of Schizophrenia.* Amsterdam: Excerpta Medica International Congress Series No. 151.
Wynne, L. C., and M. T. Singer, 1963. "Thought Disorder and Family Relations of Schizophrenics: A Classification of Forms of Thinking." *Archives of General Psychiatry* **9**(September):191–206.

Social Class and Schizophrenia: Some Requirements for a Plausible Theory of Social Influence

David Mechanic

Since the classic study of Faris and Dunham (1939) in Chicago, generations of sociologists have sought to demonstrate a link between social factors and the occurrence of schizophrenia and to argue the importance of social causation. Such arguments have varied greatly in their sophistication, and some years ago I lamented—in reviewing the field of medical sociology at a meeting of the American Sociological Association—that some sociologists seem to be willing to grasp any argument of social causation, however flimsy the evidence, but remain skeptical of the findings of biological and genetic investigations, however impressive the methods and data (Mechanic, 1966). Since that time in 1964 the evidence favoring an important genetic link in schizophrenia has impressively cumulated, while the studies on social causation have produced a mixture of results providing little confidence that we have located those social factors, if any, that play a central part in this profoundly disabling disease of great social consequence (Rosenthal, 1970; Rosenthal and Kety, 1968).

In this latest effort, Melvin Kohn, a careful researcher and long-term student of social factors in mental illness, attempts to reformulate the relationship of social class to schizophrenia in light of recent developments in genetic and epidemiological research in social psychiatry. He comes to his task with sophistication, an excellent grasp of the research literature, and an appreciation of the difficulties of the issues with which he tangles. The fact that he comes with such high credentials makes a critical appraisal of his formulation particularly compelling, since he is not one to speak lightly or without careful consideration of the issues at stake.

Put briefly, it is Kohn's hypothesis that schizophrenia is the outcome of a genetic vulnerability interacting with environmental stress and impaired ability to deal with it due to socially learned conformity orientations. He infers the existence of these orientations from the endorsement of values such as obedience, good manners and cleanliness, and suggests that underlying these is a rigidly conservative view of man, fearfulness, distrust and fatalism. Such orientations that make it difficult to adapt resourcefully, he believes, are linked with lower social-class position and account for the relatively high rate of schizophrenia found in the lowest socioeconomic strata. Kohn's discussion offers little evidence for this view, nor does he provide any observations on genetic or stress factors that are not already widely known. Thus, all we can do is evaluate the plausibility of his hypothesis and the extent to which there is existing evidence to substantiate the links necessary for the hypothesis to have merit. Too little is known about schizophrenia and mental disorders generally to take a dogmatic view on causation, but we must also be tough-minded enough to set reasonable research priorities. The major task of this discussion is not to comment on the truth or falsity of Kohn's hypothesis—for this is not known—but rather to examine his assertion that ". . . it is time to devote a larger portion of our efforts to devising and testing formulations about how and why lower-class conditions of life might contribute to schizophrenia."

To establish that a relationship exists between social class and the occurrence of schizophrenia is logically prior to developing and testing formulations as to the reasons underlying that relationship. Kohn offers little explanation in his paper for his rejection of more recent and carefully executed studies that strongly suggest that the association between social status and schizophrenia is a product of social failure or limited mobility potential resulting from the disabilities associated with the condition (Dunham, 1966; Goldberg and Morrison, 1963; Hare, 1956; Turner and Wagenfeld, 1967). Further, Kohn points out that it is reasonable to anticipate some overrepresentation of schizophrenia in the lower social classes on the basis of what we already know about the genetics of schizophrenia. Taking these considerations into account, it is hardly clear that there is a phenomenon worthy of social explanation at all. It is puzzling, therefore, that Kohn chooses to comment on the incidence rates for treated schizophrenics reported by Hollingshead and Redlich (1958). These data incorporate all of the difficulties so effectively demonstrated by recent analysts: they largely depend on social-class indices characterizing the patient rather than the family of orientation; they have the largest proportion of unreported information in the case of private psychiatrists who were most likely to provide treatment for upper-status persons; and they involve too few cases, particularly at the higher-class levels, to feel confidence in the validity of the rates.

For the sake of analysis, let us assume that Kohn's judgment—that there is a phenomenon in need of explanation—is correct and then consider the conditions that would be necessary for his hypothesis to be plausible. Kohn notes, on

From *Social Forces,* 1972, **50**, 305–309. Reproduced by permission of The University of North Carolina Press.
Supported in part by Grant 5 RO1 MH 14835, National Institute of Mental Health.

the basis of his earlier research, that the lower class encompasses an orientational system that is inflexible and ineffective in dealing with stress. Although his earlier work is competently executed and supports the contention that there are value differences associated with social class, his conception relative to his arguments concerning schizophrenia involves at least two major unexplained links. To begin with, the correlations between social class and conformity values are relatively modest (Kohn, 1969:70, table 4.8: 86, table 5.3), and thus we have no particular reason to believe that lower-class schizophrenics are very likely to have extreme values on this dimension. But if, indeed, there is any substance to Kohn's reformulation we would expect to find schizophrenics overrepresented relative to other lower-class persons among those with high conformity values. Even if orientation has no effect independent of genetics and stress, we should anticipate that among persons who are vulnerable because of genetics and stress, those most likely to develop an illness would be those with high conformity orientations. In this light, I find Kohn's statement, ". . . the family is important for schizophrenia, not because the family experiences of schizophrenics have differed in some presently undisclosed manner from those of other people of lower-class background, but precisely because they have been similar," difficult to comprehend. If all he is saying is that genetic vulnerability and stress may not be sufficient to produce an illness, then his point is obvious; but if he is saying that we should not expect to find differences in conformity orientation between lower-class schizophrenics and nonschizophrenics, then he is plainly wrong. I should add that we would also have reason to anticipate that if high conformity orientations contribute to schizophrenia, then middle-class and upper-class schizophrenics should have higher scores on this variable than their class counterparts. Kohn presents no evidence one way or the other on these issues, but even more important is his failure to provide any evidence at all for his belief that a high conformity orientation handicaps the individual in coping flexibly and effectively with people or other factors in his environment. The evidence from studies of various social pathologies suggests that deviance is most associated with neglect and "cruel parenthood" rather than with the maintenance of conformity standards. I do not wish to prejudge the issue, but I see no compelling reason to believe that Kohn is correct.

It is Kohn's attempt to conceptualize the links between social status, stress, and coping in relation to existing empirical data that I find particularly unconvincing. In making his argument Kohn depends on the findings of Langner and Michael (1963) concerning psychological disorder, which he acknowledges might not be fully appropriate to schizophrenia. My own assessment is that Kohn has taken this matter too lightly, and that the weight of existing evidence supports the contention that schizophrenia is fundamentally different from the types of entities that are the primary concern of the Langner and Michael study (Mechanic, 1969). Unlike psychological disorders in general, schizophrenia shows relatively little variation over time, from place to place, and under differing social circumstances. Although schizophrenia may be a group of disorders constituting part of a wider spectrum of related disorders, the existing evidence should make us extremely cautious in generalizing from other disorders to schizophrenia.

But let us again accept Kohn's basic assumption that the comparison is a reasonable one to make, and examine the Langner and Michael study in greater detail. The stress index used by Langner and Michael included such factors as parents' poor mental health, childhood economic deprivation, childhood poor physical health, childhood broken homes, present health status, and the like. It is important to note that they found only small differences in average scores on their stress index relative to socioeconomic status.

> The score range was 0 to 18, yet the average scores of the Lows, Middles, and Highs were 5.7, 5.3, and 4.7, respectively. Although the Lows had a slightly harder life according to these averages, the difference was not enough to account for our finding of a mental health risk ranging from .41 among the Highs to .59 among the Lows (1963:151).

It is important to note that economic deprivation was the only childhood factor that differentiated among the socioeconomic groups. Among the adult factors, lower socioeconomic respondents were more likely to report a more stressful life, were more likely to report themselves not to be in good health, were more likely to have no close friends in whom they could confide, and to report that children give more trouble than pleasure (1963:151–152).

As Kohn reports, when amount of stress is controlled, Langner and Michael find low socioeconomic status associated with mental health risk for all but the lowest stress group. Kohn wishes, then, to attribute these differences to factors other than stress such as the lower-class conformity orientation. On the face of it, however, it seems reasonable to contend that Langner and Michael's index is not an adequate sampling of types of stress, but disproportionately includes those stresses, particularly those associated with childhood, that have little relationship to social class. It seems plausible that lower-class persons who suffer from many such stresses probably are more likely to also experience related class-linked problems than middle-class persons similarly high on the Langner and Michael index. In short, the analysis is not very convincing in excluding the possibility that lower-class persons with a high stress score were under greater stress than higher-status persons with comparable scores. One facet of the problem to consider relative to the mental health measure used by Langner and Michael is the differential impact of positive events on the various socioeconomic groups. The work of Bradburn (1969) and the Dohrenwends (1969) provides a strong case that general well-being is as much a product of the occurrence of positive events as it is of social stress. Whether all this is relevant to schizophrenia is another matter entirely. Certainly there is some possibility in the case of schizophrenia that even positive arousal (i.e., activation for whatever reason) may precipitate an exacerbation of the illness (Brown *et al.*, 1962).

Theoretically speaking, the conceptualization of stress as a set of occurrences independent of the capacity for mastery creates extremely difficult research problems. Kohn notes the difficulty involved in this perspective, but then does not explore the resultant implications. The psychological impact of stress, of course, depends not alone on the occurrence of events but rather on the relationship between the demands an event makes and the individual's capacity to cope (Mechanic, 1968:294–306). It has been too readily assumed by many writers in this field that the poor are always at a disadvantage, but it seems reasonable to anticipate that the poor are equally capable or superior to higher-status persons in dealing with some kinds of misfortunes. The development of coping capacities comes frequently through experience and practice, and in some areas of living, persons of lower economic status get greater opportunity to develop skills. Moreover, successful mastery builds confidence and a sense of effectiveness, and many persons of lower socioeconomic status, despite their low incomes, develop a strong sense of self. To talk of lower-status persons as a monolithic group on the basis of modest statistical differences among the social classes is conducive to asking the wrong research questions. I personally find it more challenging to inquire why so many lower-status persons do so well in facing adversity than why some fail. For despite the contentions of some sociologists, the vast majority of lower-status persons have frequently shown themselves to be extremely resourceful and adaptive in dealing with the difficult circumstances of their lives. I think a careful review of the literature on health and social pathology would support the view that the most important dependent variables measuring health are related to social status primarily by virtue of the fact that difficulties predominate in the very lowest social segments where lives are characterized not only by low income but also by profound disorganization, deprivation, and alienation. I question whether it is appropriate to generalize from studies involving the working class, such as in Kohn's investigation, to the much smaller and more atypical population constituting the very lowest and most deprived socioeconomic stratum. Indeed, in Kohn's investigations this lowest stratum appears to have been excluded.

But let us more frontally attack the issue of schizophrenia itself. Let us assume again that Kohn sufficiently answers all of the issues already raised, and consider the logical nature of his hypothesis. He implies that one would not anticipate orientational differences between lower-class schizophrenics and lower-class nonschizophrenics (an argument which I contest on statistical grounds), but that the lower-class orientation becomes important only in its interactions with genetic vulnerability and stress. Using the same logic, it would be reasonable to cite any of the numerous findings differentiating one social class from another and positing these as contributing factors in interaction with other forces in producing schizophrenia. Kohn offers no more compelling case for his particular variable than can be offered for numerous others. But even more serious is his failure to suggest what a reasonable test of his theory would involve. The evidence presently available makes a reasonable case for rejecting the likelihood that Kohn's hypothesis is correct. A class orientation must inevitably be communicated largely through the socialization process and particularly through the types of reinforcement processes that take place within the family. We would anticipate that the vigorous study of family factors in schizophrenia would have given us some basis for Kohn's conceptualization. Unfortunately, this literature provides little to build upon despite years of effort among serious and talented investigators.

At the very least we should consider the possibility that there is a great variety of situations that may trigger schizophrenic episodes among genetically vulnerable persons. Such events may include environmental difficulties, failures in coping capacities, role changes, excitement, or any of a large number of other factors. A similar view has been developing among some investigators studying the occurrence of coronary heart disease. To a large extent it appears that vulnerability to coronary disease develops over a long period of time in relation to a variety of medical factors, including genetic characteristics, diet, and physical activity (Hinkle *et al.*, 1968). But any of a wide variety of events involving a Valsalva maneuver may precipitate a coronary attack, and such factors may occur randomly (Hinkle, 1969). As a plausible analogy among schizophrenics, one might speculate that genetic and developmental factors combine in some way to create vulnerable persons whose conditions may be exacerbated by any of a variety of alternative situations. It is conceivable that the nature of a schizophrenic vulnerability may make it difficult for such persons to tolerate extreme stimulation of any sort independent of its source or quality. I do not wish to argue that this is the case, but only to suggest that hypotheses are a dime a dozen. Hypotheses that explain data previously unaccounted for are those we must take seriously.

I cannot conclude this discussion without commenting on the nature of schizophrenic disorders in general. I disagree with Kohn's strategy of accepting a broad definition, common to American investigators, even if there are indications of a spectrum of schizophrenic disorders (Heston, 1970). Certainly there is merit for analytic purposes in separating cases that all can agree fit the concept from those more marginal. Too many of the problems in psychiatric epidemiology stem from the failure to devote sufficient attention to case-finding procedures and from the use of varying concepts of the phenomenon in question. The value of a clear concept applied similarly to different populations is exemplified by the finding that reported differences in rates of schizophrenia in the United States and England are the product of varying case-defining techniques (Cooper, 1970). We had best be careful that we do not elaborate complex theories to explain methodological artifacts.

As a sociologist, I share some of Kohn's predispositions. My own work is based on the assumption that structural and social-psychological factors play some part in the occurrence and outcome of mental illness, and I have been concerned particularly with the relevance of coping skills. In reviewing the literature, I am not particularly convinced that such factors are very influential in the occurrence of schizophrenia as defined by more conservative criteria. I do feel that such concepts are particularly fruitful in understanding more common psychological disorders and the various social pathologies. But contention divorced from evidence is somewhat sterile, and we must always be clear on what the requirements are for demonstrating that our fancies of mind have some relationship to evidence gleaned from the real world. I know there are many who still prefer to speculate on how social change increases psychoses, but take no time to consider the most careful study ever undertaken in this field which found no evidence that there was any relationship worthy of explanation (Goldhamer and Marshall, 1953).

Kohn obviously knows the literature and the issues, and he has spent his efforts over the years collecting data of importance. I regret, therefore, that I must differ so profoundly from his assessment that we need to devise and test formulations of *why lower-class conditions of life contribute to schizophrenia.* I would much prefer that we devote our resources to improving the conceptualization and measurement of various psychiatric conditions and to examining a variety of factors that may mediate their occurrence, their course, and their consequences, not only for the patient but also for society.

REFERENCES

Bradburn, Norman, 1969. *The Structure of Psychological Well-being.* Chicago: Aldine.

Brown, G. W., E. M. Monck, G. M. Carstairs, and J. K. Wing, 1962. "Influence of Family Life on the Course of Schizophrenic Illness." *British Journal of Preventive Social and Social Medicine* **16**:55–68.

Cooper, J., 1970. "The Use of a Procedure for Standardizing Psychiatric Diagnosis." Pp. 109–131 in Edward H. Hare and John K. Wing (eds.), *Psychiatric Epidemiology.* London: Oxford University Press.

Dohrenwend, Bruce, and Barbara Dohrenwend, 1969. *Social Status and Psychological Disorder.* New York: Wiley.

Dunham, H. W., 1966. "A Research Note on Diagnosed Mental Illness and Social Class." *American Sociological Review* **31**(April):223–227.

Faris, Robert, and H. Warren Dunham, 1939. *Mental Disorders in Urban Areas.* Chicago: University of Chicago Press.

Goldberg, E. M., and S. L. Morrison, 1963. "Schizophrenia and Social Class." *British Journal of Psychiatry* **109**(November):785–802.

Goldhamer, Herbert, and Andrew W. Marshall, 1953. *Psychosis and Civilization: Two Studies in the Frequency of Mental Disease.* New York: Free Press.

Hare, E. H., 1956. "Family Setting and the Urban Distribution of Schizophrenia." *Journal of Mental Science* **102**:753–760.

Heston, L. L., 1970. "The Genetics of Schizophrenia and Schizoid Disease." *Science* **167**(January):249–256.

Hinkle, L. E., Jr., 1969. Presentation at Conference on Behavioral Aspects of Disease, Department of Behavioral Science, University of Kentucky Medical School, April.

Hinkle, L. E., Jr., L. H. Witney, E. W. Lehman, J. Dunn, B. Benjamin, R. King, A Plakun, B. Flehinger, 1968. "Occupation, Education, and Coronary Heart Disease." *Science* **161**(July):238–246.

Hollingshead, August B., and Fredrick C. Redlich, 1958. *Social Class and Mental Illness.* New York: Wiley.

Kohn, Melvin L., 1969. *Class and Conformity: A Study in Values.* Homewood, Illinois: Dorsey.

Langner, Thomas S., and Stanley T. Michael, 1963. *Life Stress and Mental Health.* New York: Free Press of Glencoe.

Mechanic, David, 1966. "The Sociology of Medicine: Viewpoints and Perspectives." *Journal of Health and Human Behavior* 7(Winter):1–12.

Mechanic, David, 1968. *Medical Sociology: A Selective View.* New York: Free Press.

Mechanic, David, 1969. *Mental Health and Social Policy.* Englewood Cliffs: Prentice-Hall.

Rosenthal, David, 1970. *Genetic Theory and Abnormal Behavior.* New York: McGraw-Hill.

Rosenthal, David, and Seymour S. Kety (eds.), 1968. *The Transmission of Schizophrenia.* Oxford: Pergamon.

Turner, R. J., and M. Wagenfeld, 1967. "Occupational Mobility and Schizophrenia: An Assessment of the Social Causation and Social Selection Hypotheses." *American Sociological Review* **32**(February):104–113.

Rejoinder to David Mechanic

Melvin L. Kohn

Underlying many of the disagreements between David Mechanic and me are our divergent appraisals of the stance sociologists have taken in coming to terms with the relationship between social class and schizophrenia. He thinks we have been too quick to infer a causal relationship. From my reading of this same research literature, I think the opposite is true. I have often wondered why we have expended so much energy and imagination in minimizing the importance of one of the best-documented and most provocative findings of our science, while spending so little effort exploring its possible theoretical implications. My essay attempts to refocus sociological interest.

It was not possible in a short paper to review all the studies documenting the relationship between class and schizophrenia, to reassess the evidence for and against social selection hypotheses, to reconsider all the methodological problems and alternative interpretations. The first few paragraphs attempt to summarize the principal issues, referring to my (1968) earlier extended treatment of them and to other systematic reviews. Mechanic sees the evidence dif-

From *Social Forces,* **1972**, 50, 310–313. Reproduced by permission of The University of North Carolina Press.

ferently and certainly it is open to more than one reading; but I urge the reader to study the cited reviews. Particularly questionable is Mechanic's conclusion that "recent and carefully executed studies . . . strongly suggest that the association between social status and schizophrenia is a product of social failure or limited mobility potential resulting from the disabilities associated with the condition." His citations include studies of varied quality, favoring and disfavoring this conclusion. My (1968:158–160) own critical appraisal of these and other pertinent studies leads me to think it highly improbable that class differences in schizophrenia could result entirely or even in large part from the disabilities attendant on the disorder.

Mechanic also implies that recent evidence for genetics is somehow at odds with the possibility of social causation. The evidence for genetics has long been convincing (cf. Clausen and Kohn, 1954:144). But recent studies have made it clear that the magnitude of the genetic contribution is not so great that genetics alone can explain schizophrenia; other factors must also play an important part (cf. the very works Mechanic cites: Rosenthal, 1970; Rosenthal and Kety, 1968). Many students of schizophrenia now recognize the desirability of bringing genetic and social factors into the same formulation, for only then can we precisely define the role of either. My essay attempts to construct such a multidimensional model.

Also at issue are my conceptualization of stress and the adequacy of the studies I cite to support the belief that stress probably contributes to schizophrenia. My discussion attempts to distinguish between the possibly painful properties of the situation, as they would affect anyone who experiences them, and the individual's ability to assess and deal with that situation. Mechanic questions the desirability of treating the two separately. Given his interests, there is not much need to do so, for here, as in his (Mechanic, 1962) own research, his principal concern is how similarly situated people cope with the same threatening situation. But the question I must ask is whether differently situated people, some of whom have become schizophrenic had been differentially subjected to stressful experiences. To answer this question, one must keep the situation's potential for inducing stress conceptually distinct from the individual's ability to deal with stress.

The evidence for stress playing a part in schizophrenia is not so compelling as that for genetics or for social class, but it is a good deal better than Mechanic allows. The research most in point is not Langner and Michael's (1963) study of mental disorder in general, but studies specifically focused on schizophrenia, especially those by Rogler and Hollingshead (1965) and by Brown and Birley (1968). I do rely on Langner–Michael, though, for evidence that class differences in exposure to stressful situations do not explain class differences in the occurrence of mental disorder. Their study makes that unlikely possibility even more remote.

As for my radical reinterpretation of the role of the family in schizophrenia: the central idea is that because investigators have approached the problem from a single-factor perspective, they have pursued the wrong question. As good an example as any is my (Kohn and Clausen, 1956) own study, which looked to the structure of parent–child relationships in the vain hope of finding something unique to schizophrenia. This search has been endless and fruitless. But if one reformulates the question from a multidimensional perspective, the myriad negative findings take on new meaning. There is no longer any need to search for some essential difference between schizophrenia-producing and other lower-class families. Instead, one asks what there may be about the experience of growing up in lower-class families that might contribute to the development of schizophrenia in persons who are both genetically predisposed and subjected to stress. I suggested that because of the constricting circumstances of their own lives, many lower-class parents transmit to their children an orientational system too limited and too rigid for dealing effectively with stress and, more generally, with complexity and change. I also suggested that although the family is of great importance for transmitting orientational systems, the conformist orientational system need not be learned from one's parents. My formulation posits that a conformist orientational system contributes to the schizophrenic process; it matters not whether the orientations are learned from parents or from the individual's own experiences (cf. footnote 18).

Mechanic questions on both empirical and theoretical grounds the plausibility of my suggestion that the lower-class orientational system contributes to the schizophrenic process.

On the empirical level, he argues that the evidence for there being a relationship between class and orientation is inferential, that the correlations are too small for the requirements of my model, and that the data of my own research are based only on the working class, not the lower class. The facts are these: (1) Rather than inferring orientations from data about the characteristics parents value for children, I explicitly indexed each of the facets of orientation cited as pertinent to schizophrenia (cf. Kohn, 1969:78–82; 265–269). (2) The correlations of social class with these facets of orientation are sufficiently large to justify their inclusion in a multidimensional model; they range from *0.13* to *0.38* (Kohn, 1969:81; 83), the strongest correlate being the one most important to my formulation, "a rigidly conservative view of man and his social institutions." (3) The sample does exclude one important group of lower-class men, those who were unemployed at the time the interviewer made contact, in the spring or summer of 1964. But most lower-class men—those working at unskilled jobs, those intermittently employed—were included. Moreover, I supplemented my own research by turning to Rainwater's (1968) summary of studies specifically focused on lower-class population groups. This summary makes it evident that my generalizations are valid for the lowest social strata.

On the theoretical level, Mechanic argues that there are class differences in all sorts of things; why select orientations as being especially relevant to schizophrenia? There are three main reasons for doing so.

The first was left implicit in my essay, but perhaps it should be made explicit. Instead of searching aimlessly among the innumerable correlates of class for one or another that might help explain the class–schizophrenia relationship, I think it strategic to look to what underlies the social-psychology of class: members of different social classes, by virtue of enjoying (or suffering) different conditions of life, come to see the world differently—to develop different conceptions of social reality, different aspirations and hopes and fears, different conceptions of the desirable. Class differences in orientation are an important bridge between social conditions and psychological functioning.

My second reason for thinking orientations pertinent is that my analysis of the interrelationship of class, genetics, and stress points to the necessity of our taking account of class differences in people's ability to deal with stressful or problematic situations. It seems to me that the conformist orientational system characteristic of the lower social classes is less adequate for dealing with such situations than is the self-directed orientational system more prevalent at higher social-class levels. There is no disputing the usefulness of a conformist orientational system for meeting many of the ordinary exigencies of lower-class life. One does not have to declare an orientational system either useful or harmful. It can be useful in some circumstances and harmful in others.

My third reason, merely hinted at in the paper, is that orientations—conceptions of reality are fundamental to schizophrenia. Fearful, inflexible reactions to threat are integral to the schizophrenic experience. A conformist orientational system may provide the base on which schizophrenic conceptions of reality are built.

How would one test my formulation? Since the formulation posits that schizophrenia is produced by the interaction of genetic vulnerability, stress, and the disabilities attendant on a conformist orientation, a rigorous test clearly requires that all three elements be considered together. I speak of interaction in its precise statistical sense: the relevance of any of the three factors depends on the strength of the other two. It may also be that the critical threshold for each of the factors depends on the strength of the other two. If, for example, the genetic predisposition is exceptionally strong, less stress may be required (cf. Rosenthal, 1963:507–509); if there is exceedingly great stress, perhaps only minimal genetic vulnerability will be sufficient (cf. Eitinger, 1964); if a person's orientation is strongly conformist, even moderately stressful situations may overwhelm him. These possibilities, and the numerous variations they imply, suggest that my model may be only a simple prototype of a family of models. Fortunately, research designed to test any one of them can assess the others as well, for they are all based on the interplay of the same three factors.

If the effects of genetics, stress, and orientation were assumed to be additive, we could test any of them by comparing schizophrenics to nonschizophrenics of the same social class on that factor alone. But with an interactive model of the type I have proposed, a single-factor comparison is inadequate. Since no one factor could produce schizophrenia except in combination with the others, it would be possible for *all* members of a given social class to surpass the threshold for any factor, provided they did not exceed the thresholds for the others. Thus, an absence of difference between schizophrenics and nonschizophrenics of the same class level on any of the factors in the model is no disproof of the pertinence of that factor. Correspondingly, finding a difference provides *prima facie* evidence that the factor is pertinent to schizophrenia, but no proof that its place in the model has been correctly established. An important corollary is that different factors may distinguish schizophrenics from nonschizophrenics in different social classes.

Mechanic assumes that the moderate correlation between class and orientation means that many lower-class people do not hold a conformist orientation; he therefore predicts substantial differences in orientation between those lower-class people who do and those who do not become schizophrenic. I interpret the moderate correlation between class and orientation to mean that a conformist orientation is widely held at lower social-class levels and is far from absent, though less widely held, at higher social-class levels. I would therefore predict little or no difference in orientation between lower-class schizophrenics and nonschizophrenics. From either perspective, we should expect lower-class schizophrenics and nonschizophrenics to differ most decidedly in genetic vulnerability, perhaps also in exposure to stress, and least of all in orientation. Since present evidence indicates that the correlation between class and orientation is greater than that between class and genetics, or than that between class and stress, differences between schizophrenics and nonschizophrenics should center more and more on orientation at increasingly higher social-class levels.

Many of the remaining issues raised in Mechanic's commentary are matters on which we agree (see, for example, my discussion of diagnostic problems in Kohn, 1968:160–162). The others I see as tangential to my thesis; here I would include both his analogies to phenomena other than schizophrenia and his observations about the essential difference between schizophrenia and other psychological disorders.

Mechanic seems impatient of ideas that cannot be confirmed or disproved by evidence now in hand. I feel no embarrassment that existing data do not provide a test of my formulation. It is precisely because a long tradition of empiricism has left some of the most important questions unasked that I feel impelled to speculate. I have tried to put several previously unconnected bodies of research into a single formulation consistent with all the evidence, as best I can judge that evidence. I hope the formulation will be provocative of new research. The sooner this research leads to new and better models, the more successful will my effort have been.

ADDITIONAL REFERENCES

Clausen, J. A., and M. L. Kohn, 1954. "The Ecological Approach in Social Psychiatry." *American Journal of Sociology* 60(September):140–151.

Mechanic, David, 1962. *Students Under Stress: A Study in the Social Psychology of Adaptation.* New York: Free Press of Glencoe.

Rosenthal, David, 1963. *The Genain Quadruplets: A Case Study and Theoretical Analysis of Heredity and Environment in Schizophrenia.* New York: Basic Books.

A Comparative Study of the Personal Histories of Schizophrenic and Nonpsychiatric Patients

William Schofield

Lucy Balian

One of the currently popular views of the etiology of severe personality disruption holds that the seeds of mental illness are to be found in the life experiences of the individual. In particular, the childhood is conceived as a critical period, and certain areas, such as parent-child relationships and psychosexual development, are viewed as crucial determiners of or prodromal to later adjustment or psychopathology. Three possible forms of "historical" or biographic etiology may be distinguished: (*a*) the traumatic incident (e.g., witnessing in childhood the "primal scene"), (*b*) sequential traumata (i.e., a concatenation of emotional blows resulting finally in disintegration of the ego), and (*c*) acquired predisposition (i.e., the learning of a pattern of maladaptive response). Writing in 1893, Breuer and Freud (trans. 1957) noted that:

> The causal relation between the determining psychical trauma and the hysterical phenomenon is not of a kind implying that the trauma merely acts like an "agent provocateur" in releasing the symptom, which thereafter leads a separate existence. We must presume rather that the psychical trauma—or more precisely the memory of the trauma—acts like a foreign body which long after its entry must continue to be regarded as an agent that is still at work (p. 6).

Freud (Breuer & Freud, trans. 1957), in describing the case of Elizabeth von R., observes:

> Almost invariably when I have observed the determinants of such conditions what I have come upon has not been a *single* traumatic cause but a group of similar ones. . . . In some of these instances it could be established that the symptom in question had already appeared for a short time after the first trauma and had then passed off, till it was brought on again and stabilized by a succeeding trauma (p. 173).

Finally, we have a succinct expression of the learning hypothesis in Shaffer and Shoben (1956):

> An evident conclusion is that our distinctive attributes, even our most fundamentally human qualities, are products of our experience with other human beings. *Personality* (italics ours) is learned as a result of the events in one's history (p. 402).

The significance of the once-occurring trauma in production of later symptomatology is given less prominence now than it held during the heyday of "la grande hysterie" and when public-compulsive symptoms were viewed as more circumscribed phenomena. Likewise, a simple additive notion about accumulations of emotional "shocks" is retained today chiefly by the laity, who express this notion in the "straw and camel's back" allegory. It is currently more common to view the patient's history as either having deprived him of an opportunity to learn normal patterns of socialization or as "overtraining" him in some repertoire of abnormal responses. If varying patterns of psychopathology are differentiated, and if the biography, or certain ages or elements in the biography, are believed to have pathogenic potential, it is reasonable to assume that differential patterns of personal history might be found which are demonstrably associated with various behavioral syndromes. Research in this realm immediately involves the investigator in difficult methodological problems with respect to definition and recording of the life history.

What is a life history? As the concept is widely and loosely used in much psychological writing, it is implicitly a theoretical abstraction. It may be conceived as inclusive of all *events* in the total sequence of time-space displacements of the individual from the moment of his birth up to some time at which a summary is prepared. It may be conceived as the complete sequence of *experiences* had by the individual over such a period. It may be thought of as a "complete" collection of the events *and* experiences of the individual. Unless one wishes to assume perfect recording (and retention?) characteristics for the nervous apparatus, it is unlikely that the individual's population of events, as observable time-space dispositions, has isomorphic representation in his population of experiences or subjective events.

Without much formal attention to the theory of the life history, most of the research into biographical factors in mental illness has been content to use the framework or part of the structure of the so-called "psychiatric history." This is essentially a relatively uniform selection of significant events and experiences in the histories of research subjects. What determines the selection and what defines significance? Selection is determined in part by what data are obtainable as a function of accuracy of records and

From *Journal of Abnormal and Social Psychology*, 1959, 59, 216–225.

This study was made possible by a grant from the Frederick L. Wells Fund.

integrity of memory. Significance is expressed through clinical judgment, largely as a result of observations of apparent association between certain factors and specific outcomes (e.g., broken homes and delinquency). Significance may be also determined on the grounds of currently (and locally) popular theory. Recognizing these constraints upon the adequacy of the typical psychiatric history as a representative sampling from the theoretical population of events and experiences constituting the true life history, it is incumbent upon the investigator into the contribution of life history factors to psychogenesis of emotional disturbance to seek at least minimal insurance against these sources of error. Such safeguards are afforded in the utilization of history outlines and recording forms and in the collection of data for control samples. The development and application of detailed history schedules helps to assure uniformity and thoroughness of coverage. The study of control groups serves as a check on the associations and hypotheses of etiological factors suggested by the study of exclusively pathological samples.

The obviousness of these experimental caveats encourages an expectation that they have been well respected in researches into the life history as a source of psychopathology. A search of the literature reveals over 300 studies of life histories of psychiatric patients. Fewer than ten of these included data on a reasonably comparable control group (Aldrich & Coffin, 1948; Lane, 1955; Nielsen, 1954; Steinberg & Wittman, 1943). The bulk of the studies report simply the frequency of such items as patient's age at death of a parent as recorded in mental hospital records. Frequently, only selected items are tabulated without any attempt at a comprehensive history. When more extensive coverage of history data has been undertaken, a variety of procedures for collection has been used and efforts to study a control sample have been rare. When studied, control groups have seemed mostly to be determined by accessibility rather than appropriateness (Brockway, Gleser, Winakur, & Ulett, 1954).

PURPOSE AND PREMISES

The purpose of this study was (*a*) to determine what the life histories of "normal" persons look like if examined through the spectroscope of a comprehensive psychiatric history interview as conducted and recorded by a skilled clinician and (*b*) to determine in what ways such histories may be distinguishable from those of such psychiatric patients as schizophrenics.

The basic hypothesis of this research simply stated was: the life histories of "normal," i.e., nonpsychiatric patients, will be readily and clearly differentiated from those of psychiatric patients if equally complete and carefully collected history data are available for both. More specifically, the hypothesis is that the histories of normals will reveal markedly less occurrence of those events or experiences (trauma, deprivations, frustrations, conflicts, etc.) which have been commonly considered to have a psychogenic or prodromal role in schizophrenia. This is a formal statement of the assumption which is made, usually implicitly, in those clinical and uncontrolled studies which derive from the absolute frequency of given events in the histories of certain patients the conclusion that the event has causal import. In the absence of comparative data on the frequency of these same events in appropriate control subjects, there is not only room but need to be doubtful of such conclusions.

Table 1. *Gross Descriptive Data for Normals and Schizophrenics.*

	Normal (N = 150)	Schizophrenic (N = 178)
Age	M = 28.6 yrs. SD = 9.7	M = 28.7 yrs. SD = 9.6
Sex		
Male	44.7%	44.4%
Female	55.3	55.6
Marital Status		
Married	33.3%	26.9%
Single	64.7	69.1
Divorced	1.3	1.7
Widowed	0.6	1.7
Separated	0.0	0.6
Education	M = 12.0 yrs. SD = 3.4	M = 9.9 yrs. SD = 2.5
Home		
Urban	44.7%	50.8%
Rural	55.3	49.2
Religion		
Lutheran	38.0%	35.7%
Other Prot.	31.7	31.0
Catholic	24.0	27.0
Jewish	0.6	6.2
Moslem	0.6	0.0
No. of Siblings	M = 4.1 SD = 2.8	M = 4.2 SD = 3.4
No. of Children	(N = 53) M = 2.4 SD = 2.1	(N = 50) M = 2.8 SD = 2.4

SAMPLE AND PROCEDURE

The selection of the "normal" subjects (*S*s) for this study was determined primarily by the nature of the 178 schizophrenics with whom comparison was to be made. These patients were hospitalized at the University of Minnesota Hospitals, and comprehensive personal history statistics have been previously reported (Schofield, Hathaway, Hastings, & Bell, 1954) for them.[1] To assure comparability of the normal and psychiatric samples, the former were drawn primarily from the same population which yielded the latter, i.e., the general group of persons referred to the University hospitals for diagnosis and treatment. Of the total, 105, or 70% were University patients. An additional 14 cases were obtained from Minneapolis General Hospital. Finally, 31 physically and psychiatrically negative cases

[1] It is recommended that this report be read for further detail on the history schedule and method of data collection for the schizophrenic sample.

were obtained from sources including hospital employees, students, employees of a large industrial firm, and office workers. The term "normal" as applied to this sample specifies the absence of psychiatric disturbances under treatment at the time the histories were recorded *and* the absence of any previous mental disorder. The nonpsychiatric patients were drawn from all but the psychiatric wards and psychiatric clinics of both the University hospitals and Minneapolis General Hospital. The medical diagnoses represented covered a wide range, and no type of illness or defect was predominant.

To assure further comparability of the two groups, selection of the normals was made so as to achieve matching with the schizophrenics for age, sex, and marital status. Success of the matching is indicated in Table 1. As a further reflection of the comparability of the two samples, data on education, rural–urban origin, and religious affiliation are recorded in Table 1. The mean number of years of formal education for the normals is reliably higher than that of the schizophrenics; however, the overlap between the two distributions is approximately 50%. Also, the higher average educational level of the normals undoubtedly reflects the general increment in average educational level of the public, since they were hospitalized in 1956–1957 (of school age in 1904–1956), in contrast to the schizophrenics who were hospitalized between 1938–1944 (of school age in 1886–1944). No basic difference is indicated in the intellectual or general socioeconomic character of the two samples. The comparability of the two samples is further supported by the data on number of sibs and number of children in the married *S*s as reported in Table 1.

The life histories of the normals were collected through the medium of a comprehensive clinical interview requiring from 45 to 90 minutes.[2] Only two of the patients who were approached refused to cooperate. Satisfactory rapport was achieved in most cases, and the *S*s appeared to give reliable accounts of their backgrounds. Many of them were interested in the nature of the study, and this was briefly discussed with them at the close of the interview. Also, at the end of the interview each *S* was administered an MMPI as a further check on his psychiatric status.

Immediately after each interview, the interviewer transcribed her notes and further observations onto a detailed schedule covering over 100 distinct items pertaining to developmental, personal, social, and medical history. This was the same schedule which had been used in recording the history data for the schizophrenic sample.[3]

RESULTS

The major findings of the study are reported in Tables 2–7, which show the percentage frequency of occurrence in the two samples of various psychological relationships and adjustment variables. These range from the quality of the relationship between the *S*s parents to the degree of manifestation of a life plan and initiative in the pursuit of that plan. The reliability of the differences between the distributions of the two samples are reported in the tables.[4] Generally more notable than the presence or absence of statistical reliability of the differences are the marked *overlaps* in the distributions for the schizophrenic and normal samples.

Table 2 reveals that the relationship between the parents of *both* the normal *S*s and schizophrenic patients was predominantly one of affection. Relationships characterized as ambivalent, indifferent, or hostile were slightly more frequent between the parents of the normals. In their relationships with their fathers, the schizophrenics experienced a reliably higher frequency of unfavorable attitudes. However, two-thirds of these patients apparently received affection from their fathers, and less than one-fourth were the recipients of either rejection or domination. The maternal relationship more clearly differentiates the two samples. Again, however, it is to be noted that nearly two-thirds of the schizophrenics enjoyed the affection of their mothers. Of the various undesirable relationships which were recorded, overprotection and domination were most prominent in the schizophrenics. This is slight support for the current belief of some experts in the existence of the so-called "schizophrenogenic mother":

> Psychoanalytic students are uniform in the opinion that maternal rejection and domination are regularly found in the histories of those who are found later to have been predisposed to the development of schizophrenia. The mother of the schizophrenic is variously described as cold, dominating, narcissistic, lacking love for the child, having death wishes toward it . . . (Woolley, 1953).

However, domination or overprotection characterized the relationship of *less than one-fourth* of the mothers of the schizophrenics in the present day.

Table 2 also reports the relationship between the two samples and their respective sibs and the frequency of six factors of physical and/or psychological deprivation or trauma. The intersib relationships do not differentiate the two groups. While none of the home conditions noted occurred in more than a fifth of the homes of either sample, two of the factors, namely, poverty and invalidism, did have a reliably different rate in the two groups, and the rate of divorce approached a reliable difference. All three of these more frequently characterized the childhood homes of the normals.

The attitudes, adjustment, and achievement of the two groups in their school experiences are recorded in Table 2. All three factors show reliably different distributions for the two samples. General attitude toward the school situation was less different for the normals and schizophrenics than were achievement and deportment. Three times as many schizophrenics as normals found their school work difficult, and twice as many normals as schizophrenics easily earned good grades. The passivity of the prepsychotic

[2] All interviews were conducted by the junior author, who at the time was a senior medical student.

[3] Copies of the 12-page rating schedule for case history analysis and of the 4-page record form used with it have been deposited with the American Documentation Institute. Order Document No. 4209 from ADI Auxiliary Publications Project, Photo-duplication Service, Library of Congress, Washington 25, D. C., remitting in advance $1.25 for microfilm or $1.25 for 6 × 8 inch photocopies. Make checks payable to Chief, Photoduplication Service, Library of Congress.

This schedule was originally developed by Dahlstrom (1949) in connection with an unpublished doctoral dissertation.

[4] The chi square test was used to determine probability that the obtained distributions belong to a common population. Where indicated, Yates' correction was applied.

Table 2. *Interpersonal Relationships, Home Factors, and School Adjustment in the Early Histories of Normals and Schizophrenics.*

	Normal	Schizo-phrenic	χ^2	P
Interparental Relationship	(N = 144)	(N = 101)		
Affection	75.7%	76.2%	0.14	> 0.98
Ambivalence	6.3	5.9		
Indifference	0.7	1.9		
Hostility	17.4	15.8		
Paternal Relationship	(N = 143)	(N = 127)		
Affection	76.2%	65.3%	13.02	< .05
Ambivalence	9.8	5.5		
Indifference	4.2	3.1		
Rejection	7.7	11.8	3.91	< .05
Overprotection	0.7	1.5		
Domination	1.4	11.8		
Maternal Relationship	(N = 150)	(N = 128)		
Affection	81.3%	64.8%	32.90	< .01
Ambivalence	8.0	2.3		
Indifference	2.7	1.5		
Rejection	6.0	6.2	9.72	< .01
Overprotection	0.7	13.2		
Domination	0.7	10.9		
Neglect	0.7	0.7		
Sibling Relationship	(N = 178)	(N = 126)		
None	3.4%	3.9%	4.43	< .50
Affection	70.8	76.1		
Indifference	2.2	4.7		
Rivalry	16.3	13.4		
Domination	2.8	0.7		
Submission	4.5	0.7		
Home Conditions				
Poverty	20.7%	9.0%	8.00	< .01
Alcoholism	6.0	6.8	0.19	< .70
Invalid	12.7	0.6	18.67	< .01
Divorce	6.0	1.6	3.14	< .10
Separation	2.7	1.1	0.38	< .70
Death of parent	14.7	10.7	0.82	< .50
School Acceptance	(N = 155)	(N = 159)		
Marked hostility	7.1%	3.8%	13.64	< .01
Mild dislike	17.4	11.3		
Indifference	11.0	25.8		
Agreeable	54.8	54.7		
Keen enjoyment	10.0	4.4		
School Achievement	(N = 150)	(N = 163)		
Repeated failure	7.3%	4.9%	21.49	< .01
Work difficult	6.0	19.6		
Average performance	42.0	50.2		
Easily earned good grades	38.7	19.6		
Accelerated	6.0	4.4		
School Deportment				
Poor record	9.3%	7.9%	22.92	< .01
Usual no. of escapades	36.0	10.6		
Excellent record	54.7	81.6		

Note. In this and subsequent tables, where two χ^2 values appear for a given factor, one is based on all categories and the second is for comparison of bracketed versus unbracketed categories.

schizophrenic in the school room, which has been commonly observed by clinicians, is suggested in their clear preponderance of excellent deportment records. While nearly one-fourth of the schizophrenics experienced failure or difficulty with their school work, less than one-tenth of them had poor deportment. By contrast, while better than 85% of the normals had satisfactory or superior achievement, only half of them had excellent deportment records.

Occupational success and satisfaction distinguishes the normals from the schizophrenics as revealed in Table 3. The proportion of the two groups without any history of occupation is not reliably different. While poor occupational achievement was recorded for none of the normals with an occupational history, this rating was assigned to one-fifth of the schizophrenics. Overlap is again notable, with 85% of the schizophrenics manifesting average or good occupational success. Satisfaction with their occupations also differentiated the two groups. Over half of the schizophrenics disliked or were indifferent to their work, while three-fourths of the normals apparently enjoyed their occupations.

Table 3 indicates that the two groups were not differentiated with regard to frequency of church attendance, although the role of religion or attitude toward it was different in the two. While there was no difference in the frequency with which religion afforded a dominant source of balance to the lives of the two groups, an intellectualized or ritualistic approach to religion was found four times as frequently among the normals as among the schizophrenics. Table 3 also reports the occurrence of delinquency and criminal records; the rates are very small and not different for the two samples.

Table 4 records the dating history and marital adjustment of the two samples. Frequency of dating is not reliably different in the two groups if the "average" and "very popular" categories are combined for contrast with the "none or little" category. Although there were no schizophrenics rated as "very popular" in terms of frequency of dating, less than 5% of the normals fell into this category. Approximately a third of both samples were married (Table 1). The marital adjustment of the two groups was not

Table 3. *Occupational Histories and Religious Orientation of Normals and Schizophrenics.*

	Normal	Schizo-phrenic	χ^2	*P*
Occupation	(*N* = 150)	(*N* = 177)		
None	15.3%	21.1%	0.72	<.50
Occupational Success	(*N* = 127)	(*N* = 127)		
Poor	0.0%	14.9%	1.60	<.30
Average	38.6	31.5		
Good	61.4	53.5	18.66	<.01
Occupational Satisfaction	(*N* = 127)	(*N* = 126)		
Dislike	7.9%	9.5%	21.74	<.01
Indifference	17.3	43.6		
Enjoyment	74.8	46.8		
Church Attendance	(*N* = 150)	(*N* = 147)		
Very infrequent	22.0%	38.3%	4.77	<.10
Occasionally	36.7	31.2		
Steady	41.3	35.3		
Religiousness	(*N* = 142)	(*N* = 121)		
Intellectualized, ritualistic	18.3%	4.1%	12.31	<.01
Occasional solace	42.3	55.4		
Dominant source of balance	39.4	40.5		

Table 4. *Dating History, Marital and Heterosexual Adjustments of Normals and Schizophrenics.*

	Normal	Schizo-phrenic	χ^2	*P*
Dating	(*N* = 150)	(*N* = 145)		
None or little	49.3%	57.2%	5.98	<.10
Average	46.0	42.8	1.83	<.20
Very popular	4.7	0.0		
Marital Adjustment	(*N* = 53)	(*N* = 50)		
Extreme frustration	18.9%	16.0%	6.73	<.20
Continual conflict	15.1	14.0		
Compatibility	17.0	42.0		
Pleasure	41.5	24.0		
Chief pleasure	7.5	4.0		
Affection to Mate	(*N* = 53) 62.3%	(*N* = 51) 64.7%		
Heterosexual Adjustment	(*N* = 150)	(*N* = 171)		
Poor	36.7%	22.2%	10.49	<.01
Fair	20.7	33.3		
Good	42.7	44.4		
Adequacy of Outlet	(*N* = 150)	(*N* = 170)		
Poor	38.6%	24.7%	11.18	<.01
Fair	33.3	30.5		
Good	28.0	44.7		

different, and a third of both groups experienced frustration or conflict in their marriages. Although the normals tended to derive distinct pleasure from their marriages with somewhat higher frequency than the schizophrenics, a third of both groups evinced attitudes of affection toward their spouses.

The quality of sexual adjustment and adequacy of outlet are shown in Table 4. Sexual adjustment is reliably different in the two samples. Surprisingly, the difference appears primarily in the greater frequency of poor sexual adjustments in the normal *S*s. Likewise, the schizophrenics were rated twice as frequently as the normals as enjoying "good sexual outlets."

The quality of social adjustment and of factors affecting interpersonal relationships are shown in Table 5. The adequacy of social adjustment is clearly different for the two samples, with the schizophrenics showing a high frequency of withdrawal and a low rate of active group membership. Likewise, both the variables of social intelligence and poise show reliably inferior distributions for the schizophrenics. The overlaps between the two groups are considerable, however. Nearly 90% of the schizophrenics were rated as having at least moderate skill in interpersonal relations, and only a third of them were characterized as retiring and sensitive. Pursuit of solitary recreation was more character-

Table 5. *Social Skill and Adjustment of Schizophrenics and Normals.*

	Normal	Schizo-phrenic	χ^2	*P*
Social Adjustment	(*N* = 150)	(*N* = 85)		
Withdrawal	10.0%	61.2%	78.60	<.01
Ambivalence	7.3	14.1		
Membership	82.7	24.7		
Social Intelligence	(*N* = 150)	(*N* = 167)		
Inept and clumsy	8.7%	8.9%	29.66	<.01
Moderate skill	68.7	88.8		
Adept	22.7	2.3		
Poise	(*N* = 150)	(*N* = 170)		
Retiring and sensitive	22.7%	37.4%	12.99	<.01
Fairly articulate	51.3	49.7		
Confident	26.0	12.8		
Recreation	(*N* = 150)	(*N* = 163)		
Solitary	27.3%	40.5%	6.51	<.05
Mixed	66.0	52.2		
Social	6.7	7.3		

Table 6. *Interests, Aspirations, and Initiative of Normals and Schizophrenics.*

	Normal	Schizophrenic	χ^2	P
Breadth of Interest	(N = 150)	(N = 173)		
Narrow	20.7%	35.2%	44.30	<.01
Some outside	46.0	60.2		
Broad	33.3	4.6		
Level of Aspiration	(N = 150)	(N = 170)		
Limited	16.0%	34.7%	17.79	<.01
Interested in improving	61.3	55.3		
High	22.7	10.0		
Life Plan	(N = 150)	(N = 164)		
Vague	22.7%	46.4%	56.63	<.01
Confused	9.3	28.0		
Clear	68.0	25.6		
Stability	(N = 150)	(N = 172)		
Constant fluctuation	10.7%	13.9%	47.17	<.01
Moderate variability	78.7	42.7		
Stolid	10.7	43.4		
Initiative	(N = 150)	(N = 169)		
Apathetic	8.0%	16.0%	4.12	<.20
Appropriate	57.3	53.2		
Energetic	34.7	30.8		

istic of the schizophrenics than the normals, but over half of the former had a history of mixed or social recreation.

In Table 6 are reported five areas of early personal attitude and expression which might be broadly classed as manifestations of individual perspective and morale. Four of these variables show reliably different distributions in the two groups. Summarizing for these variables, it may be said that the schizophrenics less frequently had broad interests, a high level of aspiration, and a clear life plan; more frequently than the normals they were characterized by a stolid, nonvarying temperament and by absence of initiative.

DISCUSSION

The single most impressive feature of the data presented in Tables 2–6 is the sizable overlap of the normal *Ss* and schizophrenic patients in the distributions of the various personal history variables. Of the 35 separate tests which were run, 13 (or 37%) failed to reveal a reliable difference between the two samples. Further, on 5 of the remaining 22 variables, the distributions showed a reliably greater presence in the normals of negative or undesirable conditions. In those instances where the statistical tests did indicate a reliable characterization of the schizophrenics by prevalence of a pathogenic variable, the normals generally also showed a closely approximating degree of the same factor. Before discussing the implications of the findings, it will be well to review facets of the data collection and recording which might have had biasing effects.

The history data for the schizophrenics were abstracted from the material routinely collected and recorded clinically in the hospital charts of these patients as they were admitted, diagnosed, treated, and discharged. A variety of persons, including social workers, junior medical students, psychiatric residents, and staff psychiatrists, contributed to the recording of these data. No single person was charged with the collection of comprehensive history nor was a detailed research schedule applied as a reference in collecting the material. These facts suggest the possible underestimation of the actual frequency of certain variables in the histories of the schizophrenics. However, in abstracting the clinical material and recording it on the research schedule, no attempt was made to force the rating of a variable when clear information was not available; free use was made of an "unknown" category. This tactic has the effect of enhancing the reliability of the frequencies reported at the expense of having a varying size of sample (for example, "paternal relationships" was rated for only 127 of the 178 schizophrenics).

Reliability of the ratings of the various factors is an important consideration. This is especially true with respect to the data on the schizophrenics for whom the original clinical records were not uniform and from which, without any other source of information or contact with the patient, the rater had to abstract the material pertinent to a given variable and then assign it a rating. The definitions of the various scales were made as objective and nonambiguous as possible, and the number of steps to each scale was generally small. As reported previously, independent abstractors-and-raters achieved an 80–95% agreement over a small sample of trial cases (Schofield et al., 1954).

The reliability of the data for the normals was enhanced by providing for an immediate recording and rating of information which had been collected in an extended interview conducted with the research schedule as an implicit guide to insure coverage. Failure to find distinguishing features for the two groups might be the result of a "contamination effect" if the same person or persons had been responsible for the study and rating of both the schizophrenics and normals. Actually, two researchers working quite independently and at different periods of time collected and rated the schizophrenic and normal material respectively.[5] This avoids an artificial overlap in the distributions as a function of a common rater projecting implicit "base rate" standards from one sample to another. There remains the question of interrater reliability and the possibility of stable but different interpretations of the criteria for various ratings leading to Type I errors (Walker & Lev, 1953). This possibility was particularly suggested, for example, by the surprising distributions of the "heterosexual" adjustment variable (see Table 4). As a check on the possibility that relatively different criteria had been applied by the two raters (both single females) in assessing this variable, they were asked to give independent, free accounts of their respective interpretations of the steps on this scale and

[5] The schizophrenic records were rated by Miss Bell in 1951–52, and the normal *Ss* were recorded by Lucy Balian in 1956–57.

of the criteria they utilized in assigning the cases. They appeared to be in essential agreement in these respects. In short, within the limits of the inequalities imposed by the differences in the nature of the raw data for the two samples and the methods by which the basic history material was obtained, it would seem that the ratings of the various history factors were reasonably reliable and no obviously biasing and unbalanced factor operated which would serve to either exaggerate or diminish true differences between the two groups.

Consideration must also be given to the possibility that such differences as were obtained between the two samples might be a function of the different periods of time from which they were sampled. As pointed out in discussing the difference in mean educational level of the two groups, the schizophrenic patients were hospitalized between 1938–1944. Approximately 80% of these patients were between the ages of 20–50 when hospitalized. Using these ages as a reference point for the sample and defining childhood and early adolescence as encompassing the first 15 years of life, this period occurred for the bulk of the schizophrenics between 1890–1940. By contrast, the normals (with the same age distributions as the schizophrenics) were evaluated in 1956–1957. For these *S*s, the period of childhood and early adolescence would fall predominantly in years 1910–1950. It would be difficult to ascertain the degree to which these two periods would be characterized by distinctive patterns of parental attitude, child-rearing practices, major social upheaval, and other potential sources of psychological effects in the early life histories of individuals. Such contrast could be best drawn for the earliest period represented in the schizophrenics (1890–1910) and the most recent period sampled in the normals (1940–1950), but these periods would account for the "formative years" of only a small portion of each of the groups. The overlap in childhood years for the two samples is great, and such significant factors as the impact of Freudian psychology, the first World War, and the Great Depression occurred in the time interval common to both. It seems unlikely that broad differences in the sociopsychological cultures from which the schizophrenics and normals were drawn can be used to account for their respective distributions on the personal history variables analyzed in this study. In any event, if significant social and cultural factors did indeed differentiate the periods 1890–1910 and 1940–1950, and such factors had causal potency for personality development, they should contribute to more and larger differences between the schizophrenics and normals. The restricted number of differences obtained and the impressive amount of overlap between the two groups suggests limited existence and/or potency of differential sociological factors.

Finally, the lack of more extensive and clear-cut differences between the backgrounds of the two samples might be attributed to the fact that they did not actually represent distinct populations of the psychiatrically ill and the psychiatrically negative. No quarrel can be made with the diagnoses of the schizophrenics. They clearly suffered psychotic disturbance of sufficient magnitude to necessitate hospitalization. Furthermore, they received their specific diagnoses at a time when schizophrenia was not being used as a synonym for all psychosis without obvious brain pathology.

Some clinicians undoubtedly would take exception to the "normality" of our control group. It should be iterated that they denied any history of mental illness or psychiatric consultation, and they manifested no evidence of gross emotional disturbance at the time they were interviewed in spite of the fact that they were currently under study or treatment for serious physical illnesses. The MMPIs administered as an objective check on psychiatric status supported the clinical impression of essential normality. As shown in Table 7, the mean scores on this psychiatric screening test were well within normal limits. A further analysis of the quality of the normal group was made by identifying those *S*s whose histories included one or more of the events or experiences which are generally regarded as psychic trauma. The MMPIs of this group of 37 persons (nearly one-fourth of the normal sample) were compared with those of the remaining "nontraumatized" sample. Mean profiles of the two subgroups are reported in Table 7. Only the *K* and *D*

Table 7. *MMPI Scores Obtained by Normal Controls.*

	Mean *T* Scores				
Scale	Female ($N = 75$)	Male ($N = 57$)	"Traumatized" ($N = 37$)	"Nontraumatized" ($N = 95$)	Ratio
?	50	50			
L	53	50	4.27 ± 1.98	4.01 ± 2.21	0.6
F	50	53	3.78 ± 2.98	2.88 ± 2.13	1.66
K	59	59	14.43 ± 5.47	17.56 ± 4.00	4.35[a]
Hs	56	57	57.73 ± 9.41	55.88 ± 10.30	1.0
D	57	58	62.27 ± 11.11	54.38 ± 9.74	3.75[a]
Hy	59	60	59.95 ± 8.21	59.26 ± 8.43	0.43
Pd	55	60	57.46 ± 11.53	57.69 ± 9.08	0.11
Mf	51	55	51.76 ± 10.21	52.46 ± 8.55	0.37
Pa	56	53	54.43 ± 7.87	53.77 ± 7.93	0.44
Pt	55	56	56.62 ± 8.86	55.48 ± 8.61	0.67
Sc	55	57	56.81 ± 9.64	55.83 ± 6.86	0.56
Ma	53	55	53.68 ± 9.64	53.94 ± 10.41	0.13

[a]Exceeds the .01 level.

scales distinguish these cases. The "traumatized" group had a lower mean *K* score ($t = 4.35; P < .01$) and a higher mean *D* score ($t = 3.75; P < .01$). These observations suggest a less defensive and somewhat more depressive orientation in the *S*s with the traumatic histories. The lack of more extensive differentiation of these two subgroups throw a further doubt on the hypothesis that early traumas per se are significant predisposing factors in later mental illness.

The data of this study seem to cast serious doubt on the etiological significance of certain early life factors for which such import has been frequently claimed. These factors may in fact play a causal role in the development of personality disturbance, but not as solitary pathogenic elements. It would appear that it is the patterning or chaining of experiences rather than occurrence or absence which must be examined. While the notion of multiple causation is well established, it is more frequently stated in the context of types of etiological agent—the physical and the psychological—rather than in terms of multiplicity within a given area—personal relationships.

The surprising frequency with which certain forms of pathogenic experiences or circumstances were found in the life histories of the normal *S*s suggests the need to think in terms of "suppressor" experiences or control variables in the development of personality. Woolley (1953) found cold, rejecting, or dominating and exploiting mothers to be "regularly" present in 100 cases selected only for the adequacy of their histories, but stipulated:

> These factors constitute the background for the children who escape as well as for their schizophrenic siblings. Moreover, there are families in which no schizophrenic denouements occur. Evidently, there must be factors concerning the degree of rejection, its time of occurrence, its differential distributing among the siblings or the occurrence of reinforcing or ameliorating experiences.

May it not be that the development of serious mental disorder will be less well understood if we concentrate solely on examination of pathological processes and injurious agents, rather than examining for the nature and extent of "immunizing" experiences? It seems necessary that we turn some of our research energies toward a discovery of those circumstances of experiences of life which either contribute directly to mental health and emotional stability or which serve to delimit or erase the effects of pathogenic events. For this purpose, we will need to make extensive psychological study of the biographies of normal persons as well as of patients, with such biographies recorded so that their coverage and uniformity facilitate analysis.

SUMMARY AND CONCLUSIONS

Through the medium of extended clinical interviews the life histories of 150 psychiatrically normal subjects were collected and subsequently recorded in detail on a research schedule which had been used previously in a study of the histories of 178 hospitalized schizophrenics. Of the 150 normals, 119 were hospital or clinic patients being studied and treated for a wide range of serious physical illnesses. Selection of the normals was made so that they were drawn from the same general population as the psychiatric patients, and they were matched with the schizophrenics for age, sex, and marital status.

Separate statistical analyses were made of the reliability of the differences between the distributions of the normals and schizophrenics on 35 major aspects of early history and adjustment. Of these 35 variables, 13 (or 37%) failed to reveal a reliable difference between the two samples. On 5 of the 22 variables which yielded reliable differences, the normals were characterized by greater frequency of the undesirable or pathogenic factor. Specifically, the normals had a greater frequency of poverty and invalidism in their childhood homes, poorer heterosexual adjustment and adequacy of sexual outlet, and a greater incidence of an intellectualized, ritualized orientation toward religion. Additionally, the greater frequency of divorce in the childhood homes of the normals approached reliability.

The schizophrenics were characterized by reliably higher incidence of unfavorable relationships with mothers and fathers, poorer attitudes toward and achievement in school, less occupational success and satisfaction, higher rates of social withdrawal, lack of social adeptness and poise, narrow interests, limited aspiration, vague life plans, and lack of initiative. These personal history characteristics which are predominant in the schizophrenics are in line with the general description which has been made of the preschizophrenic personality and lend some support to the central concept of withdrawal. However, the extent to which these same characteristics were found in closely approximate proportions in the histories of the normals suggests the need for great reservation in interpreting the isolated schizophrenogenic potency of such factors as the mother-child relationship.

The notion that any single circumstance, deprivation, or trauma contributes uniformly and inevitably to the etiology of schizophrenia is called into serious question. The necessity of studying the incidence of such factors in appropriate samples is exemplified. It is suggested that the patterning of life experiences may be more crucial than occurrence or absence of specific psychic stresses. The finding of "traumatic" histories in nearly a fourth of the normal subjects suggests the operation of "suppressor" experiences or psychological processes of immunization. It is suggested that improved insights into mental illness may be afforded by careful, intensive studies of the life histories of normals.

REFERENCES

Aldrich, C. K., & Coffin, M. Clinical studies of psychoses in the Navy. I. Prediction values of social histories and the Harrower-Erickson Test. *J. nerv. ment. Dis.*, 1948, **108**, 36–44.

Breuer, J., & Freud, S. *Studies on hysteria.* J. Strachey (Trans.) New York: Basic Books, 1957.

Brockway, A. L., Gleser, G., Winakur, G., & Ulett, G. A. The use of a control population in neuropsychiatric research (psychiatric, psychological, and EEG evaluation of a heterogeneous sample). *Amer. J. Psychiat.*, 1954, **3**, 248–262.

Dahlstrom, W. G. An exploration of mental status syndromes by factor analytic techniques. Unpublished doctoral dissertation, Univer. of Minnesota, 1949.

Lane, Robert C. Familial attitudes of paranoid schizophrenic and normal individuals of different socioeconomic levels. Unpublished doctoral dissertation, New York Univ., 1955.

Nielsen, G. K. The childhood of schizophrenics. *Acta psychiat. neurol. Kbh.*, 1954, **29**, 281–290.

Schofield, W., Hathaway, S. R., Hastings, D. W., & Bell, Dorothy. Prognostic factors in schizophrenia. *J. consult. Psychol.*, 1954, **18**, 155–166.

Shaffer, L. F., & Shoben, E. J., Jr. *The psychology of adjustment.* (2nd ed.) New York: Houghton Mifflin, 1956.

Steinberg, D. L., & Wittman, M. P. Etiologic factors in the adjustment of men in the Armed Forces. *War Med.*, 1943, **4**, 129–139.

Walker, H. M., & Lev. J. *Statistical inference.* New York: Holt, 1953.

Woolley, L. F. Experimental factors essential to the development of schizophrenia. In P. Hoch, & J. Zubin (Eds.), *Current problems in psychiatric diagnosis.* New York: Grune & Stratton, 1953.

Chapter 11

Antisocial Personality

Until relatively recently, experimental and empirical data about antisocial personalities were sparse. This is surprising in view of the puzzling picture that the antisocial individual presents clinically. Here we have someone who exhibits none of the usual symptoms of neurosis, psychophysiological disturbance, or psychosis. Yet, his behavior is clearly disabling and maladaptive.

Now there is some research that begins to put the pieces of the puzzle together. Our three selections are but small samples of this research. The first experiment, which was originally the doctoral dissertation of David Lykken at the University of Minnesota, demonstrated that "primary" sociopaths showed significantly less test and laboratory anxiety than "secondary" or "neurotic" sociopaths.

Pitching his study at a somewhat more physiological level, Robert D. Hare, in the second paper, explores the cardiac and respiration and muscular responsivity of antisocial persons.

Using a novel approach to behavior modification among delinquents, Robert Schwitzgebel's paper completes this chapter with a study in which a scheme is shown for delivering rewards by a remote instrumentation system.

A Study of Anxiety in the Sociopathic Personality*

David T. Lykken

The concept of the psychopathic personality includes so heterogeneous a group of behavior disorders as to be at least two steps removed from the level of useful psychiatric diagnosis. Sociopathic personality is a more recent designation (1) which refers to a subgroup of these disorders in which the pathognomic characteristics are impulsiveness, antisocial tendencies, immorality, and a seemingly self-destructive failure to modify this pattern of behavior in spite of repeated painful consequences. This category may be regarded as a genus composed of phenotypically similar, but etiologically distinct, subtypes such as the dissocial and the neurotic sociopaths.

A third species has been described (3, 12, 13, 14, 17), which may be called *primary sociopathy*, in which neither neurotic motivations, hereditary taint, nor dissocial nurture seem to be determining factors. Cleckley (3) has reported the chief clinical characteristic of this group as a lack of the normal affective accompaniments of experience. If this observation is correct, it would point the way toward accurate diagnostic isolation of primary sociopathy as well as guiding research into the question of its etiology. Classification according to the presence or absence of defective emotional reactivity, therefore, satisfies one criterion of useful diagnosis in that it shows promise of relationship to the as yet unknown origins of the disorders to be distinguished.

The other requirement for useful diagnosis is that the criteria of classification must be objective. Clinical assessment of the "normality of the affective accompaniments of experience" is subjective and unreliable. In consequence, Cleckley's work has had as yet little real impact on psychiatric practice. By expressing this putative defect of the primary sociopath in terms of the anxiety construct of experimental psychology (18, 19, 20, 21, 22), it becomes susceptible to quantification and empirical test.

An experimental hypothesis may now be formulated. Among persons conventionally diagnosed as psychopathic personality, those who closely resemble the syndrome described by Cleckley are (*a*) clearly defective as compared to normals in their ability to develop (i.e. *condition*) anxiety, in the sense of an anticipatory emotional response to warning signals previously associated with nociceptive stimulation. Persons with such a defect would also be expected to show (*b*) abnormally little *manifest anxiety* in life situations normally conducive to this response, and to be (*c*) relatively incapable of *avoidance learning* under circumstances where such learning can only be effected through the mediation of the anxiety response.

METHOD

The Sample

The extreme heterogeneity, even on the crudest descriptive level, of persons diagnosed as psychopathic personalities in various clinical or institutional settings complicated the selection of an appropriate experimental sample. The institution psychologists[1] were given a list of 14 criteria drawn from Cleckley (3, pp. 355–392) and were asked to compare against these criteria those inmates diagnosed as psychopathic personality. Inmates who, in their opinion, best fitted the Cleckley prototype were listed as candidates for experimental Group I, the primary sociopathic group. Inmates who they felt did *not* meet the criteria in important respects were listed as candidates for experimental Group II, designated as the neurotic sociopathic group. In this selection process, the psychologists were asked to reaffirm the original diagnosis, discarding from consideration for either group those inmates who, in their present opinion, would not be diagnosed as psychopathic personality at all.

A control Group III of 15 "normals," roughly comparable in age, intelligence, and socioeconomic background,

From *Journal of Abnormal and Social Psychology*, 1957, **55**, 6–10.

*Drawn from a thesis submitted to the University of Minnesota in partial fulfillment of the requirements for the degree of Doctor of Philosophy. The author is indebted to his adviser, Professor Ephraim Rosen, and to others whose assistance aided in the completion of this research.

[1] The writer is indebted to the administrators and to the psychologists of the Minnesota State Reformatory, St. Cloud, Minnesota; the Minnesota State Reformatory for Women, Shakopee, Minnesota; the State Home for Girls, Sauk Centre, Minnesota; and the St. Peter State Hospital, St. Peter, Minnesota.

was selected from the University General College and a local high school.

Group I, composed of 12 males and 7 females, had a mean age of 21.6 years (SD = 4.3), and a mean IQ of 109.2 (SD = 10.7). Group II included 13 males and 7 females, had a mean age of 24.5 years (SD = 5.4), and a mean IQ of 104.5 (SD = 8.8). For the 10 male and 5 female normals, the mean age was 19.07 (SD = 3.2), and the mean IQ 100.4 (SD = 10.2). None of these group differences were significant.

The Measures and Testing Procedure

It was necessary to do the testing at the several institutions under varying conditions. In all cases, however, the apparatus was arranged on a large table, the experimenter on one side and the subject (*S*) seated comfortably opposite. The *S* was told that he was assisting in a psychological experiment having no bearing on his personal record and that his performance would be treated with strict anonymity. An attempt was made throughout to keep the testing on an informal basis.

As an indicant of manifest anxiety as referred to in hypothesis *b*, an "Anxiety Scale" was constructed expressly for this study to supplement the Taylor scale and Anxiety Index which appear to be more strongly loaded on a factor of neurotic self-description. In this new scale, each of the thirty-three items involves two statements of activities or occurrences, matched for general unpleasantness or undesirability according to a modified Thurstone scaling procedure utilizing 15 college student judges. One activity of each pair is unpleasant, presumably because of its frightening or embarrassing character (e.g., "making a parachute jump" or "knocking over a glass in a restaurant"). The paired activity is intended to be onerous but not frightening (e.g., "digging a big rubbish pit" or "cleaning up a spilled bottle of syrup"). The *S* is required to choose that member of each pair which he would prefer as a lesser of evils. The degree to which the "frightening" alternatives are rejected is interpreted as an index of the extent to which anxiety determines behavior choices within the range of life situations sampled by this test.

The booklet form of the MMPI was used and the answer sheets scored and *K*-corrected in the usual way (10). The Anxiety Index, or AI, was calculated according to the formula given by Welsh (23). The Heineman form (11) of the Taylor scale was given and scored by subtracting the number of "anxiety" items rejected as "least applies to me" from the number endorsed as "most applies to me."

An avoidance learning test was given to determine whether there were group differences in capacity to learn on the basis of anxiety reduction (hypothesis *c*). It involved an elaborate, electrically operated mental maze which the *S* was given 20 trials to learn (the "manifest task"). At each of the 20 choice points in this maze, choice of one of the 4 possible alternatives (always an error alternative) gave an electric shock. It was intended that social and ego rewards should reinforce performance in the manifest task. Performance on the "latent task," which was to avoid the shocked alternatives—to err instead on the unshocked alternatives—was presumably reinforced only through anxiety reduction.

The measure of anxiety conditionability (hypothesis *a*) employed the GSR as the dependent variable. A shocking electrode was attached to *S*'s nondominant hand, the GSR electrodes being already in place on the dominant hand. The *S* was told that after the blindfold had been replaced, he was to sit as quietly as possible for the next 30 to 40 minutes, during which time he would periodically hear a buzzer (which was then demonstrated) and occasionally receive a brief electric shock. When the *S* was seated comfortably and relaxed insofar as possible, the recording apparatus was started and the conditioning series (CS) begun.

Two buzzers were used which were distinguishably different in timbre rather than in pitch, the difference being one not easily labeled (to minimize verbal mediation of a discrimination between them). Buzzer No. 1 was used as the CS and was the only one reinforced; buzzer No. 2 was used to test for generalization effects. In all cases, stimuli of the conditioning series were presented as soon as GSR activity from preceding stimuli had subsided, the intertrial interval being therefore not constant within or between *S*s, but averaging between 20 and 60 seconds. (This method of stimulus timing automatically eliminates temporal conditioning.) When turned on, the buzzers sounded for a period of 5 seconds, controlled by an automatic timer.

The reinforcing stimulus or UnCS was an electric shock from a 700-volt AC supply through two 68,000-ohm series resistors, presented automatically for about 100 milliseconds just before the termination of the CS (buzzer No. 1). The shock was applied between an electrode on the palm of one hand and the GSR *ground* electrode on the palmar tip of the middle finger of the opposite hand. The shock sensation was felt mainly on the richly innervated finger tip and was a decidedly unpleasant stimulus, producing in most cases a pronounced startle reaction and in all cases a strong GSR.

The sequence of trials or stimulus presentations was as follows:

1. To permit the adaptation of unconditioned GSR to the buzzers themselves, stimuli were first presented without shock reinforcement for a total of 10 trials in the order 2, 1, 2, 1, S, 2, 2, 1, 1, 1, 1. A single preliminary shock was given in the series at the point S, separated by at least 30 seconds from the buzzers occurring before and after it.
2. Seven consecutive shock-reinforced presentations of the CS were given as the conditioning series, followed by four more reinforcements interspersed with four unreinforced trials with buzzer No. 2 in the order 1, 1, 1, 1, 1, 1, 1, 2, 1, 2, 2, 1, 2, 1, 1.
3. A total of 24 extinction trials was then given, the two buzzer stimuli being presented in the order 1, 2, 1, 1, 2, 1, 2, 1, 1, 2, 1, 1, 1, 1, 2, 2, 1, 2, 1, 1, 2, 1, 1, 1. Considering only the CS, buzzer No. 1, the series therefore consisted of 6 prereinforcement trials, 11 reinforced conditioning trials, and 16 extinction trials.

Skin resistance was measured by a modification of a circuit suggested by Flanders (6) which passed an electronically regulated constant DC current of 40 microamperes through *S*. The electrodes were curved discs of Monel metal, 15 mm. in diameter, applied to the palmar surface of the distal phalange of the first, second, and third fingers of the same hand. The skin surface was first scrubbed with alcohol and then coated with Sanborn electrode paste. The exosomatic current was applied between the first and third fingers, which were also connected to the push-pull input grids of a Sanborn Model 126 DC amplifier, driving a Sanborn Model 127 recording milliameter. The electrode on the second finger was connected to amplifier and external ground. The instrument was calibrated before each use and provided a linear record of resistance and resistance change, accurate to less than ±50 ohms.

All GSRs were recorded in terms of resistance change. A variety of transformations was then applied and tested against the usual criteria of normality of distribution, correlation with basal resistance, and homogeneity of variance across people with respect to several test stimuli (2, 8, 9, 16). The result of this analysis was that each resistance change was expressed as the logarithm of the ratio of that change to the mean resistance change produced by the first six electric shocks. This unit expresses the galvanic CR as a proportion of the individual's UnCR and, for a conditioning study, seems quite appropriate for individual comparisons.

Three GSR indices were derived from the protocols of the conditioning series: (*a*) GSR Reactivity, which is the mean GSR to the CS during the fourth through seventh conditioning trials; (*b*) GSR Conditioning, which is equal to (*a*) minus the mean GSR to the last three preconditioning trials and the last three extinction trials (this index measures essentially the slope of the conditioning curve or the increment actually produced by the reinforced trials); (*c*) GSR Generalization, the ratio of the mean GSR to buzzer No. 2 during early extinction trials 18, 20, 21, 23 to the mean GSR to buzzer No. 1 during trials 17, 19, 22, 24.

The testing sequence was as follows: (*a*) anxiety scale; (*b*) GSR Conditioning series; (*c*) Avoidance Learning test; (*d*) MMPI (given during the week following the foregoing individual testing); (*e*) Taylor Manifest Anxiety Scale, forced-choice form given later with the MMPI.

RESULTS AND DISCUSSION

Scores on all measures were converted for easier comparison to a standard score form with each distribution having a grand mean of 500 and a standard deviation of 100. Group means on all measures, together with significance test results, are given in Table 1.

It would clearly be too much to expect of the judgments based upon the Cleckley criteria that they should have perfectly separated the psychopathic sample into a "primary" species in Group I, and a neurotic or dissocial species in Group II. That the separation was reasonably good, however, is supported by the finding that Group II scored significantly higher than the normals on the Taylor scale, a great deal of evidence having accumulated (4, 7, 15) to indicate that this scale is primarily a measure of neurotic maladjustment or neuroticism rather than of anxiety level or anxiety reactivity *per se.* On the MMPI Anxiety Index, which like the Taylor scale is unquestionably polydimensional with a heavy loading on neuroticism, Group II again has the highest mean, with Group I again only slightly higher than Group III.

In contrast, the Anxiety scale, which was designed for this study and which is not loaded on neuroticism and only negligibly correlated with the Taylor scale or the AI, separated the groups in a different order. On this test, the primary types of Group I show the least anxiety reactivity, significantly less than the normals, with Group II falling in between but rather nearer to the Group III mean. This result appears to support hypothesis *b* of this study, that the subset of primary sociopaths show abnormally little manifest anxiety, i.e., anxiety reactivity to the real-life anxiety stimuli referred to in the questionnaire.

Both sociopathic groups scored significantly higher than the normals on the *Pd* scale of the MMPI, but this measure, which differentiates at the phenotypic or genus level, does not distinguish between the types or species of sociopathy represented in Groups I and II.

Schedule difficulties unfortunately led to a reduction in the number of *S*s to whom the avoidance learning test could be given. With nearly half of the total group, the available testing time was too short to cover all of the procedures; in such cases the avoidance test, requiring nearly an hour to give, was passed over. Even on the residual sample of 34 *S*s, however, rather clear-cut differences exist. As a crude, overall index of avoidance learning, the avoidance scores (shock errors divided by unshocked errors) were averaged for all but the first of the 20 trials; this is the basis of the mean scores entered under "avoidance" in Table 1. The distribution was reversed to make high values represent greater avoidance of the shock. It is impossible, of course, to summarize adequately a complex learning process by a single numerical index of this sort, but in spite of these limitations, it is striking that Group I (primaries) shows the least avoidance as expected, Group II (neurotics) next, and Group III (normals) the most. The Group I versus Group III, and Group II versus Group III differences are significant by Festinger's *d*-test (5), and the actual distribution of scores shows the groups to be remarkably well separated (only 17 per cent overlap between Groups I and III). This result supports hypothesis *c* of this study, that the primary sociopath demonstrates defective avoidance learning.

Table 1. *Group Means on All Measures: Significance Tests.*[a]

	Group			*d*-Test
Measure	I	II	III	prob.[b]
Taylor Scale	471	556	462	.01
Anxiety Index	472	557	464	.01
Anxiety Scale	470	511	529	.05
MMPI *Pd*-Scale	532	547	395	.05
Avoidance Learning	461	501	558	.01
GSR Reactivity	498	494	534	.05
GSR Conditioning	478	483	551	.05
Generalization	473	542	490	—

[a] All measures converted to a scale having an over-all mean of 500 and *SD* of 100.
[b] Probabilities given are for significance of largest difference (e.g., III—I for GSR Conditioning). Significance test was Festinger's distribution-free '*d*' test (5).

Results of the GSR Conditioning Series

Of all the tests employed here, principal emphasis should be laid on GSR conditioning. The various difficulties attending the interpretation of GSR data are well known, but one fact stands out with relative certainty: given certain necessary conditions, if an *S* does *not* produce a GSR to a stimulus, one can be sure that he has not "reacted emotionally" to that stimulus.

The two numerical indices which were derived as alternative ways of representing in a single value the conditioning indicated by the GSR protocols (anticipatory GSR to the buzzer after several pairings with shock) have already been described. As shown in Table 1, the group means are in the expected order on both indicants, with Group I significantly lower than Group III on GSR Reactivity and GSR Conditioning (.05 level, *d*-test).

A somewhat more meaningful comparison is obtained by contrasting the reactivity by trials for the three groups. Group I shows the least GSR reaction to the CS in 14 out of the 16 double trials. Group II is significantly higher (.02 level) than Group I at the end of the extinction trials. The positions of Group II and Group III interchange during the series with Group II beginning to show greater reactivity during the extinction trials, suggesting a perseveration (failure of extinction) of the anxiety response in the neurotic group. This trend was tested for statistical reliability by correlating the differences between Group II and Group III with the ordinal position in the conditioning series at which the difference was taken. The quadrant sign test (24) shows this association to be significant at the .01 level. This result supports hypothesis *a* of this study, that the primary sociopath is defective in his ability to condition the anxiety response.

The generalization scores were leptokurtically distributed, the group differences being determined by a few deviant *S*s. Group II shows the highest mean generalization score, but the differences are not significant.

SUMMARY

Forty-nine diagnosed psychopaths were divided into two groups according to the descriptive criteria of Cleckley. Fifteen normals served as controls. A battery of tests related to anxiety reactivity or anxiety conditionability were administered. As compared with normals, the Cleckley, or "primary" sociopaths, showed significantly less "anxiety" on a questionnaire device, less GSR reactivity to a "conditioned" stimulus associated with shock, and less avoidance of punished responses on a test of avoidance learning. The "neurotic" sociopaths scored significantly higher on the Taylor Anxiety Scale and on the Welsh Anxiety Index.

REFERENCES

1. Amer. Psychiatric Assoc. *Diagnostic and statistical manual: mental disorders.* Washington, D.C.: American Psychiatric Assn., 1952.
2. Bitterman, M. E., & Holtzman, W. H. Development of psychiatric screening of flying personnel. III. Conditioning and extinction of the GSR in relation to clinical evidence of anxiety. *USAF Sch. Aviat. Med.*, 1952, Proj. No. 21-37-002, Rep. No. 3, N. 232 p.
3. Cleckley, H. *The mask of sanity.* (2nd ed.) St. Louis: C. V. Mosby, 1950.
4. Eriksen, C. W., & Davids, A. The meaning and clinical validity of the Taylor Anxiety Scale and the hysteria-psychasthenia scales from the MMPI. *J. abnorm. soc. Psychol.*, 1955, **50**, 135–137.
5. Festinger, L. The significance of the difference between means without reference to the frequency distribution function., *Psychometrika*, 1945, **11**, 97–105.
6. Flanders, N. A. A circuit for the continuous measurement of palmar resistance. *Amer. J. Psychol.*, 1953, **66**, 295–299.
7. Franks, C. Conditioning and personality: a study of normal and neurotic subjects. *J. abnorm. soc. Psychol.*, 1956, **52**, 143–150.
8. Haggard, E. A. Experimental studies in affective processes. II. On the quantification and evaluation of "measured" changes in skin resistance. *J. exp. Psychol.*, 1945, **33**, 46–56.
9. Haggard, E. A. On the application of analysis of variance to GSR data. I. The selection of an appropriate measure. *J. exp. Psychol.*, 1949, **39**, 378–392.
10. Hathaway, S. R. *Supplementary manual for the MMPI. Part I, The K scale and its use.* New York: Psychological Corp., 1946.
11. Heineman, C. E. A forced choice form of the Taylor Anxiety Scale. *J. consult. Psychol.*, 1953, **17**, 447–454.
12. Karpman, B. Psychopathic types: the symptomatic and the ideopathic. *J. crim. Psychopathol.*, 1941, **3**, 112–124.
13. Karpman, B. The myth of the psychopathic personality. *Amer. J. Psychiat.*, 1948, **104**, 523–534.
14. Karpman, B. Conscience in the psychopath: another version. *Amer. J. Orthopsychiat.*, 1948, **18**, 455–491.
15. Kerrick, Jean S. Some correlates of the Taylor Manifest Anxiety Scale. *J. abnorm. soc. Psychol.*, 1955, **50**, 75–77.
16. Lacey, O. L., & Siegel, P. S. An analysis of the unit of measurement of the galvanic skin responses. *J. exp. Psychol.*, 1949, **39**, 122–123.
17. Lippman, H. S. Psychopathic behavior in infants and children: a critical survey of existing concepts. *Amer. J. Orthopsychiat.*, 1951, **21**, 227–231.
18. May, M. A. Experimentally acquired drives. *J. exp. Psychol.*, 1948, **38**, 66–77.
19. Miller, N. E. Studies of fear as an acquirable drive. I. Fear as motivation and fear-reduction as reinforcement in the learning of new responses. *J. exp. Psychol.*, 1948, **38**, 89–101.
20. Miller, N. E. Learnable drives and rewards. In S. S. Stevens (Ed.), *Handbook of experimental psychology.* New York: Wiley, 1951. pp. 435–472.
21. Mowrer, O. H. A stimulus-response analysis of anxiety. *Psychol. Rev.*, 1939, **46**, 553–565.
22. Mowrer, O. H. Anxiety reduction and learning. *J. exp. Psychol.*, 1940, **27**, 497–516.
23. Welsh, G. S. An anxiety index and an internalization ratio for the MMPI. *J. consult. Psychol.*, 1952, **16**, 65–72.
24. Wilcoxon, F. *Some rapid approximate statistical procedures.* New York: American Cyanamid Co., 1949.

Psychopathy and Physiological Responses to Adrenalin

Robert D. Hare

Physiological recordings were taken while 16 psychopaths (P), 16 nonpsychopaths (NP), and 16 "mixed" (M) Ss received an injection of saline, followed 15 min. later by an injection of adrenalin. Tonic skin conductance of Group NP was generally greater than that of Groups M and P, a difference that increased throughout the course of the experiment. There were no significant group differences in tonic heart rate, respiration rate, blink rate, or electromyogram (EMG) activity. Both saline and adrenalin injections produced sharp increases in skin conductance, blink rate, digital vasoconstriction, and EMG activity, but these changes were more persistent with adrenalin. Adrenalin also produced large and prolonged increases in heart rate, while saline had virtually no effect on heart rate. With one exception, there were no significant differences between groups in responsivity. The exception involved electrodermal activity—the increases in skin conductance following saline and adrenalin were smaller in Group P than they were in Group NP. Physiological responses given by each group were unrelated to scores on the Activity Preference Questionnaire. The results therefore do not support earlier claims that psychopaths show extreme cardiac lability in response to adrenalin. On the other hand, they are consistent with the view that psychopaths are electrodermally hypoactive.

During recent years, there has been an increasing amount of interest shown in the physiological correlates of psychopathy. Much of this research has been concerned with the autonomic responses of psychopaths to simple stimuli and mild stressors, often in the context of a classical conditioning experiment (see reviews by Hare, 1968, 1970; Hare & Quinn, 1971). Several studies, however, have used an injection of adrenalin as the basis for making inferences about the functioning of the autonomic nervous system in psychopaths.

In one study (Schachter & Latané, 1964), *S*s were given an intramuscular injection of .5 cc of a 1:1,000 solution of adrenalin chloride prior to engaging in an avoidance learning task. Pulse rate was taken by a physician prior to the injection and after *S* had completed the task (about 30 min.). Although the mean pulse rate of psychopathic *S*s increased more than did that of nonpsychopathic ones, the difference was not significant. Subsequently, continuous heart rate recordings were made from four psychopaths and four nonpsychopaths who were engaged in the avoidance learning task. The psychopaths showed a significantly larger increase in heart rate under adrenalin than did the nonpsychopaths. On the basis of these findings, along with the citation of other studies of doubtful relevance (e.g., an unpublished study by Schachter & Ono), Schachter and Latané concluded that the cardiovascular system of psychopaths is unusually responsive to adrenalin. However, it appears that not even Schachter (1971, p. 14) is entirely convinced of the soundness of this conclusion, nor of the data upon which it was based.

In a recent paper,[1] Goldman, Lindner, Dinitz, and Allen (1971) reported that the heart rate response of psychopaths to a .5-mg. intramuscular injection of adrenalin, given just prior to an avoidance learning task, was not significantly larger than that of nonpsychopaths, thus failing to replicate Schachter and Latané's (1964) findings. However, Goldman et al. stated that upon examining their data further they discovered that adrenalin produced a significantly greater increase in heart rate in those psychopathic *S*s ($n = 11$) with low scores on Lykken's (1955) Activity Preference Questionnaire (APQ) than in those with high scores ($n = 8$). On the basis of biographical data obtained from *S*s' institution files, the authors concluded that the low APQ–high cardiac lability *S*s were "simple" psychopaths, while the high APQ–low cardiac lability *S*s were "hostile" psychopaths. However, it is apparent that the labels simple and hostile and the categories they ostensibly represent are gratuitous. The differences in cardiac responsivity, reported by Gold-

From *Journal of Abnormal Psychology*, 1972, **79**,138–147.

This research was supported by Public Health Grant 609-7-163 from the National Health Grants Program (Canada), Grant MA-4511 from the Canadian Medical Mental Health Association. Derek Neale, staff psychiatrist, helped select *S*s, conducted the medical interviews, and along with Roger Brock, provided helpful comments and advice. The collection and analysis of data were carried out by Thomas Taylor and Janice Frazelle. The cooperation of the staff and inmates of Matsqui Institution is gratefully acknowledged.

[1] Essentially the same data were published in an earlier paper (Lindner, Goldman, Dinitz, & Allen, 1970), both papers being based upon a PhD dissertation by the last author (Allen, 1969).

man et al. as being significant at the .05 level, were in fact nonsignificant, as perusal of Allen's (1969) dissertation, from which the data were taken, clearly indicates. Further, only a few of the large number of reported group differences in social characteristics and criminal histories were significant, and in some cases the differences could be related to the age difference between groups. It is important to note here that virtually no physiological data, beyond a very crude summary, were actually presented by Goldman et al., nor indeed by Allen (1969).

There are several other limitations of the studies discussed so far. For example, the effects of adrenalin upon heart rate were probably confounded with the cardiovascular effects of engaging in the avoidance learning task (Hare, 1972; Lacey, 1967). Data on only a single physiological variable, heart rate, were presented. And, in the case of the Goldman et al. (1971) paper, the data were presented in a somewhat cryptic fashion.

In the present study, a variety of autonomic and somatic responses to adrenalin was continuously monitored. The *S*s were not required to engage in any specific cognitive or motor activity that could influence their physiological responses.

METHOD

Subjects

The *S*s were male inmates of the Matsqui Institution, a medium-security institution near Abbotsford, British Columbia. The selection procedure was similar to that used in earlier studies (Hare, 1968; Hare & Quinn, 1971). The concepts of psychopathy outlined by Cleckley (1964) were discussed with members of the institution's professional staff, each of whom was asked to submit the names of inmates known to him and whom he could roughly categorize as psychopathic or nonpsychopathic. The author and two of his research associates then read each potential *S*'s file and independently made a global assessment of the extent to which they were confident that a given *S* was or was not a psychopath. A 7-point scale was used for this assessment, with a rating of 1 indicating that the rater was very confident that *S* was a psychopath and a rating of 7 indicating that he was certain *S* was not. A separate assessment based upon interviews and case histories was made by the staff psychiatrist. The *S*s given a rating of 1 or 2 by all raters were designated psychopaths (P), while those given a rating of 6 or 7 were considered to be nonpsychopaths (NP). A third group of *S*s received ratings of 3, 4, or 5 and included inmates who met some of the criteria of psychopathy but about whom there was considerable doubt, usually because of insufficient data. The *S*s in this group probably represented a heterogeneous mixture of misclassified psychopaths and nonpsychopaths, as well as those who could be termed neurotic "psychopaths" or acting-out neurotics (Arieti, 1967; Hare, 1970). The term mixed group (M) seems appropriate here.

There was a total of 48 *S*s, 16 in each group. Ten other inmates refused to participate in the experiment. Seven of the 10 would have been placed in Group P had they chosen to take part.

Mean age, Revised Beta IQ, and years of education were, respectively, 31.3, 104.1, and 8.8 for Group P; 35.1, 106.1, and 8.3 for Group M; and 30.4, 105.9, and 7.6 for Group NP. None of the differences between groups was significant. Age, IQ, and education were similar to those obtained for comparable groups in earlier studies (Hare, 1968; Hare & Quinn, 1971; Hare & Thorvaldson, 1970).

Five of the *S*s in Group P, nine in Group M, and nine in Group NP were legally classified as heroin addicts. Although the proportion of addicts to nonaddicts was smaller in Group P than in the other groups, the difference was not significant.

Mean scores on the revised version of Lykken's APQ (Lykken & Katzenmeyer, 1968) were 42.1 for Group P, 43.3 for Group M, and 44.9 for Group NP, $F < 1.0$. Although these scores seem somewhat high according to the norms provided by Lykken and Katzenmeyer, the failure of the APQ to differentiate between nonpsychopathic inmates and carefully diagnosed psychopathic inmates is noteworthy.

Since there was some possibility that the physiological responses of *S*s would be related to the absorption rate of adrenalin, a number of physical characteristics of the *S*s were determined during the medical interview. There were no appreciable differences between groups in mean height, weight, arm and shoulder musculature, body type, or skinfold thickness.

Apparatus

A Grass Model 7 polygraph was used to obtain simultaneous recordings of skin resistance, heart rate, respiration rate, vasomotor activity, blink rate, and muscle tension (EMG). Skin resistance recordings were taken from Beckman biopotential electrodes attached to the first and third fingers of the left hand. Heart rate was recorded from biopotential electrodes placed on the sternum and left side of the rib cage, with the output from the polygraph being expressed in beats per minute. Changes in digital vasomotor activity were measured by placing a photocell transducer on the second finger of the right hand and passing the signal through a preamplifier with a time constant of .1 sec. EMG activity was assessed by passing the input from Beckman miniature electrodes placed on the mental and submental areas of the chin through a preamplifier with a time constant of .02 sec. The output was not integrated. Eye blinks and gross eye movements were recorded from the right eye with Beckman miniature electrodes placed at the outer angle of the eye and just below the eye; time constant was .1 sec. A chest bellows and pressure transducer were used to obtain recordings of respiratory activity.

Procedure

Before taking part in the experiment, each *S* was given a medical examination to determine whether an injection or adrenalin would be likely to have any adverse effects upon him. He was then taken into the experimental room where the general procedures to be used were explained to him, including the fact that injections of adrenalin and saline were to be administered while physiological responses were recorded.

The experiment was conducted with *S* lying on a hospital bed separated from *E* and his equipment by a screen. About 15 min. after the electrodes had been attached, *S* was given an intramuscular injection of .5 cc of physiological saline in the shoulder. Fifteen minutes later he was given an injection of .5 cc of Parke, Davis Adrenalin Solution. The experiment terminated about 20 min. after this second injection.

The saline and adrenalin solutions were administered in a single session because institutional routine made it difficult to have *S*s back for a second session. In addition, some *S*s would have been released before a second session could have been arranged. The saline was always administered first, although *S*s were not told what order the injections would follow. Since the effects of adrenalin are relatively persistent, it was felt that better separation between the effects of saline and adrenalin could be obtained by giving the saline first, rather than administering them in counterbalanced order.

RESULTS

Resting Tonic Levels

Measurements of "resting" levels of tonic activity were made at three points in the experiment prior to the injection of adrenalin. These were (*a*) the 1-min. period beginning about 2 min. after the electrodes had been attached; (*b*) the 1-min. period just prior to injection of saline; and (*c*) the 1-min. period just before injection of adrenalin. The interval between the first and second periods was approximately 12 min., while that between the second and third periods was about 14 min. A fourth measurement was taken 20 min. after injection of adrenalin, that is, just at the end of the experiment.

Tonic skin conductance. Mean tonic skin conductance (SC) of each group is plotted in Figure 1. Although the SC of Group MP was generally greater than that of the other groups, the overall differences were not significant, $F = 1.91$, $df = 2/45$, $p > .10$. However, there was a significant Groups × Periods interaction, $F = 2.64$, $df = 6/135$, $p < .05$, with Group NP showing an increase and Group P a decrease over the first three periods. Post hoc analyses confirmed that the differences between Group NP and each of the other groups were significant ($p < .01$ in each case) during the third and the fourth periods.

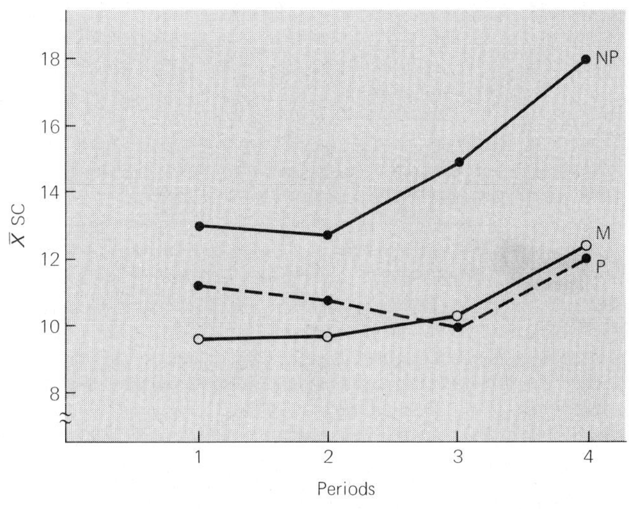

Fig. 1. Mean tonic skin conductance (μmhos/cm²) of each group throughout the experiment. (Period 1 is just after electrode hook-up; Periods 2 and 3 are just prior to injections of saline and adrenalin, respectively; and Period 4 is at the end of the experiment. P = psychopaths; M = mixed; NP = nonpsychopaths.)

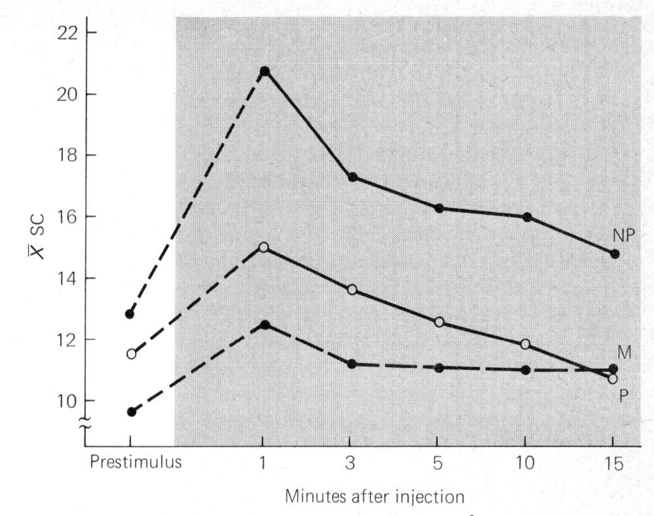

Fig. 2. Mean skin conductance (μmhos/cm²) in response to saline injection. (P = psychopaths; M = mixed; NP = nonpsychopaths.)

Tonic heart rate. Mean tonic heart rate of Group P during each period was 69.5, 67.8, 66.0, and 77 bpm. Corresponding values were 69.4, 68.0, 65.5, and 73.4 for Group M, and 68.4, 67.3, 65.2, and 76 for Group NP. There were no overall differences between groups, $F < 1.0$; however, the general decrease of about 4 bpm from the first to the third period and the increase of about 10 bpm from the third to the fourth period were highly significant ($p < .001$ in both cases).

Other variables. No significant group, period, or interaction effects were found for respiration rate, blink rate, or EMG activity.

Responses to Saline

Each record was scored for the mean heart rate, skin conductance, digital pulse amplitude (PA), respiration rate, blink rate, and EMG activity occurring during the 1-min. period preceding saline injection and during the first, third, fifth, tenth, and fifteenth minutes after saline injection.

Heart rate. The increase in heart rate produced by saline injection was extremely small (< 1 bpm) and nonsignificant. None of the differences between groups was significant ($F < 1.0$).

Skin conductance. Mean skin conductance during the period following saline injection is plotted in Figure 2. The differences between groups in the increase in conductance from the prestimulus level to the first minute after injection were significant, $F = 7.51$, $df = 2/45$, $p < .01$, with post hoc analyses indicating that Group NP showed a larger increase ($p < .01$) than did either Group P or Group M. However, since the differences in response amplitude may have been related to the differences in prestimulus skin conductance, the data were subjected to analysis of covariance, with prestimulus conductance as the covariate. The results were essentially unchanged, with the difference between groups still significant, $F = 7.35$, $df = 2/44$, $p < .01$.

The general decrease in conductance from the first to the fifteenth minute was significant, $F = 28.28$, $df = 4/180$, $p < .001$. However, the Groups × Minutes interaction, $F = 3.06$, $df = 8/180$, $p < .001$, along with post hoc analyses, indicates that the decrease was greater for Groups P and NP than for Group M, and that during the fifteenth minute, the SC of Group NP was significantly greater than that of Group P.

Digital pulse amplitude. Changes in digital PA were expressed as deviations (in millivolts) from the mean PA observed during the 1-min. period prior to injection. The vasomotor response given by each group was a marked decrease in PA (vasoconstriction) during the first minute after injection, $F = 31.17$, $df = 1/45$, $p < .001$. Recovery was rapid, being about 70% complete by the third minute. There were no differences between groups in the size of the vasoconstrictive response or in the rate of recovery, $F < 1.0$ in each case.

Respiration rate. Saline produced only about a 3% increase over the preinjection rate of 15.6 respiratory cycles/sec ($p < .10$), an increase that lasted for only a few minutes and was unrelated to the diagnosis of *S*s, $F < 1.0$.

Blink rate. The ocular response to the injection was a sharp increase in blink rate, from a mean of 13.1 in the preinjection period to a mean of 27.3 during the first minute after injection, $F = 33.53$, $df = 1/45$, $p < .001$. The return to the preinjection rate was rapid, being almost completed by the fifth minute. Group differences were small and nonsignificant.

EMG. An attempt was made to quantify muscle tension of the chin by computing, for each 1-min. period, the area of the "envelope" produced by the excursions of the EMG recording pen, and expressing the results in millivolt-seconds. EMG activity increased by about 25% during the first minute after injection, $F = 19.82$, $df = 1/45$, $p < .001$. This activity had almost completely subsided by the fifth minute. None of the differences between groups was significant.

Responses to Adrenalin

Each record was scored for the mean heart rate, skin conductance, digital PA, respiration rate, blink rate, and EMG activity occurring during the 1-min period preceding adrenalin injection and during each of the 20 1-min. periods following injection.

Heart rate. Adrenalin produced large, prolonged increases in the heart rate of all three groups. As Figure 3 indicates, the increase began shortly after the injection (especially in Group NP) and persisted for at least 20 min. The general increase over the 20-min. period was highly significant, $F = 16.69$, $df = 19/855$, $p < .001$. Although Figure 3 suggests that there may have been group differences in the rate and

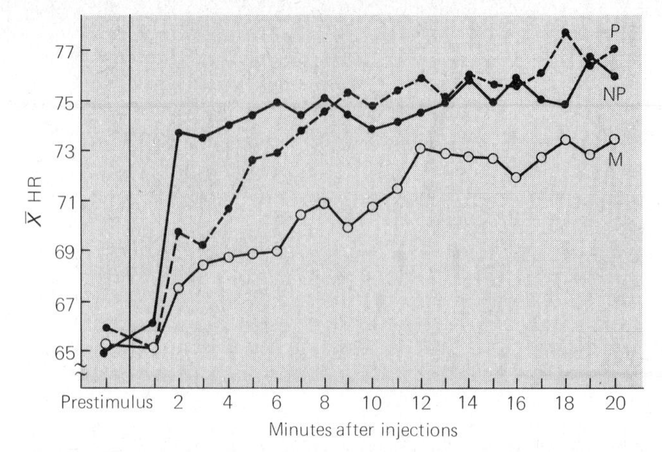

Fig. 3. Mean heart rate (bpm) in response to adrenalin injection. (P = psychopaths; M = mixed; NP = nonpsychopaths. Appearances notwithstanding, the differences between groups were not significant.)

extent of the increase shown, the Groups × Minutes interaction was not statistically significant, $F = 1.23$, $df = 38/855$, $p < .20$. Subsequent analyses indicated that there were no significant differences between groups in the magnitude of heart rate increase from the first to the second minute, $F = 1.37$, $df = 2/45$, $p > .20$. Similarly, there were no significant differences between groups in mean heart rate during the second minute, $F = 1.54$, $df = 2/45$, $p > .20$, or during any subsequent period.

An additional analysis compared the mean heart rate of each group during the first, third, fifth, tenth, and fifteenth minutes after adrenalin with that observed during comparable intervals after injection of saline. The Injections (adrenalin versus saline) × Minutes interaction, $F = 24.83$, $df = 4/180$, $p < .001$, confirmed that adrenalin produced the larger cardiac acceleration.

Skin conductance. Mean changes in skin conductance following adrenalin injection are presented in Figure 4. There was a significant difference between groups in the increase from the preinjection level of skin conductance to the level during the first minute after injection, $F = 3.52$, $df = 2/45$, $p < .05$, with Group NP obviously giving the largest response. There were group differences in mean conductance throughout the 20-min period, $F = 4.33$, $df = 2/45$, $p < .02$; it is apparent from Figure 4, confirmed by post hoc analyses, that the difference was between Group NP and each of the other groups. All three groups recovered from the effects of adrenalin at about the same rate, the Groups × Minutes interaction being small and nonsignificant.

Additional analyses indicate that the magnitude of the increase in conductance produced by saline and adrenalin was similar, $F = 1.0$. However, the Injections × Minutes interaction, $F = 3.34$, $df = 4/180$, $p < .02$, indicates that recovery from the effects of adrenalin was slower than it was from saline.

Digital pulse amplitude. Adrenalin produced a marked decrease in PA during the first few minutes after injection, F

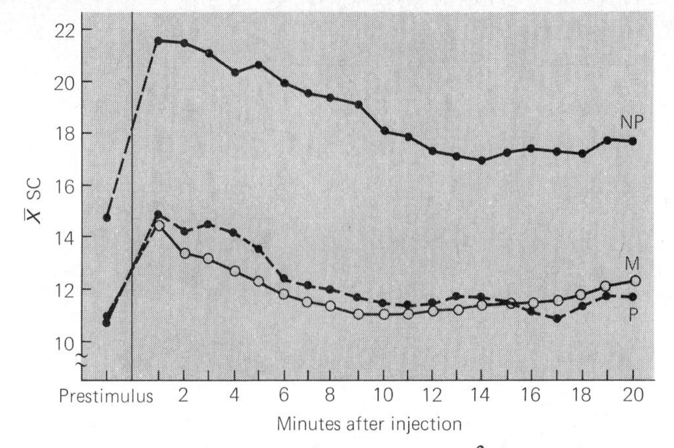

Fig. 4. Mean skin conductance (μmhos/cm^2) in response to adrenalin injection. (P = psychopaths; M = mixed; NP = nonpsychopaths.)

= 49.62, df = 2/45, $p < .001$. Although there was a gradual return toward the preinjection PA, F = 2.42, df = 19/855, $p < .001$, the effects of adrenalin were so persistent that recovery was only about 30% complete by the twentieth minute. There were no group differences in the size of the initial vasoconstrictive response or in the rate at which recovery occurred, $F < 1.0$ in each case.

The maximum response to adrenalin (a 50% decrease in PA) was greater than that to saline (a 35% decrease in PA), F = 12.29, df = 1/45, $p < .001$.

Respiration rate. Mean respiration rate increased gradually throughout the 20 min. following adrenalin, F = 1.67, df = 19/855, $p < .05$. By the twentieth minute, the number of respiratory cycles/sec was about 10% greater than the preinjection rate (15.5). The increase was unrelated to the diagnosis of *S*s, $F < 1.0$.

Blink rate. The changes in blink rate were similar to those following saline—a sharp increase of about 12 blinks/min during the first minute, F = 9.48, df = 1/45, $p < .001$, followed by a return to the preinjection rate. Again, group differences were negligible, $F < 1.0$.

EMG. EMG activity increased by about 35% during the first minute after injection, F = 16.24, df = 1/45, $p < .001$. Although it subsided somewhat thereafter, the decrease during the remainder of the 20-min. period was not significant, F = 1.28, df = 19/855, $p < .20$. during the twentieth minute after injection, mean EMG activity was still about 20% above the preinjection mean. There were no differences between groups in the magnitude of the initial increase in activity or in the rate at which the return to the preinjection level occurred ($F < 1.0$ in each case).

Addicts versus Nonaddicts

Since there were fewer heroin addicts in Group P than in the other groups (though the differences were nonsignificant), it was felt advisable to repeat the above analyses, this time with each of the three diagnostic groups subdivided into addicts and nonaddicts. The results clearly showed that the differences between groups already reported were not significantly related to the number of addicts in each group.

Responses of High and Low APQ Subgroups

Although the claim by Goldman et al. (1971) that psychopathic *S*s with low APQ scores gave unusually large cardiac responses to adrenalin was not really consistent with the data they presented, it was decided to reanalyze the present data by subdividing each diagnostic group (at the median) into high and low APQ subgroups of eight *S*s each.[2] The results of the analyses were generally negative. That is, there were no significant differences between high and low APQ psychopaths in tonic physiological activity or in physiological responses to saline and adrenalin. The cardiac responses of these two groups to adrenalin, for example, were virtually identical and were very similar to those of the other subgroups. More generally, all but one of the groups' interactions were nonsignificant. The lone exception involved the increase in skin conductance following injection of adrenalin—the high APQ *S*s from Group NP gave significantly larger responses than did *S*s from the other subgroups ($p < .01$).

DISCUSSION

Tonic Levels

The relatively low tonic SC of the psychopaths is consistent with earlier findings with *S*s from a different (though related) institution (Hare, 1965, 1968; Hare & Quinn, 1971). Especially noteworthy is the fact that the difference between psychopaths and nonpsychopaths increased from the beginning of the experiment to the point just prior to administration of adrenalin, and that adrenalin augmented this difference. Similar increases in the difference between psychopaths and nonpsychopaths during the progress of an experiment have been observed in several previous studies (Hare, 1968; Hare & Quinn, 1971), suggesting that the experimental procedures used were less arousing (at least electrodermally) to the psychopaths than to the other *S*s.

The finding that there were no differences between psychopathic and nonpsychopathic *S*s in tonic heart rate is similar to that obtained in previous studies (Blankstein, 1969; Fenz, 1971; Hare, 1968; Hare & Quinn, 1971).

Two other variables also failed to differentiate between groups, viz., tonic blink rate and tonic EMG activity.

Responses to Saline and Adrenalin

The response to saline injection was a sharp decrease in digital PA (vasoconstriction), marked increases in skin conductance, blink rate, and EMG activity, and little change in

[2] Separate analyses were also performed on the physiological responses of high, medium, and low APQ *S*s, with the diagnosis of the *S*s being disregarded. The results (available from the author) were complex and often difficult to interpret. For example, there was a curvilinear relationship between APQ scores and cardiac responses to adrenalin, with high APQ *S*s giving the largest and medium APQ *S*s the smallest responses.

respiration rate or heart rate. Only the increase in skin conductance differentiated between groups, with the psychopaths giving smaller responses than those given by the nonpsychopaths. Assuming that the needle used for the injection was a noxious stimulus, the small electrodermal response given by the psychopaths is consistent with the results of previous studies in which noxious stimuli were used (e.g., Blankstein, 1969; Hare & Quinn, 1971; Lykken, 1957). It might be argued, of course, that the large electrodermal responses of *S*s in Group NP were related to the fact that there was a relatively high proportion of heroin addicts in this group. However, whatever significance a hypodermic may have to an addict, it is unlikely that it had much bearing on the present results. As reported earlier, statistical analyses indicated that physiological responses were not related to the proportion of addicts in each diagnostic group.

As expected, responses to adrenalin were generally larger than those to saline, the exceptions being skin conductance and blink rate, and except for blink rate, the responses to adrenalin were considerably more prolonged. However, neither the amplitude nor the persistence of any of the responses to adrenalin differentiated between psychopaths and nonpsychopaths. In particular, the cardiac responses of the psychopaths were much the same as those given by the nonpsychopaths, a finding that is inconsistent with the results obtained by Schachter and Latané (1964), but in line with results reported by Goldman et al. (1971). It is possible, of course that the different results obtained were related to procedural differences. For example, *S*s in the Schachter and Latané study were engaged in a rather complex avoidance learning task, involving electric shock, whereas *S*s in the present study were presented with nothing more noxious than hypodermic injections and were not required to do anything in particular other than to lie still throughout the session. Further, the preinjection heart rate of *S*s in the Schachter and Latané experiment averaged around 90 bpm, compared with an average of about 68 bpm in the present study. It is obvious, therefore, that *S*s in the two studies were in somewhat different psychophysiological states (e.g., see Elliott, 1970). Whether this means that cardiac responsivity to adrenalin is related to some rather complex interactions between task requirements, stress involved, organismic states, and personality characteristics, is unknown. However, it should be noted that *S*s described by Goldman et al. were also engaged in an avoidance learning task involving electric shock and, according to Lindner, Goldman, Dinitz, and Allen (1970), had preinjection heart rates of around 90 bpm. In spite of these similarities to the Schachter and Latané study, the cardiac responses of their psychopaths were not significantly different from those of their nonpsychopaths. The most tenable conclusion at this point, therefore, seems to be that the cardiovascular system of psychopaths is not any more or less sensitive to adrenalin than is that of nonpsychopaths.

A similar conclusion apparently applies to electrodermal responsivity and to at least some aspects (blink rate, respiration, muscle tension of the chin) of somatic activity. It is true that the psychopaths gave smaller electrodermal responses to the injection of adrenalin than did the nonpsychopaths. However, it is doubtful whether this means that the electrodermal system of psychopaths is hyposensitive to adrenalin. The increase in skin conductance during the first minute after injection was probably in response to the activities associated with the injection itself rather than to the biochemical effects of adrenalin: the latter probably took somewhat longer to occur, and no doubt contributed to the relatively small decrement in skin conductance during the 20 min. following injection. Consistent with this suggestion is the fact that the initial response to saline injection was generally just as large as the initial response to injection of adrenalin. Presumably, both injections produced relatively small responses in the psychopaths because these *S*s were electrodermally hyporesponsive to aversive stimuli in general.

The results of the present experiment clearly indicate that the physiological responses of psychopaths to adrenalin were unrelated to the APQ scores they obtained. They serve to reinforce the comments made earlier about Goldman et al.'s (1971) discussion of "simple" and "hostile" psychopaths.

Comment is needed at this point on some of the interpretations that Schachter and Latané (1964) and Goldman et al. (1971) have placed upon their data. As noted earlier, Schachter and Latané concluded that the cardiovascular system of psychopaths was unusually sensitive to adrenalin. They also concluded that psychopaths "are more autonomically responsive to a variety of more or less stressful stimuli than are normals [p. 264]," a conclusion that suffers from the obvious dangers involved in generalizing from a single physiological variable and from an experimental situation involving a biochemical stimulus (Hare, 1968; Lykken, 1967; Plutchik & Ax, 1967). Moreover, the suggestion that psychopaths are autonomically hyperactive is inconsistent with a considerable body of empirical evidence (reviewed by Hare, 1968, 1970; Hare & Quinn, 1971). Although it is true that most of this evidence was not available at the time the Schachter and Latané paper was written, both Schachter (1971) and others (e.g., Valins, 1970) continue to show a puzzling disregard for evidence that is contrary to their conviction that psychopaths are individuals who are physiologically hyperactive but incapable of applying the appropriate emotional labels to their states of arousal. Part of the problem here no doubt arises from their tendency to equate low scores on the APQ with psychopathy. While such a procedure simplifies selection of *S*s, there is no assurance that *S*s selected are in fact psychopaths. The APQ is assumed to be a measure of anxiety reactivity (Lykken & Katzenmeyer, 1968), and although psychopaths should theoretically receive low scores on it, several studies, including the present one and a recent one by Fenz (1971), have found that they do not (see also Footnote 4). Although the reasons for this failure of the APQ to discriminate between psychopathic and nonpsychopathic inmates are not known, it is possible that the responses of psychopaths to psychological tests and inventories are relatively inaccurate indicants of their "true" psychophysiological state and are best viewed with a certain amount of suspicion. In any case, even if the APQ did reliably differentiate between psychopaths and nonpsychopaths, it is doubtful whether it could be effectively used by itself to select psychopathic *S*s.

Psychopaths are not the only persons with reduced anxiety potential, nor are those with low APQ scores necessarily psychopaths.

From a theoretical point of view, it would be rather nice if the psychopath *was* a cardiovascular hyperresponder. Cardiac acceleration is one component of a "defensive response" (e.g., Graham & Clifton, 1966) and may be associated with "sensory rejection" and cortical inhibition (Lacey, 1967). If the psychopath did respond to potentially stressful situations with relatively strong cardiac acceleration, the resultant attenuation of sensory input and reduction in cortical arousal would perhaps serve to reduce the emotional impact of the situation (Hare, 1968; Lykken, 1967). The difficulty here is that there is little evidence that psychopaths give unusually large accelerative responses to stressors and aversive stimuli. As a matter of fact, there is some modest evidence that the shift in cardiac response from deceleration (orienting response) to acceleration (defensive response) may require more intense stimulation in psychopaths (Hare & Quinn, 1971). It is still possible, of course, that the appropriate experimental situations have not as yet been used, and that under the right conditions psychopaths will prove to be more proficient than normal persons at "tuning out" disturbing stimulation, and that this process will be associated with unusually large cardiac acceleration and small electrodermal responses. Even if the latter should not prove to be the case, there is other evidence (reviewed in Hare, 1968, 1970) to support the hypothesis that psychopathy may be related to the operation of inhibitory mechanisms that selectively modulate sensory input. In effect, psychopaths

> may be able to "tune out" or at least greatly attenuate stimulation that is disturbing. The result would be that threats of punishment and cues warning of unpleasant consequences for misbehavior would not have the same emotional impact that they would have for other individuals [Hare, 1970, p. 69].

Or in Lykken's (1967) terms, psychopaths may be relatively proficient in the process of negative preception.

Goldman et al. (1971; see also Linder et al., 1970) have recently proposed that psychopaths suffer from a form of sympathetic denervation hypersensitivity, a condition in which a denervated autonomic effector becomes highly sensitive to chemical agents, including adrenalin (Cannon & Rosenblueth, 1949). This proposal rests upon the assumption that the autonomic nervous system of the psychopath is unusually sensitive to adrenalin. As the present results and discussion indicate, however, this assumption is untenable, and the arguments behind it unconvincing.

As a final point, it is worth noting that Groups P and M in the present experiment were physiologically similar. This physiological similarity between a carefully defined group of psychopaths and a "mixed" group of inmates has been found in several earlier studies (Hare, 1968; Hare & Quinn, 1971). What this suggests is that the proportion of misclassified psychopaths in the mixed groups was rather high. This should not be too surprising, however, since the selection criteria for psychopathy were relatively strict. And one of the reasons for having placed *Ss* in Group M was that although they were suspected of being psychopaths there was not sufficient information available to be certain.

REFERENCES

Allen, H. E. *Bio-social correlates of two types of antisocial sociopaths.* (Doctoral dissertation, Ohio State University) Ann Arbor, Mich.: University Microfilms, 1969. No. 70-13971.

Arieti, S. *The intrapsychic self.* New York: Basic Books, 1967.

Blankstein, K. R. Patterns of autonomic functioning in primary and secondary psychopaths. Unpublished master's thesis, University of Waterloo, 1969.

Cannon, W. B., & Rosenbleuth, A. *The supersensitivity of denervated structures. New York: Macmillan, 1949.*

Cleckley, H. *The mask of sanity* (4th ed.) St. Louis, Mo.: Mosby, 1964.

Elliott, R. Comment on the comparability of measures of heart rate in cross-laboratory comparison. *Journal of Experimental Research in Personality,* 1970, **4**, 156–158.

Fenz, W. Heart rate responses to a stressor: A comparison between primary and secondary psychopaths and normal controls. *Journal of Experimental Research in Personality,* 1971, **5**, 7–13.

Goldman, H., Lindner, L., Dinitz, S., & Allen, H. The simple sociopath: Physiologic and sociologic characteristics. *Biological Psychiatry,* 1971, **3**, 77–83.

Graham, F. K., & Clifton, R. K. Heart rate change as a component of the orienting response. *Psychological Bulletin,* 1966, **65**, 305–320.

Hare, R. D. Temporal gradient of fear arousal in psychopaths. *Journal of Abnormal Psychology,* 1965, **70**, 442–445.

Hare, R. D. Psychopathy, autonomic functioning, and the orienting response. *Journal of Abnormal Psychology,* 1968, **73**(3, Pt. 2).

Hare, R. D. *Psychopathy: Theory and research.* New York: Wiley, 1970.

Hare, R. D. Response requirements and directional fractionation of autonomic responses. *Psychophysiology,* 1972, in press.

Hare, R. D., & Quinn, M. J. Psychopathy and autonomic conditioning. *Journal of Abnormal Psychology,* 1971, **77**, 223–235.

Hare, R. D., & Thorvaldson, S. A. Psychopathy and response to electrical stimulation. *Journal of Abnormal Psychology,* 1970, **76**, 370–374.

Lacey, J. I. Somatic response patterning and stress: Some revisions of activation theory. In N. H. Appley & R. Trumbell (Eds.), *Psychological stress: Issues in research.* New York: Appleton-Century-Crofts, 1967.

Lindner, L., Goldman, H., Dinitz, S., & Allen, H. Antisocial personality type with cardiac lability. *Archives of General Psychiatry,* 1970, **23**, 260–267.

Lykken, D. T. Valin's "Emotionality and autonomic reactivity. (Doctoral dissertation, University of Minnesota) Ann Arbor, Mich.: University Microfilms, 1955. No. 55-944.

Lykken, D. T. A study of anxiety in the sociopathic personality. *Journal of Abnormal and Social Psychology,* 1957, **55**, 6–10.

Lyyken, D. T. Valin's "Emotionality and autonomic reactivity": An appraisal. *Journal of Experimental Research in Personality,* 1967, **2**, 49–55.

Lykken, D. T., & Katzenmeyer, C. *Manual for the Activity Preference. Questionnaire* (APQ). (Research Laboratories Tech. Rep. No. PR-68-3) Minneapolis: University of Minnesota, 1968.

Plutchik, R., & Ax, A. A critique of determinants of emo-

tional state by Schachter and Singer (1962). *Psychophysiology*, 1967, 4, 79–82.
Schachter, S. *Emotion, obesity and crime.* New York: Academic Press, 1971.
Schachter, S., & Latané, B. Crime, cognition and the autonomic nervous system. In M. R. Jones (Ed.), *Nebraska Symposium on Motivation, 1964.* Lincoln: University of Nebraska Press, 1964.
Valins, S. The perception and labeling of bodily changes as determinants of emotional behavior. In P. Black (Ed.), *Psychological correlates of emotion.* New York: Academic Press, 1970.

A Remote Instrumentation System for Behavior Modification: Preliminary Report

Robert L. Schwitzgebel*

There is fairly wide agreement that unwanted behavior is often the result of disturbances or unfavorable conditions in the social environment. Yet techniques for obtaining valid information about such changes, and a patient's reaction to them, are markedly inadequate. Studies by Gray (1955) and by Cartwright (1962), for example, indicated substantial differences between self-reported and observed behavior. The general lack of accurate field data means that even in individual cases we may be forced to speculate on critical factors such as the actual reinforcement contingencies or important discriminative stimuli.

Furthermore, from both a theoretical and a practical standpoint, it may be impossible to create in the laboratory or clinic the frequency, duration, and complexity of particular conditions which may be of concern (cf. Barker, 1965). Almost all treatment procedures today rely on massive transfer of behavior from the clinic to the patient's usual environment (assuming the individual will come to the clinic in the first place). Recent advances in telemetry and electronic communication systems, however, may now make feasible the investigation of aspects of the therapeutic process which heretofore have been relatively inaccessible. New modes of intervention are also suggested.

The potential value of remote instrumentation and data-recording systems in biomedical research and in medical practice has long been recognized. Among early reports are those of Einthoven (1906), who transmitted electrocardiac data over a telephone line a distance of approximately 1 mi, and of Winters (1921), who devised a radio telemetry system in order that similar data could be transmitted from a ship without a physician on board to a medical facility on shore. Efforts to introduce radio devices into psychotherapy and educational situations have been reported for at least a decade. Korner and Brown (1952) described a "mechanical third ear" to be used for supervising beginning therapists; Ward (1960) devised a similar system for the same purpose. More recently, Sanders (1966) reported an auditory prompting system. In this latter case, the therapist speaks into a microphone of an FM transmitter, and the output is fed into a wire loop encircling the perimeter of an adjoining therapy room. A person in the therapy room, wearing a wireless subminiature behind-the-ear-type receiver, is then able to hear the therapist. This system has been used to supervise trainees during interviewing and psychological testing. A more novel application was the use of the so-called Bug-in-the-Ear with parents while they were interacting with their children during play therapy (Welsh, 1966). Presumably, this prompting could facilitate generalization of certain parent-child interactions outside the clinic. Patterson, Jones, Whittier, and Wright (1965) have described an instrumental conditioning procedure with a hyperactive nine-year-old boy in a classroom in which the therapist sent messages to the child via a small radio headset. An earphone and miniature radio unit (held in place by suspenders) was given to the youngster, and he was instructed that a buzz over the earphone indicated that he had earned a piece of candy for sitting still.

The present paper reports the designing and field-testing of a prototype electronic communication system for use with adolescent delinquents in natural settings.

From C. Franks and R. D. Rubin (eds.). *Advances in behavior therapy.* New York: Academic Press, 1968.

*The author wishes to acknowledge the early contribution of his brother, Ralph Schwitzgebel, to the system design. The development reported herein was performed pursuant to a contract with the United States Department of Health, Education, and Welfare, Office of Education.

RATIONALE AND SYSTEM DESCRIPTION

Some previous work (R. L. Schwitzgebel & Kolb, 1964; R. L. Schwitzgebel, 1967) suggested that systematically arranged positive consequences for delinquents employed as

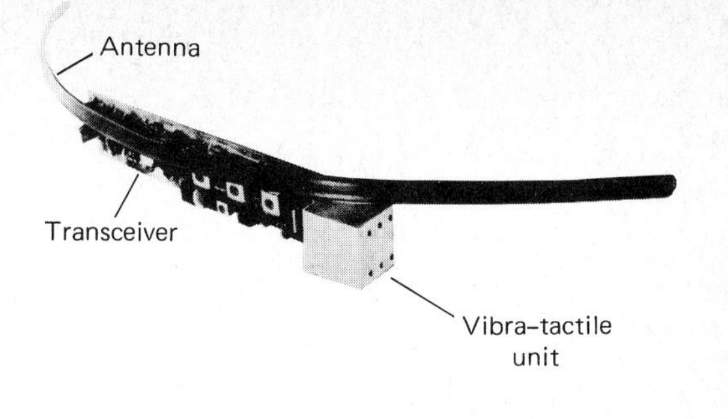

Vibra-tactile belt transceiver

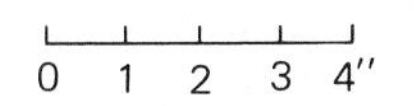

Fig. 1. Belt transceiver unit.

experimental *S*s could alter the frequency of social behaviors. *S*s who had participated in 20 or 30 hours of experimental interviewing tended to emit verbal operants at a fairly high rate. For example, on days when there were no interviews, *S*s often called the *E* on the telephone. Conversations were usually lengthy (30 min or more) and had little informative content. This behavior is certainly not atypical of adolescents; but what is therapeutically intersting is the reinforcing potential of the behavior (cf. Premack, 1965).

In psychoanalytically-oriented treatment, patient-initiated contact may be interpreted as a "transference" phenomenon and deliberately extinguished. In typical school counseling programs, contact with the counselor is either behaviorally noncontingent (e.g., on a fixed interval schedule of once a week) or contingent upon misbehavior. The remote instrumentation system to be described here was an attempt to make a high-probability behavior and positive consequences contingent on prosocial behavior by *decreasing* the *duration* and *increasing* the *frequency* of *E-S* contact. This arrangement was believed to be particularly desirable when dealing with patients characterized by impulsivity (cf. Mischel, 1958).

A two-way vibra-tactile radio communication system was designed to meet the following functional specifications:

1. Direct communication is possible within a radius of 100 yards under adverse city conditions, including normal building attenuation of the signal. The system can function with either party in his normal location. The supplemental use of local repeater stations and rented telephone lines can link extended geographical distances.
2. The communication is nonverbal in order to assure privacy and to prevent third parties from being unknowingly recorded. Messages are sent by simple arbitrary code, based on the presence or absence of a vibra-tactile or light signal or both.
3. Either party may send, receive, and initiate communication.
4. Controls are simple to operate and do not interfere with normal activity.
5. Equipment is small, lightweight, and packaged in a manner to allow, and perhaps encourage, acceptance among potential users.

Probably the most distinctive physical feature of the system is a 6 × 3 × 2 in. transceiver unit housed in a belt which sends and receives messages via a ¾ in. tactile transducer (see Fig. 1). The belt also houses the antenna. By pressing a button, the sender activates a small coil on the receiver's unit which is felt as a "tap" in the abdominal region. Information is conveyed by the number and the timing of the signals—similar to standard audio-telegraphy systems. The development of this mode of communication was based primarily on the work of Geldard (1957, 1962) and his associates. A light and a barely audible tone accompanies the vibration. A multiple-frequency relay coil in the *E*'s belt allows him to communicate with four different *S*s without the *S*s themselves being able to communicate with each other.

The system is presently licensed by the FCC to operate two 12-W base stations at a frequency of 165.395 Mc/sec. and four 1-W belt units at 164.980 Mc/sec. One base station is located at the Fernald School (a nonresidential remedial school) on the North Campus of UCLA. This station transmits to, and receives messages from, the belt units worn by students in the school area. A similar base station serves the Psychology Department area in the South Campus. A rented commercial telephone line links the ¼ mile distance between the two stations.

APPLICATION

A small pilot study was conducted to estimate the feasibility of the system in terms of mechanical reliability and social acceptability. Four male *S*s were selected from among volunteers on the basis of age (15–17 years), academic retardation, a history of antisocial aggressive behavior in the classroom, and reasonably high peer-group rating (or above-average physical size) in order to "protect" the equipment from students who might be jealous, curious, or hostile.

Because the system was designed to use code, the *S*s were given a series of five 1 hour practice sessions using telegraph practice-sets outside the classroom. Base-rate measures for classroom social and academic behaviors were obtained on a time-sampling basis from observers in an adjoining observation room and from self-reports of the *S*s. During certain hours, the *S*s were asked to report the frequency of four behaviors: 10 min or more of uninterrupted study, 10 min or more of idleness or socializing, hostile statements regarding academic work, and physical aggression toward other students. The validity of the self-reports was checked by concurrent independent observations of two lab assistants. The *E*'s signals to *S*s were limited to a query (e.g., "What are you doing now?"), acknowledgement of a communication, and notification of the *S* that he was eligible for some type of positive consequence (e.g., time out of the class visiting with the *E*). Various technical and procedural difficulties resulted in the consequences being given in what would have to be described as an unsystematic or haphazard manner.

Our work thus far has led us to several conclusions. These are undoubtedly biased by idiosyncratic factors in our particular project, but they may provide some tentative guide to therapists and researchers contemplating the use of remote instrumentation of this type.

1. **Mechanical reliability.** In general, the basic design was found to be mechanically satisfactory, i.e., functional. However, a number of limitations should be noted. Attenuation of the signal by buildings was more severe than we had anticipated on the basis of published studies (e.g., Rice, 1965; Young, 1952). The belts did not withstand well the usual abuse given by active and curious adolescents. A very limited budget required that some military surplus components such as power transformers be installed in the base stations—resulting in a number of breakdowns and on one occasion a small fire. Fortunately most of the difficulties appear to be a matter of straightforward refinement of the components. The most serious design question involves the use of vibra-tactile signalization. The vibra-tactile transducer was often not powerful enough to produce a discrete signal through a layer of clothing; thus light and tone signals became important and necessary auxiliary information channels.

2. **Social acceptability.** The belts were generally well-received by members of the class. The novelty of the devices, an opportunity to spend some study periods outside the classroom, and attention from the *E*s probably accounted for much of the willingness of the *S*s to participate. *S*s tended to fantasize themselves as being "wired-up" in a manner similar to astronauts. Verbalizations about scientific research and about "trying something new" were encouraged by the *E*s; prosthetic or therapeutic connotations were purposefully avoided. Two of the *S*s asked to continue wearing the belts after the closing of the school year.

It should be noted that the belts were used only in the classroom of the clinic school where there is considerably more tolerance for experimentation than in typical public school classrooms. On the other hand, social deprivation in terms of positive adult attention is undoubtedly greater in the public school.

3. **Use of code.** Our original plan to use Morse code was not found to be feasible due to the time and effort required to learn the code. The task appears to be roughly comparable to learning touch-typing and, of course, has less general practicality. A simple arbitrary code, conveying two or three bits of information, mutually decided upon by the *S*s and the *E* seemed to be adequate.

If verbal communication should be considered necessary, a small speaker (cordless hearing-aid style) could be added to the *S*'s unit, although the acceptance of this by adolescents is somewhat questionable. A "hearing aid"-microphone arrangement will not solve the problem, among delinquents at least, of a tendency to use socially unacceptable language. Furthermore, it may complicate, without any increased validity, eventual classification of the communications for research purposes (e.g., into digital code for computer analysis).

4. **Behavior modification.** The results of the pilot study are inconclusive in terms of demonstrating replicable behavior change. All self-reported behaviors (i.e., time spent idle or working, hostile expressions regarding school work, and physical aggression toward other students) showed an apparent increase in frequency regardless of any attempted reinforcement or extinction via transceiver communication from the *E*. Direct counterconditioning or punishment was not used. Observer-subject reliability was high on three of the four dependent variables. By observers' standards, *S*s reported too infrequently the incidents of physical aggression. *S*s typically claimed that they were "just playing." Our impression is that the *S*s tried to report accurately the behaviors of concern; they were also aware that observers might be present.

Simply requesting a *S* to report a specified behavior, which then became a condition for using the belt, seemingly prompted the behavior to a level consistently above the base rate (even for the too seldom reported physical aggression). Sensitization by frequent self-reporting and a desire to use the belt are factors associated with the use of the transceivers—beyond the usual application of contingent consequences—which might be effectively utilized to modify established response patterns. Generalization and extinction phenomena remain entirely unexplored.

DISCUSSION

A judgment as to the usefulness of this type of instrumentation system obviously depends, in part, on the replicability of procedure and results. In order to increase the feasibility of other investigators developing remote communication devices similar to the units described here, the 165 Mc/sec range was selected because of the availability of nearby multiple-use citizen bands and relatively inexpensive equipment.[1] The eventual cost of materials in the individual belt units should be under $75.

Generally, studies employing telemetry must be viewed

[1] Investigators who contemplate using radio devices outside the frequency and power limitations of the citizen bands should be prepared for a minimum of 6 to 8 months processing time for licenses. Many frequencies are crowded or reserved for special purposes. One is also advised not to invest heavily in equipment prior to licensing as the final assignment is likely to vary to an unknown degree from the original request.

with considerable skepticism. Equipment and labor costs are still high because "off-the-shelf" components do not often meet all the requirements of novel application. Furthermore, there is an unfortunate tendency to assume that mechanization in itself produces "hard" and valid data. Remote systems are quite likely to have more "noise" in them than comparable laboratory arrangements. Like any innovation, remote instrumentation has its own costs and special limitations.

In order to provide a reasonably accurate and detailed report of the actual process of intervention, the system should be designed to automatically record all transceiver communications. This verification of procedure should prove to be one of the major advantages of using electromechanical interfaces in behavior therapy. Such recording will document, not necessarily eliminate, what may be seen later as the idiosyncratic (and perhaps valuable) "style" of the therapist.

Elsewhere (R. K. Schwitzgebel, Schwitzgebel, Pahnke, & Hurd, 1964) it has been suggested that remote instrumentation systems could have a fairly wide range of therapeutic application. Often before a serious crime is committed, for example, the potential offender will have strong ambivalent feelings. At times like these, it would require very little effort to signal for help. Presumably, the "cry for help" is also common prior to suicide attempts. This suggests that similar systems could be used with psychiatric patients in crisis situations, for alcoholics beginning treatment, or for hospitalized patients on their first few trips into town by themselves. Other potential applications would involve supportive or informational communications with retarded individuals or in geriatric cases.

It has been estimated that it will be possible within the next decade to manufacture all the circuits in a television set on a single slice of silicon at a cost of approximately 40 cents (Gifford, 1967). Whether or not this actually becomes possible, we can predict with some certainty that this type of technological advance will permit us, if we wish, to record and intervene in ongoing chains of behavior in more "natural" social situations. By and large our psychotherapeutic, educational, and correctional institutions have been slow to recognize the impact of this technosocial evolution. The boundaries of therapeutic or correctional systems no longer need be confined to the bricks and mortar of the pre-electronic age. "Therapeutic learning spaces" will be increasingly defined by the *possibility of communication* rather than by the designation of physical surfaces.

REFERENCES

Barker, R. G. Explorations in ecological psychology. *American Psychologist*, 1965, **20**, 1–14.

Cartwright, A. Memory errors in a morbidity survey. *Milbank Memorial Fund Quarterly*, 1962, **16**, 5–24.

Einthoven, W. Le Telicardiogramme. *Archives of Internal Physiology*, 1906, **4**, 132.

Geldard, F. A. Adventures in tactile literacy. *American Psychologist*, 1957, **12**, 115–124.

Geldard, F. A. Virginia cutaneous project 1948–1962. Final report to the Office of Naval Research on Project NR-140-598, Psychology Laboratory, University of Virginia, 1962.

Gifford, J. The performance/economics/marketplace inter-relationships. *WESCON Technical Papers*, 1967, **2**, Part 2.

Gray, P. G. The memory factor in social surveys. *Journal of the American Statistical Association*, 1955, **50**, 344–352.

Korner, I. N., & Brown, W. H. The mechanical third ear. *Journal of Consulting Psychology*, 1952, **16**, 81–84.

Mischel, W. Delay of gratification, need for achievement, and acquiescence in another culture. *Journal of Abnormal and Social Psychology*, 1958, **57**, 13–16.

Patterson, G., Jones, R., Whittier, J., & Wright, M. A behavior modification technique for the hyperactive child. *Behaviour Research and Therapy*, 1965, **2**, 217–226.

Premack, D. Reinforcement theory. In D. Levine (Ed.), *Nebraska symposium on motivation.* Lincoln: University of Nebraska Press, 1965.

Rice, P. L. Transmission loss predictions for tropospheric communication circuits. *National Bureau of Standards (U.S.), Technical Note*, 1965, **1** & **2**, No. 101.

Sanders, R. A. The "Bug-in-the-ear": A device for training of clinical psychologists. Paper presented at the meeting of the Midwest Psychological Association, Chicago, May, 1966. (Mimeo., Northeast Nebraska Mental Health Clinic, Norfolk, Nebr.)

Schwitzgebel, R. K., Schwitzgebel, R. L., Pahnke, W., & Hurd, S. A program of research in behavioral electronics. *Behavioral Science*, 1964, **9**, 233–238.

Schwitzgebel, R. L. Short-term operant conditioning of adolescent offenders on socially relevant variables. *Journal of Abnormal Psychology*, 1967, **72**, 134–142.

Schwitzgebel, R. L., & Kolb, D. Inducing behavior change in adolescent delinquents. *Behaviour Research and Therapy*, 1964, **1**, 297–304.

Ward, C. H. An electronic aid for teaching interviewing techniques. *Archives of General Psychiatry*, 1960, **3**, 357–358.

Welsh, R. S. A highly efficient method of parental counseling: A mechanical third ear. Paper presented at the meeting of the Rocky Mountain Psychological Association, Denver, June, 1966.

Winters, S. R. Diagnosis by wireless. *Scientific American*, 1921, **124**, 465.

Young, W. R. Comparison of mobile radio transmission at 150, 450, 900, and 3700 Mc. *Bell System Technical Journal*, 1952, 31, 1068–1085.

Chapter 12

Sexual Deviation

Because of the publication of the Kinsey reports in 1948 and 1953, the topic of sex became a proper subject for discussions in learned circles. However, the Kinsey reports, in spite of their impact on our society, were fraught with numerous statistical problems that seriously flawed the accuracy of their findings.

Our lead article, which is by the three distinguished statisticians William Cochrane, Frederick Mosteller, and John Tukey, is the longest reading in this book. We present it here in its totality because it is an important critique of a popular study and because it is relatively unknown. Moreover, it is a masterpiece of critical writing.

The second paper, by anthropologist Robert LeVine, deals with sex offenses among the Gusii of Kenya. LeVine bridges the gap between the Gusii and our own culture by pointing out how the breakdown of traditional controls and barriers can result in numerous sex offenses when these controls are not replaced by other structural barriers of equal effectiveness.

Bartell's paper on group sex among mid-Americans is an interesting benchmark of some sexual practices that have characterized some Americans in the 1960s and 1970s. This anthropological report of the "swinging" practices of some Americans describes the practices and motivations of the participants and attempts a sociopsychological analysis of the phenomenon.

Our last selection is a report of aversion behavior modification of three cases of exhibitionism, two of transvestism and one of masochism. The results achieved by the therapists—Abel, Levis and Clancy—suggest that aversion therapy may be a choice form of treatment for these types of deviation.

Statistical Problems of the Kinsey Report*

William G. Cochran
Frederick Mosteller
John W. Tukey

This is the report of a committee appointed by the Commission on Statistical Standards of the American Statistical Association to review the statistical methods used in *Sexual Behavior in the Human Male.* We shall refer both to the book and to its authors (Kinsey, Pomeroy and Martin) as KPM. The committee wishes to emphasize that this report is confined to statistical methodology, and does not concern itself with the appropriateness or the limitations of orgasm as a measure of sexual behavior. The treatment of specific problems has necessitated an examination of some of the statistical and methodological problems of such studies, and the organization of frames of reference in which the statistical methods can be discussed. The committee hopes that both detailed and general considerations will be of service to Dr. Alfred C. Kinsey and his coworkers; to the National Research Council's Committee for Research on Problems of Sex, who requested the appointment of this committee; and to others facing similar statistical or methodological problems.

We have endeavored to write this report in a way that would minimize the possibility of misunderstanding. To do this, it is necessary to deal with many detailed aspects of the work, one at a time. By judicious selection of topics and attitudes, it would have been possible to write two factually correct reports, one of which would leave the impression with the reader that KPM's work was of the highest quality, the other that the work was of poor quality and that the major issues were evaded. We have not written either of these extreme reports.

Even within the present report, a reader who is trying only to support his own opinions could select sections and topics to buttress either view. In the details of this report the reader will find numerous problems that we feel KPM handled admirably. If he pays attention only to these, he would find support for the opinion that the work is nearly impeccable and that the conclusions must be substantially correct. There are other problems which we believe KPM failed to handle adequately, in some cases because they did not devote the necessary skill and resources to the problems, in other cases because no solutions for the problems exist at present. The reader who concentrates only on the parts of our report in which such problems are discussed would find support for the opinion that KPM's work is of poor quality.

Our own opinion is that KPM are engaged in a complex program of research involving many problems of measurement and sampling, for some of which there appear at the present to be no satisfactory solutions. While much remains to be done, our overall impression of their work to date is favorable.

Many details are discussed in the body and appendices of this report. The main conclusions are as follows:

1. The statistical and methodological aspects of KPM's work are outstanding in comparison with other leading sex studies. In a comparison with nine other leading sex studies (four supported in part by the same NRC Committee) KPM were superior to all others in the systematic coverage of their material, in the number of items which they covered, in the composition of their sample as regards its age, educational, religious, rural-urban, occupational, and geographic representation, in the number and variety of methodological checks which they employed, and in their statistical

From *Journal of the American Statistical Association,* 1953, **48**, 673–716. Reprinted by permission.

*This article consists of the main text, but not the appendices, of the report of a committee appointed in 1950 by S. S. Wilks as President of the American Statistical Association, to review the statistical methods used by Alfred C. Kinsey, Wardell B. Pomeroy, and Clyde E. Martin in their *Sexual Behavior in the Human Male* (Philadelphia, W. B. Saunders Co., 1948). For further details on the appointment of the committee and its charge, see Section 1, p. 676 below. For an outline of the appendices, as well as of this paper, see Section 3, pp. 678–81. Appendix G, "Principles of Sampling," will appear as an article in the March issue of this JOURNAL. The full report, including both the text given here and the appendices, will be published as a monograph by the American Statistical Association in 1954.

analyses. So far as we can judge from our present knowledge, or from the critical evaluations of a number of other qualified specialists, their interviewing was of the best.

2. KPM's interpretations were based in part on tabulated and statistically analyzed data, and in part on data and experience which were not presented because of their nature or because of the limitations of space. Some interpretations appear not to have been based on either of these. We feel that unsubstantiated assertions are not in themselves inappropriate in a scientific study. The accumulated insight of an experienced worker frequently merits recording when no documentation can be given. However, KPM should have indicated which of their statements were undocumented or undocumentable and should have been more cautious in boldly drawing highly precise conclusions from their limited sample.

3. Many of KPM's findings are subject to question because of a possible bias in the constitution of the sample. This is not a criticism of their work (although it is a criticism of some of their interpretations). No previous sex study of a broad human population known to us, medical, psychiatric, psychological, or sociological, has been able to avoid this difficulty, and we believe that KPM could not have avoided the use of a nonprobability sample at the start of their work. Something may now perhaps be done to study and reduce this possible bias, by a probability sampling program.

In our opinion, no sex study of a broad human population can expect to present incidence data for reported behavior that are *known* to be correct to within a few percentage points. Even with the best available sampling techniques, there will be a certain percentage of the population who refuse to give histories. If the percentage of refusals is 10 per cent or more, then however large the sample, there are no statistical principles which guarantee that the results are correct to within 2 or 3 per cent. The results may actually be correct to within 2 or 3 per cent, but any claim that this is true must be based on the undocumented opinion that the behavior of those who refuse to be interviewed is not very different from that of those who are interviewed. These comments, which are not a criticism of KPM's research, emphasize the difficulty of answering the question: "How accurate are the results?," which is naturally of great interest to any user of the results of a sex study.

4. Many of KPM's findings are subject to question because of possible inaccuracies of memory and report, as are all studies of intimate human behavior among broad segments of the population. No one has proposed any way to remove the dangers of recall (involving both memory and report) and KPM were superior to the nine studies referred to above in their attempts to control and measure these dangers. We have suggested still further expansions of their methodological checks.

Until new methods are found, we believe that no sex study of incidence or frequency in large human populations can hope to measure anything but reported behavior. It may be possible to obtain observed or recorded behavior for certain special groups, but no suggestions have been made by KPM, the critics, or this committee which would make it feasible to study observed or recorded behavior for a large human population. These remarks are intended as a comment on the present status of research techniques in sex studies and not as a criticism of KPM's work.

5. KPM received only limited statistical help, in part because the work was pursued during the War years when such expert help was difficult to find for non-military projects. In view of the limited statistical knowlege which was available to them, as made clear by the failure of their sample size experiment, KPM deserve much credit for the straight thinking which brought them safely by many pitfalls. Their need of adequate statistical assistance continues to be serious. Substantial assistance might come through the development of a statistical clinic at Indiana University, or through the addition of a statistical expert to KPM's own staff. Unfortunately the sort of assistance which might resolve some of their most complex problems would require understanding, background, and techniques that perhaps not more than twenty statisticians in the world possess.

6. A probability sampling program should be seriously considered by KPM. The actual gains from an extensive program are limited, to an extent unknown at present, by refusal rates and indirectly by costs, particularly by the costs of maintaining the present quality of the individual histories by KPM's approach. A step-by-step program, starting with a very small pilot study, is recommended.

7. In addition to proposing a probability sampling program, we have made numerous suggestions in this report for the modification and strengthening of KPM's present approach. The suggestions include expanded methodological checks of their sampling program, a further study of their refusal rate, some modification of their methods of analyses, further comparisons of reported vs. observed behavior, and stricter interpretations of their data. We have been informed by KPM that many of these improvements, including some expansion of their techniques for obtaining data, have already been incorporated in the volume dealing with sexual behavior in the human female.

CHAPTER I. BACKGROUND AND ORGANIZATION

1. Organization Involved

This committee, consisting of William G. Cochran, Chairman, Frederick Mosteller, and John W. Tukey, was appointed by President S. S. Wilks in September 1950 as a committee of the Commission on Statistical Standards of the American Statistical Association. This action was initiated by a request from the Committee for Research on Problems of Sex of the National Research Council, as indicated by the following excerpt from a letter dated May 5, 1950, from Dr. George W. Corner, a member of the NRC Committee, to Dr. Isador Lubin, Chairman of the Commission on Statistical Standards of the American Statistical Association.

> In accordance with our telephone conversation of yesterday, I am writing to state to you the desire of the Committee for Research in Problems of Sex, of the National Research Council, that the Commission on Standards of the American Statistical Association will provide counsel regarding the research methods of the Institute for Sex Research of Indiana University, led by Dr. Alfred C. Kinsey.

This Committee has been the major source of financial support of Dr. Kinsey's work, and at its annual meeting on April 27, 1950, again renewed the expression of its confidence in the importance and quality of the work by voting a very substantial grant for the next year.

Recognizing however that there has been some questioning, in recently published articles, of the validity of the statistical analysis of the results of this investigation, the Committee, as well as Dr. Kinsey's group, is anxious to secure helpful evaluation and advice in order that the second volume of the report, now in preparation, may secure unquestioned acceptance.

Some correspondence ensued, in which Wilks indicated the willingness of the American Statistical Association to provide counsel as requested.

Kinsey, in a letter to Wilks dated August 28, stated that

we should make it clear that we deeply appreciate the willingness of the American Statistical Association to undertake such an examination of our statistical methods, that we will give it full cooperation in having access to all of our data as far as the peculiar confidential nature of our data will allow, and that we understand, of course, that the committee shall be free to publish its findings of whatever sort.

In the same letter, Kinsey also made a number of suggestions about the constitution and work of the committee, to the effect that the persons on the committee should be primarily statisticians with experience in human population studies, that they should plan to review the statistical criticisms which have been published about the book on the male, and that they should compare methods used by Kinsey and his associates in their research with methods in other published research in similar fields.

With respect to the research on the human female, Kinsey wrote as follows:

It should, however, be made clear that all the data that will go into our volume on *Sexual Behavior in the Human Female* are already gathered, that the punch cards have already been set up and most of them punched, and that statistical work is proceeding on that volume now. While the recommendations of the committee may modify further work, it can affect this forthcoming volume only in the form in which the material is presented, the limitations of the conclusions, and the careful description of the limitations of our method and conclusions.

2. Committee Procedure

Although no specific written directive was issued to the committee, the letter quoted earlier from Corner to Lubin sets forth the task assigned to the committee. In one respect the scope was deliberately reduced as compared with that invisaged in the letter. The committee decided not to undertake any examination of the researches and data relating to the human female, in order to avoid disruption of Kinsey's proposed schedule of work.

In October, 1950, the committee spent five days at the Institute for Sex Research of Indiana University, accompanied by Mr. Robert Osborn as assistant. Subsequent meetings of the committee were held at Chicago (December 1950), Princeton (January 1951), Cambridge (May 1951), Baltimore (July 1951) and Princeton (October 1951).

In their review of previous studies of sexual behavior, the committee received major assistance from Dr. W. O. Jenkins, who prepared a series of reports which appear in Appendix B. Mr. A. Kimball Romney prepared a helpful index of the principal criticisms made of the statistical methodology used in the book *Sexual Behavior in the Human Male.*

3. Structure of This Report as a Whole [*Exhibit 1*]

KPM's program of research is a major undertaking, involving more than ten years' work. Any discussion of it which aims at thoroughness must itself be lengthy. In order to keep the main body of our report down to a reasonable length, we have relegated much of the documentation of our conclusions, and all detailed discussion, to the following series of appendices.

A. Discussion of comments by selected technical reviewers.
B. Comparison with other studies.
C. Proposed further work.
D. Probability sampling considerations.
E. The interview and the office as we saw them.
F. Desirable accuracies.
G. Principles of sampling.

Appendix A contains our discussion of the statistical and quantitative methodological content of six of the critical reviews which appeared after the publication of the KPM book. These six were chosen from among the large number of published reviews, because they concentrated their attention on the statistical aspects of the research. Appendix A also includes, where this seems appropriate, discussion of some critical points which were not explicitly raised in the reviews in question.

Appendix B, by W. O. Jenkins, contains a review of the statistical aspects of eight of the major previous sex studies which have been carried out in the United States. Also included are similar reviews of the KPM book and of one more recent study by J. E. Farris. The purpose of this appendix is to provide a basis for comparing the KPM study with the other studies as to comprehensiveness, sampling methods, interviewing methods and statistical analysis.

Appendix C begins by outlining and commenting on suggestions for further work made by the reviewers. It explains the difficulty of estimating the stability of results from a sampling procedure such as KPM's, offers some possible methods for this estimation, and suggests how more appropriate variables for expressing sexual behavior might be developed, and how compound variables might be built on these. It then explores the problem of when to adjust, giving a simple numerical procedure for making the decision, and concludes by summarizing the probability sampling suggestions derived from Appendix D.

Appendix D discusses the problems of analysis and usefulness of probability sampling as a check on a nonprobability sample, particularly when refusal rates are considered; two possible types of probability samples and a probability sampling program which KPM might undertake; and the alternative of studying restricted populations.

Appendix E discusses the interview and the office as we saw them. Appendix F discusses what seems to be known about the accuracy needed in such work as KPM's. Appendix G presents an account of the principles of sampling illustrated with general examples.

Many of the problems faced by KPM occur in most types of sociological investigation. Some are likely to be encountered in almost any kind of scientific investigation. For this reason, we have thought it advisable to present certain of the methodological issues in rather general terms.

The reader is asked to bear in mind that in general our conclusions are not documented in the main body of the report, but in the appendices to which references are given.

CONTENTS OF FULL REPORT

4. Structure of the Main Body [*Exhibit 2*]

In preparing the main body, we have stressed easy reference and have kept related matters together at the expense of fluency of arrangement and lack of repetition. Thus our main conclusions in a form intended for the general reader take 3 pages in the digest above, while more detailed conclusions, expressed for a more technical audience, take 3 pages in Chapter XI. A particular subject summarized there is also likely to be discussed once in Chapter II, where we try to point out what KPM did, once again in one of Chapters IV to IX, where we assess KPM on an absolute scale, and yet again in Chapter X, where we compare KPM with previous workers in the field. This is repetitive, but we hope that it will permit ready reference and avoid treating subjects out of context.

After this introductory chapter on background structure, the remainder of the main body falls into three parts:

(i) Chapters II and III. In the first of these, we describe, respectively, what choices KPM had to make and what they chose. In Chapter III we outline some essential principles of sampling, which seem not to have been clearly enough formulated or widely enough understood. These chapters are introductory.

(ii) Chapters IV to XI. In the first six of these, we try to compare KPM's work with an absolute standard. The order chosen (interview, sample, methodological checks, analytical techniques, complex examples, interpretation) is that in which the problems arise in an evolving study such as KPM's. Chapter X compares KPM with previous works on the basis of Appendix B, while Chapter XI summarizes the conclusions of this part.

(iii) Chapter XII. This discusses briefly various suggested expenditures of further effort.

CONTENTS

CHAPTER II. MAJOR AREAS OF CHOICE

5. What Sort of Behavior?

The purpose of Chapter II is to record in summary form the major choices made by KPM.

Certainly the choice of orgasm as the central sort of sexual behavior for study was a major one, leading to consequences whose statistical aspects will be discussed in various places, but this choice is not a matter of *general* quantitative methodology, and hence falls outside the scope of this committee's task.

6. Whose Behavior?

KPM had to choose the population to which this study should apply. This decision does not seem to have been made clearly. From the basis for the "U. S. Corrections" (p. 105) we should infer it to be "all U. S. white males." If it were the population to which the U. S. Corrected sample actually applies on the average (the *sampled* population, see Section 18), it would be a rather odd white male U. S. Population. It would have age groups, educational status, rural-urban background, marital status and all their combinations according to the 1940 census, but it would have more members in Indiana than in any other state, and it would have been selected to an unknown degree for willingness to volunteer histories of sexual behavior. We do not regard this description of the sampled population as an automatic criticism, as some critics do. We make it here as a factual statement, noting that the careful and wise choice of the sampled population, although difficult, is a relatively free choice of the investigator. More discussion relevant to this point will be found in Chapter II-G (Appendix G).

Further, KPM chose to study the behavior of many (at least 163 in tabular form) segments of this large population, feeling, apparently, both that comparisons among segments would be illuminating and that data for (clinical) application to individuals should come from a reasonably homogeneous segment. KPM's choice of a broad population created many problems, particularly in sampling. Whether they would have been well advised to confine themselves to a more restricted population, e.g., the state of Indiana, is debatable. For our part, we are willing to take their choice as given, and to discuss briefly elsewhere some alternatives for further work (Chapter IX-D).

7. Observed, Recorded, or Reported Behavior

KPM, interested in actual behavior, had, in principle, the choice of studying observed, recorded, or reported behavior. But since they selected a broad population and orgasm as the type of behavior, their only feasible choice seems to have been *reported* behavior. This situation does not seem likely to change in the foreseeable future.

The choice of reported behavior implies that the question: "On the average, how much difference is there between present reported and past actual behavior?" is seriously involved in any inferences about actual behavior which are attempted from KPM's results. The difference might well be large, leading to a large systematic error in measurement. However, use of observed or recorded behavior in order to avoid this difference does not seem to us a feasible way to measure nationwide incidences and frequencies for KPM's broad population, because it would have produced systematic errors in sampling possibly larger than the error in measurement.

8. Interview or Questionnaire, and Types Thereof

Having settled on reported behavior, KPM had to decide whether this report should be oral or written, and what methods should be used to elicit it. Their choice was oral, in a face-to-face interview whose flavor was designed to be that of a doctor or family friend. The choice of oral rather than written report:

(1) made it possible to obtain *apparently* satisfactory answers from many more subjects (the percentage of complete illiteracy in the U. S. is small, but the percentage of illiteracy on complex subjects not usually written about is undoubtedly substantial).
(2) permitted and encouraged variation of the form of the questions to suit the subject and the situation.

Those, like some critics, who believe in a repeatable measurement process, regardless of whether or not it measures something that is always relevant, find (2) bad. Those who, like KPM, feel that appropriately flexible wording improves communication and thus improves the quality of report despite the variability resulting from changes in the form of questions, find (2) good.

Given an interview rather than a questionnaire, the remaining choices of KPM follow a consistent pattern. In nearly every case their approach resembled the clinical interview more closely than the psychometric test.

9. Which Subjects?

Here there are various choices, pertaining to:

(1) selection of individuals one at a time or in clusters.
(2) keeping age, education, marital status, etc., segments in the sample proportionate to those in the population or making them of more nearly equal size.
(3) selecting individuals on a catch-as-catch-can basis, a partly randomized basis, or according to a probability sampling plan.

They chose:

(1) to select individuals in clusters.
(2) to keep age, education, marital status, etc., segments more nearly equal in the sample than in the population.
(3) to use no detectable semblance of probability sampling ideas.

The pros and cons will be discussed later.

10. What Methodological Checks?

There are choices as to the types of checks and the number of each to be made. The types of checks made by KPM, including

(1) take-retake,
(2) husband-wife,
(3) duplicate recording of interview,
(4) overall comparison of interviews,
(5) others (see Chapter V-A)

seem to cover all those easily thought of. The numbers of checks made are discussed later. Duplicate recording of interviews occurred in an unknown, but presumably small, number of cases. No comparisons from duplicate recordings were reported, perhaps because most occurred in connection with the training of interviewers.

11. How Analyzed and Presented?

In analyzing frequency and incidence of activity, KPM chose to report both raw and "U. S. Corrected" data and to make simple comparisons. Just what was done in general was clearly stated, but the steps involved in detailed computations were not explained. No attempt was made to find helpful scales or composite variables (see Chapters IV-C and V-C).

With the exception of "U. S. Corrections," most of the analysis of the tabular data is confined to straightforward description. Some attention is paid to the problem of sample-population relation in the form of standard errors (presumably underestimated because they were based on the assumption of random sampling). However, this approaches lip service, since many apparent differences are discussed with no attention to significance or nonsignificance. (Again we do not regard this as an automatic criticism, particularly since accurate indication of significance would have been difficult—see Section A-18.)

In analyzing cumulative activity, KPM's main tool was the

accumulative incidence curve, a technique which they developed independently.

12. How Interpreted?

The main choices concerned

(1) extent of warning about possible differences between reported behavior and actual behavior,
(2) extent of warning about possible differences between the sampled population (see Section 18) and the entire U.S. white male population,
(3) extent of warning about sampling fluctuations,
(4) extent of verbal discussion *not* based on evidence presented,
(5) certainty with which conclusions were presented.

Under (1) the emphasis was on methodological checks in order to indicate, as far as they could, how small this difference seemed to KPM to be. Under (2) there was little discussion. Under (3) the warnings were made early, incompletely, but not often. Under (4) the extent of discussion was substantial, most of it aimed at social and legal attitudes about sexual behavior, and descriptions or practices not covered by the tables. Under (5) the conclusions were usually presented with an air of solid certainty.

In general the observations seem to have been interpreted with more fervor than caution, although occasional qualifications may be found.

CHAPTER III. PRINCIPLES OF SAMPLING

13. Introduction

It is difficult, if not impossible, to assess the quality of any sample and its analysis without comparing it with a set of principles. This is particularly true of KPM's works. The present chapter endeavors to set down, in compact form, a few of the principles of sampling which are especially relevant to a consideration of KPM's sampling. As we have noted (Section 6), KPM chose to select individuals in groups or clusters, to divide the population into segments and keep segment sizes more nearly equal in the sample than in the population, and to use no semblance of probability sampling ideas. The discussion in this chapter concentrates on these aspects of sampling.

Many readers will, we believe, desire a more connected account of the principles of sampling, with examples and fuller discussion. These are provided in Appendix G. Any reader who finds the statements used in this chapter unclear, or not intuitively acceptable, is urged to turn to Appendix G before proceeding further. Once there, he should read through from the beginning, since argument and exposition there are closely knit and unsuited to piecemeal references.

Whether by biologists, sociologists, engineers, or chemists, sampling is often taken too lightly. In the early years of the present century, it was not uncommon to measure the claws and carapaces of 1000 crabs, or to count the number of veins in each of 1000 leaves, and to attach to the results the "probable error" which would have been appropriate had the 1000 crabs or the 1000 leaves been drawn at random from the population of interest. If the population of interest were all crabs in a wide-spread species, it would be obviously almost impossible to take a simple random sample. But this does not bar us from honestly assessing the likely range of fluctuation of the result. Much effort has been applied in recent years, particularly in sampling human populations, to the development of sampling plans which, *simultaneously*,

(i) are economically feasible,
(ii) give reasonably precise results, and
(iii) show within themselves an honest measure of fluctuation of their results.

Any excuse for the practice of treating non-random samples as random ones is now entirely tenuous. Wider knowledge of the principles involved is needed if scientific investigations involving samples (and what such investigation does not involve samples?) are to be solidly based. Additional knowledge of techniques is not so vitally important, though it can lead to substantial economic gains.

14. Cluster Sampling

A botanist who gathered 10 oak leaves from each of 100 oak trees might feel that he had a fine sample of 1000, and that, if 500 were infected with a certain species of parasites, he had shown that the percentage infection was close to 50%. If he had studied the binomial distribution, he might calculate a standard error according to the usual formula for random samples, $p \pm \sqrt{pq/n}$, which in thise case yields 50 ± 1.6% (since $p = q = .5$ and $n = 1000$). In doing this he would neglect three things:

(i) probable selectivity in selecting trees (favoring large trees, perhaps?)
(ii) probable selectivity in choosing leaves from a selected tree (favoring well-colored or alternatively, visibly infected leaves perhaps) and
(iii) the necessary allowance, in the formula used to compute the standard error, for the fact that he had not selected his leaves individually.

Most scientists are keenly aware of the analogs of (i) and (ii) in their own fields of work, at least as soon as they are pointed out to them. Far fewer seem to realize that, even if the trees were selected at random from the forest, and 10 leaves were chosen at random from each selected tree, (iii) must still be considered. But if, as might indeed be the case, each tree were either wholly infected or wholly free of infection, then the 1000 leaves tell us *no more* than 100 leaves, one from each tree, since each group of 10 leaves will be all infected or all free of infection. In this event, we should take $n = 100$ in calculating the standard error and find an infection rate of 50 ± 5%. Such an extreme case of increased fluctuation due to sampling in groups or clusters would be detected by almost all scientists, and is not a serious danger. But less extreme cases easily escape detection.

We have just described, as one example of the reasons why the principles of sampling need wider understanding, an example of *cluster sampling*, where the individuals or sampling units are not drawn separately and independently into the sample, but are drawn in clusters, and have tried to make it clear that "individually at random" formulas do not apply. Cluster sampling is often desirable, but must be analyzed appropriately. KPM's sample was, in the main, a cluster sample, since they built up their sample from groups of people rather than from individuals.

15. Possibilities of Adjustment

Often the population is divided into segments of known relative size, perhaps from a census. It is sometimes thought that the best method of sampling is to take the same proportion from every segment, so that the sample sizes in the segments match the corresponding population sizes. Such samples do have the advantage of simplifying computations by equalizing weights, and they sometimes lead to a reduction of sampling error. But modern sampling theory shows that optimum allocation of resources usually requires *different* proportions to be sampled from different segments, whether the purpose is to estimate average values over the population or to make analytical comparisons between results in one group of segments and those in another.

When there are disparities in the relative sizes of segments in the sample as compared with the population, whether accidental or planned, these disparities must be taken into account when we attempt to estimate averages over the whole population. One way in which this can be done is by adjustments applied to the segments. Such adjustments proceed as follows. Suppose that we know

(i) the true fraction of the population in each segment, and
(ii) the segment into which each individual in the sample falls.

Then we can weight each individual in the sample by the ratio

$$\frac{\text{Fraction of population in that segment}}{\text{Fraction of sample in that segment}}$$

(It is computationally convenient to weight each segment mean with the numerator of this ratio; the result is algebraically identical to that described above.)

The result of adjustment is a new "sampled population"—one such that the relative sizes of its various segments are very nearly correct (according to (i) above). Since the weight is the same for all the sample individuals in a given segment, adjustment does nothing to redress any selectivity which may be present *within* segments. If we adjust in this way, we remove one source of systematic error without affecting other sources at all. The philosophy of such adjustments is discussed further in Section G-12, and it is concluded that they may generally be appropriately made (within the limits discussed in sections C-16—C-18). Their chief danger is the possible neglect of the possibilities that they may be

(i) entirely too small,
(ii) too large,
(iii) in the wrong direction,

because of unredressed selectivity *within* the segments. When this possibility exists, extreme caution in presenting the results of adjustment is indicated.

16. Probability Samples

When probability samples are used, inferences to the population can be based entirely on statistical principles rather than subject-matter judgment. Moreover, the reliability of the inferences can be judged quantitatively. A probability sample is one in which

(i) each individual (or primary unit) in the sampled population has a known probability of entering the sample,
(ii) the sample is chosen by a process involving one or more steps of automatic randomization consistent with these probabilities, and
(iii) in the analysis of the sample, weights appropriate to the probabilities (i) are used.

Contrary to some opinions, it is *not* necessary, and in fact usually not advisable in a pure probability sample for

(i) all samples to be equally probable, or
(ii) the appearance of one individual in the sample to be unrelated to the appearance of another.

In practice, because some respondents cannot be found or are uncooperative, we usually obtain, at best, approximate probability samples (see Sections A-2 and D-13) and have approximate confidence in our inference.

17. Nonprobability Samples

Samples which are not even approximately probability samples vary widely in both actual and apparent trustworthiness. Their trustworthiness usually increases as they are insulated more and more thoroughly from selective factors which might be related to the quantities being studied. Insulation may be obtained by:

(i) adjustments applied to the segment means in the sample,
(ii) examination of the sample as drawn for signs of selection on a particular factor,
(iii) partial randomization.

Adjustment for segments, as explained in Section 15 above, corrects for any selective factor operation *between* segments, but corrects not at all for selective factors operating *within* segments. If adjustment is to be used, deliberate selectivity between segments may be exercised without danger, *so long as it does not imply selectivity within segments.*

Negative results when the sample is examined for signs for selection on a particular variable are comforting, and strengthen the reliability of the sample. The amount of this strengthening depends very much on the *a priori* importance of the variables checked to what is being studied.

Deliberate (partial) randomization is a step toward a probability sample, and may be very helpful on occasion.

18. Sampled Population and Target Population

We have found it helpful in our thinking to make a clear distinction between two population concepts. The *target* population is the population of interest, about which we wish to make inferences or draw conclusions. It is the population which we are trying to study. The *sampled* population requires a more careful definition but, speaking popularly, it is the population which we actually succeed in sampling.

The notion of a sampled population can be more clearly described for probability sampling. In order to have probability sampling, we must know the chance that every sampling unit has of entering the sample, and the weight to be attached to the unit in the analysis. The sampled population may be defined as the population generated by repeated application of these chances and these weights. The frequency of occurrence of any particular sampling unit in the sampled population is proportional to the product

(Chance of entering the sample) × (Weight used in analysis)

This product is made constant for a probability sample. Thus, with probability sampling, the sampled population consists of all sampling units which have a non-zero chance of selection.

The sampled population is an important concept because by statistical theory we can make quantitative inferential statements, with known chances of error, from sample to sampled population. It must be carefully distinguished from the target population, the population of interest, about which we are tempted to make similar inferential statements.

Even with probability sampling, the sampled and the target population usually differ because of the presence of "refusals," "not-at-homes," "unable to classify," and so on. The consequence of these disturbances is that certain sampling units, although assigned a known chance of selection by the sampling plan, did not in fact have this chance in practice.

With non-probability sampling, the situation is much more obscure. By its definition as given above, the sampled population depends on the existence of a sampling plan (which may be only a vague set of principles in the investigator's head) and on the "chances" that any sampling unit had of being drawn. These chances are not well known—if they were, we should have a probability sample. But in many cases, it is reasonable to behave as if these chances exist and to attempt to estimate them, because they provide the only means of making statistical inferences beyond the non-probability sample to a corresponding "sampled population." The difficulty comes in specifying, or sometimes even thinking about, the nature of the sampled population. It is certain to be a weighted population where, for example, Theodosius Linklater may appear 1.37 times, while Basil Svensson appears only 0.17 times.

Insofar as we make statistical inferences beyond the sample to a larger body of individuals, we make them to the sampled population. The step from sampled population to target population is based on subject-matter knowledge and skill, general information, and intuition—but not on statistical methodology.

CHAPTER IV. THE INTERVIEW AREA

19. Interview vs. Questionnaire

The committee members do not profess authoritative knowledge of interviewing techniques. Nevertheless, the method by which the data were obtained cannot be regarded as outside the scope of the statistical aspects of the research.

For what our opinion is worth, we agree with KPM that a written questionnaire could not have replaced the interview for the broad population contemplated in this study. The questionnaire would not allow flexibility which seems to us necessary in the use of language, in varying the order of questions, in assisting the respondent, in following up particular topics and in dealing with persons of varying degrees of literacy. This is not to imply that the anonymous questionnaire is inherently less accurate than the interview, or that it could not be used fruitfully with certain groups of respondents and certain topics. So far as we are aware, not enough information is available to reach a verdict on these points.

20. Interviewing Technique

Many investigators have faced the problem of attempting to obtain accurate information about facts which the respondent is thought to be unwilling to report. It is natural to inquire whether KPM, in their interviewing technique, took advantage of accumulated experience as to the best methods for extracting the facts. But it is also well to inquire how much definite experience has been accumulated.

The KPM interview impressed us as an extraordinarily skillful performance. Direct questions are put rapidly in an order which seems to these respondents hard to predict, so that it is difficult to tell what is coming next. Despite the air of briskness, we did not receive the impression that we were being hurried if we wished to reflect before replying, and supplementary questions or information were given if this seemed helpful to the memory. The coded recording of the data was done unobtrusively by the interviewer, so that the interview appeared to be a friendly conversation rather than any kind of an inquisition. These, of course, are personal impressions.

KPM evidently think highly of the virtues of this technique, because it was adopted despite limitations which it imposes on the scope and rate of progress of the study. The technique makes great demands on the interviewer. The long period of training and the personal qualities required have restricted and will continue to restrict the interviewers to a very small number. This limits the speed with which data can be accumulated and also puts restrictions on the type of sampling that can be employed.

The type of interview used by KPM differs markedly from the less directive methods which are sometimes recommended for dealing with taboo subjects. If the subject is likely to feel that his answer to a certain question will affect his prestige in the eyes of the interviewer, a less directive approach would be to conduct the interview in such a way that he gives the desired information without realizing that he is answering the awkward question. The KPM method is the antithesis of this. Research on interviewing techniques has not yet produced any substantial body of evidence as to the superiority of either the less directive methods or the KPM technique.

With regard to specific inaccuracies in the KPM data, we

believe that the interview gives an opportunity both for positive and negative bias. The KPM assumption that everyone has engaged in all types of activity seems to some likely to encourage exaggeration by the respondents. (KPM feel (personal communication) that their cross-checks are highly effective in detecting such exaggeration.) On the other hand, our impression from the interview was that a successful denial of certain types of activity would be possible if the subject was prepared to do so, although we do not know the full extent of the KPM cross-checks which would lead them to be suspicious of such a denial. KPM assert (personal communication) that they regard cover-up as a more likely source of bias than exaggeration. Our opinions on this statement are divided.

As KPM point out (p. 48), the subject's willingness to talk about certain types of activity is influenced by the attitudes of the social group to which he belongs. Until evidence to the contrary is presented, the presumption (made by some of the critics) that his final responses will also be influenced is one that cannot be cast aside. The size of these influences is still a matter of opinion. A corresponding element of doubt is present in almost all comparisons between different social levels, both those which provide some of the most interesting comparisons in the book, and those in many other studies.

CHAPTER V. THE SAMPLING AREA

21. KPM's Sampled Population

As noted above, KPM's sample was deliberately disproportionate, partly in order to cover individual segments defined by age, education, religion, etc., in an adequate manner, partly because of geographical convenience. If the results for individual segments were to be based on samples of at least moderate size, such disproportion was necessary and wise. Its effects on overall results are less clear. It seems impossible to be sure what effect it had on the variability of the final result, and its use is certainly not a demonstrable error as far as variability is concerned.

In their U. S. corrections, KPM provided adjustments for disproportion between segments defined by age, education, and marital status. As noted above (Section 17) we feel that such adjustments are usually appropriate. Due to absence of population data, they did not adjust for religion. The geographical imbalance of their sample was so great that an overall geographic adjustment was not feasible. Thus they compensated for some disproportions, and left others to produce what effects they would.

Their only examination of the sample for signs of selection within segments is their comparison of 100% groups (groups where all members were interviewed) with partial groups (groups where only part of the members were sampled). This gives some insight into the effect of volunteering as a selective factor. Beyond this, KPM report no serious effort to measure the actual effect of volunteering, or to discover what percentage of the population they would be able to persuade to be interviewed.

They made no use of randomization. They might have attempted to sample, say, college seniors from two colleges drawn at random from a large list of colleges, but they are of the opinion (personal communication) that this would have slowed up the work to an unmanageable extent.

All in all, the absence of any orderly sampling plan contrasts strikingly with their usual methodical mode of attack on other problems.

As stated briefly above (Section 6), the "sampled populations" corresponding to
(1) KPM's raw means, and to
(2) KPM's "U.S. corrected" means,
respectively, are startlingly different from the composition of the U. S. white male population. (For example, although these sampled populations have the U. S. average combination of education and rural-urban background, they have half of their members living in Indiana.) Since a complete probability sample seems to have been out of the question at the beginning of the KPM investigation, some such "sampled population" was to be expected, although it might have been somewhat less distorted. Provided that further statistical analyses of the sort indicated in Appendix C, Chapter II-C were made, it would be possible to make adequate rigorous inferences from the sample to this ill-defined "sampled population."

The inference from these vague entities to the U. S. white male population depends on:
(a) the inferrer's view as to what these "sampled populations" are really like, and
(b) the inferrer's judgment as to how (reported) sexual behavior varies within segments.
It is not surprising that experts disagree.

The inference from KPM's sample to the (reported) behavior of all U. S. white males contains a large gap which can be spanned only by expert judgment. This is a common phenomenon in social fields, but is still unfortunate. A considerable bridge across this gap would be furnished by a small probability sample.

22. Could KPM Have Used Probability Sampling?

If probability sampling could have been used, its use would have avoided one of the main gaps in KPM's present chain of inference. We have, therefore, considered this possibility carefully.

The difficulties in applying probability sampling to KPM's study lie in the expenditure of time required to make the contacts necessary to persuade a predesignated man to give a history. By adapting the mechanism of the probability sample to KPM's situation, these difficulties may perhaps be reduced (see Appendix D, Chapter V-D). It would almost certainly have been impractical for KPM to have used a probability sample in the early years of their study. If KPM's apparent "opinions" (p. 39 of KPM) as to the effectiveness of their present techniques of contact are correct, starting a probability sample would have been practical at any time since the appearance of the male volume in 1948.[1] However, KPM (personal communication, 1952) feel that such an interpretation of their written statement is unwarranted.

[1] "The number of persons who can provide introductions has continually spread until now, in the present study, we have a network of connections that could put us into almost any group with which we wished to work, anywhere in the country." (P. 39 of KPM.)

Since it would not have been feasible for KPM to take a large sample on a probability basis, a reasonable probability sample would be, and would have been, a small one, and its purpose would be:

(1) to act as a check on the large sample, and
(2) possibly, to serve as a basis for adjusting the results of the large sample.

A probability sampling program planned to serve these purposes is discussed in Appendix D, Chapter VII-D. Such a program should proceed by stages because of the absence of information on costs and refusal rates.

This conclusion about probability sampling does not excuse KPM from the responsibility for choosing geographical disproportion in order to save travel time and expense. The wisdom or unwisdom of this choice seems to depend on one's view as to the magnitude of geographical differences. Again, it is not surprising that experts disagree.

CHAPTER VI. METHODOLOGICAL CHECKS

23. Possible Checks

The primary check, if it could be made, is the comparison of *average* actual behavior with *average* reported behavior. *Variability* in the difference between actual and reported behavior is secondary in interest, because high variability merely implies the necessity of larger numbers of cases, while large average differences between actual and reported behavior represent a systematic error that cannot be adjusted without rather complete knowledge. Unfortunately this primary check does not at present seem feasible in studying human sexual behavior as it occurs in our culture.

Of secondary importance are checks of the single actual report with the average actual report, where averages may be taken over fluctuations, time, spouses, and/or interviewers. (See Appendix A, Chapter V-A) In this second category, the following possible comparisons suggest themselves:

1. Reinterviews of the same respondent
2. Comparison of spouses
3. Comparison of interviewers on the same population segment
4. Duplicate interviews by the same interviewer at various times.

24. KPM's Checks

The only comparison of observed and reported behavior which KPM found feasible was the date of appearance of pubic hair, which agreed quite successfully. This is a physical characteristic, different in character and emotional loading from the behavior of main interest. Some subjects may have had to rely upon general information, plus some assistance from the interviewer, in naming a date for themselves. Thus this check furnishes rather weak support.

At the level of rechecks on respondents, some information is available but more is needed. Similarly, comparisons of spouses have been made for a relatively selected group. The checks themselves are encouraging, but more cases are needed.

Some attempts have been made to compare the staff interviewers but since there is some selection in the assignment of cases, these comparisons do not meet the problem as squarely as interviews of the same respondent by different interviewers, or the recorded interview technique.

A comparison of early versus late interviews by Kinsey is given in KPM, but it is hard to tell, for example, whether the 12.4% drop (from 44.9% to 32.5%) in the accumulative incidence for total premarital intercourse at age 19 (single males, education level 13+) from early to late interviews is due to differing groups sampled, instability in the interviewing process, or reasonable sampling variation for cluster sampling (KPM p. 146).

KPM have made serious efforts to check their work in the aspects where checking seems feasible. However, improved and more extensive checking is needed. Although duplicate recording of interviews is mentioned, no data have been published. Even if they must be based on very few cases, such comparisons should be made available.

CHAPTER VII. ANALYTICAL TECHNIQUES

25. Variables Affecting Sexual Behavior

After introductory chapters (5 and 6) on early sexual growth and activity, KPM proceed to examine the effects of the following variables:

Age
Marital status
Age of adolescence
Social level
Comparison of two generations
Vertical mobility in the occupational scale
Rural-urban background
Religious background

In this chapter we attempt to appriase, in general terms, the analytical techniques used by KPM in their study of these variables.

26. Definition of the Variables

Some of the variables: age of adolescence, social level, occupational level, rural-urban background and religious background, involve prolems of definition. These seem to have been in the main thoughtfully handled and presented by KPM. For instance, KPM discuss the relative merits of educational level attained by the subject and of the occupational class of the subject and of his parents as a measure of social level (pp. 330–32). In their opinion, educational level is the most satisfactory criterion and this was adopted for the analysis. In the case of religious affiliation, KPM distinguish between active and inactive profession of religious faith, though the definition of the two terms is not made entirely clear.

The definition which looks least satisfactory is that of age of adolescence (p. 299), where the problem is formidable. The criteria employed by KPM appear difficult for the reader to interpret.

27. Assessing Effects of Variables

With a multiplicity of variables which may interact on each other, the task of assessing the importance of each variable individually is not easy. Examination of the variables one by one, ignoring all other variables except the one under scrutiny, may give wrong conclusions, because what appears on the surface to be the effect of one variable may be merely a reflection of the effects of other variables.

A thorough attack on this problem calls for a multiple-variable approach in which all effects are investigated simultaneously. This requires a high degree of statistical maturity and of skill in presentation.

The method utilized by KPM is a compromise. In general, with some exceptions, they regard age, marital status and educational level as basic variables, which are held fixed or compensated for in the investigation of each of the remaining variables. The other variables are disregarded for the moment. Although we have not examined the matter exhaustively, this policy seems to have been justified by events, because KPM claim from their analyses that the other variables, with the exception of age at adolescence, have had relatively minor effects.

28. The Measurement of Activity

In the KPM tables, activity is measured by "incidence" (per cent of the population who engage in the activity) as well as by frequency per week. In some tables, both mean and median frequencies are given, and also frequencies for the total and for the active population. There are advantages in presenting various measures. On the other hand, inspection suggests that all these measures are correlated: that is, to some extent they tell the same story. A complex internal analysis would probably show about how many measures are really needed to extract the information in the data and what individual measurements, or combinations of them, are best for this purpose. Perhaps a single one, or at most two, would suffice. As it is, both KPM and the industrious reader have to wade through tables and discussion of a number of different measurements, without being clear whether anything new is learned. Simplification would be pleasant, but is far from essential.

29. Tests of Significance

In the discussion of effects which they regard as real, KPM make little appeal to tests of significance. They often present standard errors attached to the mean frequencies for individual cells. Because sampling was non-random and was by groups, these standard errors, calculated on the assumption of randomness, are under-estimates, perhaps by a substantial amount. The standard errors have a kind of negative virtue, in the sense that if a difference is not significant when judged against these errors, it would not be significant if a valid test could be devised. The problem of devising a realistic estimate of the true standard errors is one of considerable complexity (see Section II-C).

We have been unable to discover from the book the principles by which KPM decide when to regard an effect as real. The size of the effect is one criterion. Size should certainly be taken into account, since an effect may be significant statistically but too small to be of biological or sociological interest. They evidently attach some importance to the consistency with which an effect is exhibited in different parts of a table. As a criterion, consistency is of variable worth. Consistency over different age groups (where age denotes age at the time of the reported activity) is of little worth, since there is inevitably substantial correlation between sampling fluctuations of reported activities at neighboring ages because the same subject appears in neighboring age groups. More weight can be attached to consistency over different educational levels, because different groups of subjects are involved.

To summarize, statements about the data in their tables lie at the level of shrewd descriptive comment, rather than at the level of an attempt to make inferential statements from a sample to a clearly defined population (even though this could not be the U. S. white male population).

We do not propose to discuss the analysis for each variable separately. Two analyses which have attracted much attention will be considered later (Sections 33 to 37).

30. U. S. Corrections

In most sampling plans it is necessary to provide a set of weights for the segments of the sampled population to recover accurate estimates for the target population (i.e. the population about which inferences are desired). That such adjustments are usually appropriate, whether probability or nonprobability samples are employed, has already been pointed out (Section 17, see Section II-G).

Since KPM have as their target population U. S. white males, we can reasonably expect them to apply weights in an attempt to correct for disproportionate representation in the sampled population of some segments of the target population.

KPM supply U. S. Corrections (p. 106–9) and use them rather consistently throughout the work. There are no examples given explaining the application of the weights. The critics, and sometimes this committee, have had difficulty in verifying computations where they have been used. Of the 13 tables where corrections could be checked completely, one checked, 10 checked except for one age group each, and two were not checked by the correction mentioned in the text. Apparently the exposition could be improved.

The U. S. Corrections should be used, but it might be possible to make a more effective choice of segments (see A-43 and V-C and II-G).

KPM did not sufficiently warn the reader that U. S. corrected figures are not corrected for selection within segments, and may be seriously biased.

31. The Accumulative Incidence Curve

KPM have a useful device for summarizing incidence data by age. This accumulative incidence curve gives the percentage of individuals in the sample (reporting for a given age) to whom a particular event has occurred before that age. Although the explanation of the concept of accumulative incidence is not as clear as most of KPM's writing, the computations made are satisfactory. When there are no generation-to-generation changes in the population and no differential recall depending on age at report, this method is particularly justified, because it packs all the incidence data neatly into one grand summary. (For discussion of the critics' comments see A-39.) No better method for overall comparisons seems to be available.

32. Other Devices

1. KPM did some extensive sampling experiments on their data, with a view to discovering the sample size needed for the accuracy they desired. These experiments turned out to be almost valueless because KPM did not take account of the necessary statistical principles (see A-19).

2. The committee had an opportunity to inspect the KPM facilities on a visit to Bloomington, Indiana. We observed that the data sheets were neatly filled out, that the files were well kept, that requests for original data were usually met in a matter of moments, and that the office was well equipped for handling the extensive data with which KPM deal.

3. The KPM volume was written while data were still being collected. Apparently KPM chose to use all the data on hand at the time a particular point was being analyzed (personal communication from KPM). Thus different tables have different totals, a source of annoyance to critics and users of the book. The reasons for this should have been pointed out by KPM. The additional interviewing was deliberately selective with an aim to strengthen weak segments (personal communication from KPM). It seems to us that, if this strengthening was necessary for later analyses, it would have been worthwhile to add the new material to the early tabulations. This would also have increased comparability and avoided the problems raised by the existence of many different sampled populations.

CHAPTER VIII. TWO COMPLEX ANALYSES

33. Patterns in Successive Generations

In this chapter we discuss briefly two analyses by KPM which have attracted much attention. Our object is to give two specific illustrations of the kind of analysis which they chose to undertake, with comments on their competence.

The first analysis was made by dividing the sample into two groups: those over 33 years of age at the time of interview, with a median age of 43.1 years, and those under 33 years at the time of interview, with a median age of 21.2 years.

Our comments deal with three topics: (i) the statistical methodology employed (ii) KPM's summary of their tables (iii) the general problem of inference from data of this type.

34. Statistical Methods

In the comparisons, educational level and age at the time of the activity are held constant and in nearly all comparisons marital status also. The method used to compare the group means seems satisfactory except for some minor points, discussed in A-25, A-33 and A-43.

It would have been helpful to present classifications of the older and younger groups according to other factors which might influence sexual activity, e.g., rural-urban background, religious affiliation, marital status at age 20 or 25. The two groups would not necessarily agree closely in these break-downs, for there has been a slow drift towards the towns, and perhaps a drift towards "inactive" rather than "active" religious affiliation. For interpretive purposes it is advisable, in any event, to learn as much as possible about the compositions of the older and younger groups. Some critics have claimed that the older generation is "atypical."

35. KPM's Summary of Their Tables

The data are presented in 8 large tables (98–105). As a statistician learns from experience, a competent summary of a large body of data is not an easy task. KPM give a detailed discussion of the accumulative incidence data for each type of outlet, followed by a similar discussion of the frequency data.

These detailed comments on what the data appear to show seem sound, except that on two occasions where the younger group showed greater sexual activity, KPM ignored or played down the difference between the two groups (Section A-45).

Their general summary statement reads in part as follows:

> The changes that have occurred in 22 years, as measured by the data given in the present chapter, concern attitudes and minor details of behavior, and nothing that is deeply fundamental in overt activity. There has been nothing as fundamental as the substitution of one type of outlet for another, of masturbation for heterosexual coitus, of coitus for the homosexual, or vice versa. There has not even been a material increase or decrease in the incidences and frequencies of most types of activity. . . .
>
> And the sum total of the measurable effects on American sexual behavior are slight changes in attitudes, some increase in the frequency of masturbation among boys of the lower educational levels, more frequent nocturnal emissions, increased frequencies of premarital petting, earlier coitus for a portion of the male population, and the transferences of a percentage of the pre-marital intercourse from prostitutes to girls who are not prostitutes.

Some critics have objected strongly to this statement, particularly the first paragraph, on the grounds that it gives a biased report by brushing aside the differences in activity, which are almost all in the direction of higher or earlier sexual activity by the younger group. The reporting does appear a little one-sided, in that the reader is encouraged to conclude that the differences are immaterial, although KPM do not state what they mean by a "material" increase. On the other hand, the catalogue of differences, given at the end of the second paragraph above, includes all differences noted either by KPM or the critics, except for an increased homosexual activity in the younger group at educational levels 0–8 and 9–12.

36. Validity of Inferences

Two objections have been made by some critics to any inferences drawn from a comparison of this type. The first is that the groups may not be representative of their generations. KPM have attempted to dispose of this objection, at least in part, by holding educational level and marital status constant. It might be possible to go further and hold other factors constant, or at least examine whether the samples from the two generations differ in these factors. But with non-random sampling the objection is not removed even if a number of factors are held constant, because one or both groups might be biased with respect to some factor whose importance was not realized. Various opinions may be formed as to the strength of the objection, but it can be removed only by the use of probability sampling accompanied by valid tests of significance.

Secondly, in a comparison of this type, the older generation is describing events which involve a much longer period of recall, with a possibility of distortion as events become distant. Further retake studies, if KPM can continue them for a sufficiently long period, may throw some light on the strength of this objection.

The joint effect of these objections is to render the conclusions tentative rather than definitely established.

37. Vertical Mobility

This analysis (pp. 417–47) shows a degree of ingenuity and sophistication which is not too common in quantitative investigations in sociology. The data are arranged in a two-way array according to the occupational class of the subject at the time of interview and the occupational class of the parents. KPM examine whether the pattern of sexual activity of the subject is more strongly associated with the parental occupational class than with that attained by the subject. They conclude (p. 419)

> In general, it will be seen that the sexual history of the individual accords with the pattern of the social group into which he ultimately moves, rather than with the pattern of the social group to which the parent belongs and in which the subject was placed when he lived in the parental home.
>
> The most significant thing shown by these calculations (Tables 107–115) is the evidence that an individual who is ever going to depart from the parental pattern is likely to have done so by the time he has become adolescent.

The amount of data which KPM present in this analysis is worth mention as evidence that they do not shirk work. Tables are given for 7 types of activity. Three age groups are shown in each table. When we classify by occupational level of subject and parent, this leads to 21 two-way tables. Five measures of the type of activity are given, so that a painstaking examination extends over 105 two-way tables.

KPM appear to have paid most attention to the frequency data. Their task is to determine whether this shows a stronger association with the occupational class of the subject or of the parent. In reaching a verdict, they rely on judgment from eye inspection. By a similar eye inspection, we agree with their verdict as a descriptive statement of what the data indicate, although different individuals might disagree as to how definitely their statement holds. Judgments made by one individual for the data on frequencies were that in 7 of the 21 two-way tables, association with subject and parent either was not present at all or looked about equal. In 9 it looked mildly more with the subject and in 5 it looked strongly more with the subject.

It would be of interest to undertake a more objective analysis. Analysis of variance techniques are available for this purpose, although some theoretical problems remain.

So far as interpretation is concerned, the principal disturbing factor is the possibility, which some critics have mentioned, that the subject's reports of his activity are influenced by the social level to which he belongs at the time of interview. KPM maintain that attitudes towards different types of activity are strongly affected by the social level of the subject. Whether they change when he changes his social level would be interesting to discover. Something might be learned by retakes for subjects who had moved in the social scale. To obtain an abundant body of data of this kind will, however, be a slow and difficult process.

CHAPTER IX. CARE IN INTERPRETATION

38. Sample and Sampled Population

In sample surveys, the inference from sample to sampled population is often relatively straightforward, although not trivial. We can usually set limits so that the statement "the sample agrees with the sampled population within these limits" has approximately the agreed-upon risk. (We may have to work fairly hard to set these limits correctly.) But we have always to remember, and usually must remind the reader steadily, that these limits are not infinitely narrow.

KPM's caution on page 153 (quoted in Appendix A, Section 48) is a caution, but it is not repeated.

In general, their statements about small differences are more forthright than we would care to make.

39. Sampled Population and Target Population

When a respectable approximation of a probability sample is involved, the step from sampled population to target population is usually short and the inference strong. Otherwise, the inference is often tortuous and weak. It depends on subject matter knowledge and intuition, and on other barely tangible considerations. These considerations deserve to be brought to the reader's attention, and to be discussed as best the authors may.

This KPM did not do adequately. Their discussion of diversification (p. 92) and 100 per cent samples (p. 93) is only a beginning.

40. Systematic Errors of Measurement

Any quantitative study offers the possibility of systematic errors of measurement. It is generally agreed that these possibilities should be placed before the reader and discussed.

In KPM's study these possibilities concentrate on the difference between present reported and past actual behavior. KPM spent Chapter 4 on this question. Their discussion is generally good, except on some questions which arise in connection with generation-to-generation comparison (see Sections A-25 and A-44).

41. Unsupported Assertions

We are convinced that unsubstantiated assertions are not, in themselves, inappropriate in a scientific study. In any complex field, where many questions remain unresolved, the accumulated insight of an experienced worker frequently merits recording when no documentation can be given. However, the author who values his reputation for objectivity will take pains to warn the reader, frequently repetitiously, whenever an unsubstantiated conclusion is being presented, and will choose his words with the greatest care. KPM did not do this.

Many of the most interesting statements in the book are not based on the tabular material presented and it is not made at all clear on what evidence the statements are based. Nevertheless, the statements are presented as if they were well-established conclusions.

42. Some Major Controversial Findings

Some KPM findings about which much scientific discussion has centered relate to:
(i) stability of sexual patterns,
(ii) homosexuality, and
(iii) the effects of vertical mobility.
In all these areas KPM have made forthright and bold statements. As discussed in more detail in Sections A-45 to A-47 (also see A-25), there are reasons for caution in every one of the three areas.

CHAPTER X. COMPARISON WITH OTHER STUDIES[2]

43. Interviewing

Good sex studies have been made using both the personal interview and questionnaire techniques. Given that just one technique is to be employed, KPM's choice of personal interview seems necessary if illiterates or near-illiterates are to be sampled. At present, it is good practice in gathering this type of data to endeavor to have all subjects give information on as many relevant points of the study as possible. No study seems to have done better on this matter than KPM.

Whether it is always good practice to standardize the questions asked is debatable. KPM did not do this and give telling arguments against the practice. Some other studies have standardized the questions, both in personal interview and in self-administered questionnaires, and they have included good arguments in favor of their procedure. In training interviewers KPM seem to have gone to greater lengths (a year of training) in preparing for the *specific* interview used in the study, than any of the other personal interview studies. Information on training of interviewers is fairly hard to come by in all these studies.

Given the choice of personal interview, it is not possible at this writing to be logically certain whether the KPM technique is better or worse than that of the other interview studies, no matter whether one approves or disapproves of the tactics of a diagnostician or medical detective. Some discussion of how the KPM interview appeared to us is given in Appendix E. Numerous cross-checks on frequency and dates of occurrences appear within the KPM interview, while they seem to be lacking in most other studies. Setting aside points on which there is no evidence, KPM's interviewing is as good as or better than that of the other studies reviewed.

44. Checks

As for checks on the interviewing process, KPM unquestionably lead the field with 100 per cent samples, retakes, spouse comparisons, early vs. late groups, interviewer comparisons, and the pubic hair study. Some authors mention casual checks with no data supplied. Bromley and Britten compare interview and questionnaire results on different groups. Davis reports a study where 50 subjects were interviewed before and after questionnaire administration, and offers a breakdown by consecutive 100 questionnaires received. Dickinson and Beam's two books speak of comparing verbal reports and physical examination results as a way of verifying the record rather than as a check—no records seem to be published. Farris' comparison of reported vs. personally recorded masturbatory rates omits the critical comparative information. Hamilton finds that different question wordings give different responses, but leaves the matter here. Landis and Bolles use several independent judges for evaluation of scales—but, instead of comparing their results, argue that agreement will be good because of experience and training. They do not compare normal with handicapped subjects. Landis checks with the psychiatric case history as a means of eliminating subjects with discrepancies, and gives data on the agreement of independent judges' ratings. Terman offers spouse comparisons. When KPM's checks are viewed with those of the other leading sex studies in mind, it is clear that a new high level has been established.

45. Sampling

All studies used volunteer non-probability samples. Some were drawn from more specifiable target populations than others. For example, Bromley and Britten drew exclusively from college volunteers, while Davis used mail-questionnaire respondents from lists of Women's Clubs and college alumnae. Others used well-to-do patients, or clinic groups. Aside from KPM, Bromley and Britten is the only study that seems to have attempted to get nationwide geographic

[2] The material in this chapter is our inference from the reviews supplied by W. O. Jenkins and presented in Appendix B. We have not personally read all the volumes concerned. The volumes are as follows:
Bromley, Dorothy D., and Britten, Florence H. *Youth and sex.* New York: Harper and Brothers, 1938.
Davis, Katherine B. *Factors in the sex life of twenty-two hundred women.* New York: Harper and Brothers, 1929.
Dickinson, R. L., and Beam, Lura A. *The single woman.* Baltimore: Williams and Wilkins Co., 1934.
Dickinson, R. L., and Beam, Lura A. *A thousand marriages.* Baltimore: Williams and Wilkins Co., 1931.
Farris, E. J. *Human fertility and problems of the male.* White Plains, N.Y.: Author's press, 1950.
Hamilton, G. V. *A research in marriage.* New York: A. and C. Boni, 1929.
Kinsey, A. C., Pomeroy, W. B., and Martin, C. E. *Sexual behavior in the human male.* Philadelphia: W. B. Saunders Company, 1948.
Landis, C., et al. *Sex in development.* New York and London: Paul B. Hoeber, 1940.
Landis, C., and Bolles, M. M. *Personality and sexuality of the physically handicapped woman.* New York and London: Paul B. Hoeber, 1942.
Terman, L. M., et al. *Psychological factors in marital happiness.* New York: McGraw-Hill Book Co., 1938.

representation (we have omitted M. J. Exner's 1915 study), while Davis has covered the eastern area, and Terman covers part of the California area. Although KPM's sample is heavily charged with college students, a broader representation of social and educational levels is offered than in the other studies. All studies reviewed have special features which make generalizations to specific populations difficult. Certainly KPM's sampling seems never worse and often better than that of the other studies.

46. Analysis

Most studies confined their analysis to simple descriptive statistics—percentages, means, and medians. A few added ranges, standard deviations, correlation coefficients, and attempted significance tests. About half used two-way breakdowns, usually on background characteristics, as a way of sharpening differences between groups. Three studies offered scales either based on judges' evaluations (Landis, and Landis and Bolles), or scoring of batteries of items (Terman). KPM restricted the use of scales to occupational classification and homosexual-heterosexual rating. They added the accumulative incidence curve, the U. S. corrections, and extensively used fine-grained (high-order) breakdowns. In general, KPM's analysis employed more devices and was more searching than the analyses offered by other studies.

47. Interpretation

We have already mentioned (33) that KPM are competent at the accurate and understandable verbal description of the meanings of a table whose entries are taken as correct. Some of the other authors have also done well, although the extent of their analysis is usually more limited. In inferring from sampled population to target population, all the studies are weak. The inferences left with the reader (if we are to judge) are much broader than the studies could possibly warrant. Every study has its own precautionary remarks to the effect that the reader must not extend the inferences beyond that of the population studied. Very little attempt is made to describe the target population, to help the reader with the step from sample to sampled population, or to remind him of sampling fluctuations. The precautionary remarks in the opening pages of a study are usually forgotten when the authors come to discuss matters of national policy, morals, legislation, therapy, and psychological and sociological implications toward the end of their book. The reader must then be left with the inference that the findings apply on at least a national scale. Bromley and Britten are more forthright than most. They argue overtly that their volunteer college sample is a representative of all U. S. individuals of college age. Of the 10 studies considered, only two, Davis and Farris, seem to have consistently exercised due caution about generalization from sample to population and warnings to the reader. The last paragraph of the section entitled, "Description of Sample and Sampling Methods" in each review in Appendix B gives one reader's opinion of the generalizations from sample to sampled population intended by the author.

Our reviewer was not asked to gather data that would give us a way of comparing the extent of unsupported statements in the other studies with those of KPM, so this aspect of interpretation remains uncompared by us. It would be very interesting if someone would collect such information, not only in connection with the present work, but with regard to general scientific writing in various fields. This would be no small task.

CHAPTER XI. CONCLUSIONS

48. Interviewing

(1) The interviewing methods used by KPM may not be ideal, but no substitute has been suggested with evidence that it is an improvement.
(2) The interviewing technique has been subjected to many criticisms (see Section A-11), but on examination the criticisms usually amount to saying "answer is unknown," or "KPM have not demonstrated how good their method is."

These conclusions can be summarized by saying that we need to know more about interviewing in general.

49. Checks

(1) The types of methodological checks considered by KPM seem to be quite inclusive.
(2) A greater volume of checks—more retakes, etc. is desirable, as is more delicate analysis. (See Sections C-15 and C-18.)
(3) The results of duplicate recording of interviews should be published.

These conclusions can be summarized by saying that KPM's checks were good, but they can afford to supply more.

50. Sampling

Given U. S. white males as the target population, our conclusions are that:

(1) KPM's starting with a nonprobability sample was justified.
(2) It should perhaps already have been supplemented by at least a small probability sample.
(3) If further general interviewing is contemplated, and perhaps even otherwise, a small probability sample should be planned and taken.
(4) In the absence of a probability-sample benchmark, the present results must be regarded as subject to systematic errors of unknown magnitude due to selective sampling (via volunteering and the like).

51. Analysis

KPM's analysis is best described as simple and relatively searching. They did not use such techniques as analysis of variance or multiple regression, but they brought out the indications of their data in a workmanlike manner.

In more detail:

(1) their selection of variables for adjustment seemed to

be a reasonably effective substitute for more complex analyses,
(2) they gave several measures of activity (giving the reader a choice at the expense of more tables to examine),
(3) they made essentially no use of tests of significance, but cited many standard errors (which were inappropriate for their cluster samples),
(4) they used U. S. Corrections and their (independently developed) accumulative incidence curve. More careful exposition of these devices would have been desirable.

To summarize in another way:
(i) they did not shirk hard work, and
(ii) their summaries were shrewd descriptive comments rather than inferential statements about clearly defined populations.

Their main attempt at inferences was a sample size experiment whose results (i) could have been predicted by statistical theory, (ii) were irrelevant to their cluster sampling.

They continued to add new interviews without redoing earlier tabulations, thus producing an unwarranted effect of sloppiness in the book, although their records were kept carefully and in unusually good shape.

52. Interpretation

(1) KPM showed competence in accurate and understandable verbal description of the trends and tendencies indicated by their tables. In stating and summarizing what the sample seems to show, they were competent and effective.

(2) Their discussion of the uncertainties in the inferences from the numbers in the tables to the behavior of all U. S. white males was brief, insufficiently repeated, and oftentimes entirely lacking. In instilling due caution about sampling fluctuations and differences between sampled and target populations, they were lax and ineffective.

(3) Their discussion of systematic errors of reporting is careful and detailed (with the exception of some questions bearing on generation comparisons).

(4) Many of their most interesting statements are not based on the tables or any specified evidence, but are nevertheless presented as well-established conclusions. Statements based on data presented, including the most important findings, are made much too boldly and confidently. In numerous instances their words go substantially beyond the data presented and thereby fall below our standard for good scientific writing.

53. Comparison with Other Studies

In comparison with nine other leading sex studies, KPM's work is outstandingly good.

In more detail,
(1) their interviewing ranks with the best,
(2) they have more and better checks,
(3) their geographic and social class representation is broader and better,
(4) their volunteer non-probability sample problem is the same,
(5) they used more varied and searching methods of analysis,
(6) only two of the nine studies (Davis and Farris) were more careful about generalization and warned the reader more thoroughly about its dangers.

Thus, KPM's superiority is marked.

54. The Major Controversial Findings

It is perhaps fair to regard these four as KPM's major controversial findings:
(1) a high general level of activity, including a high incidence of homosexuality,
(2) a small change from older to younger generations,
(3) a strong relation between activity and socio-economic class,
(4) relations between activity and *changes* of socio-economic class.

All of these KPM set forth as well established conclusions. All are subject to unknown allowances for:
(a) difference between reported and actual behavior,
(b) nonprobability sampling involving volunteering.

While their findings may be substantially correct, it is hard to set any bounds within which the truth is statistically assured to lie (see Appendix A, Section 4). Once again, we wish to point out that the same difficulties are present in many sociological investigations.

CHAPTER XII. SUGGESTED EXTENSIONS

55. Probability Sampling

Appendix D discusses the advantages, possibilities and difficulties of probability sampling in some detail.

In brief summary:
(1) Costs and refusal rates together determine the wisdom of extensive probability sampling.
(2) Information on costs and refusal rates is lacking.
(3) Hence probability sampling should begin on a very small scale, say 20 cases.
(4) A step-by-step program, starting at such a scale, seems wise, and is recommended to KPM.

56. Retakes

While retakes showed high agreement on vital statistics, and moderately high agreement on incidence, the data presented in KPM for frequencies show considerably less agreement. The data do not make clear how much better a retake agrees with a take than with a randomly selected interview for another subject with the same age, religion, social class, etc.

If the agreement is better, then retakes will provide evidence as to non-random agreement—evidence bearing on the much discussed subject of the constancy of recall. In addition, take-retake differences are clearly so large as to make retakes of two old subjects at least as valuable as a take of one new subject in determining the average behavior of groups (see Section A-24).

If the agreement is no better, then retakes will provide evidence that this was so, and every retake will be as valuable as a new take in determining the average behavior of groups.

In our opinion 500 retakes would help the standing of KPM's data more than 2000 new interviews (selected in the same old way). It would of course be important to determine and report the selective factors which influenced the selection of the retaken subjects.

57. Spouses

Separate interviews of husband and wife are a useful supplement to retakes, in that they supply the nearest approach to two independent reports of the same action, although the information is restricted for the most part to marital coitus, and is weakened by the possibility of collusion. In the book, KPM present comparisons for 231 pairs of spouses.

In an expansion of this program, various elaborations could be suggested. The first objective should probably be to interview more pairs from the lower educational levels, in order that the agreement between spouses can be examined separately for different educational levels. As in the case of retakes, the data are not wasted so far as the main study is concerned, since they contribute both to the male and female samples.

58. Presentation

As the critics point out (Chapters VII-A, I-C), parts of the book are hard to understand because of lack of clarity of presentation. In future editions, the following steps would remove the major ambiguities.

(i) KPM should explain why the numbers of cases change erratically from table to table. In future publication it would be worth substantial effort to avoid these changes.

(ii) Table headings and contents should be critically reviewed as to their lucidity.

(iii) Worked examples of the calculation of U. S. corrections should be given. References under the tables to the variables used for correction should be more precise.

(iv) More discussion should be given, with numerical illustration, of the meaning of accumulative incidence percentages.

(v) More information should be given about the questions asked, with their variations, in the interview. Although this would be extremely laborious to do for the complete interview, one or two blocks of related questions might serve the purpose. For such a block, KPM might describe (a) the variations used in the statement of the questions (b) the variations in the order of questions (c) the reasons for the variations. An illustration of this type would give deeper insight into the logical structure of KPM's interviewing technique and might go far to substantiate their claim (p. 52) that flexibility is one of the strengths of their technique.

(vi) Several critics make a strong plea that more information be given about the composition of the sample (see Chapters I-A, I-C). The specific items requested vary with the critic, and some would be a major undertaking both in preparation and publication. A minimum that seems feasible would be to present a multiple classification of the subjects according to the following items *at the time of interview:* age, marital status, occupation, educational status, religious affiliation, place of residence. In addition, more information is needed about the extent to which special groups (e.g., those in penal institutions, homosexual groups) contribute to the tables.

59. Statistical Analyses

In Appendix C, a number of statistical analyses are outlined which would be a useful contribution to the methodology of studies of this kind. The analyses would require expert statistical direction.

As has been pointed out, the standard errors presented by KPM are invalid, because they were computed on the assumption of random sampling of individuals. A method for calculating standard errors so as to take into account the actual nature of KPM's sampling is given in Chapter II-C. These standard errors would allow a realistic appraisal of the stability of KPM's means. They would indicate by how much the means determined from the present KPM sample are likely to vary from the means of a much larger sample of cases obtained by the KPM methods.

KPM described orgasm rates in terms of per cent incidence and mean or median frequency. However, other mathematical functions of these variables may be more appropriate, leading to simpler statements of the results. Approaches for investigating this question, and the related question of the use of some combination of the variables, are suggested in Chapters III-C and IV-C.

The question of applying adjustments to segment means has already been discussed (Section 17). A technique is presented (Chapter V-C) for reaching practical decisions on the appropriateness of adjustment and on the number of variables for which adjustment should be made.

60. Relative Priorities

We give here our personal collective opinion as to how further effort on the male study might best be spent (we have not tried to evaluate priorities in comparison with the female study, or any other studies which KPM may contemplate).

If the interviewer time which it would require were available, we believe that the effort required for the proposed probability sample would be worthwhile.

So long as it did not interfere with the possibility of a probability sample, available interviewer time should be concentrated:

on retakes when working in or near old areas.

on husband-wife pairs when two interviewers are available.

If the probability sample has already been ruled out, and if fewer interviewer months are available, then an attempt to retake a random sample of previous subjects would be most desirable, whenever possible, husband and wife being taken whenever either is retaken.

Effort in the form of statistical analysis and presentation need not interfere with interviewing, and should be pressed to the extent that experienced and understanding personnel can be found.

Gusii Sex Offenses: A Study in Social Control*

Robert A. LeVine

Among the Gusii of southwestern Kenya, the high frequency of rape is a major social problem and has been a source of concern to British administrators and Gusii chiefs for over twenty years. In this paper I shall inquire into the causes of that situation and attempt to formulate some general hypotheses concerning the control of sexual behavior in human societies.

Before proceeding with the inquiry it is necessary to define "rape." In the contemporary legal system of South Nyanza District, where the Gusii live, a heterosexual assault is classified as rape (or "defilement of a girl under sixteen years of age") only when an examination by the District Medical Officer indicates that the hymen of the alleged victim was recently penetrated by the use of painful force. Such cases are heard by the Resident Magistrate of the District, a European judge. When medical evidence is unobtainable due to the lateness of the examination or the fact that the alleged victim was not a virgin, the case is classified as "indecent assault" and is usually heard by one of the African Tribunal Courts presided over by Gusii judges. Most cases are of the latter kind. The Gusii themselves do not distinguish between "rape" and "indecent assault." They use the following expressions to refer to heterosexual assault: *okorwania*—"to fight" (a girl or woman), a euphemistic expression; *ogotachira inse*—"to stamp on" (a girl or woman); *ogosaria*—"to spoil" (a girl or woman); *ogotomana*—"to engage in illicit intercourse," inclusive of adultery and incest. Any of these expressions could be accurately applied to a case legally classified as "rape" or "indecent assault;" the act they refer to is universally considered illicit by the Gusii. I shall use the term rape in this paper to mean the culturally disvalued use of coercion by a male to achieve the submission of a female to sexual intercourse; this includes both of the legal categories.

Evidence for the high frequency of rape among the Gusii is not entirely impressionistic. An extremely conservative estimate of the annual rate of rape (including indecent assault) indictments based on court records for 1955 and 1956 yields the figure of 47.2 per 100,000 population.[1] During the same period the annual rate in urban areas of the United States was 13.85 per 100,000 (rural areas, 13.1). On the basis of the relatively few serious rape and defilement indictments entered at the Resident Magistrate's Court, it is possible to make a limited comparison of the Gusii with the major adjacent tribal groups, the South Nyanza Luo and the Kipsigis. During 1955–56 the Gusii (1948 population: 237,542) accounted for thirteen such indictments, the South Nyanza Luo (1948 population: 270,379) for six, and the Kipsigis (1948 population: 152,391) for four. Though the figures are small, they clearly indicate the Gusii lead over the other two groups in number of rape indictments relative to population size. Thus on a comparative basis it is possible to state that the contemporary rate of reported rape among the Gusii is extraordinarily high. It should be noted that the years chosen for comparison, 1955 and 1956, were locally recognized as being high years but by no means the worst on record. In 1937 a mass outbreak of rape created a law enforcement emergency and induced the District Commissioner to threaten a punitive expedition. In 1950 the number of rapists convicted was so great that the district prison facilities were not adequate to hold them. The great amount of rape, then, is a problem of unusual persistence in Gusiiland.

In the following sections I shall attempt to explain the prevalence of rape in Gusiiland by presenting and analyzing data on institutionalized forms of sex antagonism, traditional and contemporary limitations on premarital sexuality, the differing motivations of rapists, and the role of bridewealth rates in delaying marriage.

Reproduced by permission of the American Anthropological Association from the *American Anthropologist*, 61, 6, 1959.

*This article is an expanded version of a paper read at the Annual Meeting of the American Anthropological Association in Washington, November, 1958. The fieldwork on which this analysis is based was conducted among the Gusii from December 1955 to May 1957 and was made possible by a Fellowship from the Ford Foundation. I am indebted to Barbara B. LeVine for her large part in the collection and organization of data, to John W. M. Whiting and Beatrice B. Whiting for theoretical orientation in problems of social control, to Walter B. Miller for the concept of similarity between law-abiding and non-law-abiding behavior, and to Audrey I. Richards for helpful suggestions and criticisms. Responsibility for the statements contained herein is of course my own.

[1] I have chosen to underestimate grossly the Gusii rape rate rather than make dubious extrapolations from available figures. There are three African Tribunal Courts in Gusiiland, with somewhat overlapping jurisdictions: Manga, Kuja, Gesima. The annual rate reported above is based entirely on the indecent assault indictments entered at Manga, combined with the very few rape (and indecent assault) indictments entered at the Resident Magistrate's Court. Manga handles more cases than the others but not more than half of the total cases heard by Tribunals. By letting the Manga figures plus the RM figures stand for the entire Gusii people, I may have reduced the actual rate of rape indictments by half or more. The figure for Gusii population which was used in the computation was 270,000, which is higher than the Agricultural Department's formula of 1948 census figures plus 10 per cent. The use of the higher figure also serves to depress the number of indictments per 100,000.

SEX ANTAGONISM IN GUSII SOCIETY

The Gusii are a Bantu-speaking people practicing agriculture and animal husbandry in the Kenya highlands just east of Lake Victoria. They are strongly patrilineal and have a segmentary lineage system with a high degree of congruence between lineages and territorial groups. Before the onset of British administration in 1907, clans were the most significant political units and carried on blood feuds.[2] Each of the seven Gusii tribes consisted of one or more large, dominant clans and a number of smaller clans and clan fragments. Clans of the same tribe united for war efforts against other tribes, but feuded among themselves at other times.

Each clan, although an independent military and territorial unit, was exogamous and patrilocal, so that wives had to be imported from clans against which feuds had been conducted. The Gusii recognize this in their proverb, "Those whom we marry are those whom we fight." Marriages did not mitigate the hostilities between clans on a permanent basis; in fact, women were used by their husbands' clans to aid in military operations against their natal clans. A captive from an enemy clan might be tortured in a pillory-like device while a married woman originally from his clan would be sent to relate tearfully to her kinsmen, "Our brother is being killed!" and to urge them to save his life by a ransom in cattle. Marriage among the Gusii was thus a relationship between hostile groups and it continues to be nowadays although blood feuds are prohibited. Clan territories in some areas have been broken up into discontinuous fragments, but local communities are homogeneous with respect to clan membership. Social relations between adjacent communities of different clans are minimal, whereas neighboring communities of the same clan have a considerable common social life. Marriages are still contracted with the aid of an intermediary (*esigani*) between members of alien and unfriendly groups.

The clearest expression of the interclan hostility involved in marriage can be found in the *enyangi* ceremonial. Enyangi is the final ceremony in a Gusii marriage and can be performed either shortly after the start of cohabitation or any number of years later, even after the children have grown up. During the ceremony, iron rings (*ebitinge*) are attached to the wife's ankles and are never removed until the death of her husband or her wilful desertion of him. The practice of enyangi is rapidly disappearing in many areas of Gusiiland, partly because of its expense and partly because many girls become nominal Christians to escape the indignities described below. However, the attitudes and emotions expressed in the traditional rite persist in the contemporary situation. Mayer, who witnessed the ceremony on several occasions, has described its setting as follows:

> *Enyangi* opens with formal contests between the two groups of affines—a wrestling match for the men and a dancing competition for the women. Afterwards, a strictly obligatory seating arrangement separates bride's from groom's people, who must face each other across the space occupied by the sacred beer pots—the groom's party under the surveillance of the 'watcher' whose special task is to avert quarrels (1950a:123).

On the following day the groom in his finery returns to the bride's family where he is stopped by a crowd of women who deprecate his physical appearance. Once he is in the house of the bride's mother and a sacrifice has been performed by the marriage priest, the women begin again, accusing the groom of impotence on the wedding night and claiming that his penis is too small to be effective. He attempts to refute their insults. The next day bride and groom go to the latter's home. The groom enters the door of his mother's house but when the bride attempts to follow she is met by a bellicose crowd of women who keep her at the door for a long time. They scream insults at her, mock her, pinch her, sometimes even smear dung on her lips. Throughout it all she must remain silent. Some brides have been kept at the door for so many hours that they have given up and returned home. Usually, however, the bride is allowed in and treated with kindness thereafter. Other examples of hostile interaction between affines at enyangi could be given, but Mayer (1950a) has described them in great detail.

The enyangi ceremony allows the expression of hostility which in-laws must never give vent to under ordinary circumstances and is indicative of the interclan tensions which are involved in every Gusii marriage. Inevitably, it is the bride who experiences this tension in its most acute form. She must move from her childhood home into the enemy camp; she must sever allegiance to her native group and develop loyalty to an opposing group.[3] It is not surprising, then, that girls are ambivalent toward marriage. On the one hand, they yearn for it because women can only achieve security and prestige in Gusii society through legitimate motherhood and especially through bearing numerous sons. On the other hand, they have heard the folk tale in which the innocent bride discovers her parents-in-law to be cannibalistic ogres, and other similar tales; they all know of girls who have returned to their parents claiming that their in-laws were witches who tried to lure them into witchcraft. They are thus as frightened by the prospect of marriage as they are attracted to it.

The fears of the bride are institutionalized in her traditional resistance to being taken to the home of the groom. Among the adjacent Luo and other East African tribes, it is customary for kinsmen of the bride to fight with kinsmen of the groom and attempt to prevent her departure. With the Gusii, however, it is the bride herself who resists, or who hides herself in a nearby house, and her father, having received the bridewealth cattle by this time, may even help persuade her to go if her reluctance appears to be sincere. Five young clansmen of the groom come to take the bride;

[2] For a more complete treatment of Gusii social organization, including definitions of the terms "clan" and "tribe" as they are used here, see Mayer (1949).

[3] This can be considered a special case of a general phenomenon which has been noted by Murdock: "Where marriages are exogamous with respect to the community . . . spouses of one sex find themselves living among comparative strangers, to whom they must make new personal adjustments and upon whom they must depend for the support, protection, and social satisfactions which they have previously received from relatives and old friends. They thus find themselves at a considerable psychological and social disadvantage in comparison with the sex which remains at home (1949:18)."

two immediately find the girl and post themselves at her side to prevent her escape, while the others receive the final permission of her parents. When it has been granted, the bride holds onto the house posts and must be dragged outside. Finally she goes, crying and with her hands on her head. Her resistance is token and not really intended to break off the marriage, but it expresses the real fears of every Gusii bride.

When the reluctant bride arrives at the groom's house, the matter of first importance is the wedding night sexual performance. This is a trial for both parties, in that the impotence of the groom may cause the bride to break off the marriage, and the discovery of scars or deformities on the bride's body (including vaginal obstruction) may induce the groom to send her home and request a return of the bridewealth. The bride is determined to put her new husband's sexual competence to the most severe test possible. She may take magical measures which are believed to result in his failure in intercourse. These include chewing a piece of charcoal or a phallic pod commonly found in pastures, putting either of these or a knotted piece of grass under the marriage bed, and twisting the phallic flower of the banana tree. The groom is determined to be successful in the face of her expected resistance; he fortifies himself by being well fed, which is believed to favor potency, by eating bitter herbs, and nowadays by eating large quantities of coffee beans, valued as an aphrodisiac. His brothers and paternal male cousins give him encouragement and take a great interest in his prospects for success. Numerous young clansmen of the groom gather at the homestead in a festive mood; chickens are killed for them to eat and they entertain themselves by singing and dancing while waiting for the major events of the wedding night.

The bride usually refuses to get onto the bed; if she did not resist the groom's advances she would be thought sexually promiscuous. At this point some of the young men may forcibly disrobe her and put her on the bed. The groom examines the bride's mouth for pods or other magical devices designed to render him impotent. As he proceeds toward sexual intercourse she continues to resist and he must force her into position. Ordinarily she performs the practice known as *ogotega*, allowing him between her thighs but keeping the vaginal muscles so tense that penetration is impossible. If the groom is young (by traditional standards, under 25), the young men intervene, reprimand the bride, and hold her in position so that penetration can be achieved on the first night. An older groom, however, is considered strong enough to take care of himself, and the young men wait outside the door of the house, looking in occasionally to check on his progress. It is said that in such cases a "fierce" girl in the old days could prevent the groom from achieving full penetration as long as a week. Brides are said to take pride in the length of time they can hold off their mates. In 1957, a girl succeeded in resisting the initial attempts of her bridegroom. His brothers threatened and manhandled her until she confessed to having knotted her pubic hair across the vaginal orifice. They cut the knot with a razor blade and stayed to watch the first performance of marital coitus by the light of a kerosene pressure lamp.

Once penetration has been achieved, the young men sing in jubilation and retire from the house to allow the groom to complete the nuptial sexual relations. They are keenly interested in how many times he will be able to perform coitus on the first night, as this is a matter of prestige and individious comparison. He will be asked about it by all male relatives of his generation, and the bride will also be questioned on this score when she returns to visit her own family. It is said that the groom's clansmen also question the bride, in order to check on the groom's account of his attainment. Six is considered a minimally respectable number of times and twelve is the maximum of which informants had heard. They claimed that it was traditional to achieve orgasm twelve times but that performances were lower in recent years.

The explicit object of such prodigious feats is to hurt the bride. When a bride is unable to walk on the day following the wedding night, the young men consider the groom "a real man" and he is able to boast of his exploits, particularly the fact that he made her cry. One informant quoted some relevant conversation from the *enyangi* ceremony which is performed at a later time. At the bride's home the insulting women say to the groom:

> You are not strong, you can't do anything to our daughter. When you slept with her you didn't do it like a man. You have a small penis which can do nothing. You should grab our daughter and she should be hurt and scream—then you're a man.

He answers boastfully:

> I am a man! If you were to see my penis you would run away. When I grabbed her she screamed. I am not a man to be joked with. Didn't she tell you? She cried—ask her!

The conception of coitus as an act in which a man overcomes the resistance of a woman and causes her pain is not limited to the wedding night; it continues to be important in marital relations. Wives in monogamous homesteads never initiate sexual intercourse with their husbands, and they customarily make a token objection before yielding to the husbands' advances. The wife does not take an active role in the foreplay or coitus and will not remove her clothes herself if she has not already done so for sleeping. Most importantly, it is universally reported that wives cry during coitus, moaning quietly, "You're hurting me, you bad man" and other such admonitions. Gusii men find this practice sexually arousing. The following statement by a 36-year-old husband epitomizes the attitude of the Gusii male toward his wife's sexuality.

> During coitus the husband asks her, "What do you feel? Don't you think it's good?" The wife says, "Don't ask me that." She will never say yes. When the woman cries and protests during intercourse you are very excited. . . . We are always mystified as to whether women enjoy it. But the wives in polygynous homesteads complain when their husbands neglect them, so they must like it.

There is good reason to believe that the reluctant sexual pose of Gusii wives is not feigned in all cases. Young husbands claim to desire coitus at least twice a night, once early and once toward dawn. In a number of monogamous marriages, however, this rate is not achieved, primarily due to the stubborn resistance of wives. Every community contains some married women with reputations for refusing to have intercourse with their husbands for up to a week at a time. Such husbands are eventually moved to beat their wives and even send them back to their parents. I knew of one case of this kind in which the wife's distaste for coitus was the only major source of conflict between husband and wife. Among monogamous wives who do not have anti-sexual reputations, refusal to have intercourse with their husbands usually occurs when they have quarrelled over something else. Since family modesty prescribes the performance of intercourse in the dark after the children have fallen asleep, wives enforce their refusal by pinching a child awake if the husband is insistent. Such evidence suggests that for some Gusii wives the resistant and pained behavior in marital intercourse does not represent a conventional pose or an attempt to arouse their husbands but a sincere desire to avoid coitus.

On the basis of the Gusii case alone, it is difficult to arrive at a satisfactory solution to the problem of whether the sadomasochistic aspect of Gusii nuptial and marital sexuality is inexorably connected with, and a reflection of, the antagonism of intermarrying clans. Many of the above facts point to such a connection, but it is noteworthy that there is at least one culturally patterned form of expressing heterosexual antagonism within the clan. This is the practice of "arousing desire" (*ogosonia*) which Mayer (1953: 22–23) has described in some detail. When Gusii boys undergoing initiation are recuperating from their circumcision operation, adolescent girls of the same clan come to the seclusion huts, disrobe, dance around the novices in provocative attitudes, challenge them to have intercourse, and make disparaging remarks about the genitals of the boys. The latter are of course incapable of coitus, and the girls are well aware of this. According to Mayer, "Most Gusii think that the purpose of *ogosonia* is to cause pain. The girls have their triumph if a resulting erection causes the partly-healed wound to burst open, with acute pain to the novice" (1953:23). Here, then, is the use of sexuality to inflict pain occurring between girls and boys of the same exogamous clan. It could be argued that the adolescent girls have already developed the attitudes appropriate to the wedding night and apply them to the nearest males whom they know to be in a uniquely vulnerable sexual condition. In any event, the practice of ogosonia indicates that the antagonism of Gusii females toward male sexuality and their view of sexual intercourse in aggressive terms are components of a general pattern of behavior not limited to the marital relationship.

Regardless of what other conclusions can be drawn from the foregoing descriptions of institutionalized forms of sex antagonism, one major point has been established: Legitimate heterosexual encounters among the Gusii are aggressive contests, involving force and pain-inflicting behavior which under circumstances that are not legitimate could be termed "rape." In the following sections I shall discuss the conditions which lead to the performance of such behavior under illegitimate circumstances.

SEX RESTRICTIONS WITHIN THE CLAN

Since males are almost by definition the active participants in rape and are held responsible when its occurrence is made public, it is appropriate to examine the circumstances leading to rape from the point of view of the typical male, the potential rapist. This examination will begin with the intraclan restrictions on premarital sexual behavior which face the Gusii youth and will proceed in the next section to the situation he faces when attempting to make his way sexually with females of other clans.

Gusii parents do not tolerate the sex play of their children; they beat both boys and girls for indulging in it. Children have opportunities to escape parental supervision and engage in heterosexuality, and adults are aware that children in general do such things, though they become upset upon learning that a particular child of their own has done so. After initiation, at ages 8–9 for girls and 10–12 for boys, the situation becomes somewhat different. The boy or young man (*omomura*, "warrior") lives in a separate hut near that of his parents and is allowed considerable privacy in his sexual conduct, since a rule of intergenerational sex avoidance prohibits parents from paying attention to the sexual affairs of their initiated sons. It is just the opposite for girls, however, since their reaching puberty makes parents fearful of sexual scandal (described below) and leads to stronger parental attempts at sexual control.

Although parents generally ignore the sexual behavior of their initiated sons, the latter find their choice of sexual objects limited by restrictions operating in the community. In many East African societies young men are allowed sexual privileges with brother's wives, father's young widows, or other married women, but among the Gusii such practices are prohibited and viewed with utmost horror. No provision is made for a young man to receive sexual education from an experienced woman. Furthermore, he is barred from having intercourse with any of the married women in his clan; wives are expected to be faithful to their own husbands, with no deviations allowed. This rules out as sex objects all the married women in the local community, since they are all married to his clansmen.

The rules concerning marital fidelity are enforced by three types of sanctions. One is a supernatural sanction known as *amasangia* which can be incurred at any time after the transfer of bridewealth to the bride's parents. Amasangia literally means "sharing," and refers to the consequences of illicit sharing of a married woman's sexual attentions. Amasangia is caused by the adulterous behavior of a woman, but it directly affects her husband and children rather than herself. The Gusii believe that if a woman has sexual intercourse with a man other than her husband and continues to cohabit with her husband, then when the latter becomes ill her presence in the same room may cause his death. It is said that the sick husband begins to sweat profusely when approached by his adulterous wife; if he has cut himself, her attempt to bandage the wound will promote bleeding rather than arrest it. Some of the older polygynists will not allow their wives to visit them when they (the husbands) are ill, since they jealously suspect their wives of adultery. The "shared" wife may also unintentionally kill her child by her proximity to him when he is ill, and miscarriages are regularly attributed to adultery. Belief in amasangia appears universal among Gusii women, including Christians. They see it as punishment directed against themselves, since no woman wants to be a widow or to lose children. When a women has committed clandestine adultery, she can avoid the evil consequences either by confessing to her husband and having a purifying sacrifice performed or by running away with her lover.

The second type of sanction enforcing marital fidelity is also part of the amasangia complex but is directed at men rather than women. When two men of the same clan have had intercourse with the same married woman, regardless of whether or not she is married to either of them, it is believed that a visit by one to the sickbed of the other will result in the death of the sick one. This is unimportant if the two men are distantly related and do not in any case visit one another, but it enters significantly into the relations of brothers, half-brothers, and first cousins. If one of them has an affair with a married woman he must concern himself with whether any of the male clansmen whom he often visits has also had intercourse with her. Sometimes suspicion of adultery with a wife is aroused when a man becomes ill and finds that a particular half-brother or paternal cousin has not visited him. I knew of two young married men who were constantly seeking extramarital affairs and who would tell each other of the married women they had intercourse with so as to avoid sickbed visits if any of them were the same. Such collaboration to prevent supernatural punishment is rare; ordinarily amasangia acts as a check on male access to the wives of others.

The third sanction operating against the young man who wishes to have affairs with married women is the discovery and disapproval of the elders. Each Gusii clan is divided according to generation with respect to any individual, so that every clansman is his "brother," "father," "grandfather," "child," or "grandchild." With his "brother," "grandfather," and "grandchild," he may make sexual jokes and discuss sexual matters, but with members of adjacent generations he must avoid all mention of sex. Persons of the latter group are said to be *abansoni*, in whose presence one experiences *ensoni*, sexual shame. It is particularly shameful to have one's sexual behavior come to the attention of members of one's father's generation. Furthermore, in the case of a young man his paternal generation contains many of the lineage elders who sit as an informal judicial body with traditional power to place curses on serious offenders. A man convicted of raping a married woman in his own clan would be punished by a fine in livestock. If he refused to pay, the elders would turn their drinking tubes upside down in a pot of beer and utter a curse that was believed to result in his death. If a man repeatedly sought the wives of his clansmen, the elders might decide to slaughter his cattle as a punishment. Even apart from these formal sanctions, however, the mere disapproval of the elders is a force which cows many a young man. In engaging in sexual affaris with local married women, every effort is made to achieve the utmost secrecy. The anxiety attendant upon such affairs is too much for most unmarried men, who consider the risk not worth taking.

These three sanctions together operate to keep the amount of adultery among the Gusii at what seems a low level. The women are genuinely afraid of supernatural punishment, and the men fear supernatural punishment to some extent and discovery by the elders within the clan to an even greater extent. Widows in stable leviratic unions are bound by the same rules and sanctions as ordinary married women, although a neglected widow is likely to be sexually promiscuous until a clansman of the dead husband decides to cohabit with her regularly. Even women whose husbands are working far from home usually remain faithful, aided by the fact that their husbands return home or send for them frequently enough to impregnate them at regular intervals. Several cases were reported in which women whose husbands were away loudly rebuffed adulterous advances, accusing the embarrassed males of desiring to kill (through amasangia) the husbands they intended to cuckold. All in all, the opportunities for the average young Gusii male to have sexual relations with married women are few and far between.

Another possible category of sex objects for the unmarried Gusii male is that of unmarried girls in his own clan and local group. The desire of youths for these girls whom they are forbidden to marry is recognized in the annual institution of *ogochabera*, "taking by stealth" (Mayer 1953:31). During the initiation seclusion of a girl, the older girls sleep with her in her mother's house. It is customary for the younger unmarried men to sneak in and attempt to have intercourse with the girls on such a night. The boys hope that the girls will pretend to continue sleeping, so that coitus may be performed without interruption. Some girls acquiesce but in some cases the boys are rebuffed by the intervention of a married woman sleeping there who decides to be scandalized or by one of the girls herself who may throw things at the boys and try to drive them out. Nowadays some girls are said to knot their petticoats to prevent sexual access. Frequently even the more successful boys have premature ejaculations due to the excitement and anxiety of the occasion. Since "taking by stealth" occurs in the dark, it sometimes happens that kin as close as full brother and sister are sexually united (Mayer 1953:31), although some informants deny this possibility. Such a union would be condoned during the time of girls' initiation so long as pregnancy did not result. The initiation period covers a maximum of two months toward the end of the year in any given locality, so that the practice of "taking by stealth," especially with its inherent limitations, does not provide a substantial outlet for the sexual impulses of young men.

At other times of the year adolescent boys and girls of the same clan and even the same community do carry on sexual liaisons. It was not always so easy to do as it is nowadays, for in the past the young men lived in cattle-villages (*ebisaraati*) apart from the ordinary homesteads and were concerned with defending and grazing their own cattle as well as raiding the herds of other clans. Females were not allowed to enter the cattle-villages. This segregation was a barrier to sexual contact between young men and the girls of their own home communities. The cattle-villages were abolished by governmental decree in 1912, bringing the young men back to the family settlements and giving them more opportunity to develop relationships with girls of their own communities. Nowadays boys of fourteen to seventeen years of age have sexual intercourse with girls of twelve to fifteen in their own communities, following many patterns of premarital seduction described in the following section. As they get older, however, they become increasingly fearful of impregnating these girls whom they may not marry.[4] A clandestine affair with a related girl is a matter of little import to the community, but should it become public both boy and girl suffer some measure of disgrace. Pregnancy insures public notice of the incestuous adventures and may bring punishment in its wake. In one case a young man impregnated his classificatory daughter and she confessed it during childbirth. He was rebuked and criticized in the community on so many occasions that he did not visit other homesteads for a long time. Eventually he had to make a public confession and apology (*ogosonsorana*) to the elders. With such consequences awaiting an unfortunate youthful violator of the incest regulations, it is not surprising that boys of eighteen begin looking for sexual partners beyond the confines of the exogamous clan.

Before proceeding to premarital sexuality of an interclan nature, we must consider three other outlets for males possible within the local group, i.e., masturbation, homosexuality, and bestiality. Masturbation is punished by parents and, according to all reports, never practiced by Gusii boys except the ones in boarding schools who have learned it from members of other cultural groups. Gusii men consider homosexuality almost inconceivable and could not recall cases of it. If the practice occurs at all, it is extremely rare and certainly not socially condoned. Bestiality, on the other hand, is familiar to Gusii men. It is impossible to estimate its incidence, but everyone interviewed could recall cases of it from different localities, and one case of it appears in the records of the Resident Magistrate's court. When a boy of early adolescence, up to sixteen, is discovered having intercourse with a goat or cow, punishment is light, as it is assumed that the youth is attempting to find out if he is potent in a rather harmless way. The animal is considered defiled and is either killed or traded to an alien cultural group, the Luo or Kipsigis. If the animal belonged to someone other than the boy's father, it must be replaced. The son is warned against such activity by his father and sometimes by other elders as well. Nevertheless, it is probably performed clandestinely by many boys who are never caught at it. When a boy older than about sixteen is found having intercourse with an animal it is taken more seriously and treated in the same manner as incest within the nuclear family, or as mental disorder. The assumption in such cases is that the ancestor spirits forced the individual to commit the act by way of retaliation for some ritual misdeed such as omitting a funeral sacrifice. He is taken to a diviner (*omoragori*) who usually prescribes a sacrifice. Despite the formal assumption of supernatural responsibility, if the individual has had any history of sexual misconduct he will become the subject of hostile gossip. Furthermore, the necessity of replacing the defiled cow adds to the punishment, for cows are valuable and expensive. Thus a youth whose bestiality has been revealed on one occasion is unlikely to repeat it unless he has developed a strong preference for animals as sexual objects.

[4] Although Gusii informants claimed that the fear is based on the greater ability of eighteen-year-old boys to impregnate, it seems probable that the realistic basis of the fear is that older boys choose as sexual partners older girls who are outgrowing their "adolescent sterility." For a general discussion of the adolescent sterility of women and its implications for anthropological accounts of premarital sexuality, see Ford and Beach (1952:172–173).

The evidence presented in this section points to the conclusion that the sexual activity of the Gusii youth within his own community and even in other communities of the same clan is drastically limited. Married women are barred to him by the rules of marital fidelity and the sanctions supporting them; unmarried girls are available when he is unsure of his virility, but as he grows older he turns from them in fear of the consequences of incest. Animals are also available to him in his earlier years but are prohibited as continual sexual objects. All of these restrictions within the clan are enforced by the moral sanctions and legal penalties which the clan as an extended kin unit, and its component communities as groups of closely related kin, can use to effect conformity to group norms.

CHANGING PATTERNS OF PREMARITAL SEXUAL BEHAVIOR

With so many restrictions and sanctions operating to limit his sexual behavior within his own community and other communities whose members belong to the same clan, the unmarried Gusii male turns his attention to females of other clans. In the past, when interclan feuding was a reality, there were relatively few occasions for meeting girls of other clans. Marriage ceremonies provided almost the only legitimate situation for premarital contact. Twice during the arrangement of a marriage, a party of young men would accompany the groom to the bride's home and would sing and dance with girls there. On the second occasion the unsupervised indoor dancing would go on for most of the night and the young men and women would sleep in the same house. Informants claim that sex play such as kissing and fondling of breasts was practiced but that intercourse was forbidden and did not occur.[5] The individuals who participated in these sessions were of marriageable age and were consciously scrutinizing each other's looks, dancing ability, and behavior in terms of mate selection. Since there is considerable feeling among Gusii young men even nowadays against prenuptial intercourse with one's mate, it may be that this consideration, coupled with female resistance, acted to restrain sexuality at these marriage dances. In light of the fact that contemporary marriage dances often result in sexual intercourse, however, the allegation of their past chastity must be held in question.

It is difficult though necessary to reconstruct the premarital situation of the Gusii male prior to British administration of Gusiiland. My own findings concur with those of Mayer (1953:10–11) in placing the age at which males were circumcised and initiated in the past at sixteen to eighteen in contrast to the ten-to-twelve-year-old age of initiates today. The uninitiated boys spent most of their time at the homes of their parents, while their elder brothers were out in the cattle-villages. The boys at home received no instruction in sexual matters from their parents or other elders and had relatively little contact with the initiated youths who might have given them sexual information. Consequently, it

[5] Unlike other Kenya groups, such as the Luo, Kipsigis and Kikuyu, the Gusii did not practice partial (interfemural) intercourse before marriage, or at least the practice was not institutionalized. This is consistent with the fact that these other groups are specifically concerned with the physical virginity of brides, while the Gusii are not.

is said, adolescent boys were sexually innocent until a later age than they are today. After initiation, they became involved in the active life of the cattle-village, herding, raiding and conducting skirmishes against hostile clans. For the youths of the cattle-villages, "taking by stealth" provided an annual period of sexual activity within the clan, and the marriage dances of their friends involved them in some sexual contact with girls of other clans. For the most part, however, their interests were in cattle-raiding, not only for its own sake but because the cattle acquired could be used in bridewealth and thus help speed the day of obtaining a legitimate and steady sexual partner.

An outstanding aspect of traditional premarital relations in Gusiiland was the social and physical distance between exogamous clans. Each clan was a territorial unit separated from neighboring clans by a strip of uninhabited bush (*oborabu*). The people of a clan did not tolerate trespassing by males of other clans except in connection with marriage arrangements and ceremonies. Blood feuds could begin when a trespasser was slain or injured and when cattle were raided and women abducted or raped by men of hostile clans. Warriors were inevitably attracted to the territories of neighboring clans by good grazing land, herds of cattle, and women. Sometimes they would take their herds to graze on a good pasture of another clan in the middle of the night, hoping to return before morning and before detection by the warriors of the trespassed territory. If they were detected, however, spear-fighting would ensue. The abduction or rape of a girl belonging to another clan was a more serious offense, and some prolonged feuds are traced to such a cause. Elders tried to prevail upon warriors not to commit reckless acts which would endanger the lives of all the clan members, though they were not always successful in convincing them. Interclan rape and abduction were definitely kept in check, however, by the threat of violent retaliation and the distinct physical boundaries between clans.

The British administration eliminated the traditional system of controlling interclan sexual behavior by military deterrence and territorial separation. Under the Pax Britannica, clans were effectively prohibited from feuding, regardless of provocation. This meant that they could no longer enforce their prohibition on the trespassing of male outsiders, and they could no longer take up arms to avenge their ravished clanswomen. The judicial system introduced by the government did not substitute sanctions of equivalent force. Whereas previously a prospective rapist could anticipate the possibility of annihilation of himself and his fellows by the clansmen of his victim, nowadays he faces an indecent assault charge with maximum prison sentence of one year and a fine of $70.[6] Furthermore, two-thirds of indecent assault indictments are dismissed, mostly because the enforcement agencies cannot prevent the escape of rapists to European plantations in Kericho District where they stay and work until the charges are dropped. Thus in the present situation a rapist has only one chance in three of being punished at all, and if he is, the punishment is a light one by his standards. It is not surprising that young men do not find this as discouraging to interclan sexual activity as their grandfathers found the real threat of a blood feud.

The Pax Britannica also created many new opportunities for contact between unmarried people of different clans. With peace established and population growing rapidly, settlements filled up the previously uninhabited strips between clans. Many Gusii migrated to adjacent areas that had been no-man's-lands between the Gusii and the Kipsigis and Masai. In these new areas clans became territorially fragmented, having no military need for territorial integrity. Each community has a single clan identity which it shares with some adjacent communities as well as with many others farther away. But nowadays boundaries between adjacent communities of hostile clans are indiscernible to the untutored eye. The members of such groups use the same streams and have common paths. Boys who are watering cattle or fishing at the stream can easily meet girls from a nearby community of another clan who are fetching water or washing their clothes. They may also encounter these girls along paths running between the communities. Finally and most importantly, the government established markets, usually at or near clan boundaries, where young people of numerous clans can meet in an atmosphere free of the supervision of elders. Thus the territorial separation of clans, which in the past effected a segregation of young men from their potential mates, no longer exists and no longer acts as a control of interclan premarital sexuality.

Since most of the negative sanctions limiting premarital sexual activity within the clan are still in force while the traditional barriers to interclan activity have disappeared, young men naturally turn to girls outside their own clan for premarital sexual gratification. That they do not do so in younger adolescence is apparently due to the availability within the community of sexual partners whose adolescent sterility prevents conception and to the inexperience of the boys in approaching strange girls. When the boy reaches 17 or 18, his presence in a community of differing clan affiliation is accepted as that of a young man looking for a wife, although in fact his aim may be seduction. At this age a boy ordinarily has a confidence which allows him to approach strange girls, though he would not have done so before.

Nowadays most Gusii young people of both sexes have sexual intercourse before marriage. They may meet under a variety of circumstances, some of which have already been mentioned. When a girl visits her father's sister, it is expected that a half-brother or paternal cousin of her father's sister's son will attempt to seduce her. She may refuse, and in any case the act must be kept secret from members of the parental generation, but apparently such liaisons do occur. At marriage dances, too, youths establish contacts with girls whom they try to seduce. Both situations are only occasional, however; the boy must go to the marketplace for the more frequent social mixing which leads to sexual adventures.

Each marketplace has its day of the week when activity is greatest and trading goes on; this is when girls dress up and

[6] In the Resident Magistrate's Court, prison sentences up to 14 years can be given for rape, but such a small proportion of the rape cases are taken there that it is unlikely that its sentences have an effect on prospective offenders. African Tribunal Courts, which hear most of the rape cases (as "indecent assault") are not empowered to give sentences of more than one year in jail and 500 shillings fine. Even the 14-year sentence does not compare in severity with the traditional sanction.

go in groups to sell some family produce and be seen by boys. The boys and young men also attend, singly and in groups, looking for attractive girls. In the 1930's the young people used to perform traditional dances in the marketplace on market days but this was banned after the 1937 outbreak of mass rape and has never been resumed. Youths approach strange girls, often through girls they already know or through male friends who know them. There is an initial period of small talk in which the girl may immediately reject the boy by claiming that she is married or by assuming a cold and aloof attitude. If she is friendly and laughs, however, the boy is encouraged and may begin some sexual joking. If the girl is favorably inclined to him she will respond in kind, usually using terms of obscene abuse. The boy may grab her arm and attempt to pull her away from the group but she will refuse, at least until he buys her a present in one of the market shops or treats her to some food. Even then he may not succeed in detaching her from the other girls, and he will let her go after arranging a rendezvous and possibly promising a phonograph party. She may agree to the assignation but not show up, in which case the youth will try to woo her later with more gifts and provocative exhortations. Eventually she meets him at a small party in his house or in a secluded part of the bush or forest. The following is a story completion by a Gusii schoolboy writing in English; it is a typical account of a Gusii seduction.

Before they go into the forest Moraa [the girl] will be pretending not to be pleased with this boy for he is talking to her matters concerning sex. But as Gesimba is very serious about it, he will force her and even try to pull her into the forest. When Moraa is being pulled she will fall down, just pretending, and Gesimba having high sex now will lie with her. She will pretend to cry and Gesimba will be trying hard to get the one thing he only wants. He will just catch one of her thighs and lift it, and as a result he will get between the two thighs and push his male organ into the vagina. At this time she will be quiet and all the work will be going on smoothly. After he has spermed several times he will now be satisfied and leave her to dress properly, also himself dress, and thank her many thanks.

In this as in other accounts, it is assumed that the girl will resist and have to be forced even if she desires intercourse. The Gusii girl avoids looking into the eyes of her seducer during coitus, and some go so far as to cover their faces with their dresses. Some Gusii girls cry out of shame and revulsion after intercourse and, unlike Moraa of the fantasy, may refuse to repeat the act on the same occasion. They often become panicky about discovery of the illicit act and the possibility of a premarital pregnancy.

With respect to premarital sexual activity, three types of Gusii girls may be distinguished. The first type is stigmatized as a "slut" (*omokayayu*) because she has achieved a reputation for promiscuity. This type of girl engages in intercourse with men and boys she knows very slightly, and after relatively little persuasion. With her, resistance in coitus is probably conscious role-playing designed to please her lover. Some girls of this type occasionally take on a number of young men in succession. Although she is in demand as a sexual partner, a girl with this sort of reputation is considered highly undesirable as a wife and is ordinarily not married with bridewealth unless her marriage takes place at an early age before her reputation has spread. She is likely to elope from the home of her father or legitimate husband and live as the concubine of one man after another.

The second, and probably modal, type is that of the girl with real ambivalence about engaging in premarital intercourse. She desires it but is careful not to be taken advantage of. Thus she will not meet privately with a boy until after he has bestowed numerous gifts upon her from the market; these may be head scarves, bananas, and candy. She rejects the advances of some boys whom she finds unattractive. Her accessibility for sexual liaisons also depends on her moods and the skill of her would-be seducer. Sometimes she is unapproachable; on other occasions, such as a marriage dance, her resistance may be easily broken down, especially by a dashing young man who serenades her on the guitar. She engages in provocative behavior, mostly of a hostile sort such as sexual joking, but is determined not to be publicly compromised and not to give away her sexual favors until she has received tangible rewards and flattering attention from her prospective lover. With her, resistance in coitus is partly conscious role-playing and partly an expression of real fears and hostility. This type of girl, if her sexual activity is not discovered and does not result in premarital pregnancy, is considered desirable as a wife, for the marriage intermediary (*esigani*) will have no scandal to report to the groom. The prospective husband and his family do not want the intermediary to pry so deeply into the girl's affairs that he reports her casual liaisons; if she has been discreet enough not to acquire a reputation as a "slut," then he ordinarily informs them that she is chaste. There is no inspection of the hymen, for the husband does not desire knowledge of his wife's premarital experience so long as she is considered a proper girl.

The third type of Gusii girl is the one in whom sex anxiety and hostility toward men outweigh heterosexual desires. Such a girl may acquire a reputation for rejecting sexual advances and eventually be avoided by boys in the marketplace, though her desirability as a wife is in no way diminished. Ordinarily, a girl of this type continues going to the market with the other girls and meets numerous boys who know neither her nor her reputation. Despite her fear of sexuality she enjoys the gifts, the flattery, the attention from the boys, and thus tends to exploit her suitors without giving them the sexual satisfaction they desire in exchange. Though she may even refuse sexual overtures at wedding dances and scold the young men who make them, it appears that most girls of this type do occasionally have intercourse before marriage. When they do, their resistance and crying is probably commensurate with their real feelings, and they are more likely to cover their faces during coitus and be overcome with remorse afterwards. It seems likely, though I have no definite evidence on this point, that such girls become the difficult wives who restrict marital sexual activity and who quarrel over it with their husbands.

Although Gusii girls vary in their reactions to the premarital situation, there are common features which characterize a majority of them. They enjoy the initial phase of the relationship with a young man in which they are given gifts and fervently wooed, and many of them attempt to prolong this phase in order to obtain more goods and attention, regardless of whether or not they intend to comply with the wishes of the would-be seducer. Many of the girls seem to enjoy inflicting frustration on a male or at least putting him in a position of subordination, and this is also indicated by their provocative and hostile sexual abuse of the young men they meet in the marketplace. Premarital sexual affairs are extremely brittle, being terminated after a boy and girl have had intercourse once or twice, so the girls have opportunities to go through the early stages of seduction over and over again. Another behavior pattern common to all young Gusii females, except the most extreme girls of type one, is sexual inhibition and some degree of distaste for the act of coitus. While this is variable from one individual to another, Gusii girls as a group exhibit a greater degree of inhibition and anxiety about sexual intercourse than do girls of surrounding tribes. To understand the premarital behavior exhibited by Gusii girls in their sexual relationships it is necessary to examine briefly their childhood experiences and the pressures acting upon them before they marry at an average age of 15 to 16.

Are the childhood experiences of Gusii females substantially different from those of Gusii males whose adult heterosexual attitudes are so different? On the basis of an Oedipal hypothesis we would consider the relation of the child to the parent of opposite sex as the model for later heterosexual relationships. In exploring the implications of this hypothesis for the Gusii family, intergenerational avoidance relationships are of primary importance. Both parents practice sexual avoidance of their children, in the sense that they attempt to prevent the children from seeing their nude bodies, in coitus or at any other time. There are clearly recognized degrees of avoidance: father-daughter avoidance is most strict, father-son next, then mother-son, and finally mother-daughter. The father usually insists that any of his daughters over three or four years of age sleep in a different hut in the homestead (with the grandmother or mother's co-wife) when he is sleeping with the mother. This is not required of a son until he is about seven years old. The son has a close and dependent relationship with his mother until he is circumcised and initiated into manhood at 10 to 12 years of age. The daughter never has such a relationship with her father, who is aloof from all the children in the family, but more especially his daughters. Furthermore, the father has a greater role in punishing the children and is used by the mother as a bogey man with which to threaten misbehaving children of both sexes. Using an Oedipal hypothesis, we could say that the father-daughter relationship in the Gusii family provides the girl with training in avoiding and fearing men, while the mother-son relationship promotes in males a positive attraction toward women.

There are other specific differences in the life histories of males and females in Gusii society. Girls are required to wear dresses and to sit so that their genitals are not exposed from the age of three or four onward. Sometimes this training is begun earlier, but is never put off beyond the age of five. A girl of six who runs naked in the morning or who does not sit properly in mixed company is curtly reprimanded by one of her parents. A boy may go naked until he is circumcised. This earlier modesty training of girls may well have an impact on their adult sexual attitudes. Another difference is that the girl is under the domination and supervision of her mother and a few other women from birth until marriage, while the boy is freer of maternal supervision from the time he first goes out to herd cattle (which may be as early as the age of three), and is completely free of it after circumcision. The effect of this supervision on the Gusii girl is to isolate her from intensive contact with men and to make her accountable to her mother for her expenditure of time during the day. After the girl is initiated at age eight or nine, she begins spending time washing herself and her clothes at the stream and making little expeditions to the market place. Girls of this age are aware that they are destined to leave the parental home for that of their husband, and they are preparing for their role in courtship. This causes friction with the mother, who expects the girl to attend to cooking, fetching water, and other domestic chores more than ever since her competence at these tasks is well developed. Disobedient girls as young as nine years old are told by their mothers, "You'll probably elope and cheat your parents of the bridewealth cattle!" This aspect of child rearing is probably more pronounced now than it was in the past, when the possibility of elopement was not as great.

As the girl approaches marriageable age, her mother becomes increasingly suspicious that the time she spends away from the homestead (or from agricultural work) will involve her in sexual affairs detrimental to her reputation and desirability as a wife, and which may also result in her elopement (without the payment of bridewealth). At this point the father also steps in to use his authority to discipline the daughter and prevent her from seeing boys. A girl who returns home late at night can expect to be scolded and harangued by both parents, particularly her father if he is at home, and there are Gusii fathers who beat their daughters on such occasions. Whatever fear of sexual involvement a girl has developed in the course of her early life is strongly augmented by parental punishment during adolescence. Thus when a girl is tempted to have sexual intercourse with a young man, she is anxious about whether her parents will notice her absence, whether someone will see her going off with a male and report it to her parents, and whether she will become pregnant and be disgraced. Her premarital behavior, then, can be seen as compounded of attitudes carried over from childhood experience (some of which may not have been covered in this analysis) and feelings resulting from her contemporaneous position in the family of orientation.

To recapitulate: the spatial and military barriers to interclan premarital sexual activity in Gusiiland have disappeared as the result of British pacification of the area and rapid population growth. The barriers that now exist reside not so much in the structure of the situation as in the behavior of Gusii females, whose sexual inhibitions and antagonism to males (learned in childhood and enforced in adolescence) present young men with a different set of obstacles to premarital sexual outlet. It is possible to seduce girls, but seduction requires social and musical skills as well as money. Even the most adept seducers are rarely able to obtain sexual partners more than twice during a week, and youths who are less attractive, skillful, and wealthy may go for several weeks at a time without heterosexual intercourse. When premarital intercourse occurs, it has many behavioral similarites to rape, but so long as the eventual acquiescence of the female is won, the act will not be considered rape by Gusii cultural standards. In the following section the several conditions are described which can result in the female refusing to acquiesce.

TYPES OF SEX OFFENSES

The typical Gusii rape, so far as I can determine from anecdotal evidence (court records being deficient in this respect), is committed by an unmarried young man on an unmarried female of a different clan. There are some cases in which married men and married women are involved in rape, and also those in which both rapist and victim have the same clan affiliation, but these appear to be relatively infrequent. Furthermore, rapes of married women or of girls in the same clan as the rapist are more likely to be settled locally without resort to the courts, so that they probably form a very small proportion of the high rate of rape indictments which is in question here. Thus I shall concentrate on explaining interclan rape involving unmarried persons. On the basis of the conscious intent of the rapist, three types of Gusii rape may be distinguished: rape resulting from seduction, premediated sexual assault, and abduction.

1. Rape resulting from seduction. Since the typical Gusii seduction bears a strong behavioral similarity to rape, it is only necessary to understand the conditions under which Gusii females who are being seduced decide to bring the act to the attention of the public and eventually to the authorities. First of all, the standard reluctant pose of the Gusii girl provides many opportunities for a young man to misunderstand her motives. Although she may sincerely want to reject his advances because she finds him unattractive or because of her own current fears, the young man may confidently assume she is pretending and proceed to use physical force to achieve his aim. If her revulsion or fear is great enough she may cry for help and initiate a rape case. Such misunderstandings can be due to the eagerness of the youth and his consequent inability to perceive her subtle cues of genuine rejection, or to the girl's failure to make the signs of refusal in unequivocal fashion.

Second, fear of discovery is ubiquitous in Gusii seduction. Opportunities for privacy exist, but a couple may be seen going off together. If they are engaging in intercourse out of doors, someone may pass nearby and either actually observe them or arouse their fears of being seen. When this happens, a girl who was originally willing may decide to save her reputation by crying out (or reporting it later), pretending that she was being raped. Although this may be considered pseudo-rape, such cases appear to be common in societies in which rape is considered a crime and probably inflate the rates of rape indictments in all of them. There is no way of determining what proportion of rape cases in Gusiiland or anywhere else are of this kind.

Finally, as mentioned above, Gusii girls who have no desire for sexual relations deliberately encourage young men in the preliminaries of courtship because they enjoy the gifts and attention they receive. Some of them act provocative, thinking they will be able to obtain desired articles and then escape the sexual advances of the young man. Having lavished expense and effort on the seduction of an apparently friendly girl, the youth is not willing to withdraw from the relationship without attempting to obtain sexual favors. If the girl is of the third type described above, rape may easily result. An aggressive conclusion is particularly likely if the girl is actually married. In the early stages of marriage brides spend a good deal of time in their home communities visiting their parents. Such a girl may accompany a group of unmarried females going to the marketplace and may pretend to be unmarried in order to be bribed and flattered by the men there. No matter how emotionally and financially involved in her a young man becomes, the bride is too afraid of supernatural sanctions against adultery to yield to him sexually. After she fails to appear at several appointments in the forest or at his hut, he may rape her in desperation the next time they meet, and she will report the deed.

Thus, the similarity of Gusii seduction to rape, the communication difficulties arising out of this similarity, the girls' anxiety about their reputations and consequent fear of discovery, and the provocative behavior by girls whose motivations are not primarily sexual—all of these contribute to turning the would-be seducer into a rapist.

2. Premediated sexual assault. In some cases Gusii youths decide to obtain sexual gratification from girls by force with no semblance of a friendly approach. One or more boys may be involved in an attack on a single girl. Usually the object is to frighten her first so that she will not cry or resist; for this reason young (11 to 13 years old) and easily frightened girls are more likely to be chosen as victims. The boys disguise themselves by draping cloaks or skins over their heads, hide at a place out of hearing distance of the nearest homesteads, and dart out from behind bushes when the girl comes walking by collecting firewood or carrying a pot of water. Sometimes they beat her badly and tear her clothing. Girls are brought into court with lacerations and bites inflicted by sexual attackers. They may drag her off to the hut of one of them, and there force her into coitus. They intend to let her go eventually, but they may hold her for a couple of days. By this time her father has gone to the chief for the services of Tribal Policemen in finding the attackers. If the policemen track them down in time, the case is more likely to be brought to the Resident Magistrate's court, since rupture of the hymen and other signs of attack are common in this type of rate.

3. Abduction. When a Gusii man lacks the economic means for a legitimate bridewealth marriage and does not have the personal attractiveness or seductive skill needed to persuade a girl to elope with him, he may resort to desperate measures. Determined to obtain a mate, he enlists the aid of some clansmen in an attempt to abduct a girl from a different clan. Sometimes the girl is one he knows fairly well but who has refused to live in concubinage with him. The young men act for him as they would in a legitimate marriage, accosting the girl and taking her away by force.

Under these conditions, however, they take pains not to be seen by the girl's parents or anyone else of her community. Another difference is that the girl's resistance is sincere, since she desires a legitimate marriage or concubinage with a man she finds unusually attractive. The young men frequently are rough on her, beating her and tearing her clothes. When she arrives at the home of her would-be lover, he exhorts her in peaceful terms to remain with him until bridewealth can be raised to legitimize their union. Her refusal is ignored in the hope that she will eventually acquiesce, and the wedding night sexual contest is performed, with the clansmen helping overcome her resistance. If she does not escape and report the offense to her father, the latter will eventually come with Tribal Policemen and arrest the abductor.

The type of abduction described is not to be confused with elopement in which the girl is willing to go despite her father's ire at being deprived of bridewealth. Such cases are entered in the Tribunal Courts under a customary law offense, "Removing a girl without the consent of her parents." In the abductive rape which is of interest here, the girl is not a willing accomplice and must be forced into sexual relations not only on the first night but subsequently as well. This type of case results in an indecent assault indictment.

Of the three types of rape described above, two are unlawful versions of patterns which are normally law-abiding and socially acceptable by Gusii standards. The first type develops out of seduction, which has gained acceptance as a culture pattern when kept within the bounds of discretion; the third type is an imitation of traditional wedding procedures, but lacking the legitimizing bridewealth and the consent of the bride and her parents. In both cases there is a close parallel between the criminal act and the law-abiding culture pattern to which it is related. The question arises, why does an individual commit the criminal version of the act rather than its law-abiding counterpart? I have attempted to show how various limitations on the premarital sexual behavior of Gusii males tend to make them sexually frustrated and hence inclined to a less discriminate use of the aggressive aspects of accepted sexual patterns. The occurrence of the abductive type of rape, however, poses an important question: if difficulty of premarital access to females is what frustrates Gusii males, what prevents them from marrying at an earlier age and thus solving their problem in a law-abiding way? In the following section I shall describe the barriers to marriage in contemporary Gusii society and what effect they have on the incidence of all types of rape.

THE BRIDEWEALTH FACTOR IN SEX OFFENSES

A legitimate Gusii marriage requires the transfer of cattle (and goats) from the father of the groom to the father of the bride (Mayer 1950b; 1951). The number of animals transferred is a matter of individual agreement between the fathers but it is influenced by the prevailing bridewealth rate in Gusiiland. The rate has fluctuated throughout the years from as many as twenty cows to as little as one cow. Reduction in the rate resulted from a severe cattle epidemic, in one case, and from actions taken by traditional and British authorities, in other cases. Despite attempts by authorities to control it, the Gusii bridewealth rate has a tendency to rise which can only be understood in terms of the uses to which bridewealth is put.

The father of the bride receives in one lot most of the bridewealth animals before he allows his daughter to live with her prospective mate; installment payments are not ordinarily permitted. Bridewealth given in marriage for a girl is most often used to procure a wife for her uterine brother (or in some instances for her half-brother or father), and her father is concerned lest the number of animals he accepts for her marriage will prove insufficient to obtain a wife for her brother at a later time. Fearing that the bridewealth rate will rise between the two marriages, the father of the bride demands more cattle than the current rate and thereby helps to bring about a rise. The resulting inflationary spiral has continued in the face of temporarily effective decreases brought about by authoritative action in 1903, 1920, 1937, and 1948, and despite an apparent decrease in the total number of cattle available for marriage payments. Since the British administration prohibited inter-tribal cattle raiding in the first decade of the century, the Gusii have been deprived of one traditional source of livestock for use in bridewealth. In recent years, overcrowding of the land and unavailability of pasturage have tended to effect a reduction in Gusii herds. Yet fathers tenaciously insist on the cattle (rather than cash or other currently valued commodities) for their daughters in bridewealth, and in fact demand larger numbers of them now than fathers did 40 years ago.

One consequence of the inflation in bridewealth rates and the reduced availability of cattle is that young men who come from cattle-poor families and who do not have uterine sisters old enough to be married, must postpone their own marriages. They can wait until their sisters grow up (if they have sisters), secure a loan from close patrilineal kinsmen, or attempt to raise money to buy cattle through wage labor. (The minimal bridewealth rate in 1957 was equivalent to the total wages a Gusii plantation worker would receive in 40 months.) Meanwhile, fathers attempt to marry off their daughters as secondary wives to wealthy old men. Among the poorer young men, the enforced postponement of marriage creates a group who reach their late twenties or early thirties before they can afford marriage. A majority of Gusii males marry between 18 and 25, but there are numerous men who are unmarried at later ages and even some who never have legitimate wives. Some of these unfortunates persuade girls to elope without the payment of bridewealth, and such concubinage has been increasing despite efforts by girls' fathers and the courts. Inevitably, however, there are men who lack the economic means for a legitimate marriage as well as the attractiveness and seductive arts needed to convince a girl to elope. In desperation a man of this type may resort to abductive rape as described in the preceding section.

The relationship between excessive bridewealth demands and rape is not a conjectural one. In 1936–37, the bridewealth rates were up to 8 to 12 head of cattle, 1 to 3 bulls, and 8 to 12 goats. This was the highest they had been since before the great cattle plague of the 1890's. Many young men could find no legitimate way of getting married, and they resorted to cattle theft and all types of rape. On one market day in Kisii township, a large group of young men gathered and decided to procure mates for themselves by abduction. They grabbed girls in the marketplace and carried them off. Many of the girls returned home after being raped. The incident precipitated action by the administration. The district records report the following for November 29, 1937:

> A large general baraza [assembly] was held to deal with (1) indecent assaults on girls and defilements of girls under 16 years of age, (2) increased stock theft. The District Commissioner pointed out the bestial nature of practice (1) comparing it to that of dogs and condemned the young men. He also held the elders responsible for demanding a prohibitive marriage price.

Under the orders of the District Commissioner, the Gusii elders present at the meeting swore an oath to reduce the amount of bridewealth demanded to 6 cows, 1 bull and 10 goats. The reduction was effective until 1942, when the rate resumed its upward trend. By 1950 high bridewealth rates resulted in a serious outbreak of rape again, though without the dramatic or organized qualities of the earlier one. Further efforts at control of bridewealth have been made by the African District Council, but with ephemeral success. In 1956, one of the years covered in the figures on rate of rape indictments presented earlier, bridewealth rates averaged 10 head of cattle in the area studied, but wealthy, older men were giving considerably more. All in all, it is likely that the high rate of rape indictments in Gusiiland is in part a function of the economic barrier to the marriage of young men created by excessive bridewealth demands.

DISCUSSION

The foregoing analysis of the etiology of rape in Gusiiland may be summarized as follows: Normal forms of sexual intercourse among the Gusii involve male force and female resistance with an emphasis on the pain inflicted by the male on the female. This general heterosexual aggression appears to be related to the hostility of exogamous clans, since marriage is the prototype of a heterosexual relationship in Gusii culture. Regardless of its origin, the aggressive pattern of sexuality is not entirely pretense but shows clear signs of involving sadistic and masochistic impulses on the part of some Gusii individuals. Rape committed by Gusii men can be seen as an extension of this legitimate pattern to illegitimate contexts under the pressure of sexual frustration. The sexual frustration of Gusii young men is due to effectively enforced restrictions on intraclan sexual activity, the sexual inhibitions and provocative behavior of Gusii girls, and high bridewealth rates which force postponement of marriage. Prior to British administration of Gusiiland, rape was not such a problem because interclan controls were as effective as intraclan controls. Pacification of the district, however, has eliminated the threat of force and the spatial distances between clan settlements, increasing opportunities for interclan heterosexual contact in the face of greatly diminished penalties for interclan rape. Had Gusii girls proved uninhibited, promiscuity rather than rape would have been the consequence of pacification. However, Gusii values favor restriction of premarital sexuality and the burden of enforcing this restriction now falls upon the girls themselves rather than upon their clansmen. Thus the contemporary system of sanctions operating in Gusii society is not adequate to control the effects of the factors motivating men to commit rape.

If the above analysis is valid, there are four factors in the Gusii situation which should be found in any society with a high frequency of rape: (1) severe formal restrictions on the nonmarital sexual relations of females; (2) moderately strong sexual inhibitions on the part of females; (3) economic or other barriers to marriage which prolong the bachelorhood of some males into their late twenties; (4) the absence of physical segregation of the sexes. This last condition distinguishes high rape societies from societies in which women are secluded and guarded, where rape is not feasible and homosexuality may be practiced instead. These four factors should be regarded as necessary but not sufficient conditions for a high frequency of rape, as they may also be found in societies having prostitution or other functional alternatives.

The Gusii case raises some general points about the control of sexual behavior in human societies. Not all societies have restrictive sexual rules; in many groups nonmarital sexual relations are permitted and carried on relatively unhampered by cultural restrictions. In societies which do have severe formal limitations on heterosexual gratification, the problem of control, in the sense of enforcing conformity to ideal rules, is a great one. How can such control be achieved? Students of social organization have emphasized the role of structural arrangements and social sanctions in social control; psychoanalytic theorists have emphasized the role of repression and super-ego (acquired in childhood) in the individual's inhibition of culturally unacceptable impulses. Assuming that both types of variables play a part in the control of sexual behavior, I shall discuss their respective contributions to the control process, referring to them as *structural barriers* and *socialized inhibitions.*

A structural barrier, as I define it for sexual control processes, is a physical or social arrangement in the contemporary environment of the individual which prevents him from obtaining the sexual object he seeks. A socialized inhibition is a learned tendency to avoid performing sexual acts under certain conditions. Structural barriers are part of the settlement pattern and group structure; socialized inhibitions are the products of the socialization process which the individual undergoes in his early years. I do not assume that these two are concretely separate factors in social control but that their relative weight in a particular situation may be analytically assessed. Societies with restrictive sexual rules vary in the extent to which they depend on structural barriers or socialized inhibitions to achieve conformity to these rules.

The purest forms of structural barriers to heterosexual gratification involve spatial segregation of the sexes. There is the royal harem with high walls, barred windows, and armed guards and, less elaborately, the veiled seclusion of ordinary married women in some Near Eastern and Indian societies. Where the regulation of premarital sexual activity is the aim, it can be partly achieved by keeping males and females in separate schools until late adolescence, as among higher class groups in some European societies. These physical types of structural barriers have the effect of preventing opportunities for social contact between potential sexual partners. A somewhat less extreme form of structural barrier is chaperonage. Where it is practiced, potential sexual partners may be physically proximate and perhaps even have social contact, but only under the surveillance of one or more persons whose special duty it is to see that no sexual act occurs. Punishments for transgression of sexual rules are likely to be severe, particularly if there are any opportunities for unsupervised contact. The social rather than purely physical type of structural barrier is also found in those societies in which the entire community or neighborhood acts as chaperone. While possible violators of sexual rules may be in frequent contact, the ubiquity of the cohesive social group with its power to punish is assumed to act as a strong deterrent to misbehavior. The effectiveness of such a system is probably inversely related to the amount of opportunity for privacy which potential sex offenders have.

In a sense there is no structural barrier which does not depend on the willingness of individuals to cooperate with it, and in that sense a certain amount of socialized inhibition is involved in all of the abovementioned structural barriers. Insofar as harem walls fail to prevent adultery, it is because the guards and inmates are not inhibited in their sexual behavior. For a structural barrier to be effective in enforcing a restrictive sexual rule, it must be supported by socialized inhibitions; individuals must at least anticipate the penalties to be incurred by transgressing the barriers, and inhibit their responses on that account. While recognizing the universal necessity for a minimum of socialized inhibition, we may distinguish those societies which depend less on it for control from those which use it more. Where there is physical segregation of the sexes, the socialized inhibition required to restrict heterosexuality is less than where the sexes are in continual contact. In the former case, simple difficulty of access acts as a deterrent; in the latter, impulses are aroused which must be inhibited by the individual if conformity is to be achieved. When temptation is removed it is not difficult to be an ascetic, but when the temptation is present only the individual trained to asceticism can resist it. In societies where community "chaperonage" acts to restrict sexual behavior, individuals are ordinarily socialized to avoid public sexual performance, and in some cases their fear of discovery is so great that they inhibit sexual responses even when the opportunity for transgression arises. In societies where socialized inhibition is even stronger, individuals control their own impulses in the absence of any structural barriers to violation of sexual rules. Thus Gusii wives are trusted not to commit adultery when their husbands are working far away from home, although they have opportunities for clandestine intercourse. The question of whether sexual inhibition in the absence of structural barriers result from child training, as I have assumed, or from later socialization, is an empirical question which can be tested cross-culturally.

The analysis presented above has implications for the study of contemporary culture change and the breakdown of traditional controls of sexual behavior in many parts of the world. When, as among the Gusii, structural barriers to premarital sexual activity are removed without being replaced by other structural barriers of equal effectiveness, the socialized inhibitions of individuals are put to the test. If both sexes are highly inhibited, premarital activity may be only slightly greater than before. If females are highly inhibited but males are not, rape is likely to occur. If both sexes are low on inhibition, promiscuity will result. Since socialized inhibitions are probably more resistant to change in acculturative situations than are structural barriers,[7] it may be necessary to pay more attention to such individual factors in order to predict the direction of cultural change and the future incidence of sex offenses.

REFERENCES

Bruner, Edward M., 1956. Cultural transmission and cultural change. *Southwestern Journal of Anthropology* 12:191–199.

Ford, Clellan S. and Frank A. Beach, 1952. *Patterns of sexual behavior.* New York, Harper and Bros.

Mayer, Philip, 1949. The lineage principle in Gusii society. *Memorandum* XXIV, International African Institute.

Mayer, Philip, 1950a. Privileged obstruction of marriage rites among the Gusii. *Africa* XX:113–125.

Mayer, Philip, 1950b. *Gusii bridewealth law and custom.* The Rhodes-Livingston Papers, Number Eighteen. London, Oxford University Press.

Mayer, Philip, 1951. Bridewealth limitation among the Gusii. In *Two studies in applied anthropology in Kenya,* Colonial Research Studies No. 3. London, His Majesty's Stationary Office.

Mayer, Philip, 1953. Gusii initiation ceremonies. *Journal of the Royal Anthropological Institute* 83:9–36.

Murdock, George Peter, 1949. *Social structure.* New York, Macmillan.

[7] This statement is based on the plausible hypothesis of Bruner, "That which was traditionally learned and internalized in infancy and early childhood tends to be most resistant to change in contact situations" (1956:194).

Group Sex Among the Mid-Americans*

Gilbert D. Bartell

This paper is one in a series of special presentations for the Society for the Scientific Study of Sex, dealing with group sex. Our data were collected from a selected sample of midwestern and southwestern white, suburban and exurban couples and single individuals engaged in what they call swinging. We contacted and interviewed approximately 350 informants during the two years of our research, using data from 280 interviewees who fit into the above category.

These informants define the term swinging as having sexual relations (as a couple) with at least one other individual. Since more than a simple dyadic relationship exists whether the sexual activity involved takes place together or apart, the fact remains that more than two people had to enter into an agreement to have sexual experiences together. We therefore conclude that this must be considered group sex.

We were interested in the growth and development of the broad spectrum of activities associated with organized swinging, but we wished to concentrate specifically upon those individuals belonging to some form of sodality or swinging organization. We attempted to ascertain to what extent American cultural patterns would be transferred to this relatively new phenomenon. Since white middle class, non inner city people constitute the majority in the United States, and we assume they are the major actors within the cultural system, our sample is restricted to these informants.

Interviews lasted anywhere from two to eight hours. We eliminated individuals from the inner city, Blacks and Latin couples to keep our sample restricted. We did not misrepresent ourselves, but told them that we were anthropologists interested in knowing more about swinging. We did not use a tape recorder or questionnaires, as these people were frequently too frightened to even give their right names, let alone fill out questionnaires, or tape. We were also able to attend a large number of parties and large scale group sexual activities.

Our basic method of interviewing was the anthropological one of participant observer. Due to the etiquette and social mores of swinging as we shall detail below, we were able to observe the only act as though we were willing to participate.

Evidently the interest in swinging or wife swapping, mate swapping or group sex came about as the result of an article in Mr. Magazine in 1956. Since then it has received a great deal of attention from the semi-pornographic press. However, despite the fact that there are an estimated one to ten million people involved in mate exchange, it has received practically no attention from the scientific community. We don't have any reliable figures on how many people are involved in swinging, but a club in a midwestern city published a list with names and addresses of 3500 couples in the metropolitan area and its suburbs, who are actively engaged in mate exchange.

The impetus toward swinging usually comes from the male, but it is the contention of a number of sophisticated swingers that it is often promoted by the female who lets the male take the aggressive role in suggesting that they become involved in the swapping situation. Although we have a great deal of background material on the initial introduction of the partners to group sex activity, which includes the acquiring of magazines, self-photography, discussion, and extra marital activity, we do not feel it falls within the scope of this paper.

Within the area of investigation, there are primarily four methods of acquiring similarly minded partners for sexual exchange. Most prevalent is the utilization of an advertisement in one or more of the various magazine/tabloids catering to these specialized interests. Second, an introduction to another couple at a bar, set up exclusively for this purpose or through one of the swingers sodalities. Third, personal reference from one couple to another, and fourth, personal recruitment, seduction or proselytizing.

In the first method an advertisement is placed in one of the sensational tabloids such as the National Informer. This might read, for example:

> Athens, Georgia marrieds. Attractive, college, married, white, want to hear from other marrieds. She, 36, 5′7″, 35-22-36, 135. He, 40, 6′2″, 190. Photo and phone a must. Discretion. Box, #.

or

> Florida Marrieds. Attractive, refined, professional marrieds would like to hear from similar liberal minded marrieds. Complete discretion required, and assured. Can travel Southern states. Photo and phone please. Box, #.

Alternatively, the couple may respond to such an ad. This method is the least expensive and time consuming as the National Informer sells for 25¢ and is printed and distrib-

From *Journal of Sex Research*, May 1970, **6**, 2, 113–130. Reprinted by permission.

*In some academic circles sex research is not considered pertinent. I therefore would very much like to thank the President of Northern Illinois University Rhoten Smith, my anthropological colleagues, Drs. Pierre Gravel and James Gunnerson, and colleagues from other departments including sociology for their cooperation, assistance, and particularly their genuine moral support.

I wish, furthermore, to acknowledge the help and assistance of Carole Dick and Nancy Frank in the preparation of this article and thank them for their efforts.

uted on a weekly basis. The couple has to pay for an ad or a fee plus postage for their letter to be forwarded to an advertisee. Exactly the same method is used if the couple selects one of the large slick paged magazines, such as Swinger's Life or Kindred Spirits. The major difference between tabloids and slick magazines is that the magazines offer membership in a sodality and cater exclusively to swingers. Examples of such ads would be:

Baltimore, D.C., 60 mile radius, luscious, upper thirties, attractives, seeking couples, females to 40 for exotic French Culture etc. She, 35-27-35, 5′6″. He, husky, muscular, but gentle. Let's trade pictures and telephone and addresses.

or

New Orleans, young couple, 28 and 32. She, a luscious red head, 5′7″, 36-26-38. He, 5′9″, 175, well built. Enjoy all cultures. Attractive couples main interest, but will consider extremely attractive single girls and men. Photo required for reply.

Please note the difference in the tenor and construction of the advertisements, remembering that the magazine sells for $3.00 per copy. Additionally these magazines offer instruction on what kinds of letters to write to attract the highest results. Initial contacts are made through letters with descriptions formulated in such a way as to stimulate the interest in making a personal contact with the other couple. These would almost universally include a nude or semi-nude photograph of the female, and sometimes, but much less frequently, a photograph of the male. These photographs are considered very important. Physical dimensions, particularly of the female, usually somewhat overly abundant in the mammary zone, are frequently included. Ages are given and usually minimized. Third, the written answer usually states that the couple is fun loving, vivacious, friendly, and extremely talented sexually. This leads, hopefully, to a telephone contact with the other couple and from there to a first meeting, which is by agreement, social in nature with no obligations to swing on the part of anyone. If successful, this first meeting leads to an invitation to swing, either open or closed (see below) or an invitation to a party. If unsuccessful, it may lead only to a referral to another couple or to some club.

The second method of meeting other couples, the bar or sodality, can be the result of reference from another couple. In a few cases, the club or bar may advertise openly in either a swinging magazine or a tabloid. These units or sodalities break down into three categories. The very common, but least imminent, is the large scale semi-annual party social, advertised in one of the national swingers magazines. The magazine advertises where the social will be held, and the cost for dinner, dance, and drinks. The organizer most commonly will be some local couple who agree to do the actual work. Usually these meetings, or socials, are held at a motel. The swingers bar is one which is open on certain nights of the week only to couples, and it is known to everyone that all couples present are either active or interested in becoming swingers. The bars can be run by either an individual who has an interest in promulgating swinging or an organizer who will contract with the bar owner offering a guarantee for the use of the bar for the particular night involved. Occasionally some interested couple or couples may institute a club which charges a membership fee and rents a hall or bar one or two nights a month at which times known swingers congregate. These clubs are frequently chartered, operating as social organizations much like ski-clubs. Inducements are offered to the members for recruiting new members. The club may, for example, sponsor "Bring another couple night," and only charge half price for entrance. A number of clubs seek to go beyond the purely sexual by organizing hay rides, beach parties and picnics. Several attempts have been made within our area to organize a group tour of swingers to the Caribbean and to Las Vegas. These efforts have not been successful. In general, swinging does not take place on the premises of these bars or clubs, but instead the couples make their alliances or organize private parties and leave the bar in groups.

A third method of meeting other compatible swingers is a simple reference from another couple. If a couple has made a few contacts either by one of the two methods mentioned above or sometimes purely by accident, they can meet a number of other couples by this reference method. A knowledgeable couple who have been swinging for some time will recommend other known swingers to the new couple. This in turn, of course, can lead to other contacts without ever having to write letters, join a club or go to a bar.

The fourth method of contacting new swingers appears with the least degree of frequency in our sample. Many swingers, either due to the zeal of the convert or personal stimulus, attempts to seduce (to convert) other couples to what they call the "swinging life." We have reports of this occasionally occurring in nudist camps or with couples that have known each other on a social basis for some time. In a few cases, couples who had been bridge partners or dance partners have mutually consented to exchange.

The neophytes coming onto the "swinging scene," as it is referred to, is faced with a number of dilemmas. They must find out, with a certain degree of care, exactly what actions are appropriate to allow them to participate in this venture which is somewhat surrounded by mystery. The various books and magazines purporting to open the door and guide the novice through the intricacies of swinging, universally exaggerate its ecstasies. In fact, what swingers do is relatively prosaic. For example, one responds to an ad with a letter. This letter gives one's interests and includes a picture. The purpose of the letter is to present oneself in such a manner as to elicit further response in the form of a telephone call. Then, usually using only first names, such as Joe and Ruth, a meeting is arranged.

This first meeting we call the Mating Dance (taken directly from ethologists). The couple goes through a patterned ritual behavior. In effect what they are doing is testing each other. If one couple is baby swingers, baby swinger meaning one who has never been involved in a swinging situation before, of necessity they must permit themselves to be seduced. This role also allows one to ask questions which the experienced couple are more than pleased to answer. In most cases this is the role we took. It is also advantageous in that you have to learn the secret vocabulary of swinging in order to interview effectively. These people do have a definite secret language, or at least think it is secret. Terms most often used are TV (transvestite), S & M (Sado-masochist), A-C D-C (Homosexual and Heterosexual), Bi-sexual (enjoying both males and females and usually applied to women only), Ambisexual (the correct term, yet less frequently used for the preceding two terms), gay (homosexual or lesbian), B & D (bondage and discipline), French Culture (cunnilingus and fellatio), Roman Culture (orgies), Greek Culture (anal intercourse).

This first meeting is the equivalent of the dating coffee date or coke date. The general etiquette dictates that this first contact is without sexual involvement. Should it be decided that the foursome wants to get together they will meet later either at a motel, or at the house of one of the couples.

Once this decision to participate has been made by all four people, we arrive at the three typologies of swinging. Number one, open and closed swinging; two, open and closed large scale parties; and three, three-way parties. As defined locally, closed swinging means that the two couples exchange partners and then go off separately to a private area to engage in what amounts to straight, uncomplicated sexual intercourse. Then after an agreed upon time, all four return back to the central meeting place. Sexual behavior under these circumstances is relatively ritualized. It almost always includes fellatio, cunnilingus and coitus, with the male either dorsal or ventral. In the vast majority of cases, fellatio does not lead to orgasm. Every attempt is made by the male to bring the female to climax by cunnilingus. Climax by the male after prolonged delay occurs most frequently during coitus with the female supine.

In contrast, open swinging in a foursome means that the couples at some time during the evening, engage in sexual activity together, either in the same room, on the same bed, or as a four way participatory activity. In 75% of our cases, this will generally include the two females engaging in some form of cunnilingal activity, although in approximately 15% of the cases one of the female partners will be passive. Less than 1% of the cases reported that any male homosexual activity takes place. We have only two or three reports of males performing fellatio, and in 6 or 7 cases the male informant was passive, permitting another male to fellate him. We have no reports of anal intercourse taking place between either male or female in a swinging scene. Sometimes references are made to this fact, but we have no verification. Occasionally a foursome of the open variety may result in everyone devoting their attention to one person, three on one in effect, and again most frequently, two males and one female devoting their attention to the female. The only other variety is the so-called "daisy chain" which is alternately fellatio, cunnilingus in a circle.

The second type of swinging is the party, which can be organized in several different ways, and can be run as an open or closed party. Certain individuals are known in this area as organizers. These individuals devote a great deal of their time to the organization and promulgation of swinging activities. They may organize nothing more than social events in which people meet to make future contacts, or they may organize a party, at which sexual activity will take place. These parties are frequently held in a private home. Couples are invited by the organizer who may or may not be the owner of the home. Frequently each couple invited is asked to bring another couple who are known to be swingers. Although not always true, there is an implication that no one is required to swing. At other parties, no swinging activity takes place until after a certain time, such as 10:30. Any couple still there past 10:30 is expected to participate. In contrast to the swingers' self image, they are not nudists and they are still relatively inhibited, hesitating to initiate any positive action. Therefore, the organizer or the host or some less patient swingers may initiate a game, the object of which, obviously, is the removal of everyone's clothing.

Parties in suburbia include evenly numbered couples only. In the area of our research, singles, male or female, are discriminated against. Blacks are universally excluded. If the party is a closed party, there are rules, very definitely established and generally reinforced by the organizer as well as other swingers. These rules may even include clothing restrictions, "baby dolls" for the women and for the men, swinger's shorts (abbreviated boxer type). Or there may be a regulation that one couple may occupy a bedroom at a time or that they may stay only so long or that no one must appear nude in the central gathering area. Most parties are "bring your own bottle" parties, although in a few cases the host supplies the liquor. Food is often prepared by the hostess, but seldom consumed. Stag films are generally not shown. Music is low key fox trot, not infrequently Glenn Miller, and lighting is definitely not psychedelic. Usually nothing more than a few red or blue light bulbs. Marijuana and speed are not permitted.

The same generalized format is true for the open party, the difference being that the party is less structured. Nudity is permitted in any part of the house and couples are free to form large groups of up to 10 or 12 people in large sexual participating masses. Voyeurism is open and not objected to by the majority of the participants. Parties generally begin around 9:00 in the evening and frequently continue until 9:00 the following morning in contrast to closed parties, which generally terminate around 1 A.M. It is not infrequent that as the party proceeds and the males become progressively more exhausted, the females continue to party without males. Open parties in suburban groups appear infrequently and when they do, they are held by the younger swingers between the ages 20 and 35, who have begun swinging in the last year and a half. Culturally this younger group resembles the older closed group with the exception that they have never been under the influence of the organizers. They have no ideas as to what is considered appropriate party behavior, as does the older group. This younger group apparently either is more innovative or is learning from the now-frequent popular writings on swinging. Some of the older swingers who are now participating in open parties state that when they began swinging they "didn't know there was any other way to do it." Although most couples state an interest in the taking of polaroid pictures during sexual exchanges, in practice, this is very infrequent. Among other reasons it points out the extreme caution and fear with which the majority of our informants react to the possibility of their identities being revealed.

The third type of swinging is in a three-some, which can hardly be called menage a trois, which implies a prolonged triadic relationship. Analysis of advertisements in swingers magazines indicates that the vast majority of swingers, whether potential or experienced, advertise for either a couple or a female. Although the majority of threesomes constitute a couple and an alternate single female, 30% of our informants indicate that they have participated as a threesome with an alternate single male. (Cross-checking of informants cause our own figures to be revised upward as high as 60%.) The males report that they enjoy the voyeuristic qualities of watching their partner engaging in sexual activity with another male. Most commonly threesomes with two females include ambisexual behavior of mutual cunnilingus between the females. Although in the majority of our cases the triad is of relatively short duration, twelve couples report triadic relationships of longer duration ranging from a low of two or three weeks to a high of as long as ten years. In three of the cases the extra woman lived in the household on a more or less permanent basis. In two cases the male was a boarder, and in one case the male lived in the household for ten years, seven of which he had been involved in a menage a trois.

Few other variations of sexual activity had been reported. We have in our entire sample only two reports of bondage and/or discipline. Transvestitism has never been reported. We have observed one case of bestiality. Obviously from the preceding, homosexual males are not welcome. In a few cases, three to be exact, we have reports of a lesbian participating at a large party, however she was not discriminated against. It should be noted that to accuse a woman of being "straight-gay" is considered pejorative. Clothes fetishists are uncommon. Bizarre costume is not considered proper and clothing is decidedly not "mod," but is very middle class.

THE INFORMANTS

Ninety-five per cent were white. We included Latin Americans in this category as well. Of our Latin Americans, 10 individuals in all, each swung with a white partner. The predominant ethnic division was German. In fact, of all foreign born informants, Germans constituted the single largest group comprising twelve couples in our sample. We have only five black couples, none of whom live in the suburbs. The ages of our informants ranged from 18 to the mid forties for the women, and from 21 to 70 for the males. Median age for women, 28-31. For males, 29-34. All couples, based on our knowledge of certain societal factors, tended to minimize their age, except for the very young 21-30 age group. In general we believe the men gave younger ages when they were married to younger women. Age plays an extremely important role in acceptance or rejection for swinging. Although informants almost universally verbalize that age is unimportant, in reality they tend to reject couples who are more than ten years older than themselves. Invitations to parties are generally along age lines also. With the emphasis on youth in our culture today, it is important to appear young and our interviewees were reluctant to give exact ages.

Ninety per cent of the women in our sample remain in the home as housewives. We have no exact figures as to how many worked previous to marriage. In case where this was their first marriage, they had married between the ages of 17 and 21. Several were married as young as 15 to 17. There were seventeen female teachers in our sample. Those who had advanced schooling, both males and females, had attended small colleges and junior colleges. About 25% of our males had some college. Forty to 50% of the men could be classified as salesmen of one sort or another. Our interviewees also included one M.D., one dentist, three university professors, three high school teachers, and several owners of small service-oriented businesses. A number of swingers in this group are truck drivers and some are employed in factory work. The largest professional group was lawyers. Earnings were extremely difficult to ascertain. We based our estimate on life style, houses, and occupations. The range of income extends from $6,000 to a probable high of $75,000.

Religion was seldom discussed. These people would not admit to atheism or agnosticism. They would say that they were Protestant, Catholic or Jewish. The majority are Protestant and the proportion of Jews is the same as the general population. The proportion of Catholics is a little higher. The majority did not attend church regularly.

Universally they were extremely cautious with regard to their children, about phone calls, and visits from other swinging couples. The majority of couples would not swing if their children were in the house, and some made elaborate arrangements to have children visit friends or relatives on the nights when they were entertaining. All couples took precaution that their children did not find letters from other swinging couples, pictures, or swinging magazines. We found few instances of couples merely socializing and bringing their children together, although the children might be of the same ages, and have the same interests. Only a few in our sample said that they would raise their children with the same degree of sexual libertarianism they themselves espouse, or that they would give the girls the pill at a very early age.

In interviewing these respondents, we found that they have no outside activities or interests or hobbies. In contrast, the suburbanite is usually involved in community affairs, numerous sports, and family centered activities. These people do nothing other than swing and watch television. About 10% are regular nudists and attend some nudist camps in the area during the summer. Their reading is restricted to newspapers, *occasional* news magazines and women's magazines with the outstanding exception that 99% of the males read Playboy. An occasional couple owns a power boat and spends a few week ends in the summertime boating. Yet a striking contradiction is that fact that in their letters they list their interests as travel, sports, movies, dancing, going out to dinner, theater, etc. In reality they do none of these things. Therefore all conversational topics are related to swinging and swingers as well as television programs. Background is usually rural or fringe areas, not inner city.

Due to the exclusion in the midwest of singles from the swinging scene, we find that approximately 1/3 of the swinging couples interviewed admitted they were not married. However, to be included in parties and to avoid pressures and criticism from married couples, they introduced themselves as man and wife. We are unable to compile exact statistics of the frequency or cause of divorce in the swinging scene. At least one partner and sometimes both of the couple swinging currently had been married before. Frequently they have children from a previous marriage. We have only hearsay evidence that couples have broken up because of swinging. However, we feel in general that the divorce rate is about that of any comparable group of people in the country. As we have not followed up any couples who have dropped out of swinging, these findings are susceptible to change.

As much of the interviewing took place during the 1968 National Presidential Campaign, we had occasion to hear political views. Normally politics is never discussed. There were many Republicans and better than 60% of the respondents were Wallaceites (partially due to change from blue collar to white collar jobs). These people were anti-Negro. They were less antagonistic to Puerto Ricans and Mexicans. They were strongly anti-hippie, against the use of any and all drugs, and would not allow marijuana in their homes or people who use it if they had knowledge of it.

Based on overt statements in letters and advertisements, such as "whites only" and from the fact that Blacks are seldom, if ever, invited to parties, it is safe to say that a strong anti-Black prejudice exists. In social conversation antagonism, although veiled, is often expressed.

Informants overall reflect generalized white suburban attitudes as outlined in almost any beginning sociology text. Their deviation exists mainly or primarily in the area of sex. And even this has imposed upon it middle class mores and attitudes. For example, some men have been paying prostitutes to pose as their swinging partners. In the few cases in which this occurred and became general knowledge, a large outcry from both males and females was heard. The same attitudes prevail toward couples who are not married as well as singles, male or female. The reason is less the sanctity of marriage than the idea that the single individual or the prostitute has nothing to lose. They are absolutely terrified, even though they think of themselves as liberated sexually by the thought of involvement. If you swing with a couple only one time, you are obviously not very involved. It is taboo to call another man's wife or girl friend afterward, or to make dates on the side.

The consumption of alcohol, sometimes in large quantities, is perfectly permissible. Current fashions such as mini skirts and bell bottom trousers for men and beards are seldom seen except among the youngest of the swingers.

ANALYSIS

Obviously due to the nature of a short article, we have been forced to be overly restrictive in a descriptive sense. We have only touched on the highlights and those points that would be considered pertinent to the vast majority of readers of this journal. With all due respect to our readers, we should like to give a brief socio-psychological analysis of our research.

As stated originally, we were particularly interested in swinging as a cultural phenomenon. We feel convinced that it reflects very much the culture of the individuals interviewed and observed. They represent white middle class suburbia. They do not represent a high order of deviance. In fact, this is the single area of deviation from the norms of contemporary society, and there may be some question whether they really represent the acting out of an ideal image in our society rather than an attempt to be innovative. They represent an attempt to act out the cult of youth, the "in scene." They are, in their own minds, the avant garde, the leaders in a new sexual revolution. They see swinging as a "way of life." They refer, like the hippie, like the ghettoite, to the non-swinger as being "straight." In contrast to their own conceptualization of themselves, the majority of swingers are very "straight" indeed. The mores, the fears, that plague our generation are evidenced as strongly in swingers as in any other random sampling from suburbia. It has been said that our data reflects a mid-American bias; however, the O'Neills and the Smiths (personal communication) have indicated that the same phenomena can be found in suburbs in both the east and west coasts. What we find in these couples consistently is a boredom with marriage. Much of this problem stems from diffuse role expectations in the society. Americans have imposed upon themselves a number of possible roles, both ideal and real, which one may assume. We believe the action of the media to be crucial in the self perception of ideological roles. Most of the male swingers want to see themselves as—and many groups actually call themselves—international Jet Setters, the Cosmopolitans, the Travellers, the Beautiful people. Instead, they have become a consequence of suburban life. They sit in silence and look at television. The woman who feels restricted to the household environment believes she should be out doing things, be a career woman, but she has her obligations. The man wants to be a swinger, and to be in on the "scene" and know "where it's really at."

Within the psycho-socio-sexual context of contemporary American culture, we would like to present those positive and negative affects of swinging for the individuals involved. Please note that we have been unable to interview more than a few dropouts from swinging. Therefore, our information is based solely on those who are participants. Our interviews with people who have discontinued swinging, about six or seven couples, reflect what we shall call the negative aspects of swinging. But first, we should like to summarize what we believe to be the positive aspects of swinging. Among these, there is an increased sexual interest in the mate or partner. All of our respondents report that due to swinging they now have a better relationship, both socially and sexually. These people are replaying a mating game. They can relive their youth and for many it is advantageous. They can get dressed up, go out together, and attempt a seduction. It is a form of togetherness that they never had before. There is the desire of each partner to reinforce in the other the idea that they are better sexually than any swinger they have encountered. There is a general increase in sexual excitation of both partners due to the possibilities of new types of sexual experiences and increase in thought and discussion of actual sexual experiences. The woman receives a great deal of positive reinforcement if she is seen as the least bit desirable. She is actively committing men to her. A fifty-year-old man can "make it" with a twenty-two-year-old girl without any legal repercussions, and his wife will be equally guilty. It must be a tremendous satisfaction. Women uniformly report that they have been able to shed sexual inhibitions that they were raised with. And our society certainly has an overabundance of sexual inhibitions, mainly because we impose different standards on different members of the society. The Raquel Welches of our world can perform in one fashion, but the good little housewife must perform in another. How does one adjust to this conflict between one's model and one's own activities? The female respondents state that one way to resolve this conflict is to swing.

The partners now share an interest, which can be explored, observed, and discussed between themselves and among their new "friends." Both partners can indulge in voyeurism at parties, and thereby utilize the learning experience in their own relationship. Due to the fact that most of these people have had few, if any, opportunities throughout their lives for actually observing or learning by observation how to act and respond to sexual stimuli, the swinging scene may be an experience which could not be provided in any other way.

Swinging may be extremely exciting inasmuch as it carries certain elements of danger. Swingers may feel very avant garde in the breaking of cultural taboos or of legal codes. There is also a certain implied danger and possibility of losing the love of one's partner; however, this is usually offset by the mutual reinforcement mentioned previously. There can be a great deal of sexual excitement provided by the stimulus of profane versus sacred love. Both partners can now become conspirators in writing and hiding advertisements and letters and evidence of their interest from children, relatives, "straight friends," and business colleagues. We feel that one of the greatest advantages in the relationship comes from the fact that the couple may now spend more time together searching for new contacts and pursuing leads for parties, bars, and other compatible couples. They may now plan week-end trips together, vacations, etc. to other parts of the country to meet swingers. They feel that now they have broadened their social horizon, acquired new interests or hobbies as a by-product of their swinging contacts. Swingers seem to derive a great deal of satisfaction out of merely meeting and gossiping with other swingers, which gives them the dual role of also proselytizing. For the first time in many years, due to the restriction of early marriage, suburban environment, and the social and economic restraints of raising children, they may now have the opportunity to dress up, make dinner dates, plan for parties, acquire a full social calendar, and be extremely busy with telephone conversations, letter writing, picture taking. If they do prove to be a fairly "popular" couple and be in demand, they can now feel that they are both beautiful or handsome and desirable. They see themselves and each other in a new light. They may now feel that they are doing what the "in" people are doing and living up to their playboy image. Most swingers report unsatisfactory sexual relationships prior to swinging. Now, due to the necessity of operating as a pair on the swinging scene, they may find that they actually have an increase in perception, awareness and appreciation, sexual and otherwise, of each other.

One of the most important negative aspects, as we see it, is the inability to live up to one's own psycho-sexual myth and self-illusions. This is particularly disadvantageous in the case of the male. They read about sexual behavior in the outer world, and they realize they are not participating in this elaborate sexual life. Since the demise of the houses of prostitution, many early sexual contacts by males became hit and miss propositions. Boys usually begin by masturbating; to masturbate, one must fantasize (Simon and Gagnon, 1969). Most males have an elaborate fantasy world in their internalized sexual lives. One of the fantasies is that of having access to a bevy of females. He sees himself capable of satisfying any and all of them. He now goes to a party, particularly a party of the younger group, and he has all these naked women running around in front of him. He experiences the anxiety of being incapable of performing up to his own expectations. This very anxiety may defeat him. In American society, the male is expected to be a tremendous performer sexually, and he must live up to his own publicity. This is extraordinarily difficult. He may find he cannot maintain an erection, he cannot perform. He finds himself envying younger men who are physically more attractive and his anxiety and fears increase. For the woman, such self-doubts are less in evidence, although beyond a doubt all females upon initiation to the swinging scene go through a stage of comparison of their own physical appearance and sexual performance with that of the other females. Should the couple be both older and less attractive than the majority of swingers encountered, they may regard the whole swinging scene as a failure, and withdraw immediately. For those who remain, other negative aspects include sexual jealousy. The male may find after a number of parties in which his opportunity for satisfaction is limited and he sees the women around him engaging in homosexual activities and continuing to satisfy each other over and over again for the duration of the evening, he may feel, and this is verbalized, that the "women have the best time," that the swinging scene is "unfair to men." We find that less than 25% of the men "turn on" regularly at large scale open parties. In contrast to this, many men report that they "turn on" much more frequently at small scale parties or in small groups of threesomes. This is the major deterrent to the swinging situation. If one keeps experiencing failure, and continuously worries about this failure, one will keep failing. This is a complete feedback situation. In an attempt to "turn themselves on," the males push their women into having ambisexual relations with another girl. Most of them got the idea from either books or pornographic movies. Again, the male experiences disaster. Why? Sixty-five per cent of the female respondents admit to enjoying their homosexual relationships with other females and liking it to the point where they would rather "turn on" to the female than to males.

For a couple who are relatively insecure with each other and with themselves, swinging may invoke a great deal of personal jealousy. The man who finds he is occasionally rejected or easily tired physically, may resent his wife's responsiveness to other men. She, in turn, may feel that her partner is enjoying other women more or to a different degree than he enjoys her. These personal jealousies frequently erupt under the pressure of alcohol and the ensuing scene evolves into an event which makes all parties present uncomfortable if not antagonistic to the couple. This causes them to be excluded from future invitations and branded as "trouble makers."

Another less common negativism in swinging is the "bad experience." A couple may encounter another couple who have sexual "hang ups," habits, or attitudes that are repulsive or objectionable to the initiating couple. If they encounter two or three consecutive "bad" couples, they may decide that it is not worth taking the risk of such exposure.

Some of our respondents report that in the past there have been incidences of venereal disease that were introduced into a swinging couple by one couple and for all concerned, this provoked a great deal of fear and embarrassment due to the legal necessity of seeking medical aid from sources that would not report to health authorities. Fear of disease is always present, and discussed frequently.

For many swingers a constant negative aspect of swinging is the perpetual hazard of discovery. To professional people and to those who work for a state or national government or for very conservative business firms, there is a strong possibility of status diminution or loss of occupational position if they were discovered. All respondents consistently insist upon all possible discretion and some go so far as to not give out addresses, correct last names, place of employment, and the majority of swingers keep unlisted telephones. The upwardly mobile feel that their "life would be ruined" if the world knew they were swingers.

Although our findings are inconclusive on this last negative aspect, we feel it is important and maybe the primary reason for the dropouts among the more sensitive intellectual group of people who enter swinging. These people seem to feel that swinging in general is much too mechanistic, that there is a loss of identity and absence of commitment and a total non-involvement that is the antithesis of sexual pleasure and satisfaction. Some explicitly say that the inconsistencies between the stated objectives and the actual performance are too great to overcome. Although a couple initially report that they want new friends, interests, and activities in addition to pure sexual contact, in reality this is not so. As proof of this we offer the fact that most couples will see another couple only once, and even on those occasions when they have relationships with the other couple, their social relationship is minimal even when their sexual relationship is maximal. In much the same light their self-image of avant-garde/sexual freedomists suffers when one considers their worries vis-a-vis jealously.

Since many people have asked us where we think swinging is leading we should like to make some comments on our personal attitudes toward the future of the swingers. We feel that these individuals interviewed in our sample are not really benefitting themselves because the ideals that led them into swinging have not been fully realized. They may very well be acting out and getting positive reinforcement, psychologically and physically from their activities. However their human relationships outside of the dyad are not good. Their activities with other couples reflect mechanical interaction rather than an intimacy of relationships. As a cultural anthropologist one cannot doubt that this reflects the impersonalization as well as the depersonalization of human relationships in our culture. One would suppose that the next generation will carry a duality of purpose rather than a single-minded interest in sexual performance. What we would like to see is a freedom of sexuality, but one more concerned with human relationships, and that these human relationships rather than the sexual relationships become the primary goal.

REFERENCES

Simon, William and Gagnon, John. Psycho-sexual Development. *Transaction,* March 1969, pp. 9–18, Vol. 6 No. 3.

Aversion Therapy Applied to Taped Sequences of Deviant Behavior in Exhibitionism and Other Sexual Deviations: A Preliminary Report

Gene G. Abel
Donald J. Levis
John Clancy

In three cases of exhibitionism, two of transvestism and one of masochism, tapes were made involving descriptions of each subject's individual deviant behavior divided into three sequential segments. Five of the six subjects were placed on a schedule on which, at first, the final segment of the tape was followed by shock, at later sessions the second seg-

ment and ultimately the first. At each session the shocked tape runs were followed by runs in which the patient avoided shock by verbalizing normal sexual behavior in the place of the shocked segment. The sixth subject was given shocks out of relation to taped material, as a control. Treatment was evaluated by measuring penile responses to sexually deviant and non-deviant tapes, and by clinical reports. In the experimental subjects there was reduction of erectile responses to deviant tapes but sustained responses to non-deviant tapes. These subjects reported weaker deviant responses, less frequent deviant behavior and fewer symptoms of psychopathology in general.

Although current opinion favors the use of psychotherapeutic and correctional programs in the treatment of deviant sexual behaviors, Freund (1960) and Smith (1968) indicate that conventional approaches such as psychoanalysis and group therapy have not produced impressive results. By contrast, Feldman (1966) describes encouraging initial findings with behavior therapy.

Rachman (1966), using conditioning techniques, has developed fetishistic responses in non-deviant subjects. Feldman and MacCulloch (1965), Marks, Rachman and Gelder (1965), Rachman (1963), Raymond (1956) and Thorpe *et al.* (1964), have treated deviants by developing avoidance of deviant sexual expression or by increasing the reward value of desired sexual behaviors. Following Freund's (1960) and Davison's (1968) suggestions, both these principles were utilized in this study.

In designing our treatment procedure, we gave consideration to the following facts: (1) A deviant act is often followed and strengthened by primary reinforcement, that is, orgasm; (2) Deviant sexual acts usually involve a sequence of discrete behaviors. The fact that orgasm often follows deviant behavior is a unique feature of these disorders and may be a major reason for their persistence. To extinguish the deviant behavior, it was important to prevent the terminal reward in the form of orgasm. In addition, pairing pain with the terminal deviant act (or fantasy), e.g. exposure of the genitals, was expected to inhibit its occurrence.

The second factor, the sequence of behaviors preceding the deviant act, has been frequently overlooked as a potential relevant variable. It is not a single condition which precipitates the deviant act, but rather a chain or sequence of behaviors. This sequence is evident in the following description of a typical exhibitionist's experience.

The sequence begins with sexually stimulating memories of previous exposures. This ideational material is followed by driving to a place where he has previously exposed himself. The urge for a new experience now appears. After locating a young girl, the patient circles the area, rehearsing mentally. He then stops the car and calls the girl. As she approaches, he anticipates with pleasurable excitement her reaction to the sight of his genitals. Finally, he exposes himself and terminates the sequence by masturbating.

Every exhibitionist patient reports such a sequence with only minor variations before each deviant act. As the sequence progresses, sexual arousal increases, and so does the difficulty of self-control. These reports suggest the desirability of extinguishing as many phases of the sequence as possible. Additional advantages of separating and conditioning distinctive phases have been emphasized by Levis (1966) and Stampfl (1966). By presenting rats with stimuli ordered serially, they produced an avoidance conditioning with extreme resistance to extinction following minimal shock presentation.

In addition to the above measures designed to combat the deviant behavior, non-deviant sexual behavior is reinforced. This is especially relevant when a negative reinforcer such as pain is used. The danger exists that the pairing of deviant sexual material with an aversive stimulus may result in the generalization of aversiveness to non-deviant sexual material. In order to counteract this possibility, the patients were able to avoid punishment at some trials by substituting 'normal' for deviant sexual material.

From *Journal of Behavior Therapy and Experimental Psychiatry*, 1970, 1, 59–66. Reproduced by permission of Pergamon Press.

METHOD

Subject Selection

To facilitate follow-up, patients were solicited only from psychiatrists and legal authorities within a 75 mile radius, including three state psychiatric hospitals. These were advised of 'a new treatment program for male sexual deviants' and were asked for referrals. Excluded were patients classified by history or clinical interview as psychotic, retarded, organic or homosexual. Of ten consecutive referrals, three were excluded on these criteria. A fourth was excluded because frequent progress reports to the court were legally required, and it was feared that this might influence follow-up findings.

The remaining six subjects were three exhibitionists with histories of voyeurism, two transvestites and one masochist. They were 21–31 years old—four married, two single. Four had recent histories of arrest following deviant acts, but only one faced criminal charges. Four had had no previous psychotherapy; the remaining two had had five and seven years of intermittent psychotherapy, with 3 and 4 psychiatric hospitalizations respectively. Five subjects had had frequent heterosexual petting and intercourse; the sixth had petted occasionally but had never attempted intercourse.

Procedure

There were 4 stages.

Stage 1. Each patient's pre-treatment pathology was estimated on the basis of a clinical interview, two rating scales, and the Minnesota Multiphasic Personality Inventory (MMPI). The interview served two purposes: (1) to provide a detailed account of the patient's specific deviant behavior, and (2) to afford a general impression of personality, sexual behavior, occupational ability, and social competence. The first of the two rating scales consisted of ten phrases. Five described those deviant behaviors judged to be most sexually arousing to the patient. The other five described non-deviant behavior judged sexually arousing to most men. These latter items were of course the same for all patients. The subjects rated the 10 items from least to most exciting. The second rating scale, the Weekly (Clancy and Abel, 1967), consisted of 21 items in three categories: (a) specific deviant behavior practiced by the patient; (b) deviant behavior not practiced by him; and (c) non-deviant sexual behavior. Each of these categories was subdivided into fantasized and overt behaviors. The patients reported the frequency of each listed behavior during the week past. At the end of Stage 1, they were each given a supply of Weekly scales and asked to fill out and mail one every Sunday for the duration of the experiment.

Stage 2. A modification of the penile transducer described by Bancroft, Jones and Pullan (1966) was applied to the patient's penis. This apparatus records changes in penile diameter, and is used to measure the degree of erection. A verbal description by the patient of his activities—deviant sexual, normal sexual and general (non-sexual) daily routine—was recorded on audio tape while the penile responses were recorded. The subject described in detail the behavior sequences and thoughts involved in three actual deviant sexual experiences. In addition, he discussed normal sexual experiences and other non-sexual activities.

The experimenter then selected sections from the audio recordings of the six patients to produce for each of them six experimental tapes, each 120 sec in length. The first 30 sec of each tape consisted of a description of non-sexual behavior. The last 90 sec of three of the tapes contained deviant sexual material, and the other three contained normal sexual material. The selected passages were in all cases those associated with the greatest penile responses. Two patients did not exhibit much in the way of penile responses. For them the experimenter facilitated arousal by recounting the recorded sexual experiences, expanding on those parts of the original description which had previously produced even a minimal penile response. By this means, tapes were finally obtained that elicited marked arousal.

When the 120 sec experimental tapes were completed a 5 sec silent period was inserted after each 30-sec segment. Each 30-sec period of the last 90 sec then comprised an ideational link in a behavioral sequence preceding either a deviant or a normal sexual act. Of an individual's three deviant tapes the one producing the greatest penile response was selected for use in Stage 3—the conditioning phase (see Fig. 1).

Stage 3. Five patients were randomly assigned to a contingent shock schedule,[1] and one patient to a non-contingent shock schedule. Throughout this stage the patient wore the penile transducer, as well as two silver electrodes on the left forearm through which a painful shock could be given. The patient's selected deviant tape was then played, and he was

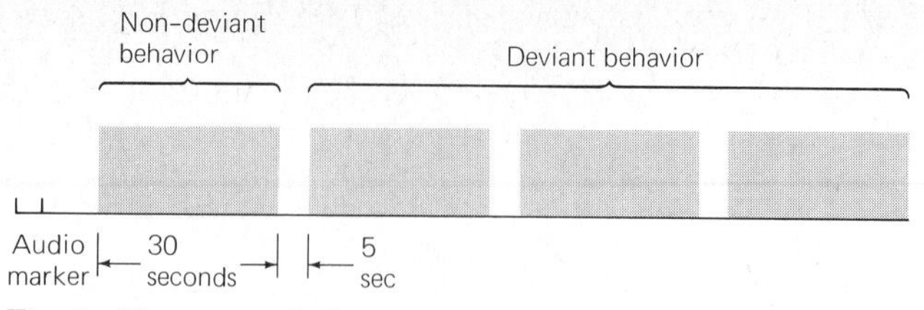

Fig. 1. Tape-recorded sequence of a sexual deviant experience.

asked to imagine the material being described. The last three 30-sec segments of the tape contained the deviant material, as described above. The tape was run 10 times at a session. In the first three runs the 4th segment was immediately followed by shock. With regard to the remaining seven runs the subject was told that he could avoid shock if at the 4th segment of the tape he would verbalize and fantasize alternative non-deviant sexual behavior. In the implementation of this the tape was stopped as soon as the patient spoke. He usually spoke for 2 or 3 min. If the patient failed to verbalize non-deviant sexual material the 4th segment was played through and followed by shock as in the first three runs.

During sessions 5 to 7 only the first three segments of the tape were presented; and for sessions 8 to 10 only the first two. Thus in sessions 5 to 7 it was the third segment that was followed by shock in the first 3 runs, and replaced by the patient's verbalizations of non-deviant sexual material in the subsequent 7 runs; and in sessions 8 to 10 it was the second segment to which this schedule applied (see Fig. 2).

Each tape run was followed by an intertrial interval of 4 minutes: 1 minute of silence, 2 minutes in which the patient did simple mathematical computation and another minute of silence. The mathematical computations were designed to inhibit thinking of sexual material so as to allow the penile response to return to a baseline level. Each session was conducted on a separate day. At the end of the ten training sessions, each subject had received a total of 30 shock conditioning trials and 70 avoidance trials.

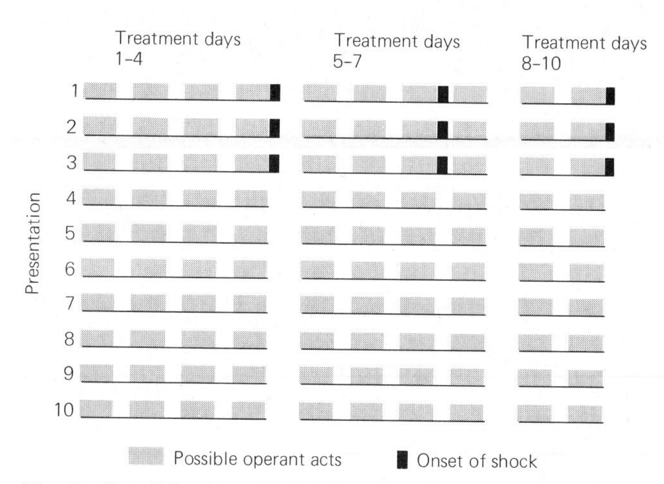

Fig. 2. Conditioning schedule for the contingent shock group during the 10 days of treatment.

[1] Delivery of shock was contingent on, i.e. followed exclusively, the presentation of a particular tape segment containing deviant material, as indicated in Fig. 2.

The non-contingent shock subject underwent the same procedure as the shock contingent group except that the shock was never avoidable and was administered at random and only during the mathematical computation period of the intertrial interval. This subject, furthermore, was matched with one of the patients in the shock contingent group for number and sequence of shocks.

Stage 4. The effectiveness of treatment was evaluated at 1, 8 and 18 weeks following conditioning. The subjects were clinically interviewed (the interviewer being unaware of the subject's treatment condition) and were given the 10 item scale and the MMPI. In addition, the six tapes constructed in Stage 2 were played back to the subject while his penile responses were recorded. The first tape presented was the one used during conditioning. The remaining five tapes (two containing deviant and three non-deviant material) were randomly presented.

The degree of sexual arousal elicited by the tapes was estimated by subtracting the highest transducer reading during the initial, neutral 30 sec period, from the highest reading during the presentation of sexual material.

RESULTS

The penile response to the deviant tape that figured in the aversive conditioning was found to be suppressed up to 18 weeks following shock-contingent conditioning (Fig. 3).

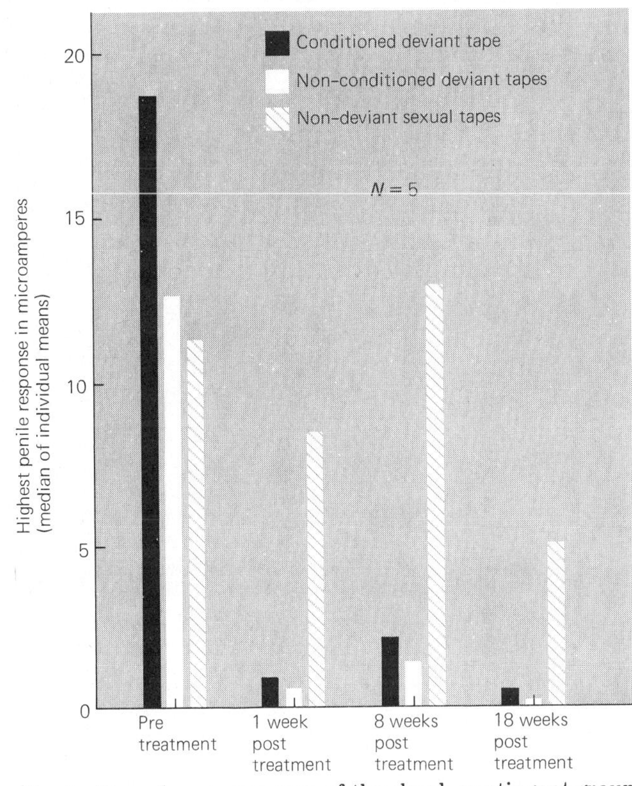

Fig. 3. Transducer responses of the shock contingent group before and after conditioning.

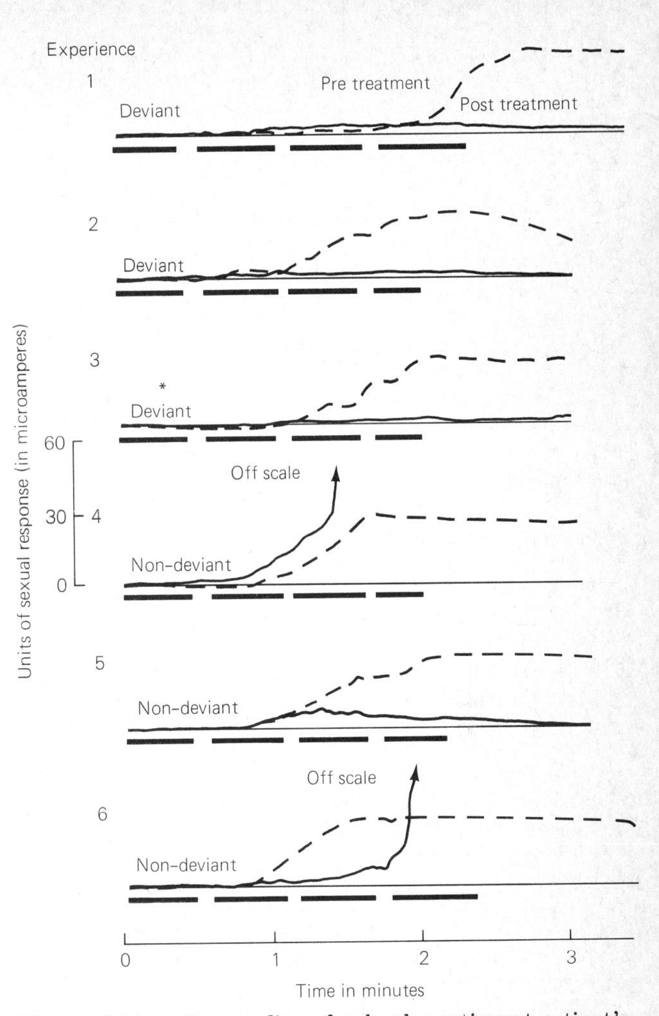

Fig. 4. Polygraph recording of a shock-contingent patient's penile responses 1 week before and 1 week after aversive conditioning. Only experience 3 was used during conditioning (marked with asterisk).

Marked suppression of response was also observed with the deviant tapes that had not been used in the treatment, indicating good generalization. Arousal to non-deviant sexual material continued, indicating that discrimination had been achieved.

Figure 4 shows the penile responses of a shock-contingent patient to the three deviant and the three non-deviant tape sequences 1 week before treatment and 1 week after treatment. The post-treatment penile response to deviant material is manifestly inhibited, while the response to normal sexual material is enhanced.

The general clinical assessment of the shock contingent group appears in Fig. 5, expressed as the median percentage of normality on a scale ranging from zero to 100 per cent. A rank of 100 means that a clinical judgment was made that the patient was free from pathology. The group's clinical status can be seen to have improved by about 35 per cent after treatment.

The shock contingent group's 10-item ranking scales

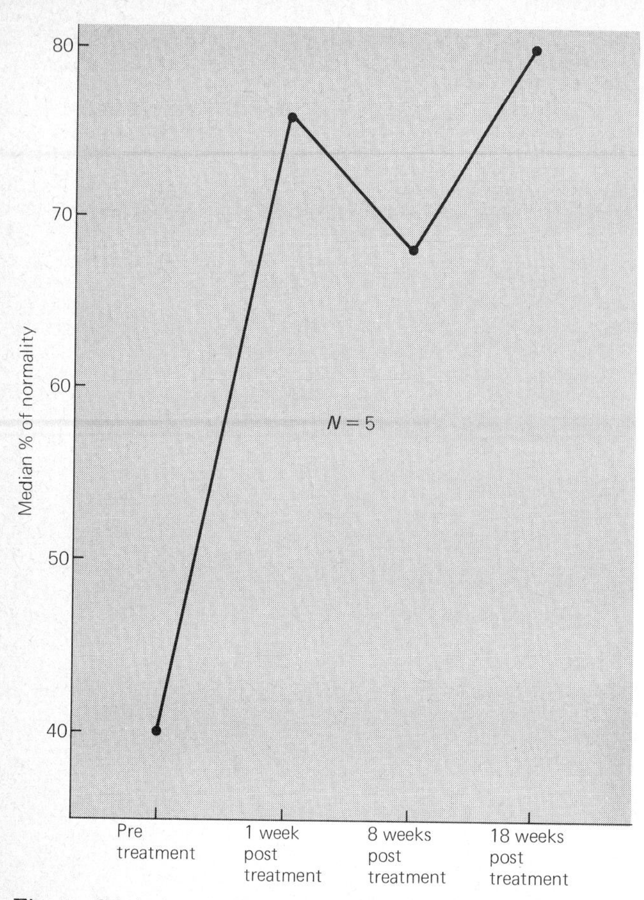

Fig. 5. Clinical assessment of the whole shock contingent group. 100 means free from psychopathology.

(Fig. 6) were determined by adding the deviant preferences and subtracting 15. If the five highest rankings all consisted of deviant items, a maximal score of 25 would be obtained (10 + 9 + 8 + 7 + 6 − 15). A considerably decreased preference for deviant items followed treatment. The group's total clinical MMPI scales (T scores) greater than 70 also declined after treatment (Fig. 6).

In the shock-contingent group only one overt incident of deviant behavior was reported during the 18 weeks following treatment. The patient, while intoxicated, had acted out one of the deviant taped experiences not used in his treatment 15 weeks after termination of the treatment. In the Weekly reports, no new patterns of overt sexual behavior were recorded. Deviant sexual fantasies were less frequent after treatment, and non-deviant fantasies more frequent. Normal sexual behavior either increased or was the same as before the treatment.

Analysis of the data obtained from the non-contingent shock subject indicated that 1 week after his treatment there was a marked reduction in his penile response to the deviant material conditioned. However, there was only minimal reduction in his response to the other deviant tapes. Moderate suppression of the penile response to non-deviant sexual material was also observed. In interesting contrast to the shock-contingent subjects, the penile response was reduced to both deviant and non-deviant tapes 8 weeks after treatment. The global clinical assessment rating and MMPI remained the same after treatment. No new patterns of sexual behavior developed. However, preference for deviant material on the 10-item scale dropped considerably after pseudoconditioning. Unfortunately, the 18 week follow-up data could not be obtained from this patient.

DISCUSSION

The object of the treatment was to extinguish the deviant sexual behavior and encourage socially acceptable, normal sexual outlets. Etiology and individual differences were not considered in the deployment of the technique. The results achieved suggest that the treatment was successful in suppressing deviant sexual behavior for at least 18 weeks. Continued follow-up may yield evidence of sustained benefit.

It is clear that in the laboratory environment deviant sexual responses were inhibited in all patients. The Weekly reports also indicate that this suppression was generalized in the shock-contingent group to the life situation.

Although the non-contingent shock subject showed suppression of his sexual response to the deviant material that was used during his treatment, this suppression did not generalize to other deviant material. There was also the

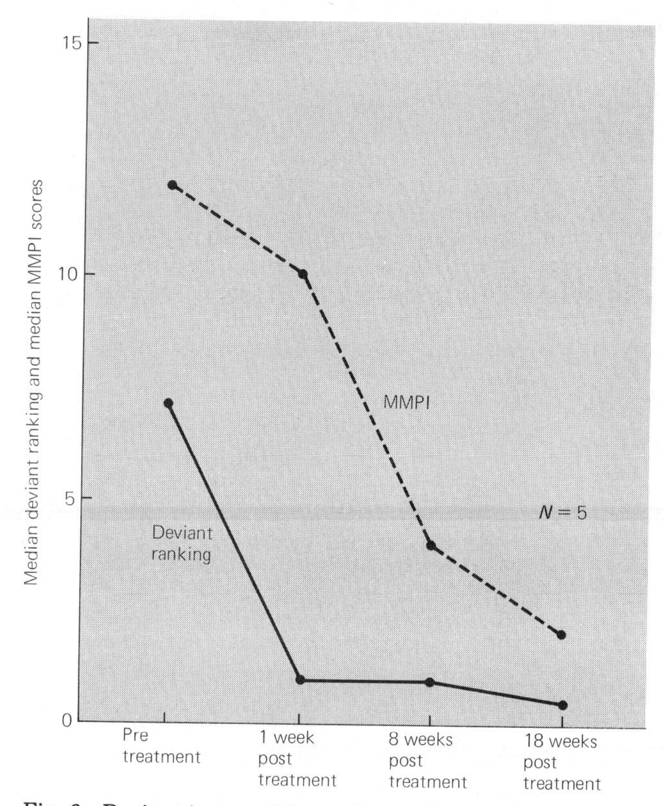

Fig. 6. Deviant item ranking scale and MMPI scores of the shock contingent group. Lower scores indicate less preference for deviant items and less reporting of pathologic symptoms respectively.

undesirable result of a reduction in his sexual responses to normal stimuli. On the other hand, it appears that he benefited from his experience, as shown by the absence of any overt deviant sexual behavior and a reduction in his 10-item scale score.

On the basis of the clinical assessment ratings, all patients were only 80 per cent 'normal' 18 weeks following treatment, indicating residual pathology. This could be due to non-sexual problems. Further investigation might have revealed the details of the remaining unadaptive behavior so that appropriate treatment might have been instituted.

Additional studies involving greater numbers of both experimental and control subjects with long term follow-ups are clearly necessary.

REFERENCES

Bancroft J. H. J., Jones H. G. and Pullan B. P. (1966) A simple transducer for measuring penile erection, with comments on its use in the treatment of sexual disorders, *Behav. Res. Therapy* 4, 239–241.

Clancy J. and Abel G. G. (1967) Unpublished material available on request.

Davison G. C. (1968) Elimination of a sadistic fantasy by a client-controlled counterconditioning technique, *J. Abnorm. Psychol.* 73, 84–90.

Feldman M. P. (1966) Aversive therapy of sexual deviations; A critical review, *Psychol. Bull.* **65**, 65–79.

Feldman M. P. and MacCulloch M. J. (1965) The application of anticipatory avoidance learning to the treatment of homosexuality. I. Theory, technique and preliminary results, *Behav. Res. Therapy* 2, 165–183.

Freund K. (1960) Some Problems in the Treatment of Homosexuality. In (Ed. H. J. Eysenck) *Behavior Therapy and the Neuroses.* pp. 331–326. Pergamon Press, Oxford.

Levis D. J. (1966) The effects of serial CS presentation and other characteristics of the CS on the conditioned avoidance response, *Psychol. Rep.* 18, 755–766.

Marks J. M., Rachman S. and Gelder M. G. (1965) Methods for assessment of aversion treatment in fetishism with masochism, *Behav. Res. & Therapy* 3, 253–258.

Rachman S. (1963) Aversion therapy: chemical or electrical? *Behav. Res. & Therapy* 2, 289–299.

Rachman S. and Hodgson R. J. (1968) Experimentally-induced "sexual fetishism": replication and development, *Psychol. Rec.* **18**, 25–27.

Raymond M. J. (1956) Case of fetishism treated by aversion therapy, *Brit. Med. J.* **2**, 854–857.

Smith C. E. (1968) Correction treatment of the sexual deviate, *Am. J. Psychiat.* **125**, 615–621.

Stampfl T. G. (1960) Avoidance conditioning reconsidered: an extension of Mowrerian theory. Unpublished manuscript. Data review in Levis D. J. (1966) Implosive therapy, Part II: The subhuman analogue, the strategy, and the technique, In (Ed. by S. G. Armitage) *Behavior Modification Techniques in the Treatment of Emotional Disorders.* pp. 22–37. V. A. Publication, Battle Creek, Michigan.

Thorpe J. G., Schmidt E., Broun P. T. and Castill D. (1964) Aversion-relief therapy: A new method for general application, *Behav. Res. & Therapy* 1, 293–296.

Chapter 13

Disorders of Childhood and Adolescence

The three papers in this chapter focus on infantile autism, sleepwalking, and symptom removal by free-operant-conditioning methods. The first article by Ornitz and Ritvo, shows that disturbances of perception are fundamental to all aspects of autism and are manifested by early developmental failure to distinguish between self and environment, to imitate, and to modulate sensory input.

Clement's paper describes a therapy program for somnambulism and shows how this behavior was extinguished in a 7-year-old boy. In this paper Clement compares a number of treatment techniques and explains why he favors conditioning procedures.

Beatrice Barrett's study describes how tics were controlled in a patient who was previously resistant to pharmacological and psychological therapies. Moreover, using conditioning therapy, Barrett was able to transfer his control of the tic symptom to a form of self-control.

Perceptual Inconstancy in Early Infantile Autism: The Syndrome of Early Infant Autism and Its Variants Including Certain Cases of Childhood Schizophrenia

Edward M. Ornitz

Edward R. Ritvo

Within the decade since the syndrome of early infantile autism was first described by Kanner (1, 2), terms such as childhood schizophrenia (3), atypical children (4), children with unusual sensitivities (5), and symbiotic psychosis (6) were used to conceptualize similar, yet apparently distinctive clinical entities. The tendency to create separate entities was reinforced by a desire for diagnostic specificity and accuracy and etiologic preference. As the symptomatology in these children varies both with the severity of the illness and age, it has been possible to emphasize distinctive clusters of symptoms and relate these to particular theories of causation. For instance, the predominance of disturbances of relating coupled with the prevailing belief in the 1940's and 1950's that specific syndromes in children must be outgrowths of specific parental behaviors or attitudes (7) led to attempts to implicate the parents in the development of early infantile autism. The notion that something noxious was done to the children, presumably by the parents, led to a teleological view of the disturbed behavior. Thus, disturbances of relating, perception, and motility have been described as defensive or protective, as a warding off or withdrawal from adverse stimulation or as compensatory self-stimulation.

The purpose of this paper is to describe a single pathologic process common to early infantile autism, certain cases of childhood schizophrenia, the atypical child, symbiotic psychosis, and children with unusual sensitivities. It will be shown that these descriptive categories are variants of a unitary disease. First, we shall describe a specific syndrome of abnormal development which is defined by observable behavior patterns that occur as clusters of symptoms. These clusters of symptoms involve the areas of: (1) perceptual integration, (2) motility patterns, (3) capacity to relate, (4) language, and (5) developmental rate. Secondly, we shall show that a pathologic mechanism underlying the syndrome can be inferred from the nature of the symptom clusters. While this pathologic mechanism may be associated with multivariant etiologic factors, it is operative at birth and makes it impossible for the child to utilize external and internal stimuli to properly organize further development. If maturational or as yet unknown self-corrective factors do not mitigate the influence of this pathologic process, a relatively complete clinical picture of the syndrome develops and persists. If maturational or self-corrective factors do mitigate the influence of this pathologic process, symptoms may wane or shift in predominance resulting in a varying clinical picture. In all such cases the child's later development will show residuals of varying severity. The relationship of these residuals to the primary pathology common to all the symptom clusters will be elaborated.

It will also be emphasized that while early infantile autism must be defined as a behavioral syndrome, it is at the same time a disease. The symptomatology will, therefore, be interpreted as primarily expressive of the underlying pathophysiology rather than being purposeful in the intrapsychic life of the child.

From *Archives of General Psychiatry*, 1968, 18, 76–98.

This work was supported by United States Public Health Service grants No. MH-12575-01 and No. MH-13517-01. Prof Henry Work and Prof George Tarjan, the Division of Child Psychiatry, UCLA School of Medicine, provided support of this study.

DIAGNOSTIC TERMINOLOGY

The different diagnostic labels which have been used to characterize the large group of young children whose symptomatology has varied from Kanner's criteria for early infantile autism have included pseudoretardation, atypical development, symbiotic psychosis, childhood schizophrenia, and infantile psychosis.

The major criteria for the diagnosis of early infantile autism were the inability to relate to people in the expected manner, failure to use language for communication, an apparent desire to be alone and to preserve sameness in the environment, and preoccupation with certain objects (1, 2).

The term pseudoretardation has been used because many of these children appear retarded while showing intellectual potential which differentiates them from the general group of retarded children.

The term atypical development was originally used to describe children (8) with histories and behavior indicative of grossly uneven ego development. Later, when it became apparent that these children shared some of the features of early infantile autism, the term atypical development became used to denote children in whom relatedness was not quite so disturbed as to make the term autistic appropriate.

The term symbiotic psychosis (6) was used to describe children whose behavior appeared to be the opposite of those with autism. That is, the child rather than being aloof, remote, and emotionally isolated was found to be emotionally fused and physically clinging to the mother.

The term childhood schizophrenia has been used by some authors as a synonym for early infantile autism (9), by others to describe a presumed separate syndrome (10), and by some to describe symptoms which others accept as those of early infantile autism without reference to that terminology (11, 12). While some authors (11) describe a continuum of abnormality in which infants and very young children with the symptoms of the autistic child represent the earliest manifestations of schizophrenia, others (10, 13) attempt to maintain a distinction between the two conditions wherein the term childhood schizophrenia is reserved for those cases in which the pathologic process appears to begin after the age of 4 to 5. They postulate that in childhood schizophrenia, a prior stage of intact psychic organization has decompensated, whereas in the autistic child, psychic organization failed to develop. However, in our experience, follow-up of some children who were diagnosed autistic prior to the age of 5 reveals the development over the years of a picture indistinguishable from schizophrenia. Brown and Reiser (14) apparently observing similar changes, reported eight different clinical outcomes (after 9 years of age) of atypical children and included a "schizophrenic" group. Also, in some cases, if detailed retrospective histories of children diagnosed as being schizophrenic after the age of 5 are taken, previously overlooked but diagnostically significant behavioral deviancies can often be elicited. For example, behaviors such as hand-flapping, hypersensitivity to noise, and the failure to adapt to solid foods may be overlooked in ordinary history taking.

Although neither Eisenberg (15) nor Rutter (10) observed paranoid ideas, hallucinations, or delusions in follow-up studies of autistic children, one would not necessarily expect to see these classical symptoms of adult schizophrenia in children. However, in our clinical experience with children, we have observed clear transitions from early infantile autism to the thought disorder characteristic of adult schizophrenia. Similarly, Eisenberg (15) found "peculiarities of language and thought" possibly characteristic of schizophrenia. The case reported by Darr and Worden (16) illustrates an acute schizophrenic reaction in a marginally adjusted adult who had been autistic as a child. When 4 years old, this patient had been examined (Dr. Adolph Meyer) and the classic symptoms of early infantile autism were recorded. At 32 years of age, this woman complained that people would be killed by the poison that was in her, that she would die because she was urinating cider, etc. Tolor and Rafferty (17) found that adolescents diagnosed as schizophrenic scored high on a checklist of symptoms of early infantile autism. While the delineation of early infantile autism from childhood schizophrenia may have prognostic and therapeutic value, available evidence suggests that the former condition can develop into the latter and that so many transitional states occur as to imply a fundamentally similar underlying mechanism in many of the cases. Difference in age of manifest onset rather than separating the two conditions, demonstrates the effect of maturational and developmental level on the way the disease process is expressed.

Reiser (13) has suggested the term infantile psychosis to describe the period from birth to 5 years of age in which the pathologic process develops. He suggests this term as encompassing and, therefore, replacing all of the other terminology just discussed. He feels that the designation "psychotic" is merited by virtue of impairment in perception, failure to test reality, social isolation and withdrawal, impaired control of instinctual energies, and disturbances of feeling, thinking, and behavior. This description overlaps the syndrome and subclusters of symptoms which will be described in the following sections of this paper. However, the terms *psychosis* and *psychotic* are also commonly used in a broader sense than is applicable to these conditions. Therefore, the terms *early infantile autism and autistic child* will be used in this paper as representative of the group of clinical states under study. Early infantile autism and the other conditions will be further considered as variants or sequelae of a basic disease.

NATURAL HISTORY

Family

When the syndrome of early infantile autism was first described by Kanner (1), it was thought that these children came from highly intellectual families in the upper socioeconomic levels. In fact, the parents were from the academic and professional communities and their family life was characterized by obsessive meticulousness and intellectualism. The corollary of these attributes was an emotional coldness often described as "refrigeration" (2). In the subsequent two decades a broader clinical experience with autistic children and their families has revealed that these children come from every socioeconomic class and that the parents may, or may not, be professionally employed. The fathers may indeed be university professors, psychiatrists, electronic engineers, or mathematicians. We have observed, however, that they may be common laborers or artists.

Wolff and Chess (9) have made similar observations. While some of the parents are reported to be cold, isolated, or refrigerated individuals, others have proven to be warm, loving, and quite capable of raising normally affectionate siblings of their autistic child. A condition of family disruption and emotional turmoil may surround the infancy or childhood of autistic children (13) or the disease process may develop in a normal emotional climate (10).

A realtive sparcity of schizophrenic parents has been noted by some observers. However, Rutter's (10) failure to find a single schizophrenic parent in his population of autistic children was not confirmed by Goldfarb (12) Wolff and Chess (9) or O'Gorman (18).

It is rare to find more than one nontwin sibling with the disease (13), and we have seen only one such case. However, J. Simmons (oral communication, June 1967) has followed five families with two nontwin autistic siblings. Dizygotic twins are discordant for early infantile autism. With one exception (19), all reported cases of monozygotic twins are concordant for the disease when monozygocity has been adequately demonstrated and the disease is not associated with perinatal trauma to one twin (20, 21).

Pregnancy and Delivery

Available surveys provide conflicting evidence as to the relative incidence of complications during pregnancy and delivery in the mothers of these children as compared to other diagnostic groups. Schain and Yannet (22) and Kanner (23) reported no increase in prenatal and perinatal complications. However, in a well-controlled study, Taft and Goldfarb (24) reviewed hospital charts of autistic children, their siblings, and normal controls. They reported a significantly greater incidence of prenatal and perinatal difficulties in the autistic group.

Postnatal

In the immediate postnatal period, some autistic children have been described as unusually quiet, motorically inactive, and emotionally unresponsive or, conversely, as unusually irritable and extremely sensitive to auditory, tactile, and visual stimuli. The same infant may alternately manifest both types of disturbance.

Following the immediate postnatal period two general courses of development may be reported. In the first, the baby shows early signs of deviant development. In the second, relatively normal development is described by the parents until the age of 18 to 26 months, at which time an apparent regression in all areas of behavior rapidly occurs. These children then look identical to the children whose development has been deviant from birth. In many cases, parents report that the "regression" is associated with some concurrent event such as the birth of a sibling, marital rift, economic reversal, or a move to a new home. In other cases, the behavioral changes are associated with factors influencing the child directly, such as illness, hospitalization, or separation from a parent. We have found in several cases where "normal" development was reported during the first 18 months, detailed history taking revealed evidence of deviant development which had gone unnoticed.

Neonatal Period

Most frequently it is reported that the autistic infant was: "a good baby"; "he never cried"; "he seemed not to need companionship or stimulation"; and "he did not want to be held." Concomitant with being "good," he may have shown a reduced activity level, torpor, and a tendency to cry rarely, if at all. When picked up, he may have been limp with peculiar posturing and flaccid muscle tone. This data obtained from retrospective questioning of parents of autistic children has been confirmed by one prospective study (25).

First Six Months

During the early months of development the mothers often report being perplexed by the baby's lack of crying or by their difficulty in relating crying to hunger or to discomfort from other specific needs. These babies seem content to be left alone a great deal. In some family constellations these factors are very disturbing to the mothers, resulting in anxiety and bewilderment which then leads to either compensatory overinvolvement or withdrawal. Either response may result in the mother's loss of self-esteem in her role as mother. In other families, the advent of such an "undemanding" baby is welcomed by a harrassed mother who then leaves the baby alone.

The first definite signs of deviant development may be the baby's failure to notice the coming and going of the mother, a lack or delay of the smiling response, or the lack of the anticipatory response to being picked up. Concomitantly, underreactivity (failure to play with the crib gym or show an interest in toys) and paradoxical overreactivity to stimulation (panic at the sound of a vacuum cleaner or telephone) may occur. Finally, failure to vocalize during the first half year may also be noted.

Second Six Months

An ominous sign of later pathology may appear when solid foods are introduced. A baby who had fed well at breast or bottle and adapted easily to strained foods may show severe distress when rough textured "junior" and table foods are introduced. Several types of response occur, including refusal to hold food in mouth, refusal to chew or swallow, or intense gagging. After dentition appears, it may become apparent that the infant avoids chewing food. Some of these children actually remain on pureed baby foods and the bottle until their 6th or 7th year.

The disinterest in toys noted during the first six months may precede the active casting or flicking away of toys. Objects placed in the hand may be simply dropped. This behavior may contrast markedly with an alternate tendency to hold an object such as a piece of string, a broken pencil, or a marble. Such a child often is panicked and upset if the object disappears. He may persist in holding onto it for years.

The sequence of motor development may be precocious or retarded or may be characterized by accelerated achievement of one motor skill followed by a lag before development of the next. Also characteristic is the tendency to give up a previously acquired motor skill; the parents often describe the child as not wanting to use an acquired ability.

Mothers frequently describe their autistic children as being unaffectionate. When picked up and held, they may either go limp or stiffen. When put down by the mother, they do not seem to notice. At this point the busy or bewildered mother may leave the baby alone because her feeling that he does not need her is reinforced. By the age of 10 or 11 months these babies do not play "peek-a-boo" and "patty-cake" games and do not imitate waving "bye-bye." The mother's bewilderment at her baby's lack of responsiveness may be further reinforced by his failure to develop communicative speech. The baby who did not "coo" or "babble" earlier may now show a crucial failure to imitate sounds and words. As with motor function, speech development may be retarded or may show precocious advances followed by failure to use words previously learned. Nonverbal communication also lags: the child does not point toward what he wants and does not look toward a desired object.

At this stage of development and later, these children are frequently thought to be deaf. This possibility is often belied by unusual sensitivity to and awareness of certain unexpected or loud sounds. A similar type of sensitivity may also be observed in the visual modality. Sudden changes in illumination may evoke panic. Often the earlier tendency of babies to regard their own writhing hand and finger movements becomes a comsuming preoccupation. Other sensory modalities may also be affected. For example, unusual tactile discrimination with adverse reactions to rough wool fabrics and preference for smooth surfaces occurs. Proprioceptive and antigravity responses may be similarly involved and come to attention when the father who enjoys tossing the child in the air is rebuffed by the baby's distress.

Second and Third Years

After 12 months, unusual sensitivity to auditory, visual, tactile, and labyrinthine stimulation is often accompanied paradoxically by peculiar and bizarrely expressed pursuit of sensations in these modalities. Noisy, vigorous, and sustained tooth grinding occurs. Some of the children scratch surfaces and listen intently to the sounds they have created. They may pass their eyes along surfaces apparently attending to patterns. They may rub surfaces with their hands, apparently reacting to textural differences. Contrasting with these behaviors, they seem to ignore more meaningful, environmentally determined stimuli.

Between 1 and 3 years of age, repetitive habits, mannerisms, and gestures may begin to develop. They suddenly cease activity, posture, and stare off into space. Frequently, this posturing involves hyperextension of the neck. Such children may begin to whirl themselves and characteristically flutter or flap their arms, hands, or fingers. The fingers may flick against stable objects or in the air. A variant of flapping is an oscillatory motion of the hand and forearm. As the child learns to walk and run, he frequently does so almost exclusively on his toes. Toe walking, whirling, and flapping may be seen as slow, consistent, repetitive mannerisms which may be suddenly interrupted by peculiar darting or lunging movements accompanied by excited gesticulation of the arms. Certain external stimuli, such as spinning objects (children's tops), may set off these explosive, yet organized patterns of activity. Continuous body rocking and head rolling are also frequently observed. These behaviors may become organized into complex repetitive sequences. Long hours may be spent spinning tops, wheels, jar lids, coins, or any available object, running back and forth across a room, switching the overhead lights repetitively on and off, and dancing around an object while flapping the hands.

By this age, it may become apparent that there is a lack of eye contact. They seem to look beyond or through people as if looking through a window. Other people can be used as extensions of the child's self, eg, taking the arm of the adult and placing it on a doorknob. In doing this, they do not look at the adult but only at the desired object. Although they may seek out objects for repetitive stereotyped activity, eg, light switches or tops, they usually show an utter lack of interest in toys offered to them.

Fourth and Fifth Years

By the time the child is between 3 and 5 years old, the unusual sensitivities to external stimulation noted above may decrease. Motor retardation, when it has occurred, is usually overcome and the child becomes capable of physical activities appropriate to his age. Yet, he may not actually engage in such activities as jungle-gym climbing or riding a tricycle because of his lack of social awareness of the activity itself. The tendency to walk on toes, flap arms, and whirl may decrease but in some cases continues for many years.

A major problem in the 3 to 5-year-old child is found in the area of language development. Speech may not have developed at all or if present may be characterized by parroting (echolalia), the parroted phrase being repeated completely out of the social context in which it had been heard. This is called delayed echolalia (26). These children often make requests by repeating what has been said to them in the interrogative form. For example, the child will say "you want to walk" rather than saying that he wants to go for a walk. Pronoun reversals using "you" or "he" for "I" or "me" are noted, and the object and subject of discourse are confused. The voice may sound atonal, arhythmic, and hollow.

SYNDROME AND SUBCLUSTERS OF SYMPTOMS

The symptoms of early infantile autism and its variants have been described in the previous section in terms of their onset of occurrence. This multitude of symptoms will now be classified into certain related subclusters in order that a unified disease process can be delineated.

It is to be emphasized that the subclusters of symptoms are defined on the basis of observable behaviors. There is no a priori assumption that one subcluster of symptoms stands independently of another. In fact, it is one purpose of this paper to show that one of the subclusters (disturbances of perception) may underlie most of the other groups of symptoms which together make up the syndrome.

The subclusters are: (1) disturbances of perception, (2) disturbances of motor behavior, (3) disturbances of relating, (4) disturbances of language, and (5) disturbances of developmental rate and sequence.

It should be emphasized that the total syndrome characterized by these five subclusters of symptoms is based upon detailed observation of over 150 cases by us. It is not implied that in any particular case all symptoms will be seen nor will every subcluster of symptoms achieve full expression. In fact, we have observed individual autistic children who show primarily disturbances of relating and only minimal suggestion of the other subclusters. In contrast, we have seen an occasional child who shows primarily disturbances of perception, with minimal expression of the other subclusters and relatively intact ability to relate.

Disturbances of Perception

Heightened awareness, hyperirritability, and obliviousness to external stimulation all may occur in the same child. All modalities of sensation may be involved. While auditory changes are most often noted, unusual perceptual aberrations may be seen in the visual, tactile, gustatory, olfactory, proprioceptive, and vestibular senses.

Heightened Awareness of Sensory Stimuli

Auditory. Attention to self-induced sounds (eg, scratching of surfaces), attention to background stimuli, ear-banging, ear-rubbing, and flicking of the ear are observed.

Visual. Prolonged regarding of writhing movements of the hands and fingers, brief but intense staring, and scrutiny of visual detail are noted.

Tactile. The auditory and visual scrutiny is paralleled by passing the hands over surfaces of varying textures.

Olfactory and Gustatory. Specific food preferences, according to taste and smell, and repetitive sniffing occur.

Vestibular. The children are unusually aware of things that spin and can become preoccupied with car wheels, phonograph records, or washing machines—far beyond the interest expressed transiently by normal children.

Heightened Sensitivity and Irritability

Auditory. Unusual fearfulness of sirens, vacuum cleaners, barking dogs, and the tendency to cover the ears in anticipation of such sounds are observed.

Visual. Change in illumination will occasionally precipitate fearful reactions.

Tactile. There may be intolerance for certain fabrics. The children often do not accept wool blankets or clothing against the skin, and show a preference for smooth surfaces.

Gustatory. A specific intolerance toward rough textured "junior" or table foods is observed.

Vestibular. A marked aversion to being tossed in the air or to ride in elevators occurs. Intense interest and pleasure in spinning objects may alternate with fearful, disturbed, and excited reactions to them.

Nonresponsiveness

Auditory. Most notable is the disregard of speech and the lack of detectable behavioral response to loud sounds.

Visual. These children ignore new persons or features in their environment. They may walk into or through things or people as if they did not exist.

Tactile. Early in the first year of life, they may let objects placed in the hand fall away, as if they had no tactile representation.

Pain. These children may not react with evidence of pain to bumps, falls, or cuts.

Disturbances of Motor Behavior

Motor behaviors can be divided into two groups, those that seem to be associated with sensory input and those that seem to be associated with discharge.

Motor Behaviors Apparently Associated With Sensory Input

Auditory. Scratching at surfaces is often accompanied by bringing the ear down as if to listen to the sound created. Banging of the ear or head may induce intense repetitive auditory and vibratory stimulation. Tooth grinding may have a similar effect.

Visual. Both the regarding of the slow writhing movements of the hands and fingers and the more vigorous flapping of the hands within the visual field may provide visual input to the child.

Tactile. Scratching at or rubbing of surfaces provides tactile sensation.

Vestibular. Autistic children tend to whirl themselves or spend long hours spinning objects, such as tops, can lids, and coins. These activities may provide increased vestibular input. The children may whirl themselves in many ways, for example, while standing up or frequently while sitting on a smooth floor, swiveling around and around on their buttocks. They spin objects in many ways too and will become excited and preoccupied with spinning metal tops or take toys completely unrelated to spinning and find ways of spinning them. They seem to be able to make tops out of almost anything. Often bizarre ritualistic activities accompany the preoccupation with spinning. They will flap their hands and engage in excited, repetitive movements, lunging at the top as if to push against it and then pulling away from it only to repeat the activity again and again. At other times, the same child will appear frightened and run away from the top. The diagnosis was clarified in the case of a 3-year-old child with relatively intact capacity to relate when he was offered a top. He reacted with increasing tension and fearfulness, gesticulating as the top was spun faster. He stared at his hands and then ritualistically patted the floor while engaging in a stereotyped dance around the top. As his excitement increased, he became oblivious to reassurance, stared at the ceiling, and then began to flap his fingers while fixing his gaze intently on the top. When told that he could stop the spinning if he did not like it, he responded by making a "stop" gesture with his hand from a distance. Then he shot at the top with a toy gun, lay down to play "dead" and finally put the top in a cupboard out of sight.

Proprioceptive. Hand-flapping deserves special mention, as it is an activity that is characteristic and almost pathognomic of the autistic child, although it may be seen occasionally in other syndromes. It may occur only transiently or may become a fixed behavior. It may be associated with states of excitement or occur over prolonged periods unassociated with external stimuli. The flapping of the arms has many modifications, such as wiggling of the fingers, flicking at surfaces, or oscillating of the hand while empty or while holding small toys. Flapping behavior often has an interesting evolution in individual children. In one case it was first noted at 11 months of age that while mouthing a small plastic airplane, the child would rhythmically flick at the wing with one hand while holding it to his mouth with the other. At the age of 5 years, this behavior evolved into a repetitive gesticulation wherein the child would start to put one hand and thumb into his mouth while flicking that hand away with the other. By 8 years of age, he had given up this activity, attempting to follow directions to suppress it; he was observed instead to repetitively flex his extended fingers at the metacarpophalangeal joints over long periods of time. Another child, 4 years old, whose variant of hand-flapping was a rapid oscillation (alternate pronation and supination) of the hand and forearm, developed a pruritic dermatitis and began scratching. As the dermititis increased, the scratching took on the oscillatory nature of his hand-flapping, and for a period of time substituted in part for the hand movements. As the pruritis abated, he gave up the scratching and again oscillated. In some of the children hand-flapping does not occur spontaneously during examination, although a history of it may be elicited by detailed questioning. It may at times be elicited by specific stimulation, eg, presentation of a top. However, under controlled conditions of observations, it is found to be a remarkably persistent behavior, neither increasing nor decreasing with time (Sorosky, A.; Ornitz, E.; Brown, M.; and Rituo, E., unpublished data).

Other Motor Phenomena

Toe walking and periodic bursts of excited lunging, gesticulating, and darting movements do not seem especially related to sensory input. The lunging and darting may appear almost seizure-like. Toe walking may occur intermittently or may be the only mode of walking.

Disturbances of Relating

Poor eye contact, delayed or absent social smile, delayed or absent anticipatory response to being picked up, apparent aversion to physical contact, limpness or stiffening when held, disinterest in looking at, casting away, or bizarre use of toys, a lack of active response to the "peek-a-boo," "pat-a-cake," and "bye-bye" games, and the general preference to being alone are all characteristic. The use of people as an extension of the self, and the more pervasive lack of emotional responsiveness are additional manifestations of disturbed relating.

Disturbances of Language

Frequently, there is a complete failure of speech to develop. When and if speech does develop, it is often poorly modulated, atonal, arhythmic, and hollow sounding without communicative or affective content. The most prominent specific type of pathologic language is called echolalia (26). Also, characteristic is pronoun reversal.

Disturbances of Developmental Rate

The rate of development may be disturbed, leading to discontinuities in the normal sequence. Altered rates of development involving motor and speech areas occur. The child may roll over precociously early and then may not sit without support until 11 months, or he may sit up without support at 5 months and not pull to a stand until 13 months. In the language area he may use a few words at 10 months and fail to use words again until 2 years old, or the early use of words may be followed by a long delay in joining them into phrases. Further, he may successfully perform some skill such as crawling and then may not ever do it again. Some of the children have been described on the one hand as slow and on the other hand as showing precocious motor and language development. The most characteristic finding on infant developmental testing is a marked scatter both between and within sectors of tests such as the Gesell (27).

Other attempts to group the many symptoms of this disease have been made. Closest to our approach is the work of Creak (28). She abstracted nine criteria from the descriptive literature on childhood schizophrenia and early infantile autism. These nine points overlap the five subclusters of symptoms described here. Impairment of emotional relations with people and preoccupation with objects have been included here with the other disturbances of relating. Speech disturbance, distortion in motility, and retardation are synonymous with the disturbances of language, motor expression, and developmental rate. Along with abnormal perceptual experience, we consider the unawareness of self-identity, the maintenance of sameness, and anxiety precipitated by change as derivatives of the disturbances of perception.

CHANGE IN SYNDROME AFTER EARLY CHILDHOOD

One of the most confusing aspects of this disease is that after the age of 5 or 6 years, symptom-complexes of early infantile autism and its variants tend to merge with other clinical entities, eg, childhood schizophrenia (see above). The manifestations of the subclusters of symptoms as they appear past the age of 5 or 6 years will now be discussed.

Relationship to the Environment and Language

Disturbances of relating and disturbances of language are best considered together; as with increasing age, the capacity to relate depends markedly on the capacity to communicate with others. It has been observed that speech may not develop by the age of 5, in which case the autistic child becomes less and less distinguishable from the large group of severely retarded children (15). Absence of speech has been correlated with low intelligence (10). Those autistic children who develop noncommunicative speech and progress no further, when seen again at 10 to 15 years of age, tend to look much as they did when younger.

If they develop communicative speech by 5 years of age, then several possible courses of development are open. First, language capacity may be quite rudimentary. Communications are literal and concrete, with minimal capacity for abstract thought. Affect tends to be flat, and they do not become emotionally involved with others.

In a second course of development, characteristics typical of organic brain disease become manifest. There may be an impulsiveness, a lack of emotional control, hyperactivity, restlessness, and irritability accompanied by some degree of mental retardation and concrete thinking.

A third developmental course seen during the school years and in early adolescence is identical to that described by others as schizophrenia. This is often an insidious process wherein the child who is diagnosed earlier in life as being autistic becomes harder and harder to distinguish from those children who are called schizophrenic. Language is characterized by loose, free, or fragmented associations leading away from social contact and communication through tangles of irrelevancy and tangential thinking. Bizarre, illusory, or hallucinatory thinking may be present. A distorted fantasy life may be elaborated around some of the earlier behaviors which have been grouped as disturbances of perception or motor expression. For example, the child who evolved hand-flapping into a complex gesticulation wherein one hand and thumb was pushed back from the mouth by a flicking action of the other hand, elaborated the fantasy that his thoughts were falling out of his mouth and that he was pushing them back into his head.

A fourth course of development may evolve either from the schizophrenic stage or follow directly from the autistic syndrome itself. Such children superficially appear to have a relatively normal personality structure or neurotic or characterologic defects. However, careful attention to behavior and a detailed history of earlier development will reveal a clinical picture suggestive of residuals of an earlier autistic syndrome. Particularly, one sees a certain oddness in character and impaired empathy coupled with a lack of social judgment and discrimination. There may be excessive preoccupying interests in mechanical things coupled with a lack of interest in human relationships.

Perceptual and Motor Phenomena. The disturbances of perception and motor behavior may persist during the school years but usually dropout. Some of the children who suffer a schizophrenic outcome still toe-walk, tend to whirl, and also may hand-flap. In the children who develop neurotic or personality disorders, one may under certain circumstances see hand-flapping or one of its variants. For example, one 10-year-old child was examined and purposely presented with a noisy spinning top; he commented that he used to get excited when he saw a top spin. While there was no overt hand-flapping, observation of his crossed hands, one pressing down on the other, revealed a rhythmic contraction of the tendons at the dorsum of the hand. It appeared that he was consciously suppressing the tendency to flap.

These relationships among diagnostic categories are illustrated in Fig. 1. Increasing diagnostic specificity as the child gets older is evident.

DIFFERENTIAL DIAGNOSIS

The differential diagnosis of early infantile autism and childhood schizophrenia has been thoroughly reviewed by Reiser (13), Rutter (10), and Ekstein (29). Discussion of different diagnosis here will be limited to those syndromes wherein certain common symptoms suggest etiologic consideration.

In the syndrome of institutionalism (30), not only are a certain limited number of symptoms common to early infantile autism, but certain aspects of the history may be common to both conditions, making differential diagnosis initially difficult. The child raised in an institution may suffer sensory, emotional, and maternal deprivation, resulting in a developing state of apathy during the first year of life accompanied by a tendency to excessive rocking, transient preoccupation with looking at objects, and athetoid-like movements of the extremities. When followed later, some of these children showed unstable and particularly indiscriminate relating to others, failing to develop a meaningful one-to-one relationship with a mother figure. They also may show deficiencies in abstract thinking. Institutionalism can occur in home settings (31) and we have observed infants with this syndrome, particularly when the mother has suffered a prolonged but inadequately recognized postpartum depression. These infants, although at home, tend to be left alone and are therefore understimulated. The autistic child may also be left alone a great deal, and this can be in response to the mother's bewilderment at his lack of interest in her presence. Thus, the isolation of the autistic child follows rather than precedes the pathologic process. The apathy of the primarily understimulated child can superficially resemble the emotional deficiency of the autistic child, and the prolonged rocking, preoccupation with objects, and peculiar athetoid-like movements can mimic transiently some of their motor expressions. The indiscriminate relating superficially suggests the disturbed type of relating seen in early infantile autism. However, the children who suffer institutionalism either in the institution or at home do not develop the complete autistic syndrome. The myriad ways in which the autistic child expresses deviant development are not seen.

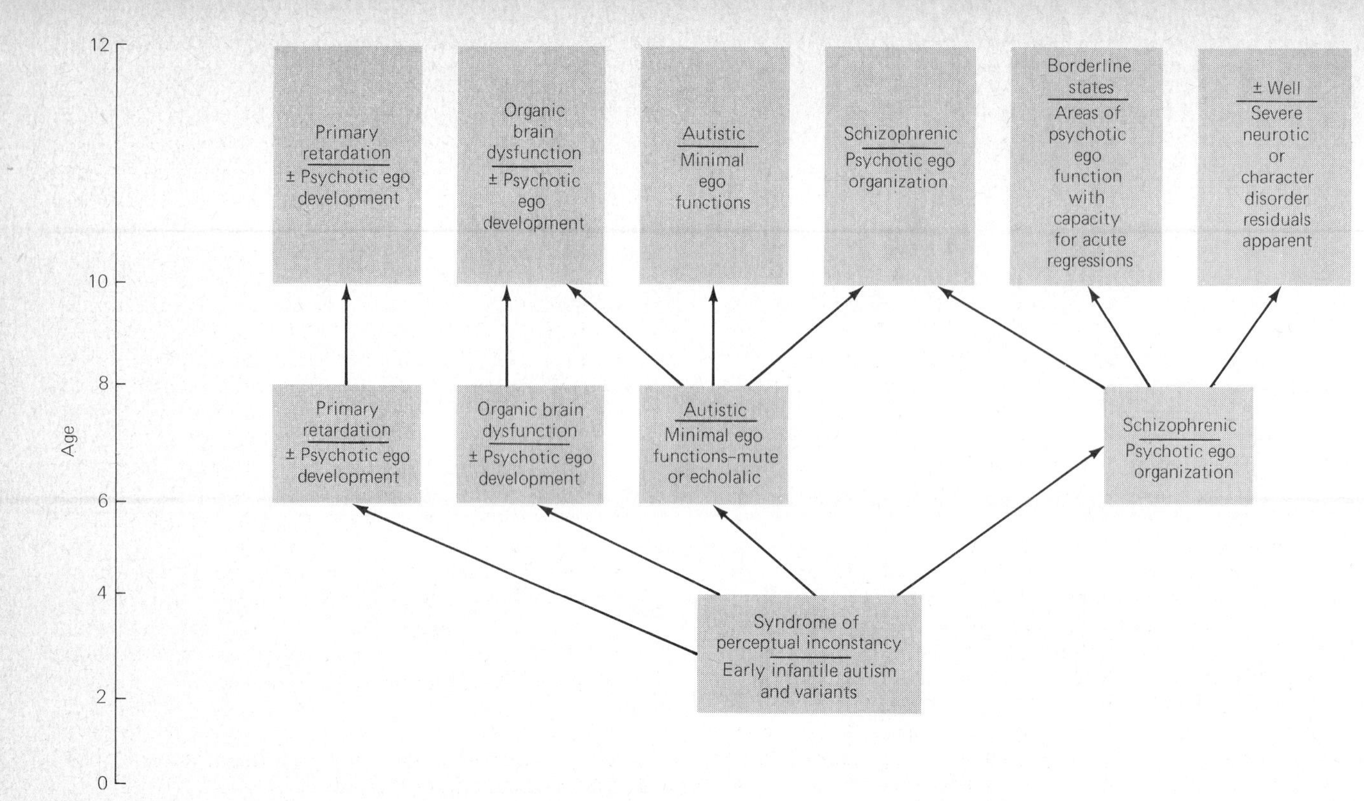

Fig. 1. Developmental relationships among diagnostic categories.

Loss of a maternal figure who has already become significant during the first year also leads to disturbed development. This has been referred to as anaclitic depression (32). Here profound withdrawal is not accompanied by the other facets of the syndrome of early infantile autism or its variants.

The absence of development of early infantile autism in children suffering from institutionalism (S. Provence, MD, oral communication, November 1966) and following loss suggest that although early infantile autism is in part a profound disturbance of relating, etiologic factors must be looked for within the child. Such factors must lie within the central nervous system; sensory deprivation may at the most be a secondary component in the etiology of this condition.

Reiser (13) has commented on the variety of chronic brain damage syndromes with or without accompanying retardation which should be considered in the differential diagnosis of early infantile autism. While the behavioral disturbance in chronic brain syndromes includes irritability, emotional lability, hyperactivity, short attention span, and lack of impulse control, at times behavior more specifically suggestive of early infantile autism may occur. Berkson and Davenport (33) observed "hand flick-shake," "hand held before eyes," and "twirling" in severely retarded "mental defectives." As these behaviors which are probably identical with the hand-flapping, regarding, and whirling of autistic children are lumped with less specific "stereotyped movements," their incidence is unknown. Since diagnostic precision was limited to "mental defective," the number of possibly autistic individuals in the patient group is also unknown. Occasionally, in brain damage secondary to specific syndromes, we have seen whirling (tuberous sclerosis) and hand-flapping (phenylketonuria). However, it should be stressed that in all children suffering from these conditions we do not see these disturbed motor expressions which are so characteristic of autistic children. It is postulated, therefore, that in those cases with known brain damage and autistic behavior, certain specific functional systems of the central nervous system, pathology of which underlies early infantile autism, may become involved. No anatomical sites for these hypothesized functional systems are at present known. In those cases of early infantile autism which are not accompanied by evidence of brain damage, it is postulated that the same functional systems are involved on a congenital basis as suggested by twin studies.

Since early infantile autism can only be diagnosed as a behavioral syndrome (34), it would seem that those cases of the syndrome where evidence of brain pathology, eg, phenylketonuria, encephalitis, birth trauma exists should be referred to as "early infantile autism associated with . . ., eg, PKU, encephalitis, birth trauma" rather than excluding those cases from the behavioral syndrome as is often done. Rutter (10) reports a high incidence of brain damage in a follow-up study of 63 autistic children.

The failure of speech development in both early infantile autism and aphasia creates diagnostic problems of both semantic and etiologic significance. While the autistic child without speech is by definition "aphasic" confusing cases of real differential diagnostic import are seen. The relationship between the two conditions has been thoroughly discussed by Rutter (10, 35). The fact that aphasic children may use gesture to communicate, while autistic children often do not, may help to separate the two conditions if the child is seen at an early age. If the child improves in all areas but speech, the diagnosis of aphasia is supported.

ETIOLOGIC CONSIDERATIONS

In the literature, the etiology of early infantile autism has been considered from several points of view: (1) hereditary tendency; (2) influence of parental personality or malignant family interaction; (3) critical or vulnerable periods in infancy; (4) possible disturbed neurophysiologic mechanism; and (5) underlying or concomitant developmental and neurologic pathology.

Various investigators have stressed different symptom subclusters as expressing the fundamental and basic nature of the disorder. For example, Kanner when first describing the disease process focused on disturbed relating to the environment. The coldness, aloofness, and withdrawal of the child was described in relationship to analogous though less severe behavior observed in the parents and even the grandparents in this particular patient sample. This lent itself initially to a genetically based interpretation wherein the autistic child was seen as the final expression of an innate tendency toward intellectualism and an associated lack of emotional expression (1). The emphasis on the disturbed relatedness, however, also lent itself to an alternative etiologic notion, namely that the children were disturbed and emotionally "refrigerated" because they were raised in an emotionally refrigerated environment (2, 36). Therefore, the etiologic emphasis was changed from faulty genes to faulty parents. A more specific emphasis on the parents' role in the development of the syndrome was postulated by Szurek (37) and by Rank (38) and has been categorically stated by Reiser (13). The emphasis shifted from the type of environment created for the child to the parent-child interaction; a state of emotional turmoil in the parents during the critical period of infancy was postulated to compromise the essential relationship. In our own experience, however, this has not been seen in all cases; moreover, in many families where great emotional turmoil has been present during the infancy of the child, that child has not become autistic. This experience has been confirmed by others (10).

The concept of symbiotic psychosis was introduced by Mahler (6) and emphasized the parent as the etiologic agent in the development of psychosis in the child, but for opposite reasons than those of Kanner (2). In the development of symbiotic psychosis, the parent was described as all-enveloping and never giving the child the opportunity to differentiate himself. However, we have seen both "symbiotic" clinging and complete physical and emotional fusion alongside of, and alternating with, emotional aloofness and cold, icy withdrawal in the same child. What is basic and common to these apparently opposite disturbances is the fluctuating capacity of such a child to perceive separateness between himself and the surrounding environment. The inability to maintain a distinction between self and nonself can be expressed as readily by fusion as by lack of awareness of the other person. Thus, both behaviors, which superficially appear to be opposites, are simply different expressions of a failure in these children to delineate the boundaries between themselves and their environment.

Emphasis on the disturbances of relating has led others to pin-point the period of differentiation from the mother between 6 and 18 months of age (34, 39) as the critical period of vulnerability in development of the disease. However, our clinical experience and direct observation (40) show that the onset of the illness can be manifest at birth or in the first months of life when other symptom clusters are considered.

Another subcluster of symptomatology which has received particular consideration with reference to etiology has been that of disturbance of developmental rate. Bender has emphasized this aspect of the syndrome by postulating a maturation lag at the embryonic level as being characteristic of and fundamental to the development of the entire syndrome (41).

The disturbances of motor expression which we have described have received mention in passing, but have not been related systematically to the syndrome as a whole. Some investigators have referred to the motor behaviors as self-stimulation (42).

Disturbances of perception have been emphasized by several authors. Bergman and Escalona (5) observed abnormal sensitivities in a small group of children, some of whom became psychotic, and postulated a low barrier to external stimulation as being of etiologic import. Goldfarb (43) has studied perception from the point of view of receptor preference in these children and has pointed up their apparent preference for the use of near receptors (tactile sensation) over far receptors (vision and audition). Schopler (44) has attempted to use near receptor preference as evidence that early sensory deprivation due to inadequate reticular arousal mechanisms is a factor in etiology. Although the linkage between near receptor preference and sensory deprivation is not made clear, an overriding consideration is that infants actually suffering known sensory deprivation exhibit an entirely different syndrome than that of early infantile autism. Contrasting with the notion of reduced arousal functions is the postulation of a chronically high level of arousal as basic to the etiology (45). Actual observation, however, of the behavior of autistic children, either individually or as a group, reveals them at times to be in apparent states of low arousal (posturing, immobility, and unresponsiveness), and at times in apparent states of high arousal (agitation, excitation, and fearfulness). Wing (46) stressed the autistic child's inability to make meaningful patterns out of sensory stimuli, thereby linking cognitive to perceptual disturbances.

Goldfarb (12, 47) has described both motility disturbances and disturbances of perception in a high percentage of schizophrenic (autistic) children whom he labels the "organic" subgroup. This subgroup is differentiated from "nonorganic" children who are relatively free of these disturbances. Goldfarb postulated a continuum of etiologic variables ranging from purely environmental to specific organic influences. These have been detailed by Sarvis and Garcia (39) who associated the illness with faulty family psychodynamics, traumatic environmental circumstances, severe physical illness, and temporal lobe and other neuropathology affecting perception. However, the absence of autistic behavior under conditions of severe environmental and organic insult, and the presence of the syndrome unassociated with such conditions suggests that a basic pathologic mechanism specific to the illness must be present. Environmental factors may determine in some cases the time at which the illness comes to clinical attention. Somatic factors may in some cases either trigger or replicate the expression of the basic pathology.

UNDERLYING MECHANISMS

Is it possible to relate the symptom clusters of early infantile autism to an underlying pathologic mechanism? All of the subclusters of symptoms can be seen as resulting from certain cardinal developmental failures occurring in the first year of life. First, many of the behaviors of an autistic infant stem from a failure to develop a distinction between himself and the outside world. Second, imitative behavior is fragmented, greatly delayed, or does not appear. Third, the autistic infant fails to develop the capacity to adequately modulate perceptual input; much of his behavior suggests that he is either getting too little or too much input from the environment. These three developmental failures can be associated and explained by assuming that autistic children do not have the ability to maintain *constancy of perception.* Thus, identical percepts from the environment are not experienced as the same each time. This is due, we further postulate, to an underlying failure of homeostatic regulation within the central nervous system so that environmental stimuli are either not adequately modulated or are unevenly amplified. This postulated failure to maintain perceptual constancy results in a random underloading or overloading of the central nervous system.

The autistic infant seems to get either too much or too little sensory input, and these states often alternate rapidly and without relation to the environment. Behaviors suggesting that sensory overload is being experienced include attention to inconsequential stimuli and scrutiny of tactile and visual detail. Such activities suggest that the trivial cannot be treated as trivial. More impressive is the tendency of so many of these children to respond with increased excitation, irritability, or apprehension bordering on panic to stimuli which may be either minimal or intense. Such stimuli may be in the auditory, visual, tactile, and proprioceptive modalities. Spinning objects may incite particularly intense reactions in these children. This suggests sensitivity in the vestibular modality as does the panic brought on by an elevator ride.

That these children also get too little external stimuli is inferred from their underresponsiveness.

What type of pathologic mechanism might interfere with the capacity to maintain perceptual constancy? While the failure of homeostatic regulation may represent a neurophysiologic deficiency, behaviors such as the tendency to rub surfaces, visual regarding of finger movements, hand-flapping, and whirling suggest a breaking through of a pathologic excitatory state or activating mechanism. Such a postulated state would have the characteristic of interfering with homeostatic regulation of perception.

Physiologic states can be characterized by degrees of excitation, facilitation, inhibition, or some combination thereof. In the behaviors which define early infantile autism and its allied conditions, we can discern expressions of both states of excessive excitation and inhibition. These states may occur independently in an individual child, may alternate rapidly with each other, or even appear to coexist. The hyperexcitatory state is manifested by hand-flapping, finger-fluttering, whirling, circling on tiptoes, sudden lunging and darting, accentuated startle, hypersensitivity to stimuli, and excited reactions to spinning objects. The overinhibitory state is manifested by posturing, prolonged immobility, and nonresponsiveness to external stimulation. To a considerable, though not complete extent, the symptoms indicative of the state of hyperexcitation include those behaviors which suggest that sensory input is not being adequately dampened. The symptoms indicative of the overinhibitory state, on the other hand, suggest excessive damping of sensory input whether from auditory, visual, proprioceptive or other sources.

In the Table, the symptomatology common to early infantile autism, childhood schizophrenia, atypical development, and the other related conditions is outlined for comparative purposes by chronological order of appearance, descriptive subclusters, developmental failure, and pathologic states of excitation and inhibition.

In summary, the behavior common to a group of related clinical entities, eg, early infantile autism, childhood schizophrenia, and atypical children, suggests a common underlying pathologic mechanism. This mechanism involves the presence of states of hyperexcitation and inhibition which interfere with the normal capacity to maintain perceptual constancy. The presence of these states may indicate a dissociation of a physiologic equilibrium between facilitatory and inhibitory systems which regulate sensory input.

CLINICAL ILLUSTRATIONS

How do these postulated pathologic mechanisms find expression in the multivariant clinical entities under consideration and how do they lead to the major subclusters of the symptoms?

If the dissociated excitatory and inhibitory states are not too severe, then percepts are available for imitation and self can be distinguished from nonself. In such cases, symptomatology may be confined primarily to disturbances of perception and motor behavior.

Case 1. This 4-year-old boy has been under psychiatric observation since 2½ years of age. His older brother was diagnosed as having early infantile autism. His parents are nonprofessional people who did not complete college. Following an uneventful pregnancy, he was born three or four weeks postterm, weighing 3,714 gm (8 lb, 3 oz). The neonatal period was not remarkable. Between 3 and 19 months of age, he had asthmatic bronchitis. Frequently, during the early months of life, his mother could not be certain when he was hungry. "Junior" foods were first introduced at 5 months, but were not accepted until 7 months.

Between 9 and 36 months, he was unusually aware of anything that would spin. He would go past the shower curtain, pressing his eyes very close to it, apparently preoccupied with the details in the printed pattern. At 36 months, he was particularly responsive to any change in his mother's appearance, such as a change in hair styling or make-up. From time to time, he would seem to stare as if he saw something that was not there. He was not exces-

The Symptomatology of Early Infantile Autism, Its Variants, and Certain Cases of Childhood Schizophrenia.

Chronological appearance of symptoms

Postnatal
- Hyperirritability
- Failure to respond
- Torpor
- Flaccidity

First 6 mo
- Failure to smile
- No anticipatory response
- Failure to vocalize
- Hypersensitivity to stimuli
- Lack of eye contact

Second 6 mo
- Unwilling to chew or accept solids
- Flicking at objects
- Casting away of toys
- Letting toys passively drop out of hands
- Irregular motor development
- Limp or rigid when held
- Unaffectionate
- Failure to discriminate mother
- Failure to play "peek-a-boo," "patty-cake," or "bye-bye"
- Lack of words
- Failure to point
- Regarding of hands
- Intolerance of sensory stimulation; cupping ears
- May appear deaf

Second-Third Yr
- Attending to self-induced sounds
- Ear-banging & flicking
- Visual & tactile scrutiny
- Ignoring meaningful or painful stimuli
- Posturing & staring
- Whirling
- Hand-flapping
- Darting, lunging motions
- Spinning of objects
- Deviant eye contact
- Use others as extension of self
- Early speech drops out
- Prolonged tooth-grinding

Fourth-Fifth Yr
- Failure to speak
- Echolalia
- Pronoun reversal
- Atonal, arhythmic voice
- Severe distress in novel situations

Subclusters of symptoms

Disturbances of Perception

Heightened Awareness
- Auditory—Attending to self-induced sounds, ear-banging, & tooth-grinding
- Visual—Regarding of hands, staring, & visual detail scrutiny
- Tactile—Rubbing surfaces
- Olfactory & gustatory—Bizarre food preferences, sniffing
- Vestibular—Spinning objects

Heightened Sensitivity
- Auditory—Fearful reactions to noise; cover ears
- Visual—To change in illumination
- Gustatory—Intolerance of "rough" foods
- Vestibular—Fearful of roughhouse, fright in elevators

Nonresponsiveness
- Auditory—Disregard of speech, ignoring loud sounds
- Visual—Disregard of surroundings
- Tactile—Let objects fall out of hand
- Pain—Failure to react to bumps & falls

Motor Disturbances
- Hand-flapping; finger-flicking
- Bizarre gesticulations
- Whirling
- Toe-walking
- Darting & lunging
- Posturing

Disturbances of Relating
- Deviant eye contact
- Absent social smile
- Delayed anticipatory response
- Limpness or stiffness when held
- Bizarre or stereotyped use of toys
- Failure to play "peek-a-boo," etc
- Use others as extension of self
- Lack of emotional responsiveness

Disturbances of Language
- Lack of speech development
- Echolalia
- Pronoun reversal
- Atonal, arrhythmic voice

Disturbances of Developmental Rate
- Retarded development
- Precocious development
- Giving up of acquired skills
- Scatter on developmental tests

Developmental failures expressed by symptoms

Failure to Distinguish Between Self and Nonself
- Lack of interest in eye contact
- Absent social smile
- Failure to play "peek-a-boo"
- Let objects fall out of hand
- Use others as extension of self
- Pronoun reversal

Failure of Imitative Behavior
- Failure to play "patty-cake"
- Failure to say "bye-bye"
- Failure to mimic sounds & expressions
- Lack of emotional expression

Failure to Modulate Input

Sensory Overload
- Attention to trivial stimuli
- Visual & tactile scrutiny
- Irritability or apprehension to inconsequential stimuli; cover ears, etc
- Panic in elevator
- Intolerance of "rough" foods

Sensory Under-Load
- Disregard of auditory & visual stimuli
- Underreactivity to painful stimuli

Dissociated Motor Excitation and Inhibition
- Excitation
- Hand-flapping
- Whirling
- Circling
- Darting & lunging
- Inhibition
- Posturing
- Prolonged immobility

Excessive excitatory & inhibitory states expressed by symptoms

Excitatory States
- Hand-flapping
- Whirling
- Circling
- Darting & lunging
- Accentuated startle
- Overreactivity to stimuli in all modalities
- Excitation associated with spinning objects

Inhibitory State
- Posturing
- Prolonged immobility
- Nonresponsiveness to stimuli in all sensory modalities

sively disturbed by auditory stimuli. Between 24 and 38 months he walked on his toes; when presented with a spinning top, he would flap his hands. Between 30 and 38 months he would whirl himself. The use of sounds, syllables, words, phrases, and sentences occurred on schedule. However, as he developed communicative speech, an excessive parroting of phrases and sentences also occurred. He particularly repeated questions directed to him rather than answering them. He developed a pleasant, responsive smile, an anticipatory response to being picked up, and good eye contact during the first half year of life. He was cuddly, affectionate, and always seemed to need his mother. His use of toys was limited, and he was preoccupied with any part of a toy that would spin. He played "peek-a-boo" and "patty-cake" and mimicked his parents' gestures and mannerisms. Motor development was not delayed.

He began psychotherapy at 3½ years of age. A relative paucity of fantasy was noted during the early phase of treatment. He tended to repetitively confuse the identities of persons, for example, calling his therapist "daddy" or "Dr. Smith Jones," a name combining that of his therapist and his father. He had some bizarre ideation: For example, when shown a microphone, he said, "Mommy is inside the microphone."

Such a case is often referred to as an *atypical child* or a *child with unusual sensitivities*.

In severe cases where perception is so unstable that imitation (and subsequent identification) and distinction between self and nonself is impossible, then disturbances of relatedness, language, and development are seen along with the disturbances of perception and motor expression.

Case 2. A 5-year, 7-month-old boy had his first psychiatric evaluation at the age of 3 years and 10 months. Since age 4 he has been an inpatient in a psychiatric hospital. He is the second child of parents whose formal education stopped at the end of high school. His father has been a truck driver and laborer. Following a normal pregnancy, he was delivered without incident at term, weighing 3,345 gm (7 lb, 6 oz). The neonatal period was not remarkable, although he was described as "irritable and oversensitive." He developed chickenpox at 12 months. The parents were first concerned at 16 months as he did not seem to respond normally. However, they had noticed that he had been preoccupied with twirling beads in his crib at 4 months and twirling ashtrays at 8 months. Furthermore, he failed to show an anticipatory response to being picked up until after 12 months. He remained on baby foods until 36 months, as he had refused to chew earlier.

He was unusually aware of visual detail and spent considerable time regarding the movements of his fingers since 15 months. He completely ignored auditory stimulation and toys presented to him. If handed objects, he let them fall out of his hand or flicked them away. From 24 months, he whirled himself, walked on his toes, and developed a repetitive, rapid oscillation of the hands. From 4 months, he rolled his head rhythmically from side to side and could only be distracted from such activity with great difficulty. Although he had spontaneously used some sounds by 6 months and some syllables by 12 months, he did not imitate either sounds or syllables. By 36 months, he had developed a 10-word vocabulary, but after that age, he ceased using words. He never combined words into phrases. He never made eye contact, and he used others as an extension of himself. The parents have said, "he pushes us to his needs." He never played "peek-a-boo" or "patty-cake." Between 18 and 24 months, he occasionally waved "bye-bye" in imitation of his father, but then abandoned this activity. He sat without support by 7 months but did not walk alone until 16 months.

In the course of extensive observation in an inpatient setting, he was noted to sustain his oscillatory hand-flapping throughout the entire day. He was never observed to use toys or other objects in any appropriate way and would only spin them.

This case demonstrates a more severe manifestation of the same basic disease than does case 1 and is usually labeled *early infantile autism.* If the development of such a child remains static, particularly when speech fails to develop, while the motor and perceptual disturbances gradually abate, he may be relabeled *pseudoretarded.*

If a child such as case 2 develops speech, particularly echolalia and pronoun reversal, he will continue to be labeled autistic.

Case 3. This 6-year-old boy has been under psychiatric observation since 4 years of age. He is the third in a family of four children, and his parents are high school graduates. His father is a salesman. The pregnancy was not remarkable. He was delivered at term by breech presentation and weighed 3,970 gm (8 lb, 12 oz). His Apgar rating was 10, and the postnatal course was not remarkable.

He has been in good physical health with no illnesses other than chickenpox at age 2 years. The early feeding history revealed he was apparently unwilling to hold solid food in his mouth or to chew. He sat without support at 7 months, but did not walk until 21 months. He showed no excessive reaction to auditory, visual, tactile, or proprioceptive stimuli, but he would become excessively disturbed when given new toys or clothes. He consistently ignored people and did not respond to sounds or to painful stimuli, eg, bumps and falls. He would let toys fall out of his hands. He maintained prolonged and unusual postures and between 2 and 3 years of age, whirled himself, flapped his hands, and walked on his toes. He never showed an anticipatory response to being picked up; he seemed to look through people, stiffened when held, and ignored affection.

He spontaneously made sounds such as "coos" and "babbles" by 4 months and later used syllables. He later ceased these vocalizations. He did not use phrases until after 36 months and never used complete sentences. Prior to 24 months, he failed to imitate sounds and words, but after 36 months, he would repeatedly parrot words and phrases he had heard in the past, but which had no relationship to the present situation. His speech was characterized by a flat tonal quality without inflection.

The echolalia and pronoun reversal are sequelae of the earlier failures to imitate and to distinguish between self and nonself (26). If, in the early arrested autistic child, the failure to distinguish between self and nonself is manifested by persistent clinging to other people, then the label *symbiotic psychosis* may be applied.

Case 4. This 4-year-old girl has been under psychiatric observation since 30 months of age. She is the third child in her family. The mother, a teacher, had considerable experience with school-age children and was a warm and affectionate person. Following an unremarkable pregnancy, the patient was born several days after rupture of the membranes. At delivery, the umbilical cord was looped around the neck. She was kept in an incubator during the first postnatal day because of "congestion in the lungs." The first month of life was characterized by projectile vomiting until pyloric stenosis was diagnosed and corrected surgically. Following the surgery she thrived on bottle feedings and gradually accepted strained foods. She would not, however, accept any chopped foods, and at 30 months, eating was limited to strained baby foods or puddings. Paradoxically, she chewed on crinkly cellophane.

She failed to cry to be held or fed, from birth on, and by 6 months of age, it became apparent that she did not smile at others. During the first and second years, she never indicated wanting to be held by her mother. At 27 months she first seemed to be aware of changes in her surroundings and at such times began to cling tenaciously to the mother. By 33 months, she showed persistent clinging. She would throw severe temper tantrums if the mother refused to hold her on her lap. However, she accepted being held by any other person in the same way, and then would seem unaware of the mother's absence. She would kneel for hours at a time on her mother's lap, pressing her chest against her mother, or she would stand on her mothers' lap, hanging onto her thumbs, vigorously rocking back and forth. She would press her fingers into her mother's eyes, with no apparent awareness that this caused pain. She would, on occasion, smile responsively when her hands were pushed together in the "patty-cake" game, but she did not actively imitate. By 33 months, she was saying "ring around" and "fall down" responsively to a "ring around the rosy" game, and she would also say "rock, rock the baby" while pantomiming rocking a doll in her arms. She would say "Mary, Mary" to her own image in the mirror but had no specific term for her mother. She would point to her nose and verbalize a word that sounded like a fusion between "nose" and "mouth" or mix up the words for "mouth" and "nose," and she often held her forearms flexed upward with her hands loosely waving in the air. She scratched at surfaces. In an elevator she would cry both at the beginning and at the end of the ride. From 15 months, she often engaged in peculiar posturing with her hands held in a "claw-like position." She did not sit without support until 12 months, but pulled herself to a standing position at that time and walked without support by 15 months.

Those cases in which communicative speech develops, the disturbance of relatedness is not too severe, and a thought disorder becomes manifest are usually referred to as *childhood schizophrenia.* In such cases, the perceptual inconstancy has not been so severe as to arrest the development of relatedness and language but results in distortion in these areas. This distortion is manifest in the thought disorder. The persistence of disturbances of motor behavior and perception are the pathologic sequelae of the abnormal or dissociated states of excitation and inhibition and reveal the fundamental developmental relationship between such cases of childhood schizophrenia and early infantile autism.

Case 5. This 11-year-old boy has been under continuous psychiatric observation since 4 years of age. His natural parents were high school graduates. Following a normal pregnancy, he was delivered at term, weighing 3,913 gm (8 lb, 10 oz). Examination at 8 days revealed good crying and color; the Moro reflex was described as "only fair." He was placed for adoption and was noted to be a quiet baby, not particularly responsive to stimulation. He entered the home of his adopting parents when 18 days old. Both adopting parents are college-educated, thoughtful, and affectionate people. The father is an engineer. A social work report at 4 months indicated a "happy and well-adjusted child." There were no early feeding problems and "junior" foods were introduced at 6 months without difficulty. He chewed well and ate everything offered until 24 months, at which time he limited his diet to liquids and soft foods. When 4 years old, he again accepted a regular diet.

From three months, he was panicked by any loud noise and startled repeatedly if one moved suddenly near him. The sensitivity to loud noises persisted until he was 6 years old. Until 15 months he became severely upset by any encounter with a strange person. He was markedly disturbed when brought into unaccustomed surroundings until 3 years old. Between 2 and 3½ years, he was panicked at any attempt to toss him in the air. He remained oblivious to any toy presented to him until he was 3 years old.

Photographs document a preoccupying interest in regarding his own writhing hand movements from 8 months and hand-flapping from 11 months. At first, he held a toy to his mouth with one hand and repetitively flapped his fingers against a part of it with the other hand. By 4 years this evolved into a stereotyped ritualistic gesticulation consisting of a rapid pushing of the fingers of the one hand against the other. At the same time, the thumb of one hand would be rhythmically pushed toward the mouth while it was pushed back by the pressure of the other hand. At 8 years of age he tried to consciously suppress this activity, but substituted a rhythmic stereotyped alternating extension and flexion of the fingers. He has always walked on his toes. When he was a baby, he would sit for hours content to be alone playing with a toy that he could spin. Later, he would say that he was inside the washing machine while he was preoccupied watching it spin.

From birth, he was described as being "very sober." When held he conformed without stiffening but did not snuggle or cuddle. He did respond to affection and to the "peek-a-boo" and "pat-a-cake" games. Although he was aware of his mother when she was present, separation evoked no response. He reacted to other children as if they were inanimate. By 4 years, he became interested in toys and began to use them functionally.

He first used syllables at 6 months and words at 9 months. He did not use speech for communication until after 4 years of age, but would parrot words and phrases up to that time. He was not able to use pronouns properly and characteristically confused and reversed the pronouns "you" and "I."

He never crawled, and while he started walking at 11 months of age, if he fell, he would not stand up again by himself. He never pulled himself up or cruised about the furniture prior to walking without support. He did not open doors or turn knobs until 3½ years old.

Once he began speaking, he revealed a preoccupation with fearful thoughts. Before the age of 6 years, he had a dream about a frightening chair and insisted on following his mother around so that he would be protected from it. He dreamed that his father or mother were in a chair costume chasing him. He became quite concrete and literal in his expressions, saying, for example, "There are so many chairs I have to be afraid of now." From 5 years to 9 years old, he thought of himself as being a car. Whenever he had to urinate, he would say that he was draining his tank. He believed that other people could control or actually think his thoughts. Between the ages of 7 and 10, he would ask his therapist, "Can you think my thoughts?" and, "Can you dream my dreams?" At 11 years, when his teacher tapped on her desk for attention he commented that her act "weakens my blood" and he often noted that everything around him seemed to grow smaller or larger.

This child experienced great difficulty in absorbing formal learning. Mastery of reading and writing was delayed and learning could only be accomplished in a special school.

The following case is presented to illustrate another clinical variant of the same basic syndrome. In this child, perceptual and motor disturbances are associated with precocious intellectual development.

Case 6. Case 6 is a 6-year-old boy. His parents, nonprofessional people, did not finish college. The child and a fraternal twin brother were born following a full-term pregnancy which was not remarkable except for a viral illness during the second trimester. The patient was the firstborn and was delivered by an easy breech extraction. He weighed 2,438 gm (5 lb, 6 oz). The neonatal period was not remarkable. The mother did not recall any early feeding difficulties. From the first months, he showed unusual awareness in all sensory modalities, including a tendency to stare at spinning objects such as the record player. He was easily upset by many types of stimuli. Hair clippers and vacuum cleaners were particularly disturbing to him. At 4 months, his sensitivity to noise was manifested by responding to his mother's voice with a startled reaction and scream. He flapped his hands and walked on his toes. Early motor development was not remarkable. While he smiled responsively, there were periods during his development when it was felt that he did not really look at people but rather looked through them, would stiffen when held, and seemed emotionally aloof. He would let objects fall out of his hands. His play with toys was limited, and he only became involved with toys that spin. He pointed to and gestured for what he wanted, and he communicated early with words, although his speech was described as being "a monotone with no inflection." He never confused pronouns and no echolalia was reported.

At 6 years of age, he had many fears and continued to panic at strange noises. He did not like to play with other children, apparently preferring to be alone and involved in fantasy. He became preoccupied with being able to name the capitols of all the countries of the world and with the relationship between the different species of animals in a nature book. He became fearful of things he had seen on television and reacted to them as if they were real. He learned to read early, read well, and was at the top of his class in a regular school.

Such a child may be labeled *autistic*, *atypical*, *borderline psychotic*, or *schizophrenic*, depending on the clinical setting in which he is seen.

These six cases illustrate the merging of clinical entities which have been described under different diagnostic rubrics.

The following case is an example of the clinical syndrome of early infantile autism in which specific neurological abnormalities were found.

Case 7. Both the mother and father of this 5-year-old boy held degrees in the physical sciences and their families had a long history of intellectual achievement. During the early years of the patient's life, his mother was depressed, agitated, and emotionally labile. The pregnancy, delivery, and postnatal course were not remarkable. During the first weeks of life, he was noted to lie very quietly, and he was described as being "apathetic." The mother felt that the baby did not want to be held. He was prop-fed and was not weaned until after his third birthday. No difficulties in chewing solid food developed. Prior to 24 months of age, he responded to many types of noise by "running and screaming" and putting his hands over his ears. He responded with equal distress to change in illumination and continued to show a sensitivity to auditory and visual stimuli throughout his life. He became preoccupied with spinning tops and pot covers before 36 months, and this behavior became a persistent activity. Before 48 months, he would often ignore both people and various forms of stimuli not related to people. At 36 months, he did not respond with pain to bumps and falls. From the time he could walk, he persistently whirled himself, flapped his hands, and walked around on his toes. He failed to imitate either sounds or words during his first 24 months, and he did not use words for communication until after 5 years of age. He also failed to communicate by gesture. He never used complete sentences. He did not show an anticipatory response to being picked up until 3 or 4 years of age and earlier he would stiffen when held. He used others as an extension of himself and actively withdrew from affection. He had not played "peek-a-boo" or "pat-a-cake."

Neurological examination revealed a spreading of the biceps reflex into the finger, active finger jerks, crossed adductor reflexes, and persistent plantar grasp reflexes at 5 years, 11 months. Two EEGs showed focal slowing appearing on the right side. A pneumoencephalogram revealed asymmetry of the frontal horns of the lateral ventricles with the right appearing slightly larger than the left. A bilateral carotid angiogram revealed the right lateral ventricle to be slightly larger than the left. The findings were felt to be consistent with focal cortical atrophy on the right side.

In this case, both the development of the child and the family history are consistent with the syndrome of early infantile autism as described by Kanner. The syndrome, however, is seen to occur in association with a specific cerebral abnormality.

The following case is presented as an example of children in whom careful history and observation does not reveal evidence of the symptoms characteristic of the syndrome of perceptual inconstancy (early infantile autism, its variants, and sequelae) yet who nevertheless have severe ideational and affectual distortion of psychotic proportions.

Case 8. This 7-year-old boy was admitted for inpatient evaluation because he refused to eat, saying, "bad people have touched my food." History revealed that at three months' gestation, the mother had a viral illness with high fever, vaginal hemorrhaging at four months, and that the patient was delivered five weeks prior to term, weighing just 2,268 gm (5 lb). He was reported to have had intermittent difficulty breathing from birth on, and at 6 months asthma was diagnosed. All motor developmental landmarks were normal. There was a good smiling response noted by 2 months, stranger anxiety at 6 months, words and phrases by 1½ years, and sentences were used by 2 years. No unusual sensitivities or mannerisms were noted. When the patient was 1½ years and 3½ years old, his mother was hospitalized for medical and surgical treatment. During these hospitalizations he was cared for by his grandfather. Six weeks following the mother's second hospitalization, the grandfather was killed in an automobile accident and

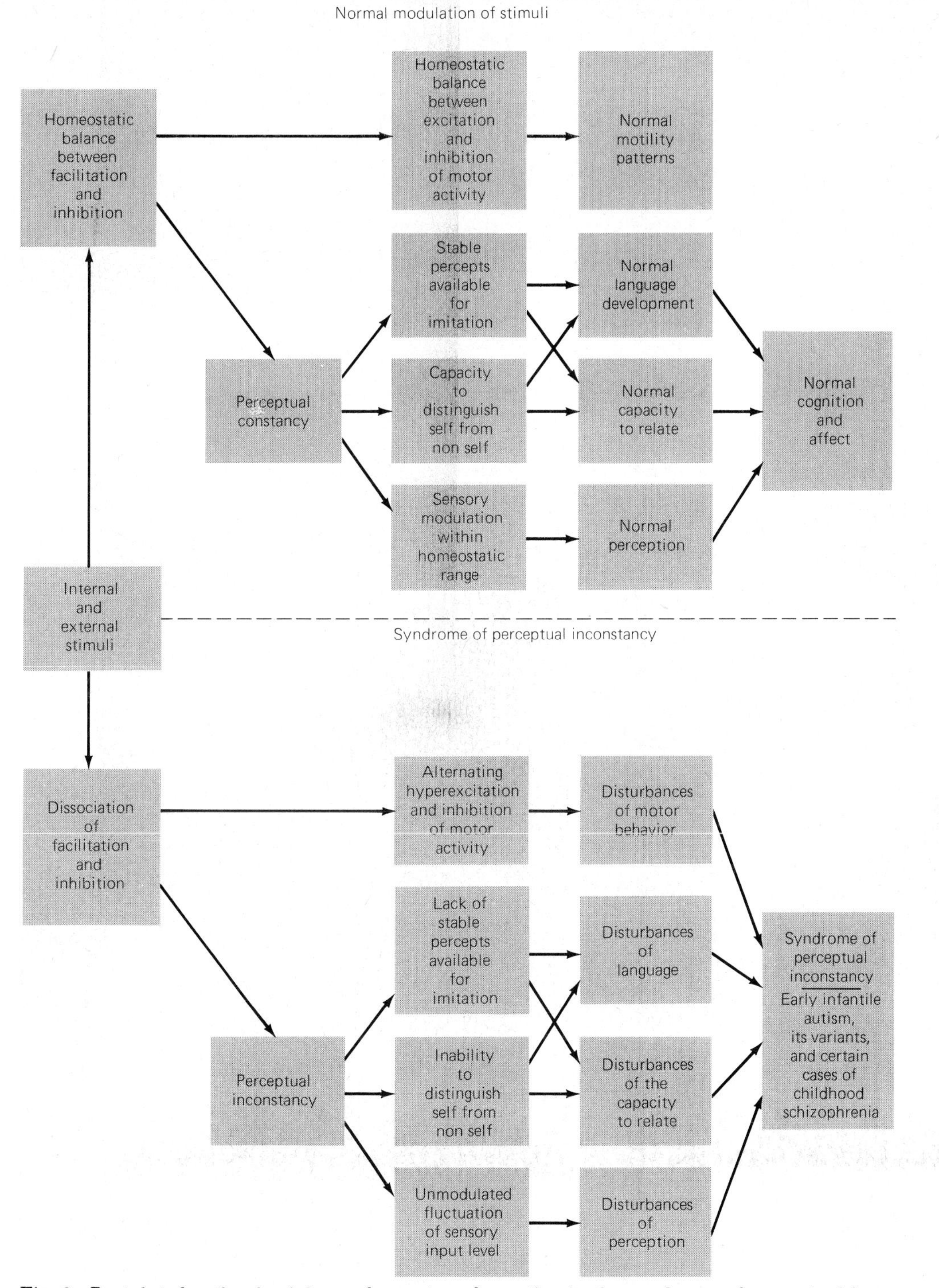

Fig. 2. Postulated pathophysiology of symptom formation in the syndrome of perceptual inconstancy compared with the regulation of sensory input in normal children.

the parents related the onset of his illness to this event. He refused to accept his grandfather's death, saying that he could see him and would speak to him. He wanted to die so that he could be with him and on one occasion released the car brake and rolled the car into the street in an attempt to get killed. He gradually withdrew interest from friends and family and evolved an elaborate fantasy world peopled by robots, devils, gods, and other powerful creatures. He became fixed in the belief that he was a mechanical robot, had switches on his body, and was impervious to pain. He was expelled from kindergarten because of unprovoked outbursts of severe hostile behavior to the other children. Psychiatric examination revealed loosening of associations, preoccupation with fantasies of being made out of steel and controlled by wires, and grossly inappropriate affect. Psychological testing revealed a psychotic ego organization with impairment of intellectual potential and no evidence of organic brain dysfunction. Prolonged observation has revealed no evidence of symptoms indicative of disturbed perceptual or motor development. Observation of his parents indicated that the mother had a severe thinking disorder; she, in fact, had frequently told her son that certain foods should not be eaten because they had been poisoned.

We consider such a case is an instance where childhood schizophrenia is not related to the syndrome of perceptual inconstancy as are other cases of childhood schizophrenia (eg, cases 5 and 6).

COMMENT

The basic pathologic mechanism underlying this syndrome is presumed to be on a neurophysiologic basis. A particular pathoneurophysiology will be postulated in a subsequent communication. The relationships between the basic dissociation of facilitatory and inhibitory influences, the resulting perceptual inconstancy, the major developmental failures, and the resulting symptom-complexes are illustrated schematically in Fig. 2.

Early infantile autism, its clinical variants, and its sequelae can best be understood as a unitary disease with varying symptoms which are expressive of an underlying pathophysiology. With maturation the symptoms undergo certain vicissitudes. In those autistic children in whom the disease process severely limits development of intrapsychic organization, these symptoms may secondarily be utilized to modulate sensory input. For other autistic children, in whom more advanced intrapsychic organization occurs, these symptoms may secondarily serve as foci for the development of bizarre or psychotic fantasies. However, neither a "need" for self-stimulation nor the child's fantasy life explain the original development or the sustained activity level of these symptoms.

Since the symptoms of early infantile autism can be understood as expressive of a pathophysiologic mechanism related to dissociated states of excitation and inhibition, it may be possible to investigate the etiology from a neurophysiologic point of view. This seems to be hopeful since these behavioral states occur concomitantly with known brain pathology, disturbed environment, or completely independent of these factors. Therefore, such factors appear to be neither specific nor fundamental to the etiology of this disease. The overt expression of the pathologic mechanism may be triggered by some of the associated conditions. As the weight of clinical evidence suggests that a schizophrenic thought and affect disorder may be one sequela of early infantile autism, the hypothesis suggested may have applicability to certain children and adults with this major psychiatric illness.

Since early infantile autism, its variants—atypical development and symbiotic psychosis—and its major sequela—some cases of childhood schizophrenia—are expressions of one disease process based on faulty homeostatic regulation of perceptual input, we could refer to children within this clinical spectrum as manifesting a *syndrome of perceptual inconstancy.*

SUMMARY

Early infantile autism and several related syndromes are described in terms of the natural history of the symptoms and their developmental relationships. Early infantile autism, atypical development, symbiotic psychosis, and certain cases of childhood schizophrenia are shown to be essentially variants of the same disease.

The symptoms of this disease have been grouped into five major subclusters: disturbances of perception, motility, relatedness, language, and developmental rate.

Disturbances of perception are shown to be fundamental to the other aspects of the disease and to be manifested by early developmental failure to distinguish between self and environment, to imitate, and to modulate sensory input.

It is suggested that these developmental failures are caused by a breakdown of homeostatic regulation of sensory input. This results in a condition of perceptual inconstancy.

The symptoms suggest that the illness is characterized by dissociated, uncoupled, and alternating states of excitation and inhibition. It is this pathophysiology which interferes with the adequate homeostatic regulation of perception and leads to a state of perceptual inconstancy.

Since the symptomatology is primarily expressive of an underlying pathophysiology, the symptoms may only secondarily in some cases come to be purposeful in the intrapsychic life of the afflicted child.

As this syndrome may be seen in children with specific organic brain dysfunction or may occur independently from birth, the pathophysiologic mechanism causing perceptual inconstancy is probably specific to the disease but may be activated in certain cases by particular neuropathologic conditions.

REFERENCES

1. Kanner, L.: Autistic Disturbances of Affective Contact, *Nerv Child* **2**:217–250, 1943.
2. Kanner, L.: Problems of Nosology and Psychodynamics of Early Infantile Autism, *Amer J Orthopsychiat* **19**:416–426, 1949.
3. Bender, L.: Childhood Schizophrenia: Clinical Study of One Hundred Schizophrenic Children, *Amer J Orthopsychiat* **17**:40–56, 1947.
4. Putnam, M. C., et al: Round Table, 1947: Case Study of an Atypical Two-and-a-Half-Year-Old, *Amer J Orthopsychiat* **18**:1–30, 1948.

5. Bergman, P., and Escalona, S. K.: "Unusual Sensitivities in Very Young Children," *Psychoanal Stud Child* **3-4**:333–352, 1949.
6. Mahler, M. S.: On Child Psychosis and Schizophrenia: "Autistic and Symbiotic Infantile Psychosis," *Psychoanal Stud Child* **7**:286–305, 1952.
7. Despert, J. L.: Some Considerations Relating to the Genesis of Autistic Behavior in Children, *Amer J Orthopsychiat* **21**:335–347, 1951.
8. Rank, B.: Adaptation of the Psychoanalytic Technique for the Treatment of Young Children With Atypical Development, *Amer J Orthopsychiat* **19**:130–139, 1949.
9. Wolff, S., and Chess, S.: A Behavioural Study of Schizophrenic Children, *Acta Psychiat Scand* **40**:438–466, 1964.
10. Rutter, M.: The Influence of Organic and Emotional Factors on the Origins, Nature and Outcome of Childhood Psychosis, *Develop Med Child Neurol* **7**:518–528, 1965.
11. Bender, L.: Schizophrenia in Childhood—Its Recognition, Description and Treatment, *Amer J Orthopsychiat* **26**:499–506, 1956.
12. Goldfarb, W.: An Investigation of Childhood Schizophrenia, *Arch Gen Psychiat* **11**:620–634, 1964.
13. Reiser, D. E.: Psychosis of Infancy and Early Childhood, as Manifested by Children With Atypical Development, *New Eng J Med* **269**:790–798, 844–850, 1963.
14. Brown, J. L., and Reiser, D. E.: Follow-up Study of Preschool Children of Atypical Development (Infantile Psychosis): Latter Personality Patterns in Adaptation to Maturational Stress, *Amer J Orthopsychiat* **33**:336–338, 1963.
15. Eisenberg, L.: The Autistic Child in Adolescence, *Amer J Psychiat* **112**:607–612, 1956.
16. Darr, G. C., and Worden, F. G.: Case Report Twenty-Eight Years After an Infantile Autistic Disorder, *Amer J Orthopsychiat* **21**:559–570, 1951.
17. Tolor, A., and Rafferty, W.: Incidence of Symptoms of Early Infantile Autism in Subsequently Hospitalized Psychiatric Patients, *Dis Nerv Syst* **24**:1–7, 1963.
18. O'Gorman, G.: *The Nature of Childhood Autism*, London: Butterworth Co., Inc., 1967.
19. Kamp, L. N. J.: Autistic Syndrome in One of a Pair of Monozygotic Twins, *Psychiat Neurol Neurochir* **67**:143–147, 1964.
20. Ornitz, E. M.; Ritvo, E. R.; and Walter, R. D.: Dreaming Sleep in Autistic and Schizophrenic Children, *Amer J Psychiat* **122**:419–424, 1965.
21. Vaillant, G. E.: Twins Discordant for Early Infantile Autism, *Arch Gen Psychiat* **9**:163–167, 1963.
22. Schain, R. J., and Yannet, H.: Infantile Autism, *J Pediat* **57**:560–567, 1960.
23. Kanner, L.: To What Extent Is Early Infantile Autism Determined by Constitutional Inadequacies, *Proc Assoc Res Nerv Ment Dis* **33**:378–385, 1954.
24. Taft, L., and Goldfarb, W.: Prenatal and Perinatal Factors in Childhood Schizophrenia, *Develop Med Child Neurol* **6**:32–43, 1964.
25. Fish, B.: Longitudinal Observations of Biological Deviations in a Schizophrenic Infant, *Amer J Psychiat* **116**:25–31, 1959.
26. Griffith, R., and Ritvo, E.: Echolalia; Concerning the Dynamics of the Syndrome, *J Amer Acad Child Psychiat* **6**:184–193, 1967.
27. Fish, B., et al: The Prediction of Schizophrenia in Infancy: III. A Ten-Year Follow-up Report of Neurological and Psychological Development, *Amer J Psychiat* **121**:768–775, 1965.
28. Creak, M.: Schizophrenic Syndrome in Childhood: Progress Report of a Working Party, *Cereb Palsy Bull* **3**:501–503, 1961.
29. Ekstein, R.; Bryant, K.; and Friedman, S. W.: Childhood Schizophrenia and Allied Conditions, in Belak, L. (ed.): *Schizophrenia: A Review of the Syndrome*, New York: Logos Press, 1958.
30. Provence, S., and Lipton, R.: *Infants in Institutions*, New York: International Universities Press, 1962.
31. Coleman, R., and Provence, S.: Environmental Retardation (Hospitalism) in Infants Living in Families, *Pediatrics* **19**:285–292, 1957.
32. Spitz, R. A.: "Anaclitic Depression," *Psychoanal Stud Child*, **2**:313–342, 1946.
33. Berkson, G., and Davenport, R. K.: Stereotyped Movements of Mental Defectives, *Amer J Ment Defic* **66**:849–852, 1962.
34. Garcia, B., and Sarvis, M. A.: Evaluation and Treatment Planning for Autistic Children, *Arch Gen Psychiat* **10**:530–*541, 1964.*
35. Rutter, M.: "Behavioral and Cognitive Characteristics of a Series of Psychotic Children," in Wing, J. K. (ed.): *Early Childhood Autism*, New York: Pergamon Press, Ltd., 1966.
36. Eisenberg, L., and Kanner, L.: Early Infantile Autism 1943–1955, *Amer J Orthopsychiat* **26**:556–566, 1956.
37. Szurek, S. A.: Psychotic Episodes and Psychotic Maldevelopment, *Amer J Orthopsychiat* **26**:519–543, 1956.
38. Rank, B.: "Intensive Study and Treatment of Preschool Children Who Show Marked Personality Deviations, or 'Atypical Development,' and Their Parents," in Caplan, G. (ed.): *Emotional Problems of Early Childhood*, New York: Basic Books Co., Inc., 1955.
39. Sarvis, M. A., and Garcia, B.: Etiological Variables in Autism, *Psychiatry* **24**:307–317, 1961.
40. Fish, B.: Involvement of the Central Nervous System in Infants With Schizophrenia, *Arch Neurol* **2**:115–121, 1960.
41. Bender, L., and Freedman, A. M.: A Study of the First Three Years in the Maturation of Schizophrenic Children, *Quart J Child Behav* **4**:245–272, 1952.
42. Simmons, J. Q., et al: Modification of Autistic Behavior with LSD-25, *Amer J Psychiat* **122**:1201–1211, 1966.
43. Goldfarb, W.: Receptor Preferences in Schizophrenic Children, *Arch Neurol Psychiat* **76**:643–652, 1956.
44. Schopler, E.: Early Infantile Autism and Receptor Processes, *Arch Gen Psychiat* **13**:327–335, 1965.
45. Hutt, S. J., et al: A Behavioural and Electroencephalographic Study of Autistic Children, *J Psychiat Res* **3**:181–197, 1965.
46. Wing, J. K.: "Diagnosis, Epidemiology, Aetiology," in Wing, J. K. (ed.): *Early Childhood Autism*, New York: Pergamon Press, Ltd., 1966.
47. Goldfarb, W.: *Childhood Schizophrenia*, Cambridge, Mass: Harvard University Press, 1961.

Elimination of Sleepwalking in a Seven-year-old Boy

Paul W. Clement

A therapy program for the treatment of somnambulism in a 7-year-old boy was described. In-therapy events such as feeling identification, modeling of self-expression, assertive training, and providing a nonthreatening, accepting atmosphere did not seem directly related to changes in the target behavior. After a conditioning procedure was introduced, clear-cut changes in the referral problem occurred. The conditioning model was similar to that used in the behavioral treatment of enuresis. The mother was trained to carry out the treatment at home. A simple associative learning model, such as Guthrie's, appeared to fit the data most parsimoniously.

Although existing clinical reports suggest that approximately 10% of all people exhibit sleepwalking (somnambulism) at some point in their lives prior to adolescence (Abe & Shimakawa, 1966; Kanner, 1957, p. 616), there has been a general failure by psychotherapists to describe techniques for eliminating this behavioral problem. The major exception was a paper by Walton (1961) in which he presented the case history of a 35-year-old man who repeatedly assaulted his wife while he was sleepwalking. Walton claimed that he was able to eliminate the man's somnambulism through assertive training (Salter, 1961) in a brief period of time.

When the present writer's first child sleepwalker was referred to him, he turned to his books on clinical child psychology and child psychiatry, but they were not helpful. Since there were no therapeutic guidelines available in the child-therapy literature, the therapist had to develop his own approach. The present paper describes the treatment procedures which were selected and the attending results.

CASE HISTORY

The client, Bobby B., was a Caucasian male of 7 years, 8 months, who had just completed the second grade at the time of the referral. The somnambulism was associated with nightmares, crying, and talking in his sleep. His mother said that he perspired heavily during these episodes. He was amnesic of these events when he awoke in the morning, except that he did remember some dream content which will be described later.

Mostly he mumbled while sleepwalking, but he had said some intelligible things, such as, "Mama, please don't leave me. I want to stay with you." On one holiday he had been spanked by his mother for misbehaving in front of company. About an hour and a half after he had gone to bed that night, he came out of his room glassy-eyed and walked in an unsteady gait to his mother who was sitting on the davenport. He put his arm around her and said, "I love you." On another occasion he walked through the living room, exclaimed, "Good-by, Jodie [his sister]," and started out the front door dressed in his pajamas. His mother stopped him and returned him to his bed. When she would ask him about such episodes in the morning, he showed no awareness of what he had done during the night.

Sleepwalking first occurred 6 weeks before the initial interview with Mrs. B. She reported that the first episode happened on a day when Bobby had been sent home from school with a temperature. Although she had not kept a written record of his sleepwalking during this first 6-week period, she estimated that he had averaged four occurrences a week. His normal bed time was 8:00 P.M., the somnambulistic episodes usually taking place 45–90 minutes after he retired.

Mrs. B.'s major request was for therapy to stop the somnambulism; however, she also said that Bobby felt inferior to other children, was not very assertive, and desired adult male companionship of which he had very little.

Bobby lived with his mother, maternal grandmother, and half-sister, Jodie, who was 6 years older than he. Mrs. B. had left her husband when Bobby was still an infant; he had no recollections of his father. At the time she and Bobby were in therapy, she did not know where her husband was nor what he was doing. Fearing that Bobby would develop sociopathic traits such as his father's, Mrs. B. attempted to be "a strict disciplinarian."

Most of the family's social activities involved going to services in a very fundamentalistic, conservative Protestant church. Bobby attended church services four times a week.

Following a comprehensive physical examination and laboratory tests which failed to identify a medical basis for the sleepwalking, the family physician had recommended psychotherapy for Bobby. His developmental history was normal, and he was of average height and weight. He was right-handed, well coordinated, and showed no signs of neurological deficit.

Although he tended to avoid most rough and tumble

From *Journal of Consulting and Clinical Psychology*, 1970, 34, 22–26.

games, he seemed to get along well with his peers both in the neighborhood and at school. Bobby had two close friends of his own age. His teachers seemed to like him, and he was making good progress in his academic work.

Bobby's mother had come alone for the first two sessions in which a complete history was taken; then he came for two evaluation sessions. His vocabulary and responses in the interviews suggested a child of normal intelligence, and there was no evidence of a perceptual-motor handicap.

The clinical data indicated a very anxious, guilt-ridden little boy who avoided performing assertive and aggressive behaviors appropriate to his age and sex. He exhibited a marked preoccupation with religious matters. For example, the following protocol for Card 8B of the Michigan Picture Test was representative of his responses:

> He is looking up into the sky and he is wondering about Jesus. He loves Jesus and he can't go to sleep without thinking of Jesus. He goes to church. He feels bad because he didn't pray to God. Well, he didn't want to pray because he thinks that he will die. God will make him die if he doesn't pray to Him. God will let him die by making the devil kill him. He worries most about dying.

TREATMENT PLAN

Phase I: Preawakening

For the first two therapy sessions Bobby was seen individually in the first 25 minutes and Mrs. B. was seen alone in the second 25. In order to allow Bobby to explore the playroom freely, the therapist was passive in the first session. In the second session the therapist modeled aggressive behaviors with hand puppets. The therapist also discussed with him the idea of having his mother join them in the future for conjoint play-therapy sessions. Bobby agreed to have his mother join them in the next session.

During the first two individual sessions with Mrs. B., the therapist explained to her that Bobby's sleepwalking was probably caused by his refusal to accept and to integrate his angry and assertive feelings. The negative effects of her own fears that he might turn out to be like his father were also explored. She agreed to participate in conjoint sessions.

Mrs. B. had been keeping a daily record of Bobby's sleepwalking episodes since the onset of therapy.

In all conjoint sessions the therapist saw Bobby and his mother together for the first 25 minutes, after which the therapist and Mrs. B. went into the adult consultation room. There they discussed what had just taken place in the conjoint session plus the events of the preceding week. Then the therapist made specific suggestions of what Mrs. B. should do in the next session. While the therapist and his mother talked, Bobby continued to play in the child-therapy room.

The first three conjoint sessions were held during the fifth, ninth, and eleventh weeks following the onset of therapy. (See Figure 1 for the spacing of all sessions.) The therapist instructed Mrs. B. (*a*) to put Bobby's feelings into words for him, (*b*) to let him decide what kind of playing he wished to do, and (*c*) to praise and approve aggressive play. While sitting in one corner of the room, the therapist modeled some verbal interventions for the mother to help her learn what was expected of her. All three discussed the angry feelings which family members tend to have toward each other.

In the third conjoint session Mrs. B. reported that no changes had taken place in Bobby's sleepwalking since treatment began. During this session the therapist also learned that Bobby usually had a nightmare just before each somnambulistic episode started. The nightmare was always about "a big black bug" which was chasing him. He fantasized that the bug would eat off his legs if it caught him. Apparently the nightmare had always been a part of the sleepwalking sequence.

The temporal sequence of Bobby's episodes ran approximately as follows: (*a*) his nightmare began, (*b*) he began to sweat heavily, (*c*) he moaned, talked in his sleep, and tossed in his bed, and (*d*) he got out of bed and began walking through the house in his sleep.

After hearing this account, the therapist hypothesized that the nightmare had become the conditioned stimulus which triggered the response of sleepwalking. This conceptualization of the problem led the therapist to look for some stimulus which would elicit a response that would be incompatible with sleepwalking.

Phase II: Awakening

For most people, waking up is a very common response to a bad dream. Waking up is incompatible with somnambulism; therefore, the therapist concluded that Bobby needed to learn to wake up when his nightmares began. The therapist explained this analysis to Mrs. B. at the end of the third conjoint session and instructed her to awaken Bobby *completely* each time he began walking in his sleep or showing clear signs of an impending episode (e.g., moaning and tossing in bed). She was to take him into the bathroom and wash his face and the back of his neck with cold water until there was no doubt in his mind that he was fully awake and aware of his surroundings. Next she was to return Bobby to his bed where he was to hit and tear up a picture of the big black bug. The therapist had instructed Bobby to make several drawings of the bug and to keep them beside his bed on the night stand.

Mrs. B. carried out these instructions during the following week, and Bobby had the fewest somnambulistic episodes since the onset of the problem (see Figure 1). During the sixth conjoint session, however, the therapist learned that Mrs. B. had failed to awaken Bobby *fully* during the preced-

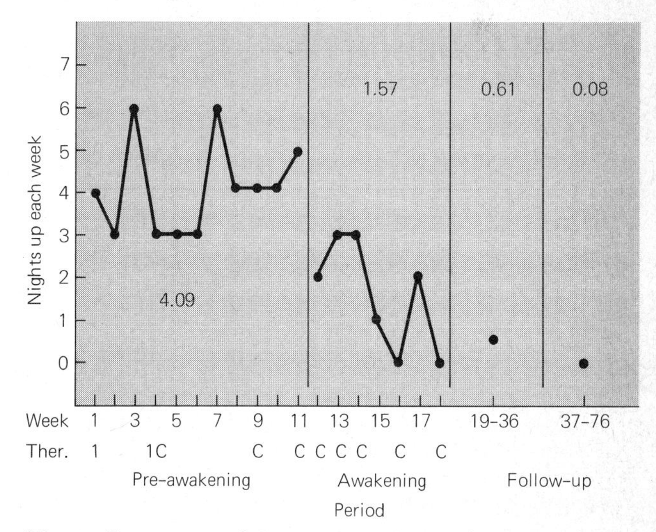

Fig. 1. Frequency of sleepwalking during therapy and follow-up. (I indicates individual therapy sessions and C indicates conjoint sessions. The numbers within the graph are mean frequencies for the indicated periods.)

ing 2 weeks. He explained to her the absolute necessity of following the therapy program exactly as specified. She agreed to do so and followed through on all instructions from then on.

Five conjoint sessions were held after the initiation of the awakening procedure, and Mrs. B. turned in a record of Bobby's sleepwalking at each session. Because prior to therapy she had not recognized that he punished himself just for thinking angry thoughts, the therapist placed special emphasis on her discriminating between angry feelings and hostile acts. She was encouraged to reinforce Bobby for the verbal expression of all of his feelings.

The final conjoint session was held in the eighteenth week following the onset of therapy. No additional sessions could be held because the therapist was moving to a new community, but follow-up was maintained for 14 months after termination. The agreement was that Mrs. B. would continue to use the awakening procedure whenever Bobby showed any signs of sleepwalking.

RESULTS

Figure 1 graphically summarizes the basic results of the treatment program. Mrs. B. did not begin systematically recording the frequency of somnambulistic episodes until the first week of therapy. In the initial evaluation, however, she had indicated that he was walking in his sleep on an average of four times a week. There was no change in this rate during the 4 weeks of evaluation; hence, for a period of about 10 weeks before therapy began, Bobby had been averaging four nights a week of sleepwalking. These estimated data, however, are not included in Figure 1.

The data presented in Figure 1 were analyzed by a chi-square test (Siegel, 1956, pp. 175–179). There were four levels corresponding to the periods of the treatment program: the preawakening period which included the two individual therapy sessions and the first three conjoint sessions (Weeks 1–11); the awakening period which included the last five conjoint sessions (Weeks 12–18); the first phase of follow-up (Weeks 19–36), during which a few episodes occurred; and the second phase of follow-up (Weeks 37–76), during which no sleepwalking occurred for the first 27 weeks (i.e., from Week 37–63) but three episodes occurred during the final 13 weeks. The difference between the four periods is highly significant ($\chi^2 = 156.70$, $df = 3, p < .001$).

Following Week 55, Mrs. B. had ceased keeping a written record of Bobby's sleepwalking; therefore, she did not remember the exact weeks of the last three occurrences. She did know, however, that they had all taken place since the start of the new school year (Week 64).

During follow-up Bobby reported that he woke himself up whenever he dreamed about the big black bug. Mrs. B. said that she had questioned him on the mornings following each episode. On the last three occurrences he denied that he had dreamed of the bug. Mrs. B. indicated that she had given him a spanking on each of the days these last three episodes occurred; on each of the nights *following* a "spanking day" he walked in his sleep. He did not remember in the mornings what had happened prior to the point at which his mother awakened him; however, he did remember being awakened and put back into bed.

At the end of follow-up Mrs. B. summarized Bobby's progress during the past year. She said that he still sometimes talked in his sleep and once in a while had a bad dream during which he usually awakened spontaneously. He usually told her about the dream in the morning. She felt that his self-confidence had improved. He had joined Cub Scouts at the end of therapy and was continuing to be active and doing very well. He had also joined Little League in the spring during follow-up. Peer relationships were not fully adequate, however, in that some children "picked on him for being a baby."

DISCUSSION

The data suggest that the awakening procedure was the most important factor leading to the reduction of sleepwalking frequency. There had been no reliable changes between the preevaluation, evaluation, and preawakening periods which covered a time span of 5 months. The drop in "nights up" between the eleventh and twelfth weeks (see Figure 1) does not seem due to an attention-placebo effect, because there had been 3 months of client contact up to that point with no systematic change in the referral problem. The first week of the awakening procedure, however, was accompanied by the lowest frequency since the somnambulism began.

The case for awakening being the most important treatment variable was further strengthened by the fact that Mrs. B. "unintentionally" altered the reinforcement contingency by not awakening Bobby during the thirteenth and fourteenth weeks. Sleepwalking increased during these 2 weeks. When awakening was reintroduced in the fifteenth week, the somnambulism again dropped.

Following this time, Bobby seemed to be moving toward a complete cessation of somnambulism, but in the seventeenth week he had two sleepwalking episodes. They occurred on a Saturday and Sunday night following his spending the day with a man he liked very much. At one time the man had been a "big brother" to him, but Bobby had not seen the man in about a year. Bobby was very excited about their day together, and there seemed to be a direct relationship between his heightened emotional arousal and the momentary increase in sleepwalking.

There were no major changes in Bobby's life which corresponded with the drop in sleepwalking. In-therapy events such as feeling identification, modeling of self-expression, assertive training, and providing a nonthreatening, accepting atmosphere did not seem directly related to changes in the target behavior. Although when therapy commenced the therapist had hoped that such factors would lead to therapeutic changes, the evidence did not support his expectation. Only after the specific conditioning procedure was introduced did clear-cut changes in the referral problem occur; however, some treatment variables had been confounded with the awakening procedure. Bobby had been instructed to make drawings of the bug and to hit and tear up the picture upon returning to his bed; nevertheless, carrying out this latter procedure seemed dependent on his waking up. Instrumental conditioning effects due to the mother's administering positive social reinforcement contingent on Bobby's awakening no doubt also played some role in his improving. Mrs. B. seemed convinced that Bobby had learned to wake up on most occasions when he was having a bad dream.

Although there are many theoretical systems which could account for the present results, an associative learning model (e.g., Guthrie, 1952) seems to fit the data most parsimoniously. All that is necessary is to elicit a response (e.g., awakening) in the presence of a stimulus complex (e.g., dream material and feedback from a high state of emotional arousal). The next time the stimulus complex is presented, the response will tend to occur. Guthrie identified three ways of breaking up a previously learned response: (*a*) initially present the stimulus below threshold for eliciting the response, then gradually increase the intensity of the stimulus while the person is behaving differently than the previously learned response; (*b*) present the stimulus repeatedly above threshold for the response until the original response is fatigued, and continue giving the stimulus so that new responses become associated with the stimulus; and (*c*) present the stimulus just before eliciting a new response which is incompatible with the original response. The present treatment procedure followed this third paradigm.

The conditioning treatment of enuresis basically follows the same theoretical model (e.g., Browning, 1967; Jones, 1960). In the conditioning treatment of bed wetting, a waking response is elicited by an intense stimulus (a bell or buzzer). This same stimulus inhibits micturition. The bell is presented in the presence of endogenous stimuli which have previously been associated with nocturnal micturition. Hence, these endogenous stimuli eventually become associated with awakening and the inhibition of micturition in place of sleeping and bed wetting.

Of course, the data of this case study are only suggestive. The efficacy of the awakening treatment approach needs to be tested in a controlled experimental study; however, the prediction is that the awakening procedure will substantially add to the treatment effects of more traditional child-therapy approaches. A second hypothesis is that "relationship" and "insight-oriented" approaches will produce little positive change in sleepwalking and/or will be slow to do so.

REFERENCES

Abe, K., & Shimakawa, M. Predisposition to sleep walking. *Psychiatria et Neurologia*, 1966, **151**, 306–312.

Browning, R. M. Operantly strengthening UCR (awakening) as a prerequisite to treatment of persistent enuresis. *Behavior Research and Therapy*, 1967, **5**, 371–372.

Guthrie, E. R. *The psychology of learning.* (2nd ed.) New York: Harper, 1952.

Jones, H. G. The behavioral treatment of enuresis nocturna. In H. J. Eysenck (Ed.), *Behavior therapy and the neuroses. New York: Pergamon Press, 1960.*

Kanner, L. *Child Psychiatry.* (3rd ed.) Springfield, Ill.: Charles C Thomas, 1957.

Salter, A. *Conditioned reflex therapy.* New York: Capricorn Books, 1961.

Siegel, S. *Nonparametric statistics for the behavioral sciences.* New York: McGraw-Hill, 1956.

Walton, D. The application of learning theory to the treatment of a case of somnambulism. *Journal of Clinical Psychology*, 1961, **17**, 96–99.

Reduction in Rate of Multiple Tics by Free Operant Conditioning Methods

Beatrice H. Barrett

The experimental investigation of neuromuscular tics has probably been most limited by difficulties in developing sensitive and reliable behavioral measurement techniques. The closest approximation to an experimental study of tics, by Yates (18), was based on a patient's records of her ability to reproduce her tic symptoms. Yates did not attempt to obtain objective records or measurement of the patient's tics.

The method of free operant conditioning, originally developed by Skinner (15) to study animal behavior and later modified by Lindsley (9) to study the behavior of chronic psychotics, has provided precise techniques of behavioral measurement and control. These techniques have been extended to the investigation of such pathological behaviors as vocal hallucinatory episodes (10, 11, 12), pressure of speech (13), and stuttering (7). By the application of free operant techniques, Ferster (5) succeeded in expanding the very limited behavioral repertories of two autistic children, and Brady and Lind (3) performed an experimental analysis

From *Journal of Nervous and Mental Disease*, 135,187–195.

This research was supported by Research Training Grant 2M-7084 and Research Grant MY-2778 from the National Institute of Mental Health, U. S. Public Health Service.

*Ogden R. Lindsley, Ph.D., Director of the Laboratory, generously supplied the diagrammatic sketch in Figure 1 and the controlling and recording equipment. His advice and encouragement were invaluable in the conduct of this experiment.

with therapeutic results in a patient with hysterical blindness.

The basic datum of the free operant method is the frequency of a specific and reliably defined response within a controlled experimental environment. The method is most readily applied, therefore, in cases where changes in the rate of a repeated movement are of primary concern. The present report describes an application of free operant methods to the control of multiple neuromuscular tics.

METHOD

Patient

The patient in this experiment was a 38-year-old veteran, hospitalized in the Neurology Service of a local Veterans Administration hospital.[1] His extensive multiple tics started approximately 14 years ago, during his term of duty in the armed services. Although a medical discharge was available to him, the patient chose to continue in the service, eventually serving overseas, until regular discharge. Since then he has been employed as an accountant by a single firm.

An interview prior to the experiment revealed that the patient knew of no traumatic experience preceding the abrupt onset of tics. He told of awakening during the night with a choking sensation accompanied by a momentary inability to breathe or swallow. He recalled this as a frightening experience and was puzzled by the subsequent development of tics. Within a few months, spasmodic movements had developed in much of his body. At the time of this experiment, his major movements included contractions of neck, shoulder, chest, and abdominal muscles, head nodding, bilateral eye blinking, opening of the mouth, and other comparatively mild facial movements.[2] The patient complained of difficulty in swallowing, hence of slow ingestion. His clear, intelligent speech was marked only occasionally by barely noticeable hesitation.

In recent years the patient was not fully aware of the presence of his tics. On occasion, when he thought himself relatively free of them, his wife reported that there was no reduction in his twitching. The patient did feel, however, that his movements were reduced in frequency while he was playing his saxophone in a local band on weekends. His greatest concern was the extent to which his tics made him conspicuous to strangers and limited his business advancement. In general, little was known of the patient's personal history.

The patient had undergone psychological counseling for a number of months and had received pharmacological treatment which included a variety of tranquilizing and muscle-relaxing drugs. Neither treatment had afforded symptomatic relief. The patient displayed no outstanding symptoms of psychopathology. His tics were considered symptomatic of an extrapyramidal system disturbance and untreatable by conventional methods.

Since he had experienced no success with other methods, the patient was highly motivated to participate in this experiment. Although he was soon discharged to return to work in a neighboring state, he voluntarily rehospitalized himself two months later for continuation of the experiment.

Arrangement of Apparatus

Patient's enclosure. A quiet, well ventilated room with observation facilities was equipped with a comfortable swivel-tilt armchair, an ashtray, a set of comfortable earphones which the patient wore throughout all experimental sessions, and a Grass EEG console (see Figure 1).

Operandum. A large U-shaped magnet, securely attached to the outside of the chair back, served as a convenient device for summating multiple tics. Although the swivel arc of the chair was restricted and the chair's casters removed, its tilt was freely operative. An induction coil rested in a "nest" of electrical tape strung between the poles of the magnet.[3] Slack in the tape was adjusted so that when the patient was seated in the chair his most noticeable spasmodic movements, regardless of locus or amplitude, created a slight movement of the coil in the magnetic field.

Response definition and recording. The current induced in the moving coil was amplified by one channel of an EEG recorder to operate a sensitive relay. The operations of this relay were directly recorded as tics. The duration and amplitude of the recorded tics were determined by setting the amplifier gain so that each strong and obvious tic would operate the response relay and cumulative response recorder. After initial selection, this amplifier gain was held constant throughout the experiment.

Response-Contingent Events

In free operant conditioning, the frequency of a response is altered by programming particular consequences contingent

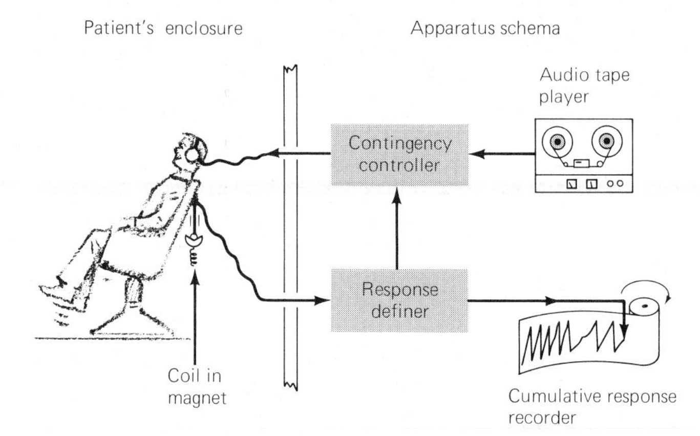

Fig. 1. Schema of apparatus used to pick up, automatically record, and program the contingent consequences of multiple tics.

[1] The author is grateful to Norman Geschwind, M.D., Department of Neurology, Boston VA Hospital, who suggested the experimental behavioral study of this patient and who arranged for space and the loan of various apparatus components.

[2] Some of the patient's movements were so strong that, when he was seated in a chair on casters, they caused slight rolling.

[3] Michael J. Malone, M.D., offered the general idea of the "tic chair" and magnetic pickup.

upon the emission of that response. Generally this method has been used to generate steady rates of responding or to increase the frequency of a given response. When *reduction* in the frequency of a symptom is desired, the event contingent upon symptom occurrence may be 1) the removal of a positive stimulus or 2) the presentation of an aversive stimulus. In this experiment, both types of tic-contingent events were used.

By the use of a tape recorder, a positive stimulus (music) could be removed or an aversive stimulus (noise) presented when a tic occurred. Pulses from the response relay were transmitted through a timer to a circuit which controlled the tape recorder output to the patient's earphones (see schema in Figure 1). All recording and controlling equipment was located in a nearby room.[4]

Music. In order to maximize the patient's interest, the music used in the experiment was selected by the patient himself from the hospital's music library. Boredom and satiation were minimized by using several selections with no repetitions.

The contingency arrangement was programed so that each tic produced a 1.5 second interruption of music. If the patient did not tic for at least 1.5 seconds, he could hear the music until it was automatically interrupted by the next tic. In effect, this schedule differentially reinforced time intervals between tics of 1.5 seconds or more.[5]

Noise. Azrin (1) found that responses could be eliminated by making the presentation of white noise contingent upon their occurrence; and Flanagan, Goldiamond and Azrin (7) successfully reduced chronic stuttering by presentation of a stutter-produced loud tone. In the present experiment a tape loop of white noise (60 db) was used as a tic-produced aversive stimulus.

The contingency was arranged so that each tic produced 1.5 seconds of noise over the patient's earphones. When the patient was tic-free for at least 1.5 seconds, the noise was automatically interrupted and did not recur until the next tic.

Contingency Testing

As a control measure to test the effect of the contingencies described above, periods of continuous music and continuous noise were used. This amounted to removal of the contingency requirement which, in the case of music, more nearly approximated the conditions of music therapy.

Self-Control

The effects of music and noise were compared with the patient's own efforts to control his tics. A signal light (60 watt bulb) was introduced and the patient was instructed to control his tics by his most frequently used methods for as long as the light was on.

[4] The cooperation, assistance, and patience of David Adkins and the staff of the EEG laboratory at the Boston VA Hospital made possible the occupancy of sufficient space to approximate good environmental control.

[5] In technical terms, this schedule is a time contingent crf drl of 1.5 seconds with an unlimited hold (6).

Experimental Sessions

The patient was informed that we would be studying the effects of various conditions on his tic rate. He had selected a lasting supply of music tapes with the understanding that he would hear them at least some of the time during the experiment. He was instructed to make himself comfortable and to remain seated in the chair, with earphones on, throughout the sessions. Aside from previously mentioned instructions concerning the signal light, no further explanation was given. The experimental room was closed, and recording was begun. Experimental conditions were changed without interruption by adjusting the controlling equipment. The duration of sessions varied from two to three hours depending on meal schedules and other hospital routines. No attempt was made to set up predetermined time intervals for each experimental condition. With a few exceptions due to time limits, each condition was run long enough to show its maximal effect when compared with the normal tic rate or operant level.

RESULTS

Cumulative records of the first four sessions showing the effects of music and noise on tic rate are shown in Figure 2.[6] These sessions were conducted during a 48-hour period prior to the patient's discharge. The remaining sessions were held two months later when the patient voluntarily rehospitalized himself for continuation of the experiment.

To facilitate comparison of tic rates under the various experimental conditions, the continuous records in all figures have been telescoped and grouped. The steeper the slope of the curves, the higher the tic rate. Rate estimates may be made by reference to the grid showing rates for representative slopes.

Operant level determinations. The patient's normal tic rate (operant level) ranged between 64 and 116 tics per minute (tpm), with some decrease in the short run at 4E during the last session in Figure 2. No diurnal variations in tic rate were noted. Although sessions were run during various hours of the day and evening to capitalize on limited time, neither fatigue nor hunger affected tic rate or response to experimental conditions.[7]

Effects of noise. There was a very slight increase in the tic rate during a brief seven-minute period when continuous white noise (60 db) was played ("noise" in Figure 2). However, when made tic-contingent, noise reduced the tic rate to about 40 tpm ("contingent noise" in Figure 2). The long tic-free intervals toward the end of the contingent noise period may have been due to dozing which the patient later reported. Because of its apparent soporific effect, noise was not used further.

[6] The cumulative response recorder feeds paper at a constant speed while each tic impulse moves the recording pen one step in a vertical direction. After 450 tics have been recorded, the pen automatically resets to the base and is ready to step up with the next tic (see Figure 1). Horizontal lines in the curves are periods when no tic impulses occurred.

[7] Sessions 2, 4, and 8 were run in the morning and terminated for the patient's lunch; sessions 1 and 3 occurred in the afternoon; sessions 5 and 7 were conducted in the evening.

Effects of music. Continuous music ("music" in Figure 2) reduced the tic rate about as much as did contingent noise (40 tpm). However, when each tic interrupted the music ("contingent music"), the rate was lowered to 15 to 30 tpm. During every period of contingent music, the effect of the contingency was an additional reduction of 40 to 50 per cent in tic rate. After the first session there was no overlap between the range of rates under continuous music and under tic-contingent interruption of music. The differential magnitude of these effects on this patient thus requires no statistical test.

The fact that contingent music produced a greater reduction in rate of ticing than did continuous music appears to be the result of longer, more frequent tic-free periods when the contingency was in effect. The improbability of fatigue effects is indicated by a comparison of the 4A rate under contingent music obtained at the start of a morning session with the 1D, 2C, and 3E rates under this condition recorded at the end of the three previous sessions.

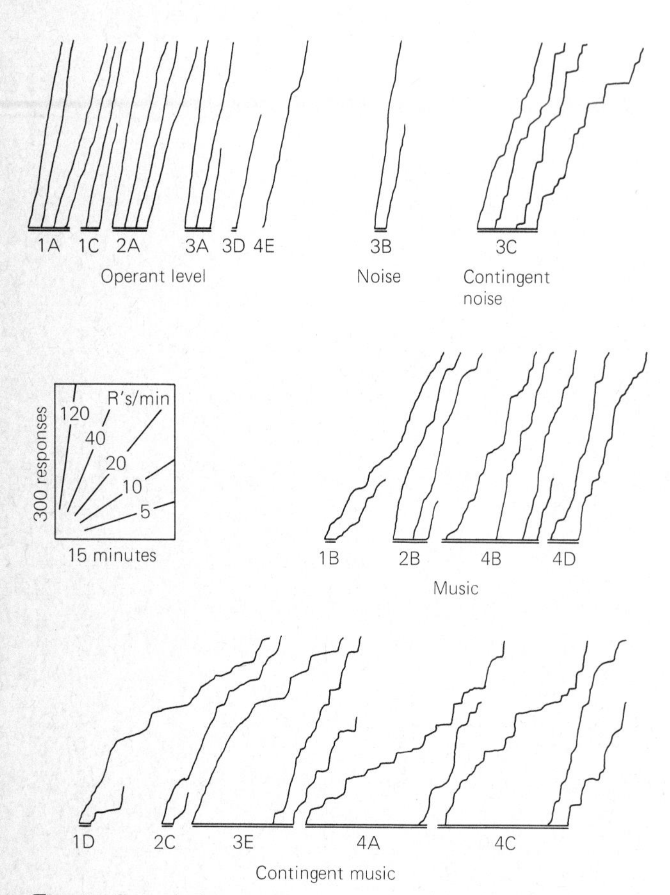

Fig. 2. Cumulative response records of the first four experimental sessions showing changes in tic rate under conditions of tic-contingent noise and tic-contingent interruption of music and control runs of both noise and music without the contingency requirement. The experimental sessions are numbered and the sequence of conditions within each session identified by letters. Double bars connect all immediately successive curves under designated conditions. Breaks in double bars indicate a change of conditions.[8]

[8] For example, the first four pen excursions labeled 1A were continuously recorded tics during a 26-minute period at the start of the first session to get an operant level. Without interruption, the 1B curves follow, showing 27 minutes of tics under continuous music. The two curves labeled 1C record a return to the operant level for 10 minutes, followed immediately by the 1D period of 34 minutes with each tic producing interruption of the music. The 2A curves show operant level rates at the start of session 2, followed by 25 minutes of continuous music (2B), then 21 minutes of tic-contingent interruption of music (2C), and so on. The same identification system is used in Figure 4 for sessions 7 and 8.

Effects of self-control. The tic-reducing effect of contingent music is compared with the patient's sustained efforts of self-control in Figure 3 (fifth session). In response to instructions and a signal light, the patient reduced his tic rate to 50 to 60 per minute. This rate is only slightly higher than that previously obtained with contingent noise and non-contingent music. Under the condition of tic-contingent interruption of music, however, rates were considerably lower, ranging from 20 to 35 per minute.[9] Again there was no overlap between the range of rates under the three conditions (operant level, self-control, and contingent music). Note the initial rapid tic rate at the beginning of the C period of contingent music. This increase in rate following a period of self-control (B) parallels what clinicians have observed in tiqueurs (17). It appears that this effect was strong enough to counteract temporarily the effect of the contingent music (C).

In addition to the differential effects on tic rate of self-control and the music contingency condition, there was

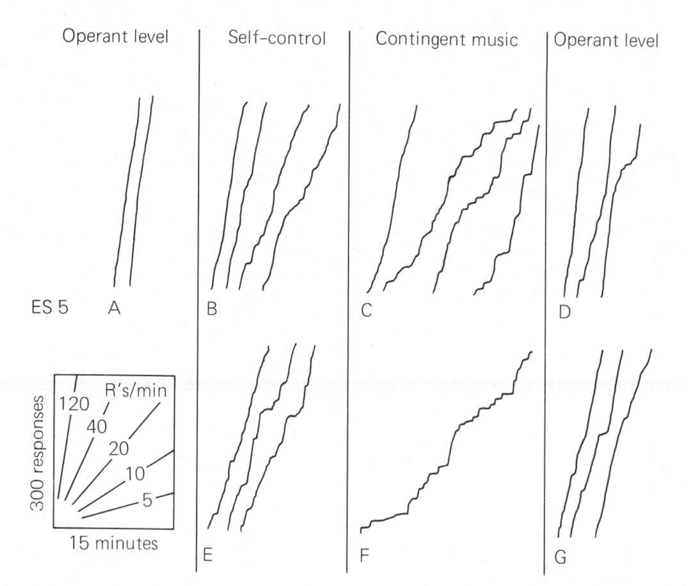

Fig. 3. A continuous cumulative record of the fifth experimental session showing rate changes under sustained self-control compared with the greater reduction under tic-produced interruption of music. The sequence of conditions is indicated by letters.

[9] This differential effect was reproduced repeatedly in session 6, which is not shown here.

also a difference in the patient's general behavior topography. In the B period of self-control, the patient was observed to engage in head-holding and general prolonged contraction. In contrast, during the E period of self-control, he engaged in relaxed tapping with finger or foot and occasional singing. This new form of behavior was first observed as the patient accompanied contingent music in the C period.

These differences in behavior topography shown during the B and E periods of self-control may account for the longer tic-free intervals in E than in B. They may also explain the differential response to contingent music in C and F. In other words, it appeared that the patient used two different methods of reducing his tics and that these two methods had different effects on subsequent tic reduction under contingent music. During B, self-control was effected by a generalized rigid contraction which was followed in C by an initial increase in rate despite the availability of contingent music. In contrast, during E self-control was achieved through release methods with the subsequent rapid and marked rate reduction under contingent music (F).

Reliability of the effect of contingent music. The previously described data from six experimental sessions showed that tic-contingent interruption of music reduced the patient's tic rate far more than did non-contingent music, tic-produced white noise, or the patient's efforts at self-control. During those sessions, the patient had approximately six hours' exposure to contingent music. Following a two-month interruption of the experiment, the reliability of the tic-reducing effect of contingent music was subjected to empirical test by a series of replications on the same patient.[10] The result of alternating operant level control periods (7A, 7C, 7E, and 7G; and 8A, 8C, 8E, and 8G) with periods of tic-produced interruption of music (7B, 7D, and 7F; and 8B, 8D, and 8F) are shown in Figure 4. The effect of contingent music on tic-free intervals was dramatically and reliably demonstrated by reductions of from 55 to 85 per cent below the operant rate on each of these six replications.

The tic-reducing effect of contingent music was more immediate and prolonged than in earlier sessions. Tic-free intervals were, for the most part, considerably longer and more frequent than previously, and only brief bursts of tics occurred with high local rate. The patient expressed irritation at the end of session 8 because he had wanted to hear the remainder of a jazz concert being played during 8F (the period with lowest tic rate: nine per minute). He commented that he was concentrating on the musical ideas and became annoyed when his brief bursts of tics interrupted it. During most of the 44-minute 8F period of contingent music he was observed to be almost motionless as he listened to the music.

The pattern of tic-free intervals followed by brief intervals of heightened local rate which developed in response to contingent music appeared to generalize to the operant

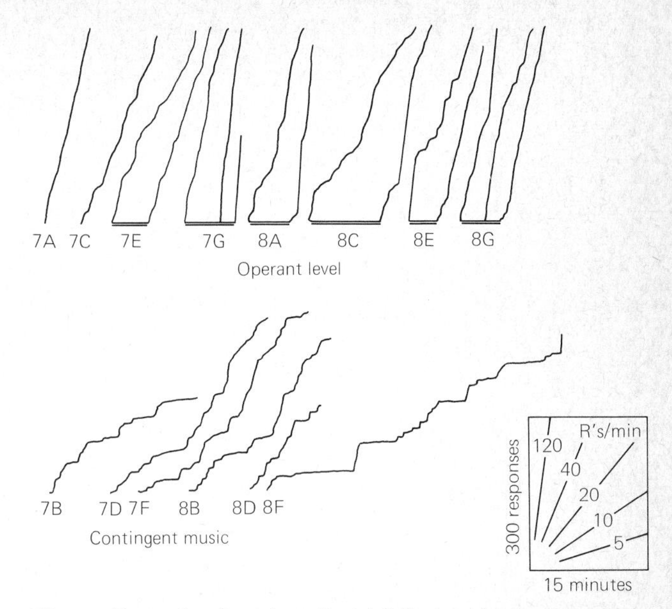

Fig. 4. Records of sessions 7 and 8 demonstrating reproducibility of the marked tic-reducing effect of tic-contingent interruption of music in six replications. Letters designate the sequence of conditions within numbered sessions.

ticing rate as early as session 4. If this was a true generalization, it may have therapeutic implications. On the other hand, it may simply represent a minor shift of unknown nature in the tic rate. Because of possible operandum unreliability (discussed below), the most valid comparisons should be limited to the differential effects of self-control, non-contingent music, and contingent music relative to the operant tic rate.

Intrasession decrease in operant level rate did appear with regularity during the last two sessions (Figure 4). Operant tic rates 7C, 7E, 8C, and 8E, which were recorded between periods of contingent music, showed somewhat longer tic-free intervals than those recorded at the beginning of these sessions (7A and 8A) or those recorded at the end of these sessions (7G and 8G). The reasons for this decrease are far from clear, but the decrease may have something to do with attention. The patient reported that during these sessions he was anticipating more music and knew he would not hear it if he had many tics.

DISCUSSION

The results of this experiment clearly demonstrate that non-contingent music and tic-contingent white noise reduced the tic rate to a level comparable with that produced by self-control. A far more powerful reduction was produced by tic-contingent interruption of music.

In evaluating the differential control of tic rate shown in these data and the possible extensions of the basic method to other symptoms for either therapeutic or research purposes, the most pertinent consideration is the design of the operandum, the device which permits the symptom to operate a switch (16). Two major requirements of a good

[10] Both Claude Bernard, in 1865 (2), and Murray Sidman, in 1960 (14), have pointed out that the most convincing test of reliability of an "effect" is the demonstration of its reproducibility in a series of replications.

operandum are the reliability of its operation and the specificity of the response class which actuates it.[11] The fragile tape arrangement of our crude operandum does not insure reliable operation for continued general application. It is not stable enough to maintain accurate calibration during repeated use. A more stable operandum might have permanently fixed pickups, preferably embedded in upholstery in different areas of a chair.

Although a chair operandum provided a relatively comfortable situation for the patient, it did restrict his motility more than might be desired. Moreover, it was not specific to tic movements alone. A more tic-specific operandum would be operated solely by tic movements. Improved specificity of tic measurement without restrictions on motility might be obtained by pickups placed at the loci of various tics which would be telemetered by transmitters worn on the patient's belt or in a pocket (8). The patient could then engage in routine daily activities while effects of interest are continuously recorded.

Once the operandum requirements have been refined, therapeutic effects can be more reliably evaluated. The use of tic-contingent interruption of music could be extended in time or otherwise modified. For example, the duration of the tic-free interval necessary to produce music could be progressively lengthened. With remote recording, the long term effects of an appropriate contingency arrangement could be evaluated by furnishing the patient with a portable contingency controller to plug into his home radio or television set for relief of his symptom. The contingencies for music and noise, already demonstrated to be effective, could be combined in a multiple contingency whereby each tic would bring 1.5 seconds of noise and pauses greater than 1.5 seconds would bring music, until the next tic impulse simultaneously interrupted the music and restored the white noise.

The observed behavior changes offered as possible explanations for differential tic rates recorded under self-control could be objectively measured to evaluate the interaction between symptomatic and non-symptomatic responses. For example, if operanda had been provided for simultaneously recording the patient's finger-tapping and singing, it might have been possible to show an inverse relationship between the rate of vocalizing and finger-drumming and the tic rate. In addition, experiments could be run to determine whether tic movements may be diminished or even eliminated by differentially reinforcing another more circumscribed and more socially acceptable motor response which serves the same discharge function as tics.

A free operant conditioning analogy to the negative practice technique used by Yates (18) could be readily investigated by positively reinforcing the patient for each tic. If this variation of the method is therapeutic, positive reinforcement of the symptom should be followed by reduction in the operant tic rate.

[11] Ferster (4) has discussed in some detail the general requirements of an accurate operandum (manipulandum). This device, which is manipulated by the subject's behavior, also defines the response being conditioned or attenuated. It is the point of contact between the subject and the automatic recording equipment. For these reasons its operating characteristics are of utmost importance.

The general aspects of the pickup and continuous recording system described here provide a method for direct and objective behavioral measurement of motor symptom frequency which would be useful in studying the effects of drugs, the influence of attention, and variations in tic rate during diagnostic or therapeutic interviews.

SUMMARY

A method for continuous automatic recording of the rate of multiple tics has been used in a demonstration of differential control of tic rate by free operant conditioning procedures.

The results showed that the multiple tics of a neurological patient, previously refractory to pharmacological and psychological therapies, could be reduced in rate by self-control, by tic-produced white noise, and by continuous music. The most dramatic, rapid, and reliable reduction resulted from tic-produced interruption of music. The power of tic-contingent environmental consequences in controlling this patient's symptom was shown, and suggestions were offered for extending and refining the basic method for more definitive investigations of this and other motor disturbances.

REFERENCES

1. Azrin, N. H. Some effects of noise on human behavior. J. Exp. Anal. Behav., **1**: 183–200, 1958.
2. Bernard, C. *Introduction to the Study of Experimental Medicine.* Paris, 1865, translated 1927. Dover Publications, New York, 1957.
3. Brady, J. P. and Lind, D. L. Experimental analysis of hysterical blindness. A.M.A. Arch. Gen. Psychiat., **4**: 331–339, 1961.
4. Ferster, C. B. The use of the free operant in the analysis of behavior. Psychol. Bull. **50**: 263–274, 1953.
5. Ferster, C. B. The development of performances in autistic children in an automatically controlled environment. J. Chron. Dis., **13**: 312–345, 1961.
6. Ferster, C. B. and Skinner, B. F. *Schedules of Reinforcement.* Appleton-Century-Crofts, New York, 1957.
7. Flanagan, B., Goldiamond, I. and Azrin, N. H. Operant stuttering: The control of stuttering behavior through response-contingent consequences. J. Exp. Anal. Behav., **1**: 173–177, 1958.
8. Hefferline, R. F. Learning theory and clinical psychology—an eventual symbiosis? In Bachrach, A. J., ed. *Experimental Foundations of Clinical Psychology.* Basic Books, New York, 1962.
9. Lindsley, O. R. Operant conditioning methods applied to research in chronic schizophrenia. Psychiat. Res. Rep. Amer. Psychiat. Ass., **5**: 118–139, 1956.
10. Lindsley, O. R. Reduction in rate of vocal psychotic symptoms by differential positive reinforcement. J. Exp. Anal. Behav., **2**: 269, 1959.
11. Lindsley, O. R. Characteristics of the behavior of chronic psychotics as revealed by free-operant conditioning methods. Dis. Nerv. Syst. Monogr. Suppl., **21**: 66–78, 1960.
12. Lindsley, O. R. Direct measurement and functional definition of vocal hallucinatory symptoms in chronic psychosis. Paper presented at Third World Congress of Psychiatry, Montreal, Canada, June, 1961.

13. Shearn, D., Sprague, R. L. and Rosenzweig, S. A method for the analysis and control of speech rate. J. Exp. Anal. Behav., 4: 197–201, 1961.
14. Sidman, M. *The Tactics of Scientific Research.* Basic Books, New York, 1960.
15. Skinner, B. F. *The Behavior of Organisms.* Appleton-Century, New York, 1938.
16. Skinner, B. F. Operandum. J. Exp. Anal. Behav., 5: 224, 1962.
17. Wechsler, I. S. *Clinical Neurology.* Saunders, Philadelphia, 1952.
18. Yates, A. J. The application of modern learning theory to the treatment of tics. J. Abnorm. Soc. Psychol., **56**: 175–182, 1958. Reprinted in Eysenck, H. J., ed. *Behaviour Therapy and the Neuroses.* Pergamon Press, New York, 1960.

THE DEPENDENCIES

Chapter 14

Alcoholism

In our society, alcohol consumption has become a generally accepted custom. One is expected to drink on joyous occasions and it is well established as a "social lubricant." However, alcohol is a psychoactive agent that causes numerous behavioral anomalies, the best known variety of which is drunkenness.

The papers of this chapter address themselves to the problem of how organisms become addicted to alcohol. Myers and his associates take an organic view and limit their research to alcohol preference among rhesus monkeys. They demonstrate that alcohol preference can be built up by infusing alcohol into the brain of an organism.

Jessor and his associates, per contra, describe alcoholism from a sociocultural vantage point and demonstrate the relationship of personality factors to drinking behavior. Specifically, they argue that drinking may play quite a different role in different cultures, depending on how it is socialized and institutionalized.

Preference for Ethanol in the Rhesus Monkey Following Chronic Infusion of Ethanol into the Cerebral Ventricles*

R. D. Myers

W. L. Veale

T. L. Yaksh†

In rhesus monkeys acclimated to primate restraining chairs, cannulae were implanted bilaterally in the lateral cerebral ventricles. Solutions of ethanol (8 or 12%), acetaldehyde (0.1%) or paraldehyde (0.1%) were infused chronically in a volume of 0.1 ml every 15 min around the clock. Each animal was offered a choice of water or a solution of ethanol which was increased in concentration from 3–30% over an 11–13 day sequence. The results showed that in three of four monkeys, the chronic infusion of ethanol evoked sudden and intermittent increases in ethanol intake which varied in terms of onset of preference as well as concentrations preferred. The other two substances had no reliable effect on preference except that in two of three monkeys, acetaldehyde infused intraventricularly evoked an increase in ethanol intake after the chronic infusions had been terminated. These findings indicate that the phenomenon of abnormal ethanol-preference induced by intracerebral ethanol is not species-specific.

As has been observed with other infrahuman species, the monkey will not consume a large quantity of ethanol under normal conditions in a self-selection situation (6). For example, Anderson and Smith (1) showed that *Macaca nemestrina* preferred only water of 5% ethanol to a 10 or 20% solution. In an attempt to induce a high level of ethanol consumption in the primate, Clark and Polish [2] found that rhesus monkeys consumed 20% ethanol during a shock avoidance procedure, but this intake did not persist after the experimental sessions had ended. When a monkey was trained to avoid shock by licking a fluid spout dispensing ethanol or a bourbon solution in concentrations of 5, 15 or 25%, the licks became shorter and the volume of ethanol consumed dropped significantly as the alcohol concentration was increased (7).

Fitz-Gerald *et al.* (3), reported that chimpanzees would drink significant quantities of a 10% ethanol solution if the taste were concealed with orange, grapefruit or grape juice, but Mello and Mendelson (7) found that monkeys given only a solution of bourbon to drink over a period of 70 days did not prefer this fluid over water in a free-choice situation.

In 1963, Myers (8) demonstrated that the chronic infusion of ethanol into the cerebral ventricles of the naive rat caused a remarkable increase in ethanol consumption. In other experiments, it was found that acetaldehyde, paraldehyde, or methanol infused similarly evoke the same shift in ethanol intake (13). Koz and Mendelson (5) explored this phenomenon in a rhesus monkey by injecting ethanol into the cerebral ventricle once a day. This animal did not increase its preference for ethanol presumably because the cerebral levels of this alcohol must be elevated continuously to induce the shift in intake (8, 10).

This paper is based on a series of experiments designed to determine whether an increase in ethanol preference could be induced in the primate by chronic infusion of ethanol, acetaldehyde or paraldehyde into the cerebral ventricles. In this study, the intraventricular infusions were given intermittently, around the clock, so that the actions of these compounds would be nearly continuous.

From *Physiology and Behavior, 1973,* 8, 431–435. Reproduced by permission.

*This research was supported in part by National Science Foundation Grant GB 24592 and ONR Contract N00014-67-A-0226-0003. The authors are indebted to P. Curzon for his valuable technical assistance.

†National Institute of Mental Health Pre-Doctoral Fellow supported by Grant TI-MH-10267.

METHOD

Naive male rhesus monkeys weighing between 4.7 and 6.5 kg were acclimated to primate restraining chairs for two weeks and maintained at 70°F; Wayne monkey biscuits were provided ad lib. At the beginning of the second week, surgery was performed. At the beginning of the third week, each animal was given access to three drinking spouts, one of which dispensed an ethanol solution, another water and a third which served as a dummy to prevent the development of a position habit (12). Inverted 1000 ml graduated cylinders were connected to the spouts and the fluid shifted each day according to the random rotation paradigm of Myers and Holman (12). The concentration of the ethanol solution, which was prepared with 95 per cent ethanol and tap water (v/v), was increased daily in steps from a low concentration of 3% to usually 30% during the 11- to 13-day preference sequence. Measures of fluid intake were recorded every day at the same time, and examinations of the behavioral state of each monkey were made at frequent intervals.

Surgery

Following rigid aseptic precautions, modified Collison cannulae were implanted bilaterally in the lateral cerebral ventricles according to procedures described previously (11), with the stereotaxic coordinates as follows: AP 13.0; L 2.0; H + 11.0. Figure 1 illustrates schematically the position of the cannula and the area reached immediately by the infusate. Following a one week recovery period, the animals were given intraventricular infusions of artificial CSF (17) (N = 1); 8% ethanol (N = 4); 12% ethanol (N = 1); 0.1% acetaldehyde (N = 3); or 0.1% paraldehyde (N = 1).

Solutions were prepared in pyrogen-free 0.9% saline and the concentrations selected on the basis of previous findings with the rat (9, 13) in which significant increases in ethanol intake were observed. Calibrated 20 cc glass syringes were mounted on a modified Harvard infusion pump which was programmed to deliver 100 μl over an interval of 75 sec every 15 min around the clock. Each syringe was autoclaved, and the polyethylene tubing which was connected to the injection cannulae was kept in 70% ethanol and flushed with sterile saline before being filled with the infusate.

Infusion of a given solution was begun 24 hr prior to the start of the ethanol-water preference test sequence (third week) and was continued throughout this sequence. Ethanol intake measures were calculated on the basis of the monkey's weight at the time of surgery; the weight of the animal at the end of the experimental sequence did not fluctuate by more than 0.2 kg. The infusion solutions were changed every 24 hr.

At the termination of an experiment, representative monkeys were used for verification of the cannula patency according to methods described previously (11). An injection of 0.1 ml of 0.5% bromophenol blue dye was injected into the ventricular cannula, the animal sacrificed with an overdose of Nembutal, and careful dissections of the ventricular cavities were carried out.

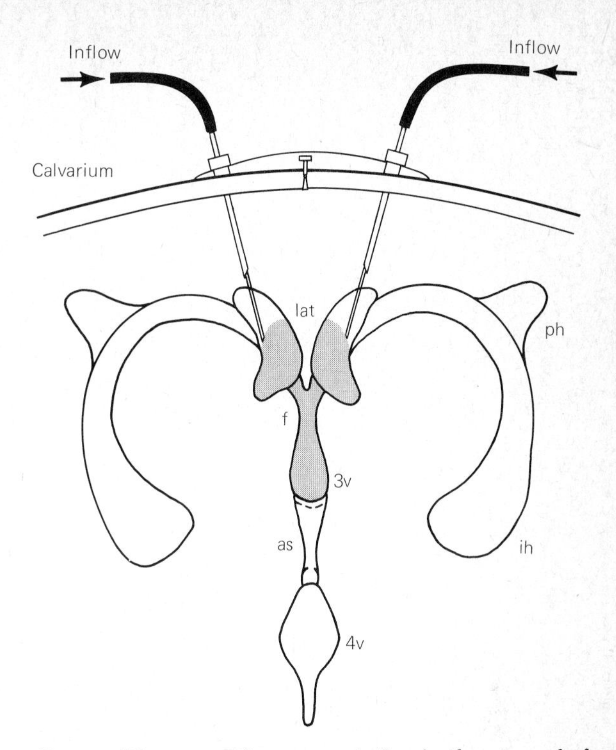

Fig. 1. Diagrammatic representation in the coronal plane of the procedure for the bilateral infusion of the cerebral ventricles of the unanesthetized monkey. The shaded area indicates the region reached immediately by the infusion. Cranioplast cement retains the cannula hubs in position together with the anchor screw placed on midline. Abbreviations are: as, aqueduct of Sylvius; f, foramen of Monroe; ih, inferior horn of lateral ventricle; lat, lateral ventricle; ph, posterior horn of lateral ventricle; 3v, third ventricle; 4v, fourth ventricle.

RESULTS

The effects of chronic intraventricular administration of ethanol on the volitional consumption of ethanol varied from animal to animal. When the volumes ingested were compared in terms of g/kg, it was found that in those monkeys in which 8% ethanol was infused into the lateral ventricles, four different drinking patterns evolved.

Figure 2 shows that the control, acetaldehyde and one of the 8% ethanol-infused animals failed to increase their intake of ethanol at any of the concentrations offered. The saline vehicle did not alter the aversion to ethanol which has been described for the same self-selection sequence of ethanol concentrations in the rhesus monkey (14). On the other hand, the chronic infusion of an 8% solution of ethanol had a significant effect in three of the four other monkeys. One animal (Fig. 2B) drank more than 2 g/kg per day at the 6, 7, 12 and 15% concentration. However, another monkey (Fig. 2C) did not consume a substantial amount until the 8th day of infusion, and then a maximum of 11.4 g/kg of ethanol was ingested at the 20% concentration. The third animal (Fig. 2D) consumed a maximum of 9.5 and 9.0 g/kg at the 4 and 7% concentrations, respectively, and then failed to prefer ethanol thereafter.

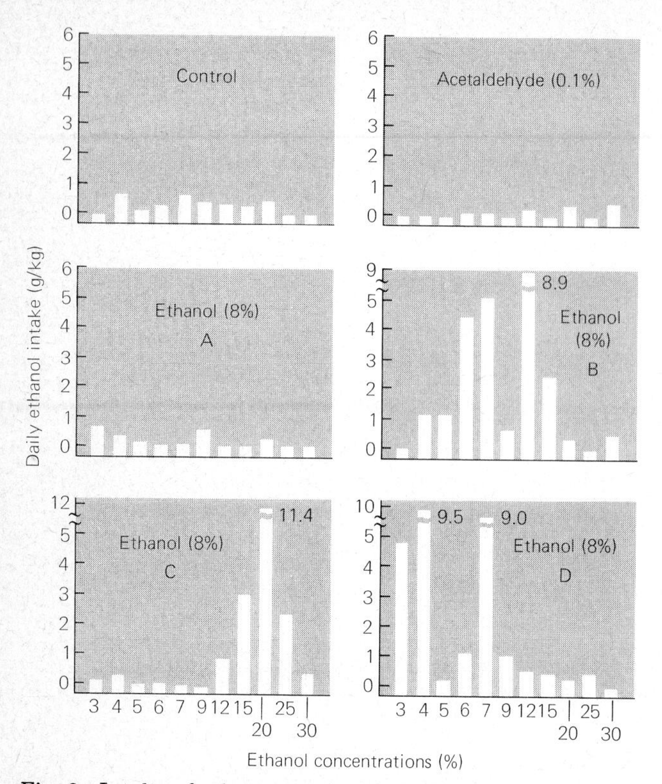

Fig. 2. Intake of ethanol in g/kg of six monkeys recorded for the specific concentration offered on each day of the ethanol–water choice sequence. Each monkey was given an intraventricular infusion of the solution as indicated (control received 0.9% saline) every 15 min, in a volume of 0.1 ml, around the clock during this preference sequence.

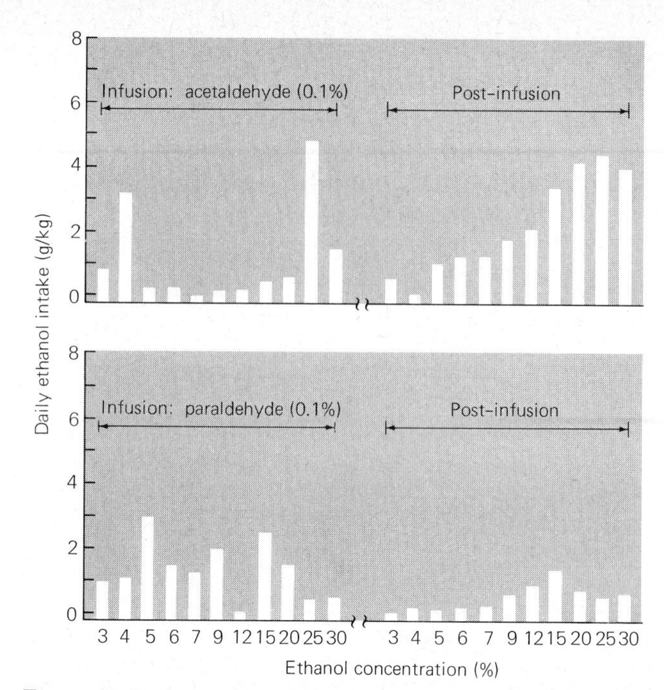

Fig. 3. Daily intake of ethanol (g/kg) for two monkeys in which 0.1% acetaldehyde (Top) or 0.1% paraldehyde (Bottom) was infused intraventricularly in a volume of 0.1 ml every 15 min around the clock during the initial preference sequence. The chronic infusions were discontinued (post-infusion) during the second ethanol–water choice sequence.

On those days of elevated ethanol intake of greater than 6 g/kg per day, each of these monkeys often displayed behavioral signs of intoxication which included muscular relaxation, loss of the threat response, docility and general motor incoordination. In fact, on several days following the relatively rapid intake of ethanol, the monkeys (Figs. 2B and 2C) were unable to sit up in their primate chairs. At all other times, the animals appeared normal and in fact would depress a lever to obtain food. Similarly, the other monkey in which ethanol was infused (Fig. 2A), the control animal, and the acetaldehyde-infused monkey did not show any effects whatsoever of receiving bilateral infusions of these solutions every 15 min.

Post-infusion

In four monkeys in which 0.1% acetaldehyde (N = 2), 0.1% paraldehyde (N = 1) or 12% ethanol (N = 1) was infused chronically, the pattern of volitional consumption of ethanol was somewhat irregular. As shown in Fig. 3 (Top), during the infusion sequence acetaldehyde evoked sporadic ethanol intake at the 4 and 25% concentrations, but in the post-infusion sequence, one week later, from 2 to 4 g/kg were selected between 12 and 20% concentration (Fig. 3, Top). The infusion of paraldehyde in another monkey (Fig.

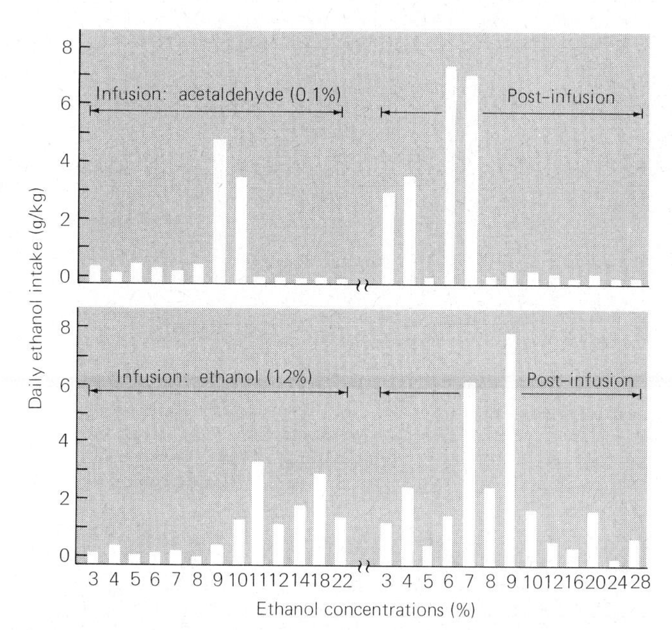

Fig. 4. Daily intake of ethanol (g/kg) for two monkeys in which 0.1% acetaldehyde (Top) or 12% ethanol (Bottom) was infused intraventricularly in a volume of 0.1 ml every 15 min around the clock during the initial preference sequence. The chronic infusions were discontinued (post-infusion) during the second ethanol—water choice sequence.

3, Bottom) evoked a slight increase in ethanol selection, but during the post-infusion period, the average intake was less than 1.0 g/kg per day.

Figure 4 shows that 0.1% acetaldehyde infused into the third ventricle also caused a marked effect on ethanol intake, but not until the post-infusion ethanol-water choice sequence. Similarly, the chronic infusion of 12% ethanol also resulted in a considerable increase in drinking of between 6 and 8 g/kg during the post-infusion sequence at the 7 and 9% concentrations. However, at the higher concentrations of ethanol offered to the monkey, the usual aversion to the fluid was observed. Finally, no signs of withdrawal were observed in any of the monkeys during or after the infusion sequences.

DISCUSSION

The results of the present experiments confirm and extend those studies in which rats increased their volitional consumption of ethanol following chronic intraventricular infusion of ethanol or its metabolite acetaldehyde (8, 9, 10, 13, 15). Thus, the effect on drinking of elevating the cerebral levels of ethanol does not appear to be species-specific. In one monkey, Koz and Mendelson (5) failed to observe a shift in ethanol preference following a single injection of 10% ethanol given once a day. Since the effects of an acute intraventricular injection in the rat or cat are imperceptible when given in the concentration used in this study (9), it would seem that the factor of chronicity is the crucial variable in the elicitation of an abnormal preference for an ethanol solution (10).

It is not clear at the present time why a shift in ethanol preference occurred in only about half of the animals which were infused. However, the effect on ethanol selection may depend entirely on several crucial variables including the site of the infusion in the ventricular lumen, the dynamics of the cerebrospinal fluid flow, or whether a structure such as the hypothalamus, septum, hippocampus, amygdala or caudate nucleus is reached by the ethanol infusate. Furthermore, from studies with the rat, it is known that the tip of the cannula must rest within the cerebral ventricle if an effect on drinking is to be evoked (9). That is, if the cannula were occluded even intermittently by glial or other tissue, then the infusion solution would, as a result, partially or wholly diffuse up the cannula track to the cortex where it would presumably exert little effect.

Why the monkey does manifest rather irregular shifts in ethanol preference during the time-course of infusion is also not clear. Moreover, in three of the four monkeys, a greater intake of ethanol occurred after the infusion had been terminated, a finding which is similar to that observed by Myers (9). In this connection, it is interesting that Jones *et al.* (4) found that a mongrel beagle drank significant volumes of 10% ethanol only once a week during a continuous infusion of ethanol rather than intermittent slow injections into the dog's lateral cerebral ventricle. In this latter study, however, a 10% solution was the only concentration offered which may have been far greater than the animal's preference threshold.

At present, there is no evidence to suggest that a monkey will become dependent on ethanol or manifest symptoms of withdrawal as a part of the *sequelae* of repeated intraventricular ethanol infusions. Additional research with this species is required to determine the longevity of the action of intracerebral ethanol, the effects of different concentrations of each infusate, and to ascertain the reasons why the apparently constant and controlled experimental conditions do not yield similar results in all animals.

REFERENCES

1. Anderson, W. D. and O. A. Smith, Jr. Taste and volume preferences for alcohol in *macaca nemestrina*. *J. comp. physiol. Psychol.* **56**: 144–149, 1963.
2. Clark, R. and E. Polish. Avoidance conditioning and alcohol consumption in rhesus monkeys. *Science* **132**: 223–224, 1960.
3. Fitz-Gerald, F. L., M. A. Barfield and R. J. Warrington. Voluntary alcohol consumption in chimpanzees and orangutans. *Q. Jl Stud. Alcohol* **29**: 330–336, 1968.
4. Jones, B. E., C. F. Essig and W. Creager. Intraventricular infusion of ethanol in dogs: Effect on voluntary alcohol intake. *Q. Jl Stud. Alcohol* **31**: 288–292, 1970.
5. Koz, G. and J. H. Mendelson. Effects of intraventricular ethanol infusion on free-choice alcohol consumption by monkeys. In: *Biochemical Factors in Alcoholism*, edited by R. P. Maickel. Oxford: Pergamon Press, 1967, pp. 158–165.
6. Mello, N. K. and J. H. Mendelson. Factors affecting alcohol consumption in primates. *Psychosom. Med.* **28**: 529–550, 1966.
7. Mello, N. K. and J. H. Mendelson. The effects of drinking to avoid shock on alcohol intake in primates. In: *Biological Aspects of Alcohol*, edited by P. J. Creaven and M. K. Roach. Austin: University of Texas Press, 1971, pp. 313–340.
8. Myers, R. D. Alcohol consumption in rats: effects of intracranial injections of ethanol. *Science* **142**: 240–241, 1963.
9. Myers, R. D. Modification of drinking patterns by chronic intracranial chemical infusion. In: *Thirst in the Regulation of Body Water*, edited by M. J. Wayner. New York: Pergamon Press, 1964, pp. 533–558.
10. Myers, R. D. Voluntary alcohol consumption in animals: peripheral and intracerebral factors. *Psychosom. Med.* **28**: 474–497, 1966.
11. Myers, R. D. Transfusion of cerebrospinal fluid and tissue bound chemical factors between the brains of conscious monkeys: A new neurobiological assay. *Physiol. Behav.* **2**: 373–377, 1967.
12. Myers, R. D. and R. B. Holman. A procedure for eliminating position habit in preference-aversion tests for ethanol and other fluids. *Psychonom. Sci.* **6**: 235–236, 1967.
13. Myers, R. D. and W. L. Veale. Alterations in volitional alcohol intake produced in rats by chronic intraventricular infusions of acetaldehyde, paraldehyde or methanol. *Arch. int. Pharmacodyn.* **180**: 100–113, 1969.
14. Myers, R. D. and W. L. Veale. The determinants of alcohol preference in animals. In: *The Biology of Alcoholism*, Vol. II. edited by B. Kissin and H. Begleiter. New York: Plenum, 1971, pp. 131–168.
15. Myers, R. D., J. E. Evans and T. L. Yaksh. Ethanol preference in the rat: Interactions between serotonin and ethanol, acetaldehyde, paraldehyde, 5-HTP and 5-HTOL. *Neuropharmacology* (in press), 1972.

16. Myers, R. D., T. L. Yaksh, G. H. Hall and W. L. Veale. A method for perfusion of cerebral ventricles of the conscious monkey. *J. appl. Physiol.* **30**: 589–592, 1971.

17. Turbyfill, C. L., M. B. Cramer, W. A. Dawes and J. W. Huguley, III. Serum and cerebral spinal fluid chemistry values for the monkey *(Macaca mulatta). Lab. Animal Care* **20**: 269–273, 1970.

Perceived Opportunity, Alienation, and Drinking Behavior Among Italian and American Youth

Richard Jessor

H. Boutourline Young

Elizabeth B. Young

Gino Tesi

A cross-cultural study of the relationship of personality factors to drinking behavior demonstrates the importance of differential socialization and institutionalization of alcohol use. A significant linkage is established, for American youth, between personality attributes reflecting frustration, dissatisfaction, and powerlessness, and measures of drinking behavior involving amount of intake and frequency of drunkenness. Neither of two samples of Italian youth provides evidence for such a relationship. A further analysis of the learned meanings associated with alcohol use shows that for American, but not Italian, youth, problem-solving or coping meanings of drinking mediate between personality-level frustration and actual drinking behavior. Italian-American culture differences with respect to alcohol clearly make a difference in the way in which an important social behavior like drinking is patterned.

In previous research on a social-psychological theory of alcohol use (Jessor, Graves, Hanson, & Jessor, 1968; Jessor, Carman, & Grossman, 1968), it has been shown that certain aspects of drinking behavior are related to attributes of personality which reflect past failure to achieve valued goals, present dissatisfactions, or the anticipation of limited future opportunity. In short, the hypothesis that drinking can serve, for some persons, as an adaptive response to frustration or as a way of trying to solve or cope with personal problems has received compelling validation within areas of American society. That alcohol can serve in this way obviously depends, however, upon how drinking behavior is socialized and institutionalized, that is, upon the experiences, the contexts, and the social definitions which accompany its initial learning and its subsequent use.

Variation in how drinking is learned and in the meanings attached to the use of alcohol should determine whether or not the relationship described above will obtain. Such variation occurs within any society, but it is perhaps most apparent across different societies or cultures; a marked example of the latter is the difference that has been described between Italian and American culture. In Italy, in contrast to America, drinking is institutionalized as part of family life and dietary and religious custom; alcohol (wine) is introduced early in life, within the context of the family, and as a traditional accompaniment to meals and a healthful way of enhancing the diet. Drinking is not, as it is in America, associated with transformation of status from adolescence to adulthood; alcohol use is not an illicit activ-

From *Journal of Personality and Social Psychology*, 1970, 15, 215–222.

This research was carried out during the first author's tenure as a National Institute of Mental Health Research Fellow at the Harvard-Florence Research Project, Florence, Italy, during 1965–1966. Analyses of the data were facilitated by a grant-in-aid to the first author from the University of Colorado Council on Research and Creative Work. The assistance of Richard M. Swanson and Stephen I. Abramowitz in completing these analyses is gratefully acknowledged.

A preliminary report of this research was presented at the 28th International Congress on Alcohol and Alcoholism, Washington, D. C., September 1968. This paper is Publication No. 131 of the Institute of Behavioral Science, University of Colorado.

ity for Italian youth; and heavy, consistent use of alcohol in Italy does not carry with it the same "problem" connotation that it does in America. Such an approach to the socialization of alcohol use should make it less likely in Italy than in America that drinking will be learned as a way of trying to solve personal problems or of coping with inadequacy and failure. In this regard, Lolli and his collaborators (Lolli, Serianni, Golder, & Luzzatto-Fegis, 1958) have asserted emphatically that "no emphasis is placed by the Italians on any 'psychological' or 'escape-providing' qualities of wine . . . [p. 129]."

The present study represents an effort to examine empirically the differential consequences of Italian and American socialization and institutionalization of the use of alcohol. While the focus is upon alcohol, the study is, more generally, a test of the role of cultural influences upon personality-behavior relationships. The general hypothesis examined was that American youth, in contrast to Italian youth, will show a significant relationship between drinking behavior and aspects of personality reflecting frustration, failure of goal attainment, and the expectation of limited future opportunity.

METHOD

Subjects

The subjects of the present study were the three samples of male youth involved in the longitudinal research of the Harvard-Florence Project. Recruited in 1957, when they were about 12 years of age, and followed closely during the intervening years, the young men were about 21 years old when the present data were collected. The three samples involved in the longitudinal research are located in three urban sites: Boston, Rome, and Palermo. All four grandparents of each subject were born in southern Italy, the families of the Palermo youth having remained in southern Italy, the families of the Rome youth having migrated north about 20 to 25 years ago, and the families of the Boston youth having emigrated to America near the turn of the century. An effort had been made to equate the three samples of youth initially for socioeconomic status (father's occupation, father's education, and condition of the home), and for intelligence (Raven Progressive Matrices). The effort was successful for the former attribute, but with respect to Raven intellectual ability scores, the Rome sample turned out to be significantly higher than the other two. Further description of the samples may be found in Young, Ferguson, and Tesi (in press).

A total of 79 subjects from the Boston longitudinal sample, 94 from the Rome sample, and 108 from the Palermo sample actually participated in the present study.

Procedure

Data were collected by means of a questionnaire designed by the first author during his fellowship year in Florence. To assure that the Italian- and English-language versions of the questionnaire were as equivalent as possible, several back-translations, with subsequent revision and adjustment, were made. The questionnaire was also pilot-tested, with both Italian and American subjects, prior to the main study. The final form of the questionnaire was administered, with some exceptions, by mail. It was felt that the subjects' prior 8-year period of test-taking experience, and their continuing involvement with the longitudinal research, would lead them to respond to a mailed questionnaire with care and accuracy. The percentage of returns was 83% for the Boston sample, 81% for the Rome sample, and 91% for the Palermo sample. These percentages are high enough to merit some confidence in the representativeness of the data.[1]

Measures

The questionnaire contained a variety of questions about the learning and context of drinking as well as a number of measures relevant to the main hypothesis of the present study. Three key measures of personality attributes were included. The first of these was a 17-item measure of *expectations of goal attainment* (perceived opportunity) in a variety of need areas (such as affection and achievement), and in a variety of life areas (such as family, work, and friendships). The second was a 13-item, Likert-type measure of *alienation* patterned after the Srole scale and emphasizing feelings of social isolation and lack of meaning in daily role activities. The third personality measure was a 12-item, forced-choice scale assessing the degree to which a subject felt he had *internal control* over his future and over the outcomes of his behavior. The main measures of drinking behavior were two: a *quantity-frequency* measure of intake, based on the average quantity (ounces) of absolute alcohol consumed per day; and a measure of the reported frequency of occasions of *drunkenness* during the preceding year. All of these or related measures are described in greater detail elsewhere (Jessor, Graves, Hanson, & Jessor, 1968).

An additional focus of the questionnaire was on the meanings, definitions, or psychological functions attributed by the subjects to their own use of alcohol. The measurement of the functions of drinking and related findings will be described later after the data on the main hypothesis have been presented.

The major hypothesis can now be stated in more specific terms. It was expected, on the basis of theory and previous research, that *lower* expectations for goal attainment, *higher* alienation, and *lower* internal control would be associated with *higher* intake of alcohol (quantity-frequency) and with *greater* frequency of drunkenness within the Boston (American) sample. These same relationships were *not* expected to hold in the two Italian samples, given the different institutionalization of alcohol use in Italian culture described earlier.

RESULTS

In each of the three samples, the personality measures evidenced similar psychometric properties suggesting that they were being responded to by the three samples in a similar way. The expectations measure showed good internal consistency (Scott's homogeneity ratio) and reliability (Cronbach's alpha) in each of the samples; homogeneity and reliability were lower but still adequate for the alienation measure; and were lower than desirable for the measure of internal control. In each sample the product-

[1] For each of the three samples, comparisons were made of the mean intelligence and socioeconomic status scores of the subjects who returned the questionnaire against those who did not. None of the t tests of the differences was significant with respect to socioeconomic status. With respect to Raven intelligence scores, there were no differences in Boston or Palermo, but in Rome, those who returned the questionnaires were higher than those who did not. They were also higher than those who returned the questionnaire from Boston and Palermo, thus reflecting the initial failure to equate the three urban samples on this attribute.

Table 1. *Mean Scores on Personality Attributes.*

Attribute	Boston (n = 79)	Rome (n = 94)	Palermo (n = 108)	p^a		
				B vs. P	B vs. R	R vs. P
Expectations	51.0	46.3	46.3	$<.01$	$<.01$	*ns*
Alienation	27.9	29.1	31.0	.10	$<.01$	$<.01$
Internal control	18.4	15.4	15.2	$<.01$	$<.01$	*ns*

[a] Two-tailed t tests.

moment correlation between expectations and alienation was strongest (−.51, Boston; −.49, Rome; −.37, Palermo), followed by the correlation between expectations and internal control (.30, Boston; .38, Rome; .28, Palermo), and then by the correlation between alienation and internal control (−.20, Boston; −.17, Rome; −.11, Palermo). The magnitude of these correlations indicates adequate independence among these three measures; the direction of the correlations supports the validity of the measures.

The data in Table 1 indicate that the Boston sample had significantly *higher* expectations for goal attainment than either the Rome or Palermo groups, the latter being identical in mean scores. The Boston youth were also *less* alienated than either of the Italian samples, although the difference is short of statistical significance in regard to Rome. Finally, the Boston subjects scored significantly *higher* on internal control than both the Rome and Palermo subjects. In general, then, the personality data show the Boston youth to have been experiencing less frustration or dissatisfaction than the Italian youth; the scores of the two Italian samples were similar, with the exception that the Palermo subjects expressed significantly greater alienation than did those in Rome.[2]

With respect to the description of aspects of the socialization of drinking behavior, the Italian samples, as expected, had wine most frequently for their first drink, more than twice as often as the Boston sample (Boston = 29%; Rome = 75%; Palermo = 64%) for the Boston sample, beer was the most frequent beverage for the first drink (Boston = 56%; Rome = 6%; Palermo = 15%). For the Italian samples, parents or family were present at the first drink in a significantly larger proportion of the cases than for the Boston sample (Boston = 56%, Rome = 88%, Palermo = 78%; $\chi^2 = 21.59$, $p < .001$). The Italian samples also began more or less regular drinking at a significantly younger age than the Boston sample (Boston = 17.7; Rome = 14.9; Palermo = 14.7; $p < .01$). These data tend to corroborate the apparent differential institutionalization of drinking in Italian and American culture.

Turning to the drinking measures of immediate concern to this study—the quantity-frequency index of alcohol intake, and the frequency of reported drunkenness in the past year—the data show, as expected, that both Italian samples had a significantly higher intake of wine than the Boston sample (Boston wine quantity-frequency = .17; Rome wine quantity-frequency = .84; Palermo wine quantity-frequency = .72; $p < .01$). However, with respect to *overall* alcohol intake, that is, a quantity-frequency index based on beer, wine, and liquor together, there is no difference between the groups, overall quantity-frequency indexes being similar in Boston, Rome, and Palermo (Boston overall quantity-frequency = 1.2; Rome overall quantity-frequency = 1.4; Palermo overall quantity-frequency = 1.4; *ns*).

Despite this similarity in overall intake, there is a marked difference in frequency of reported drunkenness between Boston and the two Italian samples. Fifty-two percent of the Rome drinkers and 58% of the Palermo drinkers reported *no* occasions of being "drunk or pretty high" in the last year; only 24% of the Boston sample could say the same thing. On the other hand, 30% of the Boston drinkers reported having been drunk four or more times during the preceding year, whereas only 9% of the Rome youth and 10% of the Palermo youth could say the same thing. The difference in the distribution of drunkenness frequencies between the Boston and the Italian samples is highly significant ($\chi^2 = 24.39$, $p < .001$), with more frequent drunkenness in the American sample.

These differences in drunkenness are also to be expected as a function of the differential institutionalization of drinking, and the present findings are entirely consistent with previous studies of Italian drinking (Lolli et al., 1958) and with the similar analysis of the role and context of drinking among Jews (Snyder, 1958). Additional data in the present study with respect to the occurrence of physical upsets associated with the use of alcohol, for example, "headaches, nausea, stomach upset . . . ," are also consistent with the drunkenness differences between Americans and Italians. Significantly more frequent physical upsets were reported in the Boston sample than in either of the two Italian samples ($\chi^2 = 9.82, p < .01$).[3]

[2] These findings cannot be treated as anything more than mere description since no firm basis for directional personality outcomes was established in advance. It is of some interest to note, nevertheless, the emphasis of several writers upon the fatalistic outlook of the southern Italian, an outlook which should be reflected at least in the internal control measure. Peterson and Migliorino (1967), in their study of child-rearing in Palermo, referred to the Sicilians as having "far less faith in the power of the autonomous individual than there is in the United States. The Sicilians have learned to be patient, to take *'il destino'* as it comes [p. 970]." Cancian (1961), in describing the southern Italian world view, referred to the peasant's "lack of confidence in his own ability to control the environment [p. 13]." The findings from the present measures may suggest their potential utility in documenting such sociocultural variation.

[3] The data cannot be interpreted simply as reflecting the operation of a differential response set in the Boston and Italian samples. When cigarette smoking rather than alcohol was inquired about, the Boston sample reported smoking significantly *more* cigarettes per day than the Italian samples but having *less* physical upsets associated with smoking than the Italians reported.

Table 2. *Correlations Between Three Personality Attributes and Two Measures of Drinking Behavior.*

	Boston (n = 65)		Rome (n = 81)		Palermo (n = 83)	
Attribute	Quantity–Frequency	Drunkenness	Quantity–Frequency	Drunkenness	Quantity–Frequency	Drunkenness
Expectations	–.27[a]	–.19	.22[b]	–.13	.18	.03
Alienation	.12	.25[a]	–.09	.00	–.19	–.14
Internal control	–.45[a]	–.03	–.00	.16	.01	.09

Note. Correlations are based on drinkers only within each sample.
[a]Correlation significant at the .05 level or better, two-tailed test. The three significant correlations in the Boston sample are in the theoretically expected direction.
[b]Correlation significant at the .05 level or better, two-tailed test. This Rome correlation is in a direction *opposite to* that hypothesized for Boston.

Although the preceding data are of interest and are, in general, as expected, they are merely descriptive of differences in personality and in drinking behavior between the American sample and the two Italian samples. They do not bear directly upon the major theoretical concern of the study, namely, *the relationship between the personality attributes and drinking behavior within the three samples.* It is possible now to turn to an examination of this issue; the relevant data, product-moment correlations between the personality measures and the drinking measures, are presented in Table 2.

Within the Boston sample, the data provide support for the main hypothesis. The lower the expectations for goal attainment (i.e., the lower the perceived opportunity), the greater the intake of alcohol and the more frequent the drunkenness. The correlation is statistically significant for quantity-frequency and almost significant for the drunkenness measure. Alienation, while not related to intake, is significantly related to frequency of drunkenness—the higher the alienation the more frequent the drunkenness. Internal control, on the other hand, is significantly associated with quantity-frequency—the lower the internal control, the greater the intake—but it has no relationship to drunkenness. Each of the three personality attributes thus relates significantly to at least one of the drinking measures, in the Boston sample, and all of the correlations are in the expected direction.

By sharp contrast, *none* of the correlations is significant within the Palermo sample. The one significant correlation in the Rome sample is actually in the opposite direction (the *higher* the expectations the more the intake). As a matter of fact, all four of the correlations larger than .15 in magnitude in the Italian samples are in the opposite direction from that specified with respect to the Boston sample. These data, therefore, reflect quite clearly the differential function of at least part of the behavior of drinking in the Italian and the American culture.

Thus far we have shown, for Boston youth only, a linkage between personality attributes reflecting frustration, alienation, and powerlessness, on the one hand, and variation in drinking behavior on the other. That linkage implies that alcohol use, or heavy alcohol use, has been learned as a way of responding to or coping with frustration, dissatisfaction, and failure. For such an implication to gain additional support, it would be necessary to show that the meanings or functions attributed to their alcohol use by those who are frustrated tend to be problem-solving, coping, or what we have called "personal effects" functions. In short, the meanings, definitions, or functions of drinking can be considered to *mediate* between personality attributes and actual drinking behavior.

In order to investigate this mediation notion, drinking function data were collected as part of the same questionnaire. A list of 40 different functions was used, and the subject checked those which were important to him in his own drinking. The functions list was largely derived from the authors' earlier work (see especially Jessor, Carman, & Grossman, 1968) which, in turn, had been influenced by Mulford and Miller (1960); it included 9 dietary, 9 positive social, 6 conforming social, 6 psychophysiological, and 10 personal effects items.[4] For present purposes, we will deal only with the 10-item personal effects scale. Examples of personal effects functions items were: "to get my mind off failures," "helps you forget you're not the kind of person you'd like to be," or "makes the future seem brighter." Internal homogeneity and reliability of the personal effects scale were good in all three samples.

The first part of examining the mediating role of the personal effects functions involves the relation of the three personality measures to the personal effects scores; the second part involves the relation of the personal effects scores to the drinking behavior measures, quantity-frequency, and drunkenness. These data are presented in Table 3.

Boston is the only sample in which *both* parts of the mediating role of personal effects functions are empirically established. On the personality side, alienation is significantly related (.27) to variation in personal effects functions: the more alienated one is the more drinking is done for personal effects reasons. On the behavior side, personal effects functions are significantly related to variation in both quantity-frequency (.41) and drunkenness (.54): the more that drinking is for personal effects reasons, the greater the intake of alcohol and the more frequent the

[4] As would have been expected, and as further evidence of the different cultural meanings attached to alcohol use, both Italian samples endorsed the dietary functions (e.g., "it makes food taste better," or "it helps digestion") significantly more often than the Boston sample. The Boston sample, on the other hand, endorsed the positive social functions of drinking (e.g., "just to have a good time," or "makes get-togethers fun") significantly more often than either Italian sample.

Table 3. *Correlations Between Personal Effects Functions Scores and Three Personality Measures and Two Drinking Measures (Drinkers Only).*

	Personal effects and personality			Personal effects and behavior	
City	Expectations	Alienation	Internal control	Quantity–Frequency	Drunkenness
Boston (n = 65)	−.16	.27[a]	−.03	.41[a]	.54[a]
Rome (n = 81)	−.06	.18	.14	.09	.13
Palermo (n = 83)	−.09	.09	.04	.37[a]	.26[a]

[a] $p \leqslant .05$, two-tailed test.

drunkenness. These data, therefore, support the implication drawn from the earlier results.

Those results showed an *overall* linkage between personality and drinking behavior. The present data show how such an overall linkage is mediated by the personal effect functions which have been attached to the use of alcohol. They show explicitly that drinking can serve as a response to or as a way of coping with frustration and dissatisfaction.

By contrast, there is no evidence at all, for the Rome sample, of a relation between personality and personal effects scores or between personal effects scores and drinking behavior. In the Palermo sample, no relation obtains between any personality measure and personal effects functions scores, but unlike Rome there is a relationship on the behavior side between personal effects scores and quantity-frequency and drunkenness. Even here, however, the correlations are smaller than those for Boston; with respect to drunkenness, the Palermo correlation (.26), while significant, is less than half that for Boston (.54). The personal effects functions data thus add support to the initial findings: not only did the Boston sample differ from the two Italian samples in showing an overall relation between personality and drinking, but it was also the only sample in which *both* sides of the mediating role of personal effects reasons for drinking could be empirically demonstrated.

DISCUSSION AND CONCLUSION

It is important to keep in mind the limitations which constrain the present data, limitations intrinsic to questionnaire data, to data derived from forms in two different languages, and to questionnaires which were self-administered and which were returned by a subsample of those to whom it was mailed. Further, even with 100% return, there would still be no basis to claim that the Boston and the Italian samples are, in any sampling sense, representative of their respective cultures. These limitations obviously suggest the need for replication of the study with more adequate and representative samples.

Despite these limitations, the findings are of interest for several reasons. First, the data represent a *direct* test of the differential role of personality attributes in drinking behavior in two different cultures. Most cross-cultural studies of variation in drinking patterns have relied on modal personality descriptions inferred from ethnographic observation rather than on the individual measurement of personality attributes by established psychometric scales.

Second, the data make clear that the same behavior—drinking—may play quite a different role in different cultures depending upon how it is socialized and institutionalized. The Boston findings support the hypothesis that drinking can serve, among other things, as a way of responding to or coping with frustration and dissatisfaction. With respect to the alienation measure of personality and the drunkenness measure of behavior, especially, the pattern of findings in Boston fits the requirements of the hypothesized mediation paradigm perfectly: (*a*) alienation is significantly related to drunkenness (r = .25); (*b*) personal effects functions are significantly related to alienation on the personality side (r = .27) and to drunkenness on the behavior side (r = .54); and (*c*) these two correlations with the personal effects mediator are both greater than the correlation between the two variables being mediated (alienation and drunkenness). Although neither the expectations measure nor the internal control measure fully replicate this paradigm, both measures do vary significantly with another aspect of drinking behavior—intake (quantity-frequency) or—in the Boston sample, thus adding further evidence for the hypothesized personality-drinking behavior relationship. The Boston evidence is consistent with the first author's previous work within American society in a small rural community (Jessor, Graves, Hanson, & Jessor, 1968) and with college students (Jessor, Carman, & Grossman, 1968).

In contrast to these findings, the Italian samples provide no evidence for a linkage between personality-level frustration and either measure of drinking behavior. As a matter of fact, in the Rome sample, the *higher* the expectations for goal attainment the greater the intake, a direction also shown for Palermo and exactly opposite to that in Boston. This could suggest that drinking in Italian culture, instead of serving to cope with frustration, covaries with or tends to mark actual success or personal optimism. To examine this possibility further, the relation of expectations to the measure of *positive social functions* for drinking, and of positive social functions to quantity-frequency and drunkenness in the Rome sample, was assessed. None of these correlations was significantly different from zero. In view of this, and in view of the absence of any relation between either alienation or internal control and drinking behavior, it seems best to conclude that no relationship between personality variables referring to frustration and drinking behavior has been established for either Italian sample.[5]

[5] It should be emphasized that this lack of *relationship* does not imply a lack of frustration or dissatisfaction at the personality level. As a matter of fact (see Table 1), both Italian samples scored *more* frustrated, alienated, and powerless than the Boston youth.

This conclusion, contrasting to the Boston findings, is nevertheless quite consistent with the ethnographic and observational analyses of Italian drinking patterns. The early learning about wine and its institutionalization in the home as part of the diet would seem to be one of the important factors in differentiating the Italians from the American youth. The present data show that the first significant drinking experience took place much earlier in life for both Italian samples than for the Boston sample (Boston mean age = 14.9; Rome = 9.7; Palermo = 11.8). It also took place in the home with family present more often in Rome and Palermo than in Boston. This differential learning is reflected further in the finding that for both Italian samples, dietary functions of drinking were not only endorsed significantly more often than they were by the Boston subjects, but dietary functions were the most frequently endorsed of any of the five function categories by the Italians.

The findings are of further interest for yet another reason; they indicate that while the Rome and Palermo samples are similar in many respects, especially in respect to the main hypothesis, there are, nevertheless, important differences between them. Such differences suggest that treating Italian culture as a homogeneous entity is likely to be misleading. The salient contrast between the Rome and Palermo samples is in the fact that for Palermo, but not for Rome (see Table 3), there was a relationship between personal effects reasons for drinking and both alcohol intake and frequency of drunkenness. The Palermo youth not only endorsed significantly more personal effects functions than did the Rome youth (Palermo M = 1.23; Rome = .68), but such endorsement also related to their actual pattern of alcohol use. What accounts for this difference between the two Italian samples is difficult to pinpoint. Although the Palermo youth were significantly more alienated than the Rome youth, there was no relation between alienation (or, for that matter, expectations or internal control) and personal effects functions (or any of the other functions). The fact that the Raven intellectual ability scores of the Rome subjects were higher than for the Palermo sample seems logically remote from the present issue, especially since there were no socioeconomic differences. Perhaps most germane is the fact that Palermo youth began drinking significantly later than the Rome youth and tended to have their first drinking experience outside the family slightly more often. These data may indicate the existence of differences between Palermo and Rome in the overall socialization of drinking, which could result in a somewhat different definition of drinking in the two locations. This possibility would seem an important focus of future research.

It is of interest to note that although there is a significant relation between personal effects and drinking in Palermo, the pattern of findings is quite different than that for Boston. In Palermo, personal effects related more strongly to quantity-frequency than to drunkenness (.37 versus .26); in Boston the reverse was the case (.41 versus .54). In addition, in Palermo the relation between personal effects and drunkenness was about the same as the relation between positive social functions and drunkenness (.26 and .29); in Boston the former relation was nearly twice the latter in magnitude (.54 and .29). Given that drunkenness is the criterion drinking measure more closely tied to a problem-solving type of drinking (than the intake measure, quantity-frequency), the results again make clear, even with respect to the personal effects data, the more benign pattern of Italian as against American drinking behavior.

Finally, it is of interest to keep in mind that the American sample is actually an *Italian*-American sample, with common ancestral, geographic, and, especially, cultural origins with the Italian samples. The Boston data, therefore, can be taken to indicate the direction of *change or shift* in a culturally established behavior pattern which can occur as a group—the Italians—becomes acculturated over time to an alternative—American—culture pattern. This interpretation provides further evidence for the importance to behavior of cultural patterning; it also points to the possibility that exists of *changing* certain socially undesirable aspects of drinking behavior by changing the way that drinking behavior is institutionalized and socialized in society.

REFERENCES

Cancian, F. The southern Italian peasant: World view and political behavior. *Anthropological Quarterly,* 1961, **34,** 1–18.

Jessor, R., Carman, R. S., & Grossman, P. H. Expectations of need satisfaction and drinking patterns of college students. *Quarterly Journal of Studies on Alcohol,* 1968, **29,** 101–116.

Jessor, R., Graves, T. D., Hanson, R. C., & Jessor, S. L. *Society, personality and deviant behavior: A study of a tri-ethnic community.* New York: Holt, Rinehart & Winston, 1968.

Lolli, G., Serianni, E., Golder, G. M., & Luzzatto-Fegis, P. *Alcohol in Italian culture: Food and wine in relation to sobriety among Italians and Italian Americans.* New Brunswick, N. J.: Rutgers University Center of Alcohol Studies, 1958.

Mulford, H. A., & Miller, D. E. Drinking in Iowa: III. A scale of definitions of alcohol related to drinking behavior. *Quarterly Journal of Studies on Alcohol,* 1960, **21,** 267–278.

Peterson, D. R., & Migliorino, G. Pancultural factors of parental behavior in Sicily and the United States. *Child Development,* 1967, **38,** 967–991.

Snyder, C. R. *Alcohol and the Jews: A cultural study of drinking and sobriety.* New Brunswick, N. J.: Rutgers University Center of Alcohol Studies, 1958.

Young, H. B., Ferguson, L. R., & Tesi, G. (Eds.) *Puberty to manhood: A cross-cultural study of development,* in press.

Chapter 15

Drug Abuse

Like alcohol, drugs exert a psychoactive effect on individuals and may impair normal functioning. Such impairment in marijuana users includes a slight increase in heart rate and an intoxicating effect upon naive as well as chronic users, although the latter's behavior is less affected.

Joel Goldstein's paper investigates the motivations for psychoactive drug use among college students and compares personality test scores among 752 drug users and nonusers. He found substantial agreement in the personality and value score patterns among those who use amphetamine, marijuana and hard liquor, on the one hand, and those who are not psychoactive drug users.

Motivations for Psychoactive Drug Use Among Students

Joel W. Goldstein

Drug usage is a complex behavior with multiple causes. Motivational causal analysis is useful in specifying who within a given demographic category is most likely to engage in this behavior. In the past, however, personality analyses of usage motivation and causation have often been used to stigmatize users and to deprecate their usage. Studies comparing degree of usage of a given drug and personality scales show impressive similarity of findings. The similarity of personality profiles of users of a wide variety of drugs with each other is also impressive and only recently has attracted the attention of investigators. For example, teenage cigarette smokers, college student marijuana users, college student amphetamine users, college student drinkers, and Haight-Ashbury multiple drug users all score lower than nonusers of these drugs on scales assessing satisfaction with self and higher on scales assessing flexibility. Detailed data on amphetamine, marijuana and hard liquor use by a university freshman class (N = 752), tested during their first days at college, was obtained as part of a major all-university drug study. Comparisons of scores and scale configurations on the California Psychological Inventory *and on the Allport-Vernon-Lindzey* Study of Values *reveal substantial agreement in the pattern of user-nonuser differences for all three substances.*

Rather than label drug-taking behavior as "pathological" it is suggested that a value-free model of approach and avoidance forces be used to better clarify the relationships between the various usage correlates discovered to date. Such an approach has the additional virtue of helping to prevent the exacerbation of personal and social difficulties (the "drug problem problem") which sometimes accompany efforts to combat drug usage. Labeling adherants of deviate behavior as pathological often is disguised circular reasoning; further, it increases the likelihood that they will be treated unjustly while not advancing understanding of causation or, where needed, treatment. To lessen the problems of drug abuse we must separate it from drug use by criteria based upon deleterious effects, not merely on unauthorized use, and when we do this we find that the amount of drug abuse which exists is but a small fraction of even illicit use. Motivational analyses which distinguish between users and abusers are now needed to guide therapy with abusers and to help us in understanding the relationships between innocuous and deleterious use.

Drug use is a behavior with causes at many levels of molarity, ranging from historical-cultural socialization of usage to genetic predispositions. Past explanations of specific episodes of drug use have tended to concentrate on a few explanatory variables, usually at the same moderate level of molarity. The upsurge in psychoactive drug usage in the United States has lead to research which adhered to this pattern of explanation at first, but which is now displaying increasing sophistication. The first reaction to greatly increased usage among youth was to conduct surveys asking, in effect, "How many people are taking these illegal drugs?" This was followed by surveys asking, "Who is taking what?" Currently, research is expanding into more sophisticated analyses of causation. Personality studies have been a favorite of psychologists. As certain forms of usage become more prevalent, relationships with personality variables can be expected to weaken, and explanatory mechanisms drawn from the study of collective behavior will become increasingly relevant.

What continuing role, then, for personality variables in understanding widespread drug use? Several possibilities exist. As the extent of usage increases, personality variables may still be of interest in delineating user-nonuser differences; however, the nonuser may become of primary inter-

Invited address delivered at the symposium, "Drugs and Society," Annual Meeting of the Eastern Psychological Association, April 15, 1971, New York, New York.

This research was supported by the Falk Medical Fund and by NIMH grant MH 15805.

est. This situation exists in some studies of alcohol usage. Further, we would expect to continue to find that degree and type of usage would still be related to these variables, with extreme patterns being most readily identifiable. It is extremely frequent use, and use of the more potent drugs, which arouses greatest public concern, of course.

Our consumption of motivational analyses should be especially cautious because drug usage is perceived with ideological overtones which are not always recognized. The problem of the investigator here exceeds considerably what has become normal concern for experimenter bias. Drug usage has strong attitudinal correlates. The early and pervasive socialization of these attitudes makes it especially difficult for him to avoid premature conclusions in evaluating the meaning of drug use behavior. Drug use comes in many types, but all of them have their adherents and their detractors who, in turn, have built up elaborate cognitive rationales for their behaviors and their beliefs. Indeed, one theory of social psychology suggests that involvement with a new behavior itself leads one to change his attitudes about that behavior (Bem, 1967).

In our study of student drug usage (Goldstein, Korn, Abel, and Morgan, 1970; Goldstein, 1971) we not only found that use was related, as expected, to benign perceptions of drug effects (perceptions which were somewhat more accurate than those of nonusers), but that users of illicit drugs tended to estimate the percentage of such users on our campus at twice the figure of the "straight students"—those who used not even alcohol—and who, incidentally, estimated the percentage almost perfectly! Perhaps seeing more usage than there is, is a way to reduce the perceived degree of personal deviance associated with one's behavior. Of course, the exaggerated descriptions of the dangers of such drugs by their opponents (see discussions in Goode, 1970; Kaplan, 1970) and by nonusers (Goldstein *et al.*, 1970, 25–26, 57) are well known.

It is essential that we remember that not all users are in trouble. That is, if one defines "trouble" as life-disturbance, produced by drug use or by a use pattern that leads to such disturbance with a high degree of probability, then most drug use in our society, including the vast majority of illicit use, does not result in such trouble. The tendency of some in the medical and other professions, therefore, to define any illicit use as abuse is not definition based upon effects of use. To be able to help those in trouble and to prevent others from having such experiences, we need to know more about those who do get into difficulties as a result of drug use. The general question for the drug usage motivation researcher is, I submit, "What is the role of usage in the life of the user?"

In investigations of the meaning of drug use from this point of view, it must be recognized that the phenomenon of interest is not static. The meaning of usage differs greatly from culture to culture. For example, Jessor, Young, Young, and Tesi (1970) found that frequency of alcohol use and drunkenness was associated with frustration, dissatisfaction, and feelings of powerlessness in a sample of Boston adolescents of Italian origin, but not in adolescents in southern Italy. They conclude that, for their American, but not for their Italian youth, heavy drinking is seen as an appropriate way to respond to personal frustration—especially that resulting from a failure to achieve one's goals. We obtained clear differences in usage patterns for students from various religious and social class backgrounds attending the same University (Goldstein *et al.*, 1970, 20–24). Data such as these suggest that socialization has considerable influence upon the manner and personal meaning of drug use. Psychological interpretations of use from the user's point of view differ widely with different cultural backgrounds, and thus inferences of the evaluation of drug use by the participants which are based upon the mere existence of use run the risk of frequently being erroneous.

The meaning of usage also changes over time within the same culture and for the same individuals. Ray (in press) indicates that the President's position on illicit drug use in our society has shifted from an emphasis on tough law enforcement in 1968 to one also advocating education and understanding in 1970. Not only governmental and public opinion, but also the characteristics of drug users change with time. The first participants in a deviant behavior are, it is proposed, highly distinguishable from the rest of the populace. We would expect to find that they are less closely tied to traditional mores and are more open to and eager for new experience. Not only do we expect their personality profiles to be distinct from the mass of adherents who follow them in the successful new trend, but we should also expect their patterns of usage to be different.

In our study of drug usage by all students at our university in 1968, we offered respondents 25 different possible reasons for using each of the 17 drugs about which we asked. For marijuana and even for the more exotic drugs, LSD and mescaline, the exotic reasons offered were usually passed by in favor of "curiosity" and "to get high, feel good." One surmises that the first entrants into the unknown utilize elaborate mystical-religious preparatory rituals as socialization vehicles to provide them with positive expectations and confidence to sustain them in their "risky" endeavor. As usage expands and experiences are shared such elaborate preparations may come to be seen as less necessary and shortcuts may be taken; ("Maybe I don't have to read *all* of the *Tibetan Book of the Dead*. . ."). Sometimes early adherents will derogate the cheap "body highs" sought by those who forego the ideological context which they used so faithfully to give meaning to their usage.

These trends toward wider use and more routine definitions of use indicate that the society generally is becoming less "straight" and that illicit drug use is becoming less deviant. As behavior can change attitudes at the individual level, changes in statistical norms produce changes in the moral norms of society. Can a majority behavior be deviant in either the statistical or the moral sense? It can, but those who view it as such are usually to be found outside of the setting in which the behavior predominates. Thus, adult drug use, largely alcohol, tends to be looked upon as less deviant than youthful use of empirically less harmful drugs such as marijuana.

Empirical studies relating personality scales to drug usage are becoming increasingly abundant. The similarity of findings of studies where comparisons can be made is impressive. Thus, several studies utilizing the *California Personality Inventory* (Haagen, 1970; Hogan, Mankin, Conway and

Fox, 1970; Blum, 1969, 236–237; Goldstein, *et al.*, 1970) with virtually the same profile for youthful users of illicit drugs. Further, where comparisons can be made to other instruments, the conceptual relationships obtained seem to be consistent with the CPI results.

A second type of similarity of findings in drug use, personality studies, is only recently being discussed (Brehm and Back, 1968; Goldstein, *et al.*, 1970): patterns of user-nonuser trait differences are very consistent for a wide variety of drugs and types of users. For example, teenage cigarette smokers, college student marijuana users, college student amphetamine users, college student drinkers, and Haight-Ashbury multiple drug users all score lower than nonusers of these drugs on scales assessing satisfaction with self and higher on scales assessing flexibility. Brehm and Back obtained congruent data on the relationship of predilection to use a wide variety of drugs and a personality battery. They suggest that drug usage motivation may be conceptualized as what may be called an approach-avoidance process. Motivation towards drug use loaded heavily on a factor they call Insecurity, and this relationship held across energizers, hallucinogens, opiates, stimulants, tobacco, intoxicants, sedatives, analgesics and tranquilizers. A factor labeled Curiosity related significantly only to willingness to use energizers, hallucinogens and opiates, but not the other substances listed. Such factors were said to indicate "dissatisfaction or feelings of inadequacy" and these, coupled with the absence of restraints against self-administered drug use, predict a willingness to use drugs in general.

Our study dealing with actual usage rather than willingness to use is supportive of the Brehm and Back findings. In agreement with the other studies utilizing the CPI we find among Carnegie-Mellon University freshmen that those with any marijuana experience score: especially high on the *social presence* and *flexibility* scales, and especially low on the *sense of well being*, *responsibility*, *socialization*, *communality* and *achievement via conformity* scales (Table 1). This pattern would seem to represent a configuration com-

Table 1. *CPI*[a] *and AVL Scores of Freshmen Who Have Never Used Amphetamines, Liquor and Marijuana Compared to Scores of Users.*

Scale	Amphetamines				Liquor				Marijuana			
CPI	Never used N = 679	Any use N = 73	t	p	Never used N = 224	Any use N = 528	t	p	Never used N = 601	Any use N = 151	t	P
1. Dominance	49.8	48.6	0.80	n.s.[b]	49.3	49.8	0.39	n.s.	49.7	49.3	0.40	n.s.
2. Capacity for status	50.1	52.5	2.06	.05	49.3	50.7	1.92	n.s.	49.8	52.1	2.66	0.1
3. Sociability	49.2	48.1	0.79	n.s.	47.1	49.9	3.35	.001	49.1	49.0	0.12	n.s.
4. Social presence	52.3	55.4	2.09	.05	48.2	54.5	6.91	.001	51.6	56.8	4.91	.001
5. Self acceptance	56.8	58.8	1.51	n.s.	54.1	58.2	4.94	.001	56.4	59.4	3.14	.01
6. Sense of well-being	41.9	37.3	2.99	.05	43.6	40.6	2.99	.01	42.4	37.9	3.94	.001
7. Responsibility	48.6	42.4	5.54	.001	51.4	46.6	6.65	.001	49.5	42.2	9.05	.001
8. Socialization	51.0	39.6	8.46	.001	54.1	48.1	6.81	.001	52.1	41.2	11.29	.001
9. Self control	43.2	39.9	2.53	.05	46.5	41.3	6.37	.001	43.9	38.9	5.28	.001
10. Tolerance	46.5	45.2	1.04	n.s.	47.9	45.7	2.70	.01	46.8	44.5	2.47	.01
11. Good impression	42.9	42.5	0.36	n.s.	45.1	41.9	4.12	.001	43.2	41.7	1.64	n.s.
12. Communality	49.1	42.2	5.18	.001	49.9	47.9	2.27	.05	49.6	43.7	6.02	.001
13. Achievement via conformity	46.3	38.9	5.90	.001	48.6	44.3	5.35	.001	46.9	40.1	7.51	.001
14. Achievement via independence	54.7	55.2	0.44	n.s.	54.8	54.8	0.07	n.s.	54.7	55.0	0.37	n.s.
15. Intellectual efficiency	48.4	45.3	2.30	.05	49.0	47.7	1.59	n.s.	48.6	46.0	2.58	.05
16. Psychological-mindedness	53.2	54.8	1.28	n.s.	54.0	53.1	1.16	n.s.	52.9	55.0	2.22	.05
17. Flexibility	54.7	61.7	4.95	.001	53.0	56.4	3.63	.001	54.1	60.2	5.82	.001
18. Femininity	55.3	56.7	1.09	n.s.	56.4	55.0	1.67	n.s.	55.4	55.5	0.10	n.s.
AVL												
19. Theoretical	44.3	44.9	0.11	n.s.	45.2	44.6	0.86	n.s.	44.7	44.6	0.18	n.s.
20. Economic	38.6	34.4	3.68	.001	38.0	38.3	0.42	n.s.	39.1	34.7	5.28	.001
21. Aesthetic	41.9	48.9	5.18	.001	41.4	43.0	1.81	n.s.	41.0	48.9	8.14	.001
22. Social	38.3	39.6	1.11	n.s.	38.3	38.5	0.35	n.s.	38.1	40.0	2.26	.05
23. Political	40.5	38.5	2.16	.05	39.1	40.8	3.10	.01	40.7	38.5	3.44	.001
24. Religious	35.6	33.6	1.60	n.s.	37.6	34.5	3.98	.001	35.9	33.4	2.77	.01

[a]CPI means were computed from standard scores not raw scores.
[b]n.s.—not significant.

patible with the approach-plus-lack-of-avoidance motivation position. When the user-nonuser differences are compared for the other two substances, amphetamines and liquor, we again find behavioral support for the attitudinal relationships of Brehm and Back. The scale mean patterns and significance levels of the comparisons are very similar. There seems to be a general predilection to use drugs which has validity across substances. Additional differentiation, not yet fully developed, should be able to predict the particular drugs of preference. Some interesting clinical suggestions of this sort have been made by Weider and Kaplan (1969) using a personal need model. An interesting note from our data in Table 1 concerns the only reversal of direction in the 24 scale means for all three substances: on the power scale of the *AVL* we find that liquor users are more concerned with power issues than nonusers, while the reverse is true for amphetamine and marijuana users.

The approach-avoidance model of drug usage motivation is suggested as an alternative to more elaborate models because it is (a) more parsimonious, and (b) it avoids the pejorative labeling inherent in almost all of these other models. The arguments for parsimony are well-known. The existence of pejorative labeling is not widely recognized. Such labeling exists within both the medical and the behavioral science literature. One psychiatrist with six years of experience of treating narcotics addicts prior to becoming director of a methadone maintenance program in 1969 suggests that the negative labeling is a result of treatment personnel seeing addicts at their worst; he reports that those in methadone maintenance programs probably exhibit no greater incidence psychopathology than the population at large (Ekstrand, 1971). Behavioral scientists, like the populace at large, have been socialized to view illicit drug usage as deviant behavior impelled by pathological motives. This socialization produces a subtle ideological bias: given personality data which indicates differences in user-nonuser personalities there is an enhanced tendency to evaluate the differences as indicative of pathology.

But what of drug *abuse?* Surely that is not to be denied! It is not, but, as suggested earlier, abuse is only meaningful in terms of deleterious effects or of behavior patterns which lead to such effects with a high degree of probability. Labeling any unauthorized use as abuse is merely circular reasoning. Further, it may create difficulties in a variety of ways: a self-fulfilling prophecy may be set up wherein drug users come to view themselves as "outlaws," and disrespect for law in general is engendered. Such labeling by fiat also exacerbates the "Drug Problem problem" as Helen Nowlis has called it (Nowlis, 1969, xii). This refers to all those difficulties created by societal responses to drug usage rather than by drug effects themselves. The cost to society of this problem is not readily calculable but it may exceed the cost of actual drug-induced problems. It includes destroyed trust between users and nonusers, police and legislative actions with unintended consequences, and the vast costs entailed in attempts to arrest, prevent and otherwise discourage certain types of drug use while other types of a more serious nature do not receive the attention they deserve. A discussion of the costs of the marijuana laws which develops this point is made by Kaplan (1970). Resistances to changing the definition of abuse to that of a criterion-dependent state may be due to our reluctance to recognize that many of our "drug problems" are, in part, a product of our drug control policies, and of other general societal deficiencies.

Motivation to begin and to continue and sustain psychoactive drug use can be clarified by using the approach-avoidance model. Following Dollard and Miller's discussion of drug effects (1950, Chap. 23) we should remember that drug use in some cases may be self-administered therapy designed to remove unsatisfying personal states. Many of the favored drugs have the effects of alleviating anxiety; thus, their usage is self-reinforcing. The chemo-therapy works—at least on a short term basis. Unfortunately, such use may provide only temporary relief in the absence of an external therapist to use the state of lowered anxiety to decondition the aversive stimulus situation of its anxiety-provoking properties. Even temporary relief, however may be seen as preferable to no relief. It may be that illicit drug use, while sometimes creating medical and psychological difficulties, may also be serving for some as a deterrent to the onset of personality disorders and more serious self-destructive behavior.

When the plea is made to define abuse in terms of effects it is acknowledged that these effects may be at the societal as well as at the individual level. Thus, if widespread marijuana use led to an overall lowering of national achievement—and it is by no means clear that it would—there would be justification, in my view, for labeling the general behavior pattern as abuse even if the effects upon individuals are not vividly destructive. Here we must recall, however, that changes in our national motivational patterns are seen outside of the arena of illicit drug usage as well as within it. The solution to abuse at the societal level would appear to lie at that level, and not in ignoring general national trends and in focusing blame on individuals.

Despite widespread beliefs to the contrary most illicit drug use does not result in obvious deleterious effects to the student user. Our data indicate, for example, that only 7% of those with use of amphetamines 10 times or more (outside of medically directed use) have had a disturbing or upsetting experience with the drug, and that only 1% of those with at least ten exposures to marijuana, and 4% of the one-time marijuana "tasters" had such experiences with this drug.

Psychoactive drug effects are determined by interactions of the characteristics of the agent, the user and the conditions and setting of usage. The interpretation of these effects, furthermore, is subject to socio-cultural as well as to psychophysiological determinants. Thus we were not surprised to find that novice users reported somewhat greater percentages of negative drug experiences than did the sophisticated users. Among the latter reactions to drug-induced experiences are flavored by more clearly defined expectations and greater objective knowledge about the drugs used.

While drug abuse is but a small part of total illicit drug use, it still is a significant phenomenon both in terms of the absolute numbers of persons involved, the trends towards usage at earlier ages, and the extremity of the reactions in some instances. In order to be able to anticipate which persons are likely potential abusers and to increase the effectiveness of therapeutic interventions with actual abusers additional research is needed. I would like to suggest that a major need is for motivational analyses which empirically differentiate between the person who uses psychoactive substances without harm to himself and the person whose use leads to personality disorder, blocked self actualization or medical problems. Given the extensiveness of psychoactive drug use in our society by both adults (Parry, 1968; Mellinger, Manheimer, and Balter, no date) and youth generally (Berg, 1970) solutions to drug abuse which aim for abstinence seen foredoomed to failure. Psychoactive drug use must be fulfilling substantial significant needs to be so widespread. Furthermore, there are serious, though often unrecognized, constitutional and moral issues lying beneath the surface of any attempts to impose bans on psychoactive drug use *per se* without regard to the consequences of use in a given person. The question of the right to pursue happiness chemically will no doubt stimulate a major debate in the years just ahead.

REFERENCES

Bem, D. J. Self-perception: An alternative interpretation of cognitive dissonance phenomena. *Psychological Review,* 1967, *74,* 183–200.

Berg, D. F. Illicit use of dangerous drugs in the United States: A compilation of studies, surveys, and polls. Unpublished manuscript, Drug Sciences Division, Office of Science and Drug Abuse Prevention, Bureau of Narcotics and Dangerous Drugs, United States Department of Justice, 1970.

Blum, R. H. & Associates. *Drugs II: Students and Drugs,* San Francisco: Jossey-Bass, 1969.

Brehm, M. L., & Back, K. W. Self-image and attitudes towards drugs. *Journal of Personality,* 1968, *36,* 299–314.

Dollard, J. & Miller, N. E. *Personality and psychopathology: An analysis in terms of learning, thinking, and culture.* New York: McGraw-Hill, 1950.

Ekstrand, J. Methadone maintenance of narcotic addicts. Address, Carnegie-Mellon University, April 1971.

Goldstein, J. W., Korn, J. H., Abel, W. H., & Morgan, R. M. The social psychology and epidemiology of student drug usage: Report on Phase One. Department of Psychology Report No. 70–18, June 1970, Carnegie-Mellon University, Project No. MH-15805, National Institute of Mental Health.

Goldstein, J. W. Getting high in high school: The meaning of adolescent drug usage. In W. M. Mathews (Chm.), Students and drugs. Symposium presented at the American Educational Research Association, New York, February 1971.

Goode, E. *The marijuana smokers.* New York: Basic Books, 1970.

Haagen, C. H. Social and psychological characteristics associated with the use of marijuana by college men. Middletown, Connecticut: Office of Psychological Services, Wesleyan University, 1970.

Hogan, R. T., Mankin, D., Conway, J., & Fox, S. Personality correlates of undergraduate marijuana use. *Journal of Consulting and Clinical Psychology,* 1970, *35,* 58–63.

Jessor, R., Young, H. B., Young, E. B., & Tesi, G. Perceived opportunity, alienation, and drinking behavior among Italian and American youth. *Journal of Personality and Social Psychology,* 1970, *15,* 215–222.

Kaplan, J. *Marijuana—The new prohibition.* New York: World, 1970.

Mellinger, G. D., Manheimer, M. A., & Balter, M. B. Patterns of psychotherapeutic drug use among adults in San Francisco. Unpublished manuscript, Family Research Center, Langley Porter Neuropsychiatric Institute, Berkeley, California, no date.

Nowlis, H. H. *Drugs on the College Campus.* Garden City, New York: Anchor Books, 1969.

Parry, H. J. Use of psychotropic drugs by U.S. adults. *Public Health Reports,* 1968, *83,* 799–810.

Ray, O. *An introduction to drugs, behavior and society.* St. Louis: C. V. Mosby Co., in press.

Weider, H., & Kaplan, E. H. Drug use in adolescents: Psychodynamic meaning and pharmacogenic effect. *The Psychoanalytic Study of the Child,* 1969, *24,* 399–431.

Part Six

TREATMENT

Chapter 16

The Psychotherapies

Theories about the meaning of psychotherapy for individuals abound, and all of these theories seem to be anchored in specific notions about the etiology of psychopathology. One such notion is Masserman's idea that anxieties are caused by man's inability to adequately anticipate in and control his environment. Therefore he suggests that psychotherapy is the alleviation of man's uncertainties.

Chris Argyris posits the breakdown of normal human functioning on the basis of a breakdown in interpersonal competence. His explorations lead him to propose various ways for analyzing and scoring interpersonal group behavior with a view toward competence training.

"The Neglected Client," our third paper, by the father and son team Jones and Jones, vividly portrays the black person as a potential psychotherapy client who is almost totally shunted in our society. Not only are blacks not easily understood by their prospective white middle-class counselors, but they are often also excluded from the faculties of universities where much of the teaching of future counselors, psychologists, and psychiatrists takes place.

The last paper, by Donald Kiesler, refutes three myths prevalent in psychotherapy research. In addition, Kiesler suggests several minimal research criteria for future evaluation of psychotherapy effectiveness. Like the critique that appeared in Chapter 12 on the Kinsey Report, Kiesler's paper is a lengthy one. But its inclusion is justified by its importance and comprehensiveness.

Psychotherapy as the Mitigation of Uncertainties

Jules H. Masserman

Whenever man becomes increasingly unsure that he can adequately anticipate and control his physical, social, or metapsychologic milieu, his anxieties mount and may engender deviant patterns of attempted mastery or retreat variously termed neurotic, sociopathic, or psychotic. More comprehensive insights into the Oedipus myths than those offered by Freud reveal that they epitomize not only superficial incest fears, but also more devastating uncertainties as to dependent, survival, and other relationships among parents and offspring, later "identity crises" in all concerned, the hubris *of asymptotic human aspirations after unattainable "truths" and man's ultimate defiance of Fate itself. Animal experiments also demonstrate the devastating effects of stressful unpredictabilities. The clinical relevance of the Uncertainty Principle is that all therapy (Greek*—therapeien, *service) is effective only insofar as it increases the recipient's confidence as to his physical well-being, alleviates his concerns about his interpersonal securities and fosters comforting theophilosophic beliefs.*

Three generations ago Sigmund Freud, in all earnestness, tried to clarify the differential etiology of the neuroses by distinguishing the "actual neuroses," supposedly due to physically debilitating sexual excesses, from "psychoneuroses" presumably caused by recent sexual traumata. When these explanations proved insufficient, he attributed his patients' sexual sensitivities to their having envied parental intercourse in the "primal scene," thereby giving rise to an "Oedipus complex" and the punitive incubus of "fear of castration." When this, too, proved unverifiable, he resorted to the postulate that illusory "screen memories" of the horrendous event could be equally devastating; finally, when the literal aspects of the "libido theory" again proved inadequate, he coupled self-preservation and procreation under the "life instinct *Eros*," as counterposed against inscrutably repetitive-compulsive tendencies (*Thanatos*) toward dissolution and death. It may be of interest to cultural historians to speculate why these simplistic formulations intrigued two generations of intelligentsia—much as, for that matter, Gall's phrenology and Mesmer's "animal magnetism" had done previously.

One factor may be that Freud based his inferences on the ubiquitous fables obligingly tendered him by his resignedly compliant patients, and then correlated these with the Helenic legends of Narcissus, Electra, Oedipus, and others. But since, as Freud frankly proposed to Einstein, *all* science is an evercontingent myth, this is in no sense a pejorative statement. Indeed, I still consider myself a card-carrying psychoanalyst—provided psychoanalysis is redefined in operational terms as (*a*) research into the motivations and vicissitudes of human behavior through an intensive study of verbal and other transactions among patient, analyst, and their joint sociocultural milieu; (*b*) a continuously contingent and modifiable theoretical structure, leading to (*c*) a dynamic approach to the rationale and techniques of therapy. In this sense, I am renegade only in that I am inclined to interpret man's cherished images of himself, individual and cultural, as expressing much deeper wisdoms concerning his doubts and tribulations than those usually associated with their eponyms. For example: Was Narcissus "in love with himself" as Freud would have it, or did he become so exclusively entranced by his autistic reflection that his friend Almeinas and his mistress Echo forsook him? Again, whether or not, as Eugene O'Neill would have it, "mourning became Electra," it certainly became fatal to her mother (Clytemnestra), her mother's lover (Aegisthus), nearly so to her brother (Orestes), and to practically everyone else involved. But perhaps the most comprehensive dramatizations of man's eternal uncertainties are epitomized in Sophocles' trilogy on Oedipus—a succession of existential tragicomedies which, far beyond connoting merely a middle-class Viennese son's supposed desire for coitus with his mother countered by freudian fear of his father's terrible swift sword, deals much more deeply with nearly all human travail and triumph from childhood survival to the ultimate denial of death. Let us review the content of these poignant parables, the significance of which is much more meaningfully "complex" than implied by Ferenczi's constricted use of that term:

From *Archives of General Psychiatry*, 1972, 25.

Laius, King of Thebes, is warned by an oracle that his son would slay him—as all children predictably displace their elders. Torn between doubt and fear, Laius avoids the onus of direct infanticide by pinning together the ankles of the newborn Oedipus ("swollen feet") and leaving him in a basket—there being no Mosaic bulrushes about—on Mount Cithaeron. However, Oedipus is found by a kindly shepherd and adopted by Polybus, King of Corinth—as indeed our own rejected children are partially rescued by babysitters, nursery school teachers, pedagogues and other parental surrogates. But Oedipus is never sure that he "really is" the true Prince of Corinth, cannot get satisfactory assurances from King Polybus or Queen Merope (for that matter, who *can* be absolutely certain of his paternity?) and is further perplexed when he learns at Delphi that he is indeed destined to slay his father and marry his mother. Trying to escape his fate (as who does not?) he vows never to see Polybus or Merope again, and leaves Corinth to wander in search of what Erik Erikson would call his "true identity." At a crossroads outside Thebes an old man blocks his right-of-way and is killed in the ensuing contest—again, as all oldsters who dare too long to challenge imperious youth will be disposed of in their turn. To display his intellectual as well as physical mastery, Oedipus then also conquers a Sphinx whose "riddle" (the old nursery puzzle about the quadri-, bi-, and tripedal locomotion of man from crawl to cane) he easily solves, and thereby emancipates the Thebans from years of sphincteric terror. For reward he is given the vacant throne of Thebes and marries the widowed Queen Jocasta. And yet, nagging doubts remain (who is free of them?) and Oedipus, after years of restless research, learns from the seer Tiresias who rescued him the awful truth that he had indeed killed his father and cohabited incestuously with his mother—"awful," of course, only because he fears that others regard it so. He blinds (not castrates) himself in expiation (and thereby becomes a pathetic rather than reprehensible figure), curses his own unwanted sons, Eteocles and Polynices, and then preempts the services of his daughters, Antigone and Ismene, in his further wanderings throughout Hellas—as many aging parents have done on the model of Agamemnon who sacrificed Iphigenia with the plea that this was the least she could do for him. Finally, at the grove of Colonus outside Athens, Oedipus defies the Fates and himself becomes a demi-god—thus acquiring the archangelic status we all believe we deserve.

There are, of course, many variations of these myths, not only in Greek but in Hungarian, Rumanian, Finnish, and even Lapland folklore. For example, Homer has Jocasta commit suicide, after which a more rational Oedipus completes his reign in relative peace. But whatever the versions, the legends are never naively monothetic; instead, they portray almost every nuance of the imperative, ceaseless seekings for order and certainty that imbue the human condition—and the temporary triumphs, tantalizing traumata, and terminal tragedies that would be unbearably terrorizing unless, however, covertly, man can believe himself to be superhuman.

Since the "Oedipus complex" is thus all-inclusive, the "libidinous drives" of the "pre-oedipal phases" also lose their supposed specificity, *except in the sense that all human longings and transactions remain charged* ("cathected" in analytic patois) *with uncertainty.* Thus "anal aggression" may meet with counterreactive hostility, "oral dependencies" are always precarious, and even "primal narcissism" itself, despite wishful philosophies or theologies to the contrary, is ever on the brink of existential obliteration. In essence, then, no one is ever quite sure of his continued health, or of the reliability of his friends or, for that matter, the verity of his beliefs—and the intensities of his anxieties are in direct proportion to unpredictabilities in any or all of these spheres.

EXPERIMENTAL INVESTIGATIONS OF THE ROLE OF UNCERTAINTY IN NEUROTOGENESIS

Methods of induction.—As first proposed by Pavlov and Shenger-Krestovnikova, persistent deviations of behavior can be induced by stressing any higher animal between incompatible attractions and aversions. In our own research 1-3 we have more recently concentrated on the central factor of uncertainty as the principal source of stress; for instance, subjecting a cat to an *unpredictable* electric shock during conditioned feeding, or requiring a monkey to secure food from a box in which, on several occasions, he had *unexpectedly* been confronted with a toy snake—an object as representationally dangerous to the monkey as a live one, harmless or not, would be. Nevertheless, counter to early freudian and current wolpean doctrines of neurotigenesis, neither actual or anticipated fear of injury need be involved at all, in that later experiments demonstrated that equally serious and lasting neurotigenic effects could be induced by facing the animal with difficult choices among mutually exclusive satisfactions—situations that parallel the disruptive effects of prolonged indecisions among equally attractive alternatives in human affairs. More recently, my associates and I have also employed inconstantly delayed auditory feedback of the animal's own vocalizations as another method of rendering its physical milieu unpredictable and thereby anxiety-provoking and neurotigenic. Finally, we have used experimental techniques that even more specifically demonstrate the devastating effects of sequential or temporal uncertainty; for example, if a monkey is taught to await a series of sensory cues in a given order before depressing a lever to secure food or avoid shock, and then subjected to bewildering variations in the required sequence and timing of the cues and lever-press, it becomes highly disturbed, refuses to feed or escape, attacks the apparatus and develops other striking aberrations of behavior as described below; however these adverse reactions are prevented or minimized if the experimental animal is permitted to profit by the guiding example of a monkey-like automaton ("pedagog," "therapist") in an adjoining compartment programmed to respond to the signals and lever in proper order and time. Conversely, if insufficiently mitigated to remain within the animal's adaptive capacities, all modalities of producing stringent uncertainty induced physiologic and mimetic manifestations of anxiety, spreading inhibitions, generalizing phobias, stereotyped rituals, "psychosomatic" dysfunctions, impaired social interaction, addiction to alcohol and other drugs, regressions to immature patterns of behavior, and other marked and persistent deviations of conduct.[4]

Human correlates and distinctions.—Admittedly, since man's perceptive, mnemonic, symbolic, and adaptive capacities are undeniably much (though not by necessity "infinitely" or "by quantum jumps") more complex than those of any other animal, it is obvious that ethologic or experimental studies alone cannot furnish data that completely "explain" human conduct. Comparatively speaking, man seems to differ from all other animals in having developed three ultimate (*Ur-*) assumptions, which are essential to motivations and transactions, but which are also vulnerable to frustrations leading to devastating doubts and uncertainties. We may review these axioms, beliefs, aspirations, categorical imperatives—no term quite expresses their ubiquitous dynamics—in briefest form, as follows:

First, an urgent seeking for the knowledge and technology with which to control the material universe and, hopefully, conquer disease and death.

Second, a persistent need for human relationships that, despite debacles of distrust, have led from the primal mother-child dyad through loyalties to the family, clan, tribe, state and nation, to a growing imperative toward universal brotherhood.

And finally, an existential faith that man's being has an enduring dignity and significance in some transcendental teleologic or eschatologic system that links the mundane with eternity. In this sense, we may have misread Michelangelo's masterpiece "The Creation of Adam" in the Sistine Chapel: also implicit in its title, Adam may be reaching up and creating God in his own wishfully omnipotent image.

Parenthetically, it is of historic-semantic relevance that the term *sanatos* implied to the ancients the indissolubility of physical and mental functions (*mens sana in corpore sano*) and that the very word "health" can be traced to the Anglo-Saxon root *hàl* or *hol*, from which are derived not only physical *haleness* and *healing*, but the greeting, "Hail, friend!" and the concepts of *wholeness* and *holiness*. Ergo, once again Greek, Roman, and Gaul have bequeathed to us, in the rich heritage of our syncretic language in which wish and "reality" merge, their penetrating recognition of the indissoluble physical, social, and philosophic components of comprehensive therapy.

APPLICATIONS TO CLINICAL THERAPY

Here enters a disconcerting thought that, despite Heraclitus' doctrine that no man can step into the same river twice, perhaps all I have said has merely been a reiteration of ancient wisdoms. We have always implicitly known that, although no sane human can ever be completely certain of his health, friends or philosophy, *adequate modicums* of security in each of these spheres are essential to his welfare; consequently, all methods of medicopsychologic therapy have been effective only insofar as they restored a sense of physical well-being, fostered more amicable interpersonal relationships, and helped parochial man amend his beliefs so as to render them more locally acceptable and useful—all without stultifying his individuality, infringing on his essential freedom, or stereotyping his intellect, imagery, and creativity.

REFERENCES

1. Masserman, J. H.: *The Practice of Dynamic Psychiatry.* Philadelphia, W. B. Saunders Co., 1955.
2. Masserman, J. H.: *The Biodynamic Roots of Behavior.* Springfield, Ill., Charles C Thomas Publishers, 1968.
3. Masserman, J. H.: *A Psychiatric Odyssey.* New York, Science House, 1971.
4. Masserman, J. H., et al: Films on experimental neuroses and therapy. University Park, Pa, Psychological Cinema Register, Pennsylvania State University.

Explorations in Interpersonal Competence–I

Chris Argyris

A set of categories is presented designed to measure interpersonal competence.

The primary plus categories on the individual and interpersonal levels are owning up to, openness, and risk taking. On the norms level they are individuality, concern, and trust.

The primary minus categories on the individual and interpersonal levels are not owning up to, not being open, and rejecting risk taking. On the norms level, they are conformity, antagonism, and mistrust.

Exploratory research suggests that the categories can be used (1) with an encouraging degree of reliability, (2) with an encouraging degree of predictive validity, and (3) as the basis to describe increases or decreases in individual and group competence during T-Group and other training.

Recently, especially with White's work,[1] there is an increasing realization that interpersonal competence is a central concept in understanding human behavior. In this paper, I should like to outline a theoretical framework that has been developed whose categories may be useful in studying the nature of interpersonal competence. Also, I will describe some empirical research, using T Groups, to explore the predictive validity of the framework.

In a careful series of studies, White has suggested that interpersonal competence may be a basic need of man. He defines competence to mean "capacity, fitness, or ability." The competence of a living organism means its fitness or ability to carry on those transactions with the environment which result in its maintaining itself, growing, and flourishing.[2] The extent to which individuals produce the intended effect is the measure of competence.[3]

In my view, the extent to which one produces an intended effect may not be an adequate measure of competence. Individuals may accomplish specific intended effects in such a way (1) as not to solve the problem permanently or (2) to solve it but decrease the probabilities of the individual's solving it again. Therefore, I should like to use three measures of interpersonal competence. They may be stated as follows:

Human competence tends to increase

1. as one's awareness of relevant factors increases (relevant factors are those that have effect),
2. as the problems are solved in such a way that they remain solved,
3. with a minimal deterioration of the problem-solving process.

Using this conception of competence as my guide, I began to develop the categories that seemed necessary (but not necessarily sufficient) to observe and understand this phenomenon.

It seemed to me that if these three criteria are to be met the individual will have to strive to verbalize his awareness of factors; to be able to *own up* to them; to accept responsibility for them. In addition, he will have to strive to be *open* constantly to new factors. Sometimes the openness will have to go beyond the limits of his present capacity to be receptive. The individual will need to *experiment* or take risks with his self-esteem in order to enlarge his awareness of the relevant factors.

The work has been supported by an NIMH grant (No. 92-31-43-5401). The author gratefully acknowledges the help of Fred Steele, Clayton Alderfer, Lee Bolman, Martin Evans, and Roger Simon. This is the first of two related articles.

[1] White, R. W. Motivation reconsidered: The concept of competence. *Psychol. Rev.*, 1959, **66**, 297–333.
[2] White, R. W. Sense of interpersonal competence. In R. W. White (Ed.), *The Study of Lives*. New York: Atherton Press, 1963. Pp. 72–93.
[3] *Ibid.*, p. 73.

THE SYSTEM OF CATEGORIES[4]

It was considerations such as these that led me to develop the categories presented in Table 1. Before they are defined, a few introductory comments seem appropriate. All the categories above the zero point are hypothesized to add to and facilitate interpersonal competence.[5] They are therefore called "plus" categories. All the categories below the zero point are hypothesized to detract from and inhibit interpersonal competence. They are therefore called "minus" categories.

The position of the category is inferred from a theoretical framework. On the minus side, the further away the category is from the zero line, the greater the degree of defensiveness involved in manifesting the behavior. On the plus side, the further away the category is from the base line, the greater the degree of difficulty in performance.

All behavior is assumed to have emotional or feeling components (f) as well as ideational (i) components. All feeling (f) behavior includes ideational (i) components, but not all ideational behavior includes feeling components. (This arbitrary division is temporary and may be helpful in beginning to understand the relationships between feelings and ideas.)

Behavior is categorized at two levels: Level I, referring to individual and interpersonal aspects; and Level II, referring to the cultural aspects of behavior which may be designated as *norms*. The categories used at each level are defined as follows:

Level I

A. Individual behavior

Owning up to (i or *f)*—That behavior which indicates being aware of and accepting responsibility for, the behavior that is manifested. The individual is able to identify his behavior, communicate it, and accept ownership of it.

Not owning up to (i or *f)*—That behavior which indicates being unable to be aware of, identify, and own up to one's actions.

Openness (i or *f)*—That behavior which enlarges the individual's scope or pushes back his boundaries of awareness and responsibility. The individual permits and encourages the reception of new information.

Not open (i or *f)*—That behavior which constricts the individual's boundaries of awareness and responsibility. The individual discourages the reception of new information.

Experimenting (i or *f)*—That behavior which represents some risk for the individual. The purpose of the risk taking is to generate new information on the i or f level. The individual may be observed manipulating his internal or external environment in order to create new

[4] Because of space limitations all the relevant theoretical and methodological issues cannot be discussed here. Those interested please see my *Explorations in Interpersonal Competence*. Unpublished manuscript, Yale University, 1964.
[5] Although present research focuses on interpersonal competence, the categories are believed to be relevant to technical or intellectual competence.

Table 1. *Categories of Behavior Related to Organizational Effectiveness.*

	Level I					Level II				
	Individual	Weight		Interpersonal	Weight		Norms	Weight		Outputs
Plus	Experimenting	i 4	f 16	Help others to experiment	i 7	f 16	Trust	i 4	f 16	Increased effectiveness (↑ Performance difficulty)
	Openness	i 2	f 10	Help others to be open	i 6	f 10	Concern	i 1	f 10	
	Owning	i 1	f 9	Help others to own	i 5	f 9	Individuality	i 2	f 8	
Zero										
Minus	Not owning	i −8	f −14	Not help others to own	i −3	f −5	Conformity	i −2	f −8	Decreased effectiveness (↓ Defensiveness)
	Not open	i −9	f −15	Not help others to be open	i −3	f −6	Antagonism	i −4	f −12	
	Rejecting experimenting	i −14	f −16	Not help others to experiment	i −4	f −7	Mistrust	i −6	f −16	

information. The risk is evaluated in terms of the probability that such explorations could upset the individual's self-esteem.

Rejecting experimenting (i or *f)*—That behavior which prevents the individual from taking risks.

B. Interpersonal behavior. The next six categories are the same as those above except that they focus on the behavior that helps or does not help others to do the behaviors described above.

Helping others to own up (i or *f)*
Not helping others to own up (i or *f)*
Helping others to be open (i or *f)*
Not helping others to be open (i or *f)*
Helping others to experiment (i or *f)*
Not helping others to experiment (i or *f)*

Level II: Norms

Sociological and anthropological theory suggest that the cultural aspects of behavior must be understood if a more complete picture of human behavior is to be developed. We believe that this is the case in the study of competence. The second or *norms* level is designated to categorize aspects of the cultural factors.

Norms may be thought of as developing from those interactions among the participants that have proved useful (to the participants) in maintaining the system. Norms may be defined as "coercive mechanisms" created by the individuals to sanction behavior which will be functional for the system. They act to enhance or inhibit competence. Norms arise in a group in the way that streets may arise in a community. Individuals desire to create some order in their transportation, so they create streets for cars. Once the streets are created they act to coerce people to drive on them. Norms therefore are commonly perceived and sanctioned patterns of behavior that act to influence the behavior of those individuals who desire to remain in or are coerced to become part of the system, be it a relationship between two people, a group, or an organization.

The definitions of the norm categories of behavior include three plus and three minus categories:

Individuality (i or *f)*—That behavior which acts to induce individuals to express their ideas or feelings. The norm acts to influence the members to protect and develop the uniqueness of the individual in a group or organization.

Conformity (i or *f)*—That behavior which acts to inhibit individuals from expressing their ideas or feelings. The norm acts to influence the members to help suppress the uniqueness of the individual in a group or organization.

Concern (i or *f)*—That behavior which acts to induce people to be concerned about others' ideas and feelings. The norm acts to influence the members to help protect and develop the uniqueness of others' ideas and feelings in a group or organization.

Antagonism (i or *f)*—That behavior which acts to induce people to reduce their concern about their own and others' ideas and feelings.

Trust (i or *f)*—That behavior which induces members to take risks, to experiment, on the idea and feeling levels.

Mistrust (i or *f)*—That behavior which restricts and inhibits members from taking risks and experimenting.

IMBALANCE

Trust is a highly complex variable which we hope to make more clear as we proceed. At this point, let us assume that trust tends to arise in a relationship when A senses that B is concerned enough about A and about their relationship to permit A to take a risk with his self-esteem.

Early in the exploratory studies we came upon behavior that had to be scored both as plus and minus. For example, individual A would say to B, "I believe in people having their say, but in this case x is true. You're wrong and you'd better change your mind if you wish to succeed here." This bit of behavior would be scored *own i* (A is owning up to his beliefs) and *conform i* (inducing B to conform to them). If B is to believe the plus-minus character of the behavior, it would communicate to him contradictory messages. A believes in individuality, yet he creates conditions of conformity for B.

Following "imbalance theories," this behavior was labeled *imbalance* (creating) behavior.[6] Brown concludes that . . . "human nature abhors imbalance. . . . A situation of imbalance is one that calls for mutually incompatible actions. . . . Imbalance in the mind threatens to paralyze actions."[7] This is our assumption about the impact of imbalance behavior upon competence striving. Plus-minus behavior creates imbalance because it communicates contradictory messages to the receiver.

Although space prohibits me from going into detail, I should like to point out that imbalance scores may be valid indicators of the changeability of an individual or group. I suggest that the unfreezing process will tend to be more difficult when the individual has high imbalance scores. The logic, in *summary*, is as follows. If man abhors experiencing imbalance behavior, then imbalance behavior may be caused by defensiveness in that person. The defenses may be personality or situationally related. Moreover, if man abhors behaving in an imbalanced manner, then those who do so must have a set of defenses that inhibit them from being aware of their own behavior. In short, the imbalance behavior may indicate that an individual has, at least, two sets of related defenses: one that "causes" the imbalance behavior; and one that inhibits the sendor from realizing that his behavior communicates contradictory messages.

Examples of imbalance scores include those combinations of Level I and Level II scores which are opposite in sign. For example, plus scores for *individual or interpersonal behavior* combined with minus scores for behavior related to *norms* would be imbalanced. This would hold if the score were for either the *i* (ideational) or *f* (feeling) category. Imbalance behavior may also exist if Level I is *i* and Level II is *f*, but not vice versa; since all *f's* include *i.* The exact nature of this latter imbalance is not clear, but is presently being explored.

[6] We are thinking of the work of Fritz Heider, Osgood and Tannenbaum, Festinger, Abelson, and Rosenberg. Our reading is presently limited to the work of Fritz Heider and the excellent summary and critical article by Roger Brown: Models of attitude change. In R. Brown *et al* (Eds.), *New Directions in Psychology*. New York: Holt, Rinehart, & Winston, 1962. Pp. 1–85.

[7] *Ibid.*, Pp. 77 and 78.

DEVELOPING INTERPERSONAL COMPETENCE SCORES

It is thought that different types of behavior contribute unequally to interpersonal competence or incompetence. A potency score was therefore developed for each category. The weight was somewhat arbitrary but was guided by the ranking of the different categories according to the degree of defensiveness or of difficulty in performance that we felt to be associated with that behavior (see weight columns in Table 1).

THE WAY THE CATEGORIES ARE USED TO OBSERVE BEHAVIOR

All behavior is coded for both Levels I and II. The observer's frame of reference in scoring the behavior may be as he perceives it described by these two sets of questions:

Level I—How is A functioning? Is he owning up to his ideas, experimenting, not helping others, and so on? What is A's behavior doing to the system? (A could be, in the eyes of the observer, "not helping others" in his behavior toward B; while B actually experiences the same behavior as helpful. This discrepancy will not be corrected unless the observer is able to show other data to support his view.)

Level II—What impact would behavior observed have on the creation of group norms? The observer also focuses on the impact of the individual's behavior upon the norms of the group. In making this decision he has some help from experience. There are certain norms that tend to be correlated with specific types of behavior. For example:

Helping others to own frequently leads to a norm of *concern* because helping others is showing concern for others.

Experimenting with one's feelings and ideas frequently leads to *trust* because experimentation includes taking risks, and this is the major criterion of trust.

Openness *could* lead to *concern*, if one is open to understanding others; to *individuality*, if he is focusing on his self.

Not helping others to own leads to conformity because it attempts to require them to behave as the actor desires.

Other guideposts that have been developed to help in scoring behavior are:

1. Any interruption is always scored as a *not helping others—(i* or *f)* followed by the scoring of the content of what the interruptor said.
2. If two or more people interrupt the behavior it is scored as the *group not helping others—(i* or *f).*
3. Whenever in doubt, the observer is told to select the category with the least potency so that the scores tend to be on the conservative side.
4. Any helping score is socred in terms of the category of the statement of the person being helped.
5. All questions receive an open score on Level I.
6. Every statement that includes the phrase, "I feel," is scored as an *f* score except when previous observation indicates that the individual is an intellectualizer who says "I feel" for "I think." Intellectualizers are identified by low feeling scores and/or by "not owning" feelings.

In the majority of the studies, tape recordings were made of all sessions. The observers scored behavior from the tapes, following these instructions:

1. Turn on the tape recorder and let it run for a specified period of time. (The time period varied with each project.)
2. Begin with the first full contribution. Score that statement as the first unit. Do not add another unit unless that person's behavior is no longer represented by the category just noted or a new person speaks. Score a unit any time a different person speaks or any time an individual's contribution changes from behavior representing one category to another.
3. Continue the scoring for a specified amount of time in accordance with the suggested sampling procedure. (This was varied with the research programs.)

INTER-OBSERVER RELIABILITY STUDIES

Three individuals (the writer and two graduate students) participated in the initial inter-observer reliability studies.[8] Eleven studies in T Groups, probelm-solving groups, executive decision-making groups, and case study groups were used. The total number of behavior units scored was 4,958. In these initial studies, in order to maximize learning, each observer scored several units separately and then comparisons were made. Disagreements were noted and then a discussion was held until agreement was reached. In five cases no agreement was possible. Under this procedure the minimum percentage agreement between any two observers *before* any discussion took place was 86 percent.

With this procedure, all one can state is that when two observers score behavior and they have periodic opportunity to compare notes, there is relatively high inter-observer reliability. Several studies were also conducted to ascertain the inter-observer reliability when all the behavior is scored by each observer and comparisons are made without periodic comparisons, thereby canceling the opportunity for mutual learning. The results were as follows:

The first study was conducted with one observer who had not scored tapes for nearly a year. He spent about ten minutes practice-scoring a tape and then began. The percentage agreement was 70 percent. There was an 18 percent disagreement on identification of units. In 12 percent of the cases the observers had missed units.

A second study was then conducted of 218 units. The percentage agreement rose to 80 percent. There was a 14 percent disagreement on identification of units. Each observer missed some units. The total for these was six percent.

No studies were made of the degree of agreement in the definition of a unit because the overwhelming majority of the units (about 90 percent) were of the type that were identified simply by a different individual speaking. However, such studies are necessary if the utility of the framework is to be ascertained.

[8] For details (including an item analysis), see reference in Footnote 5. The graduate students were Fritz Steele and Clayton Alderfer. The writer acknowledges their help given to, and patience with, the writer as well as their skill in observing groups.

THE PROCEDURE FOR ANALYZING AND SCORING INDIVIDUAL AND GROUP BEHAVIOR

After each meeting, a prearranged sample of the verbal behavior was taken from the tape recording of the session. With few exceptions the sample size remained constant for each session. Usually it was about 200 units both on the individual-interpersonal level and on the norms level.

Summary sheets were developed for each individual and the group. All categories, with appropriate idea or feeling designation, were listed; and the frequency of behavior in each category was tabulated. The frequency of behavior in a particular category was then multiplied by the appropriate weight for the category. Thus each category received a weighted score. These scores were then combined into four main scores: Level I (individual-interpersonal)—plus, Level I—minus, Level II (norms)—plus, Level II—minus.

In order to develop an *index* of competence it seemed useful to let the limit be ± 1.0. Consequently, each of the four weighted scores was divided by the highest possible (or lowest possible) scores. In each case, the highest weight was 16, and each basepoint was developed by multiplying 16 times the total number of units of behavior.

Indices developed in this manner seemed adequately to reflect, in studies to be described below, expert observer qualitative evaluations about member effectiveness in cases in which amount and quality of exposure of behavior were low, amount and quality of exposure were high, and when exposure was high and quality low. But when exposure was low and quality high, the scores suggested more growth than seemed empirically justifiable. Consequently, it seemed necessary to adjust such scores.

In addition to the empirical reason, there was another reason for developing an "adjusted" score. An individual who did not tend to say much in the group was minimizing his opportunity for learning. A silent person may enhance his scope of awareness but, from our view, he should find it difficult to translate these new awarenesses into behavior. If he could not translate them, then the others in the world around him (group members, staff, observers, and so on) would not tend to perceive him as increasing his competence.

If the individual did not expose his behavior, he was assumed to have reduced his potential for learning; although he could still learn by watching the exposure of others. How much an individual could learn depended, in part, on the behavior of others. (In part, it also depended on his ability to see what others do.) To take these views into consideration for developing quantitative scores, it was decided to weight an individual's score by the proportion that a particular behavioral unit appeared in the total group sample if the number of behavioral units for an individual was less than the average number of behavioral units per subject (excluding trainer interventions).

To illustrate the scoring procedure, one individual's score was arrived at in this way: Eight units of behavior under Level I categories and eight under Level II were observed (in this case, more than the average number of six units observed per member so that no adjustment of scores was required). Weighting these units (see Table I) yielded scores of 15 and −11 under Level I and of 3 and −22 under Level

II. The base point in this case was 128 (the maximum weight of 16 times the eight units of behavior observed). The individual's scores, computed by dividing this number into each of the four weighted scores, are .12 and −.09 for Level I categories and .02 and −17 for Level II categories.

Group competence scores were developed by summing all the scores in each behavioral category. The same four major indices, appropriate for individuals, were developed for the group (Level I plus and minus and Level II plus and minus). Similar procedures for computing the four scores were then used. Scores may be computed for units of behavior with and without staff comments.

SOME EMPIRICAL RESEARCH[9]

Describing and Predicting Individual-Interpersonal Competence

Our model suggests that the higher the plus scores, the greater the individual interpersonal competence (on the individual-interpersonal and norms levels). In order to explore this hypothesis, several studies were conducted with T Groups which have as an objective the increase of individuals' interpersonal competence.

The members of two T Groups in one executive laboratory and two T Groups in two other executive laboratories were used as subjects ($n = 51$). Their behavior was scored, and for each individual total plus and minus scores were developed. By subtracting the minuses from the pluses, an over-all competence score was developed for each member. Each individual was ranked relative to all other individuals in his T Group. These scores and rankings were not divulged to the staff or to the executives.

The rankings were divided into thirds. The top third represented the "high" interpersonally competent members. The next third were "moderate," and the next third were the "low" interpersonally competent members.

The two staff members and the observer, where possible, in each T Group were asked, at the end of the program, to rank each individual in their group in terms of the three categories. They were asked to do this independently of one another. Naturally, they were not told about the rankings that had been developed from the quantitative scores. In all cases except one, the staff were not familiar with the categorical scheme. In the one case where the staff member (the writer) was fully acquainted with the schemes, his judgments did not seem to be any more accurate than the others.

In the four groups studied, the ranking given each individual member on the basis of the quantitative scores was compared with the ranking given him by the two staff members as well as by the observer. The degree of agreement in all cases is statistically significant (beyond the .05 level). For example, in two groups evaluation in high, moderate, and low categories by observers and staff was in agreement with quantitative scores in 11 out of 15 cases. The range of quantitative scores is from 0 to 323.

[9] In this paper I will focus only on that research related to the laboratory method. Much research has been conducted with problem-solving and decision-making groups which will be described in the final report.

Interesting data was also obtained a day after the program was completed when the executives in Groups I and II of one laboratory were asked to evaluate their experience. They could, if they wished, sign their comments. Of the executives who turned in some comments, 10 in Group I and 11 in Group II were signed. The comments were read by a professional social scientist—one who was associated neither with the program nor with the research. He was asked to rank the comments into three categories, namely, very much pleased, moderately pleased, and displeased with the educational experience. These evaluations were correlated with our quantitative scores. Of the 21 for whom comparisons were possible, there was total agreement between the scores and reported satisfaction for 17. The data thus suggest that the men's perceived degree of learning and satisfaction with the laboratory experience correlated highly with the quantitative scores.

These results, although encouraging, are by no means conclusive. It could be, for example, that judgments are somehow distorted and that the distortion is in the same direction as the one that may exist in the scheme of categories. Research is also necessary to ascertain how well an observer could rate the individuals without having the benefit of the categories. It may well be that, for prediction purposes, our categories are not much more effective than an educated guess.

Describing individual growth. The next step was to attempt to develop, on the basis of the competence scores for each session, the individual's "growth curve" during the total number of sessions.

These curves must be interpreted with caution. First, there are no norms available from which to define, in precise terms, the meaning of "high," "moderate," and "low" competence. Up to this time all we have done is arbitrarily divide any given group of subjects into three sub-groups. Thus, since no norms exist, an individual who may be "high" in one group could be "moderate" or "low" in another group.

This points up another characteristic of these categories that must be kept in mind. All the evaluations of individual competence are related to the particular group in which the individual was a member. An individual's competence is highly influenced by the growth of this group. If his group learns much, then the probability that he can earn higher scores increases. The opposite is the case when an individual is in a group that has not learned very much.

Conversely, the group's growth is partially influenced by the growth of the individuals. But, the influence the individuals have upon the group is not simply the summation of their learning. There is a process of interaction which makes the group learning more than a sum of the individual learning curves. For us to hold such a position may seem odd, since our group curves are constructed by summing all the individual contributions. This apparent contradiction can be explained if we recall the two aspects of our scoring procedure. The "norm" categories are designed to "capture" the interaction effect of the interpersonal relationships. The pattern of norms that each group develops is unique to that group. The second factor is the interdependence of the individual and interpersonal categories. If many members are owning ideas (but not feelings), a norm of *individuality i* may become established which then (we hypothesize) sets to influence the individual's behavior toward more *owning i* and less *owning f*, or *openness i* or *f*, or *experimenting i* or *f*. Although we have group scores that are summations of individual contributions, these individual contributions are highly influenced by the individual contributions of others (as well as by the norms).

All our curves (so far) are limited to groups that have met for only a week or, at the most, two weeks. Time, therefore, is another crucial factor that must be taken into account.

Finally, none of our groups is preselected according to personality patterns of members. Schutz has shown, for example, that if individuals of a particular personality predominate in a group they can significantly influence the dynamics within the group.

Let us now turn briefly to Figure 1. The objective is to suggest that the scores might be capable of describing individual differences in learning in T Groups.

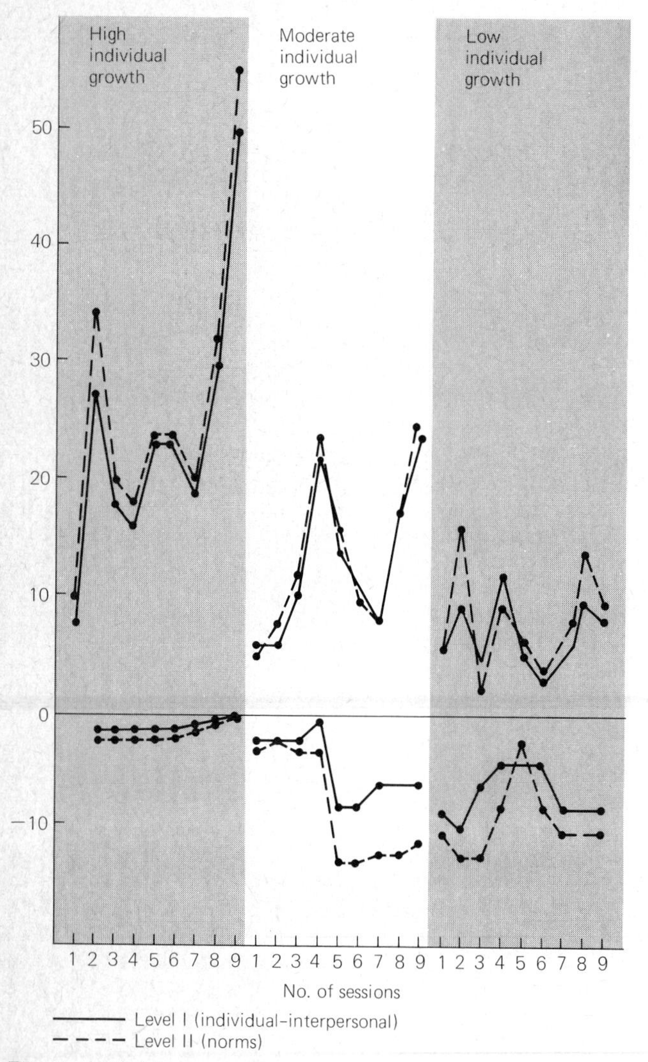

Fig. 1. Individual growth curves.

The first case represents the best individual curves that have been obtained to date (which also came from the best group we have measured). The second and third are moderate and low competence members from the *same* group. Individual curves exist from other groups whose "highest" learner is close to the bottom end of the "moderate" learners in this group.

The first aspect of interest is that all three sets of curves are not smooth, constantly increasing curves. All the individuals had periods of learning followed by periods of little or low learning. The moderate and low learners, however, had significantly higher negative scores than the high learner. Thus, although they seemed to be able to increase somewhat (and cyclically) their plus behavior, they were unable to correct their defensive behavior. The low learner had much more difficulty in this than did the moderate learner.

Although the moderate learner seemed to have corrected his defensive (minus) behavior somewhat, he did not reduce it so much as he increased his plus behavior. If this trend were to continue (i.e., the plus scores go higher but the minus remain constant or increase), he may turn out to be an example of an individual who is either "in transition" or a person who "got religion." If he is in transition, it would mean that he has learned how to increase the plus aspects of his behavior and may eventually learn to decrease the minus aspects.

An examination of the categories shows that high learners tended to have more scores, both *i* and *f*, in terms of *openness, helping others to own, to be open*, and *experimenting* than moderate or low learners. The minus scores of the high learners were very small. If they decreased in competence, it tended to be in terms of decreases in their plus scores rather than an increase in their minus scores. Perhaps they had control over their defenses so that when they began to operate ineffectively they tended to withdraw or ask for help rather than become more defensive.

The moderate learners tended to differ from the high learners in that they had lower *openness* scores, and only a few of them were related to *feelings*. Moreover, they had significantly lower *helping others* scores. It is as if they were spending most of their time worrying about their own difficulties in interpersonal competence. The moderate learners tended to have almost no *experiment* scores.

Not all moderate learners had as low minus scores as the one depicted. But where the minus scores were low, the plus scores were also low. This suggests that if a moderate learner's defenses are low his capacity to contribute to his own and others' growth may also be low. Although no systematic data are available, we would like to suggest another difference between high, moderate, and low learners. The high learners seem to have the capacity to *make* the T-Group experience a learning experience. They seem to *give to*, to *invest the group with* learning potential.[10] The moderate learner, on the other hand, is capable of

[10] I believe this finding jibes with Abraham Maslow's findings of the self-actualizors. In his terms, the high learners are able to develop "peak experiences" in a T Group.

learning, if the group culture is capable of helping him to learn. He will "take from" the environment to learn, but he does not seem to be capable of "giving to" the environment. The low learner seems unable to "take from" or to "give to" the environment.

Describing and Predicting Group Interpersonal Competence

The next step was to test the validity of the hypothesis that the higher the plus scores, the greater the group competence. Again the studies were made in two T Groups.

In Group I (Figure 2) we have a figure of the best group that we have studied to date. The curves represent the group's scores without the trainer.

The group began well, ran into difficulty, and was then able to overcome the difficulty so that it seemed to continue to increase its competence over time. (The phenomenon, "things must get worse before they get better," may be derived from the theory as being necessary for all groups that begin with relatively low competence.) The individual-interpersonal and group "plus" curves continued to go up and in about the same relationship to each other. The norm scores may be slightly higher, partially because it might be

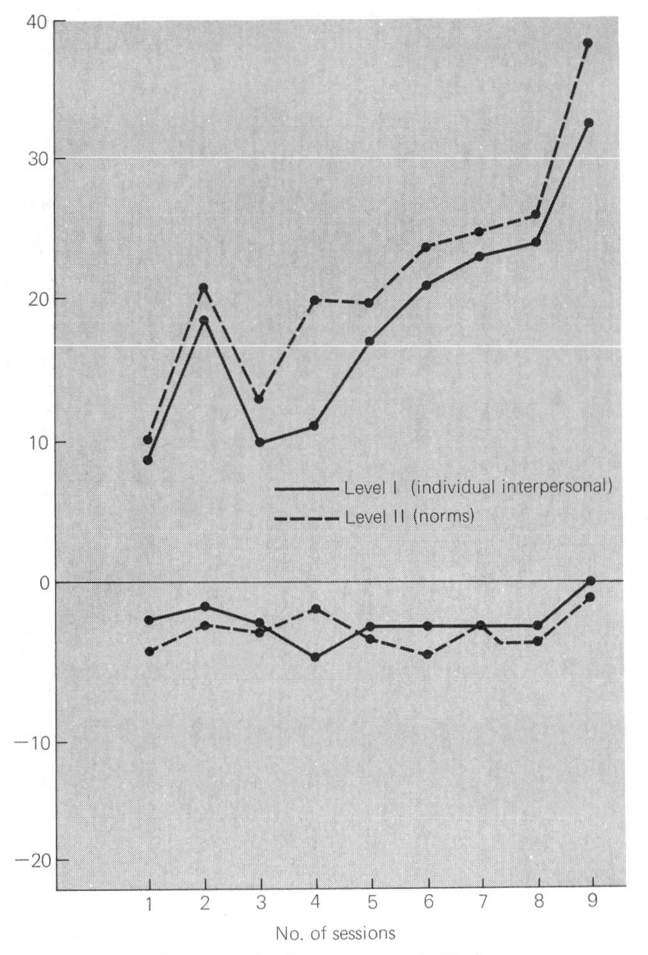

Fig. 2. Growth curves for best group studied.

easier (especially at the outset) to contribute to group growth than to one's own or to that of another specific individual.

The negative scores were much less frequent in the group. They, too, became worse, but then became better. Toward the end, the total individual negative scores reached zero; whereas the norm negative scores were almost zero.

How valid are curves like these? One method available to us to determine the validity was as follows: Since the theory suggests that the higher the plus scores and the lower the minus scores, the greater the competence of the system, then Group I should be perceived, by its members or outsiders, as becoming increasingly competent.

From our own and others' empirical experience, we developed ten indices, or criteria, of group competence. They are:

1. Contributions made within the group are additive
2. The group moves forward as a unit; there is a sense of team spirit; there is high involvement
3. Decisions are made by consensus
4. Commitment to decisions by most members is strong
5. The group continually evaluates itself
6. The group is clear about its goals
7. Conflict is brought out into the open and dealt with
8. Alternative ways of thinking about solutions are generated
9. Leadership tends to go to the individual best qualified
10. Feelings are dealt with openly.

Each of these criteria was included in a questionnaire as a dimension on a continuum of 1 through 5. The "1" represented the low end of the continuum, and the "5" the highest possible score. An alternative of "don't know yet" was included for each dimension.

At the end of each session, all the participants, the staff, and the observer filled out these questionnaires in terms of their evaluation of the group as a whole. The data were kept by the observer and were not seen by anyone. They were tabulated *after* the laboratory was completed.

In addition, each individual indicated (on a continuum of 1 through 5) how much he liked the group. This was taken as an over-all indication of his feelings about the group. Also, he was asked to predict how well he felt others liked the group.

Several analyses were made. First, the scores for all the questions per session were combined and averages were computed to indicate each individual's feelings about the group in terms of the ten indices. All these were summed so scores were developed of the total group's competence as perceived by (a) the observer, (b) the staff, and (c) the participants in terms of the ten indices.

These scores were plotted in a figure (see Figure 3). It is interesting to note that there is a large measure of agreement among the four curves. The four curves are, with one exception, highly congruent with the group curve presented in Figure 2.

In order to obtain a quantitative indication of this congruency among the curves, a correlation was computed between each of these curves and the group competence curve based on the scoring categories (Figure 2). The results are shown in Table 2.

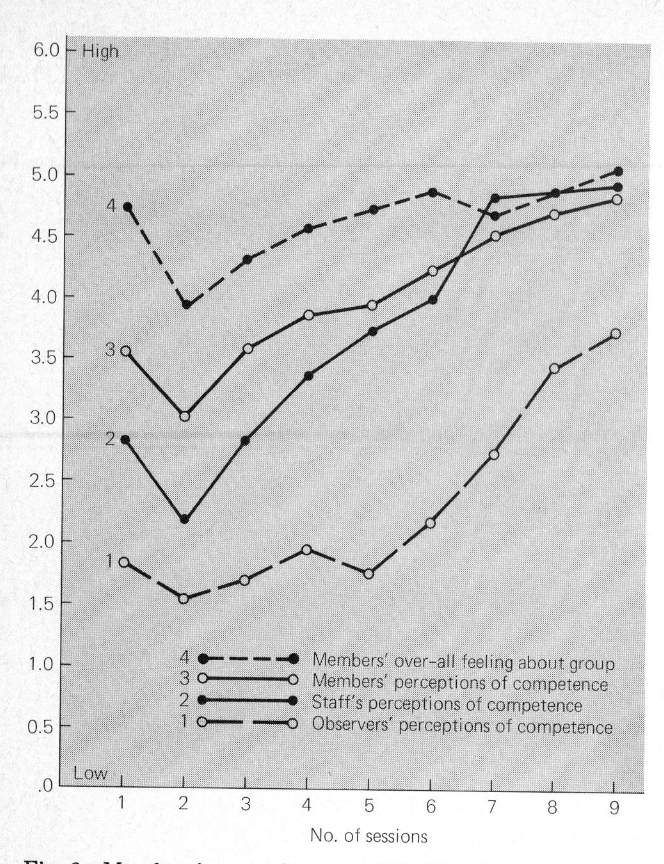

Fig. 3. Members' scores for over-all feeling about group and competence scores for group as perceived by members, staff, and observer based on the sum of ratings on the following 10 indices:

group contributions add up	group is clear about its goals
moving forward as a unit	conflict is dealt with
decision by consensus	alternatives are explored
members' commitment to decisions	leadership is appropriate to skills
constant self-check	feelings are dealt with openly

Some readers might wonder since the correlations are so high whether we may be measuring the same phenomenon or whether there is one (or two) factor(s) that underlies them all. We doubt this possibility for all the indices except 7 and 10, which we believe are overlapping.

The behavior implicit within each of the remaining factors seems significantly different. Clarity of goals, contributions "adding up," "decision by consensus," "exploring alternative solutions," "functional leadership," "strong internal commitments" seem to the writer to be criteria on different levels of analysis. This assertion may be best defended by asking the reader to visualize what would be necessary to help a group learn how to perform each of these activities effectively.

The results for the two questions regarding "liking the group" were analyzed separately. First, there was no statistically significant correlation between the individual's perception of the effectiveness of the group or the "actual" effectiveness and his liking for the group (.54). The correlation is even lower when we asked the individuals to predict how they feel others will feel about the group at the end of each session (.36).

Table 2. *Correlations of Group Competence Ratings by Observers with End-of-the Meetings Evaluations by Members, Staff, and Observers. (N equals number of sessions equals 9)*

Variable Correlated with Group Competence Scores	Correlation
Over-all Scores	
Observers' evaluations	.86[a]
Staff's evaluations	.83[a]
Members' evaluations	.93[b]
Members' over-all feelings about group	.54
Specific Indices	
Group contributions adding up	.60
Moving forward as a unit	.79[a]
Decision by consensus	.76[a]
Strong member commitment to decision	.73[a]
Constant internal check of group effectiveness	.78[a]
Clarity about goals	.84[a]
Conflict dealt with openly	.62
Alternative solutions explored	.76[a]
Leadership varied and functional	.85[a]
Feelings dealt with: not suppressed	.81[a]

[a] p .05.
[b] p .01.

In a second study, encouraging results were also obtained. Again we found a significant relationship between the members' (.83) and staff's evaluation (.77) of the group and the competence scores developed by the observers.

However, more significant results were obtained in the "liking" questions. In this study, the members' liking of the group per each session "grew" closely with the competence scores (.85). Also they predicted more accurately than the previous group members how well others liked the group (.79).

SUGGESTIONS FOR FURTHER RESEARCH

During the studies of T Groups we learned that it was possible to score an individual's behavior and to plot aspects of his learning during the T-Group sessions. We utilized the same procedure to evolve a quantitative score of the individual's competence.

Needless to say, further studies are needed to validate these findings. Aside from the obvious problem of a small number of cases (especially in terms of staff ratings), there is the problem of ascertaining whether the relatively high predictive validity of the scores remains high when the individuals who are being rated have been through a relatively poor or extremely effective T Group. It may be that we were able to obtain the encouraging results because the individual competence showed an adequate spread, which made it easier for the rators to rate and increased the probability that the predictions would be accurate. What would happen if we had to predict in groups where all the individuals learned much or little? Another possibility is that the staff variance is much greater than the amount represented within the present study. It is conceivable that another group or staff might have greater difficulty in scoring the individuals or might not, but in either case might develop significantly different ratings.

Also, studies are needed to validate the individual growth or learning curves that were presented. If such validation is obtained, then it may be possible to begin to understand the dynamics of human personality and its relationship to learning.

Studies are also needed where the categories are used to represent the more extreme of the cognitive learnings (logic, concept formation) as well as the more interpersonal and clinical learnings (therapy groups). Such studies might help to produce observations in the infrequently observed categories of our scheme. At the moment, one of the major weaknesses of our scheme as a total scheme is that many of its categories have hardly been used in the situations studied to date.

As these studies are developed, it should also be possible to begin to conduct research that focuses on learning that is simultaneously cognitive and interpersonal. This should help us to begin to understand the interrelationships between the two levels.

Turning to the small-group level, it was shown that the growth of one group's competence (which is quantitatively different from the growth of any individual in it) could also be ascertained with encouraging validity.

In the case of group learning or growth, we were able to conduct a study to explore the relationship between the curve of group learning (developed from the scoring procedure) and the members' perception of their group's development. The results were encouraging, but again the number of cases was small.

One of the interesting avenues for further research is the area between individual and group growth. For example, the same individual could be studied in groups where there is relatively great learning and in groups where there is relatively little. For example, the writer's competence scores in two T Groups were 300 and 150 respectively. Is it possible that the dynamics produced in the second T Group helped the writer to be less competent? If so, why?

Studies could also be conducted where the participants were selected according to (1) the degree to which they held the pyramidal values, or (2) their need for power, inclusion, and affection (Schutz), (3) dependence and counterdependence (Bennis and Shepard), (4) complexity versus simplification or abstract versus concrete (Harvey, Hunt, and Schroeder), to mention but a few.[11] Experiments could also be conducted where groups were permitted to develop up to a certain point, when the members would then be "transplanted" systematically.

LABORATORY EDUCATION AND T GROUPS

The research may help those practitioners interested in making laboratory education more effective. If these preliminary findings are replicated, the set of categories may provide a meaningful measurement of individual learning and group growth. It would then be possible to conduct research which would help the staff identify individual behavior styles and group conditions under which learning can be increased.

Moreover, staff members can be studied under varying conditions. The resulting knowledge might help us become more efficient in understanding how a given staff member's behavior facilitates and inhibits growth. Such knowledge should be helpful to the staff members in attempts to increase their own competence. It should also be useful in pairing staff members to develop "optimal" learning conditions for the group. Also, it may be possible to switch staff members as the groups develop so that they obtain that kind of help that they need the most at any given phase of their development.

The same kinds of alternatives can be considered for the participants. Groups could be composed and recomposed as a function of the individual pattern of scores. Participants could be matched more effectively with those staff members with whom they would probably learn the most.

Another interesting possibility is for the individual and group curves to be used to provide feedback to the members as to how their performance compares with (1) other members in their group, (2) their group as a whole, and (3) other members in other groups with or without the same pattern or same position, status, and so on. The same kind of study could be made on the group level.

The best way to use the data in order to increase learning is still not clear. One would have to be careful to try not to let the data become perceived as evaluative (i.e., whether the people are good or bad). Rather, the hope would be that the scores provide them with information which they can use to become more competent. Thus, if a man sees that his learning curve is not rising he might look at it more analytically to see why this is so. He might find out, for example, that he is manifesting much behavior that is *owning i* and *conformity i* or *owning i* and *concern i.* Examining his "scores," he may see that he could be helped if he *owned up* to his feelings more; or he could strive to become more *open* (*i* and *f* levels); or even attempt an *experiment i* or *f.* In short, the data could be used to help the individual just as the shooter uses the feedback he gets from someone who "scores" his target to show him where he is hitting. Such information can help the shooter decide what he must do to come "on target."

In comparing individual and group data, one will also have to be alert to note whether the feedback of the data tends to generate individual competition and/or group rivalry. Again, it is the writer's belief that too little is known about the positive and negative aspects of each on learning. According to Deutsch,[12] for example, competitive experience can decrease cooperation; and a decrease in coopera-

[11] Schutz, W. G. *FIRO: A Three-Dimensional Theory of Interpersonal Behavior.* New York: Holt, Rinehart & Winston, 1958; Bennis, W. G., & Shepard, H. A. A theory of group development. *Human Relations,* 1956, **9**, 415–438; and Harvey, O. J., Hunt, D. E., & Schroder, H. M. *Conceptual Systems and Personality Development.* New York: Wiley, 1961.

[12] Deutsch, M. An experimental study of the effects of cooperation and competition upon group process. *Human Relations,* July 1949, **2**, 199–231.

tion in a T Group would decrease the probabilities of individuals' helping one another and, as a result, limiting their own and others' growth possibilities.

Blake and Mouton[13] have shown that intergroup rivalries of the win-lose variety can also be harmful to learning. However, they have suggested that if such rivalries occur the staff may use them as rich data for the group members to examine and from which to begin to derive important learning experiences.

In a subsequent article, I shall use the index developed here to compare two different residential training programs for business executives.

ENCORE

"It is (men of science) who hold the secret of the mysterious property of the mind by which error ministers to truth, and truth slowly but irrevocably prevails. Theirs is the logic of discovery, the demonstration of the advance of knowledge and the development of ideas, which as the earthly wants and passions of men remain almost unchanged, are the charter of progress and the vital spark in history. And they often give us invaluable counsel when they attend to their own subjects and address their own people. Remember Darwin taking note only of those passages that raised difficulties in his way; the French philosopher complaining that his work stood still, because he found no more contradicting facts. . . . Faraday declared that 'in knowledge, that man only is to be condemned and despised who is not in a state of transition.' "—Lord Acton. *Essays on Freedom and Power.* Boston: The Beacon Press, 1949. P. 22.

[13] Blake, R. R., & Mouton, J. S. The intergroup dynamics of win-lose conflict and problem-solving collaboration in union-management relations. In M. Sherif (Ed.), *Intergroup Relations and Leadership.* New York: Wiley, 1962.

The Neglected Client

Martin H. Jones
Martin C. Jones

Meaningful knowledge of blackness does not exist because the great majority of student and academic personnel are from the white middle class. They have not lived in black communites; they are aware of black problems only superficially. It is not unfair to say that their awareness is mainly of the fact that great problems exist rather than of the problems themselves. The chief problem, of course, is the economic deprivation of blacks, but this misfortune is deeply rooted in psychological and sociological problems within the ghetto culture as well as the patterns of black-white interrelations which have been three centuries in the making. True insight leading to meaningful solutions can only come by thoroughly knowing and feeling the black person's point of view, and such knowledge can only come from an intimacy of association with the hard-core ghetto and the ghetto culture. Such association is not customarily available to the middle class, or at least they do not seek it out.

Later we were to find, most dishearteningly, that even when the opportunity to see, hear, and feel exists, many whites are unable to take advantage of it because of rigid, preformed views and because of bureaucratic structures to which they are attached. While a student, my awareness was chiefly of the great gap between the good intentions and any realistic store of knowledge possessed by white students and teachers.

This basic ambivalence, which ultimately has such a great effect on black people, is well illustrated by college teaching and texts. On the positive side are general principles of attitude and action set forth in counseling theory, such as Rogers' concept of unconditional positive regard for the client. Such a concept is certainly ideal, but its observation in practice is also conducive to the most effective practical results, as my experience has shown.

The principles of counseling, which are both practical and ideal, are universally applicable to all people in Western culture, black and white, and probably to people everywhere. As principles of human relations they extend far beyond the realm of counseling. If they had been learned and applied by the world leaders who make international policies, we would not now be faced by the dilemmas of

From *The Black Scholar,* 1970, 5, 35–42. Reproduced by permission.

neocolonialism and spheres of influence, and by the embattled color consciousness that pervades the world.

If the counselor (or physician or government official) does not recognize the person whom he faces as a fellow human being and does not listen to him as such, he cannot relate to him in any meaningful way. He cannot act constructively toward the person, nor expect the person to act constructively toward him.

For minority and ghetto groups, the negative side of this ambivalence lies in the practice of counseling as opposed to theories of counseling. As mentioned, the overwhelming majority of college teachers and textbook authors are from the white middle class. When it comes to the specifics of applying counseling theories, the application is necessarily bound up with the background and unconscious attitudes of these people. The illustrative cases in texts and journals are white middle-class people with white middle-class problems. When the cases do happen to be blacks or other minority people, it will generally be found that their problems are of white middle-class types. The actors are different, the plot remains the same.

This means that students are not trained to cope with the problems of people from the black culture. An individual is in constant psychological and sociological interchange with his environment. It is this interchange that determines personality and attitudes, and the person cannot be considered apart from it. Those trained in counseling, those who teach counseling and write about it, do not have an instinctive, internalized knowledge of ghetto culture as they do of middle-class culture. Nor is a realistic opportunity to learn provided them. The student or counselor who wishes such knowledge must find his own way to acquire it, which takes unusual determination and initiative. The blandness of good intentions must be replaced by a truly crusading spirit.

Thus the average counselor, when faced by a black or other minority person, often finds himself at a total loss. If he applied the basic acceptance of counseling and were willing to listen receptively, interaction might conceivably take place, but instead he attempts to project his innate middle-class orientations on the client. The cultural barrier becomes an immediate block to communication. The client perceives that he is not being heard or understood and mentally withdraws.

Aware that communication does not exist, the counselor resolves his frustration and bafflement by rejecting the client. He has decided that if the client cannot interact on his terms, no interaction will take place. This paranoid self-righteousness and rigidity solves the counselor's internal dilemma so that he does not feel "alone and afraid in a world he never made," but it arouses powerful negative emotions in the client. The client feels, and rightly so, that he is not being helped, and that no honest effort is being made to help him. He is the neglected client, and he knows it.

Two theoretical considerations help to throw light on this type of disrupted client-counselor communication. The first is the classic case of the Freudian concept of penis envy as a prime neurotic factor in women, which illustrates how valid psychological principles of universal scope may be invalid when reduced to certain specific corollaries which are culture-oriented. The second is the concept of libidinal diffusion, a structural theory of culture-bound human reactions as discussed by Slater (1965), Benne (1961), and James (1950).

From observing himself and his clientele, Freud made deductions which revolutionized psychology; without which, in fact, modern psychology as we know it would not exist. In broadest terms, his essential discovery was the fact that many actions of people are motivated by hidden needs of which they are not consciously aware. As a general principle, this applies to people of all cultures. When it comes to the derivation of specific subconscious motivations, however, culture plays an essential role, a fact that was not realized by Freudian psychologists for quite a long time, and even today is not as well understood by counselors as it should be.

Because of the social structure of Vienna, most of Freud's clientele were upper middle-class Jews. From facts that emerged in analysis, the keystones of the application of Freudian theories were built. One of these keystones was the concept of penis envy. Freud found that most, if not all, of his female patients had strong feelings of inferiority and suppressed envy and hostility toward their husbands, fathers, and brothers. In delving into this, Freud found that Viennese women identified the male sex organ with the strongly authoritarian position held by males in that culture. Subconsciously, and often consciously, the women felt that they had been "castrated" as infants, and thus deprived of their rights as self-determining human beings, a privilege obviously enjoyed by their fathers and brothers, who were judged to be sexually "complete."

In the Vienna of Freud's day the concept of penis envy was a valid deduction. The twentieth-century United States, however, is not a patriarchal society where the father plays the role of absolute monarch and the lowliest brother takes precedence over all sisters. For many years psychologists struggled to apply this imported concept of penis envy to their female patients, until it was finally realized that it is minor in this culture rather than being the primary cause of female neurosis. In black ghetto culture, in fact, because of the economically engendered matriarchal structure, it is the young males who are frustrated by the absurd futility of trying subconsciously to identify with their mothers rather than, as in Vienna, young females who are frustrated in being shut out of the enviable father-brother roles.

Factors of futility, despair, mistrust of hope, play a major role in ghetto culture just as penis envy did in Viennese culture. But these are not major factors in white middle-class United States culture and therefore do not appear as momentous, neurosis-producing problems in the literature of psychology and counseling, which in the main devotes itself to the problems of an essentially more leisured and economically secure class. Ghetto people have problems which stem from lack of money and life choices; middle-class whites often have problems which stem from too much money and a confusing multitude of choices.

Marijuana use provides an example of the dichotomy between textbook theory and the realities of ghetto life. The literature on marijuana has traditionally treated its use as a subconscious desire of the individual to withdraw, to escape, to turn his psychic projections inward and wreak social and personal suicide on himself. This view stems from middle-class attitudes, which see any deviation from the idealized norm as a withdrawal from society (that is, the business–military world) and a threat to it.

A University of California team sent into the East Oakland ghetto to study marijuana use at first hand discovered just the opposite. Among young ghetto people, marijuana is a social cohesion factor. It is used in conjunction with the group; to use marijuana is to belong, and its use is a factor in group acceptance. Thus it is exactly the opposite of an escape or a withdrawal, and the findings of this team contradict the traditional literature and attitudes on the subject.

This proves the value to the counselor of exerting himself to learn ghetto problems openly and intimately. When he does, he may discover new concepts diametrically opposed to standard theory and practice. At the least he will have to unlearn many textbook "facts" that have been written from the middle-class point of view, and he will have to reorient himself to a world that is bigger, more complex, and more difficult than the middle-class environment in which he supposes he finds psychological safety. However, the example of the ostrich indicates that hiding the head in the sand is the most dangerous, not the safest, thing to do.

Counselors who fail to recognize the conditional factor of acculturation in psychological concepts, the basic role of the socioeconomic environment in the psychology of the individual, cannot help ghetto people. It is probable that they cannot help anyone.

The second operative factor in this type of aborted client-counselor relationship is libidinal contraction. From Freud's several definitions of libido, the one considered here is libido as the sum total of psychic forces. Libidinal contraction is the constriction of these forces within some group with which the individual identifies for purposes of immediate self-interest and the security of clinging together. Libidinal diffusion means that the affective cognitions are directed outward toward objectives and toward persons without extreme preferential selectivity. The libidinally contracted person is socially crippled and is paranoid to some greater or lesser degree. The libidinally diffused person can, with wisdom, find in himself the resources to cope with the structural complexities of modern society and to help others.

By the very definition of the ghetto as a forced in-group structure, the ghetto person is, to a greater or lesser extent, libidinally contracted. It is the counselor's duty to help him break out of this shell psychologically and economically. If the counselor, too, is libidinally contracted, with his psychic forces frantically directed toward the traditional values of middle-class society, it will be like two billiard balls striking. Two glassy surfaces will bounce off each other, and both counselor and client will react negatively to their meeting.

The counseling situation should be like a truck tire connected to a bicycle tire. With its resources of experience and its knowledge of counseling principles, the truck tire gives the bicycle tire the air it needs to make its own way. The diffused libido of the counselor has streamed some of its own attitude and energy into the client. Like the truck tire, the counselor is continually replenished.

Very often all the client needs to diffuse his own libido and feel himself a man in this world is a job. The counselor with diffused libido, which embraces the conditionality of circumstances, will see this and will work actively for the client in that direction. The counselor with contracted libido will dispense advice and information, largely negative, which are neither helpful nor meaningful to the client, and affect him adversely. An example of this is the counselor who tells the client how limited he is as a person, that he cannot possibly handle the job or profession he wants, and then removes the burden from his own shoulders by shunting the client off to a battery of tests coached in libidinally contracted, middle-class terms.

Simultaneous operation of the two factors—culture-bound concepts accepted as general principles, and libidinal contraction—is illustrated by the occupational interest inventories which are so widely used and misused by private and public agencies.

It was not until the beginning of this decade, when the Minnesota Vocational Interest Inventory was introduced, that the authors of these inventories took serious notice of any occupations outside of the highly paid professions. Since many counselors feel they need something to go on besides their own libidinally diffused good sense, these tests have been used indiscriminantly on the presumption that they embody general principles which by extrapolation are applicable to all. In truth, they are culture-bound by the unspoken postulate that only persons educationally prepared for middle-class status occupations are worth serious concern: All others can take their chances.

Tests confined to status occupations exhibit the libidinal contraction of highly placed professors and researchers who see value in thorough investigation of professions akin to their own, but not in the great spectrum of ordinary occupations which employ the great majority of people.

The strictly limited scope of these tests gave the libidinally contracted, middle-class oriented counselor the opportunity to express his hidden needs and fears by flatly telling a client that his occupational choice had to be much narrower than he thought and hoped. Such misuse of these tests against minority clients has been and continues to be widespread.

This is not to say that such tests are not valuable when correctly used. The test literature specifically states that the tests indicate only the interests the testee has in common with the measured interests of norm groups representing a limited number of occupations. Because there is no proven theoretical connection between these interests and the occupation (the correlation is merely statistical), extrapolation to supposedly related fields is not reliable. Nor do the tests measure success potential; it is admitted that motivation is the prime success factor. The tests are not designed to make the counselor's job easier by giving him a mechanized decision-making process or to provide authority for his prejudices.

The authors have served as counselors at a public employment agency and at an industrial high school. In both places we found operative all the negative factors mentioned above. We were shocked at the great gap between counseling theory and practice. There was a nearly total lack of empathy for ghetto people and no real knowledge of their situation. Nor was there willingness and desire to learn; the people of these agencies are apathetic and often actively hostile to the needs of their clients. They collect their paychecks for appearing at work each morning and going through the day with the least possible disturbance to themselves. More social good would be done if they were paid for staying home.

There are, of course, heartening individual exceptions to this dismal picture, but on the whole, negative employee attitudes are condoned by supervisors and reflect tacitly understood, although not official, agency policy.

The taxpayers' money is not being spent constructively, in the manner intended by the legislature. Perhaps the extreme example of this disregard for human and legal values is the lady who tears up an application and throws it in the wastebasket when the applicant in some small way displeases her.

Outside of negative attitudes, the chief barrier to efficient operation of this public employment agency is the departmentalized fragmentation of its basic service, which is supposed to be finding the client a job. The applicant is shunted from employment or placement interviewer to counselor to testing service, and frequently to some time-wasting irrelevance such as watching a reading improvement course on TV. Specific instruction in the valuable techniques of filling out employment test forms and applications is not given, nor, for youth who have not had previous employment, is there instruction in what the employer will expect of them or in the social and psychological difficulties they are likely to encounter on the job.

Neither initial interviewing, job placement, nor follow-up is adequate for the client's needs. The special problems of ghetto people cause little concern and receive little understanding, although this area is supposed to be a primary objective of the agency.

During our tenure as counselors at the employment agency, we were fortunate in securing approval to experimentally apply the concept of a one-package client service. This involved both placement and counseling interviews, job development using a variety of community resources, the active seeking of suitable placement, and follow-up. The family situation always received attention as did interviews with the employer both before and after placement. When difficulties arose, such as the new employee not appearing for work or not functioning in the job, inquiry was instituted, which usually led either to a satisfactory solution in that situation or re-referral to a more suitable job.

It is my opinion that this agency could be put on a decently efficient functional basis by a two-step program. First, a training program in the principles of counseling should be instituted for the employees who deal with the public, particularly those older employees who began their employment before professional training was required. Much higher standards of agency expectation must be set: The supervisory staff must demand professional standards of conduct and attitude from all employees, and must demand that there be an active, aggressive attempt to place every applicant.

No applicant can be given up for lost. My experience was that a place could be found for even the dimmest prospect if a thorough attempt were made. One case was that of a mentally retarded, illiterate youth who was brought to the agency by his pastor and could only tell us about himself: "I want a job." After investigation and talks with his family, and an initial error in placement, he was put in a job suitable to his needs and talents and to the employer. Another case was that of a Vietnam amputee further handicapped by deep discouragement. It was first proved to him that there were many good paying jobs, such as teletype operator, that he could do without the strain of having to be on his feet all day. He was then helped to employment and to enter college.

Second, the package system of one counselor or qualified agency employee handling all aspects of a case should be adopted. The only exception would be formal testing when necessary. Because of the much higher placement rate, this system would be more efficient and less wasteful of time and money than the present departmentalized specialization. The client would be provided many personal benefits of attention and understanding he is not now receiving. The mass-production methods of Henry Ford are good for automobiles but not necessarily for black people.

Always the expressed ideals, needs, and ambitions of the client must be of serious concern to the counselor. Because motivation is the most important factor in job success, openly expressed attitudes are often much more valuable in placement than any number of hidden attitudes uncovered by formal testing. It is up to the counselor to strike the balance most beneficial to the client. To do this for black people requires intimate knowledge of the ghetto situation and a more than usual depth of understanding. When faced with frank descriptions of ghetto problems and needs, which were offered in the spirit of helpful information, the supervisory personnel of this agency demonstrated bafflement, frustration, and unwillingness to cope with reality by either withdrawing into the shell of libidinal contraction or reacting with open hostility. Neither objectivity nor the desire to help others as a prime motivation could be accepted.

The vocational high school followed much the same pattern of a tired bureaucratic structure following a rutted, timeworn path. Although educational facilities and the teaching staff are excellent, counseling as such, truly a great need for many minority and ghetto youths in this school, was nonexistent. There was no individual counseling, and only one counselor who could even be described as semiliberal. The assistant principal was the chief counselor, and his idea of counseling was discipline. He expected this type of performance from the one adequate counselor, who felt he was in a very difficult situation. Although the assistant principal maintained that there were no problems in the school, it appeared that he was disliked by a large proportion of students, and the student with problems had nowhere to turn for help or advice.

For example, there was a black math teacher in this school who realized that one of his black students was perfect college material although the boy had been recommended to a trade school. Fortunately he was able to intervene on the boy's behalf, but there seems no doubt that numerous others go down the drain. The individual loses his best opportunity in life and our society loses the best contribution he could make.

Thus the neglected client is the individual, all too often a black or other minority person, who finds himself helpless in the face of rigid, entrenched, self-serving attitudes; who receives neither help nor acceptance because of the preformed prejudices and unbending structure of dehumanized bureaucracy; and who, through lack of adequate help and understanding, is unable to find the job he needs or to make his life valuable to himself and society.

If members of the black community, as well as other ethnic groups, are to be a visible part of the mainstream, they must not be castrated members of a society. They must in turn be treated with utmost courtesy and diplomacy. In a counseling relationship individuals must not be put into a said frame of reference (i.e., slow learners, underachievers, misfits).

In a therapeutic relationship these people must be understood with clarity by knowing their culture, idiom, and jargon which is not a part of the everyday counseling setting. The counselor must be thoroughly exposed to the environmental conditions from whence his client came. In addition, there must be family consultations in the areas of school, colleges, etc. The knowledge of the family brings about the knowledge of the client and his role within the family setting. If a counselor does not meet his client on the real level, he is ineffective in his establishment of rapport. For example, "Hello, Brother, what's going down?" brings the counselor down to the real level instead of intellectual plane. Therefore, the counselor must exempt himself from formal greeting to make the therapeutic conditions comfortable.

The counselor must always bear in mind that counseling is a feeling relationship, that his effectiveness is in direct ratio to the amount of warm, positive feeling generated between him and his client. Thus counseling relations are most effective as intellectual activity *decreases.* The counselor's intellect must always be active, of course, but as an instrument for feeling, for sensing his client's emotions and needs. Too often counselors establish "intellectual fences" between themselves and their clients. These fences may take the form of preconceived theories brought to the counseling situation about the client ("Well, according to Moynihan, he's . . . " or "His records show . . . " or "The Skinner hypothesis maintains that . . . "). Or, they may take the form of highly verbal activity on the part of the counselor, which can be a form of one-upmanship. The student may walk away with his head ringing, saying, "Man, that cat's bad"—and with no effective counseling having occurred.

Effective counseling occurs with the ear—and the voice. The client must be heard and what he is *truly* saying must be heard, not filtered through what the counselor *thinks* he is saying. Most important in counseling is the pitch and tone quality of the voice. The voice tells as much as the face. It should be a soothing, friendly voice, that gives the client reassurance that he has been heard, listened to, with warmth and regard.

The black counselor should invoke and always use his knowledge of the black community. He must realize that many youngsters have been on the streets at an early age, as their families have struggled to make ends meet. Sometimes called "keychain babies," such youths have a starvation for real relationships, which can result in an intense dependency when the youth makes such a connection with his counselor. The counselor will hear statements such as, "I wish my daddy was like you," or, "I sure enjoy being here," or, "I'm glad we've got a black counselor."

In group counseling situations, black sensitivity groups can be effective. But the counselor must bear in mind that many blacks are wary of sensitivity training. Very rarely has sensitivity training been done from a black perspective, in blackness. Too often the encounters have been mixed, which creates a different kind of group content—the race problem itself, with focus on white guilt and black anger. Such encounters, while having a limited usefulness, do not provide effective counseling or therapy for the black client's deeper problems. Generally speaking, the white client has different group interaction needs than the black client; the need to touch, to feel, are not particularly black needs, nor do blacks need training in how to directly express anger to each other. Group counseling and sensitivity work can bring excellent results for black students, provided they are done from a black perspective, with an ear to particular black needs.

With the increase of black students and students of other ethnic backgrounds on college campuses nationwide, it is of the utmost importance that black counselors or counselors of other ethnic backgrounds bridge the gap for clear and direct communications. For the student it is very important that he has a counselor of his own ethnic background.

Blackness as a counseling factor avoids the time-consuming efforts of the client in testing his counselor with reference to a real, true counselor-client relationship. The client will not "shine the counselor on."

Community involvement is a function that counselors, psychiatrists, psychologists must be a part of. They should be available for talks at various churches, schools, and social organizations. This makes the community at large aware of their experts and their relationship toward their community. Community involvement also serves as a level of sensitizing the professional elite. New values and norms have to be prescribed for this individual in order for him to communicate.

In conclusion, to make a therapeutic relationship more adoptable and acceptable to black people and members of other ethnic groups, high schools, colleges, universities should adhere to the need for direct communication. For example, the hiring of more minority counselors, psychiatrists, psychologists, etc., and professional counseling programs of colleges and universities at the master's and doctorate levels should attend to the needs of the neglected client by having more ethnic faculties. At these levels courses of relevancy should be taught which make it possible to bridge the gap of disturbed communication.

Black counselors must form an association of black counselors to exchange methods and ideology with reference to the neglected client. As I envision it, such an association would be an adjunct of the National Association of Black Psychologists, with emphasis not only on counseling in academic situations, but in industry, on the job, and in the black community itself.

REFERENCES

Benne, Kenneth D. The uses of fraternity. In Warren B. Bennis (Ed.), *Interpersonal dynamics*, Homewood, Ill.: Dorsey Press, 1964.

Buscaglia, Leo. Major address "Can you hear me?" and "Your words get in your eyes," at the convention of the California Personnel and Guidance Association, San Diego, February 1970.
Clark, Kenneth B. *Dark ghetto.* New York: Harper & Row, 1965.
James, John. Some elements in a theory of small groups. In Robert W. O'Brien (Ed.), *Readings in general sociology,* Boston: Houghton Mifflin, 1964.
Lewis, Oscar. *La vida.* New York: Random House, 1966.
Segal, Ronald. *The race war.* New York: Bantam, 1969.
Thomas, Charles W. Ph.D. in psychology; past President of the National Association of Black Psychologists and Director of Education and Training at the University of Southern California's Watts Health Service. Professor of Urban and Rural Studies, University of California, San Diego.
Washington, Kenneth S. Director of the Educational Opportunity Program for the California State College System. Author of the article Black Power—Action or Reaction?
Wells, Teresa Twyla. Teaching Assistant in the High Potential Program at UCLA. Author of the article The effects of discrimination upon motivation and achievement of black children in urban ghetto schools.
West, Gerald. Ph.D.; Assistant Professor in Counseling at San Francisco State College.
White, Joseph. Ph.D.; Counseling Psychologist and Director of Black Studies at University of California, Irvine.

Some Myths of Psychotherapy Research and the Search for a Paradigm

Donald J. Kiesler

Three myths prevalent in psychotherapy research are considered and refuted. These include the uniformity assumptions, spontaneous remission of psychoneurosis, and the belief that present theoretical formulations provide adequate paradigms. Several other confusions are listed and clarified including the process-outcome distinction, the classification problem, and the expectation of the definitive study in therapy research. Finally, an attempt is made to delineate the minimal requirements of any psychotherapy research paradigm by incorporating present empirical evidence as well as by specifying common sources of confounding vis-a-vis the therapy interaction.

One of the unfortunate effects of the prolific and disorganized psychotherapy research literature is that a clear-cut, methodologically sophisticated, and sufficiently general paradigm which could guide investigations in the area has not emerged. Perhaps this is an unavoidable state of affairs in a new area of research. Yet a perusal of this literature indicates that most of the basic considerations necessary for a general paradigm have appeared, albeit in many cases parenthetically, at some place or another. But to date no one has attempted to integrate empirical findings and methodological concerns in a way that might lead to a useful research paradigm. This lack of integration of the paradigm ingredients has minimized their impact on investigators in the area. Moreover, concomitant with, and perhaps because of, the absence of a paradigm several myths have been perpetuated; and because of these myths, inadequate designs continue to appear.

This paper will first attempt to spell out in some detail several myths current in the area of psychotherapy research which continue to weaken research designs and confuse the interpretation of research findings. Secondly, it will attempt to present a minimal but general paradigm which takes into account current theoretical inadequacies and empirical learnings, and focuses on methodological considerations which can no longer continue to be ignored.

From *Psychological Bulletin,* 1966, **64**, 114–120.

SOME MYTHS OF PSYCHOTHERAPY RESEARCH

We should be wary of pseudo-quantifications and methodological gimmicks which often tend to close off prematurely an area of inquiry and give rise to the illusion that a problem has been solved, whereas the exploration has barely begun. [Strupp, 1962, p. 470].

This first section is devoted to enumerating and refuting several misconceptions about psychotherapy research which have tenaciously persisted. These myths have served the unfortunate purposes of confusing the conceptualization of psychotherapy, hence impeding research progress; and of spreading pessimism regarding the utility of further research. Let us deal with these myths in turn.

The Uniformity Assumption Myths

This misconception was first labeled by Colby (1964) although it has been alluded to by several other authors (Gendlin, 1966; Gilbert, 1952; Kiesler, 1966; Rotter, 1960;

Strupp, 1962; Winder, 1957). Colby only parenthetically mentioned the myth, and alluded to only one of its aspects, that regarding patients in psychotherapy research. This paper will extend its meaning to cover the psychotherapy treatment itself. The former is referred to as the Patient Uniformity Assumption, the latter the Therapist Uniformity Assumption.

Patient uniformity assumption. For Colby, the Uniformity Assumption refers to the belief that "patients at the start of treatment are more alike than they are different." This implicit assumption has led to a remarkably naive manner of choosing patients for psychotherapy research: patients are not selected, rather they pick themselves by a process of natural selection. In searching for patients for investigating psychotherapy, researchers have traditionally chosen available samples, such as any patient coming to a clinic over a certain period of time. In some cases patients are further divided into experimentals and controls. But, in most studies, all patients receive therapy, measures being taken pre and post in order to reflect its efficacy. In any case, the assumption has been made that by this procedure one obtains a relatively homogeneous group of patients differing little in terms of meaningful variables, and homogeneous simply because they all sought out psychotherapy (be it in a counseling service, outpatient clinic, mental health clinic, private practice, or what have you).

Far from being relatively homogeneous, patients coming to psychotherapy are almost surely quite heterogeneous—are actually much more different than they are alike. The assumption of homogeneity is unwarranted since on just about any measure one could devise (demographic, ability, personality, etc.) these patients would show a remarkable range of differences. This is apparent from clinical experience and from much of the evidence on initial patient characteristics that is available today. Because of these initial patient differences, no matter what the effect of psychotherapy in a particular study (be it phenomenally successful or a dismal failure), one can conclude very little if anything. At best, one can say something such as: for a sample of patients coming to this particular clinic over this particular period, psychotherapy performed by the clinic staff during that period on the average was either successful or unsuccessful. No meaningful conclusions regarding the types of patients for whom therapy was effective or ineffective are possible. This is inevitably the case since no patient variables crucially relevant for subsequent reactivity to psychotherapy have been isolated and controlled.

This Patient Uniformity Assumption hampered research in the area of schizophrenia for years. The assumption was that patients diagnosed as schizophrenic are more alike than different. Subsequent data showed very clearly that some schizophrenics were quite different from others, in fact more like normals than they were like other schizophrenics (Herron, 1962). In other words, extreme variability was the usual case when one lumped all patients diagnosed schizophrenic. It was only when this variability could be reliably reduced that useful research could begin to be done. The important empirical finding was that schizophrenic patients differed markedly with respect to the abruptness of onset of their disorder. Some could be reliably classified in terms of their case histories as "process" schizophrenics, those with a relatively long-term and gradual onset; while others had a quite short-term and abrupt onset, "reactive" schizophrenics. It was further discovered that the reactive schizophrenics had much better prognosis. But most importantly, the radical reduction in variability permitted by this operational distinction made possible for the first time research that could lead to replicable differences among process schizophrenics and other diagnostic groups.

Now, few would argue that for some patients psychotherapy is *not* effective. Clinical experience as well as research data point clearly to this conclusion. Many studies have shown patient differences evident at the beginning of psychotherapy which are crucially related to subsequent dropout or failure in therapy.[1] If psychotherapy is differentially effective depending on initial patient differences, as the evidence strongly suggests, then it seems clear that research should take these differences into account. This would imply the use of a design with at least two experimental groups, dichotomizing patients by one or more patient variables shown to relate to subsequent outcome; or matching experimentals and controls on these relevant initial patient measures. Meaningful results will not occur if one continues to aggregate patients ignoring the meaningful variance of relevant patient characteristics.

Therapist uniformity assumption. Perhaps an even more devastating practice in psychotherapy research has been the selecting of various therapists for a research design on the assumptions that these therapists are more alike than different and that whatever they do with their patients may be called "psychotherapy." Theoretical formulations seem to have perpetuated this assumption since they have traditionally focused on describing "The Therapy" which is ideally appropriate for all kinds of patients. The myth has been perpetuated that psychotherapy in a research design represents a homogeneous treatment condition; that it is only necessary for a patient to receive psychotherapy, and that mixing psychotherapists (whether of the same or different orientations) makes no difference.

This kind of loose thinking seems to have grown out of what Raimy (1952) has called the "egg-shell era" of psychotherapy wherein it was rare for a therapist to tape record his sessions or in other ways to make public his therapeutic behavior.

> Almost without exception . . . psychotherapists adopted the attitude that patients and clients were frail, puny beings who would flee the field if anyone except their own private

[1] In the following discussion extensive bibliographical citings will be omitted since the resulting list would be prohibitive. Fortunately, an exhaustive bibliography of the psychotherapy research literature has now appeared and is available (Strupp, 1964). From the topical index provided one can find an exhaustive bibliography of studies for each of the therapy variables discussed below. Also, several specific reviews provide some integration of the many studies and can be usefully consulted (Auld & Murray, 1955; Breger & McGaugh, 1965; Cartwright, 1957; Eysenck, 1961; Gardner, 1964; Goldstein, 1962; Grossberg, 1964; Herzog, 1959; Marsden, 1965; Stieper & Wiener, 1965; Zax & Klein, 1960). Finally, the chapters on "Psychotherapeutic Processes" and "Counseling" in the *Annual Review of Psychology* (1950–1965) as well as the American Psychological Association's two volumes on *Research in Psychotherapy* (Rubinstein & Parloff, 1959; Strupp & Luborsky, 1962) are both indispensable sources for critical reviews of research.

psychotherapist touched them. In view of the lack of evidence to the contrary, such an attitude was at one time entirely justified since, in simple ethics, the welfare of the patient does come first. The fact that the attitude also had other supports, particularly the fact that it provided defensive measures for the therapist's unsteady ego-structure, made no difference [Raimy, 1952, p. 324].

In this aura of mystery it became easy for one to think of "the One" psychotherapy which would maximally benefit all patients. As Colby (1964) relates: "As long as what went on in therapeutic sessions remained secret, myths of consensus within paradigms were easily perpetuated. For example, among psychoanalysts there grew the myth of a single agreed-upon perfect technique [p. 348]." The advent of general tape-recording has made records of the therapist's behavior progressively more available to other clinicians and researchers, and it has become apparent that differences in technique and personality exist, even within schools, and that disagreement prevails.

Despite this token admission of therapist differences, the Uniformity Assumption still abounds in much psychotherapy research. Patients are still assigned to "psychotherapy" as if it were a uniform, homogeneous treatment, and to psychotherapy with different therapists as if therapist differences were irrelevant. As Rotter (1960) observes:

Although the trend is generally away from the notion of psychotherapy as an entity, there is still too much concern with *the* process of therapy. For many there is an assumption that there is some special process which takes place in patients, accounting for their improvement or cure. . . . In a similar way the role of the therapist is conceived of as one ideal set of behaviors which will maximally facilitate the mysterious process. The alternative conception that psychotherapy is basically a social interaction which follows the same laws and principles as other social interactions, and in which many different effects can be obtained by a variety of different conditions, is frequently neglected [p. 408].

In addition, the Myth ignores the growing body of evidence that psychotherapists are quite heterogeneous along many dimensions (e.g., experience, attitudes, personality variables) and that these differences seem to influence patient outcome. Some therapy may be more effective than others; and it seems not too unlikely that some therapy may be more deleterious than no therapy at all (Rogers, Gendlin, Kiesler, & Truox, 1966). As Meehl (1955) states: "In our present ignorance it is practically certain that clients are treated by methods of varying appropriateness, largely as a function of which therapist they happen to get to. Also, it is practically certain that many hours of skilled therapists are being spent with unmodifiable cases [374]."

If psychotherapy research is to advance it must first begin to identify and measure these therapist variables so relevant to eventual outcome (personality characteristics, technique factors, relationship variables, role expectancies, and the like). One can then build therapist differences into his design by having several experimental groups, with therapists at respectively different levels of relevant dimensions. Or, one can match therapists on relevant factors. To continue the practice of assigning some patients to psychotherapy and others to a "control" group seems futile.

Unfortunately, this kind of naive conceptualization has dominated studies evaluating the effects of psychotherapy where therapy and control groups are compared. Typically, the results have been discouraging in that no significantly greater improvement has been demonstrated for the "therapy" patients (Eysenck, 1961). As Gendlin (1966) argues:

Research in psychotherapy has suffered from the fact that psychotherapy was not definable. It has meant that, if an experimental therapy group was compared to a non-therapy control group, some of the supposed therapy subjects were not really receiving something therapeutic at all. . . . The effect of averaging the changes in the "experimental" group as compared with the "control" group often showed no significant differences. To bring this home, imagine trying to investigate the effects of a drug with an experimental group taking the drug and a control group receiving a placebo. Imagine that some (perhaps half) of your "experimental" group are actually taking a preparation without the effective ingredients of the drug . . . and you don't know which ones these are. Then, too, perhaps one or two "controls" are actually getting the drug on the side. Your "experimental treatment" group is not always getting the treatment.

An implication of this consideration is that if one could analyze the variability (rather than or in addition to the mean differences) of the experimental and control groups in these many studies, the therapy groups would be expected to show a much greater range of improvement behavior than the controls. This would follow if some of the "experimental" patients indeed were exposed to some quite "bad or indifferent psychotherapy."

Sanford (1953) states this still differently: "From the point of view of science, the question 'Does psychotherapy do any good?' has little interest because it is virtually meaningless. . . . The question is which people, in what circumstances, responding to what psychotherapeutic stimuli." And Gilbert (1952) urges:

One of the extremely important problems in psychological counseling and therapy is that concerning the need for being able to describe and quantify different types of psychotherapeutic relationships. The possibility of accomplishing this is basic to further studies concerning the relative effectiveness of different types of counseling procedures. Studies of this nature will be necessary before it will ever be possible to make any scientific statements regarding such basic questions as the relative effectiveness of different counseling procedures with different types of counselee problems, or the relative effectiveness of a single over-all approach to all types of counseling problems as compared with diverse approaches based upon various diagnostic categories [p. 360].

Finally, Kiesler (1966) states in summarizing the outcome results of a 5-year study of individual psychotherapy with schizophrenics (Rogers et al., 1966):

The picture emerging is that if we compare the therapy patients as a group to the control patients no differences emerge. Yet—and this seems to me to be the crucial question for outcome studies—if we divide the therapy cases by means of a theoretically relevant therapist variable (in this case level of "conditions" offered) the results are quite consistent with theoretical expectation. Hence, my final point would be that before we can validly assess the outcome or therapy evaluation problem, it is vitally necessary that we attempt to isolate therapist dimensions that will accurately reflect the heterogeneity of therapist performance. If we continue to evaluate therapy as a homogeneous phenomenon we will continue to obtain invalid results.

In summary, it would seem quite essential and useful to bury these Uniformity Myths once and for all. Until our designs can incorporate relevant patient variables and crucial therapist dimensions—so that one can assess which therapist behaviors are more effective with which type of patients—we will continue to perpetuate confusion. Psychotherapy research must come to grips with the need for factorial designs—as recommended a decade ago by Edwards and Cronbach (1952)—wherein different types of patients are assigned to different types of therapists and/or therapy, so that one can begin to discover the parameters needed to fill in a meaningful paradigm for psychotherapy.

As a postscript, it is often not remembered that different theoretical formulations and techniques have at least originally been derived from patients of different types. As Stein (1961) observes:

> One source of difference between schools of psychotherapy that is often overlooked and which needs to be made explicit is the difference in types of patients on which the founders of the different schools based their initial observations. Maskin summarizes this point rather well when he says: "Freud used hysteria as the model for his therapeutic method, depression as the basis for his later theoretical conjectures. Adler's clinical demonstrations are rivalrous, immature character types. Jung's examples were constructed to a weary, worldly, successful, middle-aged group. Rank focussed upon the conflicted, frustrated, rebellious artist aspirant. Fromm's model is the man in a white collar searching for his individuality. And Sullivan's example of choice is the young catatonic schizophrenic." To this one might add that Rogers' original formulations were based on college students [pp. 6–7].

Assuming these theoreticians were all perspicacious and accurate in their observations, the historical fact that their different formulations were derived from experience with different classes of patients would seem to reinforce strongly the necessity and appropriateness for abandoning the Uniformity Assumption in psychotherapy research.

The Spontaneous Remission Myth

This second myth has been perpetuated primarily by Eysenck (1952, 1954, 1955a, 1955b, 1961, 1964). Despite many refutations, it has continued to muddle research regarding the effectiveness of psychotherapy, and has fostered much of the pessimism that has more recently colored this research. Although this conception was restricted by Eysenck to psychoneurosis alone, its implications seem to have generalized to most of psychotherapy. Its more specific statement takes the following form (Eysenck, 1961): "We may conclude with some confidence that about two-thirds of severe psychoneurotics show recovery or considerable improvement without the benefit of systematic psychotherapy, after a lapse of two years from the time that their disorder is notified, or they are hospitalized [p. 711]." The clear implication of this proposition is that for psychotherapy to be proven worthwhile, it has to demonstrate it can beat this two-thirds percentage, since two-thirds of the patients improve without having anything done to or for them.

This percentage represents a rather severe standard, as the evidence, such as it is, has reflected. Without this base rate for comparison most therapists and laymen might be satisfied with a two out of three success rate. But with this base rate of spontaneous remission psychotherapy needs to be almost totally successful. Apparently the assumption has taken a rather tight hold on both practitioners and researchers of psychotherapy. Yet, the surprising fact is that the entire evidence for this assumption comes from the findings of two studies, which are, at best, ambiguous. Further, the assumption contradicts clinical experience as well as some of the experimental findings regarding human and animal learning, and has been refuted in the literature on several occasions. Unfortunately, these refutations focused on different aspects of the argument, and were obscured by their connection with the effectiveness-of-therapy polemic. Hence, it is necessary to separate the spontaneous remission argument from the latter polemic, and to integrate the various arguments against spontaneous remission. This section will, therefore, seriously reconsider this assumption with the hope that this refutation will bury it permanently.

In the first place, clinical lore indicates that the phenomenon of spontaneous remission has been observed for only three diagnostic categories. The first category is acutely reactive schizophrenics, who typically experience an abrupt onset of psychosis under usually specifiable traumatic conditions, and whose premorbid history is relatively free of gross pathology. Lasting recovery is generally rapid for these schizophrenics regardless of treatment. The other two diagnostic groups include the reactive and psychotic depressions. After temporary remission of their depressive symptoms these patients characteristically exhibit a regular course of recovery, ordinarily for a period of about 2 years, after which the depression recurs. It would obviously be essential in any studies evaluating therapy with any of these three groups that these remission characteristics be considered. But, as far as can be ascertained by this author, spontaneous remission as a typical phenomenon has not been clinically observed for other types of patients. In regard to psychoneurosis, moreover, clinical tradition indicates quite clearly that, rather than spontaneous recovery, increased rigidity of symptoms tends to be the rule when the patient remains untreated. Freud was so impressed by the rigidity of the resistance encountered in the treatment of psychoneurosis that he coined the term repetition compulsion to describe the process. Secondly, no attempt has been made to explain the phenomenon in other than quite gross terms. If spontaneous remission of neurosis occurs, it must occur via some psychological and/or physiological process. What is the nature of this process? What is the stimulus which initiates the process of recovery? Are the stimulus and the process the same for all psychoneurotics, or different for various types? How does it come about that attitudes and habit systems on which one has acted for much of his life are modified so easily without rather energetic intervention of some sort? What makes an habitual maladaptive pattern of behavior suddenly begin to disappear? These are crucial questions that need to be considered regarding spontaneous remission. Thirdly, how can one reconcile spontaneous remission with the evidence in the area of learning regarding habit strength and particularly the extreme difficulty of extinguishing avoidance responses?

Since this phenomenon seems counter to clinical experience, is only grossly explained, and contradicts evidence from learning research, it would seem that the empirical evidence for its existence needs to be quite impressive indeed before its generality can be accepted. Instead, the entire argument for spontaneous remission of neurotic patients comes from two survey studies cited by Eysenck (Landis, 1937; Denker, 1947), whose results are interpreted to meet the needs of his ineffectiveness-of-therapy polemic. Let us reexamine these two studies critically to see if Eysenck's conclusion is justified.

In approaching the problem of evaluating psychotherapy, in 1952 Eysenck searched in vain for a psychotherapy research study which had included a control group in its design. This was a legitimate search, since there is always the possibility in research that some variable other than the defined treatment variable is responsible for the effects observed for the experimental subjects. To remove this possibility of confounding, one traditionally uses a group of control subjects. In the present case, if therapy patients change significantly more than controls, one can legitimately conclude that some aspect of the treatment, ceteris paribus, is responsible for the differences.

But, as mentioned, Eysenck found it impossible to find any such study in his 1952 survey. Hence, as a substitute for the missing experimental control groups he looked for evaluative studies of untreated psychoneurotics (receiving no psychotherapy) where the patients had been followed up over time to determine what, if any, improvement occurred "spontaneously" as the result of the "natural healing process." Eysenck found two published studies which seemed to satisfy these criteria. He then abstracted and used the percentage of cases who improved over time from these two untreated samples as a base line with which to compare the changes observed in the reported studies of psychotherapy in the literature at that time.

The first of these base-line studies was that of Landis (1937) who reported that amelioration rate in state mental hospitals (in New York State as well as in the United States generally) for patients diagnosed under the heading of psychoneurosis. Because of the overcrowding of state hospitals and their chronic understaffing problem, it would seem extremely unlikely that these hospitalized neurotics received much, if any, therapy. Hence, any recovery observed for them could legitimately be considered as spontaneous. Landis reported that the percentage of patients "discharged annually as recovered or improved" was 70% for New York State (during the years 1925–1934) and 68% for the United States as a whole (1926–1933). Eysenck (1961) concludes from these data: "By and large, we may thus say that of severe neurotics receiving in the main custodial care, and very little if any psychotherapy, over two-thirds recovered or improved to a considerable extent." Quoting Landis, he continues: "Although this is not, strictly speaking, a basic figure for 'spontaneous' recovery, still any therapeutic method must show an appreciably greater size than this to be seriously considered." In other words, Eysenck seems to be saying that although this is not a basic figure for "spontaneous" remission, we can still treat it as such.

The second base-line estimate which Eysenck offers comes from a study by Denker (1947). Denker's report concerns 500 disability claims taken from the files of the Equitable Life Assurance Society of the United States. These claims were made by persons who reportedly had been ill of a neurosis for at least 3 months before their claims were submitted. The claimants came from all parts of the country, had many different occupations, and included all types of psychoneuroses. During their disability (defined as inability to carry on with any "occupation for remuneration or profit") these patients were regularly treated only by their local general practitioners "with sedatives, tonics, suggestion, and reassurance, but in no case was any attempt made at anything but this most superficial type of 'psychotherapy' which has always been the stock-in-trade of the general practitioner." The disability benefits the patients received ranged from $10 to $250 monthly. Denker followed up these cases for at least a 5-year period after their illness, and often for as long as 10 years after the period of disability had begun. The criteria he used for "apparently cured" were, (*a*) complaint of no further, or very slight, difficulties, and (*b*) successful social and economic adjustment by the patient.

Eysenck (1961) reports:

> Using these criteria, which are very similar to those usually used by psychiatrists, Denker found that 45% of the patients recovered after one year, another 27% after two years, making 72% in all. Another 10%, 5%, and 4% recovered during the third, fourth, and fifth years respectively, making a total of 90% recoveries after five years [pp. 710–711].

These are certainly very striking figures. Eysenck finally concludes:

> If we take a period of about two years for each base-line estimate, which appears to be a reasonable figure in view of the fact that psychotherapy does not usually last very much longer than two years and may sometimes last less, we may conclude with some confidence that about two-thirds of severe neurotics show recovery or considerable improvement, without the benefit of systematic psychotherapy, after a lapse of two years from the time that their disorder is notified, or they are hospitalized [p. 711].

Is this conclusion justified from Landis' and Denker's findings? Is Eysenck correct when he states that two-thirds of untreated psychoneurotics will, over a 2-year period, experience spontaneous remission of their neurotic illnesses? Many individuals have questioned this conclusion, notably Rosenzweig (1954), as well as others (Cartwright, 1955; de Charms, Levy, & Wertheimer, 1954; Dührssen & Jorswieck, 1962; Luborsky, 1954; Stevenson, 1959; Strupp, 1964a, 1964b). Let us examine in detail these counter arguments.

Rosenzweig provides the most comprehensive and critical attack on the conclusion Eysenck draws from the Landis and Denker studies. His basic argument is that before these two studies can be considered as representing a base line for recovery for untreated psychoneurotics (thereby functioning as extrapolated control groups for studies evaluating the effects of psychotherapy) the data of these studies must show three experimental characteristics: (*a*) the patients used in the Landis and Denker studies must be comparable to those treated by psychotherapy—that is, the definition of psychoneurosis for the patients in these studies must be the same as that for patients in psychotherapy, and the severity of the neurotic illness must be equivalent for the contrasted groups; (*b*) the Landis and Denker base-line groups must in fact have received no psychotherapy; otherwise the essential meaning of control group here is violated; and (*c*) the criteria for successful outcome or improvement need to be equivalent, so that recovery or improvement means the same thing for the Landis and Denker patients as for typical psychotherapy patients.

Rosenzweig then proceeds to argue that the Landis and Denker studies violate all three of these necessary conditions; therefore, Eysenck's conclusion of two-thirds spontaneous recovery is unwarranted. If Rosenzweig is correct, then the purported phenomenon of spontaneous recovery for psychoneurotic patients is indeed a myth, since the Landis and Denker studies are the only evidence offered for its existence. Let us look at Rosenzweig's and others' arguments in detail as to why the two studies do not meet the three essential conditions for a psychotherapy control group.

1. *Are the Patient Groups Comparable?* In the first place, the Patient Uniformity Myth is operative in this comparison. It is quite easy, but incorrect, to assume that patients labeled psychoneurotic are more alike than different, despite the fact that they are naturally selected in both the Landis and Denker studies. From an a priori basis alone the probability seems quite small that equivalent groups resulted from these several natural selection processes. Rosenzweig further argues that

> The insurance disability cases were, as a whole, in all likelihood less severely ill than any of the others. Denker himself points out that in these cases where disability income was a factor the illness may have been prolonged by this tangible secondary gain [money]. By the same token the illness may very well have been initiated, or at least partly instigated, by conscious or unconscious prospects of such gains. To compare psychoneuroses of long standing, dating in many instances from early childhood (the typical case treated by psychoanalysis), with such disability neuroses is highly dubious, and the fact that the latter would have cleared up quickly after brief treatment by a general practitioner is thus not surprising [p. 300].

Cartwright (1955) further argues against the psychoneurotic status of Denker's insurance patients:

> Denker's study was published in 1946, and all cases were followed-up for at least five years after recovery. If it is assumed that Denker's research took one year to carry out, then, since some cases were disabled for five years and others for only one, all these cases of neurosis had their onset between 1934 and 1940. In 1933 the economic depression was at its worst in the United States. From that time on, the country's economy tended to improve except for a partial relapse around 1937–38. . . . It is evident that this period (which overlapped the period of disability of Denker's subjects) was one of general growth from a condition of severe unemployment to a condition of plentiful employment throughout the United States. These data (i.e., employment rates from 1933 to 1944) suggest that it is reasonable to ask what proportion of the variance of Denker's results may be accounted for in terms of national recovery from economic depression rather than a personal recovery from neurosis [p. 292].

And Luborsky (1954) speculates still further about the lack of comparability of the Denker patients to psychotherapy patients:

> Many of the "insurance" group would probably never have visited the doctor if it were not required. As a whole the group is probably of higher social and economic level than other groups (apparently since they were able to carry disability insurance in the first place). Very likely the choice of a general practitioner rather than a psychiatrist to treat their psychoneurosis reflects a not-to-be-ignored difference in an attitude to their illness [p. 129],

or as Cartwright has just argued, reflects the scarcity and relative expense of psychiatrists in depression years.

Regarding the lack of comparability of the patients in the Landis study, Rosenzweig makes the following comments:

> Here one could reasonably expect that the neuroses must have been extraordinarily severe in order for these patients to have become eligible for admission to these crowded institutions. In these instances the outcome of treatment would be expected to be far less favorable than for either the Denker control group or the experimental groups [p. 300].

This of course argues for less spontaneous recovery for Landis' patients, which is inconsistent with the percentages reported, at least for the questionable criterion of recovery that Landis used.

Regarding both the Denker and Landis patient groups, Rosenzweig summarizes:

> It may be concluded that, in general, the Denker base-line group was probably less seriously ill, the Landis control group more seriously ill" [than the patients who typically are seen in psychotherapy]. To the degree that this conclusion is sound it may be further inferred that the control and experimental groups fail to meet an essential criterion of comparability—illness severity [p. 300].

It seems quite clear from the above rebuttals how one can get into inextricable interpretive difficulties, by operating on a misconception as unfounded as the Patient Uniformity Assumption, (for those cases where patients are naturally selected for various studies and where one attempts to compare results). It seems quite obvious that the above itemizations represent serious patient confoundings—possible secondary gain, a concomitantly improving economic milieu, and social-class contamination of the "psychoneurotic" patients in Denker's study and the more severely ill Landis patients—and indicate at the very least feasible alternatives to Eysenck's claim of comparability of the "control" patients to those usually seen in psychotherapy. Indeed, in view of these confounding factors, the probability that the groups are comparable seems quite low; and hence the use of the Denker and Landis patients as control groups for base-line comparisons with psychotherapy seems invalid. One can approximate comparability of groups only by random selection and random assignment of patients to treatments; or by careful matching of experimental and control patients on relevant variables; or by obtaining post facto measures of relevant patient characteristics, statistically controlling for their influence. These procedures represent the reasonable alternatives to the naive selection dictated by the Patient Uniformity Myth, as well as the recommended designs for any future studies attempting to arrive at a base line of "spontaneous remission" for psychoneurotic patients. The incomparability of the control groups vitiates the case for spontaneous remission of psychoneurotic disorders based on the Denker and Landis studies.

2. *Did the Two Groups of Patients Actually Receive No Psychotherapy?* Let us look first at the Denker group, and again quote Rosenzweig (1954):

> In Eysenck's words these patients were "regularly seen and treated by their own physicians with sedatives, tonics, suggestion, and reassurance." . . . These various presumably nonpsychotherapeutic techniques mentioned include suggestion and reassurance—well-known methods of psychotherapy; and psychiatrists regularly use sedatives and tonics as adjuncts to their practice. . . . The only difference between the work of the general practitioner and of the eclectic psychiatrist that could be assumed, in the absence of detailed and specific knowledge, would be a difference in thoroughness or expertness, not a difference in kind [p. 300].

In other words, from the Denker data, legitimate comparison could be made between psychotherapy of different levels of expertness, with the prediction being that the more expert therapy would produce greater improvement than that of the general practitioner. But the crucial point is that the Denker group cannot properly be considered a control group for spontaneous recovery, since the patients admittedly received some of the elements of psychotherapy.

Similar doubt is cast upon Landis' group. Again to quote Rosenzweig:

> To maintain that neurotic patients admitted to state hospitals receive no psychotherapy is seriously open to doubt. These institutions, despite their notorious shortage of staff, usually make a special effort to treat their neurotic admissions, because these cases have a better prognosis, and because they are far more accessible to treatment [p. 301].

De Charms, Levy, and Wertheimer (1954) add: "Some of Landis' group did receive psychotherapy;" and suggest a further contamination in that "hospital confinement and treatment may themselves be therapeutic." Luborsky (1954) elaborates further on the same point:

> Also as Landis points out (in objecting himself to the use of the consolidated amelioration rate as a base-line for "spontaneous" recovery) neurotics in state hospitals are given a variety of treatments, including some psychotherapy. And, as they are relatively unusual occupants of state hospitals, they probably get unusual treatment [p. 131].

This point can be underscored further by adding that, since psychiatrists in state hospitals are very likely human, it would not be too unbelievable that they might seek out, and perhaps enjoy a little, some contact with a patient who was not divorced from reality, who could converse reasonably well, who presented some hope of recovery, and whose treatment-of-choice could appropriately be traditional psychotherapy.

One again is compelled by these arguments to agree with Rosenzweig (1954):

> It must then be concluded that the control subgroups cited by Eysenck do not sharply differ from the experimental groups in respect to the important variable of having received psychotherapy. As before with regard to illness severity, the necessary contrast between the base line and the experimental groups becomes markedly attenuated [p. 301].

Further, since the spontaneous recovery phenomenon by definition requires that control patients not be treated, the violation of this essential condition by the Landis and Denker studies by itself negates their value as evidence for the Spontaneous Remission Assumption.

3. *Are the Criteria for Improvement or Recovery Used in the Denker and Landis Studies Comparable to Those Used to Evaluate Traditional Psychotherapy?* Can the degree of improvement or recovery reported in these two studies be regarded as equivalent to that reported for traditional psychotherapy? In the first place, it is important to note that terms like improvement or recovery are at best ambiguous. As Luborsky (1954) states:

> The terms say nothing about what the patient was like at the beginning and end of treatment; they can be and are applied to patients at the entire range of mental health. A schizophrenic patient can be called "recovered"; so can a patient with a slight personality problem. Obviously the word "recovered" is used differently in each case [p. 130].

The criterion for improvement or recovery for Landis' state hospital patients was "favorable discharge" from the hospital. Rosenzweig (1954) reasons that the probability is quite low that the criteria used to come to a favorable discharge decision for hospital patients are the same as those used for termination of therapy outpatients.

> In other words, while patients residentially treated are generally considered in terms of hospital discharge and return to the community, the criterion of social recovery being highly relevant, patients nonresidentially treated, as by psychoanalysis, live continuously in the community and are worked with in terms of radical therapy which, if successful, permits them to live not only with others but with themselves. This difference in therapeutic goal is so great that percentage figures for residential and nonresidential treatment are dubiously commensurable [p. 301].

It could be added, along similar lines, that it is not too unreasonable to assume that in many hospitals, especially for voluntary, noncommitted psychoneurotic patients, factors other than personality condition—such as daily patient quotas which determine the hospital budget, pressure from relatives, pressure from the patient himself, etc.—often come to bear on the decision to discharge a particular patient.

The criteria of recovery utilized by Denker are admittedly far superior to Landis' discharge rate. Recall that Denker used two basic indices: (*a*) complaint of no further, or very slight, difficulties, and (*b*) successful social and economic adjustments by the patient. Further, he followed up these patients for a 5 to 10 year period—a procedure that would have certainly strengthened Landis' outcome data. This seems to represent a careful and sophisticated attempt to evaluate the recovery of his insurance patients. However, Cartwright (1955) asks:

It is of some interest to speculate about what evidences were available in the files of the insurance company concerning successful *social* adjustments made by persons whose disability benefits had been terminated. Such termination must certainly be taken as evidence for the making of successful *economic* adjustments. But "complaint of no further, or very slight, difficulties" may represent little more than no further supportable claims against the company [p. 291].

In other words, what motive would make an insurance company collect careful and detailed records of social adjustment of patients *after* they had withdrawn their claims. If subjective report of the patients was given heaviest weight in these indices, as seems likely, then this report seems especially susceptible to the "hello-goodbye" effect (Hathaway, 1948), particularly if one recalls the above argument regarding secondary gain (money) for these patients.

These considerations compel one to agree with Rosenzweig, that "the standards of improvement and recovery in Eysenck's various patient groups. control and experimental, bear so little resemblance to each other that, once again, the basis of his comparisons has little demonstrable validity." Since the criteria of recovery for the Landis and Denker groups seem quite divergent from those used for the evaluation of psychotherapy, the violation of this essential condition in the Landis study, and likely the violation in the Denker study as well, further destroys their utility as evidence for the Spontaneous Remission Assumption.

In summary, the discussion reported seems to lead unequivocally to the conclusion that there is no evidence for spontaneous remission of psychoneurosis. Hence, the belief seems to be nothing more than a myth propagated by a popularized and naive interpretation of two research studies. The patients used in the Landis and Denker studies and the percentages of recovery reported by these authors in no way can be considered evidence of spontaneous remission for untreated psychoneurotic patients. Consequently, Eysenck's use of these percentages as a base line of spontaneous recovery against which to compare the efforts of psychotherapy is invalid. The discussion above has shown that the control patients were very likely not comparable, in fact did receive some treatment (psychotherapy) and hence are not controls, and their recovery was very likely evaluated on significantly different criteria. As Cartwright (1955) concludes:

It is a regrettable accident that the question concerning the effectiveness of psychotherapy has been tied up with the question about spontaneous remission. It has been assumed that the question about therapy is dependent for its answer upon the answer to the question about spontaneous remission. The regrettable part of this is that the worse assumption has been made that the answer to the spontaneous remission question is already known. Of course, it is said, people do recover spontaneously from neurosis and other psychopathological states. Do they? How many? How quickly? Certainly there is no reliable evidence in the studies of Landis and Denker. Indeed, the general absence of such evidence leaves it possible to conclude that the statement asserting the existence of spontaneous remission phenomena in regard to neurosis is made on a priori grounds, rooted perhaps in loose analogy with the natural histories of coughs and colds. It seems to be an open question of fact as to whether or not there are spontaneous remission phenomena at all, and if so, what statistical characteristics they possess [pp. 294–295].

It should be pointed out that the spontaneous recovery rates reported for "psychoneurosis" are far from being reliable. Various survey studies do not agree with the two-thirds rate that Eysenck presents. As de Charms, Levy, and Wertheimer (1954) observe:

Eysenck (1952) also states that these results are typical and that they are "remarkably stable from one investigation to another." This statement is questionable in view of the reports of five year follow-ups such as (*a*) that of Friess & Nelson (1942) where one may interpret the results . . . to mean that 20% is the spontaneous remission rate, and (*b*) that of Denker (1946) where 90% is reported as the spontaneous remission rate for a five year follow-up. If these two studies differ so widely, it appears that existing figures for spontaneous remission rates are not at all consistent. Although Eysenck used a two year base, we see no reason why a five year base may not be taken in comparing two studies, especially since we found no other studies utilizing a two year follow-up with which to check Eysenck's claim of stability [pp. 234–235].

It can be added that two more recent follow-up studies report rates which are also quite different from Eysenck's two-thirds percentage (Hastings, 1958; Saslow & Peters, 1956).

Finally, it is important to emphasize that it would be quite a useful contribution if valid developmental data could be obtained for emotionally disturbed individuals. But the approach must be more sophisticated than those of Landis and Denker. One cannot operate on the Patient Uniformity Myth and report spontaneous remission rates for "psychoneurosis." Rather an attempt first must be made to develop reliable operations by which one can distinguish different types of psychoneurotics. Several more recent survey studies of remission have attempted this kind of differentiation (Hastings, 1958; Saslow & Peters, 1956), but unfortunately used traditional psychiatric nosologies (hysterics, obsessive-compulsives, etc.) which have been shown to be unreliable classifications (Arnhoff, 1954; Ash, 1949; Dayton, 1940; Doering & Raymond, 1934; Mehlman, 1952; Schmidt & Fonda, 1956; Wilson & Deming, 1927). If reliable measures can be developed which meaningfully differentiate psychoneurotic patients, then ideally one could obtain developmental data covering the entire lifespan for these respective groups. That is, it would be useful not only to have data charting the course of an untreated disorder after it has become a debilitating problem, but also to obtain data reflecting the prior development of the disorder. With data of this kind one could not only more validly assess the effects of specific therapeutic interventions, but could also be able to predict which individuals will subsequently experience which kinds of disorders.

The Myth That Present Theories Provide Adequate Research Paradigms

Most of the basic deficiencies in psychotherapy research have derived from the attempt to apply relatively unsophisticated theoretical formulations. This section will attempt to demonstrate how deficient our present formulations are, as well as the necessity for basic revision before further research progress can occur.

Three theoretical formulations have dominated the research approaches to psychotherapy: Freud's theory of psychopathology and psychotherapy, Rogers' earlier and later notions regarding the essential conditions of the therapeutic relationship, and "learning theory" via the behavior therapy approaches. Let us examine the adequacy of these formulations as guides for research in psychotherapy. It is the thesis of this section that a critical look at these systems reveals serious inadequacies: basically that the theories are not comprehensive (i.e., do not exhaust the domain of variables operative in the therapy interaction and do not incorporate existing empirical data); and secondly, do not meet the requirements for an adequate paradigm or model for psychotherapy research. Let us look at these closely related difficulties.

In order for a theoretical formulation to be adequate and useful it must first be comprehensive, covering in its explanations the known facts and variables in its empirical domain. It seems rather apparent that none of the three traditional formulations meet this basic prerequisite. The basic difficulty seems to be that none of them has explicitly built into its system propositions covering individual differences regarding either the patient or the therapist. This oversight seems to be the direct result of the Uniformity Myths. In other words, until quite recently most theoreticians and researchers have implicitly agreed that there is one ideal form of therapy for all patients, and the function of research is to tell us which of the above three best approximate this ideal. Yet, as argued above, clinical experience and recent empirical data point to the centrality of both patient and therapist individual differences in the outcomes of psychotherapy. One searches present formulations in vain for propositions incorporating these patient and therapist variables. It seems, therefore, that one is compelled to conclude that the present theories are either too specific (behavior therapy) or too general (analytical or Rogerian) in explaining the known facts about psychotherapy. In either case, these formulations are not comprehensive, and hence basically inadequate.

Another way of underlining their theoretical inadequacy is to state that the present theories do not offer an adequate paradigm or model for psychotherapy research. A research paradigm optimally should perform several useful functions. Foremost, it should focus on the apparent independent variables in a domain of research, as well as on the scaling and methodological problems encountered in attempts at operationalizing and manipulating these variables. Secondly, it should provide a similar emphasis regarding the dependent variables. Finally, it should deal with the problem of implicit and explicit confounding variables which potentially interact and covary with the dependent variables. The final product would be an explicit listing and elucidation of the total matrix of variables potentially and actually operative in the behaviors being studied in a particular research area.

Each of the three theoretical positions has failed to specify exactly what the independent or dependent variables are. None has methodically dealt with the problems of the quality or quantity of outcome expected from the respective therapeutic interventions, or of differential outcome for different kinds of patients. None has dealt with the sampling and other methodological considerations which, remaining unspecified, make it impossible to design a test of present constructs. Let us examine each of these "theories" of therapy in order to demonstrate more clearly this quite ambiguous state of affairs.

Freudian therapy. What is the heart of analytical therapy? What is the attitude, technique, or personality characteristic essential before a therapist can be said to be doing analytical therapy? The answer seems quite unclear and at best multifaceted and inexplicit. It seems to be an attitude: the therapist must present himself as a neutral and ambiguous stimulus to the patient, in order not to distort the patient's task of free-association and dream production or hamper the appearance of transference phenomena. Yet, at subsequent stages of the interaction the analyst apparently becomes quite nonambiguous, offering interpretations of childhood experiences and the transference relationship. Where does the one attitude (or complex of attitudes) end, and the other begin? What are the behavioral cues which determine the shift of set? What is the interrelationship of the various attitudes (inaction, ambiguity and/or neutrality) prevailing in the earlier stages of therapy? How do these attitudes relate to the interviewing techniques of questioning and clarification which seem to prevail concurrently? At the later stages of therapy: Does interpretation of childhood experiences need to precede interpretations of the transference relationship? Does positive transference necessarily precede negative transference in each therapy interaction? If not, what are the variables determining the sequence? Does the therapist only interpret at moderate depth, that is, just beyond the preconscious? What are the guides for the frequency at which he interprets? What are the cues for determining the optimal timing of a given interpretation? Do interpretations need to be correct in order to be facilitative of the therapeutic task? What are the cues by which the therapist determines whether a given interpretation has accomplished its purpose? Does one interpret differently (at different depths, frequencies, or with different timing) for different kinds of patients? Further, the therapist's personality seems to be crucial at all stages, in that the analyst himself should undergo therapy. But, how does one evaluate (what are the criteria?) whether an analyst has been "successfully" analyzed? What are the personality characteristics of the ideal analyst? To what extent can analytic therapy be accomplished by an unanalyzed or partially analyzed therapist? How do the personality characteristics relate to the therapist attitudes and techniques? Or are all these aspects (personality, situational, technique, etc.) essential ingredients of Freudian technique?

Stone (1951) argues that all these ingredients are essential:

It is not enough to say that psychoanalysis recognizes resistance and transference; psychoanalysis has other technical precepts which, besides the "basic rule" include the exclusive reliance upon free association, regularity of time, frequency and duration, three to five hours per week, use of the recumbent position, the confinement of the analyst's activities to interpretation, the maintenance by the analyst of an attitude of emotional passivity and neutrality in accordance with which he offers no gratification of the patient's transference wishes, abstention by the analyst from giving advice or participating in the daily life of the patient, absence of immediate emphasis upon the curing of symptoms [pp. 217–218].

It is Stone's belief that changes in any one of these features of psychoanalysis might well affect the dynamics of the transference, and hence the whole course of a treatment.

When we search for the Freudian dependent variable we encounter similar ambiguities. Is insight (or making the unconscious conscious) the crucial *in-therapy* product of the complex pattern of therapist activity in the therapy hour? If so, what are the cues by which insight is evaluated? Is insight regarding one's childhood behavior, or, regarding the transference relationship, sufficient? Or is "working through" essential? How does the therapist evaluate whether working through has been accomplished? At what level or degree of working through does the therapist begin to talk about termination: When has there been enough working through? Can working through be accomplished without the prior accomplishment of insight? Or what kind of insight and what level is required (what cues are used to evaluate these factors?) before working through can be effective? Regarding *extra-therapy* criteria of successful outcome: What specific patient characteristics or behaviors are implied by a concept of a totally reintegrated or rebuilt personality? How does the successful patient behave towards other people? What criteria does he employ in evaluating his own goal-seeking behavior? What attitudes does he hold toward himself, toward his family, toward people in general? Can he be unsuccessful at a particular job? Can he be single? Will he be involved in social organizations or civic affairs? Do different patterns of these specific extra-therapy criteria of success emerge for different patients? If so, which ones with which kinds of patients? And what are the cues by which one distinguishes the different kinds of patients?

To the author's knowledge no one has dealt with these theoretical questions methodically and exhaustively—neither Freud nor his followers.[2] What is the independent variable—the crucial therapist behavior (attitude, technique, personality characteric, or what have you) which brings about patient change in the therapy relationship? What is the crucial in-therapy patient change that occurs as the result of the therapist's behavior? How and in what manner does this in-therapy change mediate change in behavior outside the therapy hour? Since there are no theoretical answers to these questions each researcher attacks the variables most interesting to himself (e.g., interpretation, therapist ambiguity, therapist general activity, counter-transference, insight, resistance, anxiety, and the like). Although Freudian theory seems to generate many constructs, the explicit integration or description of the essential ingredients nowhere occurs.

Likewise, many methodological questions arise when one begins to investigate specific variables. Since the theory is not explicitly elaborated, one has little theoretical guidance in resolving these problems. For example, how does one decide where in the therapy sequence to study his particular variable (the problem of unit or segment location)? Is the variable operative equally in the early, middle, and later stages of therapy? Is the variable limited to a specific content of the patient, or a particular patient-therapist interaction in therapy? Does one need to study the entire interactive or content sequence, or can one sample the sequence? If one can sample, what size sample is necessary for validly reflecting the dimension in which one is interested? (What is a valid unit or segment size?) Does location in the interview hour by itself bias the kind of sample one obtains? Can a particular dimension be rated validly from the therapist's (or patient's) verbalizations alone, or does one need the preceding and succeeding comments of the other participant? (Is context necessary?) What level of clinical sophistication is needed to rate the dimension validly? What are the independent, extra-therapy criteria for the in-therapy measure? Does the patient's report of what the therapist is doing need to be congruent with the independent measure obtained?

Rogerian therapy. Rogers' theoretical statement appears in several places (Rogers, 1957, 1959a; Rogers et al., 1966) but perhaps most succinctly in his "Necessary and Sufficient Conditions" paper (1957). In this paper he specifies clearly the three therapist attitudes which must be communicated to the patient before constructive personality change can occur for that patient. The three attitudes or conditions are unconditional positive regard, empathic understanding, and congruence. According to Rogers, if the therapist communicates these attitudes to the patient, constructive personality change will occur. Moreover, he specifies the process dimension along which this patient change

[2] Fenichel made significant beginnings in the direction of systematizing the analytic theory of therapy (Fenichel, 1941, 1953, 1954) but his death interrupted the endeavor.

Recently, some of these factors have also been considered by analytic investigators. Levy (1961), reporting a large-scale research project under the directorship of Franz Alexander, recently described some of the conceptual difficulty their research has encountered: "Another important element of the therapeutic process we are investigating is the role of insight in causing changes in the patient's attitudes. . . . It is difficult, however, to be certain about both the qualitative and quantitative aspects of this feature of the therapeutic experience. Several questions need to be investigated. To what extent do cognitive—intellectual processes and/or emotional experiencing with or without awareness operate? What are their relative importance? How do they vary from case to case? To what extent is the therapist-patient relationship important primarily to provide support and relieve anxiety so that the patient can acquire insight? What are the relative roles of insight on the one hand and the living interpersonal experience with a new (substitute) parent on the other? To what extent is the learning process unconscious, and how much does conscious cognition enter into it? How important is insight into genetic factors, i.e., the re-experiencing of and understanding of the original childhood experiences in which the neurotic patterns developed? [p. 129]."

occurs, describing the seven "strands" of this process and the description of the subsequent levels of each strand (Rogers, 1959b; Rogers, Walker, & Rablen, 1960). At first glance the theoretical statement seems quite simple and easily verifiable. Therapist technique and personality characteristics are not crucial. Rather, the crucial therapist behavior is the communication of the three conditions to the patient. Hence the independent variable seems clear-cut: it is multidimensional, consisting of three therapist attitudes. Likewise, the in-therapy dependent variable is clearly delineated, as presented by the above-mentioned patient "process" construct. However, a closer examination of Rogers' theory from the same points of reference as for the Freudian framework reveals that the specificity of Rogerian theory leaves much to be desired.

What level of these therapist attitudes is necessary before constructive personality change begins to occur? Are they instead all-or-none phenomena? (The various operational definitions of therapist conditions to date all take the form of a continuum.) What is the interrelationship among the three conditions? Is it necessary for all three conditions to be at an equally high level? If so, what are the respective levels? Will a low level of one condition cancel the effectiveness of other high condition levels? Is one of the conditions a precondition? (Rogers seems to suggest that congruence may operate in this fashion.) Need the level of conditions be high at every stage of the interaction, or is it sufficient that they average at a high level for the entire interaction? How does one weight the conditions when combining them for statistical analyses? Are the conditions related to therapist personality characteristics? Is the patient's view of therapist conditions the crucial and only measure required? How will therapists' and independent observers' views agree or disagree with the patient's viewpoint, and is agreement or disagreement necessary? How is the operation of the separate conditions balanced by the others? (Is the appropriateness of congruence evaluated by empathic understanding?) Is the optimal patterning of conditions different for different patient groups or types?

Regarding Rogers' patient-process formulation, the dependent variable is his model: How are the seven strands interrelated? Does one need to utilize all seven strands in order to validly reflect constructive personality change? What function does process change take over the therapy interaction? Is it monotonic? negatively accelerated? U-shaped? or does it represent some other pattern? If it is not monotonic, what explains the points of acceleration or deceleration of the patient's process? Where over the sequence of psychotherapy does an investigator sample in order to validly reflect the process occurring? What size of sample is necessary, and from what location in the therapy hour, in order to validly represent the process occurring in an individual therapy hour? (Rogers' therapist and patient dimensions are theoretically described as content-free; hence that issue is at least resolved.) Can one measure conditions or process from the individual participant's verbalizations alone, or is it necessary that one have context, that is, the other's preceding and subsequent verbalizations? (E.g., does one need the patient's discourse subsequent to the therapist's statements in order to measure empathic understanding?) How and in what manner is in-therapy patient process related to extra-therapy criteria of successful outcome? How does a deeper level of Experiencing relate to a patient's attitudes toward his family and others, his performance on his job, his remission of symptoms, etc.?

Kiesler, Klein, & Mathieu (1966) conclude from the findings of a 5-year study of Rogerian therapy with a hospitalized schizophrenic population:

> In the future studies addressed to issues emanating from Rogerian theory will require more detailed definition and elaboration of both conditions and process factors, as well as their conceptual integration with other aspects of the therapy setting (including patient and therapist characteristics, interactional factors, and empirical phenomena). Such factors will then require more rigorous experimental control. Before this is possible, however, more extensive methodological research is necessary in order to resolve the many issues presented by the complex process phenomena. When, as in this study, theoretically central variables proved to be imbedded in a more complex framework, exploratory studies are necessary to evaluate which of the many theoretically extraneous factors in the setting require particular consideration and control. Only with such pilot information, and with validly anchored instruments for the assessment of therapy variables, can more definitive experimental studies be undertaken.

Behavior therapy. One expects the paradigm here to be quite sophisticated inasmuch as it is based on behavior theory. It is rather unexpected to find rather that the application of learning theory to the psychotherapy interaction has not led to a single behavior therapy, but rather to several kinds of behavior therapy: aversion therapy, negative practice, operant conditioning, reinforcement withdrawal, and desensitization (Grossberg, 1964). This multiplicity of products of itself makes one question the relevance of the original learning theory to the subsequent applications. As Colby (1964) ponders:

> It is often difficult to see how specific therapeutic techniques are deducible from the theory. Learning theory and behavioristic approaches pride themselves on their grounding in scientific principles. Yet different learning theorists derive different techniques from the same theory, and utilize similar techniques from different theories. The contradictory disagreement within the paradigm is obvious to all, but each fights for the exclusive truth status of his position [p. 362].

Still, at first sight, the various derivations do seem to represent greater clarity and simplicity than either the Freudian or Rogerian models. However, closer inspection reveals several inadequacies in these derivations.

Are the various techniques equally effective in the therapeutic situations where behavior therapies are traditionally applied? If they are, which are more economical? If they are not, what is the ordering of the techniques vis-a-vis effectiveness? How are the respective symptom removals or behavior reinforcements related to independent, extra-therapy indices of improvement or success (such as ability to get along with others, performance on the job, interactions with one's family and friends)? Is the particular behavior therapy technique (the independent variable) a unidimensional manipulation? Or are there other implicit facets of the technique besides the theoretically described modification? With desensitization, for example, how much of symptom removal might be the result of suggestion? Is it possible that the removal of symptoms occurs not from "desensitization" but rather because the patient has learned to discriminate his anxieties more clearly as the result of being asked to construct an anxiety hierarchy? Is it possible that by simply teaching the patient to relax, this relaxation ability generalizes to all other situations, including the one in which the phobia is apparent? Are the therapist's attitudes or other personality characteristics influencing the effectiveness of the behavior-therapy techniques? If so, how do these factors interact with the behavior technique for which patients? Given that changes in patient attitudes and feelings about himself and others are theoretically irrelevant (symptom removal is the only crucial consideration), do the various behavior techniques nevertheless affect these attitudes and feelings, and in what manner? Do the constructs used to define the technique actually lead to standardized and replicable operational procedures for different therapists applying the same technique?[3]

In an excellent critical review of the behavior therapy literature, Breger and McGaugh (1965) conclude:

> It is our opinion that the current arguments supporting a learning-theory approach to psychotherapy and neurosis are deficient on a number of grounds. First, we question whether the broad claims they make rest on a foundation of accurate and complete description of the basic data of neurosis and psychotherapy. The process of selecting among the data for those examples fitting the theory and techniques while ignoring a large amount of relevant data seriously undermines the strength and generality of their position. Second, claims for the efficacy of methods should be based on adequately controlled and adequately described evidence. And, finally, when overall claims for the superiority of behavioral therapies are based on alleged similarity to laboratory experiments and alleged derivation from "well established laws of learning" the relevance of the laboratory experimental findings for psychotherapy data should be justified and the laws of learning should be shown to be both relevant and valid [p. 339].

In summary, the basic deficiencies in prevailing theoretical formulations are that they perpetuate and do not attack the Uniformity Myths described in the previous section; do not explicitly deal with the problem of confounding variables; and do not specify the network of independent, dependent, and confounding variables in sufficient enough detail to permit researchers to solve sampling and other methodological problems. In view of these considerations, it seems evident that our formulations about psychotherapy contain serious inadequacies. Until our present theories are brought up to date by being made more comprehensive and by spelling out in much detail the variables of the theoretical paradigm—or until new formulations are introduced which meet the same requirements—it seems that psychotherapy investigators must continue to make arbitrary decisions regarding these parameters, or attempt to fill in the paradigm themselves with much exhaustive but necessary prior methodological research. As Meehl (1955) comments:

> Considering the state of our knowledge, we still do not seem sufficiently daring and experimental about therapeutic tactics. Even when practical exigencies force a certain amount of trial-and-error, doctrinaire views about therapeutic theory are likely to be left unquestioned. The lessons would seem to be that we know so little about the process of helping that the only proper attitude is one of maximum experimentalism. The state of theory and its relation to technique is obviously chaotic whatever our pretensions [pp. 374–375].

Some Miscellaneous Confusions

The distinction traditionally made between process and outcome research seems to have clouded the thinking regarding design, particularly in the latter area. The misconception seems to take the form: process is not outcome research, and outcome research is not process research. The position taken here is that these propositions are incorrect: to some extent process research is outcome research, and outcome research is equivalent to process investigation.

The traditional process-outcome distinction is made as in the following:

> The studies to be summarized here can be roughly dichotomized into those with principal concern as to *how* changes took place, therefore focusing on the interchange between patient and therapist (i.e., the process), and those that focus on the end point, to answer the question of *what* change took place (i.e., the outcome) [Luborsky, 1959, pp. 320–321].

Typically, process studies have dealt with the therapist-patient interview interaction, while outcome studies have focused on changes in the patient as the result of therapy. Process has been studied by various content-analysis procedures as well as by scales or questionnaires developed to measure therapist, patient, or interactional dimensions; whereas outcome investigations have focused on patient changes in test or other behavior from the beginning to termination of therapy.

Two unfortunate effects seem to have followed from this somewhat ambiguous distinction: "outcome" researchers have tended to focus exclusively on pre-post patient differentiations; and patient process changes have not been considered legitimate outcome.

In the first place, the exclusive reliance upon pre-post measurement in outcome designs may lead to findings that are invalid or terminate research prematurely. For example, if patient improvement (as tapped by a particular criterion measure) is not a monotonic function but rather curvilinear in some lawful fashion, a focus on only two points of time may obscure or distort meaningful patient improvement. To the extent that the function of outcome change is unknown, it seems that repeated-measures designs have just as legitimate an application to outcome studies as to interview-by-interview process changes. Further, pre-post designs demand that one have highly reliable change measures before he can expect to tap sensitively any improvement that occurs. As Chassan (1962) observes:

[3] "The 'imagination of a scene' is hardly an objectively defined stimulus, nor is something as general as 'relaxation' a specifiable or clearly observable response [Breger & McGaugh, 1965]."

It becomes apparent that mere end-point observations for the purpose of estimating change in the patient-state after, say, the intervention of some form of treatment places generally severe limitations on the precision of the estimation of the change. For random fluctuation in the patient state can then easily be mistaken for systematic change. To overcome this difficulty, frequent repeated observations must be made of each patient in the study [p. 615].

Thus, it first seems apparent that the traditional process-outcome distinction has perpetuated the relatively exclusive use of pre-post designs in outcome studies, with the unfortunate effect that information about the form of the function which represents the improvement between the two end points, as well as for follow-up periods, has not been clarified; whereas repeated-measures designs would offer this essential type of information. Secondly, the use of only two measurement points has increased the likelihood that any differences observed may be only chance fluctuations due to unreliability of the measures.

The second unfortunate result of the process-outcome dichotomy has been that patient process change within the interview has not been considered explicitly as legitimate outcome. It seems clear, however, that patient improvement manifested in his interview behavior is just as legitimately outcome as any other form of extra-therapy change. Certainly not all process investigation is equivalent to outcome—for example, if the investigator is focusing exclusively on the therapist, or on one point only of the therapy sequence. But to the extent that one is investigating in-therapy patient changes he is concerned directly with outcome; and to the extent that one is interested in outcome, he needs to be cognizant of in-therapy patient changes (a point rarely mentioned). To say this differently, there seem to be two important areas of patient change: that change manifest in the therapy hours themselves, and concomitant changes observed outside the therapy interaction (in situ). Process research begins with the in-the-interview behavior of the patient; outcome investigation begins with his outside-the-interview improvement. The crucial implication is that for either to be maximally useful, it must consider the other focus or perspective. It is necessary for both investigators to formulate some clear paradigm of the dependent variables of psychotherapy, both in- and extra-therapy, and their theoretical interrelationships.

It seems, then, that the process-outcome confusion has resulted primarily from ignoring the fact that some interview data reflects outcome (patient change); or, said differently, that some of the outcome of therapy may be evident in the interviews. Perhaps it would be helpful to discard these terms, instead referring to in-therapy (interview) studies (via direct observation, movies, tape recordings, or transcripts) and extra-therapy investigations (dealing with "in situ" observations). It must also be added that since the statistical function of these in- and extra-therapy changes is unknown, one should seriously consider the appropriateness of repeated-measures designs in attempting to evaluate the effects of psychotherapy.

A further difficulty in psychotherapy research has been connected with the scientific status of current diagnostic categories for mental illness. The problem stems not only from the fact that the classifications systems are unreliable (Arnhoff, 1954; Ash, 1949; Dayton, 1940; Doering & Raymond, 1934; Mehlman, 1952; Schmidt & Fonda, 1956; Wilson & Deming, 1927) but equally importantly from the fact that differential diagnosis makes no difference—that is, leads to no prescribed differential psychotherapeutic treatment. A suggested answer to both of these nosological difficulties is that we may be looking in the wrong places for a reliable and valid diagnostic scheme. Perhaps the answer to the classification problem lies in differential patient behavior found in the therapy hour itself. If therapists in fact deal differently in therapy with different patients, then perhaps the patient cues to which the therapist differentially responds can be isolated and reliably measured from that interaction. If the manner in which the patient talks about himself in therapy indeed provides a reliable differentiation of patients, then the likelihood seems good that the process dimensions isolated would be directly relevant to differential therapeutic techniques. It seems that this possibility has been overlooked to date.

Finally, an unrealistic hope prevailing in psychotherapy research has been the belief that sooner or later "The Definitive Study" will be published which once and for all proves the effectiveness of psychotherapy and defines the process by which it works. This belief seems to have motivated the prolific subsidization of the large outcome research projects prevalent in the last decade. One of the functions of this paper is to demonstrate the infinitesimal probability that any one-shot research attempt will ever significantly advance our knowledge in this area. The business at hand for therapy (just as for any other) research seems clear: painstaking involvement with delineated problems until repeated replication of individual findings has been demonstrated, and subsequent attack of closely related or ancillary questions. As Seeman (1961) has observed, investigators need to "dispel the notion that some single research package is likely to be devised to answer a great many questions all at once." Rather the pattern of research required is "one of plugging away at small bits of knowledge which, only after an appreciable period of time, might attain a higher order of significance."

THE SEARCH FOR A PARADIGM

In the domain of psychotherapy there is no single shared paradigm commanding consensus. With considerable overlap the leading current paradigms are the psychoanalytic, learning theory and existential. Signs of crisis are to be found in each in the increasing recognition and public acknowledgement of limitations and impasses [Colby, 1964, p. 347].

The previous section described in some detail the theoretical inadequacies present in the existent models for psychotherapy. Further inadequacy lies in the fact that (with the possible exception of Rogers) these theoreticians or their disciples have not modified their formulations in light of recent empirical evidence. For despite the fact that conceptualizations have been vague and the designs of studies leave much to be desired, there has emerged a consistent body of data at least regarding patient prognostic variables (e.g., social class, intelligence, and the like) which has not been incorporated into any theoretical system. Additional evidence is suggestive that therapist personality and expectations, as well as therapist-patient relationship factors are also critically related to therapeutic outcome. Until these various factors are incorporated into theoretical formulations (existent or new) these models cannot be utilized meaningfully in therapy research—and therapy research will remain in a state of crisis. It is the purpose of this section to spell out the minimum requirements for a useful psychotherapy research paradigm by attempting to delineate the relevant factors suggested by current empirical data, by elaborating on the methodological issues that have to be dealt with, and by doing this in a language sufficiently general to be applicable to researchers of differing orientations. The goal is not to construct an adequate paradigm, but to try to outline the minimal criteria any paradigm must satisfy before its adequacy can even begin to be considered.

The plan of the following, therefore, is to examine critically the individual psychotherapy situation in order to delineate, in general terms, the independent and dependent variables as well as the confounding variables that have been shown to be built into and complicating this system. Concomitantly, an attempt will be made to derive some suggestions regarding experimental design in light of these considerations—although this is not the primary focus since the statistical and design issues have been addressed quite competently by others (Campbell, 1957, 1963; Edwards & Cronbach, 1952; Patterson, 1956; Underwood, 1957). The "variable-model" approach used follows very closely the research model excellently presented by Underwood with, however, an exclusive focus here on the therapy research situation.

Independent Variable(s)

What is the independent variable in psychotherapy research? Clearly its choice depends upon one's particular theoretical orientation or observational hunches. Just as clearly, it is evident from the above that present formulations have not specified in sufficient detail what these independent variables are: For analytical therapy it lies somewhere among a matrix of therapist attitudinal, technique, and personality factors (e.g., ambiguity, interpretation, personal maturity). For Rogerian therapy it lies somewhere in an interactional matrix of three therapist Conditions or attitudes (positive regard, empathic understanding, and congruence). For behavior therapy it falls somewhere in the communication by the therapist of specific unlearning procedures. Obviously, more critical thinking needs to be given to the exact delineation of the therapist variable or variables instrumental in effecting patient change.

Generally, it seems clear that the independent variable in psychotherapy has to lie somewhere in the therapist and his behavior. It seems necessary that some aspect of the therapist (attitude, technique, personality characteristic, and/or the like) be communicated to the patient to some degree before one can expect the patient to change in some manner. Ideally, there would be but one therapist dimension communicated to the patient, thereby effecting beneficial changes in that patient. Practically, however, few if any theoreticians have talked of a single therapist dimension or behavior as crucial, but list several or many, emphasizing as they go the extreme complexity of the therapy relationship. Very likely, then, the independent variable for psychotherapy research needs to be multidimensional, in that more than one aspect of the therapist are crucial antecedents of beneficial patient change. An implication of this point, and an equally crucial one, is that the exact interrelationship or patterning of the variables in the multidimensional model needs to be clearly specified in any theoretical formulation.

Now, if psychotherapy were a one-time event this kind of model of independent variables might be adequate. However, since therapy is a sequential treatment procedure, one's model needs to be concerned further with the dimension of time. Are the same aspects of the therapist operative in the same pattern over the entire therapy interaction? If so, this needs to be explicitly defined theoretically. If, on the other hand, (as seems more likely) one or more therapist variables are crucial at one phase of the interaction, and others are indicated at other periods, then it is necessary to specify these time interactions. Otherwise a researcher may be sampling at the inappropriate therapy period in his attempt to investigate specific theoretical dimensions. Further, the model would be less difficult if psychotherapy were an agreed-upon perfect technique effecting changes regardless of type of patient. However, since it seems more likely that "psychotherapy" represents in practice heterogeneous therapist performance depending upon the kind of patient with whom he is dealing, then one's model must delineate differential levels or classes of independent variables which are correlated respectively with these patient individual differences.

Hence, if psychotherapy research is to progress, it seems essential that theoreticians and/or investigators first define therapist behavior in very precise terms: by specifying the dimensions along which they vary, by specifying the exact interrelationships among these dimensions at separate time-points in the therapy interaction, and by specifying their differentiations for various kinds of levels of patient disorder.

Dependent Variable(s)

Just as much imprecision has been manifest regarding the dependent variable in psychotherapy research. Here the Patient Uniformity Myth has dictated the search for the one patient "process" dimension along which beneficial patient change occurs. For analytic therapy, this dimension has resided somewhere among such variables as insight (making the unconscious conscious), working through, reduction in anxiety and resistance, etc. For Rogers, it is found somewhere among his seven strands of process or Experiencing. For behavior therapy it seems to reside somewhere in the process of anxiety reduction and symptom removal.

Many of the same concerns expressed regarding the independent variable are germane here. Does patient-beneficial change occur along one dimension or, more feasibly, along several dimensions? Are the same patient-change dimensions operative at all phases of psychotherapy? If so, what is their patterning? If not, which dimensions are changing in what manner at the different phases? Do we need different dependent variables of change for different kinds of patients? If so, what are the diagnostic dimensions involved, and what are the respective differential patient-change processes? Are these dependent variables manifest in the in-therapy verbal communications of the patient? If not, what are the extra-therapy manifestations of this change? If so, how are the in-therapy communication variables related to the extra-therapy manifestations? That is, how does the in-therapy process mediate changes in extra-therapy patient behaviors? It seems clear that the dependent variables of therapy are to be found somewhere in the in- or extra-therapy verbalizations and/or behavior of the patient, and in changes along these dimensions in a "positive" direction over the therapy sequence.

In summary, then, the basic skeleton of a paradigm for psychotherapy seems to be something like the following: The patient communicates something; the therapist communicates something in response; the patient communicates and/or experiences something different; and the therapist, patient, and others like the change (although they may like it to different degrees, or for divergent reasons). What the therapist communicates (the independent variables) is very likely multidimensional (and the patterning of this multidimensionality needs to be specified), and may be different at different phases of the interaction for different kinds of patients. Similarly, what the patient communicates and/or experiences differently (the dependent variables) is likely multidimensional (and the patterning of that multidimensionality needs to be clarified) and may be different at distinct phases of the interaction. The enormous task of psychotherapy theory and research is that of filling in the variables of this paradigm.

It should be added at this point that even if formulations were developed to the point of filling in this paradigm, there would still be many basic methodological problems before one could appropriately begin to process the raw data of therapy. These problems have been encountered in many process studies and concern such issues as unit size, segment location, context, interdependency of patient and therapist measures, data form and presentation, and parsimonious interpretation. The empirical solution of these methodological problems is necessary before one can validly test theoretical propositions. Since these issues have been dealt with in detail elsewhere (Bordin et al., 1954; Kiesler, 1966) they will not be elaborated again here. Suffice it to say that many process investigators have completely ignored these basic methodological issues.

The Problem of Confounding

Since the minimal requirements for a therapy paradigm have not been met by theoretical formulations, confounding variables have contaminated much psychotherapy research. In fact, the major value of investigations to date has been the demonstration of the multiple and varied sources from which confounding can occur. Until this contamination is dealt with, research findings will continue to be ambiguous and consequently subject to alternative interpretations. The essential goal of research is to "design the experiment so that the effects of the independent variables can be evaluated unambiguously [Underwood, 1957]."

This final section will examine the varied sources of confounding that existing paradigms have ignored. It will utilize Underwood's (1957) three classes of confounding variables (subject, task, and environmental) by applying them directly to the psychotherapy situation. Hopefully, the result will be a listing of variables or variable domains which need to be integrated into the above paradigm and/or whose contaminations need to be eliminated by experimental or statistical control procedures in individual research.

Subject confounding variables. According to Underwood, subject confounding occurs when stable or temporary factors or dimensions in the experimental subjects are per se relevant to, or inducive of, differences in the dependent variable measures. If these subject factors are permitted to go uncontrolled, one cannot unambiguously interpret dependent variable changes as a function of manipulations of the independent variable. Psychotherapy research of the past decade has shown that virtually the entire domain of patient characteristics (demographic, intellectual, motivational, semantic, perceptual expectancies) are relevant in greater and less degrees to reactivity to psychotherapy. As Luborsky (1959) notes:

> A number of studies . . . are concerned with identifying qualities of patients that are associated with staying in treatment, improving in treatment, or returning once having left treatment. There are many such studies now in the literature. They have not yet come to anything definitive, but they seem on the verge of it, for the results of all of these studies point in the same directions. To put these trends simply: Those who stay in treatment improve; those who improve are better off to begin with than those who do not; and one can predict response to treatment by how well they are to begin with [p. 324].

And Strupp (1962) observes:

> It is becoming increasingly clear that therapists have fairly specific (and valid) notions about the kinds of attributes a "good" patient should possess as well as about those attributes which make a patient unsuitable for the more usual forms of investigative, insight-producing psychotherapy. Patients considered good prognostic risks are described as young, attractive, well-educated, members of the upper middle class, possessing a high degree of ego-strength, some anxiety which impels them to seek help, no seriously disabling neurotic symptoms, relative absence of deep characterological distortions and strong secondary gains, a willingness to talk about their difficulties, an ability to communicate well, some skill in the social-vocational area, and a value system relatively congruent with that of the therapists. Such patients also tend to remain in therapy, profit from it, and evoke the therapist's best efforts [pp. 470–471].

Hence it should be now apparent that patients manifest individual differences along many outcome-relevant and likely interrelated dimensions. A tentative listing of subject confounding variables would include the following: verbal intelligence, age, motivation for therapy, level of general anxiety, level of ego-strength, type of disorder, severity of disorder, type of onset of disorder, socioeconomic background, patient expectancies, verbal expressive ability, level of occupational success, type of value system, and likely others. In view of this multiplicity of confounding factors, it should be abundantly clear why permitting patients to select themselves for research studies has made results incomparable and nonreplicable; why the Patient Uniformity Assumption is indeed a myth; why an adequate paradigm of therapy needs to incorporate these variables into its structure by tying together the patterning of these factors, and by stipulating alternative treatment procedures for patients at different levels of these dimensions.[4]

It also becomes clear why, in investigating the effects of one's independent variable or variables, it is necessary to control for these confoundings. The control problem is basically that of equivalent groups (Underwood, 1957). The experimental alternatives are random assignment of subjects to treatment groups, or prior matching of patients to form equivalent groups. The former procedure seems to be a good first solution to this difficulty. By randomly assigning patients, one is statistically assured that the various treatment groups will be comparable regarding subject characteristics, will not differ on relevant subject variables other than in chance directions. However, one needs relatively large samples and may not be able to define clearly the population from which his sample came. One also has an error term which is larger than it otherwise need be, in that much of the error variance is identifiable—can be traced directly to the kind of relevant patient variables listed above. Finally, one is not permitted to ascertain interaction effects between psychotherapy treatment (or ideally different types and/or amounts of psychotherapy) and these known-to-be relevant subject characteristics.

A more efficient procedure for controlling subject confoundings seems to be by experimental and/or statistical (partial correlation or covariance) matching procedures. By these procedures, patients in different treatment groups are matched on one or more relevant dimensions, thereby establishing group equivalency for these measures. The optimal procedure would seem to be to introduce these patient variables into the research design in the form of independent variables, so that the meaningful interactions between treatments and these organismic variables can be ascertained. For example, different depths of interpretation may be more effective for patients of low in contrast to high levels of general anxiety. Or, different levels of therapist activity or directiveness may be more beneficial for patients of low in contrast to high socioeconomic background. It seems that if the psychotherapy research paradigm is to begin to be filled in, this latter kind of interactional research (factorial designs) is essential. This seems to be the conclusion of educational research, an area having quite similar methodological and design problems. As Edwards and Cronbach (1952) observe:

> Educators spent a generation on studies of the oversimplified "Is A better than B?" type. They sought to settle by experimentation whether large classes were better than small, lectures better than laboratories, frequent tests better than few. Their studies led to endless contradiction because, as you will notice, the question did not specify the organismic variables. . . . [One investigator] showed that his Method A was better than B for bright, mediocre achievers, but that B was better for those of mediocre intelligence but good past achievement. The inclusion of both organismic variables in the design was essential if he was not to reach an over-simple, hence untrue, conclusion. . . . The writers agree that effort to isolate effects due to organismic variables can have only a beneficial effect, and that cases should be selected to represent as much variation as can be. It is far more valuable to study ten cases, two each of five identifiable subtypes, than to study a pool of fifty undescribed and undifferentiated people. . . . The most promising (i.e., the most likely to be relevant) variable should be built into the design so that gains can be assessed separately for each variable [pp. 53–54].

Task confounding variables. Task variables refer to dimensions or aspects of the experimental apparatus or stimulus, other than the experimenter-defined independent variable, which per se are relevant to, and inducive of, changes in the dependent variable measures. Task confounding comes from aspects of the experimental task (apparatus or stimulus) on which the experimenter is not focusing, aspects other than his arbitrarily defined independent variable.

In psychotherapy research, task confounding is possible whenever one arbitrarily defines the independent variable. If one's empirical hunch or theoretical framework implies that, for example, depth of interpretation is the crucial therapist dimension (leading to differences in the dependent variable, e.g., level of patient insight), then one would like to conclude that in fact manipulation of therapist depth of interpretation effected the different levels of patient insight. But task confounding occurs and confuses the situation, if, for example, the therapist's empathic understanding (rather than depth of interpretation) could also be responsible for the differences obtained. If empathy is related to insight, and if it is not controlled in the above situation, interpretation of the insight differences obtained will be ambiguous.

Recent psychotherapy research has indicated that a number of therapist variables may be related to patient improvement. A tentative listing would include: therapist experience level, prestige, occupational interest pattern, enthusiasm or confidence, verbal reinforcement, therapist expectancies, therapist "Conditions," depth of interpretation, liking for the patient, degree of ambiguity, deconditioning, therapist orientation, therapist personality, and likely others. With this extensive list of therapist or task confounding variables, it becomes essential that theoretical paradigms attempt to incorporate these dimensions, as well as explain their interrelationships.

Also, in light of the above, it should be abundantly clear that mere arbitrary definition of one aspect of the therapist as one's independent variable does not excuse an investigator from considering other therapist factors that may be concomitantly operative and of themselves producing the results obtained. One needs to tackle the arduous task of

[4] As Rapaport (1960) urges: "Therapies or therapists . . . end up by establishing their own McCarran Act: sooner or later they announce that this or that kind of patient is not the right kind for their kind of therapy. Not rarely they go further and announce that this or that kind of patient is 'not treatable.' In the long run, psychological theories of therapy must come to a point where they will make it possible to select the therapy which is good for a patient and not the patient who is good for a therapy [p. 115]."

attempting to measure and experimentally or statistically control these other factors in order to eliminate task confounding for his particular study. Or, one can incorporate these factors as additional dimensions (additional independent variables) in his design so that possible interactions between these various therapist dimensions and patient change can be determined. Quite likely the crucial therapist communications are multidimensional, and researchers need to be acutely attuned to the possible covariance and/or interaction of other therapist dimensions with the particular one in which they may be interested.

Environmental confounding variables. Environmental variables refer to all nontask (nonapparatus) variables which change concurrently with manipulation of the independent variable, and which per se are relevant to, and inducive of, changes in the dependent variable measures. Examples of this kind of confounding in psychological research would be the influence the examiner has, independent of the ink blots, in Rorschach research; or the effect humidity has on GSR responses independent of other manipulations; or time of day, in contrast to type of instruction, in educational research.

The basic reason for having a control group in traditional evaluative studies of therapy is to hold constant this possible contamination from environmental sources. This especially needs to be done for psychotherapy research since time of itself is an important variable vis-a-vis patient changes—more exactly that extra-therapy events that may be crucially relevant to patient changes can occur over time. The death of a close friend or relative may occur, causing a relapse in the patient. He may meet a new friend who may effect an important difference in the patient's perception of himself and his behavior. His job situation may change: he could be promoted, find the opening he has been waiting for; or on the other hand, he may be suddenly fired or laid off. Obviously, any number of possible interpersonal events may occur which can be directly relevant to the patient's psychopathological condition, with the result that changes apparent in a patient may have little to do with the psychotherapy he is receiving concomitantly. Hence, a control group is needed which receives no therapy, as a base line of improvement from environmental events to which the condition of therapy can be compared.

Further environmental contamination can come from the fact that some of the patients may be receiving concomitant medication which can be responsible for patient behavior changes. Other environmental variables not often mentioned would be differences in the office situation in which therapy occurs (e.g., degree of soundproofing; comfort of chairs; color of room; pictures on the wall or not, and which kinds; seating arrangement of therapist and patient; warmth of receptionist; privacy of reception room and office; etc.). These variables are likely not extensively operative in the therapy interaction, but to the extent that they are they must be controlled or varied systematically.

In short, since one can seldom have control over patients' environments (although this ability represents the real potential of institutional studies) a control group for environmental events is essential before one can be confident in concluding that either a particular therapy treatment or several treatments are more effective than no treatment at all.

Conclusion

This final section has attempted to spell out in detail the classes of variables that need to be incorporated into theoretical formulations and/or controlled for in psychotherapy research before replicable findings can result. The first crucial implication of these paradigm considerations is that theoretical formulations can no longer ignore the various domains of variables shown to be relevant to psychotherapy outcome.[5] The second, and equally vital, implication is that psychotherapy research can no longer ignore the necessity for factorial designs. Although this latter point has been emphasized in the past, few researchers seem to incorporate the recommendation. As recently as 1959 Berdie observed:

> When this author reviewed current research in counseling nine years ago, he concluded, an area of research importance to every counselor, but in which this reviewer could find no research publications, concerns the relationship between diagnosis and therapy. What diagnostic categories and techniques are most useful in selecting appropriate therapists? Near the conclusion of this nine-year period *one* group of authors reported the first substantial study of therapy that took into account the effects of precounseling attributes, differential counseling methods, and outcomes (Ashby et al., 1957). Although the results of this study were rather meager, certainly this study itself should be considered a *pioneer* one [p. 345].

In short, the research message seems clear: Current paradigms are inadequate. The time is long overdue not only to acknowledge, but also to meet head-on in theoretical formulations and research investigations the minimal requirements of a psychotherapy research paradigm.

> Now that the mystery and aura are being removed, the psychotherapy relationship is being seen by varieties of researchers as a phenomenon which is as fruitful for investigation as are the parent-child, peer-peer, teacher-student, experimenter-subject, and other important human groups. Also, importantly, it is being seen in its true perspective: i.e., as no more important or mysterious than any of these other relationships. [Matarazzo, 1965, p. 219]

REFERENCES

Arnhoff, F. N. Some factors influencing the unreliability of clinical judgments. *Journal of Clinical Psychology*, 1954, **10**, 272–275.

Ash, P. The reliability of psychiatric diagnoses. *Journal of Abnormal and Social Psychology*, 1949, 44, 27–277.

[5] For a detailed discussion of a variable model similar to the one presented here, see Levinson (1962), who presents a list of seven domains of therapy variables: (*a*) relatively stable personal-social characteristics of the therapist, (*b*) relatively stable personal-social characteristics of the patient, (*c*) characteristics of the patient-therapist pair, (*d*) stages in the treatment career, (*e*) overall treatment outcome, (*f*) the institutional setting of treatment, and (*g*) the social context of the patient's life. Levinson concludes: "If we are to forego theoretical unity, we must at least have a common framework on which to hang our differences. . . . To the extent that [this framework] in fact takes into account the events and variables dealt with in the diverse studies, it may serve to sharpen our view of the ways in which these studies overlap, converge, complement each other, and stand in direct opposition [p. 14]."

Ashby, J. D., Ford, D. H., Guerney, B. G., Jr., & Guerney, L. F. Effects on clients of a reflective and a leading type of psychotherapy. *Psychological Monographs,* 1957, 7(24, Whole No. 453).

Auld, F., Jr., & Murray, E. J. Content-analysis studies of psychotherapy. *Psychological Bulletin,* 1955, **52**, 377–395.

Berdie, R. F. Counseling. *Annual Review of Psychology,* 1959, **10**, 345–370.

Bordin, E. S., Cutler, R. L., Dittmann, A. T., Harway, N. I., Raush, H. L., & Rigler, D. Measurement problems in process research on psychotherapy. *Journal of Consulting Psychology,* 1954, **18**, 79–82.

Breger, L., & McGaugh, J. L. Critique and reformulation of "learning-theory" approaches to psychotherapy and neurosis. *Psychological Bulletin,* 1965, **63**, 338–358.

Campbell, D. T. Factors relevant to the validity of experiments in social situations. *Psychological Bulletin,* 1957, **54**, 297–312.

Campbell, D. T. From description to experimentation: Interpreting trends as quasi experiments. In C. W. Harris (Ed.), *Problems in measuring change.* Madison: Univer. Wisconsin Press, 1963. Pp. 212–242.

Cartwright, D. S. Effectiveness of psychotherapy: A critique of the spontaneous remission argument. *Journal of Counseling Psychology,* 1955, **2**, 290–296.

Cartwright, D. S. Annotated bibliography of research and theory construction in client-centered therapy. *Journal of Counseling Psychology,* 1957, **4**, 82–100.

Chassan, J. B. Probability processes in psychoanalytic psychiatry. In J. Scher (Ed.), *Theories of the mind.* New York: Free Press of Glencoe, 1962. Pp. 598–618.

Colby, K. M. Psychotherapeutic processes. *Annual Review of Psychology,* 1964, **15**, 347–370.

Dayton, N. A. *New facts on mental disorders.* Springfield, Ill.: Charles C Thomas, 1940.

DeCharms, R., Levy, J., & Wertheimer, M. A note on attempted evolutions of psychotherapy. *Journal of Clinical Psychology,* 1954, **10**, 233–235.

Denker, P. G. Results of treatment of psychoneuroses by the general practitioner: A follow-up study of 500 cases. *Archives of Neurology and Psychiatry,* 1947, **57**, 504–505.

Doering, C. R., & Raymond, Alice F. Reliability of observations of psychiatric and related characteristics. *American Journal of Orthopsychiatry,* 1934, **4**, 249–257.

Dührssen, A., & Jorswieck, E. Zur Korrektur von Eysenck's Berichterstattung über psychoanalytische Behandlungsergebnisse. *Acta Psychotherapeutica et Psychosomatica,* 1962, **10**, 329–342.

Edwards, A. L., & Cronbach, L. J. Experimental design for research in psychotherapy. *Journal of Clinical Psychology,* 1952, **8**, 51–59.

Eysenck, H. J. The effects of psychotherapy: An evaluation. *Journal of Consulting Psychology,* 1952, **16**, 319–324.

Eysenck, H. J. A reply to Luborsky's note. *British Journal of Psychology,* 1954, **45**, 132–133.

Eysenck, H. J. The effects of psychotherapy: A reply. *Journal of Abnormal and Social Psychology,* 1955, **50**, 147–148. (a)

Eysenck, H. J. Review of C. R. Rogers & R. F. Dymond: *Psychotherapy and personality change. British Journal of Psychology,* 1955, **46**, 237–238. (b)

Eysenck, H. J. The effects of psychotherapy. In H. J. Eysenck (Ed.), *Handbook of abnormal psychology: An experimental approach.* New York: Basic Books, 1961. Pp. 697–725.

Eysenck, H. J. The outcome problem in psychotherapy: A reply. *Psychotherapy: Theory, Research and Practice,* 1964, **1**, 97–100.

Fenichel, O. *Problems of psychoanalytic technique.* New York: Psychoanalytic Quarterly, 1941.

Fenichel, O. *Collected papers.* New York: Norton, First Series (1922–36), 1953. Second Series (1936–46), 1954.

Friess, C., & Nelson, M. J. Psychoneurotics five years later. *American Journal of Mental Science,* 1942, **203**, 539–558.

Gardner, G. G. The psychotherapeutic relationship. *Psychological Bulletin,* 1964, **61**, 426–437.

Gendlin, E. T. The social significance of the research. In C. R. Rogers, E. T. Gendlin, D. J. Kiesler, & C. B. Truox, (Eds.), *The therapeutic relationship and its impact: A study of psychotherapy with schizophrenics.* Madison: Univer. Wisconsin Press, 1966, in press. Ch. 21.

Gilbert, W. Counseling: Therapy and diagnosis. *Annual Review of Psychology,* 1952, **3**, 351–380.

Goldstein, A. P. *Therapist-patient expectancies in psychotherapy.* New York: Macmillan, 1962.

Grossberg, J. M. Behavior therapy: A review. *Psychological Bulletin,* 1964, **62**, 73–88.

Hastings, D. N. Follow-up results in psychiatric illness. *American Journal of Psychiatry,* 1958, **114**, 1057–1066.

Hathaway, S. R. Some considerations relative to nondirective counseling as therapy. *Journal of Clinical Psychology,* 1948, **4**, 226–231.

Herron, W. G. The process-reactive classification of schizophrenia. *Psychological Bulletin,* 1962, **59**, 329–343.

Herzog, Elizabeth. *Some guidelines for evaluative research.* (United States Department of Health, Education and Welfare, Social Security Administration Children's Bureau, pamphlet) Washington, D. C.: Government Printing Office, 1959.

Kiesler, D. J. Some basic methodological issues in psychotherapy process research. *American Journal of Psychotherapy,* 1966, in press.

Kiesler, D. J., Klein, Marjorie H., & Mathieu, Philipp L. A summary of the issues and conclusions. In C. R. Rogers, E. T. Gendlin, D. J. Kiesler, & C. B. Truox (Eds.), *The therapeutic relationship and its impact: A study of psychotherapy with schizophrenics.* Madison: Univer. Wisconsin Press, 1966, in press. Ch. 12.

Krasner, L. Group discussion: Therapist's contribution. In H. H. Strupp & L. Luborsky (Eds.), *Research in psychotherapy.* Vol. 2. Washington, D. C.: American Psychological Association, 1962. Pp. 103–104.

Landis, C. A. Statistical evaluation of psychotherapeutic methods. In L. E. Hinsie (Ed.), *Concepts and problems of psychotherapy.* New York: Columbia Univer. Press, 1937. Pp. 155–169.

Levinson, D. J. The psychotherapist's contribution to the patient's treatment career. In H. H. Strupp & Luborsky (Eds.), *Research in psychotherapy.* Vol. 2. Washington, D. C.: American Psychological Association, 1962. Pp. 13–24.

Levy, N. A. An investigation into the nature of psychotherapeutic process: A preliminary report. In J. H. Masserman (Ed.), *Psychoanalysis and social process.* New York: Grune & Stratton, 1961. Pp. 125–149.

Luborsky, L. A note on Eysenck's article "The effects of psychotherapy: An evaluation." *British Journal of Psychology,* 1954, **45**, 129–131.

Luborsky, L. Psychotherapy. *Annual Review of Psychology.* 1959, **10**, 317–344.
Marsden, G. Content-analysis studies of therapeutic interviews: 1954 to 1964. *Psychological Bulletin,* 1965, **63**, 298–321.
Matarazzo, J. D. Psychotherapeutic processes. *Annual Review of Psychology,* 1965, **16**, 181–224.
Meehl, P. E. Psychotherapy. *Annual Review of Psychology.* 1955, **6**, 357–378.
Mehlman, B. The reliability of psychiatric diagnoses. *Journal of Abnormal and Social Psychology,* 1952, **47**, 577–578.
Patterson, C. H. Matching vs. randomization in studies of counseling. *Journal of Counseling Psychology,* 1956, **3**, 262–272.
Raimy, V. C. Clinical methods: Psychotherapy. *Annual Review of Psychology.* 1952, **3**, 321–350.
Rapaport, D. The structure of psychoanalytic theory: A systematizing attempt. *Psychological Issues,* 1960, **2**, 1–158.
Rogers, C. R. The necessary and sufficient conditions of therapeutic personality change. *Journal of Consulting Psychology,* 1957, **21**, 95–103.
Rogers, C. R. A tentative scale for the measurement of process in psychotherapy. In E. A. Rubinstein & M. B. Parloff (Eds.), *Research in psychotherapy.* Washington, D. C.: American Psychological Association, 1959. Pp. 96–107. (a)
Rogers, C. R. A theory of therapy, personality, and interpersonal relationships as developed in the client-centered framework. In S. Koch (Ed.), *Psychology: A study of science.* Vol. 3. *Formulations of the person and the social context.* New York: McGraw-Hill, 1959. Pp. 184–256. (b)
Rogers, C. R., & Dymond, R. F. (Eds.), *Psychotherapy and personality change.* Chicago: Univer. Chicago Press, 1954.
Rogers, C. R., Gendlin, E. T., Kiesler, D. J., & Truox, C. B. *The therapeutic relationship and its impact: A study of psychotherapy with schizophrenics.* Madison: Univer. Wisconsin Press, 1966, in press.
Rogers, C. R., Walker, A., & Rablen, R. Development of a scale to measure process change in psychotherapy. *Journal of Clinical Psychology,* 1960, **16**, 79–85.
Rosenzweig, S. A transvaluation of psychotherapy: A reply to Hans Eysenck. *Journal of Abnormal and Social Psychology,* 1954, **49**, 298–304.
Rotter, J. B. Psychotherapy. *Annual Review of Psychology.* 1960, **11**, 381–414.
Rubinstein, E. A., & Parloff, M. B. (Eds.), *Research in psychotherapy.* Washington, D. C.: American Psychological Association, 1959.
Sanford, N. Clinical methods: Psychotherapy. *Annual Review of Psychology,* 1953, **4**, 317–342.
Saslow, G., & Peters, Ann D. A follow-up study of "untreated" patients with various behavior disorders. *Psychiatric Quarterly,* 1956, **30**, 283–302.
Schmidt, H. O., & Fonda, C. P. The reliability of psychiatric diagnosis: A new look. *Journal of Abnormal and Social Psychology,* 1956, **52**, 262–267.
Seeman, J. Psychotherapy. *Annual Review of Psychology.* 1961, **12**, 157–194.
Stein, M. E. (Ed.) *Contemporary psychotherapies.* New York: Free Press of Glencoe, 1961.
Stevenson, I. The challenge of results in psychotherapy. *American Journal of Psychiatry,* 1959, **116**, 120–123.
Stieper, D. R., & Wiener, D. N. *Dimensions of psychotherapy: An experimental and clinical approach.* Chicago: Aldine, 1965.
Stone, L. Psychoanalysis and brief psychotherapy. *Psychoanalytic Quarterly,* 1951, **20**, 215–236.
Strupp, H. H. Psychotherapy. *Annual Review of Psychology,* 1962, **13**, 445–478.
Strupp, H. H. The outcome problem in psychotherapy revisited. *Psychotherapy: Theory, Research and Practice,* 1964, **1**, 1–13. (a)
Strupp, H. H. The outcome problem in psychotherapy: A rejoinder. *Psychotherapy: Theory, Research and Practice,* 1964, **1**, 101. (b)
Strupp, H. H. *A bibliography of research in psychotherapy.* Chapel Hill, N. C.: University of North Carolina, Department of Psychiatry, 1964.
Strupp, H. H., & Luborsky, L. (Eds.). *Research in psychotherapy.* Vol. 2. Washington, D. C.: American Psychological Association, 1962.
Underwood, B. J. *Psychological research.* New York: Appleton-Century-Crofts, 1957.
Wilson, E. B., & Deming, Julia. Statistical comparison of psychiatric diagnoses in Massachusetts State Hospitals during 1925 and 1926. *Bulletin of Massachusetts' Department of Mental Disorders,* 1927, **11**, 6–19.
Winder, C. L. Psychotherapy. *Annual Review of Psychology,* 1957, **8**, 309–330.
Zax, M. & Klein, A. Measurement of personality and behavior changes following psychotherapy. *Psychological Bulletin,* 1960, **57**, 435–448.

Chapter 17

Behavior and Other Direct Therapies

As instances of the behavior therapies we have selected papers that espouse three different varieties of behavior modification: Wolpe's systematic desensitization treatment; Levis and Stampfl's implosive therapy; and Bandura's model-reinforcement technique. Each of these papers is self-explanatory, but it may be helpful to point out that all of these methods are better suited for symptom removal than for facilitating overall personality change. Of course critics of these methods, most of whom consider themselves depth theorists, are quick to object to symptom-removal procedures on the grounds that they do not tackle or solve the underlying problems. To which the behaviorists respond that the behavior is in itself often a cause of more extensive personality disturbance.

The Systematic Desensitization Treatment of Neuroses

Joseph Wolpe

That anxiety is a feature of almost all human neuroses is acknowledged by all psychiatrists no matter what theories they hold. Many believe, though without satisfactory evidence, that the anxiety is a secondary result of other processes (e.g., repression). An alternative view is that neurotic anxiety is nothing but a conditioned response. According to this view, neurotic behaviour consists of persistent, unadaptive, learned habits of reaction acquired in anxiety-generating situations; and the objective of therapy is to eliminate the unadaptive habits.

It has in fact been shown that, through the application of principles of learning, neurotic habits can be overcome both experimentally (Wolpe, 7) and clinically (Wolpe, 8, 9, 10; Eysenck, 1) with effects that are evidently permanent. In both contexts, particularly effective use has been made of the *reciprocal inhibition principle* first recognized by Sherrington (5), which is applied by arranging conditions so that the neurotic response can be inhibited by the simultaneous elicitation of a dominating incompatible response.

The therapeutic possibilities of the reciprocal inhibition principle first appeared a dozen years ago in the course of studies on experimental neuroses in cats. Unlearning of the neurotic responses was procured by feeding the animal a number of times while it was responding with mild anxiety to a stimulus slightly resembling some aspect of the conditioning situation. The strength of the anxiety response to the particular stimulus progressively declined, eventually to zero. Increasingly "strong" anxiety-evoking stimuli were successively dealt with in this way; and eventually all the conditioned anxiety responses were eliminated. Apparently, each time the animal fed the anxiety response was to some extent inhibited; and each occasion of inhibition was followed by some degree of weakening of the anxiety response *habit*.

Feeding responses were used to overcome neurotic reactions in children as long ago as 1924 by Dr. Mary Jones (3) of the University of California and also by others in recent years. I, myself, have not employed feeding responses in human subjects, particularly because my patients are mainly adults, but instead I have successfully used the following kinds of responses that inhibit anxiety responses: (1) assertive responses, (2) sexual responses, (3) relaxation responses, (4) respiratory responses (mixtures of carbon dioxide and oxygen by LaVerne's method (4)), (5) conditioned motor responses, (6) "anxiety-relief" responses (conditioning to a "neutral" stimulus of the effects of cessation of a punishing electric current), (7) conditioned avoidance responses to obsessions.

The first three of these response categories, i.e., assertive, sexual, and relaxation responses, are by far the most commonly used. The systematic desensitization method is a special way of employing relaxation responses as inhibitors of anxiety. Using *all* of these methods according to their indications, I have previously reported that nearly 90 per cent of 210 patients have either apparently recovered or been much improved after an average of about 30 therapeutic interviews. In the present paper I shall describe only the systematic desensitization method and give a separate analysis of results obtained with it.

In brief, systematic desensitization involves three sets of operations: (1) identifying the "themes" of stimuli to neurotic reactions (e.g., heights, situations of rejection), listing a considerable number of situations on each theme, and then ranking these situations in order of the intensity each arouses; (2) training the patient in deep muscle relaxation (whose autonomic accompaniments are antagonistic to those of anxiety); and (3) presenting to the imagination of the deeply relaxed patient first the weakest ranked item and repeating the presentation until no more anxiety is evoked, and dealing similarly with each stronger item until even the strongest evokes no anxiety.

In detail, the procedure is as follows. The patient is given training in progressive relaxation by Jacobson's method, but proceeding much more rapidly than Jacobson describes. All the main muscle groups are covered in the course of about six interviews, allowing about half of each interview for this training. Preliminary observations on the patient's responses to hypnotic techniques are meanwhile made, and during the same interviews steps are taken towards the construction of what is called an "anxiety hierarchy." This is a list of stimulus situations to which the patient reacts with unadaptive anxiety. The items are obtained from his

From *Journal of Nervous and Mental Disease*, **112**, 189–203.

history and from subsequent detailed probing into all identifiable sources of disturbance. The items are then ranked and the most disturbing of them are placed at the top of a list and the least at the bottom. The arrangement is based on the patient's estimation of the strength of his reactions. Multiple hierarchies are frequently obtained.

Although the construction of a hierarchy is often quite a straightforward matter, in some cases it is more difficult because the sources of anxiety are not immediately revealed by the patient's listing of what he avoids or fears. For example, it may become clear that he reacts to social occasions with anxiety, and that different kinds of social occasions, for example, weddings, parties, and musical evenings, are associated with decreasing degrees of anxiety. The inexperienced therapist may be tempted to construct a hierarchy based on these types of social occasions, with weddings at the top of the list and musical evenings at the bottom. Usually, little good would result from an attempt at desensitization based on such a hierarchy, and more careful probing would almost certainly reveal a particular facet of social occasions to be the essential source of anxiety. Frequently, fear and avoidance of social occasions turns out to be based on fear of criticism or of rejection; or the fear may be a function of the mere physical presence of people, varying with the number of them to whom the patient is exposed.

When the hierarchies have been prepared and the patient has received sufficient training in relaxation, he is made to relax as deeply as possible, sometimes under hypnosis and sometimes not. He is then asked to imagine a scene embodying the least disturbing member of an anxiety hierarchy. He is instructed to signal if he feels more than the slightest disturbance. The scene is presented two or three times and then the patient is asked to indicate, by raising a finger, if there was any disturbance on the last occasion. If there was, the same scene is presented again until it ceases to evoke any disturbance whatsoever. The therapist then proceeds to deal in the same way with the next higher scene in the hierarchy. Eventually, even the highest member of the hierarchy loses its ability to evoke anxiety.

There is great variation in how many themes, how many scenes from each, and how many presentations are given at a session. Generally, up to four hierarchies are drawn upon in an individual session, and not many patients have more than four. Three or four presentations of a scene are usual, but ten or more may be needed. The total number of scenes presented is limited mainly by availability of time and by the endurance of the patient. On the whole, both of these quantities increase as therapy goes on, and eventually almost the whole interview may be devoted to desensitization, so that whereas at an early stage eight or ten presentations are the total given at a session, at an advanced stage the number may rise to 30 or even 50.

The *frequency* of sessions is usually one or two per week. The *number* of sessions required varies according to the number and intensity of anxiety areas and the degree of generalization (involvement of related stimuli) in the case of each area. One patient may recover in about half a dozen sessions, another may require a hundred or more. For example, a patient with a death phobia, a phobia for sick people, and an agoraphobia required about a hundred sessions. To remove the death phobia alone, a total of about 2,000 scene presentations had to be used.

RESULTS

I shall present the results in 39 cases treated by desensitization. These patients, comprising about one-third of the total number so treated up to December, 1959, were randomly selected (by a casual visitor) from the alphabetical files of all patients treated. They are considered to be a representative sample of the total treated patient population.

Many of the patients had other neurotic response habits as well, that were treated by methods appropriate to them. Interspersed among the 39 cases reported were 6 others eligible for desensitization who had between 2 and 6 sessions, but who are excluded from the series because they terminated treatment for various reasons (even though usually showing some evidence of progress). It is felt proper to exclude these, as in evaluating the therapeutic efficacy of an antibiotic it would be proper to omit cases that had received only one or two doses. Also excluded are 2 cases that turned out to be schizophrenic. Psychotic patients do not respond to this treatment and receive it only if misdiagnosed as neurotic. On the other hand, every presenting neurotic case is accepted for treatment.

Outcome of treatment is judged on several sources of information. In addition to the patient's report of his reactions to stimuli from the hierarchies during sessions, there frequently is observable evidence of diminished anxious response, inasmuch as many patients display, when disturbed, characteristic muscle tensions such as grimaces or finger movements. The greatest importance is attached to the patient's reports of changed responses, in real life, to the previously fearful situations. I have in some cases confirmed these reports by direct observation.

The results are summarized in Table I. There were 68 phobias and allied neurotic anxiety response habits related to more complex situations among the 39 patients, of whom 19 had multiple hierarchies. The treatment was judged effective in 35 of the patients. Forty-five of the phobic and allied anxiety habits were apparently eliminated and 17 more were markedly ameliorated, i.e., estimated to be at least 80 per cent improved.

Among the failures, two cases were unable to imagine

Table I. *A Summary of Results of Desensitization Therapy.*

Patients	39	
Number of patients responding to treatment	35	
Number of hierarchies	68	
Hierarchies overcome	45	(91%)
Hierarchies markedly improved	17	
Hierarchies unimproved	6	
Total number of desensitization sessions	762	
Mean session expenditure per hierarchy	11.2	
Mean session expenditure per successfully treated hierarchy	12.3	
Median number of sessions per patient	10.0	

themselves within situations; another could not confine her imagining to the stated scene and therefore had excessive anxiety, but was later treated with complete success by means of another conditioning method (Wolpe, 10); the fourth had interpersonal anxiety reactions that led to erratic responses and, having experienced no benefit, sought therapy elsewhere.

The 39 patients had among them a total of 762 desensitization sessions. The mean number of sessions per hierarchy was 11.2; the median number of sessions per patient 10.0. It should be emphasized that a desensitization session usually takes up only part of a three-quarter-hour interview period, and in cases that also have neurotic problems requiring direct action in the life situation, there may be many interviews in which a session is not included.

At times varying between 6 months and 4 years after the end of treatment, follow-up reports were obtained from 20 of the 35 patients who responded to desensitization. There was no reported instance of relapse or the appearance of new phobias or other neurotic symptoms. I have never observed resurgence of neurotic anxiety when desensitization has been complete or virtually so.

DISCUSSION

The general idea of overcoming phobias or other neurotic habits by means of systematic "gradual approaches" has long been popular knowledge. What is new in the present contribution is: (1) the provision of a theoretical explanation for the success of such gradual approaches, and (2) the description of a method in which the therapist has complete control of the degree of approach that the patient makes to the feared object at every stage. The situations, being imaginary, are constructed and varied at will in the consulting room.

The excellent results obtained by this method of treatment are naturally viewed with scepticism and even hostility by those who in the psychoanalytic tradition regard phobias and allied neurotic anxiety response habits as merely the superficial manifestations of deeper unconscious conflicts. But even those who hold such views must surely agree that in many cases the onset of a phobia can be dated to a particular traumatic event. Before that time, presumably the patient already had his assumed unconscious conflicts, but did not feel any need for treatment. At the very least, then, it must be admitted that if through desensitization the patient is restored to the state in which he was before the traumatic event, something important has been gained. The reply could, of course, be made that unless the unconscious conflicts are brought to light and resolved, the patient will relapse or develop other symptoms; but in keeping with follow-up studies on the results of non-analytic psychotherapy in neurotic cases, my experience has been that relapse or the appearance of new reactions is rare, occurring only if a major group of stimuli in a desensitized area has been neglected.

At the same time, it is indisputable that since only a minority of individuals exposed to a given traumatic event develop a phobia, some predisposing condition or conditions must determine which individuals do. But we are not therefore compelled to accept the psychoanalytic version of the nature of the predisposing conditions, especially as the factual foundations of that version are far from satisfactory (Wolpe and Rachman, 11). Objective behaviour theory can also point to factors that may predispose an individual to particularly severe conditioning of anxiety. First, some people are apparently endowed with much more active autonomic nervous systems than others (e.g., Shirley, 6). Second, previous experience with similar stimulus constellations may have induced low degrees of anxiety conditioning or other possible preconditions that would sensitize a person to a particular traumatic experience. Third, there may be circumstances in the moment of trauma that may bring about an unusually high degree of focusing upon certain stimulus constellations. The second of these suggested factors is probably the most important, for patients do frequently tell of minor sensitivity having existed before the precipitating event. In the course of desensitization, these original sensitivities also come to be removed, along with whatever has been more recently conditioned.

Critics of the conditioned response approach to therapy of the neuroses frequently assert that when the desensitization method leads to recovery, it is not the method as such that is responsible, but the "transference" established between patient and therapist. If these critics were right—if desensitization were incidental to rather than causal of recovery—it would be expected that improvement would affect all areas more or less uniformly, and not be confined to those to which desensitization had been applied. The facts are directly contrary to this expectation, for practically invariably it is found that *unless different hierarchies have unmistakable common features, desensitization to one hierarchy does not in the least diminish the reactivity to another (untreated) hierarchy.* This accords with observations made in connection with experimental neuroses, in which eliminating anxiety conditioned to visual stimuli does not diminish the anxiety-evoking potential of auditory stimuli.

From the point of view of the scientific investigator the desensitization method has a number of advantages that are unusual in the field of psychotherapy: (1) the aim of therapy can be clearly stated in every case; (2) sources of neurotic anxiety can be defined and delimited; (3) change of reaction to a scene is determined during sessions (and accordingly could be measured by psychophysiological means); (4) there is no objection to conducting therapy before an unconcealed audience; and (5) therapists can be interchanged if desired.

REFERENCES

1. Eysenck, H. J. Behavior Therapy and the Neuroses (Pergamon Press, New York, 1960).
2. Jacobson, E. Progressive Relaxation (University of Chicago Press, Chicago, 1938).
3. Jones, M. C. Pedagog. Sem. **31**: 308 (1924).
4. LaVerne, A. A. Dis. Nerv. Syst. **14**: 141 (1953).
5. Sherrington, C. S. Integrative Action of the Nervous System (Yale University Press, New Haven, 1906).
6. Shirley, M. The First Two Years, Institute of Child Welfare Monog. No. 8 (University of Minnesota Press, Minneapolis, 1933).
7. Wolpe, J. Brit. J. Psychol. **43**: 243 (1952).

8. Wolpe, J. S. African Med. J. **26**: 825 (1952).
9. Wolpe, J. Amer. Med. Ass. Arch. Neurol & Psychiat. 72: 205 (1954).
10. Wolpe, J. Psychotherapy by Reciprocal Inhibition (Stanford University Press, Stanford, 1958).
11. Wolpe, J. and Rachman, S. J. Nerv. & Ment Dis. **130**: 135 (1960).
12. Wolpe, J. Amer. J. Psychiat. **119**: 35 (1961).

Implosive Therapy: A Bridge Between Pavlov and Freud?

Donald J. Levis
Thomas G. Stampfl

Learning theory and psychodynamic theory may be regarded as two of the most influential systems of thought concerning human behavior. It is surprising that the theoretical models presented by Pavlov and Freud which were developed during approximately the same period of time influenced one another to such a small degree. The independence of these two movements may be attributed, in part, to the different emphasis of the approaches. The proponents of learning theory attempted to develop laws about behavior in general, while the psychoanalytic movement strove to understand human psychopathology with the objective of devising methods of treatment. Nevertheless, theorists were quick to conclude that the goals of the two approaches need not be mutually exclusive. Attempts to apply learning theory or conditioning principles to psychopathology can be found in the early twenties (Bagby, 1922; Humphrey, 1922; M. C. Jones, 1924; Smith & Guthrie, 1922; Watson & Rayner, 1920).

A few writers even directed their efforts toward the achievement of conceptual integrations. Thus, French, 1933 (also see Kimble, 1967) pointed out that the stimulus-response analysis of Pavlov was similar to Freud's principle of the association of ideas and that Pavlovian inhibition might represent the counterpart of repression since both functioned to interfere with learned responses. Bridger (1964) linked the first and second signal systems of Pavlov with Freud's treatment of the characteristics of conscious and unconscious ideas. Other similarities or parallels have been commented on by these and other writers (e.g., Alexander, 1963).

Some theorists have utilized variations of classical conditioning principles such as Mowrer (1939) and Dollard and Miller (1950). Attempts of this nature consisted mainly of syntheses of learning models heavily indebted to Pavlov with the premises of psychoanalytic theory concerning etiology and therapy. Unfortunately, these integrations, although serving as conceptual translations, failed to suggest new approaches for therapeutic practice. It is likely that this deficiency more than anything else led to an abandonment of theoretical attempts of this nature.

From Association for Advancement of Behavior Therapy *Newsletter*, 1969, 4, 8–10. Reproduced by permission.

A systematic learning theory framework that suggests new techniques of treatment was not provided until Wolpe (1958), operating from a Hullian model, introduced the technique of systematic desensitization. Wolpe's approach was quite different from those of his historical counterparts who either tended to separate theory and application or utilized only traditional methods as a model for psychotherapy (Kalish, 1965).

It is with interest that we note that Wolpe's bold approach in deviating sharply from traditional therapeutic practice, loosened the dogmatic fetters to which current therapeutic practice was chained. However, the extremely significant contribution of Wolpe arose in part as a rebellion of the attempt to integrate traditional theoretical models with learning theory (Eysenck, 1960). This anti-dynamic orientation is extremely common among behavior therapists and even appears to be an integral part of the behavior therapy movement (see Stampfl & Levis, 1968).

Stampfl (1961) attempted an integration by extending two-factor avoidance conditioning theory (Mowrer, 1939; 1960) to the problem of psychopathology. This attempt did lead to the development of a new treatment procedure labeled Implosive Therapy. A brief outline of this approach may be helpful in understanding the rationale for the inclusion of dynamic principles in the integration provided. Rather than adopt an "active" counterconditioning model as exemplified in Wolpe's systematic desensitization, an avoidance response prevention technique which holds the patient to the CS in the absence of the US was incorporated. Basically, human psychopathology is viewed as being perpetuated by anxiety eliciting external and internal conditioned stimuli which directly or indirectly have been associated with aversive primary reinforcement (e.g., pain and/or severe states of deprivation). In an attempt to remove or reduce cues which elicit conditioned anxiety, avoidance responses in the form of symptoms and defense mechanisms are subsequently learned. To account for the persistence of the symptoms and defenses (learned avoidance responses) despite the low probability of the reoccurrence of the primary aversive stimulus, the assumption is made that the avoidance responses frequently become overlearned to the extent that they are elicited by only a fraction of the total conditioned stimulus complex. Their rapid performance prevents much of the motivating source of anxiety from being exposed and subsequently extinguishing. In addition, the total conditioned complex of anxiety eliciting stimuli is thought to consist of multiple patterns of conditioned components many of which are ordered sequentially in terms of their accessibility and aversiveness (see Levis, 1966, 1966a; Stampfl, 1961, 1966).

To facilitate the process of extinction, the implosive therapist attempts to circumvent the avoidance response by presenting as many of the avoided cues comprising the total stimulus complex as possible. In order to achieve this objective, the patient is asked to visualize in imagery various scenes suggested to him by the therapist. It is assumed that aversive cues introduced verbally or in imagery function as secondary conditioned stimuli and thus are extinguishable.

The material for the scenes which are introduced by the therapist are obtained from an analysis of the contingencies related to the patient's symptoms and from hypothesized avoided cues based on information obtained from clinical interviews. Complete accuracy of the hypothesized cues is not essential since some effect, based on the principle of generalization of extinction, would be expected when approximations are presented. The continuation of a hypothesis is determined operationally. If the cues appear to elicit anxiety, the supposition is made that the anxiety elicited occurred because of earlier conditioning to a context which involved similar cues as those presented by the therapist. The greater the degree of anxiety elicited, the greater the support for continuing the presentation of the particular hypothesized cues. These cues are repeatedly presented until a marked decrement in anxiety evocation occurs. High levels of anxiety are sought throughout this process. It is assumed that the higher the level of anxiety, the more aversive the cues introduced, the greater the extinction effect (for a more detailed presentation of the theory and technique, see Stampfl, 1966; Levis, 1966a; Stampfl and Levis, 1967a; in press, a, b).

It is in the determination of the material to be introduced by the therapists that the clinical experience and observation generated by traditional and dynamically oriented therapists is useful. It was observed especially in more severe cases of psychopathology that the introduction of scenes which included "dynamic" cues not only met the boundary condition of eliciting considerable anxiety, but also appeared to be highly correlated with standard psychodynamic interpretations of the source of pathology. Most important, the extinction of these cues also seemed to be closely correlated with symptom reduction (Hogan, 1966; Levis & Carrera, 1967).

Many of the hypothesized cues found to be effective involve dynamically significant areas such as intense fears of bodily injury, rejection, expression of aggression, guilt, and sexual conflicts. The extent to which these cues are associated with particular behavioral disorders is worthy of systematic experimentation. Support for such a relationship will determine, in part, the structures of this bridge linking Pavlov and Freud.

REFERENCES

Alexander, F. The dynamics of psychotherapy in the light of learning theory. *American Journal of Psychiatry.* 1963, **120**, 440–448.

Bagby, E. The etiology of phobias. *Journal of Abnormal and Social Psychology.* 1922, **17**, 16–18.

Bridger, W. H. Contributions of Conditioning Principles to Psychiatry. *Pavlovian Conditioning and American Psychiatry.* Symposium No. 9, 1964, Group for the advancement of Psychiatry, Reprinted in G. A. Kimble's (Ed.) *Foundations of Conditioning and Learning.* New York: Appleton-Century-Crofts, 1967, Pp. 587–599.

Dollard, J., & Miller, N. E. *Personality and Psychotherapy.* New York: McGraw-Hill, 1950.

Eysenck, H. J. (Ed.) *Behaviour Therapy and the Neuroses.* New York: Pergamon Press, 1960.

French, T. M. Interrelations between psychoanalysis and the experimental work of Pavlov. *American Journal of Psychiatry.* 1933, **12**, 1165–1203.

Hogan, R. A. Implosive therapy in the short term treatment of psychotics. *Psychotherapy: Theory, Research, and Practice.* 1966, **3**, 25–31.

Humphrey, E. The conditioned reflex and the elementary social reaction. *Journal of Abnormal and Social Psychology.* 1922, **2**, 113–120.

Jones, Mary C. The elimination of children's fears. *Journal of Experimental Psychology.* 1924, **7**, 383–390.

Kalish, H. L. Behavior Therapy. In B. Wolman's (Ed.) *Handbook of Clinical Psychology.* New York: McGraw-Hill, 1965.

Kimble, G. A. Thomas M. French on the relationship between psychoanalysis and the experimental work of Pavlov. In G. A. Kimble's (Ed.) *Foundations of Conditioning and Learning.* New York: Appleton-Century-Crofts, 1967, Pp. 581–586.

Levis, D. J. Effects of serial CS presentation and other characteristics of the CS on the conditioned avoidance response. *Psychological Reports.* 1966, **18**, 755–766.

Levis, D. J. Implosive therapy, Part II: The subhuman analogue, the strategy, and the technique. In S. E. Armitage's (Ed.) *Behavioral modification techniques in the treatment of emotional disorders.* Battle Creek, Michigan: V.A. Publication, 22–37, 1966a.

Levis, D. J., & Carrera, R. N. Effects of 10 hours of implosive therapy in the treatment of outpatients. A preliminary report. *Journal of Abnormal Psychology.* 1967, **72**, 504–508.

Mowrer, O. H. A stimulus-response analysis of anxiety and its role as a reinforcing agent. *Psychological Review.* 1939, **46**, 553–565.

Mowrer, O. H. *Learning theory and behavior.* New York: Wiley, 1960.

Smith, S., & Guthrie, E. R. Exhibitionism. *Journal of Abnormal and Social Psychology.* 1922, **17**, 206–209.

Stampfl, T. G. Implosive therapy: A learning theory derived psychodynamic therapeutic technique, 1961. In Lebarba and Dent's (Eds.) *Critical Issues in Clinical Psychology.* New York: Academic Press (To be published).

Stampfl, T. G. Implosive therapy, Part I: The theory. In S. G. Armitage's (Ed.) *Behavioral modification techniques in the treatment of emotional disorders.* Battle Creek, Michigan: V. A. Publication, 12–21, 1966.

Stampfl, T. G., & Levis, D. J. The essentials of implosive therapy: A learning theory based on psychodynamic behavioral therapy. *Journal of Abnormal Psychology.* 1967, 72, 496–503.

Stampfl, T. G., & Levis, D. J. Phobic patients: Treatment with the learning theory approach of implosive therapy. *Voices: The Art and sciences of psychotherapy.* 1967a, **3**, 23–27.

Stampfl, T. G., & Levis, D. J. Implosive Therapy—A Behavioral Therapy? *Behavior Research and Therapy.* 1968, **6**, 31–36.

Stampfl, T. G., & Levis, D. J. Implosive therapy. In R. M. Jurjevich's (Ed.) *Handbook of direct and behavior psychotherapies.* North Carolina: North Carolina Press, (in press, a).

Stampfl, T. G., & Levis, D. J. Learning theory: An aid to dynamic therapeutic practice. In L. D. Eron & R. Callahan's (Eds.) *Relationship of Theory to Practice in Psychotherapy.* Chicago: Aldine Publishing Co., (in press, b).

Watson, J. B., & Rayner, R. Conditioned emotional reaction. *Journal Experimental Psychology.* 1920, **3**, 1–4.

Wolpe, J. *Psychotherapy by reciprocal inhibition.* Stanford: Stanford University Press, 1958.

Influence of Models' Reinforcement Contingencies on the Acquisition of Imitative Responses*†

Albert Bandura

In order to test the hypothesis that reinforcements administered to a model influence the performance but not the acquisition of matching responses, groups of children observed an aggressive film-mediated model either rewarded, punished, or left without consequences. A postexposture test revealed that response consequences to the model had produced differential amounts of imitative behavior. Children in the model-punished condition performed significantly fewer matching responses than children in both the model-rewarded and the no-consequences groups. Children in all 3 treatment conditions were then offered attractive reinforcers contingent on their reproducing the model's aggressive responses. The introduction of positive incentives completely wiped out the previously observed performance differences, revealing an equivalent amount of learning among children in the model-rewarded, model-punished, and the no-consequences conditions.

It is widely assumed that the occurrence of imitative or observational learning is contingent on the administration of reinforcing stimuli either to the model or to the observer. According to the theory propounded by Miller and Dollard (1941), for example, the necessary conditions for learning through imitation include a motivated subject who is positively reinforced for matching the rewarded behavior of a model during a series of initially random, trial-and-error responses. Since this conceptualization of observational learning requires the subject to perform the imitative response before he can learn it, this theory evidently accounts more adequately for the emission of previously learned matching responses, than for their acquisition.

Mowrer's (1960) proprioceptive feedback theory similarly highlights the role of reinforcement but, unlike Miller and Dollard who reduce imitation to a special case of instrumental learning, Mowrer focuses on the classical conditioning of positive and negative emotions to matching response-correlated stimuli. Mowrer distinguishes two forms of imitative learning in terms of whether the observer is reinforced directly or vicariously. In the former case, the model performs a response and simultaneously rewards the observer. If the modeled responses are thus paired repeatedly with positive reinforcement they gradually acquire secondary reward value. The observer can then administer positively conditioned reinforcers to himself simply by reproducing as closely as possible the model's positively valenced behavior. In the second, or empathetic form of imitative learning, the model not only exhibits the responses but also experiences the reinforcing consequences. It is assumed that the observer, in turn, experiences empathetically both the response-correlated stimuli and the

*This investigation was supported by Research Grant M-5162 from the National Institutes of Health, United States Public Health Service.

†The author is indebted to Carole Revelle, who assisted in collecting the data.

response consequences of the model's behavior. As a result of this higher-order vicarious conditioning, the observer will be inclined to reproduce the matching responses.

There is some recent evidence that imitative behavior can be enhanced by noncontingent social reinforcement from a model (Bandura & Huston, 1961), by response-contingent reinforcers administered to the model (Bandura, Ross, & Ross, 1963b; Walters, Leat, & Mezei, 1963), and by increasing the reinforcing value of matching responses per se through direct reinforcement of the participant observer (Baer & Sherman, 1964). Nevertheless, reinforcement theories of imitation fail to explain the learning of matching responses when the observer does not perform the model's responses during the process of acquisition, and for which reinforcers are not delivered either to the model or to the observers (Bandura et al., 1961, 1963a).

The acquisition of imitative responses under the latter conditions appears to be accounted for more adequately by a contiguity theory of observational learning. According to the latter conceptualization (Bandura, in press; Sheffield, 1961), when an observer witnesses a model exhibit a sequence of responses the observer acquires, through contiguous association of sensory events, perceptual and symbolic responses possessing cue properties that are capable of eliciting, at some time after a demonstration, overt responses corresponding to those that had been modeled.

Some suggestive evidence that the *acquisition* of matching responses may take place through contiguity, whereas reinforcements administered to a model exert their major influence on the *performance* of imitatively learned responses, is provided in a study in which models were rewarded or punished for exhibiting aggressive behavior (Bandura et al., 1963b). Although children who had observed aggressive responses rewarded subsequently reproduced the model's behavior while children in the model-punished condition failed to do so, a number of the subjects in the latter group described in postexperimental interviews the model's repertoire of aggressive responses with considerable accuracy. Evidently, they had learned the cognitive equivalents of the model's responses but they were not translated into their motoric forms. These findings highlighted both the importance of distinguishing between learning and performance and the need for a systematic study of whether reinforcement is primarily a learning-related or a performance-related variable.

In the present experiment children observed a film-mediated model who exhibited novel physical and verbal aggressive responses. In one treatment condition the model was severely punished; in a second, the model was generously rewarded; while the third condition presented no response consequences to the model. Following a post-exposure test of imitative behavior, children in all three groups were offered attractive incentives contingent on their reproducing the models' responses so as to provide a more accurate index of learning. It was predicted that reinforcing consequences to the model would result in significant differences in the performance of imitative behavior with the model-rewarded group displaying the highest number of different classes of matching responses, followed by the no-consequences and the model-punished groups, respectively. In accordance with previous findings (Bandura et al., 1961, 1963a) it was also expected that boys would perform significantly more imitative aggression than girls. It was predicted, however, that the introduction of positive incentives would wipe out both reinforcement-produced and sex-linked performance differences, revealing an equivalent amount of learning among children in the three treatment conditions.

METHOD

Subjects

The subjects were 33 boys and 33 girls enrolled in the Stanford University Nursery School. They ranged in age from 42 to 71 months, with a mean age of 51 months. The children were assigned randomly to one of three treatment conditions of 11 boys and 11 girls each.

Two adult males served in the role of models, and one female experimenter conducted the study for all 66 children.

Exposure Procedure

The children were brought individually to a semi-darkened room. The experimenter informed the child that she had some business to attend to before they could proceed to the "surprise playroom," but that during the waiting period the child might watch a televised program. After the child was seated, the experimenter walked over to the television console, ostensibly tuned in a program and then departed. A film of approximately 5 minutes duration depicting the modeled responses was shown on a glass lenscreen in the television console by means of a rear projection arrangement, screened from the child's view by large panels. The televised form of presentation was utilized primarily because attending responses to televised stimuli are strongly conditioned in children and this procedure would therefore serve to enhance observation which is a necessary condition for the occurrence of imitative learning.

The film began with a scene in which the model walked up to an adult-size plastic Bobo doll and ordered him to clear the way. After glaring for a moment at the noncompliant antagonist the model exhibited four novel aggressive responses each accompanied by a distinctive verbalization.

First, the model laid the Bobo doll on its side, sat on it, and punched it in the nose while remarking, "Pow, right in the nose, boom, boom." The model then raised the doll and pommeled it on the head with a mallet. Each response was accompanied by the verbalization, "Sockeroo . . . stay down." Following the mallet aggression, the model kicked the doll about the room, and these responses were interspersed with the comment, "Fly away." Finally, the model threw rubber balls at the Bobo doll, each strike punctuated with "Bang." This sequence of physically and verbally aggressive behavior was repeated twice.

The component responses that enter into the development of more complex novel patterns of behavior are usually present in children's behavioral repertoires as products either of maturation or of prior social learning. Thus, while most of the elements in the modeled acts had undoubtedly been previously learned, the particular pattern of components in each response, and their evocation by specific stimulus objects, were relatively unique. For example, children can manipulate objects, sit on them, punch them, and they can make vocal responses, but the likelihood that a given child would spontaneously place a Bobo doll on its side, sit on it, punch it in the nose, and remark, "Pow . . . boom, boom," is exceedingly remote. Indeed, a previous study utilizing the same stimulus objects has shown that the imitative responses selected for the present experiment have virtually a zero probability of occurring spontaneously among preschool children (Bandura et al., 1961) and, therefore, meet the criterion of novel responses.

The rewarding and punishing contingencies associated with the model's aggressive responses were introduced in the closing scene of the film.

For children in the model-rewarded condition, a second adult appeared with an abundant supply of candies and soft drinks. He informed the model that he was a "strong champion" and that his superb aggressive performance clearly deserved a generous treat. He then poured him a large glass of 7-Up, and readily supplied additional energy-building nourishment including chocolate bars, Cracker Jack popcorn, and an assortment of candies. While the model was rapidly consuming the delectable treats, his admirer symbolically reinstated the modeled aggressive responses and engaged in considerable positive social reinforcement.

For children in the model-punished condition, the reinforcing agent appeared on the scene shaking his finger menacingly and commenting reprovingly, "Hey there, you big bully. You quit picking on that clown. I won't tolerate it." As the model drew back he tripped and fell, the other adult sat on the model and spanked him with a rolled-up magazine while reminding him of his aggressive behavior. As the model ran off cowering, the agent forewarned him, "If I catch you doing that again, you big bully, I'll give you a hard spanking. You quit acting that way."

Children in the no-consequences condition viewed the same film as shown to the other two groups except that no reinforcement ending was included.

Performance Measure

Immediately following the exposure session the children were escorted to an experimental room that contained a Bobo doll, three balls, a mallet and pegboard, dart guns, cars, plastic farm animals, and a doll house equipped with furniture and a doll family. By providing a variety of stimulus objects the children were at liberty to exhibit imitative responses or to engage in nonimitative forms of behavior.

After the experimenter instructed the child that he was free to play with the toys in the room, she excused herself supposedly to fetch additional play materials. Since many preschool children are reluctant to remain alone and tend to leave after a short period of time, the experimenter reentered the room midway through the session and reassured the child that she would return shortly with the goods.

Each child spent 10 minutes in the test room during which time his behavior was recorded every 5 seconds in terms of predetermined imitative response categories by judges who observed the session through a one-way mirror in an adjoining observation room.

Two observers shared the task of recording the occurrence of matching responses for all 66 children. Neither of the raters had knowledge of the treatment conditions to which the children were assigned. In order to provide an estimate of interscorer reliability, the responses of 10 children were scored independently by both observers. Since the imitative responses were highly distinctive and required no subjective interpretation, the raters were virtually in perfect agreement (99%) in scoring the matching responses.

The number of different physical and verbal imitative responses emitted spontaneously by the children constituted the performance measure.

Acquisition Index

At the end of the performance session the experimenter entered the room with an assortment of fruit juices in a colorful juice-dispensing fountain, and booklets of sticker-pictures that were employed as the positive incentives to activate into performance what the children had learned through observation.

After a brief juice treat the children were informed, that for each physical or verbal imitative response that they reproduced, they would receive a pretty sticker-picture and additional juice treats. An achievement incentive was also introduced in order to produce further disinhibition and to increase the children's motivation to exhibit matching responses. The experimenter attached a pastoral scene to the wall and expressed an interest in seeing how many sticker-pictures the child would be able to obtain to adorn his picture.

The experimenter then asked the child, "Show me what Rocky did in the TV program," "Tell me what he said," and rewarded him immediately following each matching response. If a child simply described an imitative response he was asked to give a performance demonstration.

Although learning must be inferred from performance, it was assumed that the number of different physical and verbal imitative responses reproduced by the children under the positive-incentive conditions would serve as a relatively accurate index of learning.

RESULTS

Figure 1 shows the mean number of different matching responses reproduced by children in each of the three treatment conditions during the no-incentive and the positive-incentive phases of the experiment. A square-root transformation ($y = \sqrt{f + ½}$) was applied to these data to make them amenable to parametric statistical analyses.

Performance Differences

A summary of the analysis of variance based on the performance scores is presented in Table 1. The findings reveal

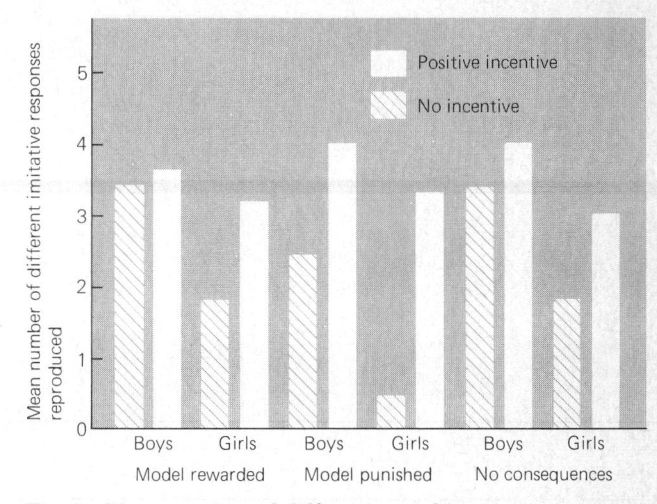

Fig. 1. Mean number of different matching responses reproduced by children as a function of positive incentives and the model's reinforcement contingencies.

Table 1. *Analysis of Variance of Imitative Performance Scores.*

Source	*df*	*MS*	*F*
Treatments (T)	2	1.21	3.27[a]
Sex (S)	1	4.87	13.16[b]
T × S	2	.12	<1
Within groups	60	.37	

[a] $p < .05$.
[b] $p < .001$.

that reinforcing consequences to the model had a significant effect on the number of matching responses that the children spontaneously reproduced. The main effect of sex is also highly significant, confirming the prediction that boys would perform more imitative responses than girls.

Further comparisons of pairs of means by t tests (Table 2) show that while the model-rewarded and the no-consequences groups did not differ from each other, subjects in both of these conditions performed significantly more matching responses than children who had observed the model experience punishing consequences following the display of aggression. It is evident, however, from the differences reported separately for boys and girls in Table 2, that the significant effect of the model's reinforcement contingencies is based predominantly on differences among the girls' subgroups.[1]

Differences in Acquisition

An analysis of variance of the imitative learning scores is summarized in Table 3. The introduction of positive incentives completely wiped out the previously observed performance differences, revealing an equivalent amount of imitative learning among the children in the model-rewarded, model-punished, and the no-consequences treatment groups. Although the initially large sex difference was substantially reduced in the positive-incentive condition, the girls nevertheless still displayed fewer matching responses than the boys.

Table 2. *Comparison of Pairs of Means Between Treatment Conditions.*

	Treatment conditions		
Performance measure	Reward versus punishment t	Reward versus no consequences t	Punishment versus no consequences t
Total sample	2.20[b]	0.55	2.25[b]
Boys	1.05	0.19	1.24
Girls	2.13[b]	0.12	2.02[a]

[a] $p < .05$.
[b] $p < .025$.

[1] Because of the skewness of the distribution of scores for the subgroup of girls in the model-punished condition, differences involving this group were also evaluated by means of the Mann-Whitney U test. The nonparametric analyses yield probability values that are identical to those reported in Table 2.

Table 3. *Analysis of Variance of Imitative Learning Scores.*

Source	*df*	*MS*	*F*
Treatments (T)	2	0.02	<1
Sex (S)	1	0.56	6.22[a]
T × S	2	0.02	<1
Within groups	60	0.09	

[a] $p < .05$.

Acquisition-Performance Differences

In order to elucidate further the influence of direct and vicariously experienced reinforcement on imitation, the differences in matching responses displayed under nonreward and positive-incentive conditions for each of the three experimental treatments were evaluated by the t-test procedure for correlated means. Table 4 shows that boys who witnessed the model either rewarded or left without consequences performed all of the imitative responses that they had learned through observation and no new matching responses emerged when positive reinforcers were made available. On the other hand, boys who had observed the model punished and girls in all three treatment conditions showed significant increments in imitative behavior when response-contingent reinforcement was later introduced.

DISCUSSION

The results of the present experiment lend support to a contiguity theory of imitative learning; reinforcements administered to the model influenced the observers' performance but not the acquisition of matching responses.

It is evident from the findings, however, that mere exposure to modeling stimuli does not provide the sufficient conditions for imitative or observational learning. The fact that most of the children in the experiment failed to reproduce the entire repertoire of behavior exhibited by the model, even under positive-incentive conditions designed to disinhibit and to elicit matching responses, indicates that factors other than mere contiguity of sensory stimulation undoubtedly influence imitative response acquisition.

Exposing a person to a complex sequence of stimulation is no guarantee that he will attend to the entire range of cues, that he will necessarily select from a total stimulus

Table 4. *Significance of the Acquisition-Performance Differences in Imitative Responses.*

	Treatment conditions		
Group	Reward t	Punishment t	No consequences t
Total sample	2.38[a]	5.00[c]	2.67[b]
Boys	0.74	2.26[a]	1.54
Girls	3.33[b]	5.65[c]	2.18[a]

[a] $p < .025$.
[b] $p < .01$.
[c] $p < .001$.

complex only the most relevant stimuli, or that he will even perceive accurately the cues to which his attention is directed. Motivational variables, prior training in discriminative observation, and the anticipation of positive or negative reinforcements contingent on the emission of matching responses may be highly influential in channeling, augmenting, or reducing observing responses, which is a necessary precondition for imitative learning (Bandura, 1962; Bandura & Walters, 1963). Procedures that increase the distinctiveness of the relevant modeling stimuli also greatly facilitate observational learning (Sheffield & Maccoby, 1961).

In addition to attention-directing variables, the rate, amount, and complexity of stimuli presented to the observer may partly determine the degree of imitative learning. The acquisition of matching responses through observation of a lengthy uninterrupted sequence of behavior is also likely to be governed by principles of associate learning such as frequency and recency, serial order effects, and other multiple sources of associative interference (McGuire, 1961).

Social responses are generally composed of a large number of different behavioral units combined in a particular manner. Responses of higher-order complexity are produced by combinations of previously learned components which may, in themselves, represent relatively complicated behavioral patterns. Consequently, the rate of acquisition of intricate matching responses through observation will be largely determined by the extent to which the necessary components are contained in the observer's repertoire. A person who possesses a very narrow repertoire of behavior, for example, will, in all probability, display only fragmentary imitation of a model's behavior; on the other hand, a person who has acquired most of the relevant components is likely to perform precisely matching responses following several demonstrations. In the case of young preschool children their motor repertoires are more highly developed than their repertoires of verbal responses. It is, perhaps, for this reason that even in the positive-incentive condition, children reproduced a substantially higher percentage (67%) of imitative motor responses than matching verbalizations (20%). A similar pattern of differential imitation was obtained in a previous experiment (Bandura & Huston, 1961) in which preschool children served as subjects.

It is apparent from the foregoing discussion that considerably more research is needed in identifying variables that combine with contiguous stimulation in governing the process of imitative response acquisition.

It is possible, of course, to interpret the present acquisition data as reflecting the operation of generalization from a prior history of reinforcement of imitative behavior. Within any social group, models typically exhibit the accumulated cultural repertoires that have proved most successful for given stimulus situations; consequently, matching the behavior of other persons, particularly the superiors in an age-grade or prestige hierarchy, will maximize positive reinforcement and minimize the frequency of aversive response consequences. Since both the occurrence and the positive reinforcement of matching responses, whether by accident or by intent, are inevitable during the course of social development, no definitive resolution of the reinforcement issue is possible, except through an experiment utilizing organisms that have experienced complete social isolation from birth. It is evident, however, that contemporaneous reinforcements are unnecessary for the acquisition of new matching responses.

The finding that boys perform more imitative aggression than girls as a result of exposure to an aggressive male model, is in accord with results from related experiments (Bandura et al., 1961, 1963a). The additional finding, however, that the introduction of positive incentives practically wiped out the prior performance disparity strongly suggests that the frequently observed sex differences in aggression (Goodenough, 1931; Johnson, 1951; Sears, 1951) may reflect primarily differences in willingness to exhibit aggressive responses, rather than deficits in learning or "masculine-role identification."

The subgroups of children who displayed significant increments in imitative behavior as a function of positive reinforcement were boys who had observed the aggressive model punished, and girls for whom physically aggressive behavior is typically labeled sex inappropriate and nonrewarded or even negatively reinforced. The inhibitory effects of differing reinforcement histories for aggression were clearly reflected in the observation that boys were more easily disinhibited than girls in the reward phase of the experiment. This factor may account for the small sex difference that was obtained even in the positive-incentive condition.

The present study provides further evidence that response inhibition and response disinhibition can be vicariously transmitted through observation of reinforcing consequences to a model's behavior. It is interesting to note, however, that the performance by a model of socially disapproved or prohibited responses (for example, kicking, striking with objects) without the occurrence of any aversive consequences may produce disinhibitory effects analogous to a positive reinforcement operation. These findings are similar to results from studies of direct reinforcement (Crandall, Good, & Crandall, 1964) in which nonreward functioned as a positive reinforcer to increase the probability of the occurrence of formerly punished responses.

Punishment administered to the model apparently further reinforced the girls' existing inhibitions over aggression and produced remarkably little imitative behavior; the boys displayed a similar, though not significant, decrease in imitation. This difference may be partly a function of the relative dominance of aggressive responses in the repertoires of boys and girls. It is also possible that vicarious reinforcement for boys, deriving from the model's successful execution of aggressive behavior (that is, overpowering the noncompliant adversary), may have reduced the effects of externally administered terminal punishment. These factors, as well as the model's self-rewarding and self-punishing reactions following the display of aggression, will be investigated in a subsequent experiment.

REFERENCES

Baer, D. M., & Sherman, J. A. Reinforcement control of generalized imitation in young children. *Journal of Experimental Child Psychology*, 1964, 1, 37–49.

Bandura, A. Social learning through imitation. In M. R. Jones (Ed.), *Nebraska symposium on motivation: 1962.* Lincoln: Univer. Nebraska Press, 1962. Pp. 211–269.

Bandura, A. Vicarious processes: A case of no-trial learning. In L. Berkowitz (Ed.), *Advances in experimental social psychology*. Vol. 2. New York: Academic Press, 1965, in press.

Bandura, A., & Huston, Aletha C. Identification as a process of incidental learning. *Journal of Abnormal and Social Psychology,* 1961, **63**, 311–318.

Bandura, A., Ross, Dorothea, & Ross, Sheila A. Transmission of aggression through imitation of aggressive models. *Journal of Abnormal and Social Psychology*, 1961, **63**, 575–582.

Bandura, A., Ross, Dorothea, & Ross, Sheila A. Imitation of film-mediated aggressive models. *Journal of Abnormal and Social Psychology*, 1963, **66**, 3–11. (a)

Bandura, A., Ross, Dorothea, & Ross, Sheila A. Vicarious reinforcement and imitative learning. *Journal of Abnormal and Social Psychology*, 1963, **67**, 601–607. (b)

Bandura, A., & Walters, R. H. *Social learning and personality development.* New York: Holt, Rinehart, & Winston, 1963.

Crandall, Virginia C., Good, Suzanne, & Crandall, V. J. The reinforcement effects of adult reactions and non-reactions on children's achievement expectations: A replication study. *Child Development*, 1964, **35**, 385–397.

Goodenough, Florence L. *Anger in young children.* Minneapolis: Univer. Minnesota Press, 1931.

Johnson, Elizabeth Z. Attitudes of children toward authority as projected in their doll play at two age levels. Unpublished doctoral dissertation, Harvard University, 1951.

McGuire, W. J. Interpolated motivational statements within a programmed series of instructions as a distribution of practice factor. In A. A. Lumsdaine (Ed.), *Student response in programmed instruction: A symposium.* Washington, D. C.: National Academy of Sciences, National Research Council, 1961. Pp. 411–415.

Miller, N. E., & Dollard, J. *Social learning and imitation.* New Haven: Yale Univer. Press, 1941.

Mowrer, O. H. *Learning theory and the symbolic processes.* New York: Wiley, 1960.

Sears, Pauline S. Doll play aggression in normal young children: Influence of sex, age, sibling status, father's absence. *Psychological Monographs,* 1951, **65**(6, Whole No. 323).

Sheffield, F. D. Theoretical considerations in the learning of complex sequential tasks from demonstration and practice. In A. A. Lumsdaine (Ed.), *Student response in programmed instructions: A symposium.* Washington, D. C.: National Academy of Sciences, National Research Council, 1961. Pp. 13–32.

Sheffield, F. D., & Maccoby, N. Summary and interpretation on research on organizational principles in constructing filmed demonstrations. In A. A. Lumsdaine (Ed.), *Student response in programmed instruction: A symposium.* Washington, D. C.: National Academy of Sciences, National Research Council, 1961. Pp. 117–131.

Walters, R. H., Leat, Marion, & Mezei, L. Inhibition and disinhibition of responses through empathetic learning. *Canadian Journal of Psychology*, 1963, **17**, 235–243.

Chapter 18

Contemporary Mental Health Services

According to Nicholas Hobbs, our lead-off author for this chapter, the mental health movement is currently in its third revolution. The first two revolutions were marked by more humane treatment of persons with personality disorders and, somewhat later, by Sigmund Freud's psychoanalytic methods. These first two mental health movements reached only small segments of those who needed its services. The current revolution, in contrast, is aimed at reaching all persons and at using all available resources of manpower for prevention, diagnosis, treatment, and rehabilitation.

Such extensive use of manpower cannot be limited to trained mental health workers; therefore the use of nonprofessionals is essential. Our next two papers, by Emanuel Hallowitz and the late Jules Holzberg, describe how nonprofessionals are best used. The first suggests an actual program of training that could be pursued; the second describes how college students were used as helpers in a hospital for chronic psychiatric patients.

Mental Health's Third Revolution*

Nicholas Hobbs

AN OVERVIEW OF THE PROBLEM

The mental health movement is in its third revolution. Training programs, both for the initial education of mental health workers and for in-service development, must be re-examined for their goodness of fit with new and demanding expectations, expectations that reflect a new conception of what society must do to nourish and maintain the mental health of its people.

The first mental health revolution may be identified with the names of Philippe Pinel in France, William Tuke in England, and Benjamin Rush and Dorothea Lynde Dix in America. It was based on the heretical notion that the insane are people and should be treated with kindness and dignity. Though 170 years old, this revolution has, unhappily, not yet been consummated. Its ideals may not yet be taken for granted and must therefore be given a major emphasis in training programs at all levels. The central thesis of Action for Mental Health, its story line, is that the mentally ill do not get adequate care because they are unconsciously rejected by family, neighbor, and professional alike. I regard this as an over-simplification, but the fact that there are still practices to support the argument of the Joint Commission's report may remind us that the work of Pinel is not yet done.

The second revolution was born in Vienna; its charismatic leader was Sigmund Freud. Its agents were the wearers of Freud's ring and other disciples who carried his ideas, making a few adjustments of their own, throughout the Western world. Freud was a giant, a companion of Darwin, Marx, and Einstein in shaping our culture, our beliefs about man. It is impossible not to include Freud in a training program today, for if his ideas were to be omitted from the syllabus they would be brought in, as the clothes they wear, by every participant who has been exposed to novels, plays, poetry, television, the jokes of the day, and even to *Infant and Child Care*, the most popular publication of the United States Government Printing Office.

Revolutions generally tend to excess, and Freud's is no exception. A counter-revolution is required to restore balance and common sense. Freud has led us to a preoccupation with the intra-psychic life of man. No; I think obsession is a better word to suggest the passionate commitment we have to the world inside a man's skull, to the unconscious, the phenomenal, the stuff that dreams are made of. Everyone must become a therapist, probing the "argument of insidious intent," stalking "ragged claws scuttling across the floors of silent seas." The psychiatrist forgets Adolph Meyer and can no longer give a physical examination. The psychologist lays down his diagnostic tools, forgets research, and gets behind a desk to listen. The social worker goes inside and waits for the patient to come. The preacher takes to his study and the teacher to the case conference. The most thoroughly trained person of all, the psychiatrist who has completed psychoanalytic training, becomes a monument of Veblenian inutility, able to treat maybe a hundred patients in his entire professional career. We owe a tremendous debt to Freud, like a son to a wise and insightful father, but to use our heritage we must break with him and discover our own, authentic idiom. The pendulum is already swinging back, and I am here trying to give it a little push.

The third mental health revolution, the one we are now challenged to further, is not readily identified with the name of a person but is evident in the common theme that runs through many seemingly disparate innovations of the last fifteen years.

The therapeutic community, the open hospital, the increased interest in children, the growth of social psychiatry, the broadened base of professional responsibility for mental health programs, the search for new sources of manpower, the quickened concern for the mentally retarded, the proposed comprehensive community mental health centers, these developments are evidences of a deep-running change, indicative of this: the concepts of public health have finally penetrated the field of mental health. Up to the last decade the mental health effort was developed on a clinical model; now we are committing ourselves to a new and more promising public health model, and are seeking specific ways to make it work in practice.

Mental health used to mean its opposite, mental disease;

From Nicholas Hobbs, *American Journal of Orthopsychiatry*, 1964, 34, 822–833.

**Mental Health's Third Revolution* was part of a symposium on *Broad Perspective of Need and Content of Mental Health Training Programs* at a regional conference on inservice training in state mental health programs, October 28–31, 1963, at Detroit, Michigan.

now it means not just health but human well-being. The revolution of our time is manifested not only in changed practices but more consequently in changing assumptions about the basic character of mental disorders and of mental health. A great stride forward was made when aberrant behavior was recognized not as madness, lunacy, or possession by a devil, but as an illness, to be treated like other illnesses. Perhaps an even greater stride forward may result from the growing recognition that mental illness is not the private organic misery of an individual but a social, ethical, and moral problem, a responsibility of the total community.

By an accident of history the problem of mental retardation is being brought into prominence, with a clear demand that the mental health professions no longer shirk their responsibility for the mentally handicapped individual. Thus the scope of the mental health field is broadening at the same time that its basic character is undergoing change. Mental retardation is also being redefined to recognize the preponderant involvement of social and educational influences in the over-all problem.

It is a paradox that the care of the mentally ill has always been largely a public responsibility but that the concepts of public health, of early detection, of prophylaxis and prevention, of adequate treatment of all regardless of wealth or social position, have never had much influence. Toward the end of the eighteenth century, the *maisons de santé* in Paris did give humane treatment to the insane, but these facilities were expensive and thus not available to the great masses of the afflicted. In America, moral and humane treatment was established in a few of the better early institutions, such as the Friends Asylum in Philadelphia; but the indigent insane continued to be neglected, to be housed in overcrowded and filthy quarters, to be bound in camisoles and forgotten. The chains that Pinel had struck off were simply turned to leather. It was in the interest of the indigent insane that Dorothea Dix launched her crusade. Of course, the situation today is much better, but the dominant theme of advantage for the well-to-do and relative neglect for those without substantial means remains depressingly evident. In June, 1963, the National Institute of Labor Education presented a report on "Issues in the New National Mental Health Program Relating to Labor and Low Income Groups" in which the following observations are central to the argument:

"While in principle the state hospital is available to the community at large, in practice its population is overwhelmingly drawn from lower income groups. To bring about a reduction in state mental hospital populations, therefore, requires that treatment and rehabilitation services be created in the community which can effectively reach lower socioeconomic groups. . . . To a larger extent, the orientation and treatment methods of existing community facilities have been based on services to middle and upper class individuals. They have neither attracted blue collar workers nor found them to be suitable clients when and if they presented themselves for help."

There are two contemporary books that present in boldest relief the character of the public health, mental health problem today. One is by Hollingshead and Redlich and the other is by George Albee.

The Hollingshead and Redlich book, *Social Class and Mental Illness*, is often quoted but not for its main point, a point so startling and so revealing of the character of much of our current mental health effort that one suspects its neglect can only be due to professional guilt and consequent repression of the disturbing facts. Hollingshead and Redlich studied all persons receiving psychiatric treatment in New Haven, Connecticut, during a specific time period, to find out what determined the kind of treatment they received. One would normally make the simple-minded assumption that diagnosis would determine treatment, that what was done for a patient would be based on what was the matter with him. The investigators found no relationship between diagnosis and treatment. They studied other variables such as age and sex, and found these unrelated to treatment. The one variable related to type of treatment received was the socioeconomic status of the patient. If he were from the lowest socioeconomic group, he received some kind of mechanical, inexpensive, and quick therapy, such as electric shock. If he were from a high socioeconomic group, he received extended, expensive, talking-type psychotherapy. If the patient were not only affluent but also a member of an old, prestigious family, so situated in life that he bestowed honor on his helper, he received extended talking-type psychotherapy, but at a discount. The relationship between socioeconomic status and type of treatment received was not manifested in private practice alone but was also evident in the treatment provided by clinics and other public supported agencies. Thus all the mental health professions are involved.

The second pivotal book is George Albee's. I regard his monograph *Mental Health Manpower Trends*, prepared for the Joint Commission on Mental Illness and Health, as a most important and instructive book for the shaping of a national mental health program as well as for the development of curricula for the training of psychiatrists, psychologists, social workers, and other mental health specialists. The book requires a fundamental shift in strategy in providing mental health services to the people of this nation.

Albee's main thesis may be stated simply: the prospective supply of people for training in the mental health professions is limited; demands for services will continue to grow more rapidly than the population of the country; and there will not be in the foreseeable future enough mental health personnel to meet demands for service.

It is widely and, I believe, erroneously assumed that the personnel shortages are a local and a temporary phenomenon. We assume that it is a matter of waiting a year or so for the training programs to catch up. Albee's point is that they will not catch up. We can't solve the problem the way we are trying to solve it.

Keep these two disturbing books in mind and then consider: (1) the geographical distribution of psychiatrists and (2) the growth of private practice in clinical psychology. Most psychiatrists are concentrated in urban centers in proportions much higher than the relative concentration of population. Over 50 per cent of the psychiatrists trained under NIMH grants go into private practice. Mental health services flow in the direction of money and sophistication. The most vigorous development in clinical psychology today is the extension of private practice, following the model of psychiatry which has followed the model of the private practice of medicine. Psychologists in private practice are a major power group in the American Psychological Association. Several universities are working toward the establishment of professional schools for the training of psychological practitioners.

Now there is nothing wrong with the private practice of psychiatry or psychology except that it does not provide a sound base for the development of a national mental health program. The one-to-one relationship, the fifty-minute hour, are a dead-end, except perhaps for the two participants or as a source of new knowledge. This mode of offering service consumes far too much manpower for the benefit of a far-too-limited segment of society. We must find a more efficient way of deploying our limited resources of mental health manpower.

These two books, more than any I know, tell us what the third mental health revolution must accomplish. We must find new ways of deploying our resources of manpower and of knowledge to the end that effective mental health services for prevention, for diagnosis, for treatment, for rehabilitation, can be made available to all of the people. Furthermore, we now have two other books that provide us with guidelines to action. They are *Action for Mental Health*, the report of the Joint Commission on Mental Illness and Health, and *National Action to Combat Mental Retardation*, the report of the President's Panel on Mental Retardation.

IMPLICATIONS FOR TRAINING PROGRAMS

To prescribe the content of professional curricula is hazardous at all times and downright foolhardy in a time of revolution. The most useful and productive thing to do is to keep up a lively debate on educational objectives for mental health professions and to leave it to local initiative, to the faculties of graduate and professional schools, and to directors of in-service training programs, to determine what to teach and how to teach it. As a contribution to the debate on goals, nine objectives should guide the development of educational programs for social work, nursing, psychiatry, medicine in general, clinical psychology, and the various adjunctive disciplines.

The changing conception of the nature of mental illness and mental retardation will require that the mental health specialist be a person of broad scientific and humanistic education, a person prepared to help make decisions not only about the welfare of an individual but also about the kind of society that must be developed to nurture greatest human fulfillment.

I am, frankly, gravely concerned about the proposed comprehensive community mental health centers. Here is a bold and imaginative proposal that may fail because top level mental health personnel (I am talking about you and me: it is interesting that in-service training is often thought of as something that is good for somebody else) may not be prepared to discharge the responsibilities of a comprehensive community mental health program. When the great state hospitals were built across this country in the 19th century, someone must have thought them to be the last word, the best way to care for the mentally ill. There is a chance that the new mental health centers will be nothing more than a product of the general urbanization of America, a movement from country to city. Twenty years from now, people may moan not of bricks and mortar but of glass and steel; there is a real danger that we shall succeed in changing only the location and the architecture of the state hospital. If the new centers turn inward toward the hospital, they too will be monuments to failure. If they turn outward to the community, as some of the testimony before the Congress said they should, who among us will know what to do? Psychiatrists have been trained primarily as clinicians, as intra-psychic diagnosticians, as listeners with the third ear; we are clinicians, not public health, mental health experts. Who among us knows enough about schools, courts, churches, welfare programs, recreation, effects of automation, cultural deprivation, population mobility, delinquency, family life, city planning, and human ecology in general, to presume to serve on the staff of a comprehensive community mental health center? The first in-service training program that we should plan should be for ourselves. We have nothing more urgent to do.

The concept of the responsibility of the doctor for patient, case worker for client, so appropriately honored in traditional educational programs for the physician, social worker, and clinical psychologist, must be reconceptualized. They must re-define responsibilities of these specialists as co-workers with other professionals who have unique contributions to make to the development of social institutions that promote effective functioning in people.

The psychiatrist might have limited himself to the treatment of the hospitalized psychotic or the acutely debilitated neurotic, leaving lesser problems of adjustment to teachers, clergymen, and counselors of various types. With respect to the mentally retarded he might have limited himself to those so handicapped as to require institutionalization, defining the rest as slow learners and thus the responsibility not of medicine but of education.

Psychiatry has, wisely I think, chosen not to take this constricted course but to concern itself with a broad spectrum of problems that are also the historical concerns of other professional groups. Most of the mental health effort, as we now define it, overlaps substantially with the domains of education, religion, welfare, corrections, and even recreation, communication, architecture, and city planning. There is nothing in most mental health training programs to provide either content or method for dealing collaboratively with other professional groups to solve problems that are legitimately defined both as mental health and as something else. Indeed, there is much in the education of the doctor, the psychologist, the social worker, that actually militates against effective collaboration in these areas of overlapping concern. For example, the honorable concept of the physician's responsibility for his patient, so carefully and appropriately nurtured in medical training, gets extended unconsciously to relationships with other professional people and becomes an issue not of responsibility but of hegemony. What the physician sees as being responsible, his colleague sees as being arrogant. The physician always seems surprised and hurt by this incongruity in role perception, this seemingly unwarranted misunderstanding of his intent. The more thorough his clinical training, the less well prepared he may be for public health responsibilities. Somehow, without sacrifice of clinical competence, the psychiatrist must be trained to meet role requirements of truly cooperative enterprises involving a variety of professional people. Is there anywhere an approved residency program in psychiatry that explicitly trains for this concept of professional responsibility?

Clinical psychology is equally vulnerable to charges of incompetence in collaborative skills. The arrogance of the psychologist is not that of responsibility but of detachment, a product perhaps of professional timidity and defensiveness, coupled with the platitudinous allegation that we need more research before we can contribute to social action programs. Perhaps only the social worker, before the advent of the sit-behind-the-desk-and-do therapy era, is prepared for public health, mental health responsibilities.

The mental health specialist must be trained in ways to multiply his effectiveness by working through other less extensively and expensively trained people. The one-to-one model of much current practice does not provide a sound basis for a public health, mental health program.

The most promising approach to this problem at the present time is the use of the extensively trained, expensive, and scarce mental health specialists to guide the work of other carefully selected persons with limited training. Such manpower is available, even in abundance, and its effective use depends on the ingenuity of the mental health specialist and his willingness to extend himself by working through other people. I would cite the work of Margaret Rioch in training carefully selected housewives to do psychotherapy under supervision; the use of college student volunteers in mental hospitals, and our Project Re-ED in Tennessee and North Carolina in which carefully selected teachers are working with disturbed children with the support of mental health and educational specialists. The place to start is in the universities, medical schools, residency centers, and in-service training programs. The challenge to the mental health specialist in training should be: after establishing his own basic clinical competence, how can he multiply his effectiveness, say by a factor of six, by discovering ways of working through other people?

Current developments will require that mental health training programs be revised to give attention to mental retardation commensurate with the degree of responsibility that the mental health professions have already assumed for the retarded. Since mental retardation is a much broader problem than it is usually considered to be in those few medical, social work, and psychological training programs that have given it attention, the inclusion of mental retardation in these curricula will require a substantial extension of their conceptual underpinnings. Slums are more consequential than galactosemia or phenylketonuria.

Few things could so radically alter the character of education in medicine, psychiatry, psychology, and social work as a serious commitment to do something about the problem of mental retardation. The health professions have laid claim to much of the problem; at least three of the institutes of the National Institute of Health are involved; a substantial portion of every state's mental health program is devoted to the retarded; yet in most training programs it receives peripheral attention.

For one thing, mental retardation is not a disease entity. It is a host of conditions manifested in impaired intellectual and social competence. It is due to chromosomal aberrations, intrauterine trauma, prematurity, metabolic disturbances, accidents, cultural deprivation, inadequate opportunities to learn, and acute emotional disturbances. Mental retardation is widely regarded as a hopeless condition; yet it is hard to think of a human affliction so amenable to productive intervention. But again, a radical reconceptualization of the problem is required. When it is in our interest to make the problem of mental retardation loom large, we cite the figure of 5,400,000 retarded in the country. Yet the major emphasis of most of our programs is on the 400,000 who have some apparent physical anomaly, to the neglect of the 5,000,000 who are primarily a challenge to the adequacy of our social institutions. We are more intrigued by galactosemia than challenged by slums and poor schools. We presume to claim the finest medical care in the world but stand eleventh among nations in infant mortality, evidence of widespread inadequate prenatal care that also produces prematurity and much mental retardation. Assumption of responsibility for the retarded will require that our major professional groups make as their cause equal access to medical services and educational opportunity by all people without regard to means or social status.

Curriculum constructors in social work, psychiatry, and psychology must come to terms with the issue of the relationship between science and practice. Are the scientist and the practitioner to be one or are their functions separable? Just at the time when psychologists seem ready to back off a bit from their insistence that the two functions should go together, there is an opposite trend developing in medical education. The issue is absolutely basic and must be clearly resolved before the content of training programs can be discerned.

The main source of nourishment for the mental health professions has been clinical practice leavened and limited by research. The shift toward a public health emphasis in mental health programs will require that the mental health specialist work through social institutions. He must acquire an appreciation of how disparate groups of people organize to achieve common goals and he must know how to encourage this process. He will need to be adept at institution building, at social invention, at the ordering of individual and community resources in the interest of mental health. I have found instructive a study by Harland Cleveland of the successful foreign service officer. The foreign service officer is in a position very much like that of the public health, mental health officer. He is confronted with a tremendous problem, his resources are limited, his staff is inadequate, and he is expected to make a difference in the lives of a substantial number of people. Cleveland found that the highly effective foreign service officer had, among other attributes, a strong institutional sense, a sense of the ways in which social groups invent institutions to serve their ends, and a notion of how this process can be furthered in the interest of his concerns. It seems to me that the public health, mental health specialist must develop a comparable sensitivity and skill.

An increased public health emphasis in mental health

programs will accentuate the need for prevention and thus lead to a greater emphasis in professional training on problems of children, on childhood disorders and early indications of later difficulties, and especially on normal patterns of development.

I feel that fully half of our mental health resources—money, facilities, people—should be invested in programs for children and youth, for parents of young children and for teachers and others who work directly with children. This would be the preferable course even if the remaining 50% would permit only a holding action with respect to problems of adults. But our resources are such that, if we care enough, we can move forward on both fronts simultaneously. This is the only way to make substantial changes in the mental health of our adult population a generation from now. I have made this suggestion on a number of occasions and no one ever takes exception to the substance of the argument. But, alas, children are unprofitable clients and, furthermore, they don't vote, so I expect them to continue to be neglected unless the public health challenge grips the mental health professions.

The new curricula should, paradoxically, reinstate an age old study, that of morals and ethics, not professional ethics but classical ethics. There are two reasons for this. First, the therapeutic relationship, whether between two people or in a broader social effort, is at heart an ethical enterprise, with respect to both method and outcome. Second, we face the awesome prospect of becoming efficient in our efforts to influence human behavior. With increasing effectiveness we must become increasingly concerned with the consequences of our work. We cannot responsibly remain satisfied with vague definitions of what we mean by mental health.

Educational programs for mental health specialists should anticipate an increasing obsolescence rate for knowledge and build habits of continuing scholarship and independent study. The more productive we are in mental health research, the more ingenious in the development of new social institutions, the more quickly will training programs become obsolete. The mental health specialist must be a continuing learner; training for independent learning must be a major commitment of mental health educational programs.

But graduate schools do not encourage independent study, not much, and medical schools are notoriously ineffectual in this regard. In our graduate program in psychology at Peabody we are encouraging students to spend a "quarter at Woolesthorpe," attending no classes, writing no papers, accumulating no credits, eschewing "guided readings," studying only because of their own need to know. I recommend the idea to other training centers, perhaps even to those concerned primarily with in-service training. What is Woolesthorpe? Well, it seems that there was a plague in England in about 1660. It was so serious they closed down the universities. There was a young and undistinguished student at Cambridge who went home to his mother's cottage at Woolesthorpe and there, without any professors to bother him, invented the calculus and began his great experiment on optics. Do all in-service training programs have to be social events? What would have happened if each member of this group had been given three days leave and fifteen dollars a day and told: "Go to Woolesthorpe and learn as much as you can about public health, mental health." But I guess it really might take a plague to get us to take the idea seriously. Learning is ultimately a lonely enterprise.

From these nine considerations, these nine objectives for the training of mental health workers, there is instruction perhaps for the improvement of in-service training programs, but there is a more insistent challenge that we re-examine the total structure of our mental health program to test its adequacy to get done the tremendous task that confronts us.

I thus come to a potentially distressing point for a speaker at a conference on training. There is a possibility that the improvement of training is not our problem at all. I see little profit, from a public health viewpoint, in the following: (1) To train better and better psychotherapists to treat fewer and fewer people. (2) To improve the training of nurses to take care of increasing numbers of hospitalized old people who are no longer ill. (3) To hone to a fine edge the group work skills of an attendant who must watch over 80 mentally retarded adults in a cyclone fence compound. (4) To improve the skills of the obstetrician in providing prenatal care to the poor in big cities when his contact with the mother is limited to thirty minutes before the arrival of the baby. (5) To train for exquisite precision in diagnosis when differentiated treatments are not available for differential diagnoses.

And so on for the social worker, the recreational worker, the occupational therapists, the community volunteer.

I come back to the possibility that we may not be able to solve the problem the way we are trying to do it, no matter how good our training. We must pay attention to the organizational structures for providing services, to the more effective deployment of our limited resources of highly trained people, to invention of new patterns for the provision of mental health services. These new patterns of organization may then have more influence on training than any other single consideration. Indeed perhaps a major goal of all in-service training programs today should be to train for the invention of new and more efficient forms for providing service, and then for skill in the diffusion of innovation.

A CASE STUDY IN INNOVATION

I should like, in concluding, to present a case study in social innovation, to illustrate the thesis that it will be of no moment simply to train ourselves to do better what we are already doing. There must be invention of new forms for the provision of mental health services, forms that will treat realistically the problems of cost, of limited resources of highly trained talent, and of the necessity of extending mental health services to all of the people and not to a privileged few. There are actually a large number of new inventions that I might cite, for the necessity of building public health concepts into mental health programs has already commanded attention and stimulated innovation; but I shall limit myself to one example simply because I know it well and can describe it fairly. I refer to our Project Re-ED, which is a compressed way of saying "a project for the Re-education of Emotionally Disturbed Children."

Project Re-ED was deliberately planned to meet a pressing social need that had been identified some eight years ago by a study of mental health resources in the South conducted by the Southern Regional Education Board. That study revealed an acute shortage in the region of specialized services for emotionally disturbed children. There were a few hospital units but most of these children in trouble were placed in detention homes, in institutions for the retarded, on wards with psychotic adults, or were left at home, festering there, occasionally seen by an itinerant teacher. The specialized services of all sixteen states would not meet the requirements of the least populous state. While the situation has improved in recent years the problem remains acute. Furthermore, it is nationwide. The problem promises to be a chronic one, for we aspire to apply the clinical model to all disturbed children, and this simply can't be done because of limitations on supply of personnel, even if it were desirable, which I question. We must turn to a public health, mental health model if we are to make any substantial headway at all. Re-ED is one such approach; there could, of course, be many others.

Two residential schools for emotionally disturbed children have been established, one in Nashville, Tennessee, and the other in Durham, North Carolina.[1] Each school will serve 40 children, aged 6 to 12, who are too disturbed or disturbing to be retained in a public school and who come from families that are too disrupted for the child to benefit from day care. The schools are staffed entirely by carefully selected young college graduates who have skills in teaching, recreation, camping, physical education, crafts and so on. They have been given nine months of specialized training for their work, and are called teacher-counselors. There is one social worker to mobilize community resources in the interest of the child and his family and one liaison teacher to coordinate a Re-ED school with the child's regular school. The teacher-counselors are backed by consultants; psychiatrists, psychologists, social workers, pediatricians, and curriculum specialists. This is a sketch of the basic plan.

Now let us look at some of the principles that guide the program and warrant, I believe, the use of Re-ED as an example of a deliberate turning away from a clinical model toward a public health, mental health model for the provision of services to emotionally disturbed children.

The program draws on a source of manpower that is in reasonably good supply and does not compromise on the quality of person who works with the child on a 24 hour-a-day basis.

[1] There are now (1968) four Re-ED schools in Tennessee. The schools in both North Carolina and Tennessee are being financed entirely by the states as an ongoing part of their mental health programs. Re-ED is thus no longer a "project."

Re-ED is basically a plan by which highly-trained mental health specialists can multiply their effectiveness by working through other less-well trained people. (If, through in-service training programs we could get most mental health specialists thinking this way, and then if we could invent the institutions to support them, the mental health personnel problem might be solved.)

Re-ED concentrates on children, aged 6 to 12, hoping to prevent more serious later difficulties by early intervention. This is the mental health analogue to the public health early case finding.

The program in Re-ED is organized around ecological rather than intra-psychic concepts. The task is not to "cure" the child (a clinical goal) but to get into reasonably functioning order the circumscribed social system of which the child is an essential part (a public health goal). The effort is to get the child, the family, the school, the neighborhood, and the community just above threshold with respect to the other. When it is judged that the system has reached a level of functioning so that the probability of its successful operation exceeds the probability of failure, the child is returned home. A little improvement in all components or a dramatic improvement in any one component may make it operational for the child. With this concept, it makes sense to plan for an average length of stay for a child in a Re-ED school of from four to six months.

A public health effort must have a public vocabulary. All of the theory of Re-ED, the objectives of the program and the processes by which these objectives are furthered, have been put into a simple vocabulary using English words as English words are commonly used.

A public health effort must be economically feasible. We think Re-ED is. The existing clinical model for the care of disturbed children costs from $25 to $100 a day with an average of around $50. We think that Re-ED schools can be operated for around $20 to $25 per day. More important than the daily cost is the cost per child returned to his family and school as described above.

I describe Project Re-ED not as the solution to the problem of the emotionally disturbed child. It obviously is not that. An array of services will be required—as in any good public health program—to do the job, including hospitals and better public school programs for the disturbed child. I see it rather as one social invention that can make a difference. For an effective public health, mental health program in America we need similar innovations in a number of fields; in the prevention of mental retardation due to inadequate prenatal care and to acute cultural deprivation; in the care of the chronic schizophrenic, the alcoholic, the drug addict; in programs to arrest deterioration in the aged and for the care of hospitalized oldsters who are no longer ill. By such innovations the concepts of public health can come to the field of mental health.

Issues and Strategies in the Use of Nonprofessionals

Emanuel Hallowitz

We have seen a spate of books and papers extolling the virtues of the "indigenous nonprofessional" not only as a new source of manpower but also as an agent of change both within the community and within the institution. Typically, new methods or techniques attract many rabid adherents and as many, usually less vocal, detractors. Also typically, the adherents tend to exaggerate the virtues of the new approach and ignore or minimize its disadvantages. In previous papers, we too have been guilty of overemphasizing the positive and paying scant attention to some of the problems created by using nonprofessionals.

Lincoln Hospital has now had three and a half years of experience with nonprofessional staff, which number fifty almost exclusively Puerto Rican and black Community Mental Health Workers, of whom 60 per cent are women and 40 per cent are men. About 75 per cent of the Workers have completed high school; a few of them have also had evening college courses; the other 25 per cent have not completed high school. In age, they range from twenty to seventy-two years, but most of them are in the thirty to forty year range.

Elsewhere (1–4) we have described in some detail the many tasks and roles they have assumed as members of our Psychiatric Clinic, Day Hospital, and Neighborhood Service Center staffs. But those reports dealt little with the special problems and stresses posed by the introduction into a community mental health center of a new source of manpower. Parenthetically, I am sure I need not point out that the situation involving fifty nonprofessionals presents problems very different from one in which only two or three such workers are introduced into an agency. This paper will therefore focus primarily upon these problems, the mistakes we have made, and the strategies we have developed out of our experience.

The Community Mental Health Workers, coming as they do from an extremely disadvantaged population, bring to the job the same strong feelings toward the power structure as are evident in the target population: suspicion, distrust, and fear that they will be exploited, fired out of hand, discriminated against because of color, ethnic background or religion, together with almost unconscious convictions that supervisors and administrative personnel have omniscience and omnipotence, and that somehow, through simple association with us, they too may become all-powerful. Countervailing this projection, however, may often be the conviction that only they really care about the poor, only they really know what is going on, only they are down to earth and reality oriented, while the professionals are "on cloud nine." Another contradictory set of attitudes we often observe is the wish to learn from the professionals combined with an anti-intellectual attitude in which reading, education, and knowledge are deprecated.

At first delighted at being accepted into the system and happy with their new status as Mental Health Workers, they soon discover that they are still low man on the totem pole. They then begin to struggle to define their role more clearly and to find steps toward higher status than they were originally assigned.

The professional himself, working with nonprofessionals, is equally subject to conflicting emotions and attitudes. He may enjoy the superior status and the assumption of omnipotence with which the nonprofessional invests him, but he feels anxious and resentful when he cannot live up to these expectations. Similarly, although he is eager to see the nonprofessional develop skills and take on more complex tasks, he is reluctant to assign responsibility or allow much independence of action or judgment to the nonprofessional. The fear that the nonprofessional cannot do a quality job with clients impels the professional to find ways of controlling and directing the worker's activity.

The professional has been taught to gather facts, diagnose, reflect, plan a course of action, and be deliberate in his interventions; the workers tend to be more active and immediate in response to client needs. The workers function informally and spontaneously; often disregarding the traditional use of channels of communication and authority. These differences in style create conflict. Perhaps the sharpest conflict arising out of the difference in style comes from the professional's traditional ways of structuring programs and offering supervision and his difficulty in adapting these traditional methods to the needs and style of the nonprofessional.

Furthermore, the professional, bringing with him an ingrained frame of reference, generally learned in professional settings, tends to view the nonprofessional's behavior, attitudes, and work performance, by the traditional standards, in spite of his intellectual awareness that the old frame of reference no longer applies.

Allow me to emphasize that I am not attributing these difficulties to either the professionals or the nonprofessionals alone, but rather to the developments that arise out of a new type of interaction that calls for major and difficult readjustments in each group. The professional, because of his greater knowledge, self-awareness, and pro-

Presented at the N.A.S.W. Symposium, National Conference of Social Welfare, San Francisco, California, May 25, 1968

fessional discipline, and in no small measure because he is in a position of power, will not only have to change himself but will also have to play a key role in helping the nonprofessional to change.

The balance of this paper will be directed toward describing some of our struggles in order to alert you to the common pitfalls inherent in this situation, and to clarify further some of the dynamics of the interactions as well as to pinpoint the internalized blocks to our own development.

First, some myths currently prevalent should be laid to rest. Specifically, the poor do not necessarily have special knowledge, insight, or intuitions not available to the more affluent; neither is the poor person ipso facto more sympathetic to others in the same plight; neither does his poverty give him special knowledge about effective administration, program planning, interviewing skills, community action, etc. He does not necessarily, despite the common assumption, understand his community or culture better than could the professional from the outside. On the whole, we found the poor and disadvantaged no more free of prejudice and snobbery than any other group in our society. The one clear advantage of the nonprofessional drawn from his community is that he understands the language, style, and customs of his neighbors.

As a matter of fact, a good sociologist or anthropologist who has gained community acceptance can understand the dynamics of the community much better than the nonprofessionals. This should not be a stunning discovery. As in most urban slum areas, individuals tend to stay in their local areas and associate with their own selected groups. Few of them have had enough experience with the community as a whole to generalize about it or even its parts in ways genuinely useful to the professional. For urban slum communities are much more heterogeneous than we tend to assume.

We were able to find that there are individuals in the target population who have developed effective survival techniques and who are capable of warmth, sympathy, and empathy. Among them are some who are vitally interested in their neighbors' welfare. When we can identify such persons and provide them with some training and supervision, they can make important contributions to our service goals.

But agencies who choose to hire nonprofessionals must decide before such a program is put into operation, whether their goal is rehabilitation of the employee or the delivery of service for, just as the nonprofessional has an inordinate fear of being fired out of hand, the professional has problems about firing. If the agency goal is to provide service rather than the rehabilitation of the worker, it must set standards for performance, being sure that the standards are realistic for the new personnel and then stick to them. Granted that the nonprofessional will need time and help to achieve a minimum standard, the question remains: how much time? And what should we do when someone slips through the selection process and we then discover that we are dealing with serious psychological deviancy? How much deviancy can we tolerate? If our therapeutic and social work interests over-ride our administrative judgment, we may delay action, particularly if the action is firing, not only at the expense of the program but also possibly at the expense of the individual. What blocks us here is our own emotionality. Our original motivation in choice of career was the wish to help, not hurt. Further, I think we are afraid of hostility and delay taking the necessary step because of our fear of other staff's reaction. Even when the issue is one of gross incompetence, we found ourselves debating whether to take such a step because we knew that to deprive someone of this job would mean, at best, difficulty in finding another and, at worst, sending him back to the welfare rolls. Speaking bluntly, such situations stimulate our guilt and we are emotionally unable to do what we know intellectually is necessary.

The uncomfortable fact is that if you decide that your agency is hiring nonprofessionals for service, you must accept your real responsibility; and that is the mandate to furnish needed manpower and create career opportunities for those able to take full advantage of them. Every incompetent retained means a competent deprived of opportunity, as well as one more unfilled task in critical services. You must use your diagnostic judgment to identify the problem, decide what might improve the situation, and how much time this process should require. Can you afford the time? After my own years of experience with this problem, I have come to the conclusion that one must set oneself a time limit and detail exactly what changes in a person's performance you would need to see at the end of that time limit. If the changes do not occur, you must set termination procedures into operation. No small element in this is the fact that, when an incompetent worker is retained for a protracted period of time, the other workers may interpret this as a signal that administration is weak and basically indifferent to its real function-service to the community. On the other hand, even taking timely action may reactivate the other workers' fears of being discriminated against or fired and produce a good deal of hostility. Nevertheless, we have found that one can depend upon the healthy part of the Workers' personalities ultimately to recognize the wisdom of the decision.

Still on the issue of whether to fire, an even more difficult situation is one in which you have hired someone whose charismatic leadership ability seems to be used destructively—in a blind hostility toward "authority." One must examine the situation diagnostically, asking such questions as: "Is this individual's need to constantly challenge authority amenable to change? Will he use it only to mobilize the other workers' latent hostility? And, even if this is true, is it worth the gamble to retain him in the hope that it will stimulate more rapid emergence of leadership among the other workers, sometimes in opposition to him?" If you decide for firing, then you risk active and hostile confrontation from the rest of the group and must be prepared to cope with it.

Temporizing over his firing tends to lead administration to simply learn to live with the situation and cope with each crisis he creates as it arises. That is why clinical judgment becomes so important for evaluating the worker's long-range potentialities and deciding how much risk you are willing to take. We must remember that we hire people for their survival characteristics: aggressiveness, assertiveness, and manipulativeness. We are delighted when these abilities are used effectively in working with other institutions, but we tend to react with anger when these same qualities are directed against us; in guarding against our counter-reactions, we must be particularly objective in evaluating those workers who frequently arouse them.

Another issue of major importance in working with nonprofessionals is the necessity to guard against giving contradictory messages: for example, encouraging them to speak out at staff meetings, but then getting angry and authoritative if they accept the invitation and express feelings or ideas that we deem inappropriate. We have also given other kinds of double messages: at one time, emphasizing all the things the workers still have to learn, and at another, telling them how much they can teach the professional, thus unwittingly feeding a growing sense of grandiosity.

Supervision presents another problem. Out of their life experiences, and probably largely out of their school experiences, they tend to see supervision not as a learning process, but as a threat. Their suspiciousness made it difficult for them to believe that criticism was meant to be constructive, and it was not unusual for them to react defensively and argumentatively. Sometimes this led to their withholding information and avoiding supervisory conferences. As we examined this, we realized that we were more comfortable with the dependent, even overdependent relationship which fed our narcissism and self-esteem, whereas the hostile reactions threatened our potency and self-image and frustrated our wish to be of service. In the attempt to avoid the hostility, we too often placated the worker, a maneuver which he tended to see as a "cop-out," or we reacted with counterhostility, which simply tended to escalate the conflict and make for a power struggle.

Paternalism too is an ever-present danger. None of us at Lincoln like to think of ourselves as paternalistic, yet as we reviewed our past experiences, we found many areas in which this had operated as an unconscious factor. The professional who chooses to work in a disadvantaged area has a stake, both personal and professional, in the success of a nonprofessional employee program. Feeling that they are his charges, he may do battle *for* them or become their spokesman, rather than encouraging them to do their own battling and speak for themselves. Or, in the attempt to make the nonprofessional's task easier, the professional may introduce changes in procedures without consulting the nonprofessionals or allowing them any participation in the decisions. If the nonprofessionals then reject or attack the changes or deem them insufficient, the professional tends to react with hurt, disappointment, or counterhostility. What passes through our minds, I think, although we quickly push them away, are such thoughts as: Don't they realize how much we've done for them? Don't they realize that we were the first to hire nonprofessionals in the Bronx? Don't they realize what a battle we had with the medical school and the university to get permission to hire nonprofessionals, to get their wages raised, their working conditions improved, etc?

Actually, in the area of participation, not only paternalism but the issue of power created special problems for us. Often, we made it clear that the program was ours, the professionals. When we did say "ours" meaning it in the sense of joint, the nonprofessionals felt that we were trying to do a "con" job on them, and I sometimes wonder whether there wasn't some truth in this. For, although on an intellectual level, we do want to have the nonprofessionals participate in decisionmaking and policy and program direction, we still have the unconscious conviction that we know better. Furthermore, we want to retain exclusive power, and the reality is that every increase in power for the nonprofessionals means a concomitant decrease for us.

The struggle to find that appropriate level of participation for the nonprofessionals involved dealing not only with our own irrationalities but with theirs. From the outset, we defined the areas in which the workers had decision-making power but specified that in others the power of decision lay with administration, although the nonprofessionals could participate in discussions directed toward determining the decision. In the first place, the workers felt that some of the areas we reserved for our own prerogative should properly have been theirs, or that, at the very least, they should have an equal share in the decision-making. A second, and even more delicate problem, arose when the nonprofessionals, having made suggestions which were solicited by the professionals, found their suggestions rejected. It was difficult, if not sometimes impossible, to make them understand that participation does not necessarily imply control. They want a democratic organization, with everyone having an equal voice and vote. It is hard for them to accept the reality that social agencies are systems of delegated responsibility and authority, and that implicit in this system is accountability to a higher authority. Similarly, they find it even more difficult to accept the political reality that the agency itself may be accountable to any of a number of governmental structures.

We have not resolved the conflict around participation, but the confrontations we have faced have taught us much and moved us further along toward genuine participation of all levels of staff than we had ever contemplated. A few examples might illustrate.

In the fall of 1965 we were invited, as an agency, to send two delegates to each of three poverty conventions being held in our area, to be composed of delegates from all agencies and resident groups in the area. Each convention was to elect an anti-poverty board. Considering ourselves the most enlightened of the agencies, Lincoln Hospital Mental Health Services decided to send a professional-nonprofessional team to each convention, although we really felt that two professionals would do a more effective job. Feeling very virtuous, we were astonished when our Community Mental Health Workers demanded to know why we were sending professionals at all, and why we felt we had the right to select the nonprofessional delegates. We explained that we, as an agency, had been invited to send delegates, and that it was an administrative prerogative to decide which personnel could best represent the agency. The workers pointed out that the conventions were essentially community affairs, that they were members of the community working in it on the kinds of problems with which the conventions were concerned, and that they were entitled to a voice in who would represent the agency. After much discussion they agreed that under the rules of the convention, administration had to be conceded the right to select three professionals, although they disapproved of the convention rules. But they insisted on the right to elect their own delegates. When one of the professionals voiced the fear that such an election would simply be a popularity contest, the workers demanded to know why we thought they didn't have enough at stake in the conventions to elect the best representatives they could.

At the subsequent caucus of the professional and administrative staff, some of my colleagues urged me not to give in, claimed that administration would lose face, that this would simply open the door to more unreasonable demands, or that an important administrative principle was at stake. Others disagreed. After much discussion and with some misgivings, we agreed to having the workers hold their own election. They accepted one of our original appointees, but substituted two others. All three were extremely effective participants—more effective, in fact, than the professionals, because they knew more people and were able to do more effective political maneuvering. One of them was elected to the board of one convention, and in another convention's election, the CMHW's politicking outside the convention was probably decisive in having the professional elected to the board, a position he probably could not have won on his own. We were, of course, officially highly gratified; I think we were also mildly chagrined.

A second such incident arose several months later, when we had received a grant for our professional staff to participate in a series of workshops and visits in Puerto Rico. At the last moment six places became available for the nonprofessional staff. This time we decided that we would permit the entire nonprofessional staff to select the six people who were to go. We worried that there would be conflict between the black and Puerto Rican members of the staff and that people would be elected on the basis of popularity rather than competency. To satisfy our curiosity the key administrators put down the names of the six nonprofessionals they thought could do the best job. And, again to our mild chagrin, the workers proceeded to select a chairman of the group, developed criteria for selection, placed names in nomination, had the nominees give two minute speeches and then voted. They selected five of the six that we ourselves would have selected. The sixth worked out quite well. In retrospect, we were forced to recognize that again we had been guilty of unreasonable paternalism.

The third situation aroused much more anxiety among the professionals. The Community Mental Health Workers requested that they be permitted to meet as a group once a month on agency time without a professional being present. This meant, in effect, the development of an independent workers group. We held a number of discussions with the group, exploring their reasons for wanting such sessions. We were afraid that their sessions would be used to reinforce hostilities toward their supervisors. Another possibility was that the meeting would be held to organize a union group—an activity we did not oppose but felt they should do on their own time. The workers assured us that our assumptions were inaccurate, that they simply wanted the freedom to talk together about such things as program development without the inhibitory effect of the presence of a professional. Further they felt that they needed some sense of identity which such a group could foster. Third they saw it as a way they could be of help to each other in sharing information about resources, programs, etc. Again, much soul-searching was involved. Not only did we have to examine the advantages and disadvantages of such a development for the future of our program but we also had to deal with our own fears and suspicions. Reluctantly, we agreed to the meetings on condition that a joint evaluation be made after six months. We also suggested that the meetings be held twice a month, since we felt that one meeting a month would not permit enough continuity of process. The workers agreed and the meetings began. At first the meetings did indeed focus and aggravate the split between the professionals and the nonprofessionals, but this allowed the acknowledgement of the split to become overt and open to much more candid discussion thus making it easier to deal with. The meetings produced much more anguish for the workers themselves. Just as the split between the nonprofessional and the professional became more open and focused, so did the suspicion and distrust between the black worker and the Puerto Rican come to the fore. It was further complicated by internal struggles for power and control within the group. After the first several meetings some of the workers asked for permission to not attend the Independent Workers Group. The professional staff took the position that attendance was required and helped them to think about ways in which they could influence the group's development. On a number of occasions we offered consultation to the group as a whole but this was adamantly refused. Things seemed to go from bad to worse and many a time, as administration, we were tempted to call the whole thing off, but recognized that if we were to do this it would be seen as an arbitrary use of power and lack of confidence in the workers' ability to handle their own differences. About the fifth month we began to see more cohesion in the group. Some of their organizational problems were resolved, others, though they were still apparent, were less intrusive. At the end of the six-month period, the joint evaluation was done. It was then clear that all the workers wanted the meetings to continue and asked that even more time be set aside for them. The workers indicated that the meetings had served the purpose of enabling some of them to speak out more easily in staff meetings, that they had gained valuable information from colleagues, and had a better appreciation of the limitations and assets of some of their colleagues. They also noted areas where the organization of the independent group needed to be strengthened. It was clear that they were guarded in making negative comments about their own organization but some of these did come through.

The professional's response was more ambivalent. They too could point to specific gains in individuals but were more concerned about the fact that the Independent Organization gave a forum to those whose attitudes toward authority were most hostile. They did recognize however that a more positive leadership was emerging but nevertheless they felt that the destructive elements were still in control, though not so much so as in the earlier phase of the group's development.

The Independent Workers Group continued and now has been in operation a little over two years. There is still no unanimity among the professionals but by and large we do feel the positive elements outweigh the negative ones. We are all in agreement that despite our fears, the confrontations forced upon us which made us rethink some of our traditional methods of organization, procedure and administration did enhance our program.

STRATEGIES

Our experience to date convinces us that the utilization of nonprofessionals from the target population has advantages that far outweigh its difficulties. To wit: in our plan for the expansion of the Mental Health Service under a National Institute of Mental Health Staffing Grant, we are planning to expand our current staff of fifty Community Mental Health workers to ninety.

In reviewing our experience, trying to look honestly at our mistakes and failures as well as our successes, we have formulated some recommendations that we hope might be useful to other agencies.

1. Before undertaking a program utilizing nonprofessionals, the professional staff needs to participate in the planning and determination of its goals. They must be alerted to possible areas of conflict and participate in developing expectations and standards of performance. They can participate in planning a training program and they can help in clarifying the role of the nonprofessional. Particularly they will need help in anticipating some of their own emotional reactions when the inevitable conflicts emerge, conflict which we maintain is an essential and a natural development.

2. It is equally essential that there be a period of preservice training for the nonprofessionals. Such training should concentrate on specific tasks, specific knowledges and skills and less on theory. There should be a heavy use of role-playing and audio-visual materials. Stress should be placed on what they already know and how it can be utilized in the new program, so that group discussions on issues rather than formal lectures should predominate.

We have found it extremely important that during this training period, individual conferences be held between the trainer and trainee which can be the forerunner of the supervisory process.

Later, in-service training in small groups can be organized on a regular basis to introduce more formal teaching of theory and application. Even here the trainer or supervisor has to be careful constantly to show the application of theory to practice.

3. For a long period of time the focus of the supervisory conference should be on "tell me about some of your exciting cases" and not on "tell me about the cases where you are having trouble." The supervisor will be well advised to note the common errors and misconceptions of her staff and to utilize these in group teaching and discussion rather than in individual sessions.

Further, it must be kept in mind constantly that the supervisor is supervising the worker and not the case. While this has always been considered an important principle of supervision we tend to lose sight of this when supervising nonprofessionals.

Wherever possible leave the worker free to accept or reject advice—really permitting the worker to learn by his own mistakes. Often we try to convince our worker that we are right, but we must keep in mind that we have better verbal facility and can always out-argue the nonprofessional. The real result then is not that we have persuaded him of the validity of our point of view but that we have forced him to submission, rather than leaving him free to develop at his own pace.

4. Just as a nonprofessional will need supervision in carrying out his assignments, so will the supervisor of the nonprofessional need help. No matter how experienced the supervisor is, he is now undertaking a different assignment that will require some readjustment. And during this period, the supervisor often needs help, whether one calls it supervision or consultation or a listening ear. To structure this from the beginning will be fruitful. As a matter of fact, we found that a group meeting of supervisors is extremely helpful and, more often than not, can replace the individual supervision of the supervisor, leaving the latter for unique problems.

5. We feel it is extremely important that the nonprofessionals be provided opportunities to make decisions. We have learned that the nonprofessionals as a group can decide on the decor and furniture of the Center, plan Open Houses for both the resident and professional community, publish their own newspaper; decide about lunch hours, the hours the Center will be open, procedures for handling people who are waiting to be seen, etc. It is important to bear in mind however that when you give a staff authority to make these decisions, you have to be willing to live with those with which you may not agree.

They also need opportunities to participate in an advisory capacity, where in a sense the administrator determines in advance that he will make the final decision but is really interested in having the benefit of their thinking. This should be made clear from the start so that the workers are not under the misapprehension that *they will decide.* As part of their development it is important as part of this process to give them opportunities to gather information and make reports. Further, it is important to create the opportunities for them to react to decisions and plans made by higher echelon, making it clear that their reactions and suggestions will be considered though not necessarily accepted. If their ideas are not accepted, we must help them to work through their feelings that they are asked to carry out decisions and plans not of their own making.

6. We must create a structure that permits the nonprofessionals to participate in the determination of personnel practices and grievance machinery.

7. It must be anticipated and accepted that in their growing sense of power they will make unreasonable, if not irrational, demands and that they will abuse their power. In coping with these phenomena, it will help us to see them in perspective and not react to the crisis with panic or counter-anger or unreasonableness of our own. We need extreme patience and flexibility. Too often, unfortunately, we simply label our own rigidity as "consistency".

8. Above all we would like to underline that merely confronting the workers with their suspiciousness or distrust or hostility, or overdependence, etc., does not make the problem disappear. We are dealing with attitudes and behaviors that have been a lifetime in the making, and our logical and rational confrontations with the worker does not undo them in a day. We are engaged in a developmental and working-through process that will have its ups and downs as it inches ahead. We, as administrators and super-

visors of such programs, have to be careful about our own swings between elation and despair and keep before us the awareness that we are engaged in a process that involves two steps forward and one and a half steps backward.

REFERENCES

1. Riessman, F. and Hallowitz, E. The Neighborhood Service Center—An Innovation in Preventive Psychiatry, *American Journal of Orthopsychiatry*, May, 1967.
2. Hallowitz, E. and Riessman, F. The Role of the Indigenous Nonprofessional in a Community Mental Health Neighborhood Service Center Program, *American Journal of Orthopsychiatry*, July, 1967.
3. Hallowitz, E. The Use of Indigenous Nonprofessionals in a Mental Health Service, presented at the National Conference of Social Welfare, Chicago, Illinois, June, 1966.
4. Hallowitz, E. The Role of the Neighborhood Service Center in a Community Mental Health Program, *American Journal of Orthopsychiatry*, July, 1968.

Chronic Patients and a College Companion Program

Jules D. Holzberg

Harry S. Whiting

David G. Lowy

Connecticut Valley Hospital's student-patient Companion Program was undertaken experimentally in the fall of 1958 as a field-work project for an undergraduate course in abnormal psychology at nearby Wesleyan University. The two institutions, both located at Middletown, Connecticut, boast a long history of close association and provide a natural milieu for programs similar to those begun earlier at Harvard and state hospitals in the Boston area. Wesleyan students, through the years, have served the hospital in a variety of volunteer activities, and have used it as an experimental laboratory for research in psychology, biochemistry, and psychopathology. The director of psychological laboratories at the hospital doubles as visiting professor of psychology at Wesleyan, and staff and students have free access to both professional libraries.

For the purpose of our experiment, we gave the psychology students a choice of writing a term paper or working with patients at the state hospital for a minimum of two hours a week—one hour with an individual patient and a second hour in supervised group activity. About forty of our fifty students elected the field work. They were organized into five groups, each with a leader from one of the mental health professions of psychiatry, psychology, social work, chaplaincy, occupational therapy, or nursing.

Our experience quickly proved that this type of volunteer work can indeed be significant for both patients and students, and can contribute substantially to the hospital's total treatment. We decided to continue and expand the program. Accordingly, during the spring semester of 1959, the hospital superintendent set up a planning committee composed of the director of volunteer programs, a continued treatment services staff psychologist, the director of psychological laboratories, and an interested Wesleyan faculty member from the department of psychology. Wesleyan students selected for positions of leadership in the program were also asked to serve on the committee.

The Companion Program that evolved from this committee's frequent meetings was further amplified and refined when the professional group leaders were selected and met with the original committee members, and the program was finally articulated in terms of actual student-patient experience when it got under way.

The committee set three major objectives:

1. To give patients the extent and kind of personal attention that is recognized as a vital factor in comprehensive treatment of chronic mental illness. We saw the Companion Program as one facet of a total rehabilitation program, designed to make social relationships less fearsome, more gratifying experiences.

2. To provide a rewarding experience, both emotionally and educationally, for the students, many of whom would become community leaders in later life. We agreed that students in the program must not be regarded as a source of unpaid manpower. We wanted them to receive a personal, maturing experience that would equip them to deal with their own adjustments to life, and, conceivably, lead some to seek careers in mental health professions.

3. To boost the morale of increasingly overburdened, often apathetic hospital personnel by bringing into the wards young, intelligent scholars, full of the social idealism, hope, and vigor of youth.

From *Mental Hospitals*, 1964, 15, 152–158. Reproduced by permission.

The program was conceived as one that would require the utmost cooperation between and integration of hospital and university activities. In practice, the hospital has accepted the role of a willing host for the students, welcoming them as real participants in its treatment and rehabilitation program. It accepts responsibility for the students' orientation and educational experiences, and maintains professional responsibility for all patients involved in the program. This responsibility is carried through the chiefs of the services on which the students operate and through the professional group leaders who supervise the students.

The university's responsibility is to recruit and organize student-participants, a function that the administration has delegated to the student body, which works through a student organization on the campus.

The director of psychological laboratories was designated as the professional coordinator of the Companion Program, and the administrative responsibility was given to the hospital director of volunteers.

Professional group leaders from the hospital staff are charged with maintaining a common philosophy and working out common problems. They meet together frequently and also meet with ward personnel in order to keep abreast of student performance and progress and patient reaction. Their interest also serves to win the support of ward personnel for the program. A university faculty member serves as advisor to the students and plays a key role in recruitment and organization.

Recruiting begins during the first days of the fall semester with the distribution of brochures and Companion Program publicity reprints, which the hospital provides. Interested students are invited to attend a meeting at the university during the first week of school to hear a discussion of the program and its benefits for patients, students, and hospital. Student "graduates" of the program, a professional group leader from the hospital, and the faculty advisor also attend.

STUDENT'S ROLE DEFINED

The role and obligations of a student-participant are made clear both at the university recruitment meeting and at the first session at the hospital. His role is defined as that of being a friend to a patient, and the importance to the patient of reliability and consistency is stressed. Once committed to the program he is obligated to spend at least two hours a week at the hospital during the academic year, except for Christmas and spring vacations.

The hospital tries to be as flexible as possible in adapting itself to the time that students have available. Most groups find afternoon visits most convenient, but occasionally we have had an evening group. The actual assignment of students to specific groups, designation of the precise hours at the hospital, arrangements for transportation, and so on, are left to the faculty advisor.

All interested students are allowed to sign up for the program, because a study comparing student companions with a control student group showed that the former differ only in terms of their higher altruistic motives, not in terms of psychopathology. However, students screen themselves informally and effectively: they do not commit themselves to the program until they have made three visits to the hospital. During this period, a student can, and occasionally does, withdraw gracefully from the program. While the primary purpose of the recruiting activities is to select students for the Companion Program, a number who are unable to devote time to this program usually volunteer for other activities at the hospital.

GROUP LEADER'S FUNCTIONS

Companions are divided into small groups, usually no more than ten, with a student leader and a professional group leader assigned to each. The first visit to the hospital is devoted to getting acquainted with its administrative procedures through a talk given by the director of volunteers and with its physical features. The Companion Program revolves around the professional group leaders. Each one has a threefold function:

1. *Supervision.* He supervises the students to make sure that the relationship is one suitable to a "companion." He helps students to keep the relationship objective and to handle problems.

2. *Support.* Typically, students require considerable support and help in dealing with their anxieties and frustrations. Their anxieties are likely to occur on their first visits to the hospital. Their frustrations occur when their ambitions for their patients stumble upon the reality of the nature of chronic illness.

3. *Education.* During the group meetings, there is usually considerable discussion of general issues pertaining to mental illness and hospitalization. This is likely to occur most intensively during the second half of the year, when the students' anxieties are sufficiently reduced.

An attempt is made to keep discussions general rather than to concentrate on the dynamics, problems, and history of specific patients. Companions do not have access to their patients' charts, but at the end of the year the group leader may discuss selected data. This is an event eagerly awaited by the companions because it permits them to test the reality of their own conclusions about their patients.

The group leader assumes considerable responsibility both in protecting the patient and in making the companion's experience a positive one. The essential qualifications for a group leader seem to be experience with patients, a dynamic approach to their problems, and a sincere interest in working with students.

At first we felt that the success of our program would depend, at least partially, on letting the students themselves choose patients with whom they thought they could become friendly. Accordingly, the chief of the service involved, the nursing supervisor, and the professional group leader selected a group of patients for the program, and for three weeks following the initial orientation period, the professional leader, the students, and the patients met at a weekly social hour held on a ward or in a special room of the service. Often the chief of the service and members of the nursing staff also attended. Students and patients mixed freely in the presence of the professional hospital staff. Coffee was served to encourage an informal, social atmosphere.

During these three weeks, the first hour was devoted to

getting acquainted with patients in this group situation; then, during the second hour, the professional group leader guided a discussion of both general issues and the students' interest in specific patients. We believed that these sessions would allay the natural anxiety of students venturing for the first time into a mental hospital. At the end of the 3-week orientation period, each student selected the patient who would be his companion for the entire year.

We have since discovered that students often prefer to have patients assigned to them, because frequently they feel guilty when they select one patient over another. Therefore, we now may assign a patient to each student, with the understanding that the assignment can be changed at any time within the first three weeks.

While most student-patient activities take place at the hospital, we also allow companions to take patients into town or on a visit to the university, if the chief of the service approves.

CHRONIC PATIENTS SELECTED

Considerable thought has been given to the question of the types of patients to be selected for this program. While the criteria developed must remain tentative, we generally agree that patients should be chronically ill but present no symptoms or behavior that would be especially disturbing to the students, nor should they be so regressed that they would be more appropriate for a remotivation program, or so socially developed and capable of tolerating an intense interpersonal relationship that they are ready for formal individual or group therapy by a professional person. We believe that the patient best suited to the companion experience is one who has responded to remotivation and is now ready for a social relationship with an individual. We are particularly interested in the "forgotten" patient who has minimal or no contact with nonhospital individuals.

The goals of the Companion Program for the patient are improvement in his level of social communication, social skill, and social responsibility that would help effect his social recovery and hopefully lead to his discharge. Patients for group therapy are often recruited from those who have been in the Companion Program.

The problem of handling separation and termination is a continuing one. The students are concerned about the effects of these on their patients, but at times more than is justified by the nature of their relationships. We have thought about this problem, but have collectively agreed that patients cannot and should not be protected from the realities of living, one of which is the movement of people into and out of their lives. The group leader's task is to help the students carry through separation and termination so that it is not traumatic, either for the patients or for the students. Separation looms as a significant problem twice a year, at the long Christmas vacation and at the end of the school year. We have found that holding a party for patients and their companions just prior to the Christmas vacation, and a picnic just prior to the end of the year serve to allay separation anxiety for both.

RESPONSE IS GRATIFYING

From its modest beginnings at one university, the program has now expanded to students at seven colleges—Wesleyan University, Trinity College, Yale University, Central Connecticut State College, University of Hartford, Hartford College, and University of Connecticut. During the past year over 150 students participated, including several who have been in the program for two and three years. They were organized into 15 groups, each with its own professional leader, and almost every service of the hospital had at least one group serving some of its patients. The groups were distributed over every afternoon of the week.

Attempts to evaluate the program in terms of its impact on patients have thus far rested on non-controlled investigations and on the observations of the professional leaders. One questionnaire study carried out on the first year's companions offers some basis for considering the experience a significant one for patients. Of the students who responded to the questionnaire at the end of the year, 84 per cent reported that their patients desired the companionship relationship and sought to maintain it. A typical student comment was "She seems to appreciate my visits and attention." Seventy-one per cent reported that students and the patients conversed more freely. Sixty-five per cent reported that the patients showed positive changes in self-confidence. Sixty-four per cent reported greater interest on the part of the patient in his surroundings. A comment of one of the students in this regard was: "She's more interested in activities at the hospital. She began helping with aged patients in the infirmary. She is generally more aware of herself and her surroundings. She began corresponding again with friends outside the hospital." Another student reported: "It has brought him out from his withdrawn state. He is first starting to show significant improvement." Fifty-five per cent of the students reported positive changes in the patient's personal appearance, and 48 per cent reported that the patient's social behavior had improved during the year.

The students also reported changes in the basic psychopathology of their patients. Forty-two per cent of the students reported that their patients showed improvement in terms of realistic thinking, and 46 per cent showed improvement in their mood state, reflected in reduction of depressive indications. Over all, the students considered that 71 per cent of the patients had shown improvement during the companionship year. Twenty-nine per cent were unchanged. We considered these data quite startling considering the fact that all of the patients were chronically ill and had been in the hospital for a substantial number of years.

Plans are currently underway to evaluate the patients more systematically. A comprehensive check list of ward behavior will be filled out by psychiatric aides at the beginning and end of a companion year. A comparable control group of patients not in the Companion Program will be similarly evaluated. This should yield information on whether the hospital behavior of patients is significantly altered by the companionship experience.

We have also evaluated the impact of the program on the students. A questionnaire administered to them in the first year of the Companion Program revealed that all felt that they had grown in their knowledge of mental hospitals and of the effects of hospitalization. Ninety-one per cent said that during the course of the year they had become less anxious in working with patients. Ninety per cent felt that they had grown in their understanding of mental illness—both its causes and treatments. Eighty-one per cent said their feelings about patients had changed: they had acquired the ability to see patients as sick people worthy of support and aid rather than derision. Eighty-four per cent reported that their feelings about mental hospital personnel had also changed and they understood better the nature of the problems experienced by these people.

BETTER UNDERSTANDING

A number of the students volunteered testimonials to the multiple values of the experience. Some of these are quoted below:

"This program is a good and effective method of letting others know the problems faced by mental hospitals today. I sincerely hope that it reaps a reward in the future generation."

"I feel that the companionship I had this year was more or less one-sided. I gained terrific insights into the mental hospital, its patients, and its problems, while my patient didn't seem to get too much out of our relationship."

"I feel quite strongly that all graduate students in psychology, and maybe even all majors in psychology, should take part in the program. It is a very valuable experience."

"The program has caused me to take a more objective view of my own emotional problems."

"Keep up the program. For me, and I think for most everyone, the experience has been most rewarding."

All told, 97 per cent of the students considered that their experience had contributed to their personal growth. It is evident that it has been a truly remarkable educational experience.

We completed one study that evaluated the changes in attitudes toward and understanding of mental illness and hospitalization in a more controlled fashion. The companions and a group of control students not in the Companion Program but engaged in other service activities were compared on a questionnaire about attitudes and understanding of mental illness, which was administered at the very beginning and at the close of the academic year. The results clearly indicated that the companions show a significant positive shift in their attitudes and understanding, while no such shift occurred in our control group.

INDEX

74 75 76 77 9 8 7 6 5 4 3 2 1